MW01040339

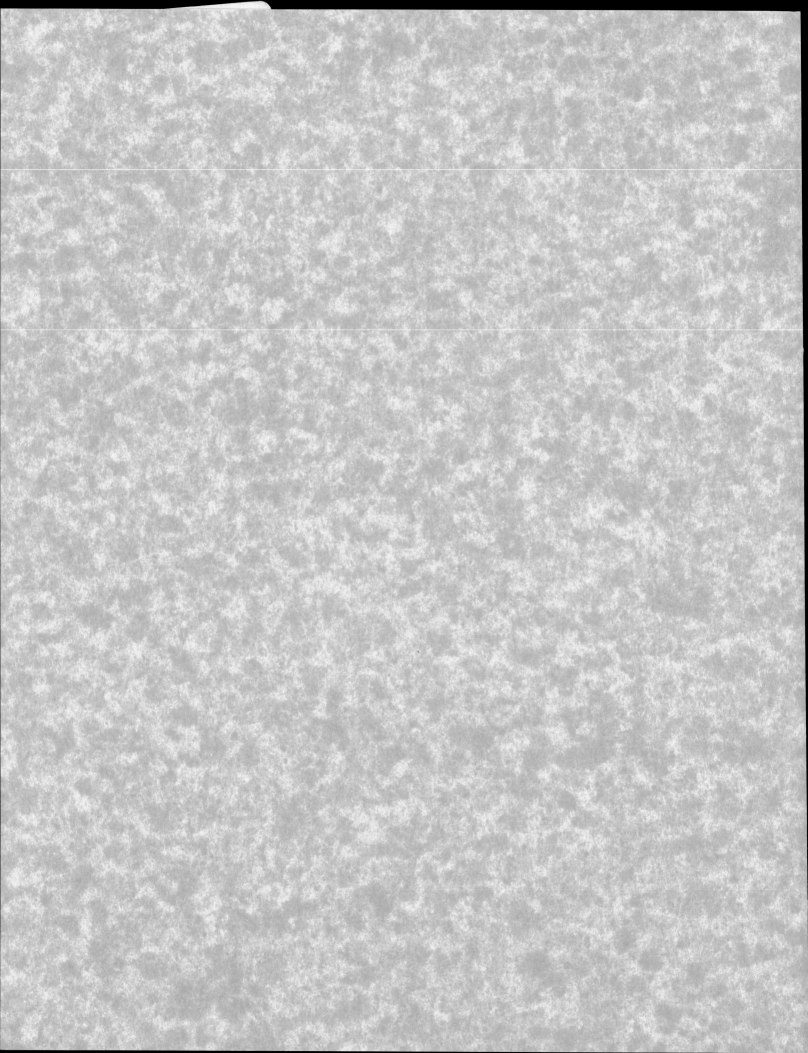

Architecture and Interior Design

An Integrated History to the Present

Buie Harwood
FIDEC, Honorary FASID, Certified Interior Designer, Virginia
Professor Emeritus, Virginia Commonwealth University

Bridget May, Ph.D.
IDEC, ASID
Professor, Marymount University

Curt Sherman
FIDEC, ASID
Professor Emeritus, Winthrop University

Prentice Hall
Boston Columbus Indianapolis New York San Francisco Upper Saddle River
Amsterdam Cape Town Dubai London Madrid Milan Munich Paris Montreal Toronto
Delhi Mexico City São Paulo Sydney Hong Kong Seoul Singapore Taipei Tokyo

Editorial Director: Vernon R. Anthony
Acquisitions Editor: Sara Eilert
Development Editor: Christine Buckendahl
Editorial Assistant: Doug Greive
Director of Marketing: David Gesell
Marketing Manager: Kara Clark
Senior Marketing Coordinator: Alicia Wozniak
Senior Managing Editor: JoEllen Gohr
Associate Managing Editor: Alexandrina Benedicto Wolf
Project Manager: Alicia Ritchey
AV Project Manager: Janet Portisch
Senior Operations Supervisor: Pat Tonneman
Operations Specialist: Deidra Skahill
Art Director: Diane Ernsberger
Cover Designer: Ali Mohrman
Cover Concept: Curt Sherman
Page Layout: Buie Harwood
Cover Art: Left image: Long Gallery, Strawberry Hill; Alamy B6E5C9. Right image: Interior, Dupont Antron Showroom, Maddox; Courtesy of Eva Maddox Branded Environments. Photographer: Steve Hall, Hedrich Blessing
Full-Service Project Management: Linda Zuk, WordCraft LLC
Composition: S4Carlisle Publishing Services
Printer/Binder: Courier Kendallville, Inc.
Cover Printer: Lehigh-Phoenix Color/Hagarstown
Text Font: Goudy

Credits and acknowledgments borrowed from other sources and reproduced, with permission, in this textbook appear on page 877.

Library of Congress Cataloging-in-Publication Data
Harwood, Buie.
Architecture and interior design : an integrated history to the present / Buie Harwood, Bridget May, Curt Sherman. — 1st ed.
p. cm.
Combined and edited version of 2 separately published works: Architecture and interior design through the 18th century, and Architecture and interior design from the 19th century.
Includes bibliographical references and index.
ISBN 0-13-509357-0 (978-0-13-509357-3) 1. Interior decoration—History. 2. Interior architecture—History. 3. Decorative arts—History. I. Harwood, Buie. Architecture and interior design through the 18th century. II. Harwood, Buie. Architecture and interior design from the 19th century. III. Title.
NK1710.H372 2011
747.09—dc22 2010029060

10 9 8 7 6 5 4 3 2 1
ISBN 10: 0-13-509357-0
ISBN 13: 978-0-13-509357-3

This book is dedicated
to our families, mentors, and students

Brief Contents

Contents

Preface

This book will be of use to students of interior design, interior design practitioners, furniture designers, design consultants, design manufacturers, and theater/film set designers, as well as students and professionals in the related fields of art history, architecture, material culture, museum studies, and history. It will also be of interest to historical/preservation societies, craftspeople, design journalists, and anyone with an interest in design history.

As a condensed volume of our two earlier publications, *Architecture and Interior Design through the 18th Century: An Integrated History* (2002) and *Architecture and Interior Design from the 19th Century: An Integrated History* (2009), it is intended to fulfill a need in interior design education. Like the others, this book allows the reader to compare and contrast architecture, interiors, furniture, and decorative arts from the past to the present. We have tried to interweave a design analysis language with that of art and architectural history. Our intent is to provide a flexible, easy-to-use, and well-organized resource for those with a variety of interests. Included also are a glossary, an extensive reference list, and an index.

Our previous two publications evolved over a number of years and developed from our university teaching experiences. We and our colleagues were continually frustrated by the lack of adequate resources to support the desired content, context, and comprehensiveness of interior design history. Many of our shared ideas have been realized in this condensed volume as we worked on the organization and presentation of the material. We hope that this effort fulfills a need for you and future generations who find the study of design history exciting.

ONLINE RESOURCES

To access supplementary materials online, instructors need to request an instructor access code. Go to www.pearsonhighered.com/irc, where you can register for an instructor access code. Within 48 hours after registering, you will receive a confirming e-mail, including an instructor access code. Once you have received your code, go to the site and log on for full instructions on downloading the materials you wish to use.

Acknowledgments

This book has been an enormous undertaking. We would like to gratefully acknowledge those who provided valuable assistance through its development. Special thanks to each of you for all of your wonderful contributions!

To our Prentice Hall/Pearson Education support team who had faith in us and made the book happen: Vern Anthony, Jill Jones-Renger, Sara Eilert, Christine Buckendahl, Louise Sette, Alicia Ritchey, Linda Zuk, Susan Watkins, Janet Portisch, Jeanne Molenar, Ann Brunner, Michelle Churma, ReeAnne Davies, and Judith Casillo.

To our many students who inspired us to undertake this project: those who had courses with Buie at Virginia Commonwealth University, the University of Texas at Austin, and North Texas State University; with Bridget at Marymount University, the University of Georgia at Athens, and Mississippi University for Woman; and with Curt at Winthrop University, San Diego State University, and Washington State University.

To the educational institutions who supported our efforts: Virginia Commonwealth University and Marymount University.

To our friends who offered their expertise, support, resources, interest, and listening ears.

To our special library resource friends: Suzanne Freeman at the Virginia Museum of Fine Arts in Richmond, who provided a wealth of information; Carl Vuncannon and his staff at the Bernice Bienenstock Furniture Library in High Point, North Carolina; and Ray Bonis in Special Collections, Cabell Library at Virginia Commonwealth University.

To our family members who offered ongoing support.

To the illustrators and photographers who recorded their environments, particularly from the 16th century through the present. As shown herein, their depictions of architecture, interiors, furnishings, and decorative arts were of enormous value in providing a resource archive.

To our wonderful and talented artist and former interior design student, Chris Good.

About the Authors

Buie Harwood, FIDEC, Honorary FASID, Certified Interior Designer in Virginia; Professor Emeritus and past Department Chair, Department of Interior Design, School of the Arts, Virginia Commonwealth University (for programs in Richmond and Doha, Qatar). Ms. Harwood has held officership and committee responsibilities in the Interior Design Educators Council (IDEC), National Council for Interior Design Qualification (NCIDQ), American Society of Interior Designers (ASID), and Foundation for Interior Design Education Research (FIDER; now called the Council for Interior Design Accreditation/CIDA) Among her many honors, she is an IDEC Fellow, received the first ASID Educator of Distinction Award in 2003, and is listed in *Who's Who in Interior Design*, the *International Directory of Distinguished Leadership*, and *Who's Who Among America's Teachers*. She has received numerous grants, published articles, and implemented research projects related to her historic research and the interior design career path. She is co-author (with B. May and C. Sherman) of *Architecture and Interior Design through the 18th Century: An Integrated History*, which won the prestigious ASID Education Foundation/Joel Polsky award in 2002, and their second volume, *Architecture and Interior Design from the 19th Century: An Integrated History*, published in June 2009. Her book, *Decorating Texas: Decorative Painting in the Lone Star State from the 1850s to the 1950s*, won awards from the American Association of State and Local History and the San Antonio Conservation Society. She has studied in the Victorian Society Summer Schools at both Rhode Island and England.

Bridget May, Ph.D., IDEC, ASID: Professor and former Chair of Interior Design, School of Arts and Sciences, Marymount University. Dr. May has held office and committee responsibilities in the Interior Design Educators Council (IDEC) and has been active in the American Society of Interior Designers (ASID). Her many honors include a Benno M. Forman Fellowship for Research in American Material Culture at Winterthur Museum and Library and a one-semester sabbatical at Marymount University. She has been listed in *Who's Who in Interior Design* and *Who's Who in American Women*. She has had many presentations, publications, and grants related to historic interiors, including one for a furnishings plan for a National Trust for Historic Preservation house as well as a 2008 IDEC Special Projects Grant for a design history symposium (with John Turpin). She is co-author (with B. Harwood and C. Sherman) of *Architecture and Interior Design through the 18th Century: An Integrated History*, which won the prestigious ASID Education Foundation/Joel Polsky award in 2009, and their second volume, *Architecture and Interior design from the 19th Century: An Integrated History*, published in June 2008. She has studied at the Victorian Society Summer School in Rhode Island and at the Winterthur Summer Institute in Delaware.

Curt Sherman, FIDEC, ASID; Professor Emeritus, Department of Art and Design, College of Visual and Performing Arts, Winthrop University. Mr. Sherman has held officership/committee responsibilities in the Interior Design Educators Council (IDEC), American Society of Interior Designers (ASID), and Foundation for Interior Design Education Research (FIDER; now called the Council for Interior Design Accreditation/CIDA), and has given numerous ASID and IDEC workshops. Three interior design programs in universities were accredited under his chairmanship. Among his many honors, he is an IDEC Fellow and is listed in *Who's Who in Interior Design*. He has won prestigious awards for his photography and furniture design, and has had his photography work included in several publications, including books on historic interiors. He is co-author (with B. Harwood and B. May) of *Architecture and Interior Design through the 18th Century: An Integrated History*, which won the prestigious ASID Education Foundation/Joel Polsky award in 2002, and their second volume, *Architecture and Interior design from the 19th Century: An Integrated History*, published in June 2009. He has also worked on several historic interiors projects and studied at the Attingham Summer School in England as well as programs sponsored by the National Trust for Historic Preservation and the Smithsonian Institute.

Introduction

The true poets of the twentieth century are the designers, the architects and engineers who glimpse some inner vision and then translate it into valid actuality for the world to enjoy.

"The Lost Worlds of the Fair," from Official Guide Book, 1939, p. 169.

We shape our buildings, thereafter they shape us.

Winston Churchill, as quoted in *Time* magazine, 1960

INTEGRATING ARCHITECTURE, INTERIOR DESIGN, FURNITURE, AND DECORATIVE ARTS

This book is a combined and edited version of our previously published *Architecture and Interior Design through the 18th Century: An Integrated History* (Vol. 1, 2002; Prentice Hall) and *Architecture and Interior Design from the 19th Century: An Integrated History* (Vol. 2, 2009; Prentice Hall). It provides a survey of architecture, interiors, furniture, and decorative arts from early cultural precedents and antiquity to the present. As with the other books, our intent in this edited version is to provide a completely integrated and interdisciplinary reference for studying the built environment, interior design, interior architectural features, design details, motifs, furniture, space planning, color, lighting, textiles, interior surface treatments, and decorative accessories. Each period is placed within a cultural, historical, social, and conceptual context so that the reader can make connections among all aspects of the aesthetic development. Examples depict buildings, interiors, and furnishings from residential, commercial, and institutional projects, such as the 17th-century high-style *Galerie des Glaces* (Hall of Mirrors; Fig. I-1) at the *Palais de Versailles* and the early 20th-century vernacular American interiors of Gustav Stickley (Fig. I-2). Later interpretations illustrate the application of each stylistic influence during later periods, including products currently available and projects recently completed, such as the late 20th-century Gothic-inspired Thorncrown Chapel by Fay Jones (Fig. I-3).

People provide our travelogue through history and our understanding of architecture and design. They shape and define our architecture, interiors, furniture, and decorative arts. Their tastes, ideas, knowledge, activities, and perceptions define the macro and micro environments. The environments discussed herein emphasize aesthetic and functional considerations—spaces that have been made by people in which to live, work, and play. The study of architecture stresses the exterior built environment—buildings within a site, structures that form shelter, forms articulating a design language—a macro view of space. The study of interior design parallels this concept but focuses on interior environments where people go about their daily activities—areas within the building, rooms and their relationship in a structure, envelopes displaying a design vocabulary—a micro view of space. The study of furniture and decorative arts offers a more detailed view of the objects and materials

▲ I-1. *Galerie des Glaces* (Hall of Mirrors), *Palais de Versailles,* 1678–1687; near Paris, France; begun by Charles Le Brun and completed by Jules Hardouin-Mansart. Louis XIV.

▲ I-2. Living room; published in *The Craftsman,* 1905–1906; United States; Gustav Stickley and Harvey Ellis. American Arts and Crafts/Craftsman Style.

within interiors. This aesthetic and functional language and vocabulary become our road map for understanding design history.

APPROACHES TO DESIGN HISTORY

There are various approaches to the study of design history, whether architecture, interior design and furniture, or a combination. Art history uses works of art such as painting, sculpture, architecture, furniture, ceramics, and metals to study the past. Its formalistic method follows chronology and stylistic development to grasp the meaning of works of art and, by extension, a society or people. Architectural history follows a similar pattern through its study of buildings. Its method addresses buildings primarily through their individual histories, functions, owners, architects, styles, sitings, materials, construction methods, and contextual environments. Material culture looks specifically at human-made objects as transmitters of ideas and values of a society or group. Objects made and used by a society may include tools, furniture, textiles, and lighting that may be high-style or vernacular. Design history studies artifacts and their contexts with a focus on their design and designers, materials, form, and function. Interior design historians bring a unique approach to design history by integrating the relationship of architecture and interiors in the context of history and design analysis. To accomplish this, the art history, architectural history, material culture, and design history approaches are merged and used as they relate to considerations of research, programming, concept, function, overall aesthetic, principles, and elements, as well as meaning and intent. As interior design educators, we have taken this last approach.

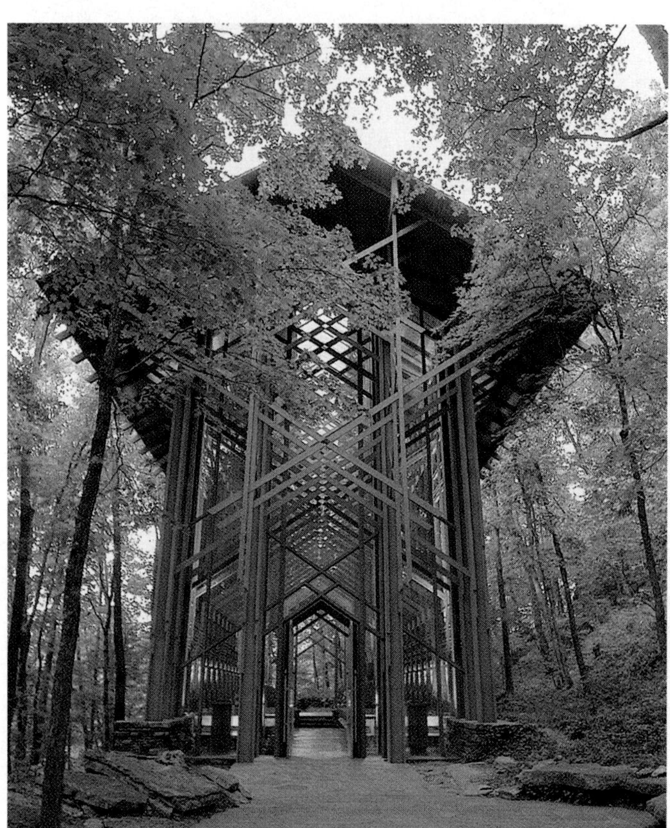
▲ I-3. Thorncrown Chapel, 1978–1980; Eureka Springs, Arkansas; Fay Jones and Maurice Jennings. Environmental Modern.

▲ I-4. Central nave crossing with dome, *S. Geneviève (Panthéon)*, 1757–1790; Paris, France; Jacques-Germain Soufflot. Louis XVI.

A stylistic approach to design history identifies forms, function, and visual features. This method, which is typically chronological, can be as simple as codifying visual characteristics with little definition of the roles of form and/or function. In a broader view, such as that of art history or material culture, style can assume that groups of people during particular times prefer particular forms and motifs as a reflection of their cultural and social qualities or particular design theories, as in the case of many modern designers. Therefore, objects, such as architecture, interiors, furnishings, and decorative arts can embody the values and/or beliefs of a society, group, or individual. In this sense, objects become historical documents or visual records. As primary documents, they can tell us much about an individual or group. Objects survive much longer than written records do and often come from a broader spectrum of society. But the most complete picture exists when objects and written records are integrated.

Styles evolve from social, cultural, economic, and/or political factors of a given time. Available materials, climate, location, technology, and historical events affect the visual image. Until the middle of the 19th century, styles originate with political or religious leaders, the wealthy, other important people, or the design elite, and then filter to the middle class through an increasing range of media as time passes. With the Industrial Revolution, mass production and communication make it possible for many to emulate high-style design. Style or movement beginnings and endings vary. Consequently, dates provided herein should be considered guidelines because resources deviate in identifying exact dates, and transitions are common as stylistic periods change. Additionally, personal preferences affect or determine the form and appearance of buildings and objects. Some people choose older styles over newer ones, especially in early periods when fashion is less important and visual resources, such as books, periodicals, or photographs, are limited.

USING DESIGN ANALYSIS

An important skill for architects and interior designers is the ability to read and understand existing exterior and interior environments. This is accomplished through design analysis—a visual language of design evaluation. This process affects aesthetic decisions and functional considerations and is most critical when evaluating historical structures and interiors and their contents. Studying these structures and interiors as historical records helps designers understand the evolution of a building, build visual literacy, and assess the appropriate design direction. Understanding historical design can also provide a wealth of design ideas for contemporary projects. A designer may enhance the original visual image, choose to reproduce it, or provide an adaptation.

Design analysis incorporates a specific language based on integrating the principles and elements of design and the architectural and interior components of a building. The principles of design include proportion, scale, balance; harmony, unity/variety/contrast; rhythm; and emphasis. The elements of design are size/space, line, color, light, texture, and shape/form (see Principles and Elements of Design definitions, page xxvi). As identified in this book, architectural components of a building embrace site orientation, floor plan, materials, construction systems, color, façades, windows, doors, roof, architectural details, and unique features. Interior components generally encompass the relationship of the interior to the exterior, materials, color, floors, walls, windows, doors, ceilings, textiles, lighting, interior details, special treatments, and unique features. Furnishings and decorative arts address specific relationships; furniture arrangements; materials; seating; tables; storage; beds; special decorative arts such as ceramics, metalwork, or mirrors; and unique features. The appearance of the exterior and interior derives from the integration of this design analysis language as applied to a three-dimensional form.

Design analysis also addresses ordering systems used to articulate buildings and interiors. The most common ordering systems are spatial definition, proportion, geometry, scale, and visual perception. Spatial definition involves wall planes enclosing space and the spatial elasticity of the surrounding space. During the 18th century, Jacques-Germain Soufflot interprets Roman influences in the S. *Geneviève* (The *Panthéon*; Fig. I-4), Paris, where he experiments with geometric shapes, spatial interplay, vaults and curved ceiling surfaces, and lighting to accentuate form. In 1929, Ludwig Mies van der Rohe creates the German Pavilion (Fig. I-5) at the International Exposition in Barcelona with open, flowing spaces that penetrate from one to another with a few walls, panels, and marble screens carefully positioned in an ordered, asymmetrical relationship. Behavioral design specialists also refer to personal and social space related to the concept of proxemics (the physical distance between people in space). These considerations can define the experience of space as being confined, tight, and restricted or spacious, expanding, and flexible, as illustrated in the design of the 1960s Action Office furniture system (Fig. I-6).

Proportion recognizes dimensions and relationships within objects. The Greeks codify the Golden Section (Fig. I-7), clarifying the specific relationship between the whole and its parts. In the 16th century, Andrea Palladio incorporates mathematical proportions based on divisions of the octave in the Villa Rotunda (Fig. I-8) with rooms in square, circular, and rectangular shapes creating cross axial symmetry and heights in a harmonious ratio. In the 18th century, Robert Adam utilizes Palladian principles in the library at Kenwood House (Fig. I-9) in London, where a rectangular plan with apsidal

▲ **I-5.** Interiors, German Pavilion, International Exposition, 1929; Barcelona, Spain; Ludwig Mies van der Rohe. The Bauhaus.

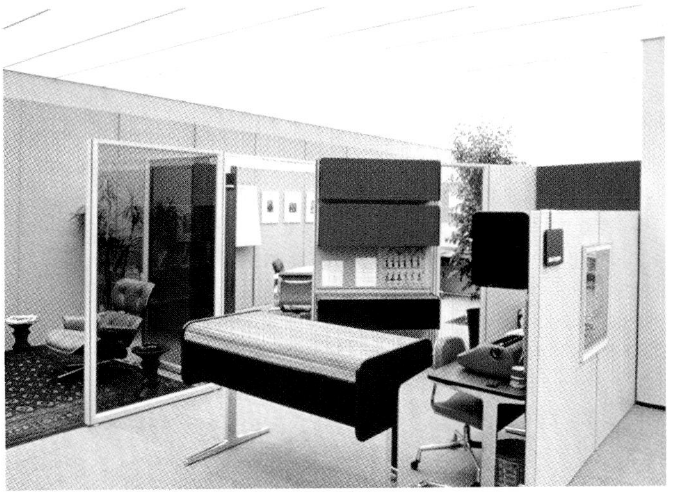

▲ **I-6.** Action Office systems furniture in polished cast aluminum, 1964–1968; United States; Robert Probst with details by George Nelson, manufactured by Herman Miller. Late Modern • 1.

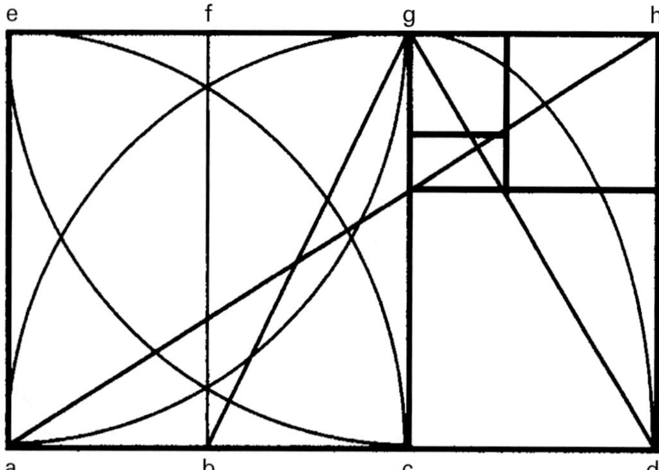

▲ **I-7.** Golden Section: aceg = square; bf = 1/2 square; bg = bd and determines smaller Golden Mean; adhe = Golden Mean.

▲ **I-8.** Villa Rotunda (Villa Almerico-Capra), 1565–1569; Vicenza, Italy; Andrea Palladio.

ends is divided by a Corinthian colonnade to extend the space, and the barrel-vaulted, compartmented ceiling displays rectangles, ovals, squares, circles, and semicircles in elegant proportions. In 1992, Donald Chadwick and William Stumpf adopt contemporary ideas of proportion in the Aeron chair (Fig. I-10) by addressing ergonomics, anthropometrics, functionality, form, materials, and movement to create a new icon in office seating.

Geometry describes three-dimensional forms in terms of standard geometric shapes to include a triangle, square, circle, rectangle, and pentagon integrated with lines. In 1924, Gerrit Rietveld favors a machine vocabulary, one stressing flat geometric shapes, unadorned surfaces, asymmetry, and the purity of the graphic language as shown in the Schröder House (Fig. I-11) in Utrecht, Netherlands. In 1983, Richard Meier envisions a language of structural geometry in Atlanta's High Museum of Art (Fig. I-12), as illustrated in the building composition, modular surface materials, architectural details, circulation patterns, and room proportions. In the 1990s, flexible office systems such as Personal Harbor (Fig. I-13) display geometry through the use of modular parts composed of panel partitions, work surfaces, storage areas, filing components, and integrated lighting.

Scale refers to the size relationship of one thing to another, such as a building to its site or a piece of furniture to an interior, based on a comparison and human dimensions. The Cathedral of the Notre Dame (Fig. I-14), a 12th- to 13th-century Gothic church in Paris, dominates it site, displays monumental interiors, and has human-scaled details on exterior and interior surfaces. Similarly, the 19th-century New Palace of Westminster (Houses of Parliament; Fig. I-15) in London, designed by Sir Charles Barry and Augustus W. N. Pugin, unites British history and heritage with Gothic design to create an imposing, grand-scaled complex along the Thames River. In 1949, Philip Johnson conceives his famous Glass House (Fig. I-16) in Connecticut as a small building placed in a natural environment, one that emphasizes the interplay of exterior and interior space and the relationship of interior space to the scale of the furnishings. In 1997, innovative architect Frank Gehry creates a unique setting for the Guggenheim Museum (Fig. I-17) in Spain by placing a large-scale sculptural structure of curved and bent forms on direct axis and proximity to the old city center of Bilbao.

Visual perception pertains to the way one views a space and the person's position within the space. The Chinese concept of perspective (Fig. I-18) presents a flat layering of images to achieve depth with the foreground at the bottom of a picture plane, the

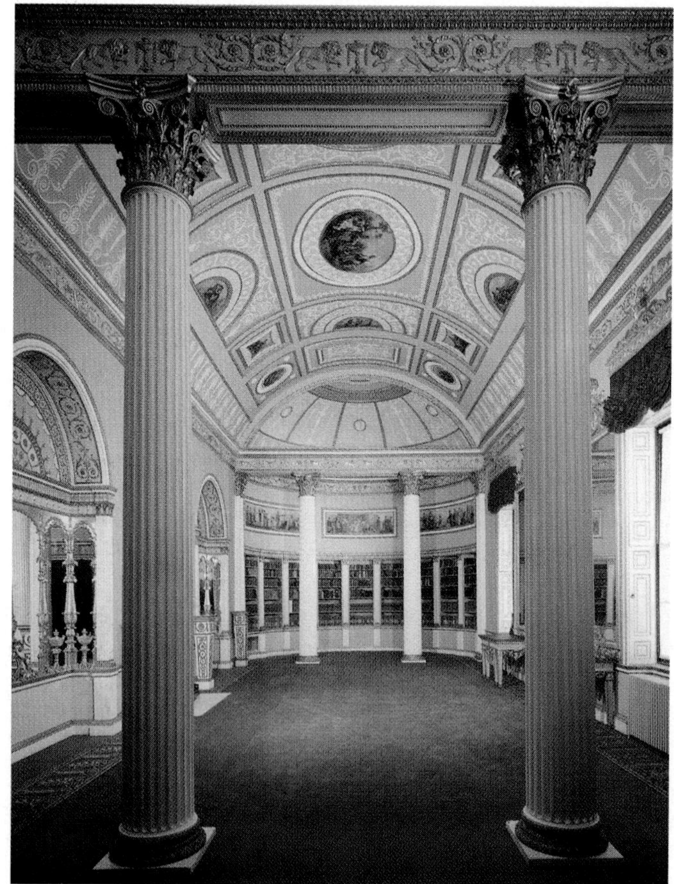

▲ **I-9.** Library, Kenwood House, 1764–1779; Hampstead, London, England; Robert Adam. Late Georgian.

▲ I-10. Aeron chair, 1992; Donald Chadwick and William Stumpf, manufactured by Herman Miller. Late Modern • 2.

▲ I-11. Schröder House, 1924; Utrecht, Netherlands; Gerrit Thomas Rietveld, in association with owner Truus Schröder-Schräder. De Stijl.

▲ I-12. High Museum of Art, 1980–1983; Atlanta, Georgia; Richard Meier. Late Modern • 1.

▲ I-13. Personal Harbor office furniture, c. 1992; United States; Paul Siebert, Mark Baloga, and Steve Eriksson; manufactured by Steelcase. Late Modern • 2.

background at the top, and with man small in comparison to the surroundings. In direct contrast, the Western use of Renaissance perspective by Sebastiano Serlio (Fig. I-19) relies on a three-dimensional convergence of angled lines to create depth with humans and objects proportionally placed within the framework, as is common in contemporary architectural and interior design perspective drawings. In 1936, Frank Lloyd Wright creates Fallingwater (Fig. I-20), his residential masterpiece in Pennsylvania that fuses the terraced building to the natural landscape, articulates the interplay of exterior and interior space, creates procession and movement, and addresses a contextual human scale.

USING THE BOOK

Within the book, the interrelationship of written narrative and graphic illustrations is considered a guiding principle. This material is integrated and carefully weighted throughout the book so that the reader can make connections between the written and visual content. One can, therefore, read the text or view the images and grasp the basic concepts of the period. A historical vocabulary and design analysis language are interwoven throughout the text.

Basic art movement sections provide an introduction to subsequent chapters that address particular historical styles. Chapters use a consistent footprint composed of headings and subheadings that offer an organized format for the presentation and sequencing of design content. This arrangement supports the idea of reviewing the content chronologically or topically. Because the book is intended to be a general survey of these periods, supplementary references, such as those in the bibliography, may assist in providing more detailed historical explanations.

The written narrative is descriptive and concise, with a combination of paragraphs and bullet-point lists to aid in the easy retrieval of information. Paragraphs present general information and bullet-point lists identify distinctive design features. Design Characteristics, including specific motifs, are noted in many chapters. The Architecture and Interiors categories are sequenced as a structure is built, from bottom (foundation or floor) to top (roof or ceiling). The Furnishings and Decorative Arts category provides an overview of the most important furniture and decorative accessories. The Design Spotlight focuses on individual examples of architecture, interiors, and furniture to illustrate specific characteristics important to a particular period, with graphic illustrations included for reference and identification of characteristics, details, and motifs.

The text synthesizes information from many sources. Primary sources (those created during the period under study), such as

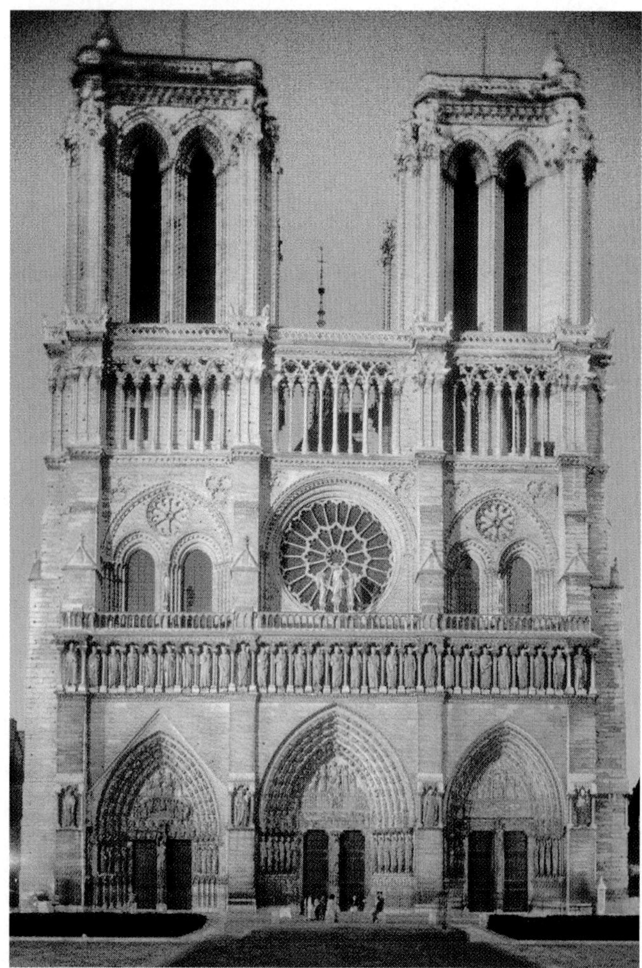

▲ **I-14.** Cathedral of the Notre Dame, 1163–1250; Paris, France. Gothic.

▲ **I-15.** New Palace of Westminster (Houses of Parliament), 1835–1865; London, England; Sir Charles Barry and Augustus W. N. Pugin. Gothic Revival.

▲ **I-16.** Living area, Glass House (Residence of Philip Johnson), 1949; New Canaan, Connecticut; Philip Johnson. Geometric Modern.

▲ **I-17.** Guggenheim Museum, 1997; Bilbao, Spain; Frank Gehry and Partners. Neo-Modern.

▲ I-18. Detail, Coromandel screen; China. China.

treatises and books, are noted where possible so that the reader can explore them individually for design ideas. Secondary sources (those describing the period under study) are numerous, and the Bibliography includes a large selection for further reading. References are grouped alphabetically by general information and by basic movement to facilitate use. A Glossary defines terms with which the reader may not be familiar.

The graphic illustrations feature a wide diversity of images, some common to the period and some less known. They include examples in black and white and color, line drawings, and material from trade catalogs, magazines, books, and journals from more recent sources and from original sources or older publications. Images are selected to convey the best representation of the place or item as it was built or used. Often this results in an illustration from drawings or photographs that may be more contemporary with the date of construction. Our preference has been to show the place or item as it looked when first developed rather than when it was first publicized or at a later point in time. This helps make clear the influence that the structure or object had on other architects or designers. Design diagramming points out major design features and characteristics of a particular style of architecture, interiors, and furniture so that the reader can make visual connections among different parts of the content.

For greater historical accuracy, some images have been slightly modified digitally from their original appearance to represent more accurately the building or object as it would have appeared upon completion or in its appropriate time frame. These actions include removing automobiles, electrical or telephone wires, and signage that are not of the original period. Older prints and negatives have also had their foxing or spotting removed. These actions have not been taken on images obtained from museums or commercial photographers.

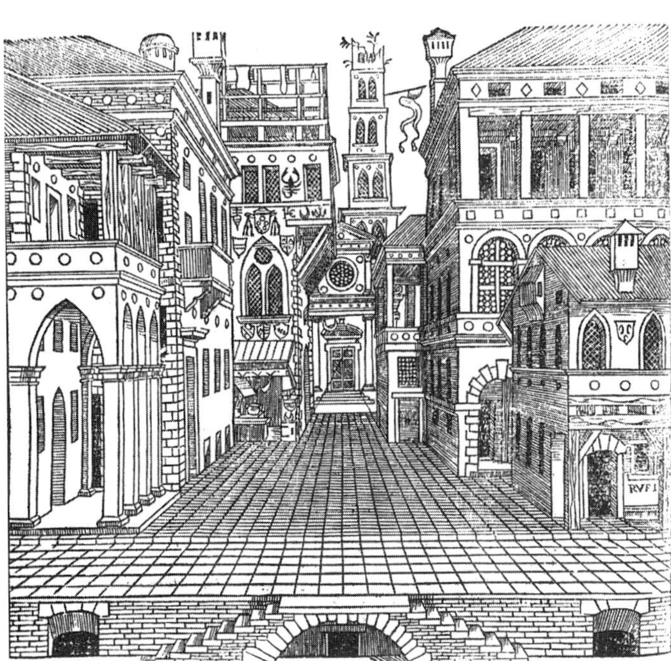

▲ I-19. Stage setting, 1540–1551; Italy; Sebastiano Serlio and published in *D'Architettura*. Italian Renaissance.

▲ I-20. Fallingwater, 1935–1937; Bear Run, Pennsylvania; Frank Lloyd Wright. Organic and Sculptural Modern.

PRINCIPLES OF DESIGN

Principles of design are the vocabulary used to measure and define design, and they are often described using the elements of design.

■ *Proportion.* The relationship of parts of a design to each other and to the whole, such as between large and small windows in a house.
■ *Scale.* A contextual relationship comparing dimensional objects, such as the proportional size of a door to all other doors, to human beings, and to the space in which it belongs.
■ *Balance.* A result when forces opposing each other achieve equilibrium. Examples include symmetrical/formal balance developing from a central axis, asymmetrical/informal balance with an irregular axis, and radial balance coming from a central core.
■ *Harmony.* The relationship of parts to each other through similarity and to an overall theme of design, such as the consistency in size and color of architectural trim on a house.
■ *Unity, Variety, Contrast.* Unity is the collection of elements seen as a visually related whole. Variety is the tension between opposing elements, such as between straight and curved lines. Contrast refers to the means of accenting a composition as through light, color, texture, pattern, scale, and/or configuration.
■ *Rhythm.* The relationship of visual elements together in a regular pattern through repetition, alternation, or progression, such as the repetition of lines and shapes in a textile pattern.
■ *Emphasis.* The importance of an item in its space that thereby makes other items less important, such as the focal point created by placing a large oil painting at the end of a narrow hallway.

ELEMENTS OF DESIGN

The elements of design are the tools for working in space.

■ *Space.* The area in which objects and people exist and move as well as a period of time, thereby establishing relationships, such as between humans and their environment. Space may be arranged through a linear, nucleus, modular, or grid pattern.
■ *Line.* The connection of two points in space, which may be straight or curved as well as directional, such as vertical, horizontal, or diagonal.
■ *Color.* Described by hue (the color name), value (its change from light to dark), and intensity (its brightness or chroma). The gradation of color indicates a transition from light to dark, such as from pink to rose to burgundy.
■ *Light.* Light defines and shapes forms and spaces so that people can view them. It typically distinguishes bright spots and shadows that create contrast between light and dark through natural or artificial sources.
■ *Texture.* The visual or tactile quality of natural and human-made objects, such as brick, velvet, or paint.
■ *Shape and Form.* Shape is two dimensional, such as squares, circles, and triangles. Form is three dimensional, such as cubes, spheres, and pyramids.

Reference: Kilmer, Rosemary, and W. Otie Kilmer. *Designing Interiors.* Ft. Worth and New York: Harcourt, Brace, Jovanovich and Holt, Rinehart and Winston, 1992.

PART ONE

A. PRECEDENTS

CHAPTER 1

Cultural Precedents

Some of them began to make roofs of leaves, others to dig out caves under the hills; some, imitating the nests and constructions of the swallows, made places into which they might go, out of mud and twigs. Finding the other shelters and inventing new things by their power of thought, they built in time better dwellings . . . at the beginning they put up rough spars, interwove them with twigs and finished the walls with mud.

—*The History of Architecture*, Vitruvius, c. 30 B.C.E.

Architecture is a building form developed by people based primarily on functional and aesthetic conditions. Early cultures create various types of architecture that become precursors or precedents for later developments throughout history. These types reflect a group's attitudes, influences, and changes in behavior, social structure, environment, climate, materials, construction, technology, and religion. Materials define the overall character and image. Interiors generally imitate the architectural form with an emphasis on the functional context rather than the decorative display. Furnishings during these early periods are few or nonexistent.

HISTORICAL AND SOCIAL

Human life has existed on earth for approximately 3 million years, but records document only some 7,000 years. The records of the earliest people, those without a written language, come from the efforts of geologists, anthropologists, and archeologists. They hypothesize how humans lived based on implements, cave drawings, and the remains of prehistoric sites. Conjectures about early architecture and art evolve from the study of this evidence and of present-day tribal groups in areas such as Peru, Africa, and New Guinea, where some people still live as those from the Stone Age.

Beginning as food gatherers, people travel in small bands and collect fruit, tubers, and wild grains. Eventually, they learn to hunt small animals, birds, and reptiles. Tools are generally rudimentary and man-made shelters are unknown, although these groups sometimes seek shelter in trees or caves.

About 50,000 years ago, hunters begin to follow migrating wild animal herds, an activity that dominates their lives. Because of the herd's importance to survival, hunters view animals as equal or superior to themselves. Cave paintings, such as those found in Lascaux (Fig. 1-1), are evidence of their beliefs. Some experts think that early peoples believed the paintings helped assure good hunting.

About 8000 B.C.E., there is a shift from hunting for survival to organized food production, which is completed in Europe by about 2000 B.C.E. The earliest farmers in Europe use the slash and burn method of cultivation, which requires them to move frequently as fields become exhausted.

Early villages originate along paths of migratory animals, and because of good land and reliable water sources, they thrive and expand. Sufficient food and the creation of goods allow the inhabitants to diversify, with some becoming traders and artisans. With the development of trade, villages also form along and at the crossroads of trading routes. Many of these pivotal villages become great cities. Some large settlements that are still extant today, such as Stonehenge in England, become religious centers focused on deities and their temples. Other large cities, such as Harappa in the Indus Valley in India, begin as farming villages in fertile areas.

About 5,000 years ago, nomads of the Great Steppes of Europe and Asia begin to herd cattle between the two continents. While on the move, they create objects of wood, fiber, and metal; tan leather for saddles, bridles, and tents; and weave coverings both for their own use and for trade. Early tribes live at a subsistence level. Food production is still an overriding concern, but as conditions improve and time becomes available, members of the tribe may begin to specialize in other tasks, such as weaving.

CONCEPTS

Nature provides the backdrop and the inspiration for all design considerations in early cultures, but initial concerns for survival are far more important than any aesthetic considerations. Later, however, art becomes more than mere decoration. It expresses people's belief systems, social orders, cultural imperatives, and sciences. Although beauty may be regarded differently than today, it does exist as a concept, with images and words of expression, and it is often associated with moral ideas such as goodness. These concepts often are expressed in symbols instead of words. The repetition of symbols comforts people and reminds their gods of their need for protection.

Because tribal groups live in a world controlled by spirits, much that governs daily activities has a spiritual connotation. The gods, whether arising from aspects of nature or existing in animal or human form, are human in conception. Consequently, they are thought to enjoy what human beings enjoy: food, drink, jewelry, pretty clothing, music, and dancing. Animals, the earth, and foods each have spirits that must be appeased. Gifts to the spirits often include decorations related to the hunt, housing, or food preparation.

▲ **1-1.** Hall of Bulls, Paleolithic cave painting, 15,000–10,000 B.C.E.; Lascaux, near Sarlat, France.

MOTIFS

■ *Motifs*. Many motifs (Fig. 1-2), seen as part of an object, reflect the forming process of the object. Geometric motifs often begin as weaves of varying materials or as color changes in basketry. Designs usually incorporate a variety of symbols, most of which have universal meanings. They include the circle (sun, moon, energy, eternity, magic), spiral (rain, prosperity, fertility), swastika (change of seasons, life giving or destroying), animal forms (propitiate the spirit of those killed), human figures (outstanding ancestors or important tribal members), or body parts (hand prints).

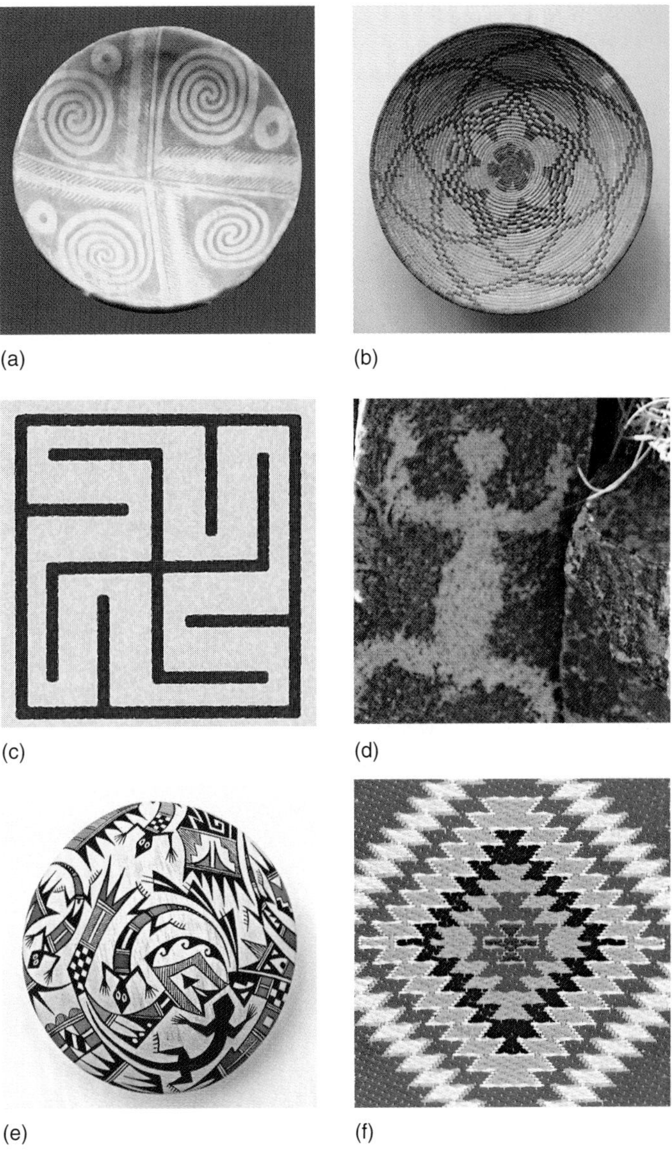

▲ **1-2.** Motifs: (a) plate with spiral; (b) North American Indian basket with spiral/wave; (c) swastika; (d) pictograph and lizard bowl with animals; (e) and (f) basket weave from Turkey.

ARCHITECTURE

Humans begin building based upon available materials and expedient construction methods, not on architectural form. Building forms develop from construction methods and available materials (Fig. 1-4, 1-5, 1-6, 1-9). The nature of the building materials and available tools impose the structure's appearance. Most shelters are rudimentary. In many cases, the physical form is less important than the relationship of the building to the home or tribal lands. People, location, climate, culture, and economy usually define the environmental considerations. In some societies, housing and shelter are more important. In others, storing and protecting foodstuffs are more critical. A building's structural envelope responds to and is shaped by these behavioral factors.

Some living environments are constructed from permanent materials such as rocks or bricks, while others use movable materials such as tree branches, grasses, and hides. Selection comes from the building site, the physical environment, and functional needs. Early tribes use naturally formed shelters such as windbreaks, rock cairns, and caves. Windbreaks, huts made of natural grasses or branches, and shelters grouped in a circle are the most common housing forms but are not suitable for all climates. Large dwellings accommodating extended families or entire villages are common in some areas (Fig. 1-9). Buildings may be grouped to face outward or inward toward a protected area or courtyard. Sun orientation is important. Because door openings often provide the main source of illumination, entries most often face the east or rising sun. This concept is evident in cultures all over the world.

▲ **1-3.** Stonehenge, c. 2600–1400 B.C.E.; Wiltshire, England.

The design image is one of simplicity, informality, irregularity, and comfort. Built spaces are small and defined by building materi-

DESIGN SPOTLIGHT

Architecture: The visual icon of the Native American Indians of North America is the teepee, although use is limited to tribes of the Great Plains. Constructed of branches and animal hides, the teepee is simple and portable, responding to the often nomadic life of Indian tribes. Parts include sapling poles, exterior cover, and sometimes an inner lining. The door flap and a hole at the top allow smoke from cooking to exit. Covers, linings, and flaps are of animal hides, so the teepee is warm in winter and cool in summer. Teepees usually are grouped together in close proximity for protection and for socializing. The land around each structure is an outside living environment and an extension of the multipurpose interior space. Conversation and dining may occur inside or outside, depending upon the climatic conditions of hot summers or cold winters. There are usually no furnishings since the inhabitants sit on the ground. Storage containers are important and include baskets and pottery jars.

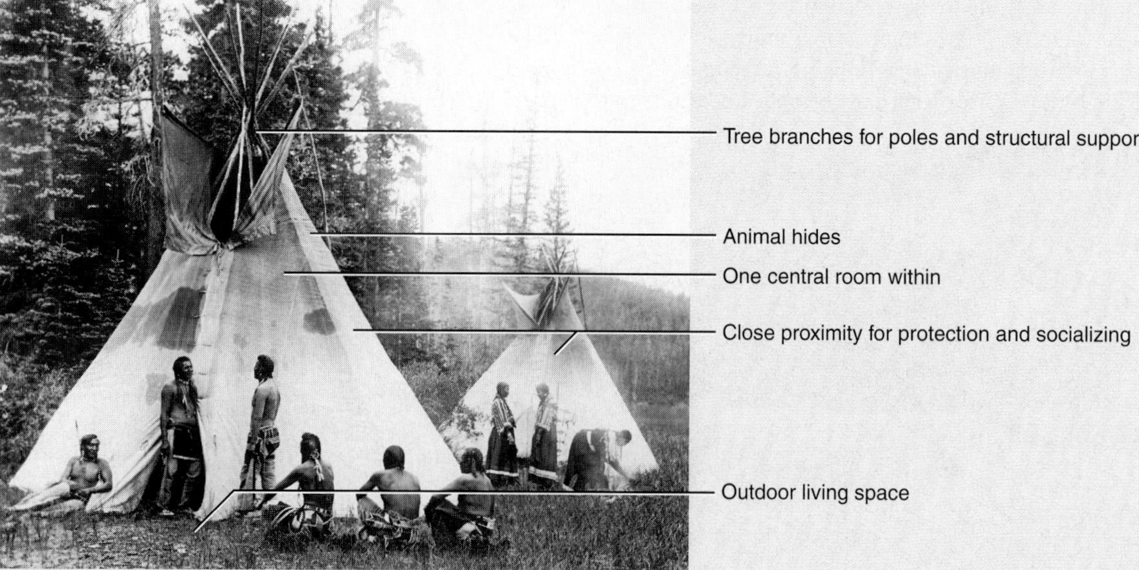

▲ **1-4.** Native American teepee.

als and human proportions. Geographic and cultural differences are apparent in architecture as well as interiors, furnishings, and decorative arts. Spiritual influences often affect the stylistic impression, with individuality shown in differing customs and beliefs.

Structural Features

■ *Interweaving Construction*. Many early structures are circular because of the flexible nature of grasses and fronds. Vegetation lends itself to an interweaving of smaller vines, twigs, or strips for coverage. Often a combination of vegetable material for structure and animal hides for enclosure is used. For example, the nomadic Plains Indians in the Americas use animal hides over long branches for their teepees (Fig. 1-4). The long poles of the teepees also provide a traverse to help move possessions as the tribe follows migrating herds.

■ *Post and Beam Construction*. The most common form of building construction is post and beam. Two vertical members such as individual posts, columns, piers, or walls support horizontal beams, as shown in the loglike basalt boulders of Stonehenge (Fig. 1-3) in England and of Machu Picchu (Fig. 1-6) in Peru. The posts may be groups of branches, logs, or walls of earth or stone. Beams are normally long branches or logs covered with smaller branches, which in turn are covered with other foliage or earth. Masonry is less common due to the limited tensile strength of the materials and the lack of tools for shaping stone.

▲ **1-5.** Traditional Nankani village; Ghana, Africa.

Public and Private Buildings

■ *Floor Plans*. Early floor plans respond to the natural environment, which imposes placement considerations for floors, walls, roofs, and openings. Plans are often round or irregular in shape depending on building materials and construction methods. Many begin small with a single central room and then gradually expand as needed. Often this expansion results in a community of small structures, with each area having a specific function: male and female quarters, food preparation areas, storage areas, or places for animals (Fig. 1-5). The rectangular plan first develops in forested countries, with the width of a rectangular plan being dependent on the length and taper of logs or branches that can span an open area. This plan evolves in size and height to provide shelter for growing families, livestock, and defense. In some climates, spatial divisions separate men and women, animals, storage, or cooking. In the United States, adobe pueblo dwellings of the Southwest become multistoried units, taking the form of early apartment houses (Fig. 1-9).

■ *Materials*. The most common building material is local vegetation including large leaves, palm fronds, and grasses. Nomadic people of the far north build homes of mammoth bones and tusks while others use snow or ice blocks for igloos. Early tribes build with stone (Fig. 1-6) or vegetation, sometimes stacking

▲ **1-6.** Machu Picchu and doorway, 15th–16th centuries; Peru.

the material in a circular fashion around the builder. Sun-dried clay or mud bricks are used extensively in countries with little timber (Fig. 1-5). In time, the discovery of firing bricks in a kiln leads to a more permanent building material.

■ *Façades*. Exteriors are simple, plain, and often unadorned except for the entryway, which may be decorated or emphasized in some way (Fig. 1-9). Informality and irregularity are common features also. In some instances, the entry to a dwelling has spiritual connotations and its compass orientation, location, or appearance may be carefully regulated (Fig. 1-7, 1-8). Generally, there are few window openings.

■ *Roofs*. Roofs (Fig. 1-5, 1-7, 1-9) may be flat, curved, slanted, or pitched at an angle. Variations depend on the building materials, construction methods, climate, and customs. Roof overhangs are important in warmer climates.

■ *Later Interpretations*. Forms and shapes of early buildings evolve over hundreds of years and gradually become more sophisticated in appearance, style, construction, and character. Later interpretations derive from the visual icons of a variety of cultures to become stage sets for 19th- and 20th-century environs such as parks, hotels (Fig. 1-10), museums, and restaurants.

▲ **1-7.** Temple at Teotihuacan, 100 B.C.E.–1525 C.E.; Central Mexico.

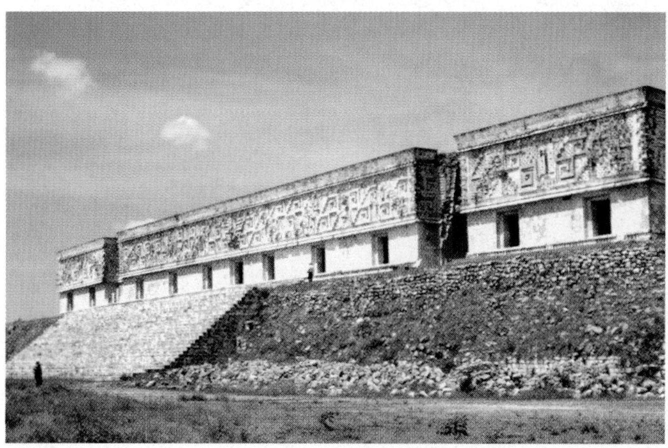

▲ **1-8.** Nunnery, Uxmal, 250–900 C.E.; Yucatan, Mexico.

▲ **1-9.** Native American pueblo houses, c. 1200 C.E.; Taos, New Mexico.

▲ **1-10.** Later Interpretation: Hotel Loretto, 1975; Santa Fe, New Mexico; Harold Stewart.

INTERIORS

Buildings typically start with one multi-purpose room that is the center of all activities (Fig. 1-11, 1-12). As tasks and functional needs increase, building forms become more sophisticated, with separate areas designated for more important activities or attendant structures assigned for specific uses, such as cooking, sleeping, storage, and entry. Public areas become separated from private ones. The organization of these spaces often reflects the social order, with separate spaces for males and females, married couples, or families. This pattern evolves to become the basic footprint of a large house, castle, or palace.

In early civilizations, interiors are simple and basic with almost all activities occurring in a common space. Each culture expresses its uniqueness in room types and designations. Items of daily use often display symbols with spiritual meanings to appease the spirits or invoke their protection and power.

▲ **1-11.** Interior of Middle Eastern Bedouin tent; Turkey.

Public and Private Buildings

■ *Color.* Construction materials provide color. Accents and applied decoration come from earth or plant materials, animal byproducts, or carbon.

■ *Floors.* Floors are most often packed earth. In hot or rainy climates, raised floors of bamboo or timbers allow cool air to pass below the living space or raise the living space above the water line. Nomadic hunting tribes may cover their floors with hides or woven rugs (Fig. 1-11, 1-12).

■ *Walls.* Walls are generally an expression of the exterior construction materials so are rarely covered or treated.

■ *Windows and Doors.* Windows are infrequent, and doors are openings left in the structure. Woven mats or hides cover both types of openings.

■ *Ceilings.* Ceilings directly convey the structural system. The space below the roof structure often is used for storage, particularly to keep food from marauding animals.

■ *Textiles.* Plaited natural grasses create mats and cover openings. Mats become textiles (Fig. 1-13) when small backstrap looms that weave narrow strips first come into being. Smaller woven pieces of cloth are stitched together to form larger pieces. Other textile techniques include appliqué, embroidery, cut-pile raffia, and leather embossing.

▲ **1-12.** Kyrgyz yurta interior of reed stems wrapped in colored wool with felt rugs on the floor, c. 1995; Kyrgyzstan; Mekenbek Osmonaliyev.

■ *Lighting.* Most people live their lives between dawn and dusk. Fires for cooking and heat provide light; animal fat is also burned for light.

(a)

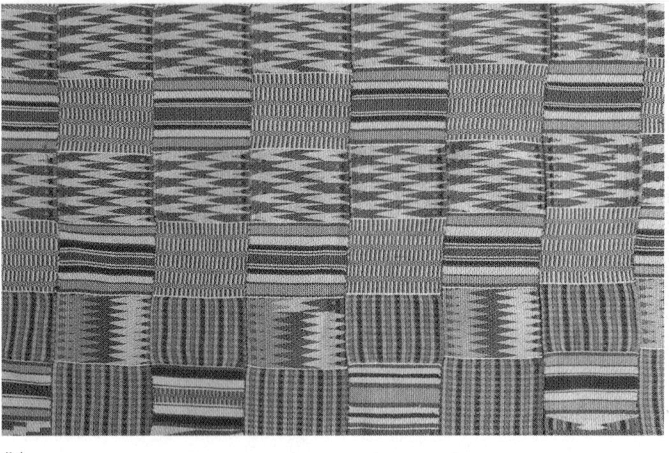

(b)

(c)

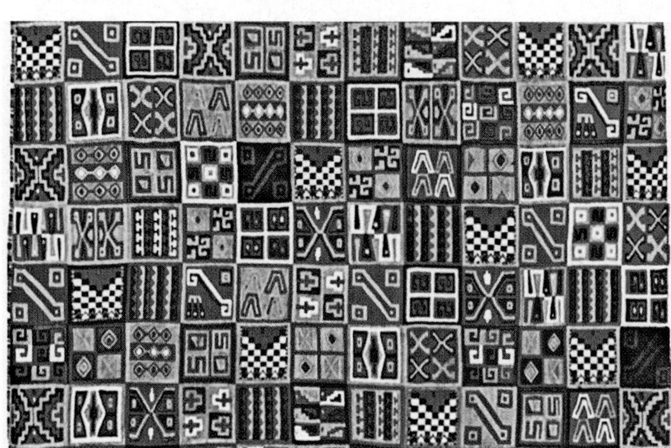

(d)

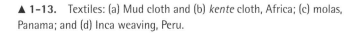

▲ **1-13.** Textiles: (a) Mud cloth and (b) *kente* cloth, Africa; (c) molas, Panama; and (d) Inca weaving, Peru.

FURNISHINGS AND DECORATIVE ARTS

Furnishings are simple but limited. Many utilitarian objects have a subtle and sophisticated sense of form, and their simplicity gives them a contemporary appearance. Design emphasis is on portability, function, and the economical use of material. As belongings increase to include clothing, jewelry, pottery, metal tools, and woven fabric, new, specialized furniture forms are necessary. Almost all furniture forms are variations of two simple forms, the platform and the box. The platform evolves into a table, stool, chair, or bed. The box becomes a chest, cupboard, or wardrobe. Specialization in crafts becomes more common in communities as time passes.

Public and Private Buildings

■ *Materials*. Common furniture materials include stone, mud, wood, grasses, bone or ivory, and to a lesser extent, metals. Wood is the most common material because of its availability and ease of working. The earliest furniture pieces develop from small branches tied together with vines or leather thongs. A larger variety of furnishings do not come into being until tools are created that allow pieces to be fitted together out of parts instead of being carved from larger trunks. Wood joinery is evident in Mesopotamia, Egypt, and China by 3000 B.C.E. Paint, carving, and applied ornament decorate furniture.

■ *Seating*. People sit in different ways because of different cultural habits, but most sit, kneel, or squat on the ground. This lower eye level, which is about 30″, affects the design of tables and stools. These objects usually have feet instead of legs.

The recognition of the tribal position of political or spiritual leaders occurs in several ways. The chief usually sits above the rest of the tribe, if only on a higher rock or a seating platform. By sitting on a raised platform the chief is symbolically supported in his decisions by the spirits of the tribe's ancestors. In many parts of the world, this platform ultimately becomes a stool (Fig. 1-14). In the absence of the chieftain, the stool itself may be the focus of veneration and may be covered with totemic figures, woven mats, or hides. When most tribal members have stools to sit on, the chief's stool acquires a back. When most chairs have backs, the chief's chair becomes a throne with a higher seat and back.

■ *Storage*. Branches and crevices in early dwellings offer places to store objects but there is little need for storage containers. The first containers are made from the hides, skins, or intestines of animals or fish hunted for food or from gourds. Much later, chests, boxes, and baskets come into use in response to needs.

■ *Beds*. Sleeping on mats of woven materials or animal hides in most instances provides some comfort (Fig. 1-11, 1-12). Raised shelves of earth, rocks, or timber are often built into dwellings. They may also protect from climatic conditions. In hot or humid climates, head or neck rests allow cooler air to circulate around the sleeper's head and protect elaborate hairstyles.

▲ **1-14.** Stool, c.1900 C.E.; Africa.

■ *Decorative Arts*. Storage containers (Fig. 1-15) are the best expression of the decorative arts. These might be made of hides or gourds or carved from wood. Many experts believe that woven baskets preceded the development of clay vessels. Clay is used to line baskets to help contain liquids. Many early pots reflect decorative patterns created by the interweaving or plaiting found in basketry as well as popular motifs.

(a)

(b)

(c)

▲ **1-15.** Decorative Arts: (a) Chalcolithic pottery, Turkey; (b) Acoma pottery, New Mexico, United States; and (c) Coloma pottery, Mexico.

B. EAST ASIA

China and Japan, the two major East Asian or Oriental cultures, both have long artistic and social histories. Each culture develops separately, yet they periodically share concepts, with China most often influencing Japan. Their arts and architecture grow out of their religious philosophies—primarily Taoism, Confucianism, and Buddhism in China and Buddhism and Shintoism in Japan. In both countries, the arts reflect a greater awareness and integration with nature than in the West. Orientation, hierarchy, placement, and structural emphasis are important. Man is generally seen in relation to nature, and buildings are carefully sited within garden settings. In China, *yin* and *yang*, the laws of the five elements, and *feng shui* guide planning and placement on both the inside and the outside of structures. In Japan, concepts of aesthetic beauty, simplicity, and *shibui* define the relationship of the exterior and interior spaces.

Both countries share common attributes related to the importance of the total environment. Harmony, unity, and careful proportional relationships articulate overall design concepts. Contrasts arising from religion and philosophy—asymmetry and symmetry, empty space and finiteness, dark and light—are significant. Respect for materials and structural honesty are constant themes. Chinese buildings emphasize strong axial relationships and hierarchy based on status. Interiors illustrate structural, applied, and/or painted decoration. Furnishings are symmetrical with elegant proportions and simple contours. Forms emphasize natural woods. Japanese buildings feature modularity in façade and plan, movable partitions supporting spatial flexibility, and natural materials. Rooms have few furnishings to allow for versatility in function. Shared motifs include lions, the phoenix, the lotus, bamboo, and geometric forms such as the diaper and fret.

The art, architecture, and designs of China and Japan have long influenced the West beginning as far back as classical Rome, diminishing in the Middle Ages, and increasing throughout the 17th, 18th, and 19th centuries as trade with Asia intensifies. Europeans use the terms *Chinoiserie* and *Japonisme* to describe what they regard as Oriental design influences, which come from their western views of Eastern Asia. In the early 21st century, cultural and artistic exchanges between the East and West continue.

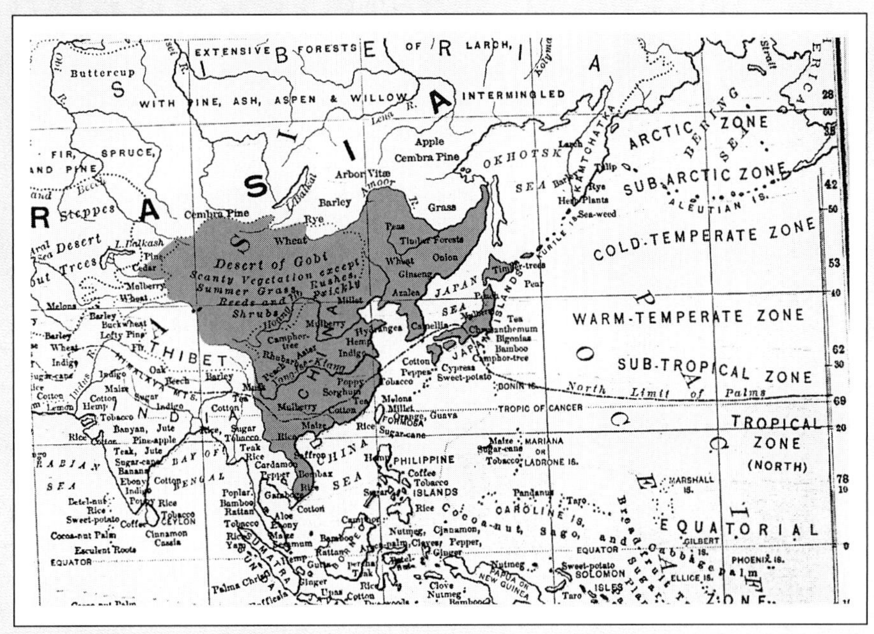

CHAPTER 2

China

Emphasis on the 12th–18th Centuries

> *The reality of the building consisted not in the four walls and the roof, but in the space within.*
>
> —Lao Tzu

China is one of the world's oldest civilizations. Forms and motifs develop early and repeat often due to the culture's respect for age and tradition. From early times, Taoism, Confucianism, and Buddhism form Chinese thought and subsequently affect its art and architecture. Separately and together, these three philosophies reflect a cultural vision that is very different from that of the West. Characteristics such as careful orientation, order, symmetry or asymmetry, and hierarchy evolve from the cultural vision. While significant in themselves, Chinese art, architecture, and culture nevertheless influence various European historical periods beginning with ancient Rome. Trade activity between Asia and Europe, and later with America, during the 17th to 19th centuries provides new and different influences affecting European and American art, architecture, interiors, furnishings, and decoration. During the late 20th century, travel, exhibits, movies, and books focused on Asia highlight the increasing interest in Chinese art, architecture, design, and health, while a booming Chinese economy supports a growing international design exchange.

HISTORICAL AND SOCIAL

Chinese history is influenced by the rise and fall of dynasties. Throughout much of this long history, emperors and their various dynasties govern an agrarian, feudal society. Trade and contacts with Europe begin during the Han dynasty (206 B.C.E.–220 C.E.). Caravan routes, established around the 1st century C.E., support trade along the "silk road," the only land route out of China. During this time, Oriental silks and lacquers arrive in Rome. Taoism and Confucianism, two seemingly opposing philosophies, develop during the period. Taoism concerns itself with the individual and his or her relationship to nature, while Confucianism focuses on ethics and groups of people. It promotes the idea that one can attain peace through correct relationships and respect for order and authority. Religions affect both philosophies.

China's first golden age occurs at the inception of the Tang dynasty (618–907 C.E.). Times are stable with economic and cultural prosperity. Emperors establish diplomatic relationships with the eastern Roman Empire, Japan, and Korea. However, civil wars end this prosperity. Buddhism, which had entered China in the 5th century B.C.E. from India, becomes the national religion during the Tang dynasty. The period of the Five Dynasties (907–1368 C.E.) ushers in a second golden age when China reestablishes trade with Europe. Venetians Marco Polo, his father, and uncle travel extensively in Asia and China in the late 1260s and 1270s. Polo's written account of his travels gives Europeans their first glimpses of China. Trade routes across Central Asia bring such Chinese innovations as gunpowder, paper, printing methods, and the compass into Europe from the 14th century onward.

During the Ming dynasty (1368–1644) in the early 17th century, the British East India Company organizes trade routes, through the port of Canton, between China, India, and England. In the late 17th century, the Dutch East India Company establishes import and export routes through Indonesia and Japan with stops in China. Soon, Chinese silks, spices, and porcelains begin flooding Europe.

During the Qing dynasty (1644–1911) in the 19th century, China and Britain clash in the Opium Wars, resulting in the loss of Hong Kong to Britain and an influx of Western influences. Later, China seeks to rid the country of foreigners during the Boxer Rebellion of the early 1900s. Also during this time, the United States and Canada bring in Chinese laborers to work on the westward expansion of the railroads, bringing a new cultural influence to North America.

Dynastic rule ends in China with the emergence of the new Republic of China (1911–1949), a period characterized by the dominance of warlords. The Cultural Revolution of 1949 brings stability, communism, and authoritative control to the country along with significant upheaval and isolation. During the late 20th century, China reopens contact with the Western world, engendering economic prosperity, design changes, new buildings, and cultural reforms. Chinese traditional ideas about health, wellness, and living spaces begin to directly affect the design of interior environments in the West. *Feng shui* is recognized and practiced by Western advocates.

CONCEPTS

Unity, harmony, and balance govern Chinese art and architecture. Forms develop early and are maintained throughout China's long history. Religious influences from Confucianism, Buddhism, Taoism, and Christianity cultivate the inner character and affect rituals, symbols, and spatial ordering. The duality of *yin* (negative, feminine, dark) and *yang* (positive, masculine, and light) guide universal life. The laws of the five elements of wood, fire, earth, metal, and water govern relationships in the natural environment. *Feng shui* (wind and water), a system of orientation, uses the earth's natural forces to balance the *yin* and *yang* to achieve harmony. All affect design components of architecture, interiors, and furnishings including relationships, spacing, color, form, and patterns.

MOTIFS

■ *Motifs*. The Chinese employ numerous motifs, many symbolic, used alone or in combinations. Common motifs (Fig. 2-1) for architecture, interiors, furnishings, and decorative arts are lions, dragons, the phoenix, fret, the lotus (purity), clouds, fruits, chrysanthemums, the *shou* (long life), and calligraphy. Others include the bat (happiness—five bats represent the Five Blessings—longevity, wealth, serenity, virtue, and an easy death), the pine or evergreen, the stork, and the tortoise (longevity). The eight Immortals are a Tao symbol. The flaming wheel, the endless knot (*ch'ang*), and state umbrella (*san*) are Buddhist emblems. Animal motifs include Lions of Buddha, the tiger, the dragon, and the phoenix. Naturalistic motifs are the lotus, peonies, chrysanthemums, and bamboo. Also evident are the meander motif and diaper patterns.

(a)

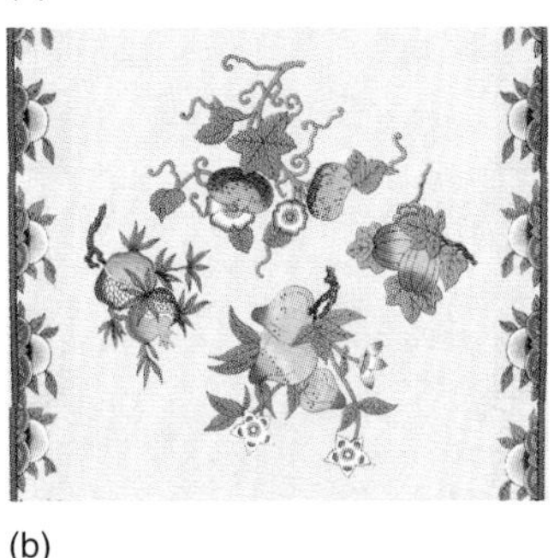

(b)

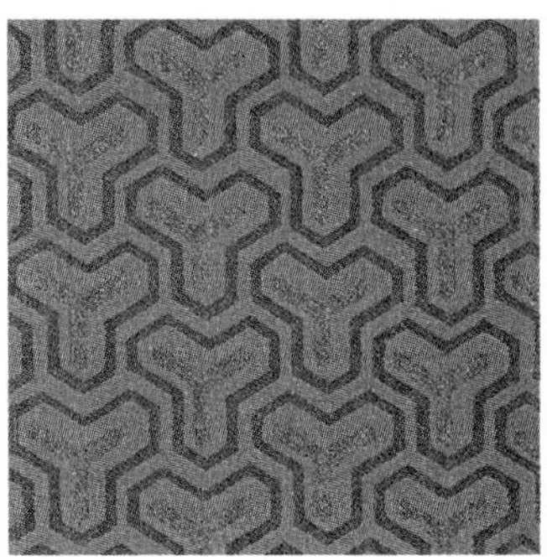

(c)

(d)

▲ **2-1.** Motifs and Architectural Details: (a) Dragons; (b) flowers; and (c, d) geometric patterns.

ARCHITECTURE

The Chinese value the site, the pattern of the building, and tradition over the building itself. Architecture, as a framework for the country's social system, is governed by ordering systems such as axiality and hierarchy. Compositions emphasize modules with definite and fixed proportional relationships. Chinese conservatism and control is evident in the repetition of forms and hierarchy in building plans. Symmetry is very important, but uneven

DESIGN SPOTLIGHT

Architecture: The Forbidden City is a walled complex of 980 public and government buildings in Beijing. During the Ming and Quing Dynasties (1344–1912), it is the Emperor's home and the ceremonial and political center for the Chinese government. Centrally located and restricted to court use, the City houses the royal residences of the emperor. The largest and most important building in this compound is the Hall of Supreme Harmony, the ceremonial center of power. Procession to the Hall is along a major north-south axis through a series of gated pavilions that lead to the Inner Court. A visual layering of pierced walls and smaller buildings accents the processional path of arrival. Behind the Hall on the same axis is the Gate of Heavenly Purity, which leads to the Palace of Heavenly Purity. The palace's name reminds citizens of the divinity and character of the emperor. The Palace houses the emperor's living quarters, and it is where he deals with matters of state. Originally constructed in 1420, the building burned several times, so the present structure dates from 1798. Built of wood and resting on a stepped marble terrace, it features a rectangular floor plan, boxy shape, nine bays with a red-columned façade, and double-tiered red-tiled roof. Ornate animals in uneven numbers related to Chinese symbolism accent the roof corners. Richly carved and painted wooden doors with latticework enhance the entry level.

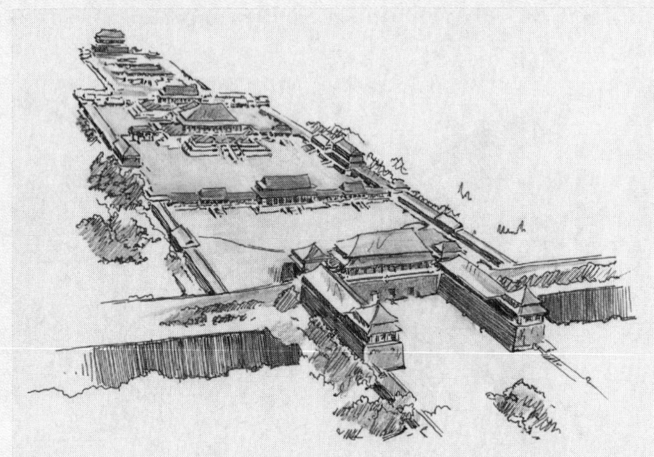

In the audience hall of the Palace of Heavenly Purity, the Emperor meets with various officials during the day. His throne and a desk area are raised on an elaborately embellished platform, which is surrounded by red columns. Above the throne are five dragons and an inscription meaning "justice and honor." Behind the throne is a richly carved five-panel wooden screen. The ceiling above is carved and accented with ornate decorative painting. The floor is composed of dark marble tiles. Gold accents signifying royalty appear throughout the space.

Entry gates, passageways, building facades, ceilings, and interiors are also richly embellished throughout other buildings in the compound. The Forbidden City became a World Heritage Site in 1987.

▲ **2-2.** Forbidden City overview, Palace of Heavenly Purity, Forbidden City passageway, and ceiling detail, and audience hall *(Qian Qing Gong)* of the Palace of Heavenly Purity, built in 1420 by emperor Yongle, rebuilt in 1798; Beijing, China.

DESIGN SPOTLIGHT

▲ **2-2.** Continued

numbering systems based on religion and nature often define roof layers, details, and spacing. Silhouettes are distinctive, but few stylistic changes appear over time. Landscapes emphasize Taoist qualities such as asymmetrical compositions, empty space, infinity, parts of elements representing the whole, and nature. This contrasts sharply with the Confucian order of symmetry, balance, finiteness, and regularity.

Traditional palace complexes (Fig. 2-2), as centers of government, continually reflect historical design features that inspire through their monumental scale and beauty. Construction, detailing, decoration, and color articulate a design language of beauty based on the principles of *feng shui*. Forms and elements grow out of construction methods and are governed by traditions that develop in the Zhou dynasty (c. 1000 B.C.E.). Characteristic buildings include *pagodas* (Fig. 2-3), shrines, temples, monasteries, mausoleums, commercial structures, and urban and rural imperial palaces and residences (Fig. 2-4).

Structural Features

■ *Construction and Decoration*. Timber-frame construction is composed of foundation, columns, and roof. A complex bracketing system creates non-load-bearing walls and adds decoration. Consequently, Chinese architecture is known for decoration that is integrated into the structure (Fig. 2-2). Bright colors often highlight the various elements. Color, form, and orientation may be symbolic. Social position and function determine the size, plan, and amount of embellishment.

Public and Private Buildings

■ *Site Orientation*. Sites and orientation are carefully chosen and planned practically and spiritually. Structures orient to the south (superiority), toward the sun, and away from the cold (evil) north from which barbarians may come. Main buildings are sited on a north–south axis with lesser structures on an east–west axis. The most important structure is the greatest distance from the entrance (Fig. 2-2). Buildings stand in isolation from one another but bridges, courtyards, gates, and other structures create a series of views and connections.

■ *Gateways*. Chinese architecture is noteworthy for its variety of gateways (Fig. 2-2). Varying in size, they serve as important focal points of entry and emphasize procession along a linear axis. Elaborate designs include geometric shapes that may be round, scalloped, rectangular, or angled.

■ *Floor Plans*. Plans are modular, consisting of rooms and courtyards, which can be added or subtracted at will. Function and respect for tradition govern the placement of individual rooms. Important public rooms such as the reception room are large, centrally located, and placed on a processional axis.

■ *Materials*. Buildings stand on foundations of earth with terraces of marble, brick, or stone (Fig. 2-2, 2-4). Wooden or stone columns rise from stone bases. Columns may be round, square, octagonal, or animal shaped. Above, a bracketing system supports the roof, which is tiled. This construction method is resistant to earthquakes and easily standardized.

■ *Façades*. Façade design varies from plain to elaborately embellished (Fig. 2-2, 2-4). Because entries are important, they usually feature decoration and color. Those on dwellings often are recessed with inscriptions to ensure happiness and protection. Windows are rectangular with wooden shutters or grilles. Doors are rectangular, made of paneled wood, and often embellished with carving, painting, and gilding.

■ *Roofs*. Upward-curving roofs are a distinguishing feature designed to deter evil spirits (Fig. 2-2). Roofs may be single or double hipped or gabled on important buildings. Ceramic roof tiles in rust, yellow, green, or blue are secured to rafters by fasteners with decorative animal motifs (*chi shou*).

■ *Later Interpretations*. Chinese influences in Western architecture are evident in styles of the 18th, 19th, and 20th centuries. Most often architects apply Chinese forms and motifs to western structures instead of designing in the Chinese manner. This begins to change in the late 19th century when some begin to exhibit a greater appreciation for Chinese architecture by directly copying architectural images for gateways and garden houses (Fig. 2-5).

▲ **2-3.** *Pagoda*, Temple of Glorious Filial Piety; Guangdong, China.

▲ **2-4.** Chinese wallpaper with house scene, Qing Dynasty (1644–1912). [Picture Desk, Inc./Kobal Collection]

▲ 2-5. Later Interpretation: Tea House at Marble House, late 19th century; Newport, Rhode Island.

INTERIORS

Chinese interiors are as carefully planned and arranged as the buildings themselves. Like exteriors, interiors reflect strong axial relationships and hierarchy based on age and status. Symmetry is important. Some rooms have large windows and doors that open to exterior courtyards and gardens. Fretwork and grilles in windows and doors provide openings that integrate interiors with the landscape. Formality and symmetry govern room shapes, the arrangement of doors and windows, and furniture placement (Fig. 2-2). Some public and important rooms are lavishly decorated. The few furnishings are of high quality.

Public and Private Buildings

■ *Color.* Colors (Fig. 2-2, 2-6, 2-12) are strong and bright because pigments are seldom combined or grayed. The palette includes red (for fire, symbolizing happiness on doors or buildings), yellow (earth), gold, green (prosperity), and blue (heaven). Walls, columns, doors, and window frames may be red. Color and gilding may highlight details and motifs. Interior color comes from applied decorations such as painting and carving.

■ *Floors.* Floors may be of dirt, wood, or masonry. Marble floors highlight important rooms in imperial palaces. Felt rugs, mats, and pile rugs may cover floors (Fig. 2-6).

■ *Rugs.* Rug weaving apparently comes late to China. The earliest surviving examples date from the end of the 17th century. Chinese rugs (Fig. 2-6) differ in colors, density of patterning, pile density, and motifs from Middle Eastern rugs. Like them, Chinese rugs may be of wool or silk and made of Persian knots with borders around an open field. But colors are brighter and clearer with much less dense patterns than Middle Eastern rugs. Motifs, which are symbolic, include flowers, buildings, and religious images. Some Chinese rugs are carved; that is, the pile around motifs is cut away to create three-dimensionality.

■ *Walls.* Walls may be plain or partially embellished. Natural wood enriches surfaces, with architecturally integrated and elaborately carved wooden grilles often defining and accenting walls, particularly in the frieze area.

▲ 2-6. Textiles: Embroidered textile and rug, late 19th–early 20th century.

■ *Ceilings.* Ceilings in important public spaces may feature repetitive geometric designs with traditional motifs (Fig. 2-2). Large beams that are elaborately carved and painted often divide ceilings into sections.

■ *Textiles.* Chinese are known for their silks, the production of which dates back 4,000 years. Traditional motifs such as clouds or the lotus are characteristic. All European silk comes from China until the 12th century, when a silk industry is established in Italy. Common fabrics exported to Europe include damasks, brocades, and embroideries.

FURNISHINGS AND DECORATIVE ARTS

Chinese furniture, like interiors, exhibits formality, regularity, symmetry, and straight lines. Furniture generally relies on simplicity, structural honesty, and refined proportions for beauty instead of applied ornament. Designs reflect boxy forms with limited diversity in visual image. Most furniture is of polished wood or bamboo, but lacquered sets are found in imperial palaces. Joinery is intricate with no nails or dowels and very little glue; mitered and mortise and tenon joints are typical. Pieces are shaped by hand instead of by turning. Most moldings are part of the furniture, not applied.

Furniture generally is against or at right angles to the wall, but is never angled. The place of honor is as far from the door as possible, facing south, and at the host's left. Armchairs are seats of honor.

As trade routes develop between China and Europe, numerous furnishings and decorative arts find their way into homes in England, France, and other countries from the 16th century onwards. Chinese influences become evident in styles of the 18th, 19th and 20th centuries. Designers adapt Chinese elements and motifs to western furniture forms, most notably in Queen Anne, Chippendale, English Regency, Art Deco, and Scandinavian designs.

DESIGN SPOTLIGHT

Furniture: Chairs are important symbols of authority and honor. Backs may be rectangular and yoked with splat, a round or horseshoe-shaped back that also forms the arms, or a fretwork back. Back splats may be pierced, carved, or painted or feature decorative panels of marble or porcelain. Trapezoidal or rectangular seats are wood, rattan, or cane and usually are higher than those of European chairs. Stretchers connect the four legs. The front stretcher often is high to raise the feet off cold, damp floors.

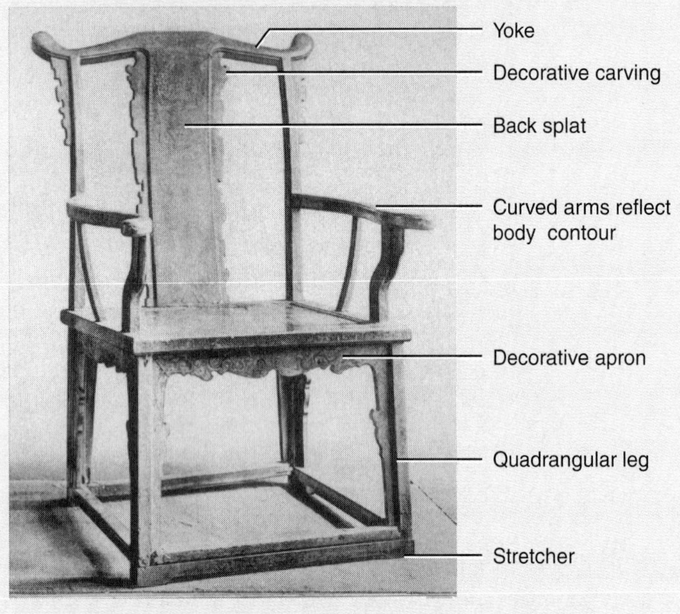

▲ **2-7.** Armchair with yoke back and solid splat, and horseshoe armchair; China.

▲ **2-8.** Side table and desk, c. late 19th century; China.

Public and Private Buildings

■ *Materials*. Most furniture is constructed of solid local hardwoods such as *tzu-t'an* (red sandalwood), *hua-li* (rosewood), chestnut, elm, or oak. Some woods, such as ebony, are imported. Several types of wood may be combined in one piece. Furniture from the south incorporates bamboo. Some pieces feature gilding or inlay. Lacquer protects against insects. Red lacquer colored with cinnabar is highly prized.

■ *Seating*. Chairs are important symbols of authority and honor (Fig. 2-7). Yokes, splats, aprons, and legs may be simple or elaborately decorated. Carving is common, and painted decoration may appear on important chairs. Stretchers hold legs together on uneven floors. Front stretchers are raised so feet are protected from cold drafts. Stools have four legs or may be cylindrical drums. Couches, also used for sleeping, are large with low backs and arms. Backs may be solid or feature fretwork. Legs may be quadrangular with soft corners, circular, elliptical, or cabriole. The hoof foot with a slight inward curve is typical. Originally, Chinese homes featured a movable or built-in platform for sitting or reclining called a *k'ang*.

■ *Tables*. Tall tables with stools support dining, writing, or form units with two chairs. Dining tables generally are square or round. Rectangular side tables (Fig. 2-8) line walls and may be used for display, writing, and painting. Some have four legs, while others have trestle bases. Stretchers, single or double, may be near the apron, which is usually shaped and/or carved.

■ *Storage*. Chests and cabinets (Fig. 2-9), small and large, store items in the Chinese house. Doors and surfaces may be plain with beautiful wood grains or elaborately decorated. Metal hardware, an important and integral part of the design, may be round, square, or bat shaped.

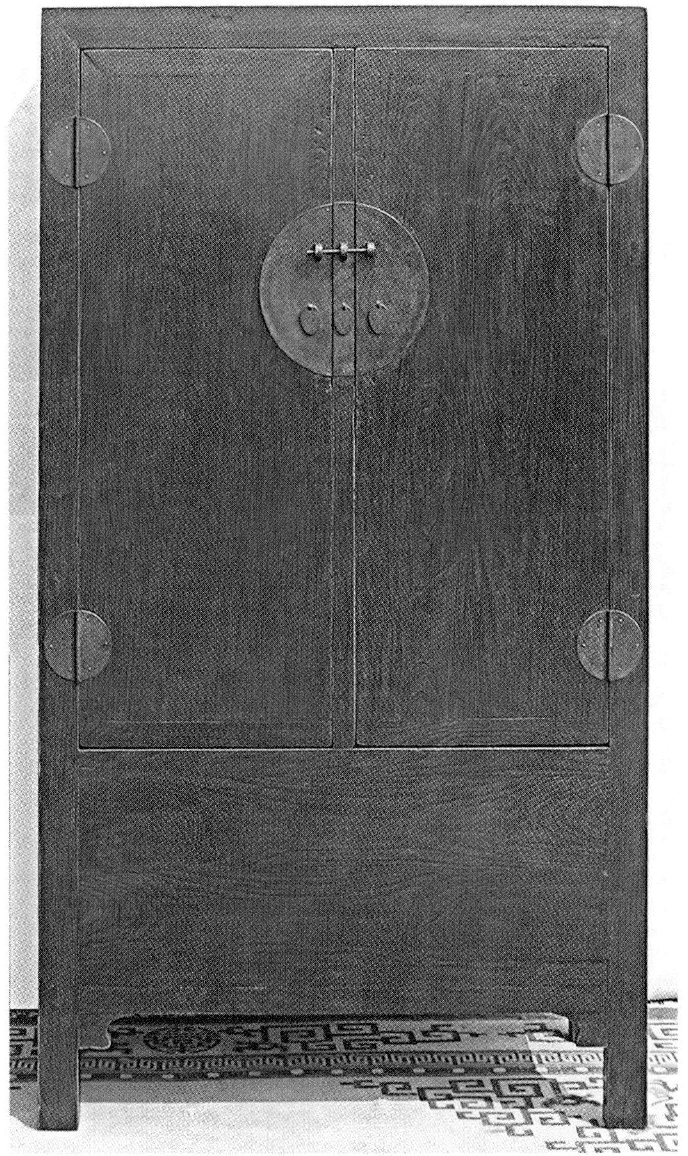

▲ **2-9.** Cabinet with brass hardware, c. late 19th century, and *Shandong* cabinet, c. early 20th century; China.

▲ **2-10.** Carved canopy bed, c. early 20th century; China.

■ *Beds*. Similar to a *k'ang* and lower than a chair seat, the movable canopy bed (Fig. 2-10) is rectangular, has low railings, features four or six posts, and is embellished with carving, latticework, fretwork, and draperies. People sit or recline in beds during the day. The short legs often terminate in hoof feet. Footstools are usually placed in front of the bed.

■ *Screens*. Interiors commonly feature screens, folding or set in a frame. They are lacquered or painted in bright colors with symbols of health and happiness. Coromandel, a polychrome lacquer with inlays of mother-of-pearl and other materials, is the best known (Fig. 2-11).

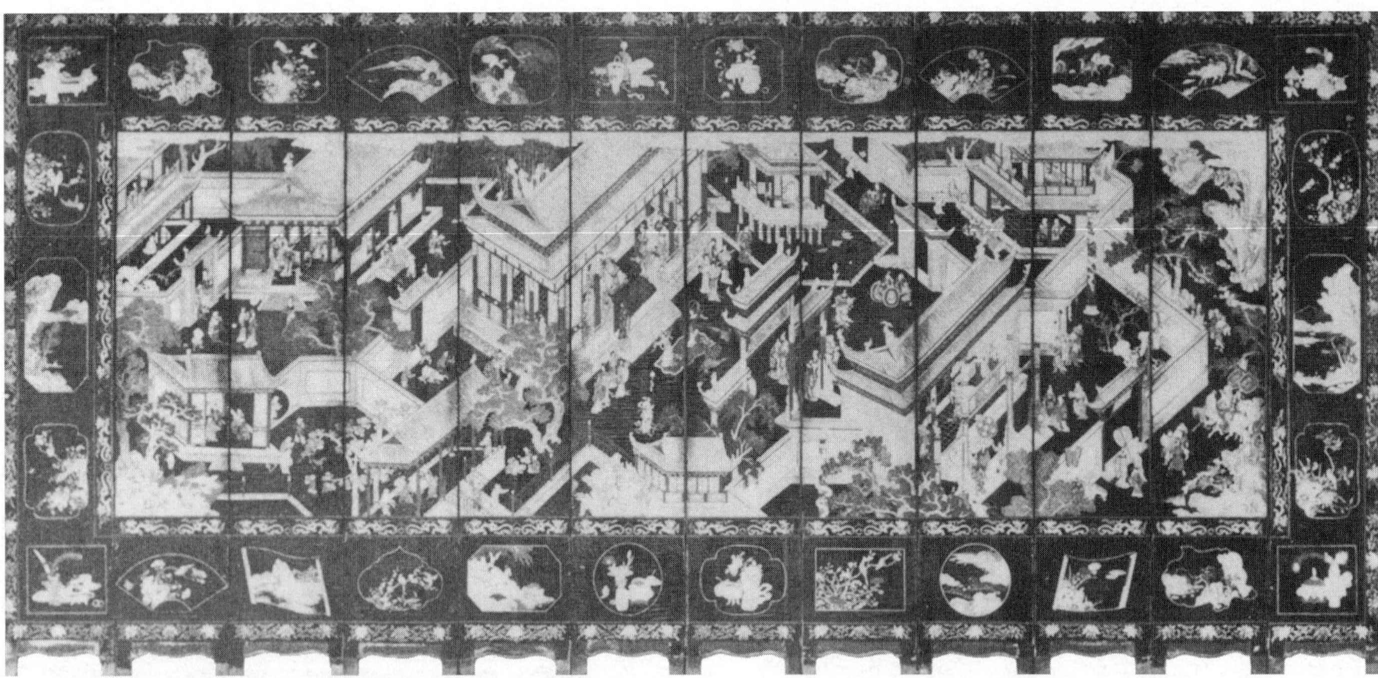

▲ **2-11.** Coromandel screen, c. 1690, and detail from a Coromandel screen.

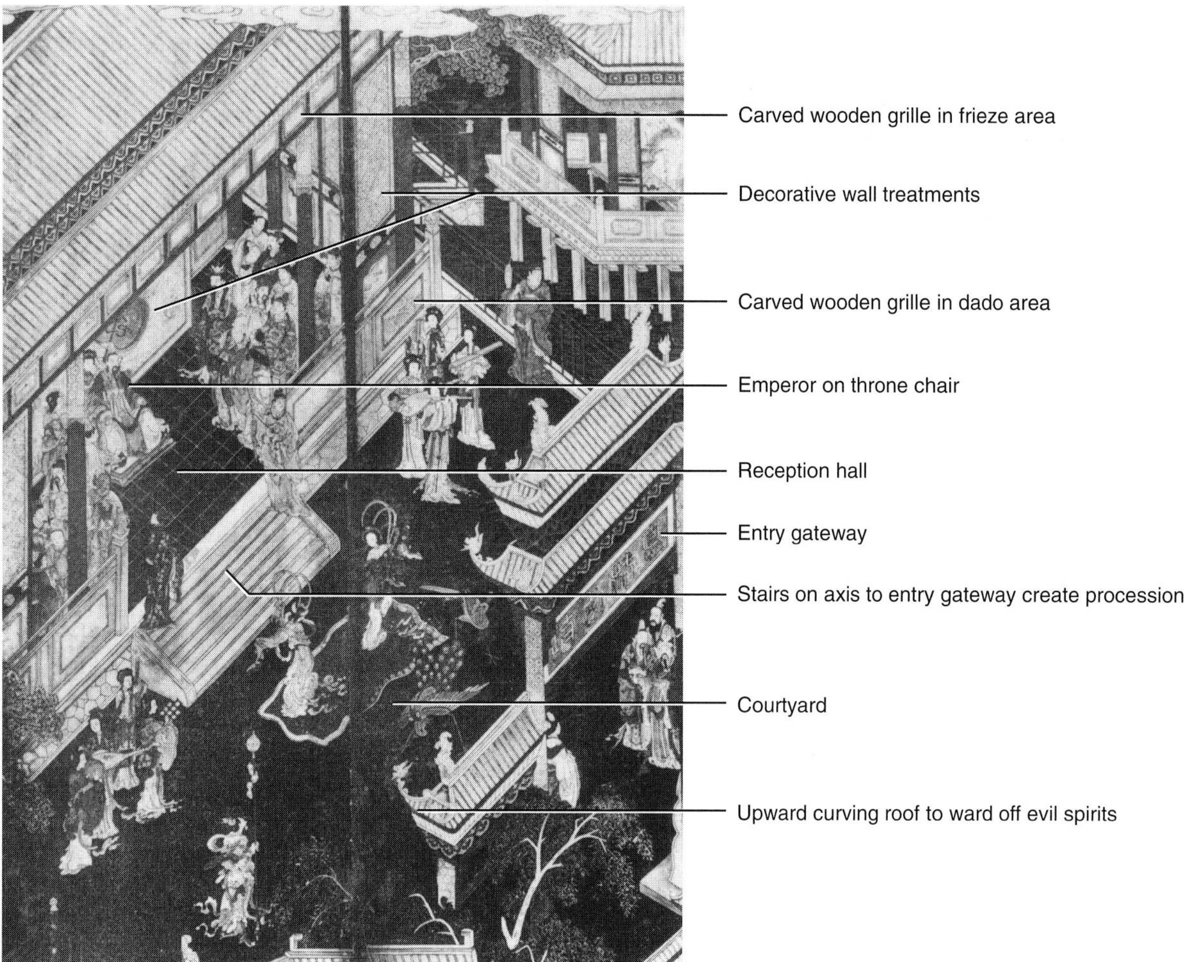

▲ **2-11.** Continued

■ *Porcelain*. Porcelain (Fig. 2-12) originates in China during the T'ang dynasty. A search for a pure white body produces true porcelain, which contains *kaolin* (china clay) and *pai-tun-tzu* (china stone). The subsequent Sung period produces many pieces of excellent design decorated with monochrome glazes, such as *celadon* (the color varies from delicate green to gray-blue). Ming period blue and white is the best known of Chinese porcelains. Reaching Europe in the 15th century, Chinese porcelains cause a sensation, particularly among the wealthy, who display them proudly. The Chinese quickly begin marketing porcelains for the Western market, known as Chinese Export Porcelain.

▲ **2-12.** Decorative Arts: Blue and white vase, 19th century, and celadon charger, Ming Dynasty (1368–1644).

CHAPTER 3

Japan

> *A west room of the main southeast hall was made ready to receive her. New curtains were hung and new screens set out, as were forty cushions, more comfortable and less ostentatious, thought Genji, than ceremonial chairs. In spite of the informality, the details were magnificent. Wardrobes were laid out upon four cupboards inlaid with mother-of-pearl, and there was a fine though modest array of summer and winter robes, incense jars, medicine and comb boxes, inkstones, vanity sets, and other festive paraphernalia.*
>
> —Lady Muraski, *The Tale of the Genji*, c. 1020

Influenced by China and evolving largely in isolation, Japan is a 2,000-year-old civilization that epitomizes the concepts of aesthetic beauty, simplicity, modularity, and attention to detail. Various religions shape activities of daily life and establish rituals that define design character, which also emphasizes relationships to nature. Within the confines of a strict society governed by hierarchy and tradition and ruled by emperors and warlords, the culture nourishes artists, designers, and scholars. Trade with Asian countries and later with the West provides numerous venues for the receipt and distribution of design influences. Elements of Japanese architecture, interiors, furnishings, and decorative arts, like those of China, are widely imitated in Western countries after the establishment of trade routes in the 17th century and continuing through the 18th, 19th, 20th, and early 21st centuries.

HISTORICAL AND SOCIAL

From prehistoric times, Japanese cultural and building traditions evolve largely independent of outside influences. However, in 552 C.E., with the introduction of Buddhism from China via Korea, a cultural transformation occurs. From China, the Japanese incorporate a centralized government, a form of writing, and Buddhism, which is the national religion by the end of the period. During the next century, Buddhism expands and peacefully coexists with the native Japanese religion, Shinto. During the 7th and 8th centuries, Chinese and Korean artists immigrate to Japan and bring with them Chinese concepts of art, city planning, and court protocol.

In the capital of Kyoto, throughout the 9th century, wealthy families surrounding the imperial court form a highly refined court culture in which good taste, manners, and carefully controlled emotions are supremely important. Art, architecture, poetry, and prose become more nationalistic as artists and writers choose and assimilate those Chinese influences that best suit their own culture. Feudalism develops around large estates of the *daimyo* (lord) who controls his domain with the help of his *samurai* (warriors).

Throughout the ensuing Kamakura period (1185–1392), *shoguns* (military dictators) from powerful families rule, maintaining political and military authority. Feudalism increases in strength, and individual ownership of land disappears. Restored contacts with China bring new architectural styles, tea drinking, and Zen Buddhism. Zen rapidly grows in popularity and becomes the dominant Buddhist sect. Warriors find its emphasis on self-reliance, simplicity, and attaining enlightenment through everyday activities, such as archery or the tea ceremony, appealing. Eventually, Zen concepts affect all aspects of Japanese life including the arts.

In the Muromachi period (1392–1568), Chinese influence brings another cultural renaissance as court nobles again become great art patrons. Traders from Spain and Holland as well as Christian missionaries arrive. In the mid-16th century, the Japanese begin exporting goods to the West, and a period of economic growth ensues. The *cha-no-yu* (formal tea ceremony) becomes a social institution. Its equalizing rituals unite host and guest in the common pleasure of conversations about everyday things, and it takes place in a specially designed tea house. The tea house's characteristic simplicity, textural contrasts, and integration with nature affect the design of dwellings.

From 1568 to 1603, civil wars devastate the country in part because the court is more interested in art and the Zen philosophy than in government. In 1603, peace comes, but at the cost of an increasingly repressive government and isolation from the world. Neo-Confucianism, which demands loyalty to the State, begins to replace Zen Buddhism as the state religion. The Edo period (1603–1868) is a golden era for the arts, and the middle class gains affluence. However, in 1635, the government fears that the influx of European traders and numerous Japanese converts to Christianity may precipitate an invasion. This leads to a prohibition of travel abroad and expulsion of many foreigners.

Throughout the 18th century, the powerful merchant class, continued peasant unrest, and an increasing awareness of the Western world contribute to the demise of feudalism in 1871. In the early 19th century, more and more traders and explorers visit Japan. In 1854, after a show of force, U.S. commodore Matthew Perry signs a treaty that permits trade between the United States and Japan, and Japan establishes trade relations and embassies in various European cities. New policies modeled after Western ones encourage industry and trade.

CONCEPTS

Through periods of isolation and contact, the Japanese acquire and assimilate outside characteristics that suit their own cultural preferences. As in China, ideas of unity, harmony, and balance govern Japanese art and architecture. *Shibui*, the highest aesthetic level of traditional Japanese design, is expressed through simplicity, implicitness or inner meaning, humility, silence, and the use of natural materials. These characteristics shape all visual arrangements and daily activities. Because an individual's relationship to nature is important, the Japanese view the physical division between nature and the man-made differently than do Westerners. In Japan, for example, houses usually open directly onto gardens so the division of space is seamless, and elements of nature appear throughout the interiors.

MOTIFS

■ *Motifs*. Naturalistic, geometric, and figurative motifs (Fig. 3-1, 3-2) embellish surface designs. Those derived from nature include flowers such as the cherry blossom, the iris, the chrysanthemum, and wisteria along with bamboo leaves, birds, waves, and whirlpool designs. Geometric designs are stripes, grids, swirls, latticework, and frets. Figurative motifs show men and women in traditional dress. The family crest, a highly stylized design appearing in art and on clothing, often develops within a circular form that may also evolve into a decorative repeat pattern.

▲ **3-1.** Motifs: *Katagami* (textile stencil patterns) illustrating fan, flower, and botanical motifs and lacquer box with landscape, 19th century.

◀ **3-2.** Architectural Detail: Walls, Kara-mon Gate, Temple Complex; Nikko, Japan.

ARCHITECTURE

Public and private buildings appear as works of art in beautiful, natural environments. Like Chinese models, architecture is governed by ordering systems such as axiality and hierarchy. Unlike the Chinese, the Japanese place greater emphasis on asymmetry than on symmetry. The asymmetric balance between right and left creates a dynamic and appealing sense of beauty. This appreciation appears in the way a building rambles as well as in roof layers, details, spacing, and overall image. Fixed proportional relationships define architecture, and contrasts dominate: simple versus ornate, traditional in relation to new, logical as opposed to contradictory.

As distinctive expressions of the country, traditional building forms vary little over time. Public complexes often are monumental in scale to impress, but may be composed of many separate buildings that individually offer personal intimacy. Construction, detailing, decoration, and color reflect the various religions and the importance of nature.

Public buildings include shrines (Fig. 3-3), temples (Fig. 3-4), pagodas, and shops. Typical domestic building types include noble residences, palaces (Fig. 3-6) or castles, townhouses, *besso* (country houses), and farmhouses. Because of the possibilities of earthquakes and fire, houses are constructed so they are easy to rebuild. Townhouses, which often include areas for shops, are generally smaller than country houses because there is less land available in the city. During the 8th through 12th centuries C.E., the appearance of rambling country houses marks Japan's first major indigenous expression of architecture.

Most dwelling complexes are situated within a landscaped garden on the edge of a pool. Gardens, which are intended for meditation and seclusion, combine natural and man-made elements and mix broad vistas with small views that surprise and delight. Unlike the Western custom, Japanese people view their gardens from verandahs as well as walking through them. Small stones comprise the paths, requiring the viewer to continually look down and consciously stop to examine the landscape, features, and buildings. Zen gardens feature rectangular forms, raked gravel grounds, and a few asymmetrically placed rocks representing natural features.

▲ **3-3.** Itsukushima Shinto Shrine, 1241–1571; Miyajima, Japan.

▲ **3-4.** Replica, Byodo-in temple from Heian period, c. 1053; original in Kyoto, Japan; Oahu, Hawaii.

▲ **3-5.** Golden Pavilion of Yoshimitsu, Kinkaku-ji, 1394–1427; Kyoto, Japan.

Structural Features

■ *Timber Construction*. Timber construction is used exclusively beginning in the 5th century C.E. Like the Chinese construction, it is composed of foundation, timber columns, and most important, the roof. After the roof is completed, the division of spaces begins within the structure. Since there are few fixed walls, movable partitions divide spaces, allowing the interior volumes and the relationship between interior and exterior to be modified easily. The openness of plan also accommodates the need for cross ventilation in the hot, humid Japanese summers. While the Chinese are known for decoration integrated into the structure, the Japanese are known for the beauty of their construction methods and joinery and their use of natural materials.

Public and Private Buildings

■ *Shrines*. The Shinto religion requires shrines (dwellings for gods) more than temples, unlike Buddhism. The shrine complex is located on a sacred site isolated by forests, mountains, and/or water. The *torii* (main entrance) gate, formed by two columns topped by two horizontal beams, introduces the complex. Constructed of wood that is often left unpainted, shrines (Fig. 3-3) are composed of a floor raised by columns, thatched or wooden gable roofs, and one or two interior spaces. Human scale and simplicity are characteristic. Although traditional form is important, shrines eventually become more formal and often attached to Buddhist complexes.

■ *Temples*. Following Chinese models, Buddhist temple complexes (Fig. 3-4) use a layering technique with entrance from a main south-facing gate that leads to the *chumon* (middle gate), which connects to a *kairo* (roofed corridor) that surrounds the sacred area. Common structures within the complex are a pagoda, a *kondo* (image hall), a *kodo* (lecture hall), quarters for priests, and storage areas. Covered walkways connect the main building to

DESIGN SPOTLIGHT

Architecture: Sitting within a carefully planned landscaped garden, the rambling Katsura Imperial Villa and tea house were constructed during the reigns of the imperial Hachijo-no-miya family and Prince Toshitada. Emphasizing Japanese principles of beauty, they exhibit a peaceful harmony between buildings and environment. The main villa was built in three connected stages: the old shoin, middle shoin, and new palace, reflecting a change from the Shoin style of the late middle ages to the Sukiya style of the early Edo period. The buildings have repeating geometric modules of natural wood on the exterior contrasted with the infills of white plaster. Verandahs and platforms, often used for moon-viewing, connect the outside garden areas with the inside spaces. A modular plan based on the *Ken* controls the order of the villa. Spaces interconnect and flow informally into one another in a zigzag pattern. *Shoji* and *fusuma* screens partition the spaces and support fluid movement. Furnishings are limited primarily to *zabutons*, small tables, and *tansus*. [World Heritage Site]

▲ **3-6.** Katsura Detached Palace (also known as Katsura Imperial Villa) with Shokin-Tei Pavilion (tea house) and Rooms of Hearth and Spear, c. 1615–1663; Kyoto, Japan; Rooms of Hearth and Spear by Kobori Enshu.

smaller pavilions. Early examples organize axially and symmetrically, but with off-center gates as in China. Later temple complexes maintain axiality, but position structures asymmetrically within the grounds. Japanese complexes integrate more fully with the landscape than Chinese examples.

■ *Dwellings*. Houses are generally one or two stories with the important rooms in the rear facing the garden. The *besso* or dwelling develops from a series of connecting rectangles that ramble to create asymmetry and informality, therefore appearing less formal and austere than palaces. Most townhouses are close to the street and have a formal entry that often becomes an area for conducting business. Townhouses usually are compact or narrow to take maximum advantage of limited space. Because of crowded conditions, they focus centrally on small gardens on one or more sides. The most private rooms face the garden. Castles may be composed of a large complex of wooden buildings, usually covered with plaster, grouped around a keep or *tenshu* (main structure) or multistoried complexes of stone with high, battered protection walls surrounding the castle complex.

■ *Floor Plans*. Early temple plans have a large central space flanked or surrounded by smaller spaces or aisles. Eventually, the need for space for worshippers dictates the addition of another space in front of the central space.

Beginning in the 12th century, house plans are usually modular based on the *Ken*, a system derived from the arrangement of structural pillars and *tatami* mats (Fig. 3-7, 3-9, 3-11). The mats are modules approximately 3′-0″ wide by 6′-0″ long and 2″ or 3″ thick with a woven rush cover and a rice straw core, and are bounded by black cloth. They are positioned parallel and perpendicular to one another in various configurations. Room dimensions derive from the arrangement of the *tatami* mats, with important rooms increasing in size accordingly and rooms labeled as to the number of mats they contain. The mats rest on the structural framework of the building and are easily removed for recovering. Spaces are fluid, interlocking, and flow one into another in a casual, informal manner with no major room defined by a specific function.

DESIGN SPOTLIGHT

▲ **3-6.** Continued

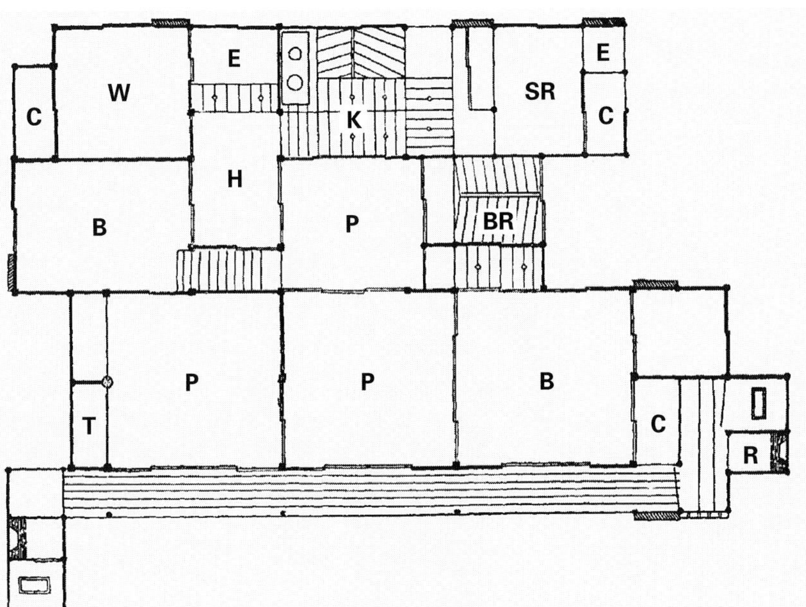

B — Bedroom
BR— Bathroom
C — Closet
E — Entry
H — Hall
K — Kitchen
P — Parlor
R — Restroom
SR— Servant's room
T — Tokonoma
W — Waiting room

▲ **3-7.** Floor plan, house, c. 1880; Tokyo, Japan.

■ *Materials*. As there are numerous forests in Japan, wooden posts and beams compose the structural framework (Fig. 3-4, 3-6). Cedar, pine, fir, and cypress are common building woods. This variety produces a deep appreciation for the diversity in wood color, luster, texture, and fragrance. Non-load-bearing walls are of plaster, wood panels, or lightweight sliding partitions. Pillar bases, foundation platforms, and fortification walls are of stone, which is less readily available for construction. Stone buildings emphasizing defensibility are common during the turbulent 16th and 17th centuries.

■ *Façades*. Façades of both public and private buildings are generally plain and unembellished and characterized by repeating modules (Fig. 3-6) composed of dark wooden frames with light rectangular center spaces. These modules surround the perimeter. Solids juxtapose with voids, light areas with dark ones, and large rectangles adjoin small ones, creating a quiet rhythm and harmony. Exterior surfaces are either of natural wood, painted black wood, or natural wood with sections of plaster infill. Large repetitively spaced columns support the verandahs (Fig. 3-5) that surround the building. In traditional architecture, the *shin-kabe* or plaster wall with exposed structure is typical. On some buildings, the wall area under the eaves has painted decoration in bright colors, such as red, blue, or yellow. Entries are important and usually feature some type of emphasis through placement, design, materials, or color.

City houses are entered through gates on the side or corner, while those for castles are larger, more important, and placed prominently on the center axis. Walls usually surround the landscaped area of large complexes and castles to ensure privacy and protection. Castle façades have small slits and/or battlements from which to shoot.

■ *Windows and Doors*. *Shoji* screens (Fig. 3-8, 3-11) serve as both windows and doors on many Japanese buildings. They shield the outer portions of a building during poor weather, establish a visual rhythm, help integrate inside and outside, and subdivide the interior spaces. Each lightweight panel is approximately 3′-0″ wide by 6′-0″ high and consists of a wooden lattice grid traditionally covered with rice paper. When open, the *shoji* frames a natural garden setting that serves as a landscaped mural. Solid sliding screens and wooden doors with latticework, carved decoration, or covered decorative painting are also common. Wooden doors are the gates separating the public and private worlds. Most doors are sliding panels 6′-0″ high. Exterior ones generally are *shoji*, as their paper coverings admit light. *Tatami* mats determine door widths.

■ *Roofs*. Roofs (Fig. 3-4, 3-5, 3-6) are low and gabled, or single or double hipped with wide, upturned overhangs to protect walls from rain. On residences, roof overhangs create verandahs that become transitional spaces between the outside and inside directions. Surfaces are either shingled or tiled. As in China, a complex bracket system usually supports the roof and provides ornament. Parts may be highlighted with color. In traditional architecture, *kokera-buki* construction usually has a *shibi* accenting each end of the roof ridge. The pagoda roof stacks in many layers with a *hosho* crown.

■ *Later Interpretations*. From the late 19th century onwards, elements of Japanese influence are shown in spatial organization, exterior design, human scale, standardization, respect for materials, and/or integration of outside and inside. These characteristics appear in the work of the Arts and Crafts Movement designers, Frank Lloyd Wright (Fig. 3-10), Le Corbusier, Mies van der Rohe, and numerous contemporary designers.

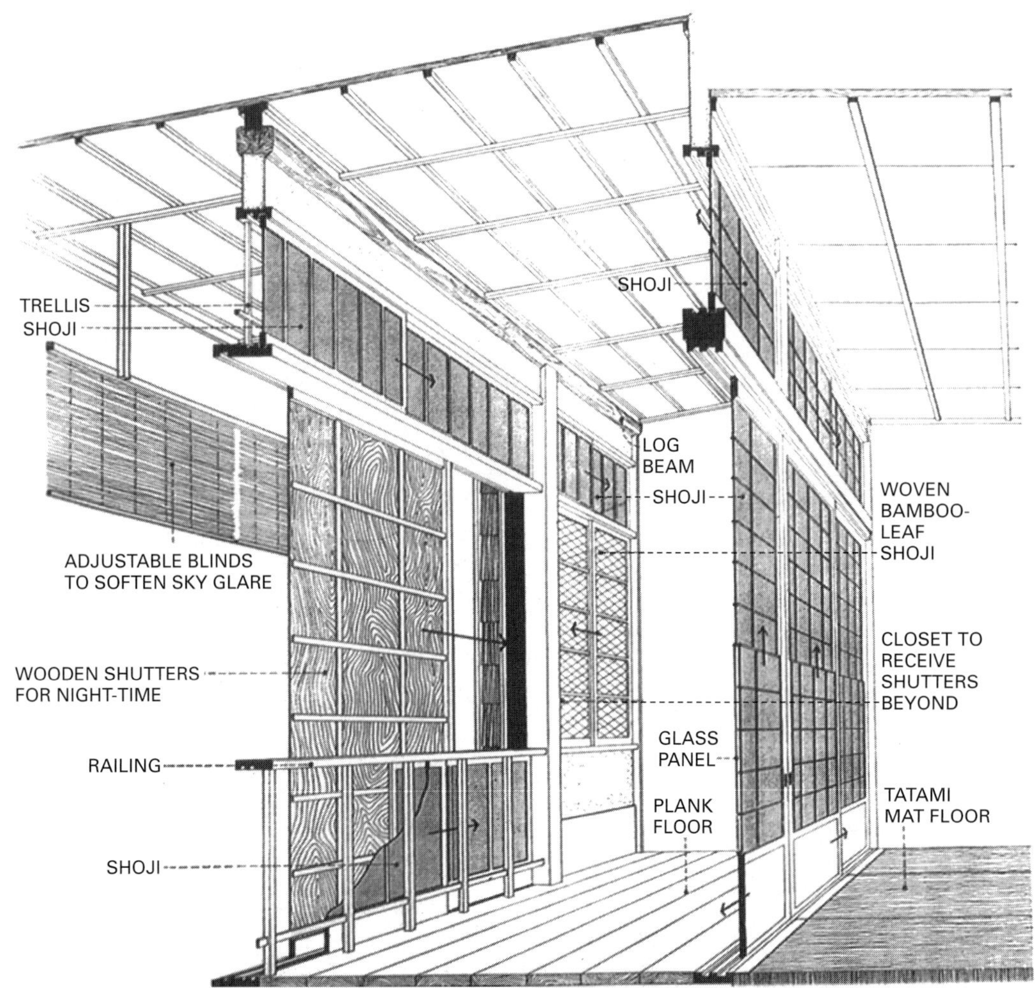

▲ **3-8.** Wall detail showing shutters, verandah, and sliding screens.

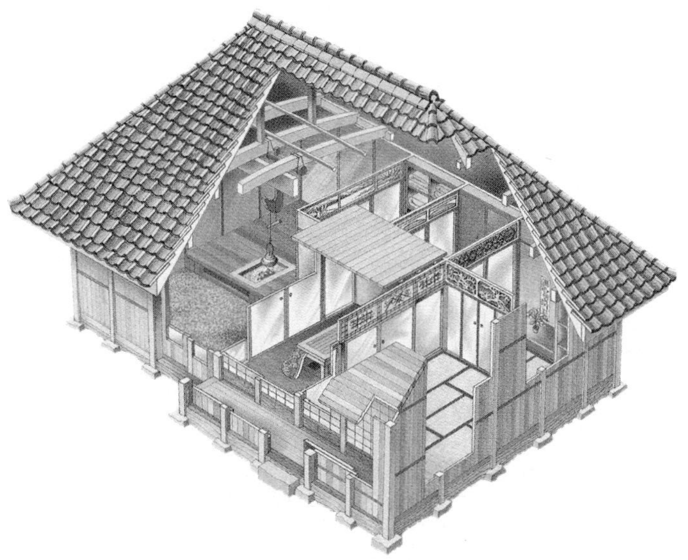

▲ **3-9.** Construction drawing, Japanese house and interior illustrating *shoji* screens, *fusuma*, and *tatami* mats.

▲ **3-10.** Later Interpretation: Robie House, 1909–1910; Chicago, Illinois; Frank Lloyd Wright; Prairie style.

INTERIORS

Defined by exposed structure, Japanese interiors express beauty, harmony, flexibility, and serenity. Economy of line, colors from nature, textural harmony with diversity, meticulous detailing, uncluttered space, and modularity are trademarks. A strong ordering system based on the positioning of *tatami* mats defines spaces. Interior walls reflect exterior design features and structural divisions. A variety of screening devices subdivide interior spaces and support spatial flexibility by enlarging the size of a room or rooms in succession or by closing off one or more rooms. *Fusumas* and *shoji* are the most common. Interior ceilings are low, as a reflection of the overall building module, the Japanese stature, and the fact that people sit on the floor rather than on chairs. Backgrounds generally are neutral with decorative objects providing color and pattern contrasts.

Interiors (Fig. 3-9, 3-11) feature the same strong geometry, respect for materials, contrasts, and harmony as exteriors. Sliding partitions open spaces to the outside (Fig. 3-11, 3-12), unlike in the West, creating little need for solid doors and/or windows. Exterior–interior relationships and harmony with the landscape create a total environment. Unlike in the West, domestic and some temple interiors are multipurpose so size, shape, and use change as needed. In residences, the formal entry serves as a separating point between the outer (unclean) world and the (clean) privacy of the home. Here, the outside life is left behind as people remove their shoes, store them, and put on slippers. Living areas generally face to the south or southeast to take advantage of the light, but may move to a darker and cooler side during summer months. The main reception space in a noble dwelling may have a raised area for emphasis and to support the noble's authority.

▲ **3-11.** Interior with *tatami* mats, table, *tokonoma*, and *shoji* screens; Kyoto, Japan.

Public and Private Buildings

■ *Materials*. Untreated natural materials, including plaster, straw, linen, wool, paper, and natural wood, are common.

■ *Color*. Colors reflect nature and harmonize with the structure. The palette contains primarily white, brown, black, straw, and gray (Fig. 3-6, 3-9, 3-11). Other interior colors, which may be bright, mainly come from the display of decorative arts.

■ *Floors*. Raised floors covered with *tatami* mats (Fig. 3-11, 3-12) are common in all areas except service spaces. Wood planks cover floors in corridors, verandahs, and lavatories. Earthen floors are typical in service areas. Temples have wooden floors instead of earthen ones.

■ *Walls*. Walls (Fig. 3-8), often composed of sliding solid partitions and paper-covered screens, may be plain or decorated. *Fusumas* partition the spaces and support movement and interchangeability in function (Fig. 3-11, 3-12). Folding screens may also temporarily divide space. Within formal or reception rooms in the Japanese house, the architectonic *tokonoma* or *tana* integrates with the wall composition and showcases changing arrangements of special items related to the various room functions. A transom area above the sliding panel features a *ramma* (Fig. 3-12), often perforated or elaborately carved for air flow and light filtration.

■ *Windows and Doors*. *Fusumas* and *shoji* become doors and/or windows (Fig. 3-11, 3-12). Other screening devices separating the outside from the inside include woven bamboo blinds, reed screens, wooden grilles, and *norens* (split curtains). These flat hanging cloth or hemp curtains can also act as shades blocking undesirable views.

■ *Ceilings*. Ceilings of traditional buildings (Fig. 3-11, 3-12) may vary in height to articulate and define spaces. They may be coved, coffered, or latticed, and may possess elaborate truss and bracketing systems. In temples, a false lower ceiling for decoration hides irregularities in the spacing of rafters. In residences, low ceilings are common, primarily because of the custom of sitting on the floor.

■ *Textiles*. Woven and dyed textiles are important sources of color and pattern in interiors. They may cover screens, hang at doors, or embellish seating. Designs are asymmetrical. Japanese woven silk differs from Chinese in its geometric motifs, such as zigzags or diapers. One of the most popular dyed textiles, *katagami* (Fig. 3-1) comes from elaborately cut paper stencils. Appearing in Japanese wood-block prints, it obtains its characteristic deep blue color from indigo dyes.

■ *Lighting*. Natural light filters softly through the translucent paper of *shoji*, adding to the feeling of serenity. Inside, lamps, usually on stands, and metal candlesticks provide artificial light. Lanterns are an important aspect of most gardens (Fig. 3-13). Those of stone are popular as well as the *chochin*, a portable spiral of thin bamboo covered by a layer of rice paper that folds flat when not in use.

DESIGN SPOTLIGHT

Interiors: This wood-block print illustrates the Shoin style of architecture, which arose in the 15th century from elements taken from Zen Buddhist religious dwellings and tea houses. Also ordered by *tatami* mats, the interiors reflect the relationship of inside to outside, sitting at floor level, the limited use of furnishings, and an architectonic character. *Shoji*, *fusuma*, and *tsuitate* screens define the spaces. The transom area features a perforated *ramma* to support air flow and light filtration. Furnishings include small tables, *zabutons*, metal candlesticks, and decorative accessories.

▲ **3-12.** Interior, *Moromasa, a House of Pleasure 18th century,* Yoshiwara. Frederick C. Hewitt Fund, 1911. (JP655). [The Metropolitan Museum of Art, New York, NY, U.S.A. Image © The Metropolitan Musuem of Art/Art Resource, NY]

▲ **3-13.** Lighting: Lanterns with curves and filigree decoration; Japan.

FURNISHINGS AND DECORATIVE ARTS

Japanese interiors feature little freestanding furniture and several carefully selected decorative accessories. People sit on their knees on *zabutons*, and often the focus of a group seating arrangement will be the *hibachi* or charcoal heater. Furnishings are often built in, and individual pieces are usually parallel to the walls. In contrast to the simplicity, strong geometry, and neutral colors of exteriors and interiors, some furnishings may have gilding or colored floral motifs. Brighter hues of red, pink, gold, green, blue, brown, white, and black in decorative arts enhance the overall color effect. The Japanese, who prefer simplicity to abundance, do not display their entire collections at once, preferring to show one or two objects at a time.

Public and Private Buildings

■ *Materials*. Oak and chestnut are common furniture woods. Lacquer-work is common and usually has a black or red background and may have floral motifs in gold. Lacquer usually covers small objects, such as writing boxes (Fig. 3-1) and accessories associated with the tea ceremony.

■ *Seating*. Because the Japanese sit on the floor, there are few chairs or stools. Brightly colored textiles often provide a soft and warm place to sit on floors. *Samurai*, because of their elaborate uniforms, sit on folding stools that may be elaborately carved or painted.

■ *Tables*. The most important table (Fig. 3-11) is the one used for dining and the tea ceremony. It is wooden, square, very low to the floor, has straight carved legs, and often features a top with a series of small curves. Small lacquer-covered tables provide surfaces for writing, presentation, or the tea ceremony.

■ *Storage*. Often works of art, chests or coffers in various sizes store possessions. The *tansu* (Fig. 3-14) is often located behind a *fusuma* as in a closet. Generally, built-in or freestanding cupboards line walls for storage. A variety of small decorative boxes may store stationery supplies.

■ *Beds*. People can sleep in almost any room where the soft *tatami* mats provide a resilient base. Thick rolled *futons* (comforters) serve as bed and bed covering; they are stored when not in use. A small box with an attached cushion becomes a pillow and provides head support.

▲ **3-14.** *Tansu* (in two parts).

■ *Screens*. The *byôbu* or decorative folding screen (Fig. 3-15), an important accessory in the interior, adds color and pattern, provides privacy, and protects from drafts. It may have two, three, or six folding panels approximately 3′-0″ to 5′-0″ high with decorative designs on both sides.

▲ **3-15.** *Byôbu* (folding screen), c. 1800; Tokyo, Japan.

■ *Porcelains and Ceramics*. Dutch traders first bring Japanese pottery and porcelains to Europe during the 17th century. Two types of porcelain (Fig. 3-16) are particularly popular with Westerners. *Kakiemon* porcelain has simple, asymmetrical designs in red, yellow, green, and blue, sometimes with gilding. *Imari* porcelain features crowded, elaborate patterns in strong blue, red, and gold.

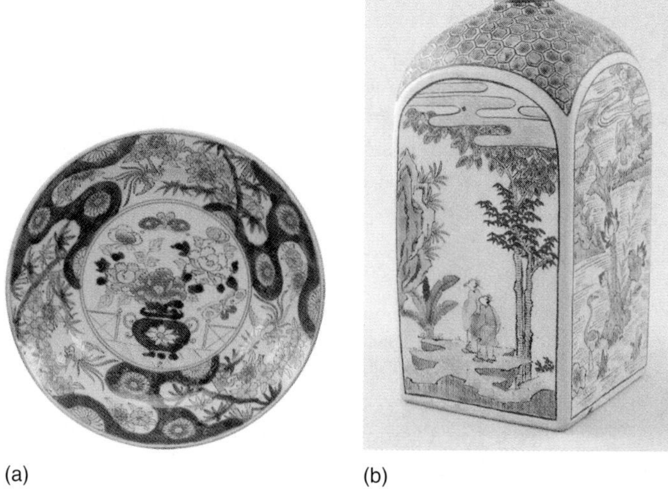

(a) (b)

▲ **3-16.** Decorative Arts: (a) Imari porcelain charger and (b) Kakiemon porcelain flask, c. late 17th century.

C. ANTIQUITY

Antiquity refers to the times following the development of written records to the beginning of the Middle Ages, when Christianity becomes the official religion in Rome. The architecture, motifs, and, to a lesser degree, interiors, furniture, and decorative arts of ancient Egypt, Greece, and Rome have long influenced Western developments. Elements and attributes from the three cultures have reappeared or been reinterpreted in nearly every subsequent period or style beginning with the Renaissance.

Although these civilizations influence each other, their arts and architecture arise within their own three individual cultures. In Egypt, surviving temples and tombs depict a society that emphasizes death and eternal life. The magnificence of its dynastic culture asserts itself in massive building projects. Greek art and architecture express a search for perfection in proportion and distribution and delineation of forms and elements. Roman visual arts glorify the Empire and express love of luxury, and its huge public building projects aim to unify diverse peoples.

Each culture makes unique contributions to architecture, interior design, and furnishings in an architectural and design vocabulary known as classicism. Classical influences define or appear in many later styles and revivals. Egypt introduces the column, cornice, pylon, and obelisk as well as various motifs, which influence Greece, Rome, and following cultures. Greek orders, temples, mathematical proportions, optical refinements, moldings, and motifs influence countless later buildings and interiors. Furniture forms also are repeated. The Romans contribute the Tuscan and Composite orders, temple and house forms, space planning, interior decoration, and furniture. Numerous later public and private buildings adopt Roman motifs, architectural details, and construction methods and have Roman-influenced interior treatments and furniture.

CHAPTER 4

Egypt

4500–332 B.C.E.

. . . as my eyes grew accustomed to the light, details of the room within emerged slowly from the mist, strange animals, statues, and gold—everywhere the glint of gold . . . it was all I could do to get out the words, "Yes, wonderful things. . . ."

—Howard Carter on opening the tomb; from *The Tomb of Tut-Ankh-Amen*, 1923

One of the most powerful and enduring civilizations in the Middle East is Egypt, whose culture evolves over a span of roughly 3,000 years. As a society immersed in religion, the country's art and architecture display a formal, ordered, and timeless feeling. The most significant buildings are pyramids, temples, and tombs—structures associated with the spirituality of life and death. Important introductions to Western architectural vocabulary include the column, capital, cornice, pylon, obelisk, and dressed stone construction. Many of these features become prototypes for later Greek and Roman developments. In addition, Egyptians are known for achievements in medicine, astronomy, geometry, and philosophy.

HISTORICAL AND SOCIAL

For most of its history, Egypt's geography isolates the country and keeps it relatively free from foreign invasions. The Nile River, the world's longest, winds through the country's interior. An essential water source, cities, villages, and cemeteries line its banks. The river supports an agrarian economy, and its annual floods nourish the land. The Nile also is an important trade and communication route. Vegetation along its banks becomes models for motifs that appear in art and architecture. For the Egyptians, the Nile is life itself.

Little is known about Egypt's origins and history before the institution of dynasties, families of rulers. About 3150 B.C.E., a single ruler unites Upper and Lower Egypt and establishes the first dynasty. The Old Kingdom (c. 2700–c. 2190 B.C.E.) spans five centuries and the 3rd through the 6th dynasties. During the period, the strong central government becomes a theocracy as people regard pharaohs, absolute monarchs, as divine. The capital is at Memphis. Pharaohs undertake massive building projects, such as the pyramids, to proclaim their power and assure immortality. Accomplishments in other disciplines match architectural and engineering feats. Turmoil, unrest, and disunity characterize the period between the 7th and the 17th dynasties. These unsettled conditions produce little significant art or architecture. The 18th dynasty begins the New Kingdom period, a golden age with numerous powerful rulers who expand territories and effect grand building programs. A new and magnificent capital is built at Thebes. Noteworthy rulers include Akhenaton and Nefertiti, Tutankhamen, and Ramesses (Rameses) II. Hatshepsut becomes the first female to rule as a pharaoh.

By the middle of the 20th dynasty, decline begins anew. Subsequently, Egypt is rarely free of foreign domination. Alexander the Great conquers her in 332 B.C.E. Under Ptolemy I, one of Alexander's generals, and his descendants, Egypt again becomes a great power. The last Ptolemaic ruler is Cleopatra VII who joins Julius Caesar and Mark Antony in an attempt to maintain power. In 30 B.C.E., the Romans conquer Egypt.

Egyptian society, headed by the pharaoh, is hierarchical. Egyptians are polytheistic, worshipping many gods and goddesses. From earliest times, they believe their rulers are divine and links to the gods. Egyptians revere both local and national gods who are depicted as humans, animals, and half-human, half-animal. Egyptian society's overarching belief is in life after death. Because that life is considered much like that on earth, those who can afford them have tombs to house their remains and the *ka*, their spirit doubles. Necessities of daily life fill the tombs as provisions for the *ka*, and walls feature painted images of the deceased in various activities. Paintings, statuettes, and mummified bodies provide dwelling places to further entice the *ka* to return. Believing that these practices ensure immortality, Egyptians carefully hide the burial chambers in tombs to prevent robbers from disturbing them. They are unsuccessful, however. The principal sources of information about royal and upper-class life in ancient Egypt are temples and tombs. The paintings and objects in them supply information about daily life and practices. Few written records survive, although apparently there were many. Archaeology has uncovered towns, worker housing near building projects, palaces, and other dwellings.

(a)

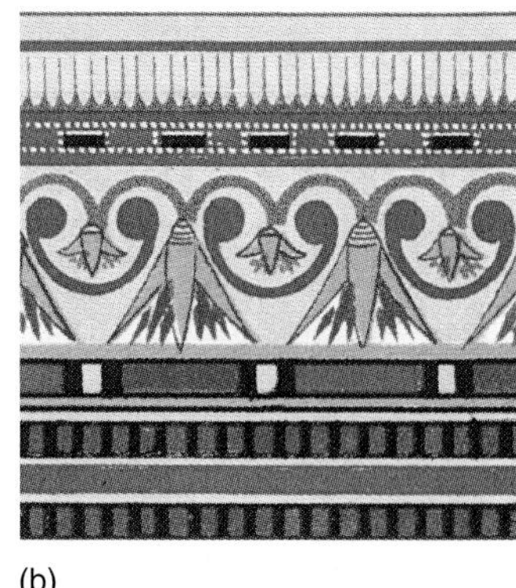

(b)

(c)

▲ **4-1.** Motifs and Architectural Detail: Egyptian ornament of (a) spirals, (b) papyrus, (c) circles.

CONCEPTS

The timeless, consistent character of Egyptian art and architecture reflects a highly religious society that sees the world in repeating cycles and unchanging patterns evident in the annual floods of the Nile, the changing seasons, life and death. In addition, geographic isolation limits foreign influence. Art and architectural patterns develop early and repeat consistently over time with minimal variations because novelty and change are not important. Far more significant are order and balance, which reflect the cultural vision.

MOTIFS

■ *Motifs*. Geometric or stylized naturalistic designs (Fig. 4-1, 4-7, 4-15) include the lotus, the papyrus, and palm; hieroglyphics (Fig. 4-9, 4-12); the sun disk and vulture, which appear frequently over temple doors to avert evil; and the sacred beetle or scarab. The Egyptians introduce the guilloche, spiral, palmette, and wave patterns.

ARCHITECTURE

Consistency is the most obvious characteristic of Egyptian art and architecture. Once created, patterns and forms repeat throughout history with little variation. There is minimal evidence of stylistic development, and similar concepts apply to almost all periods. Surviving architecture consists mainly of tombs and temples built of stone. Few domestic structures survive as they are generally built of impermanent materials. The hierarchy of buildings reflects the cultural belief in eternal life.

Simplicity, order, balance, stylization, and formality convey monumentality and a sense of eternity. Characteristic attributes include symmetry, repose, solidity, and weightiness. Axiality, simple forms, geometric volumes, rectangular shapes, and straight lines define the composition. Walls are thick, solid, and usually unbroken by fenestration. Colorful decoration highlights walls and columns. Since the climate is hot but even, structures offer protection from heat and light. In temples, grand scale, axial procession, and massive gateways dwarf humans and symbolize society's strong religious emphasis and social hierarchy. They are also visual metaphors for the power, majesty, and might of rulers and gods. Important features include hieroglyphics, the post or column, and nature-inspired motifs.

Structural Features

■ *Posts*. Egyptians consistently use trabeated or post and lintel construction. The vertical post (Fig. 4-2, 4-9, 4-11), or column, has a base, shaft, and distinctive capital. It may be either freestanding or engaged. Shafts are plain or polygonal with concave or convex channels—prototypes of fluting and reeding. Capitals are usually stylized plant forms such as the lotus bud, papyrus, or palm. Columns may feature incised and painted figures, hieroglyphics, and geometric or stylized native plant motifs. Figures may be used as columns, particularly in mortuary temples and rock tombs. Egyptians know the arch but rarely incorporate it except in the lower portions or ceilings of some tombs and buildings.
■ *Lintel*. The lintel or architrave (Fig. 4-7, 4-9, 4-11), a horizontal beam, is crowned with a cornice, the most common of which is the cavetto or gorge. Decorative moldings include the roll, scroll, and bead. Architraves (lintels) feature decorative carving and painting.

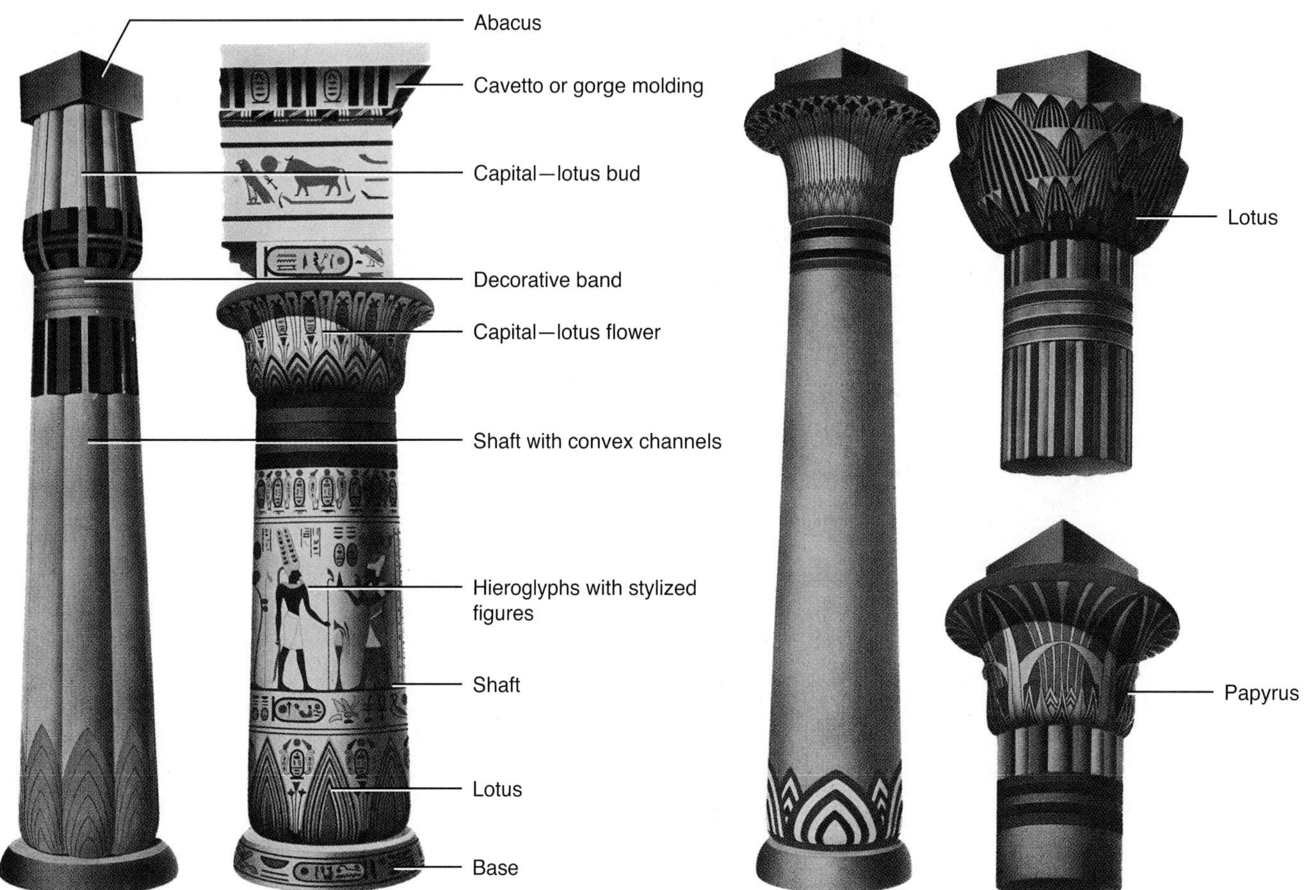

▲ **4-2.** Posts and Capitals: Posts and capitals include the lotus bud, lotus flower, and papyrus blossom.

Public and Private Buildings

■ *Tombs*. Egyptians build three types of tombs. Mastabas or funerary mounds with subterranean burial chambers are common during the Old Kingdom. The pyramids, built beginning in the 4th dynasty, are the most iconic symbol and characteristic image of Egypt (Fig. 4-3). These large structures, which protect the king's mummy, are visual symbols for his absolute and divine power. Their perfect alignment and construction reveal the Egyptians to be master builders and mathematicians. Pyramids do not prevent robberies, so rock-hewn tombs, which dominate the following periods, become common. These tombs exhibit the fundamental spaces of Egyptian architecture: an entrance with vestibule (Fig. 4-7), a columned hall, and a sacred chamber. All three tomb-types sometimes form complexes with temples, other tombs, and processional paths.

■ *Temples*. Cult temples for the worship of a god or gods follow a traditional form that responds to rituals and ceremonies. This form creates a sense of progression from small to large and from low to high, usually on an axial alignment. In some tomb and temple complexes (Fig. 4-4, 4-5), avenues of sphinxes (Fig. 4-3) lead to walled areas and serve as guardians. A typical temple plan (Fig. 4-5) has its entry past pairs of obelisks and through a huge pylon or gateway with slanted walls (Fig. 4-6, 4-8). Immediately behind is an open courtyard leading to a vestibule or hypostyle hall, a covered area filled with tightly clustered columns (Fig. 4-9) that may be decorated with figures, symbols, and hieroglyphics. Only a chosen few may enter the hypostyle hall. Behind the hall

▲ **4-3.** Great Sphinx and Pyramid of Menkaure, c. 2575–2475 B.C.E.; Giza, Egypt.

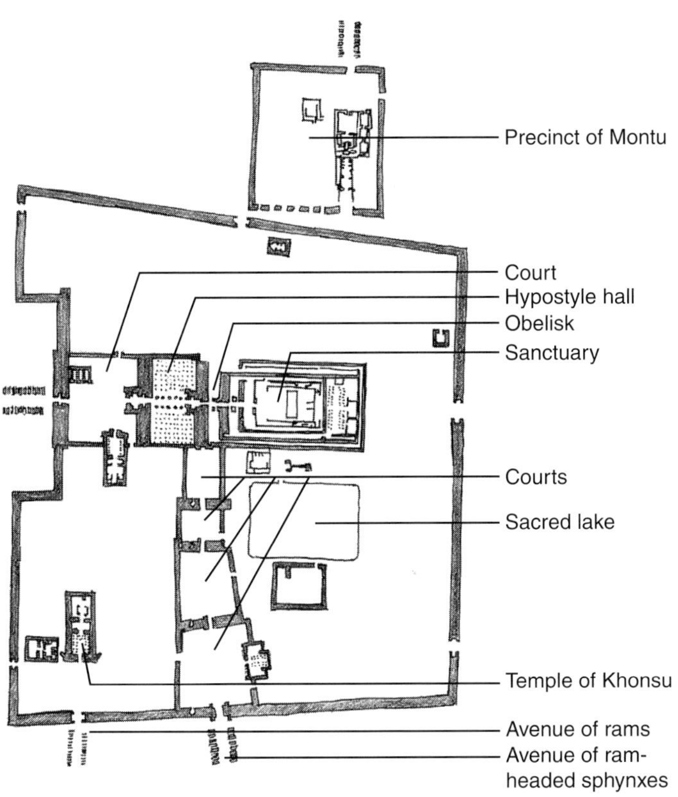

▲ **4-4.** Site plan, Temple complex, Amon-Ra, c. 1580–323 B.C.E.; Karnak, Egypt.

is a sanctuary holding the statue of the king or god. Treasure rooms surround the sanctuary, which only pharaoh and the priests may enter.

■ *Dwellings*. Few palaces and dwellings survive intact. Most knowledge of them comes from clay models, tomb paintings, and archaeology. Dwellings (Fig. 4-10) vary in size and configuration with class and wealth. Simple houses have one or two stories with three to four rooms, while great mansions have many rooms and several courtyards. Public areas, usually on the north or cooler side, include a reception room and office for conducting business. Private areas, such as bedrooms, bathrooms, and women's quarters, are usually secluded.

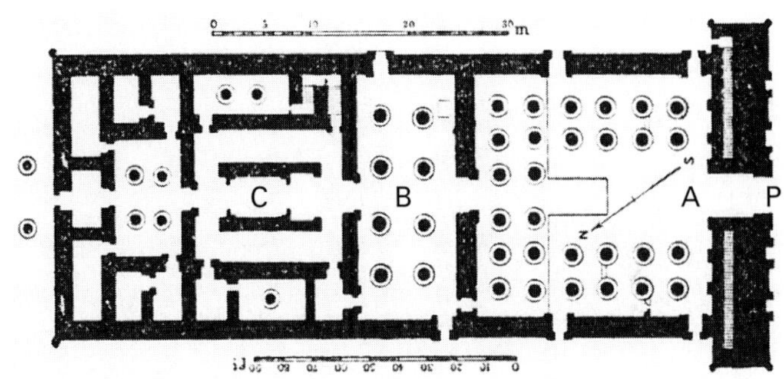

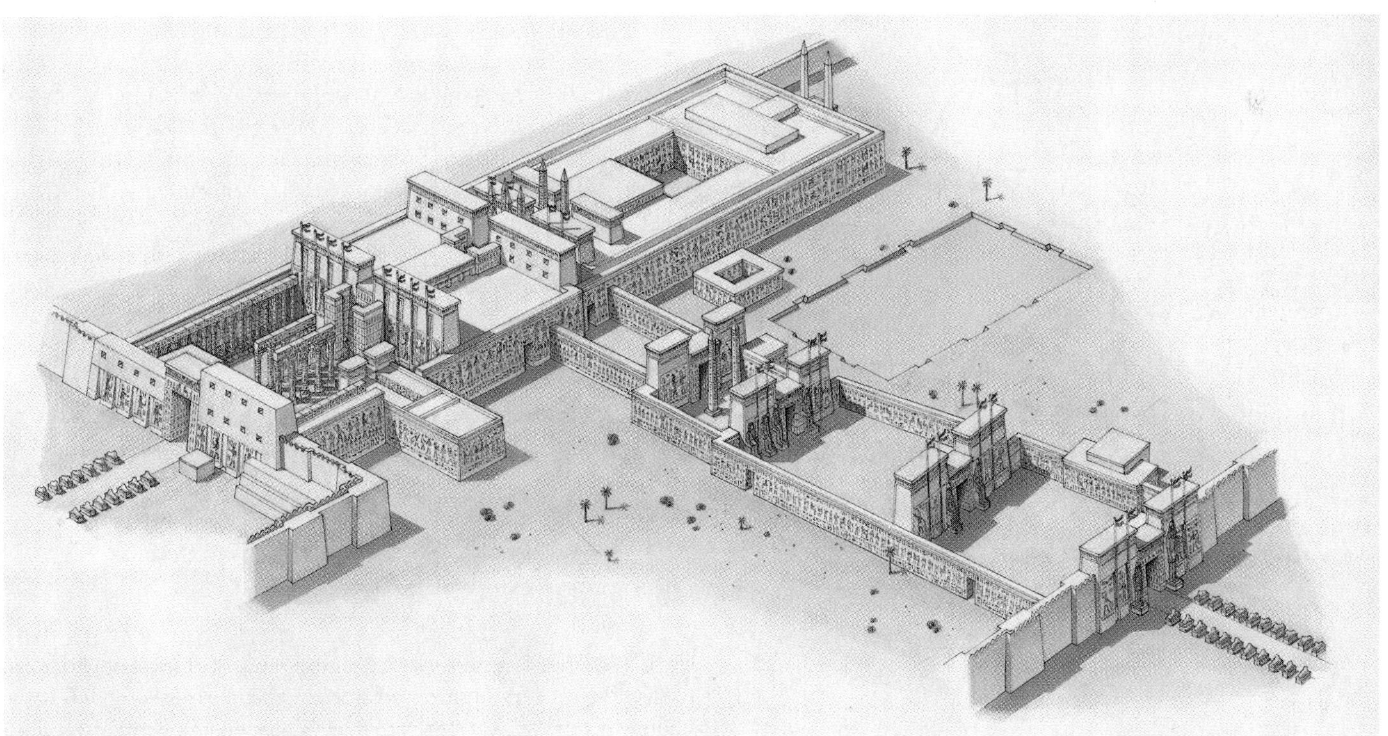

▲ **4-5.** Floor plan and section, Temple of Khons, c. 1198 B.C.E.; Karnak, Egypt. The plan (above) has the typical elements of a (P) pylon, (A) open courtyard, (B) hypostyle hall, and (C) sanctuary.

▲ **4-6.** Temple of Luxor, c. 1408–1300 B.C.E.; Thebes, Egypt.

▲ **4-7.** Entrance (reconstructed) to the Tomb of Puyemre, 15th century B.C.E.; Thebes, Egypt.

■ *Site Orientation*. Mastabas, pyramids, and temples (Fig. 4-4) are sited in axial, walled complexes with a variety of attendant buildings. Since subsequent rulers add to the complexes, relationships among structures are not planned as a whole, as Greek structures are. The most magnificent temple complex is that of Amon-Ra at Karnak.

Towns display ordered grid planning with palaces and wealthy houses sitting along wide streets. Common homes are located in more crowded areas with narrow streets. Large walled complexes of palaces and upper-class dwellings include numerous buildings, gardens, and pools. All, regardless of size, focus inward, usually toward courtyards.

■ *Materials*. Monumental and funerary architecture is built of stone, befitting its eternal purpose. Palaces and dwellings are made primarily of sun-dried mud brick, plastered and whitewashed.

■ *Façades*. Facçades are massive with thick walls that are often slanted outside for stability and rarely broken by openings (Fig. 4-6, 4-8). They are colorfully decorated with painted and incised figures of gods and rulers, hieroglyphics, and other characteristic motifs. The few doors and windows (Fig. 4-11) are usually tall and rectangular. Windows, when present, are high on the wall. Center columns in hypostyle halls and important residential spaces are taller to permit clerestory windows for light into the center. Pylons often have slits to light inner staircases. Paintings and models depict dwellings with plain façades and small windows high in the wall.

■ *Roofs*. Flat roofs are common on public and private buildings. In homes, flat roofs provide additional storage and sleeping areas in very hot weather. They often have tall vents to catch breezes.

INTERIORS

The only extant interiors are in tombs and temples (Fig. 4-9), but knowledge of domestic interiors, particularly of the wealthy, comes from excavations, painted images in tombs, and models. Rooms are rectangular with relatively straight walls, flat ceilings, few windows (often clerestory), and limited architectural details.

▲ **4-8.** Temple of Ramesses III at Medinet Habu, c. 200 B.C.E.; Thebes, Egypt.

DESIGN SPOTLIGHT

Architecture: The largest and grandest of all Egyptian temple complexes, the Hypostyle Hall site is an accretion as each ruler adds more temples and buildings. The Temple of Amon-Ra is the largest of the six temples in the site. Its massive pylons have battered walls, trabeated construction, rolled moldings, slit windows, and flagstaffs. Incised in the walls are images of the pharaoh conquering his enemies. Behind three entry pylons is an open courtyard leading to the hypostyle hall. This form emerges during the New Kingdom as a product of religious and architectural consideration. It seems to have had several functions including gatherings, coronations, and the beginnings of processions, as at Karnak, but these varied among temples. Characteristic of the hypostyle hall, as shown here, are the massive columns decorated with figures, symbols, and hieroglyphics. The hypostyle hall at Karnak measures 340′-0″ long by 170′-0″ wide. Its 134 columns in 16 rows support the roof. Most columns have lotus bud capitals and are 42′-0″ high and 9′-0″ in diameter. A double row of lotus flower columns creates the processional central aisles. These columns are 69′-0″ high and 12′-0″ in diameter, and the greater height accommodates clerestory windows, which admit light in the center aisles. This also gives an effect of lotus flowers rising to meet the sun. Decorations depict scenes of several 18th-dynasty pharaohs in processions, coronations, and other ceremonies, which are intended to reinforce the significance of the ruler. Dim and dark sanctuaries entered only by priests or pharaoh are behind the hypostyle hall. [World Heritage Site]

▲ **4-9.** Hypostyle Hall (restored and reconstructed views), Temple of Amon-Ra, c. 1580–323 B.C.E.; Karnak, Egypt.

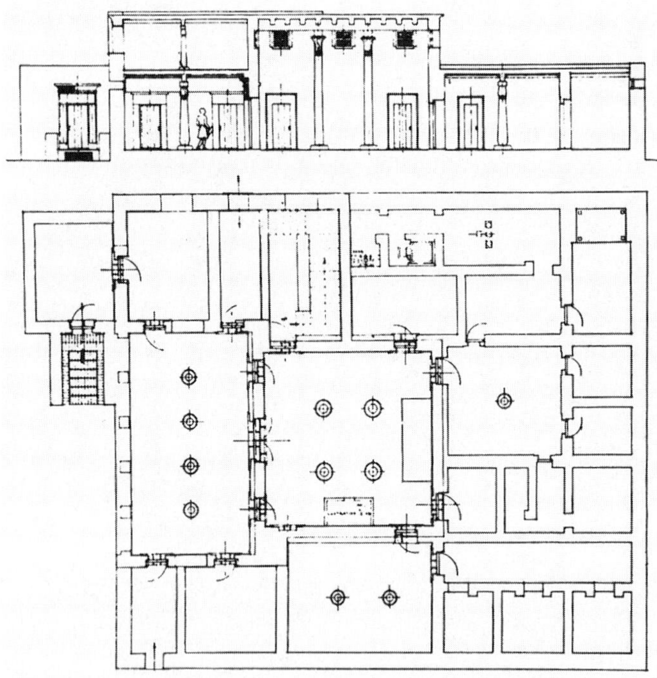

▲ **4-10.** Floor plan and section, nobleman's villa, 1500–1400 B.C.E.; Tell-el-Amarna, Egypt.

Public and Private Buildings

■ *Color.* Colors (Fig. 4-1, 4-2, 4-7, 4-11, 4-12, 4-15) include blue-green, rust-red, gold, black, and cream and are derived from earth pigments. Architectural details are often highlighted in various colors. Color may be used symbolically, especially on human figures.

■ *Floors.* Tomb and dwelling floors are mostly of pressed clay; a few are of brick or stone. Finer houses have polished plaster floors, sometimes with painted decorations. Floor mats of woven rushes are common.

■ *Walls.* Interior walls are plastered and whitewashed. Tomb decorations usually depict the deceased in various activities arranged in bands as shown in the tomb of Queen Nefertari (Fig. 4-12). In grand houses, walls in important rooms are painted. The lower portion is white, black, or dark blue with patterning above. A frieze near the ceiling displays abstractions of nature or other symbols.

■ *Windows.* Windows, which are small and rectangular, often have wood or stone grilles (Fig. 4-11) or rolled mat coverings woven of reeds.

■ *Doors.* Doors are wooden boards with pivot hinges; double doors may define important rooms. Rolled mats may also cover openings.

■ *Ceilings.* Most ceilings (Fig. 4-12) are flat; a few, often in rock-hewn tombs, are barrel vaulted. Ceilings in hypostyle halls and important rooms in some dwellings and palaces are raised by columns for clerestory windows that add light and air circulation (Fig. 4-9, 4-10).

■ *Lighting.* Common forms of lighting (Fig. 4-13) include saucers with wicks submerged in oil and torches of twisted plant material smeared with fat.

■ *Later Interpretations.* Egypt influences both Greece and Rome. The 19th- and early 20th-century Egyptian Revivals selectively use architectural details and motifs from Ancient Egypt. Examples include churches (Fig. 4-14), fraternal organizations, stage sets, movie theaters, and a few domestic spaces.

▲ **4-11.** Deep Hall of General Ra-mose (reconstructed elevation), c. 1370 B.C.E.; Tell-el-Amarna, Egypt.

▲ 4-12. Interior, tomb of Queen Nefertari, c. 1290–1224 B.C.E.; Thebes, Egypt.

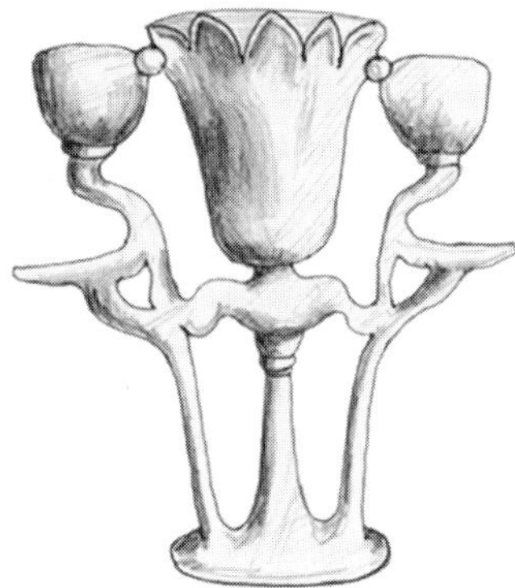

▲ 4-13. Lighting: Lamp, c. 1334–1325 B.C.E.; found in Tutankhamen's tomb.

▲ 4-14. Later Interpretation: First Presbyterian Church, 1848–1851; Nashville, Tennessee; William Strickland; Egyptian Revival.

FURNISHINGS AND DECORATIVE ARTS

Egyptian furniture is generally rectangular with few curves. It may be plain or decorated. Most surviving examples are from royal or upper-class tombs. The discovery of King Tutankhamen's tomb in 1922 provided the world with a more accurate image of the lifestyle, furnishings, and decorative arts associated with Egyptian royalty. Little is known of common furnishings, but rooms are sparsely furnished with limited types of furniture.

Defining characteristics that are unique to Egypt include front and rear animal legs positioned naturally and raised on a cylinder that is often beaded. This also is the most common leg form. Typical feet are hooves or paws.

Public and Private Buildings

■ *Materials*. Acacia and sycamore are the local woods, which are not well suited to furniture making. Better woods, such as cedar, cypress, and ebony, are imported. Poor-quality woods are often veneered or painted to imitate better woods. Egyptians develop a type of plywood composed of small wood pieces glued together. Inlay materials include ebony, ivory, Egyptian faience, and precious stones. Sheet, foil, and leaf gold or silver are common on luxury furniture. Furniture construction, which is sophisticated, primarily uses mortise and tenon, dovetail, miter, or butt joints.

■ *Seating*. The typical chair is simple and square in form with a slightly curved, sloping back supported by two or three uprights. Seats, which vary in height, may be made of plaited rushes or leather. Loose feather-filled cushions of bright colors may be added for comfort. Thrones (Fig. 4-15), as symbols of royalty, are the largest and most elaborately embellished. Stools (Fig. 4-16) are more numerous than chairs and made in various heights. Folding stools, used by military commanders, are symbols of authority. A common folding stool has legs terminating in ducks' heads and a seat of leather, canvas, or woven grass. Stools that do not fold often have a sloped wooden seat and turned or animal legs.

■ *Tables*. Small tables with rectangular or round tops are used for eating and display. Wicker stands are more common than tables.

■ *Storage*. Chests and baskets, which store possessions, linen, clothing, and food, differ in size and form based on their function. Interiors of chests sometimes are divided into small compartments to hold various objects. Decoration may include designs of ebony and gilded symbols of divine life or ivory and silver inlay (Fig. 4-17).

■ *Beds*. Beds have wooden frames and animal legs in a natural position with leather or rush webbing for support. They are richly carved and have plain or embellished footboards but no headboards. Many layers of folded linen serve as a mattress. Headrests of alabaster or wood substitute for pillows.

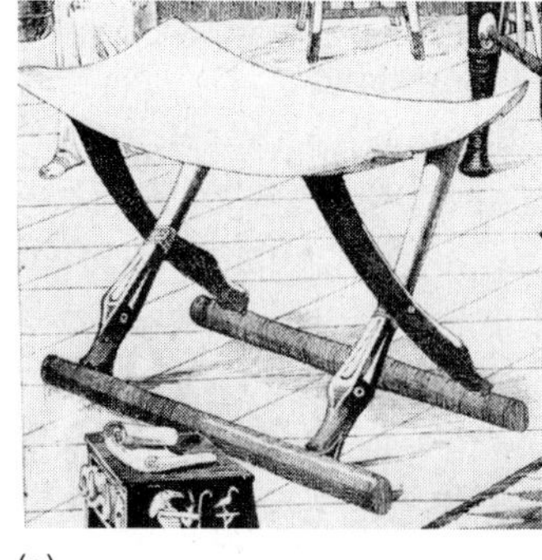

(a)

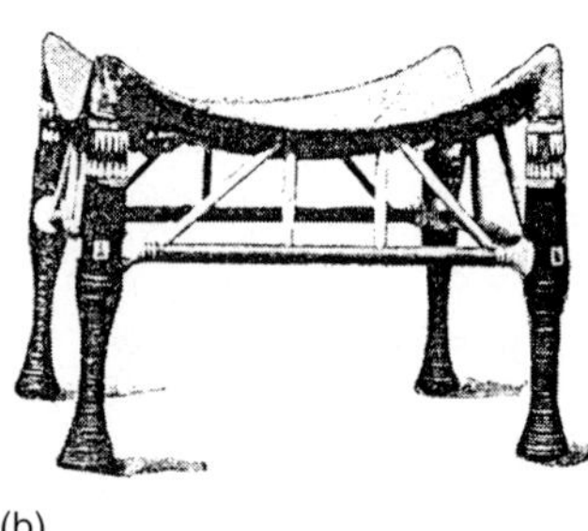

(b)

▲ **4-16.** X-form folding and rigid stools (the latter known as Thebes stool in the Arts & Crafts period), 1500–1400 B.C.E.

DESIGN SPOTLIGHT

Furniture: Although this throne was built for royalty, form and construction of this throne are similar to chairs for lesser individuals. A common style for royal chairs during the 18th dynasty, the elaborate decoration related to Tutankhamen marks it as his, as is common practice. The wood is overlaid with gold and silver foil and inlaid with semiprecious stones, Egyptian faience, and glass. Shown on the back is the king seated in a chair with a cushion and his feet resting on a stool while his queen attends him. Nearby is a stand holding a tray. Lions' heads surmount the front legs, and lions' paw feet are raised on cylinders. Colors include blue-green, red, gold, black, and cream.

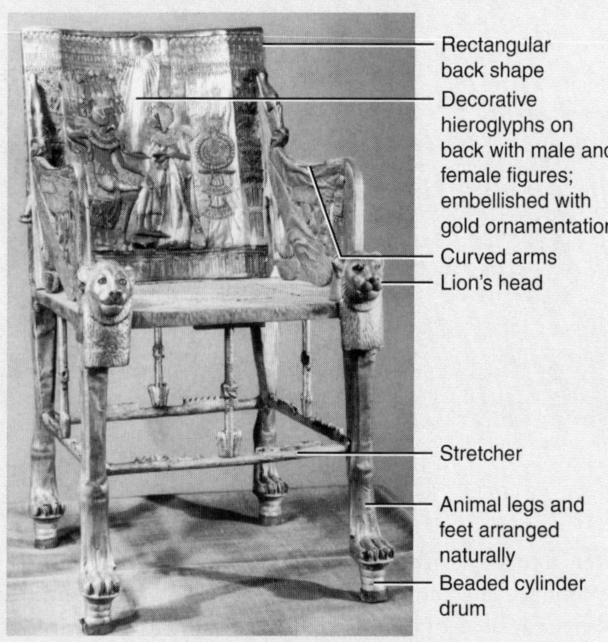

▲ **4-15.** Golden throne of Tutankhamen, 1500–1400 B.C.E.

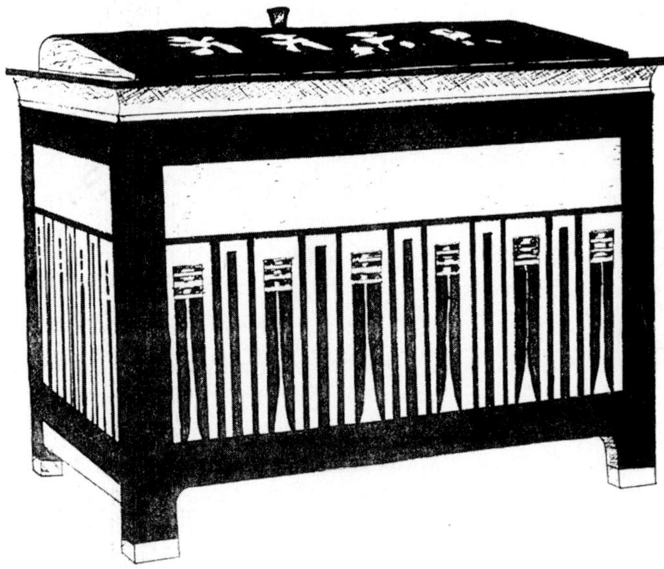

▲ **4-17.** Small chest, c. 1334–1325 B.C.E.; from Tutankhamen's tomb.

■ *Decorative Arts*. Tableware is made of pottery, alabaster, copper, bronze, gold, or silver. Common items include storage jars, bowls, jugs (Fig. 4-18), cups (Fig. 4-18), washbasins, and mirrors. Glassmaking probably begins as a royal monopoly during the 18th dynasty when the affluent begin using glass vases and jars for scents, cosmetics, or ointments. Egyptian glass is core-formed and opaque. The vessel is made around a clay and sand core that is repeatedly dipped into molten glass until the desired thickness is obtained. Colored rods applied to the hot glass may be left plain or hooked or dragged to create chevron patterns.

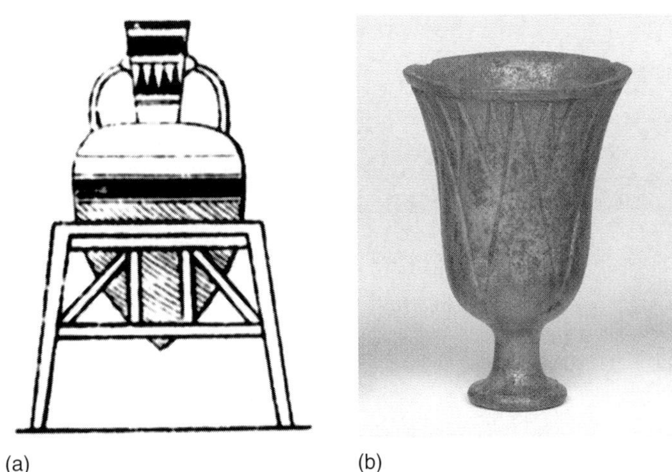

(a) (b)

▲ **4-18.** Decorative Arts: Clay jug on stand and lotus cup, c. 1500–1400 B.C.E.

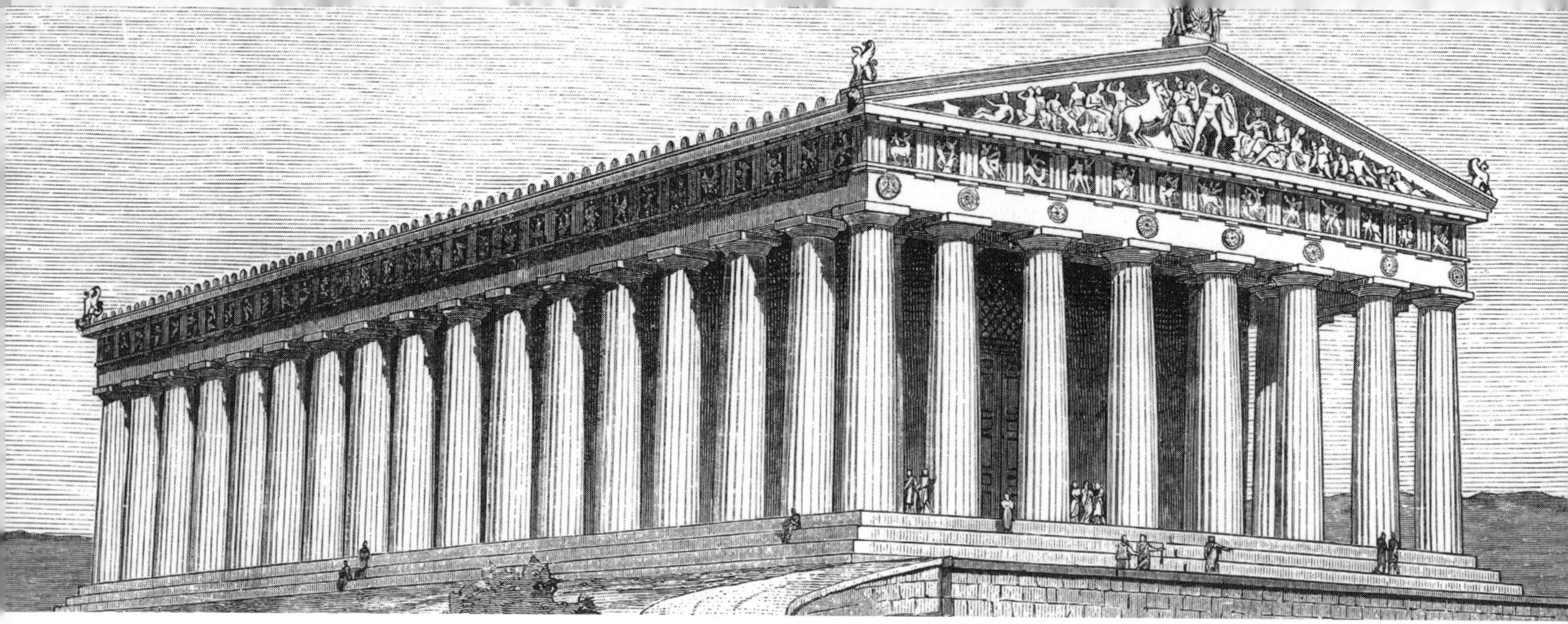

CHAPTER 5

Greece

1000–146 B.C.E.; Golden Age in the 5th Century

Take architecture. It is an art, that is a rational faculty exercised in making something. In fact there is no art which cannot be so described, nor is there any faculty of the kind which is not art.

—Aristotle, *The Ethics of Aristotle*

Greek innovations in art, architecture, literature, philosophy, and music have been sources of design inspiration since their inception. The visual images establish a language and grammar for architecture, interiors, furniture, and decorative arts copied by successive generations. Greek (and Roman) elements and forms dominate Western architecture until well into the 20th century. No other culture except Rome has had such a significant impact on the evolution of Western architecture, interiors, furniture, and decorative arts.

HISTORICAL AND SOCIAL

Greece is a peninsula with rocky seacoasts surrounded by numerous islands and mountain ranges to the north. Geographic separation from neighboring countries contributes to Greece's individual cultural identity. Early inhabitants are the Mycenaeans, who are driven out by the Dorians, a militant tribe from the north that settles in Sparta and southern Greece. Those Mycenaeans who stay maintain their identity on the peninsula of Attica, specifically in the southeastern city of Athens, and become known as Ionians. Numerous mountain ridges divide the country into small areas, which fosters the development of independent city-states, each with its own governmental, political, and economic identity. These governments encourage individual citizen participation and form models for later democracies.

Greeks are polytheistic, worshipping gods who are powerful and immortal, but have human forms and attributes. Their religion fosters respect for order, as reflected in nature and humankind. Men possess independence, wealth, ownership, and education. Women, in contrast, are their fathers' or husbands' property, being restricted by law, politics, custom, and family relationships. Their main duties are to bear children and tend the household. Few women artists are known, and nothing by those acknowledged survives.

As there is little farmland, trade is important. Not only does trade stimulate the economy, but also it brings historical influences from Egypt and the near East, Europe, and Asia. City-states establish their own colonies throughout the Mediterranean, spreading Greek culture and receiving foreign goods and effects in return. Wars waged with the Persians and Assyrians also bring new forms and ideas. The mixture of these influences produces a rich and varied culture. Later, the exploits of Alexander the Great (ruled 336–323 B.C.E.) bring additional ideas into the country as he conquers vast areas to expand his empire. During this period of cross-fertilization, Greeks call themselves Hellenes and recognize their own distinctiveness. Significant Greek contributions include the literary works and dramas penned by Aristotle, Plato, Socrates, and Homer that promote logic, questioning, and critical thinking; the first coinage system used in bartering; and the written and visual accomplishments of many artists.

CONCEPTS

Greek architecture and art search for the ideal, perfection in proportion and distribution of forms and parts, and those attributes or qualities that contribute to and enhance the ideal image. The Golden Age of the 5th century, or Classical period, has continually provided a model for the classical language of architectural form, order, and proportion. Form is characteristically expressed in the Greek temples, while order is delineated through the relationship of the parts to the whole. Proportion, tied to religion and the attainment of perfection, relates to the human body, often cited by the Protagorian axiom "man is the measure of all things." One derivative of this concept is the golden section (Fig. 5-1), developed by the Greek mathematician Euclid. He diagrammed a geometric relationship between rectangles and squares based on a system of proportioning.

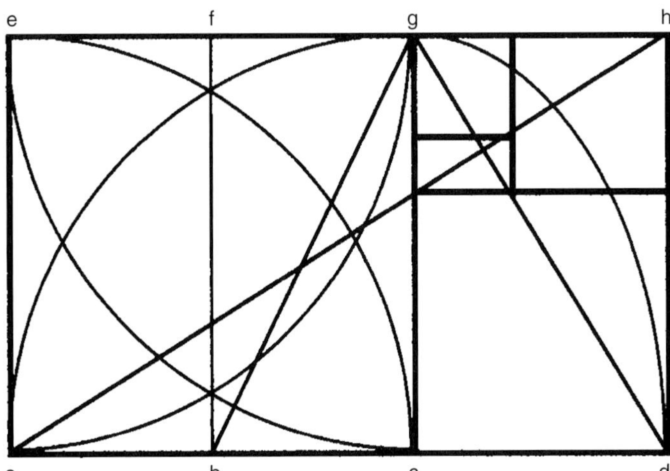

▲ **5-1.** Golden Section: aceg = square; bf = half square; bg = bd and determines smaller Golden Mean; adhe = Golden Mean.

CHARACTERISTICS AND MOTIFS

■ *Geometric or Orientalizing Period (c. 1100–650 B.C.E.).* Little survives from this early period. Mud-brick temples and tombs are chief architectural forms. Vases are the dominant surviving art form.

■ *Archaic (c. 660–475 B.C.E.).* Monumental stone architecture and sculpture originate in the 7th century B.C.E. The architectural form and vocabulary that characterize Greek buildings evolve throughout this period. The Doric and Ionic orders originate, and builders search for perfection in the proportion and distribution of parts.

■ *Classical (c. 475–323 B.C.E.).* The search for perfection culminates in the great Doric temples of the Classical period, particularly the Temple of Aphaia in Aegina and the Parthenon in Athens. Ionic temples are jewels of perfection also. The Corinthian order originates and is used only for interiors. The architectural vocabulary is fully developed, and no new innovations, only variations, are introduced. During the 4th century B.C.E., builders begin to deviate from classical forms and proportions.

■ *Hellenistic (323–30 B.C.E.).* Greek society becomes more sophisticated, and new building types appear in response. Architecture becomes more subjective, deviating even more from the Classical period architectural language. New variations of capitals appear, and proportions vary even more. Ornament becomes more important.

(a)

(b)

▲ **5-2.** Motifs and Architectural Details: (a) Acanthus plant; (b) anthemion; (c) palmette and egg and dart; (d) fret; (e) wave; (f) antefix; and (g) guilloche.

(c)

(d)

(e)

(f)

(g)

▲ 5-2. Continued

■ *Motifs*. Ornamental motifs (Fig. 5-2, 5-6), some of which come from Egypt, are often painted to enhance their attractiveness, especially when used on architecture. Those derived from nature include the acanthus leaf, anthemion, palmette, wave, antefix, honeysuckle, rosette, scroll, and rinceau. Ones created from geometry are the fret or Greek key, guilloche, dentil, egg and dart, and swastika. Mythical beasts, such as the sphinx, griffin, and chimera, are also important.

ARCHITECTURE

Greek architecture conveys a formal, refined image that emphasizes human proportions, the golden section, monumental scale, symmetrical balance, and ordered spatial arrangements. The ordering of the principal structural members distinguishes the building form. Arrangements are logical and rational, reflecting natural harmony. Parts, articulated for clarity and to emphasize the architectonics, relate to each other and the whole. Equally important principles and attributes are repose, horizontality, symmetry, stability, and clarity. In contrast to Egypt where timelessness and tradition are important, Greece continually seeks perfection in the proportion and distribution of parts. Consequently, stylistic changes occur as forms evolve.

Architectural influences from the Middle East and Egypt merge with indigenous forms to shape the building image within the Greek landscape. Bright sun alternating with rainy periods contributes to a strong emphasis on building orientation, light and dark contrast, and covered walkways. Greek designers seek to express form in the most pleasing way, so they create systems of proportions and rely on numerical relationships and geometry. Therefore, each part of a building is composed of geometric forms, each possessing its own importance and logical arrangement. Harmony among parts is achieved through the repetition of forms and numbers and carefully planned, articulated transitions. Structures display classical attributes or qualities. Thus, the term *classical* can refer to the elements (columns, pediments, and the like) and attributes (symmetry, repose, etc.) of Greek (and Roman) architecture. The addition of optical refinements to correct optical illusions and enhance the structure indicates Greek psychological understanding of architecture. Greek buildings are of trabeated construction until the 4th century B.C.E., when arches and barrel vaults are adopted but hidden behind traditional façades of some tombs and other structures. Public building types include temples (Fig. 5-8), theaters, and treasuries. Many structures, such as large civic centers for political gatherings and sports centers for athletic events, focus specifically on outdoor activities.

Structural Features

■ *Classical Orders*. The appearance of a Greek building comes from the ordering of the principal structural members according to particular and accepted modes called orders. The orders differ in proportion and details, with capitals being the most distinguishing feature. The principal structural members are the column or post and entablature or lintel. Each is subdivided into three elements. Each of these parts may be further subdivided with characteristic elements, moldings, and decorative details. The lower portions, which carry the building's load, are appropriately larger and less embellished, which gives the effect of lightening the visual weight as the composition ascends. This also creates a pyramidal form, which is perceived as more stable than is a rectangle. Renaissance architects, not the Greeks, introduce

▲ 5-3. Doric order.

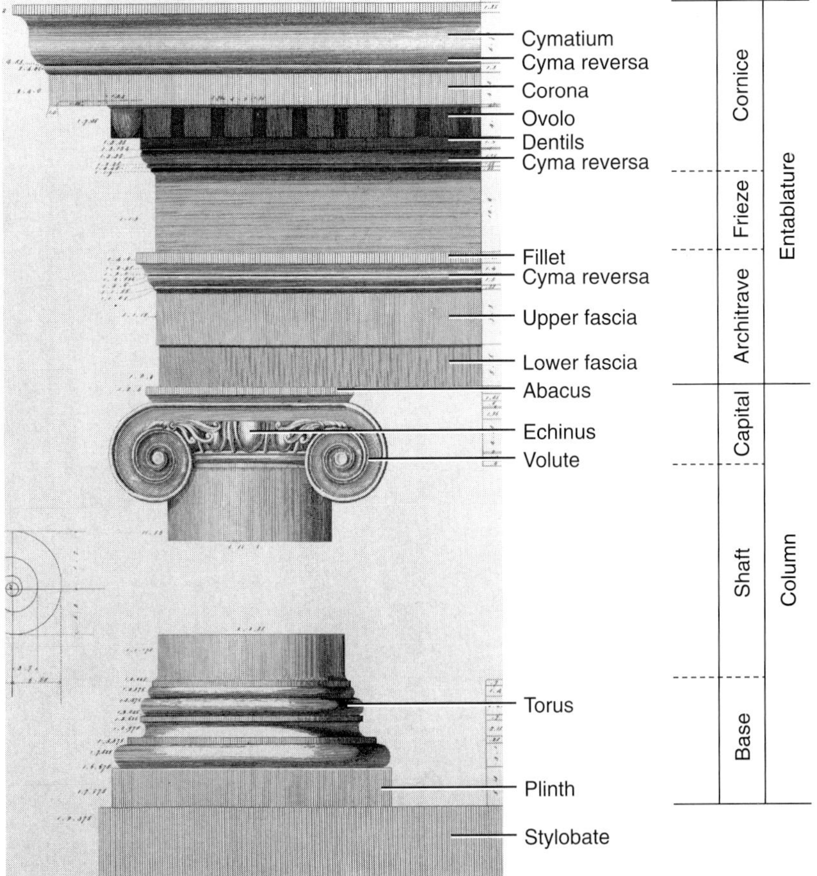

▲ 5-4. Ionic order and architectural details.

the concept of the orders based upon the work of Vitruvius and they define the five orders common in the Classical tradition today. The compositional method using the orders also appears in some Greek interiors and, following the Renaissance, will comprise the arrangement of many interior walls.

- *Column*. The column is composed of a base, shaft, and capital. The primary Greek orders are Doric (Fig. 5-3), Ionic (Fig. 5-4), and Corinthian (Fig. 5-5), which differ from each other in proportion, detail, and capital. All have fluted shafts, but Doric ones usually have entasis, a slight convex curve. Caryatids (Fig. 5-8) sometimes substitute as columns. Until the Hellenistic period, when engaged columns appear, columns are used structurally, rarely decoratively.
- *Pilasters and Engaged Columns*. Pilasters commonly adorn the corners of exterior cella walls behind the porch, corresponding to columns. Interior pilasters are rare, even in the Hellenistic period. Engaged columns appear occasionally in the 5th century B.C.E. on temple exteriors and interiors. By the Hellenistic period, they are common on temples, stoas, agoras, and other structures.
- *Entablature and Pediment*. Resting on top of columns, the entablature features an architrave, frieze, and cornice (Fig. 5-4, 5-8). The architrave is a flat, wide band; the frieze displays carved and/or painted ornamentation; and the cornice is composed of a series of three-dimensional moldings. Each order treats the frieze and cornice differently. Above the entablature is the pediment, a triangular form composed by the two slopes of the gable roof. The tympanum, or center of the pediment, may be filled with relief sculpture (Fig. 5-8).
- *Moldings*. The Greeks are the first to create and extensively use a series of moldings (Fig. 5-6) to delineate the outlines of buildings. Moldings add interest, emphasis, and contrasts of light and dark.
- *Doric Order*. The Doric capital (Fig. 5-3, 5-8) consists of an abacus and an echinus. Near the neck of the capital are three annulets or grooves. The height of the shaft varies and has flutes but no base. The earliest Doric columns are slender, but in the Archaic period they become very thick with a pronounced taper and heavy, bulging echinus. Classical Doric shafts are slimmer and not as tapered; the echinus is not so pronounced. Shafts become even thinner in the Hellenistic period. Above a plain architrave the Doric frieze is composed of triglyphs and metopes. Rules dictate the placement of triglyphs, which are centered over and between each column and must meet at the corners. Metopes may have

▲ **5-5.** Corinthian order.

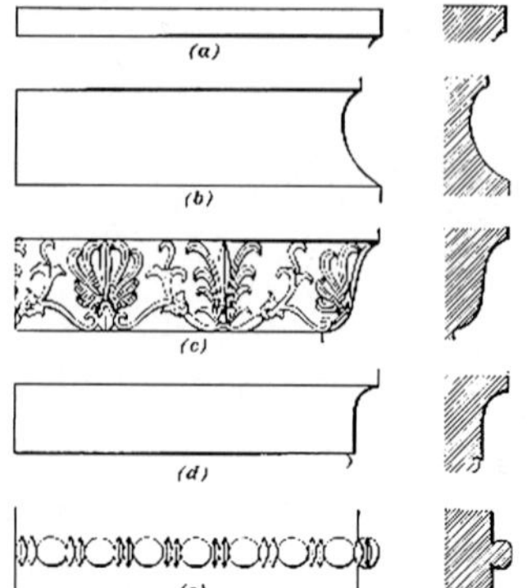

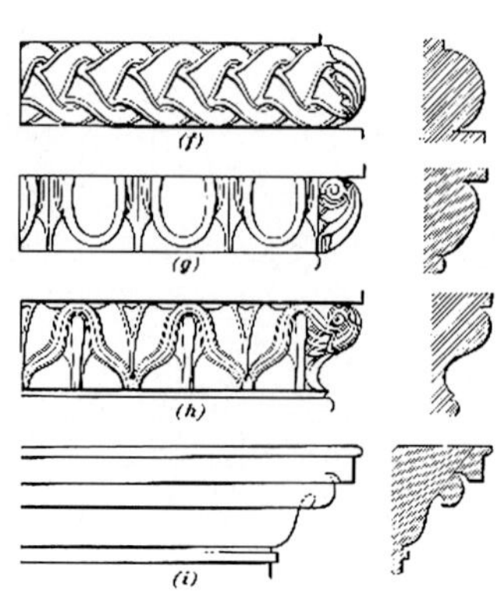

◀ **5-6.** Architectural Moldings: (a) fillet; (b) scotia; (c) cyma recta; (d) cavetto; (e) bead; (f) torus; (g) ovolo or egg and dart; (h) cyma reversa; (i) hawk's beak.

relief sculptures or painted decoration. Most large temples are Doric until the Hellenistic period, when the Ionic order dominates. Doric is often contrasted as masculine in comparison to the more feminine Ionic or Corinthian. Although characteristic of some Greek temple interiors, Doric is rarely used in later interiors.

■ *Ionic Order*. Developed about the same time as the Doric, the Ionic order (Fig. 5-4) has two pairs of volutes, one in front and one in back, joined at the side by a decorated concave cushion. The volutes usually are parallel to the architrave except on corners, when they assume a 45-degree angle for a more pleasing appearance. The smaller echinus is carved with an egg-and-dart molding and palmettes. Ionic has a taller and more slender shaft than the Doric and a contoured base. The fluted shaft is more tapered than that of a Doric column. The architrave, no longer plain, has three fascia. The Ionic frieze may be carved with reliefs. Dentil moldings delineate the cornice. The Ionic is elegant, graceful, and more flexible than the Doric because there are fewer rules, such as the placement of triglyphs. It also adapts well to curves and interiors.

■ *Corinthian Order*. Introduced as a variation of the Ionic order, the Corinthian order (Fig. 5-5) is similar to it except for the capital. Shaped like an inverted bell, the lower portion has two rows of acanthus leaves (Fig. 5-2). Curving stalks rise from the upper row of leaves. The abacus is concave on all four sides and ends in a point, and a rosette accentuates the center. The tall shaft is more slender than that of the Ionic order and the entablature is usually more embellished. Originally used inside temples because it adapted well to corners, the Corinthian order is first used on exteriors during the Hellenistic period. Even then, the conservative Greeks rarely use the Corinthian order. The Choragic Monument of Lysicrates (Fig. 5-9) may be the first use of Corinthian capital on an exterior. Like the Ionic, the Corinthian order appears in some Greek and many later interiors.

■ *Optical Refinements*. The Greek adoption of a series of architectural adjustments that enhance the building, create dynamism, and correct any perceived optical illusions indicates a psychological understanding of the art and perception of building not seen again until the Renaissance. After the 5th century B.C.E., most temples incorporate only some of the refinements, as they are costly and complicated to build. Entasis, the most common optical refinement, gives columns the appearance of responding to the weight of the entablature and counters any perception of thinness in the center of the shaft. Additionally, curves are more pleasing to the eye. Corner columns may be thicker, spaced more closely together, and lean inward slightly to avoid the appearance of weakness or outward fall. Triglyphs and metopes become closer together as they spread outward from the center. The stylobate may curve up to about 4″ to counter any semblance of sagging. The architrave, frieze, cornice, and roof gables also curve, and capitals distort to fit the architrave. Consequently, there are few straight lines or rectangular blocks in a building that uses all of these refinements, such as the Parthenon (Fig. 5-8). Inscriptions closer to the viewer usually are smaller than those farther away, so that they all appear the same size.

Public and Private Buildings

■ *Sacred Sites*. Sanctuaries with temples and other sacred buildings are often placed on high promontory points for recognition, protection, and orientation (Fig. 5-7). Unlike Egyptian processional and axial temple complexes, each building in a Greek

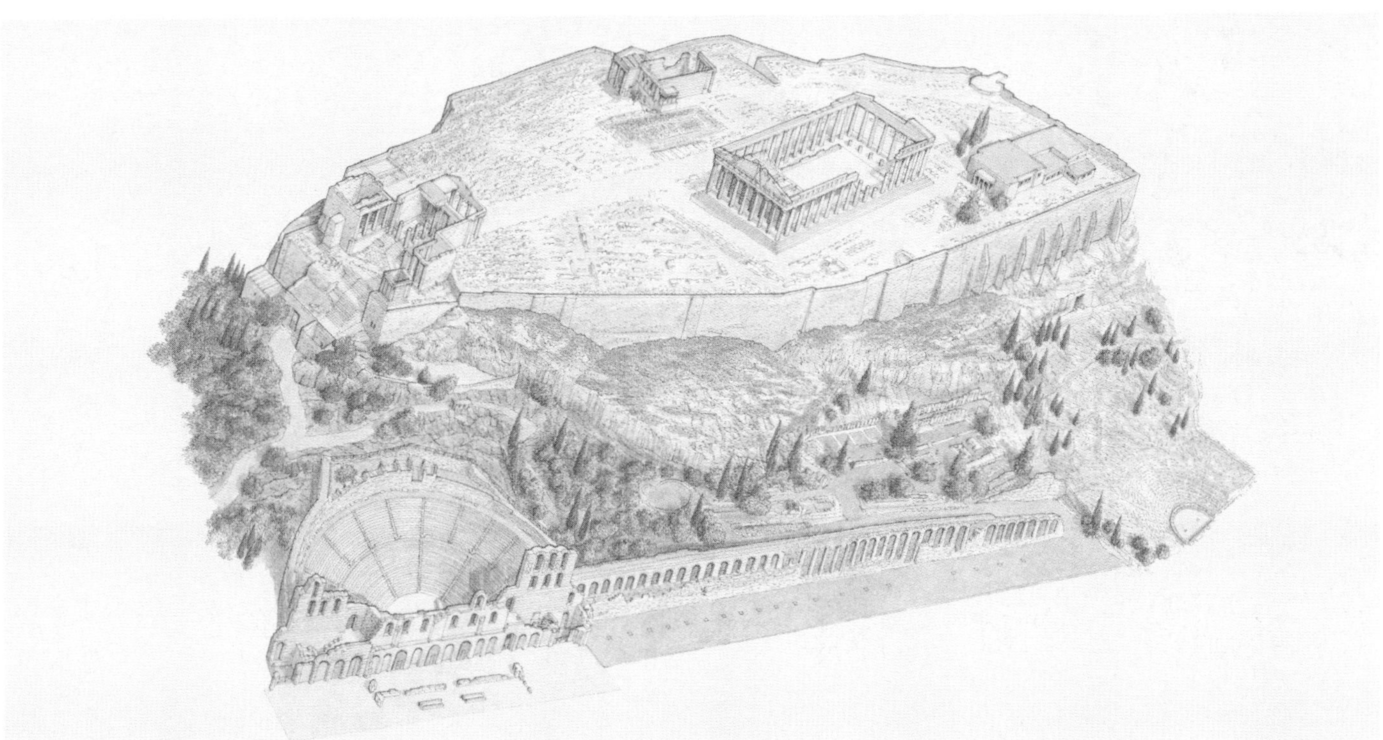

▲ **5-7.** Acropolis and site plan (reconstructed views); 5th century B.C.E., Athens, Greece.

sanctuary is an individual element integrated to natural features of the landscape. This arrangement reflects the cultural vision of each citizen as an individual who unites with others for a common purpose. Situated on a prominent plateau is the Acropolis in Athens (Fig. 5-7), the best known of Greek sacred sites. During Athens's golden age, the 5th century B.C.E., the Acropolis acquired its present appearance with the construction of the major buildings: the Propylea, a complex entrance structure designed by Mnesicles; the Parthenon (Fig. 5-8); the Erectheion (Fig 5-8); and the Temple of Athena Nike (Fig. 5-8).

■ *Temples.* Temples, the dominant building type until the Hellenistic period, pay homage to a particular god. Temples are conceived as sculpture, and their exteriors are far more important than their interiors. Worship takes place out of doors so interiors focus primarily on housing cult statues and treasures instead of decoration.

Standard floor plans for small temples include a small rectangular room (cella or naos) with columns only in front forming a portico or porch or in front and back (amphiprostyle, Fig. 5-8). Larger temples have several rooms with columns on all four sides forming a peristyle (Fig. 5-8). A single row of columns is peripteral, while a double row is dipteral. In the Hellenistic period, round temples appear.

■ *Theaters.* Often used for dramatic productions, theaters are almost circular with a stage at center surrounded by rising tiers of seats. This shape enhances acoustical quality and has been imitated in contemporary theaters. They are generally outdoors and take advantage of the natural slope of the terrain.

■ *Floor Plans.* Most residential plans (Fig. 5-10) have a symmetrical or asymmetrical arrangement of spaces around a central courtyard where most activities take place. Rooms are rectangular and include the dayroom, dining rooms with couches, bedroom, and sometimes an indoor bathroom. Cooking takes place outside. Spaces for males and females are separated, with male spaces often having entrances from the street. Some houses have shops at the street front.

■ *Materials.* Early public structures are made of wood cut from plentiful forests. Wooden construction methods and some detailing subsequently are translated to buildings of stone, which becomes the primary material for most public architecture. The most common building stones are marble and limestone because of availability, ease of cutting, sharp edges, whiteness, and reflectance in strong light. Stone blocks are put together with no mortar and only metal dowels or clamps. This demonstrates the extraordinary skill of Greek stonemasons especially in buildings with multiple optical refinements, which have few, if any, straight lines. Roofs may be supported with a wooden truss system and covered with curving terra cotta or marble tiles. Most houses are of mud brick, but some are of masonry or stucco. Roofs are tiled.

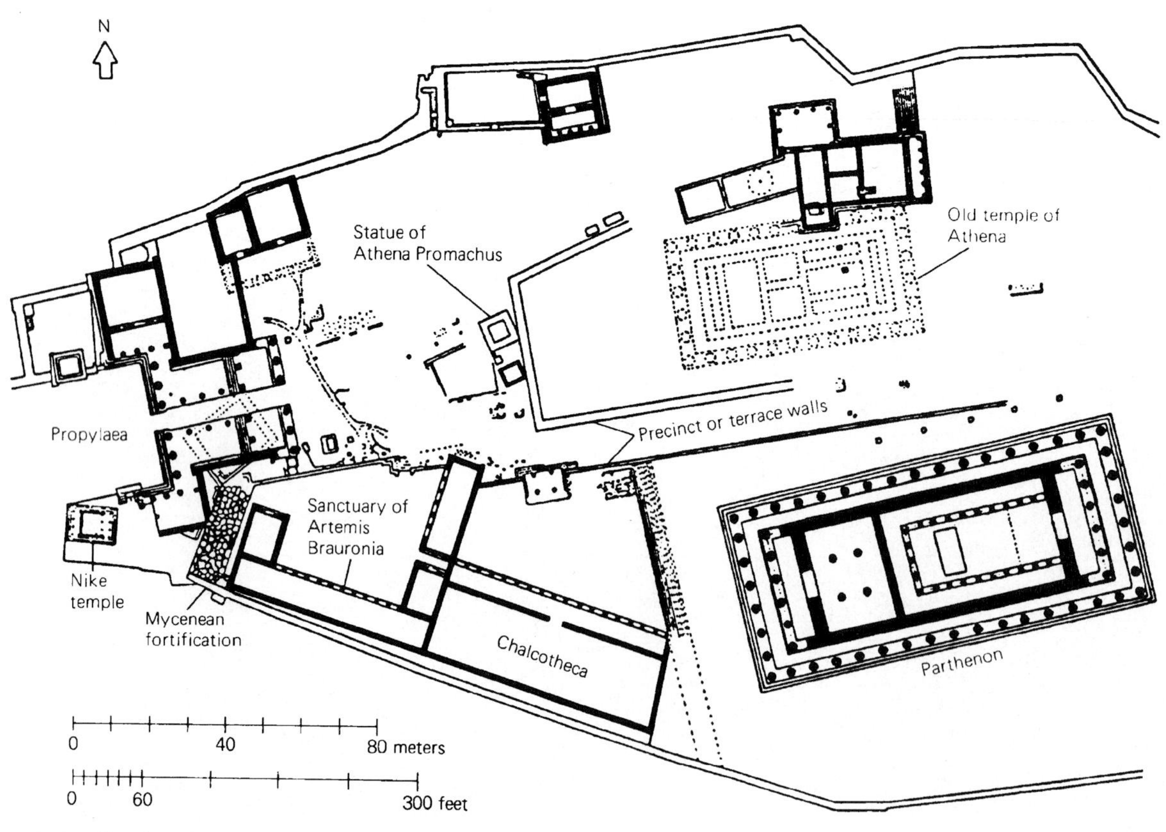

▲ 5-7. Continued

DESIGN SPOTLIGHT

Architecture: Dedicated to the goddess Athena and designed by Ictinus and Callicrates, the Parthenon represents the culmination of Classical Greek architecture and its search for perfection. Since its completion, the Parthenon has exemplified excellence in composition, proportion, unity, harmony, balance, line, detail, and ornament. Massive in scale and raised on a stylobate, a single row of Doric columns composes the peristyle. The ratio for parts is $X = 2y + 1$ (8 columns on the short sides and 17 on the long sides) and the ratio for length to width is 9:4 for the stylobate, cella, and distance between columns center to center.

Numerous architectural adjustments, more than on any other temple, correct perceived optical illusions, enhance the building and its visual impression, and demonstrate Greek understanding of overall psychological impact. The Greeks knew that curves are more pleasing to the eye; consequently, there are no straight lines in the Parthenon from the stylobate, which curves upward in the center, to the entablature that curves in response to the entasis of the columns. Additionally, the designers corrected for any supposed optical illusions that might have disturbed the sense of perfection. For example, the end columns are 2″ thicker than the rest and lean in about $2^3/_8$″ to counter any perceived sense of thinness against the sky or falling outward. More lavishly decorated with sculpture than that of any other temple, the pediment is filled with three-dimensional larger-than-life figures. All 92 metopes have reliefs, and two Ionic friezes surrounding the cella depict a procession of gods. Antefixes embellish the roof corners. The Parthenon, like many other structures, has elaborate painted decoration applied in bright flat colors, although little evidence remains.

Within the temple, the naos houses a huge wood, gold, and ivory statue of Athena (38′-0″h) by the sculptor Phidias. The space is dramatic, complex, and independent of the architectural envelope. More important, it introduces a new concept of interior space in Greece, one in which interiors become more important than previously. Wider than usual to accommodate the statue, the space becomes more pleasing and less tunnel-like in its proportions. A double row of Doric columns gives architectural importance to the walls and makes a visual connection with the exterior. Light may have filled the space from above because the roof may have been partially open. The Parthenon has long been considered the epitome of perfection in Greek Classical architecture and, as such, has been a model for numerous structures in Western architecture until the advent of modernism in the 20th century.

Named for Erectheus, a king of Athens, the Erectheion is dedicated to Athena and other gods. The irregular site and the need to retain earlier sacred portions dictated a more complex plan than found in other temples. Caryatids support the roof of the south porch. Raised on a tall parapet, the figures exhibit a relaxed contraposto pose, drapery that defines the body, and perfect symmetry. Each set of two is a mirror image of the others. Each echinus becomes the figure's abstract headdress.

Also dedicated to the goddess Athena, the Temple of Athena Nike is the first Ionic temple on the Acropolis. This small marble temple has a colonnaded portico with four slender Ionic columns on the front and rear façades. A continuous frieze of reliefs with a different scene on each of its four sides surrounds the temple. A statue of the goddess stands inside the cella. Not long after construction, a parapet is constructed around it to prevent people from falling off the bastion on which it sits. [World Heritage Site]

▲ **5-8.** Parthenon, cutaway view, and naos, 448–432 B.C.E., Ictinus and Callicrates; Temple of Athena Nike (reconstructed view), c. 424 B.C.E., Callicrates; and Porch of Maidens, Erectheion, c. 406 B.C.E.; Acropolis, Athens, Greece.

DESIGN SPOTLIGHT

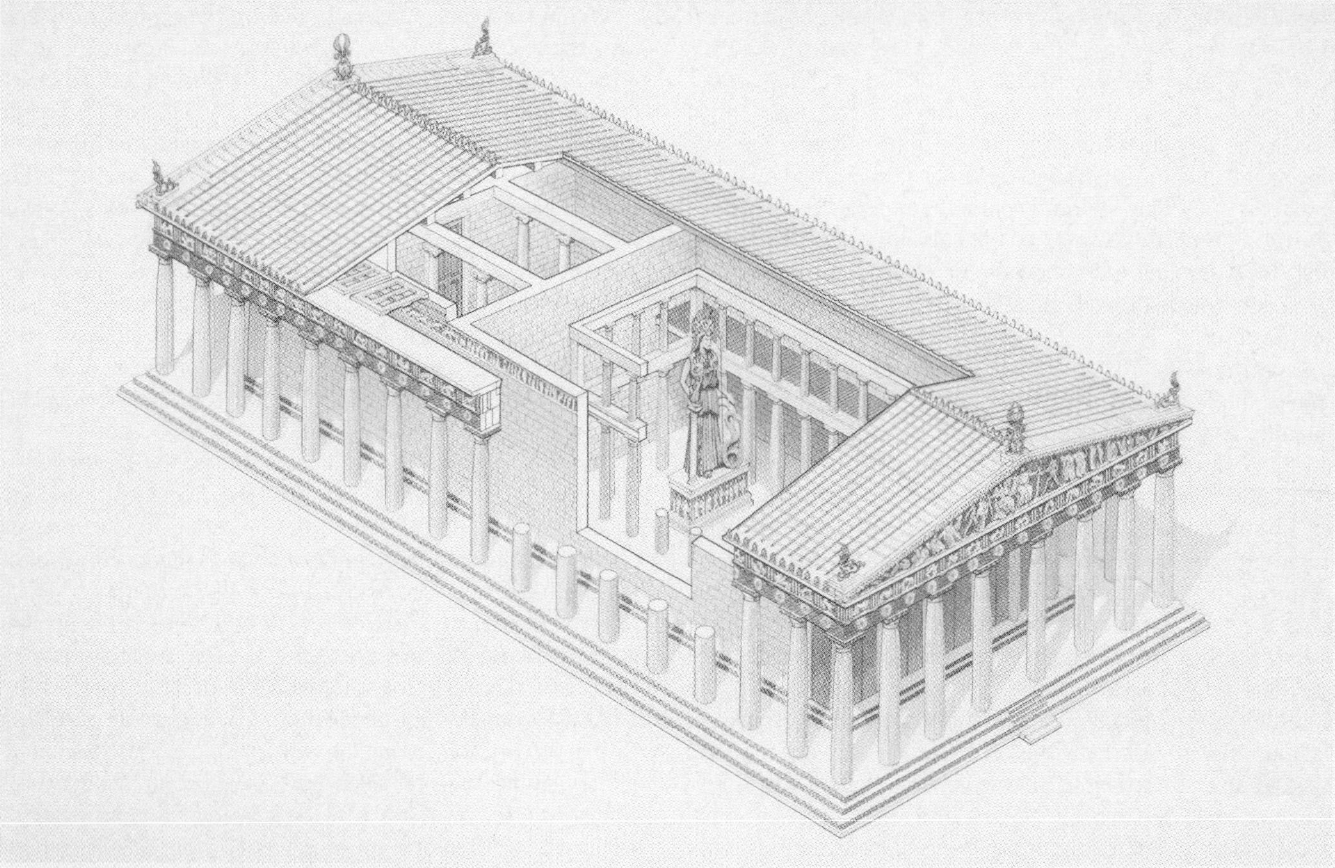

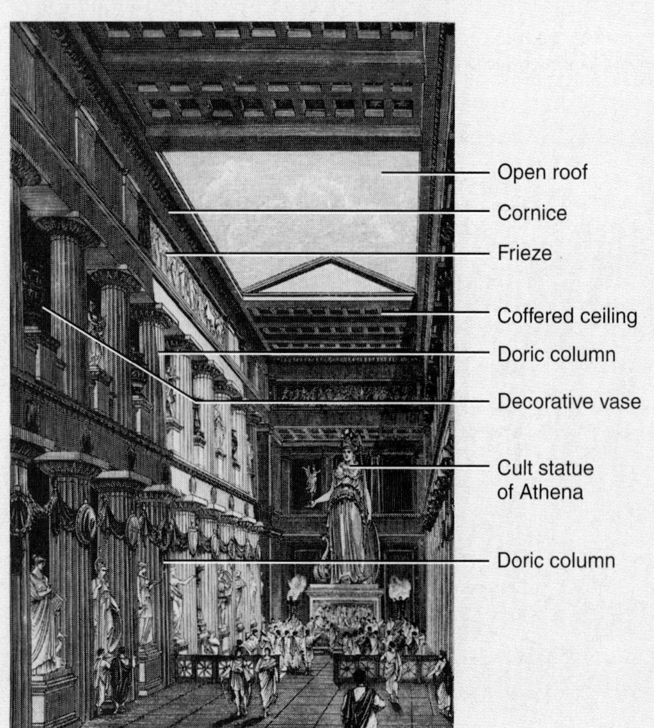

▲ **5–8.** Continued

DESIGN SPOTLIGHT

▲ **5-8.** Continued

◄ **5-9.** Choragic Monument of Lysicrates, c. 334 B.C.E., Athens, Greece.

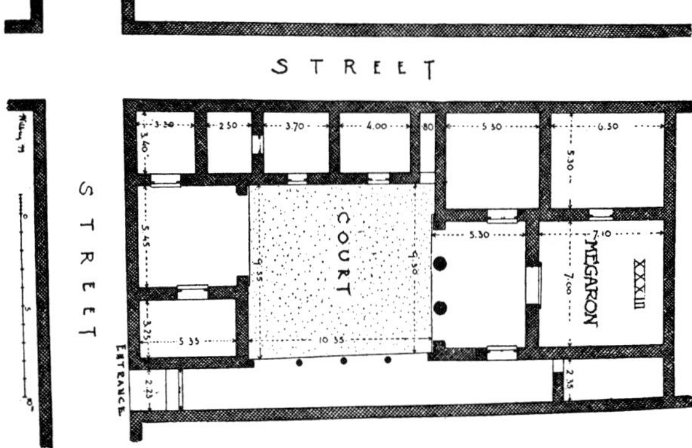

▲ **5-10.** Model of an ancient Greek farmhouse and floor plan, house c. 4th century; Priene, present-day Turkey.

■ *Color*. Color, which rarely survives, enhances and emphasizes the details of temples, such as moldings, friezes, and triglyphs (Fig. 5-3, 5-4). It is applied in flat areas or as patterns in blue, red, black, or golden yellow. Terra-cotta also contrasts in color with stonework; different colors of stone provide contrast to white marble.
■ *Façades*. Temples (Fig. 5-8) feature a columned portico, accenting the front and back of the building and providing a symbolic entry centered on a longitudinal axis.
■ *Later Interpretations*. Greek temples provide inspiration for later interpretations by the Romans and later designers such as Andrea Palladio, Robert Adam, Thomas Jefferson, Michael Graves, and many others. Examples appear in many subsequent periods, such as the 19th-century Greek Revival (Fig. 5-11).

▲ **5-11.** Later Interpretation: Andalusia, 1836–1838, Bucks County, Pennsylvania; Thomas U. Walter. Greek Revival.

INTERIORS

Public interiors express an interconnected design relationship to exteriors, repeating architectural treatments, proportion, materials, and colors. Temple interiors have more architectural details than residences do. Since few public and no private interiors survive, information about them and their furnishings comes from archaeology, literature, vase paintings, reliefs, and statuettes.

Public and Private Buildings

■ *Color*. Color palettes are primarily red, blue, and black and gradually expand as more is known about pigment mixture. Greeks use color to highlight and emphasize, as on architecture.
■ *Floors*. Floors in public buildings may be of stone or mosaic tiles. Historical studies indicate that most residential floors are of packed earth. Important rooms may have stone mosaics, a Greek innovation. The earliest tesserae are pebbles but later are made of clay, marble, or glass. Patterns may outline important furnishings, such as dining couches, or resemble rugs with borders and central medallions. Upper floors are of wood or clay.
■ *Walls*. In temples, orders inside may differ from those on the exterior. For example, the Doric Temple of Apollo at Bassae, c. 420–410 B.C.E, has Ionic columns and a single Corinthian column in the cella. Interior decoration becomes more important in the Hellenistic period and features complex painting; veneers of fine materials, such as marble or alabaster; stuccowork; or engaged columns articulating walls. Residential interior walls may be embellished with stucco and paint. Tiers of flat color often cover the surfaces; stylized horizontal or vertical bands of colored patterns may be added. Red is a favored color. No pictorial depictions have been excavated, but they may have existed.
■ *Ceilings*. Ceilings are flat and beamed or coffered.
■ *Textiles*. Greek textiles, as seen in vase paintings, are especially fine. Common documented materials include wool, linen, and some silk. In the home, textiles hang flat or gathered on walls, at door openings, or around beds, and they are often used as cushion and bed covers. Colors are rich and saturated, and designs may be woven, painted, embroidered, or a combination. Common documented dye colors are purple, saffron, crimson, violet, and green.
■ *Lighting*. Candlestands and candelabras provide some artificial lighting in addition to lamps and torches (Fig. 5-12). Fixtures are made of wood and metal with decoration of classical motifs.

▲ **5-12.** Lighting: Candelabras.

FURNISHINGS AND DECORATIVE ARTS

Examples of Greek furniture and decorative arts exist in vase paintings, grave steles, terra-cottas, theaters, and sculpture. Furniture design emphasizes function with limited embellishment. Rooms have few furnishings. Greek furniture uses three types of legs: animal (from Egypt and used early), turned, or rectangular legs. The rectangular leg featuring a cutout center accented with knobs and palmettes is a Greek innovation.

■ *Materials*. Furniture is constructed of various woods, marble, bronze, and iron. Carving and inlay are the main forms of decoration but are used sparingly.

DESIGN SPOTLIGHT

Furnishings: The *klismos*, the most important seating example invented by the Greeks, features curved back stiles, a splat, and supports contoured to the body, and front and back outward curving legs mortised into a frame with a woven seat. Its beauty comes from its proportion, silhouette, and linear quality. As in architecture, the Greeks strive for excellence in proportions and the relationship of parts to one another. Often found in the home, variations of this form appear in theaters as seating for aristocrats. The *klismos* inspires numerous later interpretations.

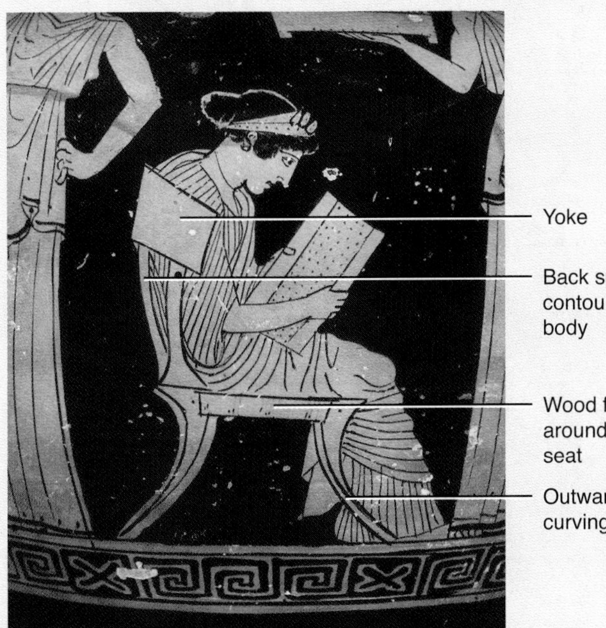

▲ **5-13.** *Klismos* from a vase painting and the grave stele of Hegeso, end of 5th century B.C.E.

■ *Seating.* An important Greek innovation is the *klismos* (Fig. 5-13), a simple light chair that reappears in varying forms in later periods. Other forms of seating include thrones, benches, and theater seats. The most common seating piece is the *diphros*, a rectangular stool (Fig. 5-14) with four turned legs and a seat of woven leather or plant thongs, sometimes topped with a cushion.

■ *Tables.* Primarily used for meals, tables have round or rectangular tops with three or four legs (Fig. 5-16). Some have stretchers. Vase paintings show a range of forms and decoration. Tables, used to serve food to individuals, may slide under couches when not in use.

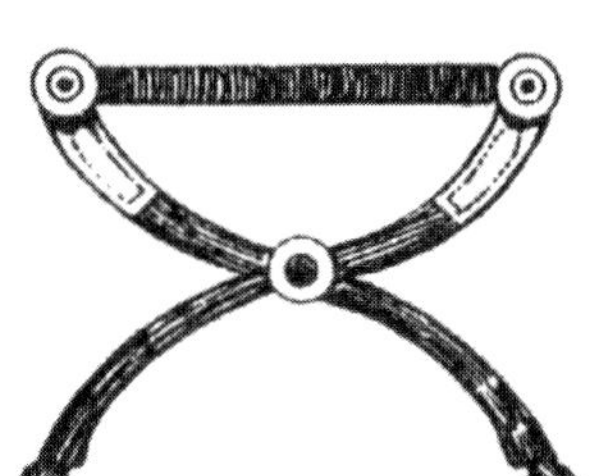

▲ **5-14.** Stools.

■ *Storage*. Chests for storage change from rectangular boxes with paneled sides to ones with arched lids. Small objects for daily use are stored on shelves or hung on walls.

■ *Beds*. The *kline* or couch, a Greek innovation, (Fig. 5-15, 5-16) is used for sleeping or for reclining during meals and at other times. Couches have legs similar to those of chairs and often are raised on bases. The head usually is higher than the foot.

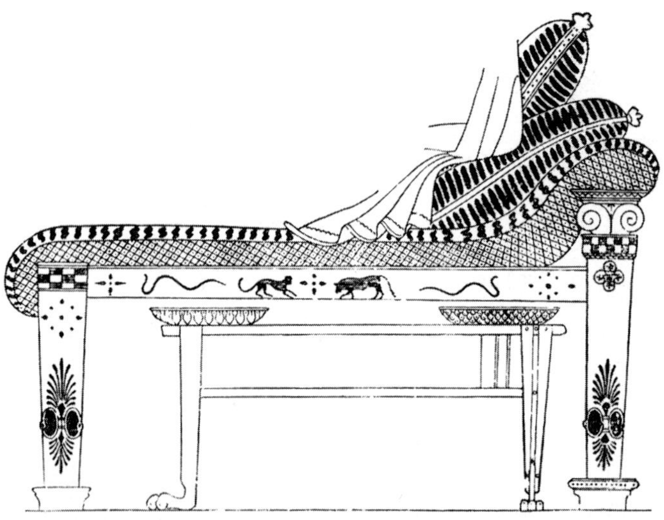

▲ **5-15.** Couches.

■ *Pottery*. The most important examples of Grecian decorative arts are the beautiful ceramic vessels, used primarily for household storage but also as grave markers or as art objects. Greek vases (Fig. 5-16) vary in shape and size according to use and may have extensive surface decoration. Black, red, and cream provide the palette depending upon the period, which includes Red Figure, Black Figure, and White Ground. Vases often depict furniture, people, and motifs and are a primary source of historical information.

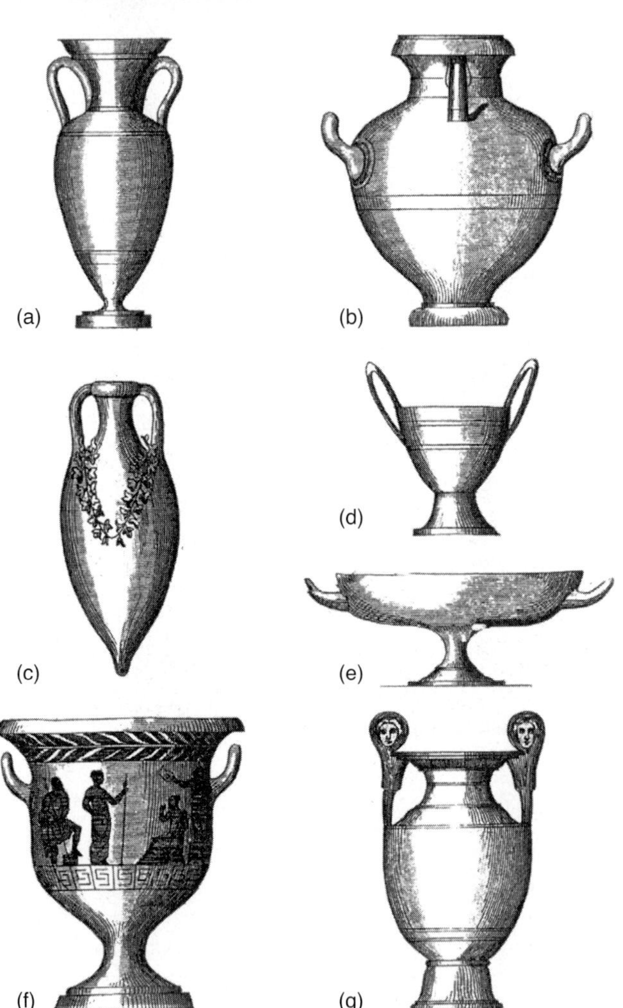

▲ **5-16.** Decorative Arts: Red-figured *pelike* vase showing couches and tables and Greek vases: (a) *amphora* (storing wine); (b) *hydria* (water jar); (c) *amphora*; (d) *kantharos* (drinking cup); (e) *kylix* (mixing wine and water); (f) bell *krater* (vessel for mixing); and (g) volute *krater.*

CHAPTER 6

Rome

509–27 B.C.E., Roman Republic; 96–180 C.E., Height of the Roman Empire

As she establishes a great empire, Ancient Rome assimilates a mixture of cultures and ideas, principally from the Greek colonists to the south and the Etruscans to the north. Roman artists, designers, and builders adapt them to Roman tastes with imagination and innovation. As with Greece, the images establish a language and grammar for architecture, interiors, furniture, and decorative arts copied by successive generations. Romans are the first to use extensively the arch and vault and concrete as a building material. The more diverse, more embellished, and monumental material culture of Rome influences Western civilizations more than that of Greece.

Architecture depends on Order, Arrangement, Eurythmy, Symmetry, Propriety, and Economy.
—Pollio Marcus Vitruvius, *The Ten Books on Architecture*, 1st century C.E.

HISTORICAL AND SOCIAL

During the 7th and 6th centuries B.C.E., the Etruscans settle Etruria (north and central Italy). Beginning in 750 B.C.E. Latin-speaking peoples inhabit the early village of Rome. By 509 B.C.E., these people overthrow the last Etruscan king and establish a Roman Republic that is governed by a Senate composed of wealthy citizens. Through various alliances and conquests, the Romans control the entire Italian peninsula by 275 B.C.E. Territorial expansion continues beyond Italy to the Mediterranean, as well as modern France and Spain.

Immense growth eventually strains Republican government and resources, and civil wars threaten the empire. In 46 B.C.E., Julius Caesar emerges victorious and establishes himself as dictator. After his assassination in 44 B.C.E., his heir Octavian takes over. In 27 B.C.E., he assumes the title of Augustus, the supreme ruler of the empire. When Augustus becomes *Pontifex Maximus*, the highest religious official, in 12 C.E., he initiates worship of the emperor as god of the state. A powerful ruler, Augustus ushers in the *Pax Romana*, 200 years of peace and stability. Rome's subsequent history is of a series of dynasties and individual emperors, tyrannical and benevolent.

The empire is at its largest under Trajan (98–117 C.E.), but internal strife and disorder, civil wars, economic instability, and sheer size contribute to its downfall. After splitting into western and eastern segments after 330 C.E., the western portion continues to decline until 476 C.E. when a Germanic chief seizes power. The eastern section survives as the Byzantine Empire until 1453, when it surrenders to the forces of the Ottoman Turks.

At its height, the Roman Empire occupies about half of Western Europe as far north as modern Scotland, most of the Middle East to the Persian Gulf, and the entire northern coast of Africa. It is a vast land area, but the city of Rome remains its heart. To further allegiance and unity, the government engages in vast building campaigns of temples, baths, entertainment structures, and public works such as roads to move troops and people and aqueducts for water. Emperor worship also intends to unite its diverse citizenry.

Society is hierarchical, with the upper and wealthiest class comprising members of the Senate. Families are patriarchal. As long as their father lives, sons cannot own property or have legal authority over their own children. Extended families make up most households. Parents arrange marriages, often for economic benefits. Women have few rights until the 1st century C.E. But many have a formal education; some become shopkeepers, physicians, or writers. Romans are polytheistic, worshipping their own and Greek gods whom they give Roman names. Some adopt the religions of their conquered peoples. Christianity becomes the empire's official religion in 312 C.E. Recreation is important to the Romans as numerous public buildings and entertainment spaces testify.

CONCEPTS

Roman art and architecture has neither the timeless consistency of Egypt nor the stylistic development of Greece. Distinctly different, its art and architecture is much like Rome itself—a melting pot of diverse influences and cultures, aggressively interpreted, and lavish in form and decoration. The Romans regard art as a means to glorify the empire, commemorate its exploits, and unify its peoples. Consequently, few artists or architects are known. The Romans synthesize their borrowings from others and invent their own classical language and forms, which are visibly expressed in architecture, sculpture, and decorative arts.

CHARACTERISTICS AND MOTIFS

■ *Republican (510–60 B.C.E.).* During this age of expansion, Etruscan influence is strong early, but Grecian forms and elements gradually increase after 146 B.C.E., when Greece is conquered. Romans adapt the Greek orders, particularly Corinthian. The main advancements in arched construction and builders' mastery of concrete occur during the 1st and 2nd centuries B.C.E.

■ *Early Imperial or Early Empire (60 B.C.E.–285 C.E.).* Builders continue to develop arcuated (arched) construction and master concrete as a building material. They introduce new building types such as basilicas and amphitheaters.

■ *Late Imperial or Late Empire (285–395 C.E.).* Interiors often become more important than exteriors as builders explore the relationships among spaces of different sizes and shapes. Large-scale public building campaigns continue. Materials are increasingly reused as the empire declines.

■ *Motifs.* Many motifs (Fig. 6-1) are adapted from Greece, such as the human figure, acanthus, rinceau, guilloche, rosette, swan, eagle, monopodium, lion, oxen, sphinx, griffin, arabesque, wave pattern, festoon, anthemion, fret, laurel wreath, and architectural details.

(a)

(b)

(c)

▲ **6-1.** Motifs and Architectural Detail: (a) Acanthus leaf with rosette; (b) rinceau from Italy; (c) mosaic, Pompeii, Italy; (d) vase and motifs; and (e) structure, Theater of Marcellus, 23–13 B.C.E.; Rome, Italy.

(d)

(e)

▲ 6-1. Continued

ARCHITECTURE

Roman architecture is a synthesis of forms adopted from its conquered peoples and its own innovations. Builders and designers adapt forms and elements to suit Roman preferences and tastes. Temple forms and the arch come from the Etruscans. The orders, other classical elements, and increased refinement evolve from Greek sources. Romans adapt the Greek classical language to their own vocabulary, resulting in a different visual image, one of lavish grandeur as compared to the more refined and spare Grecian vision.

Roman architectural history reflects developing technology and increasing sureness in construction. Unlike its precursors, Roman architecture focuses on volume, space, and spatial innovations, which are made possible by Roman engineering abilities, extensive use of concrete as a building material, and arcuated construction. Arches, vaults, and domes span large spaces, the size and scale of which are previously unknown or even imagined. Vitruvius (born c. 70 B.C.E.), official architect to the emperor Augustus, writes *De architectura* (known today as *The Ten Books on Architecture*), an architectural guidebook of design standards and codified Greek proportional systems for provincial builders throughout the empire. The earliest surviving architectural treatise, it becomes the major reference on classical architecture in the Renaissance and later.

Rome has greater variety in building types than either Egypt or Greece. Her more complex civilization demands many new and existing types such as temples (Fig. 6-7, 6-8), basilicas (Fig. 6-9), theaters, amphitheaters, circuses, baths, and aqueducts. Residential buildings include imperial palaces, *villas*, *domuses* (Fig. 6-13), and *insulae* (Fig. 6-12). Public buildings often glorify the state and the emperor, while domestic buildings reflect the Roman fondness for comfort and luxury.

Structural Features

■ *Classical Orders*. Romans adopt and adapt the classical language of Greek architecture to their construction systems. However, in contrast to the Egyptians and Greeks, they often use elements of the post and lintel system to organize exteriors or for articulation or decoration. These architectural elements include pilasters, engaged columns, and the arch order (Fig. 6-1). The Romans use all the Greek orders, but with different proportions. They introduce the Tuscan and Composite orders. Like the Greek prototypes, the Roman column has a distinguishing capital, a shaft, and a base. The base may be raised to form a pedestal.

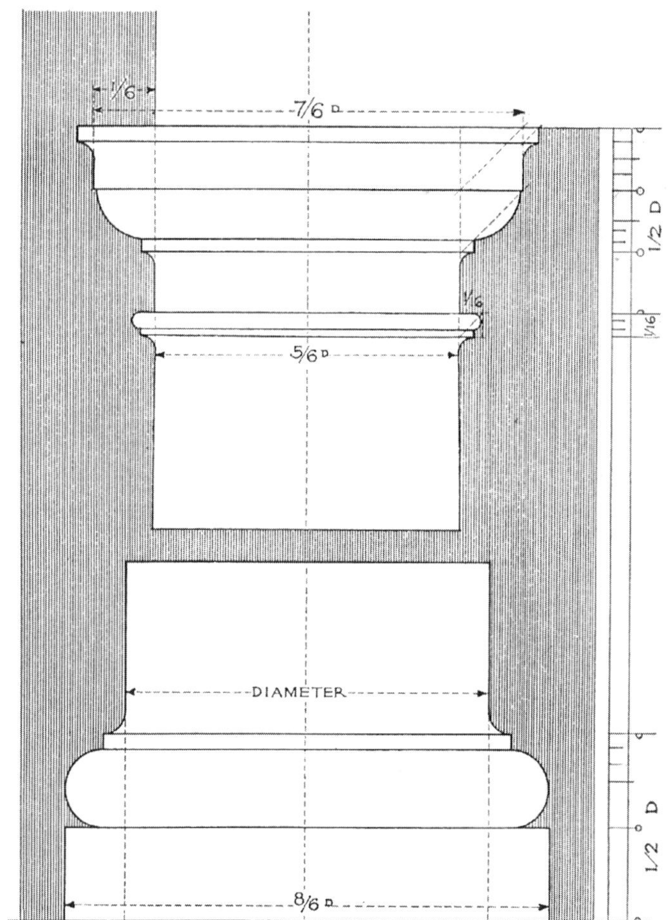

▲ 6-2. Tuscan order.

■ *Roman Orders*. The Tuscan column (Fig. 6-2), based on the Greek Doric column, has a smaller capital, a molded base, and a shaft that is not fluted. The Ionic capital (Fig. 6-3) is smaller in scale than the Greek Ionic and has a four-sided volute. The Corinthian capital (Fig. 6-4) is smiliar to the Greek one but is lighter in scale. The Composite column (Fig. 6-5) resembles the Corinthian, but the capital integrates volute forms with acanthus leaves instead of the stalks of the Corinthian.

■ *Podium*. The podium, which replaces the Greek stylobate, forms the base of many Roman temples (Fig. 6-6, 6-7) and raises them several feet from the ground. Besides emphasizing a temple's importance, it gives a single front entrance that emphasizes a frontal vista.

■ *Arches, Vaults, and Domes*. A true arch consists of wedge-shaped blocks called voussoirs, with the top center one identified as a keystone. The arch may develop into a barrel vault, groin vault, or dome. Round domes may cover small rectangular spaces or large round ones in public buildings and imperial *villas*. Romans use round arches to span openings, create space, and organize exteriors (Fig. 6-8, 6-10, 6-11). In the Late Imperial period, they introduce the arcade, which repeats arches sequentially.

Public and Private Buildings

■ *Forum*. Forums (Fig. 6-7), located in city centers, form the core of Roman civic life by housing religious and public buildings as well as markets and colonnades. Early forums have regular plans, but later ones, particularly in Rome, become irregular as each emperor adds a monument to himself. Nevertheless, strict axial alignment and vistas of individual structures are maintained. Relationships among individual buildings are not as carefully orchestrated as in Greece, and the Roman forum lacks the surrounding open space of the Greek acropolis.

■ *Temples*. Roman temples range from small and individual to large complexes. Unlike Greek ones, Roman temples create a vista or focal point by being set on a longitudinal axis with an entrance on one end. They are usually placed in the forum, but may be scattered throughout the city and countryside. Like the Greeks, Roman temples are dedicated to a particular god.

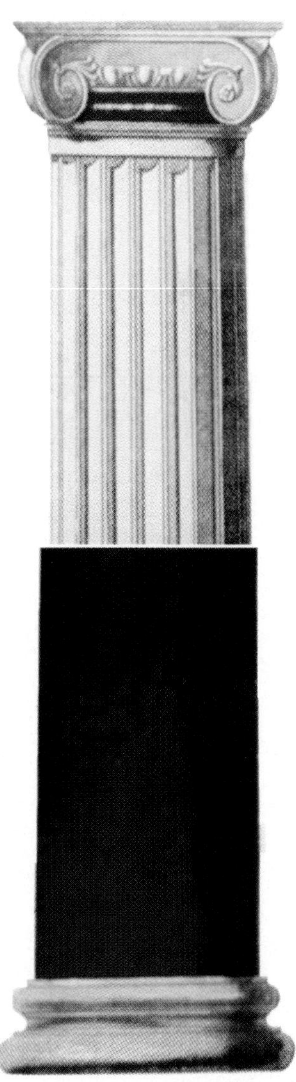

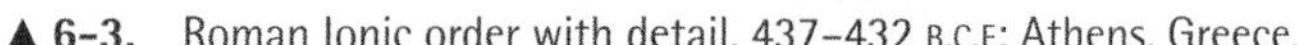

▲ **6-3.** Roman Ionic order with detail, 437–432 B.C.E; Athens, Greece.

▲ 6-4. Roman Corinthian order with capital; Ephesus, Turkey.

Temples (Fig. 6-6, 6-8) combine Etruscan and Greek characteristics into a unique form. Most rise from the ground and rest on a podium, an Etruscan characteristic. Entrance is by a single set of stairs on one end, through a porch in the Etruscan manner to a windowless cella that houses the deity and trophies of conquest. Most Roman structures have engaged columns on three sides creating the impression of a peristyle. Two of the most complete surviving Roman temples are the Maison Carrée (Fig. 6-6) and the Pantheon (Fig. 6-8).

■ *Basilicas*. Basilicas (Fig. 6-7, 6-9), used for religious, legal, and meeting purposes, have large central rectangular spaces with lower side aisles, clerestory windows, and usually an apse on one end. Originating in Hellenistic Greece and first appearing in the Roman Forum, the basilica is the model for Christian churches.

▲ 6-5. Roman Composite order.

■ *Public Baths*. Early baths are modest, but during the late Republican and early Imperial periods they become increasingly monumental and imposing (Fig. 6-10). Romans use them for bathing, exercising, relaxing, and socializing. Public baths maintain axial symmetry and sequential space planning with numerous domed and vaulted, small and large spaces. The variety of spaces within lends itself to innovations in space planning, which are first worked out in imperial palaces.

■ *Public Entertainment*. The Romans construct a variety of entertainment structures to amuse its citizens. Made possible by concrete and arcuated construction, these buildings often are monumental, accommodating thousands of people (Fig. 6-11). Types include theaters, amphitheaters for sports, and the circuses for chariot and horse racing. Roman theaters resemble Greek ones in form, and have a curved stone seating area and excellent acoustics. Unlike Greek, Roman theaters rise from the ground instead of emerging from a hillside. Some have timber roofs.

DESIGN SPOTLIGHT

Architecture: The Maison Carrée, one of the best-preserved Roman temples, was commissioned by Marcus Vipsanius Agrippa and dedicated to his sons. As an excellent example of classical Roman architecture, the rectangular temple dominated the Roman forum in Nîmes. The podium is nearly 8′-0″ high, so entrance is only by the front stairs, which creates the favored vista. The Corinthian portico leads to the small windowless cella behind it. Engaged Corinthian columns line the other three walls, giving the appearance of columns and a peripteral form. Acanthus leaves and rosettes embellish the frieze, above which is a modillioned cornice supporting the gable roof. Maison Carreé was the model used by Jefferson for the Virginia State Capitol in the 18th century and also for La Madeline in 19th-century France. [World Heritage Site]

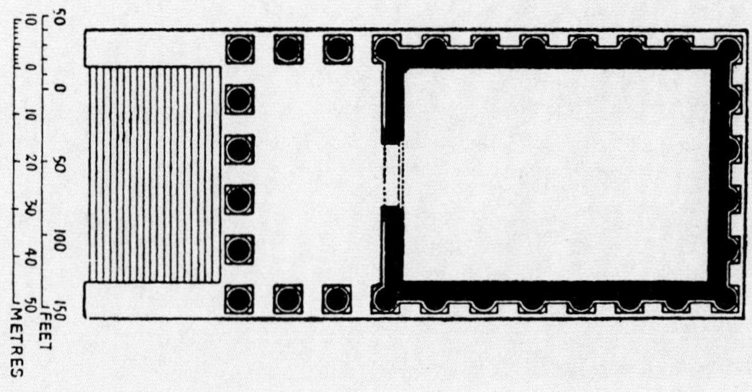

▲ **6-6.** Maison Carrée and floor plan, c. 1–10 C.E.; Nîmes, France.

▲ 6-7. Forum, Basilica, and Market of Trajan (reconstructed 19th-century view), c. 100–12 C.E.; Rome, Italy.

■ *Dwellings*. Unlike Egypt and Greece, the Romans originate several types of residences. Imperial palaces usually are vast and extremely luxurious complexes of numerous structures. *Villas* may be working farms or well-appointed country houses for the wealthy. In the city, most of the affluent inhabit the sprawling *domuses*. Some have shops on the front or sides that may or may not be connected to the house. Roman towns have numerous *insulae* (Fig. 6-12) or apartment houses where the majority of people live. *Insulae* have shops on the ground floors with apartments above. These complexes are up to four stories high and may have light wells or courtyards in the center. Apartments vary in size from one or two rooms to many rooms occupying several floors. Unlike *domuses* and *villas*, apartments have no baths or running water and often no cooking facilities because most Romans spend the majority of time elsewhere in the city.

■ *Site Orientation*. A forum, basilica, and markets (Fig. 6-7, 6-9) usually define a city center along with colonnades and additional public buildings and monuments to individual emperors. Most Roman cities are organized on a grid system, which is still emulated today.

■ *Floor Plans*. Rectangular temple floor plans (Fig. 6-6) resemble the Greek prostyle plans with columns and portico in front. Some temples have round plans with or without columns (Fig. 6-8). Basilicas have a large central space or nave that is flanked by aisles. At one end is the apse where officials sit (Fig. 6-9).

DESIGN SPOTLIGHT

Architecture: One of the best-known Roman temples is the Pantheon, dedicated to the gods. A masterpiece of Roman technical achievement and influence, the Pantheon shows the full potential of concrete as a building material and influences almost as many subsequent buildings as does the Greek Parthenon. Unfluted Corinthian columns support the pedimented portico. Behind it, the concrete rotunda culminates in a dome. In contrast to the sculptural exterior of the Greek Parthenon, the Pantheon exterior is plain and simply treated with three stringcourses and a cornice, as was common on buildings with complex interiors. The double pediments are unusual, and the reason for them remains a mystery. One possible explanation lies in the 10′-0″ height difference in the portico columns from the original plan. If the present 40′-0″ columns are raised to 50′-0″ tall as in the plan, the double pediment disappears. The floor plan shows the juxtaposition of the round domed cella and rectangular entrance porch of the building. The interior space is composed of alternating circular and rectangular niches holding statues.

▶ 6-8. Pantheon section, floor plan, and interior, 118–125 C.E.; Rome, Italy. [Samuel H. Kress Collection, National Gallery of Art, Washington, DC] (Information continues on the next page.)

DESIGN SPOTLIGHT

The interior is a hemisphere as high as it is wide. It boasts decoratively patterned marble floors, engaged columns and pilasters embellishing the walls, and a marble patterned drum below the dome, in contrast to the plain interiors of the Greek Parthenon. (The pediments in the drum are added during the Renaissance.) The entablatures visually separate the wall plane from the domed ceiling. The ceiling is coffered in geometric shapes, which not only are decorative but also lighten the weight of the dome. The coffers originally were covered with blue stucco and gilded rosettes. An oculus or opening in the center of the dome allows in light and reduces weight at a critical point. Originally constructed on the ruins of an earlier temple, the Pantheon was at one end of a columned square. As in other Roman temples, a flight of steps leads to the portico. [World Heritage Site]

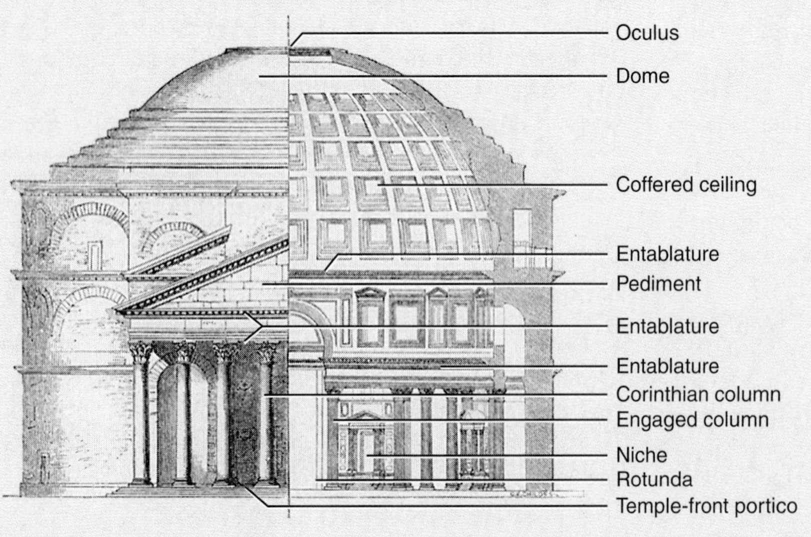

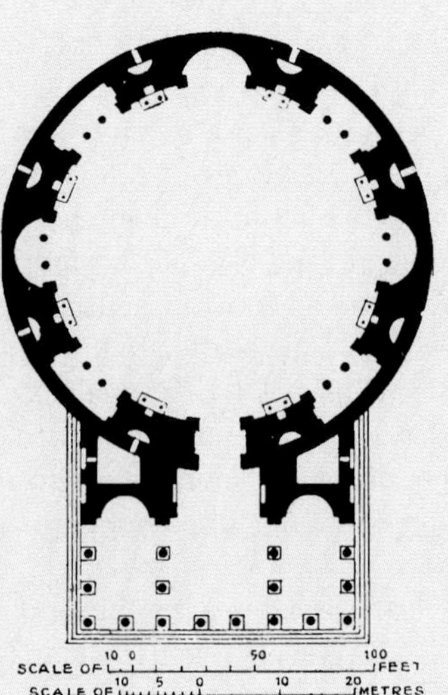

▲ **6-8.** Continued

Villa and *domus* plans (Fig. 6-13) are similar. Most extant examples come from the 1st century C.E. From the entry or vestibule, the dwelling focuses inward to the open atrium (Fig. 6-15). The atrium, which serves as a reception room and circulation space, features an *impluvium* where rainwater collects from the sloping roof. Larger atriums may have columns supporting the roof opening. Smaller rooms surround the atrium, including the *tablinium*, which is usually on the main axis and which serves as an office or master bedroom. The atrium usually connects to a peristyle, an open courtyard derived from the Greeks (Fig. 6-14), which creates a vista, adds light, and is a cool, pleasant garden space. Encircled by a covered walkway, the peristyle usually has a fountain or pool, statues, wall paintings, and mosaic floors. The *triclinium* or dining room, which takes its name from its three couches arranged at right angles to each other, usually opens to the peristyle. Various other rooms, including *cubicula* (Fig. 6-17), also open onto the peristyle, and kitchen and service areas are nearby.

■ *Materials*. Materials include brick, concrete, marble, travertine, tufa, and granite. Stucco, marble, or stone covers concrete or brick. Brick and stone are commonly used for residences. Color comes primarily from building materials, unlike Greece or Egypt where painting is more common.

■ *Concrete*. Concrete, an important and easy-to-use building material perfected by the Romans (Fig. 6-8, 6-11), gives their

Transverse Section of Basilica of Maxentius. Scale 100 ft. to 1 in.

Longitudinal Section of Basilica of Maxentius. Scale 100 ft. to 1 in.

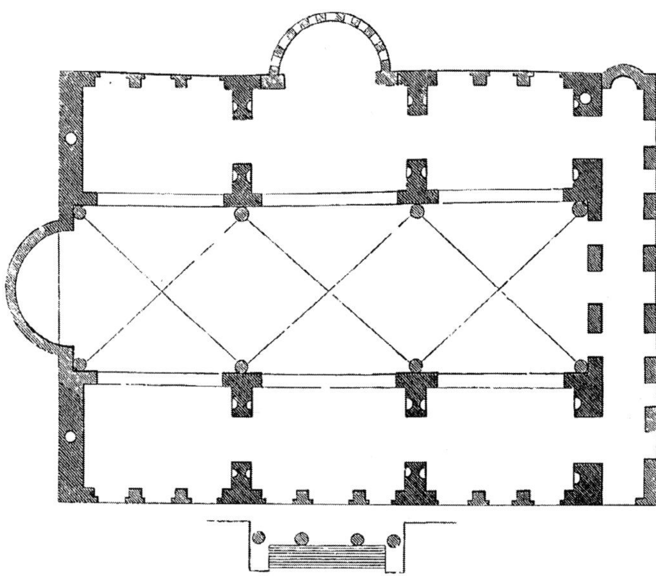

Plan of Basilica of Maxentius. Scale 100 ft. to 1 in.

▲ **6-9.** Basilica of Maxentius, plan, and sections, c. 308–312 C.E.; Rome, Italy.

▲ **6-10.** Baths of Caracalla (reconstructed drawing of frigidarium), 212–216 C.E.; Rome, Italy.

DESIGN SPOTLIGHT

Architecture: The Flavian Amphitheater or Colosseum, named for the Flavian family of emperors, is the largest setting for gladiator combat and other spectacles constructed in its day, with seating for 50,000 people. The common name of Colosseum comes from the Colosseus of Nero standing at the entrance. Four horizontal bands with arched openings compose the façade, but this exterior articulation has little to do with the interior construction. A series of arch orders on each band recalls the trabeated or post and lintel construction system on the arcuated building. Greek orders dominate the façade. Engaged columns follow typical Roman practice of Doric on the lower story, followed by Ionic and Corinthian. The plain fourth tier has Corinthian pilasters. Originally, brackets held wooden poles supporting awnings to shield spectators from the sun. Despite innovative use of a new construction system, the Romans continue the Greek practice of using orders to articulate and unify façades and give order, dignity, and formality. The stadium has a complex system of vaults, ramps, stairs, and passageways that support seating and move spectators in and out. A complicated system of pulleys raised and lowered people and animals from the rows of rooms and cages beneath the floor. This well planned, efficient, and monumental structure is a testament to Roman engineering genius.

▲ **6-11.** Colosseum and detail, c. 72–80 C.E.; Rome, Italy.

architecture a distinctive character. Concrete may be shaped in wooden frames, which is a faster and more economical building method than stonecutting. It also relies less on skilled labor. Concrete's greater cohesion can, when combined with arches and vaults, span great distances. Thus, the combination creates an architecture of space in a previously unknown scale. Marble, stucco, or brick cover concrete walls, a somewhat less honest aesthetic than Greek marble. Concrete also gives architectural unity throughout the empire.

■ *Façades*. Exteriors on public buildings usually are treated three ways: with structural or engaged columns, with arches and engaged columns on piers, or with little or no articulation. The latter is common on structures whose exterior shapes reflect complex interior planning, such as baths or the Pantheon (Fig. 6-8). Roman buildings have less sculpture than Greek buildings, but are similarly enhanced with a variety of moldings. In the 1st century C.E., the Romans deviate from Greek classical repose by intro-

▲ **6-12.** *Insula* (reconstructed view), 2nd century C.E.; Ostia, Italy.

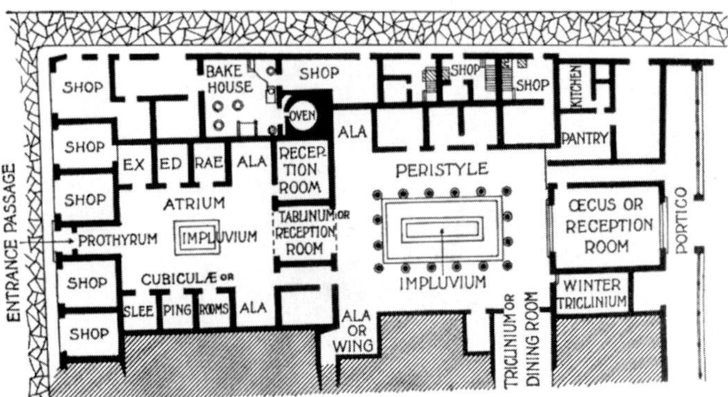

▲ **6-13.** Floor plan, House of Pansa, 1st century C.E.; Pompeii, Italy.

ducing concave and convex movement on façades, and broken pediments and entablatures. Rectangular and arched windows and openings are common on many public buildings, although some, such as temples, have none. Baths have rows of rectangular, arched, or thermae windows, a semicircular form divided by two mullions into three lights.

Exteriors of domestic buildings generally are plain with windows that are small and high in the wall. Some paintings at Pompeii depict homes with richly treated entrances and/or roof gardens.

- *Roofs*. Roofs are usually flat, double pitched, domed, or vaulted and covered with terra-cotta tiles.

▲ **6-14.** Peristyle, House of Vettii, mid-1st century C.E.; Pompeii, Italy.

▲ **6-15.** Atrium (reconstructed drawing).

INTERIORS

Although some public Roman interiors remained intact, domestic ones were relatively unknown until the discovery of Pompeii and Herculaneum, two Greco-Roman cities buried by the eruption of Mount Vesuvius in 79 C.E. Excavated beginning in the mid-18th century, these cities gave the world a detailed record of Roman 1st-century material culture. In contrast to Greek interior decoration, Roman interior decoration is more lavish and varied. Interiors and their decoration are important features of many public and domestic buildings. Spaces vary from luxurious to utilitarian in scale and treatment. Concepts of classical ordering repeat from the exterior to define many interior wall and ceiling compositions, especially in public buildings.

Public and Private Buildings

- *Color*. Bright and bold colors enliven dimly lit interiors. Typical colors include black, gold, rust, Pompeiian red, turquoise, blue, and green (Fig. 6-16, 6-17).
- *Floors*. Floor materials in public buildings vary from brick to terra-cotta, mosaics, and marble. Combinations of circles and rectangles are common.

Many types of materials cover floors in residences—brick, terra-cotta, marble, black stone (cement with charcoal dust), and

▲ **6-16.** Wall frescoes, c. 50 C.E.; Pompeii, Italy. Third Style Fresco.

mosaics (Fig. 6-17). The Romans fully develop the mosaic techniques originated by the Greeks and use many materials and patterns, including geometric forms, deities, animals, masks, and portraits. Some mosaics resemble rugs or relate to ceiling designs. Imported rugs from the East and animal skins also cover floors.

■ *Walls*. The interior relates to the form of the exterior, but usually emphasizes decoration over function. Only public buildings, the grandest rooms in *villas*, and a few domestic spaces display the orders, niches, real and painted columns, pilasters, and moldings to articulate, organize, and/or decorate the walls. Important rooms and some lesser ones incorporate brightly colored marbles, mosaics, and paintings, often with applied gilding on walls and ceilings (Fig. 6-10) along with some architectural details. Niches holding sculptures and fountains also are common. Doors in temples and other public structures are often of bronze, gilded or otherwise decorated.

Many *domuses* and *villas* have elaborate interior decoration composed of frescoes and wall mosaics to expand and lighten space (Fig. 6-1, 6-16, 6-17). Colorful frescoes in important public rooms usually enliven and divide walls into dado, fill, and frieze. Paintings vary from imitations of marble to *trompe l'oeil* renderings of architecture or landscapes, portraits, still lifes, and narratives. Wall mosaics, fashionable in the 1st century C.E., often have brighter colors and are more pictorial than floor mosaics. Another common treatment is low-relief stucco decoration of compartmentalized colored and plain backgrounds with raised designs. Imperial palaces have doors of bronze or wood that is gilded or otherwise decorated, while those in houses are of wood. Colorful fabrics sometimes substitute for doors. Draperies and awnings in the atrium and peristyle give sun protection. Shutters and blinds are more common than curtains. Glass panes appear during the 1st century C.E.

■ *Pompeiian Wall Painting*. Pompeian and other wall frescoes reveal many and varying designs. Scholars have identified at least four styles. The First Style consists of *tromp l'oeil* marble or masonry panels. The Second Style (Fig. 6-17) features architectural illusionism with realistic renderings of architectural details, such as columns, forming a frame for vistas of towns, cities, and sky. The architecture is weighty and substantial. The Third Style (Fig. 6-16) has solid black, red, blue, and white backgrounds against which small paintings and illusionistic, attenuated architecture seem to float. Crowded, complex compositions of illusionistic architecture, vistas, and wall paintings characterize the Fourth Style, which appears to combine all previous styles.

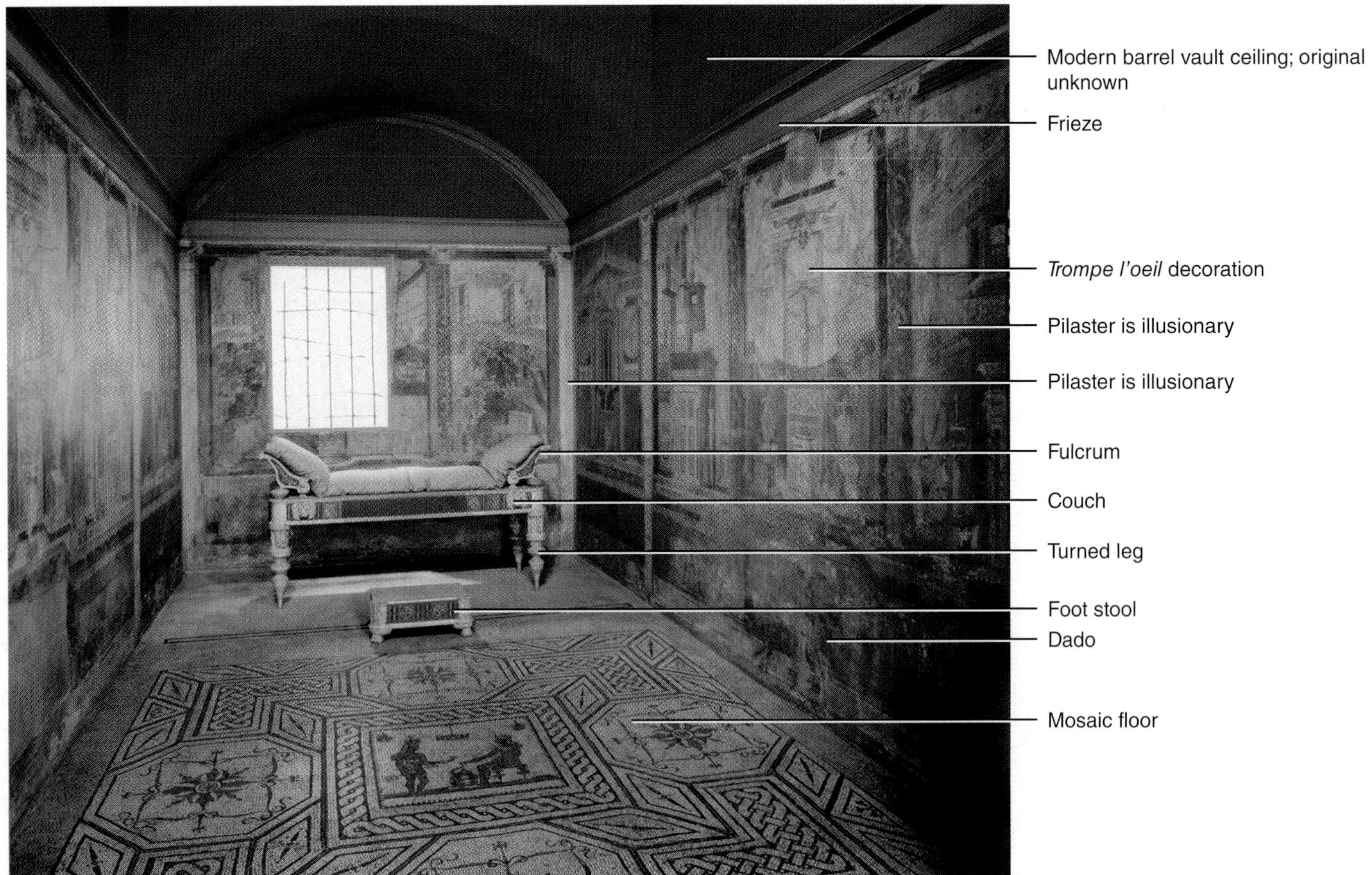

▲ **6-17.** *Cubiculum* from the Villa of P. Fannius Synistor, c. 40–30 B.C.E.; Boscoreale, near Pompeii, Italy. Second Style Fresco. [Rogers Fund, 1903 (03.14.13). The Metropolitan Museum of Art, New York, NY, U.S.A. Image © The Metropolitan Museum of Art/Art Resource, NY]

■ *Ceilings*. Most public buildings, such as baths, have barrel- or cross-vaulted ceilings. Vaults are often coffered and gilded or painted (Fig. 6-10). Those in temples and basilicas are flat and beamed or coffered. Ceilings in residences may be brightly painted, gilded, or plain. Some have mosaics or low-relief stucco decoration.

■ *Textiles*. Few textiles survive, but mosaics, paintings, and bas-reliefs show pillows, cushions, and loose coverings on furniture. Common fabrics are wool, linen, silk, and cotton in bright colors, sometimes embellished with patterns or embroidery.

■ *Lighting*. Torches, candles, and lamps provide minimal light (Fig. 6-18). Lamps are made of bronze, lead, wrought iron, gold, silver, glass, stone, or pottery.

■ *Later Interpretations*. Roman architecture, interiors, and furniture, like the Greek, influence numerous subsequent periods, beginning with the Renaissance, Late Georgian, Greek Revival, Classical Revival, Post Modern, and late 20th-century periods. Pompeiian interiors are important sources of design inspiration throughout the Renaissance and the Neoclassical periods in the late 18th and early 19th centuries. Late 19th-century designers incorporate interior features of public and private buildings such as the Roman bath (Fig. 6-19).

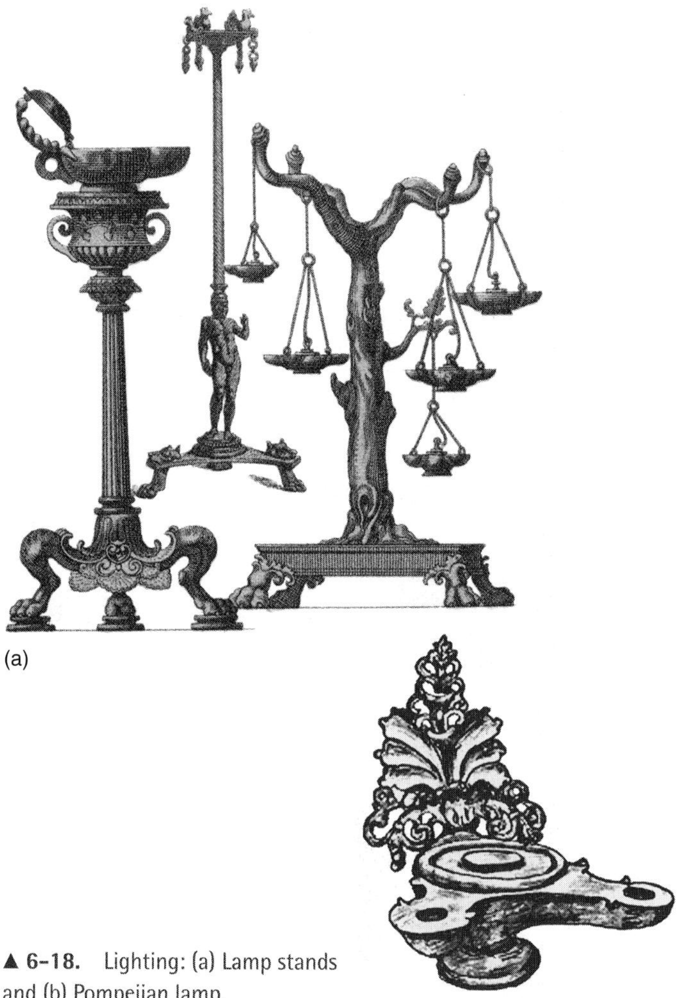

(a)

(b)

▲ **6-18.** Lighting: (a) Lamp stands and (b) Pompeiian lamp.

▲ **6-19.** Later Interpretation: Waiting room, Pennsylvania Station, 1910; New York City, New York; McKim, Mead, and White. Beaux Arts.

FURNISHINGS AND DECORATIVE ARTS

Examples of Roman furniture and decorative arts may be seen in wall paintings, sculpture, tombs, and extant pieces. Romans adapt Greek furniture forms and motifs to their taste for comfort and luxury, although rooms are sparsely furnished until the Late Imperial period. Furniture shapes and forms are similar throughout the empire. Most furniture pieces, especially luxury items, are large in scale with grand proportions. Construction is sophisticated and refined. Roman innovations include the couch with a back, barrel-shaped tub chair, and distinctive table forms.

Public and Private Buildings

■ *Materials*. Woods include maple, cedar, and oak. Citron and ebony are highly prized. Some pieces, particularly tables, are of

▲ **6-20.** *Sella curulis* (X-form stool).

metal, marble, or other stone. Decoration includes veneer, metal plating, inlay, and painting. Veneer and inlay consist of exotic and costly woods, tortoise shell, bronze, ivory, gold, and silver. Painting often disguises inexpensive woods.

■ *Seating*. Thrones, probably adapted from Greek prototypes, are elaborately decorated and important status symbols. Legs may be turned, rectangular, or shaped like animal legs. One of the most important seating examples is the *sella curulis* (Fig. 6-20), an X-shaped folding stool often used by Roman curules or city magistrates. It is more elaborate in shape and decoration than Greek prototypes. The *sella curulis* with a back replaces the Greek *klismos* in Republican times. Barrel-shaped tub chairs of plaited straw and other materials are another innovation. Like the Greeks, Romans recline on couches while dining.

■ *Tables*. Roman tables (Fig. 6-21) copy and enrich Greek forms. Particularly common are tables with a single center support, round tables with three animal legs (Fig. 6-22), and rectangular tables with slab ends, which are copied in the Renaissance. Large marble tables are used in the peristyle or garden.

■ *Storage*. Common items include chests, cupboards, and wardrobes in rectangular shapes. Wardrobes and cupboards have doors with shelves inside.

■ *Beds*. The Romans introduce the couch with a back, which is used for eating, relaxing, and sleeping. Couches, as the most expensive item in the home, have lavish decoration, particularly the rounded *fulcrum* against which diners lean. Most have turned legs of varied heights; runners sometimes connect the legs (Fig. 6-23).

DESIGN SPOTLIGHT

Furniture: New and unique tripod tables are a Roman contribution to furniture design. Roman tables are larger, bolder, and more lavishly decorated than Greek ones are. Tables with round tops have three legs in a variety of designs, from turned to animal to monopodia. One bronze Pompeiian table borrows from Greece but has a winged sphinx sitting on an animal leg with paw foot. Swags embellish the top.

▲ **6-21.** Tripod tables.

▲ **6-22.** Table with monopodia (lion) legs.

▲ **6-23.** Couch.

■ *Decorative Arts*. Glassblowing begins during the 1st century C.E., and soon becomes a major industry throughout the Roman Empire. Numerous bottles, glasses, bowls, and other objects are free- and mold-blown. Cameo glass (Fig. 6-24) is an innovation. Most Roman houses are well equipped with tableware and other metal, ceramic, and glass objects.

► **6-24.** Decorative Arts: Portland vase (copied in the 18th century by Josiah Wedgwood), 3rd century C.E. (Courtesy of British Museum, London).

D. MIDDLE AGES

C. 300–1500 C.E.

The term *Middle Ages*, "the age in the middle," describes the period between Late Imperial Rome (c. 330 C.E.) and the rebirth of classicism during the Renaissance (c. 1400 C.E.). Encompassing approximately 1,100 years, this period in Europe is characterized by invasions from Germanic tribes from the North and Moslems from Africa and the Middle East leading to social and political unrest, religious conflict, the Crusades, and artistic changes. The turbulent times turn people toward religion. The period in the Middle East marks the origin and establishment of Islam by the prophet Muhammad and its expansion by conquest of subsequent leaders.

Ecclesiastical building dominates the Middle Ages. With the exception of the Gothic period, ecclesiastical architecture in Eastern and Western Europe looks to classical antiquity in varying degrees. Early Christian churches (3rd–7th centuries C.E.) are adapted from Roman basilicas. Reinterpreted classical images appear in Christian iconography. The Byzantine Empire (c. 330–1453 C.E.) translates Roman centrally planned structures and construction techniques into a distinctive ecclesiastical architecture. The Romanesque style (8th century–1150 C.E.) uses Roman elements such as the round arch and construction techniques such as vaulting to create the first international architectural style since Ancient Rome. Gothic (1150–1550 C.E.), which strives for lightness and verticality, does not rely overtly on classical antiquity. It does, however, build on Romanesque and some Islamic innovations. In the Middle East and Spain, Islam (7th–17th century C.E.) develops the mosque, which becomes common in form throughout its empire.

Little domestic architecture from the Middle Ages survives, particularly from the early periods. Significant introductions include castles and Islamic palaces, which are combinations of residences and fortresses, and half-timber construction. Toward the end of the period as times settle, unfortified residences become more common. Except for Islamic and some Gothic examples, exteriors and interiors of dwellings do not adopt characteristics of prevailing ecclesiastical styles. Most aristocratic interiors in the Middle Ages rely mainly on textiles for warmth, color, and pattern. Furnishings are few, and portability is important as nobles move often to oversee their lands.

ROUTES OF THE CRUSADERS

CHAPTER 7

Early Christian

3rd–7th Centuries

Constantine Augustus built the basilica of blessed Peter, the apostle. . . . He made a vaulted apse in the basilica, gleaming with gold, and over the body of the blessed Peter, above the bronze which enclosed it, he set a cross of purest gold,. . . the altar itself of silver overlaid with gold, adorned on every side with gems, 400 in number. . . .

—*The Book of the Popes (Liber Pontificalis)* from the life of Pope Sylvester I

The term *Early Christian* refers to buildings and iconography related to the Christian religion, which evolve in the Roman Empire during the 3rd through 7th centuries. After Christianity receives official approval from the Roman Empire, Christians begin constructing religious structures adapted from Roman prototypes. They also create Christian images and symbols to inspire and educate believers. These building forms and the iconography define Western churches and religious structures for centuries following.

HISTORICAL AND SOCIAL

Christianity as a religion comes into being following the crucifixion of Jesus of Nazareth about 33 C.E. For the next three centuries, membership grows despite the fact that Christianity is illegal in the Roman Empire. Christians' needs consist of spaces to meet and places to bury the dead. Small, scattered, and usually poor congregations meet in private houses. Worship services are simple and informal with little ceremony. Early Christians do not believe in cremation, so they bury their dead in cemeteries or in catacombs because of the high cost of land.

In 313 C.E., Roman emperor Constantine wins a decisive battle that he attributes to the Christian God. In gratitude, he issues the Edict of Milan, which gives tolerance for all religions. The emperor's personal sanction of Christianity gives it status, which creates greater need for rituals and administrative structure. Christian churches, memorial structures, and mausoleums soon spring up in Rome, Constantinople, and other cities. Constantine himself is the patron for the construction of the first Basilica of S. Peter in Rome. Additionally, he promotes the faith and positions himself as head of the church as well as of the empire. Although emperors are no longer considered divine, he rules with the same absolute authority as his predecessors.

In 330 C.E., Constantine moves his capital to today's Istanbul, Turkey, and rules the Roman Empire from the east. His death accelerates the division of the empire into east and west. The western portion's trouble with internal strife and invaders from the north continues. Emperor Honorius moves the capital to Ravenna in 404 C.E. in an effort to prevent its being overtaken. His efforts are unsuccessful, as in 476 C.E. Odacer overtakes both Ravenna and Rome, marking the fall of the western Roman Empire. In contrast, the eastern portion prospers as the Byzantine Empire. The period marks the transition from the classical, pagan world to the Christian Middle Ages. Some regard the founding of Constantinople and the establishment of Christianity as the official religion of the Roman Empire as the beginning of the Middle Ages.

CONCEPTS

Once officially sanctioned by Constantine, Christianity requires appropriate settings and ceremonies to reflect its new importance. To avoid the pagan implications of temples, Christians adapt other Late Imperial Roman public buildings to their liturgical requirements, which include preaching and processions. They also create Christian imagery that is blended with Roman traditions. Images in paintings and mosaics adorn church walls and ceilings, which form backgrounds for worship of the Christian God, elevation of his servants, and education of believers. Church buildings and their furnishings are the most significant contribution and main extant artifacts of the Early Christian period.

MOTIFS

■ *Symbols and Motifs.* The cross is the main symbol (Fig. 7-1); others are the fish, dove, and lamb. The Greek letters chi (X) and rho (P) form the monogram of Christ. Other common images include Christ, shepherds and sheep representing Christ the Good Shepherd, Mary (the mother of Christ), and the apostles and various saints.

ARCHITECTURE

New Early Christian building types include churches, baptisteries for the ritual of baptism, mausoleums or tombs, and memorial structures at sacred sites. Roman temples, which were not intended for large congregational gatherings, are architecturally unsuited to the need for interior space for Christian worship and rituals. Consequently, builders adapt the Roman basilica, or justice hall, to suit the Christian liturgy by retaining the nave, aisles, and apse. Now, however, the aisles focus on the altar instead of screening the nave, and the apse, where the Roman emperor and judges sat, becomes the seat of the bishop or overseer. The apse, which houses the altar, faces the east because Christ is crucified in Jerusalem. The entrance is opposite it on the west side. The new Christian basilica has the singular purpose of glorifying God, which is readily apparent through the richness of its materials, decoration, and iconography. Eventually, to provide more space and house the relics of saints, a transept is added, which creates the Latin cross plan. Practical and symbolic of the faith, it becomes the most common plan for many small and large churches constructed in the eastern and western portions of the Roman Empire. Centrally planned structures, such as baptisteries, are adapted from Roman baths or tombs. Although Rome is the center for the earliest examples, Early Christian churches are built in Milan and Ravenna, Italy, Greece, Syria, and what is now Germany.

Secular public structures and dwellings constructed during the period follow late Roman forms and decoration.

(a)

(b)

(c)

▲ **7-1.** Motifs: (a) Ceiling mosaic, *S. Costanza*, Rome, Italy; (b) ceiling mosaic, *S. Costanza*, Rome, Italy; and (c) apse mosaic, *S. Giovanni en Laterano*, Rome, Italy.

DESIGN SPOTLIGHT

Architecture and Interior: On the traditional site of the Apostle Peter's tomb, the basilica's construction begins on the orders of the Emperor Constantine between 320 and 330 C.E and continues for more than 30 years. As is typical of Early Christian buildings, the plain exterior with low-pitched gabled roof belies the magnificent interior. A large forecourt or atrium called the Garden of Paradise, which is added in the 6th century, creates a gathering space and processional entry. The interior adopts elements of Roman Imperial architecture including the basilica form, transept, apse, *baldachino* or canopy, and triumphal arch. Typical basilica features are the tall nave, clerestory windows, timber truss ceiling, arcade, and lower flanking aisles. Unlike some other churches, double aisles flank S. Peter's nave. As became common, a triumphal arch frames the apse, and a screen separates the apse from the altar. The *baldachino*, columns carrying a canopy, accentuate the altar, under which is the apostle Peter's grave. Twenty-one reused Roman marble columns carry the arcade. Mosaics showing S. Peter and Constantine decorate the atrium and the nave, while frescoes of people and scenes from the Old Testament cover the walls. Over the centuries, more sculpture, new altars and chapels, and decoration fill the church. By the 15th century it is so badly deteriorated that it is torn down in 1505 and replaced by a new basilica constructed during the Renaissance and Baroque periods.

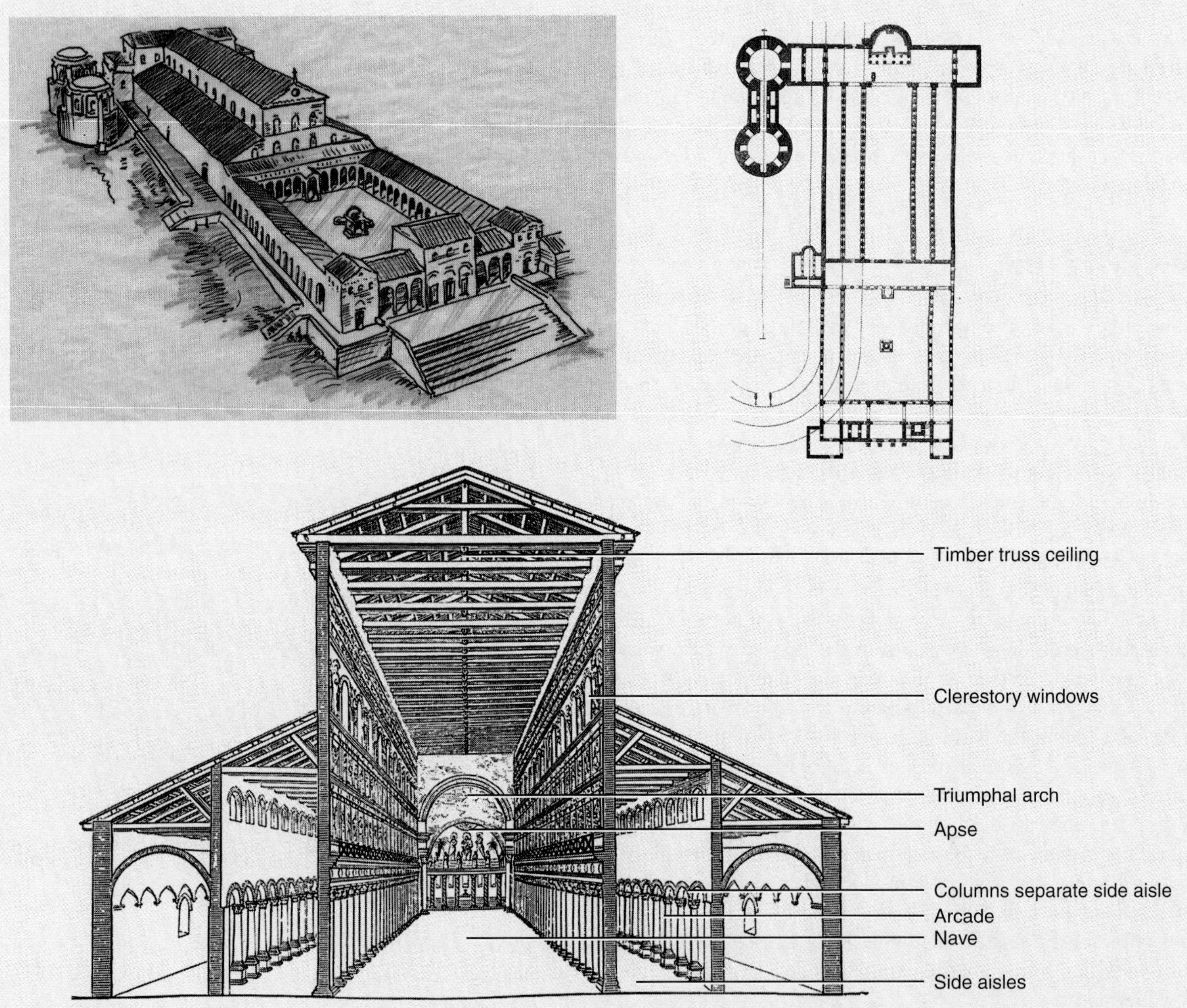

▲ **7-2.** Old Basilica of S. Peter (reconstruction drawing), floor plan, and section view, c. 320–330 C.E.; Rome, Italy; torn down in 1505.

DESIGN SPOTLIGHT

Architecture and Interior: Geometric volumes define the plain brick exterior of the early Christian S. Apollinare in Classe church. The façade composition reflects the interior taller nave and wider aisles. Round arches spread across the lower portion of the façade with entrance through the largest arch, and triple arched windows above allow light from the front into the nave. Later additions include the narthex, the building on right, and the bell tower. Twenty-four Greek columns carry the arcade, which is topped with medallions of religious figures. The semi-vaulted apse above the altar is covered with a mosaic depicting the hand of God, Moses and Elijah, a jeweled cross in a blue medallion, S. Apollinare, sheep, trees, flowers, and birds. Images of Christ and symbols of the four evangelists (Matthew, Mark, Luke, and John) fill the triumphal arch. The images above the altar, symbolic of martyrdom and triumph over death, are intended to inspire and uplift. The sidewalls were probably covered by mosaics, which may have been destroyed in the 15th century by the Venetians. [World Heritage Site]

▲ **7-3.** *S. Apollinare in Classe* and nave, c. 532–549 C.E.; Ravenna, Italy.

Public Buildings

■ *Floor Plans*. Most churches use the Latin cross plan (Fig. 7-2). Usually, the portal or main entrance is placed at the narrow end of the long section opposite the altar and apse. It opens into a large colonnaded forecourt resembling the atrium of the Roman house. The forecourt leads to a narthex that gives access to the sanctuary itself. About two-thirds of the way down the long section is a short transept at a right angle to the nave. The longitudinal axis from forecourt entry to narthex to apse forms a processional path (Fig. 7-2). Some larger churches have a wide nave flanked by double aisles like Old S. Peter's Basilica.

Some churches and most baptisteries and mausoleums have a centralized circular or polygonal plan with the altar or other sacred form in the center surrounded by a two-story colonnade (Fig. 7-4). Some mausoleums have Greek cross plans.

■ *Façades*. Following Roman prototypes, walls are plain brick or stone with little articulation except doors and windows (Fig. 7-3, 7-4). The center of the nave, raised to accommodate clerestory windows, dominates the façade composition. Windows are rectangular or arched. Unadorned exteriors, such as S. *Apollinare in Classe* (Fig. 7-3) and S. *Costanza* (Fig. 7-4), contrast sharply with the interior architectural delineation and decoration. In the poorer western Roman Empire and its remnants, buildings often reuse pillaged columns, masonry, and roof tiles. Doors, which may be single, double, or triple on the façade, may be carved wood or bronze with surface decoration enriching the surrounding portals.

■ *Roofs*. Roofs are gabled on basilicas and domed on central plans. Rust-colored clay tiles usually cover the surface.

INTERIORS

With many wall surfaces requiring embellishment, new Christian churches feature wall decoration on an unprecedented scale. This interior richness contrasts with the plainness of the exteriors. The characteristic frescoes or mosaics blend classical types and precedents with divine persons and Roman Imperial traditions in form and decoration.

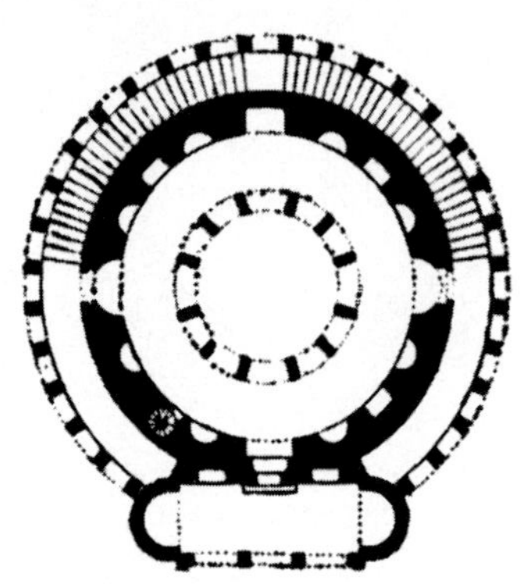

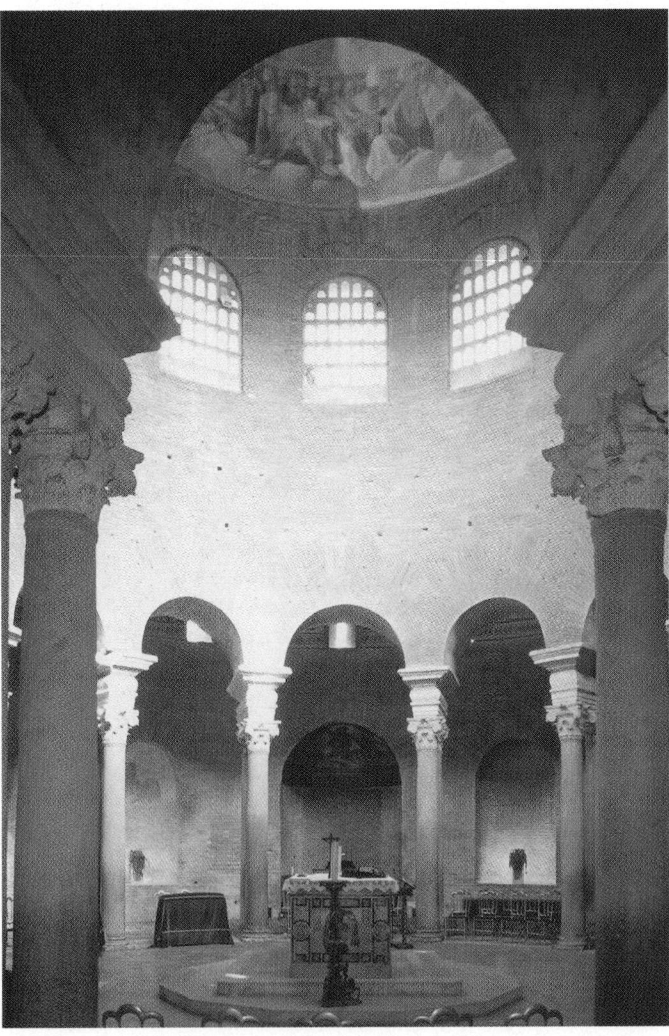

▲ **7-4.** *S. Costanza*, floor plan, and interior central area, c. 340 C.E.; Rome, Italy; built as a mausoleum.

Public Buildings

■ *Floors*. Floors are black and white, gray, or colored marble or mosaics, sometimes in elaborate patterns (Fig. 7-6).

■ *Walls*. In churches, an arcade or an entablature on columns separates the nave from the side aisles. Reused Roman (*spolia*) or new classicizing columns carry the arcade or entablature (Fig. 7-2, 7-3, 7-5, 7-6). Sometimes, capitals and columns do not match, especially when one or both are recycled (Fig. 7-5). A triumphal arch frames the apse, which has seats for clergy and a throne in the center for the bishop (Fig 7-3). Sometimes, a screen separates the apse from the altar. Columns carrying a canopy identify and accentuate the altar, under which the remains of a martyr or saint are often buried.

Marble panels, frescoes, or mosaics usually cover the nave arcade, triumphal arch, and apse (Fig. 7-1, 7-3, 7-6). Decoration is simple to maximize legibility. It also glorifies the Christian God and helps to educate believers. Frescoes and mosaics adapt Jewish, Christian, and Imperial Roman traditions and motifs. However, few early frescoes survive except in the catacombs.

■ *Mosaics*. Christians adapt Roman mosaic techniques and styles to their needs. Early Christian mosaics use glass tesserae instead of marble, which gives an intense range of colors, such as blue, green, purple, red, and gold, but little tonal variation. Tesserae, which are larger than before, are set unevenly to enhance light

▲ **7-5.** Nave, *S. Lorenzo Fuori le Mura* (S. Lorenzo Outside the Walls), c. 378; Rome, Italy, using fragments (*spolia*) of Imperial Roman buildings.

◀ **7-6.** Nave, *S. Clemente*, 11th and 12th centuries; Rome, Italy, rebuilt closely following original form and reusing materials of 4th century basilica, which burned in 1084.

reflection. The glittering glass surface dematerializes the walls and creates an illusion of heavenly realms populated with celestial beings. Although stylized, figures are solidly modeled and cast shadows. Overlap and foreshortening are common means to create depth. After intense thought and debate on His proper depiction, Christ becomes a divine, princely figure whose role is enhanced with Imperial symbols (Fig. 7-1). Some mosaics depict architectural backgrounds in the Pompeiian tradition. Later periods will use and adapt the Christian imagery from this period.

■ *Ceilings*. Ceilings may have exposed timber trusses (Fig. 7-2, 7-3) or beams. Those in centralized structures are vaulted and covered with mosaics (Fig. 7-4).

■ *Later Interpretations*. Subsequent Western European churches adopt the basilica plan with architectural features and interior decoration reflecting the period's stylistic character, such as classicism or Gothic. Later churches also may have mosaics or wall paintings and incorporate Christian symbols from the Early Christian period. In the second half of the 19th century, Early Christian is briefly revived as part of the Romanesque Revival (Fig. 7-7).

FURNITURE

Little Early Christian furniture survives but pictorial examples are found in mosaics, paintings, and illuminated manuscripts. Extant examples and depictions show that church furnishings are richly decorated with carving, gilding, and frequently, jewels. Secular furnishings, such as chairs and coffers, follow earlier Roman types and forms; they often mix pagan and Christian images.

Public Buildings

■ *Seating*. Stools are more common than chairs and resemble Roman prototypes. A manuscript illustration shows S. Matthew (Fig. 7-8) wearing a toga, sitting on a curule (X-form) stool, and writing on a lectern.

■ *Storage*. The most important pieces in churches are the storage items, which are lavishly decorated with emblems belonging to the Christian faith. Examples (Fig. 7-9) include the peacock (symbolizing immortal life), grapevines, and the cross.

▲ **7-7.** Later Interpretation: Old S. Paul's Episcopal Church, 1854–56; Baltimore, Maryland; Richard Upjohn. Early Christian or Romanesque Revival.

◀ **7-8.** S. Matthew from the *Coronation Gospels*, c. 800–810.

▲ **7-9.** Sarcophagus; Ravenna, Italy.

CHAPTER 8

Byzantine

330–1453 C.E.

So the church [Hagia Sophia] has been made a spectacle of great beauty, stupendous to those who see it and altogether incredible to those who hear of it, the beholders are quite unable to select any particular [interior] element which they might admire more than all the others. . . .

—Procopius of Caesarea, *Buildings*, c. 550 C.E.

The Byzantine, or eastern Roman Empire, maintains Roman culture and building traditions before and after the fall of the city of Rome in 476 C.E. Imperial patronage encourages growth of the Christian religion and the building of new structures. The empire sustains a long history of distinctive church architecture and decoration as well as classical scholarship. Following their development during the 3rd century, churches become the chief architectural image of Byzantium. Orthodox Byzantine churches are domed and centrally planned with distinctive mosaics.

HISTORICAL AND SOCIAL

The Byzantine Empire remains a bastion of Roman influence for nearly 1,000 years after the fall of Rome. In 330 C.E., Emperor Constantine moves his capital east to escape the aggression of Germanic tribes. He chooses Byzantium, an ancient Greek city, which he renames Constantinople (now Istanbul, Turkey) for himself. The great prosperity in the eastern empire contrasts with the decline in the west. Life in Constantinople is much like that of Rome. Citizens, who call themselves Romans, maintain Roman institutions and culture; however, they speak Greek.

As emperor, Constantine strives to protect Roman traditions, buildings, and religions, but also sanctions and promotes Christianity, creating a precedent for a theocratic state. Emperor Justinian creates that theocratic state when he declares Christianity the only legal religion in the 6th century. Because the emperor, as an earthly ruler appointed by Christ, strives to maintain the orthodoxy of the faith, court and church become synonymous. In 1054, the Eastern church separates from the Western church over doctrinal issues about which they have disagreed for centuries.

Byzantine history is one of rise and fall, growth and decline. In the 6th century Emperor Justinian attempts to recapture former holdings and reunite the former Roman Empire. His building campaigns strive to reestablish the glory of the Roman Empire. He and his wife Theodora regain much of the Roman Empire's territory but cannot maintain them. Weakened by exterior attacks, the Byzantine Empire shrinks in size and power. Another period of prosperity and expansion occurs between the 9th and 12th centuries. The Crusades, beginning in 1095, revive trade and commerce. Decline begins anew in 1203–1294 when crusaders sack Constantinople. The city eventually falls to the Ottoman Turks, ending the Byzantine empire in 1453.

In addition to maintaining Roman laws, government, and culture, the Byzantine Empire preserves ancient Greek culture by supporting a vigorous intellectual life in which classicism is a source of inspiration and renewal. Scholars safeguard and copy ancient Greek manuscripts. This scholarship lives on after the fall of the empire, especially when Byzantine scholars flee Constantinople in 1453. They help initiate the study of Greek manuscripts in Italy, which contributes to the rise of the Renaissance.

CONCEPTS

The Byzantine Empire continues classical Roman and Early Christian traditions, blending them with Near Eastern influences into a distinctive church architecture and decoration that reflects an imperial, princely Christ and saints at the head of a theocratic society. Symbolism in ornament and form is important and contributes to the Byzantine dazzling expression of Christian themes, in contrast to the more sober Early Christian. This is a Byzantine contribution to architecture and decoration.

(a)

(b)

(c)

▲ **8-1.** Motifs: (a) Decorative pattern; (b) floor mosaic, S. Vitale; and (c) ceiling detail, *Hagia Sophia*, Constantinople (Istanbul), Turkey.

MOTIFS

■ *Motifs*. Motifs (Fig. 8-1, 8-4, 8-8) include images of Christ, Mary, the apostles, rulers, and various saints, as well as foliage, frets, waves, geometric designs, guilloches, lozenges, rosettes, and animals including eagles, lions, lambs, and elephants.

ARCHITECTURE

Early Byzantine architecture continues Late Roman and Early Christian forms and volumetric spaces, which become distinctive by the 6th century with the building of *Hagia Sophia* (Church of the Holy Wisdom of God). Churches are the most common building types. Early churches follow either the Roman basilica or centralized plan, but eventually most are centralized and square with domes. By the Middle Byzantine period (9th–11th centuries), churches become smaller with more exterior ornamentation and patterned brickwork. Variations of the Greek cross and central domes are common. Taller, narrower forms; more domes; and more exterior ornamentation characterize Late Byzantine churches beginning in the 12th century. The surface decoration of interiors repeats on exteriors, and they relate more closely through pattern and ornamentation. Examples are opulent and picturesque.

Although exhibiting Roman scale and variety, Byzantine architecture does not use Roman construction methods. Architectural innovations include the pendentive, combined centralized and basilica plans in churches, and the skillful use of light as a mystical element.

Structural Features

■ *Columns and Capitals*. Columns are derived from Roman examples, particularly the Corinthian and Composite orders. Shafts are usually unfluted with an inverted pyramidal impost block. Both impost block and capitals (Fig. 8-2) usually have simple profiles but are covered with complex, elaborate, and pierced lacy undercut foliage or geometric shapes. They may incorporate anthemions, acanthus leaves, grapevines, crosses, other Christian symbols and the initials of rulers. Capitals display an infinite variety of forms and carved or painted ornament.

■ *Domes*. Domes, important elements inside churches, create a sense of space that is wholly different than earlier Roman examples (Fig. 8-3, 8-4, 8-5). Pendentives, invented but rarely used by the Romans, allow Byzantine builders to place circular domes over square spaces. The continuous surfaces of the triangular pendentives seem to create a floating dome reminiscent of heaven. This construction technique, combined with arches, vaults, and glittering ornament, creates an otherworldly atmosphere with a heightened sense of awe to inspire and remind worshippers of the power and majesty of the Christian God.

Public Buildings

■ *Floor Plans*. Church plans are symmetrical, ordered, and often complex. Centralized plans with circular and polygonal forms derived from the cube are the most common (Fig. 8-4) but the Latin cross plan continues in use with variations. *Hagia Sophia,* for example, combines the longitudinal axis of the basilica with a centralized plan (Fig. 8-3). The plan of S. Mark's Basilica is a modified Latin cross that is nearly square with four arms that terminate in rectangles or apses (Fig. 8-5).

■ *Materials*. Brick, which permits more plastic elevations, replaces Roman concrete (Fig. 8-4). Vaults and domes are of brick to eliminate centering. Iron tie-rods help reinforce arches and vaults. Brick usually is covered with stucco, marble, stone, or mosaics (Fig. 8-5).

■ *Façades*. The walls of the earliest churches are smooth, plain, and unadorned (Fig. 8-4). Architectural elements such as columns or pilasters, often from various styles, characterize later buildings. For example, S. Mark's Basilica (Fig. 8-5) combines Byzantine, Romanesque, and Gothic influences. As time passes, façades, especially those on the sides and rear, grow more complex in form following the multiplicity of interior shapes. In and out movement; circular or polygonal forms; and the repetition of windows, arches, and other elements create a lively, rhythmic pattern in Middle and Late Byzantine examples. Elaborate architecture details often enhance this patterning.

■ *Windows*. Windows with round tops punctuate walls and domes. Windows placed in the drums of domes make the domes appear to float.

■ *Roofs*. Sloped and gabled rooflines are complicated (Fig. 8-3, 8-4). Domes over centers or crossings are almost universal. Small chapels may also be domed or semi-domed.

■ *Later Interpretations*. While elements of the Byzantine style are not widely reused, a mixture of influences reminiscent of Byzantine design appears in the Cathedral of S. Basil (Fig. 8-6) in Moscow, Russia, with its array of onion domes (originally white) and arches.

(a)

(b)

(c)

▲ **8-2.** Capitals: (a) *Hagia Sophia,* Constantinople (Istanbul), Turkey; (b) S. Mark's Basilica, Venice, Italy; (c) S. Mark's Basilica, Venice, Italy.

INTERIORS

Byzantine church interiors are opulent, formal, and sumptuous. Surface decorations in rich colors and materials are characteristic. Paintings, mosaics, and/or marble panels derived from Early Christian forms cover floors, walls, and ceilings. Although decoration combines Christian iconography with classical elements, the impression is not classical but one of immense wealth and richness. Shimmering gold mosaics and natural light unite to create an otherworldly feeling.

Few secular interiors survive intact. Writings and illustrations indicate that homes of wealthy citizens and clergy followed Late Roman forms and decoration. However, treatments imitate the opulence of churches.

Public and Private Buildings

■ *Color*. The palette incorporates various shades of gold, red, green, and blue (Fig. 8-3, 8-4, 8-5).

■ *Floors*. Floors are marble, stone, or mosaics (Fig. 8-1), often in geometric patterns.

■ *Walls*. Columns, pilasters, and cornices articulate walls, which also are covered with richly colored frescoes, mosaics, marble panels, or hangings. Stylized images of divine persons, geometric forms, foliage, and Christian symbols are common (Fig. 8-3, 8-4, 8-5).

■ *Mosaics*. Byzantine churches are known for their mosaics based upon Early Christian forms and images. As in the Early Christian period, figures and forms are often modified classical and pagan

DESIGN SPOTLIGHT

Architecture and Interiors: The *Hagia Sophia* is the grandest of all Byzantine churches as befits its imperial purpose as church of the emperor. It is a masterpiece of complex vaulting and domed construction. The brick exterior is characteristically plain and devoid of articulation, but its complexity in form and outline reflects interior forms surmounted by domes and half-domes. An imperial gate marks the primary entry and establishes the main axis to the apse. The original atrium or colonnaded porch no longer exists, and the Islamic minarets are later additions. The plan is a rectangle 230′-0″ × 250′-0.″ Centered within the rectangular footprint is a 100′-0″ square, the corners of which are defined by massive piers with arches between them. Above is a huge circular dome supported by pendentives. Forty windows separated by ribs pierce the dome and filter light throughout the day so that the dome appears to float over the vast open space. On the main axis of entry and each end of the domed central space are two apsidal spaces with half domes. The main apse opposite the entry has three smaller half-domed spaces. Flanking the central spaces are square and rectangular vaulted spaces. [World Heritage Site]

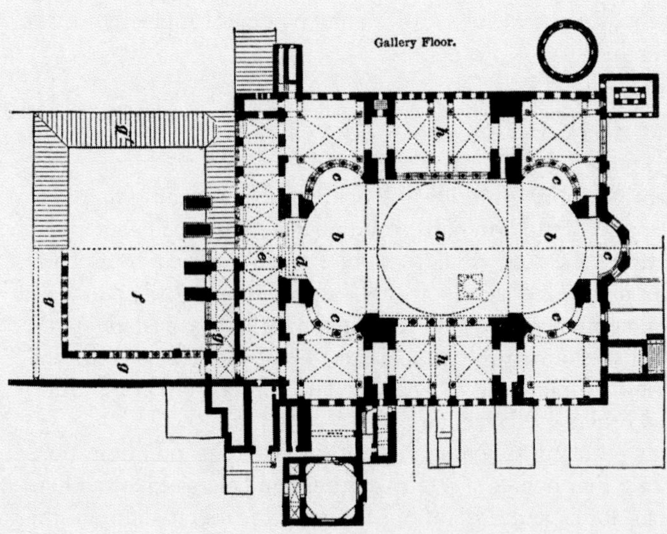

▲ **8-3.** *Hagia Sophia* (Church of the Holy Wisdom of God), floor plan, nave, detail, and section view, 532–537 C.E.; Constantinople (Istanbul), Turkey; Anthemius of Tralles and Isidorus of Miletus and built by Justinian.

DESIGN SPOTLIGHT

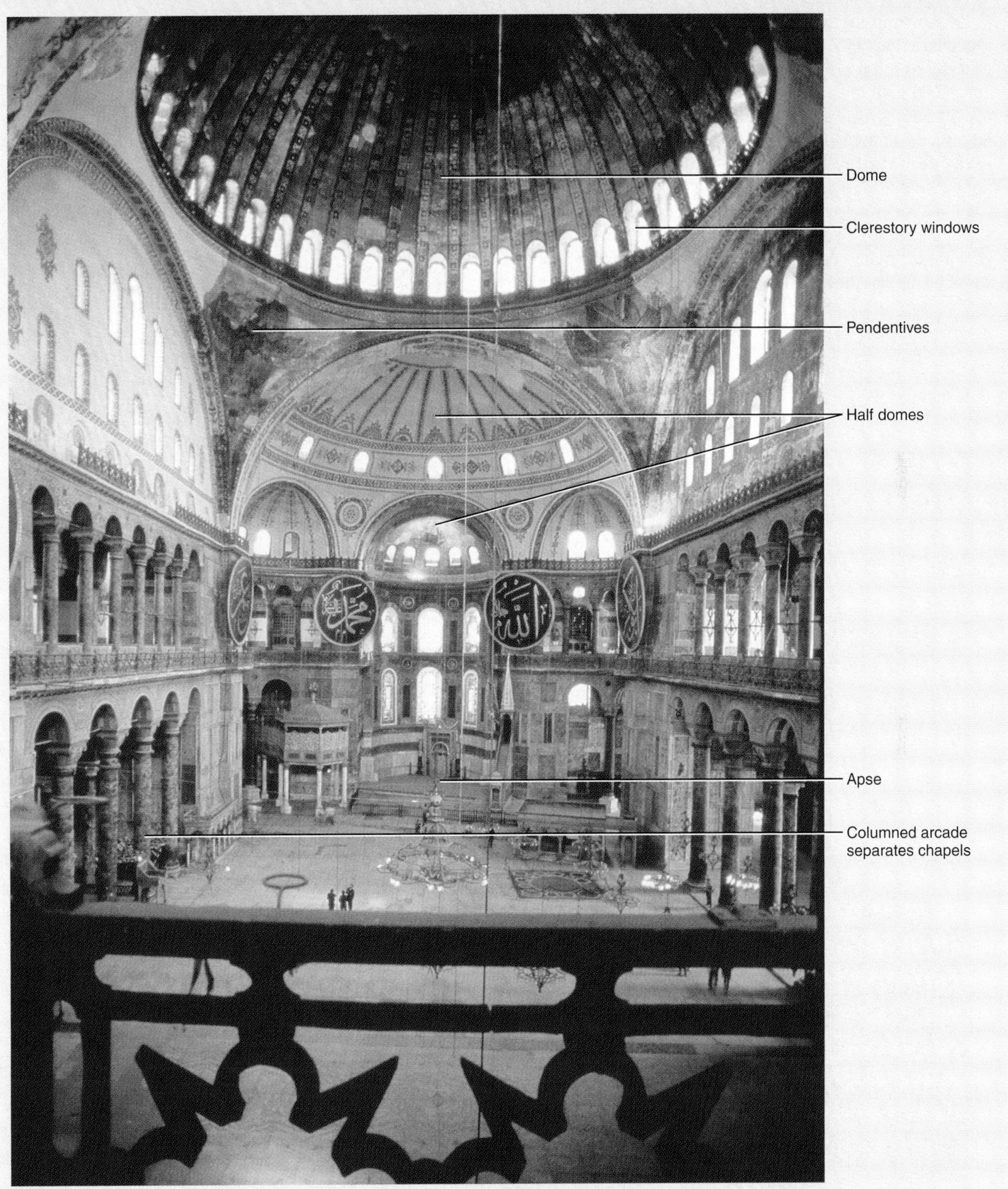

▲ **8-3.** Continued

DESIGN SPOTLIGHT

As shown in the section view, the sidewalls of the central space have double arcades carrying round arches and arched clerestory windows above. These walls screen the side chapels and, along with the apse, help create the impression of a nave and side aisles. Wall surfaces covered with color, pattern, and light seem to dissolve. Glittering gold mosaics (largely lost now) in the vaults add to the dematerialization of surface. Marble slabs carefully placed to enhance their veining add more rich color and surface decoration. Intricate mural decoration covers the spandrels of the main arches. Even the capitals of the columns are richly carved with lacy decoration that dematerializes them, too. The rich colors and decorations of mosaic and marble surfaces contrast with the plain exterior, a visual metaphor for a Christian's rich spiritual or inner life.

▲ **8-3.** Continued

ones. Unlike those of the Early Christian period, Byzantine mosaics have more gold and reflective surfaces to symbolize Christ as the light of the world (Fig. 8-5). Placement of figural decoration is hierarchical. Scenes of Christ and the Virgin Mary occupy central domes, while visions of the ascension of Christ fill the apse. Scenes from the life of Christ embellish pendentives and upper walls (Fig. 8-4, 8-5). Lesser saints and other dignitaries occupy lower walls.

Most Byzantine churches have little sculpture because of iconoclasm, a ban on figural images, beginning in 726 C.E. This prohibition results from the empire's major defeats and loss of territory at the hands of the Persians, which is attributed to ignoring the Old Testament ban on graven images. In place of figures, iconoclasm combines Christian symbols, such as the cross, with floral, geometric, and animal forms. In 843 C.E., when the prohibition of figures ends, images become flatter and more stylized to resemble human form as little as possible. Figures are linear, flat, and stylized. Forms and figures in bright colors are laid out with no overlap or perspective against shimmering gold backgrounds. Foliage, geometric forms, and Christian symbols form borders or are interspersed among the figures (Fig. 8-1).

■ *Ceilings*. Centers or crossings of churches have large domes surrounded by smaller domed and half-domed spaces. Pendentives (Fig. 8-3, 8-5) support the central dome and provide a transition from the circular dome to the vertical post of the square plan. Almost all ceilings feature painted and mosaic decorations (Fig. 8-1, 8-5).

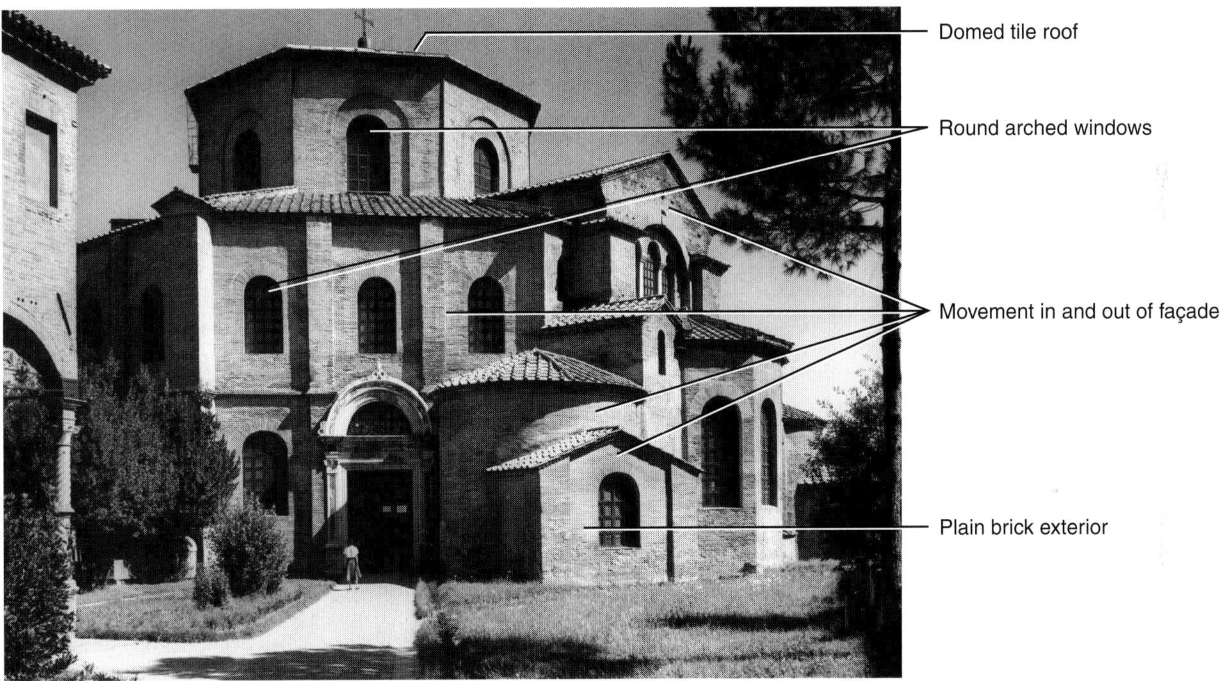

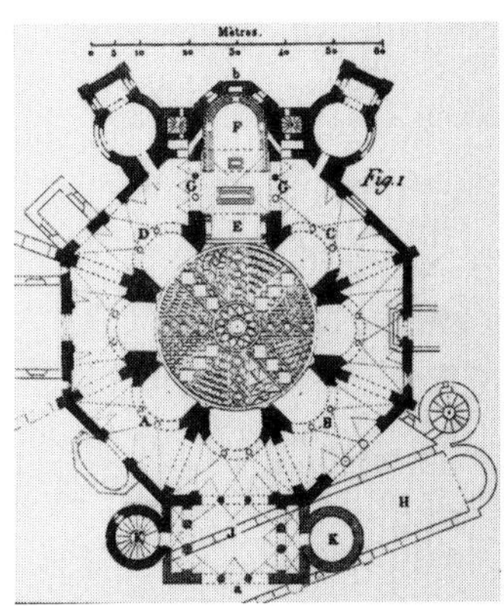

▲ **8-4.** Basilica of S. Vitale, floor plan, and interior of apse and choir, 526–547 C.E.; Ravenna, Italy.

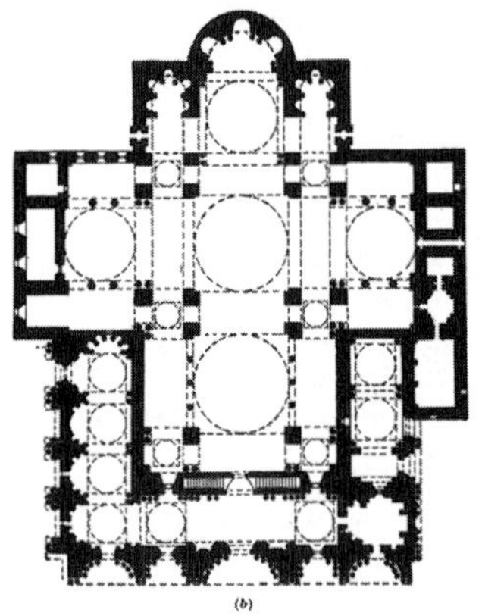

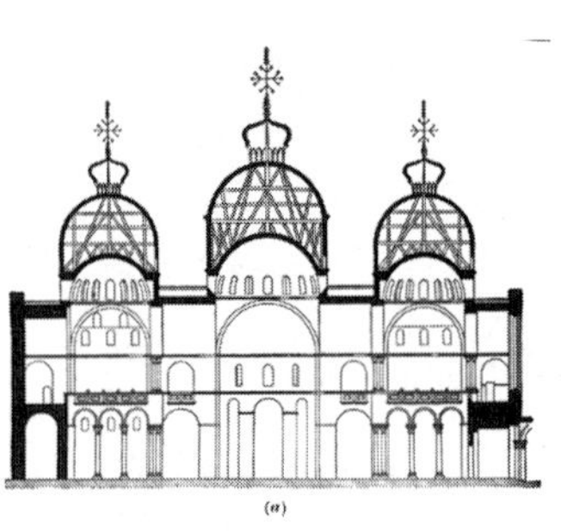

▲ **8-5.** S. Mark's Basilica, floor plan, and nave, begun 1063 from the designs of a Greek architect; Venice, Italy.

■ *Textiles*. Silk and velvet are common materials, with designs featuring animals, geometric patterns, and Persian influence (Fig. 8-7).

▲ **8-6.** Later Interpretation: S. Basil Cathedral, 1555–1561; Moscow, Russia; built by Ivan the Terrible.

▲ **8-7.** Textiles, 10th and 11th centuries.

FURNISHINGS AND DECORATIVE ARTS

Little furniture of the Byzantine era survives, but illustrations in manuscripts and mosaics show that some classical forms are retained for chairs and tables. A few pieces are draped with fabric; seating often has cushions. Surface decoration characterizes many storage pieces.

■ *Materials*. Furniture is of wood, metal, marble, and ivory and is simply constructed (Fig. 8-8). Some pieces are jeweled or have gold and silver inlay.

■ *Seating*. Architectonic thrones and chairs are often illustrated in manuscripts. The Maximianus throne (Fig. 8-8), made for Archbishop Maximianus of Ravenna, is constructed of ivory carved with animals, birds, and foliage. The panels show saints and scenes from the life of Christ. Some chairs, stools, and benches are X-shaped and often of metal.

▲ **8-8.** Maximianus throne, c. 547 C.E., and throne from gardens of Peggy Guggenheim Museum, Venice, Italy.

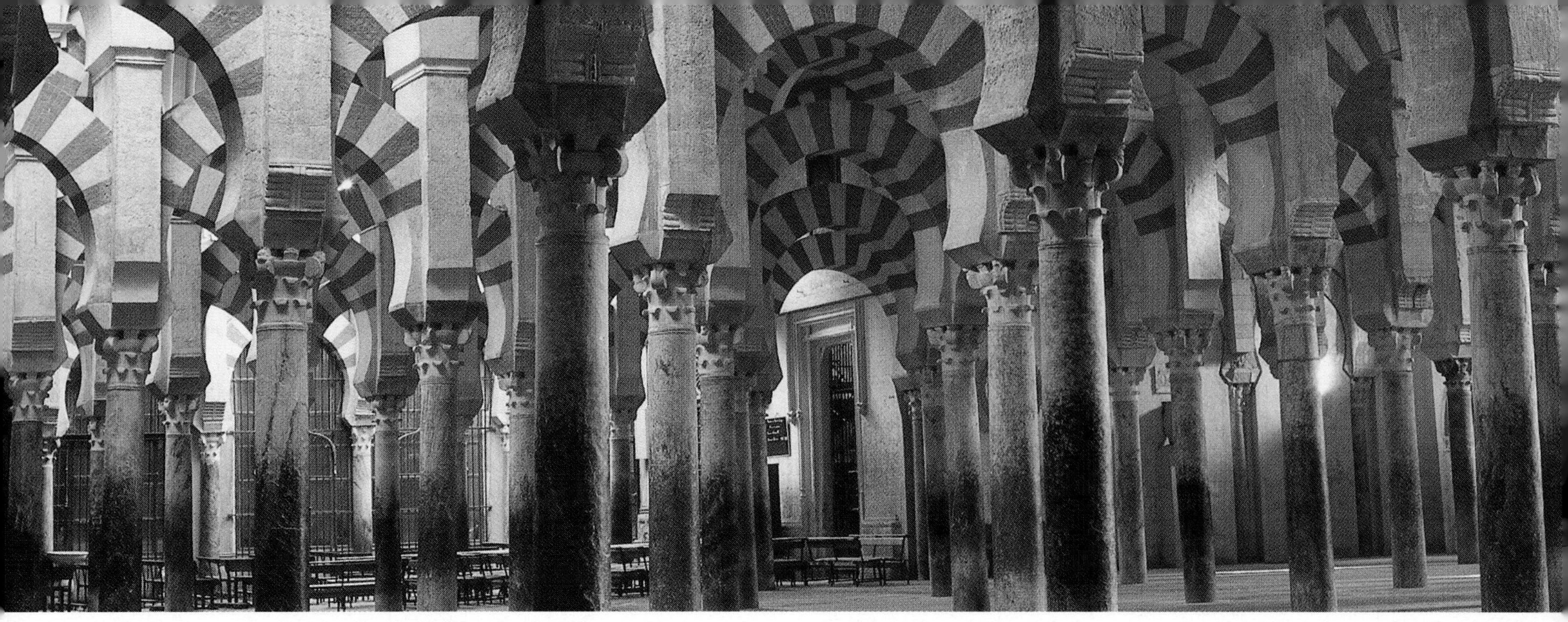

CHAPTER 9

Islamic

7th–17th Centuries

When I came within the Dore, that which I did se was verrie wonderful unto me . . . the sighte whereof did make me almoste to thinke that I was in another worlde.

—Thomas Dallam at the Sultan's Court, 1599, from Michael Levy, *The World of Ottoman Art*

The unique form and decoration of Islamic art and architecture are influenced by religion, the design traditions of its various peoples, and the aesthetic sensibilities of its artists and builders. Common to all the arts are dense, flat patterns composed of geometric forms and curving tendrils. This decoration dematerializes forms and creates visual complexity. Unique also to Islam is calligraphy, which is effectively integrated into the decoration of almost all structures and objects.

HISTORICAL AND SOCIAL

Islam, meaning "to surrender to the will of God," is the third of the great monotheistic Semitic religions following Judaism and Christianity. Established in the 7th century C.E., it derives from the teachings of the prophet Muhammad. A wealthy merchant in Mecca on the Arabian peninsula, he receives revelations from God and begins proclaiming a new faith in one god, Allah. Local citizens strongly oppose him, so Muhammad flees to Medina in 622 C.E. There he establishes the first community of followers who meet in his living compound for teachings and prayer. As converts increase, the prophet becomes a spiritual and political leader. At his death in 632 C.E., Muhammad has become the leader of a large and increasingly powerful Arab state. Subsequently, his followers continue conquests for land in the name of Islam. In just over a century, they extend their territories as far as southern France and North Africa to the west and north, and into northern India to the east.

The new faith unites the peoples of the vast territories. Believers, called Muslims, live according to the Koran (recitation), the sacred book of the prophet's revelations. There are no formal rituals or ceremonies, as each believer has individual access to God. Rules for living are simple, and members adhere to five important pillars, which include prayer and fasting. Families are patriarchal, and extended families of two or three generations are common. Islam extends some rights to women, but their freedom varies by time period and geographic location. Some women even become prominent rulers and art patrons. A few become artists and calligraphers.

The prophet establishes a new theocratic social order that replaces traditional nomadic tribal government. After his death, caliphs, who claim descent from him or his early followers, continue his model of a single ruler, in whose hands are political and spiritual leadership. The first dynasty of caliphs, the Umayyads (ruling 661–750 C.E.) in the Middle East, extend Islam's holdings to India and southern France. Builders during this period synthesize elements from their conquered cultures, resulting in structures that express great power. In Spain, the next dynasty of caliphs, also called Umayyads (ruling 756–1031), are great art patrons. The Abbasid caliphate in the Middle East (ruling 750–1258) also extends Islamic territory and promotes culture, learning, science, and the arts.

After the caliphates disintegrate in the 9th century, the empire fragments into many smaller regions. Iran and surrounding areas become the most important region politically, socially, and artistically. Noteworthy dynasties with distinctive art styles include the Seljuk Turks (ruling mid-11th century–1157), the Timurids (ruling western Iran 1378–1502), and the Safavids (ruling all of Iran 1502–1736). Between 1299 and 1922, the Ottomans rule Turkey. They expand the empire into Egypt and Syria, are great builders, and conquer Constantinople in 1453.

Between the 9th and 13th centuries, Islam expands education and science, and its university system promotes cultural development. Muslim men and women are probably more literate than others during the Middle Ages because of Islam's emphasis on studying the Koran. Scholars excel in mathematics and philosophy and make important discoveries in medicine, the natural sciences, and astronomy. Various rulers or wealthy patrons support their efforts.

CONCEPTS

Islamic art and architecture evolve from and reflect a strong societal emphasis upon religion, which creates consistency in examples across and among the various regions. Forms and ornament express a common worldview that unites the secular and the religious and art with science and mathematics. Unity and order symbolize the unity and order of nature and the universe as created by Allah (god). Repetition and repeating themes evident in architecture and decoration, specifically the *arabesque*, suggest infinity and Allah's infinite power. Bold forms, such as domes and courtyards, convey power and majesty. Emphasis upon the individual's position in society and the family creates separation of both public and private and gendered spaces in cities and public and private buildings. Consequently, much of the beauty of Islamic architecture is not visible from the outside. The lavish decoration of allover surface patterns and calligraphy expresses the geometry and precision of nature, science, and mathematics as revealed in the universal principles of Allah's creation and power. Because of the Koran's admonitions against idolatry and the matchlessness of Allah, the human figure never appears in religious art and architecture.

▲ **9-1.** Motifs: Tiles from (a) Spain, (b) Turkey, and (c) Persia; (d) Lunette, 1575 from Turkey; and (e) Calligraphy from Spain.

MOTIFS

■ *Motifs*. Common motifs (Fig. 9-1) are meanders, stars, swastikas, frets, rosettes, vines, scrolls, palm leaves, tendrils, and calligraphy.

ARCHITECTURE

Islamic architecture is consistent in form, construction, and decoration throughout its empire and across its cultures. Because nomads lack an architectural tradition, early builders assimilate construction techniques and ornamentation from their conquered peoples in Byzantium, Greece, Egypt, and the Middle East. This aids them in creating their own distinctive building types and unique forms that arise from their culture's strong emphasis on religion and climactic needs for heat and shade from the relentless desert sun. Despite differing regional resources and climates, this new architectural image is universally identifiable as Islamic.

The most common building types are those associated with religion or protection, such as mosques, *madrasahs*, mausoleums, and forts. Rulers and the wealthy build large urban and desert palace complexes (called *alcazars* in Spain) and townhouses. Often fortified, they are walled for seclusion as well as protection. Both palaces and larger dwellings have one or more interior courtyards with more rooms and courtyards added as needed. These major structures contribute forms to lesser ones such as public baths and smaller dwellings.

The architectural response to the Koran's emphasis upon hierarchy of individuals within society translates into clear distinctions between public and private sectors in cities and buildings.

(a)

(b)

▲ **9-2.** Architectural Details: (a) Door from the Blue Mosque, Turkey and (b) horseshoe (Moorish) arch.

▲ **9-3.** Dome of the Rock, begun in 688 C.E.; Jerusalem, Israel; built on the spot where the prophet is believed to have been carried to heaven.

Streets and commercial areas are public, while private houses focus inward behind plain walls. Guests, male friends, and business associates are received and entertained in the public *selamlik* or men's area. The *haremlik* or women's areas are private and secluded, and house women, children, and servants. Plans clearly separate these two areas. Similarly, building complexes are centrally organized, but often incorporate a random arrangement of separate spaces linked together. Rulers and the wealthy live splendid, luxurious lives. Others live as comfortably as their finances permit.

Distinguishing characteristics of Islamic architecture include order, repetition, radiating structures, and dense patterns covering many, if not most, surfaces. Common architectural elements are columns, piers, unique arches (Fig. 9-2), and interwoven and repeating sequences of niches and small columns. Arch forms, such as the horseshoe or multilobed arch, also are unique to Islamic buildings. Domes in various shapes also are characteristic.

Allover surface patterns and visual complexity distinguish Islamic art and architecture, giving it a unique character that is remarkably consistent among the arts and across regions. Decoration consists of dense, flat repeating patterns that are independent of structure and/or specific architectural features. Patterns cover exteriors and interiors from foundations to roofs, creating visual complexity and dematerializing form. Unity and variety within a geometric grid are common. Although there is uniformity, each element is distinguished according to its importance. There is no focal point, but infinite unity and variety exist in this intricate decorative system, known as *arabesque*, which can expand in size, direction, or form, as need demands. Patterns are generally nonfigural and derive from geometric and stylized naturalistic forms and calligraphy.

Calligraphy (Fig. 9-1) forms an important pattern on objects, architecture, and illuminated manuscripts. Because the Koran is in Arabic, copying this venerated book becomes a holy task. Designers exploit the decorative nature of Arabic script by beautifully integrating sayings from the Koran into architecture, interiors, and objects in borders, cartouches, and medallions. Islamic calligraphy assumes many styles including the early *Kufic* (vertical script) and *Muhaqqaq* (horizontal script). Manuscript illumination also is a highly developed art form practiced by both men and women.

Structural Features

■ *Arches*. Characteristic arches (Fig. 9-2, 9-6, 9-12) include the horseshoe, pointed or ogival, and scalloped or multilobed arches. These forms develop from a desire for visual complexity instead of structural innovation. Islam's pointed arches do not cover spaces of different heights, nor are they part of a structural system as in Gothic design. Surface decoration on arches is common. Elaborate stuccowork, tile work, or mosaics cover exterior and interior arches. Voussoirs may be in alternating colors (Fig. 9-8).

■ *Domes*. Domes (Fig. 9-3, 9-4, 9-5) cover prayer halls and other spaces. Squinches carry Islamic domes instead of the pendentives used in Byzantine architecture. On the exterior, domes may be melon shaped or ogival, giving rise to the Western name *onion dome*. Inside, domes may be round, octagonal, multilobed, or star shaped and have complex, nonstructural bracketing. Some feature *muqarnas*, which become more complex in form. Made of stucco, they resemble stalactites in caves. *Muqarnas* may also cover arches.

Public and Private Buildings

■ *Mosque*. Mosques are the first buildings of Islam, and the earliest are fairly simple. As Islam grows in faith and power, so the mosque evolves into a large and elaborately decorated structure that befits the faith. As the most important building, the mosque serves as a gathering place for prayer, a school, and a town hall (Fig. 9-4, 9-8). Its unique form, which is consistent throughout time and place, responds to the new faith that requires space for prayer but has neither formal ceremonies nor a priesthood. Forms and spaces develop from the open-air courtyard of the prophet's house as well as cultural requirements. Following the conquest of Syria in the late 7th century C.E., Muslims adapt the aisled spaces of basilica churches into mosques.

■ *Madrasahs*. These theological colleges or schools of religion are usually attached to the mosque. Four vaulted halls surround a center courtyard. The *qibla* side hall is the largest. Apartments, schoolrooms, and other spaces surround the halls. Exterior decoration, unlike that on other public buildings, only surrounds openings and marks the roofline.

■ *Mausoleum*. As memorials to holy men or rulers, mausoleums are centrally planned and domed. The most famous is the Taj Mahal (Fig. 9-5), built by a Muslim Indian ruler as a memorial to his wife. It features lacy marble walls, large portals, *minarets*, domes, and elaborate decoration.

■ *Site Orientation*. Religious structures are strategically located on hills, near ruler's palaces, or at the intersections of main roads. Forts and palaces may be sited on high promontory points or in defendable areas. In cities, residential districts are separate from public and commercial areas. Wealthy areas have wide streets with parks and squares. Poorer districts have narrow, winding streets.

■ *Floor Plans*. Three plans characterize mosques throughout the empire for centuries. The earliest consists of a courtyard and hypostyle hall (Fig. 9-8). The four-*iwan* mosque plan, similar to that of religious schools, has four barrel-vaulted spaces facing a central courtyard. Later mosques are centrally planned with domes. All plans are axial, oriented toward Mecca, and have similar components that include large open prayer halls, spaces for ablution or washing, at least one courtyard, and an entry. Additional spaces may include kitchens where meals are prepared for the poor, libraries, and hospitals.

When praying, Muslims face the *qibla* (prayer wall), which looks toward Mecca. Centered in the *qibla* is the *mihrab* or niche (Fig. 9-8, 9-9). A dome on the exterior often signals the interior *mihrab*. Nearby is the *minbar*, a pulpit in which the *imam* (leader) declares the *khutba* (sermon and affirmation of allegiance by the community). It may have a *maqsurea* (screen or enclosure) for protection. A screen may separate males from females in the prayer hall, or women may have their own prayer hall.

DESIGN SPOTLIGHT

Architecture: Originally in hypostyle form, the *Masjid-i-Shah* Mosque was remodeled in the 17th century into a four-*iwan* plan. *Minarets* flank the impressive recessed entrance. Plain and decorated colored tiles cover the walls. The two domes accentuate the vestibule and prayer hall. Colored tiles cover the larger, bulging dome of the prayer hall. The curving tendrils enhance the shape without obscuring it. Pierced and solid patterns dematerialize its form.

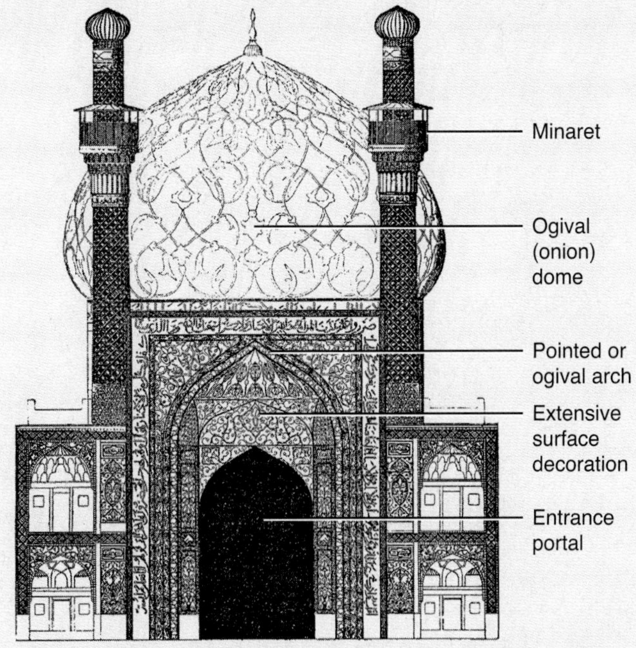

▲ **9-4.** *Masjid-i-Shah* (Great Mosque), 1612–1638; Ispahan, Iran; by Maydan Naqshi-i-Jahan.

Palaces and houses consist of groups of rectangular rooms interconnected around courtyards and gardens (Fig. 9-6). An arcaded loggia surrounding the courtyard provides a transition and filters light from the sunny exterior to the darker interior. Entrances generally open into important public spaces, such as reception halls (Fig. 9-6, 9-12), which are always located in men's quarters. The main reception hall(s) or *iwan* is located on the north (summer) or south (winter) side of the main courtyard and may have its own fountain. Enclosed on three sides, it is the most elaborately decorated room in the house and has the finest furnishings to convey the wealth and status of the household. Men's areas are separated from women's by location. Each has its own reception room(s) surrounded by sleeping rooms and storage places. Most dwellings have many guestrooms due to the Middle Eastern emphasis on hospitality. Upper floors may have balconies overlooking the garden. Ancillary spaces may include baths similar to those of the Romans, offices, and mosques. Kitchens and other service areas are separate from the main rooms.

■ *Materials*. Materials include brick, local stone, marble, stucco, glazed tile, wood, and metals for roofs, grilles, and tie-rods. Most domestic structures, even palaces, are of wood on stone or brick foundations because they were expected to last only as long as the ruler lived. Tiles (Fig. 9-1, 9-6), mosaics, marbles, and paint give much color, an important design element. Typical tile colors are blue, red, green, and gold. Tile shapes include stars and rectangles. A Muslim innovation is luster, a shiny glaze resembling metal that is used on tiles and objects.

■ *Facades*. Mosques usually have a large entrance portal (Fig. 9-4), one or more *minarets* to call the people to prayer (Fig. 9-4), an arcaded portico, and an imposing dome (Fig. 9-3). Elaborate surface decoration with Islamic motifs (Fig. 9-1, 9-4) is characteristic. Although not apparent on the façade, the interior courtyard has arcades that are lavishly embellished and carried on piers or columns, plants and flowers, and often a fountain.

Both palaces and houses focus inward for protection and privacy. Façades are plain with little architectural detailing except at the main portal and rooflines. Townhouses have two or three stories that may project over each other. Carved beams that support the projecting floors may be the only embellishment. Like palaces, private homes have plain façades that conceal the luxury within. Like those in mosques, interior courtyards are lavishly decorated with elaborate stuccowork on arches and surrounds (Fig. 9-6). Vertical surfaces have *arabesques* and calligraphy and colorful tile dadoes. Courtyards also have lush gardens in geometric patterns with fountains and water channels prominent as a type of Muslim paradise.

■ *Windows and Doors*. Windows vary in size and placement, depending on the function of the interior space, on both public and private buildings. They may be rectangular or have distinctive arched shapes. Many have tile surrounds with iron or wood grilles

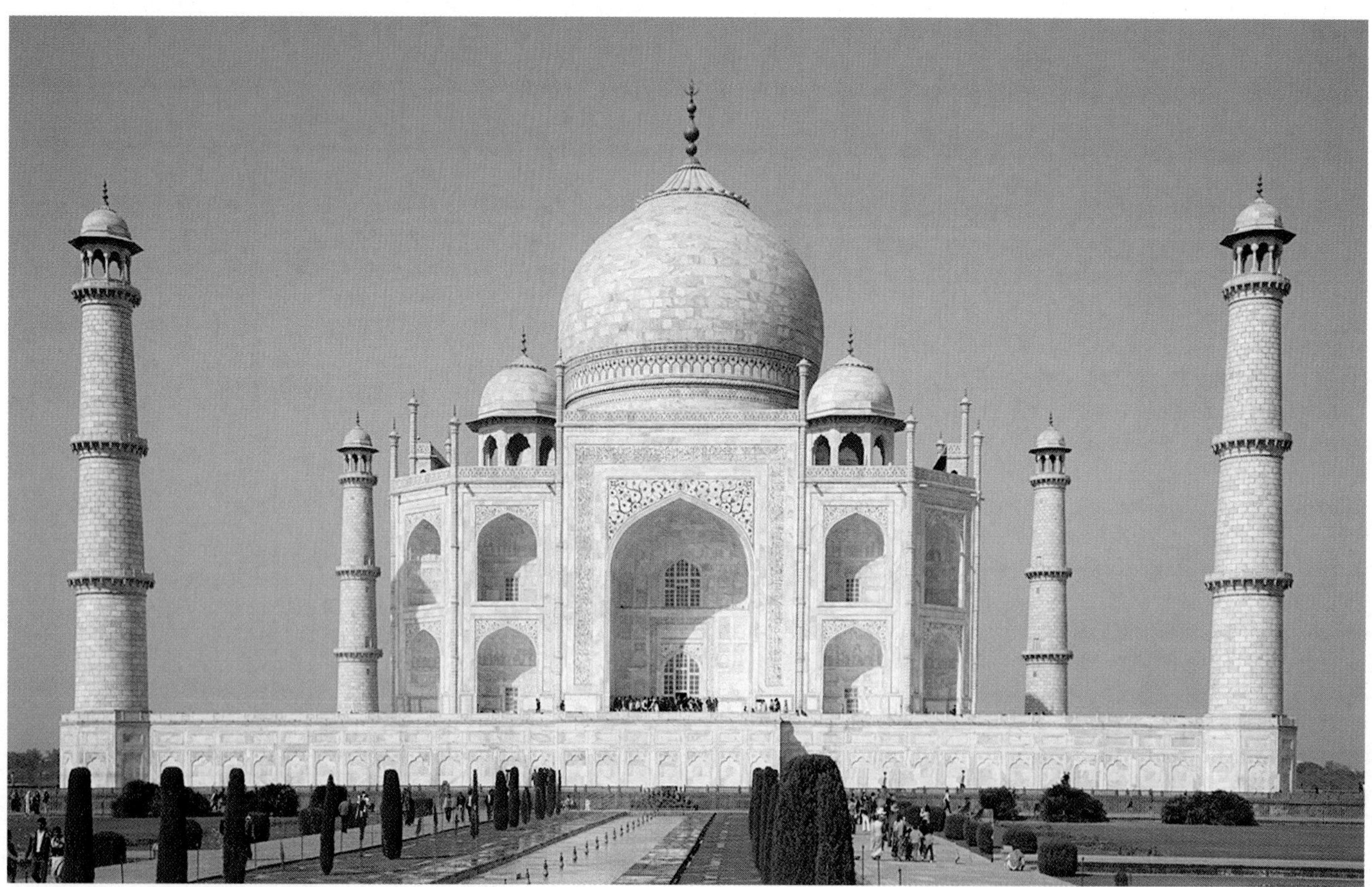

▲ **9-5.** Mausoleum of the *Taj Mahal*, 1630–1653; Agra, India.

DESIGN SPOTLIGHT

Architecture and Interiors: Once the fortress complex and later palace of Muslim rulers in Granada, the *Alhambra* (meaning red fortress) is the best surviving Moorish structure in Spain and features some of Islam's best stuccowork. As is common for Islamic buildings, the plain, austere, unembellished exterior gives no hint of the lavish courtyards and interiors inside. Proportioned according to the Golden Mean, the Court of the Lions has slender single, double, and triple columns of white marble with richly carved capitals. They carry multilobed arches covered with colored stucco decorations that obscure and deny the stonework beneath them. Pavilions projecting into the courtyard at each end have elaborately decorated walls and domed roofs. *Yeseria*, common in Spain, enhances the organic, lacy image on the gallery walls. Colored tiles pave the square and in the center is the fountain with twelve carved lions supporting an alabaster basin, which gives the courtyard its name.

Similarly, the interiors boast elaborate decoration with brightly colored tile work on walls and floors, *artesonades* ceilings, and horseshoe arches. The *iwan* or Reception Hall has the common design features of elaborate tile and *yeseria*, horseshoe arches, a honeycomb or stalactite dome, small arches in the upper wall, tiled floors, and a fountain. The color palette has rich tones of red, blue, green, gold, black, and cream. [World Heritage Site]

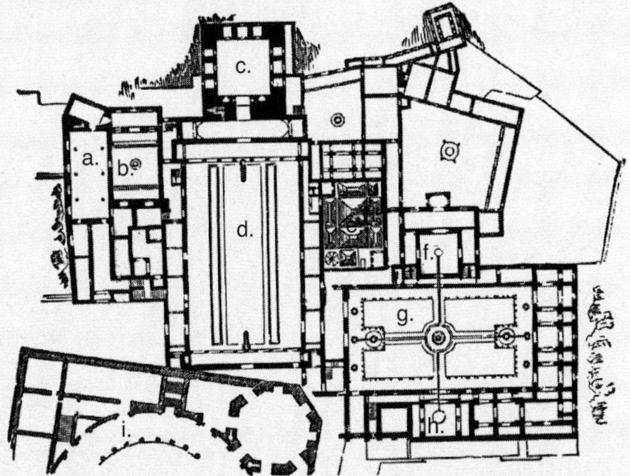

a. Mexuar b. Court of the Cuarto Dorado c. Hall of the Ambassadors d. Court of Myrtles e. Baths f. Hall of Two Sisters g. Court of the Lions h. Hall of the Abencerrajes i. Palace of Charles V

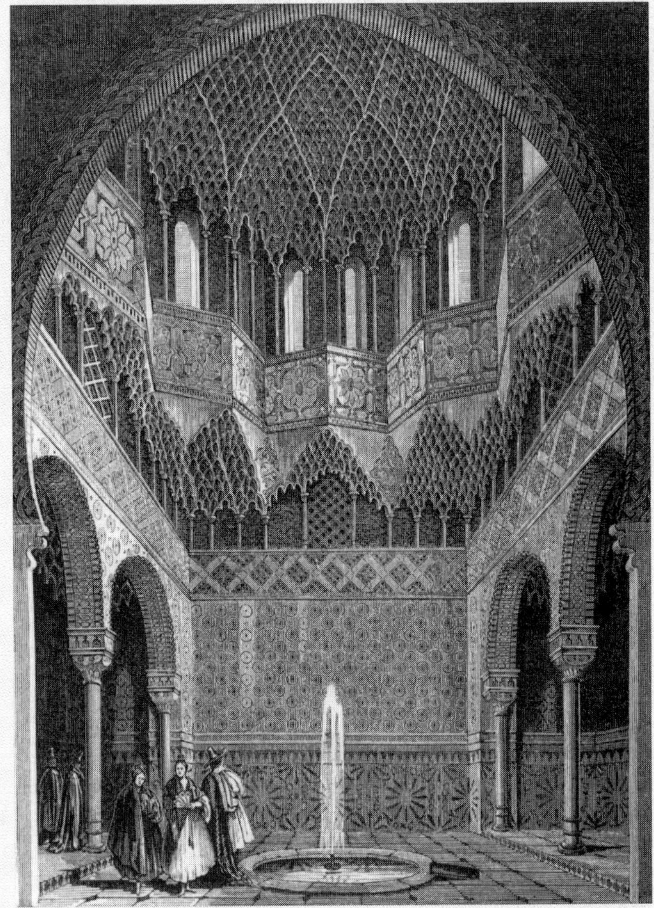

▲ **9-6.** Court of the Lions, floor plan, wall decoration, and *iwan* or Reception Hall at the *Alhambra*, 1338–1390 and later; Granada, Spain.

and shutters for privacy. Mosque windows, usually placed high in the wall, may have decorative wood, stone, or stucco grilles and/or colored glass (Fig. 9-5). Similarly, windows on palaces and dwellings are small and situated high in the wall. Wooden doors exhibit paneling or marquetry in many colors, and inlay of silver, ivory, and other materials (Fig. 9-2).

■ *Roofs*. Roofs are flat or vaulted and of masonry, wood, metal, or rusticated Mediterranean tile (Fig. 9-6). Domes and the pinnacles of *minarets* are sometimes of lead. Clay tile roofs are common on domestic structures.

■ *Later Interpretations*. Westerners do not generally copy Islamic building types because the structures are unsuitable for Western lifestyles and expensive to build and decorate. Individual elements, such as arches or domes, appear beginning in the 18th century and continuing into the 21st century. Building types are limited to those with some association with exoticism or Islam, such as some fraternal organizations. A notable example in the 19th century is the Royal Pavilion at Brighton (Fig. 9-7) in England.

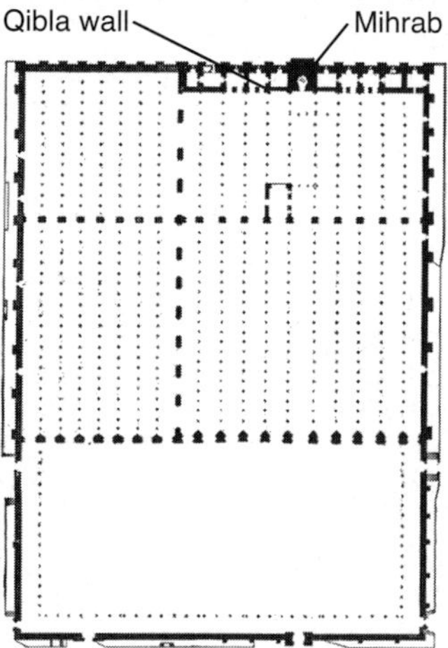

▲ **9-8.** Interior and floor plan, Great Mosque, begun in 785; Córdoba, Spain.

▲ **9-7.** Later Interpretation: Royal Pavilion, 1815–1821; Brighton, England; Henry Holland, remodeled by John Nash. English Regency.

INTERIORS

As with exteriors, most public and private interiors exhibit complex surface patterns and color on floors, walls, and ceilings and arched (Fig. 9-8), vaulted, or domed spaces. The complex, abstract patterns remind Muslims of infinity and the divine presence whose creation features eternal patterns. Although lavishly decorated, mosque interiors, intended for prayer and contemplation, neither awe nor exalt in the same manner as western churches.

In homes, the decoration of walls, floors, and ceilings conveys the owner's status. Water and light are important design elements. Room use is flexible; several activities may occur within a space. For example, the multifunctional reception room serves as a dining, entertaining, and at times a sleeping space. Public and private, male and female spaces are clearly distinguished through separation. Limited furnishings are typical in both mosques and houses.

▲ **9-9.** Interior, *Jezzar Pasha* Mosque, 1781-1782; Acre, Israel.

Public and Private Buildings

- *Color*. The interior palette mainly derives from decorative tiles, stucco, painting, and rugs. Typical colors include rich tones of red, blue, green, gold, black, and cream (Fig. 9-1, 9-8, 9-9, 9-12, 9-13).
- *Floors*. Floors feature tile or mosaic patterns, often with borders, medallions, and geometric forms (Fig. 9-12, 9-13). *Iwans* and other important spaces often have more than one level. For example, the *tazar* or main reception area in the *iwan* is a step or two higher than the entry. Rugs usually cover floors.
- *Rugs*. Originally made by nomadic tribes for many utilitarian purposes, rugs (Fig. 9-10, 9-13, 9-14) evolve into a high art form. At one time made in imperial factories, rugs are given by rulers as gifts, for recognition, or as political favors. In the 19th century, rugs begin to be woven specifically for Western markets. Rugs exhibit the same decorative system, colors, and visual complexity as

▲ **9-10.** Interior showing Ibur Sena, a poet, philosopher, and diplomat who lived 980–1037, with a Koran stand.

DESIGN SPOTLIGHT

Interior: Part of a complex of rooms, this *iwan* or main reception hall is the most elaborately decorated room in the *Alcazar*, as suits its purpose. An *afiz* or rectangular panel and molding frames the triple horseshoe arches supported by pink marble color. Above is a balcony with gilded metal balustrade. Gilded *muqarnas* accent the dome. Geometric and curvilinear stucco decoration and colored tiles create complex surface patterns and visual complexity on the walls. Red tiles with small patterned accents cover the floor. Cross-axial circulation supports movement to secondary spaces and to the adjacent courtyard. Originally the space would have had the finest furnishings, such as divans, ottomans, hexagonal tables, and Persian and Turkish rugs in rich colors, to convey wealth and status. [World Heritage Site]

▲ **9-11.** *Iwan* or Reception Hall, *Alcazar*, 1364; Seville, Spain.

▲ **9-12.** The Damascus *(Nur al-Din)* Room, 1707; Damascus, Syria. [The Hagtop Kevorkian Fund, 1970 (1970.170). The Metropolitan Museum of Art, New York, NY, U.S.A. Image © The Metropolitan Museum of Art/Art Resource, NY.]

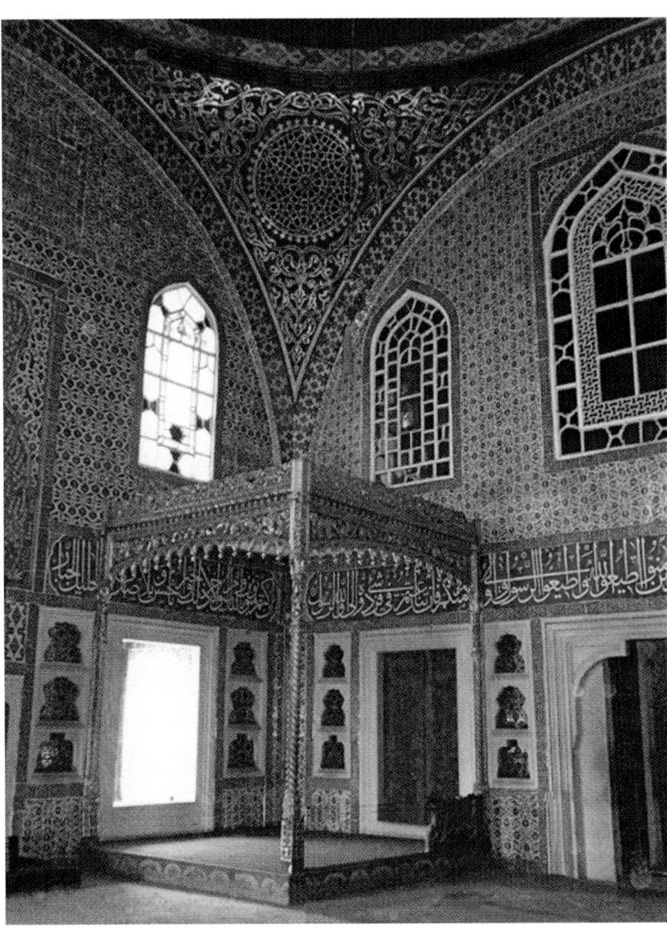

▲ **9-13.** Interiors (above and right) of the harem, Topkapi Palace, started 1454; Istanbul, Turkey.

other ornaments. Handmade rugs with a knotted pile are known as Oriental, Turkish, or Persian.

■ *Rug Construction and Decoration*. Oriental rugs have piles of wool, silk, and occasionally, cotton. The warp and weft are usually cotton. Yarns originally are colored with natural dyes, but later synthetics are used. The pile consists of numerous Turkish *(ghiordes)* or Persian *(senna)* knots (Fig. 9-14) tied around two warps. The Persian knot yields a finer pile and more defined pattern. The finer the rug, the more knots per square inch. Rugs have major and minor borders and central fields with geometric or curving patterns (Fig. 9-13, 9-14). Colors are rich and vibrant; green and yellow are rare. Patterns consist of repeated motifs, such as gulls or *meri-boteh*, all-over patterns such as garden or hunting designs, prayer patterns, and center medallions. The modern paisley motif comes from the pinecone or *meri-boteh* motif.

■ *Walls*. Walls are decorated with marble, tile, stuccowork, wood, *yeseria*, painting, and calligraphy (Fig. 9-11, 9-12, 9-13). Decoration may be in bands or panels. Often tile dadoes are at least four feet high. Poems or inscriptions in calligraphy invite closer study and remind of the divine presence. Cupboards and niches display prized objects. Small arches high on the wall filter air and light from one space to another.

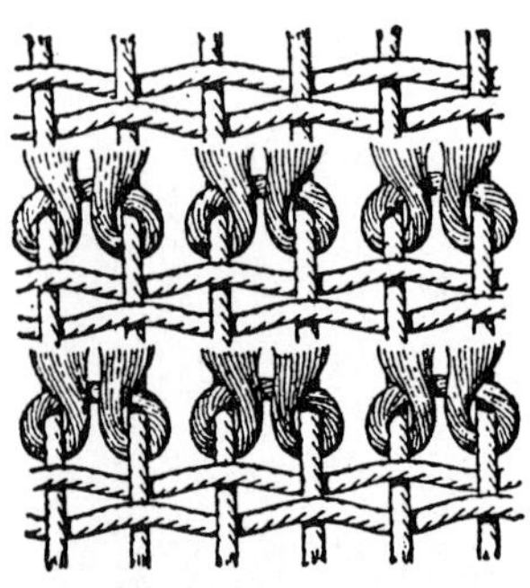

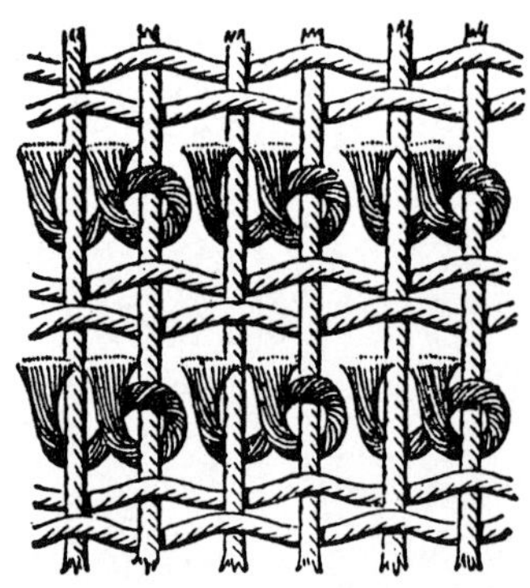

▲ **9-14.** Rugs: *Ghiordes* (e.g., Turkish) and *Senna* (e.g., Persian) carpet knots, and Persian rugs, 17th–19th centuries.

■ *Doors*. Dark wood doors, either plain or with geometric paneling or carving, are typical. They have iron hinges and door handles. Some are accented with decorative nailheads. Tiled lunettes often embellish the area over the door.

■ *Ceilings*. Ceilings may consist of domes, vaults, or beams and are highly decorated. Some are decoratively painted or tiled (Fig. 9-6, 9-11, 9-12, 9-13). In Spain, the *artesonades* ceiling is a distinctive architectural detail. A honeycomb or stalactite dome (Fig. 9-6) may cover important reception halls.

■ *Textiles*. The use of numerous textiles (Fig. 9-10, 9-13, 9-14) adds to the feeling of luxury and comfort. Rugs, hangings, curtains at doors or between columns, covers, or cushions are both functional and decorative, adding richness, warmth, pattern, and color. Patterns of textiles, ceramics (Fig. 9-16), and applied decoration on walls, floors, and ceilings are similar to architectural ones. Types include plain and embellished silks, damasks, velvets, and printed cottons in highly saturated colors.

FURNISHINGS AND DECORATIVE ARTS

Because of the nomadic heritage of the Arabs, most Islamic interiors have little movable furniture. Dining sets, beds, sideboards, and the like, are not used until European influences appear in the 19th century. Area rugs cover floors and, along with pillows, provide general seating areas. Coffers (chests) serve as storage. Important personages sit under canopies. Only rugs, basins for ablutions, Koran stands, and lamps appear in mosques.

Public and Private Buildings

■ *Seating*. Large cushions or rugs provide general seating. A divan outlines the perimeters of walls of important rooms (Fig. 9-13); its name derives from the name of the privy council of the Ottoman Empire. Seats often vary in height, and the tallest is reserved for the most important guest. Movable seating, such as chairs and stools, is rare in households.

■ *Tables*. Small movable tables (Fig. 9-10, 9-13) of wood inlaid with ivory and ebony are noteworthy for their hexagonal shape and overall decorative treatments. The Koran stand (Fig. 9-10, 9-15), which holds the holy document, is important and typically very elaborate.

■ *Decorative Arts*. Decorative arts consist of glassware, metalwork, ceramics (Fig. 9-16), and ivories. All have the same motifs and decorative systems of the architecture and interiors.

◀ **9-15.** Koran stand made of inlaid and pierced wood.

▲ **9-16.** Decorative Arts: Plate and vase with floral and Islamic motifs.

CHAPTER 10

Romanesque

8th Century–1150 C.E.

What is God? He is length, width, height, and depth.

What profit is there in these ridiculous monsters, in that marvellous and deformed comeliness, that comely deformity?

—Bernard of Clairvaux, 1127, from *Literary Source of Art History*, ed. E. G. Holt

Romanesque architecture derives its name from its similarity to ancient Roman buildings, most notably its reliance on the round arch and articulation of individual parts to create unity. Creating an international style with numerous regional variations, the builders look to older construction methods and forms for ways to respond to functional needs. Primarily appearing in churches, Romanesque structural developments, such as the rib vault, will be carried further in the subsequent Gothic style.

HISTORICAL AND SOCIAL

Institutions and precedents that significantly affect Romanesque and Gothic life and art arise during the Early Middle Ages (5th–9th centuries). After the Roman Empire disintegrates in the 5th century C.E., Europe fragments into groups of tribal alliances. The Catholic Church is the only surviving major institution. Through evangelism, Europe becomes Christianized, and the church exerts greater spiritual, political, and economic influence. The church becomes central to medieval life and thought, but its unifying abilities are limited where local rulers do not acknowledge its authority.

Beginning in the 6th century, various religious orders establish monasteries, which become important medieval institutions. These devout societies combine a strict religious rule with intellectual and artistic endeavors. Members include architecture, mathematics, and medicine in their studies. They also write books and copy ancient manuscripts, thereby preserving knowledge and culture. Their schools maintain and disseminate education. Religious rule requires manual labor, so the priests and monks also clear forests, build roads, and cultivate gardens and fields.

Feudalism and seignorialism organize society into classes of warrior-nobility, clergy, and commoners. Under feudalism, a king or noble grants a fief (usually land) to a nobleman who, in turn, swears loyalty and political and military service to the lord. The system maintains order and controls territory when governments are nonexistent or weak. Seignorialism or manorialism, closely related to feudalism, forms social, political, and economic relationships between a lord or landholder and his dependent farmers or peasants (serfs). Both systems dominate medieval society until the 14th century.

Constant warfare and poor economic conditions characterize the period before the 11th century. Consequently, there is little significant building or artistic endeavor, minimal trade, and for most people there is great hardship, numerous famines, widespread disease, and short life spans. But the 11th and 12th centuries are a turning point in Western Europe as it emerges as a separate entity from Byzantium and Islam. Eventually, the great invasions cease, but lack of political unity, widespread illiteracy, and poor communication remain. Feudalism and seignorialism continue to dominate society, while individual nations struggle to arise. Mediterranean trade routes reopen, which stimulates the economy and produces a new middle class of artisans and merchants. The expansion of towns, commerce, industry, and populations creates a building boom.

More important, Christian influence, and with it education and culture, spreads across Europe. The Catholic Church provides stability and unity through shared faith, diplomacy, and administration of justice. Monasteries flourish even more, fostering and supporting intellectual and artistic expression, with many of them becoming wealthy and instrumental in the building of numerous churches. Clergy and laypeople sponsor and join the Crusades to liberate Jerusalem from the Muslims beginning in 1095. This joining of secular and religious forces creates the ideal of the warrior-priest that, in turn, influences knighthood and its code of chivalry. Although men dominate, a few women, such as Eleanor of Aquitaine, hold power and exert influence. Illiteracy remains widespread.

Pilgrimages to favored sites such as Jerusalem and Rome reflect the period's religious zeal. Neither is easily accessible, so Santiago de Compostella in Spain becomes the most important sacred site. People, buildings, and wealth concentrate along the four main pilgrimage routes to Santiago. Stimulated by the Crusades, pilgrimages, and the needs of cities, many churches are constructed, renovated, or rebuilt. Romanesque architecture flourishes throughout France, England, Italy, Germany, and Spain.

CONCEPTS

Concepts come primarily from the period's emphasis on religion. The church guides ways of thinking about tradition, honor, chivalry, education, ceremony, and family life. These ideas shape and define social, cultural, and design progress. The Crusades, pilgrimages, churches, and monasteries give sanctuary, unity, and stability, while bringing numerous changes during this period of turmoil and unrest. For example, churches, which are often situated along pilgrimage routes, increase in size, become more multifunctional, and provide safe havens for travelers.

MOTIFS

■ *Motifs*. Important motifs (Fig. 10-1, 10-2, 10-3, 10-4, 10-5, 10-7) include the round arch, figures, corbel tables, animals, grotesques and fantastic figures, foliage, heraldic devices, linenfold, zigzags, lozenges, and geometric forms. Molding designs (Fig. 10-2) include the zigzag, star, *billet*, and lozenge.

ARCHITECTURE

Romanesque architecture, an international style, springs up across Europe as builders grapple with the problems of providing larger, structurally stable churches to accommodate crowds of pilgrims and worshippers, as well as good light and acoustics and fire resistance. Builders often look to local surviving Roman architecture and construction methods and assimilate influences

(a)

(b)

(c)

(d)

▲ **10-1.** Motifs and Ornament: (a) Norman Romanesque ornament; (b) Norman Romanesque ornament; (c) wall painting, Orvieto Cathedral, Orvieto, Italy; (d) floor, Siena Cathedral, Siena, Italy.

(a)

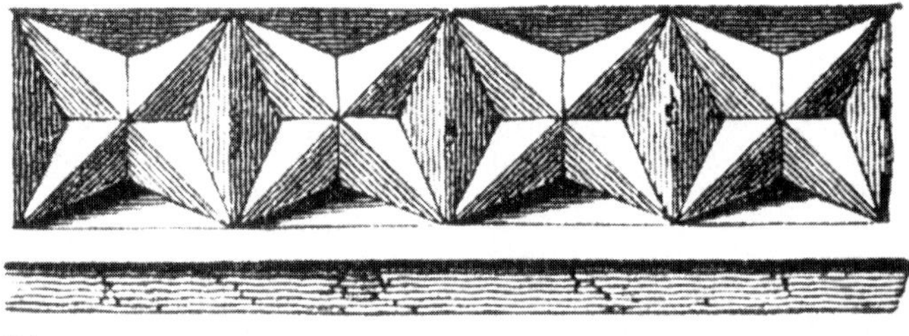
(b)

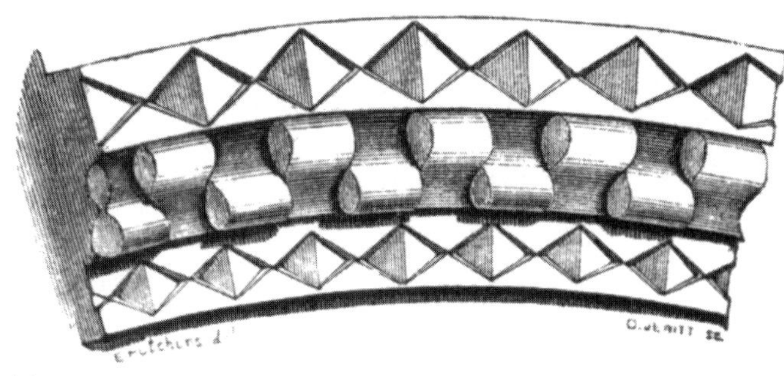
(c)

▲ **10-2.** Architectural Details and Moldings: (a) Portal, Wenlock Abbey, Shropshire, England; (b) molding; (c) molding, 11th–12th centuries.

from Byzantine, Islam, Carolingian, Ottonian, Celtic, German, and Norman design. This new approach produces a common architecture language, one that is more thoughtful and deliberate and replaces tradition and intuition. Construction innovations spread quickly as clergy, pilgrims, and master-builders travel from site to site.

Exterior and interior architectural elements provide order, unity, readability, and monumentality. Emphasis is on solidity, weightiness, architectural elements such as the arch and the pier, and moldings and sculpture to accentuate design features (Fig. 10-5, 10-7). Compositions are symmetrical and ordered, often with few openings. Romanesque revives the use of figural and nonfigural sculpture, particularly around windows, portals, and arches. Regional variations include the Lombard style in Northern Italy (Fig 10-5), the Pisan style in Italy, and the Norman style in England (Fig. 10-6).

Responses to individual needs and the variety of models produce numerous regional church styles that differ in appearance, but relate in their use of such Roman architectural characteristics as vaults and round arches, delineation of parts, and masonry construction to create larger and more fireproof structures. Innovations include variations of pier forms, original capitals, and the triforium. Other common characteristics include regularly repeated modules in plans and facades, towers, buttresses, ribbed vaults, ambulatories, and thick walls with few openings. Forms, features, and aesthetic elements partly come from technological advances in response to practical and liturgical needs.

Churches (Fig. 10-5, 10-6, 10-7) and monasteries are the primary building types. Churches serve as places of worship, eateries, and hostels. Other types of architecture include public buildings, townhouses, castles, manor houses, and farmhouses. The few secular structures that survive are mainly castles, which rarely exhibit Romanesque stylistic characteristics.

Public and Private Buildings

■ *Site Orientation*. Churches are usually located along pilgrimage routes or in town centers. In monasteries, the cloister, dormitory, refectory, and kitchen surround the church, a visual metaphor for its centrality to monastic life. Other structures include guesthouses, schools, libraries, barns, stables, and workshops. Monasteries are walled for protection and privacy.

■ *Floor Plans*. Many churches follow what is known as the pilgrimage plan (Fig. 10-7) in which the side aisles flanking the nave extend around the transept and circular apse. Besides adding needed space, this innovation allows clergy to continue their duties despite the crowds. Plans are based on a module composed of one nave bay. Aisles are half of this unit in width. Modules allow

▲ **10-3.** Portal: *Église Sainte-Foy de Moriaàs*, 1080; Moriaàs, France.

▲ **10-4.** Capitals from various churches including *S. Madeleine*, Vézelay, France.

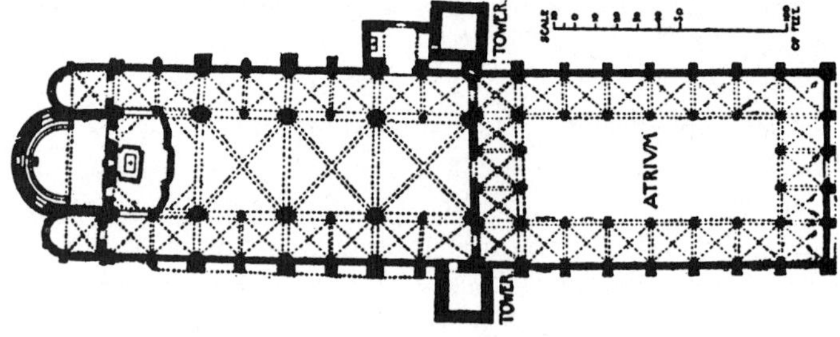

▲ **10-5.** *S. Ambrogio*, floor plan, and interior, c. 1080–1128; Milan, Italy; a significant example of the Lombard-Romanesque style.

infinite variation in size and configuration. The crossing is square or nearly so and marked by a tower or octagonal dome. Some Italian churches retain the Early Christian colonnaded forecourt or atrium (Fig. 10-5) and narthex.

■ *Materials*. Churches are primarily of masonry to prevent fires. A few retain wooden ceilings and roofs. Most use local stone because of transportation difficulties. Exteriors often feature several types in contrasting colors. Areas lacking good building stone use brick, such as in the Lombard style in Italy, which features plain brick exteriors (Fig. 10-5). A few churches are of marble.

■ *Façades*. Round arches (Fig. 10-3) and delineated architectural elements are key features. Fronts may have three parts, each with a portal that coincides with the interior nave and flanking aisles (Fig. 10-5). Twin towers are common. Buttresses, engaged columns, or pilasters, often corresponding to interior units, divide front and sidewalls into bays (Fig. 10-7). Corbel tables, a definitive characteristic, emphasize roof angles, spires, and parapets (Fig. 10-5, 10-7).

■ *Doors and Windows*. Rounded doors, windows, and arcades (Fig. 10-3, 10-7) display figural and nonfigural sculptures. Previously, stone sculpture had all but disappeared in Europe, so its revival is an important innovation. Romanesque sculpture relates to the architecture. For example, columns with sculpture form the jamb of recessed portals, and reliefs fill the tympanum and cover the *archivolts*. Sculpture programs range from simple to elaborate. To help educate the parishioners, sculpture programs illustrate biblical stories and history and incorporate Christian symbols. Windows are as large as construction permits. Stained glass emerges late in the period.

■ *Roofs*. Timber roofs are usually gabled. Chapels and towers may have conical or pyramidal roofs. The nave and flanking aisles sometimes have their own roofs.

■ *Later Interpretations*. Romanesque influences reappear in the German Rundbogenstil and Romanesque Revival elsewhere during the 19th and early 20th centuries. Characteristic elements are also evident in the work of Henry Hobson Richardson in such examples as Trinity Church (Fig. 10-8) in Boston, Massachusetts.

INTERIORS

Church interiors have many of the common Romanesque characteristics: round arches, repeated modules, ribbed vaults, compound piers, triforium, thick walls, and masonry ceilings. Like exteriors, architectural elements create identity, individuality, rhythm, and order, unlike the earlier simple basilica spaces with flat ceilings and walls. Romanesque interiors also are quite different from the glittering, otherworldly interiors of Early Christian and Byzantine churches. Like Byzantine, architectural elements delineate individual bays or units, but emphasis is on weight and mass instead of decoration. Sculpture is mostly architectonic—outlining the nave and transverse arches, windows, and moldings, and forming capitals.

Few Romanesque domestic interiors survive intact. Emphasis seems to have been on textile hangings instead of woodwork or furniture. Interiors reflect the importance of ceremony and rank through lavish appointments, textiles, and furniture. Living patterns do not change significantly from the Romanesque to the Gothic period.

Public Buildings

■ *Color*. The walls and ceilings of Romanesque churches sometimes are painted to enhance and emphasize their architectonic nature. Treatments vary from simple washes of color to extensive figural and decorative schemes. Colors include yellow ochre, sandstone, gray, or red. Contrasting color, borders, or ornamental patterns highlight architectural elements (Fig. 10-7). Some transverse arches have structural or painted voussoirs in contrasting colors (Fig 10-5, 10-7). Italian examples often continue the Byzantine traditions of mosaics and colored marble panels (Fig. 10-5).

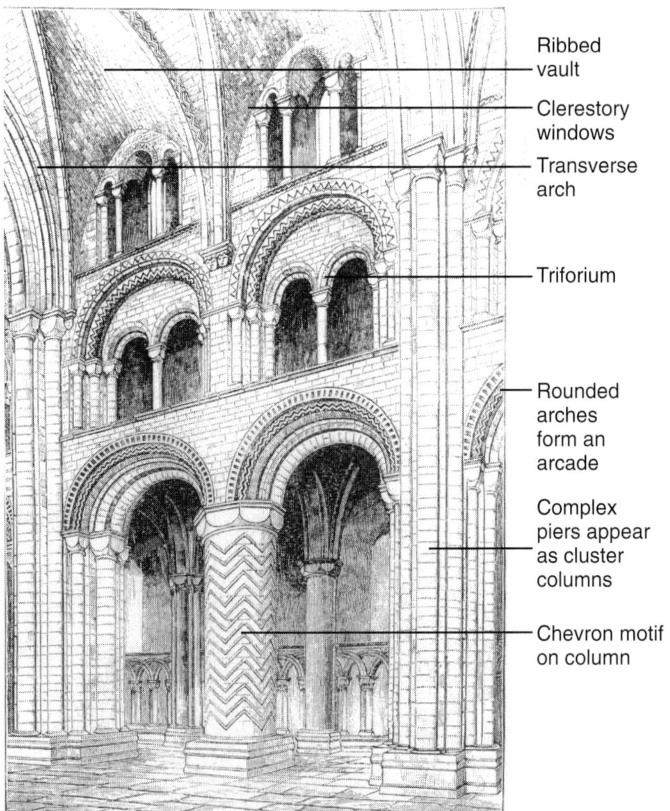

▲ **10-6.** Nave, Durham Cathedral, with arches detail, 1093–1133; Durham, England.

DESIGN SPOTLIGHT

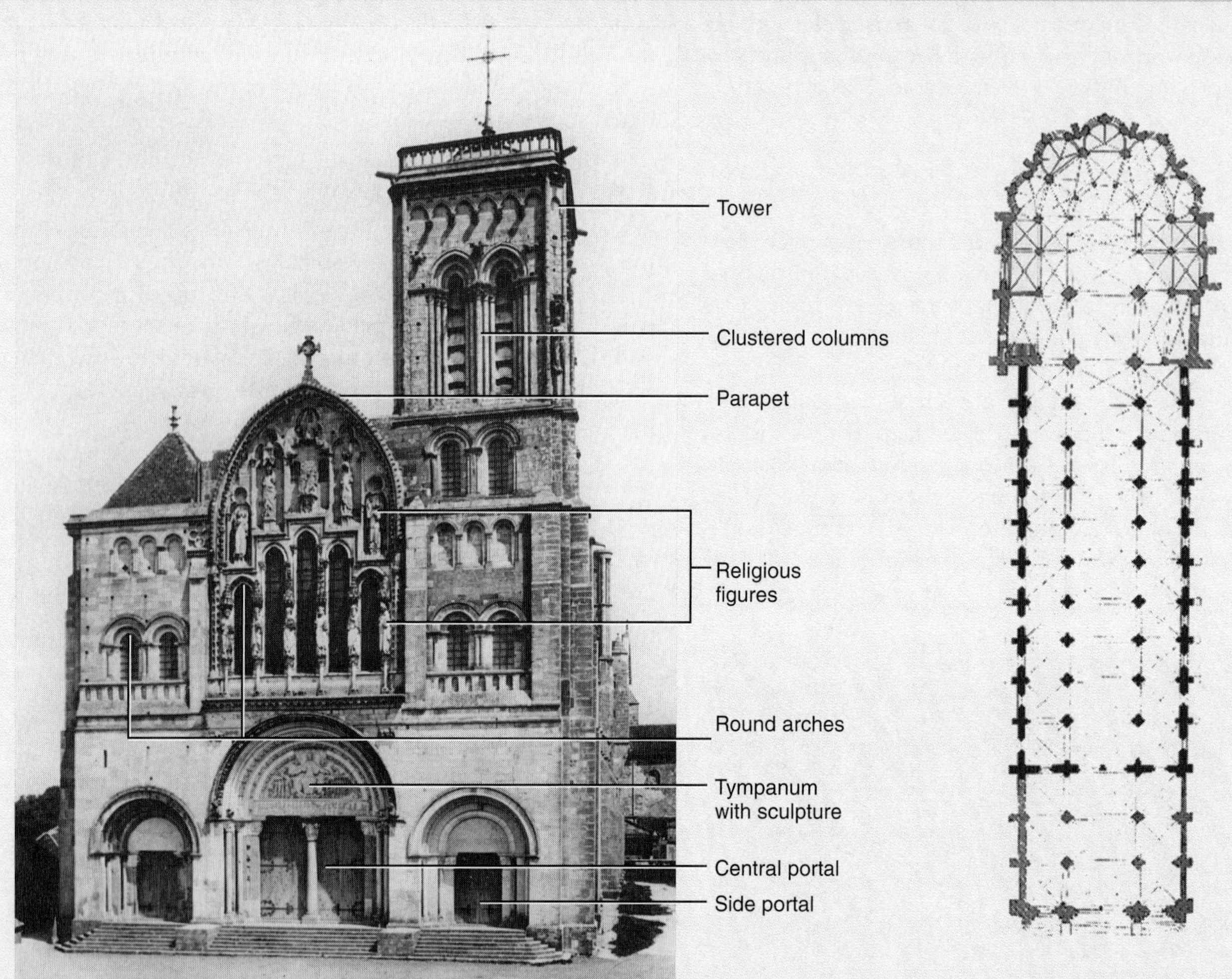

Architecture and Interior: The *S. Madeleine* basilica church claims to own the body and relics of Mary Magdalene, so it becomes a major destination for pilgrimages. Additionally, the Second and Third Crusades, 1146 and 1190, respectively, begin here. This necessitates a new and larger church, which is begun in 1104. The west front or main façade is originally Romanesque in style, but the Gothic central gable and tower are built in the 13th century. Three portals, corresponding to the nave and aisles, highlight the façade, and round arches dominate the composition. A complicated sculpture program covers the tympanum, the large arch over the central portal, and the narthex portals and continues in the interiors. Viollet-le-Duc adds the Romanesque-style tympanum of the Last Judgment in the narthex portal as part of a significant restoration in 1840. *S. Madeleine's* plan lacks the traditional transept but has chapels surrounding the apse. The original plan was extended with the addition of a narthex in 1132 to accommodate the large crowds of pilgrims.

Inside, transverse arches with colored voussoirs rhythmically delineate the barrel-vaulted nave, which is one of the oldest parts of the church, and the round-arched nave arcade. Decorative carving accentuates the nave arcade, clerestory windows, stringcourses, and transverse arches. Column capitals depict Bible stories, ancient legends, and mythological creatures (Fig. 10-2). The interior has more light than most Romanesque churches because of its carefully planned placement. Twice a year, at the summer and winter solstices, the nave is flooded with light cascading down to the altar. This masterpiece of Burgundian Romanesque art and architecture becomes a UNESCO World Heritage Site in 1979.

▲ **10-7.** *S. Madeleine,* floor plan and interior, c. 1104–1132 and later (restoration completed in 1859 by Viollet-le-Duc); Vézelay, France.

■ *Floors.* Floors are important design elements because there are no pews or seats and few furnishings. Treatments vary from plain stone or brick with simple washes of color to elaborate patterns in tile or marble.

■ *Walls.* Nave walls, which may be two or three stories, have round arches (Fig. 10-5, 10-6, 10-7), reminiscent of those used in Roman aqueducts, basilicas, and baths. The lower portion is an arcade carried by piers. Above is the triforium, composed of two

DESIGN SPOTLIGHT

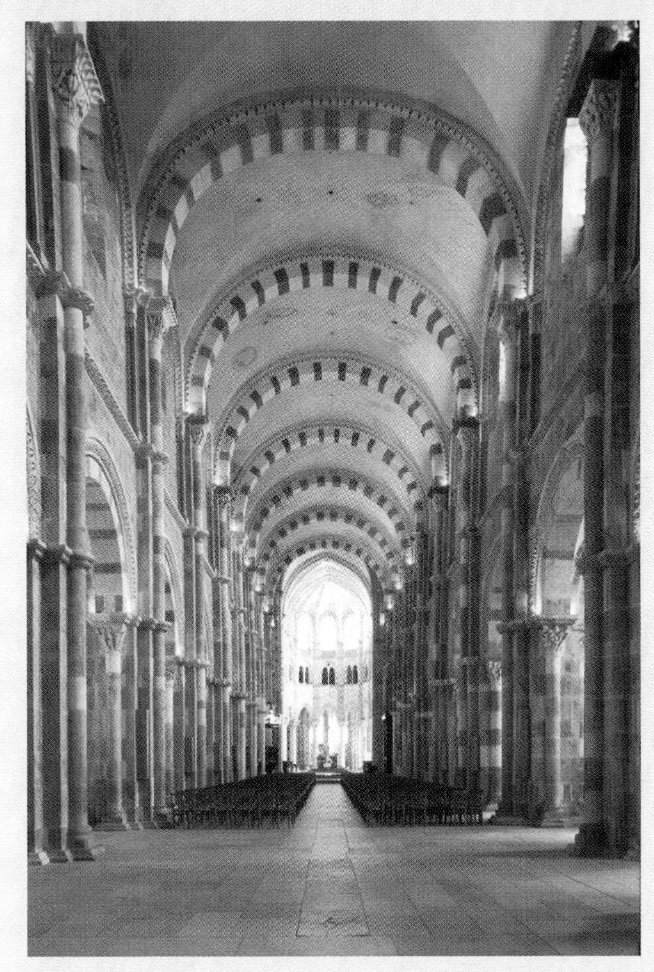

▲ **10-7.** Continued

▲ **10-8.** Later Interpretation: Trinity Church, 1873–1877; Boston, Massachusetts; Henry Hobson Richardson. Romanesque Revival.

or more round arches on columns. Clerestory windows, also with round arches, appear only in groin or rib-vaulted naves. Openings reveal wall thickness and emphasize weight. In Britain, Normandy, Germany, and Italy, churches often have passages within their thick upper walls. Largely an articulation device, columns and arches separate these passages from the main space.

■ *Nave Vaults*. The earliest nave vault is the barrel vault, which requires thick walls for support (Fig. 10-7). Consequently, there are no clerestory windows in this area. A variation is a pointed barrel vault with pointed transverse arches and a nave arcade. Besides allowing greater height, pointed forms permit the addition of a triforium and clerestory windows. Some builders experiment with groin vaults for naves, but do not generally adopt them, except in France. Ribbed vaults are a significant Romanesque innovation. One of the earliest dated instances of their use are the choir vaults and, slightly later, those in the nave at Durham, in England (Fig. 10-6). The combination of pointed arches, ribbed vaults, the triforium, and clerestory windows seen at Durham begins to dematerialize thick Romanesque walls. Gothic innovations will complete this process.

■ *Piers and Transverse Arches*. Complex piers emphasize bays and define church interiors. Piers (Fig. 10-5, 10-6, 10-7) may be compound, cluster, single spiral, double fluted, plain round, and quadrangular. Capitals (Fig. 10-4), when present, are similar in form to Corinthian capitals but are decorated with animals, figures, and foliage. They also exhibit geometric designs such as the chevron, zigzag, and guilloche. A center pier may extend upward and across the nave ceiling to form a transverse arch (Fig. 10-6). Most masonry ceilings have transverse arches, but more often for articulation than support.

■ *Ceilings*. When defense is not a concern, ceilings are flat and beamed. When defense or fireproofing is necessary, ceilings (Fig. 10-5, 10-6, 10-7) are of masonry and vaulted.

■ *Textiles*. Few textiles from the period suvive but the best is the Bayeux Tapestry (Fig. 10-9). It has embroidery of wool on linen that depicts the Norman defeat of the Anglo-Saxons at the battle of Hastings in 1066, which unites England. The tapestry celebrates William the Conqueror's victory and the beginning of Norman rule.

▲ **10-9.** Bayeux Tapestry, 1066–1082; embroidered wool on linen (230'-0" × 1'-8").

FURNISHINGS AND DECORATIVE ARTS

Church furnishings consist mainly of altars, canopies, and shrines. Accessories, such as silver chalices, are particularly luxurious and elaborate. Simple board construction, which pegs or nails boards together, is characteristic; sophisticated construction methods and decorative techniques, such as veneer and inlay, are unknown. Turning, carving, and painting in bright colors are the main forms of decoration.

Public Buildings

■ *Materials*. Local woods, such as oak, walnut, and elm, are used because transportation difficulties prevent obtaining wood from any distance.

■ *Seating*. Few chairs are used during the period. Elaborate, massive thrones (Fig. 10-10) proclaim the status of the ruler or important cleric. Other chairs are large, heavy, and simpler in design. Stools in various forms provide most seating.

■ *Storage*. Chests and ivory caskets with decorative patterns store important materials. Rosettes, animals, and figures may embellish the surface.

■ *Decorative Arts*. Illuminated manuscripts, produced in monasteries, have flat spaces, lively lines and patterns, ornamental initials, and bright colors.

▲ **10-10.** Thrones.

CHAPTER 11

Gothic

1150–1550

The outburst of the 1st century crusade was splendid even in a military sense, but it was great beyond comparison in its reflection in architecture, ornament, poetry, color, religion, and philosophy.

—Henry Adams, *Mont-Saint Michael and Chartres*

In Gothic, the great style of the Christian religion, architecture and theology combine to create a visual metaphor of a period in which religion and faith in God are all-important. The most common expressions are the great cathedrals, but Gothic architectural elements also appear in secular buildings, interiors, furnishings, and decorative arts.

HISTORICAL AND SOCIAL

A period of stability and peace begins in Europe about 1100. Newly formed central governments in England, France, and Spain facilitate economic and social growth. Cities and towns change from isolated settlements to busy and growing cosmopolitan centers as more and more people come to look for work. Trade and commerce increase, creating a prominent merchant class. Universities join monasteries as centers of learning. Feudalism declines as lords abandon their fortified residences for country or manor houses and build stately mansions in town.

By 1200, the power and prestige of the Catholic Church is at its peak, and it is the major patron for new and repaired cathedrals, parish churches, abbeys, priories, and convents. Women are admired in song and verse, and chivalry is at its height. The esteem for the Virgin Mary manifests in the many cathedrals and chapels dedicated to her. The relative peace and prosperity shatters during the 14th century with the Hundred Years War between France and England and the Black Death, a plague that eliminates over one third of Europe's population.

The Gothic style, like religion, is intimately intertwined with medieval life. The great cathedrals (from *cathedra,* meaning "seat of a bishop") are physical manifestations of Christian faith and civic pride. They serve as town halls, public meeting places, and tourist attractions, and their construction involves the entire community. Wealthy patrons or local guilds donate funds for chapels, windows, and other elements. Others give what money they are able or supply physical labor. Local clergy often direct the project. Besides a great cathedral, every village or town has one or more parish churches. Secular and religious organizations and wealthy families have their own chapels or churches.

CONCEPTS

The term *Gothic* refers to the Goths, the Germanic tribes that brought about the downfall of the Roman Empire. Originally, the style's name was a derogatory reference used by classicists of the Renaissance. In Gothic, spiritual and material elements unite and manifest visually in the great European cathedrals. Thus, they become visual metaphors for a time in which religion and faith were of utmost importance in most people's lives. The style is an outgrowth of thought regarding what constitutes a great church and its form. Church authorities often oversee ecclesiastical building projects to ensure that appropriate ideas are conveyed.

MOTIFS

■ *Motifs*. Motifs (Fig. 11-1, 11-2, 11-3) include heraldic devices, the pointed arch, trefoils, quatrefoils, cinquefoils, fantastic figures such as gargoyles or dwarfs, birds, foliage, oak leaves, crockets, and linenfold. Some geometric shapes, such as lozenges or zigzags, continue from the Romanesque period.

ARCHITECTURE

The first Gothic structure is the remodeled chevet of the Abbey of S. Denis (begun in 1135) in the Ile de France, where French nobility is interred. The intent is that S. Denis becomes the spiritual center of France and, as such, inspires, awes, and captures patriotic and religious imaginations. The elements used to accomplish this are pointed arches, slender columns, ribbed vaults, and stained glass combined with mathematical proportions. None of these individual elements is new, but their intention, combination, and use in construction enable and impart a lightness and openness not found in Romanesque architecture. They also permit more natural light. Light is a metaphor for divine illumination, and mathematical proportions represent divine order and harmony. From S. Denis, the Gothic style spreads to other areas of France. In just over 100 years, it becomes an international style.

(a)

(b)

(c)

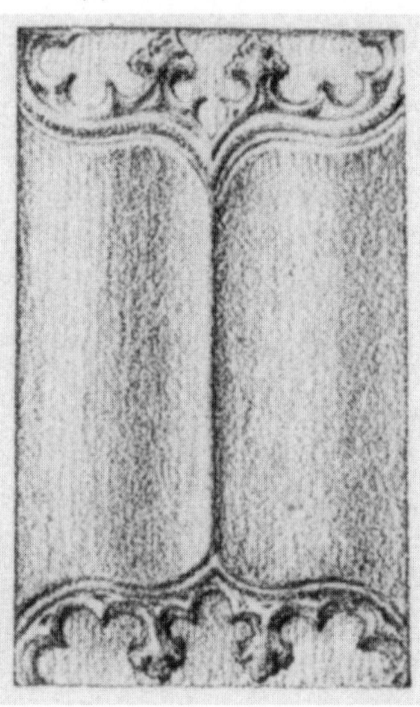
(d)

(e)

(f)

▲ **11-1.** Motifs and Architectural Details: (a) Heraldic motif, Bath, England; (b) pointed arch with tracery, Windsor Castle, England; (c) foliage diaper pattern; (d) linenfold panel; (e) rinceau with leaf motif; and (f) gargoyle.

Cathedrals (Fig. 11-4, 11-5), parish churches, and other ecclesiastical structures are the most common building types. Additionally, universities, the newly formed guilds, and prosperous towns build halls and meeting places. Images and symbols of faith and prosperity appear in cathedrals through cruciform plans with altars toward the east, soaring and vertical lines, mystical light, and decorative programs that explain faith, doctrines, and secular history to the many who cannot read. Government and university buildings sometimes resemble the design of churches with towers marking major circulation areas. Most dwellings do not resemble churches, but eventually, architectural characteristics find their way into domestic buildings and interiors as details and on furniture as motifs.

Many secular structures, including castles and walled towns, have a military or fortified nature. Function and defense, along with conservatism, construction methods, and local materials, are more important than style in determining the form and appearance of nonreligious buildings. Castles (Fig. 11-6), developing from ancient fortification techniques, are the defensive residences of monarchs, lords, bishops, and knights throughout the Middle Ages. An integral part of medieval life, their primary purposes are defending lands and maintaining order. By the 11th century, emphasis in castle planning changes from defense to comfort. Townhouses (Fig. 11-8) and manor houses often resemble castles with stone façades, roof battlements, towers, drawbridge entries, and interior courtyards.

National and regional variations in church architecture abound. Each country creates a unique interpretation of the common features: the pointed arch, groin or ribbed vaults, cluster or compound columns, large windows with tracery and stained glass, buttresses, flying buttresses, pinnacles, towers, and spires. Dimensions are mathematically related within a single structure, but not consistent among buildings. Proportions are tall, slender, and elongated. Common shapes include the square and equilateral triangle. Biblical numbers, such as 3, 7, and 12, are used in doorways, windows, exterior bays, plan bays, and other features.

■ *France*. French cathedrals (Fig. 11-4) accentuate height and verticality. Early and High Gothic (1150–1250) structures are monumental in size and height. As if in a reaction to this huge scale, subsequent Rayonnant buildings (13th–14th centuries) are smaller and more elegant. Windows, which are larger than before, feature complex radiating tracery patterns. During the 14th through 16th centuries, many structures are in the Flamboyant style with tracery on all surfaces, including vaults. Tracery patterns include adaptations from the English Decorated style and the flamelike forms that give the style its name.

■ *England*. English cathedrals (Fig. 11-5, 11-10) tend to be longer and more horizontal than French cathedrals, at least at first. Early English Gothic cathedrals are generally simple with shorter towers. This style gradually evolves into the more complex Decorated style (c. 1240–1330), which is characterized by elaborate tracery and ogee arches. The Perpendicular style (c. 1330–1530) features extravagant towers, rectilinear vertical forms with cusps, and fan vaulting (Fig. 11-10). Decorated and Perpendicular interiors have elaborate vaulting with numerous complex patterns of structural and nonstructural ribs.

■ *Germany, Spain, Italy*. Germany, Spain, and Italy synthesize Gothic characteristics with their cultures and design sensibilities to create their own unique expressions of the style in various building types, such as palaces (Fig. 11-7).

Public and Private Buildings

■ *Site Orientation*. Indicating their importance in town life, most European cathedrals are in the center of town (Fig. 11-4), surrounded by markets, other secular structures, and dwellings. In contrast, lawns and trees surround many English cathedrals (Fig. 11-5). Other public buildings in all countries may line squares or narrow streets along with shops and townhouses.

Like fortresses, castles are sited for security and protection of territory, usually on hills (Fig. 11-6) or along lines of defense, rivers, or the ancient Roman roads. Moats, sometimes filled with

▲ **11-2.** Illuminated manuscript, c. 1450–1470; Normandy, France.

▲ **11-3.** Capitals, c. 14th–15th centuries; Italy and Portugal.

DESIGN SPOTLIGHT

Architecture and Interior: Characteristics derived from the Romanesque period include the columns, buttresses, the tripartite façade, the portals, numerous figural sculptures, interior vaulting, and three-story nave. In the Gothic style, the same elements are taller, thinner, and more carefully organized, both vertically and horizontally, evidence of Abbot Suger's ideal of mathematical proportions and order. Notre Dame's façade is visually lighter because of the large windows, the height of the pointed arches, and the large openings in the towers. The verticality created by the buttresses, pointed arches, and towers is balanced by the horizontal bands, one of figures of Old Testament kings with open pointed arches with tracery above. The three parts of the façade, separated by buttresses, correspond to the nave and aisle. The central rose window with stained glass is a dominant feature that filters richly colored light into the interior. On the side and around the apse, flying buttresses, among the first in the world, provide additional support for the walls and create a graceful rhythm. The nave roof is a steeply pitched gable, while the circular apse has a conical tower. A soaring spire identifies the crossing. In the nave, single columns and square bays are reminiscent of the Romanesque period, but the lightness, verticality, and combination of architectural features are Gothic. Pointed arches lead the eye upward as do the responds or center column or pier rising unimpeded to the vault ribs. Large clerestory windows and slender architectural elements make the walls seem thin and weightless. [World Heritage Site]

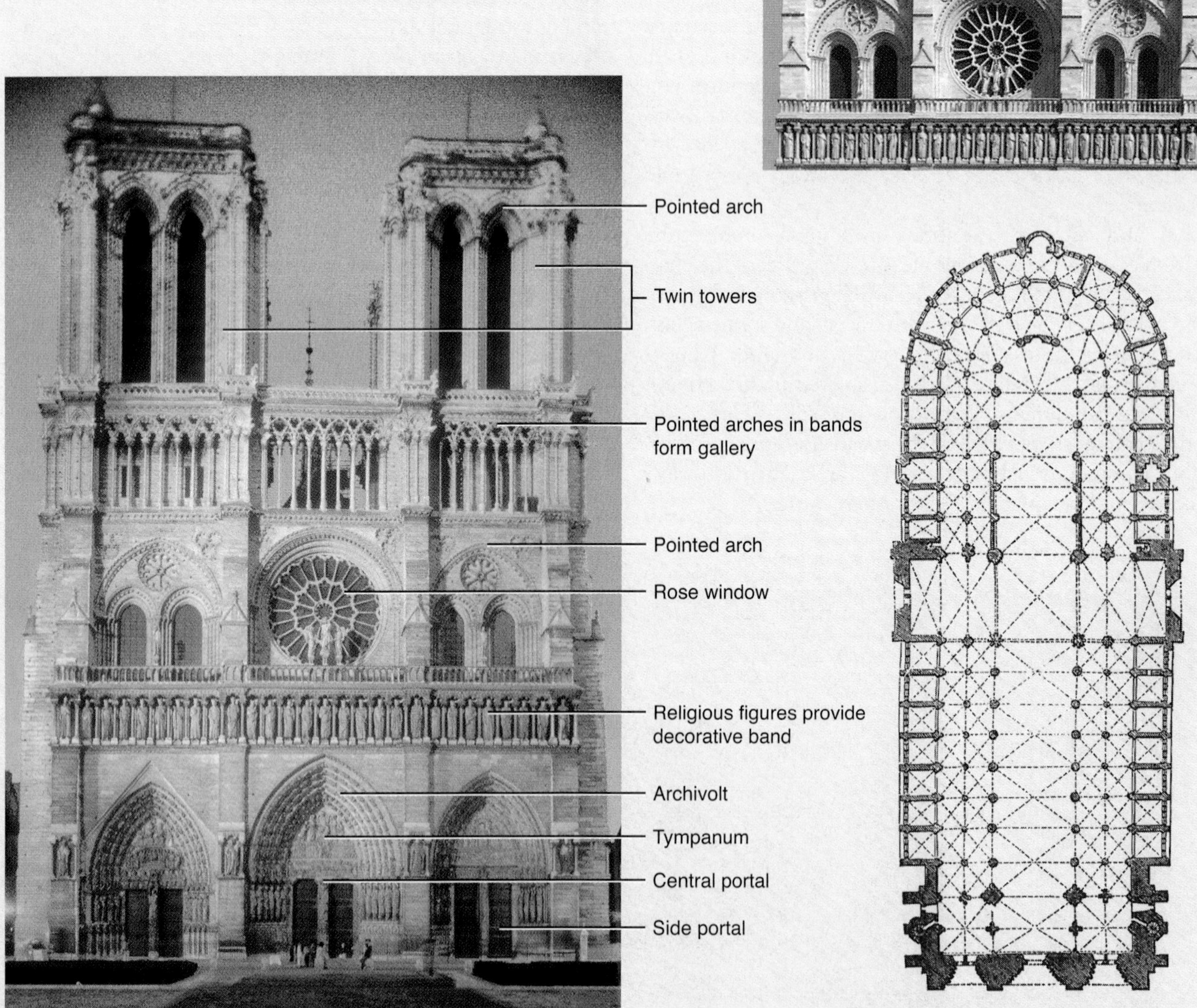

▲ **11-4.** Cathedral of the *Notre Dame;* Dome detail, floor plan, side view, and nave, 1163–1250; Paris, France. [Nave: Alinari/Art Resource, N.Y.]

DESIGN SPOTLIGHT

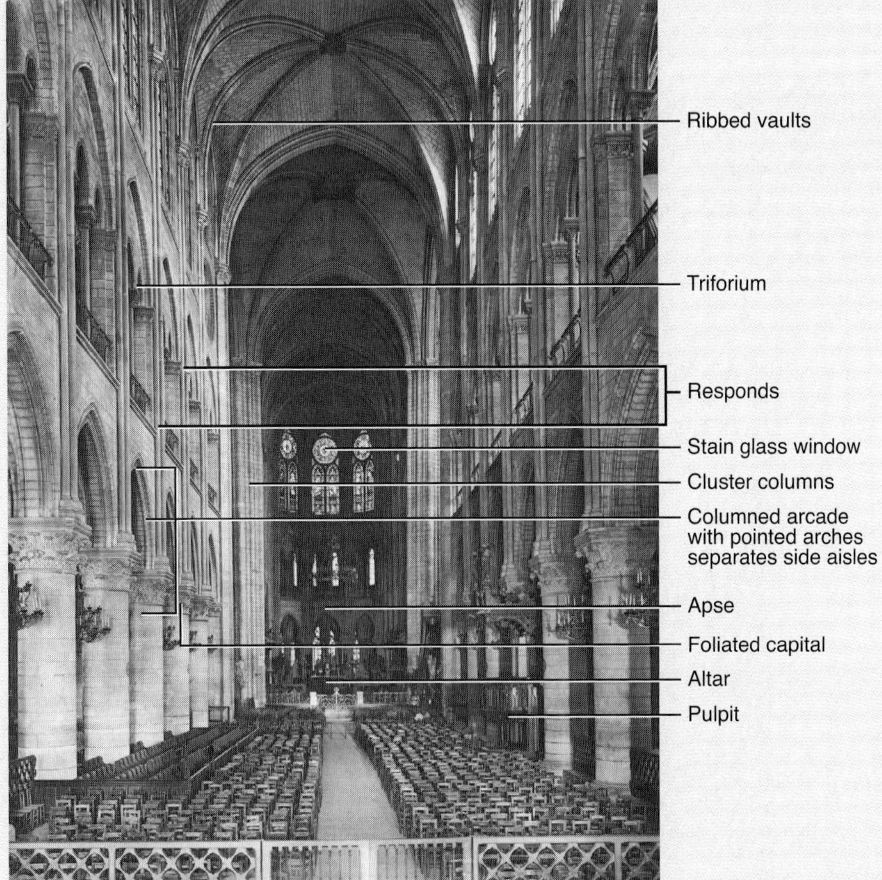

▲ **11-4.** Continued

water, and/or earthworks surround some. As times become more settled, manor houses are situated in parks surrounded by green space. Some attention is still given to protection, so usually the lawn is devoid of bushes near the main house.

■ *Floor Plans*. Cathedral plans (Fig. 11-4, 11-5) continue the earlier Latin cross/pilgrimage type composed of nave, side aisles, and radiating chapels in the apse. Plans have many square or rectangular bays, forming modules that can be added or subtracted as needed. English examples occasionally have flat eastern ends and more than one transept.

The earliest castles are erected on a raised mound (motte) with one or more walls enclosing the bailey. Support buildings, such as the stables, are in the bailey. Norman castles have a tall tower or keep, which contains living quarters for the owner and provisions for lengthy sieges. By the 13th century, castles (Fig. 11-6) grow into walled complexes with towers at the corners or other strategic locations and entry through a gatehouse. Kitchens are usually separate buildings until stone and brick construction develops. Staircases are often spirals, located in turrets with narrow windows.

Houses grow upward and outward (Fig. 11-8) in an irregular fashion, usually based on family need. Dwellings of the gentry often have two or more stories with a central courtyard. As the period progresses, rooms proliferate in number and gradually take on greater variety in function as owners seek greater comfort and lead less public lives.

■ *Materials*. Cathedrals and important buildings are of local stone or brick because transporting over distances is too difficult. Italians continue to use colored marbles in geometric patterns, colored stone arranged in stripes, and decorative Romanesque mosaics (Fig. 11-7). Originally of wood, castles are built of brick or stone. Like plans, construction becomes more sophisticated after the Crusades bring contact with military buildings in the East. Most townhouses and manor houses are of local stone or brick, and some are half-timbered with various types of infill materials.

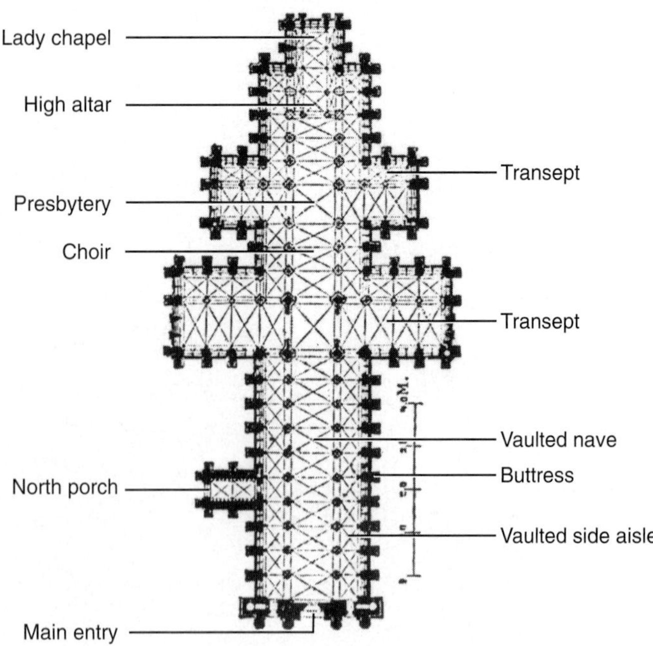

▲ **11-5.** Salisbury Cathedral, floor plan, and nave, 1220–1266; Salisbury, England.

▲ **11-6.** Bodiam Castle, 1385; East Sussex, England, and *Manzanares el Reale*, late 15th century; Madrid, Spain.

■ *Structural System*. The structural system in Gothic cathedrals is not found in ancient or earlier medieval buildings (Fig. 11-4, 11-5, 11-10). Pointed arches, ribbed vaults, transverse arches, and buttresses create a framework or skeleton. Piers and ribs are constructed first. Then, walls and the ceilings of the vaults are filled in with masonry, which gives them a weblike appearance. Buttresses add support to walls between windows and doors on façades, sides, and apses. If more support is needed, flying buttresses are added. This structural system reduces the need for load-bearing walls and allows taller buildings with larger windows that support Gothic design concepts of lightness, divine illumination, and mystical experience. It also dematerializes the surfaces and opens space, allowing larger vistas and greater continuity among and between spaces. Elements of the skeleton assert themselves by dividing the plan and interiors into units marked by columns, piers, ribs, and buttresses.

■ *Façades*. Cathedral façades display considerable variety (Fig. 11-4, 11-5). Vertical tripartite divisions, marked by buttresses, correspond to the nave and aisles inside. Sculptures; rose windows; tall, pointed arched windows; or arcades with pinnacles organize horizontal and vertical areas and may create bands. Twin towers that may be of unequal height crown fronts and emphasize height. Buttresses, instead of columns or pilasters, divide walls into bays. Flying buttresses create a graceful rhythm on side walls. Towers with spires accent crossings. Some English cathedrals are more horizontal with bands of sculpture and stringcourses. They usually have shorter façade towers and fewer flying buttresses (Fig. 11-5). Some public and private façades have architectural details common to churches, such as tracery or pointed arches (Fig. 11-1, 11-8). Irregularity achieved through the changing depths of surface planes provides movement and visual complexity (Fig. 11-6). Venetian Gothic combines pointed arches, columns, and lacelike tracery in bands (Fig. 11-7).

Castle walls are unadorned to prevent easy entrance by enemies. They are crowned with battlements composed of merlons (solids) and crenellations (openings), which offer greater defense and come from the East (Fig. 11-6). The main access is by a drawbridge to an opening containing a portcullis, a massive wood and iron-plated door. Windows, often used during battles, are tiny slits high in the walls.

Some dwellings have towers and gatehouses like castles. Windows usually vary in size and placement depending on need. They begin to exhibit tracery late in the period.

■ *Windows and Doors*. Windows on cathedrals, other public structures, and some large houses, especially late in the period, are usually pointed arches (Fig. 11-1, 11-4, 11-5, 11-7, 11-8). Cathedral

▲ **11-7.** Doge's Palace and detail, c. 1309–1424; Venice, Italy.

windows usually have two vertical lights topped by a circular or lobed form. Other window forms include the trefoil, quatrefoil, or cinquefoil. Rose windows often accent front façades and/or transepts.

Most churches have three recessed or projecting portals or doorways capped with pointed arches and pinnacles. Figural sculptures enhanced with decorative carving, usually geometric, line the jambs, lintels, archivolts, and tympanums. Doors are of wood.

■ *Roofs*. Roofs are steeply pitched and usually covered with copper or slate. Multiple roofs identify the nave, transept, and radiating chapels. Circular towers with conical roofs are common on medieval fortified castles (Fig. 11-6). Roofs on houses are steeply pitched gables or trusses (Fig. 11-8) and are of masonry, wood, or thatch. Stone houses may have parapets or dormer windows.

■ *Later Interpretations*. Gothic architecture provides a vocabulary for many styles in architecture, interiors, and furniture during the 18th, 19th, 20th, and 21st centuries. The Gothic Revival in England (Fig. 11-9) and America produces picturesque buildings that copy manor houses, churches, and half-timbered structures. Castles continue to inspire in later hospitality-fantasy environments such as Sleeping Beauty's castle in Disneyland.

▲ **11-9.** Later Interpretation: Houses of Parliament, 1836–1868; London; Sir Charles Barry and A. W. N. Pugin, Gothic Revival.

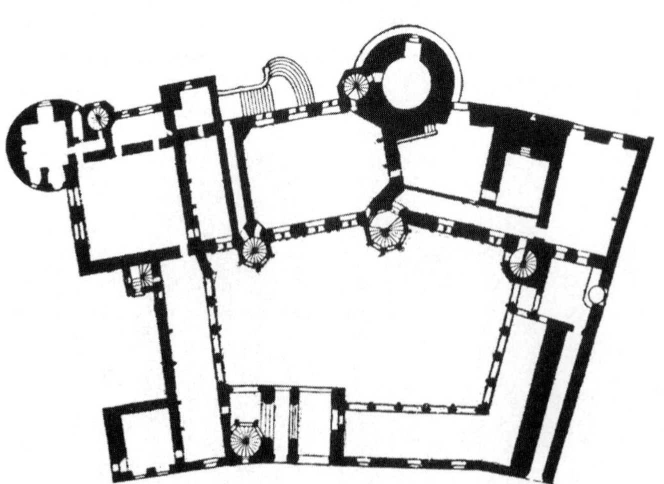

▲ **11-8.** *Hôtel de Jacques* Coeur and floor plan, c. 1442–1453; Bourges, France.

INTERIORS

Cathedral interiors (Fig. 11-4, 11-5), like the exteriors, emphasize verticality. Individual units of the interior composition are defined as in Romanesque, but the verticality, pointed arches, compound piers, and ribbed vaults allow a more open space. The effect is one of openness, weightlessness, lightness, and unity. Despite large areas of glass, cathedral interiors are dim. Stained and colored glasses continually filter light throughout the day so that it changes in color and intensity. This, together with the immense height, emphasizes the mystery of faith and gives a sense of otherworldliness. Decoration derives from the structural elements, but some interiors feature polychrome in rich, saturated colors on walls and ceilings.

Few secular interiors survive unaltered to the present. Knowledge comes from written descriptions and artistic representations, which are few and limited to the nobility or wealthy. Archaeology provides some information about vernacular interiors. Domestic and public buildings adopt Gothic details instead of the structural system with the exception of chapels or large vaulted spaces. Manuscript illustrations (Fig. 11-2, 11-12) indicate that interiors of this period are colorful and richly decorated with textile hangings but have little furniture. Lavish appointments, canopies, and furniture demonstrate the importance of ceremony and rank. Characteristic features of a private interior space, at least late in the period, include a patterned stone floor, small diamond-paned casement windows, a wood-beamed ceiling, large stone fireplace and mantel, and a few pieces of rectilinear furniture.

Public and Private Buildings

■ *Great Hall*. The hall (Fig. 11-11, 11-12), the most characteristic room in the medieval house, is a multifunctional living space until well into the 12th century in England (and later on the Continent). Evolving from an aisled space to a large vaulted or wooden-roofed room, in this space the lord demonstrates his power and wealth, entertains, and conducts estate business. It often serves as a sleeping dormitory for less important guests and servants. The upper end has a dais for the owner, his family, and their guests. At the lower end where the service areas are located, a screen, sometimes embellished with wood paneling, is a passage divider and protects people from drafts. Sometimes, a minstrels' gallery is set above the screen. Fire pits are initially set in the center of the room; later they move to a sidewall, becoming fireplaces. The number of smaller, private rooms around the hall increases during the period and includes the solar (from *sol* meaning floor or *solive* meaning beam in French), which is a withdrawing room, and the great chamber.

■ *Color*. Finishes, stained glass, and textiles provide rich, varied colors in public and private buildings. Favored colors are highly saturated green, blue, scarlet, violet, white, brown, and russet (Fig. 11-12, 11-13).

▲ **11-10.** Nave with fan vaults, King's College Chapel, 1446–1515; Cambridge, England.

■ *Floors*. Church floors are masonry, sometimes in patterns. In dwellings, floors are of dirt, stone, brick, or colored clay tiles in geometric patterns. Upper floors are usually of wood. Some woven materials, such as rush matting, cover floors in houses, but rugs are extremely rare. Oriental rugs covering tables appear in the wealthiest homes after the 13th century.

■ *Walls*. The walls of cathedrals and some important dwellings are of local stone. The English use contrasting colors of stone to delineate architectural elements in some cathedrals. Most cathedral walls (Fig. 11-4, 11-5, 11-10) are divided into three stories like those in earlier Romanesque examples. The lowest portion is an arcade of pointed arches supported by compound piers or columns. Next is the gallery or triforium with shorter arched openings into the nave. Clerestory windows are above. In the 1240s, French master masons begin to eliminate the triforium in favor of windows beneath the clerestory for more light. These windows often have lighter-colored or gray and white glass.

Walls (Fig. 11-11, 11-13) in private buildings are of stone or whitewashed or colored plaster. Natural or painted wood walls may be left as plain planks or paneled. Wainscoting, which may only cover a portion of the wall, consists of narrow panels that are often richly carved with pointed arches, tracery, and linenfold, sometimes enhanced with color. Softwood panels usually are painted; green is favored. Painted decorations on stone and plaster include imitations of stone blocks, literary or biblical scenes, and heraldic motifs in rich colors, enlivened with gold. Fabric hangings are the most common wall treatment in the period (Fig. 11-12). They transport easily; add color, texture, and pattern; and many types are available. The humblest consist of canvas, linen, or painted wool. The grandest houses of northern Europe and England adopt tapestries after the 14th century when tapestry weaving is established in Paris, Arras, Tournai, and Brussels.

During the period, the center fireplace moves to an outer wall and becomes a focal point because of its large hood to vent smoke (Fig. 11-12, 11-13). Stone hoods are lavishly embellished with heraldic devices and other carving.

■ *Columns and Capitals*. Arcade supports may be single round columns or cluster/compound columns composed of piers with engaged columns or groups of engaged columns. Capitals may have lacy leaves or plants or human and animal forms entwined in vines or foliage (Fig. 11-3). Some reveal classical influence in form and shape.

■ *Windows and Doors*. Cathedral windows have tracery and stained glass, which depicts biblical scenes, the lives of saints, and patrons or rulers in rich colors such as ruby red or dark blue. Larger single figures fill clerestories, while aisles and chapels have smaller figures and biblical scenes to invite closer inspection.

Early in the period, windows in dwellings are small square casements. As the need for protection decreases, they gradually become larger and begin to form bays, oriels, and lancets. Sizes and types vary. Glass remains a luxury so only the upper portions of windows are glazed. Most common are diamond-shaped panes with iron mullions (Fig. 11-12, 11-13). Most windows have shutters and iron

DESIGN SPOTLIGHT

Interior: The medieval great hall, as at Penshurst Place, is a multipurpose space for entertaining, dining, and sleeping. The lower end features a screen embellished with wood paneling that is intended to stop drafts and hide service areas behind it. Above is a minstrels' gallery for musicians. The oak ceiling with large trusses resembles the hull of a boat. Trusses are carved and painted. Floors are of stone. The fire pit is in the center of the room, and louvers in the ceiling allow smoke to exit. The fire, along with torches and a few candles, provide minimal illumination. The elaborate windows are later additions. The lord of the manor, his family, and guests sit at tables under a canopy upon a dais at the upper or opposite end (not shown) of the hall. Others sit at crude tables lining the walls.

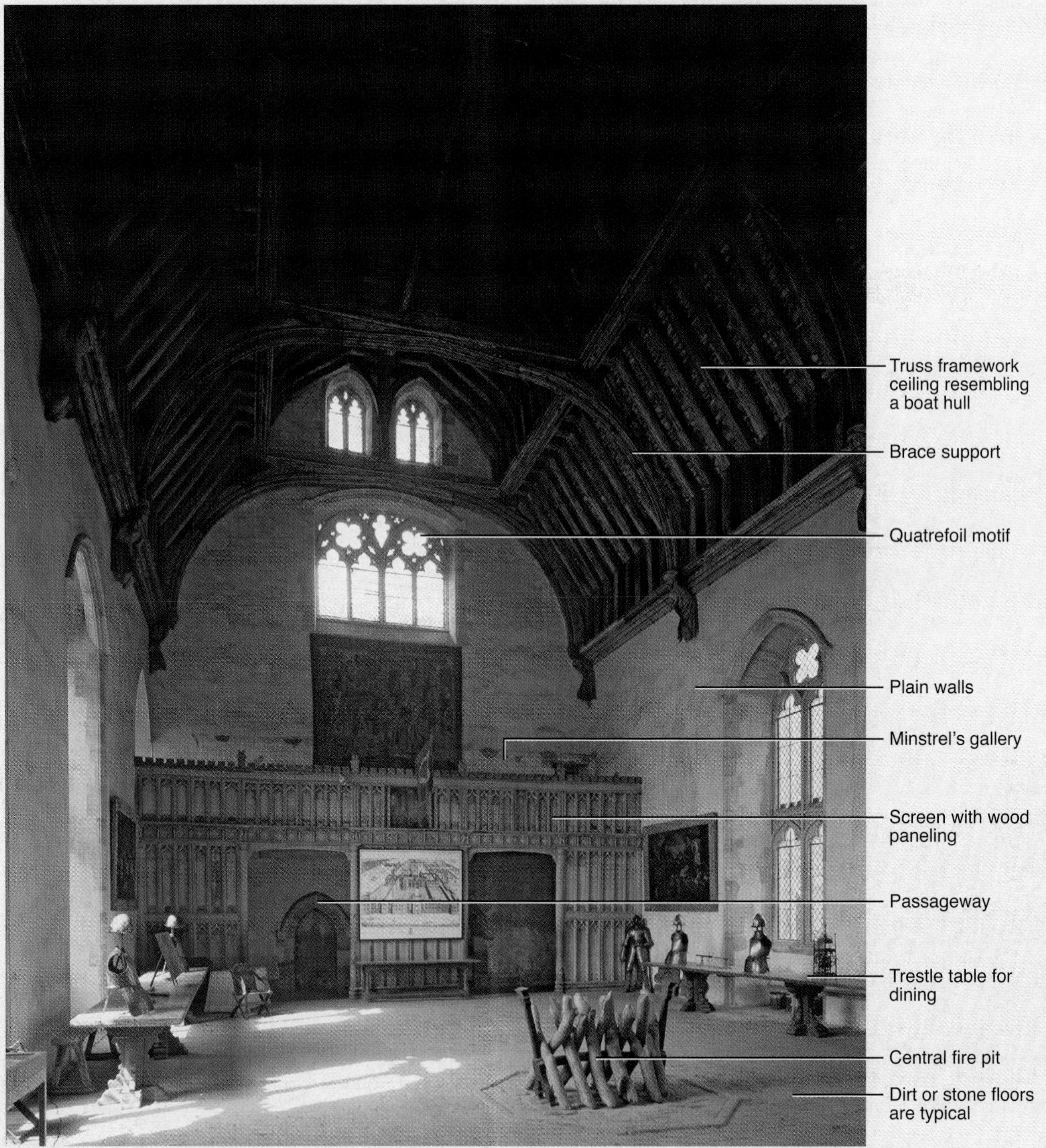

▲ **11-11.** Great Hall, Penshurst Place, 1341–1348; Kent, England.

bars for security or covers of oiled paper or animal horn. By the 15th century, stained glass appears in wealthy homes and helps to denote rank. There are no curtains.

Gothic motifs surround some doorways later in the period. Most doors are rectangular and board and batten. The wealthy have paneled doors, sometimes covered with tapestries or hangings.

■ *Ceilings*. Ceilings in churches are vaulted with four or more ribs in each bay (Fig. 11-4, 11-5). English cathedrals often have vaults with wooden ribs in complex patterns that have little to do with structure. The ribs form fans (Fig. 11-10), stars, or other shapes. The masonry between ribs may be painted blue with gilded stars or other motifs. Vaulted, beamed, or timber-roofed ceilings, sometimes decorated with carving and painting, are common in private buildings. Large halls have trussed framework ceilings of oak or chestnut that looks like inverted boat hulls (Fig. 11-11). Triangular frameworks feature multiple braces and struts by the early 14th century. Ceilings in smaller houses are beamed. A new ceiling consisting of flat boards and applied moldings with cornice emerges at the end of the 15th century (Fig. 11-13).

■ *Textiles*. Fabrics include cotton, linen, and silk in plain and twill weaves, damasks, and velvets. Wool is the most common furnishing fabric. Colors are brown, blue, green, russet, violet, and scarlet (Fig. 11-12). Plain and patterned textiles, occasionally with appliqué or embroidery, are used on walls, as canopies, for bedhangings, and on cushions in seating. Gothic tapestries have small or no borders, and figures and motifs are two-dimensional. Made in sets, tapestries feature biblical, literary, allegorical, or secular themes. Millefleurs (Fig. 11-14) tapestries, first made in France and characterized by backgrounds of numerous small flowers, become popular in the 15th century.

▲ **11-12.** Interior, Duke of Lancaster dines with the King of Portugal, from Vol. III *From the Coronation of Richard II to 1387*; Jean de Batard Wavrin.

■ *Lighting*. Torches and a few candles or lamps supply minimal lighting in churches. Homes have firelight in addition to torches and lamps. Light fixtures and candleholders usually are made of wrought iron (Fig. 11-13).

▲ **11-13.** The Annunciation, *Mérode* altarpiece showing interior, c. 1425–1433; Flanders; Robert Campin. (The Cloisters Collection. 1956. (56.70). The Metropolitan Museum of Art, New York, NY, U.S.A. Image© The Metropolitan Museum of Art/Art Resource, NY)

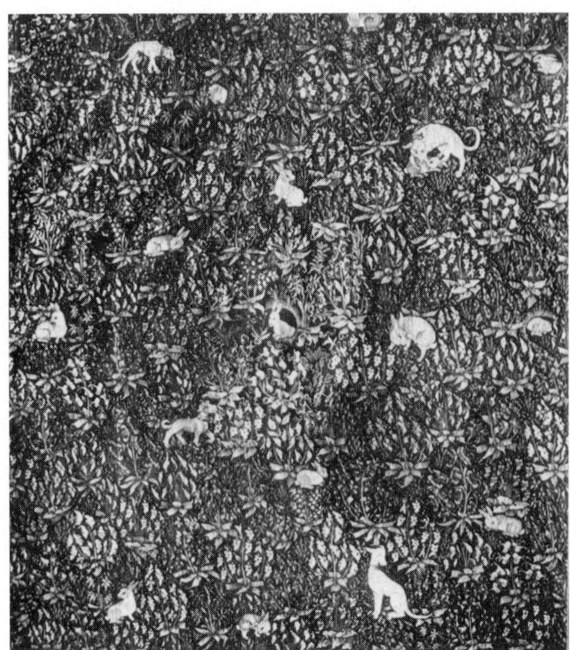

▲ **11-14.** *Millefleurs* tapestry, c. 15th century; Belgium and France.

FURNISHINGS AND DECORATIVE ARTS

Surviving examples of early medieval furniture are very rare, especially before the 14th century. Information, which comes from extant pieces, pictorial representations, and written descriptions, reflects upper-class practices. The few types include seating, tables, storage, and beds. Furniture is generally rectilinear with heavy proportions. Turning and carving are the most common decorations. Small-scale architectural motifs, such as pointed arches, show a relationship between architecture and furniture. Despite more settled conditions and a more stable economy, many nobles still move from place to place, requiring easily transportable furniture and wall hangings. Rooms may have rich treatments and wall hangings, but furniture and accessories are few. Some pieces, such as the buffet, are important conveyors of status. Cabinetmaking as a craft revives during the period. Joined (joyned) construction, introduced at the end of the 15th century, soon supplants earlier solid board construction because pieces are lighter in weight and sturdier. It uses rails and stiles to create framed panels, instead of nailing or pegging boards together as in board construction.

Public and Private Buildings

■ *Materials*. Pine, oak, and walnut are the most common furniture woods. Many pieces are painted in bright colors or gilded to highlight turning and carving. Some folding stools are of iron.

■ *Seating*. Chairs and thrones are few, ceremonial, and may feature turned elements. Common types include turned, X-frame, and choirstall chairs (Fig. 11-12, 11-13, 11-15). Choirstall chairs, derived from churches, are rectangular boxes with tall backs, solid paneled arms, and storage in their bases. Whether elaborately carved or plain, thrones and chairs demonstrate rank or precedence, particularly when placed on a dais under a canopy. However, stools and benches far outnumber chairs, even in the finest homes. Some stools resemble ancient Roman prototypes, while others are trestle forms. Attached upholstery on seating is unknown, but people add cushions for comfort.

■ *Tables*. Trestle tables (Fig. 11-11), with unattached tops that can be taken apart after meals, are common and used mainly for dining. Cloths conceal their crude construction. Tops become permanently attached during the period, but people continue to eat where it is warmest or most convenient.

■ *Storage*. Chests or coffers and boxes (Fig. 11-16) are the most common items in houses. They are chief storage pieces, but also transport goods and serve as seats, beds, and tables. Some are embellished with Gothic or other motifs, while others are plain. Display pieces, which assert rank and are associated with dining, include the buffet or dresser. The buffet originates as a set of shelves for displaying plate (silver). More shelves indicate the owner's higher rank. Linen covers hide the buffet's simple construction. The term *cupboard* refers to various pieces with doors and shelves used to store food, dishes, linen, and clothing.

■ *Beds*. Most Gothic beds are boxlike in form and crudely constructed, but surrounded by lavish draperies suspended from hooks, cords, or wooden rods (Fig. 11-2). Draperies provide warmth and privacy as well as demonstrating wealth. Some beds feature elaborate turning and carving. Bed hangings are pulled up and bagged when not in use. Pillows and bed linens are often luxurious.

■ *Decorative Arts*. Books are an important form of artistic expression throughout the Middle Ages. Illustrations in illuminated manuscripts (Fig. 11-3, 11-12) often portray figures, landscapes,

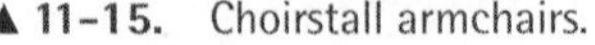

▲ **11-15.** Choirstall armchairs.

DESIGN SPOTLIGHT

Furniture: Chests are the primary storage pieces during the period, but also transport goods and serve as seats, beds, and tables. As shown here, simplicity, rectangular shapes, and decorative Gothic architectural motifs and linenfold are characteristic. Most are of oak, walnut, or pine with iron hardware. Carving is the main form of decoration. Both of these chests are of joined construction, in which panels are inserted into rails and stiles.

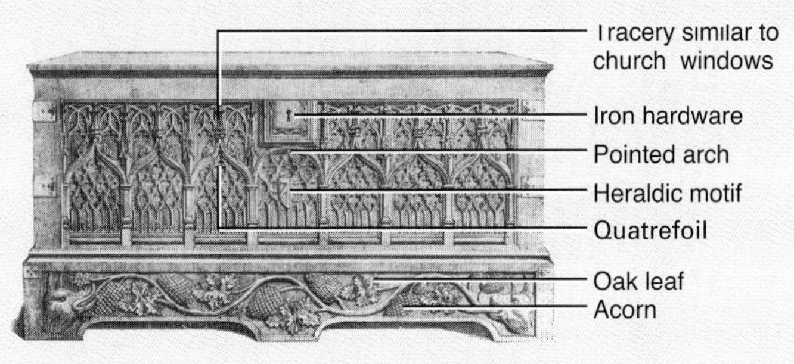

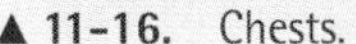
▲ **11-16.** Chests.

buildings, and furnishings, and therefore are important historical documents. Newly reformed guilds guide the production of silver during the Gothic period. Much silver made for the state and church is elaborately decorated.

E. RENAISSANCE

1400–1600

Meaning "rebirth," the Renaissance is a period of heightened interest in classical antiquity that manifests first in Italian literature, then in Italian culture and art during the 14th century. This renewed attention comes from the study of ancient texts and structures by scholars and gentlemen. Greek and Roman forms and details reappear in architecture during the 1420s in Florence, Italy, in response to demands from wealthy, erudite patrons. By the middle of the 15th century, architectural treatises create a theoretical and practical base for High Renaissance architectural developments. By the third decade of the 16th century, designers tire of High Renaissance rules, so they combine classical elements in odd or unexpected ways.

Renaissance architecture seeks to emulate, but not copy, antique examples. It adopts classical architectural vocabulary and forms, then applies them to contemporary building types and functions. In interiors, the Renaissance establishes the principle of unity in decoration and furnishings. Classical elements are less evident in interiors because there are few extant ancient examples to model, and ancient texts rarely discuss them. Similarly, since little ancient furniture is known, Renaissance furniture exhibits some architectural details and proportions along with other details.

Renewed interest in antiquity coincides with the emergence of humanism and its emphasis on the individual. Scientific studies of the body and the natural world and new inventions in navigation, mechanics, and warfare support humanist concerns and aid the rise of the Renaissance. Exploration of new continents increases contact with new civilizations and opportunities for trade and greater prosperity. After 1450, the printing press helps spread new ideas and learning. European states begin to assume their modern boundaries, and feudalism declines. Manners and fashion, products of leisure and money, become more important.

Warfare, travel, and books spread Italian Renaissance concepts to France, Spain, and England where evidence of the Renaissance first appears as decorative elements grafted onto Gothic and indigenous forms. Each country gradually assimilates Renaissance design principles, but its interpretation of them is unique. Climatic adaptations account for some design differences, particularly in Northern Europe.

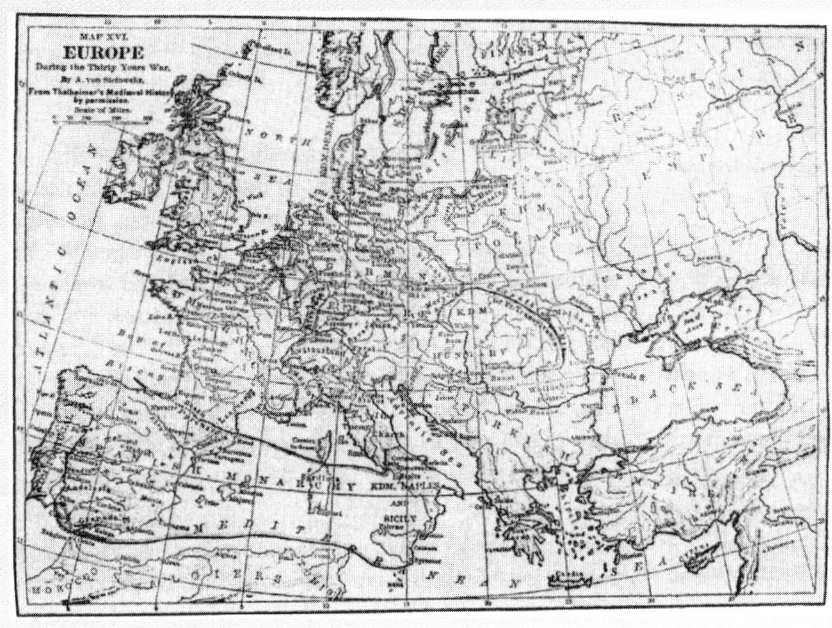

CHAPTER 12

Italian Renaissance

1400–1600

> *Beauty is "the harmony and concord of all the parts achieved in such a manner that nothing could be added or taken away or altered except for the worse."*
>
> —Leon Battista Alberti, *De Re Aedificatoria*

The Italian Renaissance is a return to classicism in culture, art, and architecture. Designers, artists, scholars, patrons, and other influential individuals in the period regard the Renaissance as a new era, separate from the Middle Ages, and a rebirth (*rinascita* in Italian) of classical antiquity. Artists and architects study Roman buildings and strive to compete with and/or surpass the achievements of the ancients. Consequently, the period is extraordinarily creative and produces numerous significant buildings, architects, and artists. Italian architecture, interiors, and furnishings are widely imitated throughout Europe and become foundations for numerous later stylistic developments.

HISTORICAL AND SOCIAL

Italy in the 15th century is a country of individual republics or city-states. Those around and north of Rome, which are ruled by bankers, merchants, and traders, are extremely prosperous. This affluent, urban, commercial society contrasts with most of Europe, which remains medieval, feudal, and rural. It also provides the ideal conditions for renewed interest in the classical past, language, poetry, history, philosophy, and humanism, which values the creative efforts of the individual.

The Renaissance begins in Florence around 1400, where prosperity in trade and banking creates a strong economy with much building activity. Great families, such as the Medici, Pitti, and Strozzi, possess the money and leisure to commission fine homes and great works of art. Their circles foster the study of classicism, which produces enthusiasm for Ancient Roman art and architecture. During the second half of the 15th century, the Renaissance spreads to other cities north of Rome. As in Florence, wealthy and powerful families in Pisa, Milan, Venice, Mantua, and Urbino embrace the Renaissance and extend commissions to artists who have studied or worked in Florence.

Despite the favor of great patrons, artists and architects still are regarded as craftsmen because their works lack a sound theoretical base. But as they associate with scholars and poets throughout the 15th century, they come to see themselves also as intellectuals and scientists. The notion of the Renaissance man who distinguishes himself in several arts or in both art and science takes hold. Artists and architects begin to write treatises espousing their ideas and theories. The invention of the printing press in the mid-15th century aids the spread of these works and the conceptual base of the Renaissance throughout Europe.

By the beginning of the 16th century, political turmoil interrupts artistic progress in northern Italy. The city of Rome becomes the artistic center, where popes and wealthy families commission architecture and works of art. Pope Julius II aspires to transform Rome from a medieval town to a modern ideal city based on clas-

▲ **12-1.** Architectural Details: Watercolor of ceiling in *Sala detta de Santi Pontefici, Appartamento de Borgia,* c. 1520–1527; Vatican, Rome, Italy.

sical forms. He wants to return the city to its former Roman glory. Subsequent popes who are scholars and patrons of the arts continue to support the transformation of the city. During this time, artists are more highly regarded than ever before. The period produces great accomplishments in art and science, as well as a few individual artistic geniuses, such as Leonardo da Vinci, Raphael, and Michelangelo.

Prosperity and progress are short lived, disrupted by the Protestant Reformation beginning in 1517, a plague in 1522–1524 that devastates Rome's population, and the sack of Rome in 1527 by Charles V, Holy Roman Emperor. Artists and architects leave Rome for work elsewhere, spreading the Renaissance throughout other parts of Italy and into the rest of Europe.

CONCEPTS

Italian Renaissance design is based on, but does not copy, classical antiquity. Designers recognize that centuries separate them from the ancients, so instead of reviving the ancient styles, they aspire to create modern works that vie with or even surpass antiquity. To these ends, they adopt classical language, classical approaches to design, and the direct observation of nature. Architects study and measure extant Greco-Roman monuments and pore over previously unknown ancient texts, such as Vitruvius' *Ten Books on Architecture* (late 1st century B.C.E). To emphasize the rational basis of art and architecture, designers use a mathematical design approach coming from linear perspective and composed of simple proportional ratios.

MOTIFS

■ *Motifs*. Classical motifs (Fig. 12-1,12-2, 12-3, 12-5, 12-8, 12-9, 12-12, 12-14) are used extensively as embellishment and include columns, pediments, moldings, the classical figure, cherub, swag, rinceau, rosette, scroll, cartouche, and geometric patterns.

(a)

(b)

(c)

(d)

▲ **12-2.** Motifs: (a) Candelabrum, Piccolomini Library, Siena Cathedral, Siena, Italy; (b) ornament, Florence, Italy; (c) ceiling painting of grotesques, *Palazzo Vecchio,* Florence, Italy; (d) Della Robbia roundel.

ARCHITECTURE

Key concepts in architecture are a return to the classical orders, the adoption of classical forms, and a mathematical approach to design. Following Brunelleschi, architects begin to relate the parts of buildings using simple whole-number proportions, usually derived from musical harmonies. Harmonious proportions and classical elements create a stable, articulate, and rational language for Renaissance architecture. A fundamental design problem for architects throughout the Renaissance is the application of classical elements and forms to nonclassical structures such as churches or chapels.

The most important building types are churches (Fig. 12-4), public structures (Fig. 12-3, 12-5, 12-6), palazzi (Fig. 12-7), and villas (Fig. 12-8, 12-9). Buildings are often large to impress, but relate to humans in scale, reflecting the humanism of designers and patrons. Classical elements and attributes, such as symmetry, regularity, unity, proportion, and harmony, are important design principles (Fig. 12-5). Designers carefully articulate parts, which relate to each other and the whole in proportional relationships.

▲ **12-3.** *Ospedale degli Innocenti* (Foundling Home), begun 1419; Florence, Italy; Filippo Brunelleschi. Early Renaissance.

▲ **12-4.** *S. Maria Novella*, Latin cross plan 1278–1350; façade begun 1456; Florence, Italy; façade by Leon Battista Alberti. Early Renaissance.

Structures and plans follow geometric forms—rectangles, squares, and circles. Important architectural features include columns, engaged columns, pilasters, arches, pediments, moldings, and modillioned cornices. Designers also use triangular and segmental pediments as decoration.

- *Early Renaissance* (1420–1500). Filippo Brunelleschi reintroduces the orders in the dome of the Florence cathedral in 1420, thus ushering in the Early Renaissance in architecture. He and others experiment with the orders, proportions, and ancient construction techniques. With the exception of palaces, which retain a fortified appearance, Early Renaissance structures look light visually because of slender architectural elements. Often there is a feeling of tension or awkwardness as designers learn to use classical design principles. Classical details sometimes are used incorrectly, and designers borrow freely from antiquity and the Middle Ages (Fig 12-3).
- *High Renaissance* (1500–1527). Following the development of architectural theory, architects have a better understanding of classicism. They begin to experiment with forms and elements but only within the rules of classicism (Fig. 12-5). Numerical ratios and geometric forms dominate designs. Although architects of the High Renaissance use the same vocabulary as those of the Early Renaissance, the feeling is very different, one of balance, repose, rationality, and stability. Architecture emulates, but does not copy, antiquity. Architects tend to fall into two categories: those who follow classical rules and a few who follow Michelangelo's inventiveness. Rome is the artistic center of the High Renaissance.

DESIGN SPOTLIGHT

Architecture: Designed by Donato Bramante and the first important example of the High Renaissance, this small, centrally planned shrine where S. Peter was supposedly crucified is one of the most influential buildings in architectural history. Bramante's design incorporates classical elements such as a dome, balustrade, and Tuscan columns and classical attributes such as stability, clarity, and repose. It follows Vitruvian concepts for proportional relationships and imitates Roman (and Greek) temples. The conical form is one of the most visually stable because it is larger at the base. The simple Tuscan columns lead the viewer's eye upward to the entablature where motifs of the papacy compose the frieze. The balusters above and the ribs of the dome continue to lead the eye upward to the apex of the dome, which is topped by a cross. Although small in size, the building appears monumental due to its geometric form, restrained ornament, and classical elements and attributes. In the manner of the High Renaissance, the Tempietto demonstrates Alberti's definition of beauty in which "harmony and concord of all the parts [is] achieved in such a manner that nothing could be added, taken away or altered except to worsen."

► **12-5.** Tempietto *(S. Pietro in Montorio)* and floor plan, 1502; Rome, Italy; Donato Bramante. High Renaissance.

■ *Late Renaissance* (1527–1600). No single city dominates the Late Renaissance. Some architects continue to follow High Renaissance principles (Fig. 12-6), while others create a parody of classicism known as Mannerism, in which they deliberately break rules and manipulate classical principles to create confusion and disorder. Classical elements are put together incorrectly or in odd ways. Classical proportions are rejected, and lightness and tension reappear.

DESIGN SPOTLIGHT

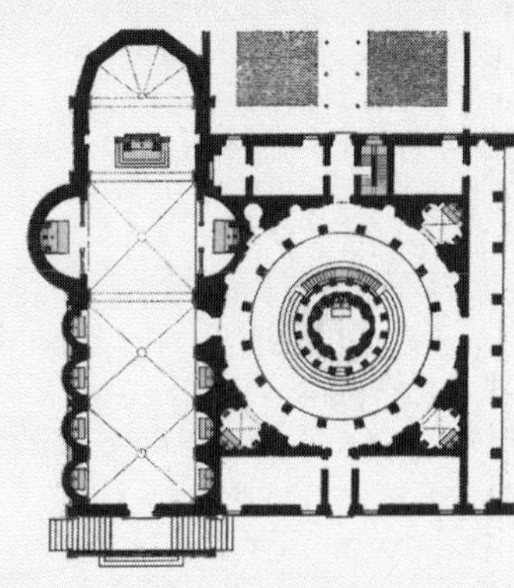

▲ **12-5.** Continued

Public Buildings

■ *Site Orientation*. Most Renaissance public buildings and urban palaces stand in self-contained isolation and do not reach out to their surroundings. Palazzi or palaces face streets or squares in towns and cities such as Florence (Fig. 12-7). Architects design villas individually in rural locales to suit function, site, region, and patron. Palladio introduces functional winged villas with central residential pavilions for Venetian noblemen who occupy and farm land in the countryside (Fig. 12-8). These villa designs consider functional needs of farmers and the landscape for the first time in Western architecture. The Villa Rotunda, best known of Palladio's buildings (Fig. 12-9), lacks wings, because it is set upon a hill giving broad vistas from each of its four porticoes.

■ *Floor Plans*. The most common church plan is a Latin cross (Fig. 12-11) composed of carefully articulated square or rectangular modules. Some architects, beginning with Brunelleschi, experiment with centralized plans but find them unsuitable for the liturgy of most churches. But small memorials, such as the Tempietto (Fig. 12-5), or chapels often have centralized plans. Public buildings, such as the *Palazzo della Ragione* in Vicenza (Fig. 12-6), have rectangular, usually symmetrical plans with rooms arranged by function.

Palazzo plans are rectangular with square and rectangular rooms that focus inward to a central courtyard or *cortile* (Fig. 12-7). Symmetry, although desirable, depends on the site. Interior walls are parallel or at right angles to the façade, and dimensions may be proportionally derived. The most important rooms are on the *piano nobile*, the first floor above ground level, particularly the *sala* or main reception room. Facing the street, these lavishly decorated spaces support entertaining and family activities. Rooms for important family members also are on the *piano nobile*, whereas rooms for lesser family members and/or servants are on the third floor. The *camera* (owner's bedroom) usually has a studio (*studiolo*, Fig. 12-14), a small private space where the most treasured possessions are kept. The apartment, a series of rooms associated with one person, appears in the late 15th century. Usually arranged in

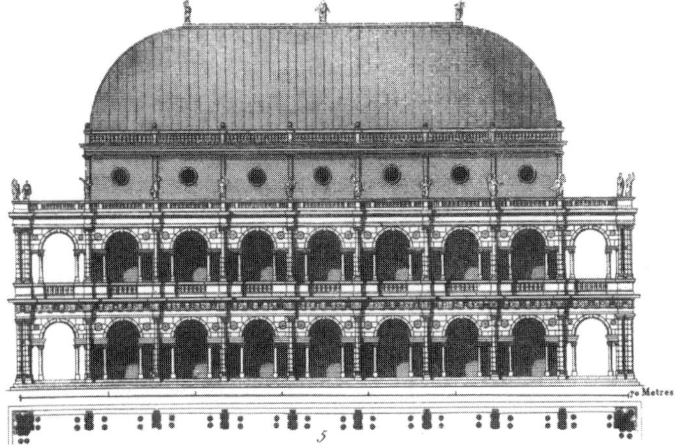

▲ **12-6.** *Palazzo della Ragione* (Basilica), 1545–1617; Vicenza, Italy; Andrea Palladio. Late Renaissance.

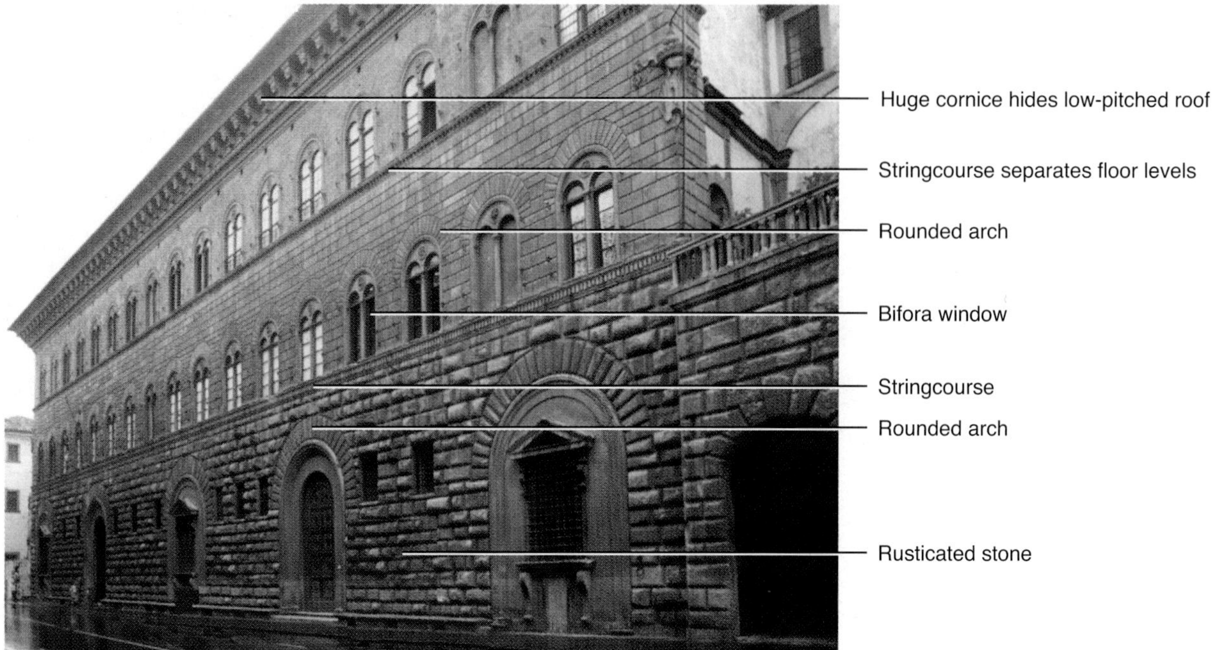

▲ **12-7.** *Palazzo Medici-Riccardi* and *cortile*, begun 1444; Florence, Italy; Michelozzo di Bartolommeo. Early Renaissance.

linear sequence, these rooms progress from public to private and from larger to smaller. Most houses have no grand staircases or hallways but do have small passages for servants near the *camera* and apartments. Shops and family businesses are on ground floors during the Early Renaissance but are later replaced by service areas.

■ *Materials*. Builders use marble, often colored, local stone, or brick for private and public buildings. They do not experiment with concrete like the Romans. The Renaissance does not introduce any new construction techniques, so the most common construction system for churches is arcuated. Dwellings are of local stone or brick. The most common construction system for houses is trabeated. Some lower stories are vaulted.

■ *Church Façades*. Classical elements and attributes typify church façades. Although designs vary, two types are common. One has a taller central portion with lower sides, which reflects the interior nave and side aisles, in the traditional manner (Fig. 12-4). Towers are not typical, however. The other is found mostly on High and Late Renaissance church façades, which resemble the gable ends of ancient temples, with triangular pediments supported by arches, pilasters, and engaged columns. Architects use repeating modules and mathematical proportions to create façade compositions. Architectural details evolve from being relatively flat in the Early Renaissance to bolder and more three-dimensional during the High and Late Renaissance. Palladian façades have superimposed temple fronts, monumentality, and strong visual organization by architectural details. Similarly, classical imagery, details, and organization are characteristic of other buildings (Fig. 12-6).

■ *Dwelling Façades*. Most palaces and villas are two or three stories high, separated by stringcourses, and capped by a large, prominent cornice. Early Renaissance palaces (Fig. 12-7) have heavy rustication on lower stories that becomes smoother and less deeply cut as it ascends; thereby appearing to lighten on each story. High Renaissance examples are less heavily rusticated and exhibit more and bolder classical details. Palladio's studies of ancient architecture lead him to believe that Roman houses had been embellished with classical details and temple fronts for dignity and distinction, so he introduces them on his villas (Fig. 12-8, 12-9). Late Renaissance façades exhibit less unity, slender proportions, tension, and confusion through studied misuse of classical details.

■ *Windows and Doors.* Windows and doors on public buildings are arched or rectangular, usually with some embellishment at least on the main story. In Early Renaissance residences, the common bifora windows (Fig. 12-7) have round arches with colonnettes dividing the lights. High Renaissance windows are pedimented or framed with *aedicula* adding three-dimensionality. Architect Sebastino Serlio is the first to publish an elaborately articulated tripartite window/door form with a centered round arch flanked by rectangular openings. Palladio adopts this form for the first time at *Palazzo della Ragione* (Fig. 12-6), and it becomes known as the Palladian window.

■ *Roofs.* Roofs on public buildings are gabled and/or domed. Brunelleschi's dome for S. Maria del Fiore (Florence Cathedral) displays the first use of the orders since antiquity. Terra-cotta roof tiles cover the roofs of many public and private buildings. Roofs on dwellings are generally flat or low-pitched and are often hidden behind cornices.

■ *Later Interpretations.* Numerous subsequent public and private buildings follow Italian Renaissance precepts including those in the Louis XIV, Baroque, Early Georgian, American Georgian, Late Georgian, Renaissance Revival (Fig. 12-10), Beaux-Arts, Colonial Revival, and Post Modern periods.

INTERIORS

Interior unity becomes important during the Renaissance particularly because artisans and craftsmen of various trades work in a common vocabulary—that of classicism. Few Renaissance architects design entire interiors. They occasionally work out a general concept and design a few details, such as chimneypieces, but for the most part, they leave interiors to artisans. Architectural treatises discuss interior planning and illustrate details, but do not focus on entire rooms. Most interior rooms are regular and rectangular, reflecting the orderly arrangement of the exterior. Designs of large architectural surfaces—walls, floors, and ceilings—usually relate to one another and feature classic detailing. Unified and often lavishly decorated, domestic interiors are sparsely furnished. Grotesques, which are Renaissance interpretations of colorful wall decorations of temples, figures, flowers, and classical details found in Roman interiors, are an important introduction (Fig. 12-2). Beginning in the 14th century, artists begin to study the few ancient Roman interiors available to them. Most of these sites are underground, so they coin the term *grotesques*, meaning derived from grottoes, to describe the ancient paintings they find on walls and ceilings. Widely published, grotesques appear in paintings, interiors, and on furniture throughout the 15th and 16th centuries.

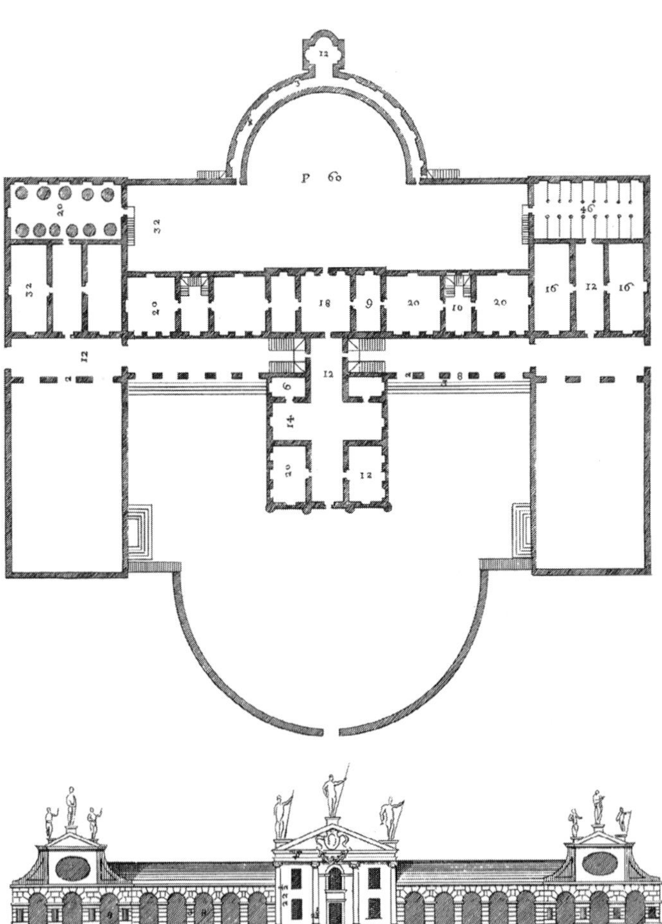

▲ **12-8.** Villa Barbaro and plan, c. 1570, from *I Quattro Libri dell'architectura* (*Four Books on Architecture*); Palladio; and *Sala*, 1550s; frescoes by Paolo Veronese. Late Renaissance.

Church interiors (Fig. 12-11) follow traditional patterns and are symmetrical, regular, formal, and majestic. Carefully planned spatial and proportional relationships are often mathematically derived with appropriate adjustments made in height and width. Early Renaissance spaces are light in scale and simply treated. In the Early Renaissance, nave arcades are often composed of round arches mounted atop slender columns. Later, large piers carry nave arcades.

Public and Private Buildings

■ *Color.* Interior color comes from construction materials and fresco paintings in public and private buildings (Fig. 12-1, 12-2, 12-8, 12-9, 12-11, 12-12, 12-13, 12-14). In residences, textiles and wallpapers give color to domestic spaces. Typical colors include scarlet, cobalt blue, gold, deep green, and cream.

■ *Floors.* Stone or tile floors are common in both public and private buildings (Fig. 12-8, 12-11, 12-12, 12-13, 12-14). Brunelleschi uses different colors of stone to define interior modules on floors in his churches (Fig. 12-11). Tiles and bricks commonly cover floors, with herringbone being the most favored pattern. Some tiles have inlaid or relief patterns in contrasting colors. The best rooms feature marble or *terrazzo*. Wood in boards or patterns is most common on upper floors. During the 16th century, floor designs often correspond to ceilings. Knotted pile rugs, imported from Spain or the Near East, cover floors and tables. Natural fiber matting usually is used on floors in summer.

■ *Walls.* Walls in public and some private buildings display a classical organization that includes a dado, fill, and entablature or cornice (Fig. 12-11, 12-12). These elements correspond to the base, shaft or center portion, and capital or cornice of ancient

DESIGN SPOTLIGHT

Architecture and Interior: Designed by Andrea Palladio and completed after his death, the Villa Rotunda is his most famous work and his only freestanding pavilion. It was built as a country retreat for entertaining, not farming, so it lacks the winged appendages common to Palladian working farms. Appearing as a visual monument, the house is situated on a hill with views of surrounding farmlands from the four porticoes. The plan features bilateral symmetry defined by internal passageways connecting the four porticoes, which are adapted from Roman temples and have statues of classical deities on the ends and apexes. Entrance to each portico is by a flight of steps in the Roman manner, and the temple fronts are the central elements of the tripartite façades. Walls are smooth stucco over brick instead of stone for economy. Pedimented windows identify the piano nobile with smaller windows on the basement and upper story. Broad stringcourses separate the stories and continue as the cornice and bases of the porticoes. Vincenzo Scamozzi completes the large dome crowning the composition after Palladio's death, so it is lower than Palladio intended.

Like most Palladian villas, this one has a symmetrical plan with rectangular or square rooms (occasionally round or apsidal) arranged around a large dominant *sala* or rotunda, as here. Proportional room dimensions are calculated using numerical ratios derived from harmonic relationships in Greek musical scales. In the Villa Rotunda, the central rotunda serves as a circulation space leading to square and rectangular rooms primarily used for entertaining. Palladio commonly places service areas in wings (also called pavilions) or below ground as here in

▲ **12-9.** Villa Rotunda *(Villa Almerico-Capra)*, floor plan, and central circular hall (rotunda), 1565–1569; Vicenza, Italy; Andrea Palladio. Late Renaissance.

columns and pedestals. Walls may be plain or embellished with painted *trompe l'oeil* decoration. During the Early Renaissance, some churches have sedate color schemes often of white with architectural details in *pietra serena*, a grey stone (Fig. 12-11), after the manner of Brunelleschi. Michelangelo uses a similar scheme in the vestibule of the Laurentian Library to accentuate important architectural details (Fig. 12-12), emphasizing the height and narrowness of the space and increasing its feelings of tension and uneasiness. In the Late Renaissance, Palladian churches are mostly white, relying on the architectural elements and details, spatial and architectural relationships, and light for interest. Many Renaissance churches have elaborate frescoes, sculptures, and decoration added to them over the years.

▲ **12-10.** Later Interpretation: Boston Public Library, 1887–1893; Boston, Massachusetts; McKim, Mead, and White. Renaissance Revival.

DESIGN SPOTLIGHT

the Villa Rotunda. The service areas in the raised basement of the villa make the building appear smaller than it actually is.

Although Palladio's intentions for the interiors are not known, Paolo Americo, the owner, commissions Giovanni Battista Maganzia and Anselmo Canera to adorn the four principal salons and central circular hall or rotunda with allegorical frescoes on walls and ceilings and add bold stucco work around doors and on ceilings. In the rotunda, *trompe l'oeil* columns frame classical figures and carry an entablature. Above a balustraded balcony, the dome soars upward to the cupola. Open arches provide entrances to the main salons, and smaller doors surrounded by aedicula lead to the staircases. (World Heritage Site)

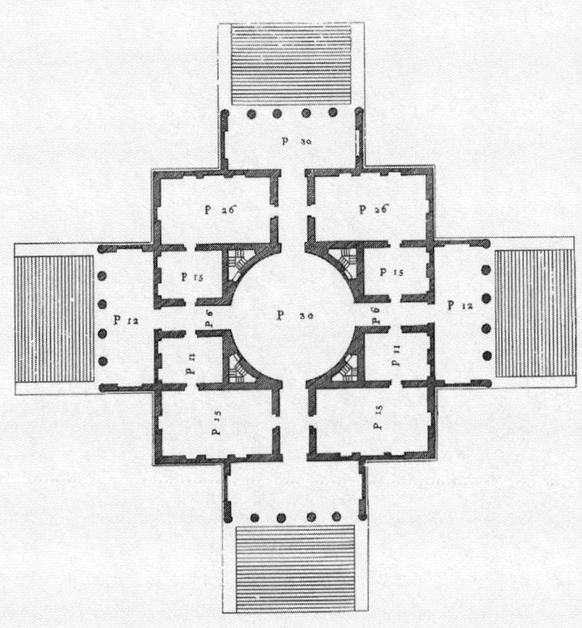

▲ **12-9.** Continued

Domestic walls may be plain stone or plaster or have architectural details, such as pilasters. Common treatments include paneling, painting, and textiles. Wood paneling either is plain, inlaid, or painted (Fig. 12-14). Plastered walls have at least a white or colored wash. Frescoes in repeating patterns, imitations of textiles or marble, *trompe l'oeil* architecture (Fig. 12-13), or actual textile hangings cover the walls in important rooms. Palaces and villas often have elaborate frescoes, executed by important artists such as Veronese (Fig. 12-8, 12-9). Fresco compositions are often allegorical depictions of the owner's virtues or accomplishments surrounded by *trompe l'oeil* architectural details and sculpture. Small panels of printed paper or larger panels of engravings sometimes are applied to walls for embellishment, although actual wallpaper develops later.

Fireplaces are a focal point for decoration. Flat pyramids or wedge-shaped hoods replace earlier conical ones because the former are easier to decorate. Embellishment includes cornices, moldings, and coats of arms (Fig. 12-13). Hoods disappear by the 16th century, and mantel decoration becomes more architectural with columns or pilasters, architrave, frieze, and cornice.

■ *Windows and Doors*. At windows, shutters block light and heat and give privacy so curtains are very rare in dwellings (Fig. 12-13). Windows have plain surrounds but some have moldings and entablatures. As important decorative features, doors are carved, inlaid, painted, or surrounded by aedicula (Fig. 12-9). Portieres of plain or embroidered cloth or woven tapestries hang at very grand doorways.

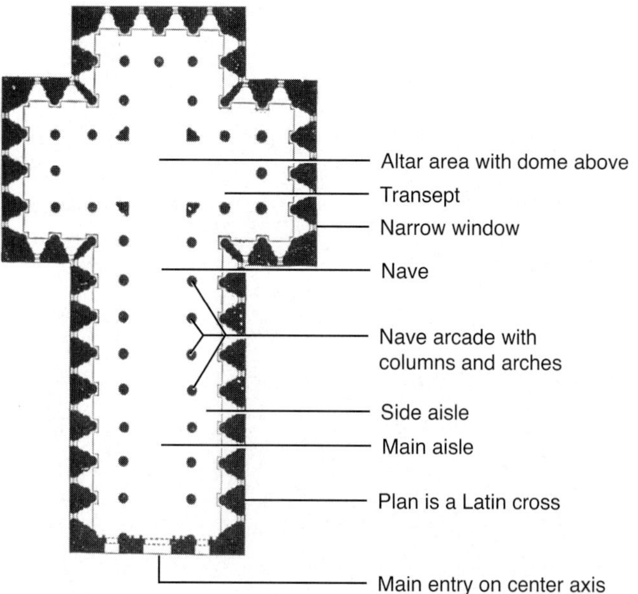

▲ **12-11.** Nave and plan, *Santo Spirito,* begun 1434 by Filippo Brunelleschi and completed 1481 by others; Florence, Italy. Brunelleschi never completed the façade, which is plain and unadorned. Early Renaissance.

▲ **12-12.** Vestibule, Laurentian Library, 1524–1533; staircase completed 1559; Florence, Italy; Michelangelo di Buonarroti Simoni. Late Renaissance.

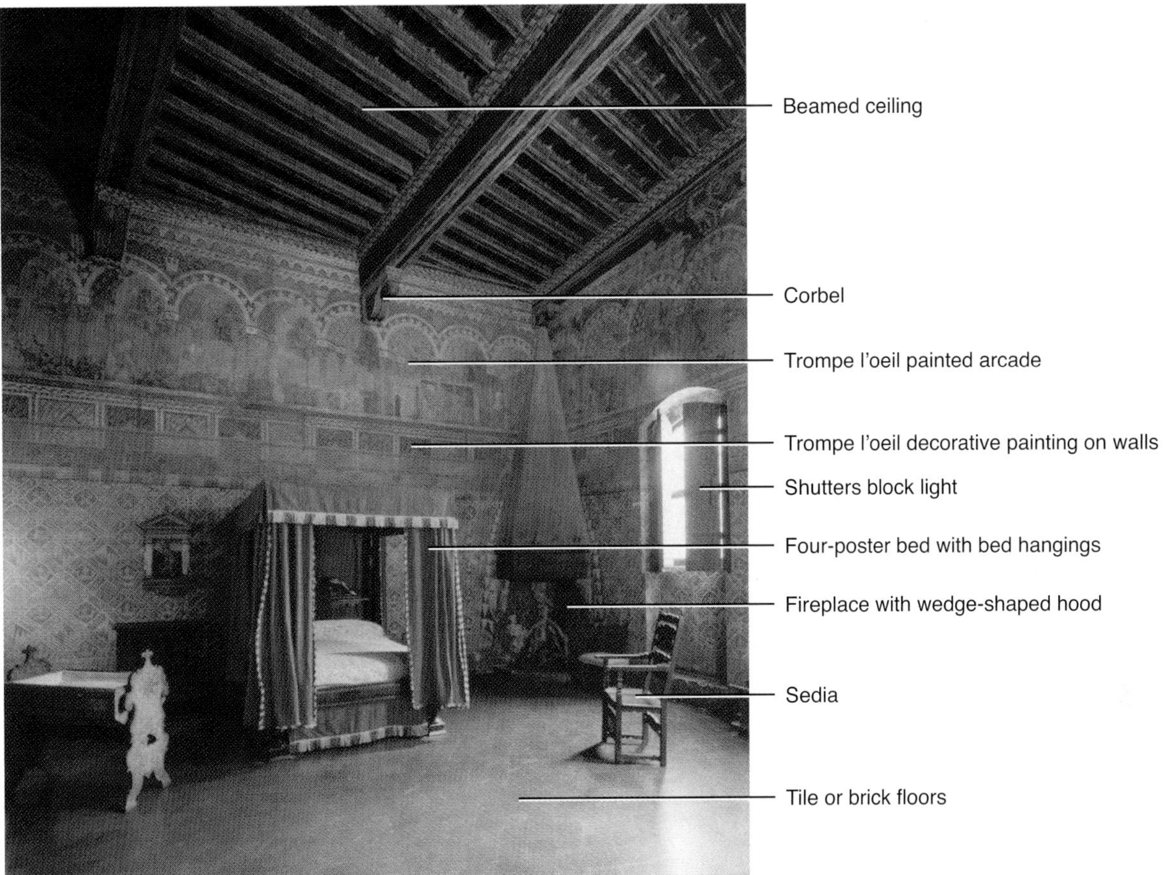

▲ **12-13.** Bedchamber and fireplace from Room of the Parrots, *Palazzo Davanzati*, mid-14th century; Florence, Italy. Early Renaissance.

▲ **12-14.** *Studiolo* of Francesco de Giorgio Martini, Ducal Palace, c. 1478–1482; Gubbio, Italy. By Giuliano da Maiano. Early Renaissance. (Rogers Fund, 1939. (39.153). The Metropolitan Museum of Art, New York, NY, U.S.A. Image© The Metropolitan Museum of Art/Art Resource, NY.).

DESIGN SPOTLIGHT

Textiles: Textiles, more expensive than furniture, include brocades, velvets, taffetas, damasks, and brocatelles. The most common are domestic and imported woolens. Ogee-repeat patterns with stylized flower and fruit designs are the most common, usually woven in deep reds, golds, blues, and greens. Important textile factories are in Lucca, Genoa, and Palermo. Royalty and the affluent in other European countries highly prize Italian textiles, which are a luxury item. Exporting textiles brings Italy great prestige and wealth.

▶ **12-15.** Textiles.

■ *Ceilings*. Most interiors in public buildings and some private ones have groin or barrel-vaulted ceilings (Fig. 12-1). Nave ceilings in churches are high to accommodate windows; some, especially in the Early Renaissance, have flat and coffered ceilings with vaulted side aisles (Fig. 12-11). Crossings are usually domed. Ceilings in churches and other public buildings may be plain, have coffers or compartmentalized ceiling paintings, or feature painted *trompe l'oeil* decoration.

Ground-floor ceilings in private buildings are usually vaulted. Those on upper floors either are beamed with large supporting corbels (Fig. 12-13), revealing the joists of the floor above, or are covered by compartments (Fig. 12-1) or coffers. Painting, gilding, or carving decorate both types. By the second half of the 16th century, frescoes dominate ceiling decoration, and wall, floor, and ceiling decorations relate to one another.

■ *Textiles*. Interiors display a variety of domestic and imported fabrics (Fig. 12-13, 12-15) at doorways, on walls and furniture, as canopies and bed hangings, and, occasionally, as window treatments. Silk in plain and damask weaves or stripes is a luxury fabric especially when woven with gold or silver threads. The affluent proudly display their costly fine linens from France and Flanders on tables and the best beds. Many types of plain and patterned woolens cover walls and some furniture. Woolen bed hangings are used in winter. Cottons, made locally or imported from India and the Near East, replace other fabrics in summer. Lace, needlework, and leather may be used on walls, for trim, or as upholstery.

Armchairs and side chairs have velvet or leather seats and decorative panels between the back uprights (Fig. 12-17). Some seat covers, cushions, and coverlets are made of tapestries. Bed hangings provide privacy and warmth (Fig. 12-13).

■ *Lighting*. Interiors in public and private buildings are usually dark both night and day. Torches, candles, and chandeliers provide some illumination in public buildings. In dwellings, candles and firelight give minimal illumination at night, so rooms have strong colors and furnishings with high reliefs and shiny surfaces. Fixtures, such as candleholders, floor stands, and wall sconces, are made of wood, iron, brass, and bronze. Candlesticks and candelabra may be placed on a table or put in a stand or *torchiera* (Fig. 12-16). Chandeliers and oil lamps are rare in dwellings.

▲ **12-16.** Lighting: *Torchiera*, candelabrum, candlestick.

FURNISHINGS AND DECORATIVE ARTS

Furniture is rectilinear and massive with classical ornament and proportions. Classical details, such as columns or pediments, first appear on church furniture and later spread to domestic examples. The most common decorations are carving, turning, inlay, painting, and gilding. Early Renaissance furniture is simple with sparse carving in low relief or inlay. High Renaissance furniture is grander and more influenced by architecture. Late Renaissance furniture derives many concepts from Michelangelo, particularly his love of figures, exaggerated scale, and unusual architectural motifs. High-relief carving dominates, while classical proportions and purity of ornament decline.

DESIGN SPOTLIGHT

Furniture: Armchairs are rare before the 16th century, but by the end of the century, they are used in most rooms, although not in great numbers. Some grand dining spaces have sets of armchairs. Size denotes high status—the larger the chair, the higher the sitter's status. Arm supports and front legs may be quadrangular or turned. Runners and/or stretchers may connect legs. Sometimes beneath the seat is an elaborately carved stretcher. Leather or fabric backs and seats may be trimmed with fringe and attached with nails. Decoration, usually carving, becomes more elaborate as the period progresses.

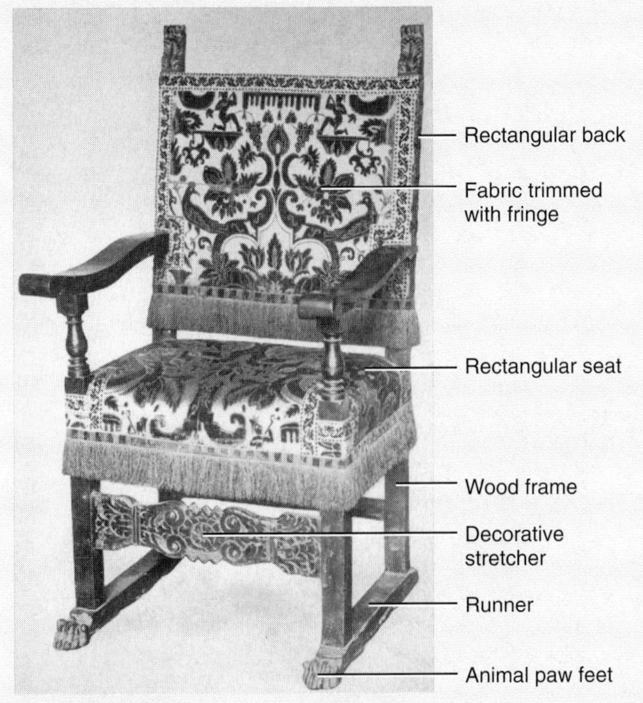

▲ **12-17.** *Sedia,* 15th–16th centuries.

Public and Private Buildings

■ *Materials*. Walnut is the main wood, but oak, cedar, and cypress also are used. Some stools are made of iron. Construction gradually increases in complexity. Inlay may be of wood (intarsia) or other materials, such as *certosina*, an inlay of ivory or bone in geometric patterns (Fig. 12-13).

■ *Seating.* Common seating pieces include the *sedia* (Fig. 12-17), folding chairs of X-form like *Savonarola* (Fig. 12-18), ladder-backs with rush seats, and the *sgabello* or stool chair used for dining (Fig. 12-19). Armchairs and side chairs have quadrangular or turned legs with side runners terminating in lion's heads. Back legs form the back uprights, and front arm posts form the front legs. Some have carved stretchers beneath the seat. Other seating includes stools, benches, and the *cassapanca* (Fig. 12-20), a long wooden bench with a seat and back and storage beneath the seat. Introduced in the mid-15th century in Florence, the *cassapanca* is sometimes placed on a dais at the end of a room to emphasize importance.

▲ **12-18.** Folding X-chair or *Savonarola,* 15th century; Florence, Italy. Named for Savonarola, a monk.

▲ **12-19.** *Sgabello,* 16th century.

▲ **12-20.** *Casapanca,* 15th century.

■ *Tables*. Tables include long, narrow, oblong trestle tables for dining (Fig. 12-21), tables with marble or *pietra dura* tops, folding tables, and small tables similar to box stools. Small side tables or sideboards help with meal service. A carved or arcaded horizontal stretcher connects dining table trestles, and some tables with rectangular tops have richly carved slab ends like Ancient Roman examples.

■ *Storage*. *Cassones* or chests (Fig. 12-22), used for storing possessions and seating, are the most important storage pieces and come in various shapes and sizes. Design and decoration vary according to intended use, such as wedding gifts, and wealth. Some have *cartouches* carved with the owner's coat of arms or initials. Large ones may rest on animal feet. Chests of drawers are introduced at the end of the 16th century. A variation is the *credenza*, an oblong cupboard with drawers in the frieze and doors beneath separated by a narrow panel or pilaster.

■ *Beds*. Beds include the *lettiera*, which has a high headboard and rests on a platform made of or surrounded by three chests; four-poster beds, and simple boards with legs like those of the Middle Ages. Bed hangings, which are often elaborate, provide privacy and warmth. Before poster beds become common during the 15th century, hangings are suspended from hooks, rods, or a dome attached by a cord to the ceiling.

■ *Decorative Arts*. Most mirrors are of polished steel until the 16th century, when Venice begins producing small glass mirrors. By 1600, most rooms have at least one print or painting. Decorative objects and informal dinnerware are made of Italian *maiolica*, tin-glazed earthenware. The Della Robbia family in Florence makes the most outstanding *maiolica*, producing monochromatic and colorful devotional reliefs and decorative tiles of religious figures, fruits, and flowers (Fig. 12-2). Della Robbia ornament appears both on exteriors (Fig. 12-3) and in interiors. Italians also highly prize Chinese porcelain and try to reproduce it. Among the most notable attempts to make porcelain is the Medici porcelain made in Florence between 1575 and 1585.

▲ **12-21.** Table, 16th century.

▲ **12-22.** *Cassone*, 16th century.

CHAPTER 13

Spanish Renaissance

1480–1650

The rediscovery of the Classical past was one of the two great adventures that informed the Renaissance. The other was the exploration and conquest of America.

—Spiro Kostof, *A History of Architecture*

Spain dominates the world politically and economically in the 16th century, but she, like others, looks to Italy for inspiration in architecture, interiors, and furnishings. Initially, the Spanish blend Renaissance design principles and motifs with 800 years of Moorish influences and a long tradition of lavish surface decoration. Major architectural projects often exhibit a blend of classical and Moorish designs. High Renaissance design concepts and details appear early in the 16th century, bringing greater severity to art and architecture, which is foreign to Spanish innate styles and tastes. Spanish emphasis on ornament quickly displaces High Renaissance plainness.

HISTORICAL AND SOCIAL

Spain's Islamic heritage, which begins with the arrival of the Moors (people from North African tribes) in 711, shapes her history, culture, and design sensibilities differently than that of the rest of Europe. Throughout much of the 800 years of Islamic occupation, Moors and Christians struggle for dominance, with Christians gradually conquering more territory and driving out the majority of Moors by the 15th century.

Spain acquires her present borders late in the 15th century. The marriage of Ferdinand V of Aragon and Isabella of Castile in 1469 unites their respective states. The conquest of Granada and the annexation of Navarre complete the unification of the country. Policies and actions of these two monarchs lay the foundations of Spain's domination as a great world power in the 16th century. One important contribution is their sponsorship of the expedition of Christopher Columbus to discover new western trade routes to Asia in 1492. Within 20 years after Columbus's arrival in North America, the Spanish are expanding their territorial holdings into the Americas. Ferdinand also makes alliances with various European royal houses. When his grandson, Charles, ascends the Spanish throne in 1516, the power of the Spanish court is unmatched in Europe.

During the 16th century, Spain leads the world in exploration, trade, and colonization. By the 1550s, she controls most of South and Central America, Florida, Cuba, and the Philippines. Newly discovered gold and silver mines in the Americas bring enormous wealth into Spanish coffers. More European territory, including the Netherlands and Burgundy, comes with Charles V's election as Holy Roman Emperor in 1519. Spain leads European politics and plays a large monetary and ideological role in the Counter-Reformation.

Charles's son, Philip II, becomes the ruler of a major world power when he takes the throne in 1556. Through his marriages to daughters of royalty in Europe, he enhances Spain's stature and financial resources with important connections to England, France, and Austria. The peace that prevails early in his reign soon vanishes in the face of religious conflicts, domestic turmoil, and epidemics that threaten economic and political stability. Maintaining territories proves costly, as does the rivalry with France, discontent in the Netherlands, and war with England. Philip's attempts at an absolute monarchy and his strong allegiance to the Catholic faith contribute to the decline of Spanish power. In addition, the Inquisition's conservatism prohibits new ideas. The defeat of the Spanish Armada by the English in 1588 marks the end of Spanish domination in both Old and New Worlds. As the 16th century ends, so does Spain's Golden Age.

CONCEPTS

The Renaissance arrives in Spain through political ties with Italy in the late 15th century. Deeply ingrained, however, are a strong medieval design aesthetic and centuries of Islamic heritage. So the sober, intellectual Renaissance has little appeal for the Spanish, who prefer lavish surface decoration composed of Gothic and Moorish forms and motifs, which convey visual complexity, emotion, and dynamism. Consequently, the classical Renaissance slowly merges with and overcomes indigenous forms and ornament. However, the monarchy and nobility prefer Italian High Renaissance classicism, which appears somewhat abruptly in the second quarter of the 16th century. Bearing little resemblance to native Spanish designs and associated with the court, it lasts only about 100 years. The Spanish love of ornament reasserts itself in the Baroque movement, which begins about 1650.

▲ **13-1.** Motifs: Renaissance tiles, 15th–16th century; Portugal.

▲ **13-2.** Door, 16th century; Seville; *Mudéjar* and door area, *Iglesia de S. Justo;* Salamanca. Plateresque.

CHARACTERISTICS AND MOTIFS

■ *Hispano-Moresque* (8th–15th centuries) reflects the Moorish architecture and decoration of Spain during Islamic domination.

■ *Mudéjar* (13th–16th centuries) appears after the conquest of the Moors by Christians. Many Christian buildings of this period use Moorish details, such as the horseshoe arch.

■ *Plateresque* (late 15th to early 16th centuries) describes the transition from Gothic to Renaissance. The characteristic minute, profuse surface ornament in low relief resembles silverwork, after which it is named. It has two sub-styles or phases. The two phases, Gothic and Renaissance, sometimes parallel each other, and some designers work in both styles.

—*Isabelline or Gothic Plateresque* (c. 1480–1504), the early phase, is Gothic in form and dominated by Gothic motifs, such as pinnacles and crockets.

—*Renaissance Plateresque* (1504–1556), the later phase, reveals more classical motifs, such as decorated pediments, pilasters, and baluster columns.

■ *Classical, Desornamentado, or Herreran Style* (1556–1650) demonstrates an understanding of classical design principles and order. Symmetrical and carefully proportioned, decoration is architectonic and emulates Italian High Renaissance forms. With the building of *El Escorial,* an even plainer, more severe expression becomes the official architectural style of Spain. It dominates Spanish architecture through the 17th century.

■ *Churrigueresque or Baroque-Rococo* (1650–1750), named for the Churriguera family of architects, flourishes after the Renaissance. The style highlights architectural ornament such as stuccowork, twisted columns, and an inverted obelisk.

■ *Motifs.* Moorish motifs (Fig. 13-1) are ogee arches, interlaced arabesques, and geometric shapes. Gothic motifs include heraldic symbols, pointed arches, pinnacles, and crockets. Decorated pediments, pilasters, baluster columns, and grotesques distinguish Renaissance Plateresque (Fig. 13-2, 13-3). Classical-style decoration more accurately copies Italian Renaissance forms and motifs (Fig. 13-2, 13-4, 13-5), such as columns, pilasters, pediments, medallions, stylized leaves and flowers, scrolls, fretwork, shells, and figures. Fewer Classical motifs are used on Spanish architecture than in Italy and France.

ARCHITECTURE

The Renaissance in Spanish architecture begins as the Plateresque style in the late 15th century. A transition between Gothic and Renaissance, its Gothic form features lavish surface decoration combining Moorish, Gothic, and Renaissance elements. Ornamentation, which concentrates around doors and occasionally windows, is not related to the structure and contrasts with surrounding blank walls. It is often complex and layered within a geometric grid as in Islamic design. Around portals, decoration extends to the roofline, resembling *retables*, the screens behind altars in churches.

By the second quarter of the 16th century, Spanish Renaissance enters a more Italian-like phase, revealing concepts of and antecedents in Italian High Renaissance and ancient buildings. Plain walls articulated with rustication and classical articulation and details replace surface decoration. Symmetry, order, and harmonious proportions are characteristic. Most structures reflect human scale. By the end of the century, design is even more severe and formal with minimal decoration. Plans and façades often reveal Italian antecedents as Spanish architects study Italian buildings and treatises. Nevertheless, some Spanish characteristics are retained, such as ornate portals, iron grilles at windows, and tile work.

Spanish building types, which are more varied than those in Italy, include churches, civic buildings (Fig. 13-3), universities, hospitals, palaces (Fig. 13-4, 13-5), townhouses, and *rancheros*. Despite a varied climate, most Spanish structures are designed for hot weather with small windows, flat or low-pitched roofs, and *patios* (courtyards) similar to those in Italy.

Public and Private Buildings

■ *Site Orientation*. Churches are dominant structures in the city or town environment. Most city buildings front on narrow streets. Public buildings and palaces may face squares or *plazas* (Fig. 13-5).

▲ **13-3.** Town hall, 1527–1534; Seville, Spain.

▲ **13-4.** Palace of Charles V, 1527–1568; Pedro Machua. Classical, *Desornamentado*, or Herreran style.

■ *Floor Plans*. Most churches have Latin cross plans. Other structures, including palaces and houses, center on *patios* or courtyards for privacy (Fig. 13-5). Like the earlier Moorish structures, rooms generally open out to one or more outdoor spaces. Rooms (Fig. 13-5, 13-6) are often long and narrow in shape or somewhat square; their dimensions are not mathematically derived. Symmetry in plan is not important until the classical period in the 16th century.

■ *Materials*. Granite, limestone, sandstone, glazed ceramic tile, and brick are typical building materials. Gray granite with contrasting white stucco details marks the classical style. The scarcity of wood limits its use. The Spanish are known for wrought-iron window grilles, handrails, and other decoration.

■ *Façades*. Walls and openings are usually symmetrical and divided into bays by architectural details. Surfaces (Fig. 13-3, 13-4, 13-5) are plain with little or no rustication until the classical period when rustication becomes a definitive characteristic. Sometimes stringcourses separate stories. Ornamentation varies in form, intensity, and motifs with the style and often reaches the roofline. Plateresque or Classical decoration usually surrounds rectangular or arched windows that have one or two lights (Fig. 13-3, 13-4, 13-5). Some have *rejas* or wrought-iron grilles. Decorative surrounds emphasize entrances and are a distinctive Spanish feature. Rectangular doors have carved wood panels, often with geometric designs (Fig. 13-2).

■ *Roofs*. Roofs are flat or low pitched. Following the completion of *El Escorial* (Fig. 13-5), many houses have corner towers to imitate it.

DESIGN SPOTLIGHT

Architecture and Interiors: Constructed over a 20-year period, *El Escorial* contains a monastery, church, college, and state apartments for Philip II. The site, a bleak, windswept, semi-wooded plain at the base of mountains, is unusual for a royal palace. The plan, which appears to resemble the famous grill on which S. Laurence was martyred, centers on spacious courtyards, some with gardens. The most likely explanation of the plan is that is it based upon descriptions of the Temple of Solomon, which centered on courtyards also, but extensively modified to suit the various needs and functions of a royal palace. Begun by Juan Bautista de Toledo and completed by Juan de Herrera, the buildings reflect the Classical, *Desornamentado,* or Herreran style with design attributes from Palladio and other Italian Renaissance architects and artists. The gray granite façade is aus-

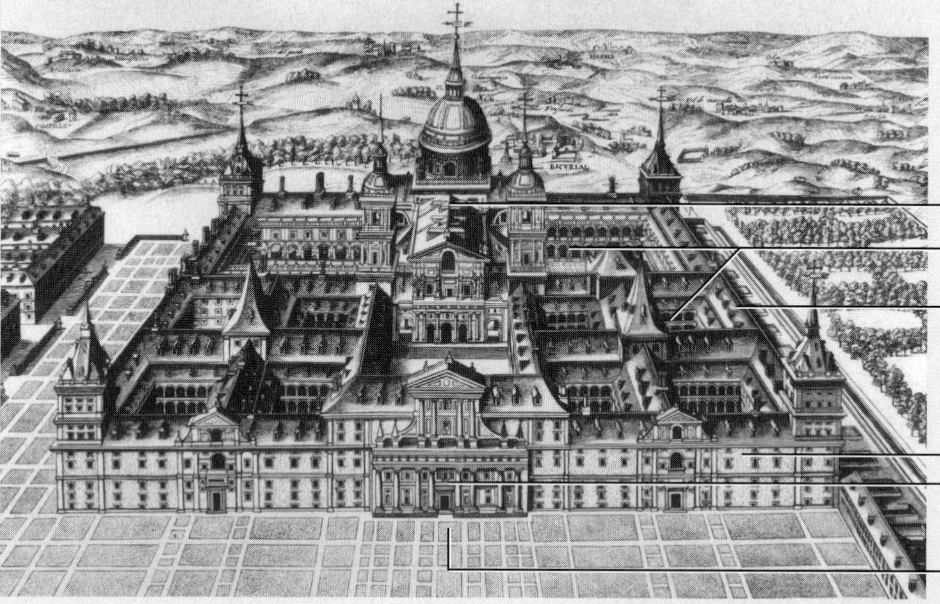

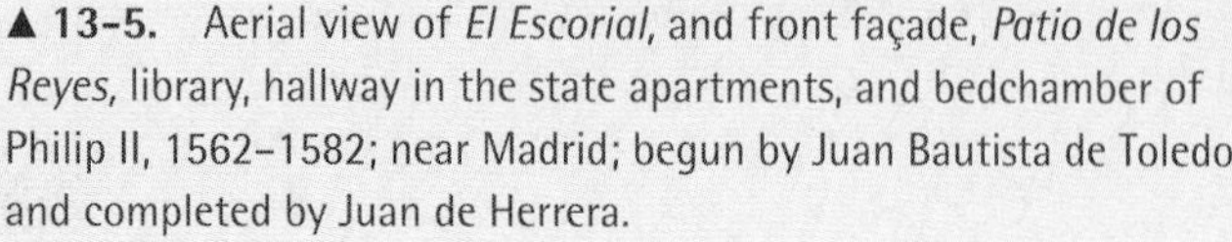

▲ **13-5.** Aerial view of *El Escorial,* and front façade, *Patio de los Reyes,* library, hallway in the state apartments, and bedchamber of Philip II, 1562–1582; near Madrid; begun by Juan Bautista de Toledo and completed by Juan de Herrera.

DESIGN SPOTLIGHT

tere and simple with little ornamentation, but major entries are highlighted with columns, pilasters, arches, pediments, and sculptures. Symmetry and impressive scale are important throughout. Within the building, the rooms vary in design, illustrating Moorish elements in the state apartments and Italian Renaissance architectural concepts in the library (below). Elaborate paintings by artists such as El Greco enhance the interior compositions. Simple furnishings are in traditional 16th-century Spanish designs emphasizing rectangular shapes, some with elaborate surface decoration. The library houses Philip II's collection plus documents and books from Spain and other countries. Ceiling frescoes depict the seven liberal arts. Philip II's rooms are small and austere, reflecting his tastes and passion for the Catholic faith. (World Heritage Site)

▲ 13-5. Continued

DESIGN SPOTLIGHT

▲ 13-5. Continued

INTERIORS

As on exterior façades, interior ornamentation concentrates around openings, and Moorish, Gothic, and Renaissance characteristics and motifs intermingle. Interior architectural features establish the design vocabulary, axial relationships, and general character. In private buildings, the most important rooms are the entrance hall, main salon, dining area, and bedchamber. Rooms have few furnishings, even in the wealthiest homes. Furniture usually lines the perimeter of the room (Fig. 13-5, 13-6).

Public and Private Buildings

■ *Color.* Colors (Fig. 13-1, 13-5), which are highly saturated, include reds, yellows, blues, and greens, and appear primarily in tile work, textiles, and decorative objects. Plasterwork is usually white. Ceilings and furnishings may be a combination of natural wood, color, and gilt.

■ *Floors.* Floors are of tile, brick, or stone, while wood is typical for upper floors (Fig. 13-5, 13-6). Knotted-pile rugs with elaborate designs and woven mats cover floors.

■ *Walls.* Walls are smooth white plaster. Colorful earthenware tiles highlight dadoes, door and window facings, window seats, stair risers, and interiors of wall niches (Fig. 13-5, 13-6, 13-7). Dining rooms often have *lavabos* made of copper, pewter, or pottery that hang on the wall or are in a niche faced with tiles. Elaborate decoration and detailing accentuate grand stairways. Aristocratic houses have wall hangings of silk, velvet, or damask (Fig. 13-6). Some are embellished with embroidery or braid and fringe. Because Spain is a leading center for leatherwork, painted, tooled, and gilded leather often is used for wall coverings. Large-scaled mantels with classical elements usually dominate the main wall in important rooms. Occasionally, plasterwork decorates chimneys. Portable *braziers* (Fig. 13-6) of elaborate brass, copper, or silver supply heat or supplement fireplaces.

■ *Windows and Doors. Yeseria* or plasterwork often frames doors and windows. Doors of wood or with iron grilles may be used to separate interiors from *patios*. Doors and shutters may be plain, painted, or carved (Fig. 13-5, 13-6). Although curtains on windows are rare, occasionally heavy lambrequins and draperies surround doorways of important rooms (Fig. 13-11).

■ *Ceilings.* Ceilings are focal points in many interiors. Most are of pine. Those in important rooms feature elaborate geometric shapes with complex ornamentation enriched with painting, gilding, and *artesonades* work (Fig. 13-5, 13-6). Beams and coffers are plain or decorated with painting and carving.

■ *Textiles.* Spanish interiors, like others, use textile wall coverings, upholstery, and bed hangings of silk, wool, or linen (Fig. 13-8). Velvet or damask, sometimes with embroidery or braid and fringe, covers walls in important rooms. Rectangular armchairs and side chairs have leather, velvet, and damask seats and backs, which may be decorated with fringe (Fig. 13-5, 13-6, 13-7, 13-11). Some chairs, benches, and stools are covered completely with fabric. Important beds, such as Philip II's, display elaborate textile treat-

DESIGN SPOTLIGHT

Interiors: These interiors of the Palace of the Duke of Alba are excellent examples of Spanish Renaissance design. Used by an important family, the impressive spaces collectively feature tile floors, off-white plain stucco walls, geometrically carved wooden doors and shutters, decorative friezes, decorated beamed ceilings, *fraileros*, tables, chests, *papalera*, chandeliers, and a *brazier*. Paintings and a tapestry cover the walls, and a simple rug accents the floor in the main salon. The windows have carved interior shutters instead of curtains. The ground floor salon window has an iron grille to prevent intrusions. The scale of the rooms as well as their furnishings contribute to their importance and grandeur, as would befit a palatial environment.

► 13-6. Main salon and ground floor salon, Palace of the Duke of Alba, 16th century; Seville, Spain.

DESIGN SPOTLIGHT

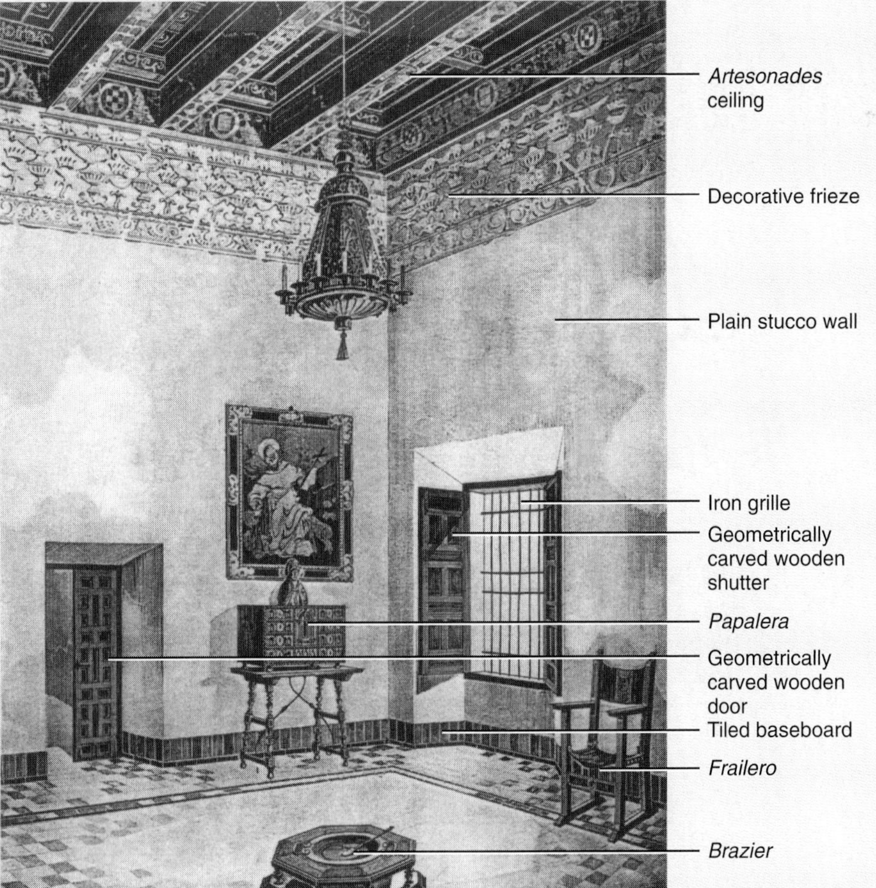

▲ **13-6.** Continued

▲ **13-7.** *Sala, Casa de El Greco,* 16th century; Toledo, Spain.

▲ **13-8.** Textiles: Fabrics of wool and silk, 16th century.

ments trimmed with lace, embroidery, fringe, or braid. A Moorish legacy in the Spanish home is an extensive use of canopies and/or cushions trimmed with braid, cord, tassels, or nailheads.

■ *Lighting.* *Torcheres* or torch stands, hanging lanterns, *braccios, candelabra,* and chandeliers are common in all types of spaces (Fig. 13-5, 13-6, 13-9). Designs may be plain or elaborate and often incorporate *Mudéjar* or classical features. Materials are iron and/or wood.

■ *Later Interpretations.* During the 16th century, Spanish forms travel to the Americas as abstracted and simplified renditions of their *Mudéjar,* classical, and Baroque precursors in Mexico, Central and South America, and the southwestern and southeastern United States. Spanish Colonial Revival (Fig. 13-10), beginning in the early 20th century, features plain walls, tiled floors, and dark-beamed ceilings of the earlier period, but with the addition of plasterwork, decorative tiles, and arches and more and varied furnishings.

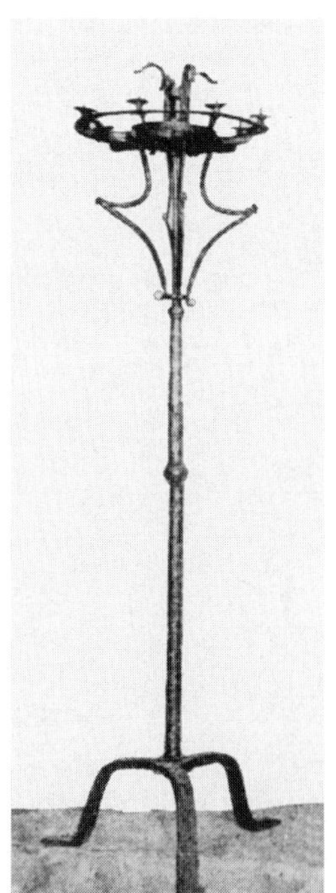

▲ **13-9.** Lighting: Iron *torchere,* chandelier, and hanging lantern.

▲ **13-10.** Later Interpretation: Foyer, McNay Residence, 1920s–1930s; San Antonio, Texas. Spanish Colonial Revival.

FURNISHINGS AND DECORATIVE ARTS

Renaissance furniture is simple in design and construction and rectilinear in form with few moldings and architectural details. The scale of Spanish furniture is often heavier than comparable Italian or French furniture. The bold, vigorous ornamentation shows Moorish and classical influence. Particularly characteristic are wrought-iron mounts, locks, and underbraces. The most important types of furniture include seating, chests, cabinets, tables, and beds.

Public and Private Buildings

■ *Materials.* Walnut is the most used wood, followed by oak, pine, and chestnut. Luxury pieces are made of exotic woods such as ebony or mahogany. Decoration includes inlay, carving, painting, and gilding (Fig. 13-12, 13-13). Inlay of bone or ivory shows Moorish influence in its intricate designs of minute details in geometric and stylized floral patterns. Silver from the New World often forms inlay or applied details.

■ *Seating.* Seating (Fig. 13-5, 13-6, 13-7, 13-11) includes the *frailero*, X-shaped chairs, the ladder-back chair, stools, and benches. Chairs are less common than benches and stools. Most chairs have medium-to-high backs with ball or leaf finials and spiral, baluster-turned, or quadrangular legs with stretchers. Trestle supports are more common than legs on benches and stools, and they may have iron braces. Many rooms have built-in seating, and ladies sometimes sit on cushions on a dais in the Moorish fashion.

■ *Tables.* Most tables (Fig. 13-5, 13-6, 13-7) are simply constructed and covered with cloths or carpets. Some oblong tables have turned, splayed legs connected with curving iron braces, which sometimes are gilded for formal rooms.

▲ **13-11.** Doorway with embroidered lambrequin, damask draperies, and *fraileros*; and *frailero, El Escorial,* 16th century; Spain.

DESIGN SPOTLIGHT

Furniture: Used for writing or to hold documents, the *vargueño* is the most distinctive piece of Spanish Renaissance furniture. It consists of a drop-front cabinet on a base. Wrought-iron mounts and locks typically provide the only decoration on the façade. Inside are numerous small drawers and doors. The most characteristic base has splayed legs and iron braces. It, like the *papalera*, was designed to travel with wealthy landowners as they moved between city and country houses.

▲ **13-12.** *Vargueños.*

■ *Storage*. Storage pieces (Fig. 13-5, 13-6, 13-7, 13-12, 13-13) include chests in various sizes, built-in cupboards, the sacristy cupboard, the *armario*, and the *fresquera*. The *vargueño* (Fig. 13-12) is the most distinctive piece of Spanish furniture. Similar to the *vargueño*, the *papalera* is an elaborate cabinet without a drop front or a permanent base (Fig. 13-6).

■ *Beds*. Spanish beds (Fig. 13-5, 13-14) have four plain wood posts and elaborately carved headboards; some posts are spirals with carving. Other beds are of iron or bronze. As in other countries, many are richly draped to demonstrate wealth. However, because of the hot Spanish climate, some beds have no canopy frames. Important beds, such as Philip II's bed, display elaborate textile treatments.

■ *Decorative Arts*. Sometimes small leather-covered chests and small boxes decorate tabletops. A Moorish legacy in the Spanish home is an extensive use of small boxes and canopies and/or cushions trimmed with braid, cord, tassels, or nailheads (Fig. 13-6).

▲ **13-13.** Chest.

DESIGN SPOTLIGHT

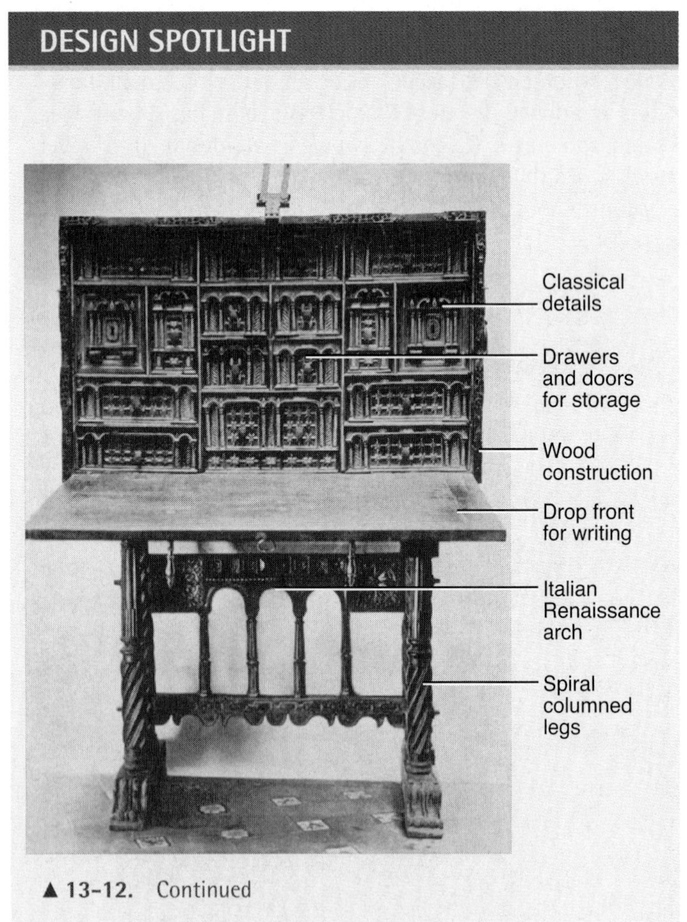

▲ **13-12.** Continued

▲ **13-14.** Bed with spiral turnings, Royal Palace, 16th century; Sintra, Portugal.

CHAPTER 14

French Renaissance

1515–1643

Que sais-je? What do I know?

—Montaigne

After becoming acquainted with Italian Renaissance designs through invasions of Italy, the French eagerly seek to adopt them in their homes and lives. Nevertheless, early expressions of French Renaissance combine indigenous characteristics, Gothic forms, and Mannerist elements to form a picturesque image most evident in the *château*. During the 16th century, the French develop their own unique classical style that features less emphasis on rules and correct proportions than in Italy and more on inventiveness and surface richness. By the end of the period, that classicism, an absolute monarchy aware of the power of art to exalt, and the demand for luxury among the nobility set the stage for the grandeur of the court of Louis XIV and Versailles.

HISTORICAL AND SOCIAL

In the mid-15th century, France becomes a single, united kingdom. At the end of the 15th century, Charles VIII invades Naples and Milan. Although the campaigns are unsuccessful, the French return home ready to adopt the new Renaissance style in all its aspects. Charles VIII himself brings Italian craftspeople to France. The next two French kings, Louis XII and François I, also attack Italy and thereby become acquainted with the Italian culture. The Renaissance flowers during the reign of François I as the country prospers and life grows more stable. A new wealthy, leisured class demands suitable accompaniments to a more refined way of life. François I supports and promotes the arts and learning. He attracts many Italian artists, such as Leonardo da Vinci and Benvenuto Cellini, and scholars to his court and builds palaces in the Loire Valley and the Ile de France. He also increases the power and prestige of the French monarchy. The marriage of his successor, Henri II, to Catherine de' Medici of Florence, enhances Italian ties. Catherine, great-granddaughter of Lorenzo the Magnificent and herself an art patron, sponsors a new wing of the Louvre and initiates the creation of the Tuileries gardens. Her collection of books and manuscripts is unmatched in France.

Religious civil wars between Catholics and Huguenots (Protestants) disrupt domestic peace and paralyze the country in the last half of the 16th century. Economic decline and political instability add to the turmoil. Henri III, who is the last of the Valois dynasty, dies in 1584. Henri of Bourbon, king of Navarre, assumes the throne in 1589 as Henri IV, the first of the Bourbon dynasty. In 1598, he issues the Edict of Nantes granting partial religious freedom to all his subjects. Henri IV restores peace, promotes economic recovery, and fosters the development of French arts and crafts. His reign marks a turning point in French cultural development. Recognizing the power of art to exalt the monarchy, in 1608 he begins the policy of providing free workshops in the Louvre for artists and craftsmen. Known as the Bourbon Art Policy, it is continued by subsequent monarchs. In addition, he brings artisans to France to create new industries, including the production of silk.

In 1610, Louis XIII becomes king following the assassination of his father, Henri IV. During his reign and with the aid of his minister Cardinal Richelieu, trade flourishes, towns expand, the power of the nobility decreases, and the Crown's power increases, ultimately creating an absolute monarchy. He lays the foundation for great luxury, grandeur, and magnificence in court life, which will ultimately lead to the opulent court of Louis XIV and Versailles.

CONCEPTS

French Renaissance design concepts come from a Gothic heritage mixed with Ancient Roman, Renaissance, and Flemish characteristics. Because the Gothic style originates in France and is best understood there, its heritage provides a rich source of design inspiration and proves difficult to overcome. As time passes, French designers increase their understanding of classical design principles because of the Italian artists and craftsmen who bring to France influences mostly from the Late Renaissance (Mannerism). Additionally, the French study Italian treatises and prints and scrutinize their own surviving Roman buildings. Some visit Rome. Through these means, they begin to formulate their own national style and write their own design treatises by the end of the 16th century.

MOTIFS

■ *Motifs.* Motifs include pilasters, columns, arches, pediments, figures in low relief (Fig. 14-3, 14-5), pinnacles (Fig. 14-4), brackets, scrolls, linenfold, tracery, strapwork, grotesques, caryatids, fruit, flowers, heraldry, *fleur de lis*, stars, and diamonds (Fig. 14-1). Crowns and initials, such as F, H, C, and L, which are symbols of royalty, appear at entrances and on ceilings, furnishings, and decorative arts. Additionally, French kings use animal motifs, such as the François I salamander and Louis XII porcupine, on entrances, overmantels, ceilings, and other places to identify their individual *châteaux*.

ARCHITECTURE

The Renaissance style gradually evolves throughout the 16th century as Gothic elements fade and classical ones assert themselves. French Renaissance, while influenced strongly by Italy, retains a unique, essentially French, expression. The French regard classicism as an ordering system. Hence, regularity, order, and symmetry are common design principles that appear early and continuously. The French generally do not emphasize mathematical relationships and the correct use of classical elements like the Italians. Instead, they value inventiveness over rules and rich surface decoration over proportions. Even as it becomes more formal and classically correct, French Renaissance architecture remains more lively, vertical, and picturesque than Italian design. Climatic differences resulting from a colder climate and softer light distinguish French Renaissance as well. These differences include more steeply pitched roofs, larger windows, and prominent chimneys. French designers also retain the traditional pavilions, distinctive structures that mark the center and ends of buildings. All of these features contribute to the individuality of French buildings.

The earliest manifestations of French Renaissance designs are Gothic in form with classical details, such as pilasters, used as decoration. This first appears on *châteaux* (Fig. 14-5), the large coun-

(a)

(b)

(c)

(d)

▲ **14–1.** Motifs and Architectural Details: (a) Initial F and salamander, emblems of François I; (b) porcupine, emblem of Louis XIII and House of Orleans; (c) *fleur-de-lis;* and (d) strapwork.

try houses of the nobility. During the first half of the 16th century, most *châteaux* resemble castles because fortification and protection remain important. Nevertheless, they freely mix Gothic, classical, and Mannerist ornament.

Italian architect Sebastiano Serlio's direct influence in France from his time there as well as the travels of French architects to Italy help institute a more confident classicism. By the second half of the 16th century, the French have become more adept in their handling of classical elements, which are no longer confined to country houses but include churches, palaces (Fig. 14-4), *hôtels*, and public buildings (Fig. 14-3). Some buildings feature adapted Renaissance and Roman details.

Public and Private Buildings

■ *Site Orientation*. Henri IV institutes Italian urban planning concepts in Paris (Fig. 14-3). Unlike Italy, where public buildings are situated in squares, French squares are frameworks for private houses. Churches usually are near the city center. *Châteaux* sit within natural landscapes featuring long vistas; many are located on high hills and/or along rivers (Fig. 14-4).

■ *Floor Plans*. Churches continue the traditional Latin cross plan. Domestic floor plans exhibit more regularity than was previously evident. The plan at Chambord (Fig. 14-4) is a fortified rectangular compound with a central courtyard and corner

▲ **14-2.** Fireplace, *Château de Blois*; Loire Valley, France.

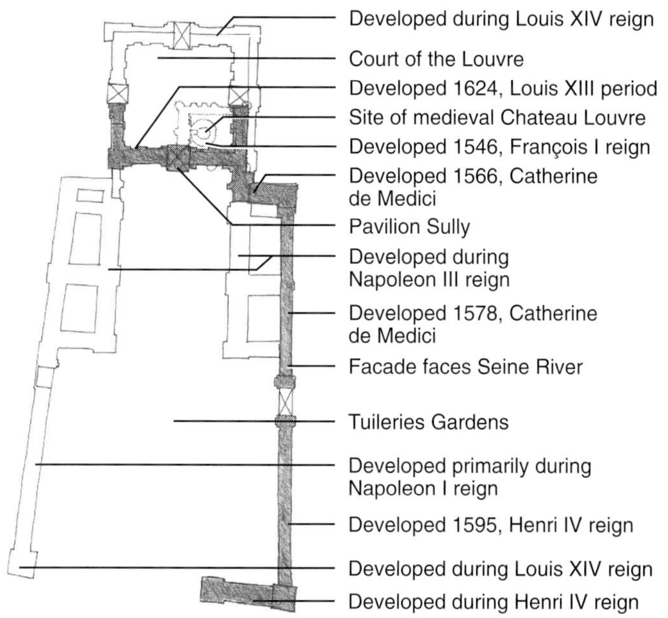

▲ **14-3.** Louvre, Square Court, elevation and site plan, 1546–1570; Paris, France; façade by Pierre Lescot.

DESIGN SPOTLIGHT

Architecture and Interior: *Château de Chambord* is a majestic stone palace built by François I to reflect the grandeur of his reign. Built as a hunting lodge, the *château* has 440 rooms, over 80 staircases, and 365 fireplaces with numerous chimneys that decorate the roof. Directly inspired by Italian Renaissance models, the design emphasizes grand scale and symbolizes the importance and value of the monarchy. Large rectangular and arched windows flanked by pilasters symmetrically order the lower façade. Stringcourses temper their verticality. The exuberant roofs feature balustrades, lanterns, chimneys, and dormers with classical columns and pilasters, lozenges, roundels, brackets, and pinnacles. Double dormer windows have parapet roofs with François's initial. The castle-like structure has a walled enclosure with four corner towers surrounding an open courtyard that contains the keep or *donjon*. The Greek cross plan has four vaulted halls with a monumental double staircase in the center. The keep also houses guard chambers, the main public spaces, and private apartments. Characteristic interior details include François's initials and other symbols, round arches, deep cornices, large stone chimneypieces, elaborate balustrades, and coffered and beamed ceilings, along with minimal but very ornate furnishings. (World Heritage Site)

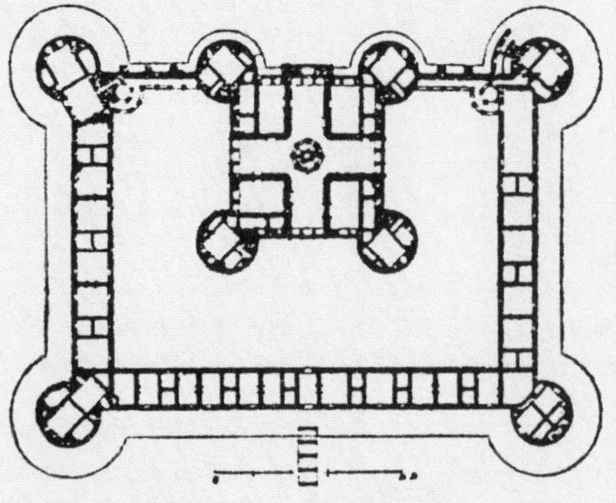

▲ **14–4.** *Château de Chambord*, floor plan, and stair hall, 1519–1547; Loire Valley, France; plan possibly by Domenico da Cortona.

turrets. The main building, which is a Greek cross, introduces the *appartement*, a suite of rooms consisting of antechamber, chambre, and cabinet. The *appartement* and the *salon* will characterize French domestic architecture for the next 200 years. Most homes have no interior hallways. Fontainebleau exhibits the first long gallery (Fig. 14-5), a long narrow space usually connecting wings, which will become common in France and England during the 16th and 17th centuries. *Hôtels* center on courtyards but have no typical plans, as sites are irregular. Shops often occupy the ground floor, with living spaces on the first floor (level above the ground) and bedchambers on the upper floors.

■ *Materials*. Stone is the most preferred building material followed by brick. Roofs are usually of slate. Vernacular buildings commonly adopt *briqueté entre poteaux* construction or *pierrotage* (Fig. 14-6).

■ *Façades*. Generally, order, regularity, and symmetry characterize the exteriors of all buildings while, in contrast, the rooflines remain steeply pitched, irregular in silhouette, and asymmetrical in organization. Façades of most public and some private buildings exhibit an Italian bay system using pilasters, windows placed directly over one another, and horizontal emphasis from cornices and stringcourses. Pavilions in centers and on ends mark the façades of public buildings and some palaces (Fig. 14-3, 14-5). Walls usually are not rusticated. Exteriors of *châteaux* (Fig. 14-4) may be fortified and have large entry gates, round turrets with conical roofs, and central courtyards. Churches retain the earlier Gothic proportions, buttresses, vaults, and pinnacles. Some *hôtels* use Gothic half-timbered construction, but with the addition of arches, brackets, and larger windows. Pilasters often frame symmetrically placed windows, and stringcourses separate different stories. By the end of the century, rusticated quoins, window surrounds, and *chaînes* are characteristic of most residences.

■ *Windows*. Windows, which vary in size, are large as in the past to allow in the maximum light. Most have mullions forming a Latin cross with four or six lights (Fig. 14-4, 14-5). Dormers often have elaborately shaped surrounds. Church windows have rounded tops, tracery, and stained glass.

■ *Roofs*. *Châteaux* roofs (Fig. 14-4) often display irregular outlines with lanterns, turrets, dormers, and chimneys decorated with classical, Mannerist, and Gothic motifs. Later, buildings have steeply pitched gables with fewer picturesque details (Fig. 14-5). Throughout the period, numerous tall, decorative, and prominent chimneys accentuate rooflines.

■ *Later Interpretations*. The Châteauesque style adapts elements from French Renaissance *châteaux* during the late 19th and early 20th centuries in France, England, and America. Biltmore (Fig. 14-7) in Asheville, North Carolina, replicates French Renaissance characteristics as well as an adaptation of the curved staircase at Blois.

INTERIORS

Italian artists Rosso Fiorentino and Francesco Primaticcio create the first French Renaissance interiors at Fontainebleau in the 1530s–1540s. They work in a Mannerist mode influenced by excavations of ancient Roman interiors. Characteristics include nymphs, garlands, scrolls, strapwork, grotesques, and stucco figures. They have few followers. Like architecture, interiors continue to feature Gothic and classical elements with classical gradually becoming dominant. Doors, windows, stairways, and chimneypieces, where decoration concentrates, are important architectural elements. As in other countries, rooms have few furnishings throughout the period, even in wealthy homes, and room use continues to be flexible.

Public and Private Buildings

■ *Color*. Colors are rich and highly saturated. Gold, deep blue, olive green, brown, cream, and crimson are important hues and most often appear in wall and bed hangings, tapestries, fabrics, tiles, painted ceilings, and decorative art objects.

■ *Floors*. Most floors (Fig. 14-5) are wood in boards or parquet patterns. A few, particularly on lower floors, are of masonry or tiled (Fig. 14-5, 14-8, 14-9). Rugs are rare.

■ *Walls*. Churches and public buildings are likely to exhibit Gothic and classical architectural details and motifs. Interior walls, particularly in houses, are often white plaster (Fig. 14-8). Other wall treatments include wood paneling (Fig. 14-5), painting (Fig. 14-9), and hangings. Tall, narrow panels retaining Gothic proportions sometimes feature carving or painted Gothic or classical decoration. Wall paintings may imitate stone or textile patterns. Gilding on architectural elements, paneling, or wall paintings is common in important rooms in greater houses. Hangings consist of plain or embellished fabric, imported and domestic tapestries (Fig. 14-4, 14-10), or leather. Some fragments of French wallpaper from the period survive.

As a focal point, the chimneypiece (Fig. 14-2) is the largest and most important decorative feature of the interior. The projecting hood is decorated with classic and Gothic details, coats of arms, and/or royal and period motifs. It does not have classical proportions, but entablatures, pilasters, and columns can shape the design.

■ *Windows and Doors*. Shutters provide privacy and light control. The few curtains, which are limited to wealthy homes, are functional, not decorative. Doorways are placed where needed and are not always symmetrical. Door panels usually match wainscoting.

■ *Ceilings*. Church and public building ceilings are often vaulted. Beamed ceilings (Fig. 14-8, 14-9) in dwellings are embellished with carving and/or brightly colored stripes, arabesques, or other repeating motifs. Coffers in geometric patterns are carved, painted, or gilded (Fig. 14-4, 14-5). Plaster ceilings are usually left plain.

■ *Textiles*. French interiors, like those in other countries, have fabric wall and bed hangings; cushions; and fabrics thrown over chairs, benches, and stools. Silk, wool, linen, and cotton textiles add warmth, color, and pattern, and great houses display more fabrics than lesser ones do. Tapestries (Fig. 14-4, 14-10) become more common in wealthy homes during the period. François I sponsors a tapestry factory at Fontainebleau, which uses Flemish and French weavers. The French also acquire tapestries from other weaving centers, such as Flanders. Renaissance tapestries

DESIGN SPOTLIGHT

Architecture and Interiors: The *Palais de Fontainebleau* is used by French kings since the 12th century as a hunting lodge before Gilles le Breton remodels the medieval *château* for François I. The grand scale and classical features reflect François's desire to emulate the Renaissance palaces he had seen in Italy. Successive rulers add to the palace to make it one of the largest of the French royal *châteaux*. Italian Renaissance design principles of symmetry, order, horizontality, and classical details including pilasters, quoins, and pedimented windows define the façade. Uniquely French are the pavilions; the large windows; the prominent chimneys; and the tall, steeply pitched roof. A large park surrounds the palace. The palace and park become a World Heritage Site in 1981.

Two Italian painters, Giovanni Battista Rosso (Rosso Fiorentino) and Francesco Primaticcio, direct and carry out the decoration of the early 16th-century interiors, which introduce Italian Mannerism to France. Characterized by slender nymphs, garlands, and classical and mannerist details, the style becomes known as the Fontainebleau style and is spread through northern Europe by drawings and engravings. Only a few remain intact in the palace, including the *Galerie de François I* (below), a long narrow space that connects two wings. Rosso directs the interior decoration. The lower walls are paneled in oak carved with classical details and cartouches with emblems of François. Above, stucco ornament and figures modeled after those by Michelangelo frame allegorical paintings of the virtues and

▲ **14–5.** *Palais de Fontainebleau, Galerie de François I*, and *Galerie de Henri II*, 1528–1540; Fontainebleau, France; architecture by Gilles le Breton.

DESIGN SPOTLIGHT

great deeds of the kings. The ceiling is beamed and coffered, and the floor is herringbone parquet. The space was used for strolling, and various craftspeople displayed their wares here.

Representing a second, later Fontainebleau style, the *Galerie de Henri II* is a formal reception room. Large round arches define its length while a monumental chimneypiece provides a focal point on the width. The opulent interior displays symmetry, classical details, elaborate gilded paneling, a carved coffered ceiling, numerous paintings by Italian artists, and a wood parquet floor. (World Heritage Site)

▲ **14-5.** Continued

▲ **14-6.** Façade, half-timbered house; Lot-et-Garonne, Caudecoste, France.

▲ **14-7.** Later Interpretation: Biltmore, 1890–1895; Asheville, North Carolina; Richard Morris Hunt. Châteauesque.

(Fig. 14-4, 14-10) have wider borders than Gothic tapestries and exhibit classical motifs or depict classical scenes. Often of wool, they may be woven with gold and silver threads.

As in the previous period, textiles are more important than furniture. Frames of chairs, stools, and beds sometimes are covered with fabric attached by gilded or brass nails. Seating often has cushions trimmed with braid and tassels. Tables may be covered with a rug or a cloth that matches other upholstery. Beds are draped with an abundance of rich, colorful fabrics.

▲ **14-8.** *Salon, Château de Chaumont,* 1465–late 15th century; Loire Valley, France.

▲ **14-9.** Bedchamber, Henri III, *Château de Blois,* 1551–1589; Loire Valley, France.

■ *Lighting.* Candles and fireplaces provide minimal artificial lighting. Fixtures include candlesticks, candelabra, and candle stands in wood and metal. Lamps and chandeliers are rare.

▲ **14-10.** Textiles: "The Lady and the Unicorn" tapestry; 'To my only desire,' depicting a maid offering a casket of jewels to her lady; one of six hangings and two fragments from two or more sets of tapestries. It has a wool warp with silk, wool, silver, and silver-gilt threads.

FURNISHINGS AND DECORATIVE ARTS

Several overlapping styles comprise furniture during the period. As in architecture, furniture continues its Gothic form but with Renaissance decoration. Gradually, more Italian influence appears in architectural details, refined proportions, and classical motifs. Desire for comfort and awareness of new artistic movements encourages the creation of new furniture types. Pattern books help spread Italian and Flemish influence in France and, later, promote French designs. As elsewhere, typical furnishings include seating, tables, storage pieces, and beds. Construction becomes more sophisticated and refined over the period. Low- and high-relief carving is the main form of decoration until the Late Renaissance when turning, veneer, inlay, painting, and gilding come into greater use.

■ *Early Renaissance or François I* (1483–1547). Furniture evolves from Gothic form and ornament to Gothic form with classical ornament. Most pieces are of oak and simply constructed following medieval traditions. Carving is the main decoration. Motifs include linenfold, strapwork, and grotesques.

■ *Middle Renaissance or Henri II* (1547–1589). French furniture begins to more closely resemble that of Italy as Italian influence increases. Walnut supplants oak as the main furniture wood. Most pieces are simple in design with good proportions. The principal decoration is carving. Human figures and animals are common.

■ *Late Renaissance or Louis XIII* (1589–1643). Massive and heavy, furniture is even more decorated and ornamental. Forms and motifs derive from Italian, Flemish, and Spanish influences. Carving and turning are common. Veneering and marquetry are introduced during the period. Paneling with heavy moldings is typical.

Public and Private Buildings

■ *Materials*. Walnut supplants oak as the main furniture wood. Cabinetmakers sometimes use imported ebony for very fine pieces, hence the term *ébéniste* for those craftsmen. Gothic polychrome falls out of favor.

DESIGN SPOTLIGHT

Furniture: Introduced in the middle of the 16th century, this armchair, used mostly by ladies, takes its name from the French word *caqueter*, meaning to chatter, cackle, or gossip. Characterized by a U-shaped or trapezoid seat, it has a tall, narrow back embellished with carved, decorative period motifs and outward-curving arms. Stretchers near the floor support the legs.

▲ **14-11.** *Caquetoire.*

■ *Seating*. Chairs include the Gothic choirstall, the X-form, the *caquetoire* (Fig. 14-11), the *chaise*, and the *chaise à bras*. Legs may be columns, baluster, or spirals and are usually connected with stretchers. Spiral carving turns left to right or in opposite directions for symmetry. Feet may be ball or bun. The *caquetoire* has a trapezoid seat, tall narrow back with carving, and outward-curving arms. Stretchers near the floor connect its legs. As the period progresses, chairs become lighter and more moveable. Stools and benches outnumber chairs.

■ *Tables*. Common to the period are trestles with removable tops and round or rectangular tables with single center supports. The table *à l'italienne* resembles Italian forms and has supports of figures, griffins, or eagles joined by a complex stretcher.

■ *Storage*. Storage pieces include chests (Fig. 14-12) in many forms, *dressoirs*, *buffets* to display plate, and *armoires*. The *armoire à deux corps* has a narrower upper portion, usually capped by a pediment, and a lower portion with doors flanked by columns, human figures, or fantastic animals.

■ *Beds*. The typical *lit* or bed (Fig. 14-9) has four elaborately turned or carved posts supporting a massive, richly carved tester from which the draperies hang. Headboards exhibit lavish carving; there are no footboards. Important beds in wealthy homes have elaborate bed hangings of Italian silk fabrics or tapestry with braiding and *appliqué*.

■ *Ceramics and Enamel*. Ceramic centers in France at Rouen, Quimper, Nantes, Nîmes, and Nevers produce *faiénce*, tin-glazed earthenware. Bernard Palissy is the most famous ceramist of the time. Known as the "Huguenot potter," his work with high-relief polychrome and naturalistic decoration are much copied. Limoges is a center for enamelware that produces cutlery with handles decorated in Renaissance motifs executed in enamel over precious metals. The little silver from the period that survives follows Mannerist traditions and shows influence from pattern books.

▲ **14-12.** Chest, 16th century.

CHAPTER 15

English Renaissance

Tudor, Elizabethan, and Jacobean 1485–1660

The ancient manours and houses of our gentemen are yet, and for the most part of strong timber. . . . Howbeit such as latelie builded are commonlie either of brick or hard stone; their rooms large and comlie. . . . So that if ever curious building did flourish in England, it is these our years, wherin our workmen excell, and are in manner comparable with skill with old Vitruvius, and Serlio. . . great profusion of tapistrie, Turkey worke, pewter, brass, fine linen, and thereto costly cupboards of plate.

—William Harrison, *The Description of England*, Book II, 1577

As in other countries, English architecture, interiors, and furniture gradually change from Gothic to Renaissance style. In England, however, design is more eclectic than in other countries and reveals more influence from France and Flanders than Italy. Mannerism, as derived from pattern books and foreign craftsmen, defines the Renaissance during the Tudor, Elizabethan, and Jacobeans periods. An exception is the more classical Renaissance work of architect Inigo Jones in the 17th century.

HISTORICAL AND SOCIAL

Wars, plagues, and internal strife dominate the 15th century. A dispute over the throne between the royal houses of Lancaster and York escalates into the War of the Roses (1450–1485). Control passes back and forth between the two houses until Henry Tudor takes the throne despite a weak Lancaster claim. A strong and capable ruler, Henry restores orderly government to England. A period of growth in trade and commerce as well as of peace and prosperity ensues. The war brings an end to feudalism, and a wealthy merchant class arises. The nobility and wealthy merchants replace their feudal castles with large, gracious manor houses set in great parks.

Henry's son, Henry VIII, also is a capable ruler, but his inability to beget a male heir tarnishes his reign. His desire for a divorce from Catherine of Aragon leads to a split with the Catholic Church and to the founding of the Church of England with Henry at its head. Subsequently, Henry dissolves the Catholic monasteries, nunneries, and friaries. He sells the land to nobles and gentry in the 1530s, which facilitates the building of more country houses. He also imports Italian, French, and Flemish craftsmen to work on the royal palaces.

Henry's daughter, Elizabeth I, takes the throne in 1558. Under her leadership, and that of Sir Walter Raleigh, England defeats the Spanish Armada in 1588. Now able to rule the seas, England supplants Spain as the major world power and begins extensive colonization, especially in the New World. Elizabeth's stable government promotes trade and commerce. Her rule encompasses a golden age in English literature and drama with works by Spenser,

Marlowe, and Shakespeare. It also is an age of luxury and splendor in the court and among the nobles. Elizabeth herself builds little, but the nobles construct new homes or enlarge existing ones in anticipation of a visit by her and the court. Elizabeth leaves no heirs, so her cousin James IV of Scotland, son of Mary Queen of Scots, becomes James I of England, thus uniting England and Scotland.

The first of the Stuarts, James wants to bring about an absolute monarchy as in France. However, England has a strong middle class and an independent Parliament who strongly oppose him. As a result, religious conflicts between Protestants and the Catholic James develop. The Puritans' disenchantment with the Church of England adds to the turmoil. Despite the religious and political differences, the first four decades of the 17th century are prosperous. The growth of England's colonies brings greater trade opportunities and more wealth. James, unlike previous rulers, ardently admires the Italian Renaissance, and England's contacts with the Continent increase during his reign.

Like his father James, Charles I admires the Renaissance and demonstrates this by collecting antique art. His marriage to Louis XIII's sister creates strong ties to France. Charles tries unsuccessfully to continue his father's policies, which plunges England into civil war in 1642. His followers, the Cavaliers, clash with the Roundheads, Puritan members of Parliament, under the leadership of Oliver Cromwell. The Puritans capture Charles, and he is tried and executed in January 1649. His son, Charles II, flees to France. Cromwell abolishes the monarchy and the House of Lords. He declares England a commonwealth. As Lord Protector, he rules with a military hand but maintains an effective foreign policy. England continues expanding her trade and colonization. As a reaction to the ostentation of the royal courts, Cromwell's rule brings simplicity and austerity. Despite the prosperity and relative peace, many despise the government and Cromwell himself for ordering the death of Charles I. Following Cromwell's death in 1658, the commonwealth collapses. Charles II returns from France and reestablishes the monarchy in 1660.

CONCEPTS

Throughout the period, Italian ideas and influences intermingle with those from France and Flanders, which creates a unique English expression. The fact that designs are assemblages from a variety of artisans further enhances the English Renaissance style's individual character and distinctiveness. As the last country to experience the Renaissance, England accepts its design principles only after a period of resistance. Because most English contacts with the Renaissance come second-hand through trade, foreign craftsmen, or architectural pattern books, examples are highly eclectic and hardly classical until the work of Inigo Jones in the early 17th century.

CHARACTERISTICS AND MOTIFS

- *Tudor (1495–1558)*. Late Gothic and a few Renaissance characteristics freely mix in the period. Some symmetry and order are evident.
- *Elizabethan (1558–1603)*. Regularity, symmetry, and combinations of classical and Mannerist elements characterize design. Decoration tends to be lavish, particularly in interiors and on furniture. Foreign influences dominate.
- *Jacobean (1603–1642)*. Named after King James, Jacobean (Latin word for James) follows Elizabethan patterns, but with less individuality and more stylistic unity than the previous period. Interiors remain lavishly decorated, but furniture design is simpler.
- *Motifs*. Motifs (Fig. 15-1) include (a) Tudor roses, heraldic symbols, (c) strapwork, roundels, portrait busts, arabesques, grotesques, obelisks, caryatids, cabochons, acanthus, and (d) vines. Interior paneling designs include (b) linenfold, (c) composite, and arcaded (Fig. 15-11). Many are copied or adapted from pattern books. Architectural features (Fig. 15-3, 15-4, 15-5, 15-6, 15-8, 15-11, 15-12) vary in design during the period and gradually begin to include classical features such as columns, pilasters, and arcades.

(a)

(b)

(c)

(d)

▲ **15-1.** Motifs and Architectural Details: (a) Tudor rose, (b) linenfold panel, (c) strapwork and composite panel, (d) pargework ceiling with vine and leaf motifs.

ARCHITECTURE

Henry VIII brings some Italian craftsmen to England early in his reign, but they have little influence. By Elizabeth's time, Englishmen know of Italian and Ancient Roman treatises, particularly those of Serlio and Vitruvius, but French interpretations of Italian Mannerism and French and Flemish architectural treatises have significantly more influence. In the Jacobean period, numerous foreign craftsmen arrive in England and spread an even more exaggerated form of Mannerism as interpreted by Hans Vredeman de Vries and Wendall Dietterlien.

A gradual increase in order, regularity, and emphasis on proportions characterizes the Renaissance in England. Architecture shows more application of Renaissance details to buildings over the period, but designs borrow from numerous sources. Architecture does not fully embrace classical design principles until later, with the exception of buildings completed by Inigo Jones. English buildings more closely resemble French than Italian buildings because of similar climatic attributes that necessitate large windows, steeply pitched roofs, and tall chimneys. The most common building types are mansions (Fig. 15-5, 15-7, 15-8), manor houses (Fig. 15-4), and townhouses in contrast to Italy where primary Renaissance expressions are churches and palaces. England has numerous churches from the Middle Ages, and the monarchs do not undertake large building campaigns.

■ *Tudor*. Houses are less fortified and formal than earlier but continue to center on courtyards. Façades are irregular and often move in and out, roofs vary in composition and height, and windows are random sizes (Fig. 15-4). Elements from military architecture, such as towers and battlements, decorate façades. Distinctive towered gatehouses form entrances. Half-timbered construction (Fig. 15-2) continues in both urban and rural locations.

▲ **15-2.** Harvard House and Garrick Inn, 1485–1660; Stratfordshire, England.

▲ **15-3.** Doorway, Ham House, 17th century; Richmond-upon-Thames, England.

■ *Elizabethan*. Horizontal emphasis and regularity on the lower portions distinguish Elizabethan buildings (Fig. 15-5). Roofs have irregular silhouettes composed of parapets, balustrades, pinnacles, lanterns, towers, roofs, and chimneys similar to those of France and Flanders. The scale of Elizabethan architecture is grander than that of the Tudor period. Plans and ornamentation come from Italian, Flemish, German, and Dutch sources. Designs are highly individual.

■ *Jacobean*. Jacobean buildings show more stylistic unity than Elizabethan buildings, although eclecticism and foreign influences remain strong. Towers, turrets, and parapets define rooflines, which are less complex than those of the Elizabethan period. Classical features, such as the orders, usually are confined to ornamental fronts (Fig. 15-5).

Private Buildings

■ *Site Orientation*. Because of more settled conditions, houses become more outward looking throughout the period. From the Elizabethan period onward, country houses are set in parks surrounded by lawns, terraces, and gardens (Fig. 15-4, 15-5, 15-8). A forecourt with gatehouse and lodges marks the entrance. On one side of the house is a formal garden, often with an intricate design of beds, paths, and fountains. Orchards and kitchen gardens occupy spaces on the other sides of the house. Garden designs relate to the house but the two are not necessarily unified.

■ *Floor Plans*. Tudor and Elizabethan (Fig. 15-5) plans consist of rooms organized around one or more quadrangular courtyards. Spaces are organized for comfort and function instead of defense as earlier, and arrangements vary greatly. Asymmetry in plan layout is common.

During the Elizabethan and Jacobean periods, courtyards are replaced by more compact H-shaped, E-shaped, U-shaped, or rectangular plans. Symmetry still is only minimally important, so plan outlines are irregular with projecting bays and corner towers. Most spaces are rectangular but not necessarily symmetrical. Symmetry in door and window placement increases in the period.

Room dimensions do not derive from mathematical formulas until Inigo Jones and his followers (Fig. 15-6, 15-7, 15-8), who use such mathematical formulas as the double cube.

Rooms vary in scale according to a hierarchy of use as well as the significance of the house. Monumentality equates with importance. The great chamber (Fig. 15-5), the most richly decorated room in the house, begins to supersede the great hall (Fig. 15-4, 15-10) in importance during the Elizabethan period. The approach to the great chamber is ceremonial and designed to impress. Attached to the great chamber are one or more withdrawing rooms, one of which usually is the owner's bedchamber. Long galleries are characteristic features of Elizabethan houses (Fig. 15-5). They occupy one side of the house on the ground or first floor and often give access to important rooms. The number of

DESIGN SPOTLIGHT

Architecture and Interior: Built for the Compton family, Compton Wynuates, a brick and half-timber manor house depicts the character of the Tudor period. Unlike earlier dwellings, the house is more outward looking and centers on courtyards. The façade projects in and out, the roofs vary in design and height, numerous chimneys highlight the steeply pitched roofs, and windows are different in shapes and sizes. The appearance is jumbled and irregular, lacking any symmetry. Elements of fortification, such as battlements and towers, punctuate the form and mingle with a few classical elements such as quoins. One enters through a small gate house roughly in the center. The interiors, which may vary in scale, have oak paneling and beamed ceilings. The banqueting hall remains largely medieval in feeling and decoration with half-timber construction, trussed ceiling, screen with linenfold paneling, minstrel's gallery, and simple furnishings. There are few colors or textiles to enliven the space.

▲ **15-4.** Compton Wynyates and Banqueting Hall, 1480–1520; Warwickshire, England.

smaller public and private spaces increases throughout the period. Suites of rooms, appropriate for royalty, distinguish homes built or enlarged to receive Elizabeth and her court as they travel during summers, making what is termed a Royal Progress. She requires a presence chamber for formal receptions, a privy chamber for private entertaining, a withdrawing chamber, a bedchamber, and a guard chamber. These spaces usually occupy two sides of a courtyard.

Staircases assume greater prominence during the Elizabethan period. Joining earlier straight forms are square or rectangular wooden stairs with landings at each turn. A more architectural form, the open-well staircase makes its first appearance at Knole c. 1605. In all types of staircases, the newels, balusters, handrails, and strings are massive in scale and covered with carved or painted strapwork and other ornamentation.

■ *Materials*. Most houses are trabeated masonry construction. Brick and stone (Fig. 15-4) begin to supplant wood during the Tudor period, although half-timbered houses (Fig. 15-2) continue to be built throughout the 16th century. Stone and brick become even more common during the Elizabethan period (Fig. 15-5). Many Jacobean houses are brick with stone quoins. Brick patterns include common bond, Dutch cross bond, Flemish bond, and England bond. The latter two are the most common.

■ *Façades*. Tudor houses (Fig. 15-4) are somewhat symmetrical with a few classical details. Common elements include battlements, towers, and gatehouses. Large, prominent windows characterize Elizabethan and Jacobean façades (Fig. 15-5). They are rarely flat because numerous bays and pavilions create a rhythmic sequence marked by stringcourses and pilasters. Lower portions of Elizabethan and Jacobean exteriors are regular and symmetrical with classical and other motifs and details. Roofs and skylines are highly irregular and picturesque in Elizabethan architecture, but become more simplified in Jacobean architecture. Both periods feature corner towers with parapets or dome-shaped roofs. Jacobean houses often have frontispieces decorated with a full range of classical and Mannerist details. Exceptions are Jones's buildings or those of his few followers (Fig. 15-6, 15-7, 15-8), which are symmetrical; carefully proportioned; and delineated with classical columns, pilasters, pediments, swags, and balustrades.

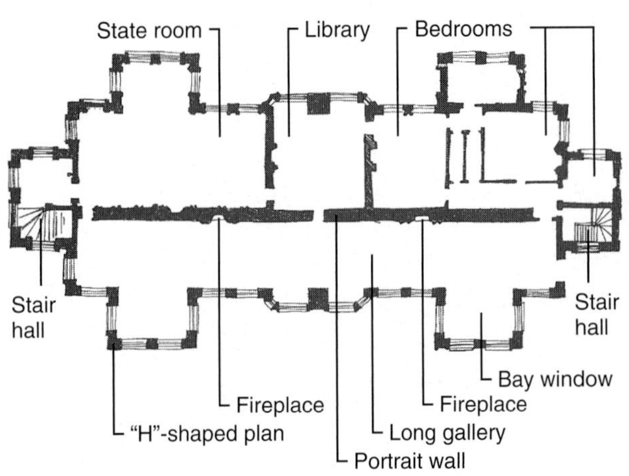

▲ **15-5.** Hardwick Hall, floor plan, Great Chamber, and Long Gallery, 1590–1597; Derbyshire, England; Robert Smythson.

DESIGN SPOTLIGHT

▲ **15-6.** Banqueting House and hall, Whitehall, 1619–1622; London, England; Inigo Jones.

Architecture and Interior: Designed by Inigo Jones and only partially completed, the Banqueting House at Whitehall illustrates his interpretation of Palladian classical theories and concepts in England. This building replaces an earlier Jacobean one, and Jones wanted to create a Palladian villa but the king wanted the entrance on one end in the medieval manner. They compromised with an insignificant side entry and classical façade. The façade has three stories with classical details and moldings distinguishing each story. Using mathematical proportions, Jones organized the symmetrical façade with bays composed of pilasters and engaged columns in the superimposed Ionic and Corinthian orders. Double pilasters mark the ends of the building, and four engaged columns accentuate the center of the two upper stories. The ground story, smaller than the other two, has the deepest rustication. Alternating triangular and segmental pediments adorn windows on the first floor, which, along with the second floor, is smoothly rusticated. Lintels supported by brackets distinguish the windows on the second floor. Above is a frieze composed of swags and masks. As with Renaissance buildings, a balustrade and heavy projecting cornice separate the roof from the walls.

Emulating the exterior, the double-cube banqueting hall uses the classical language of columns, pilasters, pediments, brackets, and a compartmented ceiling. White is the dominant color, with accents of gold. The ceiling paintings are by Peter Paul Rubens. The center shows the Apotheosis of James I. The space is used for banquets, royal receptions, ceremonies, and masques, which include music, singing, dancing, and acting.

▲ **15-7.** Queen's House, Greenwich, 1616–1635; London, England; Inigo Jones.

■ *Windows*. Windows on Tudor buildings vary from diamond-paned casements to larger rectangular examples (Fig. 15-2, 15-4). Stone mullions divide large rectangular windows into as many as 16 smaller lights in Elizabethan and Jacobean architecture (Fig. 15-5). Windows, symmetrically arranged over one another, may be flanked by pilasters or engaged columns. Bay windows and oriel windows contribute to the irregularity of plan and façade.

■ *Doors*. Door surrounds may be arched or rectangular and surmounted by a pediment or other decorative element (Fig. 15-3). Doors are located in the gatehouse of Tudor houses, centrally in Elizabethan houses, and in the frontispiece of Jacobean houses.

■ *Roofs*. Flat, gabled, parapet, and hipped roofs are common, and several may be combined (Fig. 15-2, 15-4, 15-5, 15-6, 15-7, 15-8). In addition to chimneys, parapets, and Flemish gables, Elizabethan and Jacobean houses often have towers and types with curvilinear roofs on the corners of exterior walls and interior

▲ **15-8.** Wilton House, c. 871–1653, and Double Cube Room with wall elevation (right), c. 1635–1653; Wiltshire, England; architectural addition and Double Cube Room by Inigo Jones (possibly) and John Webb; furnishings by Thomas Chippendale and William Kent, c. early 18th century.

courtyards. Roof towers sometimes become banqueting rooms where sweet wines and desserts are served after dinner.

■ *Later Interpretations*. During the English Restoration period, Jones's work influences Sir Christopher Wren. Tudor, Elizabethan, and Jacobean architecture and elements appear in English Regency, the American Stick Style (Fig. 15-9), English Arts and Crafts Movement, and Queen Anne architecture of the late 19th century. Tudor Revival houses are a popular alternative to Colonial Revival in late-19th- and early-20th-century America.

INTERIORS

Interiors of the period do not adopt the classical Renaissance characteristics as a whole, but often exhibit selected, mostly Mannerist, details that are copied from pattern books or executed by foreign craftsmen. Created as assemblages of decorative elements, these rooms lack the new unity evident elsewhere in Europe. As in architecture, the few interiors by Inigo Jones or his few followers (Fig. 15-6, 15-8) are exceptions. Throughout the period, other countries that are closer and have similar climates exert more influence than Italy. English designers and artisans rely on Italian, Flemish, French, and German pattern books for inspiration as well as specific details to embellish interior elements, such as panels, cornices, and chimneypieces.

Common spaces include the great hall (Fig. 15-4, 15-6, 15-10), great chamber (Fig. 15-5), long gallery (Fig. 15-5, 15-12), chapel, summer and winter parlors, and bedchambers (Fig. 15-11, 15-20) or lodgings.

▲ **15-8.** Continued

▲ **15-9.** Later Interpretation: Griswold House, 1862–1863; Newport, Rhode Island; Richard Morris Hunt; Stick Style.

■ *Tudor*. Interiors are largely medieval and somber in feeling (Fig. 15-4, 15-10). They exhibit few classical details, but as the period progresses, they grow more lively with colorful finishes and textiles.

■ *Elizabethan*. Interiors are exuberant with brilliant colors and nearly every surface decorated with carving, painting, gilding, or plasterwork (Fig. 15-5, 15-11). Classical details, mostly from Mannerist sources, are more evident than in Tudor buildings. Strapwork and grotesques are common motifs.

■ *Jacobean*. These interiors (Fig. 15-12) continue Elizabethan traditions of exuberant Mannerism with the exception of those by Inigo Jones (Fig. 15-6, 15-8) or influenced by him. Classically proportioned, Jones's work tends to rely more on architectural details for definition and interest than color or surface decoration.

Private Buildings

■ *Color*. Throughout the period, interiors feature highly saturated, even garish, colors in textiles and finishes. White walls are common especially if they have hangings. Occasionally, walls may be blue or green. Paneling generally is painted stone color or brown to resemble wood. Graining and marbling highlights some walls and/or architectural details. Ceilings are white or blue. As a contrast, Inigo Jones's interiors or those following his influence tend to be white or light colored.

■ *Floors*. Stone, brick, marble, and wood are common flooring materials (Fig. 15-4, 15-10, 15-11, 15-12). Hard plaster and tiles are used occasionally. The most common wood flooring is oak, either in random-width planks or parquet. All floors are usually covered with woven matting in summer (Fig. 15-5). Turkish and Persian carpets, imported since the Middle Ages, occasionally adorn floors; more often, because of their value, they cover tops of tables and cupboards. Needlepoint and other types of rugs also cover floors.

▲ **15-10.** Banqueting Hall, Haddon Hall, 1477–1545; Derbyshire, England.

▲ **15-12.** Cartoon Gallery, Knole, 1607–1608; Kent, England.

■ *Walls*. Wall paneling (Fig. 15-4, 15-10, 15-11) is usually of oak. Early in the period, panels are small and plain or with carved linenfold (called wavy work), Gothic motifs, or Romayne work. As time passes, panels become larger with more elaborate carving, and the wood is left natural or painted. Plaster walls (Fig. 15-6) are treated in a number of ways, including paint, hangings, and wallpapers. Paint may be in solid colors, stenciled in repeat patterns, embellished with elaborate arabesques and other complex designs, or decorated with mythological or biblical scenes. Hangings are of plain, patterned, or painted fabrics; imported or domestic tapestries (Fig. 15-5, 15-13); or leather. Some are embroidered or appliquéd. Use of wallpaper increases during the 16th century. A favorite pattern is heraldic devices in black and white.

▲ **15-11.** Bedchamber, Sizergh, 16th century; Westmoreland, England.

■ *Chimneypiece*. The chimneypiece (Fig. 15-5, 15-8) is a focal point in all three periods. Earlier ones have Tudor arches surrounded by paneling. By the 16th century, chimneypieces often have large rectangular openings with more elaborate mantels and overmantels of stone, marble, or wood. Columns or pilasters, strapwork, and cabochons often are taken from pattern books.

■ *Windows and Doors*. Windows may be casements, rectangles, bays, or oriels. Glass is expensive, so horn or blinds of cloth or canvas substitute for it in lesser houses. Small diamond lattice panes of glass leaded together are another alternative. Some glass is painted or stained. Great houses use curtains in winter as protection from the cold. Door panels generally match wainscoting. In larger houses, pilasters or columns supporting an entablature often flank doors. For extra emphasis, doors become a part of an interior porch that is elaborately carved and decorated with columns and strapwork. Curtains or portieres may also be used at doors.

■ *Ceilings*. Some Tudor ceilings have medieval trusses (Fig. 15-4, 15-10). Others are beamed or coffered (Fig. 15-20). During the Elizabethan period, most ceilings have elaborate plaster treatments or pargework (Fig. 15-1, 15-5, 15-11). The earliest designs are small and geometric, and later ones become more complex. Some ceilings copy Gothic ribbed vaulting with pendants. Others, and those of the Jacobean period (Fig. 15-12), display allover patterns of interlacing curved or geometric patterns with Tudor roses (Fig. 15-1), cartouches, strapwork, and scrolls. Sometimes color is applied. Plasterwork becomes compartmentalized (Fig. 15-6, 15-12) with the influence of Inigo Jones, who is thought to have introduced the cove ceiling in England.

▲ **15-14.** Textiles: Fabrics and wallpaper, 16th century; England.

▲ **15-13.** Tapestry, Hardwick Hall, 16th century; England.

■ *Textiles*. Numerous textiles (Fig. 15-5, 15-11, 15-13, 15-14) provide color, warmth, and comfort to royal and affluent interiors in all periods, but increase in luxury and refinement in the late 16th and early 17th centuries. Many types of imported and domestic fabrics and leathers adorn walls; hang at windows or doors; drape beds; and cover tables, cupboards, chairs, stools, and cushions. Types include wool and silk velvets; wool, silk, or blended damasks; satins; cut and uncut velvets from Genoa, Italy; plushes; gold or silver cloth; domestic and imported tapestries; and painted or resist-dyed cottons (chintzes and calicoes) imported from the Far East by the East India Company. Domestic linens, woolens, and imported silks are most common early in the period; cottons are rare until imported from India beginning in the late Elizabethan and early Jacobean periods. Textiles in a room do not match because dyes are not consistent. Colors include blue, crimson, russet, purple, green, yellow, pink, and black. Gold or silver fringe, lace, and tassels increase the sense of richness and luxury.

Wealthy homes often have chairs, stools, settees, and footstools completely covered with fabric and richly embellished (Fig. 15-5, 15-11, 15-17). Cushions provide additional comfort for chairs and stools. Large cushions may be used for sitting on the floor. Silk or wool damask or velvet cushions are trimmed with gold or silver lace, embroidery, braid, cord, and tassels. Table covers, which vary in length, usually are embroidered, trimmed, or otherwise embellished. In the mid-16th century, Turkey work or Norwich work, a textile that imitates Oriental rugs, becomes a common upholstery fabric. In the early 17th century, some bed hangings are made of crewel and are embroidered by the ladies of the house or by professional embroiderers. Typical patterns feature trees, flowers, and foliage rising from mounds combined with animals. Palampores, coverlets with similar painted and resist-dyed designs imported from India, occasionally are used for coverlets on beds or as hangings.

■ *Lighting*. Artificial lighting (Fig. 15-10, 15-15) is minimal, consisting of chandeliers or lanterns, wall sconces, and candlesticks in wood, brass, iron, or silver.

▲ **15-15.** Lighting: Candlesticks in iron and metal.

FURNISHINGS AND DECORATIVE ARTS

As in architecture, Renaissance design elements gradually appear. Types, which include seating, tables, storage pieces, and beds, remain limited and do not vary much from earlier times.As in other countries, English rooms have little furniture, and it lines the walls when not in use. Although declining, the practice of placing the best bed in the hall or great chamber continues until the end of the 16th century.

Joiners continue to construct Tudor furniture following simple medieval traditions. Construction becomes more sophisticated during Queen Elizabeth's reign. In the late 16th century, Flemish craftsmen reintroduce board construction, which uses dovetails to make wide pieces and enables makers to use veneer. Joined construction gradually dies out except in rural areas. Carving and inlay are the main types of decoration for furniture in all periods. Surface richness is more important than the quality of the carving.

Early in the 16th century, London becomes a center for furniture making. Numerous English, French, Flemish, Dutch, and German artisans open shops in the city and introduce Renaissance design elements and finer construction techniques. Furniture making begins to require the skills of several craftsmen instead of only the joiner as in the Middle Ages. Craftsmen begin to specialize as carvers, joiners, turners, and metalworkers.

■ *Tudor*. Tudor furniture is similar to medieval furniture in form and decoration (Fig. 15-4, 15-10). Renaissance elements mix, often incongruously, with Gothic elements. Romayne work is characteristic.

■ *Elizabethan*. Elizabethan furniture is massive with heavy proportions, rich carving, and inlay. It shows strong Flemish influence along with classical elements (Fig. 15-11, 15-16, 15-19, 15-20). The heavy, elaborately carved, bulbous support is a definitive characteristic of Elizabethan and Jacobean furniture. Originally from the Low Countries, it is called a cup and cover or melon support. Early examples are very large, but gradually decrease in size and amount of embellishment. Strapwork (Fig. 15-1), geometric decoration or inlay, and gadrooning are common details. Rooms may have more furniture than Tudor rooms, but continue relying on textiles and surface decorations for interest. A desire for comfort increases the use of upholstery.

■ *Jacobean*. Jacobean furniture continues Elizabethan traditions, but is simpler with more formal and naturalistic carving. Strapwork, arabesques, lozenges, applied pendants, and split baluster turnings are characteristic. Upholstery continues to increase in use. As earlier, rooms have few furnishings.

Private Buildings

■ *Materials*. Most furniture is of oak. A few Jacobean pieces are of walnut.

■ *Seating*. Seating includes chairs, settees, daybeds, stools, benches, and settles (Fig. 15-4, 15-5, 15-11, 15-12, 15-16, 15-17). Legs may be turned, chamfered, or fluted. They usually terminate in bun feet. Stretchers are plain and close to the floor.

Three main types of chairs are turned (turneyed or thrown, an old term for turning), X-form folding chairs (Fig. 15-11), and wainscot chairs (Fig. 15-16). The farthingale chair or back stool appears at the end of the 16th century (Fig. 15-17). During the Elizabethan and Jacobean periods, sets of furnishings in matching fabrics are introduced. *Daybed* is a modern term for a long seat with a fixed or adjustable inclined end, which resembles a chair back. They are introduced in the 16th century. Some in the 17th century have two adjustable ends and closely resemble a sofa. Joined stools, relatively common items, consist of an oblong seat, turned or fluted columnar legs, and a continuous stretcher near the floor. They may be upholstered and/or have cushions. Some Elizabethan benches are of trestle form with splayed solid supports. Settles, which may be movable or built in, have high backs and paneled arms and sides.

■ *Tables*. During the Elizabethan period, tabletops become fixed to their supports, and the drawtop is introduced. The principal table form is long, narrow, and rectangular with gadrooning on the top edges and aprons with inlay of geometric shapes. Other types include small tables imported from Flanders, Italy, and France. Tables intended to be covered with cloths or carpets are simply constructed of plain wood (Fig. 15-11, 15-20). The gateleg or falling table becomes common after its introduction in the early 17th century.

DESIGN SPOTLIGHT

Furniture: The wainscot chair, an important chair type, has a paneled back, turned legs, and stretchers. The back decoration varies to include carved motifs such as the lozenge, Tudor rose, arcaded panel, acanthus, and strapwork. Usually made of oak with open arms, the chair is often placed against a paneled wainscot wall. The more visible front legs are more ornate than the back legs. Cushions are often added for comfort.

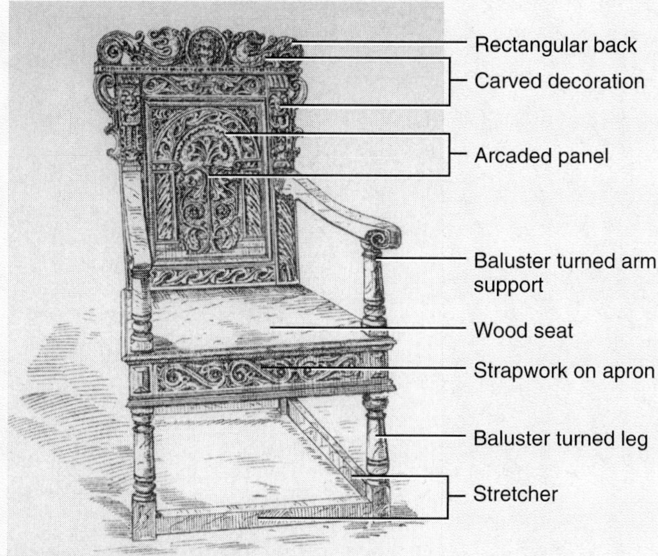

▲ **15-16.** Wainscot chair; England.

▲ **15-17.** Side chair with turned legs.

▲ **15-18.** Nonesuch chest, late 16th century.

■ *Storage.* Case pieces (Fig. 15-10, 15-18, 15-19) include chests for storage, cupboards for display in the hall or great chamber, and chests of drawers (introduced from the Continent late in the 16th century). Early chests of drawers are massive in scale, and doors conceal the drawers. The court cupboard (Fig. 15-19), coming from France at the end of the 16th century, consists of open shelves about 48″ high. Richly carved, it displays plate in the hall or great chamber. Cupboards vary greatly in design. One type has a closed upper portion resting on an open stand. On another the upper portion is divided into thirds with canted panels on either side of a central panel. A third type combines doors in the upper portion and drawers in the lower.

■ *Beds.* The most common beds (Fig. 15-11, 15-20) are wooden boxes covered and draped with fabric or draped four-posters. Some are massive with heavy turned posts and a tester with architectural moldings. The headboard usually is heavily carved with architectural and naturalistic motifs. Sometimes the two footposts are detached from the bed frame to allow draperies to enclose the bed. Because of the textiles, the bed is the most expensive piece of furniture in the home.

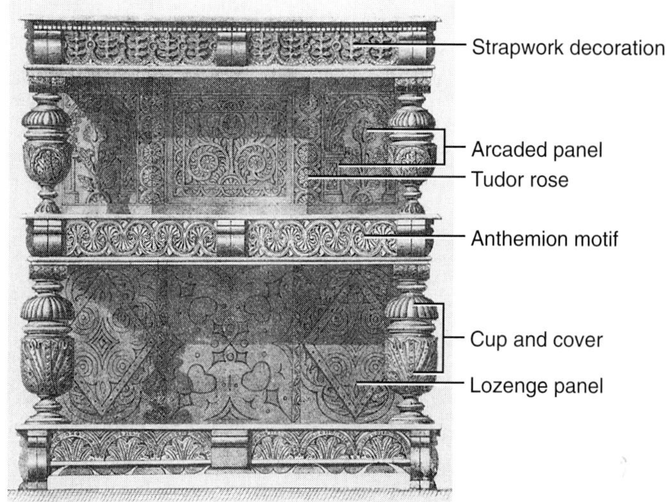

▲ **15-19.** Court cupboard, late 16th–early 17th centuries.

■ *Bed Hangings*. Rich hangings (Fig. 15-11, 15-20) not only provide warmth, but also demonstrate rank and status. A set of hangings includes the head cloth, ceiler, valances, bases, curtains on all four sides, and the counterpoint or counterpane or coverlet. Hangings do not necessarily match other textiles in the room and may combine different colors and/or types of fabrics including gold or silver cloth. Braid, tape, fringe, lace, embroidery, and tassels embellish hangings. Valances often have complicated outlines emphasized by tape and trims.

■ *Decorative Arts*. Tableware is made of wood, silver, horn, or glass. From Italy and the Netherlands comes tin-glazed earthenware (*faience* or delft, respectively). Objects made of silver or gold include saltcellars, sconces, plates, ewers and basins, flagons, drinking vessels, spoons, spice boxes, and snuffers. Many are large and elaborately decorated or encrusted with jewels. Stylistically, silver follows the other arts in slowly adopting Renaissance motifs. Other accessories are portraits, paintings, and armor. As the English begin their domination of the seas, imports include Chinese porcelains, Venetian glass, and metal work from different countries.

▲ **15-20.** Henry VIII's bedchamber, Hever Castle, c. 15th century; Kent, England.

CHAPTER 16

American Colonial: England, Spain, France, Germany, and Holland

17th–19th Centuries

> *. . . their Lord hath been pleased to turn all the wigwams, huts, and hovels the English dwelt in at their first coming, into orderly, fair, and well-built houses, well furnished many of them, together with Orchards filled with goodly fruit trees, and gardens with variety of flowers. . . .*
>
> —Edward Johnson, *Wonder-Working Providence of Sions Saviour in New England (1654), p. 211 of the 1910 edition*; from Morrison, Hugh. *Early American Architecture*. Oxford, England: Oxford University Press, 1952.

Beginning in the late 16th century, colonists from Europe begin arriving in the New World. They come for many reasons. Some immigrate to escape religious persecution. Others seek religious or political freedom or wealth. Some are aristocrats, but most are not. These English, Spanish, French, German, and Dutch settlers bring social and cultural traditions of their homelands with them. They recreate the buildings, interiors, and furnishings they had known at home, including materials (where possible) and construction methods. Most settlers are of the working classes so are not acquainted with the high-style Renaissance. Consequently, their material culture is medieval and vernacular in character, with the exception of the Spanish whose mission buildings sometimes have a more up-to-date appearance.

Each country administers its territory differently, which affects settlement patterns and material culture. Settling along the eastern seaboard of the present United States, the English are primarily farmers who raise crops or produce other raw materials to ship to the mother country. France builds outposts in strategic locations to administer her vast holdings, which stretch from present-day Canada to Louisiana. Settlers are relatively few. In the southwest and present-day Mexico, Spanish Catholic priests build missions to evangelize native people, and some colonial governors build palaces. Germans settle first in Pennsylvania, and some migrate westward to Texas and other locations. Early Dutch settlements in New York are quickly ceded to England.

ENGLAND 1608–1720

HISTORICAL AND SOCIAL

The English establish their first permanent settlement in Jamestown, Virginia, in 1607. In 1620, a group of Separatists or Puritans settle in Plymouth, Massachusetts, followed by additional colonies in Rhode Island and Connecticut. Colonies, which increase in number throughout the second half of the 17th and early 18th centuries, include North Carolina, South Carolina, New Jersey, New York (taken from the Dutch in the mid–17th century), Pennsylvania, Maryland, and Georgia. In the second half of the 17th century, immigrants from other areas of Europe comingle with the English settlers, including the Dutch and French Huguenots.

English colonists vary in wealth, social standing, and religion, which gives rise to different patterns of settlement and types of material culture. New Englanders are mainly middle-class farmers, yeomen, and artisans, many of whom have come to America for religious freedom. They live on small, self-sufficient farms united by villages until the second half of the 17th century. As they prosper through trade and commerce, they move to urban centers, such as Boston, which become populous and thriving. In contrast, Southern immigrants usually are artisans, farmers, and gentlemen with little concern for religious freedoms. Settlements form around large farms or plantations raising tobacco and other crops with few large urban centers until after the American Revolution. Busy with agriculture, Southerners import clothing, furnishings, and other items from London, so little is made in the colony.

CONCEPTS AND MOTIFS

Architecture, interiors, and furniture of the English settlers reflect the forms with which they are familiar—mostly vernacular and medieval house and furniture types that have passed from generation to generation. Most are unfamiliar with classicism as they immigrate before the general adoption of the Renaissance in England. By the end of the 17th century, however, prosperous colonists adopt the latest English fashions.

■ *Motifs*. Architecture and interiors are plain and unadorned but motifs for furniture (Fig. 16-1, 16-13) include flowers, scrolls, strapwork, or geometric shapes. Typical William and Mary motifs (Fig. 16-9) are C and S scrolls, baluster shapes, and balls.

▲ **16-1.** Panel, joined chest, 1676; Ipswich, Massachusetts; attributed to Thomas Denis.

▲ **16-2.** Bruton Parish Church and interior, 1711–1715; Williamsburg, Virginia; plans by Alexander Spotswood.

ARCHITECTURE

The earliest shelters are primitive and temporary, but as soon as they are able, colonists construct the buildings like those in their homelands. At first, public buildings and houses are small and functional with little embellishment. As times settle and prosperity increases, larger structures in the Tudor, Elizabethan, or early classical modes become more common. Plans and materials vary with region, but most structures share such medieval characteristics as steeply pitched gable roofs, casement windows, and framed construction. The most important buildings are dwellings (Fig. 16-3, 16-5, 16-6), churches (Fig. 16-2), meetinghouses, collegiate buildings, roadhouses and inns, and a few statehouses.

Public and Private Buildings

■ *Site Orientation*. New England meetinghouses often are in town centers surrounded by a green space with dwellings and other structures nearby. This stresses their importance in settlers' social and political lives. In contrast, Southern churches are in rural and urban locations. Colonists usually build their homes near sources of water and/or transportation routes. Southern houses are more

▲ **16-3.** Adam Thoroughgood House, 1636–1640; Princess Anne County, Virginia.

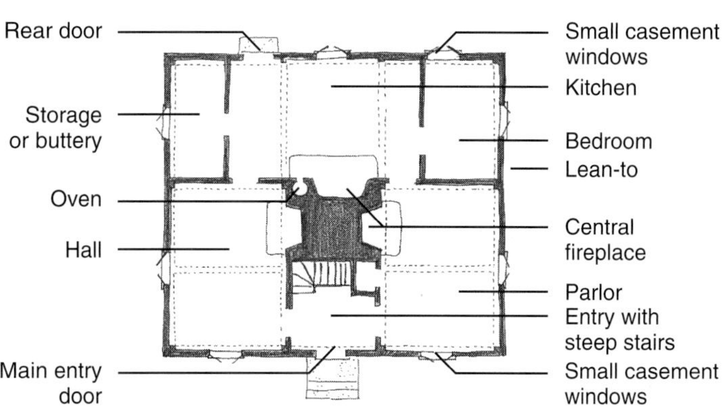

▲ **16-4.** Floor plan, hall and parlor house with lean-to, 17th century; Connecticut.

likely to have various outbuildings, such as kitchens, slave quarters, or stables.

■ *Floor Plans*. Church plans (Fig. 16-2) reflect worship patterns of Puritans (preaching) and Anglicans (preaching and ritual). Public buildings or statehouses resemble domestic structures in scale and composition.

Domestic plans (Fig. 16-4) in both New England and the South include the hall, the hall and parlor, and the lean-to within one, one and a half, or two stories. Rooms are added as more space is needed, following the additive principle of construction common to medieval-style buildings.

DESIGN SPOTLIGHT

Architecture: Representative of many New England wood-frame houses, the Parson Capen house, a 17th-century house built for Reverend Joseph Capen, reflects the English medieval tradition of a manor house in the New World. Like its English counterparts, it incorporates traditional wood-framing methods, second-story overhang or jetty with pendants on the front, another jetty also with pendants on the ends, steeply pitched roof, central chimney, and small windows (the sash windows are added later). Unlike English examples, unpainted clapboards replace half-timbering. Its excellent construction probably results from English trained artisans. Inside, the stair winds around the chimney, and the first floor consists of a hall or kitchen and parlor. They and the other interiors are plain, simple, large, and functional. Furnishings are sparse. This large dwelling asserts Reverend Capen's important position in the community. (National Historic Landmark)

▲ **16-5.** Parson Capen House, 1683; Topsfield, Massachusetts.

▲ **16-6.** Captain Thomas Newsom House, 1710; Wethersfield, Connecticut.

▲ **16-7.** Recreated interior with 17th-century fireplace and some furnishings; Ipswich, Massachusetts.

■ *Materials.* In New England, timber frame construction is common, and the spaces between timbers are filled with wattle and daub or brick for insulation. Finish materials include plaster, shingles, stone, or unpainted clapboards (Fig. 16-5, 16-6). Although surviving examples are made of brick (Fig. 16-3), most early Southern homes are of wooden timber frame construction.

■ *Façades.* Walls usually are plain and unarticulated (Fig. 16-3, 16-5, 16-6). Upper portions of New England houses are more visually complex with multiple roofs, dormers, and chimneys. The second story overhangs the first (jetty) in some houses and pendants adorn the lower portions of the jetty. Embellishment on Southern houses includes stepped chimneys, decorative brickwork, and dormers. Chimneys in both regions are large and prominent and on the ends or center of the building.

■ *Windows and Doors.* Small and placed where needed, windows may be covered with oiled paper or horn, or have shutters. Some structures have casements with small leaded diamond panes (Fig. 16-3, 16-5). Most doors are board-and-batten.

■ *Roofs.* Steeply-pitched gabled or gambrel roofs are of thatch or wood hand-riven shingles (Fig. 16-3, 16-5, 16-6).

▲ **16-8.** Hall and chamber (Hart Room), Hart House, before 1674; Ipswich, Massachusetts. [Courtesy, Winterthur Museum]

▲ **16-9.** Wentworth Room, originally second-floor chamber of John Wentworth House, late 17th century; Portsmouth, New Hampshire. [The Metropolitan Museum of Art, Stage Fund, 1926 (26.290). The Metropolitan Museum of Art, New York, NY, U.S.A. Image © The Metropolitan Museum of Art/Art Resource, NY.].

INTERIORS

Early interiors, like exteriors, follow vernacular medieval traditions. Scale is modest, function is important, and structure is visible. Textures are rough, ceilings are low, and large fireplaces dominate rooms. Rooms are multifunctional as furnishings attest. Exceptions are colonial governors who live in larger houses and bring more up-to-date furnishings with them. As times become more settled and people prosper, interiors become more refined and follow the latest English fashions. Colonists travel to England and bring back fashionable items or order them from London suppliers. Local craftsmen, who are often recent immigrants, are familiar with the newest fashions in interiors and furnishings.

In domestic structures, the hall is the center of family life, where cooking, eating, and socializing take place (Fig. 16-4). When present, the parlor or best chamber holds the family's treasured possessions, including the best bed. Upstairs rooms or chambers have few furnishings, mostly chests and beds, suggesting that people spend little time there.

Private Buildings

■ *Colors*. Most often colors come from materials such as the brown of wood, the white or cream of plaster, and the gray of a stone hearth or wall. Color accents, which come mainly from textiles and painted furniture, are earth tones of Indian red, indigo, ochre, olive, and black (Fig. 16-8). Highly saturated accent colors do not necessarily match. By the mid-17th century, paneled fireplace walls, baseboards, chair rails, and cornices are painted in various tones of brown, buff, red, gray, green, and blue (Fig. 16-9).

■ *Floors*. Floors are dirt, pressed clay, or random-width oak planks laid at right angles to floor joists. Most are unfinished; the few carpets are used as table coverings among the wealthy (Figure 16-9).

▲ **16-10.** Lighting: Lantern, betty lamps, and candlestick.

■ *Walls*. Walls are clay-daubed, plastered, or palisade (Fig. 16-7, 16-8, 16-9). Plaster is usually whitewashed. Late in the period, paneling with rectangular panel shapes and beveled edges defines fireplace walls. Wallpaper and textile hangings are rare except among the wealthy until late in the period. Huge fireplaces with no mantel dominate rooms and are used for heat, light, and cooking. A wood lintel caps the opening. Bolection mantels appear late in the period (Fig. 16-9).

■ *Ceilings*. Ceilings are low and beamed, with a sturdy center summer beam supporting the cross beams (Fig. 16-7, 16-8). Sometimes beams are painted or chamfered.

■ *Textiles*. Textiles are rare and are used mostly for cushions and bed hangings and to cover backs, seats, cupboards, and/or tables. Red, green, and blue are favorite colors. Most are imported from England; leather, linen, and wool are more common than silk.

■ *Lighting*. Fireplaces and a few candles or oil lamps provide minimal artificial lighting (Fig. 16-8, 16-9, 16-10). Iron, tin, or pewter floor candle stands and table candlesticks are unembellished. Only churches and important public buildings have chandeliers.

■ *Later Interpretations*. The earliest of English Colonial rooms are not often copied, except in kitchens, modern keeping rooms and sometimes dining rooms (Fig. 16-11).

▲ **16-11.** Later Interpretation: Dining room, Arthur Whitney House, c. 1920s; Bernardsville, New Jersey.

FURNISHINGS AND DECORATIVE ARTS

Colonists bring little furniture with them from Europe, so the earliest furniture is very simple and often quickly and crudely made. As times grow more settled, settlers begin to purchase or copy furniture in the newest modes. Furniture often has an architectural character with heavy joined construction, overhanging upper portions, and applied pendants. Like interiors, furniture is often multifunctional. Some rooms, usually the hall, are filled with furniture, particularly seating. Chairs line walls when not in use. Chambers usually have several beds.

Furniture in the Colonies closely follows English models. Early examples have Elizabethan and Jacobean forms and details with shallow carving, spiral turning, split baluster spindles, and applied bosses. Joined construction is typical. By the end of the 17th century, William and Mary characteristics, such as smaller scale and lighter weight, are evident. Trumpet legs with bun or Spanish feet replace earlier baluster ones. Furniture also employs more sophisticated cabinetmaking techniques, such as intricate joints, veneering, and inlay.

Private Buildings

■ *Materials*. Early furniture is of red or white oak and pine. Joiners often combine woods in a single piece. Chairs and case pieces may be painted in various combinations of black, red, yellow, white, and green. The William and Mary style of the later 17th century uses walnut, cherry, and maple. Turning and carving are more common than painting as embellishment.

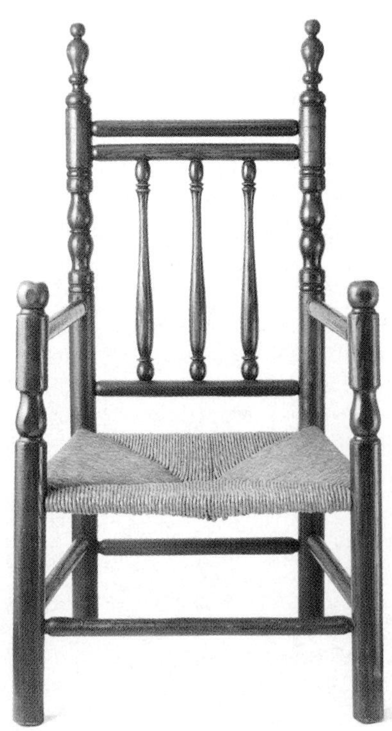

▲ **16-12.** Carver chair, late 17th century; New Haven County, Connecticut.

DESIGN SPOTLIGHT

Furniture: Chests are important storage pieces in the colonies. Made by joiners, chests follow medieval traditions in construction, form, and decoration. This rectangular chest, distinctive to the Wethersfield area of southern Connecticut, has a hinged storage area fronted with three panels over two rows of drawers. A definitive characteristic is the carved decoration of stylized tulips, vines, and Tudor roses, which are sometimes mistaken for sunflowers, in the front panels. All these motifs are found in England as are the split baluster turnings painted black that ornament the upper and lower stiles. Drawers, as here, sometimes have geometric designs and/or oval bosses. Two-drawer chests are rare in England but more common in the colonies. Oak is the preferred material for construction and paint usually accents knobs, applied decoration, and carving.

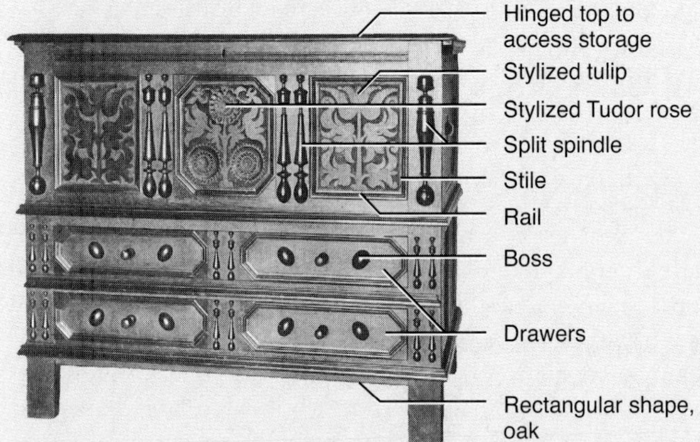

▲ **16-13.** Connecticut or Wethersfield chest, 17th century; Hartford, Connecticut.

■ *Seating*. Turned chairs with and without arms are the most common (Fig. 16-7, 16-12). Other types include the wainscot (Fig. 16-8) and farthingale (back stool) or Cromwellian chairs. Chairs with cane seats and backs are the most popular in the William and Mary period (Fig. 16-9), followed by banister-back chairs.

■ *Tables*. The most common tables are refectory, round, and oval. Gateleg tables or falling tables (Fig. 16-9) and dressing tables appear at the end of the century.

■ *Storage*. Wall pegs perform many storage functions, but boxes and chests, used for both storage and seating, are important possessions. Based on English prototypes, chests are usually elaborately carved and painted or paneled. Scholars have identified several types of chests based upon decoration and location. These include elaborately carved Hadley chests from Massachusetts, and two groups from coastal or southern Connecticut. The latter, known as Connecticut or Wethersfield chests (Fig. 16-13), are characterized by stylized English Tudor roses. Cupboards (Fig. 16-8) are luxury pieces intended to impress. Most have both open shelves and enclosed storage spaces.

■ *Beds*. Bed types (Fig. 16-8) include those with heavy posts and paneled headboards, turned types, and simple ones intended to be covered with hangings. Draped beds are the most costly item in the home and are often placed in the parlor as a sign of wealth. Trundles and palettes are common, especially for children and servants.

■ *Decorative Arts*. Decorative arts, as such, are limited to necessities in most homes, particularly early in the period. Earthenware and stoneware are most common ceramics, but English and Dutch tin-glazed earthenwares are also used. Tableware is usually wood or pewter.

SPAIN 1600–1840s

The history of Spanish Colonial architecture, over a period of nearly 300 years, embraces a span of time nearly as long as the whole history of American architecture in other regions. The Spanish also differs from all other Colonial styles in its complete departure from the medieval.

—Hugh Morrison, *Early American Architecture: From the First Colonial Settlements to the National Period*, 1952

HISTORICAL AND SOCIAL

Following the voyages of Christopher Columbus, Spain establishes her first colony in Santo Domingo, Hispaniola (present-day Dominican Republic and Haiti), in 1496. By 1600, her New World possessions include present-day Puerto Rico, Mexico, Latin America, Peru, and Chile. She also colonizes the present-day southwestern United States and Florida.

The earliest permanent settlement in the United States is at S. Augustine, Florida, founded in 1565. A military outpost, the city is sacked and burned several times, so only a few houses and other structures before 1740 survive. Following an occupation between 1763 and 1783, England formally returns Florida to Spain at the end of the American Revolution. Florida becomes part of the United States in 1821.

From the middle of the 16th to the 19th centuries, Spain dominates the Southwestern United States and Mexico (Fig. 16-15), but she will cede much of this territory to the United States after the Mexican War in the 1840s. Unlike other colonists who are farmers, artisans, and tradespeople, priests, seeking to convert locals to Catholicism, carry out much of the work of Spanish colonization, particularly in Mexico and the Southwest. Compared to the English colonies, the Southwest is sparsely populated. It also lacks the timber and natural resources found along the East Coast and in the central United States.

CONCEPTS AND MOTIFS

More than other colonists, the Spanish use impressive buildings to establish and emphasize individual, governmental, or church authority and power. Spanish buildings show more influences from the Spanish Renaissance and Baroque periods. However, these styles are interpreted in a provincial way as planners contend with local conditions, materials, and labor forces.

■ *Motifs*. Spanish Renaissance and Baroque motifs mix with those derived from the Native American culture. Common (Fig. 16-14, 16-16) are columns, *estípite*, niche-pilasters, *zapatas*, scrolls, garlands, swags, and foliated windows. Other motifs (Fig. 16-17), mainly evident in decoration, include geometric shapes, concentric circles, colored stripes, floral and herringbone patterns, shells, animals, and various symbols.

▲ **16-14.** Rose window, small chapel, *Mission S. José y S. Miguel de Aguayo*, 1768–1782; San Antonio, Texas.

ARCHITECTURE

Mission and parish churches are the main surviving Spanish public building types in the United States. Mission churches (Fig. 16-16, 16-17) in the Southwest intend to impress new converts with the power and majesty of the Christian god and the Catholic Church. Designs range from the unornamented geometric *adobe* forms of New Mexico and California to the domed and vaulted stone compositions with highly decorative portals in Texas and Arizona. Later California missions reflect the Neoclassical style with a few classical elements evident. Dwellings, which include palaces (Fig. 16-18, 16-19, 16-20), are planned for protection from the harsh, arid climate and hostile attacks rather than stylistic imitation. Materials and construction methods dictate a form that is unlike Spanish prototypes, although some characteristics, such as courtyards, are adapted.

Public and Private Buildings—New Mexico, Texas, Arizona, and California

■ *Floor Plans*. Churches may have a Latin cross or a simple plan composed only of a nave. For protection, dwellings have linear plans with a single row of rooms arranged on one side of or around one or more *patios*. As times become more settled, houses become more outward looking with more windows, doors, and porches (Fig. 16-19).

▲ **16-15.** Mexico City Metropolitan Cathedral, 1563–1667; Mexico City, Mexico.

- *Materials.* Southwestern missions adopt the *adobe* (Fig. 16-17) construction of the Native Americans who build them. Wood is scarce, so its use is limited to door and window frames and roofs. The stone churches in Mexico, Texas, and Arizona (Fig. 16-16), constructed by Spanish artisans with minimal local labor, use more sophisticated construction methods.
- *Façades.* Most mission façades (Fig. 16-16) maintain a general Spanish/European appearance with towers, parapet walls, and surface decoration concentrated around openings and contrasting with plain walls. Although some are very plain and composed of simple geometric forms (Fig. 16-17), others have more lavish ornament that may combine Gothic, Islamic, Renaissance, and Baroque characteristics. Two bell towers usually flank entrances and may serve as massive buttresses. Most windows are rectangular casements or sashes. In Texas, Arizona, and California, elaborate quatrefoil or foliated windows (Fig. 16-14) identify important interior spaces such as chapels. Decorative *rejas* are common on important structures with strong Spanish Renaissance influences. Carved wooden doors are usually set within arched or rectangular openings with simple surrounds in New Mexico. In other areas, complicated carved and sometimes painted decoration surrounds entrances and extends to the roofline as in high-style Spanish prototypes.

DESIGN SPOTLIGHT

Architecture: As in the smaller and simpler Spanish *adobe* missions, simple geometry defines the form and silhouette of *San Xavier del Bac*, but the stone structure more closely resembles examples in Spain and is more sophisticated in design. Plain walls contrast with the surface ornament that concentrates at the entrance. Stringcourses and large volutes highlight the upper portions of the bell towers. The polychrome portal ornament, composed of figures, animals, scrolls, and naturalistic elements, is low in relief but crisply carved. *Estipites* identify the façade as Baroque. Also in the Baroque tradition is the close design relationship between the portal and the *retable* behind the altar inside. (National Historic Landmark)

▲ **16-16.** *San Xavier del Bac*, 1767–1797; near Tucson, Arizona; Ignacio Gaoma.

Early façades on dwellings are plain with few windows and doors. Later examples have more windows, doors, porches, and portals with *zapatas*. *Vigas* may protrude through upper portions of *adobe* walls. Most windows are casements, which are largely replaced by sashes in the 18th century. Vertical plank exterior shutters are common in the 18th century. Doors are vertical planks or carved wood on grand houses.

▲ **16-17.** *San Diego de Alcala* Basilica and nave, 1774, rebuilt in 1803, 1812; San Diego, California. This was the first mission to be built in California.

■ *Roofs*. *Adobe* buildings have flat roofs whereas gabled or hipped roofs and/or domes are common on stone structures. Early missions have thatched roofs, replaced later with fireproof red clay roof tiles, which become the standard treatment.

INTERIORS

The theme of many Spanish public and private interiors is contrast—of colors, shapes, and light and dark. Church interiors (Fig. 16-17) often contrast their plain exteriors with voluminous spaces, plain walls, decorative paintings, and complex carved *reredos*. Some use such Baroque devices as light, sculpture, paintings, and architecture to impress or inspire. Stone churches in Texas, Arizona, California, and Mexico have barrel and groin vaulted ceilings in naves and aisles with domes at crossings and at the arms of transepts. They may use pilasters, engaged columns, and moldings to articulate and accentuate the architecture.

Interiors of houses (Fig. 16-20) usually have whitewashed walls that contrast with dark wood trim and dirt or wooden floors. They are sparsely but often luxuriously and colorfully furnished. The main spaces in the larger homes are the *sala*, chapel, dining hall, and bedchamber. The *sala* is decorated and furnished to impress. Main bedchambers are often located near the entry or open to the *patio*.

Public and Private Buildings

■ *Color*. Contrasting colors of different types of stone may accentuate architectural features on churches. Nearly all churches and a few palaces have some decorative paintings on walls, ceilings, vaults, domes, and/or pendentives when present. Colors, such as red, yellow, blue, and green, are highly saturated.
■ *Floors*. Floors may be of stone, hard-packed earth, or unglazed clay tiles in both public and private buildings (Fig. 16-17, 16-20). Upper floors in houses, when present, are of wood planks.
■ *Walls*. Walls (Fig. 16-17, 16-20) may be of plaster, *adobe*, or stone. Walls in churches usually have few architectural details. In

▲ **16-18.** Governor's Palace, c. 1610, restored in 19th century; Santa Fe, New Mexico.

houses, walls rarely are decorated with architectural details or paintings except in palaces. Dark wood beams, trim, and furniture contrast with whitewashed walls. Decorative tiles may embellish baseboards and steps.

■ *Ceilings.* Heavy cross beams or logs supported by carved wooden brackets often compose ceilings in churches and dwellings (Fig. 16-17, 16-20). Smaller logs or poles between beams are placed at a diagonal and may be painted in bands of red, yellow, white, and black. Beamed ceilings in houses may feature painted and gilded decorations.

■ *Textiles.* The local craftsmen and Native Americans provide textiles for beds, wall hangings, and rugs for floors. Textile use is limited until trade with the East Coast and the Orient increases availability. Calico commonly covers the lower portions of walls to prevent whitewash from rubbing off on people sitting on built-in benches. *Jergas*, flat woven woolen rugs in a twill weave with two colors, become common in the 19th century.

■ *Lighting.* Indirect and unexpected light sources create drama and mystery in churches. Churches with domes have windows in the drums and upper portions of ceilings to allow a mystical light to permeate interiors (Fig. 16-17). Artificial lighting (Fig. 16-20) mainly includes *torcheres*; *braccios*; and *lanternas*, candlesticks, and candle stands in iron, brass, or silver.

FURNISHINGS AND DECORATIVE ARTS

Numerous pieces of furniture and decorative arts accompany missionaries and settlers to the American colonies. At the missions, furniture production becomes the responsibility of Native Americans or local craftsmen guided by priests. Consequently, furniture follows Spanish prototypes but is more provincial and cruder. Furniture types include seating, chests, tables, and beds. Most is made of yellow pine or other local woods. Board construction for chests and case pieces continues long after it is outdated in English settlements. Simplicity in form and decoration are characteristic. Forms and supports are rectilinear, and decoration is painted or shallowly carved. Spindles are carved and often flat instead of turned. After the opening of the Santa Fe Trail in 1821, English influences appear in form, construction, and decoration.

▲ **16-19.** Thomas Larkin House, 1835–1837; Monterey, California.

Public and Private Buildings

■ *Seating.* Chairs and benches (Fig. 16-20) are the most common forms of seating. The Spanish colonial *frailero* is simpler than those of the mother country.

■ *Tables.* Wooden tables with rectangular tops and iron supports are found throughout *casas* and simpler houses. Most follow Spanish precursors and have curved or straight legs.

■ *Storage.* The most important storage pieces are the chest, *amario*, and *varqueño*.

■ *Beds.* Spanish Colonial beds are simple, plain, and utilitarian with little of the heavy decoration seen in the Spanish Renaissance examples.

■ *Decorative Arts.* The decorative arts display a fusion of Spanish and Native American characteristics. Accessories may be of Spanish Renaissance origin and design, made by local settlers, or produced by Native American craftspeople.

▲ **16-20.** *Sala*, Governor's Palace, 1749; San Antonio, Texas.

FRANCE
17th–LATE 19th CENTURIES

HISTORICAL AND SOCIAL

France establishes Quebec in 1608, a strategic location at the mouth of the S. Lawrence River that also is a gateway to the middle of the United States. For the next 75 years, she increases her holdings along the S. Lawrence River and Great Lakes and extends her territory through the entire Mississippi River Valley. France establishes forts to secure the Gulf of Mexico coast area at Biloxi in present-day Mississippi and Mobile in present-day Alabama, and, in 1708, founds New Orleans in present-day Louisiana.

France settles only a small part of her territory with military outposts and small settlements. The French eagerly engage in trading with Native Americans and do not drive them from their lands. Although the most powerful nation in Europe, France cannot maintain her colonies and territories. Conflicts and the French and Indian War cause France to cede her New World possessions to Spain and England.

CONCEPTS AND MOTIFS

As in other colonies, architecture, interiors, and furnishings in New France closely resemble those in France and derive from the settlers' classes and regions of origin. As French colonies change hands, the material culture begins to show influences of England and Spain.

■ *Motifs*. Motifs (Fig. 16-24) come from French high-style or folk traditions. Found mostly on furniture and wall paneling, popular motifs include diamond points, lozenges, flowers, rosettes, scrolls, and S curves.

▲ **16-21.** Villeneuve House, c. 1700; Charlesbourg, Quebec, Canada.

ARCHITECTURE

French settlements cross a range of climates from frigid to tropical so architecture adapts in both materials and construction. A medieval appearance characterizes all settlements until the 18th century. House types and public buildings related to particular areas, with construction and design reflecting local climate and materials, include the wood and stone houses of Quebec (Fig. 16-21) and French Canada; French log houses and structures in the Mississippi River valley (Fig. 16-22); sophisticated New Orleans townhouses and cottages; and Louisiana plantation dwellings (Fig. 16-23).The chief house type—small, with a hipped roof, and with or without a porch—appears from Canada to New Orleans.

Early plans of one or two rooms with a central chimney are similar to English ones. Later plans have two or three rooms across and one or two rooms deep. The front rooms include a *salle* or *salon* and *chambre*. There are no interior hallways, but large windows and French doors open to porches or *galeries*. Chimneys are on the ends or within walls. Dormer windows are common.

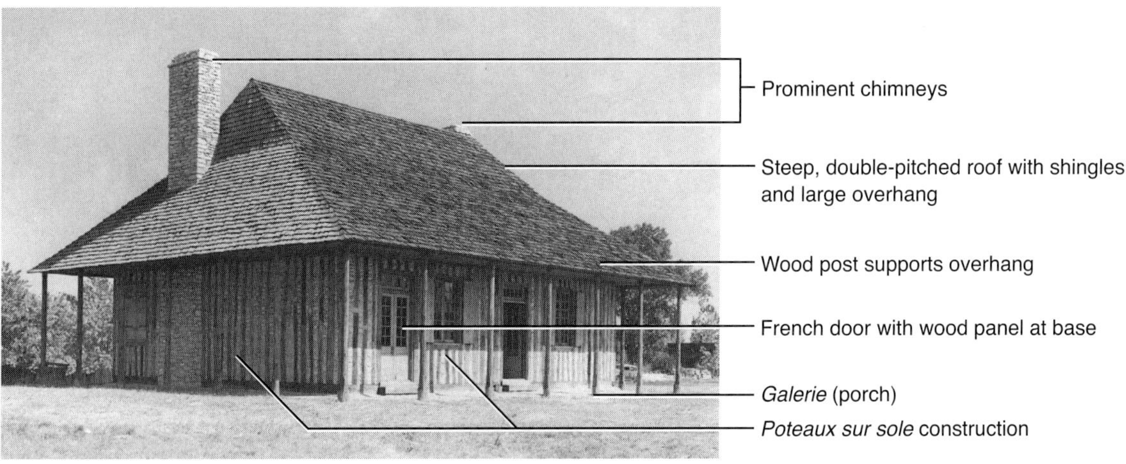

▲ **16-22.** Cahokia Courthouse, 1737; Cahokia, Illinois.

DESIGN SPOTLIGHT

Architecture: A two-story raised cottage house-type and classic example of a large French colonial plantation house in the United States, Parlange Plantation in Point Coupee Parish is the oldest surviving plantation house in Louisiana. It expresses the ambience of the vernacular Creole character on the exterior and some of the refinement of the French aristocracy on the interior. Vincent de Ternant, a French marquis, builds the house in 1750 along what is now called False River. To accommodate the semi-tropical climate the house is constructed of brick with brick pillars on the first or ground floor and mud and cypress on the second floor. Exterior and interior walls are plastered with a mixture of mud, sand, Spanish moss, and animal hair. Interior walls and ceilings are of cypress planks. A *galerie* surrounds both floors and serves as an extension of the living and service areas. As is typical in this house type, both the ground floor service areas, such as a wine cellar and food storage, and the main public and private living spaces are arranged in a double line. French doors open all around to catch the cool breezes from the river, and the roof overhang protects from frequent rains. Both exterior and interior stairs are common. Formal gardens once surrounded the house, but only the original approach of two rows of live oak trees remains. Interior architectural details are somewhat vernacular in character as are the original furnishings. Later additions are more high-style. (National Historic Landmark)

▲ **16-23.** Parlange Plantation, 1750; New Roads, Louisiana.

▲ **16-24.** Keeping Room, Louis Bolduc House, 1770–1785; S. Genevieve, Missouri.

INTERIORS AND FURNITURE

Rooms are multifunctional but specialized uses begin in the 18th century following French prototypes. Most interiors are simply treated with paneled or plastered walls and low-beamed ceilings (Fig. 16-24). Hard-packed dirt and wood plank floors are common in all areas. Ceilings are usually low in colder climates to retain the heat and higher in warmer climates to let the heat rise and keep the interior cool. Furnishings are few. Affluent homes are furnished similarly to vernacular ones but have more upholstery and textiles, and decorative arts.

Colonial furniture resembles French examples with similar construction methods, lines, legs, and details. Common styles include Louis XIII, Louis XIV, and Louis XV. Simplification, the mixing of styles and motifs, and a certain naiveté or abstraction distinguishes colonial from high-style French designs. Forms and motifs continue after the originals have passed from favor in France. Early furniture, whether built in or movable, is more architectonic with a strong rectilinear outline, symmetry, and large scale (Fig. 16-24). Later examples have more curves and a smaller, more human scale. Typical pieces include chairs, tables, large *armoires* for storage, and four-poster and built-in beds.

GERMANY 17th–19th CENTURIES

HISTORICAL AND SOCIAL

German immigrants are a diverse group that includes Germans, Swiss, Austrians, and other groups. Many early settlers immigrate for political and religious freedom along with social and economic betterment. The political freedom touted by William Penn in Pennsylvania attracts colonists from many countries including the first group of Germans who arrive in 1638. Some remain in Philadelphia, but the majority moves to the countryside in Lancaster and Bucks counties, Maryland, Virginia, Ohio, North Carolina, and Wisconsin. In the 19th century, a second influx of German settlers populates the Midwest, Texas, and later California.

Early German colonists thrive as farmers, while later ones prosper not only in rural communities but also in urban areas. Some German religious groups, such as the Amish and Mennonites, maintain a distinct separation in language, religion, and culture from other settlers.

CONCEPTS

German colonists follow traditional medieval building and furnishing patterns with which they are familiar. Rural peoples tend to maintain traditional building and furnishing patterns with little outside influence.

■ *Motifs*. Motifs (Fig. 16-27) include figures, birds, unicorns, lions, hearts, tulips, rinceaus, floral and scroll patterns, stars, and geometric shapes, such as hex signs. Designs come from many sources, reflecting the varied influences in Germany and the assimilation of English features. Motifs often have religious or symbolic meanings.

ARCHITECTURE

Rural settlers maintain medieval building traditions well into the 19th century. Some display a collective European heritage such as the German transplant of stone and log homes to America (Fig. 16-26). Although the Swedes build the first log houses in America, the Germans bring them first to the mid-Atlantic region and then to other areas as they migrate westward. Houses are the most common building type. Some rural German dwellings are of logs, while others, especially those of the affluent, are stone or brick, often with clapboard, gables, and quoins. Houses in Texas and Wisconsin mix half-timbering or *fachwerk* with stone or brick infill (Fig. 16-25). Early German dwellings often combine barns, stables, service areas, and living areas under one roof unlike other settlers. Most German houses are one and a half stories with three rooms and a loft. Usual spaces include the *stube* or parlor for socializing and dining, the *küche* or kitchen, and the *krammer* or bedchamber.

INTERIORS, FURNITURE, AND DECORATIVE ARTS

Interiors of German houses are simply treated, but colorful. Floors are made of wide boards, with wool or cotton rugs limited to the best rooms. Walls are mainly whitewashed but they are sometimes painted patterns in red, yellow, blue, green, brown, black, and white. Designs include spirals, diagonals, stippling, marbleizing,

▲ **16-25.** Klein-Naegelin House, 1846; New Braunfels, Texas. *Fachwerk* construction.

DESIGN SPOTLIGHT

German Architecture: The Swedes introduce log houses, and the Germans spread them from Pennsylvania throughout the south and, later, into the Midwest from the mid-18th through the mid-19th centuries. Horizontal log construction, like the vertical log construction of the French, makes use of readily available building materials and results in functional, albeit not decorative, architecture. Corner construction employs many different forms and is often evidence of ethnic origins of the builders. Sizes vary from single rooms to multiple rooms and stories. The inhabitants soon cover the exteriors of most log houses with clapboards, plaster, and other materials to stop drafts and prevent the logs from rotting. Logs are usually no longer than 24'-0" to 30'-0" because of their taper and weight, so expansions are common as lifestyles change or wealth increases. Log house types include the single pen, saddlebag, double pen, and dog trot. Other means of expanding space include second stories and lean-tos as shown in this example of an expanded dog trot house. It has three rooms downstairs and two rooms upstairs. Buildings in warm climates use the covered dog trot or a porch as outdoor living areas. Many interiors are plain and simply furnished. As wealth increases, interiors become more high-style and elaborate with paneled or plastered walls and ceilings, decorative finishes, architectural details, and finer furnishings.

▲ **16-26.** Muckleroy House, 1840; Round Top (now in Henkel Square), Texas.

or decorative painting with various motifs. Ceilings have exposed beams, are plastered, or have wood planks. Urban interiors follow vernacular, regional, or sophisticated English models after the 18th century.

German furniture has both rural and urban forms. Rural furniture in most areas maintains medieval traditions well into the 19th century. Urban furniture is influenced by and, in turn, influences English forms, construction, and decoration, particularly in Philadelphia. The best-known examples of German furniture are ladder-back chairs with rush seats and rural painted chests (Fig. 16-27).

Germans also are known for colorful, hand-decorated texts or documents called *fraktur*, which include hymn and scripture texts, marriage and birth announcements, and greetings often created by schoolmasters. Also distinctive are German slipware and *sgraffito* ware for their highly saturated colors and German motifs, such as tulips. Most glassmakers in America during the Colonial period are German because, unlike the English, German glassmakers face economic difficulties so they immigrate freely.

HOLLAND 17th–19th CENTURIES

HISTORICAL AND SOCIAL

The Dutch establish trading centers in New York and the Hudson River Valley during the early 1600s, but lose them before the end of the century. The Dutch West India Company founds the first Dutch colony in 1624. In 1626, a second colony is started on Manhattan Island. The colonies in Fort Orange (now Albany, New York) and New Amsterdam (now New York City) grow slowly, hampered by neglect from the founders and by conflicts with local tribes. The English encroachment on Dutch settlements on Manhattan and Long Island and the threat of invasion causes the governor to cede Dutch holdings to England in 1664. Although the English allow the Dutch settlers to remain, their influence quickly fades except in small pockets, particularly along

DESIGN SPOTLIGHT

German Furniture: The most common form of Pennsylvania German furniture, painted chests are made for men and women to store personal possessions. Retaining European characteristics, they are large rectangular storage units with lids and heavy base moldings. Most are about 24" deep and 48" wide and made of poplar and occasionally oak or walnut. Usually dovetailed at the corners, chests may have drawers and rest on straight or ogee bracket feet, runners, or no feet at all. Tops usually are flat, not paneled or arched. Forms of hinges include iron straps and tulip or heart shapes. Most chests have painted decoration that is done by the maker or a member of his family using bright hues of red, blue, green, orange, white, and black. Techniques include stencils, painting directly, drawing the pattern first, and block printing. Common decorations are birds, animals, flowers, hearts, and geometric shapes. Distinctive regional styles occur.

▲ **16-27.** Painted chest, 1795–1810; Shenandoah Country, Virginia; Johannes Spitler.

the Hudson River. Dutch settlements are more heterogeneous than English settlements because of their emphasis on commerce and religious tolerance. There, various cultures and building traditions intermingle.

CONCEPTS AND MOTIFS

As with other colonists, the Dutch recreate buildings and furnishings they had known at home, particularly in urban centers, which reflect medieval traditions instead of the classical Renaissance. Reciprocity between England and Holland is particularly strong.

■ *Motifs*. Common motifs include decorative brickwork, flowers, trees, and birds (Fig. 16-29). Dutch motifs often resemble those of the Germans, revealing a common Continental heritage.

ARCHITECTURE

Houses are the most common building type. Dutch urban rowhouses are transplanted directly from Holland. The short side of a gable-end faces the street and has a parapet wall. The wall extends above the roofline in various shapes including curvilinear or crow-step gables. Shops are below with living quarters above. In rural areas, Dutch house types are identified by their roofs, which include the staight-side gable, the flared-eave (Fig. 16-28), and gambrel. Dutch houses may be of wood, stone, or more commonly brick. Brick is often in patterns of blue, purple, or gray mixed with red. Patterns include zig zags, diamond or chevrons, geometric shapes, or florals. Many houses have a raised front door and *stoep*

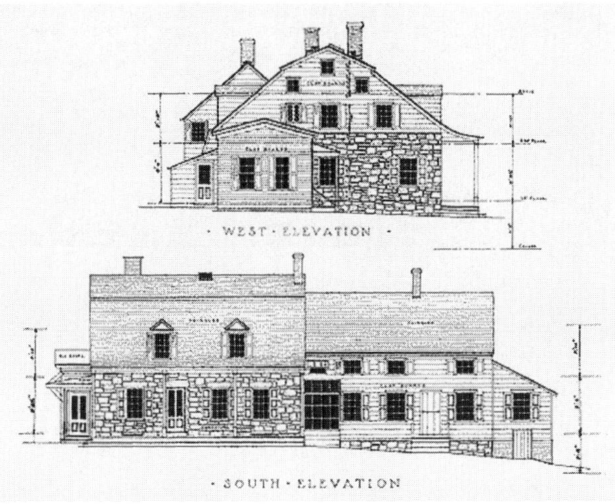

▲ **16-28.** Terheun House, c. 1670 and later; Hackensack, New Jersey. Flare-eave roof.

or platform. Floor plans, which are more linear than in other cultures, have three adjacent rooms of approximately equal size, a kitchen, a parlor, and a bedchamber. Characteristics of Dutch houses live on in the Dutch Colonial Revival of the early 20th century and later, primarily in the flared-eave and gambrel roofs.

INTERIORS, FURNITURE, AND DECORATIVE ARTS

Dutch interiors with tiles, ceramics, textiles, and paintings are more colorful than English ones. Because many settlers are merchants, interiors often exhibit objects from around the world. Interiors usually have whitewashed plaster walls. Dutch fireplaces retain the large hood over a hearth and cast-iron fireback. The surround is tiled, and a ruffled valance hangs from the hood to prevent smoke from entering the room. Ceiling beams rest on decorative brackets.

Furniture in the New Netherlands reproduces Dutch prototypes and may be brought from home or imported. Furnishings include seating, tables, and storage pieces. The *kas* is a distinctive piece made by the Dutch in the Hudson River Valley (Fig. 16-29). Used for storage, it resembles European *armoires*. Some are of dark wood with applied moldings and bosses. Others have *grisaille* paintings of fruits and flowers on their façades. Most have double doors, a heavy cornice, and bun or ball feet. Beds are sometimes built into wall paneling, usually near the fireplace.

Dutch and some English interiors commonly contain examples of tin-glazed earthenware produced in Delft, Holland, beginning in the first half of the 16th century. Blue and white and polychrome tiles produced in the 18th century are also well known.

▲ **16-29.** Bedroom, J. G. Hardenbergh House, c. 1762; originally near Kerhonkson, New York. [Courtesy Winterthur Museum]

F. BAROQUE

1600–1750

Baroque, an international style that dominates Europe in the 17th century, unites the grand scale, representational techniques, and architectural developments of the High Renaissance with the drama and emotion of the Late Renaissance. The style emerges in Rome at the end of the 16th century where it celebrates the victories of the Counter-Reformation and seeks to glorify the Christian god and the Catholic Church. At times classical and conservative, and at others plastic and exploitive, the Baroque combines monumental architecture, illusionistic painting, and dynamic sculpture to inspire, awe, and transport the viewer. Architecture, interiors, and furniture are more fully integrated and unified than during the Renaissance. The term *Baroque*, which may be from the Portuguese *barocco* or Spanish *barueco*, describes an irregularly shaped pearl. Originally derogatory, it signified a decline from Renaissance classicism.

Following Catholic military and theological victories over Protestantism, Pope Sixtus V resumes the building program in Rome in the 1580s. To construct a new city that reflects the magnificence of Christ and the Catholic Church, Sixtus institutes a vast program of urban development. Wide avenues punctuated with fountains and obelisks and highlighted by squares change the face of the city. New churches combine architecture, sculpture, and painting to create drama and inspire awe in worshippers.

From Rome where it promotes the church, the Baroque spreads to France where it becomes a tool to glorify the Sun King, Louis XIV. The magnificence of Louis's court inspires envy and the desire for comparable expressions in the nobility of other countries. Similar examples spring up in Spain, Germany, Austria, and the New World. Protestant Holland and England remain largely unaffected by the Baroque period.

Although religious conflicts predominate during the Baroque era, global colonization and scientific developments proceed. The newly invented telescope and microscope further open the universe. The 17th century is the age of Shakespeare and great theater. Opera is born. Life at court is splendid and colorful with polished manners and ornate clothing.

CHAPTER 17

European Baroque

1590s–1750

> *Imaginative, surprising, and gay, richly covered with colored marbles, carvings, paintings, and gilding, the Baroque sought to attract attention by [a] striking and picturesque appearance.*
>
> —Helen Gardner, *Art Through the Ages*

The Baroque style dominates Europe and a few American colonies throughout the 17th and early 18th centuries. An ornate, sumptuous style closely tied to religion, politics, and economics, Baroque integrates exteriors and interiors more fully than did the Renaissance style, particularly in churches. A plastic, exuberant Baroque style dominates the Catholic countries of Italy, Spain, Portugal, Austria, Flanders, and Germany where it serves to glorify the church and inspire piety. In Catholic France, Baroque, which arises from the taste of the king, demonstrates the power and majesty of the absolute monarchy of Louis XIV. Protestant countries, such as England, Holland, and northern Germany, lean toward a less monumental, more restrained style that is not closely tied to religion or politics.

HISTORICAL AND SOCIAL

The age of the Baroque is a time of contrasts in Europe. Absolute monarchies coexist with the rising nationalistic movements. The great wealth and power of monarchs and nobles contrasts with the abject poverty of the lower classes. The spread of knowledge and scientific advances continues, yet wars, famines, and plagues devastate millions. Manners grow more refined in this age of great theater, music, and opera. Royalty enjoy extravagant entertainments, masques, balls, and receptions. Commerce and trade flourish as major European powers establish colonies in the Americas. Scientists and researchers make great strides in astronomy, physics, calculus, chemistry, and medicine and invent or perfect precision instruments for observation and measurement.

CONCEPTS

The energy and tension of the Baroque mirror that of the age. The style seeks to awe and inspire, whether to greater worship of God and His church or to stronger allegiance to a nation, monarch, or noble. It also reflects an ever-expanding understanding of the universe and mind of man through various time–space devices, such as buildings that extend into surrounding spaces and require the viewer to move around and through them or vast cavernous interiors with highly illusionistic ceiling paintings that imply limitless space. These huge and monumental environments dwarf human beings while celebrating the glory of God, His Church, or a monarch.

CHARACTERISTICS AND MOTIFS

Exuberance, monumental scale, movement, seemingly limitless space, center emphasis, and complex forms, as well as sumptuous materials, characterize Baroque. Classical language, symmetry, unity, and harmony become the tools of Baroque design concepts. Contrasts, layers of elements, curves and counter-curves, and advancing and receding planes create movement, especially toward centers, energy, and dynamism. Articulation using classical elements is more three-dimensional and forceful in Baroque designs than in Renaissance designs. Forms and motifs may break, twist, and curve. Embellishment is bold and sculpturesque. Architecture, sculpture, and painting unite to create drama, inspire, or even overwhelm.

■ *Motifs*. Classical elements, such as pilasters and pediments (Fig. 17-1, 17-2, 17-3, 17-4, 17-5, 17-7, 17-8, 17-9), are common but are used more dynamically, even capriciously. Other motifs include colossal columns, C and S scrolls, shells, swags, flowers, figures, sculpture niches, and cartouches. Some Mannerist characteristics, such as pilasters that taper to the base, continue, particularly in Spain and Northern Europe.

ARCHITECTURE

The Baroque period begins in Rome under the leadership of Pope Sixtus V (1585–1590), whose major rebuilding campaign intends to celebrate Catholic victories over Protestantism and to win back and attract new worshippers. Sixtus initiates the completion of the dome and façade of S. Peter's Basilica and the addition of the piazza in front. At the same time, numerous churches are constructed, and existing ones are refurbished. Wide avenues and streets replace narrow medieval ones, and large piazzas and fountains punctuate and enhance vistas. Italian sculptors and painters create a corresponding interior style that contributes to the impact of architecture and urban planning. Although the building boom in Rome calls forth talented and well-known architects to design great and influential structures and interiors, two men primarily introduce the forms and language of Baroque. The more classical, theatrical work of Gianlorenzo Bernini (Fig. 17-2) dominates Rome. In comparison, the work of Francesco Borromini (Fig. 17-3) is more revolutionary and plastic with complex geometry. The work of both soon influences all of Europe.

Baroque buildings no longer sit in self-contained isolation, but expand into surrounding space. Often, they are part of large urban projects of which the main longitudinal axis continues into and often through the interior into a large formal garden. The monumental scale of many structures requires movement by the viewer to fully experience them.

Building types include churches (Fig. 17-2, 17-3, 17-4), palaces and palace complexes (Fig. 17-5), town and country residences, and public buildings. Papal and noble families continue to build large, impressive palaces and villas as in the Renaissance. Dwellings reflect some Baroque concepts but rarely achieve the plasticity, dynamism, and movement that characterize churches.

■ *Spain*. Spanish buildings hardly ever are as plastic as those in Italy, nor do they expand into the surrounding space (Fig. 17-5). Much of Baroque architecture in Spain features surface ornamentation, beginning with the work of the Churriguera family. Uniquely Spanish, Churrigueresque or Spanish Baroque, differs from other European manifestations in its profuse surface ornamentation reminiscent of the Spanish Renaissance Plateresque.

■ *Germany and Austria*. Germany and Austria do not adopt the Baroque until the 18th century. German Baroque combines the indigenous medieval tall façade and two towers with movement, center emphasis, layers of elements, and elaborately decorated interiors. The Germans excel in their use of dramatic light and the integration of architecture, painting, and sculpture.

■ *Holland*. Protestant Holland adopts a simpler, more classical style derived from Palladio and his follower Vincenzo Scamozzi. Scale is modest; symmetry and repose are characteristic.

Public and Private Buildings

■ *Site Orientation*. Churches, public buildings, and some palaces may be focal points of *piazzas* or in squares with impressive and monumental approaches (Fig. 17-2). Often the axis of approach continues into the interior and out to the garden. Expansive city planning is an important Baroque development.

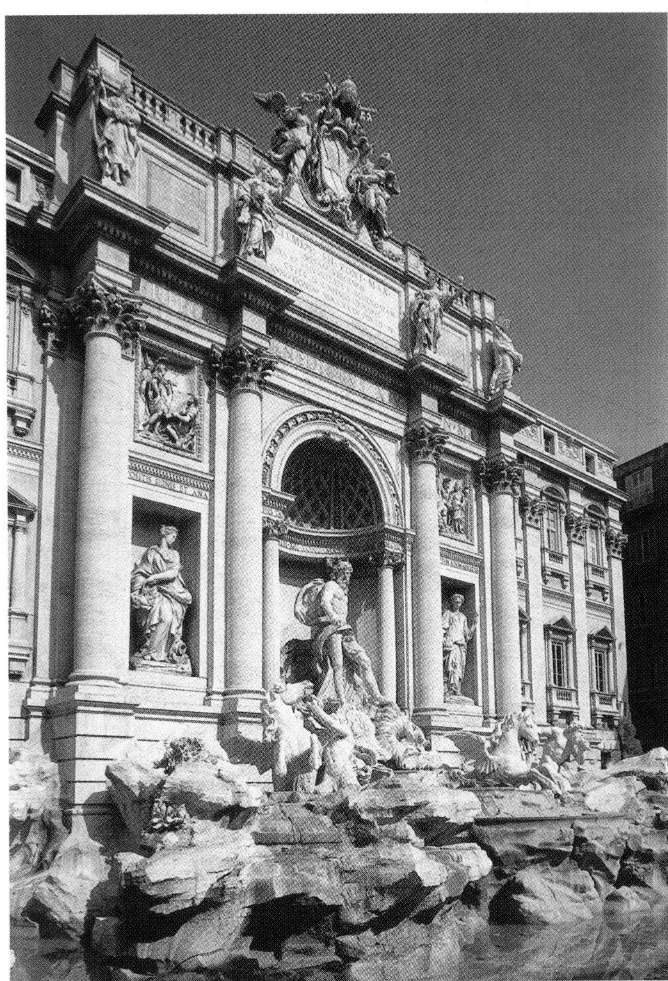

▲ **17-1.** Motifs and Architectural Detail: Trevi Fountain, 1732–1737; Rome, Italy; Noccolo Salvi.

DESIGN SPOTLIGHT

Architecture and Interiors: For S. Peter's Basilica, Carlo Maderno expands the original Greek cross of Bramante and Michelangelo to a Latin cross plan by adding several bays to the nave. Besides making it one of the largest churches in the world, the size and shape befit this, the main basilica of the Catholic faith, which many regard as one of the holiest of Christian sites. S. Peter's façade progresses outward in planes from the corners to the center, which is marked by a pediment that provides a vertical element. Pilasters become engaged columns and the layered elements break across the façade as it steps outward. Planned twin towers, which would have balanced the great width of the façade, are not completed. The monumentality of the façade obscures the vision of the dome intended by Michelangelo.

Bernini designs the *piazza*, which reaches into and encloses a vast space, a dynamic composition of oval and trapezoid that represents the welcoming arms of the church. The trapezoid form that adjoins and leads to the basilica, along with an upward gradient, creates a false perspective that narrows the façade's width. Plain Tuscan columns form the colonnade, which is crowned with sculpture. He also plans, but never completes, a smaller colonnade in the opening of the oval so that visitors will suddenly enter the huge open space of the *piazza* and be overwhelmed with the vision of the façade. The *piazza's* size complements the building and accommodates huge crowds of pilgrims and worshippers.

Bernini decorates the interiors at S. Peter's with costly colored marbles, gilding, and rich coffering on the barrel vaults. The huge scale, architectural details, and glittering surfaces unite to overwhelm the viewer who is required to move around and through the space to experience it. Monumental architectural details articulate walls and ceilings, creating a rhythm that leads the eye and the worshipper to the crossing with canopy and altar beyond. At the crossing, Bernini's *baldacchino* (canopy) attempts to bring the monumental scale to a more human size. Supported by four twisting or Solomonic columns with Composite capitals, the bronze and gilded canopy rises 100' or about nine stories. The upper portion is a valance with tassels similar to the ones used in processions. Four massive volutes curve upward to an orb surmounted with a cross. Gilding highlights elements and contrasts with the dark bronze. Light pours in from the dome, accentuating the *baldacchino* and creating a vertical axis in contrast to the longitudinal axis of the Latin cross plan. (World Heritage Site)

▲ **17-2.** S. Peter's Basilica, piazza plan, cutaway view, and *baldacchino*, 1506–1626; Rome, Italy; façade completed by Carlo Maderno; piazza plan, interior, and *baldacchino* by Gianlorenzo Bernini.

DESIGN SPOTLIGHT

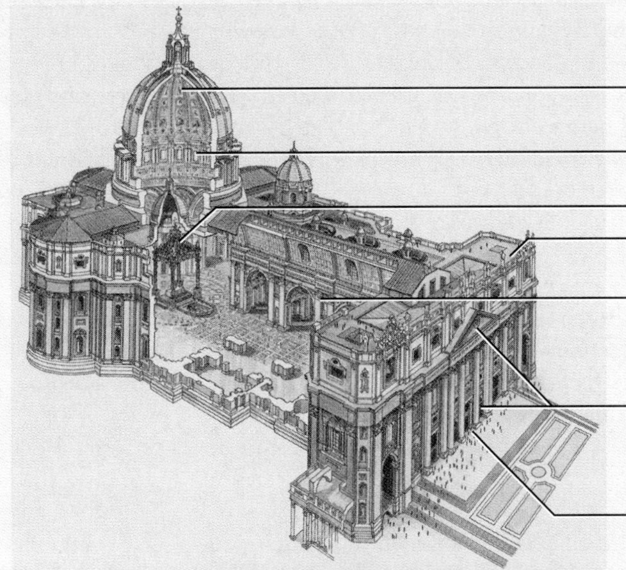

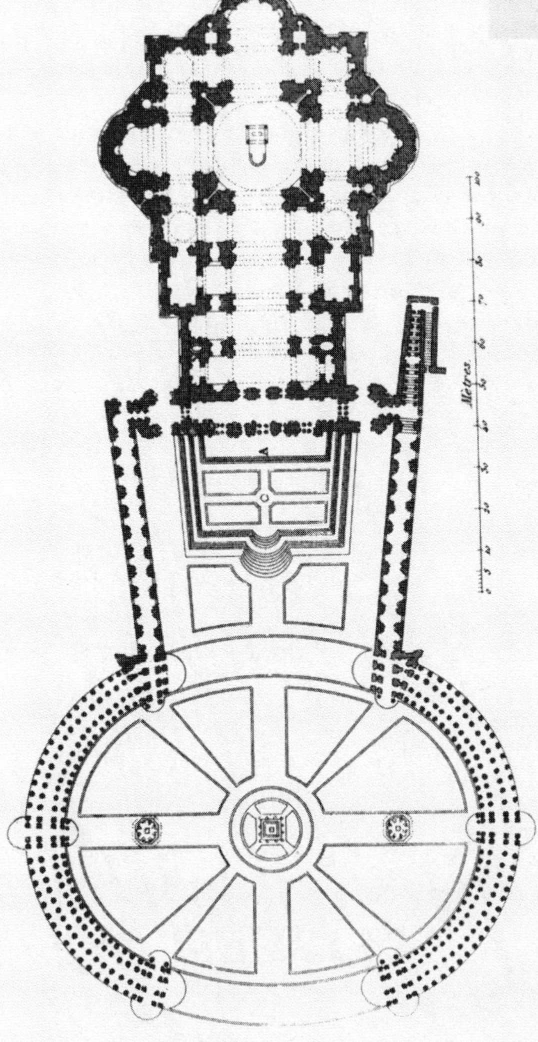

▲ **17-2.** Continued

■ *Floor Plans*. Dynamic Baroque church plans consist of complex combinations of equilateral triangles, ovals, circles, and lozenges (Fig. 17-3) instead of the simple and more static rectangles, squares, and circles of the Renaissance. Architects experiment with combining function and concepts of universality in various ways. These include basilica plans with a strong centralized emphasis on majestically domed spaces or oval or elliptical plans. Larger churches usually have basilica or Latin cross plans (Fig. 17-2) to accommodate crowds and ceremonial processions.

Domestic plans may be U-shaped, a more expansive design, or continue the rectangular block surrounding a courtyard of the Renaissance. Most rooms remain rectangular, although staircases are often oval or curvilinear. Regardless of the form, plans have grand staircases, large reception rooms, and suites of state and private apartments. In the palaces and homes of royalty, architects adopt French planning concepts in which rooms are carefully distributed to demonstrate status and to impress the visitor. Doors align on the same side of sequential rooms to create *enfilade* or vista with fireplaces opposite the entrance or the windows. These processional rooms are generally on the garden side of the home.

■ *Materials*. Designers use local stone or brick. Contrasts in color and/or material accent and emphasize parts and elements. Some Spanish examples have polychrome decoration or glazed tiles. In Holland, red brick with contrasting white stone details is common.

■ *Façades*. Classical elements, movement, and center emphasis characterize façades on churches and public buildings (Fig. 17-2, 17-3, 17-4), which are no longer in a single plane as in the Renaissance. Layers of elements; combinations of curved and straight lines; advancing and receding planes; curves and counter curves; and pilasters, engaged columns, and columns that increase in projection toward the center create movement and three-dimensionality (Fig. 17-2). Façades may undulate and/or project into space (Fig. 17-3). Classical architectural elements, such as cornices and pilasters, curve, twist, or break in response to projections and curves on the façade. They also are bolder, more three-dimensional, and forceful than in the Renaissance. Multiplication of geometric units replaces earlier mathematical modules in the work of some architects. Sculpture niches, colossal orders, pediments, and volutes highlight, define, and create contrasts of light and dark. Spanish façades often have rich surface decoration concentrated around doors and windows and spreading across the façade.

Center emphasis also characterizes palaces and dwellings (Fig. 17-5). Framing elements, such as pilasters, organize façades into bays. Fronts sometimes feature Renaissance forms of articulation, such as rustication that lightens on each successive story or superimposed orders.

In churches, light is an important design element and a visual metaphor for divine illumination. Light sources often are concealed in walls, roofs, or domes to increase the dramatic impact and/or emphasize mystery (Fig. 17-4). On exteriors, rectangular or curvilinear windows have circular or triangular pediments or complex, curvilinear surrounds. Windows on dwellings generally are larger than before.

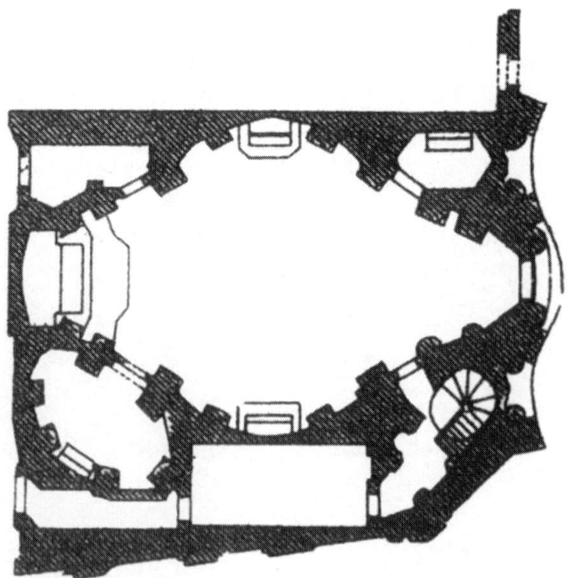

▲ **17-3.** *S. Carlo alle Quattro Fontane*, and floor plan, 1634–1682; Rome, Italy; Francesco Borromini.

DESIGN SPOTLIGHT

Architecture: Designed by Johann Fischer von Erlach and his son for Emperor Joseph I, *Karlskirche* (S. Charles's Church) is one of the finest Baroque buildings in Europe. It is unique in that von Erlach achieves unity among an eclectic assortment of classical and baroque forms and elements. The façade centers on a classical Greek temple portico that is joined by curved walls to pavilions with Roman baroque elements. A huge dome caps the composition. Two large columns, each imitating Trajan's column in Rome, sit within the façade's curving walls and define the entry. The columns display spiraling reliefs conveying messages of the virtues of S. Charles Borromeo, who helped the Viennese people during the 1576 Milan plague and to whom the church is dedicated. The heavily scaled and bold ornamentation is elaborate outside and inside. The nave continues the exterior design with marble columns, large arches, an ornate apse, classical motifs, and gold decoration. The massive dome dominates the center aisle and highlights the Greek cross plan.

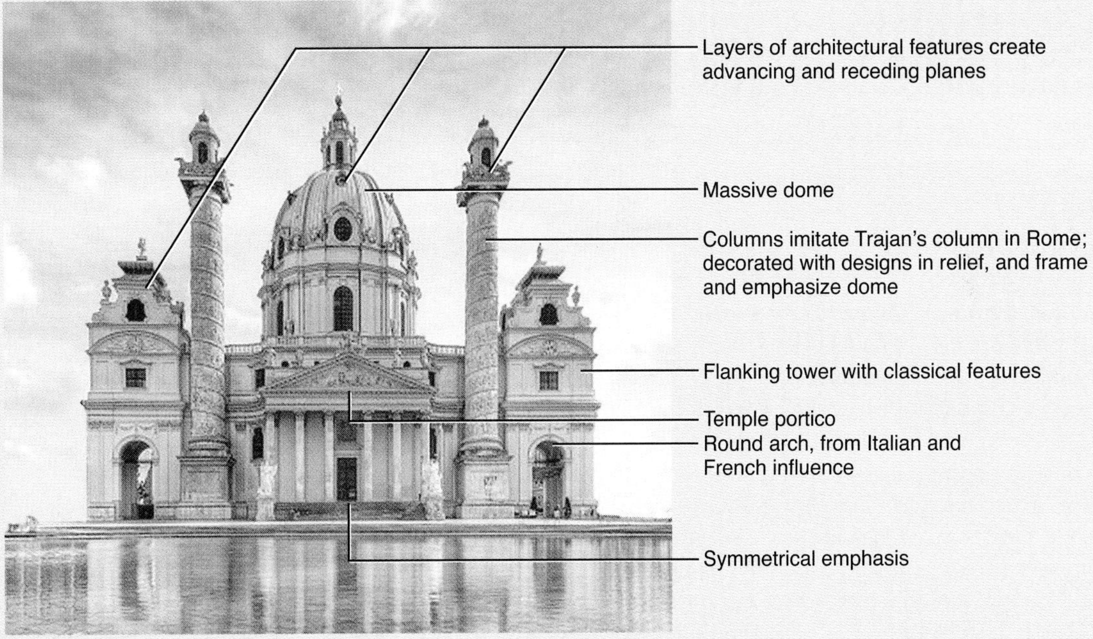

▲ **17-4.** *Karlskirche* (S. Charles's Church), 1716–1739; Vienna, Austria; Johann Fischer von Erlach and son.

Central entrances are impressive in scale and ornament (Fig. 17-2, 17-4) to accentuate them. Arches, columns, and pediments that increase in layers and project frame them. Doors are of paneled wood or heavily carved.

■ *Roofs*. Roofs (Fig. 17-2, 17-4) are usually gabled with domed crossings and chapels. Oval domes are preferred over circular domes as being more dynamic. Gables or flat roofs with balustrades and sculpture cover dwellings and palaces (17-5).

■ *Later Interpretations*. Designers adopt the scale and a few key elements, such as center emphasis, in later buildings, but literal copies of Baroque buildings are rare. A Neo-Baroque style develops in France in the 1860s, most notably in the work of architect Jean-Louis-Charles Garnier. Baroque planning concepts, scale, and surface richness continue in various forms through the 19th century. Baroque's undulating walls and complex plans influence Art Nouveau in the late 19th and early 20th centuries. Interpretations of Baroque churches continue through the early decades of the 20th century (Fig. 17-6).

▲ **17-5.** Royal Palace, 1738–1764; Madrid, Spain; Filippo Juvarra.

▲ **17-6.** Later Interpretation: Berlin Cathedral, 1905; Berlin, Germany; Julius Raschdorff.

INTERIORS

Interiors continue Baroque themes of glorification, exuberance, dynamism, drama, and/or emotionalism. To do so, they repeat the monumental scale, dynamism, contrasts, and complexity of exteriors. Integration and expansion, even to infinity, are important design principles, particularly in churches where designers experiment with traditional elements and forms to achieve these goals. Space, which features multiple vistas or diagonal focal points, is dynamic and vast. Designers strive for greater spatial unity and more openness. Light is used as a mystical element or for its dramatic impact. Architecture, sculpture, and painting unite to create drama, inspire, or even overwhelm the observer.

Opulent materials and colors, numerous classical details and embellishments, painted and gilded woodwork, illusionistic paintings, sculpture, elaborate stuccowork, and fine furnishings create dramatic settings for the ecclesiastical and social events that characterize Baroque life. European churches follow Italy's lead in designing splendid settings framed by architectural elements and exuberant wall and ceiling paintings. Decoration intends to inspire worship or greater piety and to glorify God and the church. Architecture, sculpture, and paintings, enhanced by strong contrasts of light and shadow, contribute to the drama.

Similarly, European royalty imitates the domestic magnificence of Italians and, later, Louis XIV at Versailles. They vie with one another to create the most opulent dwellings. In palaces, plans and decorations emphasize the power and authority of a particular individual, such as the owner, and also mean to astonish or overwhelm. Prominent architects, painters, and sculptors design interiors for noble families. Interior arrangements and decoration continue to show rank and precedence. Several anterooms, each more magnificent than the last, precede the lavish state and private apartments in palaces and noble homes. One's status determines how closely he or she may approach the state bedchamber. Although there is evidence of rooms set aside specifically for dining, most people take meals in entertaining rooms or wherever it is convenient.

Public and Private Buildings

- *Materials*. Rich materials and strong color contrasts create, support, and enhance the goals of inspiration and awe. Churches and dwellings alike have such combinations as white walls embellished with real or painted colored marble architectural elements, carved and gilded woodwork, and stuccowork (Fig. 17-7, 17-8, 17-9). Architectural details delineate and define spaces, but they are no longer in a single plane as in the Renaissance. Like exteriors, elements layer, curve, and break to create energy or movement or in response to undulating walls.
- *Color*. Colors (Fig. 17-7, 17-8, 17-9), which are from finish materials and textiles, are rich and highly saturated reds, greens, blues, and purples. Contrasts of color and material are common. Gilding highlights numerous surfaces.
- *Floors*. Materials include marble, brick, lead-glazed tiles, or stone. Masonry floors may be plain or patterned. Palaces and important residences use wood parquet, particularly on upper floors and/or in important rooms. People begin putting Oriental and European-made carpets on floors as well as tables. Plain, patterned, or colored rush matting sometimes covers floors, particularly in summer.

▲ **17-7.** Nave, *Rosenkranz Basilika*, S. Maria Rotunda, 1631–1634; Vienna, Austria.

■ *Walls*. Interior walls may undulate like façades. Architectural elements delineating church interiors and important spaces in palaces (Fig. 17-7, 17-8, 17-9) may be painted and/or gilded or a contrasting material to the wall. Marble often covers church walls, but is less common in dwellings, except palaces, because of its cost. A prevalent and less expensive treatment is painting wooden or plaster walls to imitate marble. Residential walls usually are divided into dado, fill, and cornice. Dadoes are painted, paneled, or left plain. The area above may be painted decoratively; paneled; or covered with costly fabrics, leather, or tapestries. Mirrors in elaborately carved frames become very important during the period.

Wall and ceiling frescoes are common in both palaces and churches (Fig. 17-7, 17-8) in most countries. Italian artists fully develop the realistic techniques of the Renaissance to create highly illusionistic frescoes with an impression of limitless space. Movement and strong diagonals unite with twisting forms, sculpturesque figures, and billowing drapery. Real and *trompe l'oeil* architectural elements, stuccowork, and paintings combine in complex compositions with religious, mythological, or allegorical themes.

Windows are important interior elements in churches and dwellings as they admit the light so important to Baroque design concepts (Fig. 17-7, 17-8). The sash or double-hung window, which develops in the 1640s, begins to replace the casement window in residences. Most windows have interior shutters to block light or give privacy. Curtains, which remain rare except in palaces, consist of two fabric panels hung on wire rods. As important design elements in the *enfilade*, doors are carved and paneled with gilding. Double doors are preferred to enhance impact.

▲ **17-9.** Bedroom, *Palazzo Sagredo*, 1718; Venice, Italy. Attributed to Abbondio Statio and Carpofaro Mazzetti. [Rogers Fund, 196 (06.1335.1a-d). The Metropolitan Museum of Art, New York, NY, U.S.A. Image © The Metropolitan Museum of Art/Art Resource, NY.].

▲ **17-8.** Nave, Church of S. Nicholas, completed 1735; Prague, Czech Republic; stucco decoration by Bernardo Spinetti; frescos by Peter Adam the Elder.

■ *Ceilings*. Architects create vast interior spaces and vistas with barrel or groin vaults, domes, and arches in both public and private buildings (Fig. 17-7, 17-8, 17-9). Unlike Renaissance architects, they intend to dwarf the viewer, thereby creating more drama and heightening impact. Round and ovoid domes create a vertical axis and a stronger centralized feeling. In churches and palaces, important ceilings are frescoed, entirely or partly. In dwellings, flat, vaulted, and plasterwork ceilings may be left white or painted and/or gilded. Carving and painting decorate beams and coffers.

■ *Lighting*. Artificial lighting is minimal except during social events. Only the wealthy can afford numerous candles, candlesticks, *candelabra*, sconces, and chandeliers in gold and silver. Design and scale complement interiors and furnishings.

FURNISHINGS AND DECORATIVE ARTS

Furnishings, used to enhance status, become increasingly important and are often designed for specific interiors or individuals. Designs reflect Baroque's massive scale and dynamism. Opulence surpasses comfort in importance. Most furniture is rectilinear with curvilinear ornamentation, which can be excessive. Sculpture and architecture influence furnishings in bold, sculpturesque carving and architectural details. Because furniture is placed against the wall, backs of chairs frequently are not upholstered for economy. Back legs on chairs and tables may be plain also. By the end of the 17th century, most European countries emulate the Baroque furniture of Italy and France, but retain some regional character. Types include seating, tables, storage pieces, and beds.

Public and Private Buildings

■ *Materials*. Local and imported hardwoods dominate furniture design, and chief decorations are carving, gilding, lacquer, inlay, veneer, and marquetry. The Flemish and Dutch are known for their excellent marquetry during the period. Cabinetmakers combine wood with other materials, such as silver or mother-of-pearl, which are often imported by merchant ships. Exotic woods and/or marble embellish many examples. European lacquer imitates that on imported Oriental pieces.

■ *Seating*. With increased emphasis on comfort, suites of furniture, daybeds, and easy chairs are more common. Armchairs (Fig. 17-10) begin to appear even in less affluent homes. Chairs with upholstered frames and lavish trims continue to mark wealth and status.

■ *Tables*. Consoles and tables with rectangular, usually marble tops feature exuberant carving and gilding. There are no tables specifically for dining.

■ *Storage*. Boldly carved figures combined with leaves, scrolls, shells, and other details often form the legs of cabinet stands and tables. Veneers of exotic woods and complex marquetry compositions in multiple colors highlight doors and façades. Prominent cornices, bases, and architectural details distinguish large case pieces. Cabinets, chests of drawers, and wardrobes supersede chests for storage. Cupboards and buffets remain the chief display pieces in spaces used for dining.

■ *Beds*. Beds (Fig. 17-9) in state apartments are raised on a dais or placed behind a balustrade. Most beds are rectangular in form with hangings completely covering them. Valances have complex curvilinear forms highlighted with gold braid or fringe. Beds of state often have vases of ostrich plumes atop the tester. Bed hangings, upholstery, and other textiles often match (*en suite*) to create unity. Rich trims enhance both hangings and upholstery.

■ *Decorative Arts*. Trade with the Orient fosters a desire for porcelains and lacquerwork. Other items from the East include lacquered furniture, screens, and some Chinese wallpaper. Baroque accessories are lavish and large in scale to suit interiors. Definitive features include curvilinear forms and classical or naturalistic carved and molded decorations and gilding.

▲ **17-10.** Armchair, 1706; now in *Ca'Rezzonico*, Venice, Italy; Andrea Brustolon.

CHAPTER 18

Louis XIV

1643–1715, France

> *"L'état c'est moi." (I am the state.)*
>
> —Louis XIV

Not only does France become the leading world power in the 17th century, but she also replaces Italy as artistic leader of Europe. Versailles, the grandest expression of French Baroque, dazzles all of Europe and sets new standards for luxury and extravagance in architecture, interiors, and furnishings. The palace exemplifies French Baroque planning concepts, design language, and intent.

HISTORICAL AND SOCIAL

When Louis XIV ascends the throne in 1643 at the age of five, France has established her position as a great European power with a tradition of art patronage by the Crown. During Louis's early years, Anne of Austria, his mother, and Cardinal Mazarin, his godfather, govern the country. Louis marries Marie Thérèse, daughter of Philip IV of Spain, which enhances relationships between France and Spain and contributes to Louis's power. After Mazarin dies in 1661, Louis himself rules France with some assistance from his economic minister, Jean-Baptiste Colbert. With Colbert's aid, Louis more firmly establishes the divine right of the monarchy begun under Richelieu and Mazarin. Louis regards himself as the greatest ruler in Europe and wants to impress others with his importance and the magnificence of court life. He likes to think that as the planets revolve around the sun, so all of life in France should revolve around him. He chooses the title *Le Roi Soleil* or Sun King.

To educate people to his greatness, Louis employs various entertainments such as festivals and fireworks and commissions statues, fountains, and palaces. To visually support his claims, he demands surroundings that embody the power and grandeur appropriate to the Sun King, his court, and court life. He reinstitutes a rigid etiquette system of formal rules to govern court relationships and further glorify himself as king. The court overflows with an entourage of nobles and Louis's relatives, descendants, and their attendants, so appropriate housing is needed. All of these factors lead to the building of the Palais de Versailles and the surrounding city as well as the construction and/or embellishment of numerous royal *châteaux* nearby.

Court policy, as established under Henri IV, supports the use of art and architecture as tools of the state, thereby ensuring a suitable climate for Louis to accomplish his goals. Italian artists brought to France contribute their artistic skills and expertise. French architects and designers study in Italy and at newly established academies of art and architecture. The result produces a unified national art expression, numerous cabinetmaking workshops, and expanded decorative arts factories. Although this has little impact outside royalty because of its lavishness and expense, it does establish France as a world leader in artistic taste.

CONCEPTS

French Baroque seeks to awe and inspire its viewer to glorify, not the church as in Italy, but the absolutism of the Sun King, Louis XIV. As the first indigenous example of French decoration, French Baroque projects grandeur and luxury embedded within a unified composition—a standard of beauty integrating landscape, architecture, interiors, furniture, and decorative arts into an elaborate statement of court taste. Created by artists and architects influenced by the Baroque style of Rome, French Baroque rejects Italian exuberance and excesses and embraces principles of reason, restraint, order, and formality. The French build on the notion of interiors composed of unified elements, which begins in Italian churches, extending this idea more fully to secular interiors.

MOTIFS

■ *Motifs*. Exteriors display classical architectural features (Fig. 18-2, 18-3, 18-4) such as columns, pediments, arches, balustrades, draped figures, niches, quoins, swags, and cartouches. Motifs (Fig. 18-1, 18-5) at Versailles include intertwined *L*s, sun faces, musical instruments, military symbols, *fleur de lis*, and crowns. Other details (Fig. 18-4) are acanthus leaves, cherubs, classical statues, cartouches, dolphins, *Chinoiserie*, *singerie*, pagodas, and landscapes.

(a)

(b)

(c)

▲ **18-1.** Motifs: (a) intertwining *L's*, (b) crown and *fleur-de-lis*, and (c) sun face and musical instruments.

ARCHITECTURE

Baroque Classicism defines architecture in France through symmetry, classical order, monumental scale, and center emphasis. The image borrows selectively from the more conservative Italian Baroque of Bernini instead of the more plastic, expressionist style of Borromini. Consequently, façades do not undulate in the Italian manner. Instead they remain relatively flat, although projecting units, especially toward the center, are common. At times dramatic and exciting, French Baroque exhibits dignity, masculinity, and vigorous, but restrained, ornament. Distinctive French features include pavilions, a projecting frontispiece with a pediment or a separate roof and sculptural ornament, and a tall hipped or mansard roof. Buildings in France are as extravagantly planned inside and out as those in Italy.

The early 17th century is a period of great building activity in France with numerous *châteaux* (Fig. 18-3) and *hôtels* built for the nobility in addition to the palace at Versailles (Fig. 18-4). During the period, the middle class increases its wealth and importance, and it, too, requires appropriate housing. The architectural design of *hôtels* exerts much influence on domestic buildings throughout Europe. Only a few churches are constructed, as dwellings are more important.

Public and Private Buildings

■ *Site Orientation*. Like Italian examples, French buildings reflect an expansive universe by integrating city, dwelling, and landscape. French urban palaces, however, are even more expansive than Italian palaces because of the *cour d'honneur* (open forecourt). Buildings, integrated with the urban and natural environment, are situated along a longitudinal axis that directs progression toward a series of goals or focal points (Fig. 18-3, 18-4). The path begins in the urban context—the city, street, or square—and continues through a forecourt to the building's entrance. Once inside, progression continues through an important interior, usually a grand staircase or salon, to the rear gardens and park. Gardens are also organized along a main longitudinal axis with smaller transverse axes and radiating patterns. The Palace of Versailles is the supreme example of this comprehensive planning.

■ *Floor Plans*. Plans (Fig. 18-3, 18-4) strive for symmetry along at least one axis, if not two. Rooms generally are rectangular, although some *salons* and stair halls are ovals. There are no interior hallways. Within this context, French architects carefully orchestrate the distribution of rooms to support formality, rank, ceremony, and the attributes of an aristocratic life. Plans are organized around public and private *appartements*. Doorways to rooms in state apartments are on the same side of the wall to create an *enfilade*, and each room is more magnificently decorated than the previous one. State *appartements* usually are located on the garden side of the house, and husbands and wives have their own. More intimate and less formal spaces are located near or behind state *appartements*, sometimes alongside them in a double row. Toward the end of the period, rooms with specialized functions become more common. This change reflects the importance of gaming and conversation, as well as the benefit of heating smaller spaces.

■ *Materials*. Typical building materials are stone, with brick used for lesser structures, and wood and plaster incorporated in vernacular examples.

■ *Façades*. Compositions are made of clearly defined classical forms occuring in repeated units with a horizontal emphasis delineated through stringcourses, cornices, or balustrades. Bays defined by pilasters create a regular rhythm and define the order as well as the edge of a unit (Fig. 18-2, 18-3, 18-4). Traditional classical features, such as rustication and quoins, help to further organize and unify façades. A series of stepped planes, usually defining interior spaces, leads to the center of the composition and the entrance. Planes may connect at right angles or, less often, in curves. A frontispiece (Fig. 18-2, 18-4) composed of superimposed orders and a pediment marks the entrance as well as the most important reception room, the salon. Pavilions (Fig. 18-2, 18-3, 18-4) mark the ends of exterior compositions, as well as indicating the placement inside the state bedchamber in the *appartement*.

The proportion of window to wall (Fig. 18-4) is greater than in Italy because windows are larger to admit more light. French windows (Fig. 18-4), a French invention, extend to the floor, becoming doors onto porches or balconies. Their use on ground and important floors creates spectacular illumination that adds to the magnificence of interior spaces. Sash windows with heavy, simple moldings are also common, particularly on smaller dwellings.

■ *Roofs*. Roofs (Fig. 18-2, 18-3, 18-4) include mansard, hipped, and flat. They are usually covered in slate with cresting at the apex. Roofs pitch steeply as before. Each unit may have its own roof.

INTERIORS

As in Italy, architecture, sculpture, and painting unite to transport and overwhelm in French Baroque rooms. Defined by classical order, language, and motifs, interiors complement the exterior design, but they are far more sumptuous than the more restrained exteriors. Baroque interiors are characterized by symmetry, formality, grandeur, large scale, rich decoration, vivid color, and luxurious materials appropriate to the rank, wealth, and rituals of court life. Rectilinear spaces arranged symmetrically reflect the organization of façades, making a stronger relationship between the exterior and interior—something new in France with this style. Important spaces align with the main, usually longitudinal, axis in the Italian manner. The frontispieces and pavilions denote important interior spaces. Pattern books and engravings spread the French aesthetic to the rest of Europe.

Ceremonial interiors (Fig. 18-4) are the most lavishly appointed and the most formal in residences. Balustrades and daises subdivide and separate spaces to support etiquette and ritual. However, most dwellings, even Versailles, have less formal, private spaces that will proliferate in the next period. *Appartements* may include an *antichambre* for eating and waiting; a *chambre de parade* for receiving and entertaining important guests; a *chambre à coucher* for receiving friends and sleeping; a *cabinet* for conducting business; and a *garderobe* for dressing, storage, and housing for servants. No room is set aside primarily for dining yet, although spaces identified as *salle à manger* appear on plans during the period. Several rooms hold dining furniture so that people can eat where they please.

The French Royal Academy of Painting and Sculpture, established in 1648, turns out many talented artists and others who can embellish interior spaces. And those at Versailles are the supreme example of sumptuous embellishment. Their grandeur and magnificence form the setting for the dazzling ceremonies glorifying the king and enhancing his absolute power. Building

▲ **18-2.** East front, Louvre, 1667–1670; Paris, France; Claude Perrault, Louis Le Vau, and Charles Le Brun.

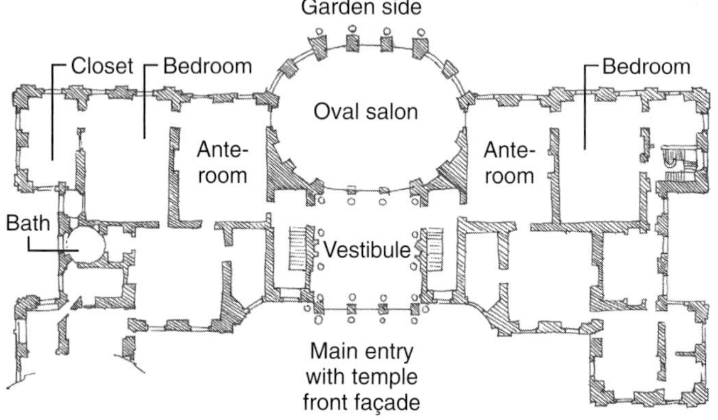

▲ **18-3.** *Château Vaux-le-Vicomte*, ground floor plan, oval salon ceiling, oval salon, and interior with tapestry, 1657–1661, near Paris, France; Louis Le Vau, André Le Nôtre, and Charles Le Brun.

DESIGN SPOTLIGHT

Architecture: Designed by chief architect Louis Le Vau, landscape designer André Le Nôtre, and architect Jules Houdoin-Mansart with interiors by Charles Le Brun, Versailles is the most important architectural statement of the period. As a completely planned building complex, it integrates landscape, architecture, interiors, furnishings, and decorative arts into a unified composition. Built on the site of Louis XIII's hunting lodge not far from Paris, it expands throughout the period to house about 10,000 people and becomes the center of the Western art world. A satellite city develops around it. The three main avenues of the city terminate in the center of the palace in the king's state chamber. André Le Nôtre's landscape plan unites *château* and landscape while providing for every activity in which the king might wish to engage. The principal axis extends from the entry court through the building into rear gardens, which progress from the formal *parterres* near the palace to less formal surrounding gardens to the natural forests beyond. Louis Le Vau's exterior shows Italian Baroque influence with symmetry, classical order, monumental scale, and center focus. Stringcourses and cornices add horizontality to the composition, while bays defined by pilasters create a regular rhythm. Typically French are the frontispiece and stepped walls leading to the center of the courtyard façade. Beginning in 1678, Jules Hardouin-Mansart encloses the rear terrace, adds rooms to each end, and designs the chapel.

Begun in 1678 by Mansart, the decoration of *Galerie des Glaces* (Hall of Mirrors) is planned by Charles Le Brun. Here, classical vocabulary supports Baroque intent as architecture, light, sculpture, and painting unite to astound, awe, and glorify Louis XIV. Light pours into and illuminates the vast space (240'-0" long, 33'-0" wide, 40'-0" high) from 17 arched windows separated by red marble pilasters. Mirrors on the opposite wall reflect and multiply the light in a manner previously unimagined. Numerous gilded surfaces throughout the space also reflect light and create glittering effects that heighten the dramatic impact. A tripartite rhythm of three arched and mirrored bays separated by red marble pilasters defines the walls. Bronze trophies delineate the end bays, while niches of classical sculpture highlight the center ones. The bases and capitals of the pilasters are gilded; the capitals are Corinthian combined with *fleur-de-lis.* A gilded, modillioned cornice supports gilded trophies carried by cherubs. The barrel-vaulted ceiling features painted scenes glorifying the reign of Louis XIV. The wood floor is *parquet de Versailles.* Tall, arched doors flanked by columns lead to the salons of Peace and War on either end. Originally, the space had solid silver furniture, three rows of crystal chandeliers, numerous *guéridons*, upholstered stools, Savonnerie rugs, and various marble and alabaster vases. Other interiors in Versailles are equally elaborate and formal as this one, including the king's bedchamber. (World Heritage Site)

▲ **18-4.** *Palais de Versailles*, floor plan, *Galerie des Glaces* (Hall of Mirrors), *Salon de la Paix* (Drawing Room of Peace), and Louis XIV's Bedchamber; Jules Hardouin-Mansart; and Grand Trianon, 1687; Versailles; France; Jules Hardouin-Mansart.

DESIGN SPOTLIGHT

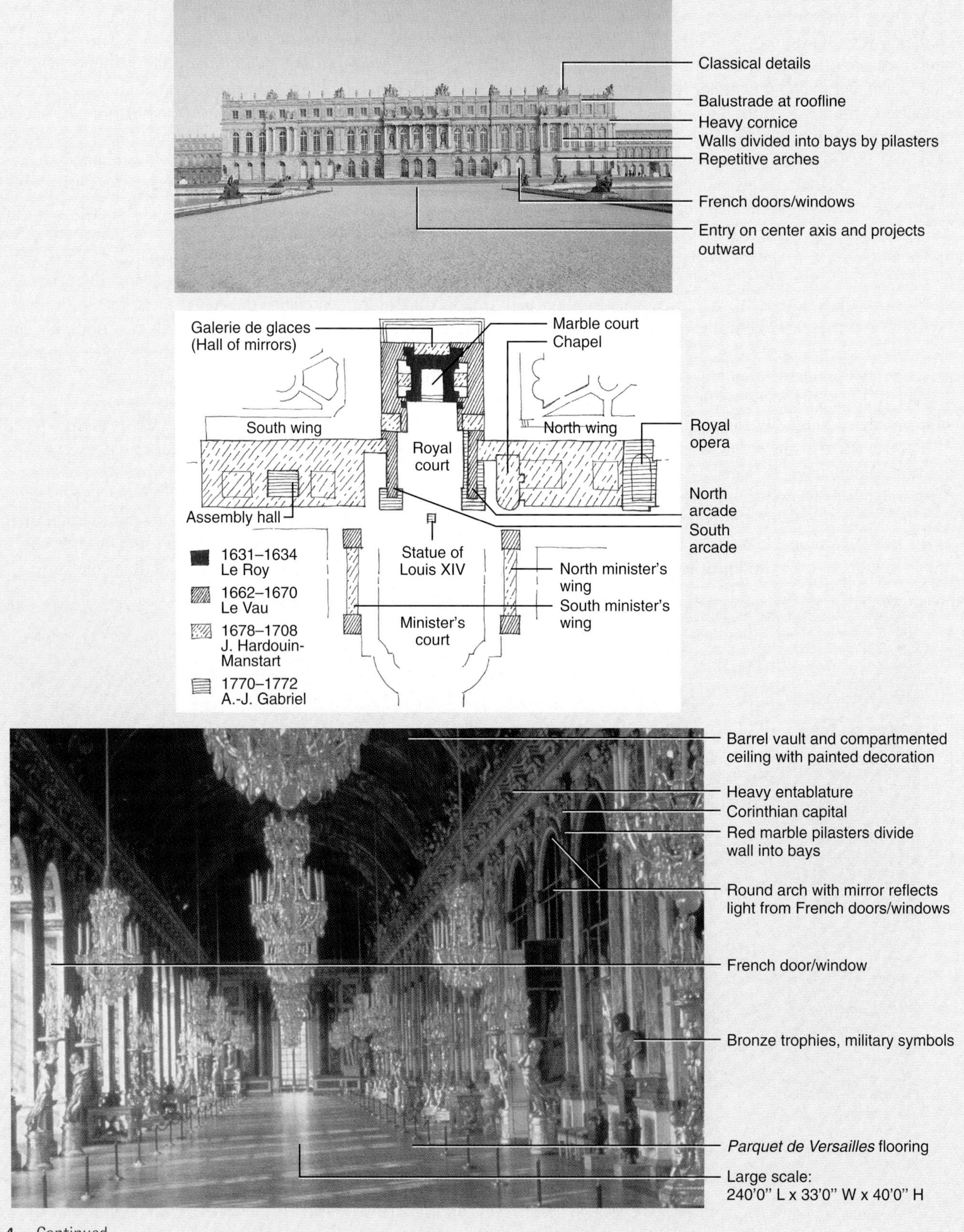

Classical details
Balustrade at roofline
Heavy cornice
Walls divided into bays by pilasters
Repetitive arches
French doors/windows
Entry on center axis and projects outward
Galerie de glaces (Hall of mirrors)
Marble court
Chapel
South wing
North wing
Royal court
Royal opera
Assembly hall
North arcade
South arcade
Statue of Louis XIV
North minister's wing
South minister's wing
Minister's court
1631–1634 Le Roy
1662–1670 Le Vau
1678–1708 J. Hardouin-Manstart
1770–1772 A.-J. Gabriel
Barrel vault and compartmented ceiling with painted decoration
Heavy entablature
Corinthian capital
Red marble pilasters divide wall into bays
Round arch with mirror reflects light from French doors/windows
French door/window
Bronze trophies, military symbols
Parquet de Versailles flooring
Large scale: 240'0" L x 33'0" W x 40'0" H

▲ **18-4.** Continued

DESIGN SPOTLIGHT

▲ **18-4.** Continued.

on principles of unity from Italy, Charles Le Brun plans and coordinates the interior design. Others execute furniture, statues, tapestries, and decorative arts under his direction. Le Brun, who possesses great power and influence, virtually creates the Louis XIV style. He is regarded as the first all-around interior decorator.

Public and Private Buildings

■ *Materials*. Rich and costly materials and classical details define interiors. Interior architectural details (Fig. 18-3, 18-4) include niches with classical figures and pilasters dividing walls into bays, similar to exteriors.

■ *Color*. The palette includes white, gold, crimson, cobalt, purple, and deep green (Fig. 18-3, 18-4). Paintings, materials, and particularly textiles supply rich, saturated colors.

■ *Floors*. Floors are of wood, marble (Fig. 18-3, 18-4), or other masonry, often in complicated patterns. Use of parquet increases throughout the period. The French favor lozenge shapes in oak. *Parquet de Versailles* is a special design composed of a diamond pattern with centers of interwoven planks. Oriental, Savonnerie (Fig. 18-7), and Aubusson rugs in harmonious designs add to the interior richness. Plain or patterned straw matting covers many floors, especially in summer. Rugs may lie on top of wood or matting, although some are still used to cover tables and cabinet tops.

■ *Walls*. Walls (Fig. 18-3, 18-4) retain classical proportions and details with an emphasis on the chimneypiece placed on the wall opposite the entrance or the windows and ornately accented above. Marble and wood mantels consist of either a bolection molding or pilasters and a cornice. Above may be a *trumeau* with a frame surrounding the mirror and painting or panel. The French use *boiserie* in important rooms as well as lesser ones, unlike the Italians. *Boiserie* usually is painted white with gold accents, especially late in the period. Symmetrically arranged wall paneling consists of a dado, center or fill, and an elaborate entablature with a decorative frieze and modillioned cornice. The horizontal portion may have rectangular panels. Walls in some rooms in Versailles are covered in polychrome marble in rectilinear patterns. A few rooms in aristocratic houses have painted polychrome grotesques and arabesques or landscapes in panels.

Textile wall coverings include damasks, plain and patterned velvets, and embossed leather. Combinations of fabrics, trims, fringe, and occasionally valances add richness and variety. Tapestries (Fig. 18-6), the most valuable wall coverings, usually hang only in important rooms, sometimes with paintings or mirrors hanging on top of them. Prints and paintings, which hang over fireplaces, doors, and inside panels, create symmetrical arrangements of form and color instead of being organized by style or subject. As important accessories, mirrors are placed over fireplaces, on piers opposite windows, or on opposite ends of the room with a table beneath them. Richly carved and gilded frames surround mirrors and paintings, which are suspended at an angle from cords with tassels.

■ *Windows and Doors*. Windows in important rooms often have draperies in velvet or silk in panels or festoons that draw up with tapes, a style newly introduced in the 1670s. Most rooms have interior wood shutters to block light. *Jalousies à la persienne* (Venetian blinds) appear in the early 18th century. Many rooms, particularly important ones, have double-entry doors. Doors match *boiserie* when present, but otherwise are paneled. Grand rooms often have *portières* that help prevent drafts and add to interior opulence.

■ *Ceilings*. Ceilings (Fig. 18-3, 18-4), especially in important rooms, are elaborately decorated and have deep moldings and cornices surrounding them. They may be flat, compartmented, coffered, coved, or vaulted with gilded or painted plasterwork. Paintings composed of illusionistic architecture and complex iconography are common in important rooms, as in Italy. French paintings are less exuberant than Italian paintings, however.

■ *Textiles*. The more important the room, the more textiles it has. French textiles (Fig. 18-3, 18-4, 18-5), produced mainly in Lyon, display Italian Renaissance influences in a predominance of brocades, velvets, and silks. Plain and patterned velvets come from Italy. Stylized flowers in urns surrounded by scrolls and garlands of fruits and flowers with large repeats are common patterns. Toward the end of the century, imported chintzes and muslins begin replacing heavier fabrics. Most chairs have slipcovers or furniture covers to protect their upholstery. Textiles also cover cushions and tabletops or shelves. People of high rank often sit beneath cloths of estate that resemble bed hangings in form and embellishment.

■ *Tapestries*. In 1662, the Gobelins Tapestry Manufactory (Fig. 18-6) begins under the influence of Le Brun and produces works exclusively for the Crown. In 1664, Colbert starts the Beauvais factory as a private enterprise under the control of the government to manufacture items for the public.

▲ **18-5.** Textiles: Textiles reflecting designs of Louis XIV; France.

▲ **18-6.** Textiles: Tapestry commemorating the visit of Louis XIV to the Gobelins factory in 1667.

▲ **18-8.** Lighting: *Guéridon* and *candelabra*; France.

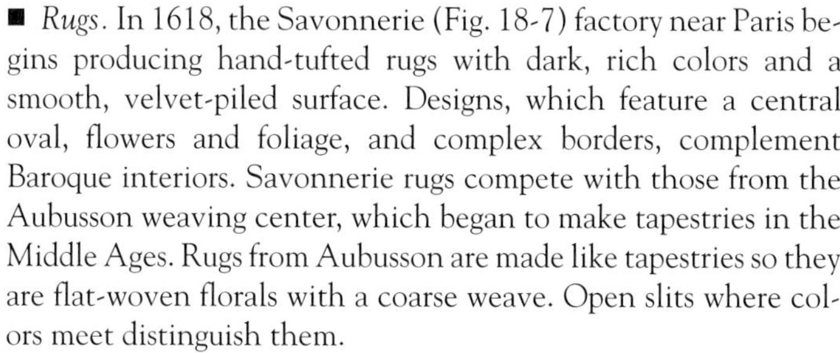

■ *Rugs*. In 1618, the Savonnerie (Fig. 18-7) factory near Paris begins producing hand-tufted rugs with dark, rich colors and a smooth, velvet-piled surface. Designs, which feature a central oval, flowers and foliage, and complex borders, complement Baroque interiors. Savonnerie rugs compete with those from the Aubusson weaving center, which began to make tapestries in the Middle Ages. Rugs from Aubusson are made like tapestries so they are flat-woven florals with a coarse weave. Open slits where colors meet distinguish them.

■ *Lighting*. Candles are the primary source of illumination, which is enhanced by crystals, gilding, mirrors, and shiny finishes. Important lighting fixtures (Fig. 18-4, 18-8) of the period include an *applique*, *flambeau*, *candelabra*, *torchère*, and *lustre à cristeaux*. They are made of gilded and carved wood, *ormolu*, and silver. Designs repeat the character of the interior ornamentation. Elaborate *guéridons* may hold either a *candelabra* or large *flambeau*.

▲ **18-7.** Rugs: Savonnerie rug, 1680; Paris, France.

■ *Later Interpretations*. Besides some imitation by the English and other Europeans in the 17th century, elements of Louis XIV character for exteriors and interiors reappears in the Beaux Arts style of the late 19th and early 20th centuries in France, England, and America. It adopts the ornate and lavish interiors of Versailles and other French Baroque dwellings (Fig. 18-9). Some wealthy Americans import French rooms to install in their own homes, a practice evident in the Newport, Rhode Island, summer "cottages" and the affluent estates in Palm Beach and other places in Florida.

▲ **18-9.** Later Interpretation: Dining room, Marble House, 1892; Newport, Rhode Island; Richard Morris Hunt.

FURNISHINGS AND DECORATIVE ARTS

Furniture of the Louis XIV period harmonizes with the interiors and through the influence of Charles Le Brun becomes an integral part of the room decoration, especially at Versailles. Most pieces, which are designed to be placed against the wall, show a direct relationship to the wall paneling in their rectilinear shape and the use of moldings and/or columns. Furniture supports ceremony, rank, and status, so appearance is more important than comfort. At court, people often stand, so there is minimal seating and an abundance of cabinets, tables, and storage pieces. Seating has a special etiquette at court. Only the king and queen may sit in armchairs. A royal child may sit in a chair with a back and no arms. Being permitted to sit on stools honors others of high rank.

Baroque furniture is symmetrical, rectangular, and often accented with large curves (Fig. 18-10, 18-11, 18-12, 18-13). Proportions are massive, and the decoration lavish. Carving, marquetry, and gilding are more important than in previous periods. Leg types include the console, term (Fig. 18-4, 18-10, 18-11, 18-12), cabriole (Fig. 18-13), turned, or round pedestal. Feet are bun, paw, carved, or turned. Many pieces incorporate heavy, ornate H or X *(saltire)* (Fig. 18-4, 18-10, 18-11, 18-12) stretchers, and seating may have curved arms with heavily carved volutes.

During the period, numerous factories are opened to produce goods for the court, the nobility, and the middle class. In 1663, Charles Le Brun helps establish and then directs the *Manufacture Royale de Meubles de la Couronne at Gobelins*, which produces tapestries, paintings, sculpture, silverwork, and furniture. In 1668, vast requirements of glass for Versailles bring about the creation of a royal glass factory nearby. In 1685, Louis XIV forbids public worship of all religions except Roman Catholic, which stifles religious freedom and results in the revocation of the Edict of Nantes. Consequently, Huguenot craftsmen leave the country, causing a setback in the production of decorative arts in France.

Public and Private Buildings

■ *Materials*. Principal furniture woods are beech, oak, walnut, and ebony. Many pieces are gilded and feature marquetry or parquetry. André-Charles Boulle develops a special marquetry of tortoise shell and brass known as Boullework that is much copied. *Ormolu* accents all cabinet pieces, especially on points of strain (Fig. 18-13, 18-14). Some Oriental influence is evident in lacquered furniture with *Chinoiserie* motifs rendered on a black background. Tables have richly grained marble tops.

■ *Seating*. Seating has tall, upholstered backs and seats embellished with fancy trims and gilded nails. Pieces (Fig. 18-3, 18-10, 18-11) include arm and side chairs, *canapés*, and stools. The *fauteuil* or open upholstered armchair is introduced during the late 17th century. Sets of upholstered chairs and sofas are very fashionable.

▲ **18-10.** Gilt *fauteuil*, late 17th century; France.

▲ **18-11.** Carved and gilded *canapé*, late 17th century; France.

■ *Tables*. Tables (Fig. 18-3, 18-12) support a variety of activities including gaming, conversation, and entertainment. The most common are *console* tables, the *bureau plat*, occasional tables, and game tables.

■ *Storage*. Rooms have no closets so clothing and other items usually are stored in *armoires* (Fig. 18-14) or newly introduced *commodes* (Fig. 18-13).

■ *Beds*. Beds (Fig. 18-4) are monumental, rectilinear, and completely surrounded with costly fabrics. Types include four-posters, beds with canopies and no posts, portable field beds, and trundle beds. In state bedchambers, a balustrade separates the bed from the rest of the room. The French prefer rectangular valances and testers, unlike the English and Dutch who use shaped ones. Testers vary in size from the half-tester or *lit d'ange* used by children and others of secondary importance to full-size ones called *lit à duchesse*. Finials or vases filled with ostrich feathers placed on top of the tester add to the opulence.

■ *Decorative Arts*. Accessories become more numerous and contribute to the dazzling display in rooms. Objects are often in pairs or symmetrical arrangements and their opulent design complements the unified composition of the space. Types include clocks, lighting, tapestries, rugs, ceramics, fireplace furniture, fire screens, paintings, mirrors, and vases. The 17th and 18th centuries are France's golden age in decorative arts because of the scope, diversity, and detail of the designs and the superb construction. Ongoing trade with the Orient provides prized pieces and stimulates new concepts in decoration, such as lacquerwork.

■ *Ceramics*. *Faience* (tin-glazed earthenware) is especially admired because its white body resembles porcelain. The Crown's support of the industry increases its importance. Chinese porcelain imports, particularly blue and white designs, continue to be vastly popular.

▲ **18-12.** Table; 17th century; France.

▲ **18-13.** *Commode*, early 18th century; André-Charles Boulle. [The Jack and Belle Linsky Collection, 1982 (1982.60.82). The Metropolitan Museum of Art, New York, NY, U.S.A. Image © The Metropolitan Museum of Art/Art Resource, NY.].

DESIGN SPOTLIGHT

Furniture: Massive in scale, *armoires* display characteristics of the Baroque style through symmetry, rectangular panels, classical motifs, marquetry, gilding, and *ormolu* decoration. Boulle, the foremost cabinetmaker of the period, supposedly introduces the one-piece *armoire* with double doors during the period. *Armoires,* as his specialty, are a particular focus for lavish embellishment. Attributed to Boulle, this one is of ebony with bold vases of floral marquetry in the center panels. Marquetry of tin and tortoiseshell fills the upper and lower panels. Exquisite *ormolu* forms the hinges and the lion heads on the base.

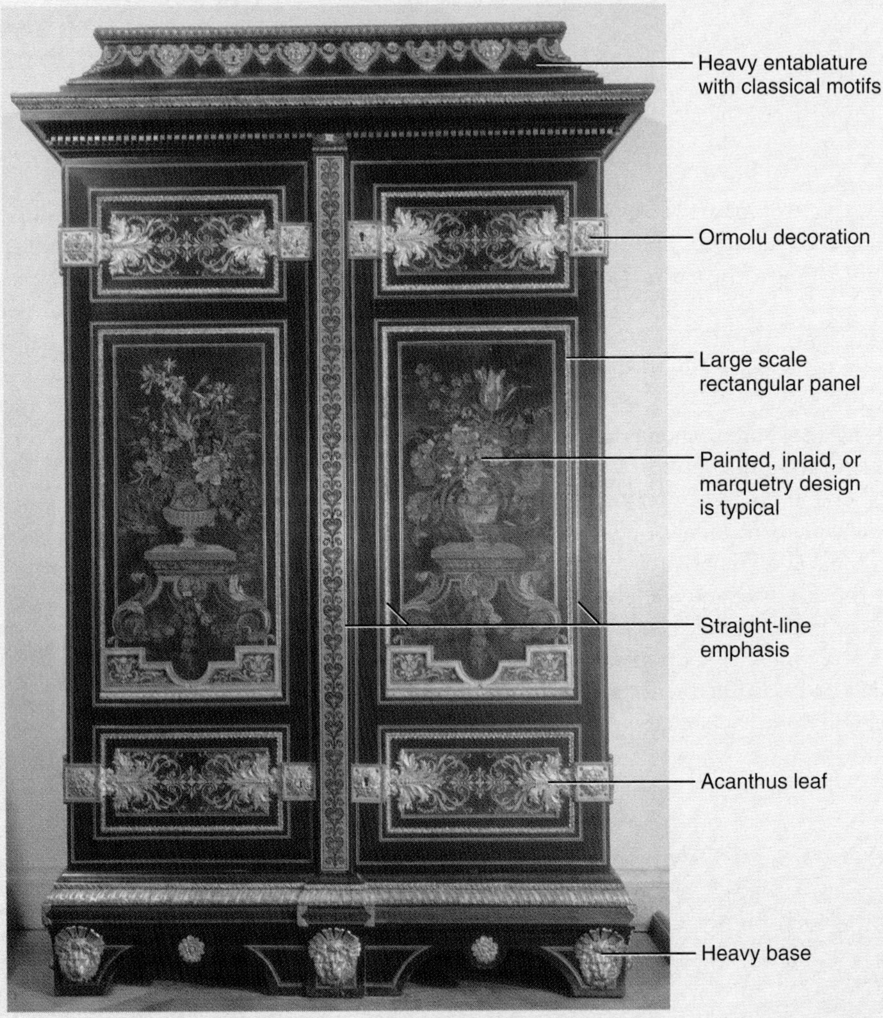

▲ **18-14.** *Armoire,* c. 1700; France; attributed to André-Charles Boulle.

CHAPTER 19

English Restoration

1660–1702

Si monumentum requiris circumspice. (If you would see this monument, look around.)

—Inscription to Sir Christopher Wren (1675–1710), S. Paul's Cathedral, London

Following the return of Charles II from France and the restoration of the monarchy, foreign influences sweep away the Elizabethan and Jacobean styles in architecture, interiors, and furniture. English Restoration architecture wholeheartedly adopts classicism, whether influenced by the Italian Renaissance, French or Italian Baroque, Dutch Palladianism, or Inigo Jones. Interiors may be exuberantly Baroque or pursue a more subdued classicism, often with rich, three-dimensional carving or plasterwork. Furniture features Baroque design principles and elements tempered by French elegance or Dutch curving silhouettes.

HISTORICAL AND SOCIAL

Oliver Cromwell is unable to establish a settled government, which enables Charles II, son of the former king, to reclaim the throne after Cromwell's death in 1660. Passionate about art and architecture, Charles II encourages foreign craftsmen to come to England to refurbish his royal palaces and the homes of the nobility. However, his reign is not peaceful because he clashes with the nobility over his Catholic faith and his belief, like his father's, in the divine right of kings to rule unaided and unassisted. Following Charles's death in 1685, his nephew, James II, tries to continue his predecessor's unpopular policies.

In 1688, the exasperated nobility invite the Dutch ruler William of Orange to invade England because they fear James II will succeed in his quest for an absolute monarchy. Following the bloodless and successful Glorious Revolution, the notion of an absolute monarchy is crushed, and a Protestant, William III, sits on the throne. As patrons of the arts, William and his wife Mary, a daughter of James II, encourage building and decoration. When William dies in 1702, Anne, his sister-in-law, who is the last of the Stuarts, succeeds him.

Despite internal conflicts, England grows in power and prestige during the second half of the 17th century. England's victory over the French at Blenheim in 1704 establishes her as a leading military power. The work of such men as Isaac Newton and John Locke give her a commanding place in science and thought. Her colonies grow and prosper, and her wealth increases.

CONCEPTS

In this period, England again develops her own eclectic expression, which is dominated by foreign influences. The Baroque style comes to England with Italian artisans who execute commissions there and the English architects and designers who visit Italy. French concepts of design arrive with Charles II and his nobles, who exile at the court of Louis XIV, and the Huguenot craftsmen who flee from France to escape religious persecution. Although these ideas stimulate a more elaborate and exuberant character in some works, they are not universally accepted. Conditions in England are not conducive to a national Baroque style as in France or Italy because most Englishmen abhor both the idea of an absolute monarchy and the Catholic Church to inspire allegiance or glorify. Instead, the most common manifestation of the Baroque is a more subdued, restrained, and conservative one than that of either France or Italy. English Baroque generally reflects a more Dutch-like character that comes from trade, commerce, and, later, the craftsmen who emigrate with William and Mary. However, there also is a more elaborate Baroque that coexists and intertwines with the more empirical classicism established by Sir Christopher Wren. Both the conservative and elaborate expressions are used to depict power and wealth.

MOTIFS

■ *Motifs*. Motifs (Fig. 19-1, 19-3, 19-4, 19-5, 19-6, 19-8, 19-9, 19-10, 19-13, 19-14) include pediments, columns, pilasters, arches, C and S scrolls, fruits, flowers, shells, garlands, leaves, swags, acanthus, and urns.

▲ **19-1.** Architectural Detail: Carved panel detail, c. 1670; England.

ARCHITECTURE

Rational classicism, along with some Baroque influences, defines the form and provides the details of English Restoration architecture. Characteristics include classical elements, large scale, symmetry, center emphasis, advancing and receding planes, and some curves. English design hardly ever exhibits the plasticity of Italy or the monumental magnificence of France. Building types include churches (Fig. 19-2, 19-3), public complexes, collegiate buildings, townhouses, country houses (Fig. 19-4, 19-5), palaces, and palace complexes (Fig. 19-6).

Following the restoration of the monarchy, architecture turns toward the Palladian classicism of Inigo Jones. However, the Great Fire of London in September 1666 brings Sir Christopher Wren to the forefront, and his work determines a different course for buildings. Wren, who has visited France, introduces Baroque concepts and motifs that move English architecture away from the restrained style of Inigo Jones. Despite monumental scale, center emphasis, and some complexity in form and plan, Wren's work rarely achieves the dynamism, forcefulness, and movement of Italy. Rather, it comes closer to the reserved classicism of France. A rationalist and mathematician, Wren uses classical elements to control and disguise the mass and form of a building while frequently borrowing from French and Italian examples. Wren's most Baroque designs are those for the royal family where glorifying the monarchy and/or imitating the French at Versailles are design goals. These works display Baroque integration of building and landscape, axial organization, and sequencing of spaces. His most creative projects are the city churches in London.

Sir John Vanbrugh and Nicholas Hawksmoor design the most obvious English versions of Baroque architecture in several country houses and city churches during the early 18th century. Integration of structure and landscape, monumental scale, center emphasis, movement, advancing and receding planes, and classical details characterize their work. Their designs reveal greater concern for mass, rhythm, and proportion than the managing of form with classical vocabulary that characterizes Wren's work.

Just before the Restoration, Sir Roger Pratt introduces the symmetrical, rectangular block house with sash windows, hipped roof, classical details, and double-pile plan that will become standard for smaller Georgian houses in England and America. Like other architects, Pratt draws elements from Italy, France, and Holland, but the resulting combination is uniquely English.

Public and Private Buildings

■ *Floor Plans*. Wren's plan for S. Paul's Cathedral (Fig. 19-3) in London is a Latin cross with domed crossing and apsidal ends of nave and transept. The dome with its considerable height creates a more centralized focus, similar to Continental examples. Plans of his London city churches (Fig. 19-2) vary because of irregular sites: some are square, others are rectangular; one is roughly oval. Wren strives for centralized designs that focus on the pulpit, a visible sign of the primacy of preaching in England's Protestant churches. Church plans by other designers are similar to those by Wren.

Most grand house plans are linear or U-shaped, although a few have H or E shapes (Fig. 19-5). Vanbrugh's dwellings usually are composed of a three-sided form with a center courtyard for the main house. The axis of approach continues into the vestibule, the grand *salon*, and the landscape beyond in the French Baroque manner (Fig. 19-6). His designs are exceptions, as most houses sit in a relatively self-contained manner within the landscape. Great houses, whether new or remodeled, adopt French and Italian *enfilade* planning and are organized around private and state apartments. Smaller houses usually are rectangular blocks with double-pile plans that are two rooms deep with a central passage or hall introduced by Pratt (Fig. 19-4). Townhouse plans become standardized: they are one or more rooms wide and at least two rooms deep, and have two or more stories.

■ *Materials*. Stone and brick, often combined, replace wood in both public and private buildings in London as a result of the Great Fire and increasing timber shortages. Varieties of stone include Portland stone, red and gray granite, and slates. Brick is the most common building material. The English bond brick pattern dominates until the 1630s, when Flemish bond replaces it. Red brick with white stone details show Dutch influence. Construction is mostly post and lintel, but churches may be vaulted and domed.

■ *Façades*. While no common or defining public exterior exists during this period, most feature classical columns, pilasters, pediments, quoins, and arches. Churches have towers or steeples (Fig. 19-2). Temple fronts define porches or form porticoes and emphasize centers (Fig. 19-3). Pilasters, engaged columns, or colossal orders define bays (Fig 19-3). On buildings without colossal orders, stringcourses delineate stories. Although there is some layering of elements, it usually lacks the forcefulness and three-dimensionality of Italy. Some compositions, especially on grander structures, build toward the center with projecting or curving architectural details, planes, or walls (Fig. 19-3).

Façades of palaces and great houses resemble Versailles or have Palladian devices such as temple fronts (Fig. 19-5). Compositions are usually symmetrical with large windows and classical details that build toward and/or emphasize centers. Colossal pilasters may divide façades into bays. Grand houses with both linear and U-shaped plans have frontispieces and/or end pavilions that often project in the French manner (Fig. 19-6). These exterior units mark important interior spaces such as the *salon* in the center, and state bedchambers on each end. Contrasts of light and dark accentuate depth and scale.

Smaller houses have restrained compositions with stories separated by stringcourses, quoins, and modillioned cornices (Fig. 19-4). Townhouses follow designs of country houses.

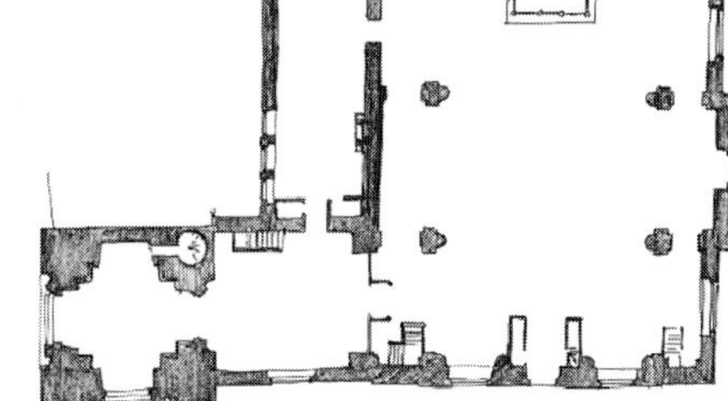

▲ **19-2.** S. Mary-le-Bow, Cheapside, floor plan, and nave, 1670–1677; London, England; Sir Christopher Wren.

DESIGN SPOTLIGHT

Architecture and Interiors: S. Paul's Cathedral is the fourth cathedral to occupy this site, and its design reflects the more sober but grand English Baroque created by Sir Christopher Wren. The broad façade has a pedimented center supported on twin columns that is reminiscent of the east façade of the Louvre, Paris. Inside the pediment is a relief of the conversion of S. Paul by Francis Bird. Recessed entries behind the columns create a strong contrast of dark and light that helps emphasize the center. Exquisite naturalistic carvings contrast with bold, layered architectural details. Flanking the portico are twin towers whose bold architecture, details, and contrasts of light and dark make them readable from a distance. The perspective windows on the towers' lower façades are like those at the Palazzo Barberini in Rome, and the tops resemble those by Borromini at *S. Carlo alle Quattro Fontane*, also in Rome. The form and shape of the dome, one of the world's largest, are reminiscent of Bramante's design for S. Peter's. The unusual three-part dome, composed of an inner dome, a brick cone supporting the lantern, and an exterior shell, is a design and engineering accomplishment unique to Wren.

In plan, Wren's design progresses through several concepts beginning with a domed Greek cross plan to the final Latin cross plan with a domed crossing. The church officials believed a Latin cross to be more appropriate to the liturgical and ceremonial needs of the building. The broad nave is used for processions and to house large congregations. A series of smaller domes mark the bays of the nave and flanking aisles, and large arches carried on piers form the nave arcade. Pilasters and deep cornices articulate the piers and lead the eye toward the altar. Coffers cover the undersides of the arches. Architectural details contrast in color to the walls to emphasize their importance. The inside of the dome at the crossing features monochrome paintings from the life of S. Paul by Sir James Thornhill, and Grinling Gibbons carves most of the woodwork, particularly the choir stalls beyond the crossing. The entire effect is one of logical planning and monumental form articulated and held in check by classical order.

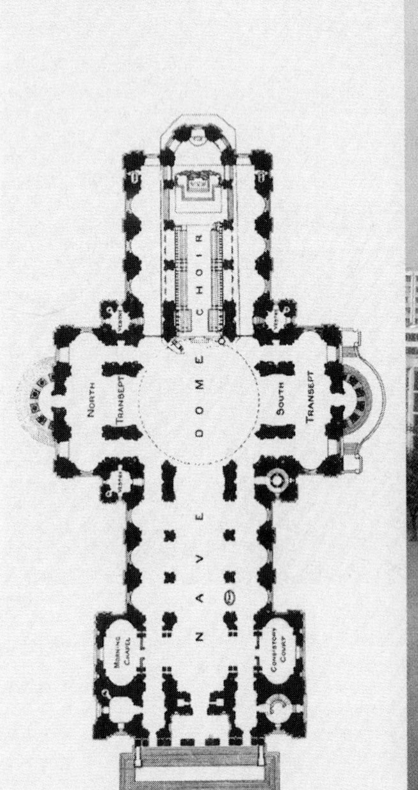

▲ **19-3.** S. Paul's Cathedral, floor plan, and nave, 1675–1710; London, England; Sir Christopher Wren.

■ *Windows*. Windows on public and private buildings (Fig. 19-3, 19-4, 19-5) remain large in size. Rectangular or arched windows have classical surrounds, pediments, and/or lintels. Wren uses as many windows as possible to fill his church interiors with light.

The most common window type on houses is rectangular with a shaped surround or surmounted with a flat lintel, triangular or segmental pediment, or a mixture of pediment shapes (Fig. 19-5). Palaces or grand houses may have combinations of arched and rectangular windows separated by pilasters or by story (Fig. 19-6). They may also have round or square windows integrated with rectangular ones. Some dwellings have small windows on the ground floor, larger windows in the story above, and square windows in the attic. Sash windows (Fig. 19-4) are introduced after the 1670s.

■ *Doors*. Entrances often incorporate classical details and bold surrounds to emphasize their importance and/or to culminate a composition. Porticoes or archways are common in large buildings (Fig. 19-3, 19-6), whereas on houses the most common devices are columns or pilasters carrying a pediment and/or an arched window (Fig. 19-4, 19-5). Door surrounds (Fig. 19-2, 19-4, 19-5) consist of triangular, or segmental, closed or broken pediments; lintels carried on columns or pilasters; and variations of round arches. Single- and double-paneled doors are either of plain or painted wood.

■ *Roofs*. Roofs on public buildings may be flat with balustrades and sculpture, gabled, hipped, or domed (Fig. 19-3). Churches without domes have gabled roofs. Smaller houses (Fig. 19-4) have gabled or hipped roofs, usually with dormers, while those on palaces and grand houses are flat with balustrades and occasionally sculptures (Fig. 19-5, 19-6). Some retain the earlier parapets. A cupola or dome may mark the center.

■ *Later Interpretations*. Restoration church forms, façades, and steeples become standard for later classical churches during the English Neo-Palladian and Georgian period in England and America. The style of large Baroque houses rarely is adopted later, although some elements reappear. However, Pratt's rectangular-block, classical houses become one of the standard house types during the American Georgian style (Fig. 19-7) and later in the Colonial Revival of the early 20th century.

DESIGN SPOTLIGHT

▲ **19-3.** Continued

INTERIORS

Both conservative and extravagant interiors characterize the Restoration period. The majority of English interiors are conservative, demonstrating a somber and unostentatious classicism in which human scale, restraint, and repose dominate. More somber than the earlier Elizabethan or Jacobean interiors, Restoration rooms have classical details, paneling, compartmentalized plaster ceilings, and wood floors. Staircases, balustrades, chimneypieces, paneling, and over doors and windows feature wood carving, the most common form of decoration during the period.

Ornate interiors express power and wealth. Found only in palatial homes, they are large in scale and display conspicuous extravagance, illusionistic wall and ceiling paintings in vivid colors, complexity, exuberant plasterwork and/or wood carving highlighted with gilding, and classical details to create drama or overwhelm. Images often reflect the Italian or French Baroque influences, and foreign craftsmen execute many of these interiors and their details.

Church interiors usually relate closely to exteriors through architectural features such as columns, pilasters, arches, windows, and ceilings. Scale is an important element in delineating the relationship of spaces and circulation paths. Large churches are more likely to have a main aisle or nave, whereas the size of the church dictates the use of side aisles. Smaller examples usually have none. Vestibules are often small, preceding entry into a large, imposing nave (Fig. 19-3).

In houses, room names and functions change under French influence. The main reception/entertaining space is now called the *salon* or saloon (Fig. 19-6, 19-9) and retains a central position on the plan. Lodgings are now called apartments, relating to French designations. Closets become cabinets, and their lavish decoration signals a new importance. Withdrawing rooms become general reception rooms and may precede an important sleeping space. Bedchambers are more public, although less so than in France. In residences, stair halls (Fig. 19-8) and vestibules become important central circulation spaces so they receive greater emphasis and design attention.

Public and Private Buildings

■ *Color.* Colors (Fig. 19-6, 19-8, 19-9) are carefully chosen to enhance the building design, sequence of rooms, and the objects within them. Expensive colors, such as Prussian blue, are used in the most important rooms. Color may also relate to a particular material; for example, wainscoting is often painted various shades of brown, emulating wood. Colors may also serve to enhance architectural details, ceilings, paintings, upholstery, or hangings.

Wall colors in churches (Fig. 19-3) are often white or the color of the building material with architectural details in contrasting colors. Ceilings or domes (Fig. 19-3) may be a painted a single color or may be frescoed. Gilding often accentuates details. Conservative rooms in dwellings tend to be dull, in browns, grays, blue grays, and olive greens, although there are some exceptions. Walls in showy interiors are often light colors, the color of the building material, or frescoed. Gilding may enhance the paneling or important decoration. Brighter colors are adopted in more intimate spaces. Sequences of rooms generally have the same wall colors.

DESIGN SPOTLIGHT

Architecture: At Coleshill, Sir Roger Pratt introduces the rectangular block, classically detailed manor house with a double-pile floor plan that will dominate smaller Georgian houses in America and Great Britain throughout the 18th century. The design incorporates English, Dutch, and French elements. The façade has two stories, nearly equal in size, separated by a stringcourse. The much lower ground story is rusticated. Quoins mark the corners, and a modillioned cornice accentuates the roofline. Large sash windows capped by lintels are distributed symmetrically across the façade. A pedimented entrance and greater spacing between windows mark the center of the composition and the stair hall within. Most of these details are Italian. The hipped roof, which is Dutch, has dormers and is capped by a balustrade and cupola in the French manner. The double-pile plan is two rooms deep and has a longitudinal hallway running parallel to the façade. Pratt transforms the medieval great hall into a ceremonial entrance hall with a grand, open well staircase. Behind is a grand salon.

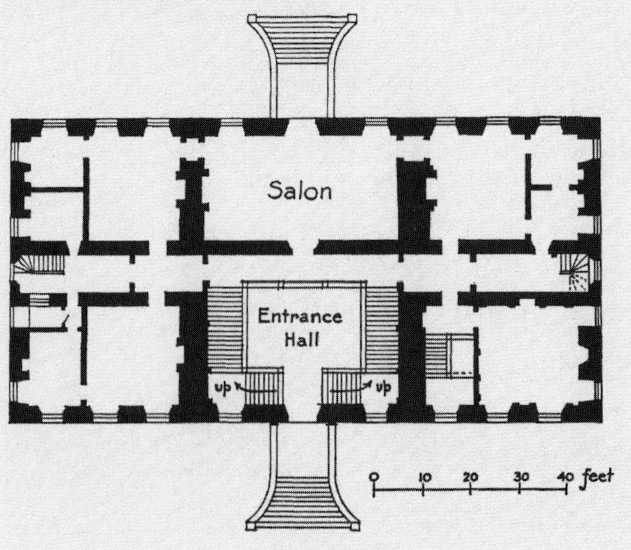

▲ **19-4.** Coleshill and floor plan, c. 1650 (destroyed 1952); Oxfordshire, England; Sir Roger Pratt.

DESIGN SPOTLIGHT

Architecture and Interior: Designed for the Brownlow family, Belton House has an elegant, classical Palladian-inspired façade. The center projects and has a triangular pediment at roofline. The hipped roof is capped by a balustrade with a cupola in the center. Quoins accentuate the corners, and stringcourses separate the stories. The H-shaped plan and large sash windows allow more light into the interiors. The somewhat outdated H plan also permits greater privacy because of easier access between and among rooms.

Characteristic of conservative interiors, the drawing room serves as an important social area and contains some of England's finest examples of the carving work of Grinling Gibbons. The symmetrical space has a dominant chimneypiece composed of a mantel with bolection molding and an overmantel. Surmounting and flanking this are Gibbons' three-dimensional carvings of fruits, flowers, and fowl. Additional carvings and walnut paneling with gilding highlight the other walls. The white, compartmented ceiling displays the richness of the Baroque style with ovals, rectangles, and heavy moldings. Furnishings are more ornate than in most conservative interiors.

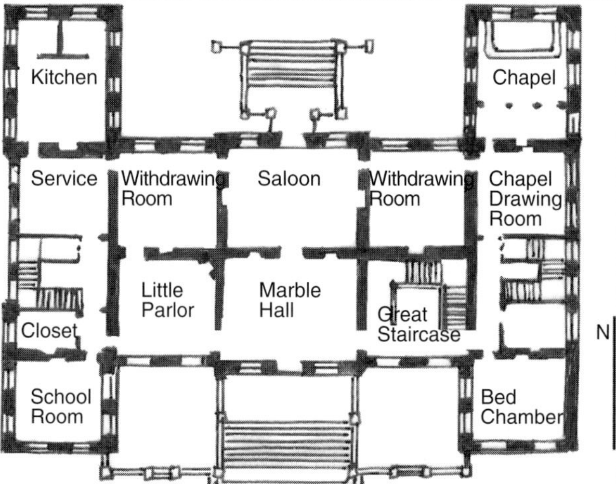

Compartmented ceiling with heavy moldings
Walnut paneling with beveled edges
Wood carving by Grinling Gibbons
Portrait over mantel
Display of Oriental porcelain
Bolection molding surrounds fireplace opening to create mantel; major emphasis is chimneypiece
Heavy scaled rug pattern

▲ **19-5.** Belton House, floor plan, and drawing room with chimneypiece detail, 1684–1686; Lincolnshire; England; house by William Stanton; drawing room carving by Grinling Gibbons.

▲ **19-6.** Blenheim Palace and saloon; 1705–1724; Oxfordshire, England; Sir John Vanbrugh and Nicholas Hawksmoor.

■ *Floors*. Floors are usually wide, unpolished boards of oak or deal (pine) in residences; public buildings more commonly use stone or marble. Polished wood parquet becomes common after its introduction from France in the 1650s. The use of rush matting continues, but finer, patterned mats are imported from North Africa or the Far East. Oriental rugs may cover tables or floors.

■ *Walls*. Classical forms and details characterize church interiors. For example, in S. Paul's Cathedral (Fig. 19-3) columns, pilasters, arches, heavy entablatures, and clerestory windows both articulate and define the interior walls and the open spaces. Walls themselves, which may be plaster or stone, are usually painted white and/or have natural wood paneling, which is usually set between pilasters. Choirstalls are often elaborately embellished with pilasters; paneling; and rich, ornate carving in the manner of Grinling Gibbons, the foremost wood-carver of the period. His work in public and private buildings is composed of fruits, flowers, and fowl rendered in a pierced, lacy, naturalistic, three-dimensional manner (Fig. 19-1, 19-5). Wren's city churches, such as S. Mary-le-Bow in Cheapside (Fig. 19-2), follow the interior detailing of S. Paul's Cathedral but on a much reduced and more intimate scale. Other church architects emulate Wren.

▲ **19-7.** Later Interpretation: Hammond-Harwood House, 1773–1774; Annapolis, Maryland; William Buckland. American Georgian.

Rooms in houses without hangings are paneled (Fig. 19-5, 19-8), which becomes more architectural and is divided horizontally into dado (standardized at 3'-0" high), wall surface, and cornice as before. Panels become larger with prominent moldings and carvings during the period. Classical moldings, such as bead, fillet, dentil, and cyma recta, are common. Important rooms may feature applied naturalistic plasterwork or wood carvings similar to the work of Grinling Gibbons around the fireplace or in paneling (Fig. 19-5, 19-8, 19-9). Paneling may be painted or left natural. Other common treatments for paneling include marbleizing, graining, and japanning. Architectural details and the stiles and rails of paneling often contrast in color or material. Panel centers may have imported or domestic lacquered panels, oil paintings, or painted designs or scenes. Gilding or silvering may highlight moldings, capitals, and other details in grand rooms. Some spaces have painted *trompe l'oeil* architectural details. Illusionistic, often exuberant, wall paintings in the Baroque manner embellish important rooms and stair halls in great houses (Fig. 19-6).

As a focal point, the fireplace (Fig. 19-5, 19-8) consists of mantel and overmantel in elaborate designs with bolection moldings or columns, pilasters, pediments, brackets, scrolls, and garlands. Oil paintings or mirrors hang above the mantel following French interiors. Naturalistic carvings in high relief sometimes flank and surmount mantels.

■ *Staircases*. Staircases (Fig. 19-9), often one of the most important features in the house, become a focus for the elaborate carving characteristic of the period. Some retain the traditional columnar banisters in the handrail, but they are now enriched with detailed carvings. Others replace banisters with panels with centers of open and lacy, curvilinear, naturalistic carving.

■ *Windows and Doors*. Doors and windows are arranged symmetrically. Most windows are sliding sashes surrounded by architectural details. They also have interior shutters that fold into the window jamb (Fig. 19-8). In important rooms, curtains in panels or the newer festoons from France adorn the windows. Sometimes, flat, shaped valances trimmed with tapes and fringe provide additional embellishment while hiding the nails attaching curtains to window frames.

Doors (Fig. 19-5, 19-8, 19-9) are paneled in dark wood, often walnut. When painted, doors match paneling. Many have paintings above them. At the end of the period, doors commonly have an architrave, frieze, cornice, and broken pediment over them. Doors in grand rooms have *portières* to prevent drafts.

■ *Ceilings*. Ceilings in churches, other public buildings, and the grandest of houses (Fig. 19-2, 19-3) are vaulted, arched, and/or domed. Compartmented, coffered, and other geometrically designed ceilings may emphasize important areas, such as the altar, the transept, and primary circulation paths. Heavy moldings provide rich surface decoration.

In houses, molded plaster, usually compartmentalized, becomes the most common form of ceiling decoration because of a new, harder plaster that dries faster and can be mounted on wire or wood. Compositions (Fig. 19-5, 19-6, 19-8, 19-9) are squares, ovals, or circles with centers left bare, or they have paintings. By the 1670s, naturalistic decorations of garlands composed of shells, leaves, and flowers similar to wood carvings form the borders and fill the centers of compartments.

■ *Textiles*. Interiors of the wealthy feature numerous colorful and opulent textiles whether as wall hangings, curtains, *portières*, cushions, or upholstery. All fabrics in the room usually match. Types include plain and patterned velvets, damasks, satins, mohairs, linens, India cottons, woolens, Turkeywork and crewelwork. Crimson is a favored color, but others include green, blue, black, white, and yellow. *Appliqué*; colored, gold, or silver embroidery; and trims embellish and add variety to curtains, wall and bed hangings, and upholstery (Fig. 19-8). Textile or leather hangings often adorn walls in state and reception rooms and may match other fabrics in the room. Trims and flat tape outline wall coverings, curtains, and the seats, backs, and wings on chairs and settees. Gilded nails secure fabric to frames. Furniture cases (slipcovers) protect expensive fabrics.

■ *Lighting*. As wax candles are expensive and tallow or rush lights are smelly and burn quickly, minimal lighting is the norm except during evening social functions or special occasions in both public and private buildings. Candleholders include candlesticks, sconces, chandeliers, and lanterns. Candles often are placed on candle stands at heights that facilitate the continual snuffing or trimming of the wicks to prevent guttering and loss of light. Most candlesticks are of wood, brass, or pewter. By the second half of the century, affluent homes commonly have silver candlesticks and candelabra or branches in Baroque designs. Sconces, usually limited to domestic use, have one or more branches and a reflecting back. Chandeliers in houses are rarer in England than in other countries, although lanterns commonly light passages, stair halls, and vestibules. Since the only sources of artificial light in houses are fireplaces and candles, room decorations strive to enhance light with gilding, shiny surfaces, and mirrors.

Between 1674 and 1676, Englishman George Ravenscroft perfects a lead glass formula, which marks the greatest improvement

▲ **19-8.** Queen's antechamber, Ham House, 1673–1683; Surrey, England.

▲ **19-9.** Stair hall, ceiling detail, and saloon, Sudbury Hall, c. 1676; Derbyshire, England; carving by Edward Pierce; plasterwork by Robert Bradbury and James Pettifer, 1691; painting by Louis Laguerre.

in glassmaking since the 13th century. The new lead glass has unsurpassed clarity. It also has excellent ability to reflect and refract light, especially when cut, which is important to chandeliers and other forms of lighting at a time when houses are dark and candles taxed. Lead glass fosters a new style in both lighting and glassware that emphasizes form over shape or applied decoration.

▲ **19-9.** Continued.

FURNISHINGS AND DECORATIVE ARTS

The nobles' desire for luxury, refinement, new forms, and finer cabinetwork transforms English furniture during the period. They reject traditional English prototypes, preferring styles from abroad. French, Dutch, and Oriental influences begin to shape high-style furnishings for the affluent. In contrast, the middle and lower classes tend to prefer plainer versions of high styles or oak furniture in the Elizabethan tradition.

Walnut replaces oak as the primary furniture wood; carving, veneer, and lacquer become more common forms of decoration. New pieces include easie chairs and completely upholstered daybeds found only in bedchambers, chests of drawers without doors, settees or sofas, cabinets on stands, and dressing or toilet tables. Furniture commonly lines the walls when not in use, following French practices. Most arrangements are symmetrical. A common grouping between windows consists of a table flanked by candlestands and a looking glass on the wall or pier above. Besides Louis XIV variations, two major furniture developments make up the Restoration period.

- *Charles II, Carolean, or Stuart (1660–1689)*. This furniture style (Fig. 19-10) features rectilinear forms, S and C curves, scrolls, and turning. Exuberant and ornate carving is the main decoration, but the use of veneers increases. Caning, carving, scrolls, and ball and bun feet distinguish Charles II furniture. The character is extravagant and Baroque.
- *William and Mary (1689–1702)*. This more conservative furniture style (Fig. 19-11, 19-12) shows more Dutch influence in curving silhouettes, cabriole and trumpet legs, spoon backs and splats, and Spanish and *pied-de-biche* feet. The style extensively uses richly figured veneers and marquetry (Fig. 19-13, 19-14). Turned, baluster, or trumpet legs and flat stretchers that repeat the shapes of aprons are definitive characteristics.

▲ **19-10.** Charles II walnut armchairs, c. late 17th century; England.

▲ **19-11.** William and Mary side chair with spoon back, cabriole legs, and *pied-de-biche* feet, late 17th or early 18th century; England.

▲ **19-12.** William and Mary dressing table, 17th century; England.

DESIGN SPOTLIGHT

Furniture: Cabinets on stands, fashionable pieces throughout the Restoration period, are a focus for the skills of the marqueter and cabinetmaker. Lacquered cabinets are imported from the Orient and placed on elaborately carved and gilded stands; others are made locally with so-called japanned finishes. This stand features spiral turned legs characteristic of France and flat, curved stretchers. The cabinet has colorful floral marquetry in oval frames on both sides of the doors. As is typical, the drawers and doors inside are as decorated as the exterior of the case. The doors and drawers inside also have more floral marquetry, oyster veneer, and crossbanding.

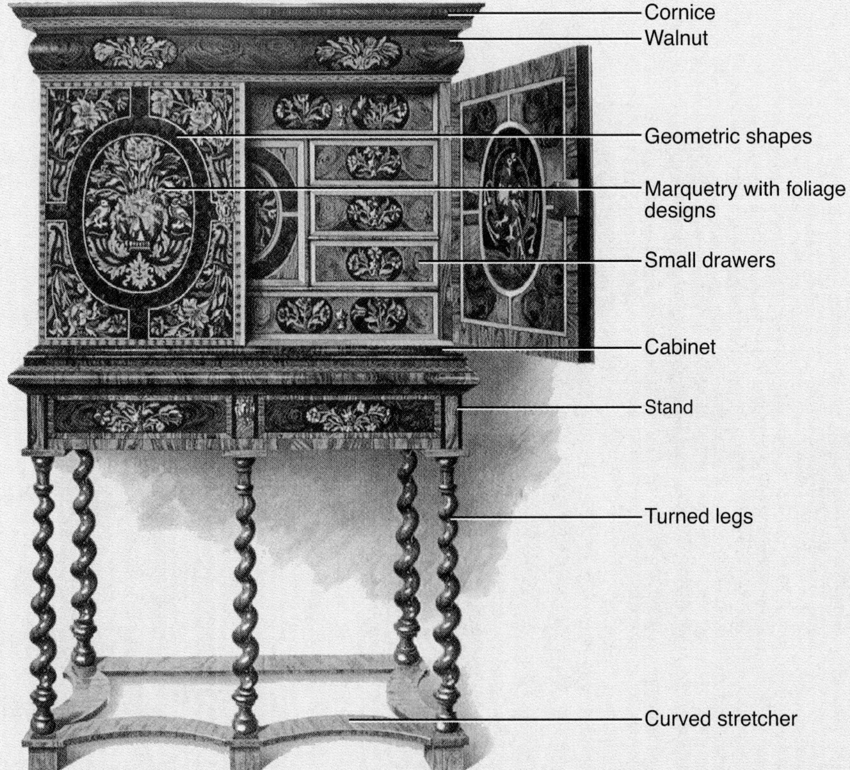

▲ **19-13.** Cabinet on stand with turned legs and marquetry, 17th century; England.

Private Buildings

■ *Materials.* Walnut is the most common wood for both conservative and extravagant furniture. Façades display figured veneers such as burl, oyster veneers, crossbanding, parquetry, and arabesque or seaweed marquetry (Fig. 19-13, 19-14). Gilding and lacquer grow in favor. Imported or locally made lacquered furniture surpasses painted examples in popularity. Japanned furniture, as it is called in England, often has black backgrounds with incongruous designs of foliage and pseudo-Chinese motifs (Fig. 19-15).

■ *Seating.* The principal Carolean chair has a high back and caned center panel framed with carving (Fig. 19-10). The seat also is caned and has an elaborately carved stretcher beneath that matches the cresting. Scroll legs terminate in ball, bun, or Spanish feet. Legs may also be baluster turned, columnar, spiral, or trumpet shaped. The latter particularly characterize the William and Mary style. About 1700, the spoon back with splat is introduced, and cabriole legs with *pied-de-biche* or cloven hoof feet (Fig. 19-11) and upholstered chairs with matching settees increase in use. Settee-backs resemble two chairs put together. Easie chairs, brought over from the Continent about 1680, have tall, upholstered backs with wings to protect the sitter from drafts. A variation known as a sleeping chair has ratchets to lower the back.

■ *Tables.* Oval or round tables supersede trestles during the period. There are infinite varieties of tables for dining, tea drinking, card playing, and dressing. Introduced in the late 17th century are dressing or toilet tables (Fig. 19-12), which are small tables with drawers. Usually, small toilet mirrors sit on top or hang above them.

▲ **19-14.** Chest of drawers, 1680–1685; England.

■ *Storage.* Cabinets on stands (Fig. 19-13), which are very fashionable, may have japanned, lacquered, or veneered façades with many small drawers and secret compartments behind doors. Some are imported from the Orient. Stands generally have four or six carved, turned, scrolled, or straight legs. After 1680, the typical chest of drawers (Fig. 19-14) has four graduated drawers resting on straight bracket feet. Tops of cabinets, desks, and bookcases (Fig. 19-15) usually are curved or hooded during the William and Mary period and often have small brackets or shelves to display Chinese porcelain or other small objects. Cabinet and drawer pulls have small brass plates with decorative drops or pendants.

■ *Beds.* Lighter-scale beds with wood frames entirely covered with fabric replace the heavy, carved Elizabethan beds. These new designs usually have tall proportions; low headboards; and heavy, complex testers. The *lit d'ange* from France has a tester hanging from the ceiling or wall instead of supported by posts. The tester

▲ **19-15.** William and Mary japanned double-hooded desk and bookcase; 17th century; England.

corners of state beds hold vases of ostrich feathers. Hangings, which still completely enclose the bed and match other textiles in the room, remain opulent to demonstrate wealth and rank. Headboards, testers, and valances often have complex shapes that are outlined with flat tape, embroidery, and *appliqué* and trimmed with fringe.

■ *Decorative Arts*. Decorative arts are similar in design to furniture with complex shapes and decoration. Particularly fashionable is Chinese porcelain, which many people avidly collect. Especially prized are looking glasses, which become more common during the period. Most are small with heavy wood frames.

G. ROCOCO

1715–1760

Great changes occur in the Western world during the 18th century. At the century's beginning, aristocrats and nobles rule politically, culturally, and socially with little influence from the middle and lower classes. Europe is largely agrarian. By the end of the century, the rising middle class expands its influence, and Europe is beginning to industrialize. Throughout the period, exploration and colonization of new lands continues, and trade increases with the Far East and the Americas. Scientists make advances in botany, biology, and the physical sciences. Women occupy positions of influence in several countries, including Madame de Pompadour in France, Maria Theresa in Austria, and Catherine the Great in Russia.

The 18th century is known as the Age of Enlightenment or the Age of Reason. The term refers to trends in thought and ideas advocating the application of reason to philosophy and life. Thinkers and writers of the period promote the scientific method; empiricism; and disciplined, rational thought over religion and myth. They believe that reason, judiciously applied, can solve human problems and generate progress. They see themselves as emerging from centuries of darkness into a newly enlightened world. Ideas of the Enlightenment come from the writings of John Locke of England. From them, Voltaire and others in France develop new ideologies and theories for humankind and society. However, these theories are only marginally accepted until the middle of the 18th century, when the Enlightenment gradually becomes an international movement. It greatly influences the French and American Revolutions.

Rococo dominates the first half of the century on the Continent. Originating in France during the late Baroque period, Rococo affects all aspects of interiors and furnishings, but has little effect on architecture. The light, asymmetrical style exhibits unity and continuity of parts in its forms and motifs, which flow in an uninterrupted manner. Complex, curvilinear silhouettes and organic ornament define the visual image. Attenuated, graceful curves suggest femininity. Rococo largely abandons the Classical language in favor of naturalism and themes and motifs alluding to love and romance, pastoral or country life, exoticism, pleasure, and gaiety.

Neither England nor her American colonies completely embraces Rococo because of its origins in and association with the French aristocracy. Also the influence of classicism in the Neo-Palladian style of architecture and the somber rationalism of the Restoration style of interiors remains strong in both areas. Rococo influences do begin to appear, shortly after mid-century, mostly in ornament and embellishment in interiors and on furniture and decorative arts. It coexists and comingles with Chinese and Gothic motifs and forms.

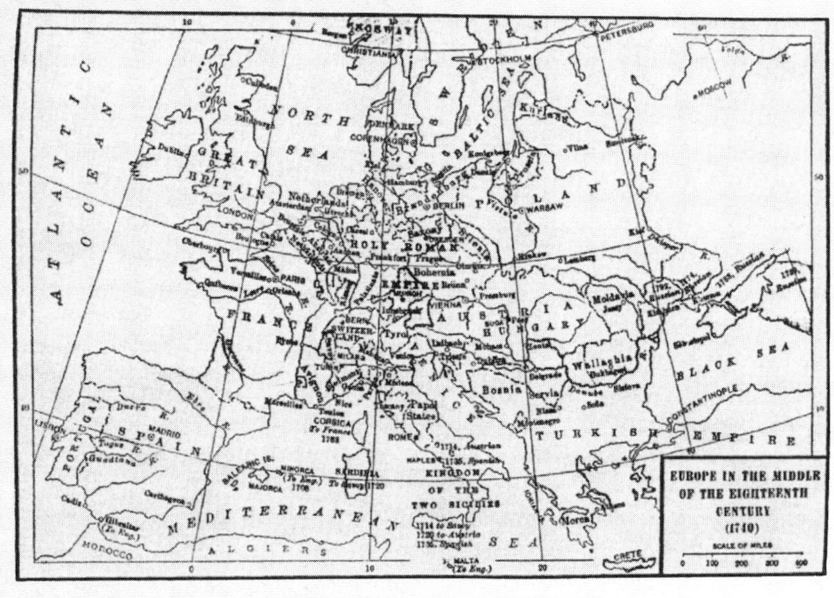

CHAPTER 20

Le Régence and Louis XV (Rococo)

1700–1760

Rococo is the style and symbol of the French aristocracy in the first half of the 18th century. The name comes from *rocaille* (small rockeries) and *coquille* (cockle shell); the latter is a common motif. The French call the style *rocaille*, *goût pittoresque*, or *style moderne*. A reaction to the stiff formality of the Baroque, the style is asymmetrical, light in scale, and defined by curvilinear, naturalistic ornament. Themes and motifs include romance, country life, the exotic, fantasy, and gaiety. The style's finest and most complete expression is in interiors, which display complete unity between decoration and furniture.

As a transition between the massive, rectilinear, classical French Baroque and the smaller, curvilinear, naturalistic Rococo, *Le Régence* features characteristics of both styles. Like Rococo, *Le Régence* primarily appears in interiors and furniture and has a minimal effect on architecture.

> *We have nothing to do in this world other than to procure for ourselves agreeable sensations and feelings.*
>
> —Madame de Chatelet, *Discours sur le bonheur*, 1740

HISTORICAL AND SOCIAL

When Louis XIV dies in 1715, his grandson, who is next in line, is only five years old. The Duc d'Orleans becomes regent until Louis reaches the age of 13. Louis XIV had left France heavily in debt from various wars and the royal building campaigns, so the Duc d'Orleans attempts to restore financial and social order. Because he lives in Paris rather than at Versailles, the court follows him, making Paris the artistic, social, and intellectual center of Europe. Louis XV obtains his legal majority and the throne in 1723. However, he fails to halt the political and economic decline begun in the last decades of his grandfather's regime. Unlike his grandfather, Louis XV has little interest in government. Along with his nobles and courtiers, he pursues pleasure and gaiety and is often influenced by his mistresses. His policies at home and abroad are inconsistent. High taxes, wars, loss of the New World colonies, corruption, and mismanagement cripple France and increase dissatisfaction and unrest among the middle and lower classes. In the last years of his reign, Louis attempts some reforms with the help of his ministers, but the new policies are reversed after his death in 1774. France and the monarchy continue their downward slide toward the Revolution.

CONCEPTS

The Rococo of Louis XV, in contrast to the Baroque of Louis XIV, reflects the taste of the nobility, not the king. Upon Louis XIV's death, the aristocracy reacts to the rigidity and formality of court life by seeking comfort and enjoyment. This polished but hedonistic society devotes itself to pleasure, fantasy, and gaiety, which are reflected in Rococo's forms, themes, and motifs of romance, exoticism, comfort, individuality, and novelty. The tastes of women, especially the king's mistress Madame du Pompadour, dictate fashions, and the feminine shape is reflected in the prevalent curvilinear forms. For the first time since the Renaissance, a style does not model itself on classical antiquity. This will help lead to its demise after mid-century.

MOTIFS

■ *Motifs*. Engaged columns, pilasters, pediments, quoins, stringcourses, brackets, and corbels appear sparingly and discretely on exteriors. Interior and furniture motifs (Fig. 20-1, 20-5, 20-7, 20-8, 20-15, 20-16, 20-17) include flowers, bouquets tied with ribbon, baskets of flowers, garlands, shells, *Chinoiserie* and *singerie* designs, romantic landscapes, Italian comedy figures, musical instruments, hunting and fishing symbols, cupids, bows and arrows, torches, shepherds and shepherdesses, Turkish arabesques and figures, pastoral emblems such as shepherd crooks, and an allover trellis pattern with flowers in the center of intersecting lines.

ARCHITECTURE

Le Régence and Louis XV architecture continue the classicism of the Baroque era, but with an increased elegance and lightness in scale and appearance. Plain walls with surface decoration concentrated around doors and windows are characteristic. Larger windows reduce wall space and help to integrate outside and inside. Classical elements, such as the orders, are less common but still adorn noble houses to demonstrate rank and wealth. *Hôtels* or townhouses built in Paris for the aristocracy are the chief Rococo building type. As in earlier periods, most sit at the rear of large plots of land in the city to create gracious *cours d'honneur* with majestic gates of entry. Architects experiment with courtyard shapes that relate to the site's shape.

Private Buildings

■ *Floor Plans*. Plans are generally symmetrical with rectangular rooms. A few plans have oval spaces. As before, designers carefully plan the distribution of rooms to give the appropriate dignity and grandeur required for the nobility while still providing comfort and privacy. As earlier, organization centers on *appartements*. Each has a variety of spaces within it. Apartments include rooms for ceremonies, such as receiving important guests, and for socializing with friends and private spaces that include bedchambers and ladies' boudoirs.

■ *Materials*. Most *hôtels* are of local stone and trabeated construction.

■ *Façades*. *Hôtels* exhibit a scale suitable for the nobility. Façades are symmetrical and horizontal with more continuity and refinement than Baroque buildings. As before, architects emphasize centers and/or ends (and important interiors) by projecting them forward and with defining architectural elements or pavilions.

(a)

(b)

(c)

▲ **20-1.** Motifs: (a) Textile detail with asymmetrical curves and flowers, (b) panel detail with shell motif, and (c) ceiling detail with *Chinoiserie* and *singerie* motifs, *Grande Singerie, Château de Chantilly,* France.

Articulation and details are subordinate to the whole to create a unified volume. To further achieve unity, façades have less movement and fewer contrasts of light and dark than in the Baroque style. Subtle rustication sometimes highlights lower stories and surrounds openings. Smooth upper stories have larger windows usually separated by plain wall surfaces. Pediments, columns, or rustication accentuate entrances, and stringcourses mark stories. Rectangular or arched windows have simple lintels above them. Curvilinear ironwork may distinguish lower portions of windows and balconies. Decorative surrounds accentuate dormer windows. For emphasis, doorways are centerpieces in compositions and surrounded by columns, pediments, coats of arms, and other ornamentation.

- *Roofs*. Mansard, hipped, or low-pitched or flat roofs with balustrades are typical.

INTERIORS

Interiors and furnishings are the primary expressions of the *Le Régence* and Louis XV (Rococo) styles. Although associated with the reign of Louis XV, the Rococo style does not confine itself to those years. Attributes of Rococo begin to manifest in the late 17th century in the published designs and ornament of Jean Bérain and others and in the early-18th-century rooms at Versailles.

The first three decades of the 18th century are a transitional period between late Baroque and Rococo called *Le Régence*. During this time Rococo characteristics begin to appear on and modify Baroque forms and details. *Le Régence* characteristics include a general lightening in the size of rooms and scale of finishes and

DESIGN SPOTLIGHT

Interior: The Varengeville Room shows the Rococo emphasis on symmetrical balance in the distribution of architectural elements such as the centered chimneypiece, arches, and double doors. The curvilinear, marble chimneypiece is smaller and projects less than before. The mantel shelf is slightly higher than the dado. The alternating wide and narrow white and gold panels have an abundance of curves and naturalistic embellishment. The door frame also curves, and above is a painting in a frame with small curves. The furniture includes a Rococo *bergère, fauteuils,* a *bureau plat,* and fire screen. *Appliqués* flank the mirror to enhance the quality of light. A Savonnerie carpet covers the *parquet de Versailles* floor. The room and its furnishings show the graceful, feminine character of Rococo.

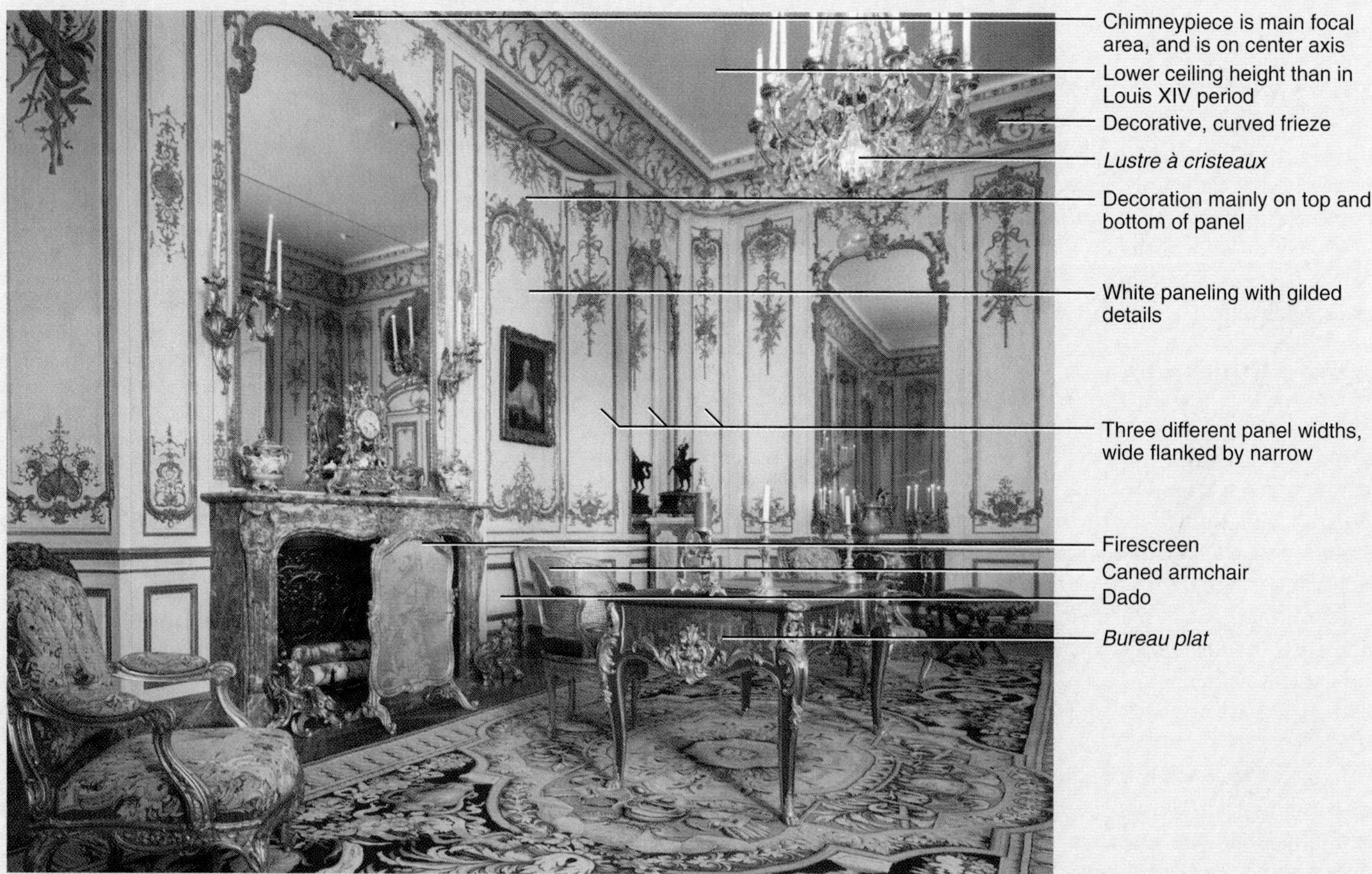

▲ **20-2.** Varengeville Room, *Hôtel de Varengeville,* 1736–1752; Paris, France. [Mr. and Mrs. Charles Wrightsman gift, 1963 (63. 228.1). The Metropolitan Museum of Art, New York, NY, U.S.A. Image © The Metropolitan Museum of Art/Art Resource NY]

decoration; asymmetry; and the appearance of naturalistic, curvilinear ornamentation. During the 1670s and 1680s, rooms become less formal. Wood paneling replaces heavy marble-paneled walls, columns and pilasters disappear, and cornices diminish in size. Corners and tops of paneling, doors, and windows begin to curve. Naturalistic, exotic, or fanciful ornamentation, which is usually asymmetrical, replaces classical.

Rocaille decoration with its asymmetrical profusion of curving tendrils, foliage, flowers combined with shells, and minute details defines the Louis XV interior. Also characteristic are themes and motifs of gaiety, pleasure, romance, youth, and the exotic. In all but the grandest and most formal rooms, classical elements are rare. Most rooms maintain a rectangular form, but curving lines, continuity of parts, and asymmetrical arrangements of naturalistic decorations characterize wall panels and finishes, ceilings, textiles, furniture, and decorative arts. Paneling may be designed to incorporate sofas, consoles, tables, beds, and/or mirrors.

Ornate Rococo interiors contrast with refined, plainer exteriors. Important and ceremonial spaces retain their monumental scale, whereas private rooms become smaller and more intimate. Some spaces are designed for special purposes, such as music rooms, but dining rooms remain uncommon. The planning and decoration of private spaces reflects a desire for comfort and convenience, whereas state apartments continue to proclaim wealth and rank. To a greater degree than ever before, Rococo achieves a complete synthesis of interior design, furniture, and decorative arts.

▲ **20-4.** *Cabinet de la Pendule* (Clock Room), *Palais de Versailles*, mid-18th century; Versailles, France.

Room decoration remains hierarchical as earlier; the more important the space, the larger its size and more lavish its decoration.

▲ **20-3.** Blue Room at *Musée Carnavalet*, mid-18th century; Paris, France.

▲ **20-5.** *Salle du Conseil, Palais de Fontainebleau,* mid-18th century; Fontainebleau, France.

As the main reception for important persons, the *chambre de parade* is the most formal and lavish room in the house and least likely to exhibit Rococo characteristics. The room has rich colors, costly materials, the orders, portraits, tapestries, antiques, and formal furniture that demonstrate and reinforce the owner's social position. Similarly, the state bedchamber and its antechamber retain their formal and opulent decor. Social rooms, such as the *salon*, usually feature Rococo themes and less formal decorations.

Private Buildings

■ *Color.* During *Le Régence*, most paneling is painted white with gilded details. By the 1730s, a yellow, blue, or green palette joins white and gold (Fig. 20-2, 20-3, 20-4, 20-5). Single hues and contrasting values of the same hue decorate paneling.

■ *Floors.* The most common flooring is wood blocks or parquet (Fig. 20-3, 20-4). Entries, halls, landings, and grand *salons* may have marble or stone in blocks or squares. Rugs (Fig. 20-2) include Orientals, Savonneries, and Aubussons. The latter two are made in Rococo colors and motifs.

■ *Walls. Boiserie* with alternating wide and narrow panels is the most common wall treatment (Fig. 20-2, 20-3, 20-4, 20-5, 20-6). French *boiserie*, in contrast to earlier French Baroque and coeval English paneling, shows a strong continuity of wall surface. Panels, moldings, and other architectural elements do not greatly project, giving little interruption in the flatness and smooth articulation of the walls. In contrast to its ornament and moldings, paneling remains symmetrical even to the point of a false door to balance a real one, and it retains the tripartite divisions of earlier, which implies an order, although no columns are evident. Asymmetrical curves, foliage, and shells soften the corners, bottoms, and tops of panels. Decoration, which at times obscures form, extends beyond moldings and borders. Curves may be free form or resemble a woman's upper lip; complex compositions feature multiple C, reverse C, and S scrolls. *Boiserie* may be left natural, painted, or lacquered (Fig. 20-2, 20-3, 20-4, 20-5, 20-6, 20-7). Panels and moldings may contrast in color or be two shades of the same hue. Panel centers may have fabrics or colorful painted arabesques with or without figures and naturalistic motifs or landscapes.

Tapestries, usually limited to grand rooms, depict Rococo themes in numerous colors and the subtle shadings of paintings. Wallpapers gain favor but are not used in rooms of state. Types include hand-painted Chinese papers, flocked English papers, and patterns imitating textiles. English papers dominate the French market until the late 1750s when war between the two countries halts their importation. Larger and more numerous mirrors with complex curvilinear frames are located on walls, over fireplaces, on ceilings, inside fireplaces in summer, and on window shutters.

▲ **20-6.** Elevation, side of a *grande salon*, mid-18th century; France.

As the focal point, the fireplace sets proportions for paneling. The mantel shelf is slightly higher than the dado. The panel above the fireplace is the same size as larger ones in the room and features a *trumeau*. The chimneypiece (Fig. 20-2, 20-3, 20-4) is smaller and projects less than before. The marble mantel itself is curvilinear, and its color may match tabletops in the room. Red is the most desired color, followed by yellow, gray, and violet.

■ *Windows and Doors*. Windows are larger than before and have curving tops. Most have interior shutters that match the paneling. Divided curtain panels and festoons are common in important rooms. Fabric valances come into general use after 1720. Door panels (Fig. 20-4, 20-5, 20-6, 20-7) match those of walls. Above most doors are paintings of pastoral, mythological, or romantic scenes in asymmetrical curvilinear frames. Important rooms have *portières* that help prevent drafts and add to the interior opulence.

■ *Ceilings*. Coved ceilings, curving corners, and *rocaille* decoration extending onto the ceiling proper are the most common treatments (Fig. 20-1, 20-4). Some ceilings are plain with a central plaster rosette.

■ *Textiles*. Heavy brocades and damasks are no longer in vogue. Silks (especially painted), linens, chintzes, and other printed cottons are used in summer, while plain or patterned velvets or damasks replace them in winter. Sets of furniture often have matching tapestry covers (Fig. 20-3). Textile colors are strong and brilliant (Fig. 20-3, 20-8, 20-16). Crimson is most favored, followed by blue, yellow, green, gold, and silver. Patterns, which are frequently asymmetrical, depict Rococo themes and motifs. In 1760, Christophe-Philippe Oberkampf opens a textile factory in Jouy-en-Josas near Versailles that quickly becomes known for its *toile de Jouy*. These fabrics (Fig. 20-8) are frequently used in bedrooms and boudoirs.

▲ **20-7.** Panel and door of the Grande *Singerie, Château de Chantilly;* France; Christophe Huet.

(a)

(b)

(c)

▲ **20-8.** Textiles: (a) Flower pattern, (b) *toile de Jouy* in a transitional style to Louis XVI, and (c) Indian palampore, mid-18th century; France.

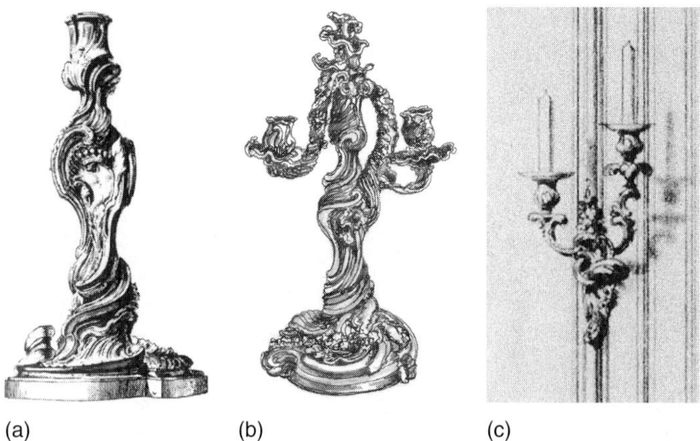

(a) (b) (c)

▲ **20-9.** Lighting: (a) *Flambeau*, (b) candelabra, and (c) *applique*, mid-18th century; France.

■ *Lighting*. Large windows, light-colored walls, shiny surfaces, and numerous mirrors, along with ornate lighting fixtures (Fig. 20-2, 20-3, 20-4, 20-5, 20-9), help to light rooms. Lanterns are more common than the *lustre à cristeaux* in *salons* and stair halls. Small and large *appliques*, *flambeaus*, and *candelabra* on mantels and tables, and *torchères* also provide light. Elaborate *guéridons* may hold either a *candelabra* or large *flambeau*. To multiply light, candles often are placed in front of mirrors. Fixtures are made of *ormolu*, porcelain, or silver in asymmetrical, naturalistic shapes. Some have crystal or lead glass drops.

■ *Later Interpretations*. Beginning in the 1840s, Rococo Revival interiors repeat the curves and naturalistic ornament of the 18th-century Rococo style, primarily in details such as mantels, wallpaper, textiles, and furniture. The goal is to evoke images of the style, not to recreate it. A more accurate rendition of Rococo occurs in the late 19th century as paneling and furnishings copy original scale, curves, and ornament. Neo-Rococo (Fig. 20-10) becomes a fashionable interior style in the early 20th century as critics and designers recommend it in place of heavy Victorian styles. The asymmetry, naturalistic ornament, and sensuous curves of Rococo also influence the *fin-de-siècle* style, Art Nouveau, of the late 19th and early 20th centuries. Human scale and curvilinear appeal ensure Rococo's continued use today.

▲ **20-10.** Later Interpretation: Bedroom, 1905; New York. Neo-Rococo.

FURNISHINGS AND DECORATIVE ARTS

Louis XV or Rococo furniture perfectly suits interiors in size, silhouette, and decoration because of its curves and naturalistic, asymmetrical *rocaille* decoration. Furnishings exhibit the highest standards of construction and craftsmanship. Matched sets of furniture may include a *canapé*; several *fauteuils*, *bergères*, and stools; a console or consoles; mirrors; a fire screen; a folding screen; and sometimes a *lit*. Pursuit of novelty gives rise to multipurpose pieces after 1750. New pieces, such as lounging furniture, that support comfort and convenience are introduced. Gaming pieces, small tables, and ladies' writing furniture are especially fashionable.

When not in use, furniture is arranged around the perimeter of the space as before. Grand rooms are sparsely furnished, but private ones are often cluttered with small pieces of furniture, such as tables and seating. Beds sit in alcoves or behind a balustrade in staterooms.

As in interiors, *Le Régence* is a transition period in which furniture combines the elements and ornament of Louis XIV (Baroque) and Louis XV (Rococo). Pieces become smaller in size, less formal, and more curvilinear. Chair backs become lower and begin to curve. Wood frames begin to surround backs and seats. Arms curve, have pads, and are set back from the seat corner. Cabriole legs replace straight ones, and stretchers disappear. Naturalistic, asymmetrical ornament highlights legs and frames. The most characteristic pieces are chairs, tables, and *commodes*.

Louis XV furniture is characterized by asymmetrical *rocaille* decoration and an absence of straight lines (Fig. 20-2, 20-3, 20-11, 20-12, 20-13, 20-14, 20-15). The period's emphasis on comfort results in smaller pieces and more use of upholstery. Any part that can curve does, including legs, backs, sides, and façades. Curves are slender, graceful, and drawn out. Seating has cabriole legs ending in whorl feet and curvilinear wooden frames around seats and backs. Joints and intersecting points are not articulated in the classical manner. Instead, the parts of the frame flow together, creating the characteristic continuity of parts. Low, upholstered backs and scrolled arms with *manchettes* also are common. Other defining characteristics of the style include *ormolu*, marquetry, undulating shapes, and ornament and moldings that flow into one another, uninterrupted across façades. Pieces are often colored and decorated for specific rooms.

Private Buildings

■ *Materials*. Cabinetmakers use more than 100 types of local and exotic woods to create colorful veneers and marquetry (Fig. 20-2, 20-3). Mahogany, first imported during Le Régence, comes into vogue after 1760. Makers also incorporate lacquered panels from the Orient into *commodes*, *armoires*, and screens. They favor Chinese, Japanese, and Coromandel lacquers (Fig. 20-15), but also develop their own lacquers in colors more suited to interiors. Although furniture sometimes is painted to match the room's colors, white or natural with painted decoration is more common. Caning (Fig. 20-12) is very fashionable for seats and backs; cushions add softness and comfort. Finely crafted curvilinear gilded bronze mounts are used for decoration, as hinges or handles, and on corners and points of strain.

■ *Seating*. Seating comes in many sizes and forms for maximum comfort. *Fauteuils* (Fig. 20-2, 20-3, 20-11) and *chaises* have either flat (*à la Reine*) or concave (*en cabriolet*) upholstered backs. The *bergère* (Fig. 20-3, 20-12) has a wider seat; a loose cushion; and closed, upholstered arms. The most common form of *canapé* (Fig. 20-14) has a back resembling three *fauteuils* or *bergères* put together. Lounging furniture becomes more important and includes the *chaise longue* and a *duchesse brisée* (Fig. 20-13).

▲ **20-12.** Caned armchair, 18th century; France.

DESIGN SPOTLIGHT

Furniture: Scaled down from Louis XIV, parts of the curving frame of this *fauteuil* flow into one another in typical Rococo fashion. The shield-shaped back is composed of small curves. The cabriole legs have whorl feet. Typical characteristics include the horizontal arms with *manchettes* resting on curving supports and set back from the edge of the seat, and asymmetrical, naturalistic carving on the frame. The Beauvais tapestry upholstery features a subject from La Fontaine's *Fables*.

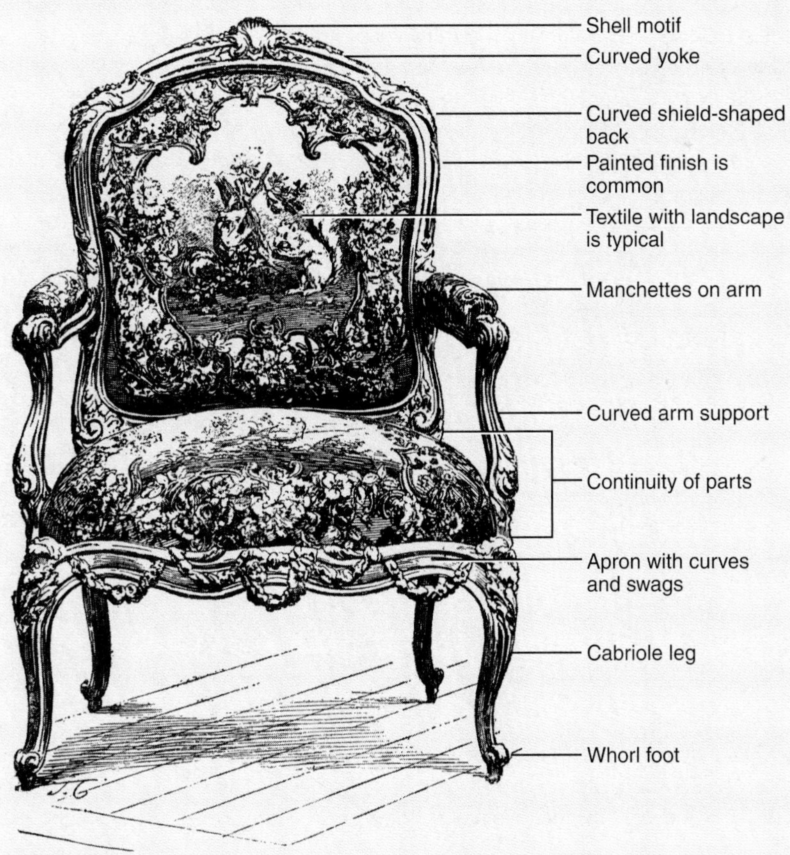

▲ **20-11.** *Fauteuil.*

▲ **20-13.** *Duchesse brisée,* mid-18th century; France; Louis Delanois.

▲ **20-14.** *Canapé,* mid-18th century; France; Jean Baptiste Oudry. [Gift of John D. Rockefeller Jr., 1935 (35.145.1). The Metropolitan Museum of Art, New York, NY, U.S.A. Image © The Metropolitan Museum of Art/Art Resource, NY]

DESIGN SPOTLIGHT

Furniture: Curving forms and decoration and asymmetrical ornament characterize *commodes*, one of the most fashionable and elaborate Rococo pieces. As is common, this *commode* has *bombé* sides and a serpentine front with complex *Chinoiserie* decoration and extravagant *ormolu*. The naturalistic, asymmetrical *ormolu* flows uninterrupted over the two drawers and inconspicuously incorporates the drawer pulls, illustrating the continuity of parts characteristic of Rococo. Typical also are the marble top and cabriole legs. It was common practice in *salons* to place pairs of *commodes* with mirrors above them on opposite sides of the room.

▲ **20-15.** *Commode* with panels of Chinese Coromandel lacquer and European black-lacquered veneer, mid-18th century; France; Bernard van Risen Burgh II. [The Lesley and Emma Shaefer Collection, Bequest of Emma A. Sheafer, 1973 (1974.356.189). The Metropolitan Museum of Art, New York, NY, U.S.A. Image © The Metropolitan Museum of Art/Art Resource, NY]

■ *Tables*. The many types of tables (Fig. 20-2, 20-3, 20-4) include game, card, work, and toilet tables. Rooms usually have varieties of *ambulantes* in many sizes and shapes to fulfill different functions. None is exclusively for eating. The *bureau plat* (Fig. 20-2) may be centered in a room. *Consoles*, an integral part of room decoration, usually are placed between two windows or opposite the fireplace. They are exquisitely carved and gilded with marble tops and mirrors in carved and gilded frames hanging above.

■ *Storage*. *Commodes* (Fig. 20-3, 20-15) first appear during *Le Régence*. During the Louis XV period, they are the most fashionable and lavishly decorated piece of furniture in the room, requiring the greatest skills of cabinetmaker and metalworker. Many have undulating horizontal (serpentine or reverse serpentine) and vertical (*bombé*) shapes that are a challenge to veneer. Some are lacquered; others have porcelain plaques. Their magnificent *ormolu* or gilded bronze mounts often obscure divisions between drawers. Besides the *bureau plat*, other writing furniture includes a *secrétaire à abattant* (drop-front desk) and *bureau à cylindre* (rolltop desk). *Armoires* remain important storage pieces, but are lighter in scale.

■ *Beds*. The most fashionable beds are the *lit à la duchesse* and the *lit d'ange*. Both have a low headboard and footboard but no posts. The *lit à la polonaise* has four iron rods that curve up to support a dome-shaped canopy. The *lit à la française* (Fig. 20-16) has a headboard and footboard of equal height; the long side sits against the wall and a canopy above supports hangings.

■ *Decorative Arts*. Decorative arts (Fig. 20-2, 20-3, 20-4, 20-17) follow the curvilinear, asymmetrical shapes and naturalistic and exotic ornament of Louis XV. Accessories include mirrors, porcelains, andirons, and fire screens. Many rooms have a lacquered, upholstered, or mirrored folding screen with three or four panels. André-Charles Boulle introduces the gilt bronze mantel clock about 1700. Mantel clocks with complex curvilinear shapes and ornament often have matching candlesticks. Tall case clocks with extravagant marquetry and *ormolu* are important pieces in Rococo interiors.

■ *Porcelain*. Although the Chinese have made true porcelain for centuries, the first porcelain created by Europeans is soft-paste or artificial porcelain beginning in the 16th century. In the 18th century, the Germans make the first hard-paste or true porcelain, and it dominates European porcelain until the mid-18th century when it is surpassed by French products. For the luxury market, Sèvres (Fig. 20-17), the premier French factory, produces table and tea services, trays, bowls and covers, clock cases, vases, potpourri, and *candelabra*. It creates exquisite biscuit or unglazed figures as part of dinner sets. The Sèvres factory uses rich ground colors, such as *rose Pompadour* (pink), *bleu de roi* (royal blue), and *vert pré* (green) with painted scenes and flowers and gilding. The factory switches from soft-paste to hard-paste porcelain after 1768.

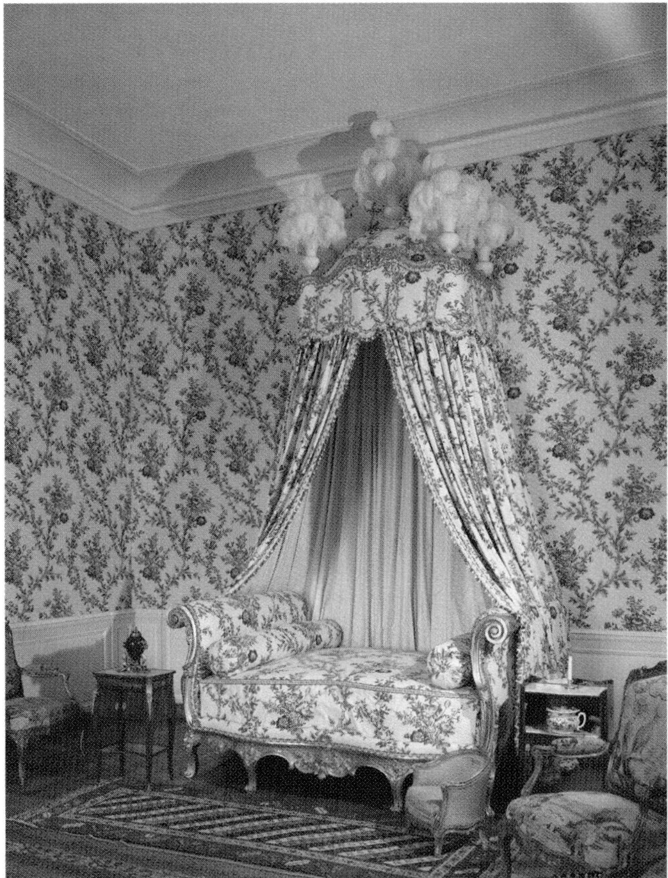

▲ **20-16.** *Lit à la française* (bed) at *Château Vaux-le-Vicomte*, mid-18th century; France.

▲ **20-17.** Covered tureen, *Sèvres;* mid-18th century; France.

CHAPTER 21

English Neo-Palladian and Georgian

1702–1770

> *In studying a design of Palladio's, which we recommend to the young architect as his frequent practice, let him think as well as measure. Let him consider the general design and purpose of the building, and then consider how far, according to his own judgment, the purpose will be answered by that structure. He will thus establish in himself a custom of judging by the whole as well as the parts; and he will find new beauties in the structure considered in this light.*
>
> —Isaac Ware, *Complete Body of Architecture*, 1756

When George I takes the English throne in 1714, members of the Whig party appoint themselves as the arbiters of taste for the nation. Believing that rational, correct, and polite should define English architecture, they promote Neo-Palladian as the only proper style. Subsequently, the style in country and townhouses becomes a visual metaphor for the owner's culture and education. Inside, classical architectural elements adorn rooms, display the owner's refinement, and highlight the collections acquired on grand tours. By mid-century, classicism coexists with Rococo, Chinese, and Gothic influences in interiors and furniture.

HISTORICAL AND SOCIAL

During the 18th century, Britain acquires most of its vast empire. Her navy rules the seas, and she establishes industrial supremacy as the period remains relatively stable and prosperous. Queen Anne, the last of the Stuarts, rules from 1702 to 1714. She has little interest in government, art, literature, or the theater, and governs through advisors. She leaves no heirs when she dies. Although others are closer in line, the Act of Settlement, passed in 1701, requires that the throne go to Anne's nearest Protestant relative, either Electress Sophia of Hanover, Germany, or Sophia's son, George Lewis. The act, designed to prevent the return of the Catholic, pro-French Stuarts, results in George Lewis ascending the throne.

The Georgian period encompasses the reigns of George I (1714–1727), George II (1727–1760), and the first years of George III (1760–1820). George I speaks little English and has no interest in either governing or artistic patronage. Unpopular largely because of a dissolute private life, he often returns to Hanover for long periods. Consequently, the Whig party comes into and remains in power for nearly 50 years. Merchants, industrialists, landed but untitled gentry, and Protestant dissenters back the party, which shifts power to the landed nobility. George II can at least speak English. But like his father, he is not interested in art and prefers Hanover to England. However, he shrewdly chooses ministers who bring prosperity to the country. George III takes the throne in 1760. Unlike his two predecessors, he is interested in ruling the country. In the first years of his reign, he regains many of the powers that the Whigs had assumed. In 1770, George

III appoints as prime minister Frederick North, Second Earl of Guilford, whose policies provoke the American Revolution.

During the period, England's colonies increase in number and wealth, and she gains power, prestige, and territory in a series of wars. The treaty ending the War of the Spanish Succession gives England the French holdings around Hudson Bay, Nova Scotia, and Newfoundland. It also expands trade with Spain's American colonies. At the end of the French and Indian War in 1763, England owns Canada, French territories east of the Mississippi River, and Spanish Florida in America, as well as India in the Far East.

The importance of education and culture increases during the period. Grand tours are fashionable for young English gentlemen. These extended visits to the European continent enable them to complete their cultural and social educations and further develop gentlemanly qualities. As they travel and study, they also collect art, manuscripts, coins, and the like. Collecting, which requires leisure, knowledge, and money, helps define the 18th-century image of the educated and cultured gentleman. An important component of this education is knowledge of architecture and design. Gentlemen frequently are as learned as the trained architects they hire to build their homes. Thus, the grand Neo-Palladian country house becomes a visual metaphor for the culture and education of the owner and a symbol of his wealth and power.

▲ **21-2.** S. Martin-in-the-Fields and plan, 1721–1726; London, England; James Gibbs. This church has great influence in America.

CONCEPTS

According to members of the ruling Whig party who consider themselves tastemakers, correct architecture is one of common sense and good taste. They reject the Baroque classicism of Sir Christopher Wren, Nicholas Hawksmoor, and John Vanbrugh in favor of the Renaissance classicism of Andrea Palladio and, more importantly, the Englishman Inigo Jones. Neo-Palladianism appeals because it is rational yet flexible, is based on antiquity, and has nationalistic associations. Two books published in 1715 help promote the style, *Vitruvius Britannicus* by Colen Campbell, a record of classical buildings in England, and an English version of Palladio's *I quattro libri dell'architettura*. As no interiors actually designed by Palladio are known to the English, interior elements come from Vitruvius, Inigo Jones, and the Venetian Baroque style as interpreted by William Kent. In the 1730s, artists, writers, and dilettantes influenced by the Romantic and Picturesque Movements rediscover England's medieval past and deem it worthy of emulation. Gothic, along with French Rococo and Chinese elements, begin to manifest, particularly in interiors and furniture.

(a)

(b)

(c)

► **21-1.** Motifs and Architectural Details: (a) Mantel detail; (b) door with classical surround; and (c) door with Chinese and Rococo surround, all from Claydon House, c. mid-18th century; Buckinghamshire, England.

DESIGN SPOTLIGHT

Architecture and Interiors: Designed by Lord Burlington and William Kent, Chiswick House, located outside of London, adopts the image, proportions, and axial alignment of the Villa Rotunda by Palladio. The Corinthian portico and symmetrically angled staircases to either side of it define the main entry, unlike the Villa Rotunda, which has Ionic columns carrying its four porticoes with straight staircases leading to the entries, like Roman temples. Flanking the portico at Chiswick House, blank walls emphasize the pedimented windows and rusticated lower story. Unlike the Villa Rotunda, all four façades are different in design but share similar elements and center emphasis. Crowning the roof is a low, octagonal dome with *thermae* windows derived from Roman baths. Lord Burlington owned Palladian drawings showing similar ones. Unlike Italian examples, tall chimneys shaped like obelisks highlight the roofline.

The square plan centers on a central octagon-shaped room known as the Tribunal. Square, rectangular, and circular rooms are symmetrically grouped around the Tribunal much like the Villa Rotunda. The composition of differently sized and shaped spaces is new in England. Of Roman and Palladian origins, it will later influence Robert Adam and the Late Georgian Neoclassical style.

The gallery, facing the rear garden, is based upon Palladio's reconstructions of Roman baths. Three spaces make up the gallery: two closets flanking the larger middle room. The central space has apsidal ends with sculpture niches and coffered ceilings from the Temple of Venus and Rome illustrated by Palladio. Arches within the apses lead to the flanking octagonal and round closets beyond, which are identically decorated. The fireplaces and compartmentalized ceilings come from Inigo Jones's Queen's House and Banqueting House, respectively. The walls of the central space are plain and unadorned to emphasize the architectural detailing, which also has gilded accents. The pedimented doors have friezes of laurel wreaths and crossed ribbons recommended by Palladio. The gallery and two flanking rooms each have a Palladian window. William Kent designs the furniture.

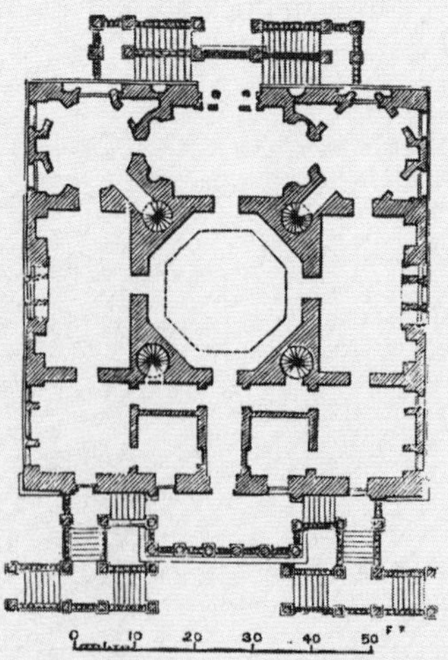

▲ **21-3.** Chiswick House, floor plan, and Gallery, begun 1725; Chiswick, London Borough of Hounslow, England; Lord Burlington and William Kent.

DESIGN SPOTLIGHT

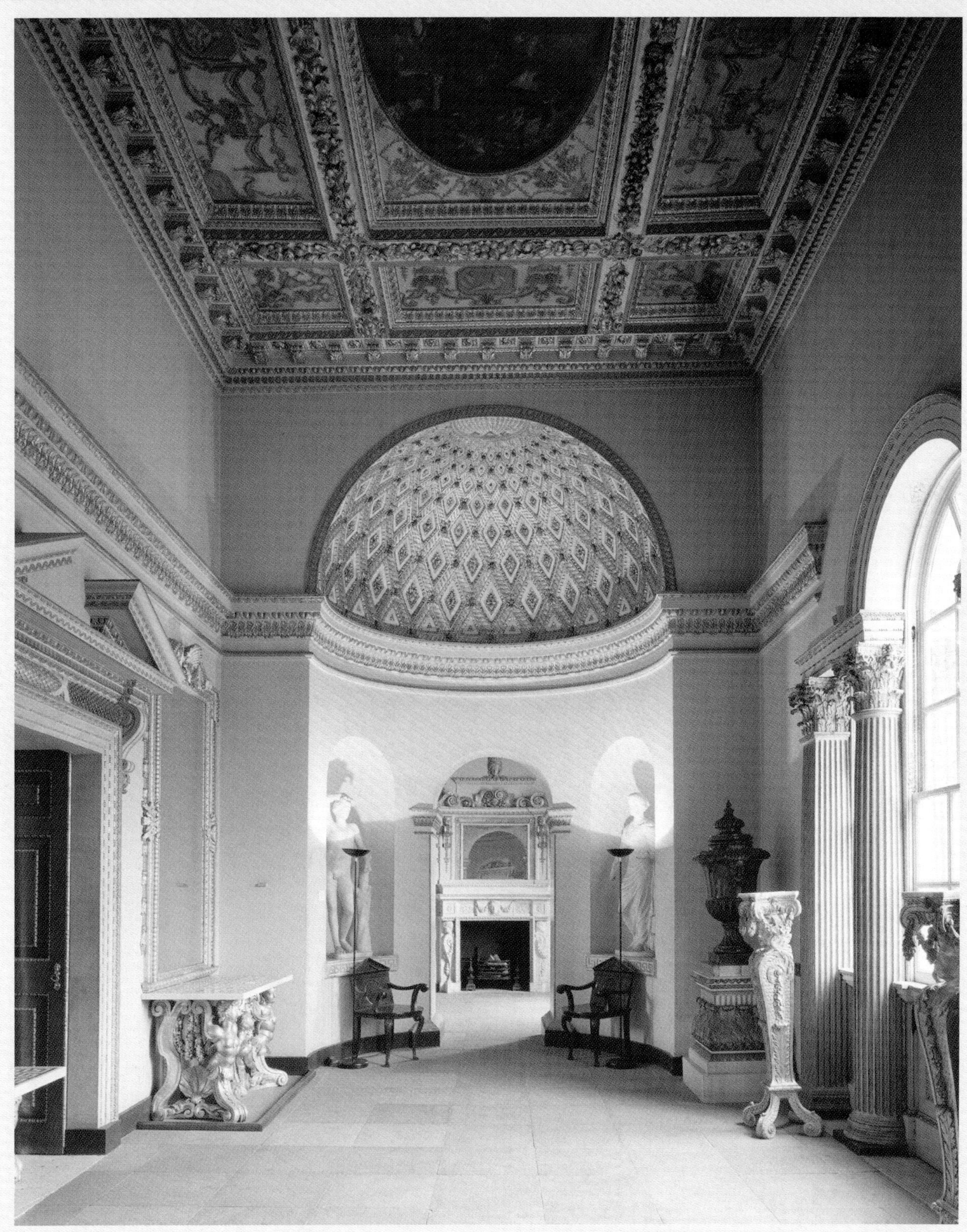

▲ **21-3.** Continued

MOTIFS

■ *Motifs.* Classical architectural details (Fig. 21-1, 21-2, 21-3, 21-4, 21-7), such as columns, pilasters, balusters, dentil moldings, and quoins, appear in architecture, interiors, and furniture throughout the period. In Queen Anne furniture, motifs include shells and acanthus leaves. Early Georgian furniture may display swags, urns, eagles, cabochons, lion masks, satyr masks, and/or foliage. Motifs in furniture and interiors after mid-century influenced by Rococo and Gothic (Fig. 21-1, 21-5, 21-12) are ribbons, leaves, shells, foliage, birds, pointed arches, quatrefoils, and tracery. *Chinoiserie* and Chinese motifs include faux bamboo, Oriental figures, and *pagodas* (Fig. 21-8, 21-17, 21-18).

ARCHITECTURE

Neo-Palladian is England's national style in the first half of the 18th century. Almost exclusively domestic, the style defines numerous country houses, smaller dwellings, and townhouses. Forms and elements draw from, but do not copy, Vitruvius, Palladio, or Inigo Jones. Symmetrical, geometric, and relatively plain, forms are simple; outlines are uncomplicated. Rules, which come from nature, antiquity, or the Renaissance, are closely observed, particularly for proportions. Distinctive are the undecorated walls or spaces around windows and the decorative architectural features that emphasize them. Other definitive characteristics include cube shapes, porticoes, temple fronts, Venetian or Palladian windows, Diocletian or thermae windows, and quoins. Each decorative element serves a constructional or aesthetic purpose. The great Neo-Palladian patron, Sir Richard Boyle, Earl of Burlington and Earl of Cork, and his protégé, William Kent, help define the form of Neo-Palladian buildings through their own work and publications of Palladio's work.

Architectural treatises that increase in number after the 1720s further refine the style and emphasize honesty of design, primacy of proportion, and harmony of the whole. This gives rise to pattern-book architecture in which designers or patrons select and incorporate images from pattern books in their work. The Earl of Burlington sets the precedent with the completion of Chiswick House (Fig. 21-3).

Beginning in the 1730s, a few structures are built or remodeled in a style that becomes known as Gothick or Gothic Revival. The

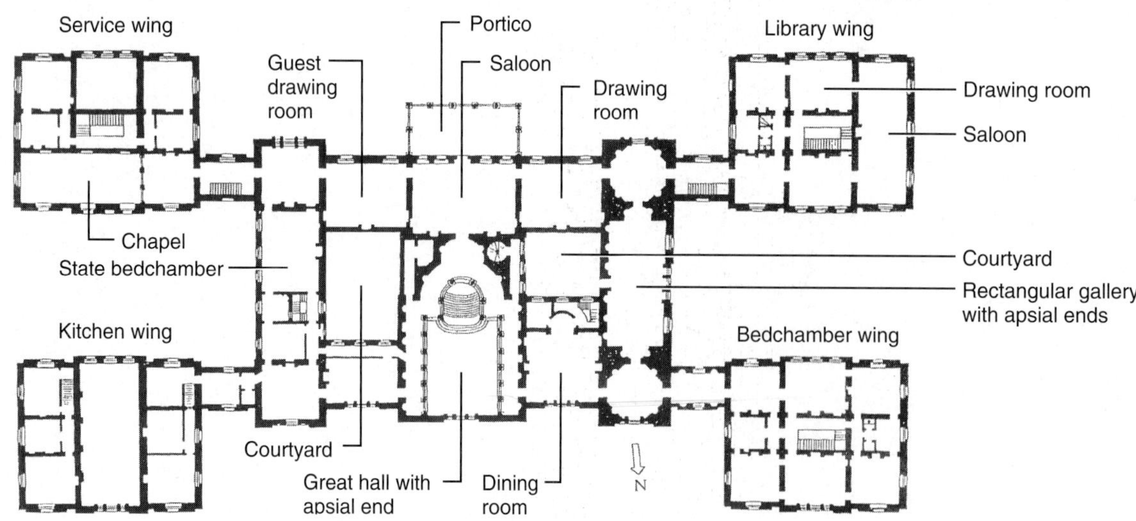

▲ **21-4.** Holkam Hall, floor plan, Marble Hall, and saloon (right), begun 1734; Norfolk, England; William Kent.

▲ **21–4.** Continued

▲ **21-5.** Strawberry Hill and long gallery, 1747; Twickenham, England; for Sir Horace Walpole.

most influential is Strawberry Hill (Fig. 21-5), home of Sir Horace Walpole. Gothic details, such as pointed arches, battlements, and tracery, applied to contemporary buildings characterize this early period of Gothic Revival. Historical accuracy is less a concern than are evoking an emotional response to the design and displaying sentiment and nostalgia. Compositions are light and visually complex, and elements often follow a classical arrangement, but with an honesty and flexibility in design. Because of the dominance of Classicism, Gothic Revival remains outside the mainstream of architecture for residences during the period.

Throughout the period, the chief building types are country and townhouses. Monumental Neo-Palladian country houses take two forms. The first, which is common for large houses (Fig. 21-4), is composed of three parts—main house, wings, and dependencies or smaller buildings—like Palladio's designs. Smaller houses, called villas, are simple rectangular blocks (Fig. 21-3). From the 1720s onward, designers treat urban row houses as one large Palladian-style structure. Some public structures, such as banks, hospitals, and churches (Fig. 21-2), adopt elements of Neo-Palladianism, such as temple fronts.

Private Buildings

■ *Site Orientation*. Gardens of the 18th century continue the formality and geometry of earlier years. William Kent introduces less formal designs that lead to picturesque compositions of winding paths, streams, and irregular plantings. By mid-century, in contrast with their orderly exteriors, country houses usually sit within irregular and wild gardens with temples, pavilions, and Gothic "ruins."

■ *Floor Plans*. Large and small houses have either double-pile plans with halls running lengthwise or adapted Palladian plans (Fig. 21-3, 21-4). Symmetry, the sequences of spaces, and the alignment of doors and windows are important planning considerations. The integration of rectangular, square, oval, elliptical, and hexagonal spaces or rooms with apsial ends used by Palladio first appears at Chiswick House but has little influence until the Late Georgian period.

The most important rooms are on the ground and first floors and are emphasized by their size and treatment on the exterior. As before, plans are organized around the grand salon, entrance hall, and suites of apartments. The stair hall and drawing room or saloon are usually on the main axis, flanked by other public rooms including a lavishly decorated dining room. In mid-century, a more circular array of rooms and doorways around a stair hall replaces this arrangement. The change is dictated by larger and more numerous social gatherings, which require more flexible plans in which stair halls become the main circulation space. Subsequently, top-lit oval or circular stairs become more important and replace other forms.

Townhouses are usually three stories high, one or more rooms wide, and two rooms deep. Kitchens and servants' quarters may occupy the basement or be in separate buildings. Drawing and dining rooms are usually on the first floor as are the parlor or family room and bedrooms of important family members. Bedrooms of lesser family members are on the second floor, and servants sleep in the attic.

■ *Materials*. Structures are of brick, local stone, or stucco (Fig. 21-3, 21-4). Early in the century, brick usually is red, but later its color varies from brown to gray, white, or cream. In the 1720s, façades begin to be stuccoed. Wood and metal portions of façades, including sashes, sash frames, shutters, doors, and door cases, are painted in bold colors whose variety and hue depend on the owner's wealth. Less affluent homeowners primarily use greens, while the wealthy can choose off-whites, browns, grays, yellows, blues, and greens. Doors are a dark color, such as green, black, or red-brown, with a light-colored door case of wood or stone. Shutters, and sometimes sashes, are painted a dark color.

■ *Façades*. Façades (Fig. 21-3, 21-4) are distinctive, having a temple front or pedimented portico at the center, Venetian or Palladian windows, and plain walls. Designers generally group windows, elements within porticoes, and other details in threes. They borrow or adapt façades and features from Vitruvius, Palladio, Inigo Jones, Colen Campbell, and the Earl of Burlington. Lower stories may be rusticated, and entry staircases may be angled to the side of the portico instead of leading directly up in the Roman/Palladian manner. Floors vary in size; first floors are the largest because they house the most important and public rooms. Stringcourses separate stories, and quoins delineate corners. A modillioned cornice generally divides the roof and wall. In the 1720s, groups of row houses, treated as one composition, have temple fronts that emphasize their centers. Gothic Revival structures (Fig. 21-5) feature towers, pointed arches, trefoils, stained glass, battlements, and other Gothic details symmetrically or asymmetrically arranged.

■ *Windows and Doors*. Most windows have uncomplicated surrounds, but some have pediments, quoins, or arched tops (Fig. 21-3). Venetian or Palladian windows (Fig. 21-4) may be used singly or in sequences with some set within relieving arches as at Chiswick House. Diocletian or *thermae* windows highlight the few domes or cupolas, such as at Chiswick House. Most windows are double hung. Most townhouse windows are plainly treated, but grander ones have pediments or lintels. Shutters flank many sash windows.

On centrally placed doorways, compositions of pilasters or columns and round or triangular pediments replace more massive and ornate Baroque treatments. Fanlights, which allow light into the hall, begin to be used above doors in the 1720s. Doors themselves have raised or recessed panels; six is a typical number for panels.

■ *Roofs*. Neo-Palladian roofs are low-pitched hipped or flat with balustrades (Fig. 21-3, 21-4). Centers or ends of compositions sometimes are domed. Gothic-style roofs (Fig. 21-5) pitch steeply and may have battlemented parapets and towers with conical roofs.

■ *Later Interpretations*. Palladian elements, such as temple fronts, are common in the American and English Queen Anne and American Colonial Revival of the late 19th century. Some English and American architects during the mid- to late 20th century design in the Palladian manner within a style that becomes known as New Classicism (Fig. 21-6).

▲ **21-6.** Later Interpretation: Richmond Riverside, 1984–1989; London, England; Quinlan Terry. New Classicism.

INTERIORS

Interiors continue 17th-century traditions until the advent of Neo-Palladianism about 1715. Neo-Palladian interiors are some of the finest created in England, and characteristics are evident in grand and lesser interiors in large and small dwellings. In contrast to the chaste exteriors, interiors may be elaborately decorated with classical and Baroque elements. Proportions of rooms in grand houses are monumental, materials rich and costly, colors bold, and furniture massive. Classical details abound, placed over and around doors and windows, on ceilings or walls, and at the chimneypiece. Designers borrow elements and ornamentation from antique models, Palladio, Inigo Jones, and Venetian Baroque. They sometimes attempt to create an antique look using assemblages derived from ancient or Renaissance sources. Attention focuses on circulation spaces, reception rooms, saloons, chimneypieces, ceilings, and furnishings. Believing that all parts of the house must be especially designed for complete harmony, William Kent (Fig. 21-3, 21-4, 21-7, 21-15) also creates the interiors and furniture for the Neo-Palladian houses he designs. His bold and flamboyant work does not become mainstream. However, large or elaborate Palladian elements, which are easily simplified for smaller homes, appear in pattern books, which include illustrations of staircases, chimneypieces, paneling, doors, and windows. Consequently, numerous middle-class houses and interiors in Britain and America adopt classically derived elements throughout the period.

Designers carefully calculate proportions of rooms, chimneypieces, door and window surrounds, and other details with com-

DESIGN SPOTLIGHT

Interiors: Houghton Hall, a Neo-Palladian country house, designed by Colen Campbell or James Gibbs and decorated by William Kent, establishes the culture and affluence of its owner Sir Robert Walpole and is one of the most important houses of its time. The Stone Hall, a grand entry space, imitates the classical character of the hall in the Queen's House in Greenwich by Inigo Jones. A 40-foot cube, it features common Neo-Palladian elements of monumental scale, rich materials, and an abundance of classical details. The chimneypiece, large doors, and niches are symmetrically aligned. Important architectural features include the elaborate *aedicula* surrounding the doors and niches, the second-floor classical balustrade with supporting brackets, and the Baroque-style ceiling by William Kent. The pedimented fireplace is a signature Kent motif that becomes very influential in both large and small houses. The white walls, mahogany doors, and black and white marble tile floor are all characteristic of the period. Kent also designs the furniture for the space.

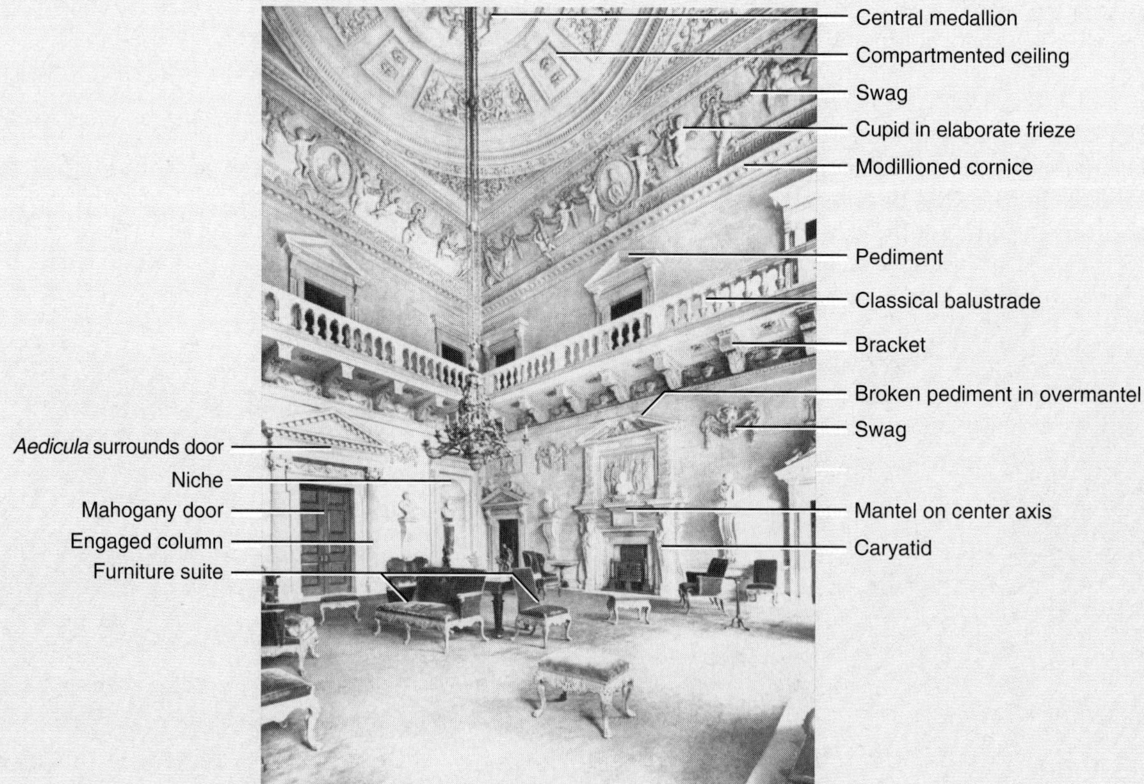

▲ **21-7.** Stone Hall, Houghton Hall, begun 1722–1731; Norfolk, England; Colen Campbell or James Gibbs and William Kent.

plex formulas given by pattern book writers or the masters, such as Palladio, or derived from antique models. Spaces often take the form of a single or double cube or a cube and a half (Fig. 21-7). Rooms are decorated according to their significance; the more important the room, the larger the scale and the more extravagant its decoration. The most lavish spaces are state apartments, reception rooms, and saloons, which reflect a formal way of life. With more emphasis on culture and learning, collectors display their assemblages in galleries or the traditional closet (a small, private room), and libraries become more common.

By mid-century, Rococo, Chinese, and Gothic forms and motifs appear more frequently on walls, ceilings, chimneypieces, textiles, wallpapers, and furniture. English Rococo, more conservative than the French, emerges mainly as ornamentation instead of form in both interiors (Fig. 21-1) and furniture. Similarly, a Chinese influenced ornament often is used in rooms in which tea is taken (Fig. 21-8, 21-12). Unlike the Rococo and Chinese styles, the Gothic style begins as an architectural style before appearing in interior details and furniture (Fig. 21-5). Rococo ornamentation mixes freely with Chinese and Gothic ornamentation, and some houses feature each public room in a different style.

DESIGN SPOTLIGHT

Interiors: The chaste Neo-Palladian exterior of Claydon House belies its elaborate, even fantastic, interiors. Home to the Verney family, it boasts a series of rooms designed in different historic influences including Neo-Palladian, Rococo, Gothic, and Chinese. The extraordinary Chinese Room is the work of master carver and decorator Luke Lightfoot, who was most likely inspired by books on Chinese designs. The alcove, which once contained a bed but now has a sofa, is ornately embellished with carved *Chinoiserie* decoration including a *pagoda,* temple bells, niches with Oriental statues, and elaborate latticework. The latticework repeats as a dado around the room. Door surrounds are equally ornate and topped with *pagodas,* Chinese figures, and latticework, all intricately carved. The door panels feature fretwork. The blue-green walls are a popular Chinese color, and matting covers the floor. The rattan furniture from Canton is sympathetic to the space, but dates to about 1800.

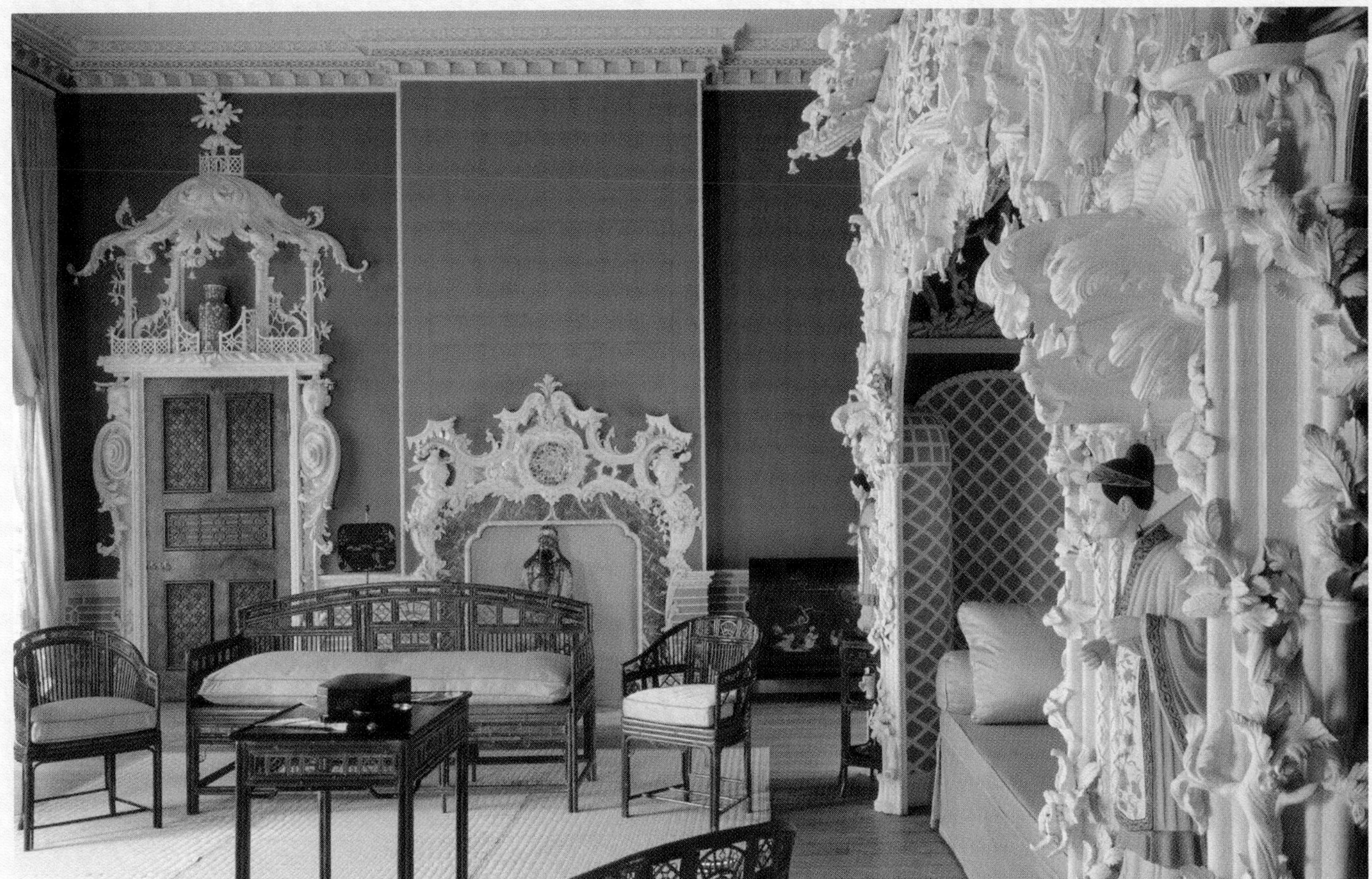

▲ **21-8.** Chinese Room, Claydon House, 1757–1768; Buckinghamshire, England; carving by Luke Lightfoot.

Private Buildings

■ *Color.* In the early 18th century, color unifies rooms. Moldings and other details match walls, except in great houses where they are sometimes gilded. By the 1720s, lighter hues, particularly white, replace earlier dark colors. The Neo-Palladian ideal of classic simplicity translates into light- or stone-colored walls (Fig. 21-3, 21-4, 21-7) that clearly reveal proportions and architectural details in the manner of Inigo Jones. Most houses have at least one important room treated in this way.

As the period progresses, more colors in various intensities and values become available, including pea green, olive green, gray green, gray, sky blue, straw yellow, and a variety of gray or brown stone colors (Fig. 21-4, 21-5, 21-7, 21-8). Stone colors are considered most appropriate for halls whereas stronger colors work better in other rooms. Libraries and dining rooms are often in reds and greens. Sometimes the color selection relates to the particular stylistic influence, such as brown for Gothic and rose for Rococo. Graining and marbling diminish as the period progresses. Doors and baseboards are painted brown or black to hide wear.

■ *Floors.* Floor materials are wood or masonry. Oak, pine, or fir board floors have random dimensions. Wood floors are not varnished, but they are scrubbed with sand or limewash that produces a silvery sheen. Parquet distinguishes the grandest rooms (Fig. 21-5). Paint, in solids or patterns, disguises cheaper woods. Stone and marble floors (Fig. 21-5, 21-7) are limited to entrances and ground-floor rooms because of their weight. They follow a variety of geometric patterns and colors, but black and white or grays are especially favored.

Painted floor cloths gain importance during the period; black and white marble patterns are preferred but other patterns are used. Carpet is more common as the 18th century progresses. Carpet types include piled carpets, such as Brussels and Wilton, and unpiled carpets such as ingrains and list carpet. Important rooms have piled carpets installed from wall to wall and often with borders. Ingrains, considered utilitarian, are reserved for halls, lesser rooms, and servants' quarters. Drugget of baize, serge, or haircloth protects carpets in wealthy homes or serves as floor coverings in humble ones. Other floor coverings include Oriental, Savonnerie, or Aubusson rugs, and reed, cane, or rush matting (Fig. 21-8).

■ *Walls.* Paneling, which is generally painted, remains a favorite wall treatment. Most panels are rectangular and recessed, but those in wealthy homes are often raised. Narrow panels flank wider ones, and paintings and pictures hang in the centers. Important rooms have elaborate moldings that are often gilded. Occasionally, paneling incorporates shelves, semicircular cupboards with shell-shaped tops, or niches, which reflect the passion for collecting. Grand rooms (Fig. 21-4, 21-7) have deep and elaborate cornices with dentils or modillions.

By mid-century, completely paneled walls are no longer fashionable. Instead, the wall over the paneled dado is painted, papered, or hung with fabric glued to the wall (Fig. 21-4, 21-5, 21-8). Walls also may have elaborate plasterwork details (Fig. 21-1, 21-3, 21-4, 21-5, 21-7, 21-8) that may be classical, Rococo, Chinese, Gothic, or a combination.

Wallpaper begins to be used in public and reception rooms during the period. The thick and heavy paper comes in squares, which are matched and glued to the wall. Backgrounds are color-washed by hand, and patterns hand-blocked. Types include flocked papers imitating cut-piled fabrics, architectural papers, papers incorporating prints or antique statues, and simple repetitive patterns. Although expensive, hand-painted Chinese or "India" papers also are popular, so English manufacturers soon produce imitations of them.

(a)

(b)

▲ **21-9.** Textiles: (a) Painted and dyed cotton *palampore*, late 18th century, and (b) English crewelwork curtain, linen and cotton twill with wool embroidery, early to mid-18th century; England.

The chimneypiece usually has two tiers, following Inigo Jones and others (Fig. 21-3, 21-7). The lower portion boldly projects into the room and incorporates a variety of classical motifs including caryatids, columns, and consoles as well as the ear motif (Fig. 21-1). Mantels are of plaster, wood, marble, or scagliola in white, black, gray, and other colors. In the 1740s, Rococo, Chinese, and Gothic motifs appear on chimneypieces. Above the mantel is a solid or broken pediment with carved wood or plaster details, such as masks, rosettes, or swags. A painting or looking glass may hang over the mantel (Fig. 21-4).

■ *Windows and Doors*. Double-hung windows are typical. Lintels, pediments, and other architectural details surround windows (Fig. 21-3) in important rooms; others are plain. Most windows have internal shutters in two or three sections that match the paneling and fold into the window jamb when not in use. Window treatments include roller and venetian blinds that block light, but work poorly. Grand houses have curtains of luxurious materials, while others use less expensive fabrics. Festoons and simple panels are the most common window treatments, which also may have valances in complex shapes with elaborate trims.

Doorways (Fig. 21-3, 21-4, 21-7) to important rooms are placed symmetrically and often have *aedicula* or other classical details, usually painted white. After mid-century, Gothic, Rococo, or *Chinoiserie* motifs (Fig. 21-1, 21-5, 21-8) may embellish the door as well as the overdoor treatment. Most doors have six or eight wooden panels with carved and gilded moldings.

■ *Ceilings*. The cove and compartmentalized plasterwork ceilings of Inigo Jones return to fashion in grand homes (Fig. 21-3, 21-4, 21-7). Alternative treatments are coffers and paintings (Fig. 21-4). Like other elements, ceilings often feature Rococo, Chinese and/or Gothic motifs (Fig. 21-5). Ceilings in lesser rooms and lesser houses are flat and a light color.

■ *Textiles*. Textile use grows during the period as new inventions increase the speed of production, produce better products, and lower costs. Carpets and curtains become more common, and bedhangings are even more elaborate. Textiles provide much of the color in rooms (Fig. 21-3, 21-4, 21-9).

Typical textiles include velvets, silks, wools, linens, cottons, and leather. Crewel embroideries and Indian *palampores* (Fig. 21-9) or similar patterns are more popular than ever for upholstery and bed hangings. Despite ongoing battles between English cotton manufacturers and importers of India cottons, printed cottons become more fashionable during the period. *Toiles*, first manufactured in Drumcondra, Ireland, in 1752, are monochromatic prints using copper plates, which allow larger and more defined repeats. Furniture covers or cases of lightweight cottons or woven checks protect upholstery fabrics. Chair backs may not be upholstered to save money.

■ *Lighting*. Artificial lighting, generally minimal, comes primarily from fireplaces, rushlights, or candles; oil lamps are rare before the 1780s. Light fixtures (Fig. 21-4, 21-7, 21-10) include candlesticks, *candelabra*, and/or wall sconces. To increase light, candlesticks and *candelabra* are placed in front of mirrors, and sconces have mirrored or shiny metal backs. Shiny textures and glossy finishes also reflect and increase light. Although chandeliers of glass, wood, or metal are available, they remain rare in most homes.

(a) (b)

▲ **21-10.** Lighting: (a) Candlestick and (b) wall sconce; England.

FURNISHINGS AND DECORATIVE ARTS

The 18th century is a golden age in English furniture. People have more money to spend on furniture and demand higher standards in craftsmanship and comfort, as well as new types for special purposes. In response, several styles of furniture rapidly succeed each other during the Georgian period, and cabinetmaking becomes a profitable business. Individual cabinetmakers achieve prominence and move into a higher social status. Thomas Chippendale is the first cabinetmaker to have a style named after him.

Furniture selection and arrangements support room function with an emphasis on formality, harmony, and stylistic integration. Symmetry usually defines the placement of major pieces of furniture. The finest furniture occupies the best drawing room and is arranged around the perimeter of the room when not in use. Common furniture pieces include chairs, sofas, tables, secretaries, high chests of drawers, dressing tables, tall case clocks, fire screens, and beds. Card tables are introduced during Queen Anne's reign, and their numbers increase with the popularity of card playing throughout the 18th century. Additional new pieces include extension dining tables, *commodes*, and new forms of tea tables.

■ *Queen Anne (1702–1714)*. Continuing the Dutch traditions of the William and Mary style, the Queen Anne style relies on silhouette and wood grain for beauty rather than applied decoration. English examples are relatively plain, but comfortable and human in scale. Curves dominate forms, and proportions are slender and elongated. Chairs (Fig. 21-11), which are definitive of the style, have a curving hoop back with plain crest. The back may be spoon-shaped to fit the body. Inside the hoop is a solid splat that has either a vase, fiddle, or parrot profile. The slip seat may be trapezoidal or curving. Slender and graceful cabriole legs may have stretchers and a shell sometimes combined with an acanthus leaf on the knee. Legs terminate in pad, club, or hairy paw feet.

▲ **21-11.** Queen Anne side chair in walnut, early 18th century; England.

■ *Baroque and William Kent (1710–1750)*. Because neither Palladio nor Inigo Jones designed furniture, designers have no precedents to copy. So, following the lead of flamboyant architect and designer William Kent, they turn to Neo-Palladian architecture and Venetian Baroque prototypes. Kent's massive, elaborate custom furniture (Fig. 21-3, 21-4, 21-7, 21-15) is limited to the large wealthy houses he designs. He designs a full range of furnishings but prefers side and pier tables with marble tops and scrolled legs or single supports in a classical shape. His favorite motifs are the shell, double shell, Vitruvian scroll, masks, swags, lions, dolphins, and brackets. Grand pieces are gilded. Kent furnishings both harmonize with and dominate their interiors and show architectural emphasis.

■ *Early Georgian (1714–1750)*. Several substyles of Early Georgian define the transition from the Queen Anne to the Chippendale style. Early in the period, Queen Anne forms continue but with more embellishment, such as lacquer, veneers, and carving. Under Neo-Palladian influence, furniture becomes more massive, and case pieces incorporate architectural details such as columns and pediments. By the middle of the period, early Georgian chairs have lower and broader proportions than those of Queen Anne, and splats boast open or pierced carving. Cabriole legs are wider and less elongated. Mahogany becomes the main wood and carving the main decoration. Common motifs and details include lion masks; satyr masks; eagle heads; dolphins; and, late in the period, Rococo influences.

■ *Chippendale (1750–1770)*. Continuing the Early Georgian form with low, broad proportions and pierced splats, this furniture style (Fig. 21-12, 21-17, 21-18) shows Rococo, Chinese, and Gothic influences. Rococo influence mainly appears in carved decoration such as leaves, tendrils, flowers, shells, and ribbons that are often combined with Chinese and Gothic motifs. Chinese influence comes from motifs such as *pagodas*, bamboo, and bells. Gothic influence manifests in cluster column legs, pointed arches, and tracery. Thomas Chippendale's book *The Gentleman's and Cabinet-Maker's Director* of 1754 illustrates, but does not originate, the style that bears his name. It is an early form of trade catalog used to solicit buyers.

Chippendale chairs have serpentine or Cupid's bow crests. Crests and splats display Rococo, Gothic, and/or Chinese motifs. Legs may be straight or cabriole. Feet include pad, club, French whorl, block, and ball and claw, although *The Director* does not illustrate the latter. Arms and legs sometimes imitate bamboo in Chinese or cluster columns in Gothic. Some Chinese Chippendale chair backs are composed of fretwork with no splat. Chinese examples may have open or solid fretwork on stretchers, legs, arms, seat rails, and tabletops.

DESIGN SPOTLIGHT

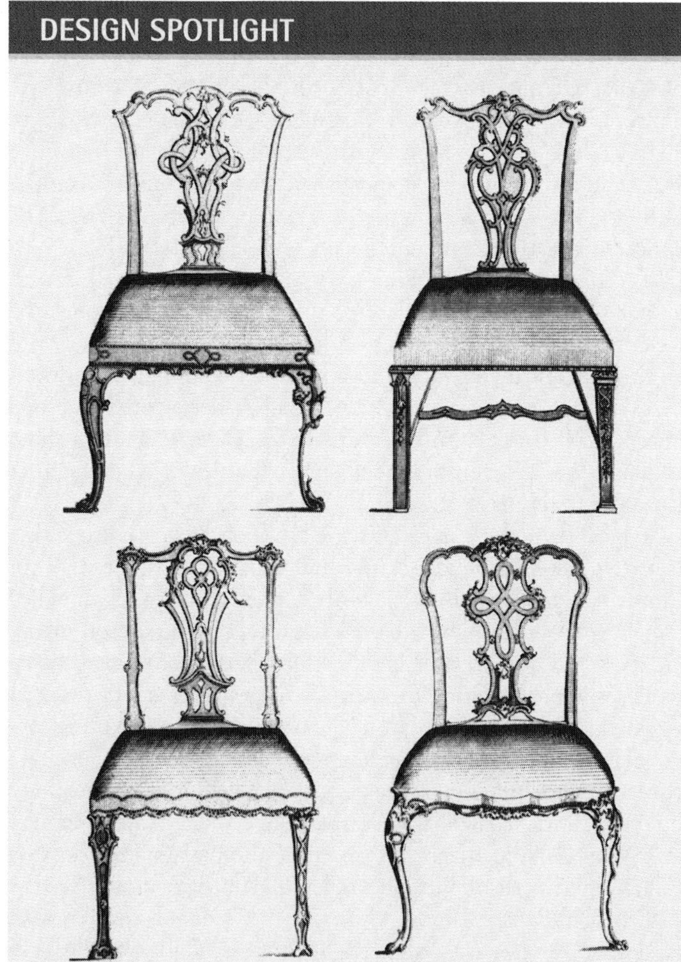

▲ **21-12.** Parlor chairs published in Thomas Chippendale's *The Gentleman's and Cabinet-Maker's Director* (or *The Director*) include side and armchairs with ribbon backs, Chippendale style, c. 1755, and an armchair, Chinese style; England.

Private Buildings

■ *Materials*. Walnut dominates Queen Anne furniture but it is supplanted by imported mahogany in the 1730s. Because mahogany has a fine grain and is easy to carve, carving replaces marquetry and inlay as embellishment. Unlike French Rococo, which influences it, Chippendale rarely features *ormolu*. Lacquering or japanning, usually in black or red, is used on some pieces, particularly bedroom furniture. Crossbanding and herringbone are favored veneer patterns.

■ *Seating*. Seating includes side chairs and armchairs (Fig. 21-11, 21-12), many forms of armchairs and armless chairs with upholstered seats and backs, *easie* chairs, settees and sofas (Fig. 21-4, 21-5, 21-7, 21-8, 21-13, 21-14). Side chairs and armchairs are more numerous and more common than settees and wing chairs. Sets of matching upholstered furniture fill important rooms in grand houses. The large, upholstered sofa, now an icon of the Chippendale style, is rare before mid-century.

▲ **21-13.** *Easie* (wing) chair, c. 1700; England.

DESIGN SPOTLIGHT

Furniture: As the first pattern book devoted to furniture, *The Director* by Chippendale is a trade catalog of prevailing fashions in the Chippendale style. It shows furniture in three "tastes"—Rococo, Chinese, and Gothic. As one of the most continuously popular styles, the Chippendale style is widely copied subsequently in the American Georgian and Colonial Revival periods in America and the Georgian Revivals of England. It remains widely adapted and reproduced today.

These chairs show the elements common on English furniture of the period. All have the low, broad proportions, carved and pierced splats, carved crests, cabriole or straight legs, and feet that characterize the Chippendale style. The illustration of parlor chairs from *The Director* shows the variety of details in backs, splats, legs, and feet from which a buyer or furniture maker could choose. The mahogany armchair has a rectangular back, modified Cupid's bow crest, a ribbon splat, cabriole legs, and intricate Rococo carving. The Chinese Chippendale armchair has a rectangular back, Chinese-style crest, an open fretwork splat, fretwork on the arm panels, imitation bamboo legs, and intricate carving. Usually in mahogany, they are elegant statements of mid-18th-century fashion.

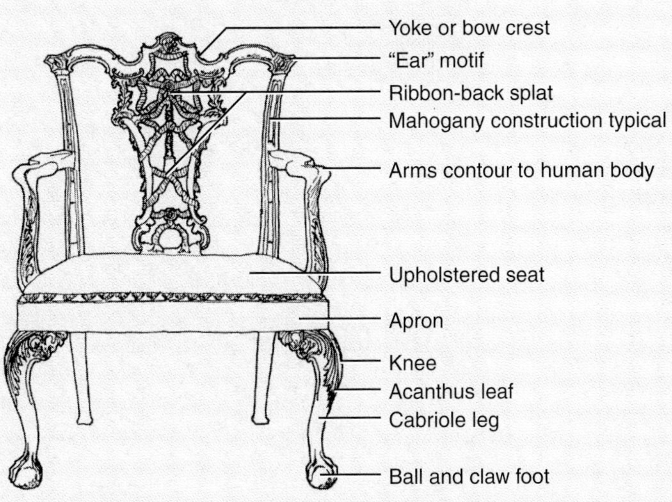

▲ **21-14.** Camel-back sofa, Claydon House, mid-18th century; Buckinghamshire, England.

▲ **21-16.** George III tilt-top tea table, mid-18th century; England.

■ *Tables*. Georgian drawing rooms have numerous small tables, reflecting society's interest in inviting friends for tea, cards, and/or conversation (Fig. 21-4, 21-8, 21-15, 21-16). Card or game tables have folding tops that rest on a hinged leg when open. When closed, they sit against the wall. Tea tables also fold down, and tops may be round, oblong, rectangular, piecrust, or polygonal (Fig. 21-16). They have legs or rest on a carved or fluted shaft terminating in a carved tripod called a claw. Dining tables have three parts: a center with drop leaves and two semicircular ends. The pieces are placed against the wall when not in use.

■ *Storage*. Every fashionable Georgian drawing room has a *commode*. It has a straight, *bombé*, and/or serpentine-shaped front and sides. Most are elaborately carved, but a few have marquetry and gilt-bronze mounts in the French manner. Large case pieces, such as desks and bookcases (Fig. 21-17), often have architectural details, such as columns, colonnettes, architectural moldings, or broken pediments for displaying sculpture or porcelain. Alternative decorations include Gothic pointed arches or a Chinese *pagoda* outline. Glass mullions in the doors may feature Rococo leaves or curving tendrils, often combined with Chinese or Gothic details.

▲ **21-15.** Side table, mid-18th century; England; William Kent.

▲ **21-17.** Desk and bookcase with *Chinoiserie* decoration, c. 1710; England.

■ *Beds*. Four-poster beds are the most fashionable. Queen Anne types follow earlier forms, but Chippendale headboards are elaborately carved with Rococo, Chinese, or Gothic details. Canopies and testers may be *pagoda*-shaped in Chinese examples, which are usually japanned (Fig. 21-18). Beds continue to have elaborate hangings with trims and tassels. A few rooms have French-style beds with no posts.

■ *Decorative Arts*. Most grand interiors display oil paintings, usually collected on grand tours (Fig. 21-4). Specially designed niches or cabinets display ancient sculptures or collections of other objects (Fig. 21-7). Accessories include painted and gilded wall brackets, folding screens, and fire screens, all of which follow the forms and decoration of furniture. Porcelain remains highly prized, and factories in Chelsea, Worcester, Caughley, and Spode manufacture it beginning in the 1740s in Chinese and European styles. Mirrors are important for decoration and to enhance light (Fig. 21-5). Queen Anne pier glasses have simple and curvilinear outlines that resemble chair backs. The wood frames may be left plain, painted, or gilded. New in the period is the chimney glass or mirror, which is horizontal in form with three parts to hang over the mantel. Architectural looking glasses with columns and pediments framing the glass are introduced in the Early Georgian period. Chippendale examples have complicated outlines; gilding; and Chinese, Rococo, and/or Gothic motifs.

▲ **21-18.** Bed for the Chinese bedroom at Badminton House, c. 1755, Gloucestershire, England; William Linnell.

CHAPTER 22

American Georgian

1700s–1780s

The houses in general make a good Appearance and also as well furnished, as in Most places you will see with many of the rooms being hung with printed canvas and paper & which looks very neat. Others are well wainscoted and painted as in other places.

—James Birket, *Some Cursory Remarks made by James Birket in his Voyage to North America 1750–1751*

During the 18th century, the traditional vernacular buildings, interiors, and furnishings with strong regional differences of the 17th century yield to a learned, tasteful, refined image based on classicism—the American Georgian style. Similar across the English American colonies, the style reflects the tastes, culture, and increasing prosperity of colonists along the eastern Atlantic coast from Canada to South Carolina who maintain strong connections to their English heritage and tradition. They copy and adapt to their needs English precedents in education, art, and architecture.

HISTORICAL AND SOCIAL

In the 18th century, times become more settled, which gives rise to greater prosperity and an increasing focus upon education and culture among English colonists. Financial independence comes from farming; exports of tobacco, rice, indigo, lumber, and iron; and trade with Britain and the West Indies. Colonists can rise socially and economically based on their own abilities, unlike in Europe where the wealthy control opportunities. Testament to this growth and prosperity are new government facilities, religious buildings, and larger domestic structures generally in towns like Philadelphia and Williamsburg and along navigable rivers. Large, grand houses built for wealthy gentleman farmers, aspiring politicians, and prospering merchants are the best illustrations of America's taste and talent. Like their English counterparts, these gentlemen consider the knowledge of architecture essential to their education and a mark of refinement. Working with local carpenters and inspired by English publications and design developments, the colonists adopt classical principles in buildings and interiors. Dwellings support formal lifestyles and refinement in social and behavioral customs that manifest in conversation, gaming, dancing, musical recitals, and socializing over tea. Vernacular interpretations imitate these models.

All is not well, however, as England continues to expect the colonies to export raw materials and import finished goods from her. Increasingly harsh government polices forced upon the colonists contribute to England's loss of her colonies along the Atlantic coast in the second half of the 18th century. Unified by ideas, language, and heritage, settlers band together to break the bonds of English political connections. Colonists want to govern themselves, more or less, because they dislike Britain's attempts at control. They eventually develop government centers and focus on the value of democracy, separate rights, and the common man. Leaders of this spiritual and political revolution include Benjamin Franklin, George Washington, Thomas Jefferson, George Mason, and James

Monroe—men who will mold a new nation. These men, influenced by the Enlightenment, become a single voice for the country, one that questions connections to Britain. Increased attempts of British domination lead to the beginning of the American Revolution in 1775 and the Declaration of Independence in 1776.

CONCEPTS

Design influences in America come from the English nobility, whose elaborate houses show their cultured tastes refined by the French court of Louis XV, trade with the Orient, and travel to Europe. Rococo, *Chinoiserie*, and Palladian designs contribute to an image based on reason and refinement. With prosperity and more settled times, colonists follow the English gentry in seeking gentility, culture, manners, and civility. Formal, classical houses and furnishings support this polite society and its activities. Knowledge about the appropriate 18th-century design language comes through immigrant artisans and architects, English pattern books, and imported furniture and materials.

MOTIFS

■ *Motifs*. Classical motifs (Fig. 22-1, 22-3, 22-4, 22-5, 22-6, 22-7, 22-8, 22-9, 22-11) defining architecture include pilasters, pediments, dentil moldings, balustrades, round arches with keystones, and quoins. Common motifs (Fig. 22-1) in interiors include the ear, shell, acanthus leaf, rosette, and pineapple or pinecone, as well as renditions of naturalistic flowers. Furniture motifs (Fig. 22-1, 22-12, 22-16, 22-17) may be classical (columns and moldings), Rococo (shells and flowers), or Chinese (fretwork and bamboo).

ARCHITECTURE

American colonists continue to look to English prototypes for architectural design inspiration. As an ordered visual unit, the buildings exhibit classical traditions inspired by Andrea Palladio, Inigo Jones, James Gibbs, architectural pattern books, and carpenter's building manuals. No longer revealing the irregular, additive, and utilitarian approach of the earlier 17th century, 18th-century structures show discipline, detailing, and preplanning. Colonial buildings become more formal with greater design sophistication and now are symmetrical, ordered, and balanced. Classical details and Neo-Palladian design influences increase throughout the period. Regional manifestations decline as a common design vocabulary develops. Public and private structures are similar in form and ornament, yet both usually maintain a smaller scale and simpler treatments than in England. Urban examples are more common in the north and rural ones dominate in the mid-Atlantic and South. While most colonists live in small, one- or two-room wooden dwellings, some build larger houses modeled after English manors.

Public buildings (Fig. 22-2, 22-3, 22-4) include government structures, churches, educational structures, and taverns. After mid-century, new types, such as hospitals and markets, increase.

(a)

(b)

(c)

▲ **22-1.** Architectural Details and Motifs: (a) Door, Westover Plantation, 1730s–1750s, Charles City County, Virginia; (b) ear motif; and (c) highboy detail with shell and rosette motifs. The doorway comes from the builder's handbook *Palladio Londinensis: The London Art of Building* (1734) by William Salmon.

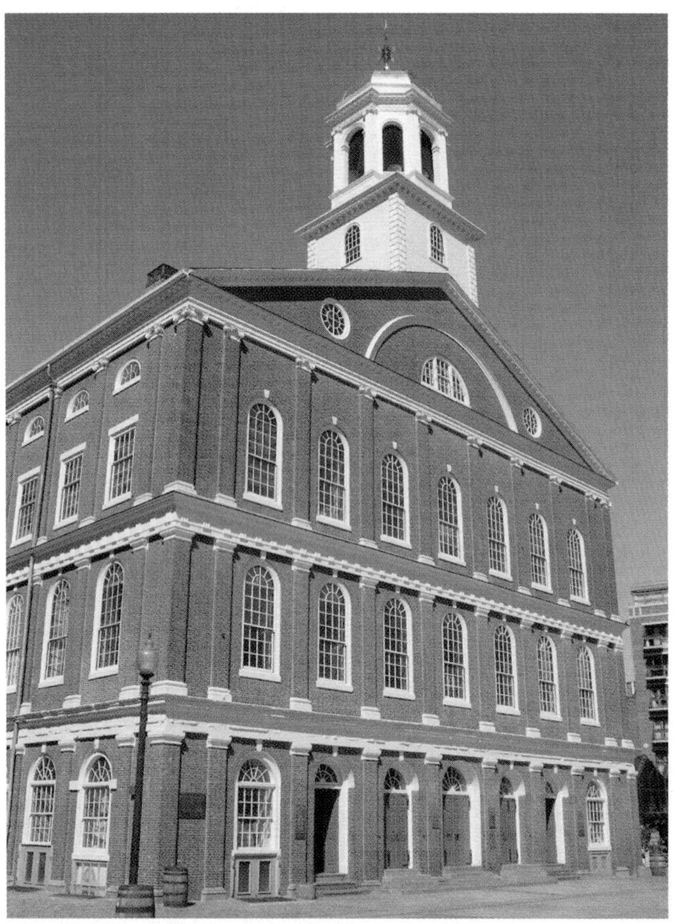

▲ **22-2.** Faneuil Hall, 1740–1742; Boston, Massachusetts; John Smibert; enlarged and rebuilt in 1805 by Charles Bulfinch.

Public and Private Buildings

■ *Site Orientation*. Government buildings and churches sit along major transportation arteries for visual recognition. Other public structures are built along dominant thoroughfares for accessibility to urban centers. Both high-style and vernacular dwellings (Fig. 22-5, 22-6, 22-7, 22-8, 22-9, 22-10) are near transportation routes within cities or are part of agricultural estates, often along rivers. In these high-style affluent dwellings, the rectangular-block main house dominates the site. Established on a center axis, the circulation paths provide an ordered arrangement of house, outbuildings, and gardens. In a plantation setting, the house often has egress in two directions, to a river or to a roadway. The outbuildings, more vernacular in character, include the kitchen, smokehouse, storage, stables, and servants' quarters.

■ *Floor Plans*. Churches follow the earlier British regional forms of a Latin cross plan in the South and a more centralized plan in New England. After mid-century, New England Protestant churches begin to abandon the traditional central meetinghouse plan in favor of the Latin cross in the Wren and Gibbs tradition. In Latin cross plans, the entry is on a center axis leading through the nave to the altar (Fig. 22-3). Crossings are usually absent. Governmental and educational buildings often have a double-pile plan or a variation.

Some imitate the tripartite compositions of Palladio and are flanked by two smaller buildings called dependencies (Fig. 22-9). These smaller structures have a similar design and may be offices or guest rooms.

Most large houses have a double-pile plan on both floors (Fig. 22-7, 22-9). The long center hall or passage, a circulation and living area, has entries at each end to catch cooling breezes and a stairway to the second floor (Fig. 22-11). The adjoining rooms (Fig. 22-6, 22-9, 22-11) for socializing, dining, and sometimes sleeping are often rectangular or square with fireplaces located on interior center walls or exterior walls. Townhouses usually have side passages with two to three rooms on one side (Fig. 22-8). Private spaces, such as bedchambers, are separated from the public spaces through placement and circulation paths.

■ *Materials*. Common building materials (Fig. 22-2, 22-3, 22-4, 22-5, 22-6, 22-7, 22-8, 22-9, 22-10) for both public and private buildings are wood, brick, and stone. Selection varies by geographic location and the availability of resources. Brick is the most common material, although some wood-frame construction with clapboard siding predominates in New England areas. Mid-

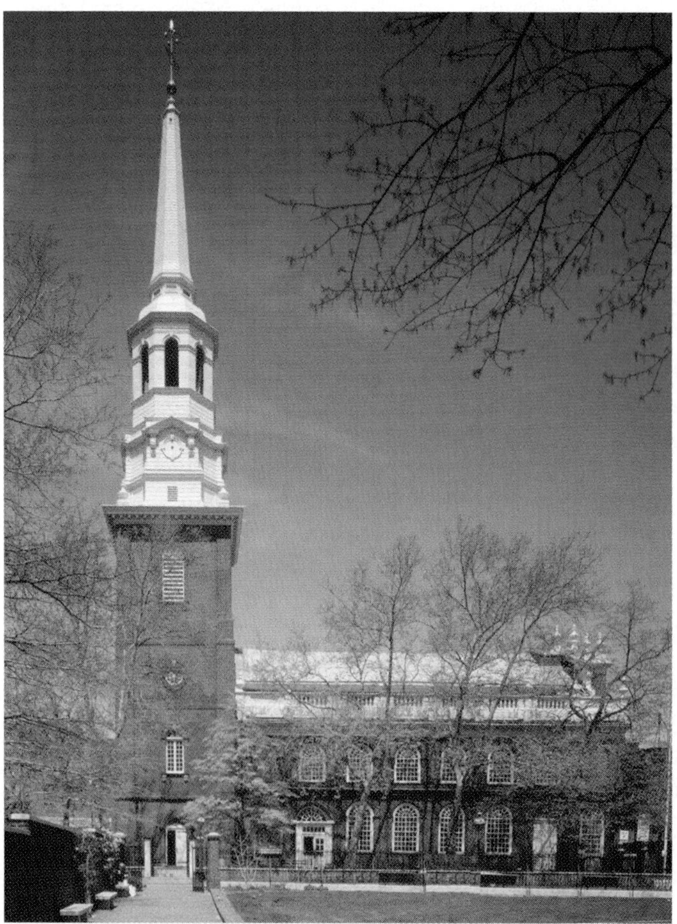

▲ **22-3.** Christ Church, 1727–1754; Philadelphia, Pennsylvania.

Atlantic and southern regions frequently choose handmade red brick or, sometimes, quarried stone. Stone contrasts in color to brick, which may alternate in color, pattern, and selection. Some public structures are of wood treated to imitate stone.

■ *Façades*. Public façades (Fig. 22-2, 22-3, 22-4) are formally organized and have two or three stories. They may resemble dwellings but are larger in size. The application of classical details increases throughout the period. Sash windows, dormers, and modillioned cornices are common except in churches, which do not have dormers. Center entrances are emphasized with *aedicula*, temple fronts, porticoes, and/or cupolas. Lower stories may be arched, and upper ones are divided into bays with pilasters in the Palladian manner. Like many of Sir Christopher Wren's city churches, steeples atop rectangular towers define entrance fronts of colonial churches rather than highlighting a traditional crossing. Rectangular towers usually have stringcourses and varieties of window shapes. Upper portions are octagonal with arches, pilasters, and clocks. After mid-century, following Wren and Gibbs, porticoes and temple fronts define tower entrances. The door may be in the tower or immediately behind a portico. Pilaster and/or windows divide side façades into bays.

Residential façades (Fig. 22-5, 22-6, 22-7, 22-8, 22-9, 22-10) have classically delineated entries. In brick homes, a belt or

▲ **22-4.** Independence Hall, 1731–1791; Philadelphia, Pennsylvania.

DESIGN SPOTLIGHT

▲ **22-5.** Drayton Hall, 1738–1742; Charleston, South Carolina.

Architecture: Probably created from pattern books, including Palladio's *Four Books on Architecture*, by the owner and a master joiner, Drayton Hall is the first Anglo-Palladian house in America. It is the county seat of Royal Judge John Drayton, a wealthy rice grower. The east front, which faces the river, has a pedimented doorway, pedimented windows on the next floor, and another pediment at the roofline. The west façade faces the road. Its design with its two-story projecting pedimented portico, nearly square in form, and symmetrical floor plan with rooms organized along a central axis resembles several villas in Palladio's book. The design differs from those in England, where two-story porticoes are rare because of the climate. The double stairs are modeled after those in Coleshill in England. On the portico, imported Portland stone Ionic columns surmount Tuscan in the Roman tradition. The space beneath the portico and the great hall inside are gathering spaces for guests as Palladio recommended. Flanking buildings, common in Palladian and English country villas, are added later but have not survived. Drayton Hall's interiors, which repeat many of the exterior architectural elements, harmonize with the exterior design. Some of the main floor rooms have very fine plasterwork ceilings. Drayton Hall is owned by the National Trust for Historic Preservation, which has chosen to preserve it as it stands instead of restoring it to a particular time in its history. (National Historic Landmark)

▲ **22-6.** Hunter House and drawing room, 1748; Newport, Rhode Island.

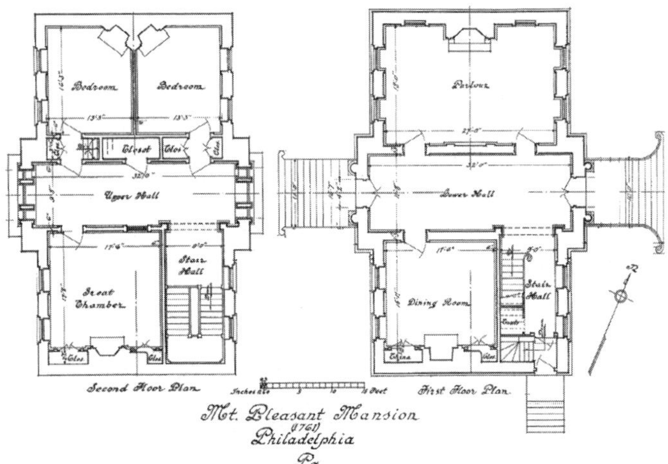

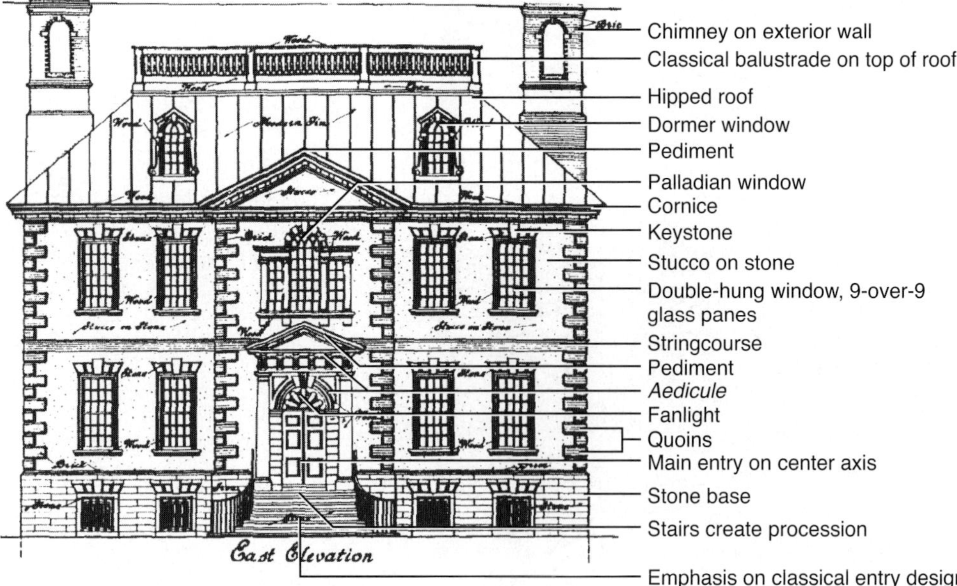

▲ **22-7.** Mount Pleasant, east elevation, and floor plan, 1761–1762; Philadelphia, Pennsylvania.

stringcourse composed of a wide, flat band separates floors. Early houses tend to be plain with ornamentation limited primarily to the doorway and roofline (Fig. 22-1). After mid-century, porticoes, pilasters, pediments, arches, keystones, and quoins create greater three-dimensionality and a more Neo-Palladian character (Fig. 22-7).

■ *Windows and Doors*. Sash windows (Fig. 22-5, 22-7, 22-9, 22-10) are typical on both public and private buildings. Six-over-six or nine-over-nine glass panes are the most common. Some churches have round-arched or round windows. Windows are often large to admit as much light as possible. Stained glass is rare, as plain glass is preferred to make nature, God's creation, visible. Windows on dwellings often have exterior shutters, especially after mid-century. Classical details define doorways on public and private buildings. Surrounds vary from simple pilasters and a pediment to Doric porticoes. Doors themselves are of paneled wood and are usually painted a dark color.

■ *Roofs*. Hipped or gable roofs (Fig. 22-5, 22-7, 22-9) are the most common on all structures. Gambrel roofs (Fig. 22-6) are also common on houses. Domes are very rare. Some roofs on houses are accentuated with a classical white balustrade, and dormer windows add variety and allow light into attics.

INTERIORS

As in architecture, interiors become increasingly formal, classical, and refined. Interiors directly reflect the symmetrically balanced exteriors, creating a classically ordered, unified image based on English prototypes. Treatments and finishes reflect English preferences. The design of public interiors varies according to function and use. Church interiors, characterized by architectural detailing and simplicity, often have seating in compartments and balconies.

Intimately scaled spaces prevail in houses, emulating the character of the Rococo in Europe, but with less ornateness. Most rooms have an impressive dominant fireplace on the main wall with a symmetrically placed door or two windows on the opposite wall. Borders and outlines are important in creating unity, outside and inside, and even appear on the furniture details of fringe, piping, and decorative tapes. Each room is usually treated as an individually designed unit with little relation to the adjoining space. Public spaces, such as passages (Fig. 22-11) and drawing rooms (Fig. 22-6, 22-8) are multifunctional with a formal character emphasizing refinement and wealth. The best room, parlor, or drawing room is used only for entertaining and formal family functions; dining occurs where convenient and seasonally comfortable. The best bedchamber, which houses the finest furnishings, may occupy a first- or second-floor position.

Public and Private Buildings

■ *Color*. Scholarship indicates that interiors used more intense colors than is commonly believed. Colors in England are also available in the colonies, although colonists are less likely to use color to depict wealth. Colors for rooms used principally in the evening are chosen with candlelight and firelight in mind. The color palette (Fig. 22-9, 22-11, 22-12, 22-13, 22-18) has medium values of russet-rose, Prussian blue, sky blue, blue gray, pea green, olive green, gray green, deep green, and charcoal gray accented with white or off-white. Walls may be painted or papered in one of these colors with details, textiles, and/or accessories in contrasting colors.

■ *Floors*. Floors in religious and government structures display variety through the use of wood, stone, and brick in various patterns. In contrast, most residential floors (Fig. 22-6, 22-8, 22-9, 22-11, 22-12) are of wide wooden boards. Some, especially those of poor quality, are painted in solids or patterns, or to resemble

▲ **22-8.** Powel House and drawing room, 1767–1769; Philadelphia, Pennsylvania.

rugs; floor cloths are common, even in the best rooms. Oriental rugs are rare until the end of the 18th century, and most often are put on tables because they are too expensive to walk on. Very wealthy homes may have wall-to-wall carpet made by narrow strips sewn together. During the summer, rush matting replaces carpet and rugs.

■ *Walls*. Classic wall divisions, common in both public and private interiors, incorporate a cornice, frieze, small architrave, shaft, dado rail, paneled dado, and baseboard (Fig. 22-6, 22-8, 22-9, 22-11). Alternative wall treatments include paint, paneling, wallpaper, or fabric. The latter two are more common in houses. Wood paneling may only highlight a fireplace wall, or it may cover the entire wall or be only below the dado. Panels are left natural, stained, or painted. Wallpaper or fabric, imported from England, covers the wall above the dado and entire walls of passages, drawing rooms, and other spaces (Fig. 22-11, 22-13). Solid colors of paper are most common, but patterns include framed paintings or prints, architectural papers, small prints, naturalistic designs resembling Oriental papers, and imitations of textiles. Matching or nonmatching borders outline architectural elements, such as doors, windows, and fireplaces.

The fireplace wall (Fig. 22-6, 22-8, 22-9, 22-12) is composed of a vertically oriented mantel and overmantel, which usually has a broken pediment, pilasters, and classic details. The chimneypiece usually projects into the room. Walls on either side might have niches called beaufats for serving or display (Fig. 22-6, 22-11), a unique feature of the period. The niche itself might be framed with pilasters and a broken pediment. Other interior walls could complement this design or be simply treated with paint or wallpaper.

■ *Windows and Doors*. Windows in many public and most private buildings usually include recessed wooden shutters on either side to block light. Curtains are rare even among the wealthy and appear only in the best rooms. Types include pairs of panels and festoons that resemble swags and cascades (Fig. 22-12). Doorways

DESIGN SPOTLIGHT

Architecture and Interior: Designed by William Buckland, an English-trained carpenter and joiner for Matthias Hammond, the Hammond-Harwood House is an Anglo-Palladian-style villa in town. An extremely sophisticated design that resembles Palladio's Villa Pisani at Montagnana, the rectangular block main house dominates the site. Re-creating the tripartite compositions of Palladio and others, it is flanked by two dependencies: the smaller buildings with half-octagon fronts. Hyphens or small connecting units join the main house and dependencies. A pediment tops the projecting three center bays of the main house. Pediments carried by engaged columns or pilasters repeat over the main doorway and smaller doors in the hyphens.

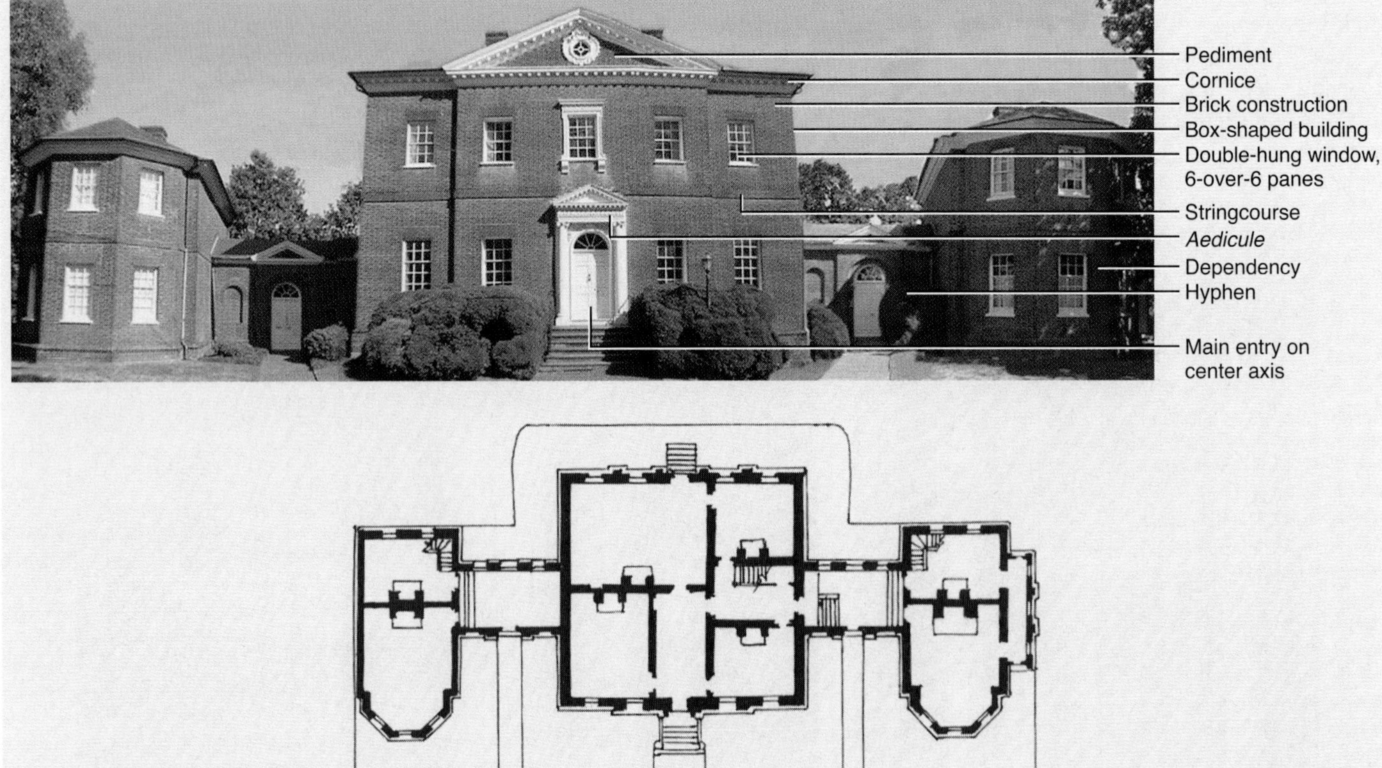

▲ **22-9.** Hammond-Harwood House, floor plan, and dining room (right), 1773–1774; Annapolis, Maryland; William Buckland.

may contribute to the classic image through broken pediments, round arches, and pilasters, and may repeat the ear motif. Wood doors with panels are common and are either painted white or, if walnut or mahogany, left natural.

■ *Ceilings*. Church ceilings are often vaulted. Classical piers or columns carry the vaults, similar to those in Wren's city churches. Ceilings in other structures usually are flat or coved. Churches and public structures are more likely to have chandeliers than are houses, even affluent ones. Often left undecorated, ceilings in houses depict an American preference for simplicity in contrast to English precursors. There are some exceptions.

■ *Textiles*. Furnishing fabrics provide much of the pattern and color, which are important, and usually all textiles in a room match (Fig. 22-12). Although textiles are somewhat more common, they are by no means greatly or universally used because they are expensive and imported. Colonists are forbidden to make their own so domestic production is limited to informal clothing,

▲ 22-10. Wythe House, c. mid-1750s; Williamsburg, Virginia; probably by Richard Taliaferro.

DESIGN SPOTLIGHT

Typical Georgian characteristics are the stringcourses, modillioned cornices, hipped roof, and sash windows. The dining room has classical architectural details and proportions, a prominent mantel and overmantel, and a mixture of Chippendale and Federal-style furnishings. [National Historic Landmark]

▲ 22-9. Continued

DESIGN SPOTLIGHT

Interiors: At Gunston Hall, the hall passage, parlor, and dining room form the public persona of George Mason, author of the United States Bill of Rights. The hall passage, which was a new space when the house was built, extends the entry for interior circulation and reception, separates the public and private spaces in the house, and is an important social and entertainment area. During the summer, it serves as a parlor and at other times as a place for servants to wait. Scholarship indicates that Plate IV in Abraham Swan's *British Architect* may have inspired the classical design treatment. Architecturally, the use of 14 pilasters, a full entablature, symmetry, and a 12′-0″ high ceiling identify it as an important space, one that conveys social refinement and taste. A double arch separates the front hall from the back stair area, and wallpaper covers the walls above the chair rail, a fashionable treatment of the period.

The parlor is architecturally the most important room in the house. The elaborate architectural details reveal both the design sophistication and the woodworking talents of William Buckland as well as the distinct divisions between public and private spaces common in houses of this time. The classical woodwork has touches of Rococo elements. Walls have classic divisions of a cornice, fill, and paneled dado. The focal point of the space is the fireplace and its flanking niches or beaufats. The mantel has shells and curving tendrils, evidence of Rococo, but the broken pediment above is classical. The beaufats, used for display, are flanked by pilasters and broken pediments above the mantel. Along with the ornamentation, other details signal the room's importance, including the red damask wall coverings with gilded borders, the carefully matched blind doweled floors and the black walnut doors with egg-and-dart moldings surrounding the panels. Rituals of entertaining assume greater importance during the 18th century, and parlors and dining rooms become the stage for the master's culture, social standing, and hospitality. [National Historic Landmark]

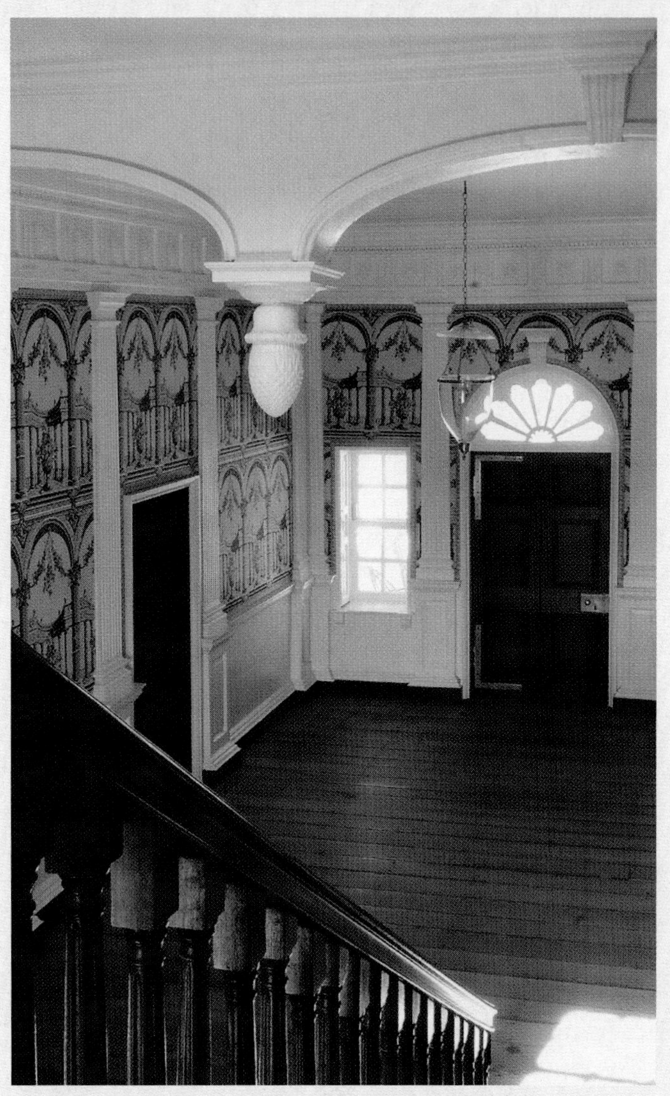

▲ **22-11.** Hall passage and parlor, Gunston Hall, 1759–1787; Fairfax County, Virginia; William Buckland and William Bernard Sears.

children's garments, and bed and table linens. English fabrics predominate, but the British East India Company imports Indian fabrics so there is no tariff. Furnishing fabrics include wools, linens, cottons, damasks, moires, chintzes, and some silks. Dominant textile colors include deep indigo blue, brown, black, purple, red, and pink. Only overprinting blue with yellow produces greens. Most colonists prefer brightly colored and highly finished wools and use silks mostly for formal clothing. Wood-block and copperplate prints include large and smaller repeats of foliage, trees, and/or birds; Rococo flowers, scrolls, and shells; *Chinoiserie* designs; indigo-resist patterns; and furniture checks. Also used are Indian *palampores* (Fig. 22-13), crewel embroidery, and *toiles de Jouy* often with patriotic subjects. Upholstery, bed hangings (Fig. 22-18), window treatments, and wall applications (Fig. 22-11, 22-13) emulate English examples, especially among colonial governors and the affluent. Furniture cases (slipcovers) of light fabrics to protect the upholstery are common.

DESIGN SPOTLIGHT

▲ **22-11.** Continued

▲ **22-12.** Readborne Parlor, c. early to mid-18th century. [Courtesy, Winterthur Museum; paneling and fireplace are originally from the Colonel James Hollyday house, 1733; Centreville, Maryland]

(a)

(b)

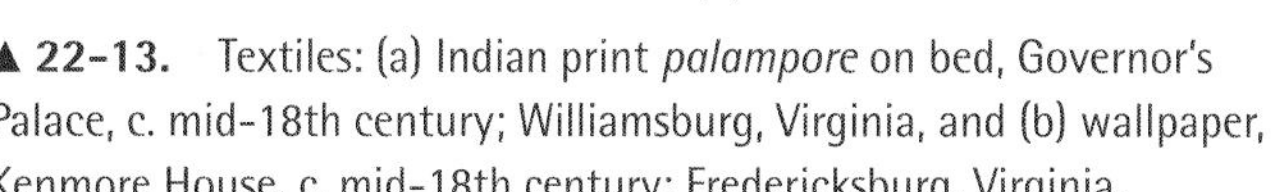

▲ **22-13.** Textiles: (a) Indian print *palampore* on bed, Governor's Palace, c. mid-18th century; Williamsburg, Virginia, and (b) wallpaper, Kenmore House, c. mid-18th century; Fredericksburg, Virginia.

■ *Lighting*. Expensive light fixtures (Fig. 22-6, 22-9, 22-11, 22-12, 22-14) of brass, porcelain, silver, and glass come from England, while cheaper ones of wood and pewter originate locally. Houses are well lit for entertainment, but the amount of light is limited compared to current standards. Strategically placed looking glasses help enhance the light quality. Families often gather around one or two candlesticks, a practice that continues until the introduction of portable lamps in the 19th century. Candlesticks enhance the light quality on game tables; wall sconces light the room perimeter; and chandeliers, which are more common in public buildings, hang from ceiling centers.

(a)

(b)

▲ **22-14.** Lighting: (a) Brass candlesticks and (b) lantern, Kenmore House, c. mid-18th century; United States.

FURNISHINGS AND DECORATIVE ARTS

Furniture design complements the building, imitates English prototypes, and has both high-style and vernacular variations. Forms and ornament are drawn from English Queen Anne, Early Georgian, and Chippendale modes. Queen Anne lasts longer in America because there is no subsequent Early Georgian development, so American styles are defined only as Queen Anne (1720–1790) and Chippendale (1750–1790). (Some American museums refer to Queen Anne as Late Baroque and Chippendale as Rococo, believing these terms to be more descriptive of the character of all decorative arts.)

Characterized by great attention to form, proportion, and detail, furniture reflects the tastes of wealthy, sophisticated clients. American examples usually are less ornate, particularly in the use of marquetry and materials, than the English models. Vernacular furnishings from rural locales mirror this fashion, but are usually made of local woods and display awkward proportions, cruder craftsmanship, less ornamentation, and painted finishes. American Queen Anne examples may combine both English Queen Anne and Chippendale elements such as Queen Anne forms with ornate carving or ball and claw feet. As in England, Chinese, Gothic, and Rococo designs are copied from pattern books such as Thomas Chippendale's *The Gentleman's and Cabinet-Maker's Director*. Embellishment on high-style pieces varies according to the buyer's tastes and budget.

Local cabinetmakers compete with English makers and contribute to a thriving colonial furniture-making industry. Within the vocabulary of English prototypes, regional variations in design, construction, and ornament characterize various cabinetmaking centers, such as those in Boston, Newport, New York City, Philadelphia, and Charleston. Smaller cabinetmaking centers spring up in other areas, such as Long Island and Williamsburg.

Furniture types include arm and side chairs, *easie* or wing chairs, sofas, tables, secretaries, high chests of drawers (highboys), dressing tables (lowboys), tall case (grandfather or hall) clocks, firescreens, and beds. As in English homes, furniture arrangements in American homes support room function, with an emphasis on formality, customs, and harmony. Symmetry and integration with the architecture are important in the placement of tables and/or pier tables and looking glasses. As before, the finest furniture occupies the best drawing room and is arranged around the perimeter of the room when not in use. This space usually holds numerous side chairs and armchairs, few sofas, no wing chairs, and several tea and/or game tables. Wing chairs, regarded as seats for the old or infirm, usually occupy bedchambers.

Public and Private Buildings

■ *Materials*. Walnut and imported mahogany are the principal woods (Fig. 22-9, 22-11, 22-12, 22-15, 22-16, 22-17) for all types of furniture, but regional woods such as maple, cherry, and pine are good substitutes. Often, local woods are stained or painted in imitation of the more valuable walnut or mahogany to enhance their appearance. Japanning is fashionable in the early part of the century.

■ *Seating*. Queen Anne chairs (Fig. 22-6, 22-12) follow English prototypes in a curving silhouette, solid splat, and cabriole legs. They may have more carving, such as shells on the knee or crest of the back, than English examples. Feet may be pad, club, ball and claw, or trifids. Chippendale-style chairs (Fig. 22-9, 22-11) feature lower and broader proportions, rectangular outlines, pierced splats, trapezoid seats, and cabriole legs. Chinese, Gothic, and Rococo ornament is common. Comfort is important, so arms curve and seats contour slightly to fit the body. Combinations of Queen Anne and Chippendale characteristics, such as a Chippendale form with a solid splat, are not uncommon in the

▲ **22-15.** Windsor chairs, c. mid-18th century; United States.

colonies. Philadelphia cabinetmakers create the most high-style chairs featuring rich Rococo carving. Sofas (Fig. 22-12) have curvilinear backs and six cabriole or straight legs. Backs and seats may be lightly tufted to hold stuffing in place. Numerous loose pillows add comfort. Easy chairs (Fig. 22-12) have tall backs, wings, and straight or cabriole legs. The first Windsor chairs (Fig. 22-15) are imported from England in the 1720s; they are made in America by the 1740s. Often found in public buildings or out-of-doors or in passages in houses, Windsors have low or high backs with spindles, saddle seats, and splayed legs.

■ *Tables.* Public rooms have numerous card and tea tables (Fig. 22-6, 22-8, 22-9), which line the walls when not in use. Card tables resemble English ones, and like them, have folding tops. Tea tables have rectangular or round tops, often with piecrust edges, and either legs or pedestals. Sideboard tables with marble tops are used for serving during meals. Dining tables (Fig. 22-9, 22-11) made in several pieces are plain because they are covered with a cloth when in use. Dressing tables frequently match high chests of drawers.

■ *Storage.* Desks with drop lids for writing and bookcases with glass doors above often display pilasters or broken scroll pediments, or they may be painted with Chinese landscapes. Newport is known for its block front furniture (Fig. 22-16), which has three panels that are convex, concave, convex, respectively. Atop each panel is a convex or concave shell carving. During the 1750s and 1760s, Boston cabinetmakers build excellent *bombé* chests of drawers, chest-on-chests, desks, and desks and bookcases. Low and high (Fig. 22-17) chests of drawers provide storage in the best bedchambers and may match beds and other pieces. Philadelphia is known for its matching high chests and dressing tables that are the most ornate in the colonies.

■ *Beds.* Poster beds (Fig. 22-18) with elaborate bed hangings define the best bedchamber. Beds in lesser rooms may be draped although some are not. Other types of beds include those with low posts, field beds with arched canopies, and press beds that fold for storage. Bedchambers often hold several beds and pallets may cover floors at night to accommodate family members, guests, and servants. Tester cornices are commonly covered with fabric to match hangings. In the South, mosquito netting surrounds the bed for protection from insects.

▲ **22-16.** Chest of drawers, c. mid-18th century; Newport, Rhode Island; John Townsend and John Goddard. [Courtesy of the Diplomatic Reception Rooms, U.S. Department of State]

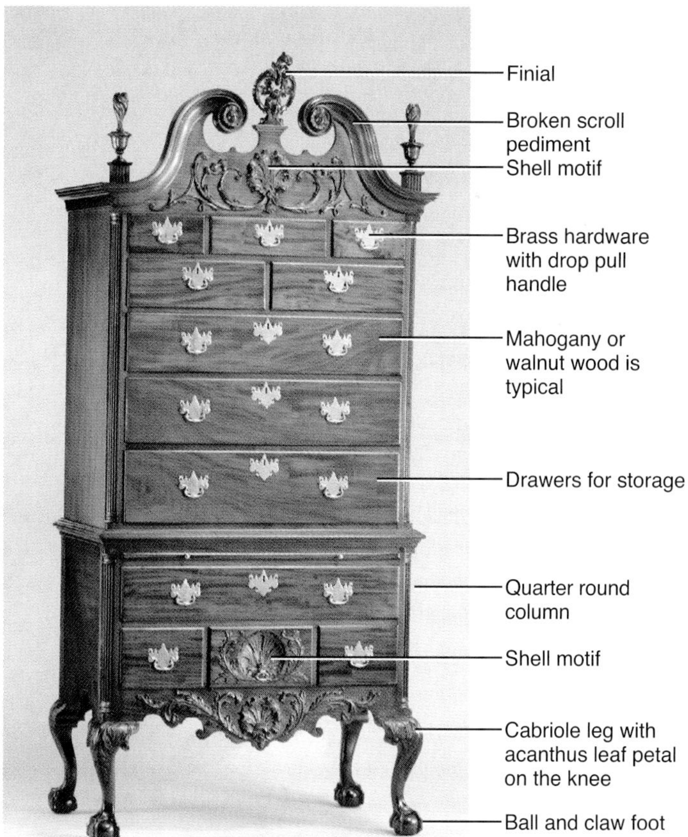

▲ **22-17.** High chest of drawers (highboy), c. mid-18th century; United States. [Courtesy of the Diplomatic Reception Rooms, U.S. Department of State]

DESIGN SPOTLIGHT

Furniture: This bed, which includes thin posts, has crewelwork bed hangings, valance, curtains, head cloth, tester cloth, base, and counterpane. Originally the bed would have had curtains at the foot, but they now form the curtain panels. Textiles *"en suite"* such as these provide essential design and color in rooms. Embroidery may be done by the ladies of the house or imported from London where it is the work of professionals. The fabric may be natural linen or cotton with embroidery imitating Indian *palampores* in colors of rust, olive, gold, indigo blue, brown, and black.

▲ **22-18.** Bed with embroidered hangings, c. early 18th century; Cecil County, Maryland. [Courtesy, Winterthur Museum]

■ *Decorative Arts*. Both imported and domestic ceramics appear in American interiors, particularly in niches and on mantels or tables. English wares dominate the market. Silver is both imported and made in the colonies and is used mainly in the homes of the wealthy. Several American silversmiths and other craftspeople become very well known, particularly Paul Revere. Items made in silver include flatware, candleholders, tea- and coffeepots, tea caddies, porringers, and serving pieces. Most Americans, however, eat and drink from pewter or wood vessels such as plates, cups, chargers, tankards, and spoons, which are relatively cheap and recyclable.

■ *Later Interpretations*. Colonial Revival of the late 19th and 20th centuries features various interpretations of 18th-century furniture designs that may or may not be true to the original model. Reproductions and adaptations of Georgian furniture and accessories remain fashionable today. In the Post Modern style, designers adapt period designs to suit modern tastes using modern materials such as plastic laminate (Fig. 22-19).

▲ **22-19.** Later Interpretation: Chippendale-style chair, 1984; Robert Venturi, manufactured by Knoll International. Post Modern.

H. EARLY NEOCLASSICAL

1740s–1790s

The Neoclassical Movement, beginning in Rome and France in the 1740s, initiates a renewed interest in classical antiquity that encompasses Europe, Russia, England, and the United States. An outgrowth of scholarship and archaeology and a reaction to the Rococo, this eclectic style seeks to imitate or evoke images of ancient Greece and Rome in art, architecture, interiors, furniture, decorative arts, landscapes, literature, dress, and behavior. Drawing on models from Egypt, Greece, Rome, and the Etruscans, the Early Neoclassical style can be plain, severe, and monumental or express the lightness, grace, and refinement of Rococo with classical forms and motifs.

Although drawing on earlier forms of classicism, the Neoclassical Movement regards antiquity differently from these previous movements. Earlier designers saw themselves as inheriting antiquity and continuing its traditions. They tried to design in the manner of the ancients. In contrast, Neoclassical designers divide antiquity into different periods and styles with differing visual characteristics. They create designs by removing individual traits from their historical context and using them to solve present design problems.

The main impetus for the Neoclassical movement are the discovery and excavations at Herculaneum (begun in 1738) and Pompeii (begun in 1748), two Greco-Roman towns near Naples, Italy, that were buried by an eruption of Mount Vesuvius in 79 B.C.E. This, the first great archaeological event of modern times, captures the imaginations of Europeans. Archaeology and the discoveries become fashionable topics for discussion and emulation. The excavations inspire numerous architects, artists, and designers. The discoveries also fill a gap in classical knowledge—that of domestic interiors. Previously there were few such examples to study so designers created what they believed were classical spaces.

Systematic scientific investigations by scholars, architects, and artists form a strong theoretical base for Neoclassicism. After studying ancient structures, many publish their analyses, theories, and drawings in architectural and art historical treatises. Designers now can more fully understand and choose from a broad spectrum of classical models. An important outgrowth of these investigations is the knowledge that Grecian art inspired the Romans. Admiration for Greece leads to the preference for Grecian models in the early 19th century.

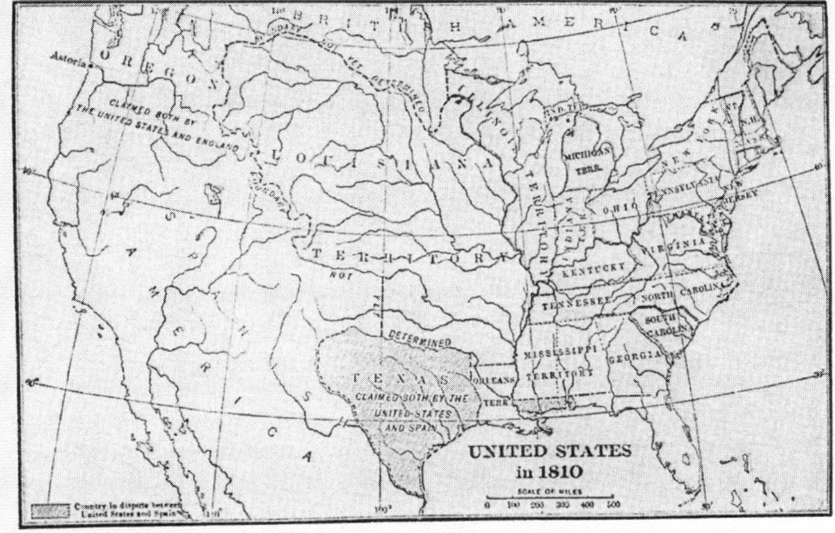

CHAPTER 23

Louis XVI and French Provincial

1774–1789

> *Amorous alcoves lost their painted Loves and took on gray and white decorations. The casinos of little* comediennes *did not glitter any more. English sentiment began to bedim Gallic eyes, and so what we know as the Louis XVI style was born.*
>
> —Elsie de Wolfe, *The House in Good Taste*, 1914

Rejecting the Rococo and responding to the renewed interest in antiquity, Louis XVI style is a return to classicism. In architecture, images can be severe and monumental or graceful and elegant. Interiors, furniture, and decorative arts maintain the scale, elegance, and charm of Rococo, but lines straighten, free-form curves become geometric, and ornament again derives from antiquity.

HISTORICAL AND SOCIAL

When Louis XVI takes the throne in 1774, he inherits an extremely troubled nation burdened by debts, inflation, and growing discontent among the people. The huge governmental bureaucracy, wars, and supporting the monarchy require vast sums of money, and because the nobles and the church are not taxed, the burden falls on the *bourgeoisie* (middle class) and peasants. As the financial crisis worsens, the government bureaucracy works less and less effectively. When the population's needs exceed agricultural output, food shortages and famines fuel greater discontent. Louis XVI attempts reforms with the help of his ministers, but the nobility blocks most of their efforts. Additionally, writers and philosophers influenced by the Enlightenment advance the idea that all people possess the right to property, life, and freedom, which governments should exist to maintain. These ideas appeal to the *bourgeoisie* and eventually filter down to the lower classes. Like the nobility, the middle and lower classes want a voice in government.

Although kind and genuinely concerned about his people, Louis is weak and ineffective, and often vacillates in making decisions. He prefers to spend time at his hobbies instead of governing. The French particularly dislike and distrust his wife, Marie Antoinette, whom they believe is more devoted to Austria, her homeland, than to France. Her extravagances and the poor reputations of her friends increase their suspicions and add to their antagonism.

In 1789, a land tax intended to avoid bankruptcy of the government brings immense opposition and forces Louis to call a meeting of the Estates General. For the first time in nearly two centuries, this representative body composed of the nobility, clergy, and commoners meets at Versailles. The Estates General assumes governing powers, a first step toward revolution. Commoners separate from the group and, declaring themselves a national assembly, vow to write a new constitution. Royal troops attempt to disperse the assembly, while an indecisive Louis XVI delays action. On July 14, 1789, the Parisians take the *Bastille*, a royal fortress, forcing Louis to give in to their demands. The king and his family soon are imprisoned at the *Tuileries* in Paris. In 1791, a new constitution forms a parliamentary government and limits the powers of the monarchy. Although Louis swears obedience to it, he continues to work against the revolution. To help restore the king's power, Austria and Prussia declare war on France. Nevertheless, on August 10, 1792, the monarchy is overthrown. In September, a National Convention declares France a republic. The king is convicted as a traitor and is executed in early 1793. The violent Reign of Terror ensues, and the queen, numerous aristocrats, priests, and even commoners are put to death.

CONCEPTS

As early as 1730, critics attack the artificiality and lack of classical order in Rococo as symptomatic of a depraved modern society. They call for a new classicism, one that is rational, truthful, and natural or derived from nature based upon ideas of the Enlightenment and contemporary architecture in Italy. They hope that association with ideal architecture of Antiquity will engender exemplary French citizens. Additionally, the unsettled times foster a desire for stability that manifests in renewed order, repose, and other attributes of classicism. By far, the greatest stimulus and influence are the archaeological excavations at Pompeii and Herculaneum. These give renewed interest in the classical past and encourage more study of ancient buildings by architects and others who publish their ideas, which gives Neoclassicism a sound theoretical base.

CHARACTERISTICS AND MOTIFS

General charcteristics include light scale, rational planning, mathematical proportions, and an emphasis on straight lines and/or geometric forms. Classical forms and details dominate architecture, interiors, and furniture. Designers employ classical attributes, such as symmetry and repose, as well as classical forms and motifs. The French call the style *goût grec* or *goût arabesque*.

■ *Motifs*. Motifs (Fig. 23-1, 23-2, 23-4, 23-5, 23-14) come from Greek, Roman, Etruscan, and Egyptian sources. Common are garlands, swags, frets, *guilloches*, palmettes, classical figures, sphinxes, masks, flowers, bouquets, baskets of flowers, shepherds, shepherdesses, farm tools, and balloons after the first successful balloon flight in 1783. Although classical motifs dominate, some Rococo themes continue, such as flowers, shepherds, shepherdesses, bows, *Chinoiserie*, and *singerie* (Fig. 23-8).

ARCHITECTURE

France never completely rejects classical influence in architecture despite the dominance of the Rococo style in the first half of the 18th century. The Royal Academy of Architecture continues to emphasize classicism. French designers and architects, visiting the French Academy in Rome, observe the work of their colleagues, who adopt a severe, structurally honest style like the Italians. Architects collect the engravings of Piranesi, read the newest architectural theories, and visit ancient ruins. French Neoclassicism, therefore, draws on French 17th-century (Baroque) and Italian 16th-century classical traditions (Renaissance), the rationalist thought of the Enlightenment, and archaeology.

Architecture develops from the rationalist views of its designers, who strive for geometric volumes, structural honesty, and simplicity. Structures are blocklike with plain façades and minimal ornamentation. The scale of buildings varies from monumental to elegant and refined. Proportions often derive from antique sources. Designers strive for horizontality, clarity, stability, and repose, those classical attributes that give feelings of dignity and grandeur. Emphasis on scale and specific design details to proclaim status and rank lessens. Although designs often are assemblages of ancient motifs, the result is clearly modern.

Neoclassical is more archaeologically correct than previous classical developments. Through their own or others' investigations and the numerous pattern books and treatises, architects are well acquainted with antique design language, methods, and concepts. Using antique models that supply form and details, designers often exactly reproduce individual parts, such as columns, but rarely copy entire buildings. Late in the century, some begin designing visionary structures with fanciful details, an influence of the English Picturesque. Following the French and American

▲ **23-1.** Motifs: Vase in *porcelaine dure de Sèvres*; decorated by Boizot and Thomire, and designs for marquetry panel vignettes, c. late 18th century; by Pierre-Gabriel Berthault.

Revolutions and new, more democratic forms of government, Neoclassicism becomes the preferred style for government buildings, which continues through much of the 20th and into the 21st centuries.

Older building types, such as churches (Fig. 23-2), palaces (Fig. 23-3), and *hôtels* continue. New types include markets, hospitals, theaters, and auditoriums.

Public and Private Buildings

■ *Site Orientation*. Most structures face streets or squares. Some residences are set in gardens that are carefully planned to look unplanned. They often feature classical and/or Gothic "ruins" in the English manner as an influence of the Romantic Movement.

■ *Floor Plans*. Architects occasionally attempt to adapt antique plans to modern needs while striving to apply logic and reason to the planning of space. Distribution of rooms in residences remains generally the same as previously, but designers pay more attention to function. Plans are generally rectangular or centralized.

■ *Materials*. Brick, stone, and marble are the chief building materials (Fig. 23-2, 23-3). Some buildings have cast-iron details. Designers use both trabeated and arcuated construction. A few reach back to Gothic construction techniques, which they consider honest.

■ *Façades*. Exteriors (Fig. 23-2, 23-3) are often composed of large geometric blocks and plain walls. Parts are clearly articulated, but ornamentation is minimal. Low-relief rustication highlights lower stories and some entrances. Upper walls are smooth and flat to emphasize volume. Pediments, columns, and porticoes accentuate entrances and ends. Columns are structural not decorative, while pilasters and engaged columns articulate façades and form bays. Civic façades are usually tripartite. Stringcourses rarely delineate stories, but most structures have a prominent cornice between wall and roof.

■ *Windows and Doors*. Windows (Fig. 23-3) are large and rectangular with plain and relatively flat surrounds. Some have straight lintels or triangular pediments above them. Designers emphasize doorways through central placement and with columns, pilasters, pediments, and rustication.

■ *Roofs*. Most roofs are flat with balustrades (Fig. 23-3).

INTERIORS

As in architecture, Louis XVI interiors return to classicism in attributes and decoration instead of changes in layout and modes of living. Aristocratic society has not changed; its members still seek luxury, comfort, and gaiety. However, some occasionally advocate the (perceived) simplicity of the ancient world as long as it does not intrude on their quest for pleasure. Interiors retain the human scale, light proportions, and charm of the Rococo. Designers now emphasize classical motifs, symmetry, straight lines, and geometric curves. As before, unity is important.

Because there were few known examples of Greek and Roman domestic architecture, previous classical interiors and furniture had been speculative at best. By this period, however, designers are able to visit archaeological discoveries to see homes in which the ancients lived. A few "Etruscan" rooms (*goût étrusque*) with decoration derived from Pompeiian examples appear in the 1760s. Late in the period, designers and cabinetmakers begin to more closely copy ancient decoration and furniture.

▲ **23-2.** *S. Geneviève (Panthéon)*, and central crossing with dome, 1757–1790; Paris, France; Jacques-Germain Soufflot.

Public and Private Buildings

■ *Floor Plans*. The trend toward smaller, more intimate spaces in residences continues. The *salon* and *salle à manger* (dining room) become separate spaces. Dining rooms and *boudoirs* are more common.

■ *Color*. Colors become lighter and cooler, dominated by pale green, white, gray blue, and pearl gray. Black and red color schemes dominate Etruscan-style rooms.

■ *Floors*. Parquet remains in vogue for most residential spaces (Fig. 23-4, 23-5, 23-6). Black and white marble also is fashionable, especially in churches and for residential vestibules, stair halls, and *salons*. The factories of Savonnerie, Aubusson, and Beauvais produce rugs in Neoclassical patterns (Fig. 23-4, 23-6). Matting usually replaces rugs in summer.

■ *Walls*. In public buildings, architectural details that contrast slightly with the walls are common. Color comes from building materials or paint (Fig. 23-2).

DESIGN SPOTLIGHT

Architecture, Louis XVI: Originally built for Louis XV as a place of escape for him and his mistress, the elegant *Petit Trianon* on the grounds of Versailles was finished after her death. Designed by architect Ange-Jacques Gabriel, the symmetrically balanced small building epitomizes architectural concepts of French Neoclassicism, including symmetry, straight lines, and geometric forms. The exterior is austere, restrained in articulation, and intimate in scale. All four façades are different but unified by common elements such as the windows and classical balustrade that hides the low-pitched roof. The southwest façade has four projecting Corinthian columns in the center with lintels above them. The large French doors allow access to the terrace and garden beyond. The other façades have Corinthian pilasters, Ionic columns, or no columns at all.

In keeping with a desire for simplicity thought inherent in the lives of people of antiquity, Marie Antoinette later has the surrounding gardens of the *Petit Trianon* transformed to an informal natural garden of winding paths and curving water features to enhance the visual setting. She also commissions Richard Mique to build the nearby *Le Hameau* (the Queen's hamlet), a rustic farm complex of farmhouse, dairy, and mill. Standing on the far side of a landscaped pond, *Le Hameau* is intended to evoke the atmosphere of a peasant village in Normandy. Marie Antoinette reigned supreme in this retreat environment, in which the *Petit Trianon*, a beautifully proportioned classical building, is in close proximity to rustic farm buildings—both clear statements of the queen's desire for simplicity and naturalness. [World Heritage Site]

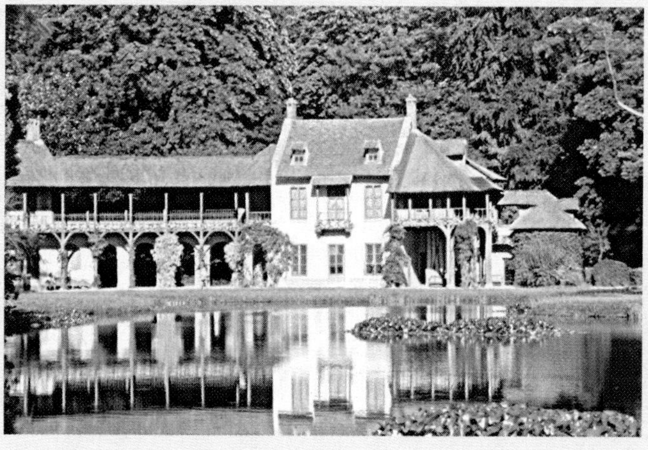

▲ **23-3.** *Petit Trianon*, 1761–1764, and *Le Hameau*, c. 1774–1783; Versailles, France; Petit Trianon by Ange-Jacques Gabriel, and Le Hameau by Richard Mique.

In dwellings, symmetry continues to define wall paneling (Fig. 23-4, 23-5, 23-6) even to the point of a false door to balance a real one as in the previous period. As before, the common form is a large panel flanked by two smaller panels; opposite walls are similarly treated; and paneling and architectural details continue to form a continuous, relatively flat surface with little variation in projection. A low dado with a field above capped by a cornice emulates the orders. Panel moldings, smaller than previously, are gilded or painted in a color contrasting with the center. Decorative painting, wallpaper, or fabric adorns panel centers (Fig. 23-5). Similar to Pompeiian and Italian Renaissance walls, French designs frequently display arabesques, grotesques, and classical figures (Fig. 23-4). Wall paintings usually have large areas of flat color articulated with borders and unobtrusive repeating patterns and/or figures inside them. *Grisaille*, which imitates relief sculpture in monochromatic grays, is especially fashionable.

Carved stucco (Fig. 23-5) becomes an alternative to wood paneling in the 1750s, and it often imitates marble or stone or forms panels. Wallpaper increases in use. Common patterns include architectural papers, colorful arabesques in the Pompeiian manner, replications of textiles, and Chinese patterns. Matching or contrasting borders outline cornices and other architectural details. Framed tapestries feature classical themes. Mirrors with classical shapes and decoration adorn fireplaces, furniture, walls, and/or piers between windows.

Protruding less into the room than before, chimneypieces (Fig. 23-5, 23-6) retain the vertically integrated mantel and overmantel of earlier. Mantels again become rectangular with a straight shelf usually supported by columns or brackets. Classical motifs, such as swags, urns, or masks, are carved on supports and beneath the shelf. Although some mantels have contrasting colors of marble, most are plain white.

■ *Windows and Doors*. French doors and windows have complete entablatures above them. Windows in important rooms (Fig. 23-4) have curtains, with festoons being the most common form. Draperies and curtains have elaborate trims and usually match upholstery fabrics.

As important components of circulation paths, doorways in important spaces in public buildings are surrounded by elaborate classical moldings. Often, their heights are greater than those in residences. Door panels (Fig. 23-5, 23-6) in palaces and *hôtels* re-

▲ **23-4.** *Cabinet doré*, Royal Apartments, *Palais de Versailles*, c. 1770s–1780s; Versailles, France; Richard Mique.

semble wall paneling. They may be painted or stained. Panel moldings may be gilded, and panel centers may have painted arabesque decorations. As in the Rococo period, paintings over doors are still in vogue, but subjects are classical themes or landscapes.

■ *Ceilings*. Public spaces (Fig. 23-2) often have vaulted and coffered ceilings enhanced with classical moldings. Domes may highlight crossings in churches or define an important area in other buildings. Residential ceilings (Fig. 23-4, 23-5, 23-6) vary from plain to ornate. Most are flat and simply painted. Ceilings in important rooms may have relatively flat combinations of geometric shapes symmetrically arranged and accented with classical motifs and flowers. Other spaces feature decorative borders with elaborate corner motifs.

■ *Textiles*. Textiles are basically the same types as in the Louis XV period, and their uses do not change (Fig. 23-7). But motifs now are classical—urns, acanthus leaves, and classically draped figures. Colors are lighter and often duller than before, such as gray or lilac, with white and gold becoming the most fashionable (Fig. 23-4, 23-5, 23-6). Cottons and linens become more common. Tapestries adorn sets of furniture, and stripes are more fashionable than before (Fig. 23-10, 23-11, 23-12). Bed hangings remain opulent and are often festoons with undercurtains (Fig. 23-15). All textiles in a room often match (Fig. 23-15).

DESIGN SPOTLIGHT

Interiors, Louis XVI: The *boudoir* of Marie Antoinette, a small room located between the bedchambers of the king and queen epitomizes the Neoclassical interior style in France. The room retains the charm and scale of the previous Rococo style but lines become straight and classical motifs replace naturalistic ones. Gold and silver paneling features symmetrical paintings of classical motifs in the Pompeiian manner. The light scale paintings in gold, pinks, and blues are composed of sphinxes, vases from which naturalistic flowers arise, classically draped figures, swags, and cameos. Bouquets of flowers decorate the dado panels. Classical moldings surround the panels and the doorway. Sculpture replaces paintings over doors in this period and is often elaborate, as here in the stucco Muses by Philippe Laurent Roland. Symmetrical mirrors with arched tops enhance the light and visually increase the size of the space. In the center of the floor is the Queen's monogram, and the ceiling is adorned with a painting of Aurora, goddess of the dawn. The furniture is by Jean-Henri Riesener, one of the Queen's favorite *ébénistes*, and it continues the gold and silver classical theme.

▲ **23-5.** *Boudoir* of Marie Antoinette, Royal Apartments, *Palais de Fontainebleau*, c. 1787; Fontainebleau, France; architecture by Pierre Rousseau.

▲ **23-6.** The *Tessé* Room, 1768–1772; Paris; France. [Gift of Mrs. Herbert N. Straus, 1942 (42.203.1). The Metropolitan Museum of Art, New York, NY, U.S.A. Image © The Metropolitan Museum of Art/Art Resource, NY]

■ *Lighting*. As before, the large windows provide bright light to rooms during the day, but the rooms are dark at night by today's standards. The use of oil lamps increases during the period, but they do not replace candles as the main artificial light source. The designs of ceiling lanterns, *lustres à cristeaux*, *flambeaux*, *candelabra*, *appliques*, and *guéridons* reflect the new taste by displaying classical elements, such as columns, urns, and lyres (Fig. 23-4, 23-5, 23-6, 23-8). *Girandoles* often feature classical figures. Ceiling fixtures hang from silk cords with tassels.

■ *Later Interpretations*. In the late 19th century, designers begin to revive Louis XVI interiors and furniture. American interior decorator Elsie de Wolfe helps reestablish a taste for French designs, starting with the renovation of her own home (Fig. 23-9). Louis XVI designs are still widely imitated today, but less so than Rococo designs.

FURNISHINGS AND DECORATIVE ARTS

Louis XVI furniture maintains Rococo's light proportions, slender forms, human scale, and emphasis on comfort as well as some motifs, such as flowers, symbols of love, hunting, and musical instruments. Straight lines, geometric curves, and classical motifs distinguish Louis XVI furniture from Rococo. Pieces are simple rectangles with outlines softened by ornament. Columns, moldings, and other details carefully articulate parts in the classical manner. Circles, ovals, and ellipses replace Rococo's asymmetrical, complex curves. Legs become straight, tapered, and/or fluted. The quiver leg, shaped like a quiver of arrows, is new. Spirals, which are extremely difficult to carve, are reserved for the legs on the finest pieces. A characteristic feature is a re-entrant corner formed by part of a square or circle with a rosette in the center; it is usually found on *commodes* and on chair frames and legs. Oval backs are new. Late in the period, pieces often have large areas of plain mahogany, a reflection of a new emphasis on simplicity. As the height of French cabinetmaking, the style's construction, excellent proportions, and harmonious ornament are rarely surpassed. Although named for him, the style appears before Louis XVI takes the throne and continues after his death. Classical influence first appears as ornamentation between 1760 and 1770, a transitional period. By 1775, the style has fully taken hold.

All types of Louis XV furniture continue. Some new table forms based on Pompeiian designs appear, especially late in the period. Dining tables are more common. The Baroque and Rococo practice of designing furniture to suit the design and colors

▲ **23-7.** Textile: Brocade; France.

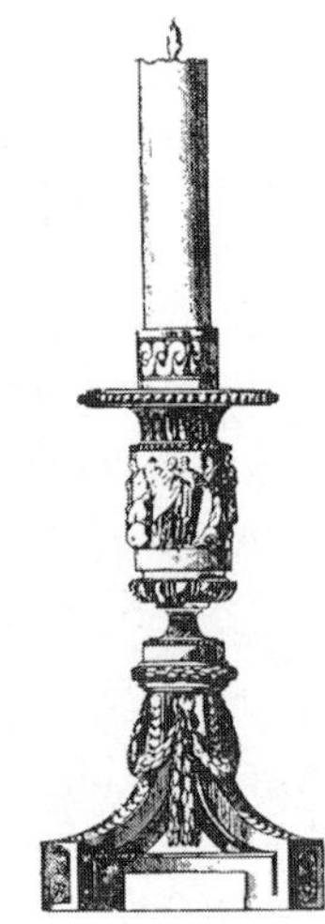

▲ **23-8.** Lighting: *Flambeau, candelabra*, and *appliqué*, France.

▲ 23-9. Later Interpretation: Dining room, Irving House (home of Elsie de Wolfe), c. 1898–1909; New York City; Elsie de Wolfe. Neoclassical Revival.

of the room persists. Form and proportions often determine the placement of a piece. Seating, beds, or storage pieces often sit in specially designed niches. Furniture is still arranged around the perimeter of the room when not in use.

Private Buildings

■ *Materials*. Mahogany and ebony are the most common furniture woods. Wood frames of seating may be left natural, partially or entirely painted, or gilded. Especially fashionable is two-tone gilding composed of shiny and flat areas. Marquetry of flowers, landscapes, and/or classical scenes and geometric marquetry in lozenges and trellis patterns are universal. Boullework is revived. Both Oriental and French lacquerwork remain in vogue but Japanese lacquer in gold and black is preferred. Dominant colors for French lacquer are red, bright blue, and green. Gilt bronze mounts of classical motifs are unsurpassed in their excellence. Also common are metal inlays, toe caps, and casters. Porcelain plaques often decorate pieces, particularly writing furniture for women. Louis XVI's love of mechanical devices assures their incorporation into many pieces of furniture. At the end of the period, plain and undecorated mahogany surfaces and metal furniture, especially for tables, become fashionable.

DESIGN SPOTLIGHT

Furniture, Louis XVI: Similar in scale and configuration to Louis XV versions, *fauteuils* appear formally or informally grouped within interiors. Retaining the wood frames, composed of straight or geometric lines, joints are now articulated in the classical manner. Backs may be rectangular and oval. Legs are straight, tapered, and/or fluted; some are spirals. Classical repeating moldings, columns, gilding, and/or painting frequently accent the frame. Arms still have *manchettes*, which now rest directly over the front legs or set back on curving supports. Upholstery may be of silk, cotton, linen, or tapestry. Patterns and motifs include swags, vases, flowers, rinceaus, urns, acanthus leaves, classical figures, and stripes; some examples feature farm motifs such as straw hats, shovels, and corn. Popular colors include gray, green, yellow, and pink on cream or white backgrounds.

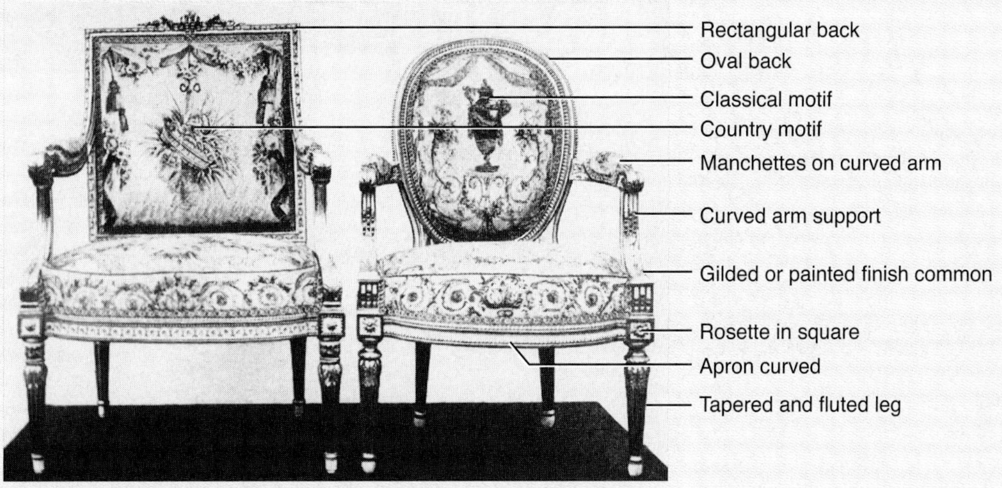

▲ 23-10. *Fauteuils* showing various tapestry designs; c. late 18th century; France.

▲ **23-11.** *Bergère*, from the *Salon de Jeux* of Louis XVI, *Château de Compiegne*, 1790; France; Jean-Baptiste Sene.

■ *Seating*. All Louis XV types of *chaises*, *fauteuils*, *bergères*, and *canapés* remain in use, but reflect Neoclassical design principles (Fig. 23-4, 23-5, 23-6, 23-10, 23-11, 23-12). Pieces retain the wooden frames around backs and seats of the Rococo style, but now have straight lines that are carved with classical running patterns, such as the bead. Continuity of parts disappears in response to classicism's demand that points of junction be delineated. Chair backs may be rectangular or oval; some have balloon shapes or splats following the first balloon flight in 1783. Back uprights may be classical columns. Arms are directly over front legs and have *manchettes*, and supports are often urn shaped. About 1785, the saber leg replaces straight back legs, and arms begin to curve back from the front of the seat.

■ *Tables*. Tables (Fig. 23-4, 23-6, 23-13), small and large, remain as numerous as before. A new form based on a Pompeiian tripod table is introduced. Dining tables, made in parts, usually divide in the center. Each portion has drop leaves. Some have casters and/or extra leaves. *Consoles* with Neoclassical designs are in vogue for drawing rooms and *salons*.

■ *Storage*. *Commodes* (Fig. 23-4, 23-14) remain fashionable, and their shapes and decoration reflect the new style as do other case pieces. Rectangles or semicircles (*demi-lune*) replace the undulating surfaces of Rococo pieces. The straight legs are tapered and fluted or vase-shaped. Small classical moldings, key patterns, Vitruvian scrolls, palmettes, *guilloches*, and garlands highlight façades. Marquetry of flowers, trophies, landscapes, architecture, or classical figures embellishes doors or drawers. Tops are of marble. Later pieces have columns or caryatids on corners. The *secrétaire à abattant* (Fig. 23-6) becomes more architectural with columns, pilasters, and pediments. Some have matching bookcases.

■ *Beds*. All types of Louis XV *lits* continue in use (Fig. 23-15). As before, they have canopies and hangings that match other fabrics in the room. Beds in alcoves are common.

▲ **23-12.** *Canapé* with tapestry designs; France.

▲ **23-13.** Table in bronze given by Marie Antoinette to Madame de Polignac.

▲ **23-14.** *Commode* with marquetry and *ormolu*, 1778; France; Jean Henri Riesener.

▲ **23-15.** Bed, Louis XVI bedchamber, *Petit Trianon* (after restoration in 1985); France.

■ *Decorative Arts*. Accessories and decorative arts reflect the classical in form and designs, particularly vases and clocks (Fig. 23-4, 23-6). Figures in classical dress are common motifs. Design and workmanship are unsurpassed. Although shapes for porcelains become severe and lines simple, decoration is sumptuous with classical landscapes and/or figures and heavy gilding. Straight sides and rectangular handles distinguish Neoclassical porcelains. Pieces are heavier and more solemn in feeling than Rococo pieces.

FRENCH PROVINCIAL

Provincial, *rustique*, or *régional* refers to houses, interiors, and furniture of the peasants and *bourgeoisie* in the rural areas of France from the reign of Louis XIII through the French Empire. Although inspired and influenced by court or high styles, provincial is simpler and less refined in design, construction, and decoration. Unlike high styles, provincial examples are less dependent upon display and rank, maintain traditional elements, and exhibit regional varieties based on climate, geography, economy, and available materials. Provincial types also are common in France's New World colonies.

HISTORICAL AND SOCIAL

By the beginning of the 17th century, relative peace and prosperity in France spread to the peasants and the *bourgeoisie*. Increased wealth fosters the adoption of more and fashionable furniture by the middle and lower classes. Traditional manners of living and furnishing remain strong. Although many continue to live simply with only a few possessions, interest in fashionable court styles of furnishing increases. Regional cabinetmakers look to Paris for inspiration; those closer to Paris show more high-style influence, and those farther away demonstrate less. Some areas, such as Alsace, exhibit influences from bordering countries.

MOTIFS

■ *Motifs*. Typical motifs borrow and adapt from high styles and include lozenges, stars, circles, fruit, flowers, foliage, shells, C and S scrolls, columns, colonnettes, fluting, urns, and lyres (Fig. 23-17, 23-20).

ARCHITECTURE

Homes of the *bourgeoisie* and peasants range from medium-sized mansions to simple, plain one-room cottages. Function and tradition are more important than style or design principles such as symmetry. Dwellings are built of local stone, brick, or wood and plaster. Roofs may be of thatch, tile, or shingles. Grander homes may be more likely to follow prevailing architectural styles and planning than peasant dwellings.

INTERIORS

Wealthier *bourgeoisie* can more readily follow prevailing decorating trends. Nevertheless, most interiors are simply treated (Fig. 23-16, 23-17, 23-21). Floors may be dirt, stone, brick, or wood. Common treatments include paneling on at least one wall, textile hangings, wallpaper, and painted decorations (Fig. 23-17). Rugs and curtains are rare.

▲ 23-16. *Salle de Ferme*; d'Ille-et-Vilaine; France.

▲ 23-17. Bedroom of Eléanore de Warns, Le Charmettes, Savoie; furniture from Louis XIII, Louis XV, and Louis XVI periods and early 19th century; France.

■ *Textiles*. Textiles range from silks, cottons, woolens, linens, and homespun. In the second half of the 18th century, rooms become more colorful with toiles and painted or printed chintzes (Fig. 23-16, 23-17). The housewife sometimes embroiders seat covers. Few pieces are completely upholstered. Window curtains are rare.

DESIGN SPOTLIGHT

Furniture, French Provincial: These *chaises*, part of a set of ten, show common characteristics of *régional* furniture, including rush seats, curved back slats, and quadrangular legs with turned stretchers. Simple and uncomplicated outlines reveal a greater concern for economy and practicality than for fashion. Scale relates to human proportions and suits smaller houses. Although the majority of *régional* furniture follows the 18th century Rococo style in curvilinear forms and naturalistic ornament, some adopt all or portions of Neoclassism. These chairs, for example, have the straight legs of Neoclassical and the curving slats of Rococo. Variations of this form may be found in Canada and the United States with the immigration of French settlers from the provinces.

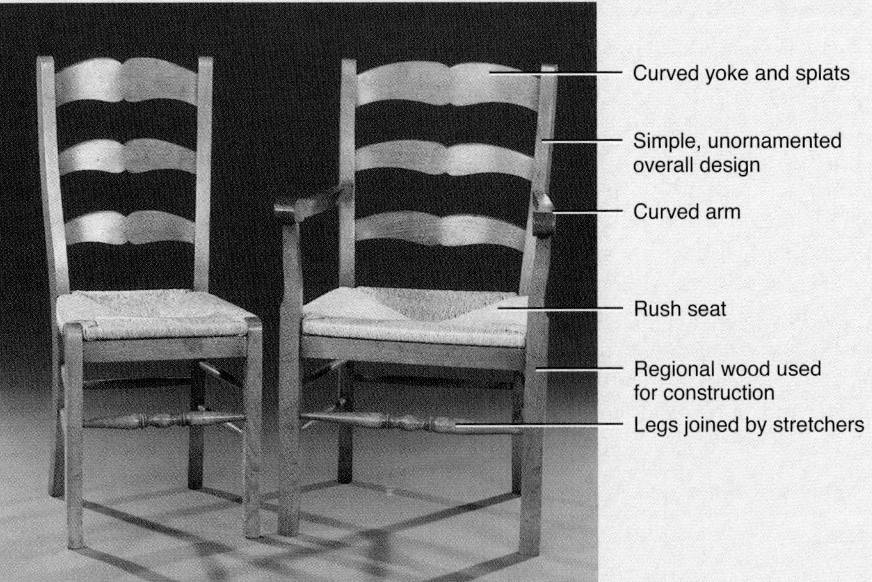

▲ 23-18. Louis XVI-style *chaise à capucines*.

FURNITURE

Provincial furniture adapts the forms, contours, and some of the ornamentation of court styles to regional needs and preferences. Local cabinetmakers are able to follow high styles, particularly in the 18th century, with help from numerous pattern books. However, clients often regard comfort, convenience, and economy as more important than fashion. Scale relates to human proportions and suits smaller rooms in smaller houses. Ornamentation is less profuse and often naive. Carving is the main form of decoration. Construction, usually simple, varies with the skill of the cabinetmaker and the region. Areas closer to style centers often see more finely constructed and ornamented examples.

Simpler lifestyles in the provinces require less furniture and fewer types of furnishings. Early pieces include chairs, beds, chests, and tables. During the 18th century, tall case clocks, writing furniture, *canapés*, and wall shelves become more universal. More practical and utilitarian, provincial furniture rarely demonstrates rank or precedence. However, people do highly prize certain pieces, such as the *armoire* (Fig. 23-20), and proudly display them in public rooms of their homes.

Regional character is stronger in provincial furniture than in high style. Although furniture types are similar throughout France because they support the similar lifestyles of provincial peoples, some regions prefer and/or more highly develop certain types. Some pieces are unique to a particular region. An example is the *panetière* (Fig. 23-21) of Provence and Normandy. Styles often last longer in the provinces and/or may mix characteristics of several high styles.

Louis XIII (reigned 1610–1643) is first of the court styles to exhibit regional or provincial character in the early 1700s; it lasts about a century in most areas. People in the Gascogne region prefer its spiral turning and geometric ornamentation much longer. Although the Louis XIV style (reigned 1643–1715) generally is too grand and opulent for provincial tastes, its influence appears most often in the panels of *armoires* and other case pieces. In contrast, much *régional* furniture follows the 18th-century Rococo style in curvilinear form and ornamentation. Rococo or the Louis XV style easily adapts to the needs of all. Its scale, charm, grace, and comfort have universal appeal, so the style dominates provincial furnishings even throughout the periods of Louis XVI, Directoire, and French Empire. Louis XVI style appears most often in classical ornamentation and mixes in shape and ornament with Rococo. Directoire and Empire have little effect in the provinces.

▲ **23-20.** Louis XVI *armoire*, with Rococo influences, Caen Region; France.

▲ **23-19.** Louis XV *commode*, c. 1780; France.

■ *Materials*. Most pieces are of solid wood. Wood varies by region, but oak and fruitwoods are common. Cherry defines better pieces. Imported mahogany is limited to very fine pieces for the *bourgeoisie* after the mid-18th century.

■ *Seating*. Seating (Fig. 23-16, 23-17, 23-18) includes turned and ladder-back *chaises*, *fauteuils*, stools, benches, and *canapés*. All regions share a preference for turning. Legs may be turned or cabriole; stretchers are characteristic. Seats in all periods are wood or rush. Backs may have spindles, slats, lattice, or splats. Contours and back shapes depend on style; Rococo slats curve, while Louis XVI types are straight. Upholstery is rare; cushions are used for comfort. Common in all regions is the *chaise à capucine* (Fig. 23-18, 23-21), a turned arm- or armless chair with rush seat and legs joined by stretchers.

■ *Tables*. Provincial homes usually do not have the card, tea, and toilet tables of grand ones. However, dining tables, small occasional tables, and work tables are common (Fig. 23-16, 23-17). Shapes and ornament follow prevailing styles.

■ *Storage*. Typical case pieces are *commodes* (Fig. 23-19), *buffets* (Fig. 23-21), wall and standing cupboards (Fig. 23-21), *armoires* (Fig. 23-16, 23-20), and chests. Outlines usually are uncomplicated, but some pieces are *bombé* and/or serpentine in form. Similarly, paneling on case pieces follows the style in shape and decoration, although asymmetrical, Rococo curves most often define panels. Aprons, cornices, and stiles often feature carved or applied decoration. Metal hinges in brass or steel often run the entire length of panels. Escutcheons are prominent. Chests are common storage pieces throughout the periods. As in high-style interiors, *commodes* (Fig. 23-19), with three drawers and brass bail handles, become common in provincial public rooms in the 18th century. Those following the Rococo style may be *bombé* or serpentine, while semicircular contours define Louis XVI examples. *Armoires* (Fig. 23-16, 23-20) are highly prized pieces. Most have two long paneled doors and a straight or arched cornice. Those influenced by Rococo designs stand on short cabriole legs and feature curvilinear panels and tops and naturalistic decoration. *Buffets* also are characteristic in provincial dining rooms or kitchens (Fig. 23-21). Variations and names differ by region.

▲ **23-21.** Louis XV chair, *buffet*, *panetière*, and various utensils; France.

■ *Beds*. Four-poster beds (Fig. 23-16) are common, but some are built into wall alcoves, particularly in colder regions. Poster and other beds have hangings for warmth and privacy (Fig. 23-16, 23-17). The *lit clos*, typical of Brittany and colder regions, resembles a cupboard with its paneled sides and doors or curtains.

CHAPTER 24

Late English Georgian

1760–1810

The present reign is indeed rendered remarkable by the multitude of magnificent buildings, fine streets, and spacious squares, that have been added, and still are adding to this metropolis.

—Anonymous, *London and Its Environs Described*, 1761

The Late English Georgian period wholeheartedly adopts Neoclassicism for architecture, interiors, and furniture. Although a continuation of the classicism of the first half of the century, the new style exhibits slenderer proportions, flatter details, and more ornamentation. Designers freely adapt elements and motifs from ancient civilizations. Robert Adam is the leading Late Georgian designer of architecture, interiors, and furniture. Following the example set by Chippendale, books by George Hepplewhite and Thomas Sheraton illustrate prevailing Neoclassical fashions in furniture.

HISTORICAL AND SOCIAL

George III assumes the throne in 1760 and determines to regain the powers of the monarchy taken by the Whigs. His lack of statesmanship and the fact that his reforms resemble absolute monarchism prevent his effecting any lasting changes. Following the loss of the American colonies in the 1760s, Britain attempts changes under the leadership of Prime Minister William Pitt, the Younger. Pitt helps reestablish the country's credibility and promotes social changes, such as the abolition of slavery. These and other moderate reforms end with the French declaration of war in 1793.

The effects of the Industrial Revolution begin to manifest during the period. Agricultural and textile production increase, and new materials, such as cast iron, are introduced. London and other cities experience unprecedented growth and development. Cities soon feature wider, paved streets; more lighting; and new housing. Industrialization creates a new, larger, and wealthier middle class that eagerly follows the latest trends in housing, clothing, and furnishings.

George III takes more interest in government than his predecessors did, but like them, he is not interested in music, the arts, or architecture. He is neither a collector nor tastemaker, so his court is not as splendid as those of Louis XV and Louis XVI of France. Nor do design innovations arise from royal patronage. Instead, they come from the nobility and middle classes. Nevertheless, British society is refined with polished manners, and grand tours of Europe remain important for young gentlemen. Members of all classes increasingly study and admire antiquity.

CONCEPTS

The previous half-century of Neo-Palladianism prepares the British to join the rest of Europe and again be inspired by antiquity. Artists, architects, and others continue their grand tours to Italy, Greece, and other ancient sites. As on the Continent, sources of inspiration expand, and designers increasingly rely on archaeology and the many authoritative studies of Greek and Roman art and architecture.

MOTIFS

■ *Motifs*. Architectural and interior details (Fig. 24-1) include swags, anthemions or honeysuckles, urns, pediments, paterae, classical figures, lyres, laurel wreaths, columns, and other classical elements (Fig. 24-4, 24-6, 24-7). Furniture motifs (Fig. 24-1, 24-10, 24-13, 24-14) also are classical, but add the Prince of Wales motif, lyres, wheat, ribbons, drapery, classical figures, architectural details, and repeating patterns.

ARCHITECTURE

English Neoclassical architecture favors simple geometric shapes and elegant classical decoration. Varying from severe to graceful, the style incorporates principles of symmetry, unity, formality, and classical elements. However, it relies on a broader range of ancient (Egypt, Greece, and Rome) and later models (Renaissance and Baroque) and often uses classical elements differently than before and usually is more archaeologically correct. Unlike French buildings, English ones sometimes have picturesque qualities, such as complicated silhouettes or in-and-out movement. Following Robert Adam, some English architects play with classical proportions and ornament, freely adapting it to their own or their patron's style and taste. Others, such as William Chambers, adhere to classical rules.

Town and country houses are the main building types (Fig. 24-2, 24-4, 24-5, 24-6), although banks, churches, and other public structures also exhibit the style. Middle-class businessmen and professionals build numerous small to medium villas in a plainer Neoclassical mode.

Public and Private Buildings

■ *Site Orientation*. Architects more carefully consider the relationship between house and landscape. Houses may be sited in irregular gardens complete with newly built ancient or Gothic ruins.

■ *Floor Plans*. Plans display a variety of arrangements. Some (Fig. 24-4) follow French prototypes in the disposition of rooms. In others, rooms in contrasting shapes and sizes are laid out in a carefully planned sequence, and are based upon such prototypes as Roman baths and Imperial palaces. In contrast, some architects, responding to the Picturesque or Romantic Movements, plan spaces as a series of picturesque views. Sometimes, rooms are organized in circular fashion around the staircase to facilitate entertaining. Toward the end of the period, plans become less formal and more loosely arranged. In townhouses, important rooms begin to move to the ground floor instead of the first floor as before. In all types of plans, rooms may be round, oval, apsidal, square, or rectangular.

■ *Materials*. Industrialization yields new materials or improves older ones. Higher firing temperatures give a wider range of brick colors (Fig. 24-2, 24-4) including yellow, gray, brown, white, and cream. No longer is red the most common brick color; white or cream brick often is used to resemble the stone used in grander houses. Improved casting techniques produce ironwork in delicate Neoclassical motifs for balconies and window frames. By the end of the period the use of structural ironwork, particularly on staircases, increases, and iron plates help create structures that are more fire resistant.

■ *Façades*. Exteriors (Fig. 24-2, 24-3, 24-4) vary from severely plain to highly decorated with classical elements. Rustication emphasizes the lower portion of some walls. Triumphal arches, niches, and other Roman elements on façades join temple fronts and other Neo-Palladian details on upper stories. As before, most have columns and pediments at entrances and on the ends, but

(a)

(b)

(c)

(d)

▲ **24-1.** Motifs and Architectural Details: (a) Wall ornament by Robert Adam; (b) stair detail at Kenwood House; (c) entablature detail; and (d) furniture details, c. late 18th century; England.

scale is lighter. The Corinthian order dominates early in the period; Doric becomes more common later. Exterior architectural features on façades indicate important interiors as before. Townhouses and smaller villas often are severely plain with little or no ornamentation.

■ *Windows and Doors*. Classically derived decoration concentrates around windows and doors with smooth, blank walls separating them. Pediments in various shapes or lintels often surmount windows. Rectangular sashes prevail, but arched, fan, round, oval, or Palladian windows (Fig. 24-3) also are used. Improved manufacturing techniques yield larger glass panes, so window sizes increase and mullions become thinner. Mullions and sashes generally are painted dark colors, such as gray, brown, or green, instead of white. Some are grained to imitate mahogany. By the 1770s, taller windows give access to balconies.

Columns or pilasters and pediments frame doors as earlier, but they are more attenuated and, when of wood, are painted light or stone colors. Fanlights become larger with delicate radiating mullions and Neoclassical motifs. Doors commonly have six panels, although some have three, five, or eight. Most are painted dark brown or green. Hardware is simple, made of brass or cast iron, and incorporates classical motifs.

■ *Roofs*. Roofs (Fig. 24-2, 24-3, 24-4) are flat or low-pitched. Slate replaces clay tiles for coverings. A balustrade often hides the roof.

INTERIORS

Late English Georgian interiors are characterized by bright colors, classical ornamentation in low relief, and refined proportions. Rooms are formal, elegant, and unified. They often are simple geometric shapes with curving ends or sculpture niches for movement. Columns sometimes delineate apses. Some designs follow antique prototypes, and occasionally designers integrate ancient artifacts into new settings. Regardless of size, the scale of elements within interiors is small and refined, and forms and details are slender and elongated. Designers adapt classical rules of proportion to the

DESIGN SPOTLIGHT

Architecture and Interior: Commissioned by Lord William Murray Mansfield, the Lord Chief Justice of England, Robert Adam rebuilds Kenwood House and redesigns its interiors in the Neoclassical style in 1764–1779. Sited on a high hill in beautifully landscaped gardens north of London, it has a three-story box-shaped central core with a temple front entrance on the north side and a defining roof pediment on the south lawn side. Hyphens with Palladian windows connect the lower-height dependencies on either side. Engaged columns with Ionic capitals order the smooth white façade. Rectangular windows with classically derived embellishment are repetitively spaced within the symmetrical composition.

Kenwood has one of the most spectacular rooms in England—the library. It displays all of the characteristic features of Robert Adam's style. The rectangular space has apsidal ends separated from the rest of the room by Corinthian columns. Adam often uses apsidal ends and/or niches to create movement within a room. Flanking the fireplace are mirrored niches with sofas. On the opposite window wall are Adam-designed pier tables and pier glasses that reflect the light. The barrel-vaulted ceiling has rectangular compartments defined by color and low relief moldings. Within the compartments, rectangles, squares, circles, and semicircles with reliefs have painted classical decorations by Antonio Zucchi, assisted by Angelica Kaufman. Colors are primarily pale shades of blue, pink, white, and gold. A frieze with anthemions borders the perimeter of the ceiling and the cornice is gilded. Pale blue walls and delicate furnishings integrate with the composition.

▲ **24-2.** Kenwood House and library (next page), 1764–1779; Hampstead, London, England; Robert Adam.

DESIGN SPOTLIGHT

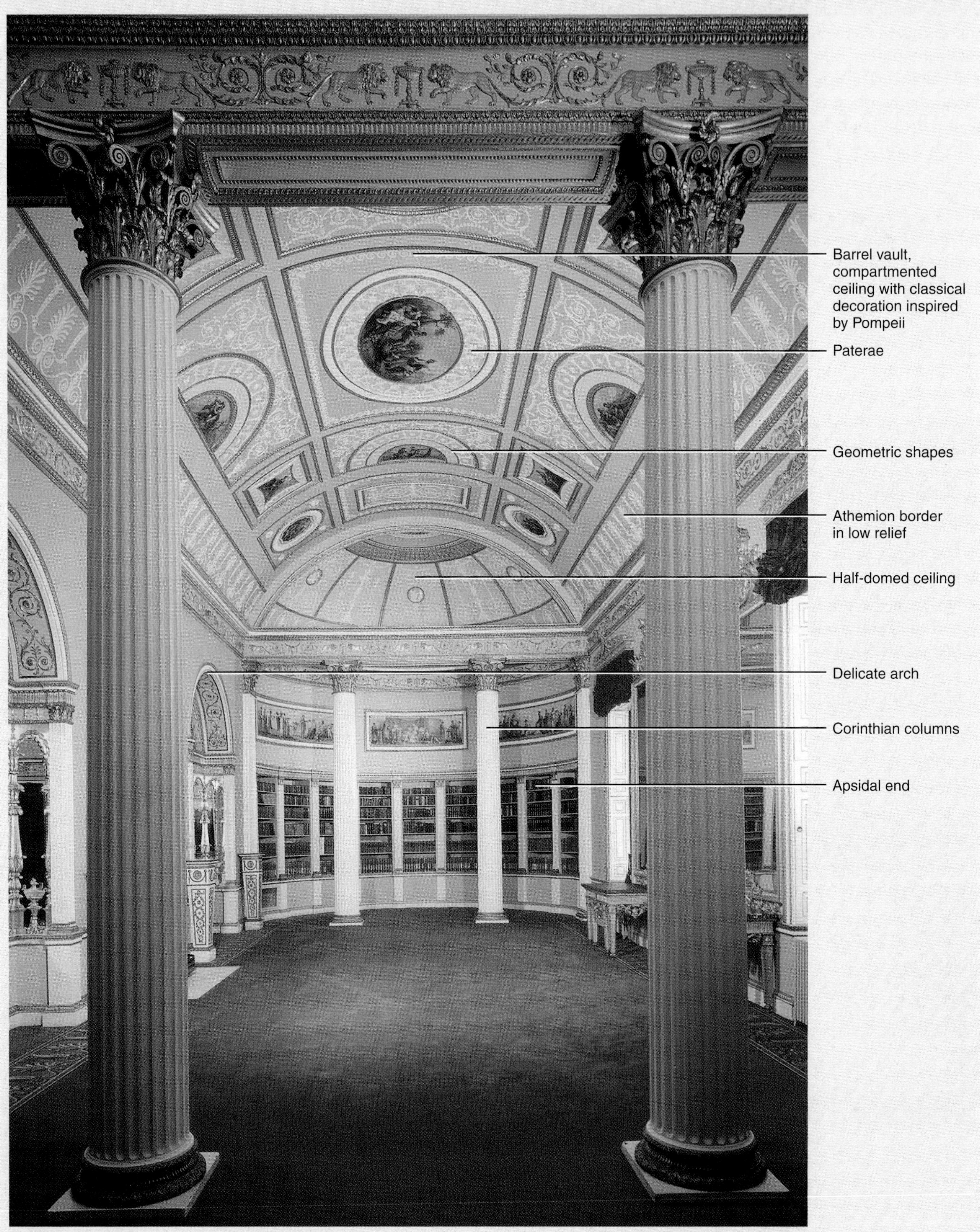

▲ **24-2.** Continued

situation. Decoration derives from the discoveries of Pompeii and the Italian Renaissance, especially the work of Raphael.

Robert Adam is the foremost and most influential designer of Neoclassical interiors. Harmonious and sophisticated, his interiors have elegant proportions and classical ornament that he abstracts and adapts to suit the particular interior. He designs all elements in the room, from walls and ceilings to furniture and accessories, to achieve unity.

Private Buildings

■ *Color*. The period adopts a vibrant palette thought to be derived from antiquity. Colors (Fig. 24-2, 24-4, 24-6, 24-15) include lilac; terra-cotta; Pompeiian red; and bright pinks, blues, and greens. Red and black, reminiscent of Grecian vases, compose so-called Etruscan color schemes (Fig. 24-6). The middle class continues using colors such as stone, gray, olive green, brown, straw, sky blue, and pea green that were fashionable earlier. Soft white remains in vogue, particularly for ceilings. *Grisaille*, marbling, and graining return to fashion. Plasterwork may be white or colored, sometimes with gilded highlights.

■ *Floors*. The grandest rooms have stone, marble, or scagolia floors (Fig. 24-5). For others, random-width stained and polished oak, pine, or deal boards are most common. Plain, uncovered wood floors may be stained, polished, painted in marble patterns, or stenciled. The wealthy continue to use parquet in important rooms, and wall-to-wall carpet grows more fashionable because it is less expensive. Axminster, Moorlands, or Kidderminster manufacture knotted pile carpets and rugs in Turkish, Persian, or Neoclassical patterns. Less expensive alternatives include woven loop pile (called Brussels or Wilton) or ingrains. Carpet and rugs (Fig. 24-4) repeat ceiling designs when following Robert Adam's example. Plain or patterned matting replaces carpet and rugs in the summer.

■ *Walls*. Walls (Fig. 24-2, 24-4, 24-6) display a variety of treatments. Completely paneled walls are out of fashion. Instead, the wall above the dado is painted, papered, or has Neoclassical plasterwork. These treatments sometimes imitate Pompeiian wall paintings (Fig. 24-6). Some walls have compartments of low-relief classical ornamentation in white or the same color as the wall. Small painted scenes are often interspersed among the ornamentation.

Alternative treatments include fabrics and wallpaper, the use of which increases during the period. English, Chinese, and French papers increasingly cover walls in numerous fashionable homes. Patterns include architectural forms, such as columns or moldings; florals; stripes; classical scenes; or landscapes. Flocked papers emulating fabrics are almost as expensive as the fabrics they resemble.

Chimneypieces (Fig. 24-4, 24-6) are usually of white, black, or gray marble or scagolia with classical motifs and slender proportions. Chimneyboards with Neoclassical motifs, flowers, or mirrors fill fireplace openings in summer. The design of coal grates, which are more common, complements interior decoration.

■ *Window Treatments*. Window treatments become more elaborate during the period. Simple panels nailed to the window continue to be used, but many now have plain or embellished valances. Single and double festoons are the most fashionable window treatments. Made in light fabrics, they resemble classical swags. In the 1780s, the French introduce draw rods (also called French rods), which gives rise to a fashion for panel curtains hanging on rings beneath festoons. By the turn of the century, elaborately swagged top treatments called drapery are fashionable. Both drapery (top treatment) and curtains (underneath treatment) are of light fabrics that often contrast in color and are trimmed with fringe and tassels. Curtains are tied back during the day. Shutters, cloth blinds, and Venetian blinds, with or without curtains, also help block light.

▲ **24-3.** Royal Crescent, 1767–1775; Bath, England; designed by John Wood before his death in 1754 and built by his son John Wood II.

■ *Doors*. Doors (Fig 24-4, 24-6) are usually paneled mahogany with brass hardware. Gilding may highlight panel moldings. Narrow moldings frame the door with a cornice and frieze above.

■ *Ceilings*. Ceilings (Fig. 24-2, 24-4, 24-5, 24-6, 24-7) are focal points, especially in important rooms in grand houses. Most are flat, but some are coved or vaulted. Decoration consists of classical motifs in low plaster relief similar to Roman stuccowork arranged in geometric shapes or compartments and repeated patterns separated by color. Most compositions center on an oval or circle of plasterwork, such as a *patera*, or a painting within it. Small paintings with classical themes and figures may be interspersed among the compartments. The rich, dark colors of these paintings contrast with the white or colored reliefs and clear, bright ceiling colors. Sometimes gilding picks out the details. Carpet may reflect or repeat ceiling patterns. Ceilings in lesser houses are flat and painted white.

■ *Textiles*. Advances in manufacturing processes make a greater number and variety of textiles available, so more people can af-

DESIGN SPOTLIGHT

Architecture and Interior: Originally a Tudor-style mansion, the house was replaced beginning in 1743. The three-story exterior of Saltram House has smooth walls and large sash windows on the ground and first floors with square windows above. A modillioned cornice separates the wall and low-pitched roof. Bays mark the ends, and a slightly projecting pediment with quoins beneath and a projecting porch added in 1818 highlight the center.

The dining room was originally designed by Robert Adam as a library for John Parker II, Lord Boringdon around 1768. Ten years later, it is remodeled as a dining room and is one of the best-preserved examples of Adam's work in England. A rectangular space with an apsidal end, it displays Adam's use of the classical language in the chimneypiece, niches (originally windows), and geometric ceiling composition. The low relief stuccowork and paintings in the ceiling are by Antonio Zucchi. Decoration by Joseph Rose accents the green walls. The rug repeats the ceiling design, a common Adam characteristic. Pedestals with urns, an Adam innovation, flank the bow-shaped sideboard, and side chairs with oval backs provide seating.

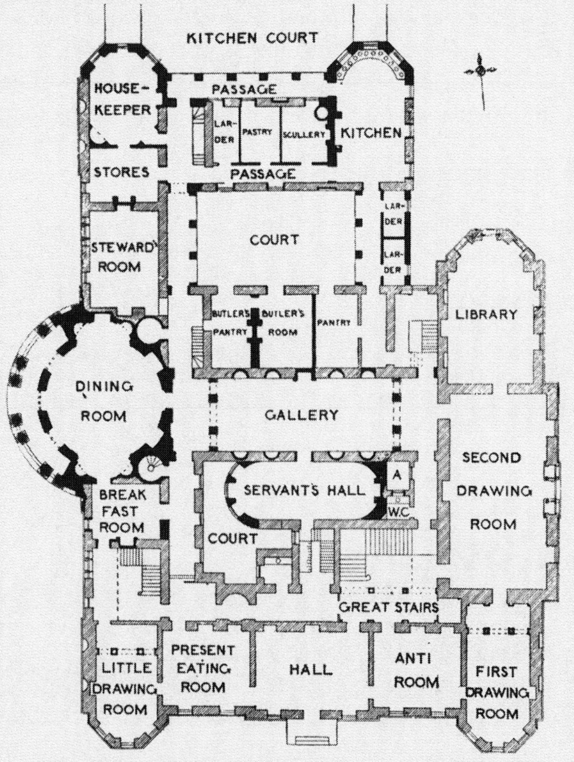

▲ **24-4.** Saltram House, floor plan, and dining room, remodeled 1743–1781; Plymouth, England; Robert Adam.

ford carpet, upholstery, curtains, bed hangings, and furniture cases (Fig. 24-2, 24-8, 24-15). In 1774, England eases restrictions on the use of domestic cotton, while imports remain illegal. By the 1780s, English chintzes and calicoes replace damasks, silks, and velvets, even among the wealthy. Multicolored English prints rival those previously imported from India. The use of linen also increases. Most cottons and linens are block printed, but copperplate printing is firmly established by 1760. Copperplate prints in a single color (red, blue, purple, black, yellow) on a light ground, known as *toiles*, increase in popularity. Especially fashionable for curtains is tabby, a silk of alternating moiré and satin stripes.

As before, textiles and wallpaper often match in color and pattern. Furnishing fabrics coordinate in color and commonly exhibit classical motifs like other materials and finishes. Upholstery during the period is not as thick and becomes squarer than previously. Tufting helps maintain shape and hold the horsehair and down stuffing in place. Shiny brass nails in geometric patterns attach fabrics to furniture frames. Furniture cases are of chintz or calico. Scarves, precursors of Victorian antimacassars, drape the backs of sofas and chairs to prevent damage from wig powder and hair grease.

▲ **24-5.** Hall, Syon House, 1762–1769; London, England; Robert Adam.

DESIGN SPOTLIGHT

Honeysuckle motif
Rosette in circle
Compartmented ceiling with classical motifs similar to Roman stuccowork
Frieze with classical swag and rosette
Mahogany door with frieze above
Niche with vase (originally side window)
Mantel with classical features
Curved sideboard flanked by urns
Oval back on chairs
Rug integrates with ceiling design

▲ **24-4.** Continued

▲ **24-7.** Ceiling design; England; Robert Adam.

▲ **24-6.** Dining room (top) and Etruscan dressing room, Osterley Park, 1766–1768 and 1775–1777; London, England; Robert Adam.

▲ 24-8. Textile: Fabric in the Adam style.

▲ 24-9. Lighting: Hanging lamp and Argand lamp, c. late 18th century.

■ *Lighting*. Candles, especially those of beeswax, are expensive, so most people use them sparingly. Those who can afford candles use them in *candelabra*; candlesticks; wall sconces; and chandeliers made of metal, ceramics, or glass (Fig. 24-4, 24-9). In 1783, François-Pierre Ami Argand invents a tublar wick lamp whose light is adjustable. Soon, Argand lamps (Fig. 24-9), called colza oil lamps in England, sit on mantels, tables, and wall shelves. The shapes and decoration of all lighting devices follow classical models.

FURNISHINGS AND DECORATIVE ARTS

Late English Georgian furniture is light in scale and rectilinear, but not necessarily classical in form. Carved, painted, and inlaid classical motifs dominate compositions. Contrasting geometric and curvilinear shapes in form and ornamentation repeat the contrasting shapes of floor plans and wall or ceiling treatments. Influences include French Neoclassical and furniture designed by Robert Adam for particular rooms. Books by George Hepplewhite and Thomas Sheraton illustrate fashionable Late Georgian furnishings. It is likely that neither author invents the styles illustrated in his publication. Although their names are associated with particular characteristics and styles, the books have some common qualities such as slender scale and decoration. Today, the term *Hepplewhite* often refers to curved backs and tapered rectangular legs, while *Sheraton* means square backs and cylindrical legs. In reality, both books show designs with these characteristics.

Because furniture still lines the walls in formal, symmetrical arrangements when not in use, designers regard it as architectonic and integral to the room. Toward the end of the period, furniture arrangements become less formal, grouping around the fireplace instead of lining the walls. Brass toe caps and casters facilitate moving. New in the period is Robert Adam's sideboard table flanked by urns and pedestals (Fig. 24-4) for dining rooms and sideboards with drawers and doors. Also new are the Pembroke table (Fig. 24-12), quartetto or trio tables, Carleton House writing table, and pedestal dining tables.

Public and Private Buildings

■ *Materials*. Most cabinet furniture is of satinwood, either solid or veneer, but rosewood or other exotic woods are also popular (Fig. 24-1, 24-2, 24-10, 24-12, 24-13). Adam usually uses mahogany (Fig. 24-6) for dining room and library furniture. Many pieces have contrasting veneer bands and inlay. *Ormolu* mounts adorn designs in the French taste. Also definitive is marquetry of classical images in a variety of colored woods. Especially fashionable are japanning in polychrome, paint in black or colors that match the room, and *grisaille*. Some pieces have gilding or porcelain plaques. Brass door and drawer pulls are round or oval.

■ *Seating*. Chairs are most typical of the style. Backs may be shield, heart, oval, wheel, camel, square, or rectangular. Hepplewhite backs include the camelback, shield, heart, oval, and wheel (Fig. 24-4, 24-10), while those of Sheraton are usually rectangular with a raised center top rail (Fig. 24-11) or trellises. Backs and splats display endless variety in carved, painted (Fig. 24-6), or inlaid ornament. Toward the end of the period, horizontal rails appear more often in chair backs, reflecting a trend toward horizontality. Quadrangular or cylindrical legs are plain, fluted, or reeded and terminate in spade or thimble feet. Other seating includes sofas in several forms and chair-back settees.

▲ **24-10.** Chairs with shield, oval, and heart backs, published in *The Cabinet-Maker and Upholsterer's Guide*, c. 1780s–1788; England; George Hepplewhite; and chair with shield back, late 18th century.

DESIGN SPOTLIGHT

Furniture: This parlor chair, shown in Sheraton's book, *The Cabinet-Maker and Upholsterer's Drawing Book in Four Parts*, has the rectangular back for which the style named after him is commonly known. Rectangular backs with various center motifs shown in the *Drawing Book* would give buyers an idea of design diversity and range of compositions available. This one has four tapered urns with inlay in the back, and the arms rest on urn shapes. The fluted legs are slender and tapered. In addition to the variety of back designs, quadrangular or cylindrical legs could be plain, fluted, or reeded and terminate in spade or thimble feet. Lightly scaled chairs such as this one are used in public and private rooms for entertaining, dining, or sleeping throughout the Neoclassical period.

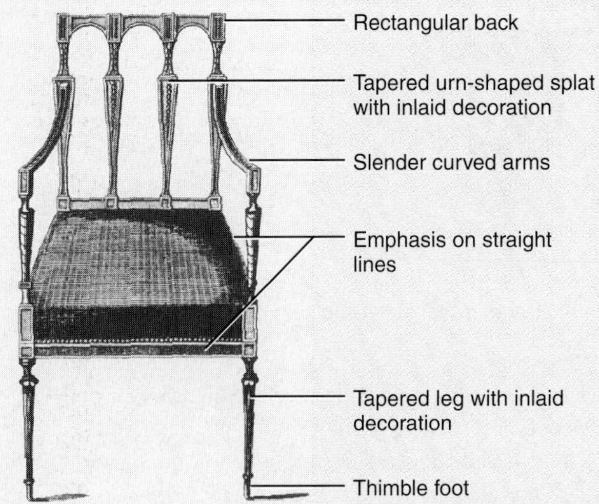

▲ **24-11.** Parlour chair, c. 1792, published in *The Cabinet-Maker and Upholsterer's Drawing Book in Four Parts*, c. 1802; England; Thomas Sheraton.

▲ **24-12.** Pembroke table, mahogany; England.

▲ **24-14.** *Commode* in the dressing room of the Countess of Derby at Osterley Park, from a colored engraving by B. Pastorini, 1770; England; Robert Adam.

■ *Tables.* Many types of small tables support various activities. Card and tea tabletops exhibit rectangular, semicircular, stepped shapes. The *demi-lune* is especially fashionable at the end of the century. Folding tops are still used so that tables can be placed against the wall. Table legs are slender and tapered with spade or thimble feet, like chairs. Pembroke tables (Fig. 24-12) serve as breakfast tables in bedrooms or as card or game tables in drawing rooms. Pedestal or pillar and claw dining tables are introduced. The pedestals have three or four outward curving legs with brass toe caps and casters. Because each pedestal is a separate unit, dining tables can be any size and are taken apart when not in use.

■ *Storage. Commodes,* featuring painted or veneer classical decoration, remain fashionable (Fig. 24-14). Semicircular or bow fronts come into vogue in the 1770s. Introduced during the period to provide storage, the sideboard (Fig. 24-13) with drawers and doors may be bow or kidney shaped with six tapering legs. Common embellishments include classical motifs, stringing, and crossbanding. Breakfront secretary bookcases, frequently in libraries, have center portions that project forward and have drop leaves for writing. New to the period and designed to be free-standing, the Carleton House writing table has a low storage unit with drawers and doors resting on its top and extending along the sides and back.

▲ **24-13.** Sideboard, mahogany with marquetry; probably by Robert Adam.

▲ **24-15.** State bed, Osterley Park, c. 1776; England; Robert Adam.

■ *Beds*. Richly draped four-poster beds continue in fashion (Fig. 24-15). Posts and testers are slender and carved with classical ornament. Some testers curve or have pediments or urns on top of them. French beds placed sideways against the wall with canopies and draperies mounted on the wall above also are fashionable. Bed hangings are as rich as before, but feature more classical swags. Hangings may be of dimity, plain or patterned silk or satin, velvet, cotton, or linen. As time passes, lighter fabrics become dominant. Rich trims continue to embellish hangings.

■ *Decorative Arts*. Sheffield plate is introduced in the 1770s, which enables even middle-class homes to have numerous silver objects, such as candlesticks, sconces, tea urns, teapots, and tableware. Silver designs are in classical shapes, such as urns or columns, with relatively flat decoration that does not interfere with profiles.

Late Georgian mirrors (Fig. 24-16) become slender rectangles, ovals, or shield shapes often surmounted with delicate metal filigree. Some rectangular ones have upper panels with engravings or *verre églomisé*. Convex mirrors with heavy circular frames also are typical.

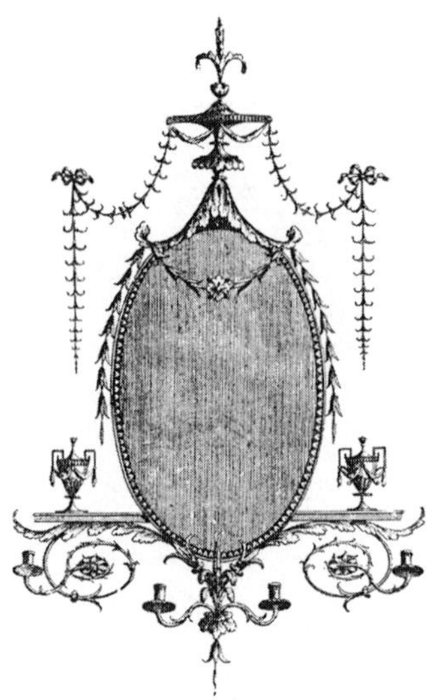

▲ **24-16.** Decorative Arts: *Girandole* (wall sconce); George Hepplewhite.

■ *Ceramics*. English factories begin producing hard-paste porcelain in the late 1760s. Josiah Spode II standardizes the recipe for bone china about 1800, and it supplants porcelain in popularity, particularly for dinner services. Straight lines, rectangular handles, classical motifs, and Greek and Roman shapes define Neoclassical porcelain. Decoration may be sumptuous, even to the point of obscuring form. Many pieces copy or are influenced by Chinese and Japanese porcelain as well as Neoclassical porcelains. The best-known Late English Georgian ceramics are those of Josiah Wedgwood. Jasperware (known as Wedgwood today) is produced in various shapes with matte colors, including blue and lilac, and white low-relief classical motifs (Fig. 24-17).

■ *Later Interpretations*. Designers reproduce and adapt Adam, Sheraton, and Hepplewhite furnishings, along with Chippendale furnishings in the American Federal period (Fig. 24-18), and again in the 1870s and 1880s in England and America. Reproductions or adaptations of Neoclassical furniture remain in fashion today.

▲ **24-17.** Decorative Arts: Vase, Jasperware, Wedgwood factory; c. late 18th century; England; Josiah Wedgwood.

▲ **24-18.** Later Interpretation: Sideboard, 1790–1800; in the style of George Hepplewhite. American Federal.

CHAPTER 25

American Federal

1776–1820

In (the) early years of nationhood, the sense of American identity demanded an American architecture for the common man as well as the privileged. Though closely derived from contemporary English hand books, Asher Benjamin's influential guide . . . published in Boston in 1806, declared American cultural independence and social egalitarianism. Architecture in America must be different from architecture in Europe, the author asserted. Americans had different materials to work with, less use for decoration, and a need to economize on labor and materials.

—Carole Rifkind, *A Field Guide to American Architecture*

The Federal style is the first phase of Neoclassicism in America. Derived primarily from English models, the style takes its name from the fact that its inception coincides with the establishment of the federal government in America. As in Europe, the style features classical details and ornament, slender proportions, and contrasting circular and rectangular shapes. However, the American Federal style generally is simpler and smaller in scale than the European Neoclassical styles in France and England.

HISTORICAL AND SOCIAL

The Articles of Confederation, the first governing instrument of the United States of America, is ratified by several states in 1781. Under the Articles, Congress represents the states, not the people. Because of its very limited powers, Congress cannot unite the country into a single political entity. Rivalries and conflicts among the states increase, threatening the stability of the young nation. In 1787, delegates meet in Philadelphia, Pennsylvania, intending to amend the Articles. Instead, they draw up the Constitution, which gives power to the people instead of the states. The Constitution also creates a three-branch government—executive, judicial, and legislative. Following many conflicts and compromises, the convention of delegates adopts the Constitution, and in 1788, it becomes the law of the land. George Washington is unanimously elected as the country's first president and is inaugurated in April 1789.

Despite its many differences, the young nation prospers. Although the Revolution severs political connections with England, many Americans, as former English citizens, want to maintain economic, cultural, and social ties with Great Britain. Commerce with England and France increases, and America initiates trade with the Orient in 1785. New state capitol buildings spring up in every state, while the new federal city of Washington is incorporated in 1799. Frenchman Pierre L'Enfant devises a formal plan for the city with wide streets, circles, and stars punctuated by important and symbolic buildings. Georgia and North Carolina establish state-chartered universities in 1785 and 1789, respectively. The population grows and spreads westward, although the country remains predominantly rural. Households are large and composed of husbands, wives, numerous children, grandparents or other relatives, boarders, servants, and/or slaves. By the end of the period, the Industrial Revolution begins to have some effects.

(a)

(b)

(c)

▲ **25-1.** Motifs and Architectural Detail: (a) Eagle inlay from card table, c. 1790–1820; Rhode Island; (b) pair of vases, c. 1810–1830, France, possibly Paris; and (c) doorway, Wickham-Valentine House, 1811; Richmond, Virginia [Table and vases Courtesy of the Diplomatic Reception Rooms, U.S. Department of State]

In 1803, President Thomas Jefferson negotiates the Louisiana Purchase with France. This acquisition of land from the upper Missouri to the Gulf of Mexico doubles the size of the nation and increases her power and wealth. Unfortunately, neither he nor his successor James Madison can keep the United States out of another war with Great Britain. Britain's continued harassment of the United States, its merchants, and its ships forces Congress to declare war in June 1812. Although the war really does not settle critical issues, it does end European dominance in American affairs and engenders strong feelings of nationalism in the young nation.

CONCEPTS

As a new nation, the United States needs an official architectural style to legitimize its emancipation and to personify its cultural identity. Leaders, such as Thomas Jefferson, who are acquainted with trends in Europe, advocate Neoclassicism, which offers models from Greece and Rome, two ancient republics. They propose a national architecture following these models because they see Neoclassicism as a visual metaphor linking these old republics with the new one. Continuing cultural ties with England assures that many Americans continue to follow English models of Neoclassicism—Robert Adam in interiors and Hepplewhite and Sheraton in furniture.

CHARACTERISTICS AND MOTIFS

Based largely on English prototypes, the Federal style has slender proportions, classical decoration, contrasts of color, and geometric forms. Emphasis is on straight lines and geometric curves, such as circles or ellipses. American designs typically are simpler than European ones. National symbols, such as the eagle, serve as important icons in establishing the cultural identity.

■ *Motifs.* Motifs (Fig. 25-1) include eagles, paterae, swags, egg and dart, palmettes, honeysuckle, classical figures, baskets, urns, and stripes. The image of George Washington and other leaders appears often, particularly in decorative arts.

ARCHITECTURE

American Neoclassical architecture differs from England's in scale, construction methods, and building materials. Scale for all buildings is domestic instead of monumental. Wood-frame construction and brick prevail instead of stone. Gentleman amateurs or master craftsmen, rather than trained architects, design and build most structures. American Neoclassicism does not have a strong theoretical base, as in Europe. Nor do Americans emphasize design dependence on classical models. Consequently, the Federal style is largely imitative, not necessarily innovative. A few immigrant builders and architects, such as Benjamin Henry Latrobe, introduce some innovations.

▲ **25-2.** Massachusetts State House, 1795–1798; Boston, Massachusetts; Charles Bulfinch.

Most Federal-style buildings are in urban areas concentrated along the eastern seaboard, although they eventually dot the entire nation. Urban houses are the main carriers of the style. But characteristics define many buildings, including most government buildings. The Neoclassical style becomes a symbol of the new nation, following the notion that buildings are to be read as models of the new republic. Structures generally retain Georgian forms, but are taller with more slender proportions. Circular or elliptical forms, windows, doors, and projecting porches usually highlight façades. Classical details, moldings, and ornamentation become shallower in relief and more delicate in scale. Public building types include statehouses (Fig. 25-2), churches, meetinghouses (Fig. 25-3), banks, theaters, and warehouses. Dwellings include detached structures (Fig. 25-4, 25-5, 25-6, 25-7) and row houses. Often, rural dwellings exhibit little change, other than slender proportions and low-relief ornamentation.

Public Buildings

■ *Statehouses (Capitols)*. Between 1785 and 1788, Thomas Jefferson designs the state capitol in Richmond, Virginia. It emulates Roman models, specifically the Maison Carrée in Nîmes, France, and, as such, is the first temple-form public building in the United States. In the Connecticut and Massachusetts statehouses (Fig. 25-2), Charles Bulfinch introduces what becomes the typical form for capitols—a symmetrical façade with a portico or temple front and, inside, a domed rotunda flanked by two chambers. The United States Capitol adopts a similar form but on a much grander scale.

■ *Churches*. Churches and meetinghouses (Fig. 25-3) continue earlier forms of the early 18th century, such as James Gibbs's S. Martin-in-the-Fields in London. However, slenderer proportions; curving forms, especially windows; and refined classical ornamentation proclaim Neoclassical influence. Interiors remain the same as before with a large open center space flanked by balconies and a choir loft opposite the pulpit.

■ *Site Orientation*. Urban public and private structures are sited on streets. Dwellings may be surrounded by lawns or have only front and rear gardens. Lawns often surround churches.

■ *Floor Plans*. Plans of public buildings and private buildings are symmetrical or nearly so. Many combine contrasting circular or elliptical spaces with rectangular ones in the English manner, and the contrasting forms repeat on exteriors. Residential plans (Fig. 25-4, 25-6) may continue the rectangular block and double-pile plan of earlier. Some rooms project, breaking the rectangular block. Occasionally, symmetrical façades conceal asymmetrical plans. Curving staircases are more common than straight ones (Fig. 25-8). Besides adding movement to interiors, they also distinguish Federal structures, particularly houses, from Georgian ones. Row houses follow standard plans of front and back rooms with side passages for entries and stairs. There are some regional forms, such as the single Charleston house featuring a room fronting on the street and others extending to the rear with a side porch or piazza and entrance.

■ *Materials*. Brick, alone or combined with wood, dominates public and private structures, but wood remains a common choice for houses (Fig. 25-2, 25-3, 25-4, 25-5, 25-6, 25-7). Brick and/or wood may be painted to imitate stone, which is used infrequently. Colors include white, cream, buff, stone, light gray, or blue. Shutters (or blinds) are usually painted dark green. Wood framing is the more common form of construction, although more arches and vaulting appear during the period in public buildings and churches.

■ *Façades*. Façades of all structures (Fig. 25-2, 25-3, 25-4, 25-5, 25-6, 25-7) are symmetrical and have contrasting circular and rectangular forms. Projecting centers, semicircular projecting porches, and/or rounded windows introduce curves and movement. Walls of public buildings may be plain or articulated with

▲ **25-3.** Meetinghouse, 1816; Lancaster, Massachusetts; Charles Bulfinch.

slender pilasters and other elements. Columns, engaged columns, and pilasters are widely spaced and attenuated, and delicate classical ornamentation is low in relief. Stringcourses may separate stories, and pediments or projecting porticoes or porches identify entrances. Church façades usually have a columned portico, behind which is a tall, multilevel steeple with columns, arched openings, and classical ornamentation. House façades (Fig. 25-4, 25-5, 25-6, 25-7) usually have fewer architectural details than public buildings do. Many are three stories, which sometimes diminish in size as they ascend. Some have pilasters on the corners and stringcourses separating the stories. Curving, projecting porches are a defining feature of the style. The exterior design often reflects room placement. Wider spaces between windows outside denote more important spaces inside.

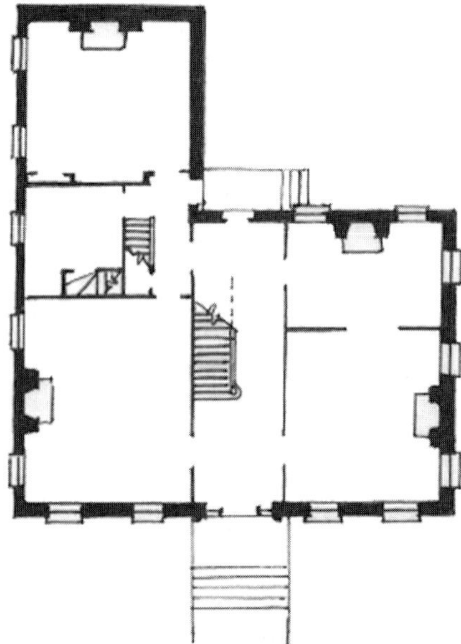

▲ **25-4.** First Harrison Gray Otis House, floor plan, and dining room, 1795–1796; Boston, Massachusetts; architecture by Charles Bulfinch.

DESIGN SPOTLIGHT

Architecture and Interior: Built in 1804–1805 from plans by Samuel McIntire for John Gardner, the Gardner-Pingree is considered the finest surviving example of McIntire's mature work in the Adam or Federal style. The imposing but austere brick façade has three stories diminishing in size and separated by wide white stringcourses. Sash windows also diminish in size; their slender mullions and the flat, white lintels above them proclaim the Federal style. A classical balustrade, also white, hides the low-pitched hipped roof. The white wooden, circular projecting porch, a Federal-style characteristic, emphasizes the entrance, and slender wooden Corinthian columns, also typical of Federal, carry its entablature. Another defining feature of American Federal is the doorway with fanlight above it and flanked by sidelights.

Elegant and formal, the Federal style drawing room was restored and redecorated following extensive research in 1989. Above a paneled dado, the wall is painted and a wall-to-wall carpet composed of flowers in a geometric design covers the floor. At the windows are red swags trimmed with fringe hanging from cornices that also have swags and are crowned by flower baskets. The white mantel, carved by McIntire, has swags, rosettes, and flowers flanking a dish of fruit. This design is repeated above the doorway separating the two parlors. Corinthian engaged columns that support the mantel have leafy tendrils twisting around them, and their design may have been based upon a plate in *Pain's British Palladio.* Furnishings are light in scale and follow the designs of Hepplewhite. The lolling chairs have furniture cases.

▲ **25-5.** Gardner-Pingree House, porch, and parlor, 1804–1805; Salem, Massachusetts; Samuel McIntire.

■ *Windows and Doors*. On both public and private structures, sash windows are taller (Fig. 25-2, 25-4, 25-5, 25-6, 25-7) with thinner mullions. Some have lintels, entablatures, or pediments above them, or they are framed with classical details. Others are set within relieving arches. Oval, round, fan, and Palladian windows contrast with rectangular openings and are definitive of the Federal style.

Door surrounds on public buildings are more elaborate than on houses and feature pediments and columns or fanlights and sidelights. Fanlights above front doors distinguish Federal houses (Fig. 25-4, 25-5, 25-7) from Georgian ones. Fanlights are often combined with sidelights, a pediment supported by pilasters, or engaged columns. Doors, which may be single or double, are paneled and painted a dark color or white.

■ *Roofs*. Roofs are low-pitched gables or flat and hidden by a balustrade (Fig. 25-4, 25-5, 25-6, 25-7). Statehouses, churches, and steeples often have domes and cupolas (Fig. 25-2, 25-3). A few houses have hipped roofs. A decorative cornice, usually with dentils, accentuates the wall beneath the roof.

INTERIORS

Federal interiors follow those of Robert Adam but are more simply decorated with fewer colors. Lavish gilding, elaborate classical reliefs, and paintings are rare, and American rooms are generally smaller than British ones but retain refined proportions. Like English Late Georgian, American Federal rooms are elegant, refined, and formal in the Adam manner. Classical motifs and architectural details dominate. Hierarchy of room decoration continues.

Important public spaces, such as those in statehouses and churches, are used for gathering, meeting, and occasionally entertaining. Domestic structures follow earlier Georgian room use and living patterns with one exception. During the period, more people set aside a room specifically for dining. Patterns of entertaining change, and lavishly appointed dinners followed by card playing become fashionable.

Americans learn about Neoclassicism from many sources including pattern books and fashion periodicals; immigrant crafts-

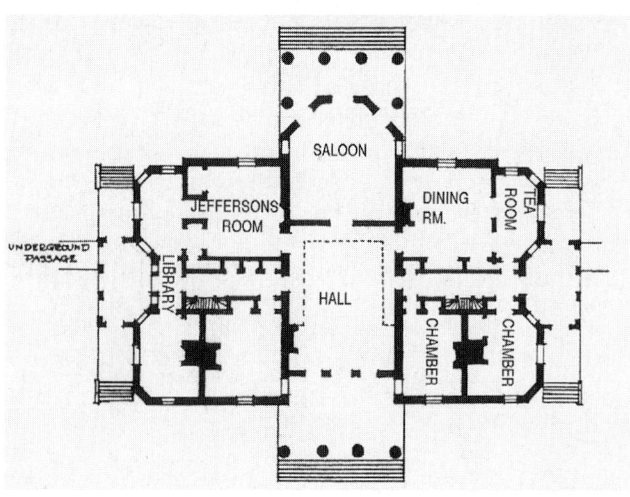

▲ **25-6.** Monticello and floor plan, begun 1777, remodeled 1793–1809; Charlottesville, Virginia; Thomas Jefferson.

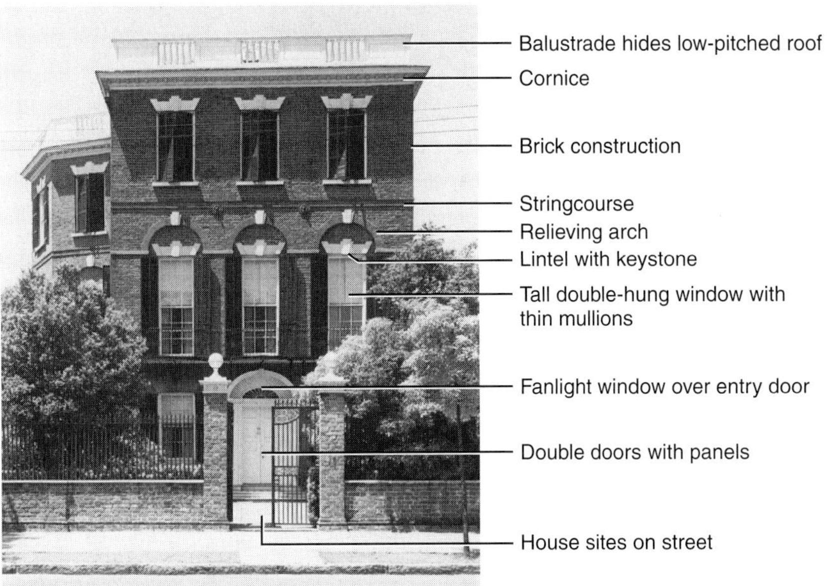

▲ **25-7.** Nathaniel Russell House, before 1809; Charleston, South Carolina; Russell Warren.

men, cabinetmakers, and upholsterers; imported furnishings; and travel. Government leaders, such as George Washington, Benjamin Franklin, and John Adams, admire Neoclassical beauty and import furnishings in the style from France and England. Continuing cultural ties with England assures that many Americans follow English models of Neoclassicism—Robert Adam in interiors and Hepplewhite and Sheraton in furniture.

Public and Private Buildings

■ *Color.* Colors are light, bright, and clear. White, off-white, buff, gray, and many shades of blue and green are common (Fig. 25-4, 25-5). Marbling and graining remain fashionable.

■ *Floors.* Masonry floors are rare in America; softwood floors are the most common. Wooden floors are sometimes painted in solid, usually dark, colors or in patterns that imitate marble or other materials. Floor coverings include floor cloths, matting, and commercial and homemade carpets. Painted floor cloths in geometric patterns continue to be fashionable, particularly in entrance halls. Brussels and Wilton wall-to-wall carpets are expensive, so many Americans purchase less costly ingrain, Venetian, and list carpets. Especially favored in all carpets are patterns composed of geometric shapes with classical motifs (Fig. 25-4, 25-5, 25-17). Carpet and rugs are removed in summer and replaced with matting. Drugget or baize crumb cloth beneath the dining table and a small hearth rug in front of the fireplace protect expensive carpets (Fig. 25-4).

■ *Walls.* Plain plaster replaces paneling for walls (Fig. 25-8). Most rooms have a baseboard, dado, and cornice (Fig. 25-4, 25-5). The most important rooms have pilasters, columns, and plasterwork ceilings. Classical moldings form cornices and chair rails. The dado, when present, is usually paneled with paint or wallpaper covering the upper portion of the wall. Wallpaper, increasingly fashionable, comes from England, France, and China

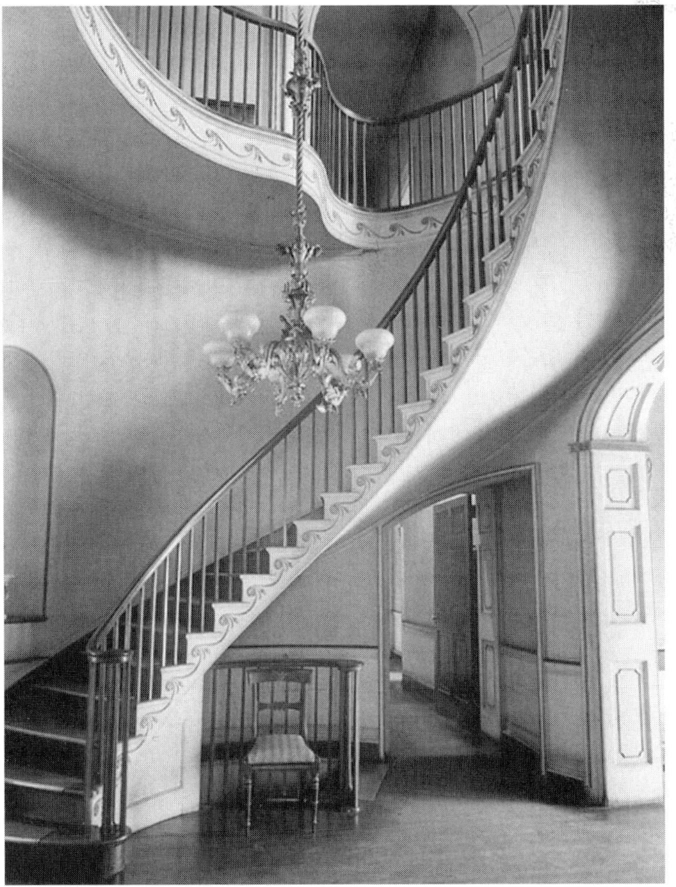

▲ **25-8.** Stair Hall, Wickham-Valentine House, 1811; Richmond, Virginia; Alexander Parris.

but is also made in America. Patterns include architectural details, scenic or landscape papers, drapery patterns, rainbow or shaded papers, textile imitations, small repeating patterns, and Neoclassical designs. Borders, essential on painted and papered walls, come in many patterns, including some that match wallpapers (Fig. 25-4). They outline all architectural features as before.

Wooden and white, gray, or pink marble mantels are simple with classical motifs (Fig. 25-4, 25-5). Elaborate overmantel treatments are no longer fashionable but decorative looking glasses or chimney glasses are common.

■ *Windows and Window Treatments*. Windows may be left plain or have interior shutters or window treatments (Fig. 25-4, 25-5). The latter become more common and elaborate as the period progresses. Interior shutters fold into the window jamb as before. Window treatments consist of a single or multiple festoons with floor-length curtains beneath them and sheer white cotton panels next to the window. Trims and contrasting linings often enhance single and double festoons, which may hang over a classically inspired rod or cornice. Floor-length curtains are lopped back over curtain or cloak pins during the day. Blinds in several forms also are used at windows. Slat or Venetian blinds are fashionable but expensive. Roller blinds, which usually do not work well, are more reasonably priced. Other shades are made of plain or pleated silk or cotton. Roller blinds or fabric shades may have decorative paintings.

■ *Doors*. Important doors are paneled and either painted or of a polished hardwood such as mahogany. Those in major rooms have classical surrounds (Fig. 25-1, 25-4).

▲ **25-9.** Textiles: *Toile de Jouy* print with symbols of the new American republic.

▲ **25-10.** Lighting: Argand lamp, c. late 18th century; United States.

■ *Ceilings*. Most ceilings are plain, flat, and light in color (Fig. 25-4, 25-5). Those in affluent homes may have carved or cast plaster decorations in the center and near the cornice imitating the work of Robert Adam. A few ceilings feature painted or stenciled designs.

■ *Textiles*. Federal is the last period in which all textiles in a room match. As the period progresses, a greater variety of textiles (Fig. 25-4, 25-5, 25-9, 25-17) becomes available because of advancements in manufacturing processes. Now, more people can afford furnishing fabrics, so they use more textiles throughout the house. Types include silk, wool, linen, and cotton. Many have shiny surfaces to enhance light. Most fabrics are imported from England, France, India, and China, but English textiles dominate. Around 1790, because cottons are cheaper and more widely available, it becomes fashionable to use printed or white cottons at windows and dressing tables or for slipcovers and bed hangings. Horsehair is commonly used on chair seats and sofas. Chairs and sofas sometimes have fabric festoons beneath the seats. Bed hangings become more complicated in design (Fig. 25-17), and valances are no longer flat and shaped, but feature trimmed swags and festoons. Most people remove window treatments and bed hangings entirely in summer or replace them with lighter weight cottons.

■ *Lighting*. Forms and decoration of lighting fixtures are Neoclassical. Candlesticks and *candelabra* in both silver and brass adopt classical shapes, particularly columns. Whale oil and Argand lamps (Fig. 25-4, 25-10) become more common in the last two decades of the century. Pairs of Argand lamps sit on mantels or tables and are also used on wall brackets or as chandeliers. Shiny surfaces and strategically placed mirrors maximize light, but many rooms are dark even during the day.

■ *Later Interpretations*. Beginning in the late 19th century, Colonial Revival interiors adopt features of the Federal style (Fig. 25-11). Particularly evident are classical details in cornices, paneling, and mantels. Wallpapers from the Federal period are reproduced, and decorating books and periodicals illustrate Adam-style rooms. Elements of Federal interiors continue to highlight public and private interiors to the present. A mixture of furniture styles from Queen Anne to Federal is common in these later rooms.

▲ **25-11.** Later Interpretation: Dupont Dining Room, Winterthur Museum, c. 1930s; Wilmington, Delaware; Colonial Revival. [Courtesy, Winterthur Museum]

FURNISHINGS AND DECORATIVE ARTS

Federal furniture adopts the scale, contrasts, and classical ornament of European Neoclassical styles including Adam, Hepplewhite, and Sheraton from England and the Louis XVI style in France. American furniture usually is simpler than European and incorporates national symbols, such as the eagle, which help to establish and maintain cultural identity.

Light scale, slender proportions, straight and usually tapering legs, reeding, fluting, spade feet, thimble feet, and contrasts of circular and rectangular forms characterize Federal furniture. Emphasis is on straight lines and geometric curves, such as circles or ellipses. Veneers, inlay, marquetry, and classical motifs dominate. Brass toe caps or casters are commonly used on chairs, sofas, and tables. Designs and motifs come from fashionable pattern books, such as *The Cabinet-Maker and Upholsterer's Drawing Book* by Thomas Sheraton.

New kinds of specialized furniture include work and sewing tables, night tables, cellarettes, and knife boxes. Large dining tables that seat 20 or more increase in use. Card tables are more common than tea tables. Sofas and suites of furniture are more fashionable than previously. As before, furniture lines the perimeter of the room when not in use, and the finest pieces fill the most important spaces.

Some cabinetmaking centers, such as Philadelphia and New York, retain their importance. Regional differences continue, although they diminish as the period progresses. Furniture making becomes more specialized to meet increased demands for furniture, so many different artisans work on a piece. Industrialization begins to affect the furniture industry. New sawing techniques produce thinner veneers, and makers increasingly use machines to save time and reduce costs. Large furniture warehouses with stock pieces increase in number, but smaller firms specializing in custom furnishings continue to predominate.

DESIGN SPOTLIGHT

Furniture: Emulating the style of English cabinetmaker George Hepplewhite, these chairs display common characteristics of both Late English Georgian and the American Federal style of the late 18th century. Proportions are light and slender, and details are classically derived. The heart back is composed of three loops. It, along with shield, wheel, and oval backs, is characteristic of prevailing fashions shown in Hepplewhite's book, *The Cabinet-Maker and Upholsterer's Guide*. Here, the splats have carving and a chain of inlaid bellflowers in the center and terminate in an inlaid paterae. The tapered, fluted legs have no feet. Modern horsehair secured to the frame with a double row of nails with gilded heads covers the seats. The shield back, which resembles a Roman shield, is commonly associated with Hepplewhite, although Robert Adam and Sheraton have examples. The shield back has slender bars, and the chair has slender tapered legs terminating in spade feet. The arms curve softly.

▲ **25-12.** Heart-back side chair and shield-back arm chair (next page) in the style of George Hepplewhite, c. 1800; Maryland or Virginia. [Heart-back chair Courtesy of the Diplomatic Reception Rooms, U.S. Department of State]

DESIGN SPOTLIGHT

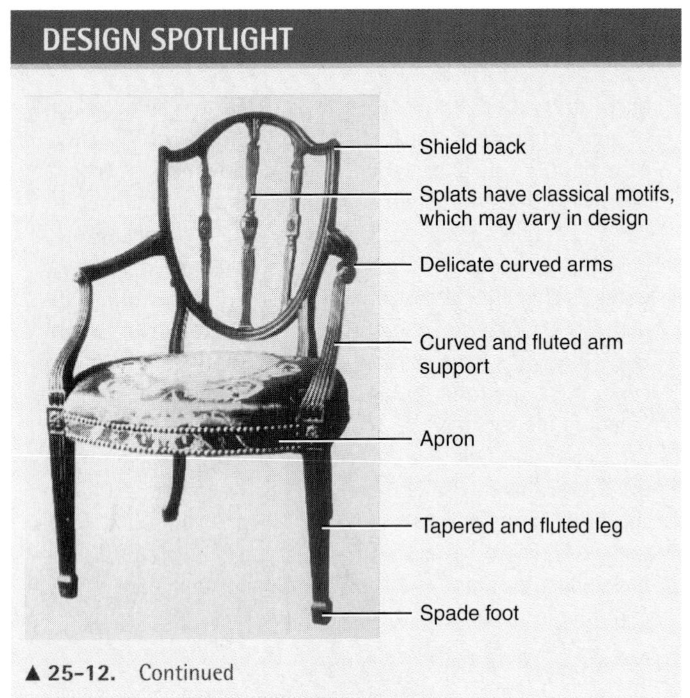

▲ 25-12. Continued

▲ 25-13. Phyfe Room, Winterthur Museum; Wilmington, Delaware; furniture in the Federal style made by or attributed to Duncan Phyfe. [Courtesy, Winterthur Museum]

Private Buildings

■ *Materials*. Woods include such native types as cherry, birch, and maple as well as imported mahogany, ebony, satinwood, and rosewood (Fig. 25-8, 25-12, 25-13, 25-14). Veneers create contrasts of circles, ovals, squares, and rectangles in different colors and grains on façades and tops (Fig. 25-15, 25-16). Light and dark contrasts are common, especially in New England, Philadelphia, and Baltimore. Crossbanding and stringing outline drawers, cabinets, doors, and legs. Marquetry or inlay of classical figures, urns, swags, other classical motifs, eagles, and patriotic symbols embellish façades or tops (Fig. 25-1). Metal pulls for drawers and doors are imported, and most have round or oval shapes. A few are lion masks. Gilded nails, sometimes in swag patterns, secure upholstery to frames (Fig. 25-12).

■ *Color*. Contrasting colors of woods characterize much Federal furniture, but painted furniture also is fashionable. Pieces may be painted completely or have painted flowers, fruit, and classical motifs mixed with other decoration and highlighted with gilding. Colors include black, white, yellow, blue, and red. Baltimore is known for its painted furniture.

■ *Seating*. Chairs and sofas generally follow Hepplewhite and Sheraton forms, but a few emulate Louis XVI (Fig. 25-4, 25-5,

▲ 25-14. Sofa, c. 1810–1815; New York City, New York; attributed to Duncan Phyfe.

▲ **25-15.** Chest of drawers, c. 1795; Maryland. [Courtesy of the Diplomatic Reception Rooms, U.S. Department of State]

25-12, 25-13, 25-17). Chair and settee back shapes include camel, shield, oval, heart, and rectangular. Lolling (or Martha Washington) chairs (Fig. 25-5, 25-17) have tall, upholstered backs and slender legs and arms. Chairs are still more common than sofas or settees. Sofas (Fig. 25-14) have square or curving backs and slender, tapering quadrangular or circular legs. Upholstery is stuffed with horsehair, straw, and other materials, but no springs, resulting in a strong silhouette with sharp edges.

■ *Tables*. Americans use many types of tables including game and card tables, tea tables, breakfast tables, and dining tables (Fig. 25-4, 25-5, 25-13, 25-17). Most have slender, straight tapered legs with fluting, reeding, or stringing. Tops vary in size and shape according to function. Work tables have a bag beneath the table for sewing, a drawer for writing, and occasionally a game board. Pembroke tables are common in bedchambers. Sofa tables sometimes are placed in front of sofas. Dining tables, made in several sections, may have pedestals or slender, tapered legs and are often semicircular with drop leaves. The sections sit against the wall when not in use. Card tables exhibit the greatest variety of forms. Shapes for tops include round, semicircular, oblong, serpentine, ovolo, or canted corners. Painted or inlay urns, eagles, bands, paterae, or husks may highlight the apron. Card tables may have slender, tapered legs with stringing or marquetry or pedestals in the form of lyres, columns, eagles, or dolphins.

■ *Storage*. Chest of drawers, *commodes*, bureaus, and desks and bookcases reflect Neoclassical influence in scale, form, and ornamentation, particularly in contrasts of circles and rectangles or colors of wood (Fig. 25-15, 25-16). Ladies' desks are new. Most have four tapered legs and small drawers and openings sometimes hidden by tambour doors. Sideboards (Fig. 25-4), which display prized decorative items, usually have three or four sections of doors and drawers adorned with veneer patterns and stringing. Shapes include bow, kidney, and serpentine. Legs are slender and tapered.

■ *Beds*. The typical bed has four slender, turned, carved, reeded, or fluted posts and a flat or serpentine tester (Fig. 25-17). Beds remain expensive pieces because of the elaborate hangings.

■ *Decorative Arts*. Americans make their own and import accessories from Europe and China. Tall case clocks often are the most expensive piece in the house, but less expensive wall and shelf clocks gradually supplant them. *Girandole* mirrors with round, gilded, heavy frames and convex glass become fashionable during the period. They may have candleholders and be topped with an eagle. Also fashionable are looking glasses with delicate, gilded moldings and crestings of urns, arabesques, or flowers (Fig. 25-18). In 1785, America initiates trade with China, and soon Chinese export porcelain, silver, and furniture are proudly displayed in American homes. Porcelain designs consist of monograms and American motifs, such as eagles and the United States seal. Americans also import great numbers of English ceramics made for the American market including porcelain, transfer ware with American scenes, and Jasperware (Fig. 25-1). Silver and other metal wares also have classical details, if not classical or classically inspired shapes and forms (Fig. 25-18).

▲ **25-16.** Secretary, c. 1805–1810; New York City, New York. [Courtesy of the Diplomatic Reception Rooms, U.S. Department of State]

▲ **25-17.** McIntire Bedroom, Winterthur Museum; Wilmington, Delaware; furniture of the Federal period. [Courtesy, Winterthur Museum]

(a)

(b)

▲ **25-18.** Decorative Arts: (a) Looking glass, c. 1800–1825; New York, New York, and (b) coffee and tea service, c. 1794; Philadelphia, Pennsylvania; John Le Tellier. [Courtesy of the Diplomatic Reception Rooms, U.S. Department of State]

PART TWO

I. REVOLUTION

From its inception in the mid-18th century, the Industrial Revolution transforms economies, societies, and cultures as well as business, industry, and technology. Industrialization profoundly affects architecture, interiors, furniture, and the decorative arts in form, materials, and technologies. It also changes the way that the creators and consumers think about and produce them and use them in their environment. The relationship or lack thereof to mechanization affects design over the next century and a half.

One of the most significant effects of industrialization is the democratization of design, style, and fashion as a greater variety of goods becomes more available to all levels of society. Individuals learn about the newest fashions and products through World's Fairs, exhibitions, and the print media. Eventually this creates a consumer culture to which designers, producers, and retailers must respond. By the mid-20th century, consumerism increasingly drives design in both creation and production.

The spread of mechanization raises questions about the design of buildings and objects, both in terms of their appearance and their effects on people. Artists, artisans, architects, designers, and others will grapple with these issues for many decades. An early consideration is whether to accept or reject the machine, and then there are debates about how to counter its effects on both design and society. Some concentrate on the negative changes in society from industrialization and prescribe transformations in design to bring reforms. Others want to improve the quality and design of goods as well as the taste and discernment of the consumer. Through their writings and/or work, architects, designers, and theorists strive to define a design language for the machine and seek to identify what it means to be modern—how buildings and products should express their own time. Results are numerous and varied, and they change over time with new theories and ideas, and new art and design movements, and as mechanization is accepted and even embraced.

By altering the way that people live and work, the Industrial Revolution affects the appearance and planning of communities and public and private buildings, ushering in new types, new construction methods, new technologies, and new materials that increase comfort and convenience for all levels of society. Architecture and interior types develop or evolve in response to changes in social patterns, business, and industry. Numbers and types of commercial interiors multiply and focus more upon the needs of function, productivity, workers, and users. In residences, the middle class generally lives less formally and has fewer social rituals, which inspires new types of rooms and modifications in planning. Although taste and fashion continue to drive the design of most spaces, function becomes an important design concept, particularly for kitchens and baths. In both public and private buildings, new types of furnishings develop or older ones evolve in response to changes in working methods, different lifestyles, and new technologies.

Because of rapidly changing fashions and the sheer number of goods available, people need help in making choices. Books and periodicals giving decorating advice proliferate. Interior decoration services spread beyond architects and artists to include large furniture firms, department stores, individual decorators, and, ultimately, interior designers and design firms. With the increased importance of specialization and professionalization throughout the 19th and early 20th centuries, architecture raises its standards for education and practice and separates itself from engineering, artisans, and builders. Interior decoration breaks away from architecture and those who make furniture in the second half of the 19th century. By the mid-20th century, the interior designer with education and training emerges in response to increased emphasis on commercial design and improvements in technology. Additionally, the new professions of furniture and industrial design emerge in the early 20th century. By the beginning of the 21st century, architecture, interior design, furniture design, and industrial design are recognized, separate professions. Additionally, the practice of architecture and interior design requires rigorous professional standards with a strong emphasis on the health, safety, and welfare of the public. Legal recognition and licensing become common practice.

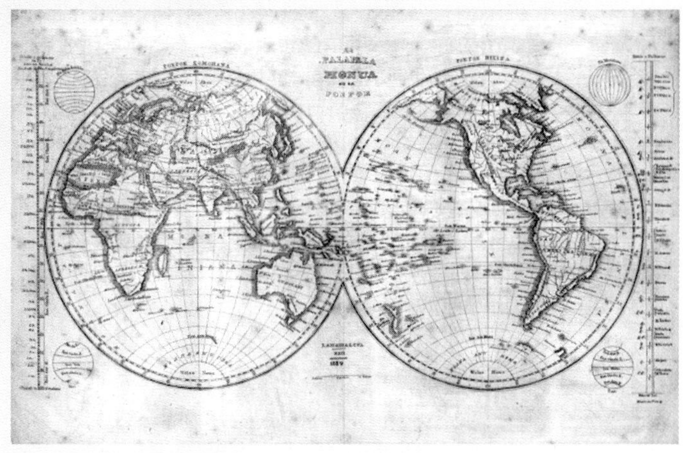

CHAPTER 26

Industrial Revolution

1750–1900s

Buildings, as things made by man, as artifacts, are conditioned by their designer's knowledge and inspiration and by prevailing trends in construction techniques and in aesthetics.

—Dennis Sharp, *Twentieth Century Architecture: A Visual History*, 1991

The Industrial Revolution begins in England in the second half of the 18th century and spreads throughout Europe, North America, and British territories worldwide. Continuing through the 19th century and into the 20th with rapid growth and significant urban expansion, societies are transformed from agrarian economies to industrial ones. New developments in transportation, engineering methods, industrial mechanization, factory production, and construction materials create a new integration of art and technology. Changes in ideas, tastes, and attitudes fostered by the Industrial Revolution lead to innovations in the aesthetics of architecture, interiors, and furnishings.

HISTORICAL AND SOCIAL

Industrialization gradually but profoundly alters economies and societies. Major centers of production such as England, France, and North America see the most significant impact. Improvements in transportation such as expanding railway systems decrease regionalism, promote homogeneity, and support cultural communication. Factories increase in number, size, and complexity, and mass-produced products become more diverse in number and decrease in price. Urban growth gives rise to larger commercial buildings with more varying types of use. Townhouses and apartment buildings multiply in cities.

The wealthy elites continue as the tastemakers, but society is no longer governed by aristocratic ideals. Old class divisions begin to disappear. Members of the newly rich, rapidly expanding middle class who are avid consumers become the trendsetters. They direct more attention to their work and home environments, creating a greater demand for goods and services. At the same time, improvements in industrialization and transportation help distribute manufactured products to wider segments of society. Consequently, shopping through catalogs, popular magazines, retail boutiques, and department stores becomes a common leisure activity as the century progresses. Greater availability tends to make goods disposable; most people no longer have to reuse or make do.

Society continues to be male dominated, and family units remain important, although they are changing in response to urbanization. Distinct gender-role separations are evident in public and private areas of activity. Men go out to work daily, and legally the sole authority for decisions rests with them. Women remain subservient in the workplace and at home. Regarded as nurturers of the family and guardians of domesticity, they are expected to create homes that are shelters and refuges from the negative effects of industrialization and urbanization. Ideas of home as the expression of the wife's creativity and artistic nature, as well as the

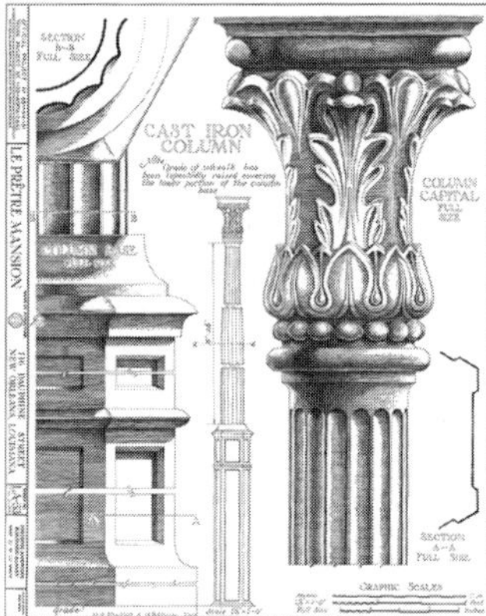

▲ **26-1.** Architectural Details: Wrought iron gate and cast iron column details.

culture and character of the family, help organize society, create its rituals, and legitimize shopping.

CONCEPTS

Besides profoundly changing the economy and society, the Industrial Revolution introduces new materials, techniques, and forms to architecture, interiors, and furnishings. It fosters novelty, innovation, and alteration. Although industrialization makes more goods available, it does not ensure that they are well made or well designed.

Throughout the 19th century, exhibitions and expositions are innovative testing grounds for new design ideas and the introduction of new products. They also are fresh sources for the introduction of new concepts in interior decoration and furnishings. Their displays introduce new styles and trends, which are important to consumers who want to be up-to-date and fashionable. Manufacturers create their finest, most innovative pieces for these exhibitions, and architects design impressive new buildings that affect architectural development. In 1851, the Great Exhibition of the Works of Industry of All Nations held at the Crystal Palace (referred to as the Great Exhibition, and herein as the Crystal Palace Exhibition; Fig. 26-3) in London becomes the largest international exhibition ever held to display machine-made goods as well as handcrafted products. The Great Exhibition establishes Great Britain's industrial supremacy in the world. More exhibitions follow in prominent European and American cities.

Consumer tastes, speed of production, and distribution dictate the look of manufactured goods. Customers want comfort or at least its appearance. Objects must look expensive, which demands visual complexity. Most people are proud of technological advances and regard them as evidence of progress. Despite widespread admiration for the machine and new goods and materials, for most of the 19th century, buildings, interiors, and furnishings look backward in design instead of forward, almost an antithesis of progress. They rarely incorporate new materials and products, but instead rely on those of earlier periods. Old forms, designs, and construction techniques are familiar and therefore less threatening, so new technology is largely ignored, except to address comfort and production.

Ultimately, a reaction begins as those who recognize the poor design and quality of manufactured goods look for ways to improve them, reform taste, and address social problems. Throughout the 19th century, many reformers advocate rejecting the machine and returning to handmade techniques.

MOTIFS

■ *Motifs.* Historical features from past styles shape the visual language from the mid-18th century well into the 20th century. Motifs generally relate to the period influences and vary within developments and countries. Details that emphasize technology (Fig. 26-1, 26-14, 26-18) appear later in architecture and interiors, as illustrated on gates, porches, balconies, columns, hardware, chimneypieces, and furnishings.

ARCHITECTURE

Social, economic, and technical changes in the 19th century lead to new building types, such as railway stations, shopping arcades, office buildings, and factories. These progressive commercial environments require new materials and construction methods and demand the expertise of engineers to achieve the necessary wide expanses of free open space. A split emerges between engineering and architecture as the century evolves. Engineers focus on the new, functional, and innovative structures, whereas most architects continue designing with traditional styles, materials, and techniques.

Engineering feats provide landmarks and set the stage for significant changes in the direction of design throughout the 19th century. Reflecting improvements in transportation and new

▲ **26-2.** Iron bridge, 1779; Coalbrookdale, Shropshire, England; Thomas F. Pritchard and Abraham Darby III.

construction materials, England leads the transformation. In 1779, the country announces the first iron bridge at Coalbrookdale (Fig. 26-2). In 1825, railway systems begin in England and expand rapidly there and in other countries as the century progresses. In 1851, gardener Joseph Paxton, using his knowledge of greenhouse construction, designs the Crystal Palace Exhibition building (Fig. 26-3) in London with prefabricated parts for construction, standardized sections of iron and glass, and large expanses of open space. In 1889, Gustav Eiffel leaves his mark through the design of the Eiffel Tower for the Paris Exposition (Fig. 26-4).

Throughout the century, new building types and techniques gradually transform the appearance of architecture into one that integrates engineering technology as a part of the built form. Examples include railway stations (Fig. 26-13), exhibition halls (Fig. 26-3), shopping arcades, department stores, office buildings (Fig. 26-5, 26-11), factories, warehouses, and industrial buildings. Within this evolution, architects design monumental commercial building façades with embellishments of past styles while creating interiors with innovations in structural form and space.

Changes brought by the Industrial Revolution also transform residential construction so that home building becomes an industry after midcentury. Eventually, prefabricated housing comes into being. Both balloon framing and prefabricated housing require standardized parts (Fig. 26-6, 26-7), but use wood construction rather than iron or steel. They offer inexpensive housing alternatives that can be ordered from catalogs, cater to the ex-

DESIGN SPOTLIGHT

Architecture and Interior: The design concept of the Crystal Palace is new and innovative, and derives from greenhouses and conservatories of the time. The largest building ever constructed of cast iron and glass, it features a modular design and prefabricated parts that allow factories to easily mass-produce the quantity of components needed. Parts arrive at the site preassembled, allowing the construction at an unprecedented rate of months instead of years. Promoted and organized by Prince Albert, husband of England's Queen Victoria, the structure showcases the first international exhibition for the display of machine-made goods and handcrafted products. The Exhibition has more than 10,000 exhibits from many countries. Interior space encompasses the enormous area of 770,000 square feet. Successful, fast construction and public acclaim open the door for more buildings like it. After the fair closes, the Crystal Palace is reassembled in a park outside of London. Fire destroys it in 1936.

▲ **26-3.** Crystal Palace and exhibition hall, 1851; London, England; Sir Joseph Paxton.

panding middle classes, and require no architect for implementation. Both help expansion in Canada and the United States, particularly as settlements move westward.

For most of the century, compositions of all building types display a distinct historical flavor, whether through revivals of past styles, direct quotations from precursors, or applied ornament. But toward the end of the 19th century, commercial buildings appear with little or no reference to past styles and traditional imagery. Often designed by architects, these structures integrate engineering technology, exhibit simplicity in design, emphasize structure and iron or steel-frame construction, and display extreme verticality.

Public and Private Buildings

■ *Mail-Order Houses*. House designs copied or ordered by mail from pattern books, trade catalogs, architectural journals, and manufacturing companies become more common as the 19th century progresses (Fig. 26-6). Publications feature exterior and interior designs, floor plans, and architectural details. Construction materials to build a complete house can be ordered from a variety of catalogs or companies, including Sears, Roebuck & Company.

DESIGN SPOTLIGHT

Architect and designer Owen Jones decorates the interiors with red, blue, yellow, and white. The vast interiors are filled with displays of industry; machinery; manufactured products such as furniture, fabrics, and wallpapers; and numerous consumer goods from England, Europe, and other parts of the world. A series of courts exhibit art and architecture from ancient Egypt to the Renaissance. Among them are the Medieval Court by A. W. N. Pugin, and Alhambra Court by Owen Jones.

▲ **26-3.** Continued

▲ **26-4.** Eiffel Tower, 1889; Paris, France; A. Gustav Eiffel, with elevators by Elisha Graves Otis.

■ *Site Orientation*. In the 1840s and 1850s, as city centers become overcrowded and overdeveloped, new housing spreads to the suburbs where houses are grouped along smaller streets to create self-contained residential neighborhoods.

■ *Floor Plans*. Plans for factories, railway stations (Fig. 26-13), shopping arcades, and other building types grow out of function. Most buildings continue traditional planning patterns with central vertical circulation cores (Fig. 26-11) and partitioned walls, but large public areas begin to encompass huge open areas of space delineated with iron columns. Classical attributes such as symmetry, regularity, unity, and harmony continue to be important design principles in plans.

Dwellings often have more and differentiated spaces with public and private areas more carefully separated. Large houses frequently have double parlors, a library, and a conservatory. As the century progresses, kitchens (Fig. 26-15) reflect greater attention to appliance selection, better storage, and functional planning. Bathrooms (Fig. 26-16), which become more common throughout the century, incorporate a sink, tub, toilet, and possibly a bidet and shower to add convenience and comfort. Elevators (Fig. 26-11) gradually supplant stairs as the main source of vertical circulation in multistory apartment complexes.

■ *Materials*. New materials include brick in more colors and artificial stone. Improved manufacturing processes increase the use of wrought and cast iron decoratively and structurally (Fig. 26-1, 26-3, 26-4, 26-10, 26-11). New manufacturing techniques, developed in France, increase the availability of glass in many forms, particularly in large sheets.

■ *Construction*. Many commercial buildings use iron and glass for the entire structure or only for roofs and walls. Prefabricated standardized parts derived from the Crystal Palace (Fig. 26-3) are more commonplace as the century progresses. In the 1840s, the cast-iron skeleton essential for tall buildings makes its appearance in New York City. By 1853, Elisha Graves Otis introduces the safety elevator in New York. Toward the end of the 19th century, the Chicago School architects introduce iron and steel structural skeletons covered by masonry façades (Fig. 26-5).

■ *Balloon Frame Construction*. Residential construction methods, primarily in North America, change during the second half of the 19th century from timber framing with mortise and tenon joints or stacked brick methods to balloon frame construction (Fig. 26-7) with prefabricated parts and standardized sizes of lumber. The new technique incorporates a frame of wooden studs that forms the height of the building, rests on floor joists, and is nailed in place.

▲ **26-5.** Reliance Building, 1890–1894; Chicago, Illinois; Daniel H. Burnham and John W. Root.

DESIGN SPOTLIGHT

Architecture: The Albert Trinler House is a mail-order house, a type of new residential construction prevalent during the late 19th and early 20th centuries. Offered by many companies and illustrated in paperback booklets, this new house type appeals to an expanding middle class seeking inexpensive homes. The Palliser brothers begin their business in Bridgeport, Connecticut, in the 1870s building speculative housing and then begin to offer houses by mail. Their catalogs provide plans, elevations, details, and specifications for a set fee. After purchasing the plans, clients then hire a local builder to construct their new houses. This process becomes common throughout the United States for numerous houses in suburb developments.

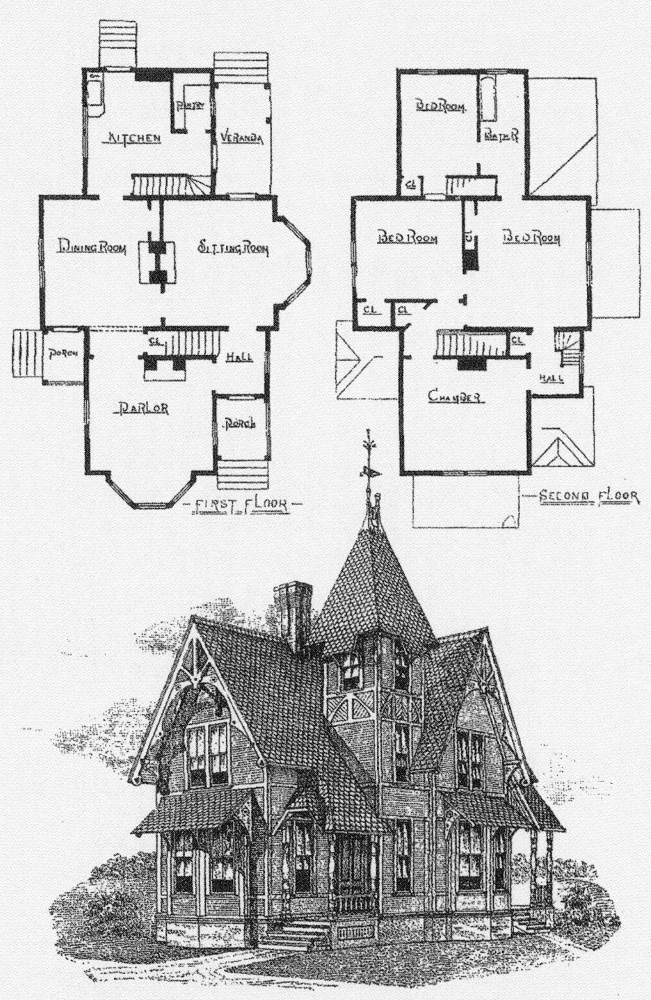

▲ **26-6.** Albert Trinler House; New Albany, Indiana; house and plans published in *American Cottage Homes*, 1878; George and Charles Palliser.

■ *Paint*. For most of the 19th century, individuals mix their own paint, either from pastes or dry pigments supplied by manufacturers. Ready-made paint generally is not available until the third quarter of the 19th century because manufacturing, storing, and shipping paint presents many difficulties that must be overcome. Additionally, a great deal of capital is required to make and supply mixed paint. By the late 1860s, manufacturers offer ready-mixed paint in a variety of colors, including earth and stone colors and sanded finishes. Expanded transportation systems bring these products to more consumers. Consequently, color schemes for exteriors and interiors become complex with a multiplicity of colors, and paint makers begin to advertise their products with colorful paint sample cards.

■ *Façades*. Façades of large commercial buildings exhibit architectural features from past styles, classical ordering, design regularity, unity, harmony, and monumental scale (Fig. 26-3, 26-5). Those that develop primarily from engineering concepts reflect diversity in appearance, form, and scale and often lack ornamentation (Fig. 26-4). Windows generally are symmetrical in scale, shape, and placement. Grand, prominent entry doors define the front façade and announce the public circulation path. Houses vary in design, but generally represent the popular historical revival styles and influences common to the period, whether they are architect or builder designed or ordered by mail (Fig. 26-6).

■ *Roofs*. Roof types and heights vary based on the particular building type and location. Office structures have flatter rooflines with cornices, and railway stations display multiple roof heights and forms.

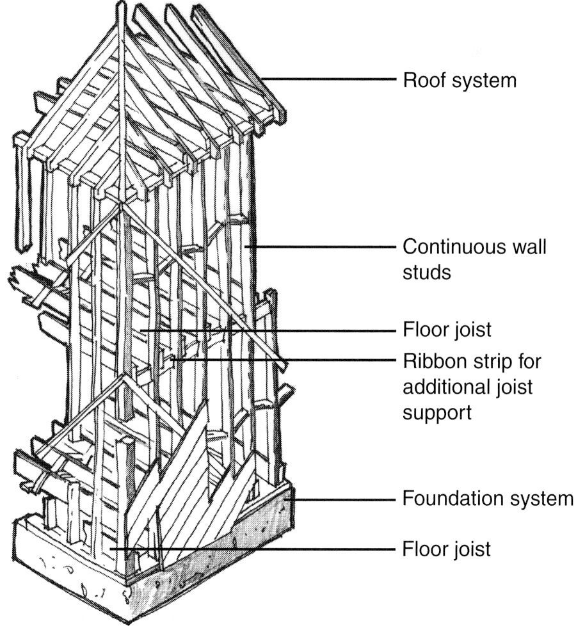

▲ **26-7.** Balloon frame construction.

▲ **26-8.** Later Interpretation: Lloyd's Building, 1978–1986; London, England; Richard Rogers. Late Modern.

■ *Later Interpretations.* As the 20th century progresses, architecture and engineering technology integrate fully in various types of structures, such as the Lloyd's Building in London (Fig. 26-8). Buildings continue to illustrate more technological advancements through construction, materials, furnishings, heating and ventilating, and lighting. Additionally, apartment buildings and houses of the 19th century are excellent design sources for residential developments into the 21st century. Designers and consumers draw inspiration from past styles to establish cultural identities, character, and human scale.

INTERIORS

The Industrial Revolution brings new technology that significantly improves the quality of life for many and revolutionizes both work and home environments. Interiors increasingly emphasize function, efficiency, and comfort—considerations that become standard for appearance and beauty in the 20th century. Conveniences derived from better lighting, heating, and plumbing increase throughout the century. Manufacturers produce more furniture, decorative objects, textiles, and wallpaper for an expanding consumer market. Improvements in rail and ship transportation make products that result in comfortable interiors available to more people. Consequently, rooms have more upholstered seating, carpeting, and practical conveniences.

Commercial interiors evidence technological innovations that integrate historic revival influences or new and later reform design ideas. Most feature at least one or two prominent, large-scaled spaces conveying the character and richness of the interior design. In these spaces a central axis defines the major circulation path from outside to inside. Sometimes users must go through small vestibules, up grand staircases, or through long corridors to access the more important space. This procession, which is a component of historical influence, adds to the awareness of arrival and may be similar to entering a grand space such as a Gothic cathedral. Architectural details, surface applications, furnishings, and lighting enhance the unified interior. Important public spaces include the main concourses of railway stations (Fig. 26-13), chief display areas of exhibition halls (Fig. 26-3), and the foremost lobbies and central stairwells of office buildings (Fig. 26-10, 26-11).

Some of these interiors become noteworthy because of their prominence in the community, popularity with the public, individual impressiveness, technological advances, and/or the recognition given the architect or designer (Fig. 26-9, 26-10). Less important commercial interiors may not show as much attention to design but often incorporate the functional aspects required to provide service, convenience, and efficiency for the users. As the 20th century progresses, offices (Fig. 26-12) exhibit significant improvements with better work areas, furnishings, equipment, and lighting. Factories and industrial complexes also focus on function over design and improved production systems.

Residential interiors usually reveal references to past historical periods. Some interiors feature new materials, such as iron and glass, but forms and motifs generally remain historical until the late 19th century. During this period, architects and designers create residential interiors for wealthy clients who want to convey their status to society. This is also true for design intellectuals who see themselves as innovators in taste and messengers of reform. The expanding middle class, however, looks to other sources for help and advice in decorating. As a result, books related to the design of interiors and their furnishings increase dramatically, especially after midcentury. Written by architects, artists, and

DESIGN SPOTLIGHT

Interior: The Main Reading Room in the *Bibliothéque Nationale,* an important architectural interior, illustrates an early use of iron, an innovative structural design, meticulous planning, and large scale. Slender iron columns and arches support nine domes of terra-cotta tiles, each pierced with a glass oculus (skylight). For the first time, modern structural materials are given a decorative and functional role in a significant interior. The vaults and wall surfaces above the built-in bookcases display elaborate Pompeian wall decorations, which offer colorful accents to a generally monochromatic color scheme. Natural lighting penetrates downward from the skylights, and task-oriented lamps on table surfaces provide artificial lighting. The impressive interior maintains a sense of order and organization through its simplicity and lack of clutter.

dilettantes, these volumes help in the quest for what is perceived as the correct home decoration. In larger homes, new rooms include double parlors, music and ballrooms, a library, breakfast room, and conservatory. Kitchens and bathrooms gain importance in the house as more attention is given to function, comfort, and appearance.

Public and Private Buildings

■ *Heating*. Wood-burning fireplaces remain common, but other types of heating appear, such as coal grates, Franklin stoves, and central heating (Fig. 26-14) in public and private buildings. Although stoves are used from the middle of the 18th century onward, they do not supplant fireplaces because of the associated smells. Central heating systems, in which a wood or coal furnace heats several rooms, are invented in the 1830s. Steam heat emerges in the 1850s. Critics favor fireplaces throughout the century, however, believing that stoves and furnaces create bad air.

▲ **26-10.** Main lobby, Rookery Building, 1885–1888; Chicago, Illinois; Daniel H. Burnham and John W. Root, with interiors modified or redesigned by Frank Lloyd Wright.

DESIGN SPOTLIGHT

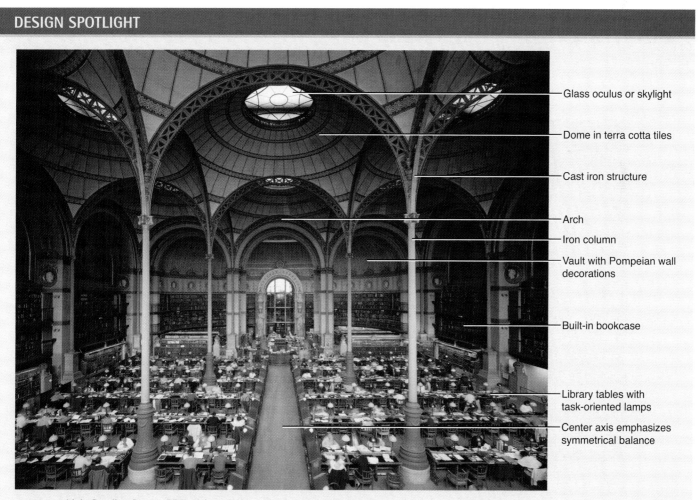

Glass oculus or skylight

Dome in terra cotta tiles

Cast iron structure

Arch

Iron column

Vault with Pompeian wall decorations

Built-in bookcase

Library tables with task-oriented lamps

Center axis emphasizes symmetrical balance

▲ **26-9.** Main Reading Room, *Bibliothéque Nationale*, 1858; Paris, France; Pierre-François-Henri Labrouste.

▲ **26-11.** Central court, Bradbury Building, 1893; Los Angeles, California; George H. Wyman. This office interior illustrates an extensive use of wrought iron in the central court and an open elevator cage.

▲ **26-12.** Office, American Type Founders Company, 1902; New York City, New York.

▲ **26-13.** Concourse with steel frame support system, Pennsylvania Railroad Terminal Station, 1906–1910; New York City, New York; McKim, Mead, and White.

▲ **26-14.** Heating Sources: Chimneypiece with coal grate and Franklin stove, mid- to late 19th century; England and the United States.

■ *Kitchens*. New appliances, better storage, and efficient planning increasingly define the kitchen as the 19th century progresses (Fig. 26-15). Cast-iron cooking ranges, introduced in the 1840s, improve in design and make cooking easier. Refrigeration remains primitive throughout the 19th century with iceboxes placed in convenient locations, such as porches, for ice delivery instead of in consideration of cooks. The first commercial freezing machine appears in Europe in the 1860s, but practical, compact units for the home are not available until the 20th century. Until municipal waterworks bring running water into the home, servants or housewives either carry water into the kitchen in buckets or use a hand pump in the kitchen. Metal or cast-iron sinks materialize in the second half of the 18th century and become more evident throughout the 19th century. Built-in kitchen cabinets arrive in the 1920s.

■ *Bathrooms*. Throughout the 19th century, people use outdoor privies and bathe at bedroom washstands with a bowl and pitcher or in small tubs brought inside for that purpose. Although some hotels have water closets and bathtubs in the early 19th century, they are rare in homes. Concerns for health, sanitation, and convenience provide the impetus for bathrooms to be incorporated into the house (Fig. 26-16), but this cannot be accomplished until there is an adequate water supply and sewerage. The first patent for a water closet that empties the bowl is given in 1772 to Alexander Cumming. Improvements continue, but water closets remain expensive, and people distrust having them inside their homes until the later 19th century. In the mid-19th century, houses begin having built-in bathtubs. By the early 20th century, most bathrooms have toilets, tubs, and sinks, and by the 1920s, bathrooms appear as they do today with more multifunctional areas.

▲ **26-15.** Kitchen: Stove, late 19th century; United States.

▲ **26-16.** Bathroom: Sinks, tubs, and toilets, late 19th century; United States.

■ *Materials*. The interior materials may repeat the exterior materials in architectural form and details. Interior surface treatments, however, vary depending on the type of structure, with expensive, impressive materials used for important and/or public spaces (Fig. 26-9, 26-10, 26-11, 26-13) such as hotel and office building lobbies and less expensive, plainer materials reserved for factories and industrial complexes.

■ *Color*. Hues are brighter and come from synthetic pigments, which offer a wider range of colors than earlier. New hues include chrome yellow, ultramarine blue, and bright green. Colors also reflect changes in lighting, so with dim light in earlier periods, colors are intense. As illumination increases with the introduction of electric lighting, colors become paler. This also reflects an increasing emphasis on health and sanitation concerns because white is regarded as sanitary. Customs change too, with more social activities in the home at night, so there is a preference for rich, cheerful colors that are attractive at all times. Various publications promote the use of certain colors for particular spaces and to replicate historical styles.

■ *Floors*. Floors (Fig. 26-10, 26-12) are of wood, tile, stone, and masonry in simple or complex patterns in both public and private spaces. Wall-to-wall carpeting is used more and more because of the need for acoustical control and due to consumer taste. Industrialization reduces its price and makes less-expensive forms, such as ingrains, more widely available.

■ *Wallpaper*. With the introduction of continuous rolls of machine-made paper and roller printing in the first quarter of the 19th century, wallpaper becomes cheaper and more readily available than earlier hand-blocked papers are. Machine-made papers have smaller repeats printed with thinner inks on standard sizes of paper. Decorating and advice books promote wallpaper, so its use increases throughout the 19th century.

■ *Textiles*. Mechanization of textile production begins in the second half of the 18th century. By the first half of the 19th century, power looms and improvements in cylinder printing and dye technology are producing a greater variety of cheaper textiles, so their use increases. Textiles are hand-block printed until about 1818 when machine roller printing begins to take over. About midcentury, wall-to-wall carpeting becomes common for important rooms, opulent window treatments are more universal, upholstered furniture increases, and a variety of textiles appear in a rooms.

■ *Lighting*. Industrialization brings significant improvements in artificial lighting (Fig. 26-9, 26-12, 26-17) in the form of kerosene, oil, gas, and electric lighting fixtures for public and private interiors. At the beginning of the 19th century, oil lamps are more common because they offer flexibility and give greater illumination than candles do. The Argand lamp (Fig. 26-17), invented by François-Pierre Ami Argand in 1781, is a tubular wick lamp with an oil reservoir that greatly enhances overall illumination, but its reservoir casts a shadow. Because of this, improved designs, some using alternative fuels, soon follow.

Introduced in England in 1787, gas lighting becomes more common in factories and public buildings because it is a cheap, readily available lighting source and offers even brighter illumination. By midcentury, it begins to be slowly adopted for residences when means are invented to lessen smoke and odors, however, gasoliers (Fig. 26-17) and gas wall brackets have limited flexibility because of the rigid stem that houses the gas pipe. Tubes attached to a gas source and a table lamp permit limited portability. Kerosene, a hydrocarbon lamp fuel patented in 1854, replaces oil fixtures, offers greater portability, and increases in popularity until the end of the century. Invented in 1879, the electric lamp provides increased illumination but has limited portability because of its connection to an electrical outlet. Early fixtures combine gas and electricity, a reflection of the uncertainty of consumer acceptance and the early unreliability of these power sources. Electric lighting does not come into general use until the early 20th century.

(a)

(b)

(c)

(d)

▲ **26–17.** Lighting: (a) Argand lamp, (b) astral lamp, (c) hanging oil lamp, and (d) gasolier, late 18th to 19th centuries; United States.

FURNISHINGS AND DECORATIVE ARTS

The furniture industry gradually mechanizes during the 19th century. Standardized parts and machine-carved ornament replace much handwork. By midcentury, large manufacturers begin to replace small shops. Some workshops of individual craftspersons making furniture at customers' requests manage to survive into the 20th century. Factories, located near large stands of timber, water, and railways, produce quantities of furniture and ship it to retailers, furniture shops, and department stores that sell it to consumers. Catalogs, which support a growing interest in selection, quality, and price, become a popular source of furnishings for the middle class. Through books, periodicals, and exhibitions, the middle and working classes see the latest fashions and attempt to copy them in less expensive ways such as do-it-yourself methods.

Furniture for the home, the workplace, and the garden (Fig. 26-18) becomes more movable and flexible, reflecting changes in lifestyles. Office furniture (Fig. 26-12, 26-20) becomes more diverse in function, type, selection, and materials. Furniture for the home offers more flexibility, and new and various types increase throughout the 19th century. Built-in furniture becomes more popular. Arrangements continue to take advantage of natural lighting, but new, portable sources of illumination permit greater placement variety. With new types of lighting, furniture assumes a more fixed location to garner the most illumination possible. For example, in offices, desks are placed next to a gas wall sconce or window; in a parlor, a table with chairs may center directly under a gasolier with other chairs located by windows. With the advent of electric lighting, furnishings are grouped near electrical outlets.

▲ **26-18.** Garden Furniture: Chair in cast iron, mid-19th century; United States.

DESIGN SPOTLIGHT

Furniture: In the 1830s, Thonet patents a method for mass-producing bentwood furniture made of beech rods in standardized sizes and shapes. The curved, contoured frames have no complicated carved joints, so they are easy to assemble. Variations of the main chair design include the popular Vienna Café chair, bentwood rocker, and several tables. Chairs are shipped all over the world and are frequently used in restaurants because they are light, strong, and portable. In 1851, Thonet shows his furniture at the Crystal Palace Exhibition and later at the Philadelphia Centennial International Exhibition in 1876. Both exhibitions help popularize his furniture throughout Europe and North America.

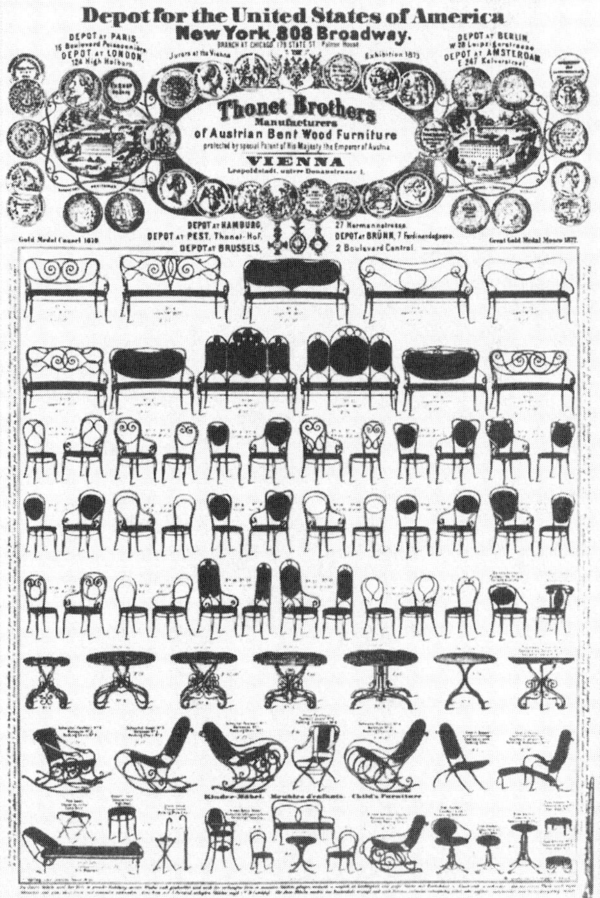

▲ **26-19.** Chairs, sofas, rockers, and tables, mid- to late 19th century; advertisement poster from 1847 for Thonet Brothers, Manufacturers of Austrian Bent Wood Furniture; Vienna, Austria; Michael Thonet.

Public and Private Buildings

■ *Mail-Order Furniture*. In the late 19th century, mail-order furniture allows the middle class to be stylish at reasonable prices. In North America, companies such as Sears, Roebuck & Company; Montgomery Ward & Company; the Hudson Bay Company; and manufacturers in Grand Rapids, Michigan, market their goods through catalogs that feature all types of furniture for both the office and home. These catalogs provide the foundation for a major furniture industry that flourishes throughout North America and Europe in the 20th century.

■ *Materials*. While wood is still the most common material, new materials include papier-mâché, coal, iron, zinc, steel, and rubber. Cane, rattan, and wicker furnishings, although not new, are fashionable. Cast iron is popular for garden furniture (Fig. 26-18), beds, umbrella stands, and hallstands. Metal becomes common for use in furniture parts.

■ *Construction*. Machine-made furniture gradually replaces handmade throughout the 19th century. Patents for new inventions such as planers, band and circular saws, lathes, and carving and boring machines facilitate the process.

■ *Seating*. New types of seating emerge throughout the 19th century, reflecting the new types of interior spaces for work, play, and home. In the 1830s, Michael Thonet in Austria pioneers mass-produced bentwood furniture that is shipped unassembled (Fig. 26-19). Exhibited widely, his furniture becomes popular throughout Europe and North America. Multipurpose furniture, auditorium seating, ice cream parlor chairs, metal rockers, and barber chairs become more commonplace. The invention of coil springs in 1822, by George Junigl of Vienna, gives rise to overstuffed upholstered furniture with rounded edges and deep tufting, which is fashionable during the Victorian period and into the 20th century.

DESIGN SPOTLIGHT

Furniture: The Wooten desk, an ingenious piece of patent furniture, is wildly popular in the 1870s and 1880s in North America. Shown in the Centennial International Exhibition in 1876, it has numerous drawers, files, and pigeonholes to assist with paper organization and becomes a symbol of status and orderliness for the prosperous businessman. The functional design emphasizes efficiency, flexibility, and practicality. The invention of the typewriter and other forms of office equipment renders Wooten desks less functional, so they decline in popularity.

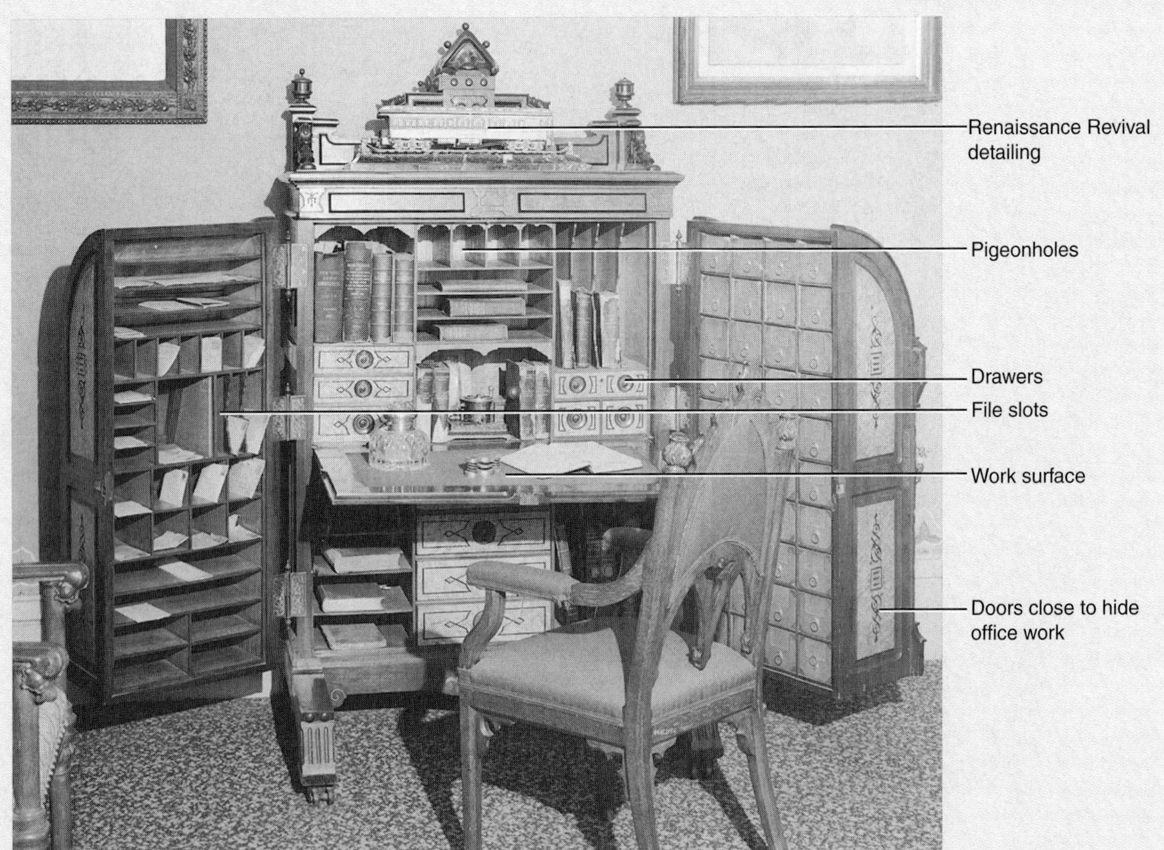

▲ **26-20.** Wooden desk (cabinet secretary), Centennial International Exhibition, 1876; Philadelphia, Pennsylvania; manufactured by the Wooten Desk Company in Indianapolis, Indiana. Renaissance Revival.

J. LATE NEOCLASSICAL

Late Neoclassical begins in France in about 1790 when it sheds its Roman complexity and ornament for an image that is simpler, often more politically appropriate, and more inspired by ancient Greece than ancient Rome. By this time, scholarship indicates that ancient Greece influenced Roman art to a far greater extent than was previously thought. Increased admiration and appreciation for ancient Greece leads to a preference for the simplicity of its art and architecture. Drawing from scholarship and archaeology, architects and designers emphasize archaeological correctness and often copy or adapt antique examples for architecture, interiors, furniture, and decorative arts. Following the French and American Revolutions, Neoclassicism aligns with the new, more democratic forms of government and becomes a favored style for government buildings and artistic propaganda. By the 1820s (earlier in England), designers begin to tire of the limitations of classicism and seek inspiration in other periods, such as the Middle Ages, and even different cultures, such as that of China.

Under Napoleon I, Late Neoclassical France resumes her leadership in art and design. Like the Bourbon monarchs, Napoleon recognizes the importance of art to the state. His principal architects, Charles Percier and Pierre-François-Léonard Fontaine, create what becomes the Empire style to glorify the emperor and help legitimize his reign. The Empire style in France largely manifests in interiors and furniture because little noteworthy building takes place. In imitation of Napoleon I, other European sovereigns and nobles adopt the Empire style for their surroundings. The middle classes in Germany and Austria follow a simplified Empire style known as Biedermeier. Lacking an emperor to glorify, neither England nor America develops a strong Empire interior style, but French Empire furniture is fashionable in both countries.

Greek Revival originates in England as the first of the great architectural revival styles of the 19th century. However, it is more popular and lasts longer in Scotland, Germany, and America. The style in all countries is associated with new building types, such as museums that are regarded as temples of art. In Germany and America, Greek Revival acquires political overtones. In the United States, it becomes a visual metaphor for the democratic government, whereas Greek Revival represents the German spirit in Germany. In contrast, the Picturesque or Romantic Movement in England promotes a greater taste for other cultures and modes. Empire or classical is but one aspect of England's Regency period, which also shows influences from Greece, Rome, Egypt, China, India, and Gothic.

During the early 19th century, the changes brought on by the Industrial Revolution increase, making its influence felt more than ever before. New technology and inventions facilitate mass production, which makes an increasing array of goods available to more people. Periodicals join books as the means of spreading the newest styles and fashions.

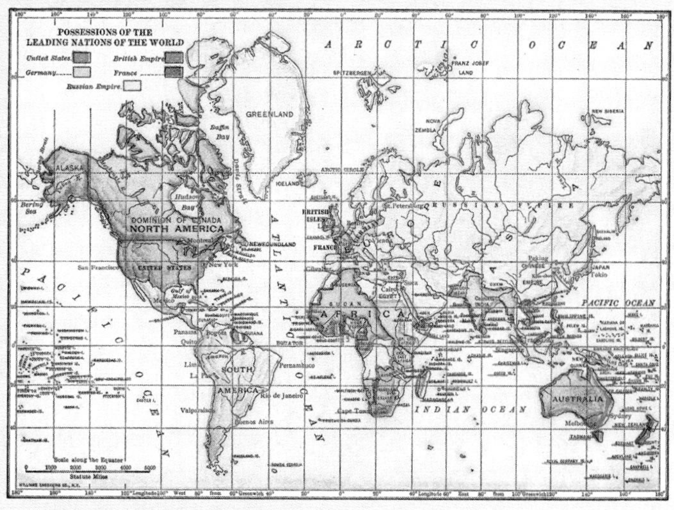

CHAPTER 27

Directoire, French Empire

1789–1815

Persuaded as we are that this sickness, which is that of modern taste . . . , must find its treatment and cure in the examples and models of antiquity—followed not blindly but with the discernment suitable to modern manners, customs, and materials—we have striven to imitate the antique in its spirit, principles, and maxims, which are timeless.

—Percier and Fontaine, *Discours préliminaire, Recueil de décorations intérieures*, 1801

Neoclassicism dominates the period, although it changes in response to political and social developments. Little important building takes place, so interiors and furniture are the main purveyors of style. In interiors and furniture, the simple, plainer Directoire defines the beginning of the post-Revolutionary period and evolves into the heavier, more majestic Empire. Architect–designers Charles Percier and Pierre-François-Léonard Fontaine create the Empire style, as dictated by Napoleon Bonaparte as Emperor of France.

HISTORICAL AND SOCIAL

The French Revolution, which begins with great hopes of changing injustices in the political and social systems, deteriorates into terror, violence, and random destruction. Ultimately, for real and trumped-up crimes against the people, members of all classes are executed, including King Louis XVI and his queen. Between 1789 and 1795, new regimes rise and fall quickly, leaving the country in shambles—its political, economic, and social systems all but destroyed.

A five-person Directory, as stipulated by the new constitution, governs France between 1795 and 1799. Although it makes some progress in restoring the country economically and socially, its incompetence and dishonesty limit its effectiveness. Additionally, conflicts between the Royalists, determined to restore the monarchy, and the Jacobins, who want a democratic republic, threaten the fragile peace. Hoping to increase financial stability, the Directory authorizes military aggression abroad and appoints Napoleon Bonaparte as commander-in-chief. Military victories reap some success while earning Napoleon national recognition and helping to restore French confidence.

During the years of the Directory, a different social life and structure evolve in France. A *nouveau riche* class of businessmen, financiers, and speculators begins to display its wealth in newly purchased and refurbished townhouses that once belonged to the aristocracy. Times that are more settled foster tastes for luxury and pleasure, and fashionable society once again attends concerts, plays, games, and fireworks. The middle class assumes a new and greater importance.

By 1799, the power and influence of the Directory are so deteriorated that Napoleon, along with others, easily seizes power in a *coup d'état*. Napoleon sets up the Consulate, with himself as *Premier Consul*, and strives to unify France, heal the wounds of the Revolution, and create a stable government. Gradually, he increases the powers of the Consulate, while decreasing those of the various legislative bodies. In 1802, he revises the constitution to declare himself Consul for life. In 1804, Napoleon declares himself Emperor, and thereby dissolves the Consulate and establishes a hereditary monarchical regime in France. He reigns as Napoleon I from 1804 to 1815. Although he presents himself as a man of peace and defender of the Republic, Napoleon believes that the way to peace is through military might. In 1805, he renews aggression against the nations of Europe. However, his efforts to enforce a blockade against Britain and to invade Spain and Russia lead to the Empire's downfall. Napoleon abdicates in 1814 but retains the title of Napoleon I until 1815. Louis XVIII, younger brother of Louis XVI, then becomes king.

French society during the time of the Empire is as glittering and magnificent as when the Bourbons reigned. Realizing the advantages to the Empire and society as a whole, Napoleon requires brilliant entertainments, although he rarely participates himself. Court etiquette and dress again become as rigid and codified as in the days of the French monarchy. Following the lead of Empress Josephine, Empress Marie Louis, Madame Récamier, and other noble women who are aware of the latest innovations in design commission the finest of furnishings for their homes. They host *salons*, gatherings of eminent people, which are once again fashionable. As the period progresses, women's freedoms, acquired during the Directoire period, diminish. Napoleon opens more schools for women, but their learning is restricted to such things as painting, dance, and sewing. The *Code Napoleon* reestablishes the husband as head of the house, so women again take a secondary role and are expected to remain at home.

CONCEPTS

Neoclassicism characterizes French architecture throughout the period. In contrast, three styles—Directoire, Consulate, and Empire—define interiors and furniture. Like architecture, they stem from Neoclassicism, but each has a different focus and appearance that reflects the political and social climate of its day.

Directoire, or *Le Style Républicain,* is named for the Directory that rules France from 1789 to 1799. A transition style, it links Louis XVI and Empire and reflects a more spare and Grecian classicism. Designers eliminate all references to the former Bourbon kings and strive to emulate more closely antique (primarily ancient Greek) concepts and designs.

During the time of the Consulate (1799–1804), the early years of Napoleon's rule, designers interpret classicism by emphasizing Imperial Roman and Egyptian influences over Grecian ones. During this period, increased formality, monumentality, and ornamentation reflect France's increasing stability, wealth, and confidence.

The fully developed Empire style, coinciding with the reign of Napoleon I, glorifies him and his empire. Recognizing the value of art to educate people about his greatness and legitimize his rule, very early in his reign Napoleon calls for writers and artists to create an image of him as a man of destiny, a modern Caesar, a hero who has earned the right to rule France. Paintings and images of the Emperor present a heroic character to reinforce the military origins of the empire. Architect–designers Charles Percier and Pierre-François-Léonard Fontaine document their design ideas in their book *Recueil de décorations intérieures*, published in 1801, 1812, and 1827.

MOTIFS

■ *Motifs*. Classical motifs common through 1815 (Fig. 27-1, 27-6, 27-7, 27-8, 27-9, 27-11, 27-13) include the classical figure, acanthus leaf, swag, rinceau, rosette, anthemion, scroll, arabesque, cartouche, vase, and lyre. Common during Directoire are lozenges, rosettes, spirals, and symbols of the Revolution, such as the oak leaf and clasped hands. During the Consulate years, Roman motifs emerge, such as animal legs, swans, caryatids, chimeras, and monopodia. They are joined by military symbols, such as stars, swords, spears, helmets, and X shapes. In 1798, after Napoleon's Egyptian campaign, Egyptian motifs (Fig. 27-13), sphinxes, obelisks, pyramids, and headdresses of pharaohs, come into vogue. Additional Empire motifs (Fig. 27-6, 27-7, 27-8, 27-11, 27-14, 27-19, 27-20) are military icons, swords, and symbols associated with Napoleon and his wife Josephine, such as the honeybee, laurel wreath, letter *N*, eagle, rose, and swan.

ARCHITECTURE

Most building activity occurs after the 1790s because earlier times are too uncertain and prominently displaying one's wealth is unwise. As the period becomes more stable, the newly rich begin to purchase and renovate the *hôtels* that once belonged to the aristocracy. Recently formed governments remodel older structures to accommodate their needs.

Designers and architects study, measure, draw, and publish information on ancient structures, which subsequently become the models for new buildings. As a result, the assembling of forms is more deliberate than it was before. Architectural theory emphasizes form and structure over ornament, and education continues

▲ **27-1.** *Détails et adjustements tirés de l'Atélier de Peinture du C. I.*, c. 1827; France; Charles Percier and Pierre-François-Léonard Fontaine.

▲ **27-2.** *Arc de Triomphe de l'Etoile*, c. 1808–1836; Paris, France; J.-F.-T. Chalgrin.

to center on ancient models. The *Académie Royale d'Architecture* closes in 1793, but its successor, *L' École des Beaux-Arts*, opens in 1819. A concept unique to France, the school strives to prepare architects to design monumental public buildings. This education system makes France a center for theory development and architectural debate in the 18th and 19th centuries.

Architecture, bold but stylistically unadventurous, continues the plain, geometric, and classical trends of the late 18th century. Greek influence is particularly evident in severity or plainness, but exteriors also may exhibit Roman or Egyptian attributes and motifs. New state architecture under Napoleon is monumental in scale and sited in open space or in prominent vistas to emphasize its monumentality (Fig. 27-2). Most of Napoleon's personal commissions are for the restoration and enlarging of palaces, *châteaux*, and *hôtels* for himself, his family, and government dignitaries.

Public and Private Buildings

■ *Site Orientation*. To create a more imperial Paris, Napoleon commands that the areas around the Louvre (Fig. 27-3) and the Tuileries palaces be cleared to open the space. This effort extends the size of the Louvre and initiates new buildings along the *Rue de Rivoli* (Fig. 27-5). To enhance the settings of public buildings and palaces, Napoleon also orders the restoration of public gardens.

■ *Floor Plans*. Most public and private building plans are rectangular in form with rooms symmetrically distributed at least along one axis (Fig. 27-4). In residences, the orientation and layout of rooms follow earlier patterns, continuing the emphasis on formality, rank, and status as was common during the Louis XIV period. Plans are organized around public and private *appartements*. Doorways to connecting rooms in state apartments are aligned on the same side of the wall to create an *enfilade*, with each space more ornately decorated than the last one.

■ *Materials*. Most new buildings are of stone with iron balconies at windows. Napoleon promotes new materials in architecture such as cast iron, which is used for bridges, domes, and structural support.

■ *Façades*. Grecian severity defines monumental buildings (Fig. 27-2, 27-4), which means that these buildings have little ornament and few details. Most buildings are raised on podia to emphasize their importance. Arcades or columns may completely surround the building or only articulate the façade. Columns, engaged columns, or pilasters combine with other details to form repeating units.

■ *Windows and Doors*. Rectangular windows, large and small, delineate façades of both state and lesser buildings (Fig. 27-5). French windows allow access to porches or balconies. As during previous periods, their use on important floors marks that floor on the exterior, enhances inside illumination, and adds to the magnificence of the interior spaces. Doorways are imposing for all buildings with columns or pilasters and pediments identifying them. Some entrances have a monumental portico (Fig. 27-4). Arcaded walkways are common (Fig. 27-5).

■ *Roofs*. Roofs are flat with balustrades, pyramidal, or gabled with a low pitch in the antique or Grecian manner (Fig. 27-4).

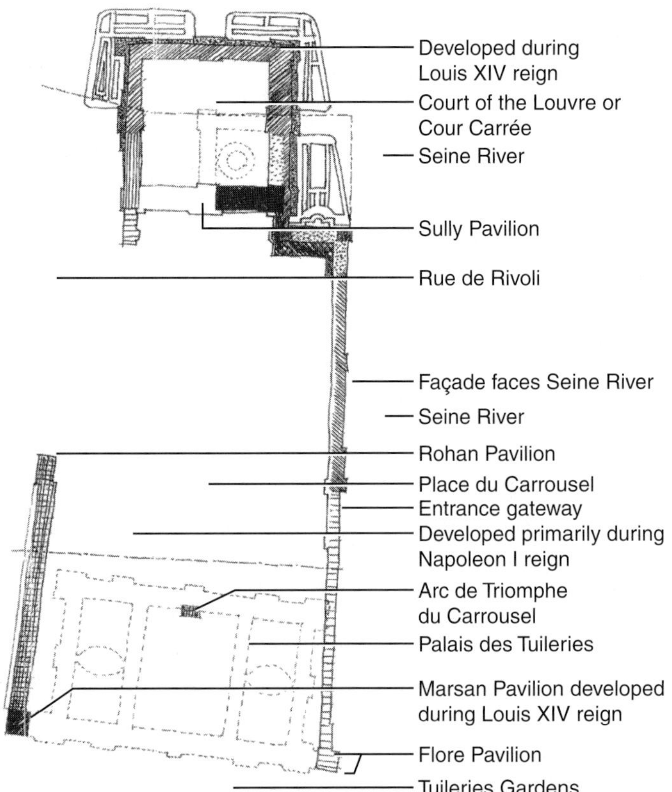

▲ **27-3.** Site plan, Louvre and the *Palais des Tuileries*, begun c. 1200 with many later additions; c. 1790s–1820s additions include the *Cour Carrée*, wing linking Rohan and Marsan Pavilions, and enlargement of *Place du Carrousel;* Paris, France; c. 1800 additions by Charles Percier and Pierre-François-Léonard Fontaine.

DESIGN SPOTLIGHT

Architecture: Inspired by Maison Carrée, and originally intended as a church, *La Madeliene*, in Nimes, France, had a short life as a Temple of Glory to Napoleon's army before returning to its original use as a place of worship. The open site and podium convey monumentality and significance. Corinthian columns surround the exterior and form the portico. A sculptured pediment announces the entry, which is approached from the front in the Roman manner. Contrasting with the relatively plain exterior, the opulent interior derives its character from Roman baths. The Corinthian columns carrying round arches and a sequence of three coffered domes are reminiscent of Byzantine and some Romanesque structures. The design of the exterior and interior serves as a visual link between the Napoleonic and Roman Empires.

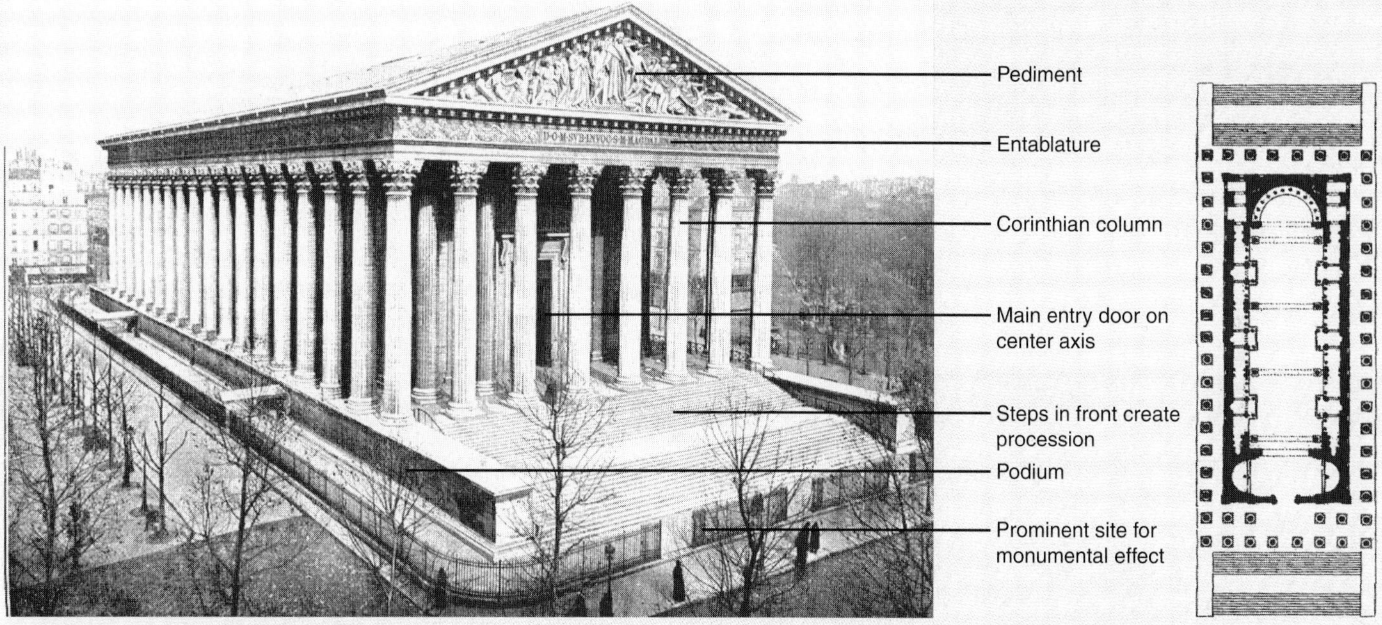

▲ **27-4.** *La Madeleine* and floor plan, 1804–1849; Paris, France; Pierre Vignon and interiors by J.-J.-M. Huvé in 1825–1845.

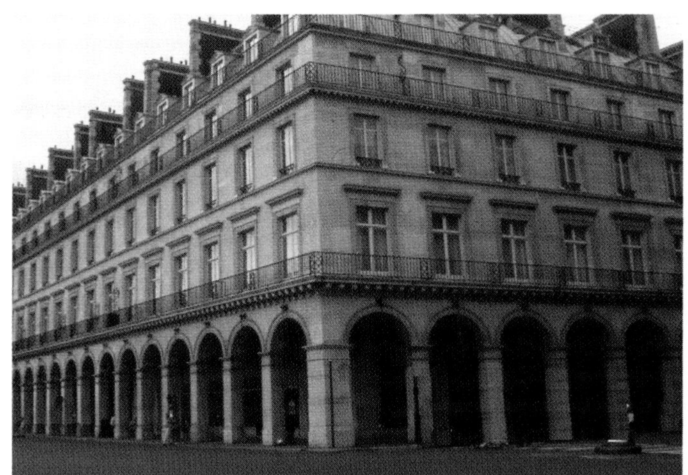

▲ **27-5.** *Rue de Rivoli*, 1802–1855; Paris, France; Charles Percier and Pierre-François-Léonard Fontaine.

INTERIORS

Classical attributes and motifs drawn from Greek, Roman, and Egyptian sources characterize interiors from the Directoire years through those of the Empire. The image changes from one of lightness and delicacy to majesty and pompousness. Common to the entire period are wall decorations based upon those uncovered in ancient Pompeii.

Directoire interiors continue the scale and treatments of the last years of Louis XVI's reign but with noticeable simplicity, muted colors, more delicate decoration, and additional antique details. In the 1790s under the Consulate, a new richness and formality begin to permeate interiors as an outgrowth of increasing prosperity. Scale and color grow bolder. Imperial Roman and Egyptian motifs appear as wall decorations and on chimneypieces, fabrics, furniture, and porcelains.

Empire interiors are masculine, formal, and richly detailed. Classical decorations; rich colors; and large, formal furniture arranged stiffly around the walls characterize interiors. Court architects Charles Percier and Pierre-François-Léonard Fontaine

▲ **27-6.** *Le Salle du Trone à Napoleon* (throne room of Napoleon), *Palais de Fontainebleau,* c. 1800; Fontainebleau, France.

create the style for Napoleon using the forms and motifs from ancient Roman models. They design all elements in the magnificent, masculine settings that glorify the Emperor and reinforce his heroic image.

Rectilinear spaces arranged symmetrically reflect the organization of façades and emphasize the integration between the exterior and interior. Floor plans and room types change little during the period because modes of living do not vary much from earlier times. Rooms of state and private *appartements* dominate residences (Fig. 27-7), and the trend of the previous period toward smaller, less formal rooms continues. Dining rooms are slightly more common than they were before.

Public and Private Buildings

■ *Color.* Directoire colors are softer with more muted blues, grays, and greens than those of Louis XVI. During the Consulate years, colors move toward richer reds, blues, and greens. Empire colors are highly saturated and include deep red, magenta, blue, green, yellow, and purple (Fig. 27-6, 27-7, 27-14, 27-20). Some have poetic names such as fawn or lemon wood.

DESIGN SPOTLIGHT

▲ **27-7.** *Salle de Conseil* (Council Chamber) and *Cabinet de travail-bibliothéque* (Library), *Château de la Malmaison,* c. 1800; near Paris, France; Charles Percier and Pierre-François-Léonard Fontaine; library published in *Recueil de décorations intérieures,* 1812, 1827.

DESIGN SPOTLIGHT

Interiors: While Napoleon is fighting in Egypt, Josephine purchases the *Château de la Malmaison,* a rundown early-18th-century *château.* She directs Percier and Fontaine to refurbish it in the opulent Empire style, which contrasts with the plain, simple three-story exterior with a slate roof. Revealing a strong masculine image, the design of the Council Chamber and the library emphasizes the large scale, symmetry, geometric forms, crisp lines, and classical details that define Empire. The striped-fabric walls and celing of the Council Chamber resemble a tent, which recalls the military origins of the Empire. The *X*-form dado, reminiscent of military uniforms, and spears add to the military character. Painted trophies and Roman-style helmets embellish the panels. A Roman-style table with monopodia supports occupies the center of the room. The library features mahogany Tuscan columns on pedestals, saucer (shallow) domes, round arches, and painted ceiling decorations composed of portraits of the Roman emperors, a reminder of the link between the Roman Empire and Napoleon. Mahogany bookcases by the firm Jacob Frères line the walls. Rich colors of red, blue, and gold enrich the interiors and complement the furnishings. As a reflection of his tastes and demand for a heroic image, these rooms are typical of the interiors with which Napoleon surrounds himself—masculine, sober, and replete with classical details and reminders of the historic nature of the empire.

▲ **27-7.** Continued

■ *Floors*. Floors are wooden boards or parquet. Entrances, bathrooms, and dining rooms are sometimes black and white marble tiles. In most rooms, Savonnerie and Aubusson carpets and rugs in bold, bright colors with classical and Empire motifs lie on wood and masonry floors (Fig. 27-6, 27-7, 27-20). Borders are added or removed to adjust width.

■ *Walls*. Walls retain classical proportions and details with an emphasis on the chimneypiece (Fig. 27-6, 27-7, 27-8, 27-20). Symmetrical compositions of paneling in classical proportions with plain or decorated centers are typical. A dado forms the base, and the wall is capped by a frieze and cornice. During the Directoire, walls display panels or friezes with painted Pompeian decorations that are composed of light-scale grotesques, arabesques, foliage, flowers, or figures in brighter colors against softly colored backgrounds. Rooms of this time usually display a simple geometric rhythm, whereas richer materials and bolder decoration characterize later Empire-style rooms.

Architectural details, such as pilasters, columns, and pediments in marble or stone, create greater formality and majesty required in official or important Empire rooms. Graining and marbling are also common treatments for walls, dados, moldings, or baseboards. Wall paneling may have large mirrors, painted or gilded stucco ornament depicting classical motifs, or painted decorations in the centers. Heavy moldings or pilasters outline the panels. Painted classical compositions resemble those of earlier times but are even bolder and more colorful.

Textile wall treatments (Fig. 27-6, 27-7, 27-20) become opulent during Empire, helping to soften stiffness and increase richness and majesty. Walls loosely draped with fabrics and/or valances are thought to look antique. Tent rooms, reminiscent of the military origins of the Empire, are fashionable during the period. Percier and Fontaine are among the first to use them at Malmaison.

■ *Wallpaper*. The use of wallpaper (Fig. 27-9) increases, particularly in public buildings and in the homes of those who cannot afford more expensive treatments. Patterns include small repeating designs, stripes, borders, architectural details, imitations of textiles and drapery, flocked papers, and shaded papers. Introduced in the first decade of the 19th century, *papiers panoramiques* or scenic papers feature exotic themes or idealized worlds block printed in lavish detail and numerous, rich colors. French wallpapers dominate European markets despite the Napoleonic Wars.

■ *Chimneypieces*. Mantels (Fig. 27-7) usually are of white, black, red, or brown marble with a shelf supported by columns, pilasters, consoles, caryatids, or winged lions. Simpler mantels are rectangular forms with applied gilded bronze or stucco classical motifs such as swags, draped figures, or sphinxes adorning them in the manner of Empire furniture. Above the mantel, there is a large painting or mirror. Objects on the mantelshelf, such as clocks or *candelabra*, are large and showy.

▲ **27-9.** Wallpaper: Panel from "Psyche and Cupid," 1814; France; Dufour.

▲ **27-8.** *Lit exécuté à Paris*, c. 1827; Paris, France; Charles Percier and Pierre-François-Léonard Fontaine; published in *Recueil de décorations intérieures*, 1812, 1827.

▲ **27-10.** Window Treatments: Wallpaper showing drapery treatment and actual drapery example, c. 1815–1820s.

■ *Window Treatments*. Like other decorative details, window treatments (Fig. 27-10) become more opulent and layered during the period. They are composed of elaborate fringed and tasseled swags and festoons draped over rods or attached to decorative cornices. Rods shaped like spears, lances, or other similar forms terminate in large finials. Beneath are curtain panels that may puddle on the floor. Muslin or other thin fabrics hang next to the glass. Pairs of windows may be treated as one with continuous drapery. Curtains may open and close using the new French draw rod introduced in 1790, or they can be tied back with ropes and tassels or looped over holdbacks during the day.

▲ **27-11.** Textiles: Upholstery fabrics with period motifs; France.

■ *Ceilings*. Ceilings in rooms of state and important residential areas are the most heavily decorated with carved wood or stuccowork enhanced with paintings or gilding (Fig. 27-6, 27-7, 27-20). Sometimes, the carpet repeats the ceiling decorations. Lesser rooms have plain ceilings, some with a central rosette. Some may be painted to look like the sky.

■ *Textiles*. Napoleon's large commissions revive France's silk and cotton industries, which had almost completely disappeared during the Revolution. Typical furnishing fabrics (Fig. 27-6, 27-7, 27-11, 27-13, 27-14, 27-16, 27-20) are brocades, damasks, velvets, moirés, lampas, and printed cottons. Printing methods include hand-blocks, copper plates, and cylinders. Patterns are numerous, but most come from classical sources. Ensembles consisting of *fauteuils*, *chaises*, *canapés*, and stools are upholstered alike in tapestry, silk, satin, or damasks in vivid colors or horsehair in black, red, green, plum, and light blue.

■ *Lighting*. Lighting fixtures of the period (Fig. 27-6, 27-7, 27-12) include candlesticks, *candelabra*, *appliqué*, *lustre*, lanterns, *guéridon*, and oil lamps. Classical motifs embellish the surfaces repeating interior ornamentation. Many fixtures emulate those of classical antiquity. For example, hanging fixtures may imitate ancient oil lamps. In progressive, wealthy homes, oil lamps begin to replace candles. Most *candelabra* are of gilded bronze with darker bronze figures.

▲ **27-12.** Lighting: (a) *Candelabra*, (b) *cristeaux* (hanging lamp), and (c) *guéridon* (floor lamp), c. early 1800s; France.

FURNISHINGS AND DECORATIVE ARTS

Classical attributes, forms, and motifs define furniture from Directoire to Empire. For inspiration, designers rely on surviving examples from Pompeii, ancient vase paintings, and stucco reliefs. Copying and adapting ancient Greek and Roman furniture continue during all periods. Directoire advances trends evident in the last years of Louis XVI's reign, such as slender proportions, greater severity, and angularity. During the Consulate period, furniture becomes heavier in scale, gilding and ornament increase, and Egyptian motifs are more evident. Empire furniture continues classical emphasis and its architectonic feeling, but becomes masculine, stiff, and majestic as design supersedes comfort. Pieces are intended to be seen primarily from the front and to support formal living. Symmetry is an important design principle in all periods.

Although furniture still lines the walls when not in use, toward the end of the period it begins to migrate from the perimeter, centering on the fireplace in less-formal rooms (Fig. 27-6, 27-7). By the end of Napoleon's reign, industrialization is affecting furniture making. Individual cabinetmakers begin to disappear, replaced by large firms. Overall design quality begins to deteriorate as furniture becomes larger, bulkier, and more curvilinear.

Although much of Directoire closely resembles Louis XVI, distinguishing characteristics in seating include the rolled-over back, saber leg (Fig. 27-13), greater emphasis on Grecian prototypes, and motifs associated with the Revolution. During the Consulate years, furniture begins to assume characteristic Empire features such as heavier scale, frontality, and Roman and Egyptian motifs (Fig. 27-15). A clean, simple silhouette with sharp corners and no attempts to soften them distinguishes Empire furniture. Large areas of flat mahogany veneer with little carving, few moldings, and heavy bases enhance the blocky appearance. Makers leave off door handles and keyholes to achieve an unbroken surface. Applied ornamentation may appear on large flat surfaces, such as those of *commodes* and beds (Fig. 27-19, 27-20).

Public and Private Buildings

■ *Materials*. Directoire furniture is of wood native to France because of hostilities; imported materials are impossible to obtain. Often a painted finish disguises common woods and coordinates with interior colors and decoration; there is little marquetry, inlay, or applied embellishment. During the Consulate and Empire, both solid and veneer mahogany dominate furniture (Fig. 27-19) until 1806, when a naval blockade imposed by France's enemies prevents its importation. After that, most furniture is made of native woods, such as walnut, beech, pear, ash, and elm. Darker woods rule before 1806; after that, lighter-colored woods replace them. After 1810, white paint with gilding or gray paint with white details is typical for furniture. Important or official rooms have gilded furnishings (Fig. 27-6, 27-7, 27-20), while plain or painted pieces fill lesser rooms. Tables and case pieces throughout the period have marble tops in black, gray, blue, dark green, purple, brown, or white. Pewter, ebony, or ivory inlay in bands and/or gilded bronze or brass mounts in classical motifs characterize Consulate or Empire casepieces.

■ *Seating*. Sets of upholstered chairs and sofas are very fashionable. Directoire seating is light in scale, often painted, and reveals delicate classical decoration. Legs are tapered and quadrangular, turned, or baluster-shaped. Backs may feature trellises or lyre splats. A rosette in a square accentuates the junction of leg and seat rail.

Designed to be sat in erectly and be seen primarily from the front, Empire *chaises* and *fauteuils* are stiffly rectilinear with some curves in backs, legs, or seats (Fig. 27-7, 27-13, 27-14, 27-15). Backs may be flat and rectangular or rolled-over. Front legs are straight and fluted, turned, sabers, or flat and reminiscent of Greek rectangular leg designs. Back legs most often are sabers.

DESIGN SPOTLIGHT

Furniture: This *fauteuil* repeats the large scale of Empire interiors. Its rolled-over back and continuous line of back and legs are reminiscent of the Greek klismos, while the turned front legs resemble those of Roman thrones. Sphinxes, common after Napoleon's Egyptian campaign in 1799, form the arm supports. The upholstery and carvings highlight classical motifs and geometric shapes common to the period. The trim and tassels under the seat add further opulence.

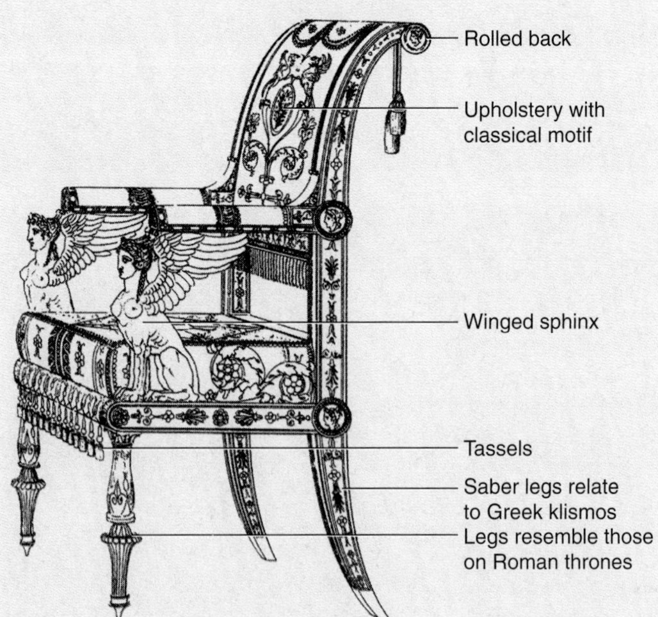

▲ **27-13.** *Fauteuil et Siege à deux places*, c. 1800; Paris area, France; Charles Percier and Pierre-François-Léonard Fontaine; published in *Recueil de décorations intérieures*, 1812, 1827.

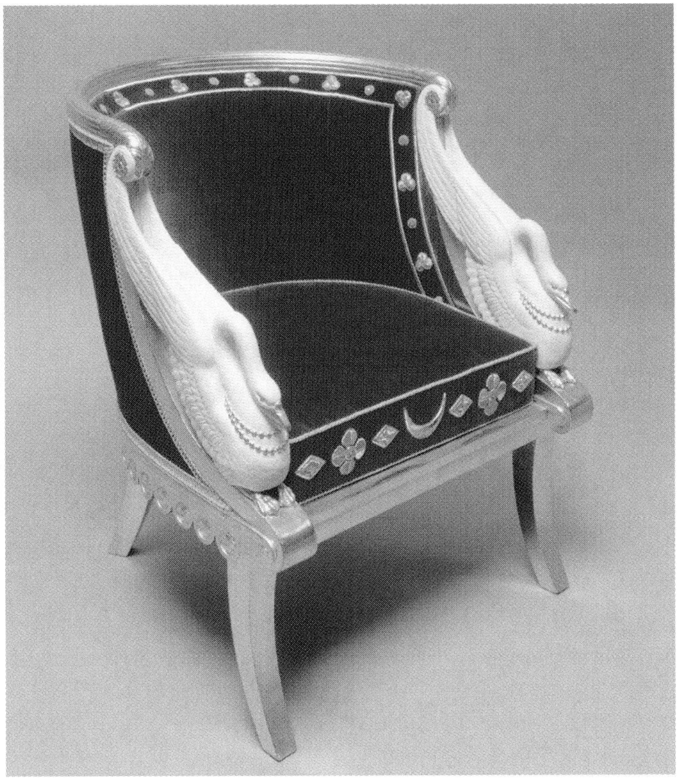

▲ **27-14.** Gondola chair with swans, c. early 1800s; France.

Arm supports may be flat, turned, or animal shaped. The boxy upholstery has sharp corners. Curule or X-shaped chairs and stools copy antique examples (Fig. 27-6, 27-15). Gondola chairs (Fig. 27-14) are popular during the period (Figure 27-14). *Canapés* (Fig. 27-16), beginning in the Consulate period, closely follow antique forms with outward scrolled arms equal or unequal in height and either turned or outwardly curved legs. A variation is the *méridienne*.

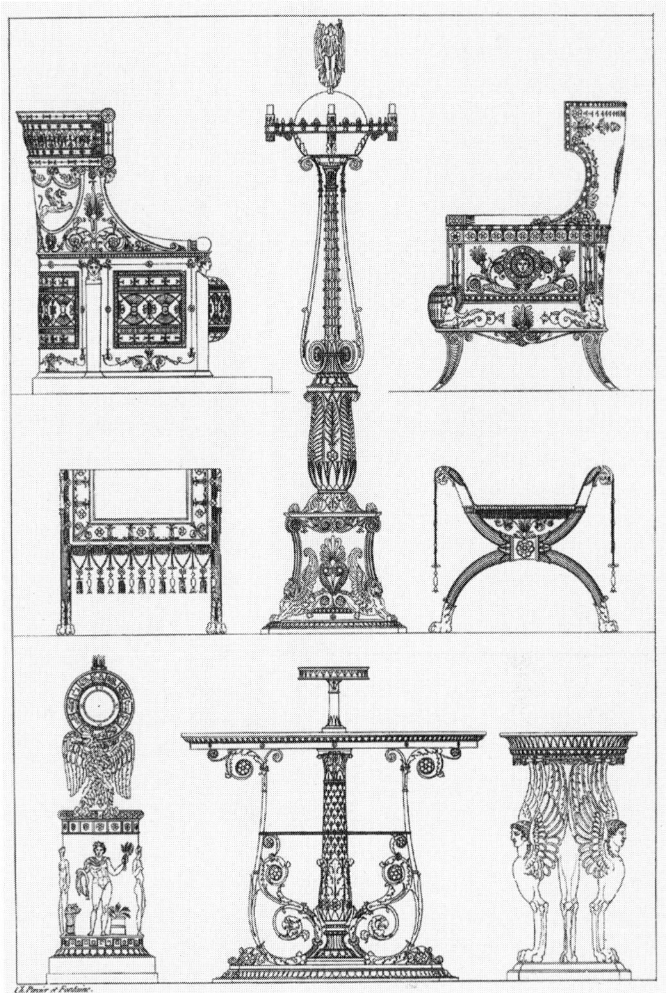

▲ **27-15.** *Fauteuils, tabourets, candelabra, côté du tabouret, petit pendule,* and table, c. 1800; Paris area, France; Charles Percier and Pierre-François-Léonard Fontaine; published in *Recueil de décorations intérieures*, 1812, 1827.

▲ **27-16.** *Canapé*, c. 1790s–1810s; France.

■ *Tables*. Empire rooms boast a variety of tables (Fig. 27-7, 27-15, 27-17, 27-18, 27-20), many of which copy or emulate antique prototypes. All of the table types and stands of the 18th century continue in this period. Particularly fashionable are small round or polygonal tables with single center supports or three or four columns on a concave-sided base. The front legs of pier tables may be columns with gilded capitals, caryatids, terms, or animal legs. Mirrored backs double the apparent size of the table and reflect light as well as the Empire-style carpeting on the floor. Inlay and applied classical motifs embellish the aprons of pier tables and consoles. Large *bureau plats* are more common than rolltop desks.

■ *Storage*. Directoire *commodes* (Fig. 27-19) are rectangular and severely plain. Simple moldings define drawers, and the pulls are plain, metal rectangles. The short, tapered legs are fluted. Tops may have stringing or cross banding. Empire case and storage pieces are massive and architectural in form with large expanses of mahogany veneer and bronze mounts depicting classical motifs and figures. Corners may have columns, caryatids, or terms. *Commodes*, used in nearly all rooms, have three drawers in the main body, a fourth in the apron, and a marble top. The corners may have columns, caryatids, or *égyptiennes en gaine* in gilded bronze or wood that is painted green *à l'antique* or gilded.

■ *Beds*. Directoire beds, simple in form and design, feature low pediments carried by fluted columns and geometric carving in low relief. In contrast, beds are the most creative designs of the Empire period (Fig. 27-8, 27-20, 27-21). The *lit en bateau* commonly has scrolled or animal-shaped ends and rests on a solid dais with bronze mounts in classical or military designs. Beds are placed in alcoves or lengthwise on the wall with a canopy above and heavy silk and muslin hangings draping over the ends. Night tables resembling classical pedestal tables flank either side of the bed.

▲ **27-18.** Pier table, c. 1800s–1820s; France.

■ *Decorative Arts*. Napoleon's commissions also revive the decorative arts. Porcelain becomes large, monumental, and completely covered with applied or painted decoration. Classical scenes, cities, sites important to the Empire, classical figures, and scenes from the Renaissance and Middle Ages embellish table services, tea and coffee services, centerpieces, vases, and other porcelain objects.

■ *Later Interpretations*. Empire furnishings are revived in the 19th century during Second Empire and in the 20th century during Art Deco (Fig. 27-22), and interpretations continue today.

▲ **27-17.** Round table with pedestal base and animal legs, c. early 1800s; France.

▲ **27-19.** *Commode* with *ormolu* decoration, c. 1800s–1820s; France.

▲ **27-20.** *Lit, Chambre a Coucher de l'Impératrice* (Josephine's bedroom), *Château de la Malmaison*, c. 1800; near Paris, France; Charles Percier and Pierre-François-Léonard Fontaine.

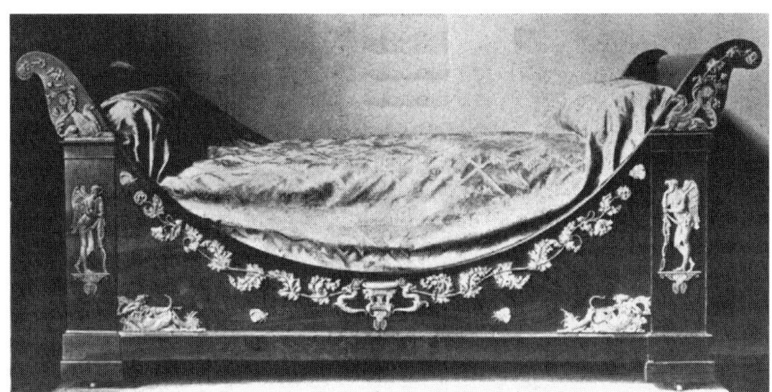

▲ **27-21.** *Lit en acajou garni de cuivres dorés* (bed in mahogany with gilded bronze *appliqués*), c. early 1800s; France.

▲ **27-22.** Later Interpretation: Table and chair, 1926; Jacques Ruhlmann. Art Deco.

CHAPTER 28

German Greek Revival, Biedermeier

1815–1848

> *The term* Biedermeier, *first used in 1853, was given to a political caricature appearing in the "Fleigende Blätter" who typified a well-to-do middle-class man without culture. Biedermeier furniture, marked by its commonplace forms, is a potpourri of early nineteenth-century classicism—Sheraton, Regency, Directoire, and especially French Empire—with certain traits of its own.*
>
> —Louise Ade Boger, *Furniture Past and Present*, 1966

Early-19th-century architecture in Germany and Austria continues the Neoclassical development first in the Greek Revival style, which is followed by a more eclectic approach that encompasses the Italian Renaissance, Byzantine, Early Christian, and Romanesque. The term *Biedermeier* applies mainly to middle-class interiors and furniture in Austria and Germany during the period of 1815 to 1848. This style, an adaptation of French Empire, replaces formality and majesty with comfort and function.

HISTORICAL AND SOCIAL

The German states, including Austria and Prussia, wage war against France for nearly 18 years before defeating Napoleon in 1813. In 1814, the Congress of Vienna convenes to decide the fate of Napoleon's empire. To help alleviate Germany's social, political, and economic problems, the Congress establishes the German Confederation to replace the Germanic remnants of the Holy Roman Empire and Napoleon's Confederation of the Rhine. The German Confederation unites 39 German states and Prussia under Austrian rule. Each state retains its independence and government.

As Minister of Foreign Affairs, Prince Clemens von Metternich of Austria strives to preserve the alliance by suppressing liberalism and nationalism. He institutes strong censorship and authoritarian rule, maintained by surveillance and repression. At the same time, he brings about economic recovery, which sustains his political stranglehold. Eventually, the growth of the middle class and the prosperity brought by the Industrial Revolution bring change in the form of revolutions beginning in 1848.

With political activism prohibited, people turn inward, focusing on their homes and families. They pursue tranquil, informal lifestyles in which visiting and entertaining friends are commonplace activities. Family members engage in hobbies and pastimes, such as reading, needlework, letter writing, or making scrapbooks. Practicality and coziness are more important than display and opulence are.

The period is a golden age for music and literature. Opera houses and music halls are filled to capacity. Those who can afford it own a clavichord and/or other type of musical instrument. Germans also highly esteem literature, owning numerous books and/or borrowing from local libraries. However, censorship and repression extend even to favored musicians and writers and their works.

CONCEPTS

As elsewhere in Europe, Neoclassicism, which begins in the second half of the 18th century in Germany, is the style of choice. German architects favor Greek architecture over Roman because they believe it exhibits honesty of structure. They and their patrons also think that the German spirit is embodied in Greek architecture; thus, architecture fulfills a political and social role as in France. German nobility embraces the formal and majestic French Empire for important interiors to express rank, status, majesty, and grandeur. In contrast, the middle class adopts a simpler style that becomes known as *Biedermeier*. The expression combines *bieder*, meaning plain or unpretentious, and *meier*, a common German last name. Biedermeier interior planning centers on function and comfort instead of rank and display. Middle-class values, such as the importance of family, modesty, and simplicity, are common themes in rooms and furnishings.

MOTIFS

■ *Motifs*. Architecture and furniture exhibit classical motifs (Fig. 28-1, 28-2, 28-3, 28-4) including columns, Egyptian terms, pediments, Greek key or fret, acanthus leaves, palmettes, lyres, urns, hearts, arrows, and a stylized Prince of Wales motif.

ARCHITECTURE

Although not stylistic innovators, German architects synthesize ancient Greek and Roman, French, and English influences and their own past styles into a unique German vision. They extensively use Greek and Roman temple forms; the Greek orders; plain walls; clean lines; and minimal, classically derived ornament. Buildings show classical attributes such as symmetry, repose, and a concern for proportion. French inspiration is evident in rationalism, geometric forms, Gothic-type structures, and visionary architecture. An underlying Romanticism stems from England, particularly in gardens and settings.

DESIGN SPOTLIGHT

Architecture: *Schauspielhaus* is an important early building by Schinkel, who receives a commission from the king to design a new theater to replace an earlier one that burned. The king requires that Schinkel follow the footprint of the previous theater and reuse some elements, such as the Ionic columns. Schinkel devises a three-part structure with a prominent main center façade approached by processional front steps and crowned by a temple front using the Ionic columns. He further articulates the image of Neoclassicism with classic ordering, rustication, straight lines, rectangular windows, and plain walls. The front vertical planes are layered to achieve depth and movement. Additional classical motifs highlight the prominent points of the roof and reiterate the classical language. Because of its frequent use and its location in an important Berlin square, the building becomes a symbolic statement of German Greek Revival architecture.

▲ **28-1.** *Schauspielhaus* (Royal Theater, now called *Konzerthaus*), 1821; Berlin, Germany; Karl Friedrich Schinkel.

The geometric forms that make up buildings retain their individuality instead of blending into a whole. Some structures copy ancient edifices, while others exhibit an antique flavor. Greek Revival is favored for the first two decades of the 19th century. After that, an increase in ornament and number of styles signals a move away from the single classical vision toward a broader, more eclectic approach, revealing attributes and details from the Italian Renaissance, Romanesque, and Byzantine. Karl Friedrich Schinkel and Leo von Klenze are the most outstanding of the German architects. Schinkel in Berlin and von Klenze in Munich design a variety of building types in the Neoclassical style, transforming those cities and affecting architectural design of their day and exerting continued influence. Building types include theaters (Fig. 28-1), museums (Fig. 28-2), monuments, gateways, galleries, prisons, factories, markets, squares, row houses, apartments, and palaces. German architects design the first Greek Revival ceremonial gateways and the first museum designed for sculpture.

Public and Private Buildings

■ *Site Orientation*. Monuments and important buildings are surrounded by open spaces to enhance their importance (Fig. 28-1, 28-2). For some, ceremonial gateways and entrances contribute to their significance. Other structures are located along streets or in squares that are carefully planned. Palaces are situated in picturesque gardens.

■ *Floor Plans*. Most plans are symmetrical and composed of rectangular, square, and/or round or apsidal spaces. For palaces and monuments, progression, ceremony, and status are important concepts in space planning.

■ *Materials*. Northern Germany favors brick, while other areas use local building stone. Schinkel introduces colored brick, terracotta, and cast iron.

■ *Façades*. Podia with front or angled staircases, porticoes, temple fronts, or colonnades announce important buildings (Fig. 28-1, 28-2). Greek prototypes inspire the designs of these porticoes and

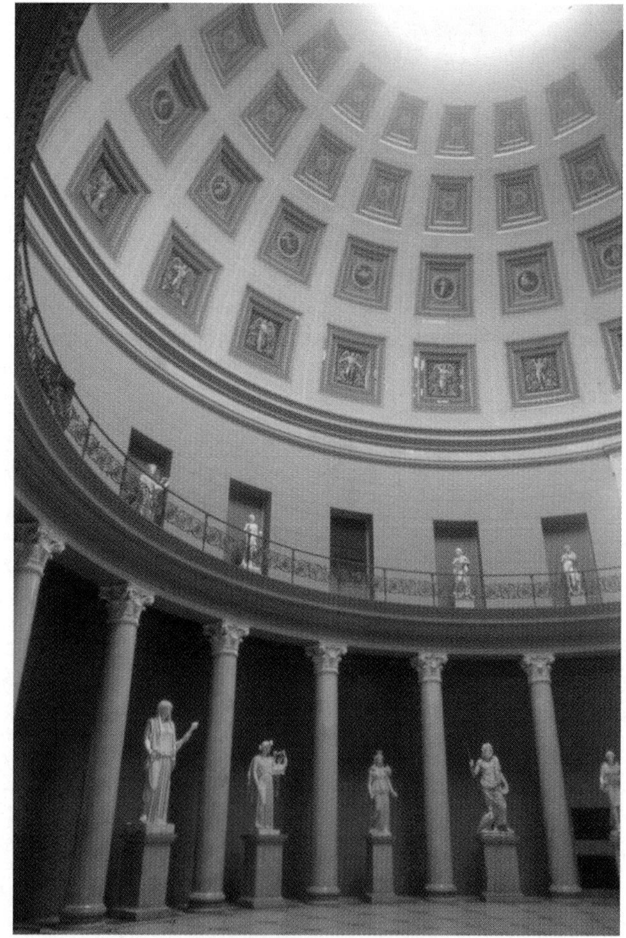

▲ **28-2.** Altes Museum and rotunda, 1823–1830; Berlin; Karl Friedrich Schinkel.

▲ **28-3.** Drawing room, Greymuller Schlossl House, c. 1820s–1830s; Germany.

colonnades. Greek Doric is the most common order followed by Corinthian. Alternatively, some façades have round arches instead of columns. In keeping with Neoclassical design, walls tend to be blank and smoothly finished or lightly rusticated.

■ *Windows and Doors*. Columns, pilasters, or plain lintels may accentuate rectangular windows and form a rectangular grid across the façade (Fig. 28-1, 28-2). Arched or round windows are more common during the third decade of the 19th century. Porticoes, temple fronts, or *aedicula* define and emphasize entrances.

■ *Roofs*. Low-pitched gabled roofs in keeping with Greek architecture are typical. Some structures, such as museums and churches, may have domes (Fig. 28-2).

INTERIORS

Following the lead of the French, German and Austrian nobility choose the Empire style especially for ceremonial spaces in their homes, palaces, theaters, and museums. Middle-class members, however, find it too opulent and expensive. They do not share the Empire vision of grandeur. Instead, they want rooms that focus on comfort and simplicity. They find these ideals in the Biedermeier style.

Biedermeier interiors display bright colors, good lighting, warm woods, plants, and flowers, contributing to an inviting atmosphere. Rooms and furnishings are small in scale, and some pieces derive from classical prototypes. Typical spaces are the drawing room, dining room, bedrooms, one or two dressing rooms, a study or library, service areas, and servants' quarters. Attention focuses on the drawing room (Fig. 28-3, 28-4) as the center of family life, so it often has a lot of furniture, especially chairs. Spaces are small, so planning requires zones for activities such as reading, hobbies, or letter writing. Furniture lines the walls and fills corners, leaving the center of the space open, but pieces can be moved where needed. Collections of glassware, needlework, or other prized possessions, and family silhouettes or portraits attest to the importance of the family and personalize the spaces. In contrast, bedrooms often have little furniture.

Private Buildings

■ *Color*. Colors are light and bright. The typical palette contains green, blue, yellow, gray, or brown (Fig. 28-3, 28-4, 28-10).

■ *Floors*. Floors (Fig. 28-3, 28-4, 28-10) are wood planks or, occasionally, parquet. Wall-to-wall machine-made carpet or area rugs in brightly colored geometric or floral patterns are common floor coverings.

■ *Walls*. Typical wall treatments are paint or wallpaper (Fig. 28-3, 28-4). Painted walls usually are a solid, light color. The use of wallpaper increases during the period because industrialization reduces the cost and increases availability. Patterns include stripes, geometrics, florals, or imitations of textiles. Occasionally, walls are draped in the French manner, as in the bedroom of Luise von Mecklenburg-Strelitz in Charlottenburg Castle (Fig. 28-10). Baseboards, cornice moldings, and trim around doors and windows usually contrast with the wall color. Doors are plain, paneled, dark wood with simple, painted surrounds.

▲ **28-4.** Drawing room, c. 1820s–1840s; Germany.

▲ **28-5.** Later Interpretation: Living room; published in *The Room Beautiful*, 1916. Biedermeier interpretation.

■ *Window Treatments*. Window treatments vary from simple white muslin swags with fringe to multiple swags in brightly colored fabrics trimmed with braid, fringe, and tassels. Floor-length curtains and glass curtains may hang beneath the swags.
■ *Ceilings*. Ceilings are usually plain gray or white. Some have painted decorations, wallpaper borders, plasterwork, or plaster rosettes (Fig. 28-3).
■ *Textiles*. Local textiles dominate Biedermeier furnishings because imported ones are too expensive. Common upholstery textiles include horsehair, needlework, velvet, printed cotton, linen, or wool. Only the nobility can afford silk. Abstract patterns in strong colors are favored.
■ *Lighting*. Most rooms have good natural lighting from large windows. Artificial lighting comes from ceiling fixtures (Fig. 28-10), such as lanterns or small chandeliers, sconces, and candlesticks. A few people can afford oil lamps.
■ *Later Interpretations*. The simple, sparsely furnished Biedermeier interior appeals to designers of the late 19th and 20th centuries (Fig. 28-5). Later designers who adapt the basic forms of Biedermeier include Josef Hoffman, Peter Behrens, and Elsie de Wolfe.

FURNISHINGS AND DECORATIVE ARTS

Like the interiors, Biedermeier furniture is human scaled, comfortable, functional, and simple in design. Like architecture, it is composed of geometric solids, and may display classical attributes or copy or adapt antique prototypes. French Empire, English Regency, Sheraton, Louis XVI, and Rococo influence designers. Although designs are volumetric, furniture maintains a planar and frontal appearance, an angular silhouette with sharp corners and smooth surfaces. It is light in scale and often multipurpose to suit small spaces. Mostly made by artisans, it reflects a high degree of craftsmanship and concern for the material. Consequently, large areas of veneer emphasize the grain of the wood on most furniture.

Early examples (1815–1830) are rectangular in form with minimal decoration. Beauty and interest lie in the grain of the wood and the geometric or curvilinear composition. Classical restraint defines the image. Later furniture (1830–1848) moves away from classical restraint to greater exaggeration with more ornament, curves, and bulges. Innovation and fashion replace function and simplicity as industrialization takes hold. Unlike French Empire, there is little gilding, few bronze mounts, and no feeling of pompousness or majesty.

Public and Private Buildings

■ *Materials*. Cabinetmakers use local woods, predominately light-colored fruitwoods, maple, birch, ash, or cherry (Fig. 28-6, 28-9, 28-10). Imported or exotic woods are too expensive for most people. Some pieces have inlay; marquetry; porcelain or glass plaques; or painted, stenciled, or transfer-printed decorations. In-

DESIGN SPOTLIGHT

Furniture: This side chair typifies the simplicity and elegance of Biedermeier furniture, with minimal decoration and classical restraint. The curved open back is inspired by French Empire and English Regency examples. Front legs are straight and tapered, while the rear legs are delicate sabers. Beauty and interest lie in the grain of the wood and the curvilinear composition. Fruitwood and mahogany are the most used woods. The seat is upholstered in a fashionable textile composed of plain stripes alernating with Greek key motifs.

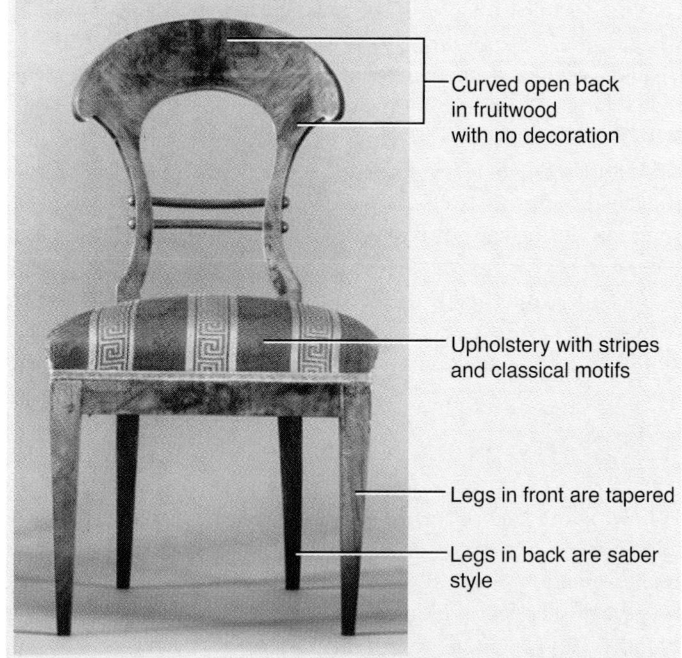

▲ **28-6.** Side chair in fruitwood, c. early 19th century; Germany.

▲ **28-7.** Armchair, c. 1825; Austria.

lay and stringing in ebony or other dark woods outline or accentuate legs, backs, drawers, and doors.

■ *Seating*. Unlike Empire, Biedermeier seating looks comfortable and inviting with its curves and deep, overstuffed seats. Seating (Fig. 28-3, 28-4, 28-7, 28-8) comes in many forms with numerous details. Side chairs outnumber armchairs because they are more easily moved. Front legs may be turned, sabers, or straight and tapered with or without a slight outward curve near the floor. Rear legs are sabers. Trapezoid or round seats are upholstered, whereas backs usually are not. Backs exhibit the greatest variety of design from ladderbacks to interpretations of the Greek *klismos*, shield shapes, fan shapes, splats, trellises, lyres, balloons, rectangles, and other geometric shapes. Sofas often correspond in design to chairs.

■ *Tables*. Biedermeier drawing rooms or libraries are filled with many tables (Fig. 28-3, 28-4, 28-10) for work, games, writing, and display. Also common are sofa tables and pier or console tables. Tables display infinite variety in shape, form, and leg styles. Round and rectangular tops have inlay, stringing, or veneer patterns such as stars or sunbursts. Tables may have a single center support or three or four scroll-shaped, turned, straight, or tapered legs.

▲ **28-8.** Sofa, c. 1820–1840s; New York; Anton Kimbel.

■ *Storage*. Storage pieces are important in drawing rooms and bedrooms. Nearly every drawing room has a secretary or drop-front desk (Fig. 28-4, 28-9) that may be tall and rectilinear or exhibit a creative shape. Inside the drop front are numerous drawers, secret drawers, and pigeonholes. Tops may have pediments or rectangular boxes diminishing in size. Doors of secretaries and wardrobes may have veneer patterns such as sunbursts. Chests with three or four drawers also store possessions in drawing rooms and bedrooms. Vitrines or display cabinets show off prized possessions of the family. *Étagères* hold books and/or display collections.

■ *Beds*. Like other furniture, beds display great variety in design (Fig. 28-10). Poster or French beds with equal-height head- and footboards are common, but four-posters are most favored. Beds are usually draped.

■ *Decorative Arts*. Mirrors, numerous pictures, family portraits, or silhouettes hang on walls (Fig. 28-3, 28-4). Proudly displayed, porcelain has classical or urn shapes with naturalistic plants and flowers in colored panels or surrounded by borders. Blown and cut glass, plain or colored, is particularly prized.

▲ **28-9.** *Secrétaire*, c. early 19th century; Germany; Karl Friedrich Schinkel.

▲ **28–10.** Bedroom for Queen Luise von Mecklenburg-Strelitz, Charlottenburg Castle, 1776–1810; Germany; furniture by Karl Friedrich Schinkel.

CHAPTER 29

English Regency, British Greek Revival

1790s–1840s

England's Regency is a creative and productive period for both architecture and the decorative arts. Designers borrow and synthesize forms and influences from classical, medieval, and exotic sources. Neoclassicism continues to dominate the arts and architecture, but the Romantic and Picturesque Movements also affect design. Consequently, formality and symmetry through classicism shape the main character, and eclecticism and asymmetry enliven the building context. This mixing of influences contributes to a unique and distinctive design image, one that offers more variety than is evident in earlier periods.

Whether the house be Grecian or gothic, large or small, it will require the same rooms for the present habits of life, viz. a dining-room and two others, one of which may be called a drawing-room, and the other a book-room, if small, or the library, if large: to these is sometimes added a breakfast room, but of late, especially since the central hall, or vestibule, has been in some degree given up, these rooms have been opened into each other, "en suite," by large folding doors; the effect of this enfilade, or "visto," through a modern house, is occasionally increased by a conservatory at one end, and repeated by a large mirror at the opposite end.

—Humphry Repton, 1816, from *Regency Style*, 1996, p. 29 by Steve Parisien

HISTORICAL AND SOCIAL

The term *Regency* can refer to several periods. Politically, it designates the time between 1811 and 1820 when George, Prince of Wales, serves as Prince Regent for his father who is too ill to reign. Artistically, Regency covers the years between 1790 and 1830, although characteristics of this style appear as early as the 1780s and continue well past 1830.

George, Prince of Wales and eldest son of George III and Queen Charlotte, is a great patron and collector of art and architecture. Unlike his forebears, he sees himself as an arbiter of taste. He gives numerous commissions to architects and designers, including the remodeling of the Royal Pavilion at Brighton. Hugely unpopular, he becomes one of the most despised English monarchs because of his excessive spending and dissolute, immoral lifestyle.

The period is largely one of luxury, prosperity, and growth despite social unrest, violence, and injustice. Following the loss of the American colonies, Great Britain looks to the south (Africa) and east (India) for colonization to increase trade and commerce and enhance prosperity. The British victories over Napoleon stimulate nationalism and patriotism. The Congress of Vienna, which meets in 1814 to bring order back to Europe following the defeat of Napoleon, increases Britain's territorial holdings by adding former Dutch possessions.

The nobility become wealthier as does the larger middle class whose demand for houses and furnishings creates a building boom. Fashion begins to surpass taste as the driving force in art and design, and fashions change quickly. Consumers of the new commercial classes face a vast array of stylistic choices. Numerous books and periodicals assist them in furnishing their homes with the latest fashions.

(a) (b)

▲ **29-1.** Motifs: (a) Ornamental motifs published in *Household Furniture and Interior Decoration*, 1807; Thomas Hope; and (b) *Pot-à-Oille éxécuté à Paris, pour S. M. l'Imperatrice*, c. 1827; Charles Percier and Pierre-François-Léonard Fontaine.

CONCEPTS

During the Regency period, classicism dominates architecture, interiors, and furniture and follows two paths. One thread maintains the flow of the Neoclassical, continuing its lightness and advocating stylistic purity and archaeological correctness. A second, later trend adopts elements from other classical sources, such as the Italian Renaissance. French influences are strong in England.

The Romantic and the Picturesque Movements influence design thinking throughout the period. Romantics believe in the unity of reason, nature, and antiquity, and they rigorously seek the beautiful and the sublime or the awe-inspiring or terror-filled experience of nature. Because feelings are supreme, Romantics esteem past styles for their visual and symbolic associations, and they evoke an emotional response. The Picturesque Movement also admires nature and the visual qualities of landscapes, such as asymmetry. These two movements open the door for a broader range of design resources and greater eclecticism. Their reliance upon links and relationships leads eventually to designing in a particular style based upon that style's historical associations, which characterizes design throughout the Victorian period. Known as associationism, this manner of thought values a work of art beyond beauty, which may be shown by intrinsic qualities such as form, to the pictures, memories, and thoughts that it may conjure up in the viewer's mind.

MOTIFS

■ *Motifs*. Motifs (Fig. 29-1, 29-3, 29-4, 29-5, 29-7, 29-8, 29-11, 29-15, 29-20) include pediments, columns, arabesques, lion's heads, urns, classical figures, vases, trellises, Chinese motifs, pointed arches, fan vaulting, rose windows, stars, and Egyptian designs.

ARCHITECTURE

Regency architecture follows two paths, Neoclassicism and the Picturesque Movement, with each producing many variations. Architects possess a large body of architectural theory, the classical being the best understood. Consequently, most public buildings are Neoclassical and feature typical classical elements and attributes like symmetry, order, balance, concern for proportion, and monumentality.

During the 18th century, classical Greek buildings become objects of scrutiny by architects, dilettantes, and others who measure, draw, and publish them. The most famous treatise is Stuart and Revett's *Antiquities of Athens*, published beginning in 1762. Although imitations of temple ruins are common in picturesque landscapes, tastes do not run to the Grecian, so few buildings are constructed in the style during the period.

By 1800, however, appreciation for things Greek has increased. Lord Elgin's importation into England of the Parthenon

▲ **29-2.** Athenaeum, 1829–1830; London, England; Decimus Burton. British Greek Revival.

▲ **29-3.** British Museum, 1823–1846; London, England; Sir Robert Smirke. British Greek Revival.

sculptures focuses popular attention on Greece. Thomas Hope, who prefers Greek designs to Roman, issues a strong call for buildings of pure Greek design. As a result of these sequential influences, the Greek Revival style develops in England. Examples feature bold, simple massing; flat, unbroken walls; minimal, refined, and flat ornament; the Greek orders, particularly the Doric; heavy proportions; porticoes; colonnades; and Greek or Roman temple forms. Many museums, libraries, art galleries, and university buildings are Greek Revival and stand as Temples of Learning or Temples of Art, structures created for educating humankind about the accomplishments of the ancients. Largely supplanted by Gothic Revival by midcentury in England, Greek Revival continues well into the 1860s in Scotland.

Beginning in the 1820s, designers, having reached what they believe are the limitations of the Greek Revival, turn to the Italian Renaissance, Italian vernacular, and Andrea Palladio for inspiration. Renaissance Revival, adopted first for gentlemen's clubs, copies and adapts forms and details from Italian Renaissance palaces.

The Picturesque Movement in architecture emerges from landscapes designed in the second half of the 18th century. These landscapes feature asymmetry, meandering paths, ponds with irregular shapes, and ruins or small buildings for contemplation as designers strive to create a series of views or pictures reminiscent of ancient history, literature, or lyrical paintings. In architecture, this translates to unity with the landscape, asymmetry in plan and form, as well as the integration of nature inside and outside. These attributes contrast with Neoclassical and for the most part characterize domestic structures.

Romanticism and the Picturesque expand sources of inspiration to include the Middle Ages—Gothic, Tudor, and Elizabethan. Elements from such exotic sources as China, India, and Islam also appear, although rarely are entire structures designed in these modes. During this period, architects make a distinction between architecture and engineering. They do not consider utilitarian buildings, such as factories, as architecture.

The period produces a variety of building types such as monuments, banks, gentlemen's clubs (Fig. 29-2), museums (Fig. 29-3), markets, churches, factories, and warehouses. Villas, which are somewhere between a mansion and a cottage in size, and townhouses are common in the period. Townhouses (Fig. 29-4, 29-5), often called terraces in England, are tall and narrow in width and exhibit classical characteristics. The most important buildings are classical or Greek Revival in style.

Public and Private Buildings

■ *Site Orientation*. Some public and private apartment buildings are part of Picturesque urban developments, and their relationship to each other and the street is carefully considered to create focal points or scenic views. John Nash's design for Regent's Park (Fig. 29-4) in London is an example.

■ *Floor Plans*. Plans do not change a great deal. Symmetry continues to govern the disposition of spaces. Important buildings often have spaces in various sizes and shapes suited to their functions. House plans influenced by the Picturesque are asymmetrical and may have angled wings and/or center on verandas or towers. These plans are more likely to be arranged in circular patterns around the staircase. New additions to house plans include the breakfast room (Fig. 29-5), adjoining parlors with sliding doors to create a more open plan, and the conservatory to bring nature into the house.

■ *Materials*. Brick is the dominant building material followed by local stone. New methods of firing give a greater range of colors for brick. Yellow, gray, cream, and white brick replace red in popularity. Stucco often covers brick and is colored and scored to resemble ashlar masonry. However, stucco is not very durable, so builders develop Portland cement in 1814 as a substitute. Its name comes from its resemblance to a stone quarried on the Isle of Portland. Ironwork is especially characteristic for balconies, verandas, windows, and roofs.

■ *Façades*. Usual classical characteristics for façades (Fig. 29-3, 29-4) include temple fronts, porticoes, colonnades, pediments, clean lines, smooth or rusticated walls, geometric forms, and symmetrically disposed wings. Greek Revival strives to create a Grecian image using the Doric, Ionic, or Corinthian orders; minimal ornament; and compositions of geometric solids derived from ancient Greek prototypes. Later, architects begin to add elements from the Italian Renaissance and Andrea Palladio. As a result, the Italian *palazzo* becomes the model for gentlemen's clubs (Fig. 29-2) and banks.

Town and country houses have wider and taller sash windows, bow and bay windows, simpler door cases, and/or stucco walls and applied details. Indian-style buildings (Fig. 29-6), which are few, feature cupolas, lacy arches, and onion domes. Verandas, a concept

DESIGN SPOTLIGHT

Architecture: These townhouses are centerpieces in Regent's Park. The design of Cumberland Terrace treats the terrace as a single unit. The building has triumphal arches in the center joined by two wings on either side. Although Grecian details embellish the building, its long wall is broken by a series of projections that create repetitive movement and visual interest, vital ingredients in the Picturesque. Projecting pavilions with balustrades carried by pairs of Ionic columns define the ends of the wings and middle section. A large two-step projection distinguishes the building's center. This pavilion is composed of a central portico with a pediment flanked by smaller stepped-back Ionic porticoes. The tympanum has terra-cotta figures of Britannia flanked by the arts and sciences. Ionic pilasters divide the recessed portions of the building into bays. The entire lower story is rusticated and has sash windows. French windows highlight the middle story, and smaller square sashes define the third and fourth stories. Nash places the main entrances and service buildings at the rear so as not to disturb his composition and to further the illusion of one long building.

▲ **29-4.** Cumberland Terrace, 1825; in Regent's Park, London, England; John Nash. English Regency.

DESIGN SPOTLIGHT

Architecture and Interiors: The cream-colored exterior of Lincoln's Inn Fields, remodeled by Soane, features a projecting façade on the first two stories with triple arches and classical details. A single projecting arch and statues define the third story, while the fourth story has square windows separated by pilasters. A balustrade caps the composition and hides the roof.

The breakfast room shows Soane's personal style that includes Neoclassical as well as Picturesque design elements. The room's location creates a series of vistas common to the Picturesque that draw the eye into the dome, across the space, and into the Monument Courtyard outside. The shallow canopy dome seems to float lightly above the space, making it appear more intimate in scale. Contributing to this effect, natural and artificial light from light wells illuminate the room perimeter, making the walls brighter than the dome is. Hundreds of small mirrors in the dome, in the pendentives, and underneath the arches multiply light and views to enhance the feeling of Neoclassical lightness. The incised lines and Greek key motifs that embellish the dome are typical of Soane's style. The house showcases his interior architecture and vast collection of artifacts, books, and artwork.

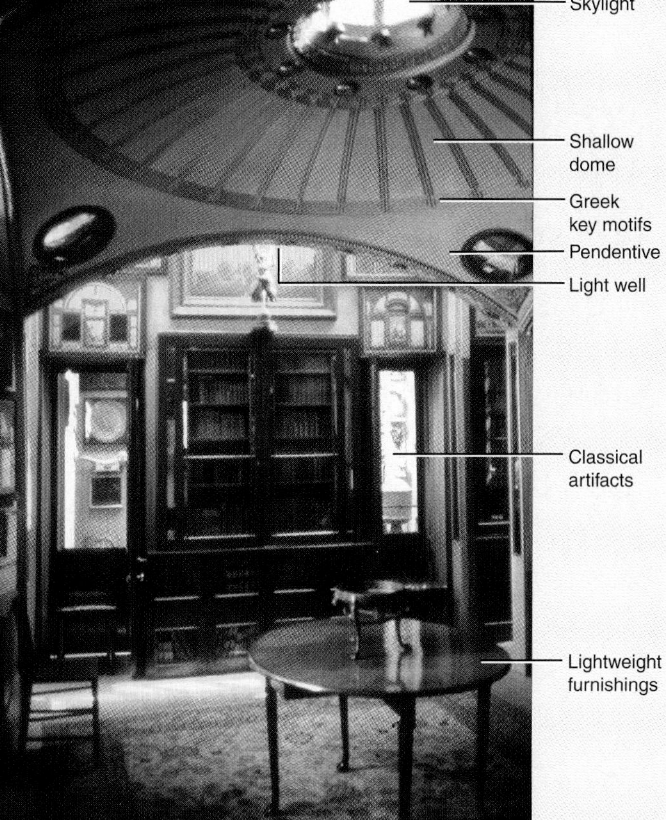

▲ **29-5.** No. 13, Lincoln's Inn Fields (Soane's house, now the Soane Museum) and breakfast room, 1812–1813; London, England; Sir John Soane. English Regency.

DESIGN SPOTLIGHT

Architecture and Interiors: Originally classical in style, the Royal Pavilion represents the exotic, eclectic aspects of Regency as envisioned by John Nash for the Prince of Wales. Nash creates a building without parallel in Europe that sets the standard for fantasy resort architecture. Taking advantage of new materials, he enlarges the building with a cast-iron frame. Highly irregular in form, the Pavilion combines Chinese, Islamic, medieval, and Indian details and motifs. Curving and rectangular forms create a picturesque outline. Chinese-style lattice in a Gothic pattern fills Islamic horseshoe arches and edges the balconies. French windows with multifoiled arched tops allow access to the outside or the balconies. Minarets, onion domes, chimneys, and pointed battlements punctuate the roofline. The minarets and domes are iron covered in stucco.

The Pavilion's interiors are equally exotic and ostentatious in design. Exterior influences repeat inside, but Chinese details predominate. Lavish materials, rich colors, gilding, bamboo, fretwork, flowers, foliage, and dragons characterize wall, floor, and ceiling treatments as well as furnishings throughout the Pavilion. The most magnificent of the rooms are the Banqueting Room by artist Robert Jones and the Music Room decorated by Frederick Crace.

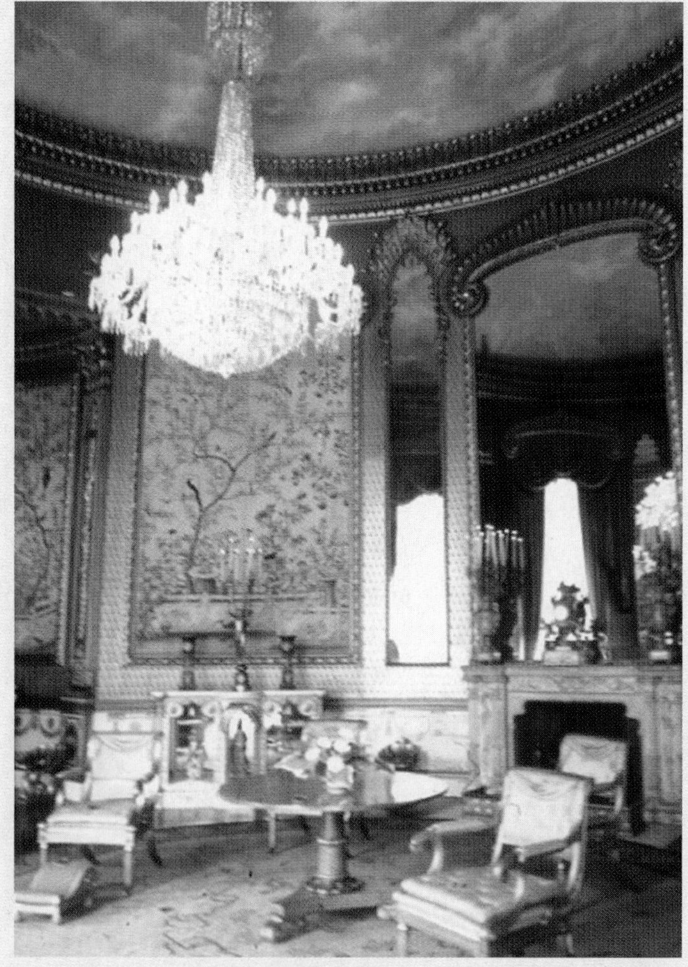

▲ 29-6. Royal Pavilion, Music Gallery, and Banqueting Room, 1786–1787, remodeled 1815–1821; Brighton, England; Henry Holland, remodeled by John Nash. English Regency.

arriving from India, may surround a medieval- or exotic-style house or be integrated into one or more façades, creating a Picturesque image and taking advantage of light and views.

■ *Windows and Doors*. Windows (Fig. 29-2, 29-4, 29-5) may be rectangular or square, small or large. Typical sash and French windows are arranged symmetrically across the façade, usually with blank walls in between. Some have rounded tops, lintels, or pediments. Exterior shutters may be brown, black, or green. Doors are wood paneled, and are painted dark colors unless they are made of mahogany or oak. Surrounds appropriate to the style include columns, pilasters, porticoes, pointed arches, and foliated arches. Fanlights are smaller with simpler glazing patterns than before. In the 1830s, doors with glass panes emerge.

■ *Roofs*. Roofs (Fig. 29-3, 29-4) of classical styles may be flat, gabled, hipped, vaulted, or domed. Medieval and exotic styles may be battlemented, parapeted, or domed in exotic shapes (Fig. 29-6). Italian villa roofs may have overhanging eaves.

INTERIORS

Like architecture, Regency interiors are eclectic and borrow from the same sources—classical, medieval, Italian, French Empire, Chinese, and Indian. Classically inspired rooms are the most common, followed by medieval examples, and, last of all, those inspired by exotic sources. Sometimes interiors repeat exterior styles, but often they do not. On occasion residences mix styles from room to room. Public interiors and important domestic rooms have more ambitious treatments that include architectural details such as moldings, the orders, or fan vaulting. Other rooms have flat, decorative treatments such as paint, fabric, or wallpaper. Each room is treated as a unit with its own color scheme or theme and is usually designated as such (Chinese Room or Yellow Room). Displayed wealth is more important than inherited rank so many rooms are ostentatious or sometimes even garish.

DESIGN SPOTLIGHT

▲ **29-6.** Continued

During this period, room use and associations become more prescribed as family and business relationships change in response to the Industrial Revolution, and etiquette and manners increasingly define roles and interactions. Residential entry halls regulate social status as friends, acquaintances, suitors, and social climbers leave their calling cards to be reviewed by the family. Parlors, where guests are received and entertained, give impressions of status and culture through formal, usually feminine, décor. An important symbol of wealth and hospitality is the dining room (Fig. 29-6), which is found in more middle-class homes. Its décor is masculine. The library evolves from a singularly masculine domain to a room used by the entire family. Commercial buildings generally continue to use the same types of room spaces, but offices become more important and increase in number. Completely architect-designed interiors decline as many people begin decorating their own rooms aided by furniture and interior pattern books. Some call in upholsterers or furniture-making firms. A few antiquarians conduct more scholarly restorations of homes.

Public and Private Buildings

■ *Color.* Color inside public buildings generally comes from the materials, such as stone or marble, but otherwise Regency colors tend to be rich and vivid.

Homeowners can choose from a broader array of colors than ever before. Usual colors (Fig. 29-5, 29-6, 29-9) include crimson, saffron yellow, blue, and gold. Color schemes come from many sources, including a motif or pattern used in the room. Usually walls, curtains, and upholstery match, another change from previously. The colors of the ancients, which form Etruscan or Pompeian color schemes, are terra-cotta, red, and black, sometimes mixed with blue or green. Chinese color schemes, such as those at Brighton Pavilion (Fig. 29-6, 29-8), may be based on the blue or green backgrounds of imported Chinese wallpapers or the red, black, and yellow of imported Chinese lacquer.

▲ **29-7.** Interior with Egyptian influence; published in *Household Furniture and Interior Decoration,* 1807; London, England; Thomas Hope. English Regency.

▲ **29-8.** Wallpapers: Papers in vogue include those with Chinese decorative patterns, often finished with matching borders.

Newly developed color theories advocate color schemes based upon the use of the room, such as green for drawing rooms or orientation, or blue for south rooms. By the 1830s, lighter hues, such as French gray, lilac, or light blue, are fashionable. As before, baseboards or skirting are painted or grained a dark color.

■ *Floors.* Most floors are wood boards cut in random lengths and widths. The best woods are left uncovered. Other woods are painted, stenciled, or covered with carpet or rugs. Parquet floors, especially those that imitate Roman flooring patterns, briefly return to fashion. Stone, scagliola, and marble cover only lower floors because of the weight of the materials.

■ *Floor Coverings.* Industrialization makes machine-made rugs (Fig. 29-6) and carpets more readily available for the middle class, although some types, such as Brussels and Wilton, remain beyond the reach of many. A less expensive alternative is ingrain, a reversible woven pileless carpet that is also called Kidderminster or Scotch carpet. Ingrains typically cover hallways, staircases, servants' rooms, sitting rooms, and parlors of those unable to afford more expensive carpet. Carpet is made in strips that are sewn together and laid wall-to wall. Usual patterns include designs after Roman pavements, stone, tile, geometric, or floral patterns in three or more colors with or without borders. Although Oriental rugs are largely out of fashion, Turkish and Persian patterned carpets are used in libraries and dining rooms. Grass matting, plain and patterned, is especially popular for Chinese rooms and summer use in all rooms.

Floor cloths are still used, but they are not cheap or durable. Composed of heavy canvas or similar tightly woven fabric and several layers of paint, patterns include black-and-white marble, stone, tile, flowers, and Turkish or Persian patterns.

▲ **29-9.** Window Treatments: Designs for draperies with fringe, c. 1820s–1830s.

■ *Walls.* In public buildings, architectural details, such as columns, pilasters, and pediments, articulate the walls. Most have a dado, fill, and cornice or frieze. Spaces between details are often painted or paneled.

In all houses, important rooms have more elaborate wall schemes (Fig. 29-5, 29-6, 29-7). Each style has its own appropriate treatments. Plaster, *papier-mâché,* or stucco decorations may adorn walls. In wealthy homes, gilding highlights these details. Architectural elements in the average residential Regency interior are lighter in scale, more restrained in design, and simpler than before because they are designed to show off furnishings and fabrics, not the moldings.

Paneling adapts to any style. Oak and pine are the most common woods. Very wealthy people choose imported mahogany for paneling. Centers of panels may be grained; marbleized; painted a solid color; or painted with classical, medieval, or Chinese motifs (Fig. 29-6, 29-8), trellises, foliage, or landscapes. Alternatively, fabrics may fill panels or be draped in folds with valances on walls. Interior doors are paneled.

With improvements in its manufacture, the use of wallpaper (Fig. 29-8) increases. Early in the period, it is block-printed in rolls called pieces. By the 1830s, most wallpaper is roller-printed. With so many patterns available, advice books recommend certain types for certain rooms, such as stone imitations for halls. In vogue are papers imitating stone, marble, textiles, or drapery; architectural papers; papers with small floral patterns; and small prints. Many papers have matching borders. Papers from China, although expensive, remain highly fashionable.

■ *Chimney pieces.* Rectangular chimneypieces are simply treated with reeding instead of columns, brackets, or caryatids. Mantels are made of colored marble, scagliola, stone with or without *ormolu* or bronze details, or, for simpler ones, painted pine or plaster.

■ *Windows and Window Treatments.* Most windows have simple molding surrounds, and many continue to have folding interior shutters. Curtains become universal during the period. Fabrics for curtains include velvet, silks, satins, damasks, moreen, moiré, and calicoes or other printed cottons. Treatments, especially in important rooms, are composed of layers of fabric (Fig. 29-9). Swags or valances (called drapery) hang from or drape over wooden or brass rods or carved and gilded cornices. Contrasting linings and a variety of trims add interest and richness. Floor-length or longer curtains hang beneath the swags with sheer white or tinted muslin curtains behind them. Blinds or shades hang next to the glass to block light and protect furnishings from fading.

■ *Doors.* Mahogany doors have a clear finish, while other woods are painted to match the rest of the decoration. Double doorways signal important rooms.

■ *Ceilings.* Ceilings (Fig. 29-5, 29-6, 29-7) are important areas for design in both public and private buildings. In public buildings, and a few houses, ceilings may be compartmentalized, beamed, vaulted, or domed with coffers, in essence more architecturally significant. In houses, ceilings may be plain white or a paler version of the walls. Ceilings in Gothic- or Tudor-style rooms may have real or imitation beams or brackets.

■ *Textiles.* Upholstery fabrics include velvet, silk, damask, chintz, and leather for dining rooms and libraries. Braid, tape, tassels, and/or fringe embellish many pieces. Also, festoons of fabric with eye-catching trim hang between furniture legs or arms, across backs, under seats or rails, and over tables and beds. Loose slipcovers to protect expensive fabrics or tabletops are more common and elaborate than ever before. Plain-woven machine-made fabrics become increasingly common throughout the period in contrast to the hand-woven silks of earlier. Printed textiles are highly prized.

■ *Lighting.* Interiors are more light-filled than ever before. Larger windows allow in more natural light. Advancements in artificial lighting brighten rooms after dark. The Argand lamp is in common use during Regency, but the Sinumbra lamp, invented in 1809, begins to rival the Argand in popularity because it has no reservoir to cast a shadow. Oil lamps may be made of silver, brass, bronze, glass, and crystal in many shapes and sizes. Chandeliers (Fig. 29-6, 29-10) with candles continue in important spaces, along with decorative wall sconces and *torchères.*

▲ **29-10.** Lighting: Chandeliers from the Royal Pavilion, c. 1775–1790; Brighton, England.

FURNISHINGS AND DECORATIVE ARTS

Eclecticism, large areas of veneer with applied or inlaid decoration, and a shiny finish characterize furniture throughout the period. Dark and exotic woods dominate, and many pieces have metal parts, ornament, details, and/or casters to facilitate mobility. Regency designers synthesize forms and motifs from classical, French Empire, medieval, and exotic sources. As in architecture, classicism is the dominant influence.

Early Regency furniture is graceful, movable, and light in scale, as in the previous period. Sheraton and Hepplewhite forms continue from before. Forms are typically rectangular and symmetrical with restrained ornament. Many classical pieces copy or adapt them from ancient sources. Medieval and exotic designs apply motifs to contemporary forms rather than copy earlier pieces. About 1810, furniture becomes heavier, more eclectic, and more embellished as form becomes subordinate to decoration. Toward the end of the period, much more furniture is machine-made, and the dominance of classicism declines in favor of other styles.

Furniture pattern books and treatises, important during Regency, show the scores of resources, styles, and approaches to design available. New pieces of furniture common to the style include sofa tables, X-form stools (Fig. 29-14), Grecian couches (Fig. 29-17), nesting tables, work-tables, chiffoniers, and dwarf bookcases. Also new to the period is the whatnot, a stand of open shelves for display.

Comfort becomes increasingly important. Less formal living patterns bring about modern space planning for use and convenience. Furniture no longer lines the perimeter of the room when not in use, except in important rooms. Sofas sit at right angles to or in front of the fireplace. Many have sofa tables in front of them. Center tables, introduced from France, become a gathering place for the family. Unique to Regency are the many additional small tables placed around the room for a variety of functions. Furniture variety indicates wealth instead of position in society.

DESIGN SPOTLIGHT

Furniture: This armchair with lion heads showcases Hope's main ideas of furniture design: to design in a close imitation of the antique. Emulating his friends Charles Percier and Pierre-François-Léonard Fontaine in Empire France, Hope copies extant ancient furniture or illustrations from vase paintings and relief sculpture. The heavy chair with lion heads derives from the Greek *klismos* and closely resembles a design by Percier and Fontaine. Massive in scale, the front supports are monopodia, a Roman form. The back legs are sabers. The solid curvilinear back is embellished with Greek frets and a laurel wreath. Decorative fringe hangs beneath the seat, as is common during the period.

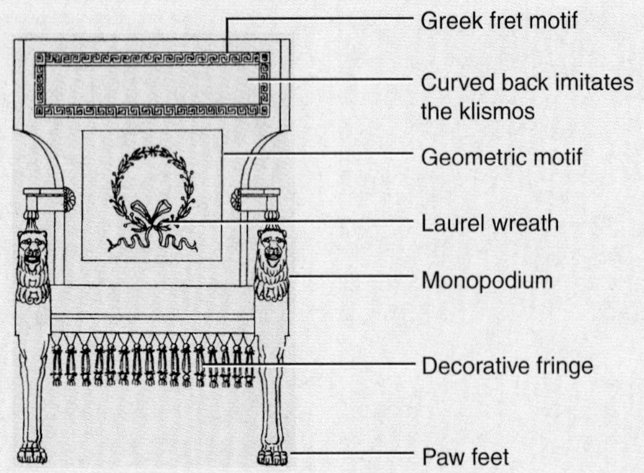

▲ **29-11.** Armchair with lion heads; published in *Household Furniture and Interior Decoration*, 1807; London, England; Thomas Hope.

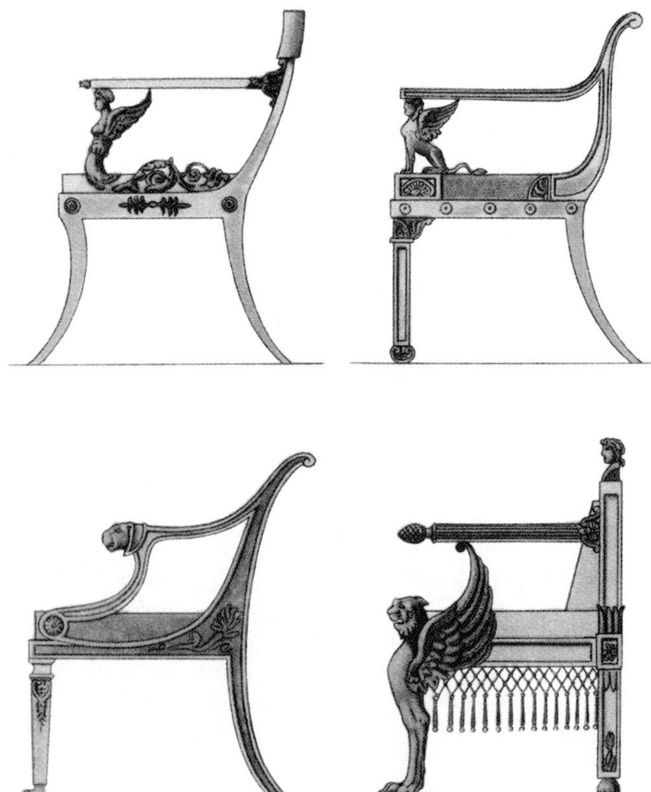

▲ **29-12.** Drawing room chairs; published in *A Collection of Designs for Household Furniture and Interior Decoration*, 1808; London, England; George Smith.

▲ **29-13.** Elbow chair with saber legs, c. 1810; England.

▲ **29-15.** Armchair of bamboo, early 19th century; England.

Public and Private Buildings

■ *Materials.* Expensive furniture is made of mahogany or oak. Highly prized are exotic woods, such as rosewood, tulipwood, or zebrawood, which are often used as veneers. Less expensive woods are grained or stained to imitate more expensive ones. Pieces may be painted green to imitate bronze, be painted like bamboo, or feature classical or *Chinoiserie* scenes (Fig. 29-20). Much furniture is painted black with gilding or japanned. Especially distinctive in Regency furniture are brass and other metals used as furniture mounts, inlay, trellises or grilles, or paw feet.

■ *Seating.* Most seating is classical in design. Some chairs imitate the earlier work of Sheraton or copy the Greek *klismos* (Fig. 29-11, 29-12). Others adapt the classical language with saber front and back legs, caned seat, and back and legs in a continuous curve (Fig. 29-6, 29-13). Arms are graceful scrolls. The horizontal backboards may be painted or gilded. Alternatively, the front legs may be turned or in the form of Roman monopodia (Fig. 29-8, 29-11, 29-12). Paw feet are common. Another much-imitated ancient form is the X-shaped or Roman curule chair or stool (Fig. 29-14) popularized by Thomas Hope. Chinese examples, which are more prevalent among exotic styles, have fretwork, *pagodas*, or lacquered finishes (Fig. 29-15).

Sofas and couches (Fig. 29-16, 29-17) inspired by antiquity or French Empire are very fashionable during the Regency. Most drawing and dining rooms have one, and many have two. Sofas have outward-scrolled arms and legs ending in paw feet. Cornucopia-shaped legs are common. Backs may be rectangular or curved, or have an asymmetrical panel not as long as the back. Seats have a bolster on each end and sometimes cushions across the back.

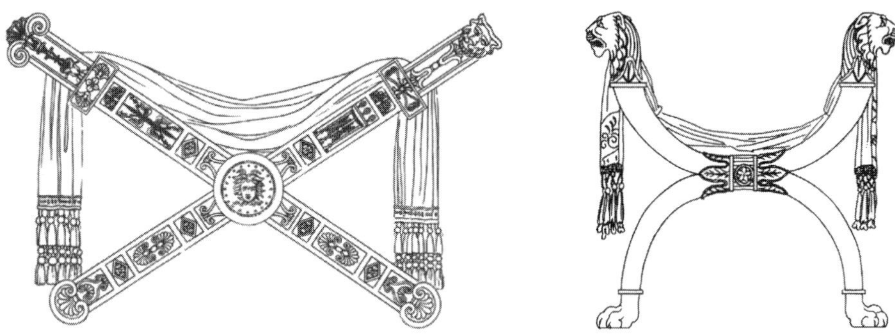

▲ **29-14.** X-form stools; published in *Household Furniture and Interior Decoration*, 1807; London, England; Thomas Hope.

▲ **29-16.** Scrolled-end sofa with representative leg detail, c. 1805–1810; England.

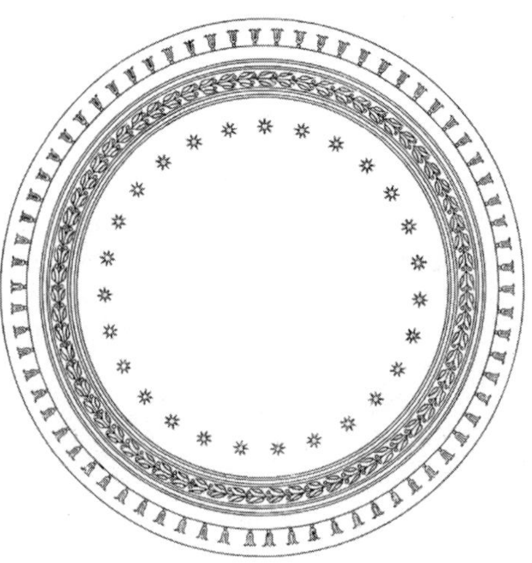

■ *Tables*. Pier tables, circular tables, and stands frequently copy antique examples in wood or metal. Supports may be turned, columnar, or monopodia. Most terminate in paw feet. Nests of tables, usually slender, may have three (trio tables) or four (quartetto tables) small tables that slide into one another. Work tables, often for sewing, are small with drawers and a silk pouch for scraps and threads. Some small tables open to reveal game boards. Sofa tables, placed in front of the sofa, are oblong and supported by trestles that are usually lyre shaped. They often have drop leaves and drawers. Dining tables (Fig. 29-5) may be in several parts as in earlier periods or may be extension tables with several pedestals or claws, as they are called. Pedestals (Fig. 29-6, 29-18) have a single center support and outward-curving legs ending in metal paws.

▲ **29-18.** Pedestal table; published in *Household Furniture and Interior Decoration*, 1807; London, England; Thomas Hope.

▲ **29-17.** Grecian-style couch; published in *Household Furniture and Interior Decoration*, 1807; London, England; Thomas Hope.

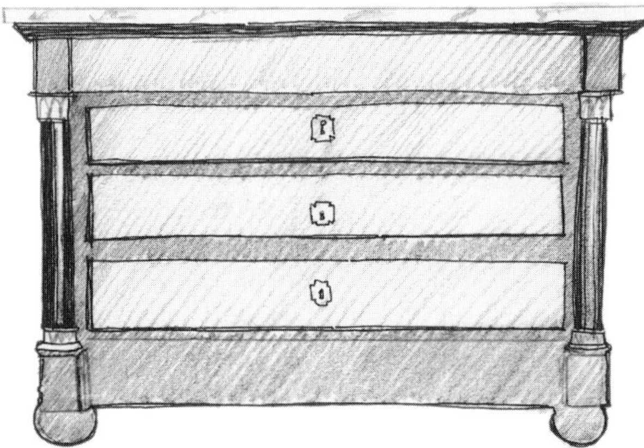

▲ **29-19.** *Commode*, mahogany, c. 1820; England.

▲ **29-20.** *Chinoiserie* cabinet, early 19th century; England.

■ *Storage*. Fashionable *commodes* (Fig. 29-19) are massive with eclectic designs and marble tops. Painting, veneers, and metalwork are common embellishments. Double chests with *Chinoiserie* decoration (Fig. 29-20) are popular and bring the exotic influence into a room.

■ *Beds*. Several types of beds are fashionable, including the four-poster, the half-tester, and the French bed or *lit en bateau*. All have carved and applied details. The four-poster with complex hangings is most fashionable, but all types of beds display opulent hangings with rich trims.

■ *Decorative Arts*. Most rooms contain at least one looking glass or pier glass (Fig. 29-6), which is carefully placed with an eye to their reflections in and among rooms. Newly fashionable for Regency is the convex mirror with a heavy circular frame that is usually gilded. Paintings, prints, and silhouettes hang on walls, usually in gilded frames.

Meals are lavish, so tables and sideboards display many pieces of silver, silver plate, china, and cut glass. Nature comes into the house through the plants, flowers, and caged birds that often decorate Regency rooms.

■ *Later Interpretations*. The scale and simplicity of some Regency furniture appeal to followers of the Aesthetic Movement in the 1860s and 1870s. Regency furniture revives along with interiors at the end of the 19th century. In 1917, the sale of Thomas Hope's personal furniture prompts a continued revival of Regency furniture in the 20th century. The form, scale, and curving lines of Regency chairs and sofas continue to appeal to designers and clients today. Some manufacturers reproduce Regency sofas and chairs; others adapt Regency designs (Fig. 29-21).

▲ **29-21.** Later Interpretation: Anziano *klismos* chair, 2004; New York; John Hutton, manufactured by Donghia. Modern Historicism.

CHAPTER 30

American Greek Revival, American Empire

1820s–1860s

Regarding it as an expression of democracy and national culture, America wholeheartedly embraces Greek Revival for numerous structures ranging from banks to courthouses, cottages to mansions. The most common expression is a temple form with a portico built of masonry for public buildings and white-painted wood for houses. Architectural details derived from Greece, Rome, and Egypt and simple wall treatments signal Grecian interiors. American Empire furniture is characterized by classically derived ornament and wood-grain patterns, often of veneer. It is heavier proportioned and more archaeologically correct than was Federal, the previous style.

The public sentiment just now runs almost exclusively and popularly into the Grecian school. We build little besides temples for our churches, our banks, our taverns, our court houses and our dwellings. A friend of mine has just built a brewery on the model of the Temple of the Winds in Athens.

—James Fenimore Cooper, as stated by Aristabulus Bragg, *Home as Found*, 1828

HISTORICAL AND SOCIAL

A great wave of nationalist feelings follows the War of 1812 with Great Britain. This period of strong national unity precedes four decades of strife between regions of the country that will culminate in the Civil War beginning in 1860. The northern, southern, and western sections have very different outlooks, societies, and economics, and each wants to control and determine national policies to its own benefit. They argue over banking, tariffs, annexation of territory, and, ultimately, slavery.

Stimulated by the Industrial Revolution and the westward migration of farmers, manufacturing dominates the Northeast. Factories using steam or water power to produce goods spring up throughout the region, transforming quiet farm towns into bustling industrial cities. New roads, canals, and railroads help transport goods to the western territories and abroad. Boston, New York, Philadelphia, and Baltimore rapidly increase in size and population.

The South remains agrarian with cotton as its chief crop. Consequently, states' rights and slavery are important issues there. Because cotton is most often grown on large plantations using slave labor, the movement to abolish slavery that arises in the North angers Southerners. Slavery becomes a major issue in the annexation of western states and settlement of western territories such as Texas, Oregon, California, and New Mexico. Southerners also greatly resent the tariffs that protect northern manufactured goods.

Migration westward accelerates, and increases when gold is discovered in California in 1848. It is caused in part by Manifest Destiny, the notion that expansion is not only inevitable, but divinely ordained. However, most settlers simply desire to own their own land or to explore new territory. Although bringing benefits to the nation, expansion also increases disputes and controversy, particularly over slavery.

Greater production of wheat, cotton, and manufactured goods increases wealth in the Midwest, South, and North, respectively. Affluent northern businessmen and manufacturers and southern plantation owners live in large, well-furnished mansions. Slaves and settlers who live in one-room hovels, log cabins, and sod houses are at the opposite end of the scale. In between these groups is the sizable middle class, which has become sufficiently large and wealthy that merchants and manufacturers begin to provide goods and services for it.

CONCEPTS

In America, the adoption of Greek Revival in architecture and American Empire in furniture coincides with a period of nationalistic fervor and enthusiasm for progress and personal liberty. Following the American Revolution, leaders such as Thomas Jefferson see classical antiquity as the source of ideal beauty and regard American citizens as models of civic virtue and morality. Thus, they choose classical-style architecture and furniture for themselves and for the architecture of the new nation and its model civilization.

Furthermore, classical studies form the basis for liberal arts education, and many see the Greek struggle for independence (1821–1830) as a parallel to America's ongoing fights with Great Britain. As a visual metaphor for beauty, democracy, republican government, liberty, and civic virtue, Greek Revival defines numerous buildings, both rural and urban, high style and vernacular across the nation. It is America's first national style.

Continuing the Neoclassical mode, American Empire furniture develops from French Empire and English Regency influences. Americans learn of European designs through widely circulated pattern books and pamphlets, when they travel abroad, or when they import furniture from abroad.

MOTIFS

■ *Motifs*. Architectural details (Fig. 30-1, 30-4, 30-12, 30-13) and motifs come primarily from Greece, but also from Rome and Egypt. They include egg and dart, bead, and dentil moldings; triglyphs and metopes; honeysuckles; anthemions; acanthus leaves; and the fret or key. Interiors, furniture, and decorative arts exhibit a greater range of motifs from more sources, including Egyptian, Greek, Roman, and Renaissance (Fig. 30-13, 30-14, 30-15, 30-17). These include sphinxes, battered or pylon forms, paw feet, Egyptian or classical figures, lyres, harps, swans, dolphins, eagles, caryatids, serpents, arabesques, and columns.

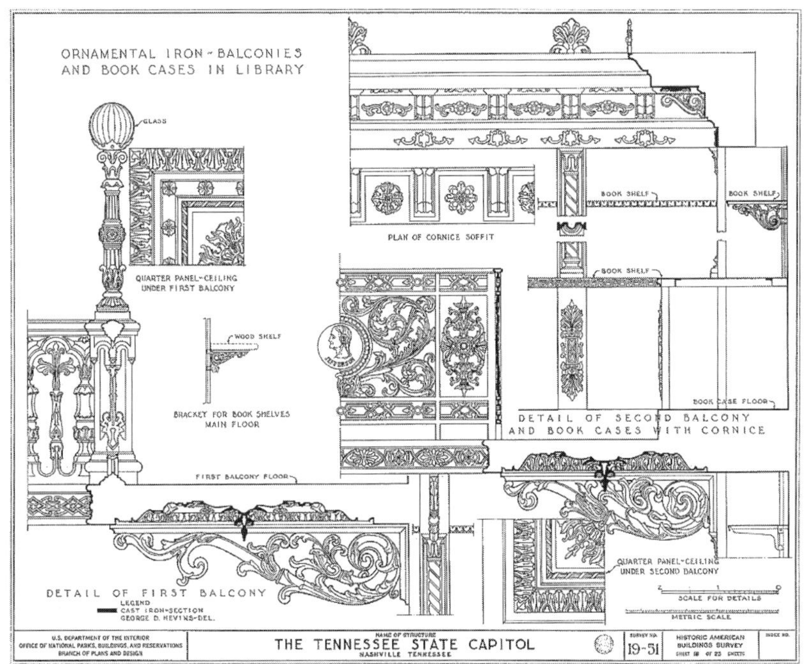

▲ **30-1.** Architectural Details: Details from the Tennessee State Capitol, 1845–1859; Nashville, Tennessee; William Strickland; and doorway, c. mid-19th century; Louisiana.

ARCHITECTURE

As in other countries, American Greek Revival architecture relies on forms and elements derived from a few classical models adapted to contemporary requirements and ornament taken chiefly from Greece, but also Rome. Inspired by earlier English buildings and publications, America alters the style to suit its national consciousness, resulting in nationalist expressions and cultural symbolism unique to America. Various building types adapt temple forms, often in wood, usually with a plainer appearance than the prototypes. Designers may deviate from classical canons for creativity, individuality, or for distinction. This design variety sets the American Greek Revival apart from its European counterparts.

In egalitarian America, everyone can be a patron. Consequently, the Greek Revival temple form becomes the most com-

▲ **30-3.** Fairmount Waterworks, 1812–1822; Philadelphia, Pennsylvania.

▲ **30-2.** First Church of Christ, Congregational, 1814; New Haven, Connecticut; Ithiel Town.

▲ **30-4.** First Baptist Church and nave, 1822; Charleston, South Carolina; Robert Mills.

mon architectural icon for high-style government, commercial, and institutional buildings designed by architects and builders as well as numerous residences. The temple form becomes a symbol of order, repose, and stability. Many Americans live in temple-form houses, believing them to be the only proper dwelling for citizens of revived classical governments. High style, vernacular, or folk interpretations of white temple-form houses dot the landscape, creating an image of Greek simplicity. In towns named for Greek cities, such as Athens, Syracuse, or Troy, temple fronts often line quiet, tree-shaded streets. Because the style's inception coincides with the population explosion and territorial expansion, vernacular examples are far more numerous in America than they are in Europe.

Numerous Greek Revival banks (Fig. 30-5), retail establishments, government and public works buildings (Fig. 30-3), offices, institutions, colleges, bridges, monuments, and memorials

DESIGN SPOTLIGHT

Architecture: The Second Bank of the United States is the first major example of Greek Revival architecture in the United States. William Strickland's design, which derives from the Parthenon for the first time in America, wins the competition held by the bank's directors. Because he has not been to Greece, Strickland uses the restored views of the Parthenon from Stuart and Revett's book, *The Antiquities of Athens and Other Monuments of Greece* (1762, 1787, 1794), as the model for the Doric porticoes on each end of the rectangular structure. In order to accommodate the windows, the design does not repeat the columns on the sides of the building. Marble veneer faces the entire structure. The gable roof conceals the barrel-vaulted banking room in the center of the plan. The building is very influential because the bank is one of the most important financial institutions in the country until the 1830s. [National Historic Landmark]

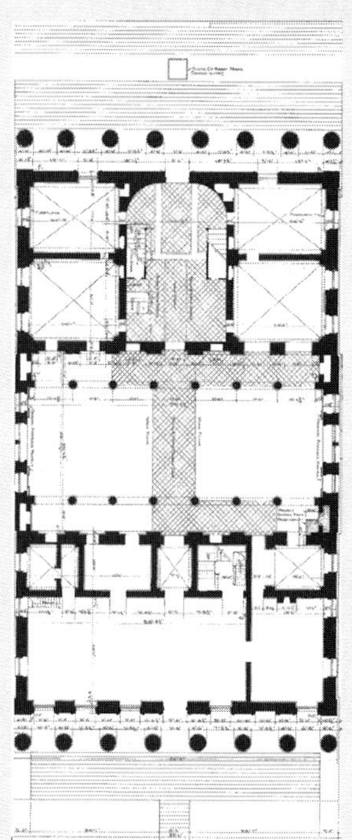

▲ **30-5.** Second Bank of the United States (later known as the Customs House) and floor plan, 1817–1824; Philadelphia, Pennsylvania; William Strickland.

▲ **30-6.** Merchant's Exchange, 1832–1834; Philadelphia, Pennsylvania; William Strickland.

proclaim the uniqueness of the new nation. Some states, such as Tennessee, build Greek Revival capitol buildings (Fig. 30-7). Pagan associations render the style inappropriate for churches, so only a few are built (Fig. 30-2, 30-4), mostly for reformed denominations. Common house types include the temple form with or without wings (Fig. 30-8, 30-9), the gable end (Fig. 30-10), and peripteral forms that are common on Southern plantations and mansions. Numerous classical porches, pilasters, and columns are added to existing houses for an updated Grecian appearance.

Public and Private Buildings

■ *Site Orientation.* Designers strive to isolate public buildings in the manner of the Greek acropolis instead of the Roman manner of relating buildings to each other. Although buildings in complexes relate to each other visually, they assert their individual character, such as the Fairmount Water Works (Fig. 30-3) in Philadelphia. Structures in cities often face important streets or parks. Houses may be sited in rural landscapes, along tree-lined streets in cities or towns, or as urban row houses. A typical image for many today, but uncommon during the period, is a long double row of trees leading to the large columned plantation house.

■ *Floor Plans.* Plans (Fig. 30-5, 30-9) are generally rectangular and suitable to building function. Most are symmetrical and oriented around important circulation spaces. Rooms vary in shape from square to round. Designers use great ingenuity in creating functional plans within the temple form but generally do not try to adapt ancient plans to contemporary needs. For larger houses, the symmetrical, double-pile or Georgian plan of central hall with flanking rectangular rooms, common in the 18th century, remains typical. To accommodate entrances on one side, plans of gable-end houses are often asymmetrical.

■ *Materials.* Building materials, particularly for public buildings, are usually local stone, granite, marble, and brick (Fig. 30-3, 30-5, 30-6). Most houses are of wood. Both public and private buildings are painted white, and brick may be covered with stucco and scored to resemble stone. Public buildings often combine trabeated and arcuated construction by using columns along with vaults and domes. Cast iron may be used for details or handrails of steps.

■ *Façades.* Temple fronts depicting the classical image and the Greek orders define Greek Revival façades (Fig. 30-2, 30-3, 30-4, 30-5, 30-7, 30-8, 30-9). Doric is the most common order, followed by Ionic and Corinthian. Most public buildings have porticos on one if not both ends, thereby emulating the Roman temple form. Others may give that impression with pilasters that continue the column rhythm, divide walls into bays, and simulate the post and lintel building system. Many houses have temple fronts and may have columns on fronts only, front and sides, or surrounding them. Proportions and scale often are very different from those of ancient structures. Because the classical idea is more important than archaeological correctness is, many liberties are taken in the designs. Walls are flat with few projections other than porticoes. Basements sometimes are rusticated. Fenestration may be symmetrical or asymmetrical.

Some public buildings closely imitate specific prototypes, such as Strickland's Second Bank of the United States (Fig. 30-5), which emulates the façade of the Parthenon (447–436 B.C.E.; Athens, Greece). Others do not copy earlier structures, so they vary greatly from the original Greek ones or display strong Roman influences. Some public structures, notably courthouses and state capitols, have domes and/or cupolas and apsidal ends or projections. The cupola of the Tennessee State Capitol (Fig. 30-7) in Nashville is modeled after the Choragic Monument of Lysicrates. Ornament on all building types is minimal and Grecian, most

▲ **30-7.** Tennessee State Capitol, 1845–1859; Nashville, Tennessee; William Strickland.

commonly a Doric frieze, the anthemion, or Greek key. Architectural details are larger and bolder than Federal ones are.

Churches (Fig. 30-2, 30-4) continue the traditional form of porch with a tall steeple behind it, but with Grecian columns and other details. Steeples, which combine rectangular and cylindrical shapes, are modern creations because vertical Grecian prototypes are rare.

■ *Windows and Doors*. Windows (Fig. 30-6, 30-8, 30-9, 30-10) are rectangular and double hung. Triple sashes are common on dwellings. Arched, round, or Palladian examples are extremely rare because arches do not characterize Greek architecture. Decorative surrounds may be plain and rectangular or have pilasters, lintels, or pediments. Exterior shutters are typical on houses. Entrances on all buildings are important and may be grandly treated with pilasters or columns. A common treatment on residences is a rectangular light above the door with flanking glass sidelights (Fig. 30-1). Tops above doors may have lintels or pediments. Often there is a balcony above. Surrounds may be further embellished with classical moldings, such as egg and dart, triglyphs, Greek key, acanthus leaves, or palmettes. Doors themselves are wood panels, and they may be single or double.

▲ **30-9.** Francis M. Dimond House, 1838; Bristol, Rhode Island; Russell Warren.

DESIGN SPOTLIGHT

Architecture: Andalusia was originally designed in 1805 for John Craig by Benjamin Henry Latrobe. The main house was enlarged in 1835 by Thomas U. Walter for Craig's daughter Jane and son-in-law Nicholas Biddle, a prominent early 19th-century Philadelphia banker. Walter's addition, which faces the Delaware River, creates the Greek Revival temple front façade with its large Doric portico and pediment. The portico reinforces the symmetrical balance of the addition, which was built to create double parlors on the first floor. Floor-length sash windows in the parlors allow access to the porch. Important architectural features are painted white, while the body of the house is a pale gold. Inside, bold classical details around doors, windows, and chimneypieces connect interior and exterior. Together with prominent cornices, plain and decorated ceilings, and unarticulated painted walls, the interiors provide formal settings for the rituals of entertaining guests and family. Colors on interior walls are the popular whites and grays of marble and stone common to the period. Family furnishings include late 18th- and 19th-century French, English, Chinese, and American furniture collected by the Biddles. [National Historic Landmark]

▲ **30-8.** Andalusia, 1806–1835; Bucks County, Pennsylvania; 1805 by Benjamin Henry Latrobe, 1835 by Thomas U. Walter and Nicholas Biddle.

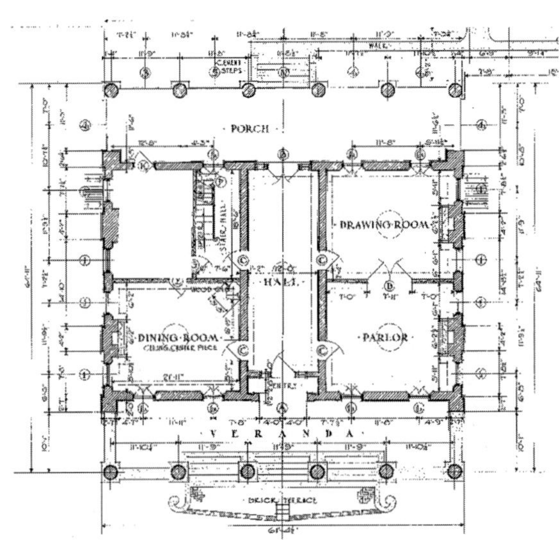

▲ **30-10.** D'Evereux and floor plan of first floor, 1840; Natchez, Mississippi.

▲ **30-11.** Later Interpretation: "The Magnolia," c. 1918; model house available through Sears, Roebuck & Company catalog. Neoclassical Revival.

■ *Roofs*. Roofs (Fig. 30-3, 30-5, 30-7, 30-8, 30-9, 30-10) are usually low-pitched gables resembling ancient temples. Some gables are steeper than the prototypes to allow for rain or snow. A few structures have flat roofs with balustrades or hipped roofs. Domes with cupolas and cupolas alone often denote important spaces.

■ *Later Interpretations*. Neoclassical Revival houses (Fig. 30-11) and public buildings sometimes replicate Greek Revival forms and details, but with larger scale and different materials.

INTERIORS

Greek Revival interiors do not replicate those of the past because few examples survive. Public interiors have large and bold classical details rather than purely classical forms and treatments. Important rooms are grandly treated with columns, pilasters, moldings, and coffered ceilings. Spaces are generally rectangular, and those with domes may be round or octagonal. Symmetry and regularity are important design principles. A few spaces feature apsidal ends with a screen of columns separating the curving portions from the rest of the space. Domestic rooms are mostly rectangular spaces, but usually with an overall simpler character than is evident in public interiors. Both public and private interiors project a dignified and somber presence. Americans are less likely to imitate Etruscan or Pompeian modes than are the English and French, and they do not have an emperor to glorify like France. Furnishings may or may not be classical because the Rococo and Gothic Revivals gain popularity toward the middle of the century.

In houses, halls or passages remain summer living spaces early in the period, but eventually become service areas or spaces for regulating social relationships. Many homes have double parlors, separated by sliding or pocket doors when needed or accented by columns. The front parlor (Fig. 30-13, 30-14), used for entertaining, is feminine and elegant in a manner to impress visitors. The rear or family parlor is less formally decorated and serves as a repository for older furnishings. Dining rooms are more common

▲ **30-12.** Rotunda, Customs House, New York City, 1834–1841; Town and Davis.

than they were before. Service areas are at the rear, in the basement, or completely separated from the house. The best chambers, located on the ground or second floor, often have elaborate, four-poster beds and large wardrobes to display wealth and prosperity.

Public and Private Buildings

■ *Color.* In public buildings, most color comes from materials such as the whites and grays of marble or stone (Fig. 30-4). Somber colors for walls, such as stone, gray, or drab (gray-brown), are common. Many walls are marbleized. Drapery, upholstery, and carpets provide accents of stronger, saturated colors in deep reds, blues, greens, and golds.

In houses, the Romantic interest in nature appears in colors with names like moss green, fawn brown, or stone gray. Early in the period, light values and neutral tones predominate (Fig. 30-13, 30-14, 30-15). By mid-century, colors such as lilac, peach, bronze green, sage, and salmon are fashionable. Dining rooms may be red or green. Emphasizing the importance of placement, writers call for light ceilings, darker walls, and woodwork that is lighter or darker than the walls. Critics believe that bedrooms should be cheerful with light-colored walls and simple patterns.

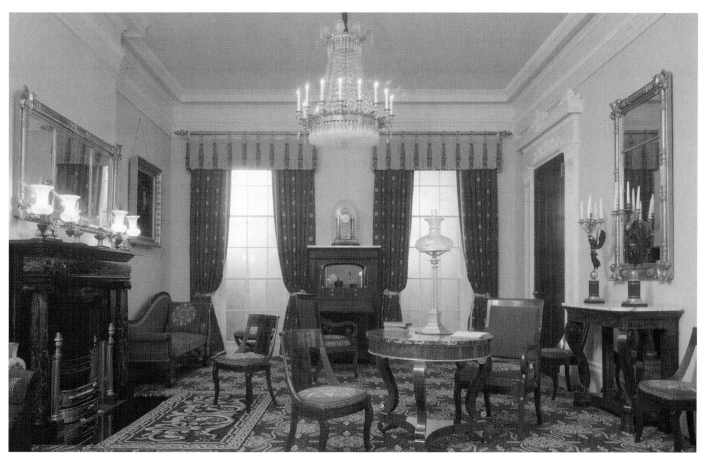

▲ **30-13.** Greek Revival parlor, c. 1835; New York City, New York; furniture by Duncan Phyfe for Samuel A. Foote. [Parlor gift of Richard and Gloria Manney. The Metropolitan Museum of Art, NY, U.S.A. Image © The Metropolitan Museum of Art/Art Resource, NY]

■ *Floors*. Floors may be masonry, marble, or wood that is painted or covered with floor cloths or carpets.

■ *Floor Coverings*. The use of carpets increases dramatically as a result of industrialization. Carpets (Fig. 30-13, 30-14) usually are installed in narrow strips that are pieced together. Wall-to-wall carpets include Brussels, Wilton, ingrain, tapestry, and list. Brussels and Wilton remain expensive. Less costly carpets include ingrain, list, tapestry, and Venetian carpets. Early in the period, carpets have geometric designs and classical motifs in red, blue, green, or gold. Combinations of red and green are especially fashionable. Later patterns include trellises and stripes with flowers, imitations of Oriental rugs, and realistically shaded flowers.

■ *Walls*. Bold architectural details articulate walls (Fig. 30-4, 30-12, 30-13, 30-14, 30-15), particularly in important spaces in public buildings. Some walls are treated as one broad expanse with paint or wallpaper, whereas others are divided by a dado, fill, and cornice, or are divided into bays with engaged columns or pilasters. Baseboards are higher than before. Rectangular, stone mantels, usually black or white, resemble exterior door surrounds.

■ *Wallpaper*. As in Europe, wallpaper (Fig. 30-14, 30-16) use increases in American homes. Continuous rolls are common after 1830; machine-made paper becomes available about 1820 but does not dominate the market until the 1840s. Most papers continue to be hand-block-printed, although roller print examples increase. New colors for papers include chrome yellow, French blue, and bright green.

Wallpaper in many patterns comes from England, France, China, and America. Landscape or scenic papers from France, particularly, are fashionable. Other patterns include architectural, ashlar, fresco, landscape, and textile or drapery imitations. Archi-

DESIGN SPOTLIGHT

Interiors: Constructed between 1831 and 1834, Shadows-on-the-Teche is owned by sugarcane planter David Weeks. The two-story gable-roofed house has a symmetrical façade of brick with double-hung windows. Colossal Tuscan columns carrying a Roman Doric frieze create the gallery or porch that runs across both stories, and an exterior stair on one side provides vertical circulation. Originally, the house was painted white with green shutters.

This interior museum installation reproduces the parlor of an upper-middle-class house where guests are received and various rites and ceremonies take place. Fresco paper in buff damask adorns the walls, its borders forming a paneled or compartmentalized design. On the floor is a multicolored wool Brussels carpet in a geometric-floral pattern. The window treatments are green damask with shaped valance and are tied back under curtains. A center table with an astral lamp and American Empire–style gondola (or *seignouret*) chairs provide a place for people to gather. Additional furniture includes American Empire pier tables, side chairs, armchairs, and a sofa. The bold cornice, door surrounds, and rectangular marble with *ormolu* mantel clock and *girandoles* are common details in Greek Revival houses. [National Historic Landmark]

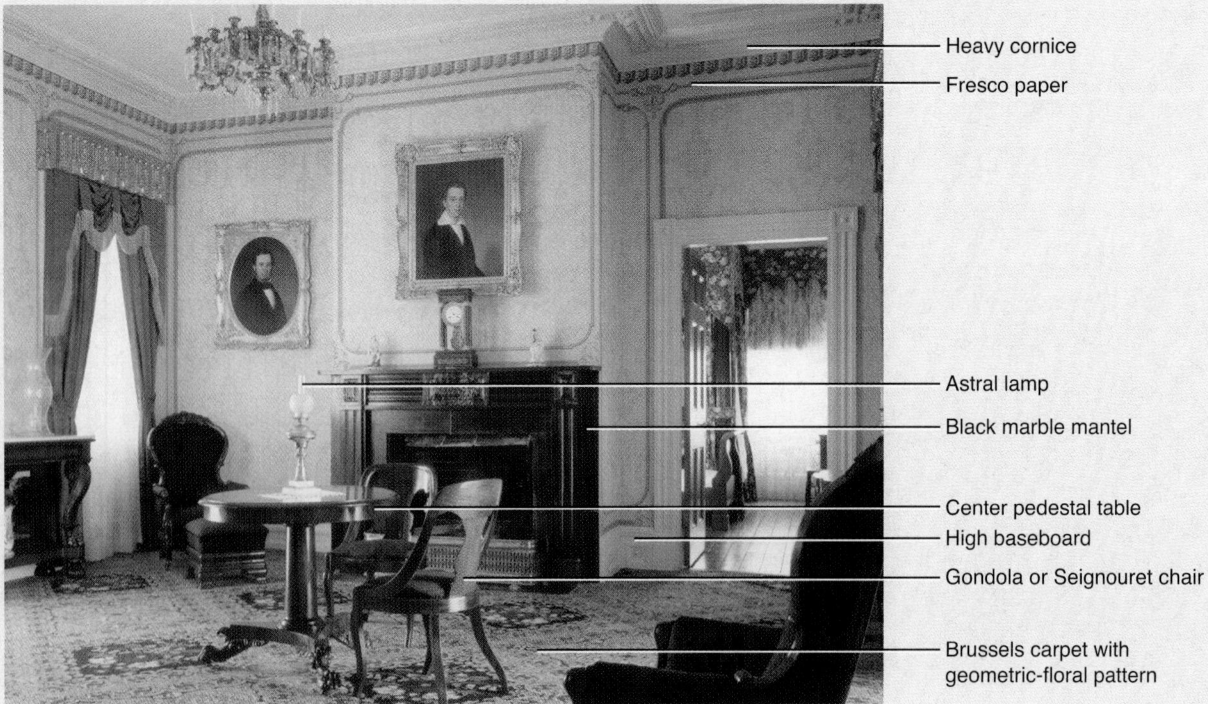

▲ **30-14.** Parlor, Shadows-on-the-Teche, 1834; New Iberia, Louisiana.

tectural papers imitate architectural details such as columns, coffered ceilings, cornice moldings, or dadoes. Ashlar papers, simulating masonry or stone in appropriate colors, are recommended for passages and hallways. Borders complement all patterns.

■ *Windows and Window Treatments*. Plain or complicated moldings surround rectangular windows, depending upon the room's importance in both public and private buildings. Those in important rooms have lintels or pediments surmounting them. Window treatments (Fig. 30-13, 30-14, 30-15), when present, are composed of swags and festoons suspended from a gilded classical cornice, under-curtains of damask or velvet that are tied back, and a thinner material such as muslin next to the glass. Simpler treatments consist of panels hanging from rings on wooden rods. Many rooms continue to have interior shutters that fold into a shutter box in the window jamb when not in use. Shutters block light and provide privacy. Roller blinds made of white cotton or unbleached linen (called Holland cloth) debut in about 1825.

■ *Doors*. Doorways (Fig. 30-13, 30-14) into important spaces have grand treatments with columns or pilasters or larger moldings with entablatures above. Doors may be single or double in paneled wood painted to match moldings, grained to imitate other woods, or sealed with a clear finish. Common woods are mahogany, walnut, or rosewood.

■ *Ceilings*. Some ceilings (Fig. 30-4, 30-12, 30-13, 30-14) are plain with a plaster rosette, while others, especially in public buildings, may have coffers or may be compartmentalized combinations of circles, ellipses, and rectangles. Paint or gilding may highlight details.

(a)

▲ **30-16.** Textile and wallpaper: (a) appliqued quilt, c. 1860; New York; and (b) wallpaper. [Quilt gift of Miss Eliza Polhemus Cobb, 1952 (52.103). The Metropolitan Museum of Art, New York, NY, U.S.A. Image copyright © The Metropolitan Museum of Art/Art Resource, NY]

▲ **30-15.** Music room, Rosedown Plantation, c. 1834–1859; St. Francisville, Louisiana.

(b)

▲ 30-16. Continued

■ *Textiles*. People increasingly use more fabrics (Fig. 30-13, 30-14, 30-15, 30-20) than they did previously. Curtain fabrics and upholstery may be silk or chintz in the parlor, moreen in the dining room, and cottons for bedrooms. Fashionable rooms may have several patterns of textiles instead of only one, as in earlier periods. The most common upholstery fabrics are horsehair, plush, silk, wool, and leather. Some covers have a central medallion for the back and seat and running decorative details for edges. Furniture covers protect fabrics both in the summer and winter. Quilt making becomes popular for women. Quilt designs are pieced together or embroidered on a fabric surface (Fig. 30-16). Flowers and eagles are popular motifs. Quilts usually cover beds.

■ *Lighting*. Interiors are lit with a combination of candlesticks, Argand lamps, astral lamps, lanterns, and hanging lamps (Fig. 30-13, 30-14, 30-15, 30-17, 30-20). Candlesticks, *candelabra,* wall sconces, and lamps may be of glass, silver, bronze, and brass. Lead glass prisms embellishing the fixtures enhance light. Large windows admit natural light, and fireplaces also may provide illumination.

FURNISHINGS AND DECORATIVE ARTS

American Empire furnishings are heavier, plainer, and more sculptural than the earlier Federal. Carving, gilding, and classically inspired forms, such as the *klismos* and curule, define the image. Also characteristic are dark woods, carving, and brass mounts. The *style antique*, as it is called, borrows heavily from, but does not copy, French Empire and English Regency. French and English designers particularly important to the development of American Empire are Percier and Fontaine, Thomas Hope, and George Smith. Pillar and Scroll or Late Classical is a later version of American Empire that is characterized by simple forms, massive pillars, scrolls, and large expanses of mahogany veneer with no *ormolu* or gilding. Both American Empire and Pillar and Scroll pieces are heavy and solid looking with good proportions. Case pieces tend to be rectangular, while chairs and sofas are more curvilinear.

Regional variations evident in American Empire disappear in Pillar and Scroll, which is usually machine-made. Furniture maintains a relationship with architecture because many cabinetmakers learn proportion, scale, and relationships using the classical orders as models. Most furniture is placed around the perimeter of a room, but chairs increasingly move to the center when not in use (Fig. 30-13, 30-14, 30-20). Sofas may be at right angles to the fireplace, and center tables are common.

Technology and industrialization influence both styles. The new circular veneer saw slices veneers much thinner than before, enabling cabinetmakers to use rare exotic woods such as rosewood and apply veneers to curved surfaces without it splitting. The steam-driven lathe, introduced in the 1820s, contributes to the popularity of turned Roman legs. Cabinetmakers also adopt the French polish, a high-gloss and more quickly applied lacquer-based finish. At the end of the 1830s, the steam-driven band saw that can cut intricate curves in any thickness of wood comes into general use. The period also marks the beginning of mass-produced furniture. People continue purchasing custom furniture from small cabinetmaking shops but now can buy other furniture from auction houses, merchants, upholsterers, and large retail establishments.

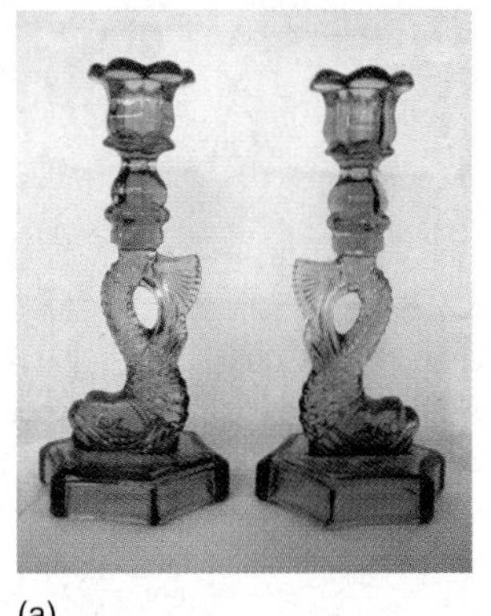

(a)

(b)

(c)

▲ 30-17. Lighting: (a) Dolphin candlesticks, (b) Argand lamps, and (c) urn chandelier, c. 1830s–1860s.

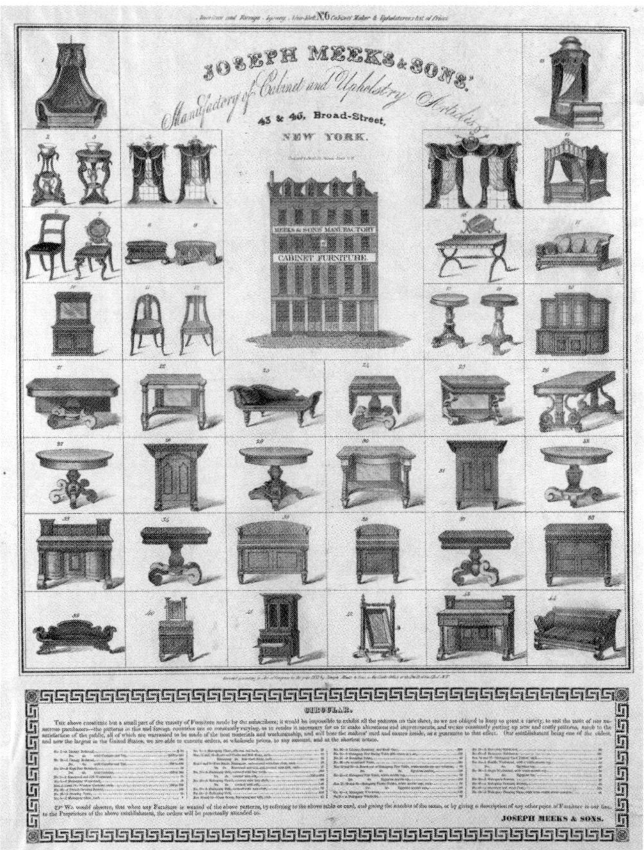

▲ **30-18.** Cabinet and upholstery articles, © 1833; New York City, New York; manufactured by Joseph Meeks and Sons. [Gift of Mrs. R. W. Hyde, 1943 (43.15.8). The Metropolitan Museum of Art, New York, NY, U.S.A. Image copyright © The Metropolitan Museum of Art/Art Resource, NY]

Public and Private Buildings

■ *Materials*. Mahogany is the most popular wood for furniture followed by cherry, maple, and exotic woods, such as rosewood (Fig. 30-13, 30-14, 30-15, 30-20, 30-21, 30-23). Many pieces are veneered; others are painted or grained to imitate marble, ebony, or rosewood. Brass mounts and other details are common on Empire examples, but rare on Late Classical or Pillar and Scroll, which is very plain and relies on line for interest. Painted furniture (Fig. 30-19) remains fashionable. Pieces may be painted completely or have color or ebonizing accentuating feet, drawers, or column supports. Typical colors include yellow ochre, red, green, blue, and black. Pressed glass knobs appear on furniture soon after patents for them are awarded in 1825 and 1826.

■ *Seating*. Seating furniture (Fig. 30-13, 30-14, 30-15, 30-18, 30-20) often is part of suites of furnishings that include chairs, sofas, window seats, card tables, and pier tables in matching designs. Most rooms have numerous chairs of which the Greek *klismos* is the most common antique form. Examples may closely or loosely follow the *klismos* form. Leg types include turned, X-shaped, cornucopia, saber, and quadrangular. Chair backs may have horizontal, vase, eagle, or lyre splats. Animal feet, brass-paw toecaps, and casters are common. Reeding and carved or painted classical motifs may highlight backs and rails. Gondola and *Seignouret* chairs derived from French Empire forms are also fashionable. Grecian cross-legged chairs and sofas have X-shaped or curule legs that may face either the front or sides.

Fancy chairs are popular versions of *klismos* or Sheraton styles. They have rush seats, turned legs, and stenciled decorations and may be painted black, yellow, or green. To simulate gilding, bronze dust may be sprinkled onto still-wet varnish. Although many firms make them, those by Lambert Hitchcock (Fig. 30-19) in Connecticut are the best known.

Every elegant parlor has at least one sofa (Fig. 30-13, 30-15). Plain sofas, as they are called, have identical scrolled ends, a long wooden crest, and lion's paw or cornucopia feet. Expensive examples feature carving, reeding or fluting, and veneer. Box types are rectangular with heavy turned legs and feet. Grecian sofas, derived from Greek prototypes, have complex scrolls, backs often not as long as the seat, and saber legs.

■ *Tables*. Center tables (Fig. 30-13, 30-14, 30-18) with round wooden tops often have central pedestals that may be carved or fluted, resting on a circular, triangular, or a rectangular base with paw or rounded feet. Some center tables have caryatid, dolphin, scrolled, or bracket supports. Card tables have pedestals that may be fluted or shaped into lyres, eagles, or caryatids. Dining tables continue to be made in pieces so that they can be taken apart when not in use. Rectangular pier tables may be used for serving food or holding dishes, decorative objects, or lighting and are placed symmetrically, usually between windows, in the parlor and dining room. Heavy columns or scrolls support the marble tops. Mirrored backs double the apparent size and reflect light.

▲ **30-19.** Hitchcock chair, 1826–1843; Hitchcocksville, Connecticut; Lambert Hitchcock.

▲ **30-20.** Parlor, Old Merchant's House, 1830s; New York.

DESIGN SPOTLIGHT

Furniture: The sideboard is the most impressive piece in the Greek Revival dining room. Intended to proclaim wealth and to display objects, silver and glass are carefully arranged on its top. Most have drawers and cupboards for storage of items associated with dining. Broad expanses of mahogany, classical details, and large scale define the American Empire sideboard. The Gothic arches may signal a transition to the Gothic Revival style. This example illustrates the variety in form and design.

▲ **30-21.** Sideboard, c. 1830s–1860s; Baltimore, Maryland.

▲ **30-22.** Wardrobe, c. 1820s–1850s; Louisiana.

■ *Storage*. The sideboard (Fig. 30-21), which dominates the dining room, is one of the most impressive pieces in the house. Used for display and storage, it has drawers and doors on the sides and a long drawer in the center with pediment above. Some sideboards have columns or pilasters on the corners and paw feet. Chests of drawers in bedchambers, or bureaus (Fig. 30-15, 30-18), as Americans call them, have three or four drawers with an overhanging top and columns on each side. The piece may rest on paw feet. Desks and bookcases have flat tops, glass doors, and a rectangular base with a drop front that reveals the writing surface. Wardrobes (Fig. 30-18, 30-22) are tall and massive with two doors. Columns and/or paw feet may embellish them.

■ *Beds*. Four-poster beds continue in use, but posts are heavier and carved with classical ornament and other motifs. A heavy canopy with curved moldings often rests on the posts. A tall, carved headboard and/or pediment add to the grandeur. Bed hangings remain opulent with swags or other complicated designs forming valances. French or sleigh beds (Fig. 30-18, 30-23) have head- and footboards of equal height. They are of dark wood with bright brass mounts. Over the bed, a rounded canopy may attach to the wall and support draped hangings of richly trimmed silk, cottons, or wool, sometimes with a contrasting lining.

▲ **30-23.** Sleigh bed, c. 1820s–1850s; Washington, D.C.

■ *Decorative Arts*. More accessories and pictures appear in interiors during the period (Fig. 30-13, 30-14, 30-15). Pictures and paintings hang symmetrically by slender cords from picture moldings mounted below the cornice. Mirrors reflect Empire design characteristics such as heavier proportions and rich carving. The *girandole* mirror (Fig. 30-24), a round mirror in a heavy frame with a convex glass and an eagle motif, remains very fashionable. English, American, and Chinese export porcelains, large in scale and classical in form, decorate mantels and pier tables and form large dinner sets.

▲ **30-24.** Decorative Arts: *Girandole* Mirror, c. 1830s–1860s; United States. [Couresty of the Diplomatic Reception Rooms, U.S. Department of State]

K. VICTORIAN REVIVALS

The period between 1830 and 1900 is named for Queen Victoria of the British Empire who ascends the throne in 1837. She rules until 1901, longer than any other monarch before her. Her reign sees a transformation of life and society as the Industrial Revolution completely and dramatically changes how people live, work, play, build, decorate, and furnish. Class structure now depends on work and wealth instead of rank. Family and gender roles change as men work away from home and women remain at home. Leisure activities such as shopping, traveling, and going to the theater, clubs, and pubs increase substantially. Consequently, numerous new building types must be designed, built, decorated, and furnished.

Before the 19th century, most people, even the wealthy, own few objects and keep the ones they do have for generations. Leisured, cultured aristocrats patronize individual craftsmen or guilds. Both makers and customers have generations of cultivated tastes and notions of excellence in design behind them. Styles develop slowly and continue for years.

In contrast, the Victorian period is characterized by numerous European and non-European styles swiftly succeeding one another and by an explosion of goods. New styles or revivals demanding attention rapidly appear throughout the period. Industrialization creates a consumer class by introducing choice, both of style and quantity. With factories producing so many new goods, outmoded objects no longer appeal, creating the notion of the disposable. Furnishings are imbued with social and cultural messages that change quickly, so middle-class Victorians, who have unprecedented spending power, continually strive to be up-to-date and in fashion to keep up appearances. Signals of middle-class affluence include wall-to-wall carpet, layers of window curtains, carved furniture, large mirrors, and a variety of accessories from wax flowers to Parian-ware busts.

Most Victorians take great pride in the machine and new materials, which they see as modern and progressive. They admire the scientific knowledge and technical achievements that produce these new objects. Most favor machine-carved ornament because it resembles hand carving but is done faster, more perfectly, and, presumably, more cheaply. Particularly admired are newly introduced and/or novel materials that imitate other materials, especially those associated with wealth, objects made of previously unknown materials, or old materials used in new ways, such as papier-mâché furniture. And these latest materials often are more durable, colorful, and cleanable than older ones are. New manufacturing techniques and materials also inspire novelty and innovation, which are highly esteemed. Manufacturers and sellers respond with a plethora of goods and styles, which increases their sales and profits.

Also characterizing the period is historicism, which stresses history as a standard of value. Its importance comes from the belief that age and longevity sanctify certain characteristics, making them respectable and ascribing both education and taste to the owner and maker. This, in turn, suggests gentility and acceptability, qualities that are very important to most Victorians. So, as evidence of their culture, status, and good taste, they seek to surround themselves with historical styles or revivals, such as Grecian, Gothic, Rococo, Renaissance, or Egyptian. These revivals rarely are historically correct. A romanticized view of history and associationism, which refers to a style's links, notions, or images it conjures up in one's mind, are more important than imitation. Although past styles become more clearly understood as the century progresses, stylistic distinctions and designations for material culture remain unclear. Nevertheless, the era is one of specialization with Rococo Revival in the parlor, Gothic Revival in the library, and Renaissance Revival in the dining room. Similarly, styles for public buildings convey their purpose or their associations. For example, some regard Gothic Revival as a Christian style that is more appropriate for churches than pagan classical temples are. Exotic styles, such as Egyptian, characterize cemeteries, prisons, and libraries to give a sense of eternity, permanence, security, or superior intellect.

Women's roles radically change during the period. The cult of domesticity pictures women as models of refinement, virtue, and piety who are keepers of the home and family. The task of decorating the home now becomes a female role and is particularly difficult because a woman must choose among an abundance of styles, each with its own historical and cultural associations and correct uses. In addition, reformers who are concerned with the effects of industrialization on the home and family insist that the home is the antidote to mechanization's negative effects. Women, they insist, are biologically suited to create homes that are refuges and places of culture, taste, and education. The notion of domestic environmentalism assumes that the home affects the inhabitants positively or negatively; this pervades writing and thinking throughout the 19th and into the early 20th century.

Additionally, the home represents the family to visitors and business associates and is the setting for life's social rituals. The objects with which people surround themselves reveal the sophistication and good taste of the family, and each object also serves as a learning experience for the children. Consequently, what a woman buys reflects who she is and what her family becomes. Not only is what she buys important, but also where she buys it and how she displays it are vital because they can affect her social status, her husband's advancement, and the moral health of her children. The Victorian period is the first to ascribe moral attributes to the style of objects and buildings. The prevailing notion is that good design represents good morals.

Gothic Revival consciously strives to emulate the Gothic style of the Middle Ages. Elements of Gothic architecture are applied to contemporary forms in architecture, interiors, and furniture beginning in the middle of the 18th century. Throughout the 19th and 20th centuries, expressions vary in response to scholarship, associations, and reform movements.

In contrast to other revivals, Second Empire is a contemporary architectural style in France that becomes fashionable in England and North America because of its associations with culture and cosmopolitanism. Also associated with culture, Rococo Revival strives to evoke the French Rococo of the 18th century. Its curvilinear compositions are bolder than the original and adopt new materials and construction methods. It is one of the most popular revival styles.

Italianate and Renaissance Revival architecture look back to the high style and vernacular architecture of Italy to create formal and informal compositions for public and private buildings in Europe and North America. The interiors and furniture are among the most eclectic of the revivals and borrow from the Renaissance in Italy, France, Germany, and England.

Exoticism looks to non-Western sources for inspiration, including Egypt, the Middle East, and the Far East. Styles include Egyptian, Turkish, Moorish, and Indian Revivals. Although manifest in architecture, interiors, and decorative arts, complete expressions are rarer than other revivals. Often people choose to decorate a room or particular furnishings instead of doing an entire house in an exotic style.

The Stick Style, an architectural style that is unique to America, looks to the Middle Ages, informality, and half timbering for inspiration. Queen Anne architecture originates in England as an attempt to avoid creating a style by adopting vernacular elements from the 16th through the 18th centuries. Most interiors follow other fashionable styles, but furniture may show some elements from the 18th century. The United States interprets Queen Anne in wood.

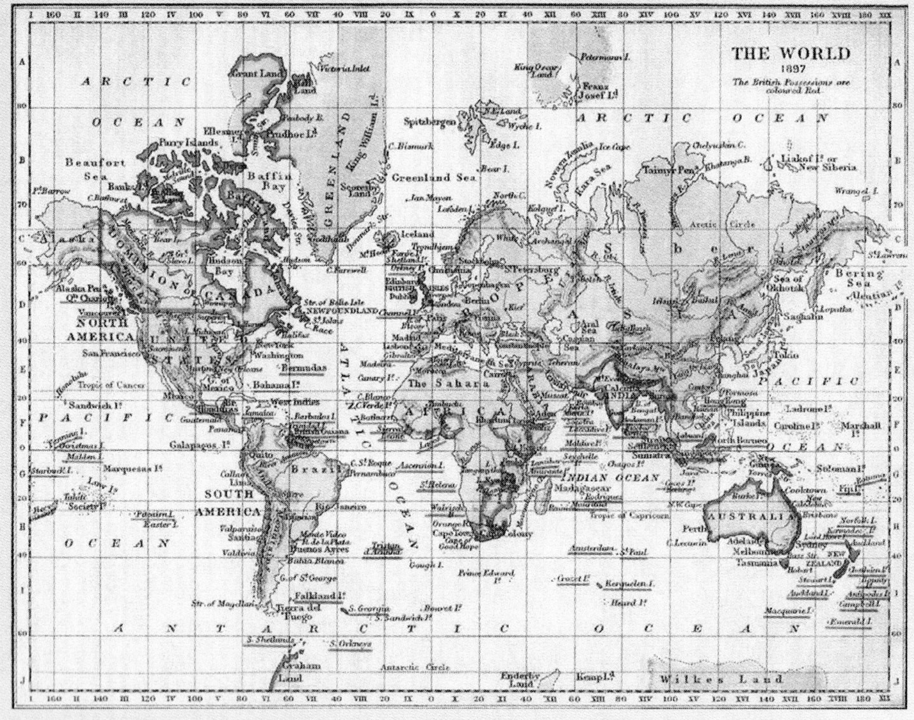

CHAPTER 31

Gothic Revival

1830s–1880s

Do not be afraid of incongruities, do not think of unities of effect. Introduce your Gothic line by line and stone by stone; never mind mixing it with your present architecture; your existing houses will be none the worse for having little bits of better work fitted to them; build a porch, or point a window, if you can do nothing else; and remember that it is the glory of Gothic architecture that it can do anything.

—John Ruskin, Lectures on Architecture and Painting, 1854
(Quote from *The Englishman's Castle*, 1945; John Gloag)

Gothic Revival deliberately revives Gothic and other styles of the Middle Ages. Beginning in England about the middle of the 18th century, it challenges the supremacy of Neoclassicism within 50 years. In its earliest manifestations, Gothic Revival applies ecclesiastical architectural motifs to contemporary forms. Following the growth of scholarship, the style begins to develop from medieval prototypes, eventually forming a unique expression indicative of its time. Elements of Gothic Revival theories become foundations for later design reform movements.

HISTORICAL AND SOCIAL

Gothic survives as a style for churches and in renovations and additions to medieval structures until the 1700s, especially in England and Germany. Gothic Revival as a style appears after the mid-18th century, when European designers, influenced by the Romantic and Picturesque Movements, turn to the Middle Ages as a source of inspiration. Influenced by literary themes, they find the gloom, melancholy, and the supernatural linked to Gothic very appealing. By redefining beauty to include not only form but the images conjured in the viewer's mind, they come to regard the medieval period as worthy of emulation like classical antiquity. Thus, Gothic becomes an alternative style to classicism.

In the early 19th century, times favor a return to the medieval past as industrialization and political changes interrupt lives and transform countries. People who are seeking stability, meaning, and continuity begin to look longingly toward an idealized past. At the same time, in reaction to the Enlightenment of the 18th century, religious fervor increases, which in turn promotes renewed church construction and discussions of what should constitute a model church building. Architects, theorists, and believers see Gothic as more fitting for the Christian church building than a classical (or pagan) temple is. Some denominations and religious groups adopt the Gothic Revival as a visual metaphor for their faith. Continuing the tradition of earlier Romance novels, 19th-century writers, such as Victor Hugo and Sir Walter Scott, write stories set in the Middle Ages, which capture the imaginations of readers in England, France, and North America.

■ *England.* The Gothic Revival in England begins earlier than in other countries and continues a sustained development throughout the 19th century. Interest in Gothic as a style for modern buildings and furnishings begins in the mid-18th century with fanciful and lighthearted manifestations that appeal mostly to the affluent. By the early 19th century, serious scholarship, investigations of medieval buildings, and a religious revival bring a more accurate Gothic Revival to the forefront of stylistic choices for numerous new and remodeled churches and their interiors, furnishings, and priestly vestments. The most important early Gothic Revival theorist and designer is Augustus Welby Northmore Pugin, who believes passionately in the superiority of Gothic. His writings form a theoretical base for Gothic Revival, and his design work is a model for others. Many of his defining principles also will significantly affect subsequent design-reform movements. Unlike others and his own earliest work, Pugin bases his designs on primary sources and strives to design in a Gothic manner instead of merely copying or applying architectural details to contemporary forms. His insistence upon correctness coupled with the newly developed stylistic chronology and scholarship leads to expanded use by others of forms and details from various English medieval, pre- and post-medieval styles.

About 1850, finding that re-created medieval prototypes cannot meet contemporary functional requirements and seeking more creativity and flexibility, some designers move toward greater eclecticism, more boldness, and an emphasis on color and surface decoration. At the same time, the views and writings of John Ruskin, an art historian and art critic, create a theoretical basis for High Victorian Gothic of the 1870s and 1880s. Ruskin praises the liveliness created by surface decoration and colorful materials of the buildings of Venice, which he sees as ideal, particularly the Ducal Palace with its Roman, Italian, and Moorish influences. In addition, English designers exchange ideas with those in France and Germany, which increases the range of design resources beyond Italy.

Also during the mid-19th century, Gothic Revival becomes a tool of the design reform movements. Recognizing the lack of taste and discrimination of the majority of contemporary society, the emphasis upon materialism, and the poor designs of most machine-made goods, reformers call for change. Like Ruskin and Pugin, they regard the architecture and material culture of medieval or preindustrial times as honest in material and construction and suitable for their purpose, unlike contemporary ones. Adherents also strive to design in the spirit of the medieval instead of relying solely upon Gothic forms or details as before.

■ *France*. In the 18th century, French Neoclassicists become interested in Gothic as a method of construction. Jacques-Germain Soufflot uses a form of Gothic construction in S. Geneviève (Panthéon, 1757–1790) in Paris, although the exterior displays the purity of Greek classicism. Although he is applauded for his integration of Gothic and classicism, there is little popular interest in Gothic beyond "ruins" in picturesque landscapes and gardens.

In the early 19th century, scholarship indicates that Gothic had originated in France, and French nationalistic pride in the style swells, especially among the clergy and aristocrats. Gothic Revival begins to convey an image of French heritage and nationalism. With the restoration of the Bourbon (and Catholic) monarchy in 1815, Gothic becomes an antidote to earlier Napoleonic imperialism. Between 1830 and 1845, the Flamboyant Gothic (14th–16th centuries) forms the basis for a more Romantic Gothic Revival that is visually complex and asymmetrical. By 1845, French designers, like the English, are producing a more correct Gothic Revival derived from earlier examples.

Eugène-Emmanuel Viollet-le-Duc is the main theorist and one of the most important designers of Gothic Revival in France. An architect and restorer, he develops his ideas from his restorations and re-creations of numerous medieval buildings. He favors Gothic over classicism as a universal architectural language. With the hope of creating a style for his own time, Viollet-le-Duc strives to design in a medieval manner instead of copying and applying Gothic details.

■ *Germany*. As in England and France, early German manifestations of Gothic Revival are picturesque and irregular. Greatly influenced by classicism, Gothic Revival innovations in Germany are the Romantic castles along the Rhine River. Unlike in England and France, the Romanesque and Renaissance modes exert greater influence on German architects than Gothic does.

■ *United States*. The United States has little Gothic architecture to study, restore, or emulate. Consequently, there is little interest in Gothic Revival and few manifestations of it before the 1830s. In the 1840s, Americans begin to build modest Gothic Revival wooden cottages and villas. The style is not as common as in England mainly because of the dominance of Greek Revival. As in Europe, American designers strive for a more archaeologically correct Gothic, particularly in churches, during the 1850s. Throughout the 1870s, High Victorian Gothic is mostly used for public and collegiate buildings and a few churches. Gothic Revival is never as popular or pervasive as in England.

In the United States, two men primarily advance Gothic Revival and its theories, Alexander Jackson Davis in practice and Andrew Jackson Downing through his writings. Both downsize and simplify European architecture to create a modest, practical Gothic Revival, often in wood, that they believe is more suitable for Americans.

CONCEPTS

Nationalism as well as religious, literary, and historical associations interweave with the ascent of Gothic Revival in architecture and design in the late 18th and early 19th centuries. England, France,

▲ **31-1.** Architectural Detail: Wall detail, S. Giles Church, 1839–1844; Cheadle, Staffordshire, England; Augustus W. N. Pugin.

and Germany all claim to have originated the medieval Gothic, in contrast to classical antiquity, which clearly comes from Greece and Rome. Consequently, each country regards it as a national style and expressive of its heritage and traditions. Largely used for churches and castles at first, the visual complexity and fanciful image of the Early Gothic Revival appeal to the senses and contrast with the rationality of classicism. Rarely is there any emphasis upon correct use of forms and motifs, proper context, and structure because essence and image are more important than accuracy.

Stimulated by their interest in the medieval period and realizing that little is known about the period, antiquarian and other learned societies begin to research a variety of medieval structures from cathedrals to cottages and other medieval sources such as illuminated manuscripts. Soon, books with histories of buildings and picturesque illustrations intensify public interest while providing architects and designers with sources of inspiration. As a result, Gothic Revival becomes more sober and archaeologically correct as designers strive for correct use of the original forms and motifs. They begin to distinguish between the various styles of the Middle Ages, often choosing one over others for personal and patron preferences or for particular associations. No longer do they limit themselves to the medieval styles of their own countries. By the 1850s, Gothic Revival has become increasingly eclectic and less directly dependent upon precedents.

MOTIFS

■ *Motifs*. Motifs (Fig. 31-1) come from medieval precedents. They include pointed arches, pinnacles, battlements, crockets, stained glass, tracery, rose windows, trefoils, quatrefoils, cinquefoils, cluster columns, oak leaves, and heraldic devices. Early buildings may have Tudor or ogee arches, while later ones may combine round arches and details from other medieval styles (Fig. 31-2 through 31-10, 31-15 through 31-17).

▲ **31-2.** Trinity Church and nave, 1841–1846; New York City, New York; Richard Upjohn.

ARCHITECTURE

Gothic forms and motifs adapted or copied from medieval churches, houses, and castles characterize Gothic Revival architecture in all phases and all countries. The extent, intent, and accuracy of borrowings vary throughout its long history.

■ *Early or Picturesque Gothic Revival (mid-18th–mid-19th centuries)*. In the first decades of the 18th century, Gothic (or Gothick until the 1750s) "ruins" set in irregular and contrasting landscapes are the earliest evidence of Gothic Revival in England. By the 1750s, the style is part of the architect's repertoire, although it is used only occasionally. From that time through the early 19th century, buildings are asymmetrical assemblages of Gothic architectural elements intended to convey a picturesque or Romantic vision. The few Gothic Revival homes belong to wealthy antiquarians who wish to make a particular design statement about themselves or proclaim a religious or ancient heritage.

Early Gothic Revival is visually complex, asymmetrical, irregular, linear, thin, and light in scale. Compositions consist of architectural motifs applied to contemporary forms, and the forms and/or details may be used in ways that are different from the originals or their intentions. Most examples reveal little concern for historical accuracy, although some show references to parts of or entire medieval sources or monuments.

■ *Gothic Revival (1830s–1880s)*. In the early 19th century, scholarship and theory broaden the appeal and advance the development of Gothic Revival. Assisted by publications and a stylistic chronology of the Middle Ages, Gothic Revival sheds its lighthearted approach as accuracy in form and detail becomes the main design goal during the 1830s. Pugin and the Ecclesiologists, a reform group, attempt to define the form and quality of religious architecture. They push for English medieval prototypes, such as the 14th-century local parish church, which becomes the model for numerous English and American churches (Fig. 31-3). The rebuilding of the Palace of Westminster (Fig. 31-4; Houses of Parliament) beginning in 1840 moves Gothic Revival from primarily an ecclesiastical and domestic style to one considered appropriate for government and commercial buildings. During this time, Pugin and others begin to promote Gothic Revival as a moral style and an antidote to industrialization and its negative effects on design and society. Pugin himself advocates late-13th- and early-14th-century manifestations of Gothic. Asymmetry, irregularity, and details derived from Gothic architecture remain characteristic.

■ *High Victorian Gothic (1850s–1880s)*. By the second half of the century, Gothic Revival enters a new phase in which bold geometric forms; simpler outlines; structural polychrome; and elements from Italian, French, German, or other medieval styles characterize structures. Architects now use Gothic on a wider range of building types, including commercial and civic (Fig. 31-5, 31-6). They may directly quote parts of earlier buildings or use them as a point of departure for their own designs. French architects, unlike the English, begin to use cast iron in Gothic Revival and restorations of earlier buildings. Roofs of iron to prevent fires are the most common use for the material, but cast and flat iron structural and decorative components are used increasingly.

■ *Gothic Revival and Design Reform (1850s–1920s)*. After becoming associated with various design reform movements in the mid-19th century, Gothic Revival architecture shows the application of principles that designers believe characterize medieval buildings, such as honest construction and ornament derived from structure. Less overtly Gothic Revival, structures nevertheless use medieval details and simplified forms and are often polychromatic.

Early Gothic Revival buildings in England are mostly churches (Fig. 31-3). By the mid-19th century, Gothic becomes an accepted style for museums, national monuments, university buildings, town halls, hotels, train stations, and commercial buildings (Fig. 31-5, 31-6). In North America, Gothic Revival is rare for government (Fig. 31-7) and commercial buildings but is commonly adopted for churches (Fig. 31-2), prisons, and cemeteries.

Gothic Revival public buildings always outnumber domestic ones because the style is difficult to adapt to residences. At first, Gothic Revival residential buildings are mostly large houses in England or *châteaux* in France. Some resemble castles with battlements, towers, and asymmetrical massing (Fig. 31-9), whereas others look like medieval abbeys. Most simply have Gothic details and asymmetry. Only a few try to re-create a medieval house because Gothic was rarely used domestically, and medieval houses no longer suit contemporary lifestyles.

American innovations are the wooden versions of Gothic in country churches and modest villas or cottages (Fig. 31-8). Unlike England, wood is plentiful, so American designers become adept in shaping Gothic form and details to the material. Following the lead of Alexander Jackson Davis and Andrew Jackson Downing, American architects and builders freely adapt Gothic elements and motifs to wood in numerous unpretentious houses, giving rise to the so-called Carpenter's Gothic. Gothic-style wooden ornament becomes easier to make following the invention of the scroll saw. Promoters of the style believe that the vertical board and batten expresses honest construction advocated by Pugin. A few affluent people build Gothic Revival mansions, such as Lyndhurst (Fig. 31-9).

Public and Private Buildings

■ *Site Orientation*. Rural churches in England are modeled after the ideal 14th-century parish church building surrounded by a lawn and graveyard nearby. American rural churches are similar. Urban structures in all countries sit on streets with little or no surrounding yards. Houses, particularly large ones, generally are set in parks or have lawns and gardens (Fig. 31-9). American Gothic Revival houses are usually rural because writers promote them as such.

■ *Floor Plans*. Plans for public buildings vary with the type of structure. Most churches retain the basilica or Latin cross plans, which adapt well for worship and liturgical functions. For other building types, Gothic Revival enables architects to design asymmetrical plans that address function, but they do not attempt to re-create Gothic ones in either public or private buildings. A few residences, such as Fonthill Abbey in England, have plans modeled after churches or castles. Residential plans vary, but comfort and function are considerations. Plans may be symmetrical, double pile or Georgian, or asymmetrical (Fig. 31-9).

■ *Materials*. Designers use many building materials including stone, brick, stucco, or cast iron. Structures before 1850 are monochromatic, although stone detailing around doors, windows, and other elements may contrast in color with walls. American structures are often of clapboards or vertical board and batten siding. Iron and terra-cotta may be used for details such as cresting or applied ornament. For painted exteriors, Downing advocates stone, buff, or gray instead of white. Details contrast in color to the walls.

After 1850, Gothic Revival buildings, particularly in England and North America, feature structural polychrome in which stone, terra-cotta, brick, and other materials form stripes, horizontal or oblique bands, diapers, or other patterns (Fig. 31-3, 31-5). Details that contrast with walls contribute to the colorful appearance. Red, black, white, and yellow are common colors. Also during this period, architects begin to incorporate cast-iron and glass interiors, which are often concealed behind masonry exteriors (Fig. 31-7). French architects are more likely to use cast iron than are the English.

■ *Façades*. There is great variety in design throughout the period in public and private buildings. Medieval forms and/or details, including pointed arches, buttresses, and battlements, characterize all (Fig. 31-2, 31-3, 31-4, 31-5, 31-6, 31-7, 31-8, 31-9). Round or square towers with pinnacles or dormers may highlight corners or centers of buildings. Ground floors may have an arcade of pointed arches. Pointed-arch lancet windows form rows on upper stories, which may be divided by stringcourses or hood moldings. Portions of walls may project, creating a regular rhythm across the façade. Earlier examples seek to evoke a Gothic spirit by using Gothic details, lightness in scale, and asymmetry. By the mid-19th century, greater accuracy is desired. Forms and details may come from newly identified Gothic stylistic designations such as Early Gothic, Decorated Gothic, Perpendicular Gothic, Romanesque, Norman, or Tudor in England. High Victorian Gothic buildings are more colorful, bolder, and more forceful, even brutal at times.

▲ **31-3.** All Saints Church and entry detail, Margaret Street, 1849–1859; London, England; William Butterfield.

Domestic façades are usually smooth with symmetrical or asymmetrical massing that is articulated with buttresses, bay windows, or towers. American houses usually have a full- or partial-width porch composed of pointed or Tudor arches and decorative trim imitating tracery (Fig. 31-8, 31-9).

■ *Church Façades*. Some church façades resemble medieval precedents with three doorways marking the nave and aisles, central rose window, and two towers with battlements and pinnacles. A tower and steeple may define the crossing, a wing, or the entry (Fig. 31-2). Some façades are triangular in shape, formed from the gable end of the building. Some French or German churches have rounded arches and corbel tables derived from Romanesque. Horizontal rows of niches with pointed arches may stretch across upper areas. Buttresses and flying buttresses may divide fronts and sides into bays. Gothic Revival churches usually do not have the educational sculpture and stained glass programs of the prototypes. Following Pugin's advice, elevations usually develop from the plan to provide clarity. Consequently, significant parts, such as the choir and presbytery, are evident on the façade. High Victorian Gothic façades are bold, muscular, and colorful. Lacking the complex silhouettes and lacey appearance of earlier examples, they reveal fewer details and more patterns.

■ *Windows and Doors*. Defining the style, windows, which are large and numerous, may be bay, oriel, lancet, rose, or pointed arches (Fig. 31-2, 31-3, 31-4, 31-5, 31-6, 31-7, 31-8, 31-9). American houses often have large pointed-arch windows extending into the triangle formed by the gable roof. Pinnacles and flat or pointed hood moldings crown some windows. Diamond panes, tracery and stained or painted glass are common in churches, large public buildings, and high-style affluent residences. Window tracery varies from simple to complex and derives its appearance from earlier Gothic styles. In High Victorian Gothic, the size and number of windows sometimes are reduced, giving more wall space.

Doorways may be recessed as in Gothic churches, have Gothic-style surrounds with pointed or Tudor arches, or have Gothic-style porches (Fig. 31-3, 31-5, 31-6, 31-7, 31-8, 31-9). Doors are wood and plain or carved with Gothic details and elaborate strap-metal hinges and locks. Entrances may be in a gatehouse in English examples.

■ *Roofs*. Steeply pitched gable roofs with slate tiles are definitive (Fig. 31-2, 31-3, 31-4, 31-5, 31-6, 31-8) for both public and private buildings. A few are flat or hipped. Many secular structures have picturesque rooflines composed of towers, dormers, and chimneys. Some have battlements or parapets and/or iron cresting. Towers may have rectangular or round roofs. Tall, prominent chimneys emphasize verticality. American houses often have one or more steeply pitched gables with bargeboards featuring Gothic motifs.

DESIGN SPOTLIGHT

Architecture and Interiors: The New Palace of Westminster is the first major public architectural statement of the Gothic Revival. Its design unites the Gothic style with British history and heritage and establishes Gothic as a proper style for government buildings in England and abroad. In October 1834, fire almost completely destroys the original complex, which is composed of buildings dating from the late 11th century. The competition held for the design of the new complex stipulates Gothic or Elizabethan as the style to harmonize with nearby Westminster Abbey. Charles Barry's design featuring Perpendicular-style details and grand scale wins the competition. The building's river side is symmetrical with buttresses, tracery, pointed arches, and pinnacles for details. Short towers or pavilions mark the ends and center of the composition. Buildings that survive the fire, including Westminster Hall and the Jewel Tower, dictate the asymmetrical, tall towers.

A. W. N. Pugin assists Barry with the design and completes the working drawings for exterior details. He is completely responsible for the interiors, which are designed after the fashion of a medieval residence. Pugin designs all parts to create a coherent whole. The interiors are far more influential than is the building itself. As befits its importance, the Lords' Chamber is the most lavishly decorated space in the Palace of Westminster. Here, ceremonies take place and the three parts of Parliament—the monarch, the Lords and the Commons—assemble. The space resembles a medieval great hall with paneled walls, a gallery, large clerestory pointed arch windows with stained glass, and a compartmentalized timber ceiling. The paneling is carved with ogee arches and linenfold. The arms of various rulers beginning with Edward III appear beneath the gallery. Statues of the sixteen barons and two bishops present at the signing of the Magna Carta stand between the windows. Pugin's original stained glass windows, which depicted monarchs of England and Scotland, were lost during World War II. The present windows have the coats of arms of peers between 1360 and 1900. The eighteen ceiling compartments have carved, painted, and gilded ancient emblems. On each end of the chamber are three allegorical frescoes representing Justice, Religion, and Chivalry. Pugin also designs the furnishings including the solid brass gates at the entrance to the chamber, the dais, and the Royal Throne, which is based upon a 14th-century coronation chair in Westminster Abbey. In the center of the space is a large cushion know as the Woolsack on which the Lord Speaker sits. Filled with wool and supposedly introduced in the 14th century, it reflects the importance of wool to England's economy. Red dominates the furnishings in the Lords' Chamber, in contrast to the Commons Chamber furnishings, which are green.

DESIGN SPOTLIGHT

▲ **31-4.** New Palace of Westminster (Houses of Parliament) and the Lords' Chamber, House of Lords, 1835–1865; London, England; Sir Charles Barry and Augustus W. N. Pugin.

▲ **31-5.** Midland Grand Hotel, 1868–1874; London, England; Sir George Gilbert Scott.

INTERIORS

Gothic Revival interiors relate to exteriors through Gothic elements and motifs. As on exteriors, verticality, asymmetry, pointed arches, and deep moldings define the style. Gothic may appear architecturally as in fan vaulting or decoratively as in wallpaper. Rooms are often more colorful and richly detailed and/or patterned than exteriors are. Furniture and decorative objects usually display Gothic details also. Gothic Revival interiors rarely emulate the originals, which are not clearly understood, so only a few are vaulted or of stone in the medieval manner. Unlike medieval ones, contemporary rooms rely on fixed decorative details and furniture instead of movable hangings and furnishings.

Entry and stair halls frequently convey the Gothic style (Fig. 31-10) through architectural details. Most large English Gothic Revival houses have a great hall like those of the Middle Ages. Decorated in a medieval manner, the space, which serves as a living room, is usually two stories with a large fireplace. However, sometimes it is rarely used because it is difficult to heat. Like other houses, Gothic Revival ones may have libraries or studies, billiard rooms, conservatories, smoking rooms, art galleries, or chapels.

▲ **31-6.** Royal Courts of Justice (Law Courts), 1874–1882; London, England; George Edmund Street.

▲ **31-7.** Old State Capitol and stair hall, 1847–1849, 1880–1882; Baton Rouge, Louisiana; James H. Dakin.

■ *Early or Picturesque Gothic Revival (mid-18th–mid-19th centuries)*. In the 18th century, Gothic motifs are arranged in a classical fashion or combined with Rococo in a lighthearted or fanciful manner. Some interiors have details derived from medieval prototypes. In the Regency period, Gothic Revival is one of several stylistic choices for interiors. Picturesque Gothic expressions continue throughout the 19th century.

■ *Gothic Revival (1830s–1880s)*. As in architecture, concern for greater accuracy in interiors arises in the 1830s. Forms and details often come from one of the styles of medieval Gothic such as the French Flamboyant style (14th–16th centuries) or English Perpendicular (c. 1330–1530). Following Pugin's example, Gothic Revival rooms become polychromatic and richly detailed. Also in this period, designers begin using two-dimensional, stylized patterns with no shading, as Pugin advocates. Like him, they abhor shading and three-dimensionality, which they believe inappropriate for flat surfaces such as walls or floors.

■ *High Victorian Gothic (1850s–1880s)*. Although there is not a corresponding interior style, rooms in High Victorian Gothic buildings often have structural polychrome and numerous patterns. Details are bolder than previously. Many pieces of furniture have colorful inlay, tiles, or paintings.

■ *Gothic Revival and Design Reform (1850s–1920s)*. At midcentury, the Reformed Gothic interior appears. Like architecture, it may be more accurate, borrowing 14th- or 15th-century elements. However, these interiors usually have more discrete references to medieval sources as designers move away from literal Gothic details, striving for a fresh interpretation. Decoration is simpler with less ornament.

Public and Private Buildings

■ *Color*. Crimson, blue, and gold, singly and together, dominate from the mid-18th to the early 19th centuries. Colors increase in variety throughout the 19th century but remain rich and glowing. Highly saturated red, blue, green, and yellow mixed with white, brown, or gold appear in patterns and on architectural details in public and private buildings in later Gothic Revival (Fig. 31-1, 31-7, 31-9, 31-11, 31-12, 31-13). Contrasting colors, borders, and stenciling may be used on architectural details, walls, and ceilings, Marbling and graining remain fashionable. In some public and private buildings, colors are those fashionable at the time instead of ones associated with Gothic Revival.

■ *Floors*. Floors may be wood or masonry. Tiles in rich colors and medieval patterns are more common in public buildings (Fig. 31-12). Some floors, particularly in residences, have ingrain, Wilton, or Brussels carpet. Patterns may be Gothic motifs, small repeating motifs, or florals in blue, crimson, green, yellow, or black.

■ *Walls*. Walls receive a variety of treatments including paneling, painting, wallpaper, textile hangings, leather, and structural polychrome (Fig. 31-4, 31-9, 31-11, 31-13). Some rooms incorporate antique architectural fragments such as paneling. Wood paneling, often of oak, may cover the wall completely or partially, or serve as a dado. Panels are stained dark to look old and may be carved with pointed arches, tracery, quatrefoils, linenfold, oak leaves, heraldic devices, or other medieval motifs. Centers of panels may

DESIGN SPOTLIGHT

Architecture: The Rotch House, a modest Gothic-style villa, is one of many that A. J. Davis designs throughout the 1840s. Houses like this one introduce the Picturesque to North America and depict characteristics that will become common for other small Gothic houses by architects and builders. A defining feature is the center steeply pitched gable with finial and bargeboard. Other definitive characteristics include the porches and tall, prominent chimneys. The tracery-like bargeboard has quatrefoils, cusps, and crockets. Above an oriel window with stained glass, a small pointed window extends into the gable. The entrance and porches have Tudor arches. The porch supports and cresting resemble tracery. Wooden details like these, which are typical of Carpenter's Gothic, are an American interpretation of Gothic Revival in wood made possible by the introduction of the steam-powered scroll saw. [National Historical Landmark]

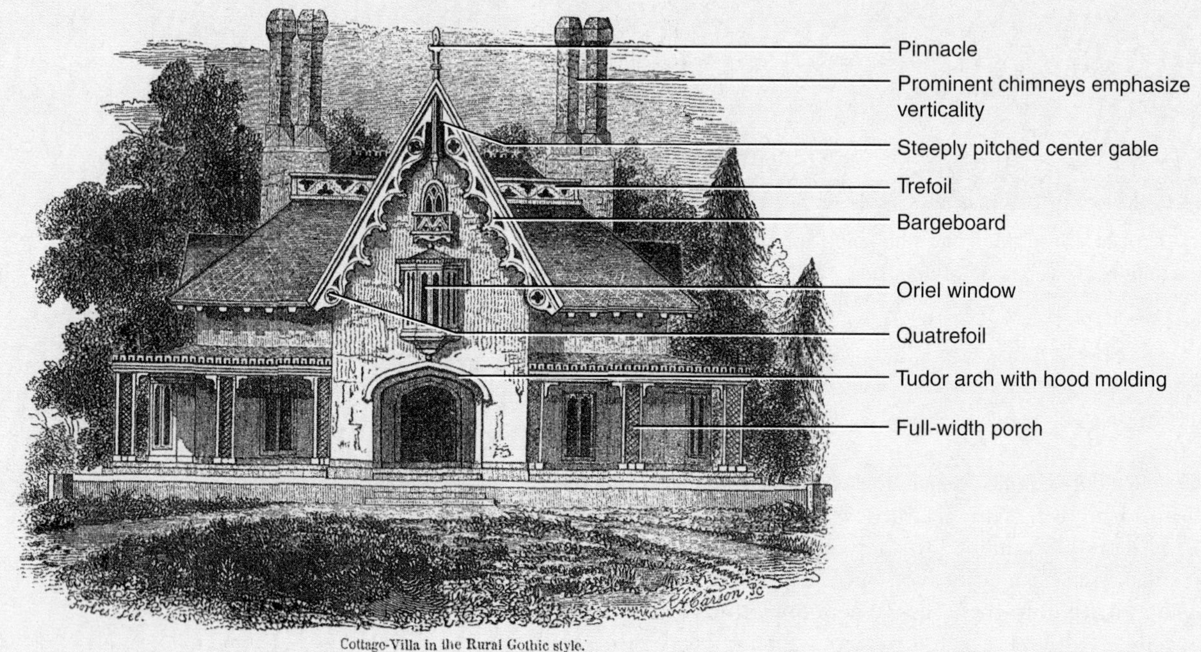

▲ **31-8.** Rotch House, 1846; New Bedford, Massachusetts; Alexander Jackson Davis.

DESIGN SPOTLIGHT

Architecture and Interiors: Architect A. J. Davis designs the original house or villa, called Knoll, in 1838 for William Paulding and enlarges it in 1864 for George Merritt who renames it Lyndhurst. It is a magnificent example of Gothic Revival villa that is somewhat rare in the United States because of its monumental size and stone building materials. Influenced by English sources, such as Pugin, characteristics include asymmetry, battlements, pointed arches, pinnacles, quatrefoils, rose windows, and stained glass. The veranda is an American detail.

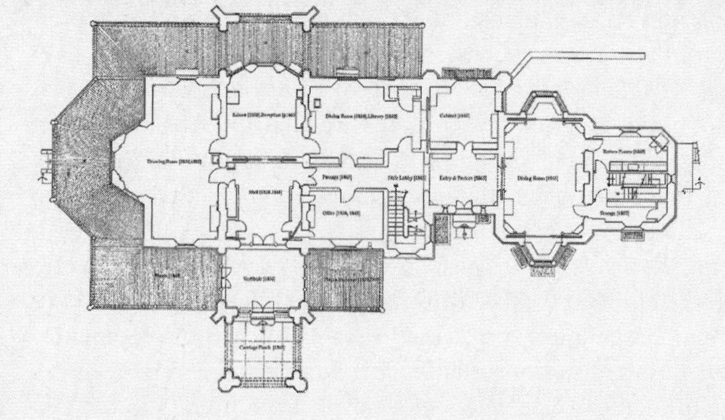

The dining room is part of the 1864 addition. As previously, Davis designs the architecture, interiors, and some of the furniture to integrate the interior with the exterior design. The interiors reflect the more opulent, robust yet sober Gothic of the

DESIGN SPOTLIGHT

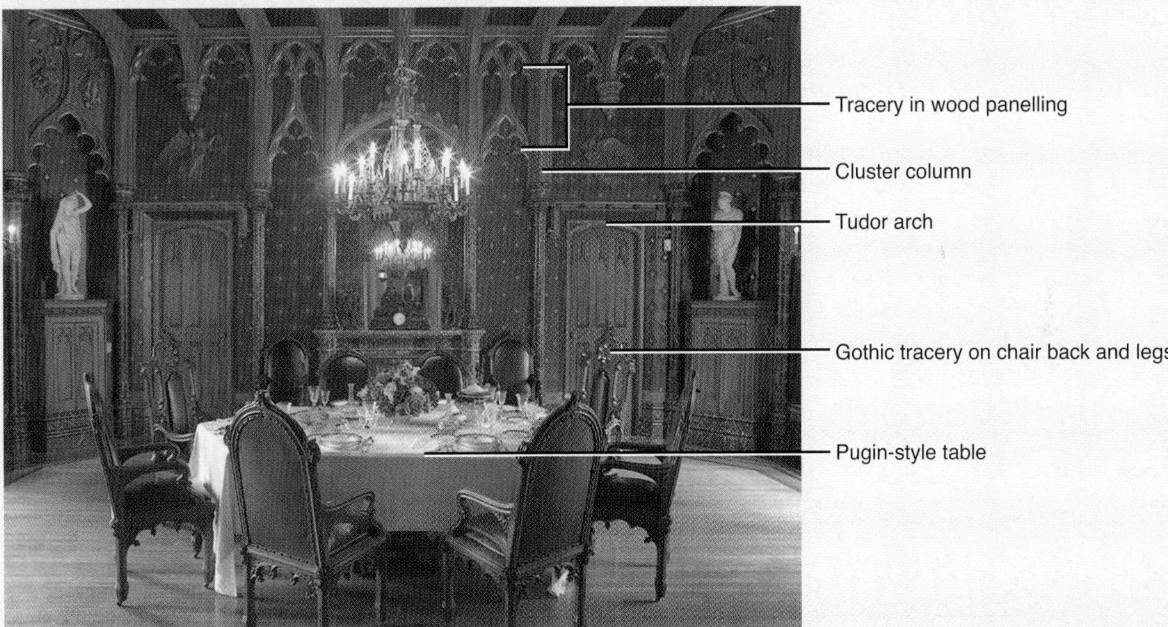

post–Civil War period. Pointed arches, crockets, tracery, and cluster columns, typical of Gothic and Gothic Revival, abound throughout the space recalling the exterior. The heavy ceiling beams terminate in corbels and cluster columns flanking the doorways and fireplace. The column shafts and baseboards are marbleized. The red wallpaper color is common for both Gothic Revival and for dining rooms. The doorways have Tudor arches with hood moldings above them and panels with tracery. Davis designs the chairs, which are heavier and less fanciful than his earlier chairs. [National Historical Landmark]

▲ **31–9.** Lyndhurst, floor plan, and dining room 1838–1865; Tarrytown, New York; Alexander Jackson Davis.

▲ **31-10.** Main entry hall, Kingscote, 1841; Newport, Rhode Island; Richard Upjohn.

have painted decorations or wallpaper. Pugin popularizes dark paneling with centers of rich, glowingly colored patterns. Cluster or compound columns may divide walls and rise to fan vaulting. Columns contrast in color to walls. Pugin sets the fashion for layers or rows of patterns painted, stenciled, or in wallpaper in rich colors (Fig. 31-1, 31-4). William Burges (Fig. 31-11) continues this fashion but draws from more sources than Pugin does. Sometimes plaster walls are painted and scored to resemble stone. Common wallpaper patterns (Fig. 31-13) include Gothic windows or pointed arches or castles in imaginary landscapes. Leather and textile hangings, including tapestries, adorn walls in some rooms.

Like exteriors, High Victorian Gothic interiors are very colorful with structural and applied colors in layers or bands. Reformed Gothic rooms may have simple wallpaper or painted stylized patterns. Paneling is dark and reveals its construction. Hangings, considered more medieval, are preferred.

Church walls often resemble originals with tripartite compositions of pointed arches carried by compound columns, a triforium above, and stained glass clerestory windows (Fig. 31-2). The nave may terminate in a semicircular apse with stained glass windows or, in Protestant churches, an altar and pulpit.

▲ **31-11.** Dining room, Cardiff Castle, c. 1870–1875; Cardiff, Wales; William Burges.

■ *Chimneypieces.* Some rooms have large or hooded chimneypieces in the medieval manner (Fig. 31-11). Smaller chimneypieces feature Gothic details such as pinnacles, pointed or Tudor arches, quatrefoils, or rosettes. American rooms often have rectangular mantels with a flat shelf (Fig. 31-9). The cast-iron grate inside the mantel often has a Tudor arch.

▲ **31-12.** Tile floors, 1860s–1880s; England; Augustus W. N. Pugin and William Butterfield.

▲ **31-13.** Wallpapers: Various patterns and motifs related to the period, mid- to late 19th century; England and the United States.

■ *Windows and Doors*. Gothic-style moldings may outline windows and doors (Fig. 31-9, 31-10). Surrounds may be elaborate with pointed or Tudor arches carried by slender cluster columns and surmounted by pinnacles. Some have hood moldings or battlements above them. Doors are wooden and may have carved or painted Gothic motifs. Like paneling, doors are stained dark to look old (Fig. 31-9).

Window treatments are usually cloth panels hanging from rings and rods. They usually are tied or looped back during the day. A cornice with crockets or cusps may hide the rods. Pelmets or valances with Gothic points replace earlier complicated types. Many windows have roller blinds painted with medieval scenes. In America, only important rooms have curtains.

■ *Ceilings*. Several types of ceilings are found: vaulted, timber ceilings in the medieval manner, or flat ceilings with beams or compartments (Fig. 31-9, 31-10, 31-11). In vaulted ceilings the spaces between the ribs usually are painted blue with gold stars. Important rooms in public and private buildings may have wood or plaster fan vaulting. Large two-storied interiors often have timber ceilings especially in England. Timbers, bracket supports, beams, and the spaces between them may be carved or painted and stenciled in rich colors. In compartmented ceilings, the point of junction typically has a pendant or rosette. Some ceilings in residences have applied beams and ribs to achieve a medieval effect. In most interiors, a cornice with pointed arches or other Gothic details separates the wall and ceiling.

■ *Textiles*. Gothic Revival interiors have a variety of plain and patterned textiles such as horsehair, cottons to silks, damasks, and woolens. Prints and wovens often have Gothic details that vary from literal to loose interpretations. Some prints mix traceried windows or other architectural details with flowers and foliage, while others have geometric medieval motifs in rich colors. Patterns may be shaded and naturalistic or flat and stylized.

■ *Lighting*. Neither public nor private interiors are lit with torches, candles, or fires as the originals were. Contemporary hanging lanterns, chandeliers, lamps, wall sconces, and candlesticks, which may be oil, gas, or electric, employ Gothic forms and motifs (Fig. 31-9, 31-14).

(a) (b)

▲ **31-14.** Lighting: (a) Candlesticks and (b) wall sconce.

FURNISHINGS AND DECORATIVE ARTS

As in architecture and interiors, most Gothic Revival furniture has Gothic and other medieval architectural details, such as pointed arches, applied to contemporary furniture forms (Fig. 31-15). There is less Gothic Revival furniture than architecture or even interiors. Few original Gothic pieces survive, so not much is known about medieval furniture, and there is little to copy. There is less built-in furniture than in the Middle Ages. A great deal of Gothic Revival furniture is custom designed and made for specific rooms in Gothic Revival houses. Not all furniture in a Gothic Revival room is Gothic Revival. Many rooms have only one or two pieces of Gothic-style furniture. There are no specific types for Gothic Revival because the style appears on all typical pieces of the time including church furnishings.

Early Gothic-style furnishings often combine Gothic with Rococo, but Rococo characteristics disappear in the 19th century. During the 1830s, following his study of primary resources, Pugin tries to design in a true Gothic manner instead of merely using

▲ 31-15. Side chairs; published in *Ackermann's Repository of Arts;* July 1823; England.

Gothic motifs. He strives for medieval forms and details, honest and visible construction, and truth to materials. Only a few furniture designers adopt his ideas; most continue using Gothic architectural details on contemporary forms and pieces.

By the 1850s, reform designers begin to follow Pugin's lead and create a simpler, less obvious style derived from Gothic. Reformed or Modern Gothic furniture relies more on form than architectural details. Its characteristics include simplicity, rectangular outline, chamfering, incised or shallow-relief carving, spindles, painted or inlaid geometric or naturalistic decoration or painted scenes with medieval themes (Fig. 31-19). Some furniture after 1850 has inlaid or applied color, tiles, or painting, reflecting the High Victorian preference for structural polychrome.

▲ 31-16. Carver chair and armchair, c. 1820s–1870s; England.

Public and Private Buildings

■ *Materials.* Much Gothic Revival furniture is of oak following the originals. Other woods include mahogany, walnut, and rosewood. Some pieces are ebonized because it is thought ebonizing was a medieval practice. Painting, inlay, or gilding highlights or embellishes details or surfaces. Pugin, Burges, and later reform designers reject veneers and marquetry, declaring them dishonest.

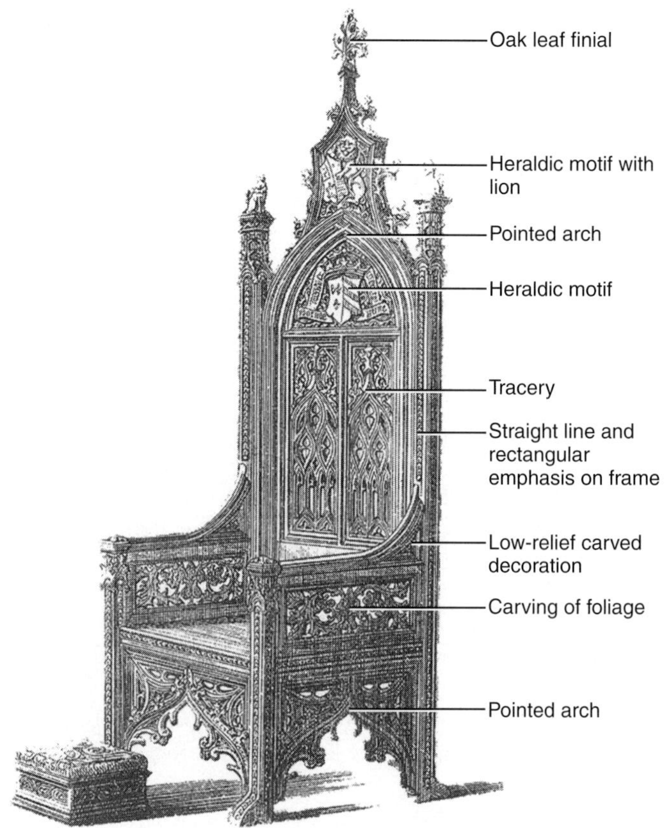

■ *Seating*. Backs of chairs and settees, with or without upholstery, often resemble rose windows or windows with tracery, or have pinnacles or quatrefoils (Fig. 31-15, 31-16). Legs are cluster columns, turned, spirals, or balusters. Pugin introduces a chair with curving Xs on the sides and a rectangular back (Fig. 31-16). Shallow carving covers the wood frame. Reformed Gothic seating is rectangular with turned or chamfered legs. Incising and naturalistic carvings embellish the frame.

■ *Tables*. Tables vary in size and shape according to their function. Tops may be round, octagonal, or rectangular. Legs are usually cluster or compound columns, but baluster-turned or spirals may be substituted. Pointed arches, crockets, or cusps may appear on aprons.

■ *Storage*. Pieces include chests, bookcases, cabinets, secretaries, wardrobes, and sideboards (Fig. 31-17). Forms are rectangular and decidedly vertical. Façades often have tracery, linenfold, rose

▲ **31-17.** Bookcases and chest, c. 1850s–1870s; England and the United States; and Andrew Jackson Downing and Augustus W. N. Pugin.

DESIGN SPOTLIGHT

Furniture: William Burges designs this washstand for the guest bedroom in Tower House, his own interpretation of a medieval house. The washstand of painted and gilded oak has a simple rectangular outline with Gothic details such as quatrefoils and long, strap hinges. The top, wash basin, and soap dishes are of alabaster. The inlaid silver fishes in the basin appear to swim when the basin is filled with water. The tap copies a bronze medieval *aquamanile*, the ewer and basin used by priests for ceremonial hand washing, a detail derived from Burges's scholarship. Mirrors embellish the back and lower portions of the washstand, a very unmedieval feature also typical of Burges.

▲ **31-18.** Washstand, c. 1880; London, England; William Burges.

windows, and/or quatrefoils in panels. Tops may have steeply pitched gables or pinnacles. Cresting, when present, has oak leaves or pointed arches. Glazing bars in glass doors form pointed arches and/or tracery. Some pieces, such as those by Burges and some reform designers, have painted decorations with complex medieval iconographies (Fig. 31-18).

■ *Beds*. Bed types include four-posters (Fig. 31-20), often with cluster-column posts, half-testers, or full canopies with pointed arches or crockets. Headboards and footboards may have carved Gothic decoration. Reform Gothic beds (Fig. 31-19) have low posts and headboards and footboards with incising and simple carving.

■ *Decorative Arts*. Gothic Revival pervades all decorative arts from ceramics to silver to clocks to fireplace furniture. Most examples have Gothic motifs applied to contemporary forms.

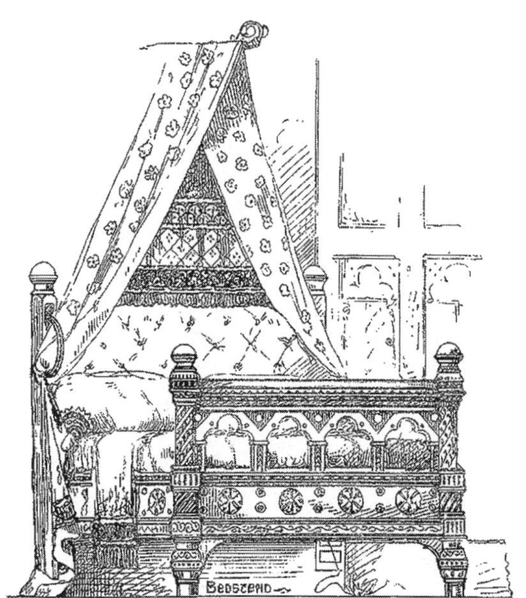

▲ **31-19.** Bed and wardrobe, c. 1870s; England; Bruce Talbert.

▲ **31-20.** Bed, c. mid-19th century; United States.

■ *Later Interpretations*. Gothic-style furniture is designed for Gothic Revival buildings into the 20th century. Historical, antiquarian, or other contexts continue to inspire Gothic Revival furnishings today (Fig. 31-21).

▲ **31-21.** Later Interpretation: Gothick bench, 2004; Hickory Chair. Modern Historicism.

CHAPTER 32

Italianate, Renaissance Revival

1830s–1870s

Italy provides the models for Italianate and Renaissance Revival architecture, interiors, and furnishings beginning in the 1830s. Various titles describe the architectural style, including Italianate, Renaissance Revival, Palazzo Style, and Italian Villa Style. Public and private buildings rely on two Italian building types: formal, classical urban palaces; and picturesque, asymmetrical farmhouses or other vernacular structures. Renaissance Revival interiors and furniture are highly eclectic, mixing characteristics from various periods and countries in addition to Renaissance Italy. The style goes by many names, such as Henri IV, Louis XIII, François I, Tudor, and Free Renaissance, the latter in Great Britain.

There is also far greater latitude and variety in the ornaments of the different modes of the Italian architecture . . . than in the purely classical style. It addresses itself more to the feelings and the senses, and less to the reason or judgment, than the Grecian style, and it is also capable of a variety of expression quite unknown to the architecture of the five orders. Hence, we think it far better suited to symbolize the variety of refined culture and accomplishment which belongs to modern civilization than almost any other style.

—Andrew Jackson Downing, *The Architecture of Country Houses*, 1850

HISTORICAL AND SOCIAL

Italianate and Renaissance Revival of the 19th century look back to the Renaissance, the rebirth of interest in classical antiquity that appears first in Italian literature, and then in culture and art in the 14th century.

■ *Italianate or Italian Villa Style*. In the early 19th century, the Picturesque Movement inspires English designers to explore alternatives to classicism, Gothic, and other styles of the Middle Ages. Some turn to Italian vernacular farmhouses whose asymmetry, irregularity, and rambling forms are appealing and picturesque, yet Italian. By the 1830s, Italian Villa–style country houses and train stations become more common in England. In the 1840s, the style is given royal approval by Osbourne House, a seaside home for Queen Victoria and Prince Albert enlarged in the style beginning in 1845.

Publications spread the Italianate style to North America, with the first examples appearing in the late 1830s (Fig. 32-6, 32-7, 32-8, 32-9). During the early 1840s, its use increases after writer and design critic Andrew Jackson Downing (Fig. 32-7) begins to advocate the style as a rural alternative to classical and Gothic. He publishes examples by Alexander Jackson Davis of what he calls Italian Villas, Italianate, Tuscan Villas, Lombard Style, or the Bracketed style in several of his books beginning with *Cottage Residences* (1842). Although he regards Italianate as somewhat inferior to Gothic, Downing nevertheless praises it for its interesting appearance, freedom in planning, and refined cultural ties.

■ *Renaissance Revival.* In the early 1830s, Sir Charles Barry initiates the Renaissance Revival (or Palazzo Style) in England by turning to Italian Renaissance urban palaces for inspiration (Fig. 32-2). By the end of the decade, High-Renaissance-style palaces define gentlemen's clubs, a few country houses, banks, and commercial buildings across England. The style spreads to North America during the 1840s where it soon is used mainly for public buildings and commercial structures (Fig. 32-3).

CONCEPTS

Although both are derived from Italian models and develop during the same period, Italianate or the Italian Villa style is asymmetrical and picturesque, whereas Renaissance Revival is classical, symmetrical, and refined. Both have associations of Italian culture and sophistication in design. Italianate, which draws from vernacular Italian farmhouses, villas, and churches, is a picturesque style that becomes an alternative to Gothic Revival. It offers asymmetry and freedom in design without the religious or moral overtones associated with Gothic. Renaissance Revival architects are not primarily interested in the order, harmony, and proportions of Italian Renaissance examples. Instead, they view them as expressions of Italian refinement and culture as well as wealth and luxury. Renaissance Italy further appeals because it is nearer to their homelands and time than the remote, somewhat obscure, classical antiquity.

Unlike architecture, Renaissance Revival interiors and furniture draw upon Italian, French, German, English, and Northern European Renaissance and Mannerist forms and motifs. But, like architecture, they express refinement and culture. Designers adapt and reuse forms and motifs, not to replicate past glories, but to create something new and uniquely of the period.

MOTIFS

■ *Motifs*. Classical motifs in Italianate and Renaissance Revival architecture and interiors include pediments, stringcourses, quoins, hood moldings, brackets, columns on porches or verandas, swags, acanthus, arabesques, and round arches (Fig. 32-1, 32-2, 32-3, 32-4, 32-5, 32-6, 32-7, 32-8, 32-9). Additional motifs (Fig. 32-11, 32-12, 32-13, 32-17, 32-18, 32-20) for interiors and furniture are fruit, game, animals, masks, strapwork, Greek key, sphinxes, lotus blossoms, palmettes, urns, roundels, cabochons, pendants, and applied bosses or lozenges.

(a)

(b)

▲ **32-1.** Motif and Architectural Detail: (a) Ceiling detail, 1892, from *The Practical Decorator and Ornamentist*; George A. Audsley, and (b) bookcase and chimneypiece detail, Great Exhibition, Crystal Palace, 1851; London, England; T. A. Macquoid.

ARCHITECTURE

As an outgrowth of a search for alternatives to classicism and Gothic, the Italianate or Italian Villa style originates in England with John Nash's Cronkhill in Shropshire (1802). Evoking images of Italian vernacular buildings, Cronkhill's picturesque, rambling forms highlight an asymmetry in which additions are built where needed with little thought to symmetry or overall design. The style soon defines other country houses as well as public buildings.

During the 1830s and 1840s, the Italianate Style spreads across England, and then to North America. The first Italian Villa in the United States is a residence designed in 1837 by John Notman for

DESIGN SPOTLIGHT

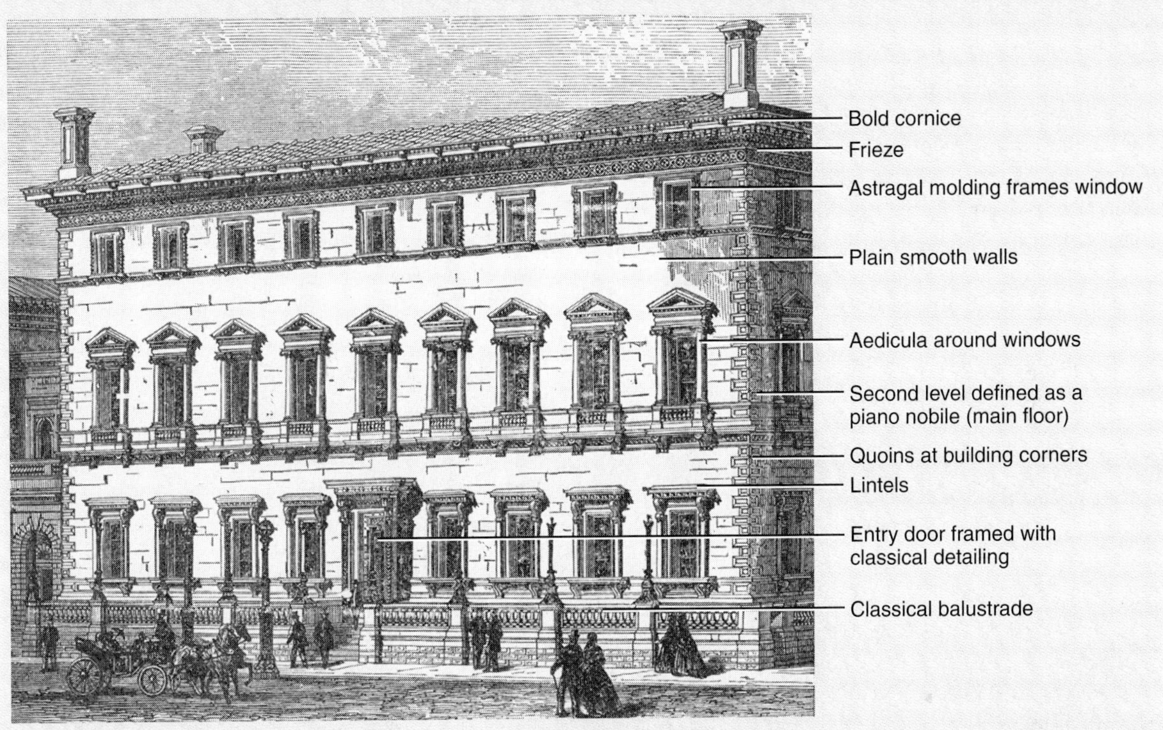

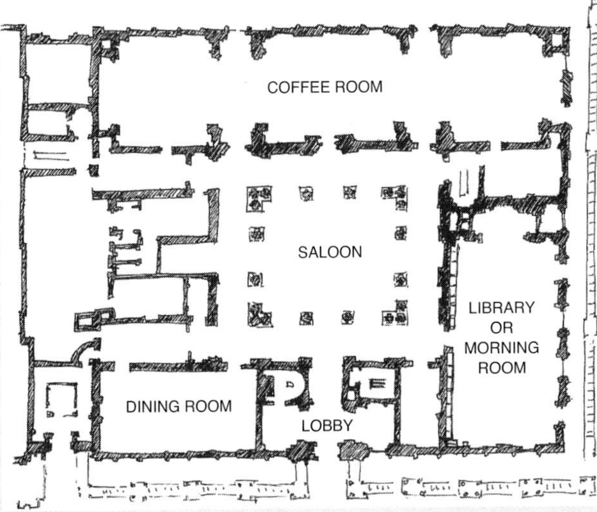

▲ **32-2.** Reform Club, floor plan, and central saloon, Pall Mall, 1837–1841; London, England; Sir Charles Barry. Palazzo style or Renaissance Revival.

Architecture: Inspired by the High Renaissance Palazzo Farnese (begun 1517; redesigned 1534, 1541, 1546; completed 1589) in Rome, the Reform Club is a rectangular block with three stories separated by bold stringcourses. Quoins highlight the building's corners. Smooth stone walls form backgrounds for the crisp details. Lower-story windows have lintels, while those on the second story have *aedicula* to identify the *piano nobile* or main floor. Attic windows are small rectangles framed with astragal moldings. A bold frieze and cornice cap the composition. The symmetrical floor plan centers on a central two-story saloon (next page) instead of the typical Italian *cortile*. The saloon is bordered by Ionic columns on the ground floor and Corinthian columns on the main floor. Pilasters with arches between them divide the saloon walls into bays on both levels. Classical architectural detailing embellishes the ceiling, balustrade, frieze, and Italian Renaissance–style marble floor to enhance the formal appearance. Colors are in the rich palette of the style. This building and the Travellers Club are the first buildings of the Renaissance Revival in England and inspire similar examples in other countries.

Rt. Rev. George Washington Doane in New Jersey. After A. J. Downing praises the style for country residences (Fig. 32-7), Americans begin building the Italian Villa style in wood like the Greek Revival or Gothic Revival. There are a few urban examples in masonry. By the 1860s and 1870s, the robust, highly embellished masonry of Italian Villa expresses wealth for the newly arrived captains of industry. Italianate is enormously popular in the United States because of its adaptability. Variations are endless.

Definitive characteristics for Italianate or the Italian Villa style (Fig. 32-6, 32-8, 32-9) include brackets beneath the low-pitched roof and individual and/or groups of round arched windows surmounted with pediments or hood moldings. Also common is a tower, usually asymmetrically placed. Other characteristics include asymmetrical massing, bay windows, balconies, porches or verandas, and round arched doorways. Interiors usually are revival styles, such as Rococo Revival and Renaissance Revival.

The Italian Renaissance again offers new inspiration for designers, who are weary of the Neoclassical columns and porticoes and are searching for a richer, more plastic alternative to the spare Greek Revival. High Renaissance Roman, Florentine, and Venetian urban palaces become models for the Italianate or Palazzo Style in England and Renaissance Revival in America, collectively known as Renaissance Revival (Fig. 32-2, 32-3, 32-4, 32-5). Structures closely resemble Italian urban palaces, particularly those of the High Renaissance. The rectangular blocklike forms usually have no columns or protruding porticoes, porches, or bay windows. Lower stories may be rusticated, and quoins are common. Windows have pediments, lintels, or *aedicula*. A prominent cornice defines the roofline. Interiors often have bold classical details and may be Renaissance Revival or other revival styles.

The first example of Renaissance Revival in England is the Travellers Club in London (1831), which is modeled after the *Palazzo Farnese* (1517–1589) in Rome. Sir Charles Barry chooses it as a sophisticated and cultured alternative to Neoclassical and a more embellished image than the plain Greek Revival. Thus, he maintains a classical style but a different, novel appearance. The choice of Italian Renaissance carries associations of Italy, culture, wealth, and leisure, highly appropriate for a men's club that is a gathering place for those returning from Grand Tours. Barry and others continue to design in the style for banks and commercial buildings. As the 19th century progresses and tastes change, architects turn to the more embellished and three-dimensional Northern Italian and Venetian examples, such as the Library of Saint Mark's (begun 1537; Venice). Publications spread the style.

DESIGN SPOTLIGHT

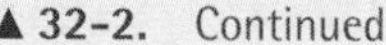

▲ 32-2. Continued

▲ 32-3. Athenaeum, 1845–1847; Philadelphia, Pennsylvania; John Notman. Renaissance Revival.

▲ **32-4.** Royal Albert Hall, c. 1871; London, England. Renaissance Revival.

As in England, the Renaissance Revival in North America recalls Italian Renaissance palaces and defines gentlemen's clubs, and government and commercial buildings. In the 1830s, the United States introduces Renaissance Revival cast-iron façades modeled on Venetian palaces for commercial buildings and department stores. Units are individually cast and bolted together to form entire front façades. Inside, a structural cast-iron skeleton eliminates the need for thick masonry walls and allows larger windows. This commercial image expresses Italian culture, wealth, taste, and a regard for the past yet a modern, progressive attitude. The Venetian style rarely affects houses until the 1890s.

Many building types, including clubs (Fig. 32-2), athenaeums (Fig. 32-3), offices, department stores, warehouses, mills, factories, post offices, custom houses, city halls, train stations, and theaters (Fig. 32-4), are Renaissance Revival. In contrast, only a few train stations and town halls display the towers, round arches, and bracketed roofs of the Italian Villa. Mansions, row houses (Fig. 32-5), and urban villas (Fig. 32-6, 32-8, 32-9) are usually Renaissance Revival in both England and the United States, whereas country villas (Fig. 32-7), houses, and cottages may be Italian Villa style or Italianate.

Public and Private Buildings

■ *Site Orientation*. Most Renaissance Revival public and private buildings occupy large portions of a city block and seldom are part of a city plan (Fig. 32-2, 32-3, 32-4). They are large rectangular blocks with no protrusions such as porches or entryways. Both Italianate and Renaissance Revival rural examples usually have surrounding lawns and gardens that combine formal and informal areas (Fig. 32-6, 32-8, 32-9). In the 1840s, architects begin to plan Italianate and Renaissance Revival row houses as long units of repetitive and uniform designs that form streetscapes (Fig. 32-5).

■ *Floor Plans*. Barry's plan for the Reform Club in London (Fig. 32-2), drawn from Italian precedents, is the model for many subsequent buildings. Symmetry and an open central courtyard or *cortile* are characteristic of these buildings. Commercial and other public building plans are generally symmetrical, developing from the function of the building. Residential floor plans do not change much with either architectural style, although some asymmetry may be evident (Fig. 32-7). Many houses maintain the traditional double-pile or Georgian plan of a central hall flanked by two rooms on each floor. Square, formal plans are typical for Renaissance Revival, but projecting rooms, porches, and verandas help break up strict symmetry in Italianate or Italian Villas. Staircases often are curvilinear.

■ *Materials*. Materials are chosen to emphasize heaviness and give rich texture and contrast. Public structures are of brick, stone, or cast iron (Fig. 32-2, 32-3, 32-4). Because smooth wall surfaces are desirable, façades may be stuccoed for a flat appearance. Details may be of different materials.

Houses are built of stone, brick, brownstone, or wood (Fig. 32-5, 32-6, 32-7, 32-8, 32-9). Wood and brick may be stuccoed and scored to resemble stone. A cheaper substitute is a paint mixed with sand, which suggests stone. In the United States, polychrome of three or more colors is common with a lighter body and darker details. The individual components within architectural details also may contrast in color to create highlights and shadows for more three-dimensionality. Typical colors include buff, straw, or stone, brown, red, olive, gold, green, and blue. One often recommended color scheme includes a buff body, light olive trim, reddish-brown sashes, and green shutters. Some residences have painted cast-iron hood moldings, brackets, porches, and other details.

▲ **32-5.** Townhouse, c. 1850s; Cincinnati, Ohio. Renaissance Revival.

▲ **32-6.** Edward King House, 1845–1847; Newport, Rhode Island; John Notman. Italinate/Italian Villa.

■ *Façades*. Façades of Renaissance Revival public buildings resemble or directly imitate Italian High Renaissance palaces (Fig. 32-2, 32-3, 32-4). Lower stories may be rusticated. Quoins delineate corners. As in the prototypes, the most important floor is the largest and usually on the second level, while on successive stories the room height may diminish. A large cornice, usually with modillions, separates walls and roof. Walls serve as backgrounds for windows, doors, and other details. Bold details, such as lintels or triangular or segmental pediments, emphasize rectangular windows and doorways. Balconies or *loggias* are common. In commercial structures, wall space is greatly reduced to allow larger windows for display and more light in the interiors. Façades based on Northern Italian or Venetian models are more embellished with round arches, pilasters or engaged columns, swags, acanthus leaves, arabesques, and other classical ornament.

Dwelling façades vary from close depictions of Italian High Renaissance palaces to asymmetrical examples that are boldly decorated with classical and nonclassical details. Renaissance Revival residences closely resemble Italian prototypes and are formal, symmetrical, rectangular blocks (Fig. 32-5). In both England and America, some Italianate/Italian villa houses and public buildings may have a centered gable or be a rectangular block with a cupola (Fig. 32-6, 32-9). Others have a tall, rectangular tower on one corner or occasionally two corners to emphasize verticality, and are asymmetrical in massing (Fig. 32-7, 32-8). In both versions, wall surfaces are smooth to provide a neutral background for windows and doors, and there may be *loggias* or balconies. Verandas or porches are common. A large cornice and heavy brackets emphasize the roofline. Italianate row houses have rounded windows with or without hood moldings, rounded doorways, and bracketed cornices.

■ *Windows*. Bold details surrounding windows and doors give three-dimensionality, contrast, and a richness not found in Greek Revival. Rectangular windows with lintels or triangular and/or segmental pediments above them characterize Renaissance Revival structures (Fig. 32-2, 32-3, 32-5). Some windows have stained glass in them. Windows may diminish in size on each story and have simpler treatments on successive stories. Second-story windows usually are the largest and have the boldest surrounds. Stringcourses often form bases for windows, which alternatively may rest on brackets or consoles. Early examples feature the rectangular windows of Roman palaces, while later ones exhibit the round-topped windows typical of Northern Italian or Venetian modes.

The Italianate and Italian Villa styles feature round-arched two-over-two windows (Fig. 32-6, 32-8, 32-9); some structures may mix rectangular windows with round-arched ones. Some residences have bay windows. Windows may be single or in groups with and without shutters or blinds. Hood moldings or pediments over windows are a definitive characteristic of the Italianate and Italian Villa styles.

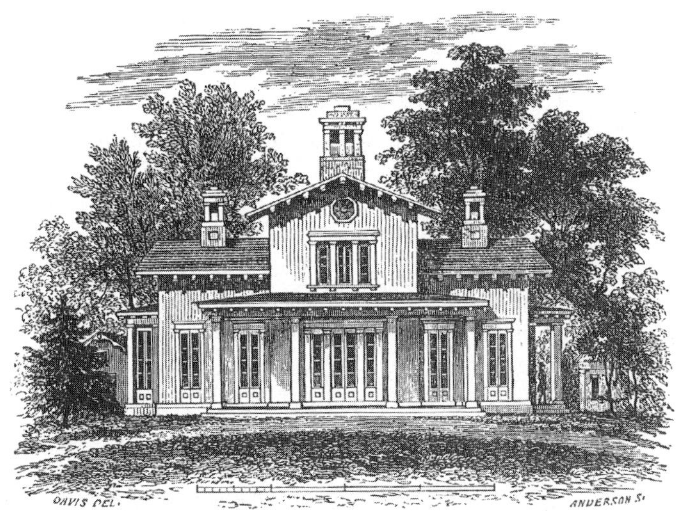

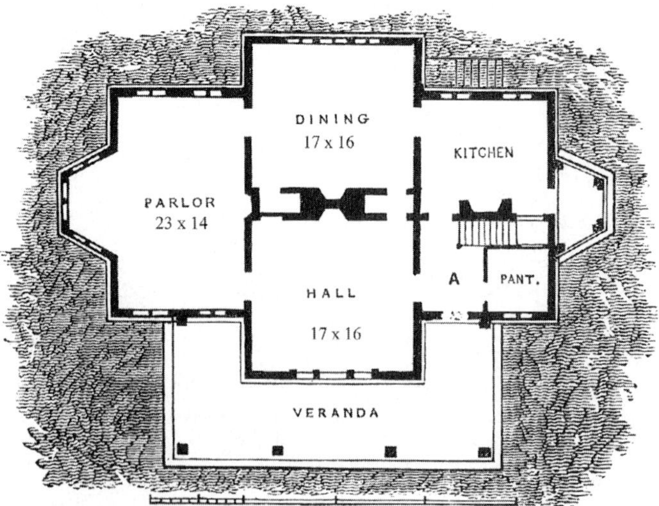

▲ **32-7.** "Design for a Small Classical Villa," published in *The Architecture of Country Houses* by Andrew Jackson Downing, 1853; Alexander Jackson Davis. Italinate/Italian Villa.

■ *Doors*. Single or double doors, of paneled wood, are often centered on the main façade to signal their importance (Fig. 32-2, 32-3, 32-4, 32-8, 32-9). They usually have rounded tops. Some may be grained to imitate more expensive woods; a few have glass in the upper portions. Doorway surrounds may include pilasters or engaged columns carrying an entablature or pediment.

■ *Roofs*. Downplayed as in the originals, roofs may be flat or low pitched. Some examples have balustrades. Tower roofs are hipped or gabled and low pitched. Brackets beneath the roof identify the Italinate or Italian Villa style (Fig. 32-6, 32-9). Grand houses may have a cupola instead of a tower.

INTERIORS

Renaissance Revival characterizes a wide variety of rooms, usually those of importance such as entry halls, atriums, court rooms, and legislative chambers in public buildings and parlors, dining rooms, and bedrooms in dwellings. Interiors exhibit classical or Mannerist architectural details, deep moldings, beamed or compartmented ceilings, rich and warm colors, numerous heavy textures, and fashionable patterns on walls, floors, and window treatments. Similarly, ornament comes from Renaissance and Mannerist sources. Interiors are highly eclectic, drawing from many sources. Renaissance

DESIGN SPOTLIGHT

Architecture: In contrast to earlier and simpler examples, the Morse-Libby House expresses richness and wealth with its masonry building materials, abundance of textures, and robust details. The asymmetrical façade is composed of geometric forms and has a marked verticality that is emphasized by the tower. Rusticated quoins and deep hood moldings and pediments stand out against the smooth walls and create strong light and dark contrasts. Large ornamental brackets beneath the roof and round-arched windows and doorway complete the Italianate/ Italian Villa characteristics.

As is typical in many homes, the interiors are in several styles, including Renaissance Revival in the parlor, Rococo Revival in the music room, and Gothic Revival in the library. As in the exteriors, the owner's wealth is evident in the bold architectural details, painted and gilded wall and ceiling decorations, costly materials, lavish textiles, and furniture in rich finishes. [National Historic Landmark]

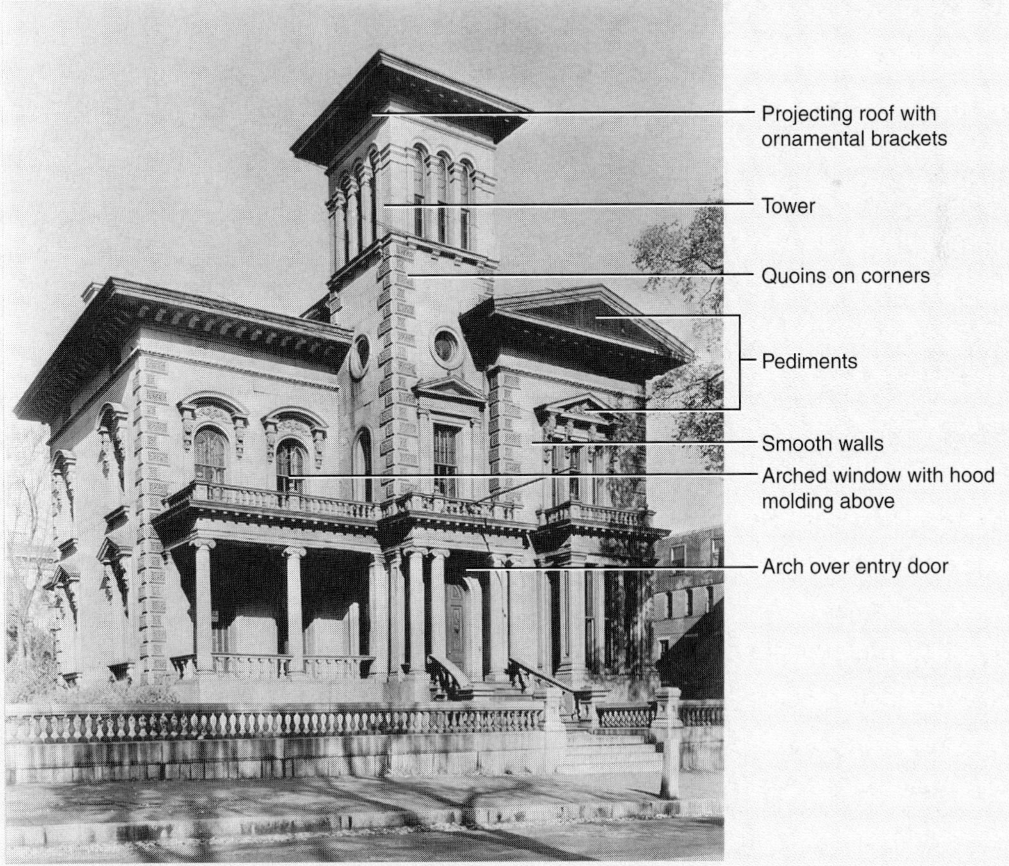

▲ **32-8.** Morse-Libby House (Victoria Mansion), 1858–1860; Portland, Maine; Henry Austin. Italianate/Italian Villa.

▲ **32-9.** Castle Kilbride and interior, 1877; Baden, Ontario, Canada. Italianate/Italian Villa.

Revival furniture has massive proportions, a rectangular or jagged outline, architectural details, dark woods, rich carving, and contrasts of form and materials. Furniture may still line the walls in rooms in public buildings as well as the entry hall and important rooms in homes. A particularly impressive piece of furniture may dominate a room, such as the center table in the parlor, the hallstand in the entry hall, and the sideboard in the dining room.

Italianate or Renaissance Revival public buildings usually have interiors with Renaissance or classical architectural details. Following Barry's design of the Reform Club (Fig. 32-2), many English public buildings center on two-story halls with superimposed columns defining floors and with skylights above. Renaissance Revival rooms, particularly important or public ones, have bold architectural details, rich textures, a variety of materials, and lavish classical and naturalistic ornament derived from Renaissance and Mannerist sources. In contrast, houses may have rooms decorated in Rococo Revival, Gothic Revival, and/or Renaissance Revival (Fig. 32-11, 32-12, 32-13).

Although the Renaissance heritage of a country often defines the style of that country, eclecticism prevails. Interior decoration and furnishings are chosen as symbols of wealth, taste, and civilization, and the Renaissance styles imply a long, genteel, sophisticated heritage. Displays of wealth frequently characterize Renaissance Revival interiors in public and private buildings.

Public and Private Buildings

■ *Color*. Renaissance Revival palettes are warm and rich (Fig. 32-2, 32-11). Crimson is favored, particularly for dining rooms, followed by green, brown, gold, and blue. Gilding may highlight details. Wood trim and paneling are stained a rich brown. Ceilings are white or a lighter tint of the wall color.

■ *Floors*. Floors may be of wood planks, parquet, marble, terrazzo, or tiles in colorful patterns (Fig. 32-2, 32-10). Masonry floors are common in public buildings and domestic entry halls. Carpets and rugs cover floors in both public and private buildings (Fig. 32-11, 32-12, 32-13). Floor cloths or oil cloths, as they are called in America, still appear in less-formal rooms. Patterns imitate carpet or masonry.

■ *Carpets*. Brussels, Wilton, or tapestry carpets in large-scale floral or geometric patterns with naturalistic shading are common in Renaissance-style rooms (Fig. 32-11, 32-12, 32-13). Typical colors are maroon, red, olive, brown, cream, and blue. Although the jacquard mechanism and steam-powered loom increase carpet production, Brussels and Wilton remain expensive because their construction methods demand a great deal of wool yarn. Less expensive tapestry carpets use preprinted wool warp threads on the surface and less expensive threads for the body. Because an unlimited number of colors can be printed onto surface threads, tapestry carpets exhibit great details and realistic shading. Ingrain carpets, used in less important rooms, have large scrolled or circular patterns in green, red, brown, and white. Plain and patterned grass matting usually replaces carpet in summer.

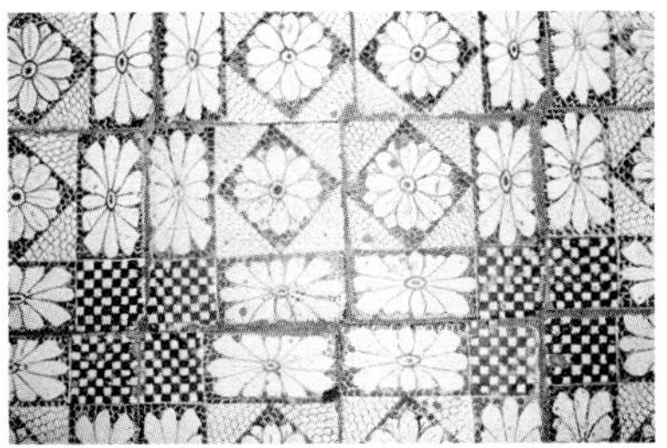

▲ **32-10.** Floor tiles, 1860s–1880s; Virginia.

DESIGN SPOTLIGHT

Interior: Like the other rooms in the Wilcox mansion, the Renaissance Revival parlor is designed *en suite*; that is, the mantel, overmantel mirror, window cornices, light fixtures, and furniture match. The white marble mantel has paneled columns, acanthus leaf carving, rosettes, and a cartouche in the center. The mirror above the mantel and the door surrounds have similar details. The carpet is typical of the period in color, and its scrolling geometric motifs recall Renaissance arabesques. It is a reproduction of a carpet from Paris found in a New York City house. Window treatments of boldly shaped lambrequins hang from ebonized cornices that match the mirror. The painted ceiling has flowers and rosettes. Made by John Jelliff and Co. of Newark, New Jersey, the Renaissance Revival parlor suite features similar details to the room's architecture. It is made of rosewood with mother-of-pearl medallions.

The exterior of the house is Second Empire and displays the style's characteristics of mansard roofs on the house and its tower, brackets supporting the roof, dormers, and round-arched windows with hood moldings. An 1870 newspaper description of the house called the style Franco-Italian and noted that the architect was Augustus Truesdell.

▲ **32-11.** Renaissance Revival parlor, Jedediah Wilcox House, 1870; Meriden, Connecticut [Gift of Josephine M. Fiala, 1968 (68.133.4, 7); American Wing Restricted Building Fund, 1968 (68.143.5); Purchase, Annonymous Gift, 1968 (68.207ab). The Metropolitan Museum of Art, New York City. NY, U.S.A. Image copyright © The Metropolitan Museum of Art/Art Resource, NY].

▲ **32-12.** Dining room, James Whitcomb Riley House, 1872; Indianapolis, Indiana. Renaissance Revival.

■ *Walls*. Common wall treatments include architectural details, paneling, paint, and wallpaper (Fig. 32-2, 32-9, 32-11, 32-12, 32-13). Pilasters, engaged columns, brackets, niches, and other architectural details define important rooms in public and private buildings. Plaster or *papier-mâché* strapwork, roundels, cabochons, bosses, and other Renaissance or Mannerist details may embellish paneling or walls. Panels may have Renaissance motifs carved or painted in the center or may be composed of contrasting colors of wood. Deep cornices exhibit brackets, leaves, foliage, or flowers.

■ *Wallpapers*. Wallpapers with Renaissance motifs may cover walls, although there are fewer Renaissance patterns than other styles. Patterns include textile imitations, flock designs, fresco styles that imitate moldings, and gilded elements and motifs. Leather in embossed and gilded designs often is used in dining rooms because it is thought that leather will not absorb smells.

■ *Chimneypieces*. Mantels are commonly of slate or marble, with white the preferred color (Fig. 32-11). Other colors are black, gray, rose, brown, dark green, or two colors such as black and white. Most mantels are rectangular with an arched opening and a shaped shelf above. They may have carved cartouches, tablets, brackets, caryatids, or columns. Heavy or decorative moldings surround the opening, and a centered keystone carved with shells, fruit, acanthus leaves, or scrolls accents it. Moldings and carvings may decorate the spaces over the opening and the sides. Plainer mantels are used in less important rooms.

▲ **32-13.** Mrs. A. T. Stewart's bedroom, c. 1870s–1880s; published in *Artistic Houses*, 1883. Renaissance Revival.

▲ **32-14.** Lighting: Gasoliers from Rhode Island and Indiana.

■ *Staircases.* Staircases may be straight, rectangular, or curved with a mahogany handrail. The large and prominent newel post may be polygonal or baluster shaped. In wealthy homes, staircases may have niches for sculpture. Some staircases are lit from above with skylights.

■ *Window Treatments.* Deep lambrequins or pelmets hanging from gilded cornices replace the complicated swagged drapery of earlier (Fig. 32-11, 32-13). Lambrequins often have complex shapes and fringe trim. Beneath them hang a pair of fabric panels and muslin or lace curtains next to the glass. Curtains may be tied or looped back over cloak or curtain pins during the day. Plain panels hanging from rings on rods are a simpler treatment for less important rooms. Heavy plain or patterned fabrics are usual for lambrequins and curtains. Also common are roller blinds in linen or brown Holland cloth painted with scenes or designs.

■ *Doors.* Doors may be arched or rectangular and are generally paneled in dark mahogany, walnut, or rosewood (Fig. 32-2, 32-12, 32-13). Sliding or pocket doors in double parlors may have frosted or etched glass panels. Robust moldings, pediments, or entablatures surmount doors in public buildings or important rooms in homes. Doorknobs may be white or decorated porcelain, glass, silver plate, or solid silver.

■ *Ceilings.* Flat ceilings may be plain with a plaster rosette, have beams, or be compartmentalized with strapwork, pendants, bosses, or other patterns inside them. Some ceilings are painted to imitate compartments (Fig. 32-9, 32-11). Gas fixtures hang from plaster rosettes.

■ *Textiles.* In contrast to the prototypes, Renaissance Revival rooms usually have a great many textiles. Carpets or rugs cover floors. Walls may have leather or textile coverings, and windows are elaborately draped. A wide variety of textile types and patterns are common. There are few distinctive Renaissance Revival textiles, but some resemble earlier Renaissance designs, such as damasks with large repeats in undulating patterns with naturalistic flowers and leaves. In the 1850s, textiles emulate the arabesques and grotesques of Ancient Rome and the Renaissance. Upholstery fabrics include damasks, moreen, horsehair, leather, and velvet, plain and patterned. Bed drapery may be of damask, velvet, satin, or moreen.

■ *Lighting.* As in other styles of the period, candles, oil lamps, and gas fixtures illuminate both Renaissance Revival and Italianate interiors (Fig. 32-9, 32-11, 32-13, 32-14). Unlike Gothic Revival or Rococo Revival, only a few feature distinctive Renaissance forms or motifs. Some forms copy ancient Greek vases or have classical motifs.

■ *Later Interpretations.* In the late 19th century, Renaissance architectural details, paneling, and other elements again define interiors in wealthy homes. These versions are more correct because the Renaissance is better understood than in the previous revival styles. Wealthy Americans import entire Renaissance rooms or specific architectural details from Europe and install them in their homes. In the 20th century, there is less direct importation of rooms and more reinvention of stylistic features. As an example, various hotels incorporate designs based on Renaissance Revival influences (Fig. 32-15).

▲ **32-15.** Later Interpretation: Grand Hall, Venetian Hotel, 1999; Las Vegas, Nevada. Hotel by Wimberly, Allison, Tong, & Gao with interiors by Trisha Wilson, Wilson Associates, Texas. Modern Historicism.

FURNISHINGS AND DECORATIVE ARTS

Renaissance Revival furniture gains popularity in nearly all European countries and North America beginning in the 1860s. Nationalist motivations are particularly strong in Germany and Italy, but less so in England and North America. Each country interprets the style in light of its own past. Nevertheless, certain features are common, including massive proportions, an irregular silhouette, architectural motifs, opulence, and Renaissance or Baroque motifs from the 15th, 16th, and 17th centuries (Fig. 32-11, 32-12, 32-13, 32-17, 32-18, 32-20). Also distinctive are competing elements instead of a unified whole, heavy cresting often in the form of a pediment, tapered legs, and carved or applied ornament. Finials, drops, or pendants highlight tops, legs, and other features.

The Renaissance Revival style does not seek to copy Renaissance forms or motifs, but instead adapts and reinvents them to create a new style in keeping with contemporary tastes that are suitable for contemporary rooms. Furniture in this style is common in gentlemen's clubs, smoking rooms, dining rooms, libraries, and entrance halls as well as the parlors and bedrooms of wealthier homes. Although all types of furniture may be Renaissance Revival, sideboards, pedestals, easels, wall pockets, and hanging cabinets are commonly in the style.

Neo-Grec, New Greek, or Modern Greek is a variation of Renaissance Revival that the French introduce in the Great London Exposition in 1862. More two-dimensional than its counterpart, Neo-Grec features less carving; more incising; and Greek, Roman, and especially Egyptian motifs (Fig. 32-11).

Public and Private Buildings

■ *Materials*. Walnut, mahogany, and oak are the most common woods (Fig. 32-17, 32-18, 32-19). Veneer, marquetry, inlay, *ormolu*, gilding, or porcelain may embellish furnishings. Burl veneer contrasting with plainer veneer is a frequent characteristic. Neo-Grec pieces (Fig. 32-11) usually are ebonized and have incising highlighted with gilding. Carving on more expensive pieces may be excessive and in high relief. Applied ornament, such as bosses, is common on cheaper furniture. Drawer pulls may be turned or teardrop pendants. More expensive pieces have large brass and ebony pendants for pulls. Cabinet tops are often marble or scagliola.

■ *Seating*. Like other styles, Renaissance Revival seating (Fig. 32-11, 32-12, 32-13, 32-16) comes in sets and shows great variety in form and details. Some seating is large and richly carved and ornamented, while other examples have simple forms with turned legs, ladder backs, and caned seats. Legs are usually turned with a large ring at the top that tapers to a smaller ring. Most have casters. Some legs are modified cabriole shapes. Back legs are commonly reversed cabrioles like Rococo Revival. Neo-Grec pieces (Fig. 32-11) may have saber, *klismos*, or curule legs and hoof or paw feet. The round or trapezoidal seats of parlor or dining chairs are upholstered, whereas hall chairs have wooden seats, which are suitable for their less important users. Backs are rectangular with a wooden frame that flares out at the top, forming ears and a large crest, usually in a pediment shape. Common embellishments include incising, carving, finials, and applied ornament such as pendants. Sofas may have double or tripartite backs. Unlike Rococo Revival, each part is treated separately and does not blend into a unified whole. Backs and seats often are deeply tufted to add to the opulence and appearance of comfort.

■ *Tables*. Like seating, Renaissance Revival tables take many forms (Fig. 32-11, 32-12, 32-13, 32-17). Tops may be round, oval, oblong, or rectangular. Most tops are of marble, and expensive tables may have inlay or marquetry. Bases and legs form complicated shapes and silhouettes. Turning, animal forms, lyres, urns, brackets, or a combination are typical for legs and bases. Pendants,

DESIGN SPOTLIGHT

Furniture: This furniture suite from the McDonough Company exhibit the variety of form and details in Renaissance Revival parlor suites. Common characteristics include the turned legs; rectangular forms; and jagged, complex outlines. Deep tufting and added embellishments contribute to an image of comfort and opulence.

▲ **32-16.** Suite of seating furniture; published in McDonough, Price & Company catalog, Chicago, 1878.

▲ **32-17.** Center table in the Italian style, mid-19th century. Renaissance Revival.

finials, drops, incising, and carving add interest and complexity. Extension dining tables with one or more pedestals replace the drop-leaf tables of earlier. In the hall or parlor, large pedestals and plant stands resembling columns decorated with Renaissance motifs hold sculpture, flowers, or plants.

■ *Storage*. Hallstands dominate the hall. Their form and embellishment are designed to create an impression of wealth and refinement for visitors. Formal and massive, they may be 6 to 10 feet tall. Characterized by a complicated silhouette topped by a pediment, the hallstand has knobs for hanging outerwear, a mirror to check one's appearance before entering the parlor, an umbrella stand, and a marble top on which to leave calling cards, a common social ritual.

Similarly, the massive sideboard dominates the dining room and is lavishly embellished with carving, *ormolu*, porcelain, marble, marquetry, inlay, and gilding (Fig. 32-12). Its main function is to display the family's wealth, culture, and good taste. The basic form features a plinth or block base with three or four doors or drawers above, a marble top, and a large wooden back with shelves and a mirror. Capped by a large pediment with finials, the sideboard may have realistic carvings of food, game, or hunting motifs. Cabinetmaking firms commission impressive Renaissance Revival sideboards, large cabinets (Fig. 32-18), and pianofortes with much carving and complex iconographies as exhibition pieces for expositions. Dressers (Fig. 32-19) and wardrobes for smaller houses may have these characteristics, but are often simpler in design. Renaissance Revival *étagères* show marked verticality, undulating forms, unusual cutouts, mirrors, shelves, pediments, cartouches, and other embellishment.

▲ **32-18.** Cabinet, c. 1866; New York; Alexander Roux. Renaissance Revival. [The Edgar J. Kaufmann Foundation Gift, 1968. (68.100.1). The Metropolitan Museum of Art, New York City, NY, U.S.A. Image copyright © The Metropolitan Museum of Art/Art Resource, NY]

▲ **32-19.** Dresser with mirror, mid-19th century; Texas. Renaissance Revival.

■ *Beds*. Renaissance Revival beds also have massive proportions (Fig. 32-13, 32-20). Headboards may be up to eight feet tall and often resemble Renaissance church façades or are capped with a tall pediment. Panels have carvings of fruit, flowers, and Renaissance motifs. Not to be outdone, the lower footboards also have carved panels. Canopies are largely out of fashion, but when present, they have deep moldings and applied ornament. Bed drapery is complicated in form and lavishly trimmed with fringe and tassels. Matching night tables, dressers, gentleman's chests, wardrobes, washstands, shaving stands, boot jacks, and towel racks complete the bedroom suite (Fig. 32-13). All match the bed in size and details.

■ *Decorative Arts*. Classical figures, busts, and urns stand on pedestals, mantels, and in niches in Renaissance Revival interiors (Fig. 32-11, 32-13). Pictures are important. Rarely from the Renaissance, subjects vary from classical to contemporary themes. Revived Italian *maiolica* with Italian, French, and Flemish motifs is especially popular. Glass and porcelain objects may decorate mantels and tables (Fig. 32-21). Large mirrors hang over fireplaces or between windows (Fig. 32-11). Wooden frames may be stained, ebonized, and gilded and are carved with Renaissance motifs. Wall pockets, hanging cabinets, canterburies to hold magazines, all in Renaissance forms, commonly accessorize interiors.

▲ **32-21.** Decorative Arts: Glass and porcelain, International Exhibition, 1862; London, England.

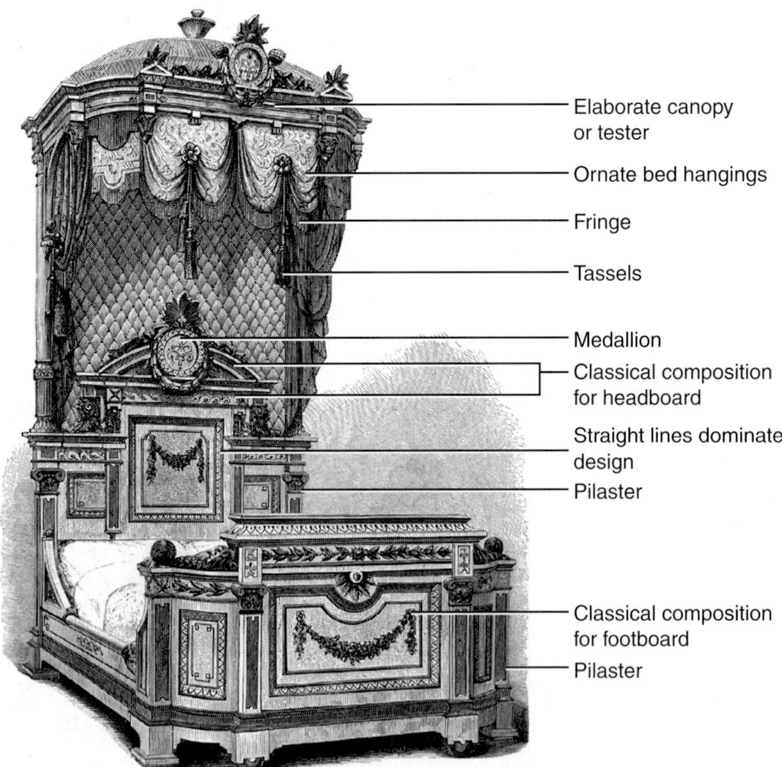

▲ **32-20.** Bed, 1876; England. Renaissance Revival.

CHAPTER 33

Second Empire, Rococo Revival

Second Empire 1855–1885, Rococo Revival 1845–1870s

Modern French furniture . . . stands much higher in general estimation in this country than any other. Its union of lightness, elegance, and grace renders it especially the favorite of the ladies.

—Andrew Jackson Downing, *The Architecture of Country Houses*, 1850

This style is exemplified in the new portions of the Louvre at Paris, at once the most extensive and elegant of the public works with which the genius of the present emperor has enriched that attractive city. From the great intrinsic beauty of this style not less than from its extreme readiness of adaptation to the wants and uses of the present day it has attained universal popularity in Europe and in the chief cities of our own country.

—*Report of the Committee on Public Buildings*, *City Document No. 44*, Boston, 1880, pp. 15–16

Developing in France, Second Empire is an international architectural style characterized by a mansard roof, pavilions, and bold details. Although evident in earlier buildings, these elements come together in the New Louvre in Paris built during the reign of Napoleon III (1852–1870). In Europe and America, the style carries associations of elegance, sophistication, and cosmopolitanism.

Rococo Revival, based upon the 18th-century French Rococo, is the most popular of all revival styles for both interiors and furniture in the 19th century, particularly in England and North America. Its curving forms and feminine grace make it suitable for parlors, drawing rooms, and boudoirs. As a style of the Industrial Revolution, Rococo Revival uses interior surface treatments, textiles, furniture, and decorative arts that often are machine-made and utilize newly developed and patented techniques.

HISTORICAL AND SOCIAL

Following the defeat of Napoleon I in 1812, France remains unsettled. A series of governments, beginning with Louis XVI's brother, neither solves problems nor resolves conflicts. More important, with the exception of the first five years of the reign of Louis Philippe (1830–1848), the new regimes do not help the country to industrialize like the rest of Europe. Finally, in November 1848, Charles Louis Napoleon Bonaparte, nephew of

Napoleon I, wins the presidency by a landslide vote. In 1851, he secures dictatorial power by a *coup d'état*. A year later, following in the footsteps of his uncle, he takes the name Napoleon III and establishes what he calls the Second Empire. He maintains a dictatorship, suppresses freedoms, and censors news until 1860 when intense opposition forces him to begin reforms. Ultimately, he sets up a limited monarchy. Nevertheless, Napoleon III has a positive effect on the country by encouraging industrialization, attempting to help the poor, and modernizing Paris.

One of his most enduring achievements is the reconstruction of Paris directed by Baron Haussman. Well acquainted with the glories of the First Empire under his uncle Napoleon I, Napoleon III and his wife, Eugénie, lead a glittering society with lavish entertainments that take place in opulent surroundings. Thus, France again becomes the model for wealth and luxury throughout the world. Despite domestic improvements, Napoleon III's foreign policies and wars ultimately lead to his downfall, like his uncle. He is overthrown following France's defeat in the Franco-Prussian war in 1870.

Initiated as a reaction to the simplicity of Neoclassicism, Rococo Revival, which adapts elements of French Baroque and Rococo, first appears in Regency England where eclecticism demands new sources of inspiration. Despite war with Napoleon, the English remain captivated by French design and decoration. The Prince of Wales, an early advocate of French antiques, collects furniture and architectural elements from French *hôtels* and *châteaux* destroyed in the Revolution. English cabinetmakers copy pieces of imported French furniture. By the 1820s, a French style called (incorrectly) *Louis Quatorze* has emerged. Confusion exists because the style, which is based largely upon Louis XV or Rococo, depicts some elements of Louis XIV or Baroque, such as symmetry and bold carving. Consequently, literature of the period may refer to Rococo Revival as Louis XIV, Louis XV or *Louis Quinze*, Neo-Louis, Modern French, or Old French.

Queen Victoria signals her approval of the style when she commissions *Louis Quatorze* furniture for Osborne House on the Isle of Wight and for Balmoral Castle in Scotland. Capitalizing on her influence, publications and pattern books popularize the new look for the expanding middle classes. Uncertain in matters of taste, they favor styles with references to the past, believing that these elements indicate a liberal education, taste, and gentility. Stylistic associations are extremely important because people believe that their homes display their family's culture and character.

In France, Rococo Revival gains popularity during the reign of Louis Philippe (1830–1848) and becomes known as *le style Pompadour*. It is fashionable during the reign of Napoleon III (1850–1870) where it shares the limelight with a revival of Louis XVI (1760–1789). Rococo Revival is fashionable in the German-speaking countries from the 1840s. First grafted onto Biedermeier forms, a full-blown Rococo Revival soon arises and is eagerly adopted by the prosperous middle class. Like the British, Americans are enamored with things French, so Rococo Revival enjoys its greatest success in the United States beginning in the 1840s.

Upholsterers and cabinetmakers, instead of architects and progressive designers, purvey Rococo Revival interiors and furnishings to create the correct image of respectability, taste, gentility, luxury, and refinement. Individuals rely on books, such as *An Encyclopedia of Cottage, Farm and Villa Architecture and Furniture* (1833) by Englishman J. C. Loudon, and periodicals, such as *Godey's Lady's Book* in the United States, to decorate their Rococo Revival rooms. Their approach emphasizes image and associations, which appeals to a broad segment of society. Despite its great public esteem, design reformers in England and North America despise Rococo Revival for its air of artificiality, fussiness, and naturalistic patterns, particularly in carpets and wallpapers. By the mid-1860s, taste for Rococo Revival declines in favor of new styles.

CONCEPTS

An international architectural style, Second Empire becomes an important expression of sophistication, cosmopolitanism, and French culture outside of France. The adoption of Second Empire in England and North America coincides with building booms and economic prosperity, so the style comes to symbolize affluence, elegance, sophisticated taste, authority, and power. Similarly, interiors decorated for Napoleon III and Empress Eugénie are models for the affluent or nobility in Europe and America. There is no corresponding furniture style called Second Empire.

Reflecting the prosperity of the aristocratic and middle classes, Rococo Revival depicts a French look associated with noble tastes, which becomes extremely popular for home decoration in all Western countries between the 1830s and the 1860s. Rococo Revival also portrays the feminine character advanced by critics for public and private parlors and other spaces associated with women or those requiring elegance. Rococo's curving forms and visual complexity communicate comfort and prosperity, which are highly desirable in the mid-19th century. Rococo Revival has no corresponding architectural style, like its 18th-century counterpart.

▲ **33–1.** Architectural Detail: Roof detail, Southwest corner tower, Iolani Palace, 1879–1882; Honolulu, Hawaii; T. J. Baker, C. J. Wall, and Isaac Moore.

MOTIFS

■ *Motifs*. Motifs common in Second Empire buildings (Fig. 33-1, 33-2, 33-3, 33-4, 33-5, 33-8) are columns, swags, cartouches, pediments, and relief sculpture. Rococo Revival motifs (Fig. 33-8, 33-9, 33-10, 33-11, 33-14, 33-16, 33-17, 33-18) include C and S scrolls, female masks, vines, shells, grapes, roses, flowers, leaves, acorns, nuts, and birds.

ARCHITECTURE

Unlike other 19th-century revival styles, Second Empire reflects contemporary architectural developments in France in the 1850s and 1860s when Napoleon III undertakes a major rejuvenation of Paris. Wide boulevards and grand buildings transform the city into a modern, elegant metropolis. The world soon strives to emulate Paris, particularly the most famous of its buildings, the new

DESIGN SPOTLIGHT

Architecture: The *Palais du Louvre* is a former royal palace originally built in the Middle Ages. Numerous subsequent additions by various French monarchs create the vast complex it is today. The Old Louvre rests on the site of the original 12th-century fortress and is primarily Renaissance in style. When Louis XIV moves the royal residence to Versailles, additions cease and the Louvre houses artists and their studios. Louis XV begins the practice of displaying royal art in the Louvre, which becomes a public museum during the French Revolution.

The New Louvre is composed of buildings built by Napoleon I and III. The sections added by Napoleon III initiate and embody the Second Empire style. After forming the Second French Empire, Napoleon III calls for the addition of two wings, one on the end of the west front of the Old Louvre, to accommodate elements of his new government. Built around two internal courtyards, they are designed by Ludovico Tullio Johachim Visconti and completed by Hector Martin Lefuel on Visconti's death. The mansard roofs, pavilions, arched lower stories, classical details, and rounded pediments with relief sculpture are reminiscent of the work of Renaissance designer–architects Pierre Lescot and Jean Goujon, and they tie old and new buildings together. The bold three-dimensional elements, columns, figural sculpture, and profuse decoration are new. Expansions to the building continue until 1876. In 1983, French President Mitterrand has the building renovated, and the French government moves out, and displays of art spread throughout the building. In 1988, I. M. Pei adds the glass pyramid to the central courtyard.

The Grand Salon of Napoleon III epitomizes Second Empire taste for lavish interiors. The decoration shows ties with the First Empire of Napoleon Bonaparte as well as earlier French monarchs, including Louis XV. Room treatments embody the magnificence of the Second Empire with bold, classical architectural details; rich finishes and materials; lavish stucco work and gilding; and allegorical ceiling paintings. Furnishings are equally lavish with deep carving, gilding, and rich upholstery. Rooms display a mix of old and new furniture in various French styles. Despite their expensive materials, splendid decoration, and rich colors, the interiors often are cold, uninviting, and overly grand. [World Heritage Site]

▲ **33-2.** New Louvre, pavilion, site plan, and Grand Salon of Napoleon III, 1852–1857; Paris, France; L. T. J. Visconti and H. M. Lefuel. Second Empire.

DESIGN SPOTLIGHT

PAVILLON TURGOT

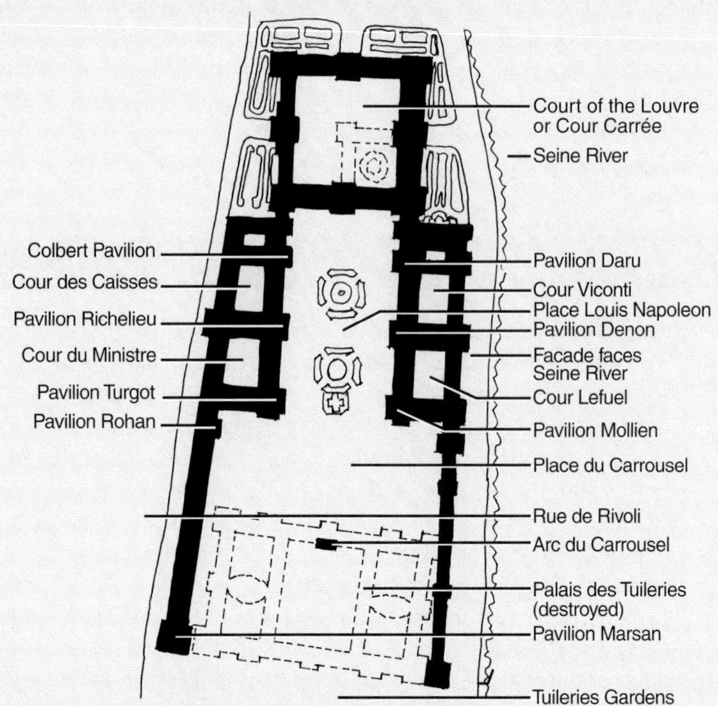
Court of the Louvre
or Cour Carrée
Seine River
Colbert Pavilion
Cour des Caisses
Pavilion Richelieu
Cour du Ministre
Pavilion Turgot
Pavilion Rohan
Pavilion Daru
Cour Viconti
Place Louis Napoleon
Pavilion Denon
Facade faces
Seine River
Cour Lefuel
Pavilion Mollien
Place du Carrousel
Rue de Rivoli
Arc du Carrousel
Palais des Tuileries
(destroyed)
Pavilion Marsan
Tuileries Gardens

▲ 33-2. Continued

▲ **33-3.** Opera House and grand staircase, 1862–1875; Paris, France; Jean-Louis-Charles Garnier. Second Empire.

Louvre. Its mansard roof, pavilions, and classical details have appeared on French buildings since the 17th century. The greater richness, three-dimensionality, and plasticity of these elements are new in the 19th century.

The definitive characteristic of Second Empire is a mansard roof (Fig. 33-1, 33-2, 33-4, 33-5, 33-6, 33-7, 33-8), which is combined with other elements that may be found in other styles such as Italianate and Renaissance Revival. Other characteristics include wall and/or roof dormers, hood moldings, round arches, stringcourses, columns, high-relief sculpture, and classical details. Pavilions characterize public buildings but are rare in private ones. Buildings project an air of grandeur and formality. European Second Empire characterizes government and commercial buildings (Fig 33-2), offices, town halls, art galleries, retail structures, theaters (Fig 33-3), railway stations, and grand hotels. In residences, the style is mostly limited to urban style mansions, apartment buildings, and row houses. However, some smaller suburban or rural examples exist in the United States.

International Expositions held in Paris in 1855 and 1867 acquaint visitors with the new style. Images in numerous professional and popular periodicals also help to inspire Second Empire buildings in Great Britain, her territories, North America, Germany, Austria, Australia, and Latin America. In Great Britain, designers find that Second Empire is eminently suitable for new railway stations, office buildings, and grand hotels to create an image of refinement and affluence. Following the Civil War in the United States, Second Empire characterizes many government buildings (Fig. 33-4, 33-5). Because this period coincides with the administration of Ulysses Grant, the style is sometimes called the General Grant style. The ornate Second Empire particularly

▲ **33-4.** Philadelphia City Hall, 1871–1881; Philadelphia, Pennsylvania; John MacArthur, Jr., and Thomas U. Walter. Second Empire.

appeals to the newly affluent and powerful American leaders of commerce and industry who choose it for their offices and homes (Fig. 33-6, 33-7, 33-8). Because it is an expensive style in which to build, Second Empire dies out following world economic reverses in the 1870s.

Public and Private Buildings

■ *Site Orientation*. As parts of urban settings, public and private buildings sit along streets in prominent locations in cities (Fig. 33-3, 33-4, 33-5). Lawns may surround dwellings, especially grand ones (Fig. 33-6, 33-7, 33-8). Sometimes they are part of large urban developments as in Paris (Fig. 33-2). Row houses may be treated as single units with each house uniform in design or they may vary.

■ *Floor Plans*. Floor plans for public buildings are usually symmetrical with formal planning reflecting the function of the building. Similarly residential plans are formal and may be symmetrical or asymmetrical. Rooms are rectangular, and some have bay windows (Fig. 33-8). Upper floors generally repeat the plan of the first floor, so supporting walls and mechanical connections align vertically.

■ *Materials*. Stone, granite, marble, brownstone (in the United States), brick, and iron details are common building materials for both public and residential buildings (Fig. 33-2, 33-3, 33-4, 33-5,

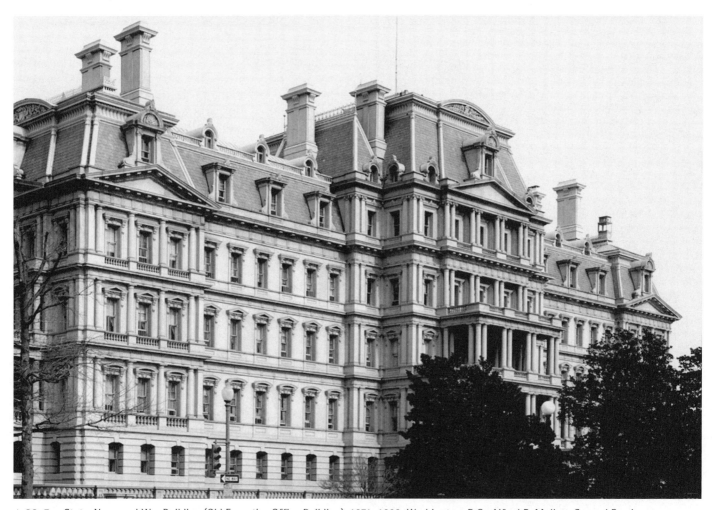

▲ **33-5.** State, Navy, and War Building (Old Executive Office Building), 1871–1888; Washington, D.C.; Alfred B. Mullett. Second Empire.

33-6, 33-7). Sometimes walls and details contrast in material and color, or the building may exhibit structural polychrome. Some Second Empire buildings, particularly multistory ones, have cast-iron façades. Shingles may be polychrome slate, tin, or wood. Some houses in the United States are of wood painted in polychrome schemes of three or more colors. One of the more frequent color combinations is a body in fawn or straw, brown quoins, olive windows and porch, and Indian red sashes. Sometimes the house is painted stone or gray to create the impression of stone. Details may be green, red, gold, or blue. Shutters, when present, are dark green or brown. Cresting and stair rails usually are of cast iron.

■ *Façades*. Façades of public buildings are formal, usually symmetrical, and majestic with projecting centers and ends defined by paired columns or pilasters in the traditional French manner (Fig. 33-2, 33-3, 33-4, 33-5). Multiple forms, architectural elements, and details, particularly on pavilions, give a plastic or layered appearance, enhancing the three-dimensionality of the façade. Superimposed orders may organize façades with prominent stringcourses providing horizontal emphasis. Some façades have numerous bays defined by single or paired columns or pilasters. Quoins may accentuate corners, and lower stories may be rusticated. Bold relief sculpture with complex or symbolic iconographies highlights important buildings. Tall, ornamented chimneys emphasize verticality.

▲ **33-6.** Governor's Mansion, 1871; Jefferson City, Missouri; George Inham Barnott. Second Empire.

▲ **33-7.** *Château-sur-Mer,* 1852, remodeled 1872; Newport, Rhode Island; Richard Morris Hunt. Second Empire.

DESIGN SPOTLIGHT

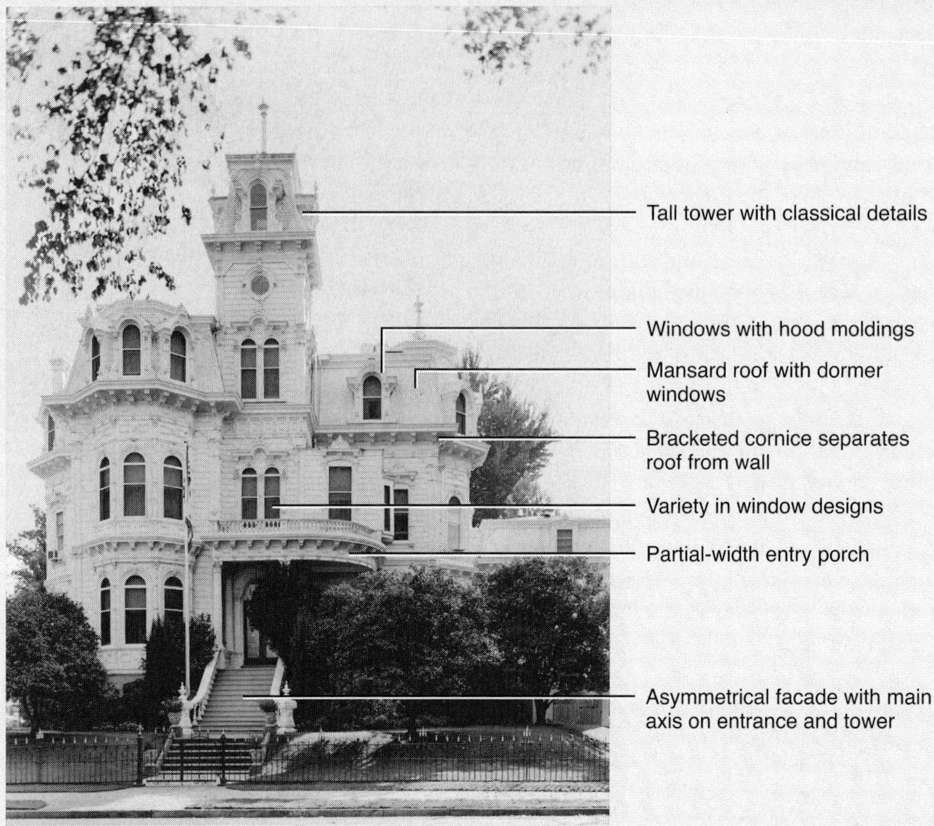

Architecture: Built by U. M. Resse from the designs of architect Nathaniel D. Goodell in 1877 for local hardware merchant Albert Gallatin, the house exemplifies Second Empire style in residences. Richness characterizes the composition and conveys the sophistication and culture of French design. Definitive characteristics of Second Empire are its mansard roof, tall tower, and bold details. Other characteristics, which appear in Italianate and Gothic Revival, include the bracketed cornice separating roof from wall, variety of windows with hood moldings, bold dormer windows, and polychrome slate roof. The asymmetrical plan contains double parlors, a music room, dining room, and kitchen on the first floor. Bedrooms, as private spaces, are on the second floor. From the enclosed vestibule with tile floor, one enters the stair hall with its spiral stair. The prominent newel post is characteristic of the period, and the ceiling has its original gilded plasterwork ornament. The northeast parlor, immediately off the entrance hall, is the most formal space in the house as befits its use for entertaining. Gallatin imports the polychrome marble mantel, one of seven in the house, from Italy and the large mirror above it from France. The parlor ceiling has gilded plasterwork like the stair hall. The fancy curtains, thought to be original, are in keeping with the opulent window treatments of the period. The mansion is sumptuously furnished in a variety of fashionable styles.

The state of California purchases the house in 1903 for use as a governor's residence and remodels the interiors. The last governor to inhabit the mansion is Ronald Reagan in 1976. The house is now a museum.

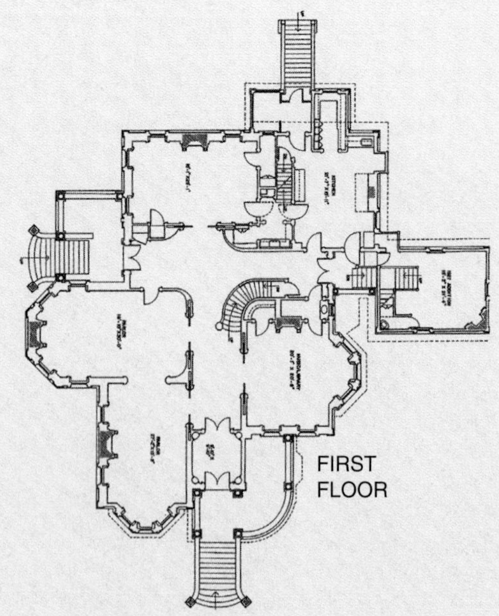

▲ **33-8.** Albert Gallatin House floor plan, stair hall, and northeast parlor, 1877–1880; Sacramento, California; Nathaniel Goodell.

House façades, usually one to four stories, may be symmetrical or asymmetrical (Fig. 33-6, 33-7, 33-8). Irregular massing and rectangular or angular projections create the three-dimensional appearance found on public buildings. Affluent houses have more projections and bolder architectural details. The center may project forward like the pavilion on a public building. The central bay, containing the entrance, often has a tower. Elements in common with Italianate or the Italian Villa styles include hood moldings, single and groups of rectangular and round-arched windows, quoins, and prominent stringcourses. A few examples exhibit stick work like the Stick style or a mixture of textures and materials like Queen Anne. Porches, usually smaller than Italianate, may be the full or partial width of the façade. Rectangular porch supports have scrollwork banisters and brackets. Towers and tall, decorated chimneys emphasize verticality.

■ *Windows.* Second Empire buildings exhibit a variety of windows (Fig. 33-2, 33-3, 33-4, 33-5, 33-6, 33-7, 33-8). Two-over-two windows may be single or grouped and rectangular or round arched as in Italianate. Most have lintels, triangular or segmental pediments, or hood moldings or a combination. Some have shutters or blinds. Windows may diminish in size, with attic or top-story windows being the smallest. Small round windows may accentuate towers or other areas. A few residences have bay or oriel windows. Wall and/or roof dormers are a defining feature and may have circular tops, pediments, or lintels.

■ *Doors.* Columns, porches, pediments, and changes in shape emphasize major doorways, which may be located in the center of the building in a pavilion or beneath a portico or porch (Fig. 33-2, 33-4, 33-5, 33-6, 33-7, 33-8). On residences, doors are often to one side if there is a tower. Moldings, pilasters, and columns form the surrounds and stress importance. Doors may be rectangular or round arched with glass panels. Grand entrances have double doors.

■ *Roofs.* The distinctive mansard roof, named for 17th-century French architect François Mansart, defines the style (Fig. 33-2, 33-3, 33-4, 33-5, 33-6, 33-7, 33-8). Its tall, full shape allows another story when legal restrictions do not, so mansards become common in both remodeling and new construction. Each portion of the building or pavilion may have its own roof. Roofs exhibit several profiles: straight, straight with a flare, concave,

DESIGN SPOTLIGHT

▲ **33-8.** Continued

convex, or S-shaped; these may be combined in one building. Iron cresting or curbing often tops the roofs. Rooflines may have a picturesque appearance with a multiplicity of shapes, layers, forms, and details. Some houses have a cupola instead of or in addition to a tower. Shingles of slate, tin, or wood may form colorful patterns in red, green, blue, tan, and/or gray. Roofs nearly always contrast in color to the rest of the house. Brackets emphasize the roofline as in Italianate but are smaller, and the eaves do not project as much as Italianate ones do. Shingles may be polychrome.

INTERIORS

True Second Empire interiors are those created for Napoleon III in the Louvre and Tuileries (Fig. 33-2). Opulent and showy like interiors of the First Empire of Napoleon I, they are in keeping with the majestic Second Empire image. These rooms usually mix old and new furniture in Louis XIV, XV, and XVI styles as a visible tie to previous French monarchs. Like the First Empire, their grandeur often makes them cold and uninviting despite expensive materials, splendid decoration, and rich colors. And, like their predecessors, they are generally considered too grand for the rest of the world. Interiors in Second Empire buildings often display bold classical architectural details. Those in public buildings or homes of the wealthy have rich textures and lavish materials. Rooms may be decorated in Rococo Revival, Renaissance Revival, Gothic Revival (more rarely), or a combination.

Enormously popular in most countries, Rococo Revival rooms appear in Greek Revival, Renaissance Revival, Italianate, and Second Empire buildings. Because it conveys an image of French culture, it is the most fashionable style for parlors, bedrooms, boudoirs, and ladies' retiring rooms in public buildings. The style is rare in dining rooms and libraries, which are considered masculine spaces. Rococo Revival combines elements of French Baroque of the 17th century and French Rococo of the 18th century. Although curvilinear, the revival style is bolder, more symmetrical, and more sculptural than its predecessors. New technology facilitates replication of the opulence, if not the elegance, of Rococo (and Second Empire) with plaster moldings, wallpapers, carpets, textiles, and richly carved furniture.

Public and Private Buildings

■ *Color*. Second Empire adopts colors of the period, which are highly saturated and rich. Crimson, green, blue, and gold are most common (Fig. 33-2, 33-3). Parlors or drawing rooms may be white and gold with furniture covered in blue, red, or green.

Rococo Revival parlors are white and gold, or pearly white or lavender. After 1850 and in contrast to its Rococo predecessor, colors become highly saturated blues, crimsons, greens, and golds (Fig. 33-9, 33-10). Shades of red, relating to roses and the Louis XV period, are very fashionable. Carpet, wallpaper (Fig. 33-11), drapery, and upholstery have numerous colors and patterns.

■ *Floors*. Floors are marble or ceramic tiles in Second Empire public buildings (Fig. 33-2, 33-3) and wood or parquet with rugs in residences (Fig. 33-8, 33-9, 33-10). Both have wall-to-wall carpet in important rooms. Public buildings and wealthy homes use Brussels, Wilton, and tapestry carpets, whereas ingrains are more common in middle-class residences. Second Empire carpets have bold classical and other motifs in rich colors. They often feature black, which intensifies colors. Rococo style carpets have scrolls, curving forms, and flowers. Much to the distaste of design critics and reformers, the public adores patterns that are three-dimensional with naturalistically shaded flowers, foliage, ferns, and/or leaves in a profusion of colors. Critics dislike these patterns because they believe that flat patterns are more appropriate for flat surfaces. Some carpets used in Rococo Revival rooms have geometric patterns in red, green, black, and white.

▲ **33-9.** Parlor, General Mariano Guadalupe Vallejo's Home, 1851–1852; Sonoma Valley, Sonoma County, California. Rococo Revival.

■ *Walls*. Prominent architectural details and deep cornices typify Second Empire interiors (Fig. 33-2, 33-3). Some rooms have paneled dadoes or paneled walls. Second Empire rooms in Napoleon III's various palaces often have rectangular paneling. Panel moldings are gilded or painted a contrasting color to the centers. Walls may be painted or wallpapered in Renaissance or Neoclassical patterns.

Walls in Rococo Revival interiors (Fig. 33-8, 33-9, 33-10) are treated as a single unit with no dado, unlike those of the earlier Rococo or Louis XV style that were paneled with dado, fill, and frieze. Between the cornice moldings and baseboards, walls may be painted or papered. Mass-produced or hand-blocked wallpapers (Fig. 33-11) are nearly universal, with French papers the most highly prized. Types include fresco papers, large florals interspersed with scrolls, satin (shiny) papers, flock papers, and imitations of textiles. As in carpet, flowers and foliage are realistically rendered and shaded.

■ *Chimneypieces*. Mantels, which are focal points in Rococo Revival rooms, are usually of white or black marble and often have curving shapes similar to those of the 18th century. However, the most common mantel form, rectangular with a shaped shelf and round arched opening, has no earlier precedent (Fig. 33-10). A heavy molding surrounds the opening, the center of which may feature a scroll, shell, or cartouche. The perimeter of the molding and/or face of the mantel may be carved with flowers, fruit, leaves, and/or female masks. The mantel shelf holds an array of decorative objects and candlesticks with prisms. Large, heavy gilded mirrors, which reflect the light, often accent the wall area above the mantel.

■ *Window Treatments*. Windows in Second Empire rooms have prominent surrounds and opulent layered, trimmed, and tasseled drapery. From richly molded and gilded cornices hang trimmed valances, curtains, and glass curtains, usually of lace (Fig. 33-2).

DESIGN SPOTLIGHT

Interiors and Furniture: The Metropolitan Museum of Art recreates the southwest formal parlor of the Italianate-style house of Horace Whittemore. The space, which contained much seating, is decorated in what was called the "French Taste" or Rococo Revival. This curvilinear and graceful style is considered appropriate for the feminine parlor. Architectural details, such as the cornice, are prominent and lavish. The mantel is of marble ornately carved with scrolls, shells, and flowers, all typical Rococo and Rococo Revival motifs. Walls are covered with a reproduction damask wallpaper that is divided into panels by *trompe l'oeil* architectural moldings. A strongly colored and patterned English tapestry carpet covers the floor. Fancy window treatments matching the upholstery hang from curving cornices and feature elaborate valances trimmed with fringe and tassels. Beneath the matching curtains are sheer embroidered glass curtains. The gasolier and lamp on the center table are of blue overlay glass.

The Rococo Revival rosewood parlor suite consisting of a sofa, two armchairs, two side chairs, and a *tête-à-tête*, along with the center table, is attributed to John Henry Belter. A German immigrant, he perfects a method of bending laminated wood that allows it to be curved in shape and carved and pierced, as on these examples. The chair, like its 18th-century predecessor, has cabriole legs and a wooden frame composed of C and S scrolls. The resemblance ends with the heavy scale; reverse cabriole rear legs; and the profuse carving and piercing of roses, flowers, leaves, and scrolls. The upholstery is a reproduction of a blue and gold brocatelle from the mid-19th century. Although the firescreen is not part of the set, it also is by Belter, whose furniture adorns the homes of America's wealthiest families.

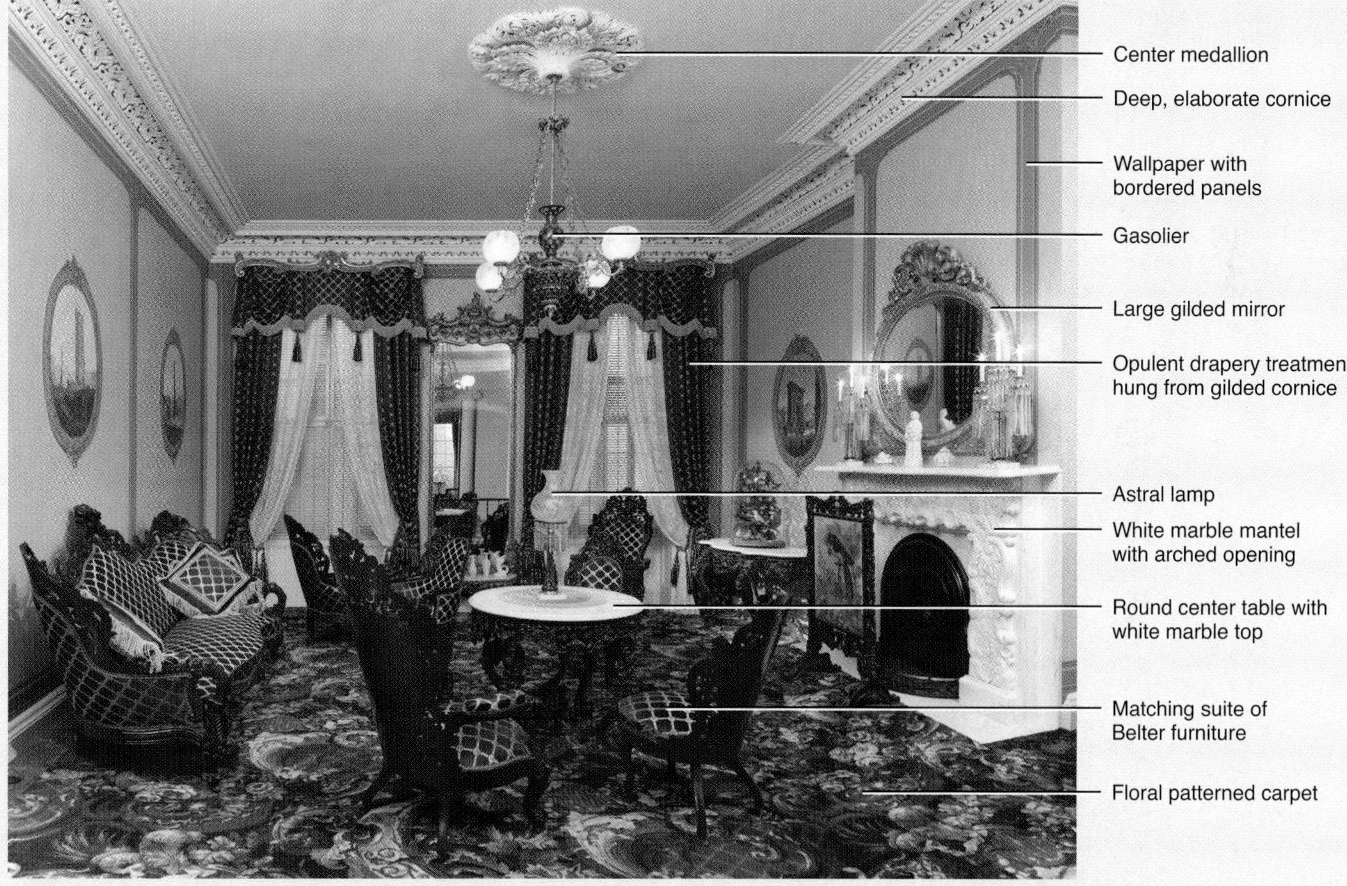

▲ **33-10.** Rococo Revival Parlor, c. 1852; Astoria, New York; parlor suite by John Henry Belter, 1845–1860. Rococo Revival. [Architectural elements from the La Roque Mansion. The Metropolitan Museum of Art, New York, NY, U.S.A. Image copyright © The Metropolitan Museum of Art/Art Resource, NY]

Similarly, windows in Rococo Revival rooms often have prominent surrounds. The typical window treatment for parlors and other important rooms consists of a lambrequin with an intricate, curving shape (Fig. 33-8, 33-9, 33-10, 33-12). It hangs from a gilded cornice that is composed of scrolls. Undercurtains, usually tied back with lace or muslin beneath them, and a roller blind next to the glass complete the ensemble. Trims, fringe, and tassels embellish lambrequins and curtains alike. Simpler treatments of panels hanging from rings are found in other rooms or lesser houses. Drapery fabrics, usually patterned, include damask, satin, brocatelle, brocade, velvet, and plush.

■ *Doors*. Doorway surrounds in both Second Empire and Rococo Revival rooms are impressive combinations of moldings with doors in dark stained or grained woods. Double doors indicate important rooms. Unlike its precedent, the Rococo Revival door does not have a painting or panel with an asymmetrical frame above it. Doorways to important rooms in affluent residences sometimes have *portières* to add to the opulence (Fig. 33-2, 33-8).

■ *Ceilings*. Ceilings may be plain, painted, or compartmentalized in Second Empire public buildings and wealthy homes (Fig. 33-2). Most ceilings in Rococo Revival rooms are flat with a plaster rosette or medallion in the center from which a chandelier or gasolier hangs (Fig. 33-8, 33-10, 33-13). Where wall and ceiling join are deep, cast-plaster moldings composed of repeating designs, foliage, and/or flowers. The 18th century cove ceiling with abundant curvilinear forms and foliage repeats in some rooms.

■ *Textiles*. Both Second Empire and Rococo Revival interiors have many textiles including wall-to-wall carpet, fabrics on walls and at windows, upholstered furniture, and bed hangings (Fig. 33-2, 33-8, 33-9, 33-10, 33-12). Additionally rooms are filled with doilies, antimacassars, mantel and shelf lambrequins, lamp mats, and table covers made by the ladies of the house. Embroidery often embellishes smaller chairs and ottomans. Typical textiles include damask, velvet or plush, brocatelle, satin, silk, cotton, linen, and horsehair for upholstery. Common patterns have naturalistic flowers, birds, fruit, and foliage in scrolling surrounds or foliage only. Flowers and leaves usually are realistically shaded. Sometimes Renaissance or Gothic-style patterns, especially when combined with flowers or scrolls, appear in Rococo Revival rooms and on furniture. Cotton or chintz in floral patterns covers furniture and hangs at windows in summer.

▲ **33-12.** Window Treatments: Single and double window draperies from *Godey's Lady's Book*, 1875; United States.

■ *Lighting*. Chandeliers and *candelabra* in Second Empire rooms are large to suit the scale of the space and may be of polished metal or cut glass with hundreds of crystals (Fig. 33-2). *Candelabra* sit in front of mirrors to reflect and intensify the light.

Candlesticks, oil lamps, gas lamps, sconces, gasoliers, and chandeliers have C and S scrolls, curving outlines, and naturalistic ornament (Fig. 33-10, 33-13). They are among the most elaborate of all styles. Lamps and candleholders often have glass prisms to reflect light and add to the air of opulence and wealth.

▲ **33-11.** Wallpapers: Patterns with roses (adaptation) and ogee motifs; England and the United States.

▲ **33-13.** Lighting: Lamp and gasolier, mid-19th century; England and the United States.

FURNISHINGS AND DECORATIVE ARTS

Like its prototype, Rococo Revival furniture has a curving silhouette, C and S scrolls, cabriole legs, and naturalistic ornament, but in contrast to its predecessor, it is larger and heavier with symmetrical, carved decoration; pierced work; and reverse cabriole legs. The revival often lacks Rococo's continuity of parts in which elements flow together with little interruption and no articulation. The style attempts to capture the spirit of Rococo instead of mirroring its image. Curving and carved silhouettes are complicated, often flamboyant. Rococo Revival ornament usually is symmetrical, higher in relief, and more profuse than that of its predecessor. With coil springs for comfort, upholstery is sumptuous. The revival style introduces furniture that is unknown in the 18th century, such as the *étagère* or *tête-à-tête*. Curves; C and S scrolls; cabriole legs; and carved, naturalistic ornament distinguish Rococo Revival from other styles.

Rococo Revival in the United States is more flamboyant and embellished than in Europe. American cabinetmakers develop new methods for shaping wood for backs and beds. John Henry Belter, a Rococo Revival cabinetmaker, perfects a process of laminating and bending woods that can be elaborately carved (Fig. 33-10, 33-16). His name becomes synonymous with high-quality furniture that integrates machine and handcrafted production methods. Designers and manufacturers find that Rococo Revival is infinitely adaptable to suit many tastes and price ranges. Expensive furniture is made of costly wood and has abundant carving, often executed by hand. Cheaper furniture resembles the expensive, but is simpler in shape, often machine produced, and made of inexpensive woods with less carving.

Public and Private Buildings

■ *Materials*. Dark woods are characteristic. Costly pieces are of rosewood and mahogany (Fig. 33-10, 33-15, 33-16), while other furniture is of walnut or maple. In the most expensive rosewood furniture, the grain emphasizes the sense of movement. Veneers are used often. In America, cabinetmakers apply veneers of costly woods to laminated backs, the tops of which may be carved or pierced, or have applied ornament. Carving of laminated woods

▲ **33-14.** Parlor chair and *papier mâché* drawing room chairs; 1830s–1850s London, England; drawing room chair by Jennens and Bettridge of Birmingham and London. Rococo Revival.

reveals the layers and enhances the visual complexity. Wood furniture has a high-gloss finish known as French polish. English and French furniture (Fig. 33-2) has gilding, *ormolu*, or porcelain plaques unlike in the United States.

New to the period is furniture made of *papier-mâché* (Fig. 33-14). Although known in Europe since the 17th century, the *papier-mâché* manufacturing process improves in the late 1830s. Thus, it becomes suitable for furniture, although structural parts are made of wood or metal. *Papier-mâché* furniture, which enjoys great popularity in Great Britain, is often lacquered or japanned in black with painted decoration or mother-of-pearl inlay.

■ *Seating.* Elaborate upholstery supports the cultural vision of comfort and expensiveness (Fig. 33-8, 33-9, 33-10, 33-16, 33-17). Particularly suited to Rococo Revival is the typical deep tufting in diamond or star patterns covering seats and backs. Tufting, piping, and puffing add visual complexity and enhance the prized expensive look. More and deeper tufts indicate a more expensive piece. Long, heavy bullion fringe may adorn the skirt, and tassels may decorate the back and arms. Adding to an expensive appearance are textiles in a variety of patterns. Some pieces are upholstered in two different fabrics: one covers the inside arms, back, and seat;

▲ **33-15.** Drawing room chair with the image of Queen Victoria; exhibited at the Great Exhibition, Crystal Palace, 1851; London, England; manufactured by Henry Eyles firm in Bath. Rococo Revival.

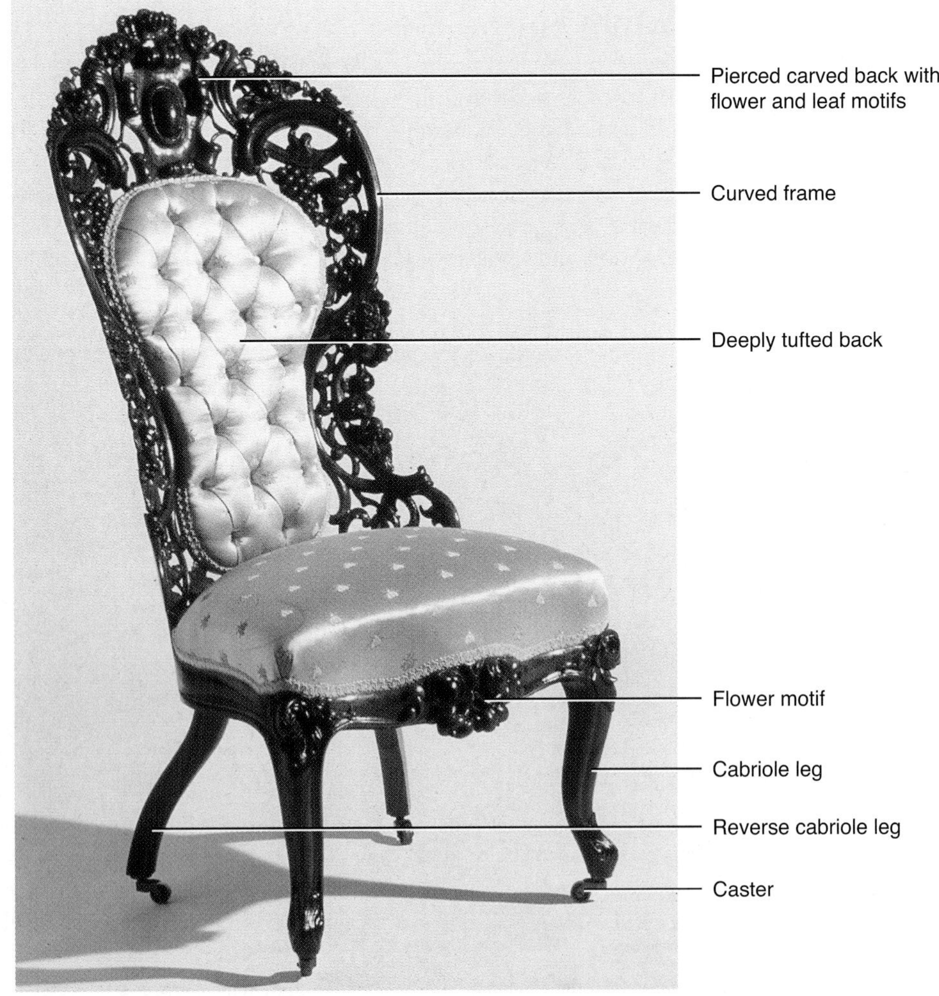

▲ **33-16.** Side chair, 1845–1860, New York, New York; attributed to John Henry Belter. Rococo Revival. [Courtesy Winterthur Museum]

another covers the outside of the back and arms. No parlor is complete without a parlor set, which has a sofa; a gentleman's chair that is larger, more thronelike; a smaller lady's chair with a wider seat; and three or more wall or side chairs (Fig. 33-9, 33-10).

Sofa backs have three forms: triple arches, serpentine (Fig. 33-9, 33-10), and double or tripartite backs composed of three separate curvilinear medallions. The most fashionable Rococo Revival parlors have a *tête-à-tête* and a *méridienne* (Fig. 33-10). The pouf or *pouffe*, a stool with deeply tufted coil spring upholstery, is introduced from France about 1830.

Rococo Revival chairs take many forms (Fig. 33-8, 33-9, 33-10, 33-14, 33-15, 33-16). Most have balloon backs composed of a single curve that flares out at the top and tapers inward at the seat, are usually upholstered, and feature cabriole legs ending in a whorl foot or cone. Some dining or parlor chairs have a wooden back with a splat or cross rail. Dining chairs sometimes have turned legs. All back legs are reverse cabrioles, and most have casters to facilitate moving.

The most ornate and expensive chairs and sofas have laminated backs that curve in two planes with hand-carved, pierced flowers, fruit, birds, and foliage along the back edges and forming the crest. Like the Louis XV prototype, seat and back rails undulate, and knees of cabriole legs are heavily carved. Belter, one of the best-known cabinetmakers of the period, creates parlor sets with lavish carving; laminated veneer surfaces; and complicated, curving forms (Fig. 33-10, 33-16). His costly furniture is highly prized and often imitated.

▲ **33-18.** Bed, mid-19th century; United States. Rococo Revival.

▲ **33-17.** *Étagère* with armchair, mid-19th century; the United States. Rococo Revival.

■ *Tables*. Convoluted shapes and lavishly carved naturalistic motifs are common on expensive tables, whereas cheaper ones have undulating shapes and less profuse carving (Fig. 33-2, 33-9, 33-10). Center tables are oval, round, or oblong in shape with marble tops and heavily carved aprons with Rococo Revival motifs. Many have four cabriole legs that are joined by arched, curving stretchers with a finial in the center. Instead of a single curve, legs may be composed of several C or S scrolls. In contrast to their 18th-century prototypes, consoles often have four legs instead of two and may be joined to a monumental pier glass with carved embellishment. Like other tables, consoles usually have shaped marble tops and heavily carved aprons.

■ *Storage*. The *étagère* features a complex curvilinear outline, pierced and solid carving, shelves, mirrored back, and marble top (Fig. 33-9, 33-17). As a showy focal point for the parlor, it displays all available contemporary techniques for ornamentation. The bedroom dresser, usually serpentine or kidney shaped, has three to four large drawers surmounted by a marble or wood top with small drawers or shelves, above which is attached a tall mirror with carved crests. Moldings outline the drawers, and, on expensive pieces, drawer pulls are hand-carved flowers, fruit, or leaves. Chests of drawers are similar in form and decoration to dressers.

■ *Beds*. Rococo Revival beds have tall headboards, low footboards, and rounded ends (Fig. 33-18). Footboards on very expensive beds undulate. Carving of flowers, leaves, and foliage adorns head- and footboards. Some beds have half or full testers with hangings. The underside of the canopy is upholstered in complicated patterns. In warm climates in the United States, lightweight mosquito netting hangs around the perimeter of the canopy for protection. The use of bed drapery declines during the period because people begin to regard it as unhealthy. In addition, central heating is more prevalent, so hangings are no longer needed for warmth or protection from drafts. Bedroom suites include the bed, night table, dresser, gentleman's chest, and washstand. Less common pieces are a shaving stand, towel rack, and wardrobe.

■ *Decorative Arts*. Rococo Revival interiors have many accessories, most of which have the complicated forms and curving silhouettes of furniture. Sitting on mantels or shelves of the *étagère* are Parian ware busts, allegorical figures, and classical sculpture; porcelain figurines and vases with curving forms and embellishment; boxes; jars; clocks; candlesticks; and candlesticks (Fig. 33-9, 33-10). Vases of dried flowers under tall glass domes highlight consoles and tabletops. Numerous etchings, engravings, lithographs, chromolithographs, and/or paintings hang on walls suspended by decorative ropes from picture moldings below the cornice (Fig. 33-9). Large mirrors with carved and gilded frames hang over the mantel and on the piers between windows (Fig. 33-10). Many parlors have a stereoscope to examine views (images) of unusual scenes or exotic lands. Decorative screens, plants, and flowers fill corners.

■ *Later Interpretations*. In the late 19th century, Rococo furniture is again fashionable. Examples more closely follow the 18th-century predecessors. Cheaper adaptations appear in mail-order catalogues. In the second half of the 20th century, Victorian Rococo furniture revives in simpler form and may appear as an inexpensive suite of furniture with traditional upholstery or as a single chair or sofa covered in an updated textile. In the early 21st century, various manufacturers experiment with old forms in new designs, some created with connecting parts (Fig. 33-19).

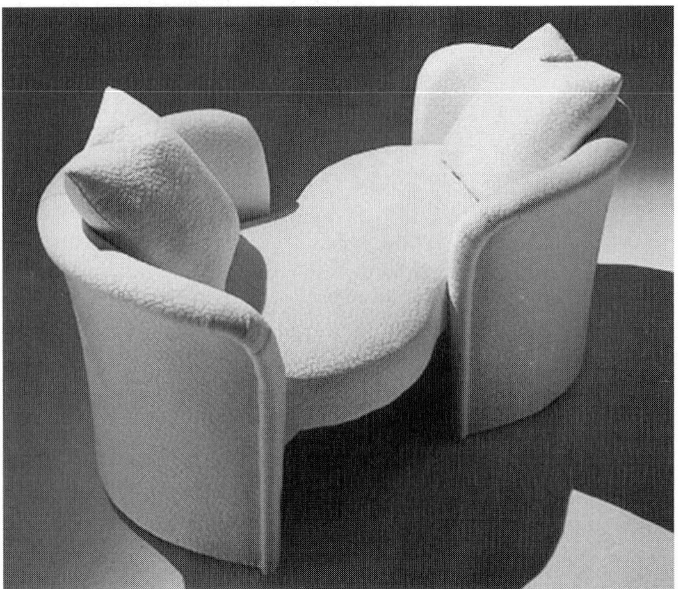

▲ **33-19.** Later Interpretation: *Tête-à-tête*, 2004; manufactured by Thayer Coggin, High Point, North Carolina. Modern Historicism.

CHAPTER 34

Exoticism

1830s–1920s

In this room Messrs. Louis C. Tiffany and Co. have made an elaborate attempt to assimilate the Moresque idea to modern requirements, and no expense has been spared to attain the most perfect result in every respect, even the grand piano being made to assume a Moresque garb. . . . The fireplace is lined with old Persian tile in blue, blue-greens, and dark purplish-red on a white ground, making a valuable sensation in the surrounding opal tile, of which the hearth is composed. . . . All the woodwork above [the floor] is executed in white holly, the panels in which are filled with various incrustations of stucco in delicate Moresque patterns re-enforced with pale tints, gold, and silver. Such portions of the walls as are not otherwise occupied are covered with stamped cut and uncut velvet on satin ground, in tones of pale buff, red, and blue. . . . The furniture is all of white holly, carved, turned, and inlaid with mother-of-pearl, making rich effects with the olive plush coverings embroidered in cream and gold-colored floss.

—A. F. Oakley, *Harper's New Monthly Magazine*, April 1882, describing the salon in the George Kemp House, New York City

Inspired by revivalism, eclecticism, and a quest for novelty in the second half of the 19th century, Exoticism looks to non-Western cultures for inspiration and borrows their forms, colors, and motifs. International expositions, books, periodicals, travel, and advances in technology acquaint Europeans and Americans with other cultures while creating a romantic and mysterious image of faraway lands and people. Egyptian Revival, Moorish or Islamic, Turkish, and Indian join, yet never completely surpass, other fashionable styles.

HISTORICAL AND SOCIAL

Non-Western cultures during the 19th and early 20th centuries inspire several Exotic revivals, including Egyptian Revival and Turkish or Moorish Revival. Each is an assemblage of motifs applied to contemporary forms. Few, if any, attempts are made to live as other cultures do because associations and evoking an image are more important. The forms and motifs of the culture define the style.

By the middle of the 19th century, Europeans and Americans begin to lose interest in the prevailing styles, such as Greek Revival and Gothic Revival. Their desire for new and novel styles opens the door for a wave of exotic influences. At the same time, designers are looking for new sources of inspiration apart from the rampant historicism. Eclecticism, a dominant force in design during the period, encourages the exploration and appreciation of the architecture and decorative arts of other cultures. Although exotic-style public and private buildings, interiors, and furnishings manifest in the British Empire, Europe, and the Americas, they are not overridingly popular.

Exotic influences are not new in Europe or even North America; they have been present in varying degrees since the Middle Ages. What is new is the widespread fascination, coming from art, travel, literature (such as guidebooks, novels, and travelogues), international expositions, trade with other countries, and colonialism (particularly in France and England). Equally important are archaeology, scholarship, and publications, which increase interest in and create design resources for exotic cultures. This intense scrutiny engenders myths about the life styles, people, customs, architecture, and objects in other countries. Exotic styles come mainly from the Egyptian and Islamic cultures, which have centuries of artistic traditions that are largely unknown to Westerners until the 19th century.

■ *Egyptian Revival.* Characteristics of Egyptian architecture appear in and influence art and architecture as early as classical antiquity and continue in varying degrees through the Renaissance, the Baroque, and into the 18th century. In the middle of the 18th century, some interest in Egypt appears after Giovanni Battista Piranesi's creation and publication of Egyptian-style interiors in the *Caffeè degli Inglese* (English Coffee House) in Rome and his prints of Egyptian-style details. At the same time, Neoclassical architects, influenced by French theories, adopt the forms, geometric volumes, and some details of Egyptian architecture to express clarity, severity, and integrity. Subsequent interest in Egyptian art and architecture usually corresponds to events that bring attention to the country.

The earliest widespread adoption of Egyptian forms and motifs in architecture and the decorative arts begins following Napoleon's conquest of Egypt in 1798–1799. Napoleon's scientists, cartographers, engineers, and artists study and record tombs, temples, and other buildings, and the newly established *Institut d'Egypte* examines all aspects of Egyptian civilization. These sources provide a wealth of information about Egypt, of which little is known in the West. A few Egyptian-style buildings and interiors are designed, and Egyptian details appear in furniture.

Egyptian Revival in architecture and the decorative arts begins in the mid-19th century, aided by new technology, which makes emulation of artifacts easier, faster, and more practical. Knowledge of Egyptian and other cultures increases through developments in communications that make the world seem smaller and allow almost anyone to visit faraway lands through photographs and stereo views. Museums and individuals collect and exhibit artifacts unearthed in numerous archaeological sites, further acquainting and stirring more interest. The successful Egyptian Court at the Crystal Palace Exhibition of 1851 leads to similar displays at later expositions. Egypt even finds a place in the design reform movements of the mid-19th century as the adherents admire the stylized forms of its ornament and sturdy and honest construction of its furniture.

A new wave of Egyptian Revival begins in the 1870s, inspired by the opening of the Suez Canal in 1869, Giuseppe Verdi's opera *Aida* of 1871 with its colorful Egyptian-style sets, and the installation of Egyptian obelisks in London in 1878 and New York's Central Park in 1879. The revival continues until the end of the 19th century when interest begins to wane, although use of Egyptian forms and motifs never completely ceases. In 1922, the discovery of the tomb of Tutankhamen immediately stirs renewed interest in and emulation of ancient Egypt.

■ *Turkish, Arab, Saracenic, or Moorish and Indian Styles.* Europeans are somewhat acquainted with Turkey, Persia, Syria, Morocco, Moorish Spain, and India before the mid-19th century. In the 1830s, a religious revival in England focuses attention on Palestine where Jesus Christ had lived. Painters, artists, and architects go to the Middle East to study, paint, and sketch. Upon their return, many publish their work. Design reformers admire the intricate, stylized, and colorful designs and motifs of the Middle East and promote them in their work and publications. Panoramas, a popular form of entertainment; photographs; travel books; and stereo views depict Cairo, Jerusalem, Paestum, Karnak, and Pompeii along with other exotic sites.

Like Egyptian Revival, expositions acquaint people with Islamic art and decoration. The Alhambra Court at the Crystal Palace Exhibition of 1851 is very successful, as is a smaller version in the New Crystal Palace four years later in London. Both are important models for designers. At the Centennial International Exposition of 1876 in Philadelphia, several buildings are Islamic in form, if not visual character. Turkish bazaars, cafés, and entertainment pavilions at successive expositions provide places for shopping, eating, and amusement. Not to be outdone, department stores and warehouses, such as Macy's in New York and Liberty's in London, import goods from the Middle East and display them in bazaars or use them in tearooms throughout the 1870s and 1880s. This inspires a domestic craze for Turkish or Cozy corners (Fig. 34-13) and other Turkish furnishings, accessories, and details.

Closely aligned with the Turkish, Moorish, Saracenic, or Arab (as it is called) in Britain is the Indian or Mogul style, a Victorian interpretation of Indian art and life. The English colonists and military returning home bring ideas, architecture, and objects from India, an important British possession. India also exports many goods to the mother country. Additionally, displays of Indian wares are well attended at the Crystal Palace Exhibition of 1851. The style is limited to a few examples in Great Britain.

CONCEPTS

Fascination with non-Western cultures gives rise to Egyptian Revival, Turkish or Islamic styles, and the Indian or Mogul style with various intensities throughout the 19th century and into the 20th in the British Empire, Europe, and the Americas. Common to all of these styles is adaptations of characteristics of the culture for which each is named to Western tastes and needs. Because associations and symbolism strongly influence stylistic choices and the visual image, each exotic style is associated with particular building types, rooms, and furniture, and conveys a particular image, such as timelessness, monumentality, or a touch of the exotic in an otherwise ordinary Victorian house.

▲ **34-1.** Motifs: Turkish, Persian, Indian, and Egyptian designs published in *The Grammar of Ornament*, 1856, by Owen Jones.

MOTIFS

■ *Motifs*. Characteristic Egyptian motifs (Fig. 34-1, 34-2, 34-3, 34-4, 34-5, 34-6, 34-10, 34-17, 34-20) are geometric forms common in Egyptian architecture, columns and other architectural details, as well as real and fake hieroglyphs, scarabs, Egyptian figures or heads, Egyptian gods and goddesses, lotus, papyrus, crocodiles, cobra, sphinxes, and sun disk. Islamic or Turkish motifs (Fig. 34-7, 34-8, 34-9, 34-11, 34-12, 34-14, 34-15) include onion domes, minarets, lattice, horseshoe arches, multifoil arches, ogee arches, peacocks, carnations, vases, arabesques, and flat and intricate patterns.

ARCHITECTURE

Examples of Exoticism in architecture are few, when compared to other styles, and are especially rare in residences. Designers apply exotic styles to a few particular public building types. This comes from the 19th-century idea that a building's design should convey its purpose, which, in turn, governs stylistic choices. So certain styles are regarded as appropriate for particular types of buildings. Symbolism, acknowledged through form and motifs, becomes an important design context and characteristic.

Although Egyptian forms and motifs appear in architecture beginning in antiquity, the first conscious revival occurs about 1810. Egyptian Revival architecture adopts the monumentality, simplicity, column forms, battered sides, and other architectural details and motifs of the surviving buildings of ancient Egypt. Architects rarely try to re-create authentic Egyptian or Middle Eastern buildings, preferring instead to apply forms and motifs to contemporary forms. These details mix with other styles. The belief that Egypt influences Greece prompts Egyptian details in Greek Revival. Islamic patterns sometimes mix with Gothic Revival in the work of some designers, such as William Burges, and the Queen Anne style in the late 19th century.

The Egyptian style becomes strongly associated with particular building types from the mid-century onward. The ancient

▲ **34-2.** Architectural Detail: Wall elevation, mid-19th century. Islamic influence.

▲ **34-3.** Philadelphia County Prison, Debtors' Wing, 1836; Philadelphia, Pennsylvania; Thomas U. Walter. Egyptian Revival.

Egyptians' strong belief in life after death makes their art and architecture appropriate for cemeteries and funerary buildings. Themes of justice, solidity, and security give rise to Egyptian Revival courthouses and prisons (Fig. 34-3, 34-4). The perceived superior knowledge of the ancient Egyptians deems the style appropriate for libraries and centers of learning. Medical buildings (Fig. 34-5) often feature the style because of the 19th century's belief in Egypt's advanced medical knowledge and practices. Freemasons, secret societies, and fraternal lodges see Egypt's mysterious image and wisdom as ample reason for choosing its style. For bridges and train stations, Egyptian Revival symbolizes advancements in technology. Less obvious is the choice of Egyptian Revival for churches (Fig. 34-6) and synagogues. In the early 20th century, Egyptian movie theaters (Fig. 34-10) support the exotic or mysterious experience of the newly introduced moving picture.

Often evident in Turkish, Arab, Saracenic, Moorish, and Indian Styles are the architectural details and complex layered ornament of Islamic art and architecture. European and American designers sometimes strive to use forms and motifs more correctly, although still copying and adapting them. Access to more information enables them to design with greater archaeological correctness. In architecture, fully Turkish or Moorish expressions are extremely rare, but many buildings display some architectural details (Fig. 34-7). Never achieving a full revival, Turkish or Moorish details may define homes (Fig. 34-8) and a wide range of

DESIGN SPOTLIGHT

Architecture: The Tombs is one of the most significant Egyptian Revival structures in the United States. The attributes and visual characteristics of ancient Egyptian buildings are intended to convey security, monumentality, terror, and the misery awaiting those to be incarcerated there. Reminiscent of the massive gateways at the entrances of Egyptian tombs, the façade features symmetry, volume, simple geometric forms, and minimal ornament. Two wings with battered walls and a center entrance portico supported by Egyptian-style columns compose the façade. Slanted moldings carrying a lintel form the window surrounds. A plain or half-circle molding emphasizes the corners and the cavetto cornice that caps the composition. Haviland derives the architectural vocabulary from several scholarly books on ancient Egypt that he owns. The building also is a model prison for its day, incorporating fireproofing, natural light and air, sanitary facilities, a hospital, and individual cells for inmates. The building are replaced in 1902 but retain the name The Tombs.

▲ **34-4.** New York City Halls of Justice and House of Detention (The Tombs), 1835–1838; New York City, New York; John Haviland. Egyptian Revival.

▲ **34-5.** Egyptian Building, Medical College of Virginia (now a part of Virginia Commonwealth University), 1844–1845; Richmond, Virginia; Thomas S. Stewart. Egyptian Revival.

public buildings from the 1860s onward. Picturesque, hedonistic, and erotic allusions limit the Turkish context for use in those building types possessing romantic ideals or some tie to the Middle East, amusement, or entertainment.

Public and Private Buildings

■ *Floor Plans*. There is no typical Egyptian Revival or Turkish floor plan. Designers do not re-create accurate floor plans of any exotic style but instead develop the plan from function or an attribute such as symmetry.

■ *Materials*. Materials include stone, brick, or wood, particularly in America (Fig. 34-3, 34-4, 34-5, 34-6, 34-7, 34-8). Brick may be stuccoed to render the smooth walls desirable in Egyptian Revival. Details such as columns or domes may be in cast iron, terracotta, or ceramic tiles. Turkish or Moorish structures have brightly colored tiles, details, and intricate patterning composed of stars, flowers, or arabesques. Common colors include neutrals, blues, turquoises, greens, purples, oranges, and reds.

■ *Façades*. Façades reveal Egyptian influence through such visual characteristics as geometric forms, smooth wall treatments, battered walls, Egyptian reed-bundle or papyrus columns, cavetto cornices, round moldings, and Egyptian motifs (Fig. 34-3, 34-4, 34-5, 34-6). Characteristic attributes include massiveness, solemnity, solidity, and timeless or eternal feeling. The Egyptian gateway or pylon is a common form for entrances or entire façades. Domes, Moorish arches, minarets, and colorful tiles define Moorish-style buildings (Fig. 34-8). Islamic arches may create bays across the façade and/or be superimposed on each story (Fig. 34-7).

■ *Windows and Doors*. Windows have slanted sides or surrounds on Egyptian Revival buildings (Fig. 34-3, 34-4). Doorways feature slanted sides and Egyptian columns (Fig. 34-3). Islamic-style arches may frame or form windows. Some have colored glass panes. Doors in Islamic-style structures may be located within horseshoe, multifoil, or ogee arches carried by piers or columns (Fig. 34-7).

■ *Roofs*. Roofs usually are flat or low pitched on Egyptian Revival structures. Islamic buildings may have multiple roofs with onion domes and minarets.

▲ **34-6.** First Presbyterian Church and nave, 1848–1851; Nashville, Tennessee; William Strickland. Egyptian Revival.

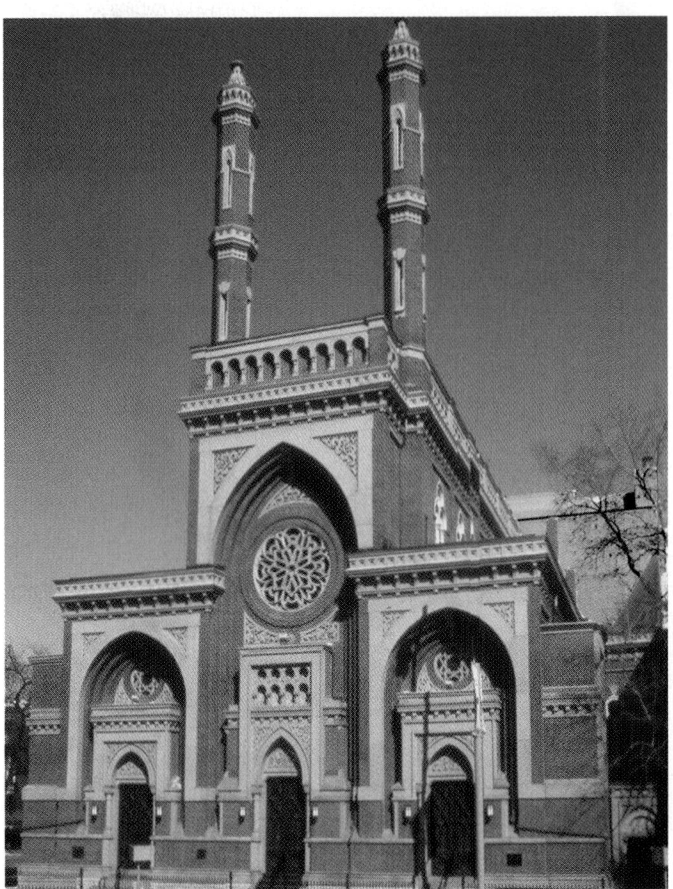

▲ **34-7.** Isaac M. Wise Temple, 1866; Cincinnati, Ohio; James K. Wilson. Turkish Revival.

INTERIORS

Exotic interiors often are the most eclectic of all rooms, combining architectural details, motifs, furniture, or decorative arts of several cultures or styles. Although this enhances their appeal, they usually define only a room or two within houses or a particular building type. As in architecture, associations are important for choosing an exotic interior style, and particular rooms are deemed appropriate for a particular style. Often exotic interiors reflect current fashion trends combined with exotic elements, motifs, colors, and furniture (Fig. 34-12).

Egyptian Revival interiors (Fig. 34-6, 34-10) are far less common in residences but typify rooms in public buildings of the style, particularly in fraternal temples and early-20th-century movie theaters. Museums, zoos, and collectors decorate interiors housing their Egyptian or Middle Eastern artifacts and animals in the appropriate style.

Smoking rooms, billiard rooms, Turkish bathrooms, male-related spaces in hotels and houses, tea rooms, and conservatories may exhibit Turkish, Islamic, or Indian designs and details (Fig. 34-9, 34-12). Turkish or cozy corners (Fig. 34-13), thought exotic, are a craze in American and English homes during the 1870s through the 1890s. Occupying a corner or small portion of the room, the Turkish corner is identified by curtains and/or a canopy of Turkish fabrics or rugs, divans or built-in seating with piles of pillows, Oriental rugs, and numerous accessories such as potted palms, ceramics, spears, swords, pipes, small tables, lamps, and candlesticks. Periodicals carry instructions for making cozy corners to aid owners of modest houses in following the fashion.

Public and Private Buildings

- *Color.* Rich, highly saturated colors (Fig. 34-1, 34-8, 34-11, 34-12) are associated with exotic styles. Blue, green, gold, yellow, red, and black are common for Egyptian. Turkish colors include blues, greens, purples, turquoises, reds, oranges, white, and black. Bold colors are usually seen against a neutral, often beige or earth-toned background.
- *Floors.* Wood floors with Oriental rugs are common in Turkish and Egyptian Revival interiors (Fig. 34-8, 34-9, 34-12). Alternative floor coverings include animal skins and furs. Decorative tiles in various patterns may embellish vestibules, large halls, and conservatories.
- *Walls.* Walls feature motifs of the style chosen. In public spaces, Egyptian architectural details, such as columns or relief sculpture, may articulate walls (Fig. 34-6, 34-10). Spaces between architectural details may be decorated with colorful Egyptian motifs or figures. Bands of Egyptian patterning, figures, or hieroglyphs may decorate walls and columns. Wallpaper and borders with Egyptian figures and motifs are available but not common. A few landscape wallpapers in the early 19th century depict Egyptian architecture.

DESIGN SPOTLIGHT

Architecture and Interior: Home of the Hudson River School painter Frederic Edwin Church, Olana's Islamic design results from Church's extended visit to the Middle East in 1867. Church designs the exterior and interiors with the help of architect Calvert Vaux. He makes numerous sketches for the exterior and each room, its architectural details, and decoration. The asymmetrical exterior is constructed of multicolored brick with tile accents and Islamic pointed arches. A tower, porches, balconies, and numerous windows take advantage of the magnificent surrounding countryside. The house adapts Middle Eastern forms and elements to an American 19th-century lifestyle.

In the stair hall, Oriental rugs cover the stairs and floors and form the drapery at the first landing. A small columned niche holds a golden Buddha. At the second landing, pointed arches are accented above with stenciling in rich colors derived from a book of Eastern designs. Light from a window with yellow glass behind the arches illuminates the staircase. Furnishings include a Moorish-style table and numerous upholstered chairs. Decorative arts in the stair hall include some of Church's finest objects, including Persian ceramics, brasswares, and sculpture. He uses them to direct attention to great past civilizations. [National Historic Landmark]

DESIGN SPOTLIGHT

▲ **34–8.** Olana and stair hall, 1870–1872 house, 1888–1891 studio wing; Hudson, New York; Frederic E. Church, with consulting architect Calvert Vaux. Exotic/Moorish Revival.

▲ **34-9.** Hotel lobby, 1902; United States.

Islamic-style arches in plaster or paneling may articulate walls or divide spaces in Turkish rooms (Fig. 34-8, 34-9, 34-11). An alternative is ceramic tiles with flat, intricate, stylized Islamic patterns, which cover walls or embellish fireplace openings (Fig. 34-11). Flat or draped textiles, such as shawls, kelims, or carpets, adorn walls of Turkish interiors. Wallpapers and borders with Islamic patterns are an alternative for textiles. Islamic patterns (Fig. 34-2) influence reform-minded wallpaper designers, such as William Morris, who adopt their flat, colorful, and curvilinear patterns in the second half of the 19th century. Fabrics in complicated patterns or rugs hanging from fretwork, Moorish-style arches, or spears frequently define the Turkish or cozy corner (Fig. 34-12, 34-13). Niches, called

▲ **34-10.** Proscenium, Ada Theater, 1926; Boise, Idaho; Frederick C. Hummel. Egyptian Revival.

▲ **34-11.** Arab Hall, Lord Leighton House, c. 1865; London, England; George Aitchison. Islamic Revival.

▲ **34-12.** Smoking room, John D. Rockefeller House, c. 1885; New York City, New York. Turkish Revival.

▲ **34-13.** Elsie de Wolfe in her cozy corner, Irving House, 1896; New York. Turkish Revival.

Damascus niches, are a common Islamic characteristic for displaying ceramics or sculpture. Rooms often appear crowded with objects collected from many exotic locations (Fig. 34-9, 34-12).

■ *Window Treatments*. Lavish, layered window treatments are characteristic of exotic rooms. Some are of Turkish textiles, such as kelims, or European imitations of them.

■ *Doors*. Egyptian doorways (Fig. 34-6) may have slanted surrounds or be painted with Egyptian motifs. Islamic-style doors may have stenciled or inlaid decoration in geometric patterns or arabesques. Some have panels shaped like horseshoes or pointed arches (Fig. 34-9). Interior doorways have *portières* made of rugs, fabrics with Turkish motifs, or bands of fabrics hanging from rings (Fig. 34-12). Above may be fretwork with Moorish-style arches.

■ *Ceilings*. Ceilings (Fig. 34-6, 34-9, 34-11, 34-12) may have wallpapers or painted or plaster decorations in highly saturated colors and Egyptian or Turkish motifs, arches, and/or patterning. Ceilings in public spaces may be compartmentalized and decorated with colorful Egyptian motifs or Islamic patterning (Fig. 34-6, 34-9).

■ *Textiles*. Textiles (Fig. 34-8, 34-9, 34-13) include damasks, velvets, cut velvets, brocades, satins, silks, Oriental rugs, cottons or other fabrics either plain or with Egyptian and Turkish motifs or patterns, and leather. Egyptian motifs mixed with flowers and foliage characterize Egyptian revival fabrics. The flat patterns of Indian chintzes and embroideries influence European textile and wallpaper designers from the 17th century onward. The European reinterpretation of the Indian elongated leaf pattern becomes known as paisley (Fig. 34-14). Islamic patterns especially appeal to reform-minded textile designers who advocate flat, stylized patterns. Textiles are important in Turkish-style interiors where Oriental carpets and rugs cover floors, pillows, or seating, or hang on walls or at doorways (Fig. 34-8, 34-12, 34-15). Turkish-style interiors, like Egyptian and Islamic ones, use European textiles with Turkish patterns. In the 1880s, Liberty and Company in London sells hugely popular silk textiles with anglicized Middle Eastern patterns in pastel blues, greens, corals, yellows, and golds.

■ *Lighting*. Lighting fixtures exhibit forms and motifs common to exotic styles. Often fixtures acquired on foreign travels are adapted to contemporary use. Mosque lamps may illuminate Turkish interiors (Fig. 34-9), for example.

▲ **34-14.** Textiles: Paisley patterns, mid- to late 19th century; England and the United States. Islamic Revival.

▲ **34-15.** Rugs: Examples from the mid- to late 19th century; Turkish, Persian, and Caucasian. Islamic Revival.

FURNISHINGS AND DECORATIVE ARTS

Exotic rooms usually have the same style of furniture, such as Egpytian Revival furniture in Egyptian Revival rooms. The exceptions are Turkish-style upholstery, which commonly mixes with other styles, and wicker, used on porches, conservatories, and other rooms. Western overstuffed upholstery has no prototype in the Middle East as do many Egyptian Revival pieces, such as pianos and wardrobes.

Egyptian character manifests in furniture as motifs in classical styles, as a deliberate revival, or as copies of extant ancient pieces. Early in the 19th century, Egyptian motifs appear in French Empire, Regency, and Biedermeier. The later Neo-Grec, a substyle of Renaissance Revival, combines Greek, Roman, and Egyptian elements. Mid-19th-century design reformers adopt the slanted back with double bracing of Egyptian chairs as a sturdy and honest method of construction. Egyptian Revival furniture (Fig. 34-17) applies Egyptian motifs to contemporary forms with varying degrees of accuracy. Most display the forms and motifs of ancient Egyptian architecture, such as slanted sides, columns, obelisks, and hieroglyphs. Some pieces are gilded or ebonized with incising. Beginning in the 1880s, the Egyptian collections at the British Museum inspire English copies of stools and chairs.

Moorish- or Turkish-style furnishings (Fig. 34-8, 34-9, 34-12, 34-16) are introduced in the 1870s. Some are imported; some are made in England and North America. Imports include screens, small tables, and Koran stands (Fig. 34-8, 34-9). In the United States, the most common manifestation of Turkish style is in upholstery or built-in seating. Deep tufting and fancy trims distinguish Turkish upholstery and give the impression of comfort and opulence (Fig. 34-16). Other Turkish-style furniture is light in scale and often has fretwork in typical patterns. Seating adopts Turkish names such as divan or ottoman. Imported furniture, rugs, and decorative arts from the Middle East easily add a touch of the exotic to any interior.

▲ **34-16.** Turkish parlor and armchair (next page), late 19th century; United States; parlor from the 1876 Centennial International Exhibition in Philadelphia; armchair by S. Karpen Brothers, exhibited at the World's Columbian Exhibition in 1893. Turkish Revival.

Wicker (Fig. 34-19), which carries associations with Exoticism, becomes extremely fashionable in the second half of the 19th century. Manufacturers experiment with forms, materials, colors, and motifs known since antiquity from China, Japan, and Moorish Spain. Wicker has numerous patterns, including Egyptian, and it can vary from very plain to highly decorative with curlicues, beadwork, and various forms of patterning. All types of furniture are made of wicker, including wheelchairs, cribs, cradles, baby carriages, and outdoor furniture.

Public and Private Buildings

■ *Materials*. Egyptian Revival and Turkish furniture usually is of dark woods, such as mahogany or rosewood. Less exotic woods are grained to imitate other woods. Embellishments consist of inlay, gilding, ebonizing (Fig. 34-12), incising, *ormolu* mounts (Fig. 34-17), or painted decorations. Inlay in Turkish furniture is of bone or ivory. Wicker is made of straw, willow, rattan, and other fibers, although most is of rattan. It is painted red, yellow, brown, black, green, or white. Some pieces have gilding or combinations of colors.

■ *Seating*. Egyptian Revival chairs (Fig. 34-17) and parlor sets have wooden frames with carved and sometimes stylized Egyptian details and upholstered backs and seats. Legs may be animal shaped with paw feet or hooves or tapered with Egyptian-style capitals or heads. Turkish-style overstuffed upholstery has deep tufting, fringe, and/or trim that covers the legs (Fig. 34-16). Chairs and sofas often have an extra roll of stuffing around the arms and backs. Cording, puffing, and pleating add visual complexity and give an impression of comfort. Turkish *divans* or *lounges* refer to deeply tufted couches without backs or arms (Fig. 34-9, 34-13). Turkish ottomans are large and round with tufted

▲ 34-17. Side chair and armchair, c. 1875; attributed to Pottier and Stymus Manufacturing Company, active c. 1859–1910. Egyptian Revival. [Funds from various donors, 1970 (1970.35.1). The Metropolitan Museum of Art, New York, NY, U.S.A. Image copyright © The Metropolitan Museum of Art/Art Resource, NY]

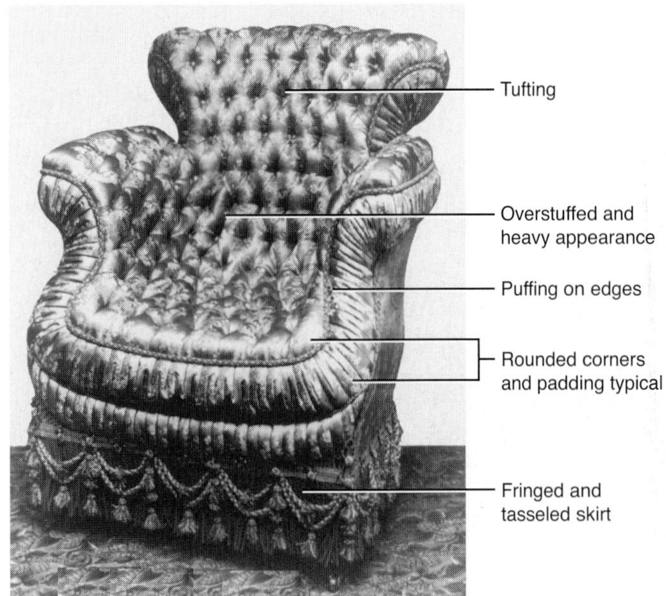

▲ 34-16. Continued

▲ 34-18. Horn chair, late 19th century; California.

▲ **34-19.** Wicker seating, c. 1880s–1910s; United States.

backs and a space for a potted palm or sculpture in the raised center. Often used in grand spaces, they are intended as a momentary seat rather than a place of relaxation. Variations of the Turkish style include chairs or sofas with round or oval backs not attached to the seats and round or oval seats. Often small and fragile, these chairs are upholstered in silk or satin and are used in parlors. Americans love Turkish-style rocking chairs. Some Turkish interiors use pillows on the floor for seating (Fig. 34-9). Others, particularly men's smoking rooms and libraries, incorporate horn chairs (Fig. 34-18) upholstered in animal skins or other types of horn furniture. Common in the western United States, horn furniture conveys a rugged, manly character.

Indoor and outdoor seating in public and private buildings, including parlor sets, sometimes is of wicker (Fig. 34-19). Solid portions may be plainly woven or have patterns, such as stars or dippers. Crests, backs, legs, and arms often display such complicated or curving forms as fans, lattice, strapwork, arabesques, ogees, or curlicues. Some wicker seating has upholstered backs and seats, although most rely on added cushions for comfort. Ladies add their own decorative touches, such as ribbon threaded through openwork, bows, or tassels.

■ *Tables*. Egyptian Revival tables exhibit Egyptian motifs, such as figures, heads, or sphinxes. Some have slender tapered legs with incising and stylized carving. Obelisks or pylon-shaped pedestals display sculpture or plants. Hexagonal or octagonal occasional tables imported from the Middle East are of dark woods with ivory or mother-of-pearl inlay in geometric patterns (Fig. 34-8, 34-12). Small stands, originally designed to hold the Koran, rest upon tables and hold books. Wicker tables and stands may match seating.

■ *Storage*. Wardrobes, cupboards, and *commodes* may have the slanted sides and fronts of Egyptian gateways, Egyptian columns or figures, and other Egyptian motifs. Tops may have cavetto cornices or rounded moldings. Some pieces are ebonized with gilding, incising, and painted decorations (Fig. 34-12). Wicker cupboards or chests of drawers are not as common as wicker seating is.

■ *Beds*. Egyptian or Turkish-style beds are very rare. Beds for children, cribs, and cradles may be in plain or fancy wicker.

■ *Decorative Arts*. Egyptian Revival decorative arts (Fig. 34-20), such as clocks, porcelains, or vases, have Egyptian architectural details, including obelisks, and motifs, such as sphinxes. Sevres and other porcelain factories make dinner sets painted with Egyptian motifs and architecture throughout the 19th century. Egyptian mantel sets consisting of a clock and vases or obelisks are common in the second half of the 19th century. Imported brass objects, ceramics, folding screens, spears, daggers, plates, tiles, and potted palms fill Turkish or Moorish interiors (Fig. 34-8, 34-9, 34-12, 34-13). Ceramics from India and the Middle East inspire tiles and other ceramics with intricate flat patterns in turquoise, blue, green, and red. The glass of Louis Comfort Tiffany and others draws inspiration from the shapes, forms, and colors of Egyptian, Islamic, and Oriental glass and ceramics. Wicker mirrors, plant stands, birdcages, and the like, add a touch of exoticism to many rooms.

▲ **34-20.** Decorative Arts: Clock and vases, exhibited at the Centennial International Exposition of 1876 in Philadelphia; United States. Egyptian Revival.

■ *Later Interpretations*. Furnishings and decorative arts reflecting an Exotic influence rarely appear in later periods, unless with custom-designed Exotic interiors. Art Deco in the 1920s and 1930s adapts Egyptian motifs and colors. The most common application in Europe and America in the late 20th century or 21st century appears in entertainment facilities focused on fantasy, romance, and mystery or in libraries. Upholstered sofas and chairs are often tufted like Turkish ones (Fig. 34-21). However, they are usually covered with plain fabrics or leather and do not have the visual complexity, fringe, and tassels of earlier furniture.

▲ **34-21.** Later Interpretation: Late Victorian club chair, late 20th century; Baker Furniture. Modern Historicism.

CHAPTER 35

Stick, Queen Anne

Stick Style 1860s–1880s, Queen Anne 1880s–1910s

Ah, to build to build! That is the noblest art of all the arts. Painting and Sculpture are but images, are merely shadows, cast by outward things. On stone or canvas, having in themselves no separate existence. Architecture, existing in itself, and not in seeming a something it is not, surpasses them as substance shadow.

—Henry Wadsworth Longfellow, from *Palliser's New Cottage Homes and Details*, 1887, by George and Charles Palliser

Unique to the United States, the Stick Style in architecture combines the character of medieval half-timbered buildings with the new balloon framing construction method in its use of wooden planks or sticks that form decorative surface patterns on exteriors. Queen Anne architecture originates in England as an attempt to create an image of home, tradition, and middle-class comfort. Highly eclectic, the style mixes elements from the 16th, 17th, and 18th centuries. Queen Anne appeals to Americans also, who translate it into wood instead of the brick of England. Neither Stick Style nor Queen Anne has a corresponding interior or furniture style, but some interiors and furniture in Queen Anne buildings vaguely recall 18th-century prototypes.

HISTORICAL AND SOCIAL

After the 1850s, a second generation of the middle class in England comes into maturity. These individuals from affluent households possess the advantages of both education and culture. Consequently, they regard the creation of beauty as very important in addition to the cultivation of classical Greek virtues, refinement, and manners to create a gentlemanly or ladylike image. This group leads sophisticated lives, traveling, attending plays and cultural events, and socializing with friends and family in well-appointed houses. During the 1860s, these English socialites begin to look back to their Stuart (late 17th century) and Georgian heritages (18th century) for the desirable attributes of refinement and gentility. Their interest in a later past rather than the earlier medieval one of Gothic Revival contributes to the creation of the Queen Anne architectural style.

Although American architects are aware of English architectural developments through publications and travel in England, they do not wholeheartedly follow them. However, the 1876 Philadelphia Centennial Exhibition acquaints the American public with both the Stick Style and English Queen Anne, and they subsequently become popular styles for residences. Americans look back to their own 17th- and 18th-century past more as an antidote to contemporary industrial life than an ideal of gentility. This nostalgia opens the way for wider acceptance of Stick and Queen Anne. Rejecting the shady values demonstrated in contemporary politics, the middle class flees the corrupt, scandalous cities of the present and escapes to the perceived purer and simpler rural life along with the imagined past. Popular travel destinations are summer resorts filled with picturesque Stick and Queen Anne structures amid tranquil landscapes.

CONCEPTS

■ *Stick Style*. Creating a half-timbered appearance rendered in wood on American buildings, the Stick Style develops during the 1850s from concepts of the Picturesque, historicism, and Gothic Revival theory. Early-19th-century Picturesque suburban architecture in England and late Gothic vernacular buildings in England, France, and Germany form the model for this uniquely American style. Also influential are Swiss chalets and the board and batten cottages of A. J. Davis and A. J. Downing published in *Rural Residences* (1837) and *The Architecture of Country Houses* (1850). Architectural historian Vincent Scully coins the term Stick Style to refer to its characteristic geometric patterning of flat boards.

■ *English Queen Anne*. Introduced in the 1860s, English Queen Anne strives not to revive a past style or to create a new historical style like the Greek or Gothic Revivals, so it has no strong conceptual basis. Although its name suggests the early 18th-century period of Queen Anne (reigned 1702–1714), the eclectic style combines characteristics from English vernacular, Elizabethan, Tudor, and Japanese architecture as well as that of the 17th and early 18th centuries. Consequently, there is confusion, even among practitioners, about what exactly constitutes Queen Anne. By the 1890s, the name Queen Anne is applied to almost anything that is not Gothic Revival.

■ *American Queen Anne*. The American middle class and design critics find the English Queen Anne image of home and ancestry very appealing, which ensures the style's immediate adoption. A variation is Victorian Vernacular, which translates Queen Anne, Stick, and other styles into common or folk versions for the American middle and working classes.

MOTIFS

■ *Motifs*. Motifs that are mostly associated with Queen Anne include sunflowers, pediments, columns, spindles, scrollwork, quoins, Flemish gables (Fig. 35-3) strapwork, swags, cherubs, flowers, and foliage (Fig. 35-1, 35-5, 35-8, 35-9, 35-10, 35-12, 35-13, 35-15, 35-16, 35-17).

ARCHITECTURE

Primarily architectural styles, Stick and English and American Queen Anne all look back to the Middle Ages, English Renaissance, and vernacular buildings for inspiration. The three are eclectic and adopt asymmetry, irregularity, verticality, forms, and details of earlier buildings.

Mostly residential, the Stick Style emerges on the East Coast of the United States during the 1850s and is more popular in pattern books than in practice, according to the actual number of buildings built. Stickwork or flat boards in geometric patterns within panels and framing windows and doors characterize structures in this style. Additional stickwork appears in the bracket supports beneath the roof, decorative trusses in the gables, and ornamental cresting. Full- and partial-width porches have supports with diagonal stickwork braces. The style conveys a half-timbered, medieval feeling.

The first example of the mature style and a prototype for others is the John N. A. Griswold House (Fig. 35-5) designed by Richard Morris Hunt and built in Newport, Rhode Island, during the Civil War. Most other examples are in summer resorts, including Newport, where the style's informal, rustic appearance is appealing. An exception is San Francisco, where the style continues well into the 1880s, corresponding to the city's rapid growth. The so-called Painted Ladies (which may be Stick, Queen Anne, or Italianate) form a colorful regional style for row houses with stickwork, brackets, and other wood decoration.

▲ **35-1.** Architectural and Interior Details: Stained glass window and doorway screen, 1870s–1880s; Texas.

▲ **35-2.** New Jersey Pavilion, International Centennial Exhibition, 1876; Philadelphia, Pennsylvania. Stick Style.

In England, the foundation for Queen Anne is laid during the 1850s and 1860s by renewed interest in the Stuart and Georgian periods, a rejection by some architects of the moral and religious nature of Gothic Revival, and a move toward a less literal interpretation of Gothic evident in the work of some architect–designers such as Philip Webb. Believing that buildings during Queen Anne's reign were basically medieval in form with classical ornament applied, designers turn to the pre-Georgian period. The style coalesces in the work of William Eden Nesfield and Richard Norman Shaw following their study of vernacular Elizabethan and Jacobean architecture. By the 1870s, the visual language becomes fully developed as more buildings in the style are built and published in architectural and building magazines.

Queen Anne does not have a strong theoretical or scholarly base but adopts the irregularity, open planning, truth in construction, and honesty of material of Gothic Revival without its moral or religious overtones. Striving for freedom in planning, design, and decoration, the style derives its red brick, sash windows, cupolas, shutters, and fanlights from 18th-century architecture. Gables, pediments, white trim, and prominent coves come from 17th-century buildings. Traditional earlier English buildings contribute a homey, friendly appearance; half-timbering; tiled façades; pargework; overhangs; casement windows; and plans and elevations that appear to have evolved over time with additions as needed. Some buildings reveal elements of the Aesthetic Movement and Japanese design. Human scale and the visual language speak of refinement, simplicity, comfort, and hominess, qualities appealing to the middle class instead of the wealthy or landed gentry.

The style is very popular in England during the second half of the 19th century for all types of buildings, including houses (Fig. 35-6), row houses, offices (Fig. 35-3), schools, colleges, shops, pubs, coffee houses, hospitals, hotels, and even a few churches. Only a few country houses adopt Queen Anne because it is not pretentious enough for the wealthy. England's Bedford Park, one of the first garden suburbs, features green settings for its small and large, single or duplex, simplified Queen Anne houses. It also includes schools, shops, pubs, and a church. Three of the most influential buildings are Leys Wood (Fig. 35-6), a large country house in Sussex resembling Elizabethan mansions; New Zealand Chambers, an office building in London, both by Richard Norman Shaw; and the Red House (demolished) in London by J. J. Stevenson.

The first American example of Queen Anne, the Watts Sherman House (Fig. 35-8) in Newport, Rhode Island, by H. H. Richardson, closely resembles Shaw's Leys Wood. It sets the stage for other early architect-designed structures, which tend to be more horizontal and differently massed than English examples are.

▲ **35-3.** Allied Assurance Company, 1–2 S. James Street, c. 1882; Pall Mall, London, England; Richard Norman Shaw. Queen Anne.

▲ 35-4. Hotel del Coronado, 1886–1888; Coronado, California, Reid Brothers. Queen Anne.

Other American differences include more open space planning, varying room heights and floor levels, and greater integration of exterior and interiors through porches, larger windows, and use of exterior materials inside. This early version of Queen Anne evolves into the Shingle Style, but the variety, eclecticism, and quasi-medievalism of English Queen Anne continue in numerous wooden residences in suburbs and cities across America. The style's large rambling forms and residential appearance also make it suitable for hotels (Fig. 35-4) and a few commercial buildings. The widespread adoption of the style is made possible by house pattern books, the expanding railroad system, balloon framing, standardized lumber sizes, and factory-made precut architectural parts.

Variety is a key characteristic of American Queen Anne. Irregular massing and a variety of forms, materials, textures, colors, and door and window types is typical—anything to avoid a plain or flat wall surface. Towers or turrets, prominent chimneys that are usually decorated, and a multiplicity of roofs and roof types are also characteristic. Interiors and furnishings may be Gothic or another revival style or follow Aesthetic Movement or Arts and Crafts principles. The latter is contemporary with the Queen Anne style's height of popularity in the United States.

Public and Private Buildings • Stick Style

■ *Floor plans*. Stick Style houses have large, rambling, asymmetrical floor plans similar to those of Queen Anne. Plans often open and center on large living halls (Fig. 35-5).

■ *Materials*. Wood is the primary building material for all building types. A few examples may mix brick, stone, or masonry with wood.

■ *Façades*. Stickwork, composed of flat boards, creates panels that organize the façade and emphasize the structure (Fig. 35-2, 35-5, 35-7). Applied over wall surfaces (usually upper stories), stickwork may be horizontal, vertical, and/or diagonal. The pattern of sticks may reflect the balloon framing beneath or simply decorate the surface. Although resembling half-timbering, the wall beneath the stickwork is covered with traditional American clapboards instead of plaster. The verticality, asymmetrical massing, and irregular silhouette of medieval buildings are common characteristics. Additional characteristics include square or rectangular towers and rectangular bay windows. Single-story porches, which lighten the mass of the structure, may be partial or full width and extend on one, two, or three sides. Porch supports have diagonal brackets. Some houses may be polychrome with colors emphasizing stickwork. Some have elements from other styles or cultures.

■ *Windows*. One-over-one or two-over-two sash windows are most common, although some have bay windows (Fig. 35-2, 35-5, 35-7). A few examples have casements or triple sash windows. Shutters are not used.

■ *Roofs*. Multiple steeply pitched roofs may be gabled, cross-gabled, or hipped with wide eaves and large brackets beneath to support them (Fig. 35-2, 35-5, 35-7). Ends of rafters may be exposed in gables. Also typical is a decorative truss in the apex of the roof that repeats stickwork on the facade. Dormers, cresting, and pendants are common. Slate or wooden shingled roofs may be polychrome.

Public and Private Buildings • Queen Anne

■ *Floor Plans*. Commercial structures do not have typical floor plans but are designed to accommodate space allowances and functional needs.

English and American houses usually have irregular floor plans centered on living halls, which are large spaces with stairs, a fireplace, and often an inglenook or area with built-in seating around the fireplace (Fig. 35-8). American plans have tall and broad openings between the living hall and surrounding spaces, which gives a more open feeling and allows space to flow between and among rooms. Balloon framing and central heating make these new, open plans feasible. The large windows and ample porches characteristic of American houses help bring the outside into the house.

■ *Materials*. English Queen Anne buildings most often are of brown brick with red brick trim or only red brick (Fig. 35-3, 35-6). Windows and other details are painted white. Ornament may

DESIGN SPOTLIGHT

Architecture and Interiors: The John N. A. Griswold House is one of the earliest examples of the Stick Style and one of Richard Morris Hunt's first buildings in Newport, Rhode Island. The house shows the definitive characteristics of the style, which are stickwork, porch supports with diagonal braces, bracket supports beneath the roof, decorative trusses in the gables, and ornamental cresting. Another defining feature is the medieval character. Here, it is influenced by rustic vernacular houses in Europe that Hunt had seen while studying at the *L'École des Beaux Arts* in France, wooden American Gothic Revival buildings, and the balloon framing construction method. Hunt's design, which is more cottagelike and picturesque than his later monumental work, creatively combines medieval character with 19th-century inventions and design intentions. Multiple steeply pitched gables, asymmetry, bay windows, casement windows, and the half-timbered appearance recall medieval styles. But the multiplication of sticks—flat boards—applied to the façade over clapboards, projecting beneath the roof, and forming porch and windows supports are new. Their structural logic and linearity unite the lightness of the body of the house and dark voids of the porch into a picturesque whole that is clearly 19th-century.

As on the exterior, the house's interiors continue the medieval character mixed with 19th-century functional needs and aesthetic preferences. Sticks outline doorways, architectural elements, and the shape of the ceiling in the stair hall. The dark wood brackets, panels, pendants, and flat trim contrasts with white walls. Carving in the stair rails recalls Gothic tracery. The flat wood trim and X-shapes in the panels like the stickwork on the exterior call attention to the decorative wall surface. [National Historic Landmark]

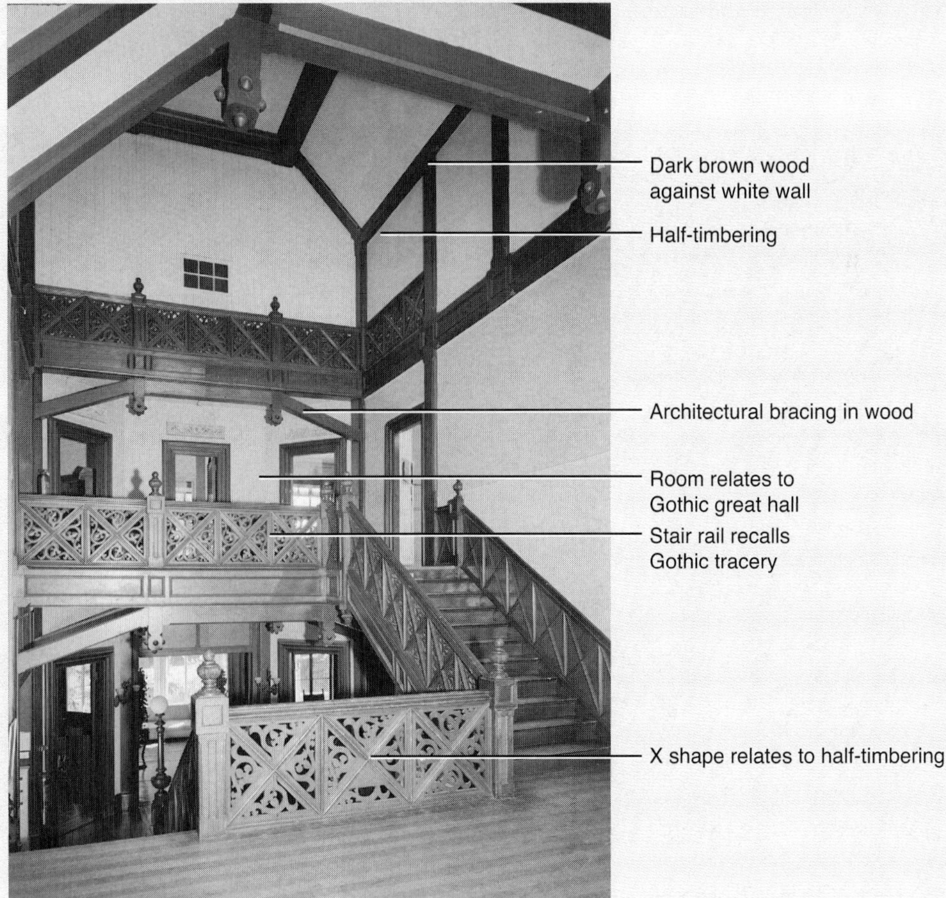

▲ **35-5.** John N. A. Griswold House and stair hall, 1862–1864; Newport, Rhode Island; Richard Morris Hunt. Stick Style.

▲ **35-6.** Leys Wood, 1866–1869; Sussex, England; Richard Norman Shaw. Queen Anne.

consist of terra-cotta plaques with naturalistic motifs, tiles, and pargework. Balcony supports may be of wood painted white, stone, or wrought iron. Roofs usually are slate.

Wood is the dominant building material for American Queen Anne houses and hotels (Fig. 35-1, 35-4, 35-9, 35-10). Timber is plentiful, and the scroll saw and balloon framing make wooden buildings cheaper, easier, and faster to construct. Some homes have a mixture of materials such as terra-cotta, brick or stone, and wood (Fig. 35-8). Board and batten, clapboards, or shingles may

DESIGN SPOTLIGHT

Architecture and Interior: The Watts Sherman House is considered the first American example of Queen Anne. Richardson models Shaw's work, which he is familiar with through publications of it. However, he creates something new and uniquely American. More horizontal than British examples, the house masses around the central open floor plan with monumental living hall. Horizontal bands of windows highlight the hall on the exterior and form a glass wall. Richardson rejects the red brick and white paint of England for a combination of granite, brownstone, stucco, and shingles in various shapes. Tall chimneys, leaded casement windows, and half-timbering resemble English medieval examples. Although lacking the ample porches characteristic of later examples, Richardson's design greatly influences the Queen Anne, Colonial Revival, and Shingle styles in the United States. The house has had several additions since its initial construction, the earliest by Stanford White in 1881. The open floor plan centers on a large staircase and living hall from which space flows through broad openings into the dining room, library, and drawing room. Details from the Middle Ages are used on the stair and in the hall and include beamed ceilings, wainscoting, a large hooded fireplace, and stained glass windows. [National Historic Landmark]

▲ **35-7.** Mark Twain House, c. 1874; Hartford, Connecticut; Edward Tucker Potter. Stick Style.

DESIGN SPOTLIGHT

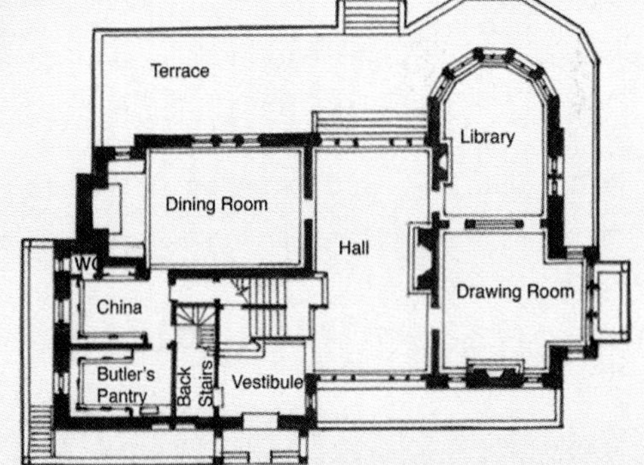

▲ **35-8.** Watts Sherman House, floor plan, and stair hall, 1874–1875; Newport, Rhode Island; Henry Hobson Richardson. Queen Anne.

cover wall surfaces. Roofs have wooden or slate shingles and, sometimes, iron cresting (Fig. 35-9, 35-10).

American color schemes are composed of several colors that contrast the body of the house with structural details, such as windows, brackets, and eaves. Multiple contrasting colors cause elements to apparently advance and recede, creating highlights and shadows. Dark, rich colors from nature are popular, including brown, terra-cotta, and olive green (Fig. 35-1, 35-9).

■ *Façades*. Queen Anne buildings in both England and the United States are asymmetrical and varied in form and design but convey a similar feeling to late medieval, 17th- and 18th-century, and/or rural houses. Both English and American public and private buildings may be self-contained or rambling depending upon the site and function. Façades, rarely flat, have a variety of projections, protrusions, and volumes (Fig. 35-1, 35-6, 35-8, 35-9). Although larger in scale than residences, public buildings have a similar character to residences (Fig. 35-3, 35-4).

English structures, particularly commercial buildings, usually have brick pilasters dividing fronts into bays. Common characteristics of both public and private buildings are straight and Flemish gables, tall and decorated chimneys, half-timbering, tile work, jetties, and combinations of windows (Fig. 35-3, 35-6). Somewhat less typical are quoins, stringcourses, columns, pediments, and arched lower stories. Houses sometimes have niches to display blue and white porcelain or other decorative objects.

▲ **35-10.** Eldridge Johnson House (The Pink House), 1892; Cape May, New Jersey. Vernacular Queen Anne.

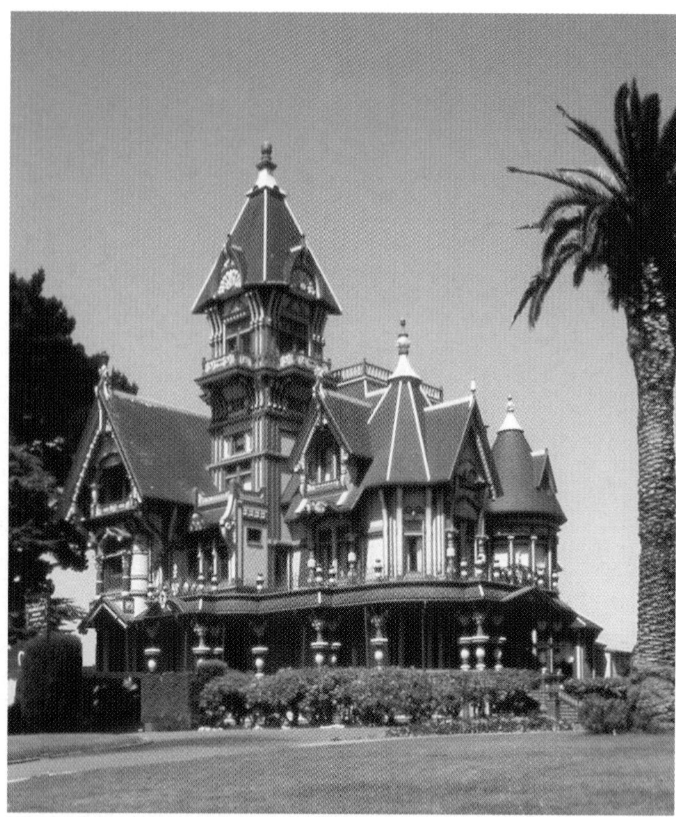

▲ **35-9.** Carson House, 1884–1886; Eureka, California; Samuel Newsom and Joseph C. Newsom. Queen Anne (or Eastlake).

Important buildings, such as town halls, may have centerpieces, clock towers, or a cupola.

American Queen Anne houses have round, polygonal, or angled towers, usually on corners; half-timbering; decorative stone or terra-cotta panels; and wooden scrollwork highlighting porches, walls, gables, and windows. Rooms, balconies, walls, and roofs interlock (Fig. 35-1, 35-8, 35-9, 35-10). Rooms may project over porches or bay windows. Spindles embellish gables, porch supports, and cornices. A variety of colors, textures, and materials is common. In the 1890s, a version of Queen Anne called Free Classic, with classical columns, colonnettes, pediments, and Palladian windows, appears in the United States. Like the Stick Style, Queen Anne houses have single-story full- or partial-width porches surrounding them. Some have additional smaller porches on their upper stories. Some examples have the latticework and/or horseshoe arches of Islamic architecture. Townhouses or flats have similar details usually organized in multiple components for unity. American Queen Anne hotels resemble large-scale houses with bays, towers, prominent chimneys, and porches (Fig. 35-4).

■ *Windows*. Use of a variety of windows is characteristic of all Queen Anne structures in England and the United States (Fig. 35-1, 35-3, 35-4, 35-5, 35-6, 35-8, 35-9, 35-10). Casements with leaded panes or white-painted sash windows with small panes are frequent. Some sashes have a single pane below with small panes above. Other types include round, square, Palladian, and arched. Shop windows often have a single pane of glass to display merchandise more effectively. Windows may be single, double, or triple, and one, two, or three stories tall. Some are small and unobtrusive, while others dominate the facade. Bay and oriel windows may be angled with three to five sides, curved, or curved with flat fronts, and exhibit endless variations. Details for bays are numerous, including arches, pediments, and pargework. Glazing bars may be of wood, lead, or stone. Bays may project beneath overhangs or have balconies above them. Stained, leaded, etched, and colored glass is common in American Queen Anne (Fig. 35-1).

■ *Doors*. Entry doors may be prominent or unobtrusive, centered or to one side (Fig. 35-3, 35-8, 35-9, 35-10). Formal porches with pediments and columns or simple surrounds composed of columns or pilasters carrying lintels, a pediment, or fanlight may define the entry. Doors are wood paneled painted dark green or black. Doorways in American buildings usually have simple or less complicated surrounds than those in England do. American doors may be single or double and have plain, etched, or stained glass in the upper portions (Fig. 35-1).

■ *Roofs*. Most buildings have a multiplicity of steeply pitched roofs that may be gabled or hipped (Fig. 35-3, 35-4, 35-6, 35-8, 35-9, 35-10). Townhouses usually have flat roofs, sometimes with a false gable. Dormers, usually embellished, are common in all styles in both countries. Flemish or straight gables are common in English Queen Anne. Jerkinhead roofs may appear in American Queen Anne (Fig. 35-4). Towers may have angled or conical roofs or onion domes. Starbursts, shingles, tiles, flowers, or foliage may decorate the apex of roofs in American Queen Anne (Fig. 35-8). Bargeboards and decorative trusses are common adornments. Towers and gables may have finials or pinnacles. Large chimneys may resemble Elizabethan or Tudor examples (Fig. 35-8).

■ *Later Interpretations*. In the late 20th century, Queen Anne Style houses adapted for modern living appear in upscale American housing developments. Often clad in vinyl siding, the contemporary versions have a tower and a porch but fewer decorative details and colors than their predecessors did. Hotels also exhibit Queen Anne and Stick Style characteristics, particularly those located near water (Fig. 35-11).

▲ **35-11.** Later Interpretation: Grand Floridian Resort and Spa, c. 1990; Lake Buena Vista, Florida; Wimberly, Allison, Tong, & Goo.

▲ **35-12.** Dining room; published in *Decoration and Furniture of Town Houses*, 1881; by Robert William Edis, London and New York. Queen Anne.

INTERIORS

Stick Style buildings do not have a corresponding interior style, but some rooms may reflect the general exterior character through paneling with stick-like patterns. Otherwise rooms feature fashionable revivals such as Rococo, Renaissance, Medieval, or Gothic (Fig. 35-5). Like architecture, interiors in Queen Anne houses do not replicate those of the 18th century. Most follow revival styles or the Aesthetic Movement or Arts and Crafts Movement. A few, particularly in England, recall 18th-century interiors with classical columns, pediments, low relief plasterwork in classical motifs, or wall paneling (Fig. 35-12). However, they are even more eclectic than are exteriors. In keeping with common practice, each room may be a different style with masculine styles, such as Jacobean, defining dining rooms and halls and feminine styles, such as Adam, in the parlor and morning room.

Living halls become characteristic during this period as formal living begins to give way to informality. They serve as living rooms, entrance halls, and circulation spaces. Many homes still retain the parlor, which varies from comfortable family rooms to carefully decorated, maintained, and seldom-used monuments to formal living (Fig. 35-13).

Public and Private Buildings

■ *Color*. Colors vary with the interior style chosen (Fig. 35-15, 35-17). Renaissance, Egyptian, Rococo, and other revival-style colors tend to be more saturated or dark and rich, especially after midcentury. Aesthetic Movement colors are mainly tertiary hues. Queen Anne colors lean toward those of the Neoclassical (late 18th, early 19th century) and as such may be saturated lighter tints. Arts and Crafts interiors use colors of nature.

■ *Floors*. Most floors are wood with rugs following the admonitions of design critics (Fig. 35-13). Middle and lower middle classes cling to wall-to-wall carpet, which they can readily afford. Some continue replacing carpet with grass matting in the summer. Other types of flooring include decorative tiles and linoleum.

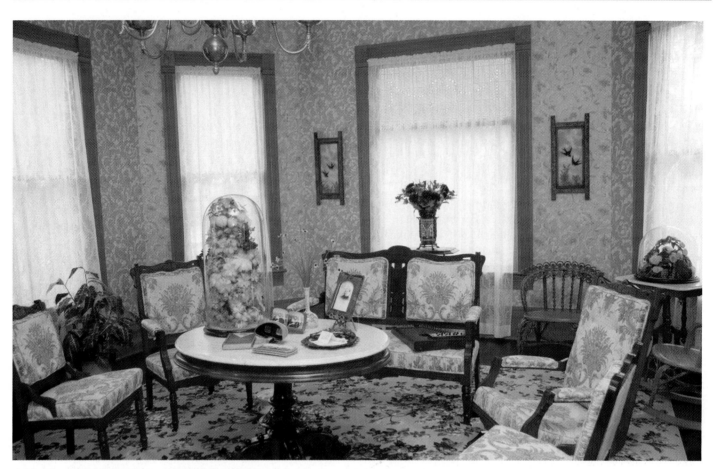

▲ **35-13.** Parlor, Davis House, 1890s; Richmond, Texas.

▲ **35-14.** Mantel, late 19th century; United States and England. Queen Anne.

■ *Walls*. Walls are decorated according to the interior style chosen (Fig. 35-5, 35-12, 35-13, 35-15). In revival interiors, wallpaper and paint are the most common wall treatments. With wallpapers, the working classes can easily imitate more sophisticated and expensive treatments. Those influenced by the Aesthetic Movement favor tripartite painted, paneled, or papered walls. British houses sometimes have tiled dadoes in the hallway, bathrooms, and kitchens. Plate rails high on the wall show off collections of china. A cove or delicate cornice molding with a wallpaper border below separates the wall and ceiling.

■ *Chimneypieces*. Fireplaces are still focal points (Fig. 35-8, 35-12). English Queen Anne chimneypieces sometimes have broken pediments surmounting shelves for display. Tiles, usually blue and white, surround the fireplace opening (Fig. 35-14).

■ *Window Treatments*. Window treatments vary from simple panels hanging from rings on plain rods to layers of treatments typical of revival styles (Fig. 35-16). Lace curtains continue to be fashionable (Fig. 35-13).

■ *Doors*. Doors have simple surrounds and are paneled and stained a dark color (Fig. 35-12). Doorways and openings to public rooms usually have *portières* that match the room's décor and sometimes the window treatments. Upper portions of openings may have spindle grilles (Fig. 35-1, 35-16).

■ *Ceilings*. Ceilings in revival-style and some other interiors are usually a lighter tint than are the walls (Fig. 35-5, 35-12). Those influenced by the Aesthetic Movement have painted decorations or wallpapers (Fig. 35-17). Queen Anne ceilings may have low-relief plaster decorations in white or other colors.

■ *Textiles*. Rooms boast a variety of textiles embellishing mantels and shelves and covering floors, windows, doorways, pianos, seating, and/or backs and arms of upholstery (Fig. 35-13, 35-16). Pillows, shelf lambrequins, and antimacassars made by the lady of the house are proudly displayed. Common fabrics are silk, linen, cotton, damask, velvet, leather, and for upholstery horsehair and tapestry. Rooms have many different types and patterns of fabrics in contrast to *en suite* rooms of the earlier 19th century (Fig. 35-13).

▲ **35-15.** Wall designs and color schemes; published in *Painting and Decorating*, c. 1898; by Walter Pierce, London.

▲ **35-16.** Wood screen and *portières*; published in the *Practical Handbook on Cutting Draperies*, by N. W. Jacobs, 1890.

▲ **35-17.** Ceiling patterns in paint, late 19th to early 20th centuries; Ohio.

▲ **35-18.** Gasolier, late 19th century; United States.

■ *Lighting*. Most homes have gas light in gasoliers, sconces, and portable lamps in brass or wrought iron (Fig. 35-18). Americans also use kerosene or oil lamps. Electric fixtures come into use late in the period. Designs for fixtures may adapt characteristics of Neoclassical, the Aesthetic Movement, Arts and Crafts, or Revival styles (Fig. 35-12, 35-13).

FURNISHINGS AND DECORATIVE ARTS

As in interiors, furniture has no corresponding style to architecture and, as a result, eclecticism rules. Use of new and sometimes old furnishings in various styles characterizes most rooms, which may combine Japanese prints, English porcelain, Oriental or Middle Eastern folding screens, Art Furniture, cottage furniture, and Sheraton, Chippendale, and Jacobean pieces, and/or overstuffed upholstery.

A few architects and others design furniture inspired by English traditional styles. This so-called Queen Anne furniture displays a range of forms and motifs from the 17th, 18th, and 19th centuries (Fig. 35-22) such as broken pediments, fretwork, turned balusters, columns, and pilasters. Characteristics of Sheraton, Adam, and Chippendale may mix together. Designers pay little heed to correct use of forms and motifs. Characteristic of many pieces are shelves and brackets to display objects and collections.

In the United States, Victorian vernacular furniture is a cheaper, machine-made version of high styles such as Renaissance or Rococo Revivals. Golden-brown-finished oak, applied carving, and embossed decoration characterizes much of this furniture, which is purchased in department stores or through the mail (Fig. 35-19, 35-21, 35-23, 35-24). Because much of the country remains rural, many furnish their homes through mail order using Sears, Roebuck & Company or other catalogs. Suites of furniture for the parlor, the dining room, and bedrooms are most popular. For the parlor, factories make affordable three-piece suites consisting of a sofa or settee, an armchair, and a rocker. Dining room suites have extension tables, chairs, and a china cabinet. Typical for bedrooms are beds, dressers, night stands, and wash stands. Factories also produce oak furniture for offices.

DESIGN SPOTLIGHT

Furniture: These chairs illustrate the many stylistic choices for dining chairs available to consumers at the end of the 19th century. Turning, spindle work, and caned, wood, or leather seats are common features. Incising and pressed and applied wood decoration embellish some models.

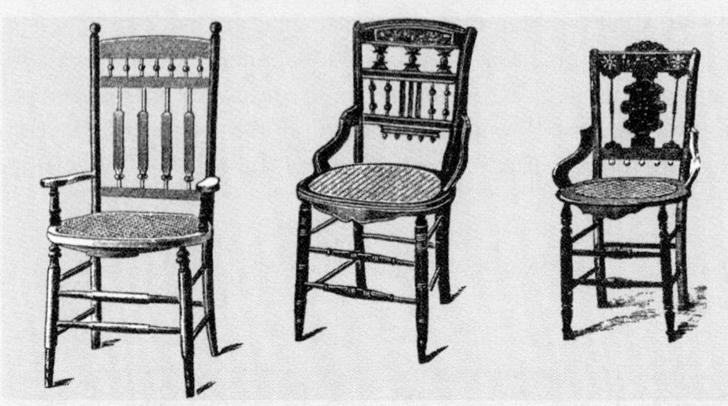

▲ **35-19.** Mail-Order Furniture: Side chairs; published in F. E. Stuart; Sears, Roebuck & Company; and Montgomery Ward & Company catalogs, c. 1900; United States.

Public and Private Buildings

■ *Materials*. Mahogany and fruitwoods in a dark finish are favored for Queen Anne style furniture. Manufactured American furniture is oak or walnut. Oak is cheaper, more readily available, and strong enough to withstand packing and shipping (Fig. 35-19).

■ *Seating*. Queen Anne–style seating (Fig. 35-12) may closely resemble the original or blend characteristics from later styles such as Chippendale or Sheraton, with modern upholstery techniques. Manufactured oak chairs have many styles identified by their details. Curving legs and carved flowers signal Rococo Revival. Renaissance Revival chairs and rockers (Fig. 35-13) have baluster legs, spindle backs, and applied moldings. No matter what the style, seats are solid wood, leather, or caned. Most common are pressed-back chairs and rockers with elaborate details (Fig. 35-19, 35-20). A metal die, heat, and pressure apply designs to backs, giving the impression of hand-carved embellishment. Made in several price levels, they have turned legs and solid seats and backs with designs that are usually curvilinear with flowers and foliage on the crest or splat. Windsor chairs also are a popular choice.

■ *Tables*. Queen Anne–style tables usually resemble Chippendale or Late Georgian ones in form and details. However, dining tables now have solid or extension tops instead of being made in pieces as was common in the 18th century. Like other furniture, tables are produced by American manufacturers in many different types, styles, and price levels (Fig. 35-13, 35-21). Dining tables in oak usually are monumental in scale with a single center support that is turned or rectangular. Four legs with paw feet or rounded ends provide support and embellishment. Round tables usually have several leaves. Fancier tables have four turned legs or melon supports with paw feet. Stretchers and aprons feature pressed

▲ **35-21.** Mail-Order Furniture: Tables; published in F. E. Stuart and Sears, Roebuck & Company catalogs, c. 1900; United States.

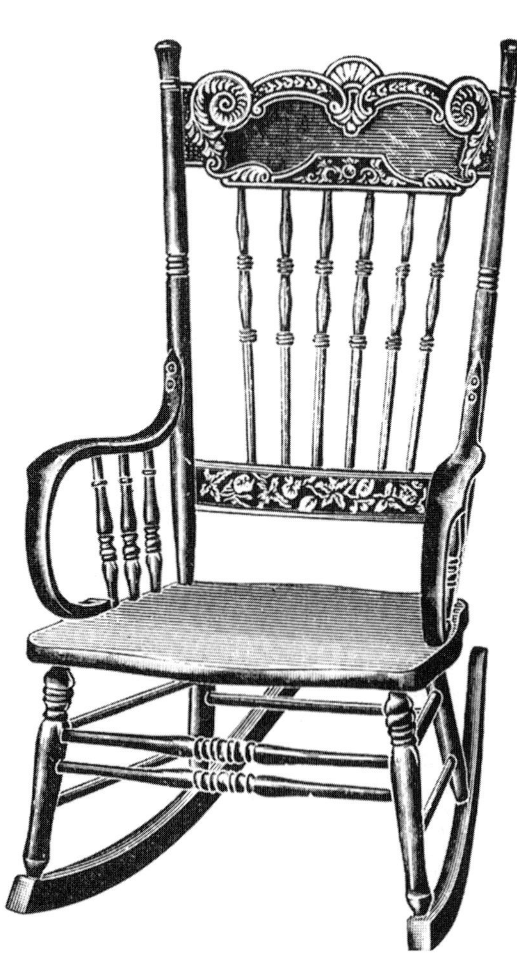

▲ **35-20.** Mail-Order Furniture: Rocker; published in Sears, Roebuck & Company catalogs, c. 1895, 1902; United States.

▲ **35-22.** Cabinet in the Queen Anne style; published in *Art Furniture*, c. 1877; England; designed by Edward W. Godwin.

decorations. The most expensive parlor tables have marble tops and a center support composed of three or four legs and a central member. Legs are rectilinear in form with incised or pressed decoration. Other parlor tables have rectangular wooden tops, turned splayed legs connected to a lower shelf, and ball and claw feet in wood or glass (Fig. 35-21).

■ *Storage*. Queen Anne–style desks, bookcases, and sideboards with cabinets on top have broken pediments and brackets to display *objets d'art* (Fig. 35-22). The bases have slender, straight, tapered legs in the Late Neoclassic manner. A lower shelf provides additional display space. Swags, paterae, urns, arabesques, husks, and stringing decorate the drawers, doors, and legs.

Factory-made oak storage pieces include sideboards, china cabinets, desks, bookcases, desk and bookcase combinations, and kitchen cabinets (Fig. 35-23). They are rectangular in form with wood, brass, or glass pulls and pressed, applied, or carved decoration on the crest. China cabinets have high, mirrored backs with shelves and lower drawer and doors. Fancier examples have applied or pressed decoration.

■ *Beds*. Wooden beds have tall solid backs with carved, pressed, or applied decorations (Fig. 35-24). Tops may be flat, arched, curved, or pedimented. Solid footboards repeat the headboard design but are shorter. Iron or brass beds may be composed of plain, round, and turned rods topped with balls or curving rods (Fig. 35-25). Bedroom suites include matching dressers, chiffoniers, washstands, wardrobes, and night stands.

▲ **35-24.** Mail-Order Furniture: Chamber suite; published in the New England Furniture Company catalog, c. 1902; United States.

■ *Decorative Arts*. Numerous brackets and shelves on furniture, the mantel, and wall shelves display blue and white porcelain and other ceramics (Fig. 35-12, 35-14, 35-22). Japanese fans and peacock feathers may add an exotic touch. Stands hold plants and flowers. Mirrors, paintings, and prints may cover walls (Fig. 35-13).

▲ **35-23.** Mail-Order Furniture: Desk; published in the Sears, Roebuck & Company catalog, c. 1900; United States.

▲ **35-25.** Bed, c. 1868; England; published in *Hints on Household Taste* by Charles L. Eastlake.

L. ACADEMIC HISTORICISM

The term *Academic Historicism* refers to a more studied method of design that is usually acquired in an academic or educational setting as opposed to learning through an apprenticeship or work experience. This approach characterizes much high-style work during the late 19th and early 20th centuries in Europe and North America. Reacting to the rampant eclecticism, vagaries, and licentiousness in the earlier part of the century, some designers return to a more disciplined and sober design process that comes from and actually uses elements of classical antiquity and the Renaissance. Many of these participating designers study at *L'École des Beaux-Arts* in France, which emphasizes study and emulation of the best examples of the past. Consequently, they reintroduce the classical idiom as a means of bringing order, unity, and restraint to design. Although eclecticism still remains supreme in the design world, it becomes more thoughtful and carefully considered or more scientific and systematic under Academic Historicism. Overt connections to the past replace the loose, haphazard borrowings of earlier.

Study of the best examples of the past becomes easier in the second half of the 19th century because past styles are better understood from previous scholarship and designers have greater access to ancient and Renaissance buildings and their images. The disciplines of art and architectural history have classified past styles and trends according to the scientific method. Museums and individuals collect and display artifacts and art works. With easier travel, more designers and their clients visit important sites. New developments in publishing and photography provide images and information for both those who travel and those who do not.

Classical eclecticism is the unifying element among late-19th-century and early-20th-century architecture, interiors, and furniture despite a large number of individual styles, such as Romanesque Revival, Chateauesque, Beaux-Arts, Neo-Renaissance, and Neoclassical Revival. Designs reveal clear and sometimes discrete references to earlier buildings. The period is one of grandiose scale and monumentality to express prosperity, culture, and nationalism in buildings and furnishings for nations and the affluent. Beaux-Arts-trained designers are readily able and willing to produce works that communicate these qualities. Collaboration among architects, artists, sculptors, landscape architects, and others to create monumental works of architecture is at an all-time high. Trained in a classical vocabulary, they create classical and, often, restrained exteriors and lavish interiors of which many rooms feature period designs in expensive materials and finishes.

Academic Historicism, the Arts and Crafts Movement, and other factors help inspire renewed interest in local or regional styles. In the United States, this gives rise to the Colonial Revival, which is based upon English Colonial and dominates the eastern part of the country, and the Spanish Colonial Revivals that derive from Spanish and Mediterranean architecture and are immensely fashionable in the southwestern United States.

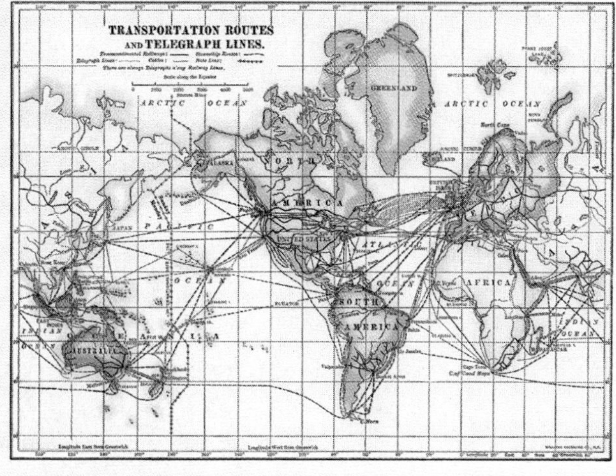

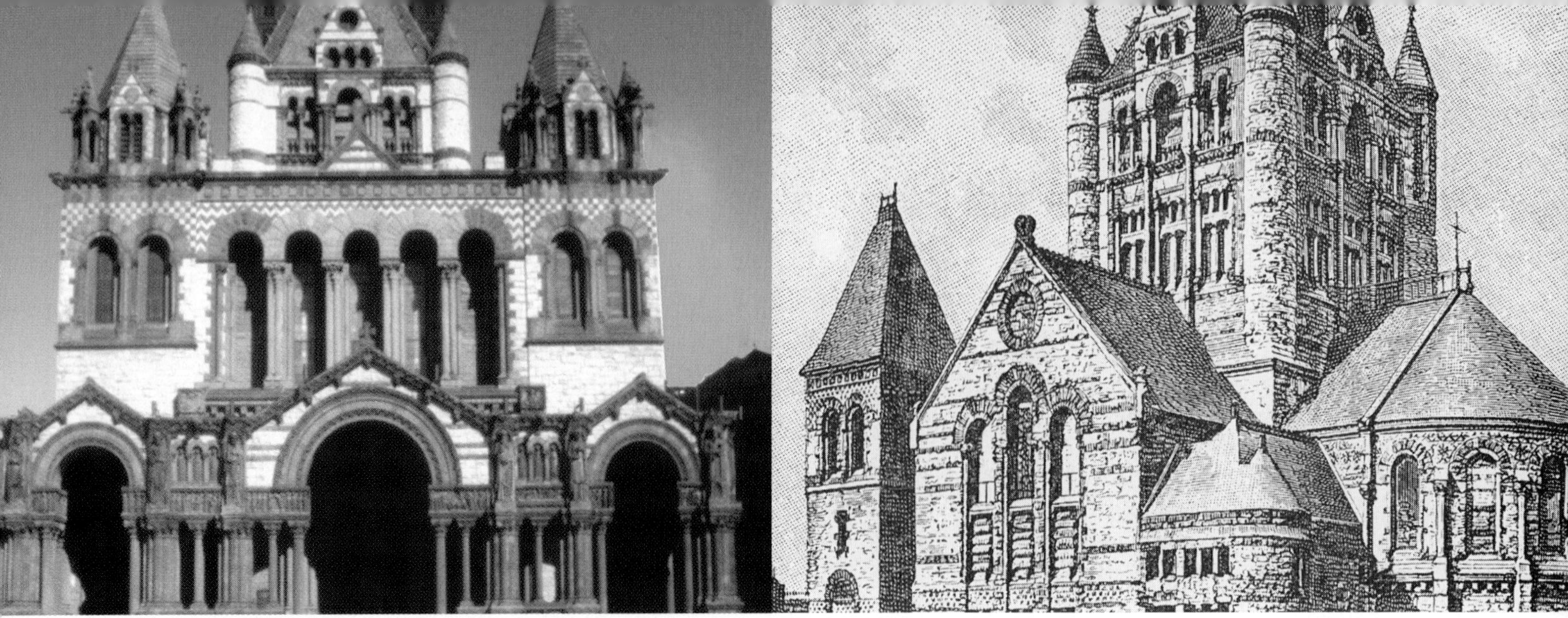

CHAPTER 36

Romanesque Revival, Richardsonian Romanesque

Romanesque Revival 1820s–1860s, Richardsonian Romanesque 1860s–1900s

The manner of Richardson is worthy of the name of an original American style if the Americans are pleased to say so. Its primary elements are these: rough rustic stonework for the wall facing wherever eligible; exceedingly bold and massive Romanesque detail, Italian, French or Spanish at pleasure; the wide, heavy, low-browed, semicircular-arched doorway, as a specially favourite feature, with its deep voussoirs strongly emphasized and its dark shadowy porch within—the focus of the composition and the foundation of its motive; then the arcade to correspond; the campanile rising like a cliff in unbroken breadth and stern repose.

—James Fergusson, *Modern Styles of Architecture*, 1899

Corbel tables and round arches distinguish buildings in the Romanesque Revival or the Round-arched Style, which originates in Germany in the early 19th century. Developing from similar medieval impulses as the Gothic Revival, Romanesque Revival is a less popular alternative to Gothic Revival in England, Europe, and North America. Its use diminishes by the 1860s. During the 1870s, American architect Henry Hobson Richardson creates a personal architectural style that becomes known as Richardsonian Romanesque. Based upon Romanesque structures and other sources, massiveness, round arches, and rough-faced stone define the style, which is the first American style to be taken up in Europe. Neither the German nor American versions of Romanesque Revival have a corresponding interior or furniture style. Like Richardsonian Romanesque, they are often medieval in appearance and feeling.

HISTORICAL AND SOCIAL

In late-1820s Germany, Romanesque Revival develops out of discussions about selecting an appropriate national style from among medieval alternatives to classicism, a resurgence of religious fervor, and the study and publication of medieval and Romanesque architecture (8th century–1150). Seeking a national style with medieval precedents that expresses their move toward unification, the Germans investigate Romanesque with great intensity and depth. Not only do scholars and architects scrutinize Germany's medieval buildings, but they also study those of Byzantium and Italy, which gives a strong Italian flavor to the revival.

Rulers Ludwig I of Germany and Friedrich Wilhelm IV of Prussia see religion as essential in the revitalization of their countries following the Napoleonic wars. Both advocate a strong church–state system and support the restoration of medieval churches and the building of new churches, many of which are Romanesque Revival. New social institutions emerge from the universal church movement, which strives to support contemporary life and confront problems of progress and modernization. Within the movement is a general push for a return to the simplicity in faith of early Christianity, which in turn supports plainer, less expensive church buildings. At the same time, religious revivals prompt a return to doctrinal simplification based upon models of Early Christianity, of which the use of Early Christian and medieval models for contemporary churches is a visual expression.

Royal family ties, visits by German architects and theorists, prints, and pattern books bring the Romanesque Revival to England. Queen Victoria's marriage to the German Prince Albert aligns the two families and creates trade and diplomatic exchanges. As in Germany, a Protestant Revival and subsequent turn toward simplicity in doctrines and buildings focuses some attention on Romanesque Revival over Gothic Revival. Nevertheless, Gothic Revival dominates English architecture, interiors, and furniture.

A similar pattern prompts the rise of Romanesque Revival in North America. The style's inception coincides with the immigration of thousands of Germans during the 1830s and 1840s, which creates an atmosphere receptive to German culture. Royal patronage plays a role in the transmission of Romanesque Revival because Ludwig I and Friedrich Wilhelm IV fund the building of churches and monasteries in America for German immigrants. Immigrant architects and architectural treatises from Germany also help advance the revival, which briefly surpasses Gothic Revival in popularity in the 1850s. In both England and North America, Romanesque Revival inspires a picturesque image that is not so tainted by associations of Catholicism or elitism as is Gothic Revival.

In the second half of the 19th century, one of the foremost architects working in Romanesque in the United States is Henry Hobson Richardson, who studies at *L'École des Beaux-Arts* in France beginning in 1860. While there, he travels in England, France, Italy, and the Mediterranean regions. When he returns to Boston in 1865, he is familiar with contemporary architectural developments in France, early medieval churches in England and France (particularly Normandy), and recently discovered Early Christian churches (c. 500–1500 C.E.) in Syria. Drawing from these and other influences, Richardson works out his own personal interpretation of Romanesque and contemporary European design. By adapting the vocabulary of Romanesque, including the round arch, to many building types and using load-bearing masonry walls, Richardson gives them a particular weightiness and monumental scale, while maintaining delicacy of ornament and attention to detail. Most Richardsonian Romanesque examples come from his office until his death in 1886. Afterward, the style as designed by other architects becomes especially strong in Chicago and the Midwest.

▲ **36-1.** Architectural Details: Capitals with faces, and arches with columns, mid- to late-19th century; Toronto and Massachusetts; arches by Henry Hobson Richardson.

CONCEPTS

German architect Heinrich Hübsch lays the theoretical foundation for Romanesque Revival in his 1828 work *In welchem Style sollen wir bauen? (In What Style Shall We Build?)*. Advancing Romanesque as superior to Gothic, he declares that it is simpler to construct and more economical than Gothic Revival. He also notes that the style is rational like classicism, can use German building materials, and suits the German climate. Hübsch probably coins the term *Rundbogenstil* or Round-arched Style by which Romanesque Revival is known in Germany. His writing sets the stage for the development and adoption of *Rundbogenstil* in Germany and later in other countries.

Richardsonian Romanesque draws from Spanish and southern French Romanesque, Norman, and Syrian Early Christian sources instead of the German *Rundbogenstil*. Although eclectic in inspiration, Richardson does more than copy forms and motifs from medieval buildings. He absorbs their character and personalizes the details of Romanesque, and creates an individual style so distinctive that it bears his name. Defining grand public buildings and residences of the affluent, Richardsonian Romanesque conveys a majestic, strong, powerful, and enduring appearance.

MOTIFS

■ *Motifs*. Common motifs (Fig. 36-1, 36-2, 36-3, 36-4) include round arches, corbel tables, hood moldings, battlements, and rose windows for Romanesque Revival. Round arches, floral capitals, lozenges, chevrons, and terra-cotta panels of floral ornament identify Richardsonian Romanesque (Fig. 36-1, 36-5, 36-6, 36-8, 36-9, 36-10, 36-11).

ARCHITECTURE

Romanesque Revival and Richardsonian Romanesque look to the past for inspiration. Deriving from several styles, including Romanesque, expressions are largely limited to architecture and feature masonry walls, symmetry, columns, round arches, and towers.

Like the medieval Romanesque, Romanesque Revival originates as an ecclesiastical style (Fig. 36-2). In Germany, *Rundbogenstil* first appears in less affluent Protestant suburban churches in Munich and Berlin. As the two cities grow, architects also easily adapt the style to other building types, particularly schools, hospitals, and other structures associated with social reform.

As in Germany, Romanesque Revival in other countries, including England, largely characterizes ecclesiastical and Protestant structures, although some museums (Fig. 36-3, 36-4), libraries, train stations, and courthouses are built in the style. In America, Romanesque Revival–style schools reflect the Americans' study of German educational methods and schools. Andrew Jackson Downing depicts an example called a Norman villa in *The Architecture of Country Houses* (1850), but few American residences are influenced by German Romanesque Revival. Alternative names for Romanesque Revival include Norman (as a precursor to Gothic) or Lombard.

Definitive characteristics of Romanesque Revival are round arches and corbel tables used as stringcourses or to define rooflines. Additional characteristics include smooth walls, round doorways and windows, a gabled façade on churches, deeply recessed doorways with layered colonnettes, and towers. *Rundbogenstil* and Romanesque Revival borrow forms or details from Early Christian (c. 500–1500), Byzantine (330–1453), Italian Romanesque (8th century to 1150; especially in Lombardy), or Early Italian Renaissance (1420–1500; especially in Florence). Buildings often exhibit structural polychrome, color that is inherent in the materials, delineating important elements.

Henry Hobson Richardson's Trinity Church (1873–1877; Fig. 36-5) in Boston, Massachusetts, is the building that transforms the Romanesque concept from German prototypes to French and Mediterranean sources as created by Richardson. Over the next 15 years, Richardson's public and private buildings

▲ **36-2.** Church, mid-19th century; Stuggart, Germany. *Rundbogenstil.*

▲ **36-3.** Smithsonian Institution, 1847–1855; Washington, D.C.; James Renwick, Sr. Romanesque Revival.

move away from direct quotations of medieval structures to a more simplified, unique style. Buildings are of rough-faced stone that gives a weighty, massive appearance. Voussoirs, lintels, capitals, ornament, and other details are often a different color than the walls. Also characteristic are round arches for doors, windows, and other openings, and arches carried by squatty columns. Façades usually are asymmetrical with one or more towers and bands or groups of windows. Embellishment is derived from medieval sources and includes foliage capitals, carved moldings, and terra-cotta panels of flowers and other details.

▲ **36-4.** Natural History Museum, 1860s; London, England; Alfred Waterhouse. Romanesque Revival.

DESIGN SPOTLIGHT

Architecture: Henry Hobson Richardson wins the competition for Trinity Church in 1872, although the final design is very different from the competition drawings. The result is considered the first full example of Richardsonian Romanesque. Richardson draws inspiration from French, English, Spanish Romanesque, and Norman examples. In the Beaux-Arts manner, the exterior design articulates the plan with its rounded apse and short nave and transept. A large porch with twin towers and pyramidal roofs defines the entrance façade, but the heavy tower marking the crossing dominates the composition and resembles the tower of Salamanca Cathedral, Spain. In the 1890s, Sheply, Rutan, and Coolidge add the arched entry and picturesque spires and windows of the towers that are derived from English sources. Trinity's walls are of ashlar-faced granite in a light color with darker sandstone highlighting such architectural details as *voussoirs* and capitals and forming stripes and geometric patterns across the façade to emphasize horizontality. Roofs of orange clay tiles cap the towers. Carved ornament in foliage and naturalistic patterns reveal Richardson's creativity, while reflecting English sources of the period. Phillip Brooks, rector of Trinity, may have had a large part in its design and choice of Romanesque. Brooks is a major exponent of the larger movement to return Protestantism to its earlier roots and away from ritualistic, Catholic practices. Romanesque, with its primitive simplicity, expresses the goals of the movement. Numerous important designers contribute to the building, including future architects Charles F. McKim and Stanford White; artist John LaFarge; and sculptor Augustus Saint-Gaudens. Trinity brings Richardson to the forefront of American architecture.

Richardson designs the nave to support the eloquent preaching of Phillip Brooks. The triple vaults with tie beams and colorful decoration come from English sources, particularly William Burges, whom Richardson admires. Although the design provides little wall space for paintings, Old and New Testament figures highlight the spandrels of the arches in the crossing. Along the nave are biblical murals within frames. Daring in a nonresidential context, the rich terra-cotta red walls unify the space. Painted and stenciled decorations in blue, green, brown, and gold

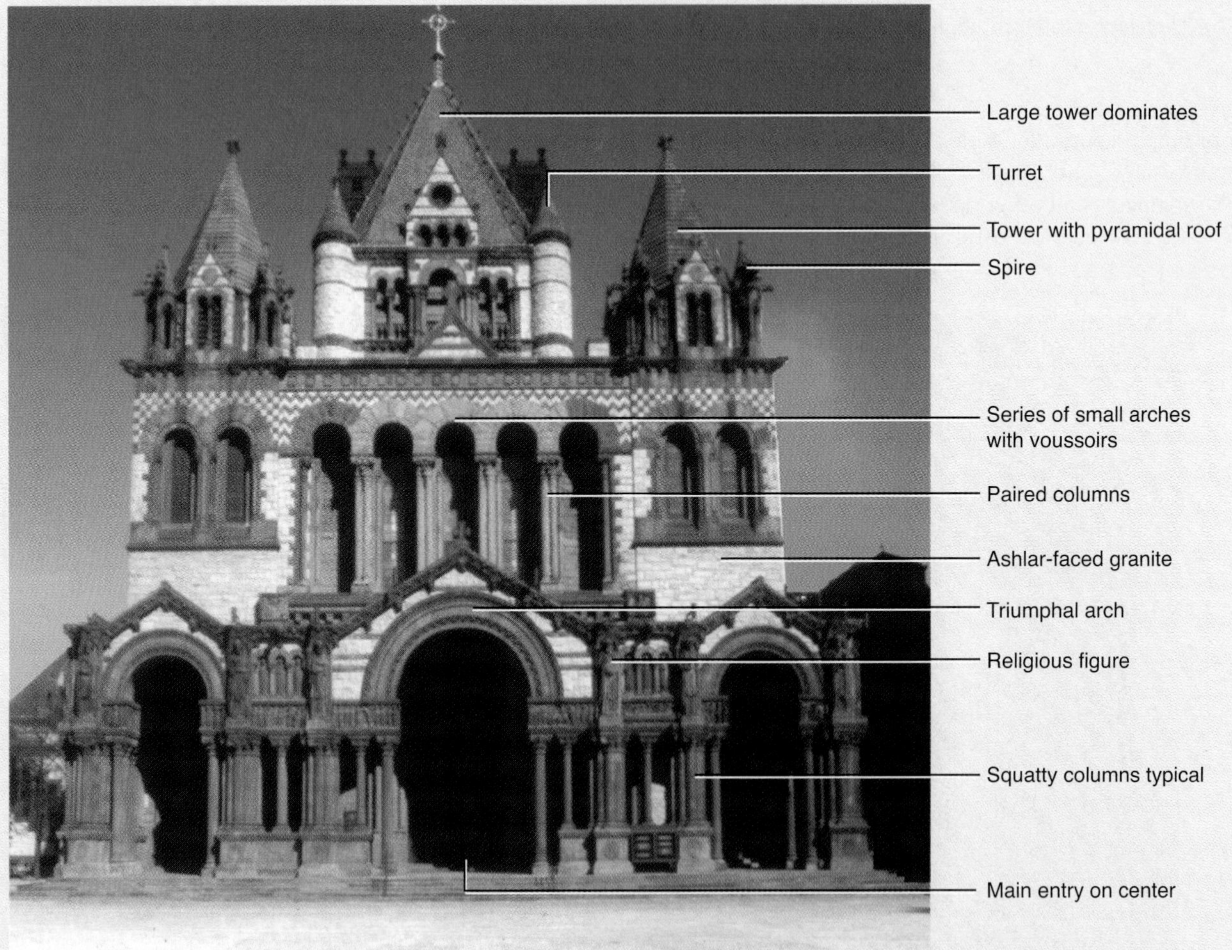

▲ **36–5.** Trinity Church and nave, 1873–1877; Boston, Massachusetts; Henry Hobson Richardson. Richardsonian Romanesque.

Richardsonian Romanesque defines more building types than Romanesque Revival does, including offices, warehouses, train stations (Fig. 36-8), libraries, churches (Fig. 36-5), and bridges. Its impenetrable and fortresslike character makes Richardsonian Romanesque a suitable choice for statehouses, courthouses, and prisons. Residences may be architect-designed single-family (Fig. 36-10) and row houses or speculatively built row houses. Because the style is expensive, it does not become part of the builder's repertoire. Following Richardson's death, as other architects take up the style, it becomes fashionable for affluent residences (Fig. 36-11). Often the style is not as successful in the hands of Richardson's followers. Interest fades during the 1890s.

Public Buildings • Romanesque Revival

■ *Site Orientation*. Public structures in all countries usually are located outside city centers as a part of newly developing suburbs. In suburban Munich, Friedrich von Gärtner designs several Romanesque Revival buildings for Ludwig I on a street called *Ludwigstraβe* (*Ludwigstrasse*). They include a state library, salt works, university, and girls' school. Prussian churches in the style sometimes are part of picturesque complexes of supporting buildings such as rectories, parish houses, schools, and bell towers.

■ *Floor Plans*. Floor plans serve the function of the building. Churches may have one of three different plans: basilica, Latin cross, or Greek cross. A few have open auditoriums with pulpit and altar on one end to facilitate Protestant preaching. Hospitals and schools usually have long corridors with rooms on either side.

DESIGN SPOTLIGHT

emphasize architectural details. Ceilings are gilded and richly painted in a similar fashion to the walls. The gilding now dominating the chancel is added in a 1937 renovation, and it separates the chancel from the rest of the space in a way the designers did not intend. The original plain windows allowed in too much light, which interfered with the color scheme. Later, John Lafarge adds the large stained glass windows, and William Morris and Edward Burne-Jones provide smaller windows. The pews feature simple spiral turning, reeding, and foliage carving in a medieval manner. [National Historic Landmark]

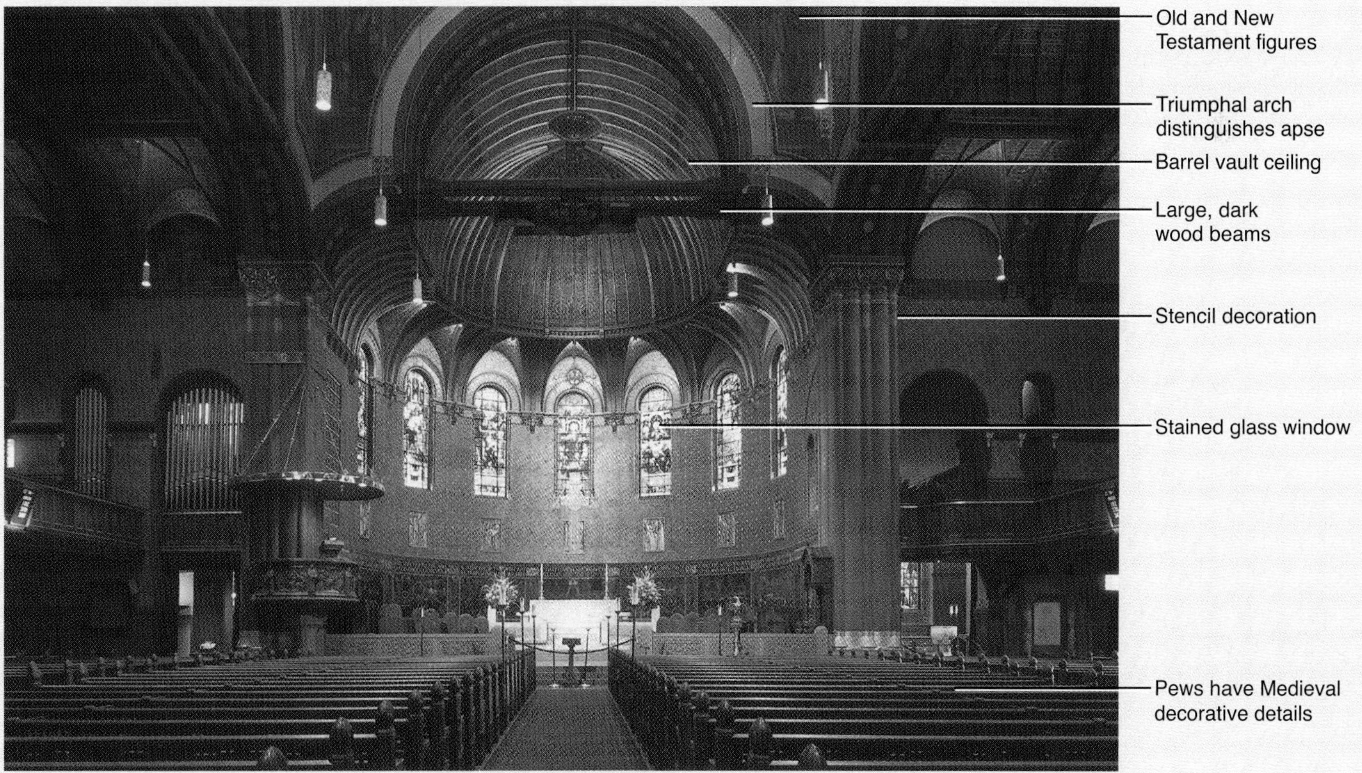

▲ **36-5.** Continued

■ *Materials*. Romanesque Revival structures are most often of brick in various colors for economy and ease of construction (Fig. 36-2). Details and ornament may be of different colored brick than walls or of stone, terra-cotta, or ceramic tiles.

■ *Façades*. Churches (Fig. 36-2) usually have one or two towers flanking a central portion, which is crowned by the triangular shape created by the gable roof. Arched or rose windows often extend into the gable. Contrary to the earlier Romanesque, each tower often has a different design. Plain wall surfaces may be articulated with buttresses, windows, hood moldings, and corbel tables. A few churches in Germany replicate the colonnaded forecourt of Early Christian churches. Public buildings (Fig. 36-3, 36-4) usually have symmetrical façades composed of rows of round-arched windows with a central entrance. Some are very plain with little or no detailing, while others have stringcourses, occasionally with corbel tables, to separate stories and/or quoins highlighting corners. Larger structures, such as schools or museums, often have towers flanking the entrance and/or on the corners (Fig. 36-3, 36-4).

■ *Windows and Doors*. Most windows (Fig. 36-2, 36-3, 36-4) are composed of round arches, but a few are rectangular or pointed. Windows may be single or grouped in doubles, triples, or more. Some are bifora, and others have hood moldings. Churches (Fig. 36-2) often have a rose window or a row of arched windows highlighting the main façade above the doorway.

Plain and carved wooden doors, like windows, usually are set within round arches. Some churches have the three traditional entrances corresponding to the nave and aisles, while others have a single center entrance. Doorways (Fig. 36-2, 36-3) may be deeply recessed with layers of colonnettes as in Romanesque. Entrances may be in a series of three or four round arches carried by pilasters or engaged columns. On public structures, larger, more prominent arches announce the entrance. Some have towers flanking the entrances to give them additional significance (Fig. 36-4).

■ *Roofs*. Roofs are usually flat or gables and/or cross gables. Church domes are rare. As a defining feature on churches and other structures, a corbel table emphasizes the roof line. Some, particularly large structures designed to resemble castles, have battlements. Towers may have conical or pyramidal roofs with spires and/or gables and spires (Fig. 36-2, 36-3, 36-4).

■ *Later Interpretations*. Very few interpretive examples of Romanesque Revival appear in later periods. In the late 20th century, some commercial buildings exhibit large round arches with new materials reminiscent of the revival character (Fig. 36-12).

Public and Private Buildings • Richardsonian Romanesque

■ *Site Orientation*. Public buildings usually are located in an urban setting near city centers or on avenues for transportation (Fig. 36-5, 36-6, 36-7, 36-8). Urban residences (Fig. 36-10, 36-11) front on streets but may have gardens on the side or in the rear. Lawns surround those in the suburbs. Some examples reveal a direct connection to the landscape through horizontal orientation, rugged textures, and natural building materials, such as rocks or boulders (Fig. 36-9).

■ *Floor Plans*. Richardson's plans have a new and original openness and fluidity of space. Plans of some large public buildings show his assimilation of Beaux-Arts planning concepts using modules or units arranged along main and secondary axes and façades that develop from the ground plan. Residential floor plans

▲ **36-6.** Marshall Field Wholesale Store, 1885–1887; Chicago, Illinois; Henry Hobson Richardson. Richardsonian Romanesque.

▲ **36-7.** Allegheny County Court House, 1884–1888; Pittsburgh, Pennsylvania; Henry Hobson Richardson. Richardsonian Romanesque.

▲ **36-8.** Union Station and waiting room, 1892–1894; St. Louis, Missouri; Theodore C. Link with interiors by Thomas Rudd. Richardsonian Romanesque.

are usually asymmetrical with rooms arranged around the stair hall (Fig. 36-11). Some have the living hall with fireplace introduced by Richardson in the Watts Sherman house (1874–1875).

■ *Materials*. Although Richardson knows about developments in the use of cast iron for structure, he favors load-bearing masonry walls and chooses rusticated or heavily textured stone or boulders to give signature heaviness to his buildings (Fig. 36-5, 36-6, 36-7, 36-9, 36-10). Veneering techniques have not yet been developed, so walls are as thick and solid as they appear. Ashlar masonry, fieldstone, brownstone, rocks, boulders, and granite are used for both public and private buildings. A few examples are brick, usually to blend with surrounding structures. Contrasts of color, material, or texture are common because lintels, voussoirs, and other architectural details are of different colors or materials. Decorative plaques in terra-cotta or stone add embellishment. Other architects follow Richardson's lead.

■ *Façades*. Façades of public buildings are usually asymmetrical with a horizontal emphasis. Rustication, rough textures, bold details, and deep reveals in windows and doorways convey massiveness (Fig. 36-5, 36-6, 36-7, 36-8). Interest comes from the structural polychrome, contrasts of texture, rhythms of windows, and carved ornament. Compositions range from picturesque and embellished to severely plain. Walls may be flat or have projections such as windows, bays, pavilions, or towers. On tall buildings, stringcourses may separate several rows of windows. Structures often have a water table or battered base, which adds to the weighty appearance. State buildings, courthouses (Fig. 36-7), and city halls usually have asymmetrically placed tall towers to signify civic authority as in the Middle Ages. Towers, which may be circular or rectangular, sometimes resemble Italian campaniles or bell towers (Fig. 36-7, 36-8). Columns, which vary from tall and slender to the more typical short and heavy, carry arches. Shafts may be unfluted, and capitals feature lacy foliage derived from Byzantine or Romanesque examples (Fig. 36-1). Chimneys are usually simply treated. A heavy cornice, corbel table, or corbelling defines the roofline.

Like public buildings, residences range from the severely plain to more picturesque compositions with lavish embellishment, and walls are rusticated stone with contrasts of color or material to emphasize architectural details (Fig. 36-9, 36-10, 36-11). Rectangular or round towers are common on suburban examples, whereas row houses substitute bay or oriel windows. Porches with round arches may define the entrance or extend on one or more sides of a house. *Port-cochères* are common. Stringcourses may separate stories, and a heavy cornice or corbelling defines the roofline. Some examples have battlements.

■ *Windows*. Windows on both public and private buildings may be round-arched or rectangular or a combination of the two (Fig. 36-5, 36-6, 36-7, 36-8, 36-10, 36-11). On both types of buildings, windows with deep reveals, often in bands, form a regular and horizontal rhythm across the façade. Single or multiple columns with foliage capitals sometimes separate windows. Deep reveals give a punched-out appearance to rectangular windows, which are usually tall and narrow with stone mullions. Many have quoins or smaller transoms, square windows, or lintels above them. The moldings surrounding arched windows may have carved ornament derived from medieval sources, such as lozenges, zigzags, or foliage. Wall dormers (Fig. 36-8), common on large public and private buildings, often have parapets with patterned brick or stonework, and carved ornament and finials, or they may be severely plain. Residences have stained or colored glass windows. Most residential windows have a single-pane lower sash with either a single-pane or multipaned upper sash.

■ *Doors*. A large round arch or triple arches often announce the entrance on public and private buildings (Fig. 36-5, 36-7, 36-9, 36-11). Some entries are recessed within arches, or as on residences, an arcade may form a porch or portico. Others have three arched doors with deep reveals and colonnettes like a Romanesque church. Doorway arches have carved ornament on public buildings to add to their importance. Doors are wood and may be carved or plain with a window.

▲ **36-10.** J. J. Glessner House, 1885–1887; Chicago, Illinois; Henry Hobson Richardson. Richardsonian Romanesque.

■ *Roofs*. Gable roofs, sometimes with side parapets, define most Richardsonian Romanesque public buildings (Fig. 36-7, 36-8). A few examples have pyramidal roofs (Fig. 36-5). Gable roofs may have decorative cresting, while pyramid roofs have finials. For residences (Fig. 36-9, 36-10), gable roofs are most common and may be front or side gables with or without cross gables. Urban row houses may have hipped or mansard roofs. Round towers have conical roofs with finials and rectangular towers have pyramidal roofs (Fig. 36-11). Some have rectangular or circular buttresses. Slate or clay tiles cover roofs, which are steeply pitched in the medieval manner. Some roofs have eyebrow dormers (Fig. 36-9).

▲ **36-9.** F. L. Ames Gate Lodge, 1880–1881; North Easton, Massachusetts; Henry Hobson Richardson. Richardsonian Romanesque.

INTERIORS

Romanesque Revival interiors often have a medieval appearance created by architectural elements and ornament from Early Christian, Romanesque, or Byzantine sources (Fig. 36-8). Many public building types, such as courthouses, and/or their interiors, such as governmental chambers, were unknown in the Middle Ages, so they have no exact prototype. As a result, these interiors may appear vaguely or even strongly medieval with a similarity to the exteriors that is defined by architectual details such as columns. Some rooms have large, hooded fireplaces such as those of the Middle Ages. Churches come closer to replicating the predecessors than do other public buildings or residences. Romanesque Revival church interiors often emulate Early Christian (c. 500–1500) or Romanesque (8th century–1150) prototypes in a large nave with a tall trussed or coffered wooden ceiling. An arcade composed of round arches separates the aisles from the nave, and clerestory windows above the arcade admit light. A triumphal arch may define the apse. A large open space with pews facing an altar and pulpit is common for Protestant churches where preaching is more important than rituals and processions are.

Interiors in Richardsonian Romanesque public buildings usually have a medieval appearance with characteristics similar to the exteriors (Fig. 36-5). Round arches carried by squatty columns and medieval-style carved ornament define stair halls and important spaces. Residential interiors often feature revival styles or characteristics of the Aesthetic Movement (Fig. 36-11, 36-13).

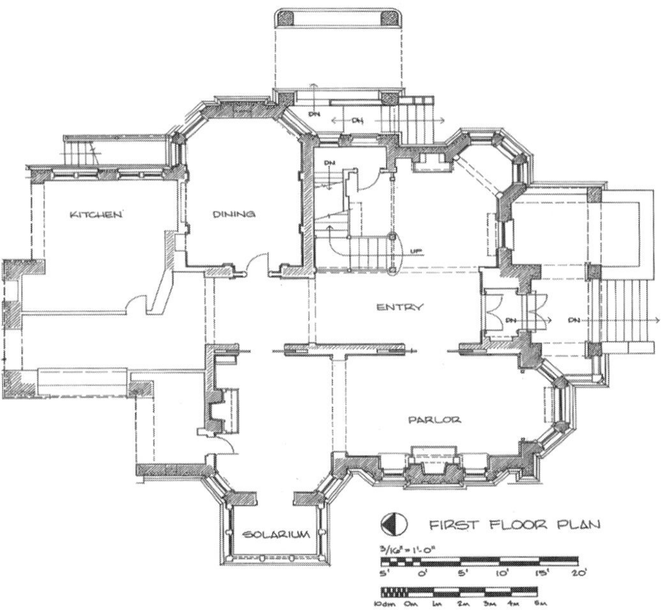

▲ **36-11.** Elizabeth Plankinton House, floor plan, and stair hall, 1886–1888; Milwaukee, Wisconsin; attributed to Edward Townsend Mix. Richardsonian Romanesque.

Public and Private Buildings

■ *Color.* The palette for public and private interiors includes terra-cotta reds, greens, blues, golds, and browns in both Romanesque styles (Fig. 36-5, 36-8). Gilding emphasizes important elements.

■ *Floors.* Floors may be stone, polished marble, encaustic tiles in colorful patterns, or wood. Carpet in period colors and patterns often covers floors in important spaces in both public and private buildings (Fig. 36-13).

■ *Walls.* Wall treatments include stone, marble, tile, dark wood paneling, wallpaper in medieval patterns, and embossed leather (Fig. 36-13). Some interior walls have large round arches. In Germany, *Rundbogenstil* initiates a revival of the art of mural painting, so in many German churches and some later American ones, murals of religious scenes embellish the walls (Fig. 36-5). Additionally, ornamental painting composed of geometric and naturalistic interlaced shapes may accentuate architectural details (Fig. 36-8). Forms, motifs, and colors are derived from medieval and Romanesque sources. Decorative balustrades in wood and iron are typical (Fig. 36-11).

▲ **36-12.** Later Interpretation: Washington State History Museum, 1996; Tacoma, Washington; Charles Moore and Arthur Anderson. Modern Historicism.

▲ **36-13.** Parlor, R. H. White House; Boston, Massachusetts; published in *Artistic Houses*, 1883; Peabody and Stearns.

■ *Windows and Doors*. Round-arched windows may have stained or colored glass in all building types. Curtains follow related period styles with heavy curtain panels and fancy valances. Doors are carved wood. They may often feature columns on the sides and carved lintels above.

■ *Ceilings*. Ceilings may be beamed, trussed in the medieval manner, coffered, vaulted, or flat (Fig. 36-5, 36-8, 36-11). Dark wood beams may be carved and painted with gilding highlighting details. Heavy corbels with carved medieval ornament may support ceiling beams. Residences may have painted ceiling decorations.

■ *Lighting*. Medieval-style lighting fixtures in brass, iron, or copper are used.

▲ **36-14.** Armchairs, c. 1870s–1880s; Henry Hobson Richardson.

FURNISHINGS AND DECORATIVE ARTS

Romanesque Revival and Richardsonian Romanesque rooms usually have medieval-style furniture, although there is no exactly corresponding furniture style for either. Richardson is one of the few American architects of his day to design furniture (Fig. 36-14). Like others before him, Richardson believes that no detail is too small for the architect's attention. So he and/or members of his office design furnishings for many of his public buildings and residences. It is not known how much actually came from his hand. Richardsonian furniture varies in design from a heavy, rugged appearance like the exteriors of his buildings to a slender form with spindles recalling early vernacular pieces. Designed to suit particular spaces, the furniture repeats the form and elements of the architecture. Designs are eclectic and medieval in character. Mostly of oak, carving is its main form of decoration. Little furniture remains in its original context, so its design relationship to the architecture is lost.

CHAPTER 37

Classical Eclecticism

Neo-Renaissance, Beaux-Arts, Neoclassical Revival, and Châteauesque 1880s–1940s

It is therefore all the more encouraging to note the steady advance in taste and knowledge . . . [that] is chiefly due to the fact that American architects are beginning to perceive two things . . . first that architecture and decoration, having wandered since 1800 in a labyrinth of dubious eclecticism, can be set right only by a close study of the best models; and secondly, that . . . these models are chiefly to be found in buildings erected in Italy after the beginning of the 16th century, and in other European countries after the full assimilation of the Italian influence.

—Edith Wharton and Ogden Codman, *The Decoration of Houses*, 1897

During the late 19th century, Classical Eclecticism, as espoused by Beaux-Arts-trained architects and designers, begins to dominate the design of public buildings and the mansions of the well-to-do in Europe and the United States. Four stylistic variations emerge: Neo-Renaissance, Beaux-Arts, Neoclassical Revival, and Châteauesque. Relying on forms and motifs from classical antiquity, the Renaissance, and/or the Baroque, the architectural compositions declare a classical or cosmopolitan European heritage, civic or national pride, or personal culture and prosperity. Inside, a team of designers creates richly decorated, often authentic, period rooms. In keeping with the period's emphasis upon professionalism, interior decoration becomes known as a profession.

HISTORICAL AND SOCIAL

The end of the 19th and beginning of the 20th century is a period of relative peace and prosperity for Europe and North America. The Industrial Revolution continues to transform lives and societies. Capitalism creates enormously wealthy persons and nations that, among other things, undertake large building campaigns. Governments and individuals alike seek to create an image of prosperity, culture, and national pride. At the same time, increased specialization within industry and business demands a more skilled approach within each. Consequently, the era sees further development of architecture as a profession and the beginnings of interior decoration as separate from architecture and a design specialty and profession in its own right. During the period, more women enter the field as career guides and other literature promote decorating as a woman's profession. They, along with males, further the devolopment of decorating through their work, writing, speaking, and activities within new professional organizations.

L'École des Beaux-Arts (School of Fine Arts), which replaces the French Academy in 1819, is the world's premier architectural school throughout the 19th century. The curriculum emphasizes study of the classical traditions, especially of ancient Greece and Rome; axial design; and formal, monumental planning. Students analyze functions of the building according to the program and organize them in units along a main circulation axis with minor cross axes. Plans show a clear ranking of axes, functions, and distinctions within the building. The façade develops from the plan, and parts of the composition are articulated with a distinct hierarchy like the ground plan. Location and site also are methodically designed with the relationships between and among structures considered.

Students at *L'École des Beaux-Arts* work in *ateliers* or studios under the direction of a practicing architect or *patron* who teaches design principles as exemplified in the best examples of classical design. The school hosts lectures in history, art, and construction and competitions through which students progress through the program of study. Presentation drawings, a hallmark of the Beaux-Arts training, are beautifully and artistically rendered plans and elevations. These drawings lead to Modernist criticism that structure and construction are ignored at the expense of creating pretty presentations. However, drawings are important to the process of developing, explaining, and completing the design solution. Beaux-Arts-trained architects strive to integrate architecture of the past with contemporary needs, materials, and technology.

Graduates of the school return home and continue these practices. Steeped in the classical vocabulary, architects and artists collaborate on the grand-scale designs that define the period. Consequently, there is a general return to classical modes in architecture and design in most countries at the end of the 19th century, signaling a rejection of the Victorian styles. The World's Columbian Exposition of 1893 in Chicago, Illinois, introduces the world to Classical Eclecticism on its grandest scale. The layout and buildings surrounding the Court of Honor (Fig. 37-4) exemplify Beaux-Arts planning principles, and the buildings'

(a)

(b)

(c)

▲ **37-1.** Architectural Details: (a) Building corner, Missouri; (b) porch ceiling detail, The Parthenon in Nashville, Tennessee; and (c) Grand Hall, Library of Congress, Washington, D.C.; c. 1880s–1930s.

gleaming white, classical façades fascinate visitors and designers from all over the world. The exposition establishes Classical Eclecticism as the standard for subsequent international exhibitions and large-scale governmental and commercial projects. The layout of the fair inspires the City Beautiful Movement, which affects city and civic centers in the United States and Europe. By 1900, Neo-Renaissance and Beaux-Arts are the fashion in North America, Great Britain, and Europe as designers turn to order and rationale in reaction to the irregularities of Victorian Revivals and curvilinear irregularities of Art Nouveau.

The patrons of Classical Eclecticism are wealthy industrialists and businessmen, such as Americans John D. Rockefeller, W. K. Vanderbilt, Andrew Carnegie, and Henry Clay Frick, who build enormous, lavishly decorated and furnished homes like the "cottages" (Fig. 37-10) in Newport, Rhode Island, and sponsor museums and other public institutions. In England, too, wealthy landowners, aristocrats, and industrialists, such as Samuel Courtauld and Sir Joseph Whitworth, build or acquire large country houses and found galleries and similar institutions. Although the middle classes cannot emulate the scale and demonstration of wealth of the affluent, some strive to follow the principles of classicism and the notion of careful choices based upon the best examples of the past in their own homes.

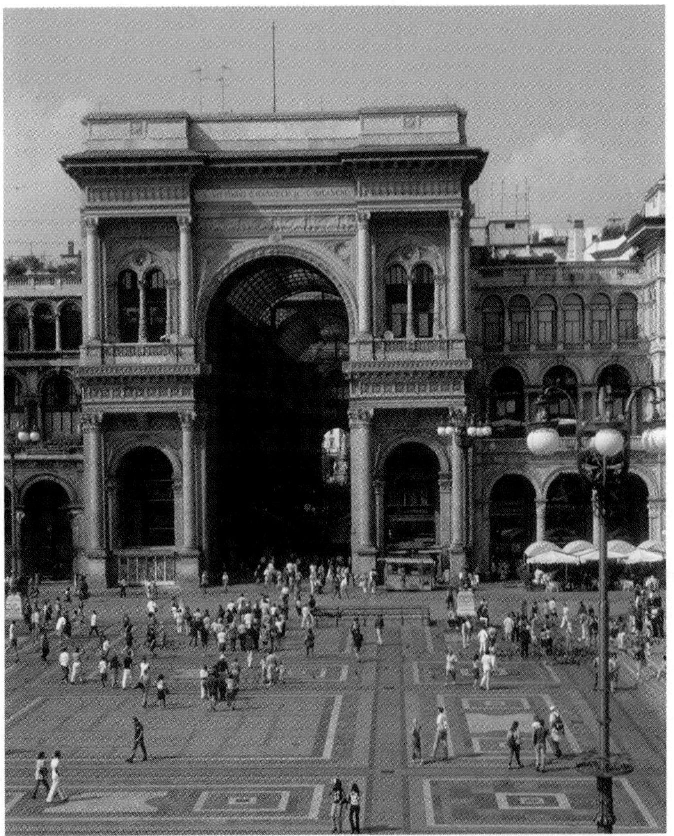

▲ **37-2.** *Galleria Vittorio Emanuele II*, 1865–1867; Milan, Italy; Giuseppe Mengoni. Neo-Renaissance.

CONCEPTS

Rejecting High Victorian picturesque irregularity, polychrome, and loose borrowings from and revivals of the past, Classical Eclecticism seeks to restore order, unity, and restraint to architecture and interiors. To accomplish this, architects and designers study and model the finest examples of history. Stylistic associations remain important as before, but compositions are more archaeologically correct and usually reveal specific borrowings of form or details from particular prototypes. The Beaux-Arts education encourages unity of appearance within classical traditions but allows for individual interpretations. Using a specific idiom of classical vocabulary from antiquity to the 17th century, Neo-Renaissance, Beaux-Arts, Neoclassical Revival, and Châteauesque architecture emulates past examples and displays monumental planning while addressing contemporary functions and using contemporary materials. Architects, designers, artists, sculptors, and landscape designers work together in the Renaissance manner to create comprehensive architectural solutions, grand-scale designs, and lavish interiors that proclaim a classical and/or European heritage. The middle classes strive to copy them in a greatly reduced manner.

MOTIFS

■ *Motifs*. Neo-Renaissance motifs (Fig. 37-1, 37-2, 37-3, 37-5, 37-8, 37-9, 37-10, 37-12, 37-13, 37-22) features egg and dart, bead, and dentil moldings; cartouches; roundels; and classical motifs such as pilasters, lintels, and stringcourses. Beaux-Arts (Fig. 37-4, 37-6, 37-7, 37-15, 37-16) motifs include swags, acanthus leaves, cartouches, figural and relief sculpture, flowers, cherubs, shells, C and S scolls, and wreaths. Neoclassical Revival motifs (Fig. 37-1, 37-8, 37-14, 37-17, 37-18, 37-23, 37-25) include egg and dart, bead, and dentil moldings; triglyphs and metopes; cartouches; honeysuckles; anthemions; acanthus leaves; the fret or key; swags; lyres; vases; drapery; and classical figures. Typical Châteauesque motifs (Fig. 37-11) are tracery, pointed arches, pinnacles, fireplace hood moldings, floral panels, griffins, and gargoyles. Motifs for interiors and furniture are similar to those for architectural styles. Classical motifs, such as columns, pediments, swags, vases, acanthus leaves, and cartouches, are common in Neo-Renaissance, Beaux-Arts, and Neoclassical Revivals interiors. Those that are French in style may have Rococo motifs, such as *rocaille* decoration, flowers, shells, and foliage, or Neoclassical ones. Interiors in Châteauesque buildings usually come from the medieval, Gothic, or Early Renaissance periods.

ARCHITECTURE

All architectural examples of Classical Eclecticism are monumental in scale and show an academic spirit, while drawing upon various classical traditions, either a specific prototype, a variety of prototypes, or a particular style. Some buildings and interiors reveal no specific prototypes in favor of the designer's or client's personal attitudes or individuality. Four architectural styles develop based upon the prototypes chosen.

■ *Neo-Renaissance*. Architects McKim, Mead, and White initiate the Neo-Renaissance (or Second Renaissance Revival) in the United States with the design of the Villard Houses (Fig. 37-9), six speculative townhouses in New York City. Based on the *Palazzo della Cancelleria* in Rome, a 16th-century palace, the individual townhouses look like a single house. The firm, seeking a style that unifies urban ensembles, finds it in Italian Renaissance palaces, which they and other firms adopt for numerous other buildings along the east coast of the United States.

Like the mid-19th century Renaissance Revival, Neo-Renaissance emulates Italian 16th-century palaces or villas. However, late 19th-century structures are larger in scale and more strongly identified with the originals. Definitive characteristics include rectangular block forms, rusticated lower stories, arched or rectangular openings, quoins, a modillioned cornice, and a flat or low-pitched roof.

■ *Beaux-Arts*. The first examples of Beaux-Arts architecture appear in Europe during the 1860s. The style does not become pervasive until the last two decades of the 19th century and first two decades of the 20th century when Beaux-Arts-trained architects disseminate it to affluent and powerful nations and individuals. In the United States, Beaux-Arts manifests largely on the east coast until the 1893 World's Columbian Exposition in Chicago in which numerous exposition buildings in the style (Fig. 37-4) inspire others across the United States.

Beaux-Arts architecture in all countries aspires to emulate the classical traditions of ancient Rome, the Italian Renaissance, the Baroque, and 17th- and 18th-century France. Examples are more exuberant and highly embellished than other styles. Definitive characteristics include symmetry, a five-part façade with center emphasis, rusticated ground story, smooth stone upper stories, advancing and receding planes, layers of elements especially on corners, paired columns, dramatic skylines, roof balustrades, grand staircases, and lavish ornament that highlights important parts.

DESIGN SPOTLIGHT

Architecture: McKim, Mead, and White's success with the Villard Houses wins the firm the commission for the Boston Public Library. To help unify Copley Square with its colorful Gothic buildings and Richardson's Trinity Church and to express Boston's cultural heritage, Charles Follen McKim chooses a classical Italian Renaissance style. There are few models for a structure that houses the largest circulating library collection in the world, so McKim draws upon several sources. The building is a rectangular block with an open central courtyard. The arched façade of Milford granite recalls *S. Geneviève* (1844–1850) in Paris by Henri Labrouste and *San Francesco* (c. 1450) in Remini, Italy, by Alberti. Above a rusticated basement, arched windows emphasize horizontality and create a regular rhythm across the façade. Patrons enter through one of three arched doorways. A deep cornice and low-pitched, hipped tile roof cap the composition. Many artists collaborate for the interiors, including sculpture by Augustus Saint-Gaudens, bronze doors by Daniel Chester French, mosaics in the vestibule by Maitland Armstrong, and murals by Puvis de Chavannes and Edwin Austin Abbey. [National Historic Landmark]

▲ **37-3.** Boston Public Library, 1888–1892; Boston, Massachusetts; McKim, Mead, and White. Neo-Renaissance.

▲ **37-4.** Administration Building and the Court of Honor, World's Columbian Exposition (White City), 1893; Chicago, Illinois; Richard Morris Hunt. Beaux-Arts.

■ *Neoclassical Revival.* The World's Columbian Exposition plays an important role in initiating not only Beaux-Arts but also the Neoclassical or Classical Revival in the United States because many state pavilions are in the style. Uniquely American, the Neoclassical Revival has few parallels elsewhere in England or Europe.

The Neoclassical Revival emulates either Neoclassical buildings of the 18th and early 19th centuries or the Grecian idiom in the spirit of Greek Revival (Fig. 37-1, 37-8). A quieter alternative to the more embellished and baroque Beaux-Arts, Neoclassical Revival characteristics include symmetry, the Greek orders, rusticated basements, smooth upper stories, flat roofs, porticoes with and without pediments, a balanced rhythm between walls and openings or walls and columns or pilasters, and limited ornament. Some examples closely resemble early Greek Revival types but are grander in scale with a more monumental feeling.

■ *Châteauesque.* Between 1878 and 1880, Richard Morris Hunt designs the first Châteauesque mansion for W. K. Vanderbilt in New York City. Hunt, the first American architect to study at *L'Ecole des Beaux-Arts*, creates the style from his sketches of numerous French *châteaux*, such as Blois and Chambord, in the transitional François I style, which intermingles Gothic and Renaissance. Châteauesque is an expensive style and one requiring design expertise; therefore, the limited number of examples are architect-designed urban or suburban affluent residences. Although too expensive for most people, some Châteauesque features, such as towers with conical roofs, appear in American Queen Anne and later houses. In England, despite the popularity of French interiors and furniture, there are few buildings in the so-called French Châteaux style that copy the French Renaissance. France has a François I Revival somewhat earlier in the 19th century.

Vertical and picturesque, Châteauesque (Fig. 37-11) features asymmetry, smooth stone walls, towers or turrets, pointed- or ogee-arched openings, bay or oriel windows, tracery, hood moldings, multiple wall or roof dormers, and tall and steeply pitched roofs with cresting or spires or pinnacles.

▲ **37-5.** Ritz Hotel, 1906; London, England. Charles Mewès and Arthur Davis. Neo-Renaissance.

Classical Eclecticism in its various manifestations, with the exception of Châteauesque, defines numerous building types including capitols, courthouses, town halls, government buildings (Fig. 37-8, 37-12), libraries (Fig. 37-1, 37-3, 37-13), train stations (Fig. 37-6, 37-15), hotels (Fig. 37-5), symphony halls, clubs, university buildings, memorials, and monuments. Although a few grand hotels are Châteauesque, it is primarily a residential style (Fig. 37-11). Dwellings in all four styles may be townhouses (Fig. 37-9), row houses, apartment buildings, residential hotels, or country houses (Fig. 37-10, 37-11).

Public and Private Buildings

■ *Site Orientation*. Context, grand scale, and comprehensive planning are important to all styles of public and private structures (Fig. 37-2, 37-3, 37-4, 37-7, 37-10, 37-11). Large public buildings with gleaming classical façades become part of urban ensembles that line boulevards or define civic or city centers. A formal, ceremonial approach is important and often characterized by a monumental staircase. Similarly, many residences have ceremonial entries created by curving drives and/or *porte cochères*. Formal gardens with engaging vistas, fountains, *parterres*, sculpture, monuments, and memorials surround both public and private structures.

■ *Floor Plans*. Floor plans (Fig. 37-9) in both public and private buildings are usually symmetrical and organized along axes with clearly defined, hierarchical spaces. Sequencing is important, so public spaces are emphasized. Because circulation spaces are also important, staircases are prominently located (Fig. 37-1, 37-10, 37-13). Rooms may be various shapes, such as circular or elliptical.

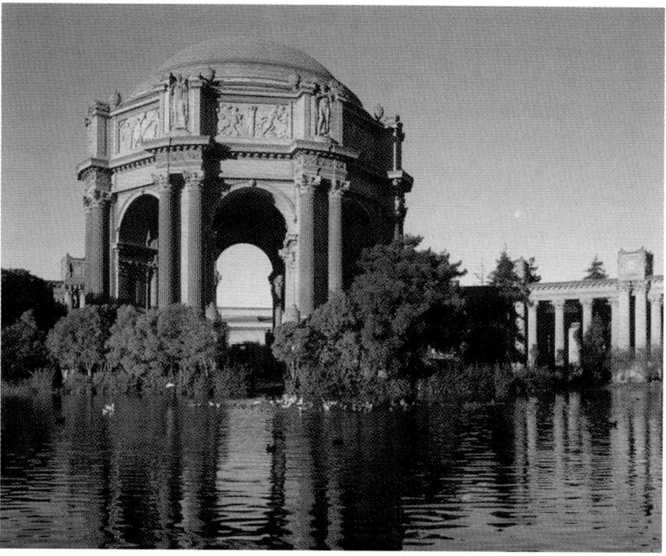

▲ **37-7.** Palace of Fine Arts, Panama Pacific International Exposition, 1913–1915; San Francisco, California; Bernard Maybeck. Beaux-Arts.

■ *Materials*. Buildings are of light-colored masonry such as marble, limestone, or sandstone (Fig. 37-2, 37-3, 37-5, 37-6, 37-8, 37-9, 37-10). Some Châteauesque structures are of darker-colored masonry (Fig. 37-11). A few public and private buildings are of brick. Decorative wrought iron, copper, aluminum, or bronze grilles and other details add embellishment.

▲ **37-6.** Union Station, 1908; Washington, D.C.; Daniel Burnham. Beaux-Arts.

▲ **37-8.** United States Supreme Court, 1935; Washington, D.C.; Cass Gilbert. Neoclassical Revival.

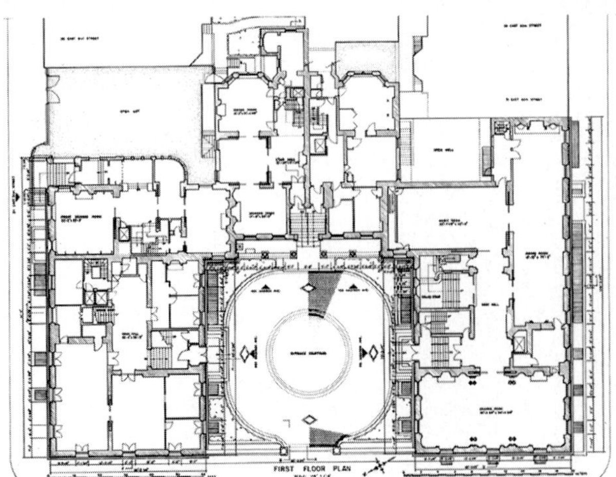

▲ **37-9.** Villard Houses and floor plans, 1882–1885; New York City, New York; McKim, Mead, and White. Neo-Renaissance.

DESIGN SPOTLIGHT

Architecture and Interiors: Designed by Richard Morris Hunt, the new Breakers (Cornelius Vanderbilt House) replaces an earlier wood-framed house that burned in 1892. Hunt's models are 16th-century *palazzos* in Genoa and Turin. Cruciform in shape with projecting porches on each end, the plan centers on a two-story hall. Monumental in scale and richly detailed, the façade facing the sea has arched *loggias* between two pavilions. Engaged columns articulate the pavilions and *loggias*. Other Renaissance details are the arched and rectangular windows, richly detailed friezes, stringcourses, and quoins. Supported by brackets, a low-pitched, hipped roof crowns the composition. This 70-room mansion is the epitome of Beaux-Arts monumental and elegant design. The Vanderbilts use it about six weeks a year, during which time it is a center of life and entertainment for the wealthiest of the wealthy.

The two-story hall has a monumental stairway, lavish finishes, and rich ornamentation. Arched openings separated by colossal Corinthian pilasters on pedestals create a series of vistas. Swags, cartouches, and roundels in various colors of marble embellish the walls around the openings and above the arches. Smaller marble Corinthian columns highlight the upper walkway leading to private rooms. Above a modillioned cornice, a gilded coffered ceiling finishes the composition and adds to the richness of materials and detailing. The French firm of Allard and Sons selects finishes and fixtures. The private family rooms are decorated by Ogden Codman in French Rococo and Louis XVI as in a Lady's bedroom (next page). The room is lavishly furnished with Rococo-style furniture and decorated with a bold damask print used on the walls, curtains, and bed hangings. [National Historic Landmark]

DESIGN SPOTLIGHT

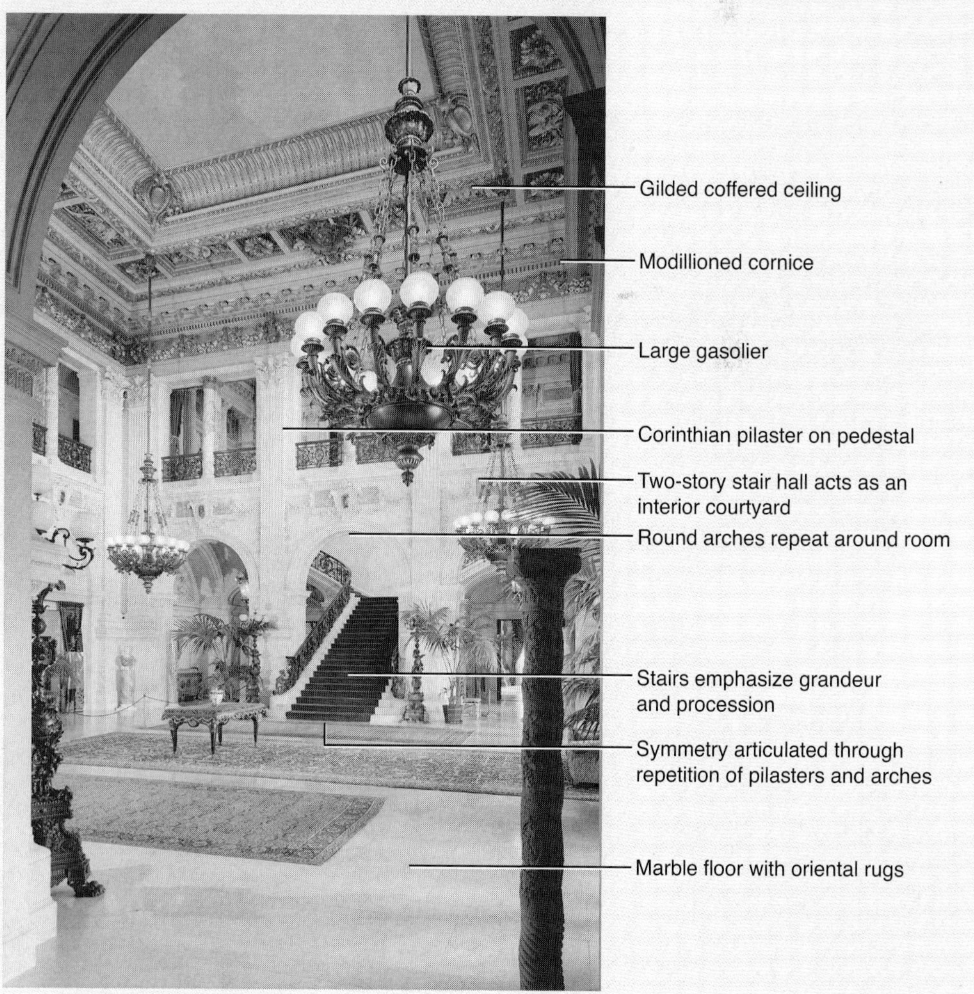

▲ **37-10.** The Breakers (Cornelius Vanderbilt House), stair hall, and a Lady's bedroom (next page), 1892–1895; Newport, Rhode Island; Richard Morris Hunt. Neo-Renaissance.

■ *Façades*. Urbane and dignified, Neo-Renaissance public and private façades (Fig. 37-1, 37-2, 37-3, 37-5, 37-8, 37-9, 37-10) present an image of stately authority through symmetry, horizontality, and classical details. Like their Renaissance models, forms generally are rectangular blocks with few projections, although residences may be U-shaped like Italian villas. Basements or ground stories usually are rusticated. Upper stories are smooth and may diminish in height. The main floor or *piano nobile*, usually the tallest story, has the largest windows and carries the greatest detail, including pediments, pilasters, *aedicula*, and stringcourses. Bold details give three-dimensionality to façades like the prototypes and earlier Renaissance Revival. Openings may be round, rectangular, or a combination, and quoins define corners. A prominent cornice caps the composition. On residences, second-story *loggias* and side porches provide outdoor living spaces.

Beaux-Arts public and many private buildings (Fig. 37-4, 37-6, 37-7) usually have five-part façades composed of pavilions, joining units, and frontispiece. As the climax of the composition, the center or frontispiece is emphasized, often with a dome. Basements, or ground floors, of public and private structures usually are rusticated and upper stories are smooth. Planes may curve or advance and recede, elements may be layered, and corners may feature multiple angles, pilasters, or quoins. Openings are round, rectangular, or a combination of the two. Pairs of columns or pilasters, balconies, and balustrades are common. Sometimes a complete entablature separates stories. Figural sculpture sometimes accents rooflines. Relief sculpture, flowers, foliage, cartouches, swags, and other carved ornament decorate façades and surround or surmount fenestration. Prominent cornices with modillions or balustrades may cap compositions. The image is one of classical, formal exuberance.

Neoclassical Revival façades (Fig. 37-1, 37-8) are plainer with far less ornament and fewer arches than the other styles. Façades exhibit a balance of rhythms in the relationship of wall to window or wall to column or to pilaster. Symmetry, center emphasis, porticos, pediments, temple fronts, and relief sculpture are characteristic. Façades may present an image of heavy solidity, if Grecian, or lightness and delicacy when reflecting Roman or French or English Neoclassical influence.

Châteauesque façades (Fig. 37-11) are asymmetrical, picturesque compositions defined by verticality, complexity, pointed or ogee-arched openings, oriel or bay windows, balconies, towers,

DESIGN SPOTLIGHT

▲ **37-10.** Continued

wall dormers, parapets, and tall chimneys. Some exhibit a nearly classical symmetry and horizontal emphasis with a picturesque roofline.

■ *Windows*. Beaux-Arts windows, whether round or rectangular, are usually lavishly embellished with quoins, lintels, shells, or foliage (Fig. 37-4, 37-6, 37-7). In contrast, Neo-Renaissance and Neoclassical windows have triangular segmental pediments or lintels over them (Fig. 37-9). Round-arched windows are typical on Neo-Renaissance buildings (Fig. 37-2, 37-3, 37-10). Palladian, round, or fan windows may highlight Neo-Renaissance and those Neoclassical Revival buildings influenced by France and England. Some Neoclassical Revival residences have triple sashes like their Greek Revival prototypes. Others have bay windows. Châteauesque windows (Fig. 37-11) often have pointed or ogee-arched tops. Some have hood moldings and stained or colored glass.

■ *Doors*. All styles have prominent entries usually as the climax of a formal, ceremonial approach. Entries, which may be recessed beneath porticoes or porches, feature pilasters, columns, pediments, or arches (Fig. 37-2, 37-3, 37-5, 37-6, 37-8, 37-9, 37-10). Beaux-Arts door surrounds may be composed of engaged columns or pilasters, pediments, or cresting, and entrances have more carved, decorative ornament than the other styles do. Neoclassical Revival structures in North America usually have full-height, full- or partial-width porches carried by colossal or two-story columns (Fig. 37-8). These porches may be rounded or rectangular with pediments. The doorways may have trabeated lights with a balcony above in Greek Revival fashion. Châteauesque-style buildings have pointed arches and cresting (Fig. 37-11). For all styles, doors are wooden and may be carved and stained or painted.

▲ **37-11.** Biltmore Estate and Banqueting Hall, 1890–1895; Asheville, North Carolina; Richard Morris Hunt. Châteauesque.

■ *Roofs*. Neo-Renaissance and Neoclassical Revival buildings usually have flat, gable, or hipped roofs sometimes hidden by a classical balustrade (Fig. 37-2, 37-3, 37-8, 37-9, 37-10). Some Neo-Renaissance examples have tile roofs supported by large brackets. Beaux-Arts residences occasionally have a mansard roof, while domes are common on public buildings (Fig. 37-7). Steeply pitched, hipped roofs; parapets; and wall and roof dormers identify Châteauesque (Fig. 37-11). Towers have conical roofs. Decorative cresting and pinnacles are characteristic.

INTERIORS

Interiors during the period follow two paths: the Aesthetic Movement or Classical Eclecticism. In the 1870s and early 1880s, Aesthetic or Artistic interiors, some of which appear in more classical buildings, show visual complexity through decoration or pattern on all surfaces and free eclecticism, borrowing from past styles and exotic cultures.

Classical Eclecticism in interiors initiates a move toward simplification, which reduces the number of patterns and eliminates clutter. Architectonic interiors reappear as surface decoration, complexity, and contrast are rejected. At the same time, an emphasis on archaeological correctness supplants the random eclecticism and helps create the period room or period-style decoration in which interiors more closely replicate past styles than earlier interior revivals had. Concern for order, balance, excellent proportions, and discipline again becomes important.

Like exteriors, interiors adopting Classical Eclecticism are monumental in scale and inspired by a variety of classical and past traditions. As in architecture, designers and decorators seriously study and hold up as exemplary the best examples of the past. French and Italian Renaissance styles are common choices. The Baroque and Rococo of Versailles and the Neoclassicism of the Petit Trianon are greatly admired, as are the palaces and villas of the Italians. The Louis styles of France (Louis XIV, XV, and XVI), regarded by many as high culture, are much copied (Fig. 37-10, 37-16, 37-17). Architecture, furnishings, painting, and sculpture combine for grand effects. Lavish and expensive materials and finishes demonstrate prosperity, wealth, and culture. In North America, houses of the wealthy incorporate entire rooms or parts of rooms from Europe.

Spatial types respond to function in public buildings. They include entrance lobbies, courtrooms, senate chambers, executive offices, art galleries, library reading rooms, music halls, and restaurants. Staircases and circulation spaces (Fig. 37-12, 37-13, 37-15) are focal points in public and private buildings. Types of rooms in residences include imposing public spaces (Fig. 37-10, 37-11, 37-16), especially drawing and dining rooms; conservatories; galleries to display art collections; clearly defined masculine spaces, such as billiard, smoking, or reading rooms; and feminine spaces (Fig 37-10, 37-18), such as morning rooms, *boudoirs*, or drawing rooms. Gendered spaces visually portray the prevailing idea of separate roles for men and women. Servants' quarters are relegated to separate wings, attics, or basements. Affluent clients demand the latest technology, such as elevators and central heat, and recreational spaces, like bowling alleys and swimming pools. Public rooms are grand with lavish furnishings, while private rooms may be simpler but richly furnished. Built-in closets and richly appointed bathrooms are pervasive in residences.

In keeping with their increased professionalism, architects often control the decoration of interiors, particularly of important buildings or for important people. They may create the designs themselves and supervise designers, artists, sculptors, and others who carry them out, or they may hire firms or individuals for this task. Interiors in public and private buildings are often works of art to which many contribute (Fig. 37-13). Frequently displayed are collections of antiques, paintings, sculpture, manuscripts, and other artifacts.

As in architecture, the wealthy are at the forefront as tastemakers. Like princely patrons of the Renaissance, they have fine homes displaying their affluence, social standing, and erudition. The extravagant and elaborate rooms exhibit their collections and become settings for lavish gatherings and entertainments. They have

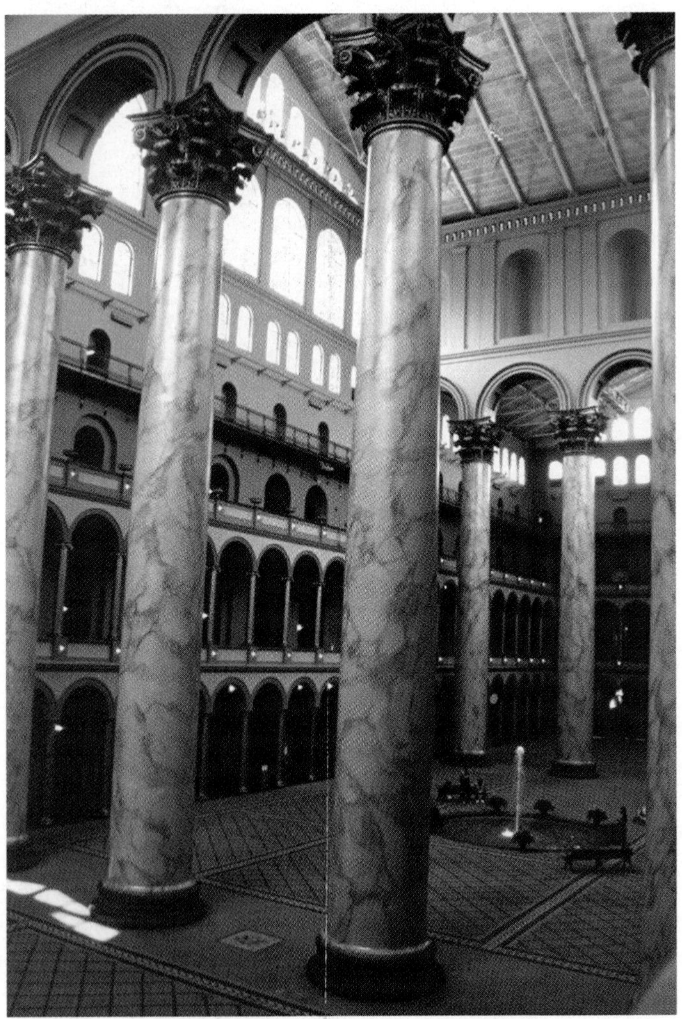

▲ **37-12.** Central Court, Pension Building (National Building Museum), 1882–1887; Washington, D.C.; General Montgomery C. Meigs. Neo-Renaissance.

▲ **37-13.** Great Hall, Library of Congress Building (Jefferson Building), 1897; Washington, D.C.; John L. Smithmeyer and Paul J. Pelz. Neo-Renaissance.

sufficient wealth to use the best Beaux-Arts-trained architects and artists and professional decorating firms. Believing that they have a moral obligation to educate the masses in matters of culture and taste, the wealthy sometimes open their homes to the public or publish them in vanity publications or catalogs. In addition, they are the chief providers of funds and/or collections for public museums.

Classical Eclecticism does not filter down to the middle classes until the first decades of the 20th century, when principles of lavish decoration diminish and less expensive means develop to carry them out. Decorating advice manuals, such as *The Decoration of Houses* (1897) by Edith Wharton and Ogden Codman and *The House in Good Taste* (1913) by Elsie de Wolfe (Fig. 37-17), advance this trend. The authors espouse the importance of careful proportion and simplicity, pale colors, light-scale furniture, and fewer objects. They insist that good taste is bound to past styles, particularly those of France and Italy. Many follow their advice, especially interior decorators who create period-style rooms for their affluent clients.

▲ **37-14.** Trellis Room, The Colony Club, 1906; New York City, New York; Elsie de Wolfe. Neoclassical Revival.

Public and Private Buildings

■ *Color*. Colors return to primary hues away from the tertiary hues of the 1870s. Colors in French rooms vary from the whites, blues, and greens of Rococo and Neoclassical to the rich tones of Baroque (Fig. 37-10, 37-16). Renaissance colors are deep reds, blues, greens, and golds (Fig. 37-13). Gilding covers or highlights many surfaces, including moldings, beams, and door panels.

■ *Floors*. Floors in public buildings are usually masonry, with marble or terrazzo most common (Fig. 37-1, 37-12, 37-13, 37-15). Homes have marble, mosaic, tile, and parquet wood floors. Area rugs include Orientals, Savonnerie, Aubusson, and other hand-woven or hand-knotted types (Fig. 37-10, 37-11, 37-17). Bedrooms and *boudoirs* often have wall-to-wall carpet in solid colors (Fig. 37-10, 37-18).

■ *Walls*. Marble or limestone usually covers the walls in important rooms and circulation spaces in public buildings (Fig. 37-13, 37-15). Alternative treatments include painted murals, wood paneling, or painted plaster. In residences, marble walls also are common in entrances, stair halls (Fig. 37-10), and principal public rooms (Fig. 37-16). Some replicate the colorful geometric marble designs of the French Baroque at Versailles. Wood paneling is used in drawing rooms, dining rooms, libraries, and some bedrooms (Fig. 37-18). For authenticity, antique or new paneling is imported from Europe. Rococo paneling features the curving shapes and foliage of the 18th century, whereas the Neoclassical style has rectangular panels with delicate repeating moldings and classical motifs (Fig. 37-18). Plaster details, such as acanthus leaves and swags, add richness to paneling and walls. Some rooms, including bathrooms, have painted murals by well-known artists. Antique or new leather or imitations may cover dining room or library walls. Tapestries become a popular wall covering during the period (Fig. 37-11). Imported from Europe, they may be antiques or reproductions of old patterns. Their popularity ensures that cheaper forms will soon be available for the middle classes. Bedrooms and *boudoirs* may have wallpapers in large formal floral or textile patterns (Fig. 37-10, 37-19). The middle classes emulate these treatments in a simpler way or with less expensive materials.

Elsie de Wolfe, one of the champions of good taste, pushes lighter, less cluttered, and more modern interiors for public and private buildings. The Trellis Room and her own dining room at Irving House exemplify these principles (Fig. 37-14, 37-17).

▲ **37-16.** Dining room, Marble House, 1892; Newport, Rhode Island; Richard Morris Hunt. Beaux-Arts.

▲ **37-15.** Waiting room, Pennsylvania Railroad Terminal Station, 1906–1910; New York City, New York; McKim, Mead, and White. Beaux-Arts.

■ *Chimneypieces*. Fireplaces vary in design from the hooded examples of the Renaissance to rectangular mantels with columns or caryatids and carved marble over treatments (Fig. 37-11, 37-16).

■ *Windows and Window Treatments*. Window treatments, particularly for public rooms, remain lavish with complicated or swag valances with trims and tassels, under-curtains, and glass curtains (Fig. 37-10). During the 1870s and 1880s, stained glass is an important decorative treatment in public buildings, wealthy homes, department stores, and even Pullman railroad cars. By the end of the century, stained and colored glass becomes common in all homes. Stained glass compositions substitute for draperies in drawing rooms; provide softly colored light in entrances and stair halls; and, with appropriate iconography, give interest and elegance to dining rooms, libraries, and studies. American designers, such as John La Farge and Louis Comfort Tiffany, experiment with ancient glass techniques, opalescent glass, multiple layers of glass, and adding different materials such as gold. Stained glass soon takes on never-before-imagined depth of shading, variety of textures, and multiplicity of tones, becoming itself a work of art.

■ *Doors*. As important elements, single and double doors to principal rooms have elaborate surrounds composed of moldings, engaged columns, pilasters, pediments, entablatures, and fancy over-door compositions of swags, cherubs, flowers, shells, and the like (Fig. 37-18). Doors are wood panels that may be stained or painted to match the rooms. *Portières* are universal early in the period but gradually decline in use.

■ *Ceilings*. Ceiling treatments vary and include painted murals, beams, coffers, and plaster designs (Fig. 37-10, 37-11, 37-12, 37-13, 37-14, 37-15, 37-16). All may have carving, painted decoration, and gilding.

■ *Textiles*. In the 1880s, textiles cover every available surface from mantels to wall shelves. By the turn of the century, this trend fades, so rooms display fewer textiles. Used for wall treatments, window treatments, and upholstery are damasks; brocades; velvets; plush; tapestry; lampas; silk; satin; cashmere; and, in lesser rooms, elaborately patterned cretonne or highly polished chintz (Fig. 37-10, 37-18).

■ *Lighting*. Gas lighting is common, but newly introduced electric lighting rapidly increases in use during the period. Some fixtures combine electricity and gas because of the limitations of both. Types include chandeliers and sconces with cut-glass prisms, and brass and glass ceiling lights, sconces, and lamps (Fig. 37-1, 37-10, 37-11, 37-14, 37-15, 37-17, 37-18, 37-20). Some fixtures reproduce earlier lighting fixtures or are antique ones that are wired for electricity.

■ *Later Interpretations*. During the late 20th century, some Classical Eclectical interiors are redesigned for new uses, such as the original rooms in the Villard Houses converted into bars and restaurants (Fig. 37-21). In other instances, designers borrow from the period influences to create new interpretations for hotels, restaurants, and other hospitality environments.

DESIGN SPOTLIGHT

Interior: In the redecoration of the rooms in Irving House between 1898 and 1909, Elsie de Wolfe transforms them from dark, cluttered Victorian spaces into lighter, less cluttered, and simpler ones. She says in *The House in Good Taste* that "light, air, and comfort" are the most important elements in a room and emphasizes them here. In the drawing room and dining room, she eliminates chests, tables, plants, and bric-a-brac, including the 19th-century Turkish corner of the drawing room with its layers of fabrics, pillows, and pictures. In both spaces, she lightens the color schemes, using the rose, cream and pale yellow of the area rug in the drawing room and a more urbane gray, white, and ivory in the dining room. Ms. de Wolfe chooses French furniture for both spaces because she believes it conveys sophistication, dignity, and graciousness. The Louis XV furniture in the drawing room gives it a lighter, more feminine air. The Louis XVI chairs with cane backs and lightweight frames painted ivory in the dining room convey simplicity and lightness, unlike the former dark, heavy furniture. The other dining room pieces—additional chairs, the table, and *console*—are different 18th-century styles, but they have the lightness and simplicity of the Louis XVI chairs. The dining room, like the drawing room, has very few decorative accessories. Mirrors, which add sparkle to the room, frame the doors and cupboards and are unusual and decorative elements. Electric wall sconces, which are mounted on mirrors, replace the gasolier over the table. An old Chinese rug in rose with blue and gold medallions and border complements the design.

▲ **37-17.** Dining room, Irving House, c. 1898–1909; New York City, New York; Elsie de Wolfe; published in *The House in Good Taste*, by Elsie de Wolfe, 1911, 1913. Neoclassical Revival.

▲ **37-18.** Bedroom, Mar-a-Lago, c. 1920s–1930s; Palm Beach, Florida. Louis XVI influence/Neoclassical Revival.

▲ **37-19.** Wallpapers in period patterns, c. 1900–1930s; Tennessee and Texas.

(a) (b)

▲ **37-20.** Lighting: (a) Lamp and (b) floor lamp, c. 1870s–1910s; New York and Rhode Island.

▲ **37-21.** Later Interpretation: Bar, Le Cirque 2000, Palace Hotel, (Villard Houses), 1996–2004; New York City, New York; Adam Tihany. Renovation and Redecoration.

FURNISHINGS AND DECORATIVE ARTS

Classical Eclecticism gives rise to period styles that will dominate popular furnishings throughout the early 20th century. Furniture is most often large in scale, formal, majestic, and carved or painted to suit a specific room. Many public and private rooms are filled with antique and reproduction furniture that follows French Renaissance, Baroque, Rococo, Neoclassical, Italian Renaissance, and Venetian Baroque (Fig. 37-11, 37-16, 37-22). In private rooms, styles in a more human scale are fashionable, including the French styles of Rococo, Neoclassic, and Empire and the English styles of Chippendale, Adam, Hepplewhite, and Sheraton (Fig. 37-10, 37-17, 37-18, 37-23, 37-24). Suites of furniture are common, although some rooms may mix a variety of styles for a more individual look (Fig. 37-10, 37-18). Often supplied by decorating firms, furniture in homes of the affluent may be designed specifically for the room it occupies. Decorative techniques include ebonizing, inlay of many types of materials, carving, gilding, and

▲ **37-22.** Cabinet with ebony inlay, exhibited at the Philadelphia Centennial, 1879; manufactured by S. Coco in Italy. Neo-Renaissance.

painting. A variety of upholstery fabrics adds color and pattern. This period witnesses the rise of the antique trade in much of Europe and America. Antique dealers and art gallery owners often offer suggestions for interior decoration along with architects, upholsterers, cabinetmakers and furniture houses, department stores, and interior decorators.

■ *Decorative Arts*. The wealthy display their collections of art or sculpture in special galleries or in important rooms in residences. Large mirrors with lavishly embellished and gilded frames hang over the mantel or on walls between windows (Fig. 37-17). The mantel usually holds a large clock flanked by *candelabra* or porcelain vases (Fig. 37-17, 37-25). In 1893, the World's Columbian Exposition in Chicago highlights art and handicraft by women, such as Candace Wheeler, and includes embroidery, decorative screens, vases, and other decorative objects. These items are usually prominently displayed in public and private interiors.

Along with these decorative arts, gigantic floral arrangements highlight the entry hall and drawing rooms (Fig. 37-10). Also on display are porcelains, large silver or brass pieces, and elaborate cut glass. Between 1880 and 1914, America leads the world in cut glass production. Known as Brilliant Cut Glass, glass of the period features deep cuts, curving lines, and elaborate patterns. It is made of lead glass, and the high cost of crafting it makes it a luxury item that only the wealthy can afford. Sets of glassware and tableware are popular items of conspicuous consumption.

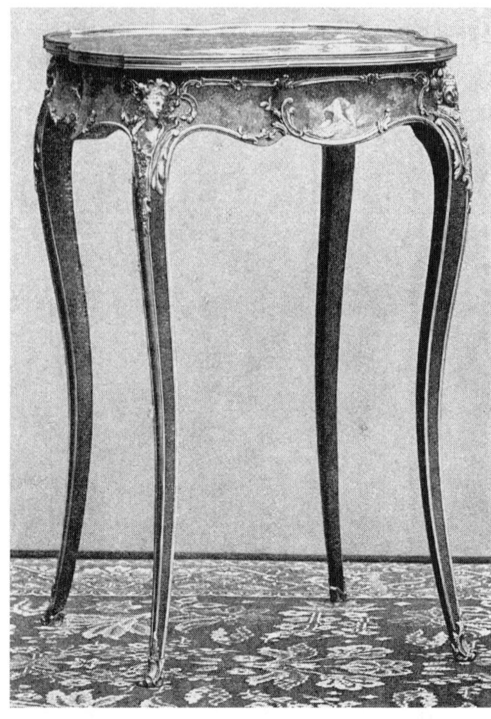

▲ **37-23.** Table in Louis XV style; published in *Art and Handicraft in the Women's Building of the World's Columbian Exposition,* 1893; Chicago, Illinois; decoration by Mme. Gabrielle Nieter, France.

▲ **37-24.** Twin beds; published in *The Practical Book of Furnishing the Small House and Apartment,* 1922. Neoclassical Revival.

▲ **37-25.** Polychrome painted vase; published in *Art and Handicraft in the Women's Building of the World's Columbian Exposition,* 1893; Chicago, Illinois; made in France by Mme. E. Apoil.

CHAPTER 38

Colonial Revival

1880s–1930s

> *Within the last decade, however, there has been an increasingly noticeable swing back to American furniture and American styles. This is partly due to the revival of nationalism that came after the world war and to a widespread desire to build into our surroundings the qualities that we consider purely "American."*
>
> —Nancy McClelland, *Furnishing the Colonial and Federal House*, 1936

Originating in the second half of the 19th century in the United States, Colonial Revival consciously strives to emulate the architecture, interiors, furniture, and decorative arts of English and Dutch settlements in North America. The style adapts elements from America's colonial past to contemporary lifestyles. Conveying associations of heritage, patriotism, and anti-modernism, the style rapidly becomes fashionable first among the wealthy and then the middle class. Colonial Revival is one of the most enduring of all styles, even maintaining popularity today.

HISTORICAL AND SOCIAL

Throughout its long history, Colonial Revival consciously attempts to imitate, but not necessarily copy, the architecture, interiors, and furnishings of the 17th, 18th, and early 19th centuries. Its character and appearance come from the material culture of the English and the Dutch colonists in North America from the first settlements up to about 1840. The American Georgian image is the one that is most often repeated in Colonial Revival, although Federal-style architecture, interiors, and furniture also are common. The revival occasionally relies on the 17th century for inspiration. Colonial Revival examples often mix attributes from several different periods and differ in design to accommodate modern lifestyles, materials, and technology.

In some parts of North America, particularly New England, 17th- and 18th-century styles never really die out. People continue to live in, build, and furnish houses in the styles of their ancestors. Colonial Revival has roots in nationalism, the Picturesque Movement, and a greater interest in the nation's history beginning in the early 19th century. Some of the early United States histories focus upon events, heroes, founding fathers and mothers, other important people, and their material culture. During the 1860s, newspapers and magazines carry stories about the colonial past and colonial towns, such as Newport, Rhode Island, which are often filled with picturesque illustrations. New England areas soon become fashionable sites for seaside vacations. The articles, along with fiction writers such as Washington Irving, begin to create an imaginary golden age filled with warm and cozy houses and fine people. At the same time, an antiquing craze leads some to scour the countryside for old furniture and other so-called relics of the past.

Often considered the initial and main impetus for the Colonial Revival, the 1876 Centennial Exhibition in Philadelphia acknowledges the past, but its main theme is progress, and it focuses more on modern inventions. Nevertheless, some colonial artifacts are exhibited, and several exhibition halls, such as the

Connecticut Pavilion, are vaguely Colonial in style. One of the most popular exhibits is the New England kitchen, which is inside a log cabin and features a real New England dinner served by ladies in colonial costumes. However, much of the importance of the exhibition lies beforehand in the articles and stories about colonial times, the founding fathers, and the Revolution that appear in popular periodicals; the local celebrations and expressions of ancestry, such as Martha Washington teas and colonial balls; and plays that occur around the country.

Contemporary architectural and design movements, such as Queen Anne and Arts and Crafts, also provide additional impetus for American designers to examine the English Colonial past, particularly on the East Coast. By the 1870s, following the lead of their English counterparts in the Queen Anne movement, American architects and builders in New England begin exploring their Colonial and/or vernacular heritage. Examples of 17th- and 18th-century architecture in professional publications, such as the *American Architect and Building News*, inspire designs by architects. A few, such as Charles Follen McKim of McKim, Mead, and White, remodel houses from the Colonial period. Colonial Revival in this period is largely architect-designed residences for the wealthy.

Beginning in the final decade of the 19th century, knowledge about Colonial architecture and design becomes available from an array of publications, including *Old Colonial Architecture and Furniture* (1887) and *American Architecture, Decoration, and Furniture* (1895) by Frank E. Wallis; *The Georgian Period* (1898) by William Rotch Ware; *Colonial Furniture in America* (1901) by Luke Vincent Lockwood; *Domestic Architecture of the American Colonies and of the Early Republic* (1922) by Fiske Kimball; *Furniture Treasury* (1933, 1949) by Wallace Nutting; *American Furniture* (1952) by Joseph Downs; Sears, Roebuck, and Company catalogs (c. 1910s); and *House Beautiful* and *House and Garden* magazines.

After the Centennial, the collecting of antique furniture and ceramics, especially blue and white china, increases (Fig. 38-1). By the first decades of the 20th century, individual collectors, such as Henry Francis DuPont in Delaware and Ima Hogg in Texas, are amassing large collections of American interiors, furniture, and decorative arts. Both will later open their homes, Winterthur and Bayou Bend, respectively, to visitors. Additionally, American museums, such as the Metropolitan Museum of Art in New York City, also begin collecting and exhibiting colonial artifacts, signaling their approval of the American past.

During the first decades of the 20th century, Colonial becomes a tool for simplifying the Victorian house with its multiplicity of styles, furniture, and bric-a-brac. Decorating magazines of the time use the term *Modern Colonial* to describe Colonial-style houses. Although visual qualities come from America's Colonial, Georgian, and Federal periods, the planning, layouts, and decoration emphasize simplicity, function, and efficiency, which reflect modern lifestyles and health concerns. Examples differ from the earlier precursors in size, proportion, and planning, resulting in buildings with open plans, more daylight, and up-to-date kitchens and bathrooms. By 1920, the Colonial Revival has its own aesthetic and becomes increasingly popular with the middle class (Fig. 38-8, 38-14). The style also occupies a prominent place in the period house and period decoration trends as practiced by architects, interior decorators, historians, and home owners of the time.

By the mid-20th century, the Colonial or Early American, as it is sometimes called, again becomes a traditional and American style that contrasts with Modernism, which is sweeping the nation. This antithesis lessens as the century progresses. With the advent of eclecticism in design from the 1970s onward, Modernism and the Colonial more comfortably coexist as expressions of personal taste.

As a style and a phenomenon, Colonial Revival is often complex and contradictory as it affects nearly all aspects of American life and material culture. Its enduring popularity comes from its associations as an American style; its reflection of American views and lifestyles; and its ability to adapt to changing fashions, times, and technologies. No matter how it changes, it still provides a sense of place, tradition, ancestry, and heritage along with an expression of personal taste.

■ *Colonial Revival and the Historic Preservation Movement.* Colonial Revival also occupies a prominent place in and contributes to the historic preservation movement in the United States. Although some efforts occur earlier, activity increases in the second half of the 19th century when preservation of the past begins to merit serious consideration by individuals and private

▲ **38-1.** "Grandmother's Cupboard"; published in *The House Beautiful*, 1878, by Clarence Cook.

groups. Women comprise many of the groups, such as the Mount Vernon Ladies Association and the Daughters of the American Revolution (DAR). In this early period, buildings are preserved and restored primarily because of their associations with founding fathers and mothers, rather than any aesthetic or other considerations.

By the early 20th century, scrutiny of colonial art and times stimulates preservation of the buildings, not only because of association, but also because of their artistic value. Groups, like the Society for the Preservation of New England Antiquities (now Historic New England) led by William Sumner Appleton, begin developing preservation plans and processes to more accurately protect and restore original historic buildings and materials. In the late 1920s, William Archer Rutherford Goodwin and John D. Rockefeller come together to restore Colonial Williamsburg (Fig. 38-3) in Virginia. A team of architects, engineers, archaeologists, historians, and furniture experts succeeds in carrying out the first and largest attempt in the United States to preserve and re-create an entire community. Their work affects the preservation movement for decades to come. An unanticipated effect is the huge public interest in the project as a model for home design and furnishing. Following the official opening of Williamsburg in 1934, the reproduction of Colonial-style furniture, historical wallpapers, fabrics, and decorative objects accelerates. During this period, interiors in museums and restorations reflect Colonial Revival more often than actual interior and furnishing practices.

CONCEPTS

From the mid-19th century onward, many see Colonial Revival as symbolizing America's heritage through a spirit of nationalism within the context of tradition and middle-class values. Colonial times are regarded as simpler and more stable, and Colonial people are believed to be finer in character and taste. These ideas are a response, in part, to the sweeping social and cultural changes brought by the Industrial Revolution and resulting decline in design and taste that alarm designers, reformers, and others. Supporters believe that living in Colonial-style houses will engender the same admirable qualities of the Colonial ancestors in contemporary people. This reverence for ancestors, as a reaction to the influx of immigrants and increased nationalism, causes many, particularly in New England, to build and furnish in the Colonial style to tangibly demonstrate their heritage and separate themselves from newcomers. By the end of the 19th century, Colonial Revival becomes firmly established as an American style that adapts to current ways of thinking about the home and the nation as well as trends in architecture and design.

CHARACTERISTICS AND MOTIFS

Colonial Revival houses, interiors, furniture and decorative arts adopt or adapt the types, forms, arrangements, ornament, and motifs from English Colonial (1608–1720), Dutch Colonial (17th–19th centuries), American Georgian (1700s–1780s), and American Federal (1780s–1820). Examples often mix attributes from several different periods and differ in design to accommodate modern lifestyles, materials, and technology. For example, Colonial house types used as modern houses often have larger windows; rooms unknown in the period, such as the living room; modern kitchens and bathrooms; and garages or carports. Similarly, interiors and furniture usually display characteristics of earlier examples but differ in materials and forms, or they may have been unknown in earlier times. Decoration, which comes from precedents, is usually simpler and different in proportion. It often combines elements from different periods. Colonial Revival inspires adaptations and reproductions of period artifacts and finishes. To accommodate contemporary use and conveniences, adaptations may alter scale, proportions, materials, construction techniques, colors, uses, details, and motifs. In contrast, reproductions copy as closely as possible, within the limitations or abilities of modern technology, a historical prototype, which can be a house, interior, piece of furniture, textile, or floor or wall covering. (However, some late-19th- and early-20th-century uses of the term *reproduction* do not fit this definition.)

■ *Motifs*. Motifs come from precedents, but they may be simplified with less detail (Fig. 38-1, 38-2, 38-5, 38-6, 38-8, 38-22). Examples include columns, pilasters, pediments, engaged columns, lintels, stringcourses, quoins, urns, acanthus leaves, shells, rosettes, palmettes, and eagles.

ARCHITECTURE

Some of the earliest Colonial Revival examples are an outgrowth of architects' investigations of New England's 17th-century buildings. McKim, Mead, and White undertake a sketching trip through New England in 1877. Soon after, they design broad interpretations of 17th-century houses and conduct restorations of 18th-century houses in Newport, Rhode Island. Other architects, such as Arthur Little and Robert Peabody, follow suit as they explore

▲ **38-2.** West Virginia State Building, World's Columbian Exposition, 1893; Chicago, Illinois; J. S. Silsbee.

the vernacular past emulating English architects in the Queen Anne style (1880–1910s) and the regionalism promoted by the Arts and Crafts Movement (1870s–1900). By the 1880s, with the influence of Classical Eclecticism and greater knowledge of precedents, high-style houses begin to more closely imitate their Georgian and Federal predecessors, although they are more eclectic and sometimes larger in scale than the originals. As before, these examples are designed by architects, such as the firm of McKim, Mead, and White (Fig. 38-4) and architect–designer Ogden Codman, for the affluent in New England and the Mid-Atlantic. Also evident during the period are Queen Anne and Shingle houses with Colonial details in the same areas of the country.

By the beginning of the 20th century, scholarship and new printing methods, which permit the wider distribution of photographs,

▲ **38-4.** H. A. C. Taylor House, 1886; Newport, Rhode Island; McKim, Mead, and White.

DESIGN SPOTLIGHT

Architecture: The Governor's Palace in Colonial Williamsburg is a result of accumulated efforts of scholarship to present an accurate depiction of a historically significant building. Begun in 1706 and finally completed in 1751, the house was intended to be a visual metaphor for the king's immediate representative in the most important capital of England's largest American colony. Two stories with prominent entrance and a tall, hipped roof with cupola distinguish the building. It is flanked by smaller dependencies and surrounded at the rear by formal gardens and a naturalistic park to the north. Upon entering the iron gates, visitors follow a carefully planned succession of spaces across the courtyard, into the building, and up the steps to the governor's chamber. Elaborately furnished as befits its purpose and status, the palace is the scene of elegant balls and other festivities until it is destroyed by fire in 1781. After the Civil War, the property passes to the College of William and Mary.

Colonial Williamsburg purchases the property in 1928. The Governor's Palace is reconstructed accurately from a copperplate engraving found in England in 1929, a floor plan drawn by Thomas Jefferson in 1779, Virginia General Assembly records, and foundations of the original building uncovered in archaeological investigations. Some elements, such as the coats of arms, are conjecture. As an important first step, the palace fosters more work in the historic section of the city and supports more research and documentation of the architecture, interiors, furnishings, and decorative arts of Colonial Williamsburg.

▲ **38-3.** Governor's Palace, 1705–1749, reconstruction in 1930s; Williamsburg, Virginia.

DESIGN SPOTLIGHT

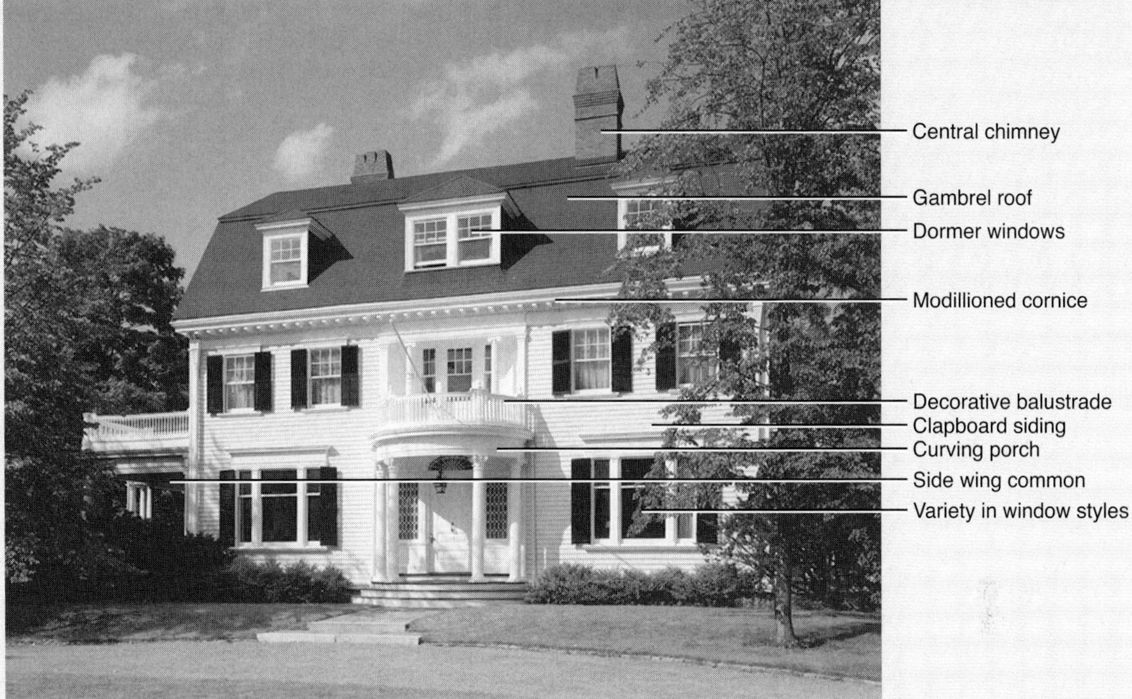

Architecture and Interior: One of the earliest Colonial Revival houses in Boston, the Annie Longfellow Thorpe house displays typical Colonial-style features. From precursors of several periods are symmetry, clapboards, gambrel roof with dormers, prominent entrance, projecting semicircular porch, doorway accented with fanlight and sidelights, and modillioned cornice defining the roofline. The house is larger and differs in proportions, particularly in the entrance porch and other details, from Colonial examples. Signals of Colonial Revival are the side porch (with *porte cochère* beyond), picture windows on the first floor, windows on the second story with single-pane lower and multipane upper sashes, prominent recessed picture windows above the front door, and wide sidelights flanking the door. Designed by Alexander Wadsworth Longfellow, family ties and the nearby Longfellow House (1759) underlie this conscious emulation of earlier architecture.

Staircases, such as this one in the hall, include elements from the precursors freely interpreted. Although many 18th-century houses had center halls, none is as broad as this one or has such wide openings, which reflect a late-19th-century preference for open planning. The staircase is made grander than was usual in the 18th century by centering it at the rear of the hall just beneath an arch. Arches like these commonly delineated front and back portions of 18th-century halls. The stair rises to a landing and splits with steps to the right and the left in a manner that was not usual in the American Georgian house. The elaborate newel post and banisters have 18th-century precedents. Large Oriental rugs on floors were rare in the 18th century.

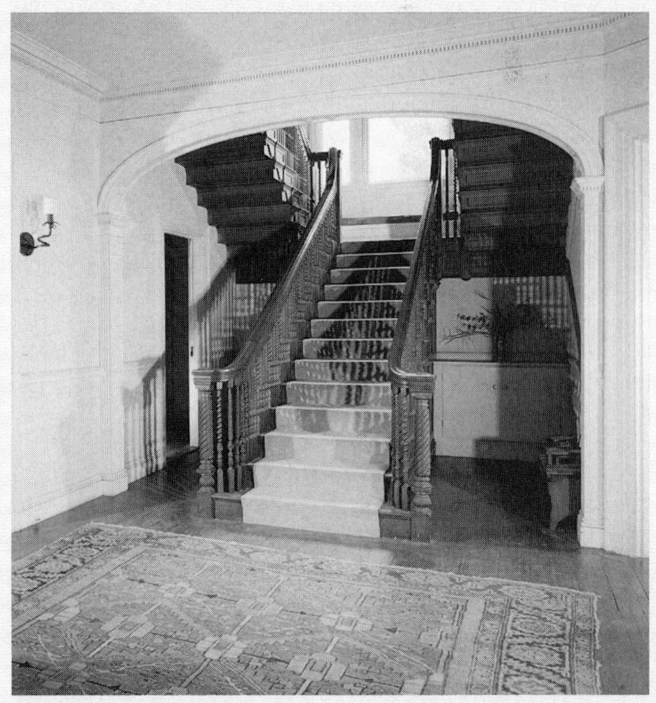

▲ **38-5.** Annie Longfellow Thorpe House and stair hall, 1887; Cambridge, Massachusetts; Alexander Wadsworth Longfellow.

▲ **38-6.** James W. Allison House (now known as the President's House, Virginia Commonwealth University), 1895–1896; Richmond, Virginia; Percy Griffin and Henry Randall.

foster designs with more correct proportions and details. Frequent publication of plans and designs for professional and popular audiences ensures wide dissemination (Fig. 38-7, 38-10). Subsequently, anonymous builders begin producing houses for middle-class suburbs (Fig. 38-8, 38-11), which proliferate throughout North America, especially in the building boom of the 1920s.

Colonial Revival adapts well to a variety of building types and sizes from small houses to large mansions. Although houses are the most common expression of Colonial Revival (Fig. 38-4, 38-5, 38-6, 38-7, 38-8, 38-10, 38-11), the style is used for exposition buildings (Fig. 38-2), civic buildings, banks, schools, and even gas stations. The most common, but not the only, house type found in Colonial Revival is the double-pile or Georgian rectangular block with center hall floor plan (Fig. 38-11). Particularly suitable for small houses is the adaptation of the 17th-century small, single-story house into the Cape Cod house. Appearing about 1910 is the Dutch Colonial house identified by its gambrel roof. There also are Colonial Revival bungalows and four-squares.

Public and Private Buildings

■ *Site Orientation*. Buildings do not replicate the surroundings of the originals. Houses may sit along quiet, tree-lined suburban streets and even form complete subdivisions (Fig. 38-6, 38-7). Commercial buildings may have large areas of formal green space (Fig. 38-3).

■ *Floor Plans*. Plans for public buildings do not replicate similar originals because the originals are more domestic in scale. Instead, public buildings develop from function and contemporary requirements. Exterior designs may reflect interior plans. House plans (Fig. 38-9) often are open and asymmetrical and do not always support the delineation of the architectural envelope. The earliest plans for Colonial-style houses have the living halls and openness of Queen Anne and Shingle styles. Later examples are likely to have variations of the Georgian plan with center halls (Fig. 38-5) that may be straight or L-shaped with rooms in various sizes and shapes on either side. Prominent stairways are typical but vary in scale and design depending on the house size and importance. Level changes may also occur on the first floor as in mid-century split-level houses. Most houses before World War I have one-story loggias or side porches on one or both sides (Fig. 38-5, 38-7, 38-8), which become outdoor living or sleeping areas to promote health and well-being and assist in the transition of inside to outside space. During this time, a single large living room replaces the front and rear Victorian parlors, reflecting the trend toward fewer rooms and multipurpose spaces. Dining rooms have direct access to serving areas and kitchens. Service areas, such as the kitchen, often are located in an ell on the rear of the house.

■ *Materials*. Brick, stone, and wood are typical, but new materials such as concrete block and stucco may be featured (Fig. 38-3, 38-4, 38-5, 38-6, 38-7, 38-8, 38-10, 38-11). Wood may be painted white or the traditional colors promoted in Williamsburg or non-Colonial palettes. The most common color scheme is a white body with dark green shutters.

■ *Façades*. Buildings reflect symmetry or asymmetry; combine details from several styles; and incorporate one, one and a half, two, or three stories (Fig. 38-4, 38-5, 38-6, 38-7, 38-8, 38-10, 38-11).

▲ **38-7.** House; Newport, Rhode Island; Aymar Embury II; published in *Inexpensive Homes*, 1912. Dutch Colonial.

▲ **38-8.** "A Colonial Home at Oaklane, Pa."; Pennsylvania; published in *House Beautiful*, October 1913.

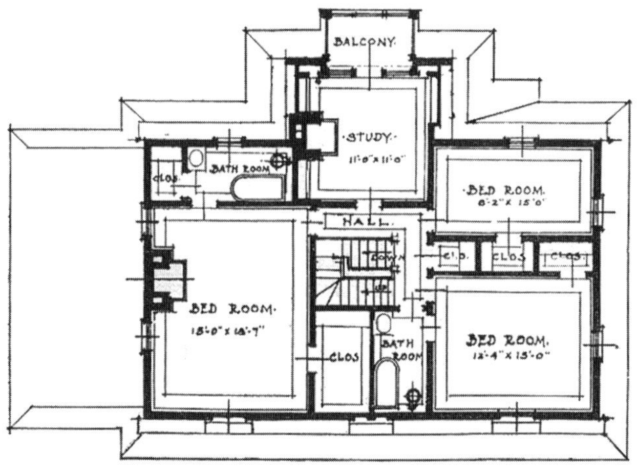

SECOND FLOOR PLAN

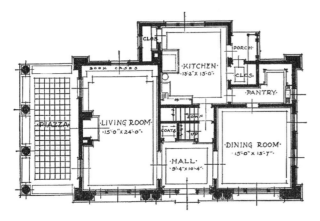

FIRST FLOOR PLAN

▲ **38-9.** Floor plans for house, c. 1920s–1930s; Virginia.

Some examples have front gables; smaller houses tend to have side gables (Fig. 38-8). Formal façades are symmetrical with projecting centers capped with a pediment or small entry porches (Fig. 38-2, 38-5, 38-6, 38-7, 38-8, 38-11). Architectural details include columns, pilasters, pediments, engaged columns, lintels, stringcourses, quoins, modillioned cornices, balustrades, and decorative brickwork. A defining feature for the style is the cornice separating wall and roof with dentils or modillions. The open eaves and exposed rafters on some Colonial Revival buildings are never found on the precursors. Full- and partial-width front porches may be on four-squares and Dutch Colonials. Some make a distinction between the Colonial Revival and the Georgian Revival (Fig. 38-11). Buildings emulating English Georgian are larger and more formal than Colonial Revivals and may incorporate elements and details associated with the Italian Renaissance. Most are of brick or stone with a projecting center that may have a pediment and quoins. Stringcourses separate stories, and quoins highlight corners.

■ *Windows*. Double-hung windows emulate precursors, except in the variety of pane patterns and sizes. Types never seen on the originals include sashes with multipane uppers and single-pane lowers, double and triple windows, picture windows, and bay and bow windows (Fig. 38-4, 38-5, 38-6, 38-7, 38-8, 38-10, 38-11). Larger buildings may have oval, round, fan, or Palladian windows like the originals. Lintels, moldings, or pediments may surmount windows on larger, affluent houses. Shutters frame most windows.

■ *Doors*. Doorways are a defining feature of the style and most often resemble Georgian or Federal prototypes (Fig. 38-5, 38-6,

▲ **38-10.** "The Martha Washington," 1921–1937; model home manufactured by Sears, Roebuck & Company in Chicago, Illinois.

▲ **38-11.** Houses, c. 1930s; Virginia.

38-8, 38-10, 38-11). Most common are paneled doors topped by fanlights and flanked by sidelights, sometimes with a projecting rectangular or circular porch with Tuscan, Ionic, or Corinthian columns. Somewhat rare on the originals, full or broken triangular and segmental pediments are common on expensive Colonial-style buildings and may be combined with fanlights. High-style or architect-designed buildings often have formal, ceremonial entrances approached through sweeping exterior staircases. Doorway surrounds are bolder and more elaborate.

■ *Roofs*. Common roofs are gable, hipped, or gambrel (Fig. 38-4, 38-5, 38-6, 38-7, 38-8, 38-10, 38-11). The latter characterize Dutch Colonials.

■ *Later Interpretations*. Following World War II, a need for housing and changing fashion dictates a simpler Colonial Revival house with form and details that only suggest its origins. Colonial elements and simple details appear on ranch houses and split-level houses in numerous suburban developments across North America. Also popular is a variation of the 17th-century jettied house in which the upper story, usually in a different material, overhangs the lower. Late-20th-century Colonial houses continue these forms and revive the larger mansions of early Colonial Revival (Fig. 38-12). Commercial buildings also continue to reflect America's love for Colonial and Georgian design.

▲ **38-12.** Later Interpretation: Suburban house, 1990s; North Carolina. Modern Historicism/Suburban Modern and Regionalism.

INTERIORS

As with the exteriors, the interiors rely on historical precedents, but they do not copy the originals except in museum restorations. Even then, early restorations are more romantic than authentic because they are often based upon imagination and extant interiors with their layers of uses and change. Throughout much of its history, Colonial-style interior decoration and treatments come from popular notions of Colonial lifestyles rather than any real understanding of them. Consequently, most interiors maintain a Colonial flavor in keeping with the exterior design. Larger and more formal Colonial Revival interiors beginning in the early 20th century often are created by designers and professional decorators. They base their work on classical ideas, including the importance of an axis, exterior and interior harmony, symmetry and order, careful proportions, and authentic architectural details. The middle class favors Colonial interiors that capture the spirit of the Colonial while retaining contemporary amenities such as asymmetrical furniture groupings, larger-scaled spaces, larger windows, and higher ceilings. No room types are particularly associated with Colonial Revival because plans follow contemporary developments, such as the addition of the living room. However, *keeping room* becomes a popular term for an informal room with a large fireplace in the 17th-century manner that may be combined with a kitchen.

In the 1930s, Colonial Williamsburg inspires somewhat more authentic 18th-century houses and interior decorations. Manufacturers quickly market house plans, architectural elements, wallpapers, paint, textiles, rugs, furniture, and decorative accessories either copied or adapted from period resources. Also during this time, the Early American room appears. Loosely based upon 17th-century and/or vernacular sources, Early American rooms are casual alternatives to the more formal 18th-century Colonial or Georgian. Colonial Revival does not commonly appear in kitchens or baths until very late in the period. Because of the absence of servants in middle-class houses, kitchens are likely to be simple and efficient, reflect scientific planning, and incorporate progressive technology. Baths, too, follow this trend, emphasizing the importance of hygiene with easily cleaned fixtures and materials.

Public and Private Buildings

■ *Color*. Colors either loosely follow precedents or the color trends of their time (Fig. 38-13, 38-17). Light colors, such as ivory, white, gray, or yellow, dominate in the 1920s. A grayed palette of tans, browns, yellows, blues, greens, and reds copied from existing 18th-century colors becomes fashionable following the restoration of Williamsburg in the 1930s. White appears extensively during the early 20th century, reflecting a concern for hygienic interiors.

■ *Floors*. Floors (Fig. 38-5, 38-13, 38-14, 38-15, 38-17), based loosely on earlier treatments, are wood planks, usually in a dark stain. Oriental rugs, although rare on floors in Colonial periods, are typical. Alternatives, some of which are unknown in early times, include braided rugs, rag rugs, rugs with simple floral or geometric patterns, unpatterned rugs, wall-to-wall carpeting, and linoleum.

■ *Walls*. Paneling, wallpaper, and paint are the most common treatments in Colonial-style houses like the precursors (Fig. 38-5, 38-13, 38-14, 38-17). In larger, more expensive Colonial and Georgian houses, interiors follow 18th-century prototypes more closely with paneling, moldings, baseboards, and cornices deriving from precursors. Paneling may be stained or painted. A less expensive alternative to paneling consists of moldings applied to the wall to simulate panels. Architectural details and moldings often contrast in color to walls. Wallpapers in old-fashioned or Colonial-style patterns also are favored (Fig. 38-16). Reproductions and adaptations of Colonial wallpapers appear beginning in the 1890s. They have a range of patterns from small geometrics

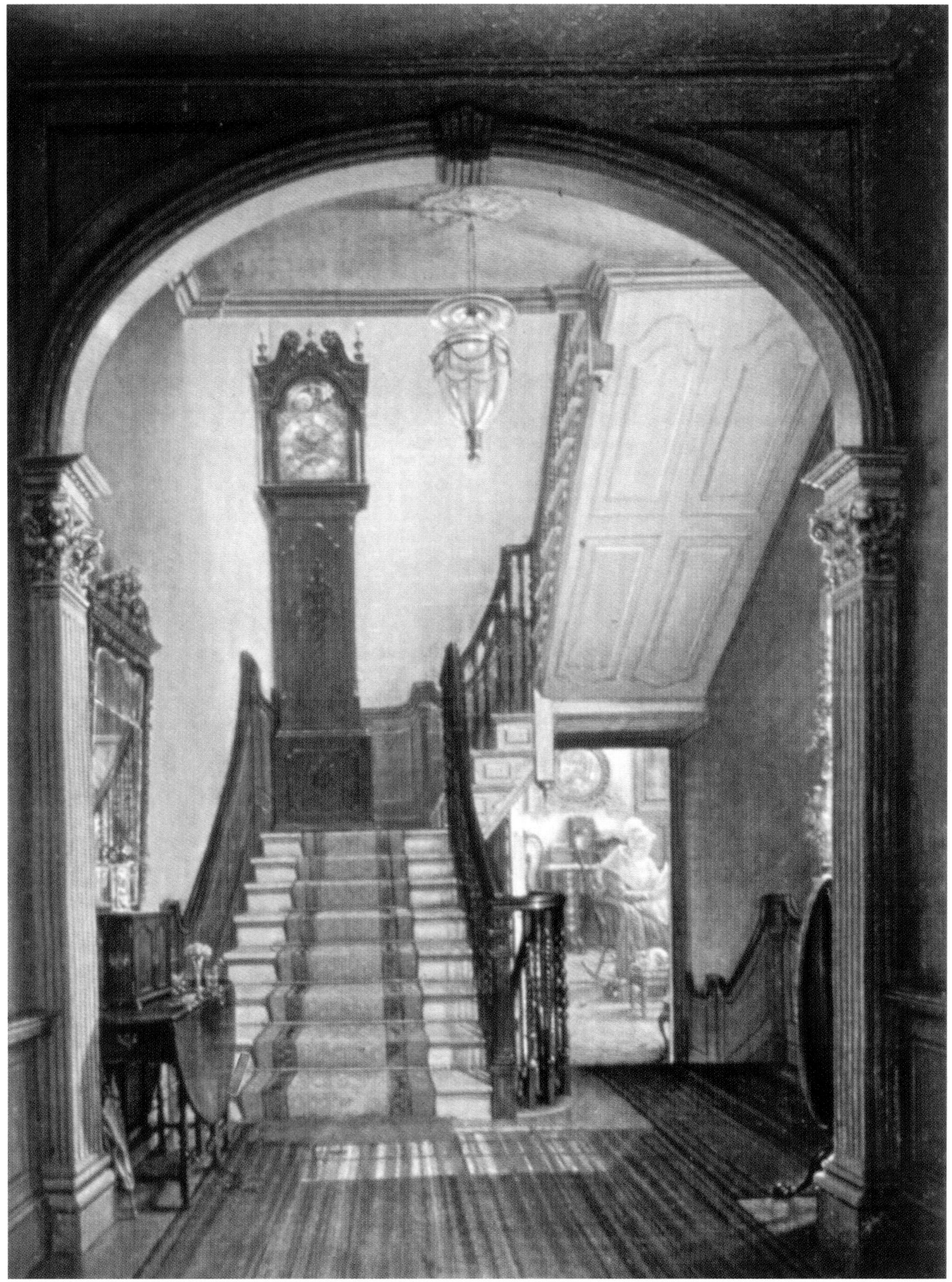

▲ **38-13.** "The Old Clock on the Stairs," 1868; painting by Edward Lamson Henry. Inspired by a Longfellow poem, the painting was exhibited at the 1876 Centennial Exhibition.

and florals to large florals and stripes. Scenic papers are more common in Colonial Revival than in the original period because they survived in greater numbers than other papers. Williamsburg inspires numerous reproduction and adaptation wallpapers.

■ *Chimneypieces*. Fireplaces (Fig. 38-17), typical in public rooms despite central heating, are usually simpler than the prototypes with plain mantels and no overmantels. Public rooms in architect-designed houses usually have more elaborate mantels composed of pilasters or engaged columns with pediment overmantels.

■ *Windows and Window Treatments*. Interior windows rarely have surrounds or interior shutters derived from historical precedents except in high-style examples. Most have simple moldings, if anything. Important rooms in more expensive or architect-designed Colonial-style houses have large cornices of classical moldings and bold surrounds. Window treatments range from simple panels hanging from rings on a decorative rod to elaborate swags, cascades, and/or cornice boards and tied-back draperies (Fig. 38-15, 38-17). The practice of universal, often elaborate, window treatments is a Colonial Revival characteristic that does not reflect 17th- and 18th-century practices when textile window treatments were rare and used only in the most important rooms in homes of the affluent.

▲ **38-15.** Living room, Mrs. William G. Langley House, Long Island, New York; published in *The Practical Book of Wall Treatments*, 1926, by Nancy McClelland. Colonial Revival.

DESIGN SPOTLIGHT

Interior: The dining room of Little Home shows typical features of a Colonial Revival interior of the early 20th century. These include paneling painted white, an Oriental rug on the floor, and the 18th-century-style furniture. Rooms of the time often mix antiques and 18th-century-style furnishings with contemporary pieces. The limited number of accessories reflects the Colonial virtue of and modern emphasis on simplicity.

▲ **38-14.** Dining room, Little Holme (Harry B. Little Residence), 1916; Concord, Massachusetts; Harry B. Little.

▲ **38-16.** Wallpapers; published in *Upholstery and Wall Coverings*, 1903, by A. S. Jennings.

■ *Doors*. Like windows, door surrounds may be bold and classical or simple depending upon the importance of the room and cost of the house (Fig. 38-5, 38-14). Doors may be six or eight panels or plain and painted or stained. Door knobs are brass, white porcelain, or glass. Some early Colonial Revival doorways have *portières*.

■ *Ceilings*. Most ceilings are plain and painted white or a lighter tint of the wall colors (Fig. 38-5, 38-14), but ceiling medallions may be used. Some ceilings may have beams and more elaborate designs.

■ *Textiles*. Reproduction and adaptation textiles for window treatments, upholstery, and bed hangings include damasks, moirés, toiles, crewels, needlepoint, chintzes, silks, solids, checks, and resists. Reproductions copy the originals as closely as possible but come in a wider diversity of color palettes. Adaptations, sometimes inspired by an historic document, vary in scale, proportion, design, and colors. They may be of materials unknown in Colonial times, such as rayon or polyester. Sometimes, apparel fabrics are adapted for furnishing textiles.

▲ **38-17.** Chinese parlor, Winterthur Museum, c. 1930s; wallpaper c. 1770; Wilmington, Delaware. Historic re-creation is by Henry Francis DuPont, owner and collector. [Courtesy Winterthur Museum]

▲ **38-18.** Lighting: Chandelier published in *House and Garden*, 1925, and wall bracket published in *Use and Design of Lighting Fixtures*, 1909, by the International Textbook Company.

■ *Lighting*. Lighting (Fig. 38-13, 38-14, 38-15, 38-17, 38-18) comes from contemporary or reproduction fixtures, sconces, or Colonial-style lamps. Chandeliers, common in dining rooms, entries, and large spaces in public buildings, often hang from central ceiling medallions. However, the use of chandeliers in Colonial Revival does not reflect Colonial practice when chandeliers were limited to some public spaces. Additionally, there is more illumination than in the Colonial periods. In the early 20th century, some Colonial Revivalists advocate only candles in Colonial-style rooms, but this quickly changes.

FURNISHINGS AND DECORATIVE ARTS

Colonial Revival furniture, which is distinguished by its resemblance to previous styles, varies from reproductions to adaptations to free interpretations of 17th-century, Queen Anne, Chippendale, Federal, and American Empire styles. Copying of historical pieces begins as early as the 1840s but does not constitute a true revival at that time. The revival occurs in earnest in the 1880s when manufacturers begin producing Colonial-style furniture, some of which they call reproductions. Most are not overly concerned with historical accuracy because the intent is to capture the spirit of the precursor image. Some do not hesitate to "improve" extant pieces in proportion or detail. Nevertheless, the best reproductions are made by hand in small cabinetmaking shops. From the 20th century forward, reproductions, particularly those licensed by museums such as Winterthur or Williamsburg, maintain as complete accuracy to the original models as possible. In its early years, Colonial Revival has certain icons or signals, such as grandfather clocks (Fig. 38-3)—a result of Henry Wadsworth Longfellow's poem "The Old Clock on the Stairs;" paintings; and other images; rifles hanging over fireplaces; and spinning wheels. Their importance begins to fade during the 1920s.

DESIGN SPOTLIGHT

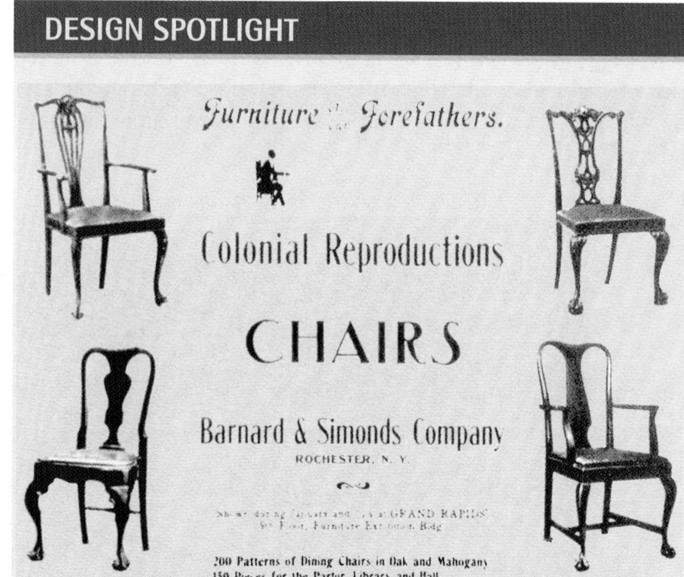

Furniture: Colonial-style chairs in varying degrees of accuracy are produced by many manufacturers. This late-19th-century adaptation of a rocker (next page) in the Chippendale style shows that many manufacturers are not overly concerned with historical accuracy. It reveals an 18th-century character in its overall design, although the proportions are incorrect, particularly in the legs. The splat resembles Philadelphia examples, and the carving on the splat and knees is similar to but coarser than 18th-century prototypes. Although rocking chairs existed in the 18th century (the exact origin is uncertain), rockers would never have been made into a formal parlor chair with ball and claw feet. The rocker, produced by C. F. Meislahn & Company in Baltimore, is a product of an imaginary past.

▲ **38-19.** Colonial reproduction chairs and rocker, 1875–1902; New York and Maryland.

Colonial Revival rooms usually have more furniture in comparison to early spaces and feature more upholstery. Antiques are often freely integrated with Colonial Revival and other furniture within room settings. Furniture may mix characteristics from several styles or bear little resemblance to the earlier prototypes. Some pieces, such as coffee tables, have no earlier precedents. Colonial-style furniture often has different proportions from the prototypes because of ignorance of earlier features or design license, or because contemporary rooms are different in scale. Furniture groupings do not follow earlier examples of lining the walls. Instead, furniture is arranged throughout a space to create comfort and convenience.

Public and Private Buildings

- *Materials*. Colonial Revival furniture is made of mahogany, walnut, oak, cherry, and maple (Fig. 38-13, 38-14, 38-15, 38-17, 38-19, 38-21, 38-23); the latter is characteristic of Early American pieces and may be stained dark to emulate age. Forms of embellishment include carving, inlay, marquetry, and painted decoration.
- *Seating*. Chairs, settees, and sofas copy, adapt, or freely interpret Queen Anne, Chippendale, Sheraton, Hepplewhite, English Regency and American Empire (Fig. 38-14, 38-15, 38-17, 38-19, 38-20). Pieces inspired by English Regency are often known as Duncan Phyfe after the popular New York cabinetmaker of the early 19th century. Early American chairs include ladderbacks and Windsors in various forms. Some chairs bear no resemblance

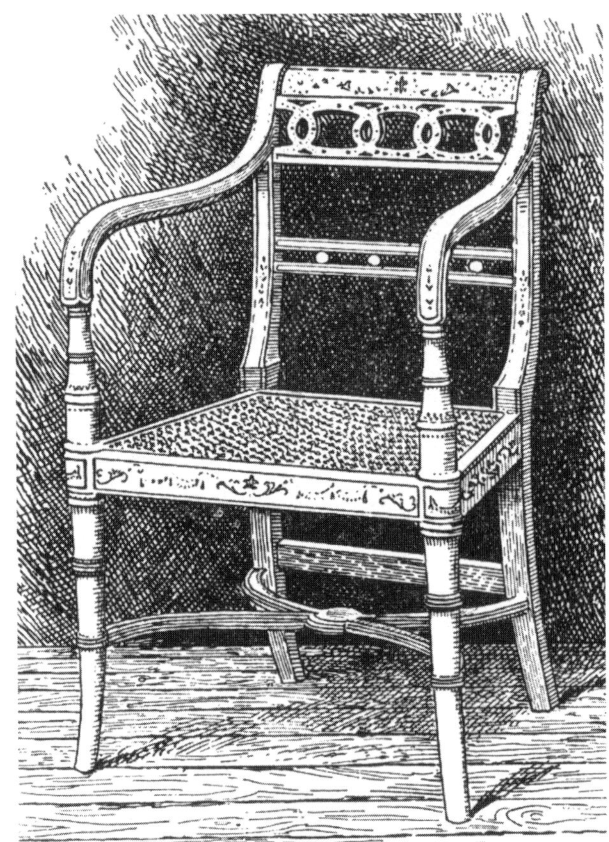

▲ **38-20.** Fancy chair, c. 1922; Sheraton-style.

DESIGN SPOTLIGHT

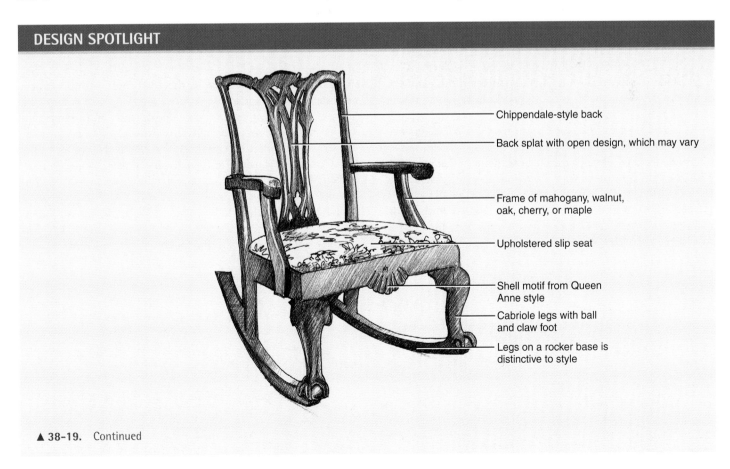

Chippendale-style back

Back splat with open design, which may vary

Frame of mahogany, walnut, oak, cherry, or maple

Upholstered slip seat

Shell motif from Queen Anne style

Cabriole legs with ball and claw foot

Legs on a rocker base is distinctive to style

▲ **38-19.** Continued

▲ **38-21.** Tables, c. 1910s–1930s.

▲ **38-22.** Chest of drawers; published in *The House Beautiful*, 1881, by Clarence Cook.

to these 18th- and 19th-century styles but may have elements of Tudor, Elizabethan, or Italian Renaissance. Spinning wheel chairs, popular in the last decades of the 19th century, are constructed of parts of spinning wheels with the wheel itself forming the back. Wing chairs are the most common fully upholstered piece from Colonial times. Unlike their predecessors that were used only in bedrooms or as invalid chairs, wing chairs are often in living rooms, family rooms, and bedrooms. Chairs with upholstered seats and backs are revived and given Colonial names. Thus, the 19th-century Lolling chair becomes a Martha Washington chair. Chippendale and Sheraton sofas also are adapted for contemporary tastes and needs in proportions to suit contemporary rooms.

■ *Tables and Storage*. New pieces of furniture include lamp or end tables and coffee tables placed in front of sofas to hold drinks and refreshments (Fig. 38-15, 38-21). Some tables common in the 17th and 18th centuries reappear in contemporary rooms, including gateleg tables, nesting tables, and drop-leaf tables (Fig. 38-13).

Blockfront chests (Fig. 38-22), dressing tables or lowboys, and high chests of drawers or highboys are commonly used in bedrooms or entrance halls. The typical Colonial-style secretary (called a desk and bookcase in the 18th century) has a broken pediment top with glass doors and a drop front with drawers that rest on ogee bracket feet or short cabriole legs. Dining tables most commonly resemble pedestal extension types that appear in the late 18th and early 19th centuries (Fig. 38-14). New in the 1920s are Colonial-style dinettes, small sets of table and chairs for breakfast nooks or kitchens. A popular dining room accessory, unknown in Colonial times, is the tea cart. Other new pieces in Colonial styles include radio cabinets; Victrolas; china cabinets; bedside tables; office furniture; bookcases; and, in the late 20th century, entertainment and computer units.

▲ **38-23.** Beds, c. 1920s–1930s.

■ *Beds*. Most Colonial-style beds have posts and a broken pediment headboard (Fig. 38-23). Posts may be short or tall enough for a tester or canopy. Canopies may be flat or curved. Although not draped in the 18th-century manner, most canopies have at least a net or cloth valance, if not curtains at the head of the bed. Beds are made in sizes unknown in Colonial times such as queen or king.

■ *Decorative Arts*. There are more decorative accessories in Colonial Revival interiors than was common in earlier periods (Fig. 38-13, 38-14, 38-15, 38-17). Rooms often display new items not previously known such as throw pillows and modern art. Antiques and/or reproductions of Colonial metalwork, ceramics, prints, mirrors, and clocks usually mix with new, contemporary examples. Formerly utilitarian objects, such as bed warmers, become decorative objects and are proudly displayed.

CHAPTER 39

Spanish Colonial Revival

Mission Revival, Spanish Colonial Revival, Monterey Style, Pueblo Revival 1880s–1930s

Originating on the west coast of the United States in the late 19th century, Spanish Colonial Revival is a counterpart to the English Colonial Revival in the eastern half of the United States. Encompassing a range of Spanish and Mediterranean styles, forms, and details, the movement responds to renewed interest in the Spanish past in California, the southwestern states, Texas, Florida, Mexico, and the Caribbean. Architecture emulates the Spanish missions in the United States as well as Spanish and other Mediterranean architecture of all periods, including vernacular. Interiors and furniture strive to capture a Spanish flavor or replicate aspects of those in Spain, including the use of Spanish imports and antiques.

Los Angeles is the first place in America where I have found original architecture. . . . Many of the houses are in the style of the Spanish Renascence—"Mission style,"—with almost flat roofs of red tiles, little round towers surmounted by Spanish-Moorish domes, and arcaded galleries, like the Franciscan cloisters of the past century. Others mingle the Colonial with the Mexican style, imitating the coarser construction of the adobe. All are very attractive and possessed of individuality.

—Jules Huret, "Mission Architecture," published in *The Craftsman 1903–1904*, Vol. 5, Oct. 1903, March 1904

HISTORICAL AND SOCIAL

Like Colonial Revival, interest in and reverence for Spanish colonial heritage are the inspirations for Spanish Colonial Revival. The style originates during the 1880s in the areas of the United States with a Spanish past, such as California, New Mexico, Arizona, Texas, and Florida. Writers and stories, such as Helen Hunt Jackson in *Ramona* (1884) and Charles Fletcher Lummis in *The Spanish Pioneers* (1929), create a vision of an idealized past in which fine people lived simple lives in harmony with nature and free of the daily cares of industrialism. Similarly, dime novels and popular periodicals create images of a mythical Old West filled with cowboys and brigands and heroes, like Wild Bill Hickok.

Critical to the development of Spanish Colonial Revival is the preservation of Spanish missions in the western United States. Spanish Franciscan and Jesuit missionaries establish these missions in California, New Mexico, Arizona, and Florida in the 17th and 18th centuries to convert natives to the Catholic faith and educate them in Spanish life and culture. Although outposts, the missions often have impressive churches and other buildings in the Late Spanish Renaissance and Baroque styles. Largely abandoned, most begin to fall into ruins during the early 19th century.

Texas makes the first step in the preservation of the missions when it declares the Alamo (built in 1724) an historic site in 1883. In California, Father Angel Casanova begins to restore Mission *San Carlos Borromeo del Carmelo* (church built in 1793) in 1884. His work inspires others in California, which has more missions than other states do and a larger population to support preservation activities. These early restorations are far more conjectural than accurate; nevertheless, they inspire further study of Spain and her colonial buildings. Enthusiasm for restoring the missions soon branches out to include Spanish *haciendas* and *ranchos*. As with other styles, publications, museum collections, and newly formed heritage and preservation organizations fuel interest and support stylistic development of Spanish Colonial Revival. The revival style can be subdivided into several phases or styles based upon historical context and characteristics.

The earliest phase of Spanish Colonial Revival, known as Mission or Mission Revival, comes directly from the preservation of the Spanish missions. Originating in California, the style tries to adapt the character, if not the details, of California missions, which are thought to be indigenous. After becoming the official style for railroad stations and resort hotels, Mission Revival spreads across the Southwest. An ensuing tourist boom increases fascination with the missions and early California. However, the limited number of sources, difficulty of adapting missions to contemporary structures, and a new movement toward more accurate period design contribute to the style's demise. Mission largely dies out by World War I (1914–1918).

The next phase of Spanish Colonial Revival, which adapts elements from Spain, Italy, and other Mediterranean countries, makes a first, important appearance at the Panama-California International Exposition in 1915. This exposition is planned as a celebration of the completion of the Panama Canal and a way to stimulate trade and growth for San Diego. The city chooses a Spanish theme and commissions Bertram Grosvenor Goodhue to design the buildings. Goodhue's plan attempts to create an ideal Spanish city with impressive buildings. The Indian Arts building is Mission Revival, but the others draw from Spanish, Spanish Colonial, Mexican, and Mediterranean sources. Widely disseminated by visitors and through postcards, publications, and even movies, the exposition buildings inspire a new, more sophisticated form of Spanish Colonial Revival. This beginning coincides with a resurgence of historicism and scholarship that inspires more studied, knowledgeable period styles. Books and periodicals with photographs of Spanish buildings and architectural vocabulary aid the stylistic development.

(a) (b)

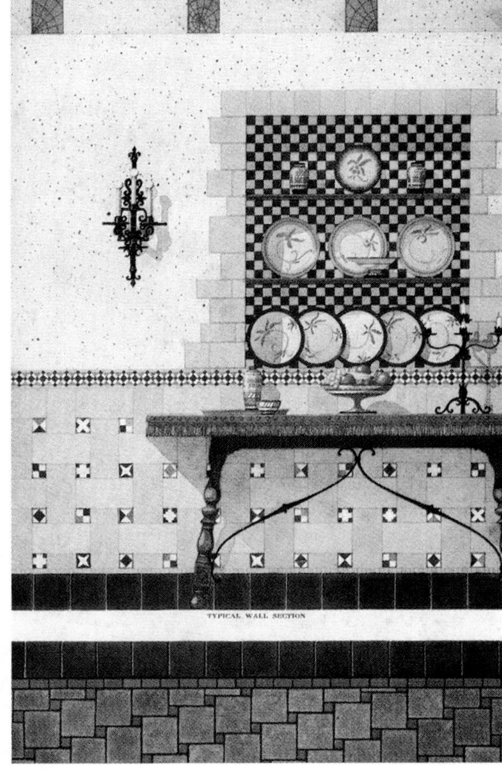

(c)

▲ **39-1.** Architectural Details: (a) Columns, Indiana Theater, 1927; Indianapolis, Indiana; (b) stairs with decorative tiles, Miami, Florida; and (c) wall with decorative tiles, late 1920s.

During the 1920s, the style proliferates across the United States, although it is more fashionable in states with Spanish heritage than those without it. Movies, which glamorize the Spanish and western or cowboy past, and the fact that many movie stars live in Spanish Colonial Revival mansions increase the style's popularity. During the period, developers and architects of the affluent choose Spanish Colonial Revival for place identity or to suit lavish lifestyles. Real estate developers adopt Spanish styles in their promotion of California as a land of sunshine and great living to attract new residents and tourists. Many cities in California, such as Santa Barbara, Pasadena, Palm Springs, and San Diego, reinvent themselves with Spanish-style public and private buildings to create a stronger city identity. Addison Mizner almost single-handedly creates a Spanish Colonial Revival in early-20th-century Florida through his mansions for the wealthy and real estate developments in Boca Raton, Palm Beach, and Coral Gables. In addition, Mizner forms his own companies that produce Spanish-style tiles, architectural details, furniture, and accessories. House plan books and mail-order companies carry a variety of Spanish Colonial Revival houses from small cottages to large mansions so that members of many economic classes can choose Spanish-style residences. The advent of modernism slows the popularity of Spanish styles, although they never completely die out.

CONCEPTS

Spanish Colonial Revival in all its forms proclaims Hispanic background or place identity, whether of an individual or particular locale or region. The architecture, interiors, and furnishings of exotic and romantic Spain appeal to those who possess or wish to possess a Hispanic heritage. The concurrent Arts and Crafts Movement's emphasis upon local or regional styles, natural materials, and integration of nature and the landscape helps to create a climate conducive to a revival of Spanish architecture in California and other states with Hispanic legacies. Also stemming from the Arts and Crafts Movement is the notion of Spanish Colonial architecture as expressing an idealized, simple, preindustrial lifestyle in which happy people live and work unencumbered in buildings of natural materials that suit the landscape. Thus, at least at its inception, the Spanish Colonial Revival shares the same motivation as Arts and Crafts and Colonial Revival movements. Additionally, Spanish Colonial Revival carries associations of the exotic culture of Morocco and North Africa, the imagined splendor of the Spanish empire in the Americas, and the rustic simplicity of Native American or Mexican design.

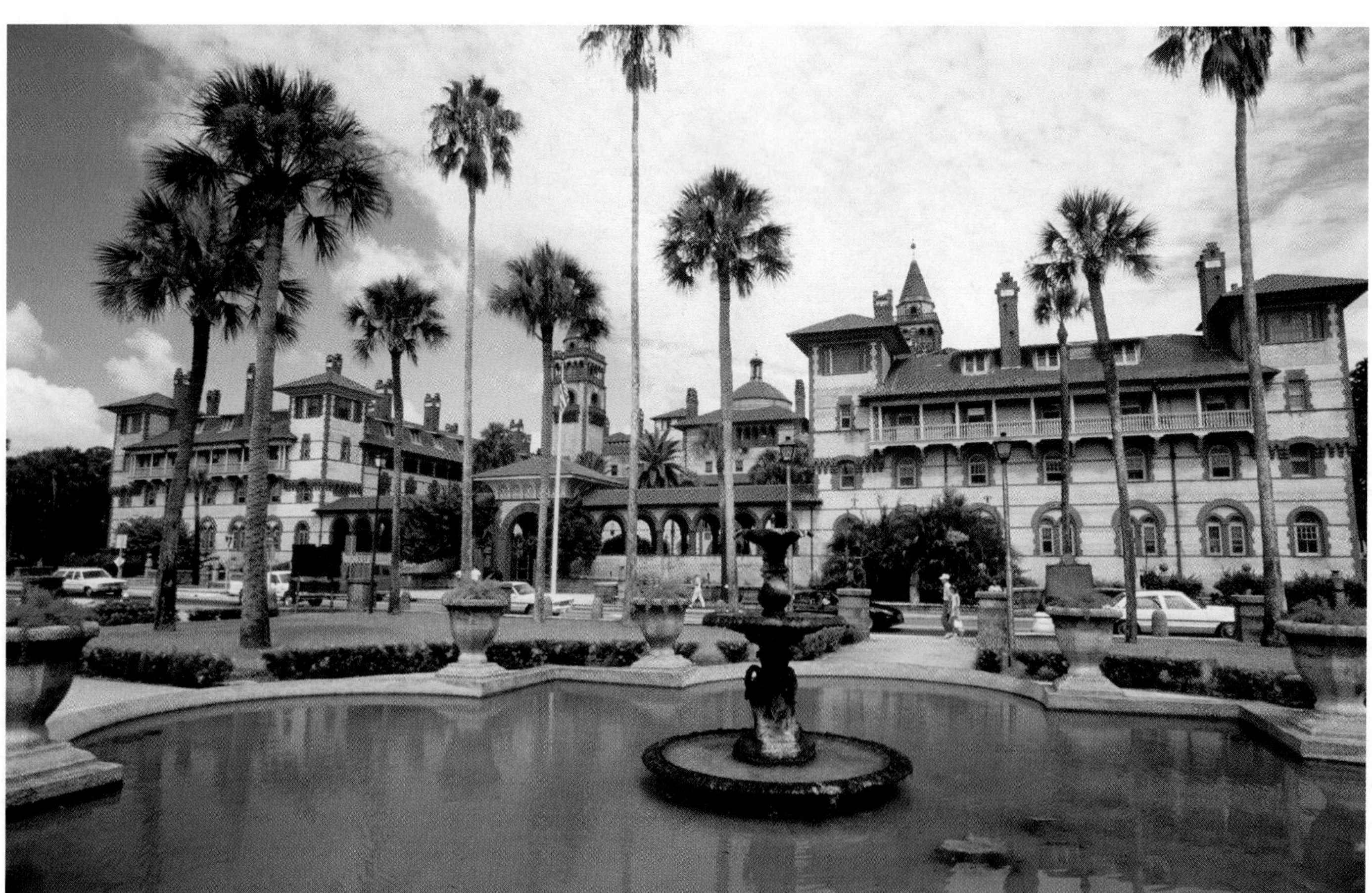

▲ **39-2.** Hotel Ponce de Leon (now Flagler College), 1888; St. Augustine, Florida; Carrere and Hastings. Spanish Colonial Revival.

CHARACTERISTICS AND MOTIFS

Forms and characteristics of Spanish Colonial Revival come from several centuries of architecture, interiors, and furniture of Spain and her colonies in North America. The revival and its subphases borrow selectively from one or more of the Spanish and Mediterranean styles of the past. Styles include the *Plateresque* (late 15th to mid-16th centuries); Classical, *Desornamentado*, or Herreran Style (1556–1650), *Churrigueresque* (1650–1750); and Spanish Colonial (1600–1840s). The intent is to evoke, not copy, the past in most cases.

■ *Motifs*. Motifs (Fig. 39-1, 39-3, 39-4, 39-5, 39-6, 39-10, 39-13, 39-21) include ogee arches, interlaced arabesques, geometric shapes, heraldic symbols, classical architectural details such as pilasters and pediments, twisted columns, *estípite*, niches, niche-pilasters, *zapatas*, foliated or quatrefoil windows, scrolls, garlands, swags, flowers, and foliage.

ARCHITECTURE

The term *Spanish Colonial Revival* covers several architectural styles derived from Spanish sources, including Mission or Mission Revival, Spanish Colonial or Mediterranean Revival, Monterey Style, and Pueblo Revival. Architectural and decorative vocabularies of Spanish Colonial Revival develop from Spanish Renaissance and Baroque styles as well as vernacular examples, particularly those from southern Spain. Revival structures range from relatively plain buildings based upon folk houses to examples with the lavish ornament from Spanish, Moorish, and other Mediterranean sources. The style is especially popular for residences. Architects design grand mansions and manor houses for the affluent in the southwestern United States and Florida. In addition, the Spanish architectural vocabulary readily adapts to bungalows, four-squares, and smaller houses. Common exterior characteristics include stucco walls that are usually white or off-white; round arches used in arcades, windows, and doors; and flat or low-pitched roofs covered with red tiles.

Spanish Colonial Revival is used on many building types, including city halls; courthouses (Fig. 39-6); hotels (Fig. 39-2); motels; museums; stores; offices; commercial buildings; school and university buildings; movie theaters (Fig. 39-5); motion picture studios; gas stations; apartments; high-style, architect-designed mansions (Fig. 39-10, 39-12, 39-13); and vernacular builder residences (Fig. 39-9, 39-14).

■ *Mission Revival (1885–1915)*. Mission Revival (Fig. 39-3) is the first of the Spanish Colonial Revival styles. Originating in the late 19th century, it uses elements of the California Spanish missions, including plain walls, minimal ornament, arcades, domes, bell towers, or courtyards. Particularly characteristic are a curvilinear parapet roof and quatrefoil or foliated windows. The style lasts until World War I; its downfall is its superficial application of features of the original missions to contemporary buildings and its inability to adapt to residences. Nevertheless, it defines many building types and even some cities.

■ *Spanish Colonial Revival (1915–1940s)*. This style (Fig. 39-4) first appears at the Panama-California Exposition in San Diego, California, in 1915, as a more urbane and sophisticated approach to architecture. World War I (1914–1918) gives additional thrust to the style because it prevents American architects and designers from making the usual Grand Tours to France and Italy. They visit Spain instead, particularly the southern part, where they become acquainted with vernacular structures, thereby adding more models to their repertoire. Accuracy is made easier by the greater number of photographs, instead of sketches or drawings, in publications. Designers demonstrate their increased understanding of Spanish architecture in compositions that recall a variety of prototypes, a broader range of materials, and a more accurate depiction of Spanish massing and ornament. Buildings, which draw more directly from Spanish and other Mediterranean sources than from the missions, are usually more ornamented than other styles are, with decoration concentrating at doors and windows. Other defining characteristics include arched doorways and windows, wrought iron or wood grilles, colorful tiles, and round or octagonal towers (Fig. 39-2, 39-5, 39-6, 39-7, 39-9, 39-10, 39-12, 39-14).

▲ **39-3.** Carnegie Library, c. 1903; Riverside, California; Burnham and Bliesner. Mission Revival.

The California Ranch house, developed and promoted by designer-builder Cliff May, becomes extremely popular during the 1940s and is the most common house form after World War II. It gives new life to Spanish Colonial Revival during a time when it is being eclipsed by the Modern movement.

■ *Monterey Style*. This style develops during the 1920s in California from the restoration and rehabilitation of Spanish ranch houses and large country estates. Freely mixing forms and details from both Spanish Colonial and English houses, the Monterey style is used for many suburban houses in California and the rest of the United States after the second quarter of the 20th century. This stylistic variation tries to replicate the 18th-century Spanish Colonial houses or those in northern California that incorporate elements of English/Anglo buildings such as porches, balconies, fanlights, transoms, sash windows, New England–style moldings and columns, wooden floors, and picket fences. Examples may mix adobe with clapboard or brick, and each story may be of a different material. Roofs may be wood or tiles.

DESIGN SPOTLIGHT

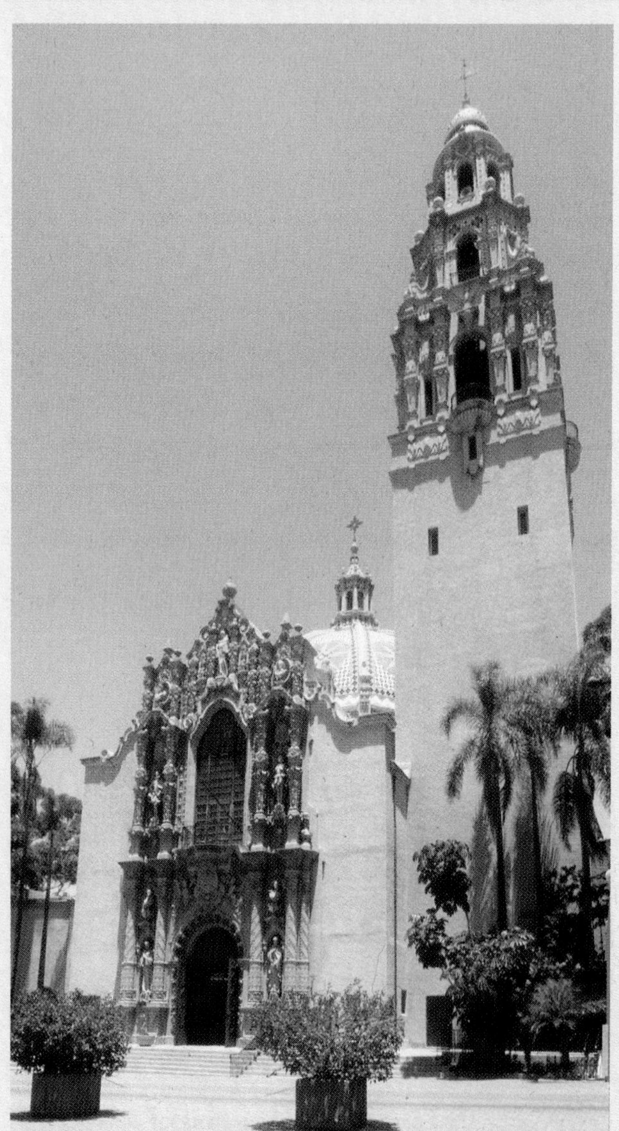

Architecture: The California Tower, one of four buildings designed to be permanent, is Goodhue's excellent interpretation of Spanish Baroque or *Churrigueresque*. The Tower is of stone and concrete, and the domes are covered with colorful ceramic tiles that follow historic precedents. The bold ornament surrounding the doorway and capping the tower consists of scrolls; foliate arches; spiral columns; *estipite*; and figural sculpture that includes Father Junipero Serra, Franciscan priest and founder of the San Diego mission, and King Philip II of Spain, under whose rule Spain establishes colonies in the United States. The New Mexico Building, in contrast, recalls Spanish missions of New Mexico, such as *San Estevan*, Acoma, and churches in Colorado, such as *San Buenaventura* with its simple outlines and adobe-like forms. Typical mission characteristics include the twin towers and the balcony between them. While respecting the character of the past, the architects better integrate the building parts and balance the composition than in early examples. The building, much transformed, is now the Balboa Park Club. [National Historic Landmark]

▲ **39-4.** California Tower and New Mexico Building, The Panama-California Exposition, 1915–1916; Balboa Park, San Diego, California; Tower, Bertram G. Goodhue; New Mexico Building, Rapp and Rapp Architects. Spanish Colonial Revival (Tower) and Mission Revival (New Mexico Building).

■ *Pueblo Revival or Santa Fe Style (1912–present)*. Like others, this style is inspired by Spanish Colonial architecture (Fig. 39-8, 39-11). But unlike others, it blends these precedents with elements of Native American structures. Although the style first appears in California, it becomes extremely popular in Arizona and New Mexico where the Native American precedents are located. Pueblo Revival is a common house style, especially in historic districts, in states throughout the southwestern United States. Architecture displays the blocky, geometric adobe forms of Native American and Spanish Colonial buildings. Plain and usually unornamented, structures have flat roofs with a parapet, *vigas*, and stucco walls. Corners are usually softly rounded like those of adobe Spanish Colonial architecture.

Public and Private Buildings

■ *Site Orientation*. No particular orientation is associated with Spanish Colonial Revival. Urban public buildings sit upon primary streets or prime locations in cities and towns (Fig. 39-3, 39-5, 39-6, 39-7). Spanish Colonial Revival residences and apartments fill suburbs and line city streets. Adopting the Spanish/Islamic emphasis upon gardens, some public and many private buildings have surrounding lawns, terraces, and gardens with lush plantings and fountains (Fig. 39-9, 39-10, 39-12). Spanish-style houses and apartments often are arranged around central courtyards for green space. Most houses, whether small or large, incorporate patios, which are a signature of the style. Large-scale mansions and manor houses sometimes are surrounded by Italian-style landscapes incorporating terraces, fountains, pergolas, and patios.

■ *Floor Plans*. Floor plans come from the building function. However, many structures, including residences, center on or have courtyards and patios (Fig. 39-9). Small houses and ranch houses usually have simple rectangular or horizontal floor plans.

■ *Materials*. Walls are of smooth or rough stucco, stone, brick, adobe, or concrete (Fig. 39-2, 39-3, 39-4, 39-5, 39-6, 39-7, 39-8, 39-9, 39-10, 39-11, 39-12). Colors include white, cream or buff, gray, ochre, pale yellow, or pink. Details and ornament may be

▲ **39-5.** Indiana Theater and lobby, 1927; Indianapolis, Indiana; Rubush & Hunter. *Churrigueresque* of Spanish Colonial Revival.

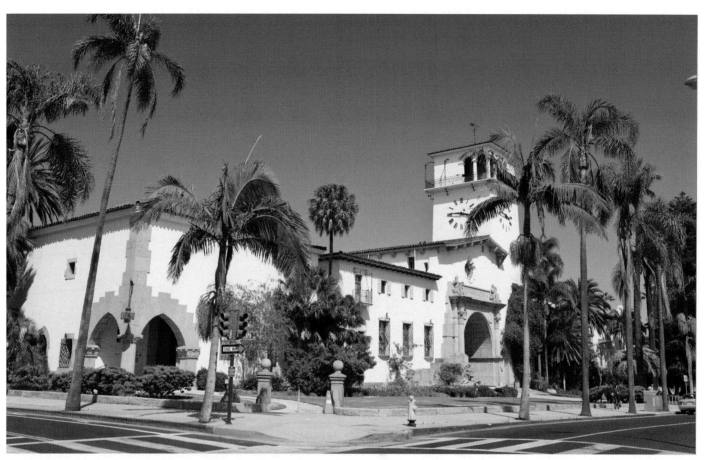

▲ **39-6.** Santa Barbara County Courthouse, 1929; Santa Barbara, California; William Moser III. Spanish Colonial Revival.

DESIGN SPOTLIGHT

Architecture and Interior: Conceived as the gateway to Los Angeles and the last great railroad station in America, the Union Station Passenger Terminal in its heyday hosted numerous prominent passenger trains, movie stars, and GIs returning from World War II. Architecturally it evokes the Spanish heritage of Southern California with its round arches, arcades, white stucco walls, prominent clock tower, red tile roof, and beamed ceilings. The façade is composed of bold geometric forms with minimal ornament. Inside, however, is a more complex interior that reflects the Streamline Moderne style through light fixtures, decorative details, artwork, and some furnishings. Native American features appear as well, particularly in the decorative floor patterns. Interior colors convey the character of these influences, with a palette primarily composed of cream, gold, rust, black, turquoise, and brown.

▲ **39-7.** Union Passenger Terminal (Los Angeles Railroad Station) and ticket room, 1934–1939; Los Angeles, California; John Parkinson, Donald Parkinson, J. J. Christie, H. L. Gilman, and R. J. Wirth. Spanish Colonial Revival and Streamline Moderne.

DESIGN SPOTLIGHT

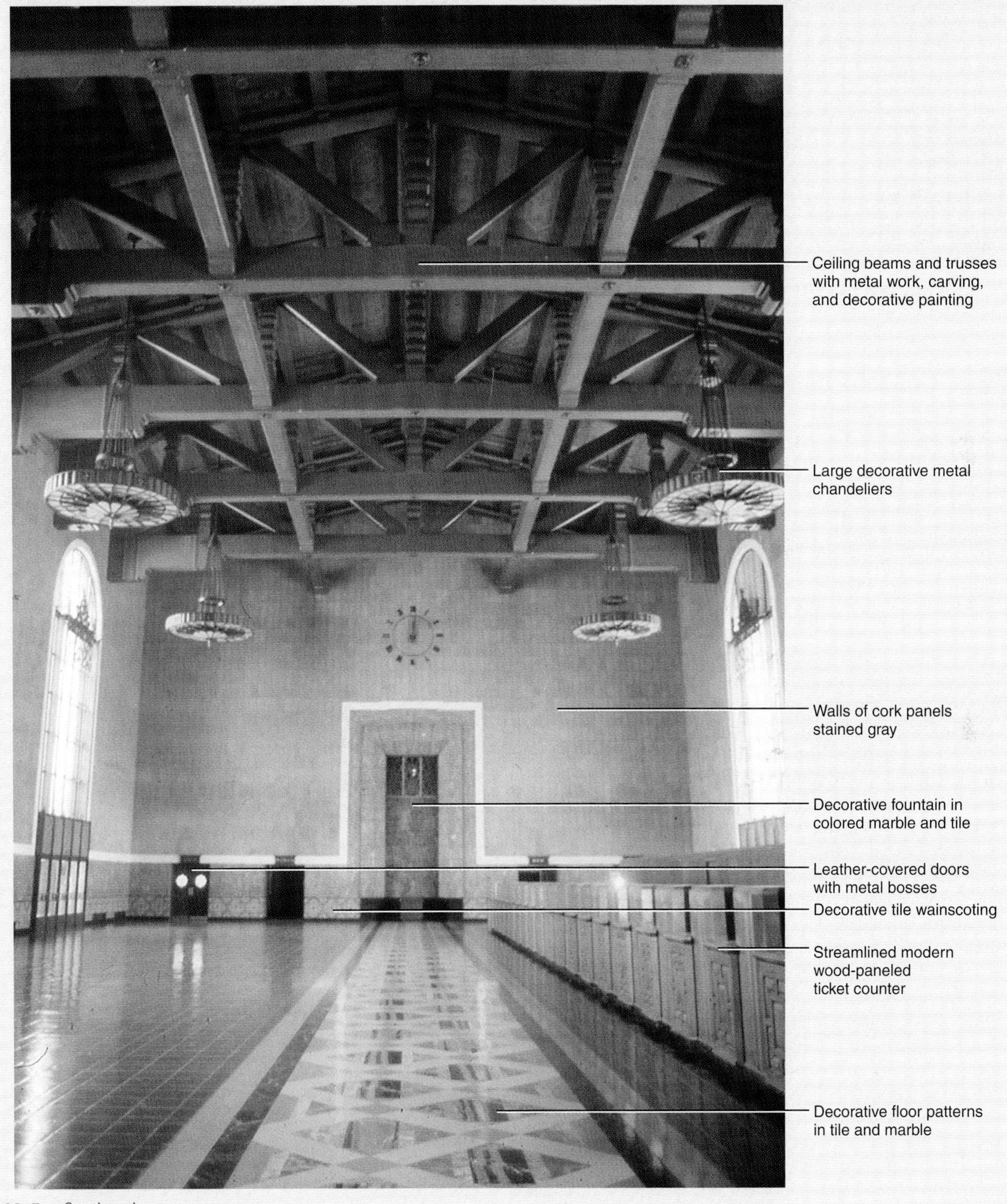
Ceiling beams and trusses with metal work, carving, and decorative painting
Large decorative metal chandeliers
Walls of cork panels stained gray
Decorative fountain in colored marble and tile
Leather-covered doors with metal bosses
Decorative tile wainscoting
Streamlined modern wood-paneled ticket counter
Decorative floor patterns in tile and marble

▲ **39-7.** Continued

▲ **39-8.** *Cristo Rey* Church, 1939–1940; Santa Fe, New Mexico; John Gaw Meem. Pueblo Revival.

another material, such as stone, and/or it may contrast in color to walls. California architect Irving Gill pioneers the use of concrete. He finds that it adapts well to his simple geometric style with a Spanish flavor. Grilles at windows and doors are of iron or wood (Fig. 39-13) and may be painted bright colors. Ceramic tiles have ochre pictorial or Moorish designs in blue, turquoise, red, yellow, orange, green, black, and buff (Fig. 39-1). Roofs (Fig. 39-2, 39-13, 39-14) are of clay tiles, usually red, in round or half-rounded shapes. Some Monterey style buildings have wooden shingles and different materials on each story. Wood clapboards may be combined with stucco or brick. Pueblo examples have stuccoed surfaces to imitate the original adobe (Fig. 39-8, 39-11).

■ *Façades.* Façades may be symmetrical or asymmetrical. Mission-inspired façades feature mission forms and/or details (Fig. 39-3, 39-4). Although a few high-style, architect-designed examples attempt to replicate missions, most compositions bear little resemblance to the originals. Mission favors smooth, flat walls like the original adobe walls. Façades tend to be unornamented, although arcades, cloisters, and full- and partial-width porches are typical. Important buildings have towers, although most do not have domes like Spanish churches often do. Most examples have a gable or parapet roof, a definitive feature.

Spanish Colonial Revival facades often are larger, more sophisticated, and more ornamented than other styles (Fig. 39-2, 39-4, 39-5, 39-6, 39-7, 39-9, 39-10, 39-12, 39-13, 39-14). Walls may be flat and smooth or covered with rough-faced stucco. Decoration, which usually is derived from Spanish *Plateresque* or *Churrigueresque* sources, concentrates at windows and doorways. Some buildings have floral or geometric ornament in terra-cotta panels. As in other styles, arcades, courtyards, and patios are common in Spanish Colonial Revival. Supports may be spiral or twisted columns, classical columns, or wooden posts with bracket capitals. Full- and partial-width balconies with wooden or iron railings in many sizes and shapes also are a characteristic feature, particularly for houses. Important public buildings often have towers that are usually rectangular with low-pitched, hipped roofs. Houses may have circular towers forming the entrance or defining a corner. Sometimes a side wall extends to create an entrance to the garage or simulate a side entrance. Examples after World War I reveal a more vernacular character in the seemingly random organization and massing that emulates growth over time through additions placed where needed with little regard for symmetry or classical organization.

Monterey-style buildings have full- or partial-width porches supported by pillars or columns and a second-story balcony under the main roof.

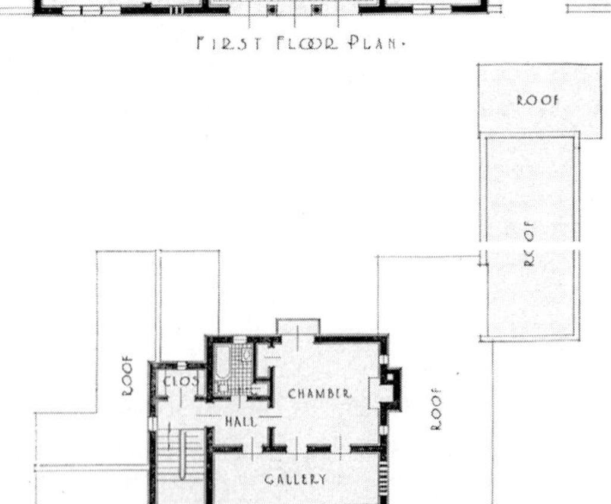

▲ **39-9.** House and floor plan from Coral Gables Gateway suburb, c. 1920s; Coral Gables, Florida; Walter C. De Garmo and Robert L. Wood. Spanish Colonial Revival.

▲ **39-10.** *La Casa Grande*, Hearst Castle (home of William Randolph Hearst), 1919–1920s; San Simeon, California; Julia Morgan. Spanish Colonial Revival.

Pueblo Revival buildings have plain, smooth walls with rounded corners like the adobe prototypes (Fig. 39-8, 39-11). Rough wooden beams may protrude near the roofline in imitation of the *vigas* of Spanish Colonial buildings.

■ *Windows*. In Mission Revival and Spanish Colonial Revival, at least one, if not all, windows are rounded arches, although they may mix with rectangular sashes or casements (Fig. 39-2, 39-3, 39-6, 39-7, 39-12). Foliated or quatrefoil windows in gables or parapets characterize Mission Revival (Fig. 39-3). More elaborate or important structures may have windows set in foliated or horseshoe arches or parabolic windows (Fig. 39-4, 39-5, 39-10). Houses often have picture windows or bay windows. Wrought iron or wooden grilles, *Plateresque* or *Churrigueresque* ornament, or colorful ceramic tiles surround or surmount many windows (Fig. 39-9, 39-13). Some have colored or leaded glass, often designed to look ancient.

Sash windows identify the Monterey style. Also typical are paired windows and shutters. Windows in the Pueblo style are rectangular, usually deeply recessed, and may have exposed wooden lintels over them (Fig. 39-8, 39-11).

■ *Doors*. Doors may be recessed or within porches and have red or colorful tiled walkways or steps leading to them (Fig. 39-2, 39-3, 39-4, 39-7, 39-8, 39-9, 39-12, 39-13). Most doorways are round arches, but some are within foliated or horseshoe arches (Fig. 39-4, 39-10). Important Spanish Colonial Revival public and private buildings often have spiral or twisted columns or pilasters and/or *Plateresque-* or *Churrigueresque*-style decoration around them. Doors are dark wood, usually carved. Some have glass in the upper portions. Hinges, strap hinges, door knobs, and knockers are of wrought iron. When garages are shown, their wooden doors are often heavily paneled.

■ *Roofs*. Geometric or curvilinear parapet roofs copied or adapted from mission churches identify Mission Revival (Fig. 39-3, 39-4). Low-pitched gable or hipped roofs are most common in all Spanish Colonial Revival styles (Fig. 39-2, 39-4, 39-5, 39-6, 39-7, 39-9, 39-10, 39-12, 39-13, 39-14) except Pueblo, which always has flat roofs (Fig. 39-8, 39-11). Some public buildings, particularly churches, may have domes. Red ceramic tiles in round or half-rounded shapes cover all Spanish Colonial Revival roofs.

▲ **39-11.** House in adobe, c. 1920s–1930s; Santa Fe, New Mexico. Pueblo Revival.

▲ **39-12.** *Mar-a-Lago* and fireplace in the Spanish Colonial room, c. 1920s–1930s; Palm Beach, Florida. Marion Syms Wyeth, architect; Joseph Urban, interior decoration. Spanish Colonial Revival.

INTERIORS

Interiors in Spanish Colonial Revival structures may be Arts and Crafts, particularly in early Mission and Spanish Colonial Revival; may replicate the character of Spanish rooms; may show aspects of Italian or French Renaissance and Mediterranean design; or may even have a rustic character. Common features in all Spanish Colonial Revival styles are tile or wood floors, plastered white or off-white walls, arched openings, and coffered or dark wooden-beamed ceilings. Colorful ceramic tiles and textiles, contrasting with stark walls, add interest. The wealthy sometimes import entire rooms or architectural elements from Spain. Antique and/or imported furniture often mixes with contemporary. Kitchens and bathrooms display a Spanish flavor in colors and materials. Similarly, furniture may be Arts and Crafts, Italian or French Renaissance, or Spanish style. Antiques may integrate with contemporary pieces.

No particular room types are associated with Spanish Colonial Revival. However, front and interior courtyards and patios are characteristic. Interiors often display an eclectic Spanish or rustic feeling related to the exterior.

Public and Private Buildings

■ *Color.* Walls usually are white, off-white, gray, pale yellow, ochre, or pink (Fig. 39-1, 39-7). Ceramic tiles, textiles, and decorative ceilings in bright blue, turquoise, yellow, orange, red, and/or green add accents of color (Fig. 39-1). Woods usually are stained a dark, rich brown.

■ *Floors.* Floors are tiles or dark wood planks (Fig. 39-7, 39-12, 39-15, 39-16, 39-17). Tiles are rectangular, hexagonal, or octagonal in unglazed red or brown clay. Sometimes tiles in other colors or patterns create repeats, borders, or *trompe l'oeil* area rugs; form

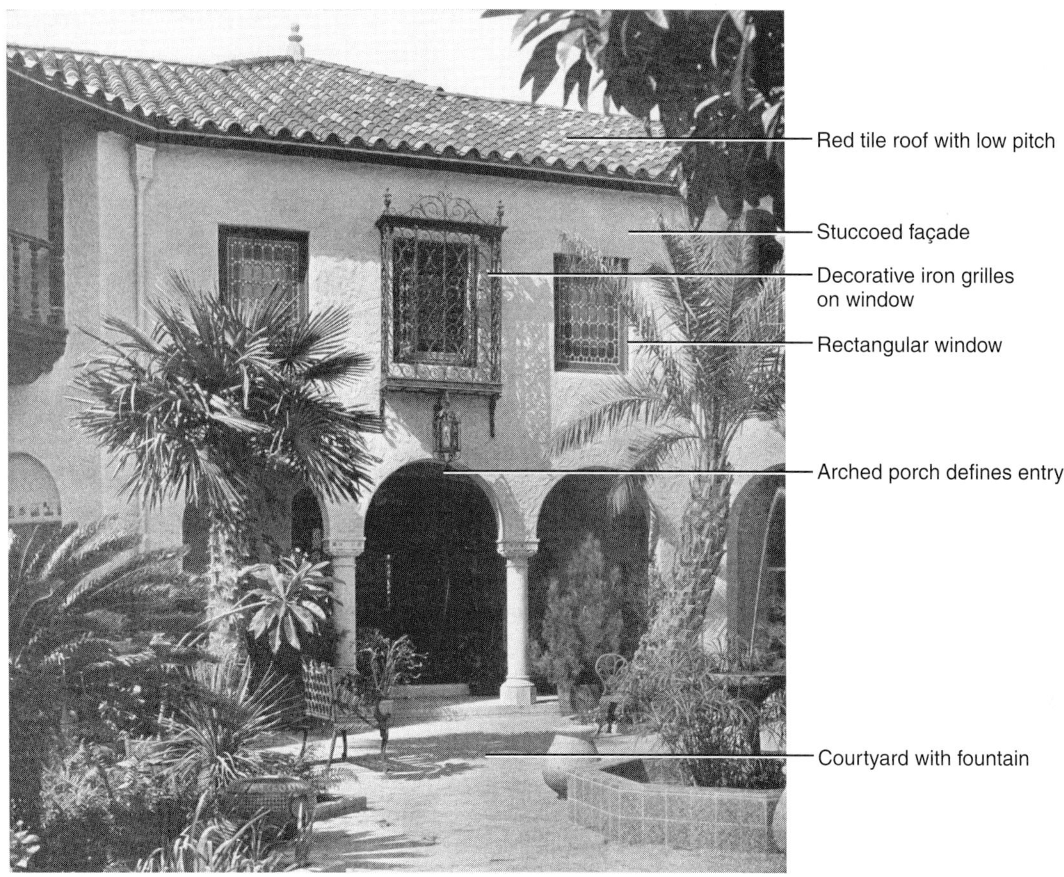

▲ **39-13.** D. T. Atkinson House; San Antonio, Texas; published in *Pencil Points*, 1930; Atlee B. Ayers and Robert M. Ayres. Spanish Colonial Revival.

baseboards; or cover risers and treads of stairways. Orientals, kelims, dhurries, or Native American rugs may cover floors, but many floors are left bare for an authentic look. Wall-to-wall carpet is rarely used except in bedrooms.

■ *Walls*. Walls usually are smooth or rough plaster with few moldings in both public and private buildings (Fig. 39-1, 39-7, 39-12, 39-15, 39-16, 39-17). Ceramic tiles, Native American rugs, and/or other textile wall hangings supply color and interest. Tiles may be used for dadoes or as surrounds for the insides of niches, fireplaces, doors, and windows. A few rooms, especially those influenced by the Arts and Crafts style, have wallpaper or paneling. High-style rooms, particularly public buildings such as hotels or theaters, may have elaborate plasterwork decorations like the original Spanish examples or extensive painted decoration such as murals or geometric designs. Fireplaces are rectangular, hooded, corner, or beehive, which is rounded in form with a rounded opening. Mantels range from stone with bold Baroque or Renaissance details to simple rough wood (Fig. 39-12, 39-15, 39-16, 39-17).

■ *Windows*. Interior windows are relatively plain with few moldings. Curtains of plain or patterned fabrics hang by rings from iron rods. Elaborate, layered treatments are not typical except in some high-end buildings. Red velvet or damask, often trimmed with fringe and/or braid, are common materials for curtains when present. Off-white curtains in muslin or linen are also popular.

■ *Doors*. Doorway surrounds are rectangular, round arches, or foliated arches (Fig. 39-15, 39-17). Sometimes ceramic tiles surround them. Doors are of dark paneled or carved wood with wrought iron hinges and knobs. Colorful painted decoration and/or gilding may highlight details or panels.

▲ **39-14.** House, c. 1920s–1930s; San Diego, California. Spanish Colonial Revival.

■ *Ceilings*. Ceilings may be plain and flat, or sloped or arched plaster (Fig. 39-17). Many have wood beams supported by brackets or are compartmentalized with carved and painted decoration (Fig. 39-12, 39-15). Some rooms have sloped ceilings with revealed trusses in the Medieval manner (Fig. 39-5, 39-7, 39-16). Important rooms in public and private buildings often have elaborate ceiling treatments.

▲ **39-15.** Vestibule, c. 1920s; California; Wallace Neff. Spanish Colonial Revival.

■ *Textiles*. Common fabrics include velvets, damasks, leather, corduroy, or canvas. They are used for curtains, bed hangings and upholstery. Large nailheads in iron or dull brass secure upholstery to wooden-framed pieces (Fig. 39-15, 39-16, 39-19).

■ *Lighting*. Electric table and floor lamps, chandeliers, lanterns, and sconces in wrought iron are most commonly used (Fig. 39-5, 39-7, 39-12, 39-15, 39-16, 39-17). Other materials include wood, dull brass, hammered copper or brass, silver, or ceramic. Some fixtures have stained glass shades. Hanging lamps may replicate Spanish or Moorish types, such as mosque lamps. Sconces and lamps sometimes have *Plateresque* or *Churrigueresque* ornament. Candlestands in iron or heavy wooden holders add an exotic or romantic touch.

■ *Later Interpretations*. The Mediterranean style of the 1970s uses the white walls, dark floors, and ceiling beams of Spanish Colonial Revival. Rich colors, such as red, orange, avocado green, brown, and black; crimson-flocked wallpapers; and heavy furniture of dark woods also identify the style. Late-20th-century Spanish Colonial Revival interiors, often in Mexican or Mediterranean restaurants or hotels, continue the smooth plaster walls, tiled floors, dark woods, and colorful accents of textiles, ceramic tiles, and decorative iron work of earlier (Fig. 39-18).

FURNISHINGS AND DECORATIVE ARTS

Dark woods, carving, inlay, wrought iron details, applied ceramic tiles in bright colors, Spanish and Moorish motifs, and a Renaissance or rustic character identify Spanish Colonial Revival furniture. Types associated with Spanish high-style and vernacular furniture of the Renaissance or Baroque are popular for Spanish Colonial Revival. These include the *frailero*, X-form chair and stool, spindle-back chairs, the *amario* or wardrobe, and the *vargueño*.

Mission Revival and early Spanish Colonial Revival interiors, particularly in houses, often have Arts and Crafts or Mission-style furniture. Later furniture replicates or more closely resembles the Spanish originals, at least in wooden or metal pieces. Revival interiors have contemporary-style upholstery because it gives greater comfort and convenience than do the originals. Imported Spanish, French, or Italian antiques may be mixed with contemporary furniture, sometimes incongruously. In areas where Spanish Colonial Revival is fashionable, antique collecting, a popular national pastime, focuses on Spanish Colonial furniture, and museums collect and display important examples.

In the 1920s, manufacturers respond to interest in Spanish architecture by producing Spanish Colonial Revival furniture. Most

▲ **39-16.** Living room, c. 1920s; California; Wallace Neff. Spanish Colonial Revival.

▲ **39-17.** Dining room, *Casa Flores*, c. 1920s; Pasadena, California; Carleton Winslow. Pueblo Revival.

pieces are adaptations of Spanish Renaissance or Baroque or Mexican pieces, but some companies reproduce 16th- and 17th-century furniture. Similarly, individual cabinetmakers create reproductions and/or adaptations of Spanish Colonial pieces, usually for wealthy clients. The Arts and Crafts Movement inspires the preservation and fostering of local craft traditions, so vernacular examples also are copied or adapted. One example is the Monterey Furniture, a fashionable line derived from Mexican folk pieces and produced by Mason Manufacturing in Los Angeles between 1929 and 1943. Some rooms display unusual furniture, such as rustic pieces made of vines and/or tree trunks or limbs, or Cowboy furniture that is made of wagon wheels or barrels.

Public and Private Buildings

■ *Materials*. Walnut, yellow pine, oak, and chestnut, usually in a dark stain, are typical woods (Fig. 39-15, 39-16, 39-17, 39-19, 39-20, 39-21). Luxury pieces may be of ebony or mahogany. Chairs and tables also may be of wrought iron or bronze. Decoration includes inlay, carving, painting, gilding, ceramic tiles, and leather. Mexican or folk furniture may be decorated with geometric or naturalistic motifs in bright colors such as blue, red, yellow, green, and white. Wooden pieces are also artificially aged by bleaching or sandblasting to make them look like antiques.

▲ **39-18.** Later Interpretation: Dining Room, *Casa de Pico* Mexican restaurant, 2009; La Mesa, California.

■ *Seating*. Chairs, stools, and benches are the primary examples of Spanish Colonial Revival (Fig. 39-5, 39-15, 39-16, 39-17, 39-19). Arm and side chairs may reproduce or adapt Renaissance types such as rectangular or the X-form (Fig. 39-12). Occasionally, more ornate and heavier-scaled Baroque-style chairs appear in interiors of the affluent (Fig. 39-16). Also evident are ladder-back and spindle-back chairs, which often reflect a more vernacular character. They usually have turning, rough carving, and/or painted decoration. Stools usually are X shaped. Window seats and built-in seating appear in living and dining rooms, kitchens, and patios and are often embellished with ceramic tiles.

▲ **39-19.** Spanish upholstered bench, c. 1927; manufactured by Kittinger Company. Spanish Colonial Revival.

▲ **39-20.** Table with iron supports, c. 1927; manufactured by Hastings Company. Spanish Colonial Revival.

■ *Tables*. The Spanish table with four scrolled, turned, or columnar splayed or slanted legs and curvilinear wrought iron braces is sometimes copied (Fig. 39-20). Lamp tables, coffee tables, and extension dining tables, although unknown in the Renaissance or Baroque periods, reflect the form and character of earlier pieces with dark stains, inlay, turning, carving, wrought iron braces; and wrought-iron braces (Fig. 39-12, 39-16, 39-17). Tops are round, rectangular, square, hexagonal, or octagonal and may have ceramic tiles or leather secured with large brass nail heads.

■ *Storage*. Chests, credenzas, and desks reflect a Spanish spirit in form and design (Fig. 39-16, 39-17). Proportions are usually heavy and the carving lavish. The *vargueño* or drop-front desk is frequently copied or adapted for contemporary rooms (Fig. 39-21). Like the originals, the base may have turned or spiral splayed legs with wrought iron supports.

■ *Beds*. Beds vary in design from heavily carved four-posters in dark woods to headboards with ornate shapes composed of C and S scrolls and details highlighted with gilding or paint.

■ *Decorative Arts*. Accessories in Spanish Colonial Revival rooms draw from Spanish, Native American, Mexican, and Islamic sources. Pieces include Mexican tinwork, Moorish braziers, Native American pottery, Arts and Crafts pottery, Native American baskets, wrought iron and hammered brass or copper candlesticks, and other decorative objects.

▲ **39-21.** *Vargueño*, c. 1927; manufactured by Kittinger. Spanish Colonial Revival.

M. REFORMS

Throughout the 19th century, the Industrial Revolution coupled with consumer demands produce innumerable goods that are poorly designed and constructed. A few forward-thinking people recognize this problem and begin seeking ways to ameliorate it during the second quarter of the 19th century. For many, a strong catalyst for change is London's Great Exhibition of 1851. Dominating the exhibit are overornamented, shoddy, and badly colored items that confirm the design critics' beliefs that design, in the hands of manufacturers and aimed at the minimally educated, has declined to the lowest point imaginable. Further contributing to this disintegration is the lack of a suitable design language for machine-made goods and the emphasis upon fashionable trends, historicism, and sentimentalism. Manufacturers are more concerned about getting goods fabricated and to the consumer than they are about design and quality. Consumers, largely uneducated in matters of taste, cannot demand better designs, so the reformers attempt to do it for them or, at least, teach them to do this for themselves.

Pleas for and attempts to change the quality of design come from many sources, including schools, such as South Kensington Museum's school in England; reform movements or groups with a common outlook, such as the Aesthetic and Arts and Crafts Movements; and design companies, such as Morris and Company. Particularly significant are the writings of John Ruskin and William Morris, who call attention to the deficiencies of design and prescribe remedies. Setting forth theories for design, architecture, and ornament, they advocate that well-designed goods should be available for all levels of society. Echoing A. W. N. Pugin, they strongly equate moralism and design. Always condemned in writings, lectures, and practices are materialism, conspicuous consumption, and what advocates consider bad taste.

Because the Industrial Revolution increasingly affects family life and relationships, a move to counter its effects through the design of the home develops. Critics, architects, and other writers regard the family and, by extension, the home as instruments of reform, so they promote what they believe to be the ideal dwelling. Most believe that the home should be a refuge from the outside world and the place to educate and strengthen the family. Women, they insist, are better suited than men are to create these nurturing environments. By the second half of the 19th century, advice books proliferate, and writers specify rules for decoration that they believe will improve both the home's decor and family life.

Individuals and groups propose different strategies to bring change depending on their outlook. Although not design reformers, the American Shakers model change through their simple, faith-dominated lifestyles in which they derive joy from labor. They, unlike others of their time, do not use machine-made goods and reject materialism. Their material culture, made in their communities to support their beliefs, demonstrates simplicity, functionality, and a respect for materials that is greatly admired by the reformers and others.

The Aesthetic Movement attempts to change design through education of artistic principles and historic precedents. Not a style but an attitude, its tenets center on beauty and usefulness for all forms of expression, particularly in the home. Followers, who are artists, designers, architects, and dilettantes, establish rules to assess the beauty of an object or artwork and espouse them through their own practices or writings. Like others of their day, they do not separate the fine and decorative arts. In contrast to others, they absolve the arts of a higher or moralizing purpose, so "Art for Art's Sake" is the movement's motto. In contrast to the Arts and Crafts Movement, the Aesthetic Movement does not reject the machine, advocate the formation of guilds, or emphasize craftsmanship or social reform. It does introduce the idea of art and beauty as important and desirable, elevates furnishing to an art form, and stresses the importance of education. The movement is also important for women as writers and practitioners.

The English Arts and Crafts Movement focuses on reform through well-made goods for all and improving the life of the worker. Like the Aesthetic Movement, it does not promote a single style but fosters an attitude toward design embodied in excellent craftsmanship, delight in and honest use of materials, simplicity, functionality, and regionalism or a sense of place. Followers form guilds, modeled after medieval ones, in which like-minded artists, architects, and designers come together to promote their work and ideas. The guilds give the movement in England cohesion, in spite of a strong emphasis upon the creative expression of the individual designer.

The American Arts and Crafts Movement shares similar goals to that of England. However, American expressions are broader, are more individualistic, and reveal a greater diversity of sources. Americans stress Arts and Crafts ideas as part of a larger reform movement intended to transform life and the family, so there is less emphasis upon the worker. Additionally, Americans use mass production to a greater degree to democratize design.

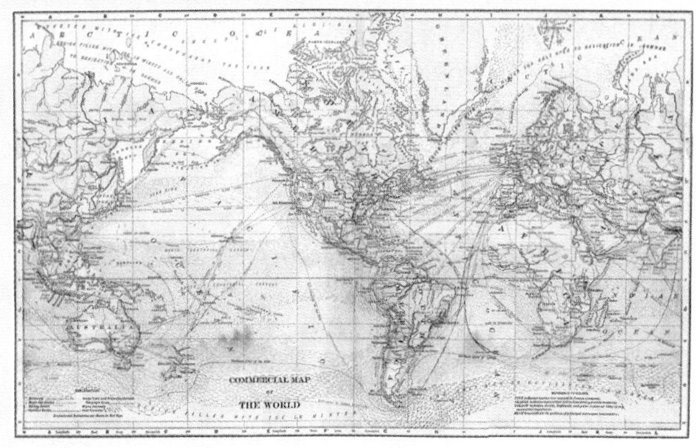

CHAPTER 40

Shakers

1774–1900

> *Beauty rests on utility. That which has in itself the highest use possesses the greatest beauty. Any thing may, with strict propriety, be called perfect which perfectly answers the purpose of which it was designed.*
>
> —Shaker saying

The architecture, interiors, and furniture of the American Shakers, a 19th-century utopian religious group, grow out of their belief system and worldview. Minimal ornament, simple forms deriving from function or utility, perfected proportions, and excellent craftsmanship reflect the communal, labor-focused lifestyles of the Shakers and anticipate aspects of Modernism of the 20th century.

HISTORICAL AND SOCIAL

The Shakers, or the United Society of Believers in the First and Second Appearance of Christ, are the largest and best known of the 19th-century communal utopian societies in the United States. Establishing 19 communities from Maine to Georgia, the Shakers practice celibacy and lead simple lives revolving around worship, community, and work. The society originates from the French Camisards, a millennium group that immigrates to England in the late 17th century to escape persecution. They unite with a Quaker group and become known as the "Shaking Quakers" (Fig. 40-1) because of their vigorous, trembling worship. Eventually, the name shortens to the Shakers. Ann Lee, an illiterate, working-class Englishwoman, becomes the first leader of the American group. Along with seven others, she arrives in America in 1774. The early years are extremely difficult for them as British pacifists during a time of conflict with the Mother country. Life is hard, and converts are few.

In 1775, the group purchases land in Albany, New York, and the move to inhabit it yields relative stability and income. Between 1781 and 1783, Mother Ann and others begin to travel and preach. Many people find Shaker beliefs appealing and convert. Of particular importance is new member Joseph Meacham, a former Baptist minister who leads the group following Mother Ann's death in 1783. Under Meacham's leadership, missionary trips throughout the region expand Shaker influence and set up new villages. Established in 1787, Mount Lebanon in New York becomes the parent community and model for others. By the middle of the century, the Shakers reach their peak with about 6,000 members in 19 communities in New England, the Midwest, and the South. The uniformity of Shaker architecture, interiors, and furniture, which is striking for so large a group, develops from the shared belief systems as well as the similar backgrounds of members. Other factors include the travel of artisans and craftspeople among communities to teach and assist each other, the sharing of ideas and forms among members, and training through apprenticeships.

Following the Civil War, membership declines as public fascination with utopian societies and religious fervor wanes. The simple and celibate Shaker way of life no longer appeals. Economic woes plague some communities, and they begin to disband and sell or abandon their buildings. Membership continues to dwindle through the 19th and 20th centuries. Today, one active community remains, and a few villages are museums or preservation sites.

▲ **40-1.** "Shakers, a Quaker sect, performing their distinctive, trembling, religious dance"; Currier and Ives.

CONCEPTS

Shaker doctrines of separation from the world, communal living, lives centered on worship and work, equality between the sexes, and celibacy shape their material culture. Members isolate themselves physically in villages to escape worldly or outside influences. They see the physical environment as a means of creating a heavenly kingdom on earth and believe surroundings can positively affect people who live and work in them. The Shakers' emphasis on community before individuals; lives that revolve around unity of purpose; and shared experiences of community, life, and work drive the form of their villages, dwellings, workshops, barns, interiors, and furnishings. Their communities are deliberate advertisements of the better world to be had through the Shaker lifestyle.

All members share equally in the community, so order, uniformity, and consistency dominate daily life, including dress, schedules, tasks, housing, and furnishings. The parent group in Mount Lebanon defines the appearance and organization of Shaker communities. In 1821, the first of the Millennial Laws, rules for life and conduct, are circulated among Shaker communities. Subsequent leaders expand the laws in 1845 and 1860. These later versions specify rules for planning architecture, interiors, and furnishings that are intended to shape Shaker life and labor and to further group identity.

Shaker buildings, interiors, and furniture are planned primarily for work, division of labor by task and gender, and celibacy. Mother Ann equates work with worship, so her followers see labor as a positive force in their lives. Consequently, economy, efficiency, and function are important life and design principles that become the guidelines for beauty. Believers are innovators in labor-saving forms and devices, many of which they freely share with the world. These include the flat broom, the circular saw, and the coat hanger. Well ahead of their time, believers regard men and women as equal in power and position; nevertheless the sexes assume different tasks based upon traditional labor divisions. For example, men farm while women weave. Celibacy within the group determines architectural forms and the distribution of space to separate men and women. Rules stress order, neatness, and cleanliness, so the few furnishings are designed for easy maintenance and to avoid pride in ownership. Other defining principles thoughtfully applied to life and physical surroundings include purity of mind and body, honesty, integrity, prudence, diligence, humanity, and kindness.

Shakers believe that to fulfill a task wholeheartedly is evidence of love for God and the group. It is also a means of asserting individuality in a group that dresses alike; worships alike; and arises, eats, works, and retires at the same time. Shakers value learning new skills and taking on different labors. Versatility is esteemed as evidence of God-given talents.

MOTIFS

■ *Motifs*. Because the Shakers regard decoration as worldly, thus forbidden, no motifs are associated with them other than flowers and hearts that appear in their paintings (Fig. 40-2, 40-13). Buildings, furniture, and decorative arts rely on materials, function, and form for beauty.

▲ **40-2.** Motifs and Architectural Details: Wooden boxes, mid- to late 19th century; and door and window details, Kentucky.

ARCHITECTURE

Shaker architecture, whether domestic or utilitarian, eschews fashion and style in favor of neatness, efficiency, function, and easy maintenance. Thus, most buildings have unembellished forms, refined proportions, and a discreet emphasis upon beauty in materials, which contributes to a similar appearance in the communities. Some differences come from the size of the community, its location, the available materials, and members' backgrounds. Converts, most of them working class, bring their previous building and carpentry skills to the community, so they build in the simple forms that they know.

Shakers abstract and adapt the character of 18th-century Georgian and Federal and 19th-century Greek Revival styles to community needs and preferences. However, awareness of prevailing high styles sometimes appears in proportions and a few details. Following the Civil War, Shaker buildings to some extent begin to adopt Stick, Queen Anne, and Shingle styles as the Shakers, always progressive, seek to modernize. Public and private buildings also feature symmetry and efficient planning that supports Shaker work and worship and reinforces expected behaviors. For example, buildings often have separate entrances for male and female believers.

Communities usually have a meetinghouse, dwelling houses for families, and a variety of utilitarian support buildings such as barns, stables, sheds, laundries, shops, workshops, privies, and bath houses. Most villages have a trustee office that links them to the outside world through commerce and/or accommodates visitors and tourists. Architectural innovations include dwellings that house large numbers of people and adapting the form and construction of meetinghouses, barns, and utilitarian buildings to the community needs. Always frugal and efficient, Shakers remodel and renovate buildings to meet the community's changing needs.

▲ **40-3.** Meetinghouse, Canterbury Shaker Village, 1792; New Hampshire; Moses Johnson.

Public and Private Buildings

■ *Meetinghouses*. Meetinghouses (Fig. 40-3) are the physical and spiritual center of Shaker villages because lives and worship centered on God are the foundations on which the group is built. Symmetry, order, and architectural perfection symbolize the hope of salvation and the new kingdom on earth that the Shakers strive to create. Most early meetinghouses follow the original at Mount Lebanon with two or three stories, white painted clapboard, two entrances, and a gambrel roof. Later structures are more diverse. The first floor of the meetinghouse is a large open space with no interior columns so that the Shakers can perform their ritual dances during worship. Upper stories have living quarters for ministry leaders who do not associate with regular believers.

▲ **40-4.** Village area, Sabbathday Lake Shaker Village, 1884; New Gloucester, Maine.

DESIGN SPOTLIGHT

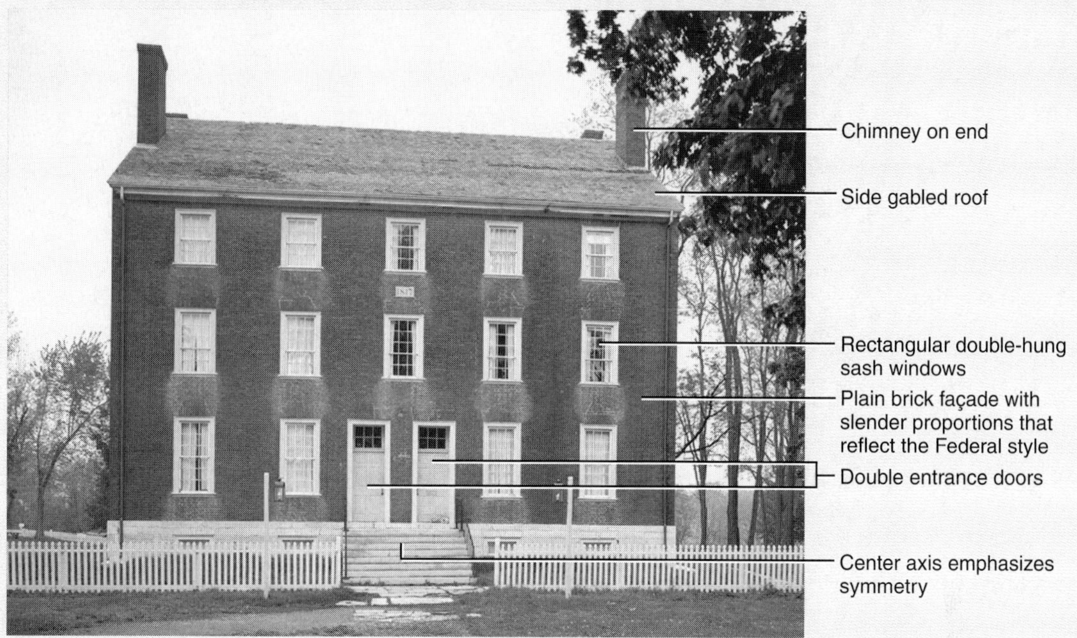

Architecture and Interiors: Established in the 1820s, the Shaker Village of Pleasant Hill has one of the largest Shaker communities in the country. As is common for Shaker villages, the community centers on the meetinghouse with dwelling houses, workshops, and barns arranged nearby. The buildings illustrate common features of plain architecture, neatness, and orderly planning. Built by Micajah Burnett in 1820, the Family Dwelling Houses follow early Shaker prototypes. The rectangular block structures have side gable roofs, chimneys at each end of the buildings, a plain brick façade with slender proportions, and double-hung sash windows. The main façades have the usual double entrances. The left one is for the Brothers and the right is for the Sisters.

The stair hall, hall, and sleeping room exhibit the Shaker characteristics of uniformity, simplicity, function, and ease of maintenance through design, materials, and furnishings. Wood plank floors, wood trim, white plaster walls, and wooden pegboards for hanging clothes are common. Shaker-built cast-iron stoves, not fireplaces, provide heat. Rooms are sparsely furnished because accumulating possessions is believed to engender worldliness and pride. Furnishings are simple, utilitarian, movable, and undecorated, which reflects the Shaker belief system and supports their lifestyle. Household textiles, which often appear in sleeping rooms, are homemade or purchased. Patterns are nonrepresentational and colors are bright, but not flashy. Decorative accessories are rare. [National Historic Landmark]

▲ **40-5.** Family Dwelling Houses and hall, stair hall, kitchen, and sleeping room, Shaker Village of Pleasant Hill, 1820s–1850s; Harrodsburg, Kentucky; Micajah Burnett. (*Continued on next page*)

DESIGN SPOTLIGHT

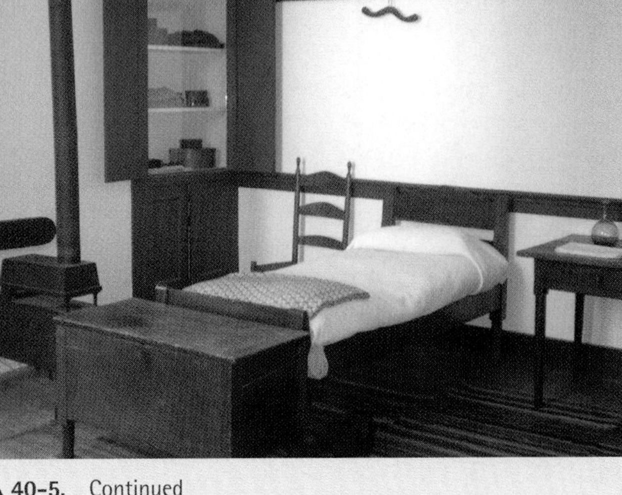

▲ **40-5.** Continued

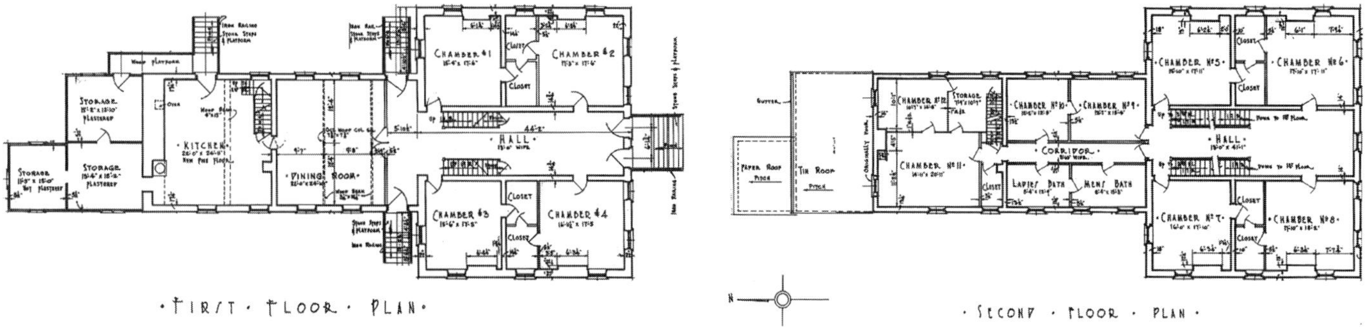

▲ **40-6.** Floor plans, Shaker Centre Family Dwelling House, Shaker Village of Pleasant Hill, 1820s–1850s; Harrodsburg, Kentucky; Micajah Burnett.

■ *Dwelling Houses.* Dwelling houses (Fig. 40-5) support the group's organization into families, which disregard blood ties to further group identity. These large communal or family residences are designed to conform individual behavior to Shaker laws. Each family builds its own house, which reflects its character. Children (orphans or those brought by converts) and the elderly live separately from others. Larger, wealthier families build stately dwellings of stone or brick with two to six stories and 40 to 50 rooms to house up to 100 members. Southern dwellings have higher ceilings, wider hallways (Fig. 40-5), and larger rooms than those of other communities. Within dwellings, four to eight members with similar labor roles share rooms. Elders and eldresses live in first-floor quarters near an entrance to permit them to observe behavior. Movement within and between dwelling houses is frequent as members change roles, leave, or grow older.

Despite diversity in appearance, dwellings are similar in plan organization (Fig. 40-6). Usually there are two sets of stairs, one for men and another for women. They may be near each other or side by side. In eastern communities, kitchens, bakeries, pantries, storage rooms, and communal dining rooms are in basements. Those in the west usually place these services in a rear ell or in a separate building behind the main house. The first floor has a meeting room (Fig. 40-7) that is used for family worship, lectures, or socializing. The communal dining room and waiting rooms may be on the first floor. Upper floors have symmetrical, separated retiring (sleeping) rooms (Fig. 40-5, 40-8, 40-11) and sitting rooms for men and women. Some dwellings have small weaving or spinning shops on upper levels. Finished attics usually have built-in storage for out-of-season bedding and clothing.

■ *Site Orientation.* Shaker villages (Fig. 40-4) often begin on the farm of a new convert. Members vigorously adapt the landscape by clearing trees and brush, building ponds, diverting streams, and planting crops. They usually align with or intersect a main road in rural areas to maintain isolation from the world but still have access to a town. Generally, main buildings line the major road with secondary buildings behind them. The meetinghouse is centrally placed, and the dwelling of the First or Central Family is across from it or nearby. (The Central Family is made up of people most devoted to the faith, hence their location near the house of worship.) Other dwellings, also named by their locations, scatter throughout the community. Workshops and support buildings surround each dwelling. Diversity in layout as well as the number and types of buildings in Shaker villages reflects the makeup of each group.

■ *Materials.* Building materials vary with regions (Fig. 40-2, 40-3, 40-4, 40-5). Following the example set at Mount Lebanon, meetinghouses are of clapboards, although other materials are occasionally used. Dwellings may be wood, brick, limestone, or granite. Kentucky and New Hampshire Shaker families build in brick and limestone. Ammi B. Young, a prominent but non-Shaker architect, designs a granite dwelling house for the Enfield, New Hampshire, group. Meetinghouses are painted white to stand out among the other structures. Dwellings and other structures may be yellow, red, brown, or tan. In the late 19th century, most buildings are painted white despite earlier prohibitions. Wooden barns may be painted black.

■ *Façades.* All façades are plain and unadorned like the Shakers and their lives (Fig. 40-2, 40-3, 40-4, 40-5). Millennial Laws mandate rectangular forms and straight walls. There are no pilasters, quoins, columns, or fancy moldings. Some buildings in western communities reveal a bit of embellishment such as cove or bead moldings. Façades of meetinghouses and dwellings are symmetrical to reflect order. Workshops and other utilitarian buildings have windows where needed. Most dwelling houses have a cupola or belfry for the bells that announce times for rising, dining, working, meeting, and retiring.

■ *Windows and Doors.* Large sash windows with shutters are typical (Fig. 40-2, 40-3, 40-5). Stone lintels surmount windows in brick or stone buildings. A few Palladian or arched windows appear in the 1840s.

Of the typical two entrances, the left is for Brothers and right for Sisters. The Mount Lebanon meetinghouse has a third door for the ministry leaders. A few entries, such as in Pleasant Hill, Kentucky (Fig. 40-2, 40-5), have fanlights or side lights; others have rectangular transoms above them to let in light. Porches are rare, but eastern buildings have shed roofs over the entries in the Anglo-Dutch tradition. Unique to Canterbury, New Hampshire, are small gable roofs with supports of curved brackets above doorways. Paneled doors have simple surrounds.

■ *Roofs.* Early meetinghouses have gambrel roofs with dormers (Fig. 40-3). Some later ones and those in the west have gable roofs. Dwelling houses usually have gable roofs with dormers (Fig. 40-5). The Mount Lebanon meetinghouse has an unusual and innovative curved roof.

INTERIORS

Shaker interiors exhibit uniformity, simplicity, function, and ease of maintenance through materials and furnishings. The most common types of spaces are worship areas (Fig. 40-7), meeting rooms, and retiring rooms (Fig. 40-5, 40-8, 40-11), which are planned to facilitate work and worship and to separate the sexes. Most rooms have white plaster walls with brightly painted trim, built-in cupboards and drawers, wood strips with pegs for hanging clothing or objects, and a cast-iron stove (Fig. 40-8). Shaker-built cast-iron stoves that protrude into the room space are preferred over fireplaces. Shaker built-ins and peg rails are one of their most distinctive characteristics and one of their design legacies. Built-in cupboards and drawers provide storage and a way of controlling behavior through limiting storage space, which encourages sharing and discourages accumulating possessions. Most rooms are sparsely furnished with a mixture of Shaker-made and other furniture brought by new converts. The Millennial Laws define room furnishings for uniformity and specify rules for their placement to prevent individuals from arranging spaces for themselves. Exceptions are the spaces for visitors located in trustee office buildings, which may have wallpaper, carpet, and horsehair upholstery as well as walnut or mahogany furniture. By the end of the 19th century, other Shaker interiors also begin to have wallpaper, carpet, and more upholstered and ornamented furniture.

Public and Private Buildings

■ *Color.* Common colors for wood trim include Prussian blue in the meetinghouse, blue, brown-red, yellow ochre, green, and black in other spaces (Fig. 40-5, 40-8, 40-11). Walls are always pristine white in dwellings and meetinghouses.

■ *Floors.* Floors are wood planks (Fig. 40-5, 40-7, 40-8, 40-11). Millennial Laws prescribe that floors, if painted or stained, should be reddish yellow. Only those in the meetinghouse are polished. Kitchens and other utilitarian spaces may have stone floors for easy cleaning. Linoleum becomes typical in the second half of the 19th century. Rag, braided, woven, hooked, knitted, or crocheted rugs may cover floors. Linen, wool, or cotton rugs are colorful combinations of orange, yellow, green, black, brown, rose, and purple. Blue and red are especially favored. Rugs may be round or rectangular and come in many sizes from long runners to rectangles shaped to fit various spaces. Painted floor cloths sometimes cover floors in the first half of the 19th century, whereas some rooms have ingrain carpets in the late 19th century.

■ *Walls.* Walls are white plaster with painted wooden trim (Fig. 40-5, 40-7, 40-8, 40-11). Some rooms have paneled dadoes. About three-quarters of the way up the wall is a narrow board with pegs for hanging clothing, possessions, lighting, and even chairs. Although function is primary, the peg board adds an architectonic element to interiors. Most spaces, including attics, have built-in storage drawers and cabinets.

■ *Windows and Doors.* Most windows have simple wood trim surrounding them (Fig. 40-5, 40-7, 40-8, 40-11). They often have simple curtains hanging from rods in the lower half. Curtains usually are plain white linen or cotton, although some are green or blue. The color red, checks, plaids, and stripes are prohibited. Interior doors are usually wood and have simple wood molding surrounds that contrast in color to walls. Many have transoms to allow light into interior rooms. The Center Family Dwelling House in Pleasant Hill, Kentucky, has arched doorways.

▲ **40-7.** Meeting room, Family Dwelling House, 1824; New Lebanon, New York; Moses Johnson.

■ *Ceilings.* Ceilings are plain white (Fig. 40-5, 40-7, 40-8). Most are flat, although one in Pleasant Hill, Kentucky, is arched. Meetinghouse ceilings are often beamed to support large open spaces.

■ *Textiles.* Household textiles may be homemade or purchased. Those made by the Shakers are well executed and carefully planned with symmetry and nonrepresentational patterns. Colors are bright, not drab, and never flashy. Other textiles include splash cloths behind washstands and wall cloths near beds for warmth.

■ *Lighting.* Light is important to the Shakers, so large windows illuminate spaces during the day. Interior windows in strategic spots bring light into rooms without windows. Like others of their time, Shakers use lamps and candles for artificial lighting. Fixtures and holders are simple in design. Always progressive, Shakers install gas and electricity for lighting when available.

FURNISHINGS AND DECORATIVE ARTS

Shaker furniture, like architecture and interiors, reflects their belief system and supports their lifestyle (Fig. 40-5, 40-7, 40-8, 40-9, 40-10, 40-11, 40-12). It relies on materials, form, silhouette, and function for beauty. The simplicity reflects the simple lives as well as the humble, working-class backgrounds of most members who are unfamiliar with high-style furnishings. Furniture is practical and easy to clean and maintain. Shaker belief in work as worship yields perfection of proportion and craftsmanship. Materials are used appropriately and honestly. Because ornament is considered worldly, furniture has little of it. Nothing superfluous is allowed to disturb the beauty of proportions and craftsmanship.

Plain and utilitarian, movable and built-in furniture is uniform in appearance and distribution among members. Craftspeople work in standard furniture types but adapt them to community and individual needs. Because Shakers equate beauty with utility, furniture is designed to suit the user or users and the task. Dimensions are adapted to individuals or community requirements. For example, dining tables are made in different sizes, and some can accommodate up to 20 diners. Craftspeople often make multiples of pieces for uniformity and invent new forms to accommodate changes in technology or work requirements.

The Millennial Laws prescribe what furnishings each member should have so that no one has more or less than anyone else. All furnishings belong to the community, although some pieces are made for individuals, such as older members. Rooms are sparsely furnished because accumulating possessions is believed to engender worldliness and pride. Shaker artisans do not sign their furniture but often apply number and letter codes to indicate in what room a piece belongs and/or for whom it is made.

There is little distinctive Shaker furniture before 1800. New converts usually bring furniture with them, so little is needed. After that time, Shaker craftspeople begin to adapt standard types to their lifestyles. After 1860, furniture is no longer made in the western communities, but some is marketed to the world in New England and New York. Following the Centennial International Exhibition in 1876 in Philadelphia, interest in handcrafted furniture sparks great interest in Shaker furniture, the sale of which becomes a major source of income for the group. Market furniture is offered in fewer types. Chairs and rockers are the most common and come in several standard sizes and different finishes. A distinctive aspect of Shaker seating is the variety of colored tapes used for seats and cushions. Worship spaces have little furniture except seating located on one end. Meeting rooms may have benches or settees, or believers

DESIGN SPOTLIGHT

Interior: The walls in this dwelling room have the common Shaker treatments of white plaster and painted woodwork. Reflecting Shaker concern for neatness and cleanliness, the peg board or rail holds furniture, clothing, and other items. A small Shaker-designed cast-iron stove supplies heat. The storage wall is a Shaker innovation. These built-in arrangements of drawers and cupboards allow the many believers residing in dwelling houses to store out-of-season clothing, bedding, and other possessions. Larger communities often have entire rooms devoted to storage. As is usual, no patterned fabrics, framed pictures, mirrors, decoration, or excess furniture mar the simplicity or encourage pride or worldliness among the members who live here. All Shaker interiors emulate these concepts to encourage uniformity of design and behavior, which creates an integrated whole among buildings, interiors, and furnishings.

▲ **40-8.** Dwelling room with storage wall, Family Dwelling House, 1841–1846; originally from Enfield, New Hampshire. [Courtesy Winterthur Museum]

may bring their own chairs. Retiring or sleeping rooms (Fig. 40-5, 40-8, 40-12) have a bed, a chair, and storage for each inhabitant, and a communal washstand and a table or candlestand (Fig. 40-10). There is no padded upholstery until the late 19th century.

Public and Private Buildings

■ *Materials*. Eastern furniture is of pine, maple, birch, ash, cherry, hickory, and butternut (Fig. 40-5, 40-7, 40-8, 40-9, 40-10, 40-11, 40-12). That made in western villages is of walnut, cherry, beech, or poplar. Shakers use no veneer, inlay, marquetry, or graining. Sometimes, drawer fronts, tabletops, or entire pieces are of figured woods, such as curly maple or flame cherry. Early furniture is stained or painted red, blue, or yellow. Later pieces are simply varnished. Mushroom-shaped knobs for cupboards or drawers are of wood because brass is considered worldly.

▲ **40-10.** Candlestand, Shaker Village of Pleasant Hill, early 19th century; Harrodsburg, Kentucky.

DESIGN SPOTLIGHT

Furniture: Although similar to American Colonial or vernacular furniture, simplicity and refined proportions characterize the Shaker rocking chair, reflecting the community's belief in purity and a simple life. No carved embellishment, veneers, or painted decorations obscure form or multiply housekeeping tasks. The plainness of the chair encourages unity by discouraging individuality. Following the Civil War, Shakers find a ready market for their chairs in the outside world.

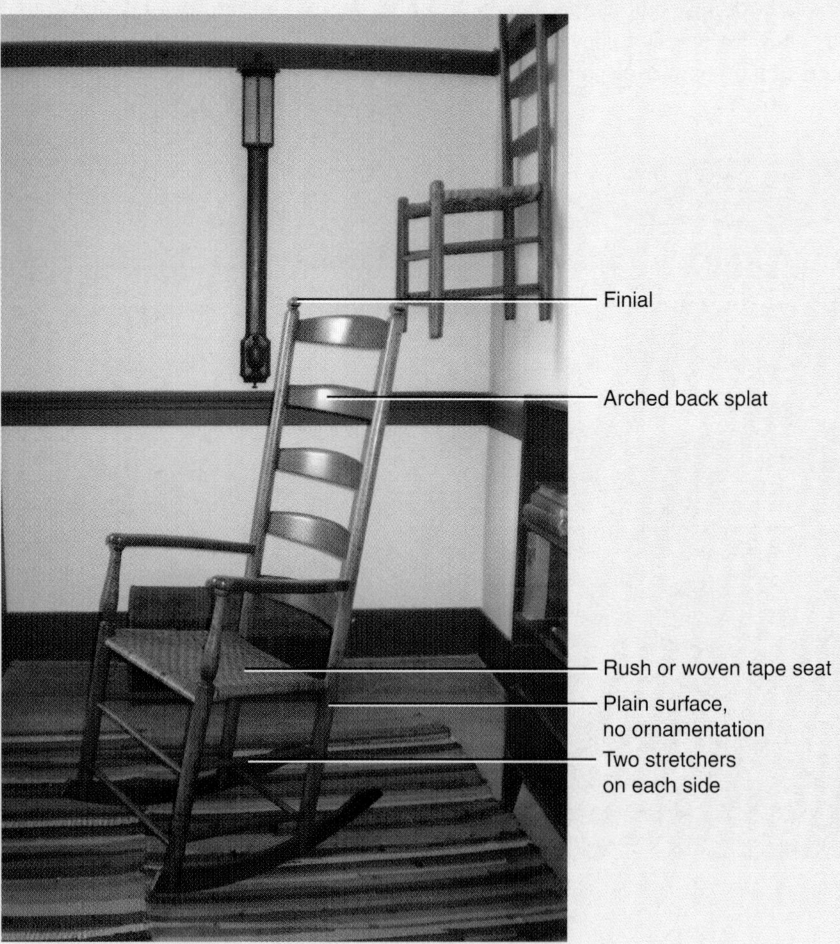

▲ **40-9.** Rocking chair, early to late 19th century.

▲ **40-11.** Interior with bed, early to late 19th century.

■ *Seating*. Shaker seating includes chairs, rockers, settees, and benches (Fig. 40-5, 40-7, 40-8, 40-9, 40-12). Ladder-back chairs and rockers, the most common type of seating, display regional differences in materials and appearance. Other types include low-back chairs with one or two slats to enable them to be pushed under dining tables or hung from the peg rails; high-legged chairs used by weavers; and revolvers, which have rotating seats. Legs usually are cylindrical, of one piece of wood, and may taper near the floor. After 1825, back legs often have a tilter, a Shaker innovation of a flat bottom ball that allows the chair to lean backward yet remain stable on the floor. Two stretchers on all four sides is typical. Back slats are usually arched and may graduate in size. A rounded cushion rod may surmount the uppermost slat. Finials, used as hand grips, vary in shape, and their distinctive shape may indicate where the chair is made. Arms may be flat, slightly curved, or rolled with mushroom-shaped or round handholds. Seats are planks, rush, cane, splint, or colored tape. Shakers weave cotton tape for seats until 1850 when they begin to purchase it. Colorful tapes may form patterns such as checkerboards or herringbone. Rockers with and without arms resemble chairs. Benches and settees, used in meetinghouses and rooms, have shaped seats, tapering legs, and spindle backs.

■ *Tables*. Shakers make and use many different types of tables (Fig. 40-5, 40-7, 40-8). Some designs are unique and used for particular tasks. Trestle tables are used for dining. Early trestles are chamfered with flat, tapered feet. Later ones are rounded or quadrangular with arches. Lighter than traditional examples, Shaker trestle tables have a heavy stretcher under the top. Most

▲ **40-12.** Chest of drawers, early to late 19th century.

▲ **40-13.** Decorative Arts: Shaker gift drawings, 1860; Hannah Cohoon.

candlestands (Fig. 40-10, 40-12) have round tops, a baluster support, and spider or arched legs. Drop-leaf, work, and sewing tables usually have four slender, tapered legs and sometimes a drawer in the apron. Some work or sewing tables have a pull-out work surface and two sets of drawers on opposite sides to accommodate two or more users. Sewing desks, unique to the Shakers, rest on short legs and have several drawers with smaller drawers in the top gallery.

■ *Storage*. Shakers use both movable and built-in storage (Fig. 40-5, 40-8, 40-11, 40-12). Large Shaker families require great amounts of storage, so built-ins may fill attic spaces and be fitted into odd or small spaces such as corners or under stairs or eaves. Built-ins may consist of only drawers or can combine drawers and cupboards (Fig. 40-12). Function determines the arrangement and size of drawers and cupboards. Drawers are plain with no moldings or embellishment and simple wooden knobs. Early cupboard panels are raised, whereas later ones are flat with quarter-round edges for greater simplicity and ease of cleaning. Chests of drawers have simple silhouettes and no embellishment, including no escutcheon plates around keyholes.

■ *Beds*. Beds parallel developments in Shaker history (Fig. 40-5, 40-8, 40-11). Early on, two adult brothers or sisters or several boys or girls sleep in double beds to accommodate as many people as possible in little space. Trundle beds are common during the height of Shaker membership to conserve space and to help care for the sick. As membership declines, narrow, single beds prevail. Simple in design, beds have cylindrical legs, low headboards, and stretcher footboards. They are often on wheels to make moving easier. The Millennial Laws prescribe green for bed colors. In the infirmary, adult-sized cradles gently rock the sick and help prevent bed sores.

■ *Decorative Arts*. Accumulating and displaying possessions are incompatible with Shaker beliefs and lives, so rooms have no decorative accessories. Occasionally Shakers give drawings or paintings as gifts (Fig. 40-13). The Millennial Laws forbid pictures and paintings, although they do permit one small mirror in retiring rooms for grooming. At first, clocks also are forbidden, but later the elders realize that time pieces help maintain orderly lives. Many communities have a tall case clock in the hall of their dwelling houses and in their shops and barns. Shakers do not make their own tablewares, but purchase plain, white utilitarian ceramics. The Shakers are known for the elegance and beauty of their baskets and oval boxes (Fig. 40-2) that they make in various sizes and shapes. Toward the end of the 19th century Shaker dwellings have more accessories, a reflection of the loosening of rigid laws.

■ *Later Interpretations*. During the mid-20th century, designers such as Paul McCobb (Fig. 40-14) interpret the concept of Shaker simplicity in their furniture designs. During the early 21st century, Shaker-style furniture is extremely popular, as reproduced or adapted by various manufacturers. Plain, unadorned, simple Shaker forms are adapted for dining rooms, living rooms, and bedrooms and made in types and materials unknown in their day.

▲ **40-14.** Later Interpretation: Planner Group chest of drawers, 1960s; Massachusetts; Paul McCobb, manufactured by Winchendon Furniture Mfg.

CHAPTER 41

Aesthetic Movement

1860s–1890s

> *The ceiling is frescoed in bold work of black and gold of unsymmetrical design. The walls are paneled with Japanese painted stuffs framed in gilt bamboo, and the frieze is a continuous band of brilliant figures on paper crêpe. Over the doors, and in the spaces where the tint of wall is flat, fans of brilliant colors have been tastefully displayed. A table in blue and white, and red lacquer saucers inserted in the dull black wood of the furniture, help the effect.*
>
> —William A. Hammond House, *The Art Amateur*, June 1879 (description of Japanese bedroom)

The Aesthetic Movement attempts to reform design by educating consumers about artistic principles. Not a single style but an attitude or philosophy, the movement draws upon many styles and cultures for inspiration and largely rejects the idea that art should serve a higher, moral purpose. Followers see no division between the fine and decorative arts, so they introduce principles of Art into interiors, furniture, textiles, accessories, and other areas. Primarily focused on the ordinary home, the movement inspires artistic interiors and furniture in England and the United States. Lasting only about two decades, the Aesthetic Movement brings changes with immediate and far-reaching influences.

HISTORICAL AND SOCIAL

The Aesthetic Movement stems from the desire to reform the home and its design following London's Crystal Palace Exhibition, 1851. The movement takes form when poet Charles Algernon Swinburne and writer Walter Pater bring the cult of Aestheticism to England from France in the 1860s. Finding a sympathetic audience in the artists and designers of the Pre-Raphaelite Brotherhood and others, their discussions of aesthetics begin to take a different, less moralistic tone in contrast to other reform ideas and movements.

Many members of the Aesthetic Movement follow Matthew Arnold's *Culture and Anarchy*, which defines two groups according to their taste and ability to appreciate art. The more important group is the Aesthetes, who enjoy "artistic" sensibilities. In contrast are the Philistines, members of the middle class, who possess little or no appreciation for or capacity to assess beauty. Crass materialists, Philistines lack the high-minded, artistic natures of the Aesthetes. The most aesthetic Aesthetes, such as James A. M. Whistler and Oscar Wilde, reject everything admired by the Philistines. They esteem delicacy, refinement, soft colors, anything old, and the young. Although the more radical group remains small, many others in England during the 1870s are inspired to cultivate their artistic sensibilities in order to live in beautiful surroundings. In the United States, the Aesthetic Movement is at its height in all levels of society from the mid-1870s to the mid-1880s. The Centennial International Exhibition of 1876; publications; and visits from Aesthetes, such as Wilde, introduce the American public to English artistic precepts.

Aesthetic discussions of what constitutes beauty inspire various artists, designers, and architects to establish design principles based on usefulness, color, form, and ornament to assess the beauty of an object or artwork. With missionary passion, followers set out to reform taste through example and publication. The movement stimulates artistic activity and opportunities for collaboration among designers in both England and the United States. Designers, artists, and architects come together to create Artistic architecture, interiors, furniture, and decorative arts. Their roles change and expand. Architects not only routinely design the building but also the interiors, furniture, wallpaper, textiles, and accessories. Painters and sculptors also design interiors or furniture. Some designers publish books of ornament drawn from every culture, while others advance the movement through lectures, plays, and novels.

The terms *Art* and *Artistic* signal aesthetic sensibilities early in the movement's development. By the late 1870s and 1880s, the terms become synonymous with the latest fashion, and anyone and everyone uses them to appeal to consumers. Architecture, interiors, furniture, and accessories are never described as *Aesthetic*, but rather as *Artistic*. Consequently, firms, artists, and designers create Artistic rooms and design Artistic furniture. The well-known Liberty's Department Store in London, as well as other department stores, sell "Art Furniture," and local and imported "Artistic" goods reflective of the Aesthetic taste.

Numerous books and periodicals serve as guides and educate the public on matters of design and taste. *Hints on Household Taste* by Charles Locke Eastlake, published in 1868 and running to numerous editions, begins a deluge of books by artists, designers, and dilettantes offering advice on decorating and furnishing the home. Artistic journals include *The Decorator and Furnisher*, New York, and *The House, An Artistic Monthly for Those Who Manage and Beautify the Home*, London. The movement also inspires various art societies and groups in England and America who spread its tenets. One outgrowth of the Aesthetic Movement's passion for education comes from the affluent who, believing in *noblesse oblige*, sometimes open their homes for tours by lesser folk. In addition, during this period wealthy patrons' collections of art and objects often form the basis for public museums. The Aesthetic Movement also inspires the Household Art or Art at Home Movement.

Women are especially important in the Aesthetic Movement as both the focus and transmitters of reform. Critics, many of whom are female, devote much attention to housewives, who now have the duty of decorating their homes artistically. Writers emphasize that decorating is a very important task because the design and furnishings must demonstrate the family's culture and taste and create a wholesome environment and refuge to counter the negative effects of contemporary life. This new role, coupled with greater emphasis upon education, prompts many women to become artists, designers, decorators, and critics. Not only do they create artistic goods and interiors, but they also write books and articles to assist other women in doing the same. They form and participate in art groups, such as china painters or embroidery societies, as leisure activities or to produce an income. Some of these groups exert important and longlasting effects on art education by establishing art schools or museums.

▲ **41–1.** "My Lady's Chamber"; published in *The House Beautiful: Essays on Beds and Tables, Stools and Candlesticks*, 1878; Clarence Cook.

Regarded by some as an excuse for excess and self-indulgence, Aesthetes and the Aesthetic Movement frequently are ridiculed in the press and become the subject of numerous satirical articles; cartoons; songs; and even an opera, *Patience* by Gilbert and Sullivan. Nevertheless, the movement has positive effects on design; the home; and, more important, the way people think about them. The deemphasis of styles helps loosen the grip of historicism. Promoting principles of Art increases awareness that art is important in all areas of life, which in turn helps to promote the worth of an object as deriving from its intrinsic beauty instead of its associations. By the 1880s, the Aesthetic Movement begins to move in other directions, such as the Arts and Crafts Movement and Art Nouveau. However, discussions about beauty and the pursuit of excellence in design continue long after the Aesthetic Movement declines and its ideas influence subsequent movements.

CONCEPTS

The Aesthetic Movement advances the idea that good taste is not ostentatious display, but careful planning based on educated knowledge of artistic principles and historic precedents. Consequently, good taste can be acquired through learning the principles of art and applying them to everyday life. Developing from various artistic theories, the movement does not distinguish between the fine and decorative arts but emphasizes beauty and usefulness for all forms of expression, particularly the home. Thus, it elevates decoration and furnishing to a high Art, ennobling them with purpose above mere fashion, novelty, or conspicuous consumption. Adherents believe that each surface, object, or pattern provides an encounter with Art and, as such, must be carefully chosen and placed or arranged. Some reject the idea that art should have a moral purpose and avow a credo of "Art for Art's Sake"—the idea that art and beauty, above all, should give pleasure in which one should freely indulge. In contrast to the English, Americans cannot completely reject the moral purpose of art, but they do accept the notion that Art is good for them.

Preferring no style above any other and avoiding historicism, the Aesthetic Movement internationalizes design by drawing upon scores of styles and cultures, most of which are preindustrial, a signal of its rejection of contemporary values. Sources of inspiration include Greece; Rome; the Middle Ages; Italian Renaissance; vernacular traditions; and the arts of Japan, China, India, and the Near East. From nationalistic fervor and to promote its own culture above that of others, the English movement scrupulously avoids anything French as the embodiment of false principles of design in its curvilinear silhouettes and decoration, veneers and graining, naturalistic shading of flowers and plants, and over-ornamentation.

MOTIFS

■ *Motifs*. Motifs (Fig. 41-1, 41-2, 41-5, 41-6, 41-10, 41-12, 41-19, 41-20) include sunflowers, peacock feathers, lilies, paisley, flowers, leaves, Japanese forms, insects, butterflies, and birds.

ARCHITECTURE

Although there is no specific architectural style called Aesthetic Movement, Queen Anne and Old English in England and Queen Anne in North America are associated with it. Architects and designers working in those styles often reveal Aesthetic concerns in their designs. The movement inspires far-ranging effects in architecture and subsequent stylistic developments in both England and America. Immediate changes include a new diversity of sources, including Japan and vernacular traditions. New open planning and simplicity in the United States will affect later styles such as Shingle and Arts and Crafts. The emphasis upon vernacular traditions also helps open the door for the Colonial Revival in the United States and the preservation movements in both England and America. Garden suburbs, inspired by the Aesthetic Movement, profoundly affect urban planning and landscape. In 1876, Bedford Park on the west side of London becomes the first garden suburb and a haven for Aesthetes.

▲ **41-2.** Motifs: Sunflower decorative screen, 1876, by Barnard, Bishop, and Barnards; England; and mantel lambrequin and decorative arts, c. 1870s–1890s.

INTERIORS

Because there is no corresponding architectural style, public (Fig. 41-3, 41-4) and private (Fig. 41-5, 41-6) interiors are the main conveyors of the design characteristics of the Aesthetic Movement. Important design principles include asymmetry, unity, harmony, and contrast. Simplicity, as defined by the period, and eclecticism also are definitive. Other definitive characteristics of Artistic interiors include tertiary colors; a variety of patterns on walls, floors, ceilings, furniture, and accessories; wooden floors with area rugs; *portières* and banded curtains hanging from rings on rods; and furniture and accessories from different periods, cultures, and styles. Art Furniture, inspired by the Aesthetic Movement, has Anglo-Japanese, Eastlake, and vernacular expressions. Also important and characteristic are needlework and other crafts that show off the talent of the lady of the house.

The natural focus for the Aesthete is the home because it is the repository for the badly designed, poorly made goods that pervade the domestic market. Homeowners purchase them in great numbers. Reformers believe that consumers have little, if any, notion of good taste and are more concerned about price and being in fashion. Like other reformers, Aesthetic Movement adherents and writers advance the notion that choosing and arranging furnishings and finishes are critical to the comfort and well-being of the family. They insist that the home and its furnishings both demonstrate and advance the family's culture and social status, help to educate children, and influence character. For assistance in achieving these very important decorating goals, the wealthy call upon architects; decorating firms such as Morris, Marshall, and Faulkner in London and Associated Artists in New York; or cabinetmaking firms such as Herter Brothers in New York (Fig. 41-3, 41-4, 41-8, 41-9, 41-19). To assist them in correctly decorating their homes, the middle class relies on the numerous decorating books and department stores like Liberty's in London that actively promoted Aesthetic ideas.

As designers and writers specify rules for decorating, they also encourage personal expression through eclecticism balanced by

▲ **41-3.** Green dining room, 1867; located in the Victoria and Albert Museum in South Kensington, London, England; Philip Webb.

▲ **41-4.** Veteran's Room in the Seventh Regiment Armory, 1879–1880; New York City, New York; published in *Scribner's Monthly*, 1881; interiors by Louis Comfort Tiffany and Associated Artists, and the building by Charles V. Clinton.

unity and harmony. They especially emphasize principles of arrangement and composition, which are to be carefully studied and planned to give the most artistic result. As a result, juxtapositions and contrasts are common, and simple forms often contrast with complex or multiple patterns. Patterns usually layer upon each other from floor to walls and their components to ceilings as well as to furniture and accessories. The movement advocates simplicity, but its highly patterned rooms seem cluttered and complicated to modern eyes. When compared with revival styles, Artistic rooms are somewhat simpler and may have fewer furnishings, but use a greater variety of patterns throughout.

Pattern is so important that it becomes the focus of intense discussions to define the best types. Prominent artists and architects often create designs for wallpapers, textiles, floor coverings, or embroidery (Fig. 41-10, 41-12). Naturalistic or geometric artistic patterns usually are flat, two-dimensional, and stylized with a bold outline and no shading following Pugin's earlier admonitions. Some examples may be more realistic, but the subtle shadings typical of French patterns are rigorously avoided. Asymmetrical patterns reflect the interest of designers in things Japanese.

In the 1870s and 1880s, Japan and the Aesthetic Movement are nearly synonymous. English and American designers, who avidly collect Japanese prints and ceramics, are inspired by their inherent simplicity, asymmetry, and unity. Japanese motifs, details, and decorative arts soon freely mix with other interior details and furnishings (Fig. 41-5, 41-9). No one considers a room

▲ **41-5.** Japanese bedroom, Dr. William A. Hammond House, 1873; New York City, New York; published in *Artistic Houses*, 1883.

complete without some Japanese pottery or porcelain, and one or more parasols, fans, kimonos, and/or lanterns. Textiles and wallpapers with Japanese motifs and asymmetrical designs add an exotic touch to Western rooms. Designers, such as Edward W. Godwin and Charles F. A. Voysey, create Anglo-Japanese furniture inspired by Japanese design principles (Fig. 41-15, 41-17). Furniture manufacturers also produce popular versions that bear little, if any, resemblance to Japanese design (Fig. 41-18). Following or adapting principles of Japanese design or simply using motifs is more important than re-creating Japan's material culture.

Because of the influence of the Aesthetic Movement, the term *living room* begins to replace the term *parlor*, signaling a move to an inclusive and informal lifestyle. Similarly, the entrance hall becomes less formal than before, with open planning and inglenooks, reminiscent of settles, flanking a fireplace. The affluent tastemakers continue to incorporate conservatories and smoking rooms in their homes during the period. Writers promote asymmetrical furniture arrangements as more useful and convenient and, therefore, beautiful. So, large case pieces and cabinets may line walls, while seating and tables are dispersed throughout the space in informal groupings that are intended to look unplanned.

DESIGN SPOTLIGHT

Interior: Thomas Jeckyll originally designs the dining room as a setting for Whistler's *Princesse de la Pays du Porcelain* and the shelving to accommodate Frederick Leyland's collection of Oriental porcelain. When the room is almost done, Jeckyll consults Whistler about the colors for the shutters and doors. James A. M. Whistler, believing that the wall color clashes with the painting, volunteers to overpaint the walls and decorate the cornice. Like a true Aesthete, Whistler spends eight months redecorating the room in the manner he thinks appropriate, largely without Leyland's approval. He paints the antique Spanish leather wall coverings the present blue-green; gilds the shelving; and decorates the ceiling with gilding and a pattern of peacock feathers. On the shutters and doors, he paints gold peacocks with lavish tails. He also invites friends and acquaintances to view his accomplishments while in process, which further antagonizes Leyland. When Leyland refuses to pay him what he asks, Whistler exacts revenge by depicting two fighting peacocks with a sack of gold coins at their feet. The downtrodden bird represents the artist and the angry one Leyland. The blue-green here is first used by Morris and Company in the South Kensington Museum and becomes a signature Aesthetic Movement color. Also characteristic of the Aesthetic Movement are peacocks, lavish patterns, Oriental porcelains, and the sunflower andirons adapted by Jeckyll.

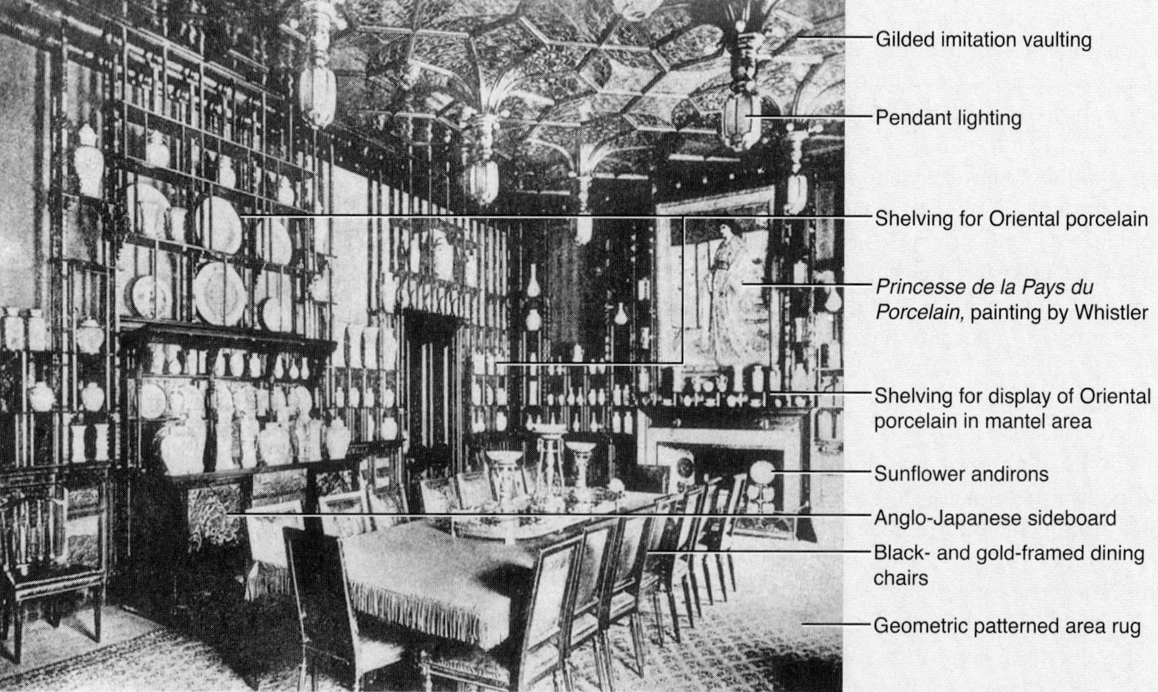

▲ **41-6.** Dining room, Frederick Leyland House, 1876–1877; London, England (now located in the Freer Gallery, Washington, D.C.); Thomas Jeckyll and James A. M. Whistler.

Public and Private Buildings

■ *Color*. In reaction to the brilliant, almost gaudy, hues obtained from the newly introduced synthetic dyes introduced in the 1840s and 1850s, Artistic colors are muted. Tertiary colors, such as blue-green, old gold, olive, terra-cotta, and drab or khaki, dominate the palette (Fig. 41-3, 41-6, 41-10). Some secondary colors are used. Japanese-inspired colors include golds, yellows, and reds (Fig. 41-12).

Writers advocate certain colors and color schemes for particular rooms. Because entrance halls have little light, they require lighter colors than other rooms. Appropriate dining room colors are rich and dark, although if used as family rooms, lighter colors are more appropriate. Drawing rooms, parlors, or living rooms should have light colors to create an Artistic atmosphere.

■ *Floors*. Aesthetic writers, beginning with Eastlake, advocate wood floors and area rugs despite the fact that manufacturers are producing inexpensive carpet (Fig. 41-1, 41-6, 41-7). Reformers insist that wall-to-wall carpet is wasteful and cannot be reused in other rooms. Particularly important, carpet is difficult to clean. During the 1870s, germs are discovered to be the cause of disease, and reformers promote the idea that dirt and dust harbor germs and are a reason for discarding wall-to-wall carpet. If a house's wood floors are unappealing, then parquet should replace them. If the homeowner cannot afford parquet, then writers suggest a wood carpet on the existing floor. Wood carpets, new on the market, are inexpensive thin strips of wood glued to muslin backing.

Hand-knotted Oriental rugs are preferred (Fig. 41-4). They are considered Artistic because of their irregularities and jewel-like colors. Geometric Turkish rugs are appropriate for the dining room and more curvilinear Persians are suited to the drawing room. In response, manufacturers produce Brussels, Wilton, and ingrain in Oriental designs, which are called Art Squares. If a homeowner prefers wall-to-wall carpet, critics recommend small geometric, stylized patterns in muted colors. The naturalistic and shaded floral floor coverings that Aesthetic and other reformers so despise continue as a popular choice of the middle class. Plain and patterned grass matting remains a summer or year-round floor covering.

Alternative floor coverings include ceramic tiles, linoleum, and kamptulicon. Frederick Walton invents linoleum in 1863 in England.

DESIGN SPOTLIGHT

▲ **41-6.** Continued

▲ **41-7.** Design for a drawing room, plate no. 35; published in *Examples of Ancient and Modern Furniture, Metalwork, Tapestries, Decoration*, 1876; Bruce J. Talbert.

▲ **41-8.** Japanese room, W. H. Vanderbilt House, 1879–1882; New York City, New York; published in *Artistic Houses*, 1883; Charles B. Atwood at Herter Brothers.

It soon is used in kitchens and stairs in England and North America. Patterns imitate tile, wood, and ingrain carpet. Kamptulicon is the more expensive and less popular version of linoleum.

■ *Walls*. Aesthetic rooms usually have tripartite walls with three horizontal divisions (Fig. 41-1, 41-3, 41-4, 41-5, 41-6, 41-7). The dado or lower portion is 3′-0″ to 4′-0″ high. Darkest in color, the dado provides a background for furniture. Dados can be covered with wood paneling, tiles, matting, or wallpaper. Above the dado in the middle of the wall is the fill, which varies in height. Because pictures hang there, it usually has an unobtrusive pattern. The frieze, lightest in color, is above the fill near the ceiling. Moldings, wallpaper borders, or changes of paint color mark divisions among the dado, fill, and frieze. Sometimes drawing rooms have only a wide fill and frieze with no dado if large furniture sits against the walls (Fig. 41-8, 41-9). Late in the period, plate rails become fashionable for dining rooms.

DESIGN SPOTLIGHT

Interior: This dining room in Louis Comfort Tiffany's apartment epitomizes Aesthetic Movement principles as espoused by Tiffany and Associated Artists. Contrast and eclecticism characterize the space, which is of no particular style but brings together numerous styles and cultures. Japanese wallpapers adorn the wall, frieze, and ceiling, with a different flat, stylized pattern on each. In contrast, the large, naturalistic harvest painting over the fireplace is in strong yellows, blues, and reds. The circular shapes of the ceramics differ from the rectangular shapes of the walls and shelves. The plates on the mantel shelf repeat the shapes of the painting above them. A few pieces of simple, vernacular American furniture contrast with the many decorative objects in the space.

▲ **41-9.** Dining room, Louis Comfort Tiffany apartment; published in *Artistic Houses*, 1883; Louis Comfort Tiffany.

Critics prefer wood paneling as a wall treatment, especially for halls and dining rooms where furniture would not hide it. Paneling in a dark stain shows Japanese influence. Rails and stiles sometimes are darker than the panels. Painted woodwork is especially recommended for kitchens, bathrooms, and bedrooms because it is easier to clean than is stained or natural wood. In important rooms, wood trim may be painted in two or more coordinating colors that are darker than the walls. Graining, to imitate wood, is less fashionable than before because critics condemn it as dishonest. Not everyone can afford paneling. Alternatives include wallpaper, moldings with different colors of paint on either side, or ready-made wainscoting made of wood strips glued to heavy cloth and available in the 1880s.

■ *Wallpaper.* Most people choose wallpapers in coordinating patterns for dado, fill, frieze, and borders (Fig. 41-1, 41-5, 41-10). Wallpaper sets even come in angled shapes for stairways. In keeping with most reform precepts, patterns are geometric, stylized, and two-dimensional in secondary or tertiary colors. Papers designed by William Morris and his associates have similar characteristics interpreted in rich, naturalistic patterns. Naturalistically shaded wallpapers still abound in middle-class homes despite reformers' efforts to eliminate them. Some of Godwin's designs, influenced by Japanese art, are asymmetrical.

Wallpapers with raised or embossed patterns also may appear in Artistic interiors. Japanese leather paper, an inexpensive paper made in Japan, is one of several similar means of imitating the more expensive leather used on the walls in wealthy homes. Made of heavy paper, it can be embossed, painted, and varnished to enhance its leatherlike appearance. Lincrusta Walton is an English product that successfully imitates the appearance of leather, plaster, or even carved architectural details. Patented by Frederick

▲ **41-10.** Ceiling paper and wallpapers, 1876-1880s; England; ceiling paper by Walter Crane, wallpapers by Jeffery and Company (left), Bruce J. Talbert produced by Jeffery and Company (center), and Edward W. Godwin (right).

Walton in 1877, Lincrusta is made from solidified linseed oil and comes embossed with various designs, including Renaissance, Japanese, Moorish, Byzantine, Greek, Gothic, and Modern. It is painted after hanging. Then the excess paint is wiped away and gold is generously applied. Lincrusta proves to be indestructible, so it is used for stairways and other high-traffic areas. Anaglypta, introduced in 1887 and made of embossed cotton pulp, is lighter in weight than Lincrusta and is an affordable competitor to it.

■ *Mantels*. The mantel is a focal point because writers insist that the hearth should be the center of the home (Fig. 41-1, 41-2, 41-5, 41-6, 41-9). The Artistic mantel unites the useful and the beautiful by having cabinets, niches, shelves, and brackets above it to display Oriental ceramics, porcelain, glass, and other carefully chosen objects. Art Tiles in plain and embossed designs and subdued colors surround the fireplace opening. Andirons shaped like sunflowers are popular (Fig. 41-6).

■ *Window Treatments*. Usually hanging from rings on plain rods, Aesthetic-inspired curtains have horizontal bands of contrasting plain, printed, or embroidered fabric or *appliqué* that correspond to the wall divisions (Fig. 41-11). Unlike before, they are not tied or looped back. Fabrics for curtains include velvet, plush, silk, satin, damask, serge, moreen, cretonne, chintz, and Oriental or other exotic fabrics. Underneath, next to the glass, are lace or muslin glass curtains. A few rooms have roller shades or Venetian blinds beneath the curtains. Some people still use layered curtains with complicated valances.

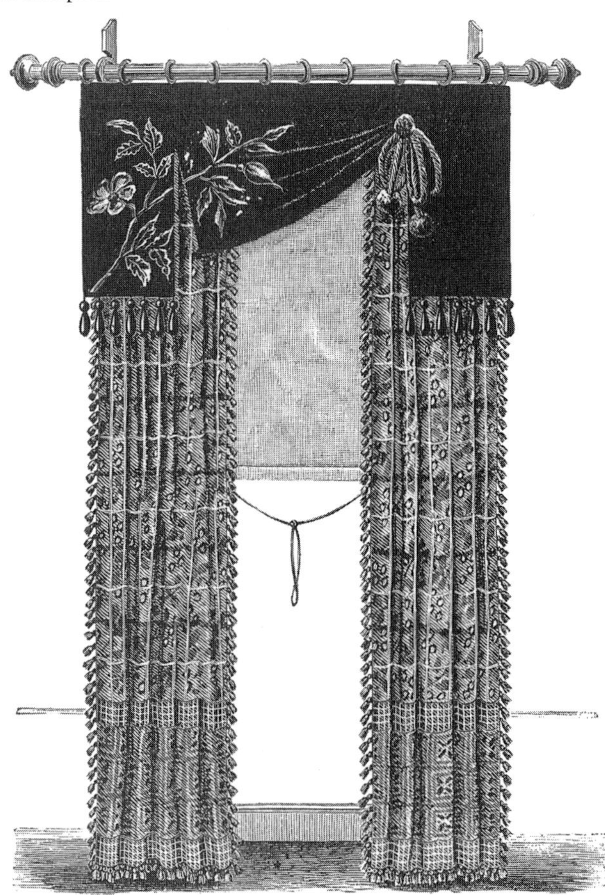

▲ **41-11.** Window treatment; published in *Needlecraft, Artistic and Practical*, 1890.

▲ **41-12.** Textiles: Butterfly brocade furnishings fabric (above) and Victorian crazy quilt or slumber throw (next page) c. 1870s–1880s; England and the United States; fabric by Edward W. Godwin.

■ *Doors*. Most doors are paneled and may be stained or painted wood to match the rest of the woodwork. Rails and stiles usually are lighter in color than panels are. Some panels have painted decorations, and occasionally the designs continue from panel to panel. Doorways to most public rooms have *portières* to shut out drafts and enhance comfort (Fig. 41-5, 41-8). Hanging from rings on rods, *portières* may be more elaborate than window curtains. They come in a variety of fabrics including chenille, Indian dhurrie rugs, or exotic fabrics. Each side may be different to match the room it faces. Reflecting Japanese influence, the space above *portières* may be filled with wooden openwork grilles composed of balls and spindles or other carved decoration.

■ *Ceilings*. Critics condemn white ceilings and insist that they at least should be painted a lighter tint of the wall colors. Consequently, most ceilings are very decorative (Fig. 41-3, 41-4, 41-5, 41-6, 41-7, 41-8, 41-9). Painted decorations include flowers, foliage, clouds, stenciling, and stripes in various colors and widths. Artistic three-dimensional ornament in wood, plaster, or *papier-mâché* comes in sets with central medallions, cornices, and details for corners. Japanese influence appears in coffered or beaded-board ceilings. Ceiling papers are a common and inexpensive way to decorate ceilings (Fig. 41-10). These specialty papers have patterns that look the same from all over the room. Forming the fourth element in wallpaper sets along with the dado, frieze, and fill, ceiling papers typically are lighter colors such as cream, light olive, light blue, and light gray. If the ceiling is low, its treatment may continue down the wall. A few homes use tin ceilings, although these ceilings are more common in commercial buildings. Once in place, tin ceilings are painted and otherwise ornamented to suit the taste and style of the room.

▲ 41-12. Continued

■ *Textiles*. Textiles abound in Artistic interiors to add comfort and interest, and to display the needlework talents of the lady or ladies of the house. A combination of plain and patterned upholstery is common to avoid matching window treatments or wall coverings and to deliberately contrast with other textiles (Fig. 41-8, 41-12). Bands of contrasting fabric or needlework may outline backs or seats. Furniture cases to protect expensive fabrics still are common in summer or year-round, but bed hangings are no longer fashionable for health reasons.

In addition to the usual rugs, curtains, and upholstery, scarves, fabrics, and shawls may drape seating, tables, pianos, the mantel, shelves, wall cabinets, and pictures (Fig. 41-2, 41-5, 41-8). White or colored antimacassars cover backs of chairs and sofas to protect and embellish them. Shelf and mantel lambrequins or table covers, purchased or made at home, are decorated with embroidery, *appliqué*, fringe, or beading. If the back of an upright piano faces into the room, it has its own set of curtains to hide its back. Another set of curtains can hide an ugly fireplace and be opened when a fire is needed. Appearing in the 1870s in America, crazy quilts or Victorian slumber throws display feminine creativity (Fig. 41-12). They are derived from Japanese *kiri-hame*, a complex form of patchwork *appliqué*.

■ *Lighting*. Candles, oil lamps, and gas lamps continue to light the home (Fig. 41-1, 41-3, 41-4, 41-5, 41-6, 41-9, 41-13). Although electric lighting becomes available in the 1880s, few homeowners use it because it is notoriously unreliable. Most writers recommend candles over oil or gas lamps because candles produce a softer light and do not smell. Fixtures are made of glass, brass, bronze, wrought iron, or silver. Many have shades in the new Art Glass in unusual shapes, colors, and finishes.

▲ 41-13. Lighting: Wall sconce and chandelier, Seventh Regiment Armory, 1879–1880; New York City, New York; published in *Scribner's Monthly*, 1881; interiors by Louis Comfort Tiffany and Associated Artists.

FURNISHINGS AND DECORATIVE ARTS

The Aesthetic Movement shuns historical styles and sets or suites of furniture for a more personal expression and a new informality. Consequently, Artistic rooms display numerous pieces of furniture in a variety of styles and from different cultures. Although simplicity is a precept, rooms still may be cluttered with armchairs, side chairs, footstools, small tables, large tables, plant stands, music stands, shelves, wall cabinets, and folding screens (Fig. 41-8). Bay windows and inglenooks often have built-in furniture. Because of a lack of well-designed furniture on the market, the movement advocates using antique furniture with its honest construction and appropriate ornament that does not obscure its form. Chippendale and Sheraton are favored. The Aesthetic Movement does not introduce new types of furniture. As adherents redesign existing types, all types of furniture may exhibit Artistic characteristics; and the movement inspires several furniture variations.

One variation is Art Furniture, which initially is designed by architects and artists and exhibits elements of honest construction and craftsmanship. Later, manufacturers apply the term to any style and type of furniture they sell. Art Furniture varies in design but has some common characteristics. They include slender, usually turned or quadrangular legs often with casters; spindle supports and uprights; numerous brackets and shelves on cabinets and tables; ebonized woods or black or green stains; coved or arched panels; mirrors with beveled edges; and limited decoration such as gilding, incised patterns, and painted figures or foliage in panels (Fig. 41-14, 41-15, 41-16, 41-18).

Anglo-Japanese furniture exhibits Japanese design principles of asymmetry, balance of solid and void, brackets, fretwork, faux bamboo, dark finishes, spindles, and Japanese motifs such as cherry blossoms or chrysanthemums (Fig. 41-15, 41-17, 41-18). Eastlake furniture, enormously popular in America, comes from principles established by Charles Locke Eastlake in his treatise on decoration (Fig. 41-14). However, manufacturers so debase it that Eastlake rejects any association with it. Eastlake furniture emulates Medieval influence in its rectilinear form that expresses honest, strong construction; reeding; incising; spindles; balusters; finials; chamfering; and low-relief, carved geometric or stylized naturalistic motifs.

Public and Private Buildings

■ *Materials.* Most people favor walnut or mahogany in a dark stain and oak in a light stain. Japanese pieces often are lacquered. Faux bamboo, usually made of maple, may appear on Anglo-Japanese furniture. Art Furniture is often stained blue or blue-green. Ebonizing with gilded incising also is common, and veneers and faux finishes are avoided. Marquetry and inlay of various woods and materials, such as mother-of-pearl, embellish expensive furniture and are imitated in paint on cheaper versions. Carving is generally out of favor but still accents some pieces. Eastlake advocates low-relief carving and walnut veneers because of walnut's increasing scarcity. Art Tiles may adorn beds or cabinets.

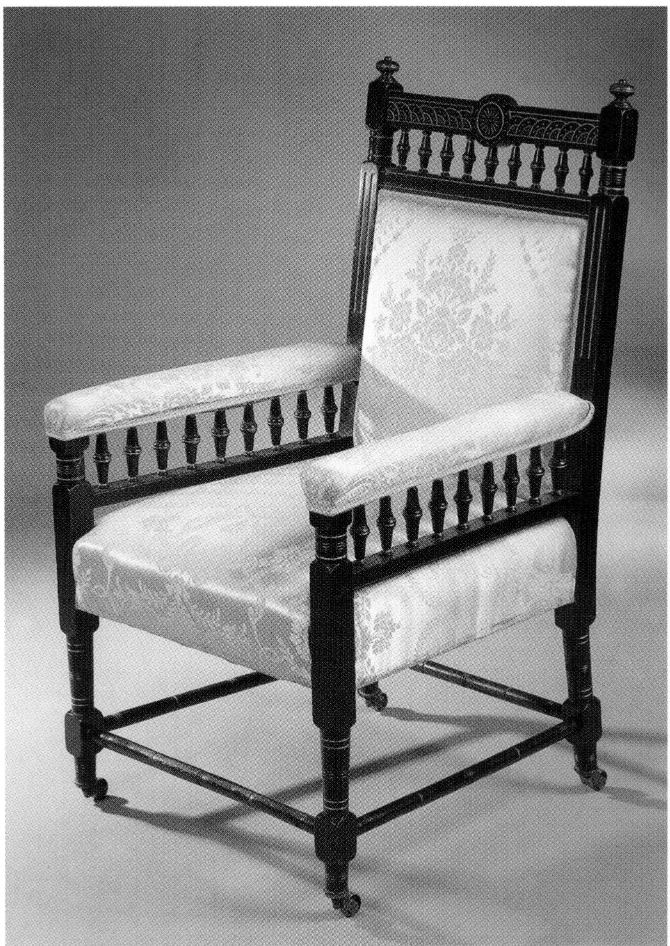

▲ **41-14.** Armchair based on an example from *Hints on Household Taste* by Charles Eastlake, c. 1860–1890s; England.

■ *Seating.* Manufacturers continue to produce seating with stylistic designations and in matching sets even though critics decry them. To reduce costs, the number of pieces in a parlor set decreases. Three or five pieces become the norm instead of six to eight. In the United States, most parlor sets have at least one rocker. Chairs and sofas have simplified, angular silhouettes and turned legs (Fig. 41-6, 41-14, 41-15). Backs and seats have wooden frames and tufting. Rows of spindles top backs or appear below arms. Incising and low-relief carving add decoration. Individual chairs are usually slender, somewhat spindly, with ladder- or spindle-backs, and are stained green or black. Seats may be upholstered, caned, or rush. Some rooms have overstuffed upholstery, although critics condemn it.

■ *Tables.* Most Aesthetic rooms have many small tables for convenience and displaying objects, although the center table disappears from use (Fig. 41-15, 41-16). Tops are wood because marble is considered cold and uninviting. Desks and other tables have many shelves and brackets supported by spindles and/or have galleries composed of spindles. Anglo-Japanese tables are characterized by an asymmetrical arrangement of shelves or brackets and legs, aprons, stretchers with brackets or fretwork, and faux bamboo carving.

■ *Storage*. Still an important piece, the drawing room cabinet or *étagère* displays a carefully chosen collection of vases, plates, tiles, Oriental porcelains, and other objects (Fig. 41-8, 41-18, 41-19). Rectangular in form with a façade composed of solids and voids, it is made up of shelves, brackets, spindles, cabinets or arched niches, and mirrors with beveled edges, and may be topped with a spindle gallery or a coved panel. Decoration may include painted or carved sunflowers, lilies, or foliage. Anglo-Japanese cabinets are rectilinear with a balanced, often asymmetrical, arrangement of vertical and horizontal lines, solids, and voids (Fig. 41-15, 41-17). Minimal surface decoration and no elaborate carving, ornament, or moldings are characteristic. Eastlake cabinets feature incising, spindles, and simplified ornament usually derived from Medieval sources. Many Artistic rooms have Eastlake-style or Anglo-Japanese wall cabinets for additional display space. Like other pieces, sideboards and secretaries reflect Aesthetic design principles.

■ *Beds*. Most beds (Fig. 41-5) have tall rectangular headboards and lower footboards. Paneled head- and footboards may have diagonal boards, plain or printed textiles, Art Tiles, or painted decorations. Cresting is made up of galleries of spindles or rooflike projections. Anglo-Japanese beds have bamboo spindles or moldings. Eastlake beds have incising and diaper or sawtooth edging. Matching the bed are dressers with matching tops, washstands, armoires, night stands, and shaving stands.

DESIGN SPOTLIGHT

Furniture: Inspired by Japanese woodcuts, Edward W. Godwin's composition for this Anglo-Japanese sideboard is a careful balance of horizontals and verticals, and solids and voids like Japanese architecture. The simplicity and elegance also reflect the Japanese aesthetic. Japanese leather paper covers the doors, and silvered handles and hinges add a touch of decoration. Like most Japanese-style furniture, the sideboard is ebonized. Godwin succeeds in capturing the essence of Japanese design in this piece, in contrast to many others who simply add Japanese motifs and some forms to Western furniture.

▲ **41-15.** Table, c. 1890s; United States.

▲ **41-16.** Anglo-Japanese cabinet, c. 1860s–1890s.

DESIGN SPOTLIGHT

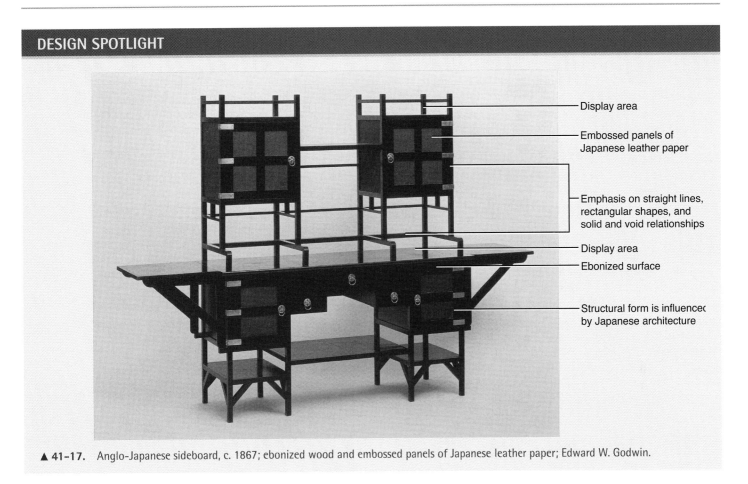

Display area

Embossed panels of Japanese leather paper

Emphasis on straight lines, rectangular shapes, and solid and void relationships

Display area

Ebonized surface

Structural form is influencec by Japanese architecture

▲ **41–17.** Anglo-Japanese sideboard, c. 1867; ebonized wood and embossed panels of Japanese leather paper; Edward W. Godwin.

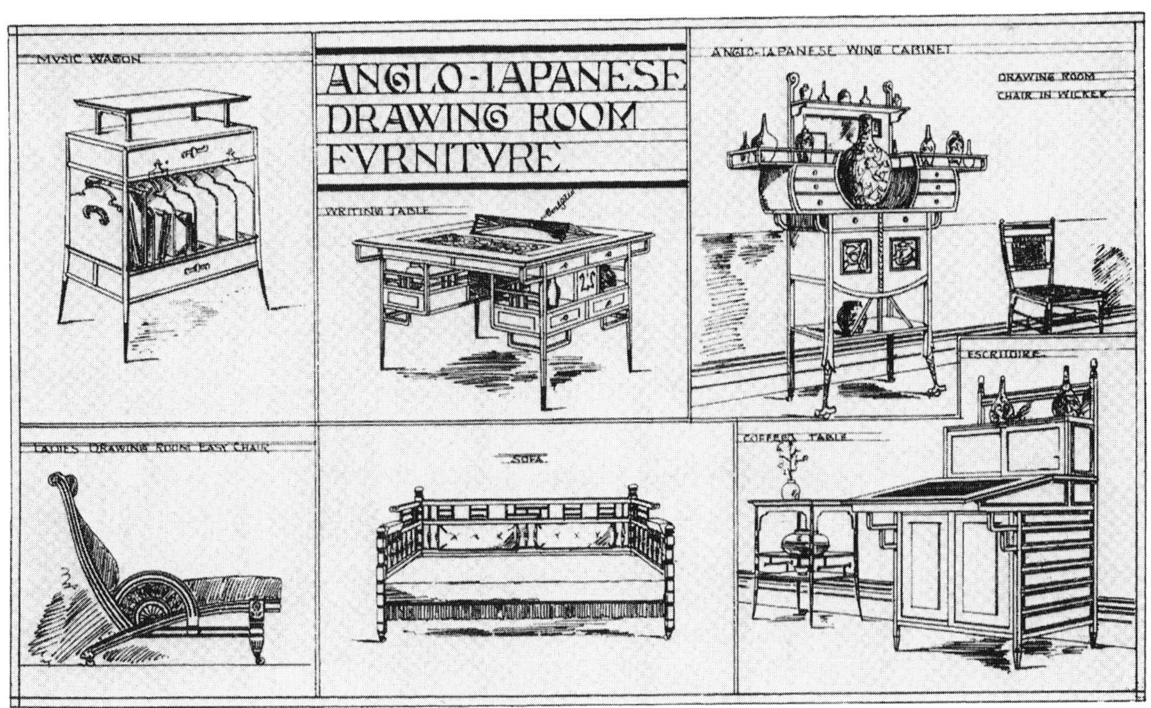

▲ **41–18.** Anglo-Japanese drawing room furniture, 1877; Plate 8 in *William Watt's Catalogue of Art Furniture*; London, England; Edward W. Godwin.

■ *Decorative Arts*. Accessories are extremely important and an integral part of Aesthetic interiors (Fig. 41-1, 41-5, 41-6, 41-8, 41-9, 41-21). Collections showcase the artistic sensibility and culture of the family, and each piece is regarded as a lesson in taste for the children. Pictures hang in symmetrical arrangements from picture moldings near the ceiling. The dining room usually displays oil paintings, while the living room features prints, photographs, and watercolors of artistic subjects. Tastemakers especially favor Japanese prints and Oriental ceramics. Artists and others avidly collect the much esteemed blue and white porcelains from China and Japan. Folding screens (Fig. 41-20); bookcases; and canterburies holding magazines and plants; and flowers enhance the Artistic interior.

■ *Art Pottery*. During the 1870s, a mania for china collecting explodes (Fig. 41-6, 41-8, 41-9). In response, manufacturers, such as Royal Doulton and Wedgwood in England and a number of individual potteries in the United States, such as Rookwood in Cincinnati, begin producing Art Pottery. Designers of these ceramics experiment form, colors, glazes, and surface decoration. Artistic precepts and creativity are important design principles. Manufacturers often employ art students, artists, or industrial designers to create unique designs derived from ancient Greek vases, Islamic pottery, and Oriental ceramics. Oriental-style ceramics copy or adapt the forms, glazes, and motifs of the originals. Glazes or colors often imitated are celadon (gray-green to blue-green), *sang-de-boeuf* (deep red), deep blue, apple green, mustard yellow, and peach bloom. Motifs include cranes, butterflies, lotus blossoms, and chrysanthemums. Islamic Art Pottery replicates forms, such as mosque lamps; colors like cobalt blue, red, green, or turquoise; and Islamic motifs. Some pottery has applied relief decoration or surface enameling with gold outlines. Minton, Wedgwood, and others revive Renaissance *maiolica*, renaming it majolica (Fig. 41-21). Its figurines and naturalistic forms in shiny colorful blue, yellow, pink, and green glazes have great appeal.

■ *Art Tiles*. Art Tiles often cover floors, fireplaces, sideboards, cabinets, beds, stoves, and clocks (Fig. 41-1). Decoration, which follows artistic principles, is in relief, painted, transfer-printed, imprinted, or glazed. Sunflowers, butterflies, latticework, hexagons, fan shapes, and figures in Greek or Japanese dress are typical motifs. Colors, which are compatible with interiors, include brown, gold, yellow, blue, or green.

▲ **41-19.** Cabinet and secretary in ebonized cherry inlaid with gilded woods, c. 1880–1882; New York; Herter Brothers.

▲ **41-20.** Screen; London, England; exhibited at the Centennial International Exhibition, 1876.

▲ **41-21.** Decorative Arts: Cameo glass vase and majolica *jardinière*, late 19th century; England.

■ *Art Glass*. In contrast to Art Pottery, which may be made by individuals, Art Glass production is always industrial. Like Art Pottery, Art Glass experiments with form, color, and surface decoration, but it is not as enthusiastically collected as ceramics are. Like ceramics, models include Roman, Oriental, and Islamic glass. Experiments with color yield shaded wares like Amberina, which changes from amber to deep ruby, and Burmese, blending from yellow to pink with a shiny or matte surface. Makers revive early techniques such as cameo glass, which depicts relief ornament in contrasting colors to the body (Fig. 41-21). Japanese Art Glass often features enameled surface decoration of grass, flowers, or birds, while Islamic Art Glass replicates the form of mosque lamps and arabesques or rosettes in blue, red, or gold. Because much Art Glass is too expensive for the middle class, pressed glass is made in artistic colors and patterns with names like Queen Anne or Lily.

▲ **41-22.** Later Interpretation: Country occasional chair #0337-23; manufactured by Hickory Chair in Hickory, North Carolina.

■ *Later Interpretations*. Art Furniture and Eastlake are not revived in later periods, but Japanese influences continue in furniture, varying from close approximations to those including various characteristics (Fig. 41-22). Bamboo furniture remains a popular choice. Art Pottery and Art Glass are avidly collected in the late 20th century. Artists continue to make ceramics and glass following Artistic design principles, particularly in the Studio Glass Movement.

CHAPTER 42

English Arts and Crafts

1860s–1910s

If you want a golden rule that will fit every body, this is it: have nothing in your houses that you do not know to be useful or believe to be beautiful.

—William Morris, 1880 lecture, "The Beauty of Life"

The Arts and Crafts Movement, a reform development in England, strives to change the working conditions of craftspeople while improving the quality of design. It emphasizes preindustrial values and medieval-like craft guilds in the midst of rapid industrial growth centered on machine production. The ideal concept promotes intelligent space planning, allowances for human needs, design unity, harmony with the natural environment, and honesty of materials. Individual designers blend these principles with concepts derived from the vernacular, Japan, and a variety of sources.

HISTORICAL AND SOCIAL

The Arts and Crafts Movement builds on the principles and theories of Augustus Welby Northmore Pugin, a Gothic Revival architect; John Ruskin, an art historian and critic; and, more important, on the theories and practice of William Morris. Pugin is the first to apply a moral dimension to art and calls for designs that develop from function and appropriate context, structural honesty, and an honest use of materials. He also is instrumental in the revival of Gothic craft techniques, such as stained glass.

John Ruskin admires Gothic, functionality, and honesty, but he also reveres the Middle Ages. He equates good design with joy in labor, which lays the foundation for reforming the work process. Ruskin believes that industrialization has dehumanized the laborer, resulting in badly designed and poor quality manufactured goods; and purchasing these goods debases the society itself. He therefore advocates a return to hand craftsmanship, guilds patterned after those of the Middle Ages, and the elimination of false and applied ornament. He establishes the Guild of S. George in 1871, the first of the 19th-century guilds modeled after medieval ones. It quickly fails but sets an important precedent. Ruskin's writings, especially *The Stones of Venice* (1853) and *The Seven Lamps of Architecture* (1851), are important to the movement.

William Morris has the greatest influence on the Arts and Crafts Movement through his writing, his lectures, and his work. Influenced by Ruskin, Morris comes to advocate simplicity in design, structural honesty, medieval-inspired treatments, and handcrafted production. Morris calls for unity between the fine and decorative arts and advances the Ruskinian idea of an individual craftsperson conceiving and executing an object. He puts these ideas into practice through his design company, Morris, Marshall, Faulkner and Company, founded in 1861 and later known as Morris and Company. A Socialist, he advocates well-designed goods for everyone but largely rejects the means for achieving this goal, the machine. In a further paradox, the goods produced by him and his firm are only affordable by the affluent. Besides Morris, the firm includes Sir Edward Burne-Jones, Ford Maddox Brown, and artist Dante Gabriel Rossetti, all of whom are members of the Pre-Raphaelite Brotherhood.

In the 1870s, Morris's ideas find sympathetic ears in many progressive architects, artists, and designers. Regarding all creative endeavors as equal in value, they strive through a variety of means to restore harmony between designer and maker, art and craft. One method is to form guilds. These organizations of the Middle Ages had governed a craft or trade. In contrast, Arts and Crafts guilds, beginning with the Century Guild in 1882, are commercial enterprises intended to promote the work and ideas of a group of like-minded architects, artisans, and designers. Few are commercially successful, but they give structure and cohesion to the movement and are able to achieve more as groups than individuals can. Interdisciplinary works, professionalism, and a sense of unity and brotherhood characterize Arts and Crafts guilds. They spread their ideas through meetings and discussions; exhibitions of their work; and publications, such as *The Hobby Horse* (1884–1892) put out by the Century Guild. The first exhibit of the Art Workers' Guild in 1888 gives the movement its name.

England's Arts and Crafts Movement is vastly influential, providing models for design reform in the United States, Scandinavia, and Continental Europe. Nevertheless, by the turn of the century, the Arts and Crafts Movement begins to lose momentum. Morris dies in 1896, and the guilds prove to be commercially unsuccessful. As society loses interest in the Arts and Crafts Movement, the marketplace for handcrafts disappears. Great Britain exports fewer goods, and the prosperity of the middle and upper classes declines. Ideals begin to change and a return to classicism and formality replaces medieval informality. The death blow to the movement comes following World War I when Modernism gains favor in Britain.

▲ **42-1.** "Flora," 1886; England; Edward Burne-Jones, executed by Morris and Company.

CONCEPTS

The Arts and Crafts Movement attempts to reform both design and society by uniting art and craftsmanship. Not a single style, the movement reflects an attitude that develops in response to the effects of industrialization on mass-produced goods and the quality of life. Not all followers adhere to all precepts, but most believe that well-designed goods should be available to all and that resurrecting craftsmanship is the means to achieve this goal. Other key concepts stemming from the ideas of Pugin, Ruskin, and Morris include simplicity, suitability to purpose, structural honesty, honest use of materials, excellent craftsmanship, functionality, elimination of the unnecessary, and regionalism or a sense of place. The movement has a variety of expressions that are informed by the past but do not attempt to copy or revive it. Indeed, followers reject the very notion of style in favor of individual freedom in design and concern for and delight in materials, which underlies all creative endeavors from architecture to textile design. Excellent craftsmanship is of utmost importance, so some architects and designers become makers to more fully understand the process of design and creation as well as the qualities of the materials involved. Also underlying the movement is a strong sense of nationalism in its admiration for vernacular traditions and the simple, rural life. Although the vernacular influences design, the result is not a copy but an abstraction of its elements and forms. Despite regarding itself as rural, the movement largely takes place in urban settings.

Many Arts and Crafts adherents believe in Socialism and strive through example to improve the life of the worker and effect change in working conditions. Although progressive in its concern for the worker, the Arts and Crafts Movement looks back to the preindustrial past. Instead of reforming the design and manufacturing relationship, adherents largely reject the machine in favor of handmade goods. In reality, the machine produces goods that most can afford, despite the drudgery and repetition in the manufacturing process. The notion of the individual craftsperson creating an object reflects an elitist ideal.

DESIGN SPOTLIGHT

Architecture: Following his marriage, William Morris commissions his friend Philip Webb to design a house for him. Webb and Morris collaborate in the design of this first example of Arts and Crafts architecture, which is very influential. The Red House, conceived from the inside out, has an L-shaped floor plan that gives a feeling of welcome and hospitality. The plan also is practical with its line of rooms and secondary corridor to the rear. Façades reveal the function of rooms within, and windows are placed to give maximum light and air instead of according to the dictates of style. Although there are a few Gothic details, such as the steeply pitched roof and pointed arches in windows and doors, the house is not Gothic. Rather it has a medieval and centuries-old feeling. The plain red brick is unusual at the time because brickwork was most often covered with stucco. Webb carefully selected the brick for its color variations and to give a handmade appearance. No applied ornament detracts from the form.

The stair hall conveys the simplicity, attention to detail, and informality that is important to Arts and Crafts interiors. Straight lines, rectangular forms, white walls, and wood floors and trim contribute to the handcrafted appearance, rural character, and sense of place. Unable to find suitable furnishings, Morris founds Morris and Company to supply them. On weekends, friends and guests assist the Morrises in decorating the house.

▲ **42-2.** Red House, floor plan, and stair hall, 1859–1860; Bexleyheath, Kent, England; Philip Webb.

DESIGN SPOTLIGHT

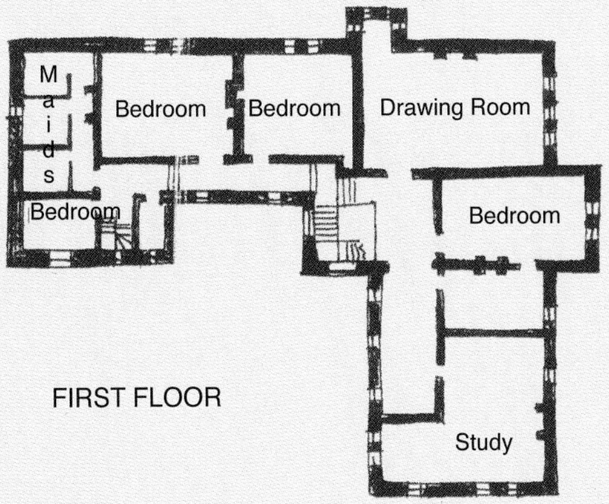

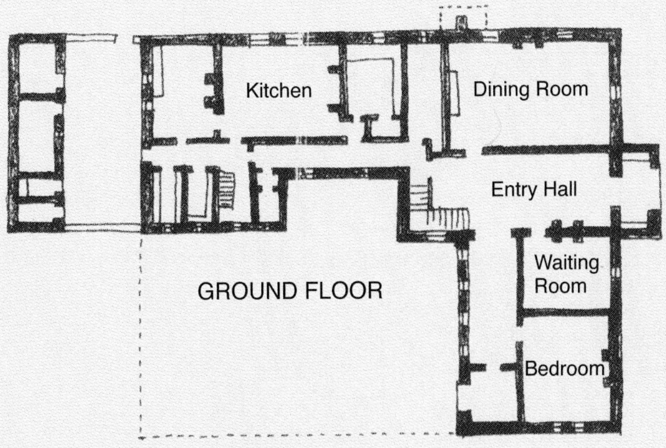

▲ **42-2.** Continued

CHARACTERISTICS AND MOTIFS

Arts and Crafts architecture, interiors, and furnishings in England maintain a strong, visible relationship to each other in their reliance upon common precepts. Two varieties of expression are most common. One comes from rural vernacular traditions, whereas the other relies more strongly on the medieval or Renaissance past. Whether rural or medieval inspired, some examples are simple and plain with little or no ornament, applied or inherent. Others are visually complex, revealing excellence in execution.

Stylistically, early Arts and Crafts examples of interiors, furniture, textiles, wallpapers, and book art exhibit the colors, forms, and interest in surface decoration of the Aesthetic Movement. Soon, the movement evolves to a more structural, rational approach to design that more closely relates to architecture.

■ *Motifs*. Typical motifs of the period are sunflowers, lilies, birds, images and letters from medieval manuscripts, Gothic details, and Oriental images (Fig. 42-1, 42-7, 42-8, 42-10, 42-11, 42-12, 42-13, 42-14).

ARCHITECTURE

Arts and Crafts architecture has many variations because it is produced by individualist architects who believe in freedom of expression and frequently experiment with form and materials. Most examples are country houses for the prosperous upper middle class. Buildings exhibit no imposed style but appear to grow out of the surrounding landscape and to have been there for centuries. Architects strive to maintain a sense of place through regional or local forms and materials. The visual language uses individual forms and elements to symbolize home, family, refuge, and shelter. Materials and structure depict the function of the building and the interiors within. Architects search for the finest materials and use local artisans to ensure that the building expresses timelessness. Emphasis upon texture, color, pattern, harmony with nature, and catching light and casting shadows reflects the architect's delight in materials and the process of design. Overall, buildings are clean and sparse with little ornament. They generally have an informal character blended with natural building materials, medieval imagery, and Japanese design.

An important outgrowth of the Arts and Crafts Movement is the founding of the Society for the Protection of Ancient Buildings (SPAB) by William Morris in 1877. Formed in reaction to the damaging restorations of the time, SPAB strives to preserve old buildings, restore old buildings gently, and inspire new construction. As a meeting place for architects and others interested in old buildings, it becomes a vehicle for such ideas as the study of past building traditions, contemporary work that looks new but harmonizes with the old, and use of quality materials in restoration.

Most Arts and Crafts structures are country houses (Fig. 42-2, 42-3, 42-4), although some churches and parish houses exist. Urban examples of Arts and Crafts architecture are few because cities lack the strong sense of place of rural villages. Freedom of expression is particularly difficult for terraces or row houses because sites and codes prescribe their forms and arrangements. Consequently, the main urban manifestations are garden suburbs that use vernacular cottages as models. In London, for example, architects begin designing low-density garden suburbs for the middle and professional classes to counter the city's unplanned approach to urban worker housing. These planned environments, such as Hampstead Garden (Fig. 42-5), are filled with picturesque, sanitary, detached houses set within their own individual gardens.

Public and Private Buildings

■ *Site Orientation.* Unity and harmony between building and landscape are expressed through architectural features (Fig. 42-2, 42-3, 42-4, 42-5). Architects try to make the house appear to be growing from the land. The surrounding landscape becomes almost as important as the design of the structure, thus leading to a revival of garden design. Designers believe that a formal garden balances the informal planning of the house. Planned and random plantings, walks, and trees are carefully organized with an eye toward vistas. Features, such as sundials and fountains, are integrated into the design.

DESIGN SPOTLIGHT

Architecture: Broadleys, which overlooks Lake Windermere, embodies Charles F. A. Voysey's distinctive style that simplifies and abstracts elements of traditional buildings. Seeming to grow out of its site, the house is long and low with a horizontal emphasis. Typical Voysey details include the battered corner buttresses; deep, hipped roof with broad overhangs supported by iron brackets; and bands of tall, narrow windows. The L-shaped house has an entrance courtyard from which a long corridor opens and allows access to the line of rooms on the other side of it. On the lake side are three curving bay windows extending through the roofline. Besides anchoring the house to the land like the tapered buttresses, they give vertical accents and light the dining room, two-story hall, and drawing room. At one end, the roof extends over a verandah. The marked horizontality, clean lines, and plain surfaces give an air of repose and domesticity.

▲ **42-3.** Broadleys, 1898–1899, Lake Windermere, England; Charles F. A. Voysey.

▲ **42-4.** The Orchards and second floor hall, 1897–1899; Surrey, England; Sir Edwin L. Lutyens.

■ *Floor Plans.* Plan layouts (Fig. 42-2, 42-6) develop from use rather than a prearranged order, resulting in asymmetrical designs and open flowing movement. Courtyards are common. Floor plans are composed of an *L*, *T*, or an elongated rectangular shape to provide clear and direct circulation. A series of rooms directly behind one another with a side corridor is a common plan for country houses. Economical in space, the corridor allows access to individual rooms without passing through one to get to another. A variation is the butterfly plan in which the corridor plan is bent to form a symmetrical *V* with a central core. It symbolizes arms of welcome or hospitality. The formal Victorian drawing room or parlor becomes an informal sitting area or living room. Some plans revive the medieval great hall, a communal living space that forms the hub of the home.

■ *Materials.* Stone, brick, and wood convey textural harmony and simplicity of appearance (Fig. 42-2, 42-3, 42-4, 42-5). Architects, favoring local materials over exotic or imported ones, carefully select them considering combination of colors, textures, light, and shade. Variations of material on the façade often indicate function of rooms or articulate different parts of the structure. Sometimes more contemporary materials, such as concrete or stucco, are used structurally or functionally.

■ *Façades.* Exteriors feature a horizontal emphasis, structural repetition, and an asymmetrical silhouette and fenestration (Fig. 42-2, 42-3, 42-4, 42-5). Façades are largely unornamented, having few architectural details such as stringcourses, columns, pediments, and the like. Interest and variety come from forms, textures, and materials. Structures may be rambling with multiple gables and roofs or self-contained under a single, deep roof. Designs strive to recall, but not copy, the past, so forms and details often are simplified or abstracted. Walls may be rough or smooth in texture; be plain and flat; or have half-timbering, crow-step gables, and/or projections or overhangs. Individual features, such as a corner chimney, buttresses, or stair halls rising from the ground, may be exaggerated to emphasize function or construction, or to integrate with the landscape. Changes of material or color around doors and windows highlight these elements and add interest.

■ *Windows.* A variety of window types alternate in size and placement (Fig. 42-2, 42-3, 42-4, 42-5). Single, groups, or bands of casements or mullioned windows are placed where needed to provide light or views instead of according to the dictates of style. Also arched, bay, or oriel windows add variety and a sense of place. Windows appear in repetitive horizontal bands directly under long overhanging roofs, reinforcing the union of the building to the land.

■ *Doors.* Entry doors (Fig. 42-2, 42-4) defined by low-hanging projections are usually placed asymmetrically on the façade

▲ **42-5.** House, begun 1906; Hampstead Garden suburb, London, England; Parker and Unwin.

composition. Deeply recessed, arched entrances symbolize shelter and refuge.

■ *Roofs.* Roofs frequently alternate in height and have planes at many angles to catch the light (Fig. 42-2, 42-3, 42-4, 42-5). To further symbolize shelter and refuge, architects often use a single, deep roof with deep overhangs. Some revive thatched roofs but combine them with more practical, weatherproof materials such as concrete.

INTERIORS

Arts and Crafts interiors integrate elements of architecture along with the furnishings and decorative arts into a unified whole. Meticulous attention to details and handcrafted work complement the concept of the parts blended into the whole. Emulating the exterior design, the interior appearance is informal portrayed in intimate scale, free-flowing space, asymmetrical organization, horizontal movement, rectangular shapes, and straight lines. Bands of windows invite the outside in; rough textures and naturalistic color schemes and patterns further integrate interior and exterior. Built-in furniture gives rooms an architectonic appearance and emphasizes structure. Some interiors display a vernacular appearance while others recall medieval or Gothic rooms. A few architects revive the great hall as a living room. Less-formal living rooms replace formal entertaining spaces. Richard Norman Shaw reintroduces the inglenook in the 1860s, and it becomes a common feature in large stair halls that are used as living rooms in Arts and Crafts houses.

Architects frequently design the interiors and furniture for their buildings and oversee the creation of them by local artisans, the guilds, or commercial firms such as Morris and Company. However, these services are limited to the wealthy. By the early

DESIGN SPOTLIGHT

Interiors: The Orchard, built as a house for himself, expresses Voysey's personal concepts of simplicity, honesty, and plainness. The exterior, following other Arts and Crafts models, has long, horizontal windows; low, deep gables; wide porches for shelter; and vernacular appearance. The entrance hall illustrates his innovative use of purple and white walls, all white woodwork, and white ceiling combined with large expanses of glass windows to bring in light. Not only is the interior cheerful and bright, but it also follows Voysey's principles of easy cleaning and inexpensive maintenance. Distinctive features include a large scale mantel with green fireplace tiles, a vertical slat screen by the stairs, green or patterned carpets, plain wood furniture, and crafts-style metal door hinges. The dining room continues these innovative ideas through its simplicity of design, olive-gray and white walls, white ceiling, large scaled mantel, purple and green rug, and plain wood furniture. Ornament and decoration consist only of a few decorative accessories, mainly placed on the mantel shelves. This design statement contrasts with earlier dark and cluttered Victorian interiors and consequently appeals to those seeking a more contemporary home environment. As such, it is widely copied and garners significant recognition for Voysey.

▲ **42-6.** Entrance hall (1901 image in black and white and 2007 contemporary color interpretation by Chris Good), dining room (1901 watercolor by Wilfrid Ball, as published in *Modern British Domestic Architecture and Decoration,* by Charles Holme), and 1901 floor plans, The Orchard, 1899–1900; Chorley Wood, Hertfordshire, England; Charles F. A. Voysey.

DESIGN SPOTLIGHT

Voysey-designed clock
White upper wall, white ceiling, white screen
Crafts-style strap metal hinge
Purple lower wall
Large mantel with green fireplace tile
Simple, unadorned oak furniture

The Orchard
Chorley Wood

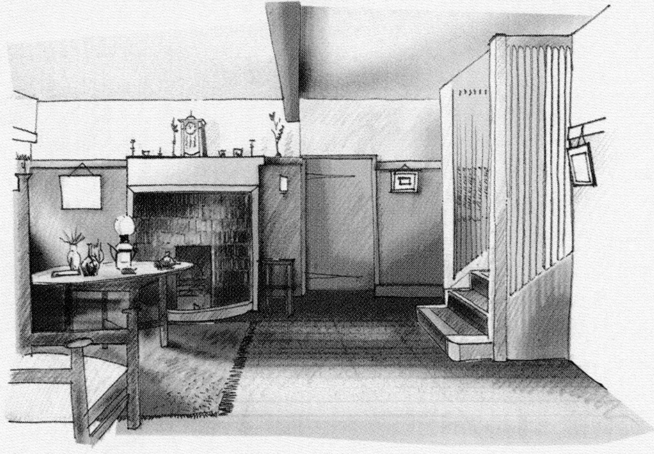

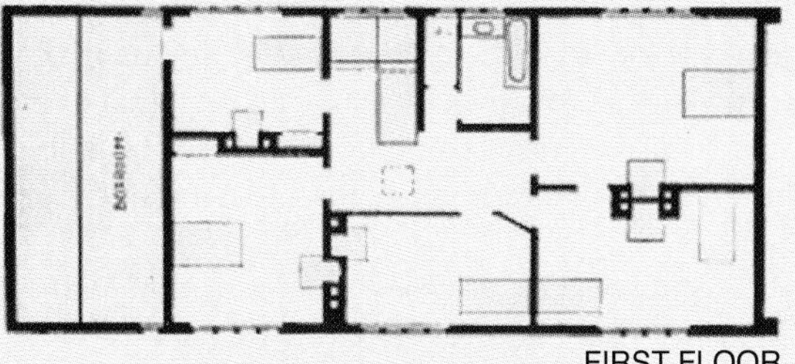

FIRST FLOOR

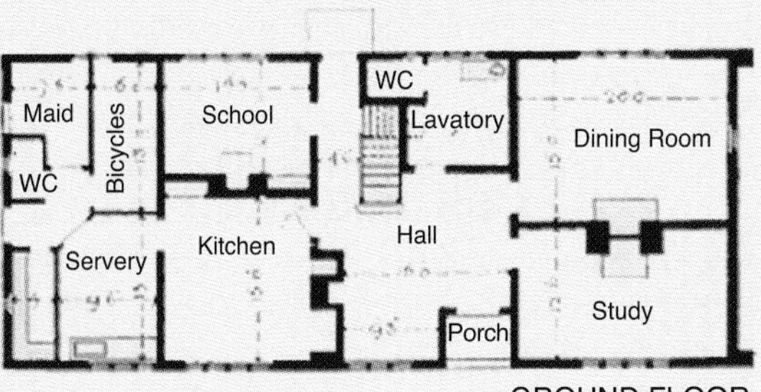

Maid
Bicycles
School
WC
Lavatory
Dining Room
WC
Hall
Kitchen
Servery
Porch
Study
GROUND FLOOR

▲ **42-6.** Continued

▲ **42-7.** Interior; England; published in *The International Studio, An Illustrated Magazine of Fine and Applied Art,* 1900; M. H. Baillie Scott.

20th century, department stores begin offering handcrafted or machine-made goods and decorating services that are affordable for more people. Arts and Crafts principles evolve into the Cottage or Vernacular style for popular consumers.

Public and Private Buildings

■ *Color.* Designers advocate color schemes derived from nature to further integrate interior with exterior (Fig. 42-2, 42-4, 42-6, 42-7, 42-8, 42-10, 42-13, 42-14, 42-15). Brown, ochre, buff, and off-white are typical wall colors with brighter ochres, blue-greens, olive-grays, roses, russets, and black incorporated in wallpapers, textiles, stained glass, and accessories. Wood often is left unstained or is lightly stained for a natural appearance. Philip Webb and Charles F. A. Voysey stress off-white color palettes in public and private spaces, which is noticeably different from other designers.

■ *Floors.* Naturally finished wood-planked floors covered with decorative area rugs are common, along with tile and painted wood floors (Fig. 42-2, 42-4, 42-7). Wall-to-wall carpet is rare. Leading architects and practitioners, such as Morris and Voysey, design carpets commercially or for individual clients. Hand-knotted or machine-made designs have graceful and flowing lines and stylized plants and flowers in bright colors. Handmade Oriental or scatter rugs may be used.

■ *Walls.* Stucco walls with rough wood posts, half-timbering, or wood paneling with a clear finish are usual treatments (Fig. 42-2, 42-4, 42-6, 42-7). There are few applied architectural details, such as moldings. However, built-in furnishings are common, including benches or settles in inglenooks, bookcases, and window seats. Stucco or plaster walls may be white- or color-washed. Leading architects and practitioners, such as Morris, design wallpapers with stylized plants and flowers in bright colors (Fig. 42-7, 42-8). Frieze papers and plate rails divide walls into two parts instead of the three favored by the Aesthetic Movement. Other less common wall treatments include murals of medieval scenes or landscapes or painted decoration, such as folk designs. Tapestries or embroidered wall hangings may add warmth and color (Fig. 42-1).

(a)

(b)

(c)

▲ **42-8.** Textiles: Fabrics and wallpapers, c. 1870s–1890s, (a) "Honeysuckle," (b) "Pimpernel," and (c) "Strawberry Thief"; Morris and Company, London, England; William Morris.

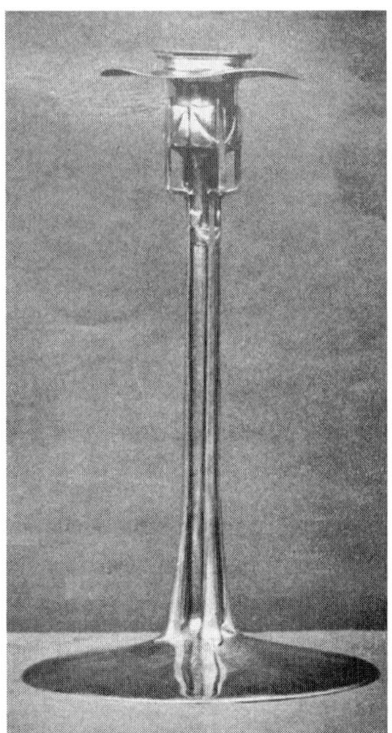

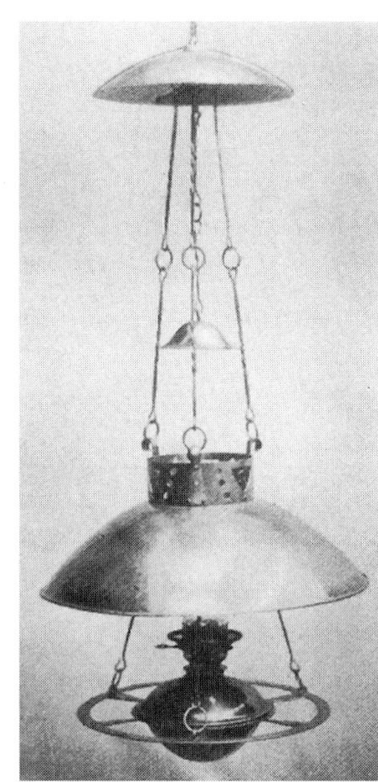

▲ **42-9.** Lighting: Candlestick, table lamp, and hanging lamp, 1900–1907; England.

■ *Chimneypieces*. Public rooms usually center on the fireplace or hearth as a symbol of home and family (Fig. 42-6, 42-7). Some chimneypieces are large and prominent with deep hoods, while others are smaller with handmade tiles, copper or brass detailing, or rustic wooden mantel shelves. Mottos, sayings, and proverbs may be inscribed or painted beneath the mantel shelf or in the frieze.

■ *Windows and Doors*. Surrounding moldings, when present, are simple and either contrast or blend with the wall color (Fig. 42-2, 42-4, 42-6, 42-7). Stained glass appears frequently as a decorative element. Simple drapery treatments composed of panels hanging from rings complement plain window designs (Fig. 42-6). Fabrics may be plain, patterned, or embroidered. Large, wood-planked doors with iron hardware, expressing a medieval image, are common. Doors may be left unpainted or be painted with a medieval scene or landscapes.

■ *Ceilings*. Ceilings may be low and beamed or higher with other decorative treatments (Fig. 42-4, 42-6, 42-7). Designs generally enhance the wall composition with wooden beams; coffers; pargework; or plain, painted cream surfaces.

■ *Textiles*. Textile design relies upon geometric repeats; natural objects transformed into abstracted shapes; and flat, two-dimensional treatments (Fig. 42-1, 42-8, 42-10, 42-14). Compositions may be flat with little depth, in the manner advocated by Pugin and Owen Jones, or more naturalistic and complicated, as Ruskin recommends. Fabrics created by Morris and Company usually have tightly clustered foliage motifs rendered in natural colors printed on cotton or linen grounds. Textiles include cretonne, cotton, velvet, plush, linen, wool, and leather with little decoration. Hand-blocked printing replaces mechanized roller techniques for printed fabrics and most wallpapers, making them available only to the affluent. Needlework and other handmade pieces may be purchased or made at home.

■ *Lighting*. Natural light fills the interiors, particularly in social spaces. At night, candlesticks; table lamps; wall brackets; and hanging lamps and fixtures of wood, ceramic, copper, iron, or brass, with a rustic appearance, illuminate spaces (Fig. 42-9). Fixtures frequently have hand-blown or stained glass shades.

FURNISHINGS AND DECORATIVE ARTS

Arts and Crafts furniture displays similar concepts to architecture and interiors, including revealed structure, truth of and delight in materials, and compositions based upon vernacular or traditional forms. Freedom in expression and marked individuality define compositions, which are frequently designed by architects for specific clients or interiors. Individual pieces are human scale and often have unique design features. Vernacular or medieval forms inspire designers, but imposed style is rigorously avoided. Consequently, within the body of work for a guild, firm, or individual, there may be few common elements. The work of individual designers is distinctive depending upon use of form and materials, construction methods, application of decorative details, and sources of inspiration.

Designs range from simple, plain, rectangular, and rustic to refined, sinuous in line, and complicated with inlay, carving, or painted decorations. Decorative, painted symbolism, an extension of medieval storytelling (Fig. 42-13), is a common characteristic feature. By the turn of the century, furniture manufacturers hire prominent designers to create furnishings utilizing Arts and Crafts principles, which become known as the Cottage style. Department stores, such as Liberty's, and commercial firms such as Heal and Sons and Wylie and Lockhead offer mass-produced Arts and Crafts furniture.

DESIGN SPOTLIGHT

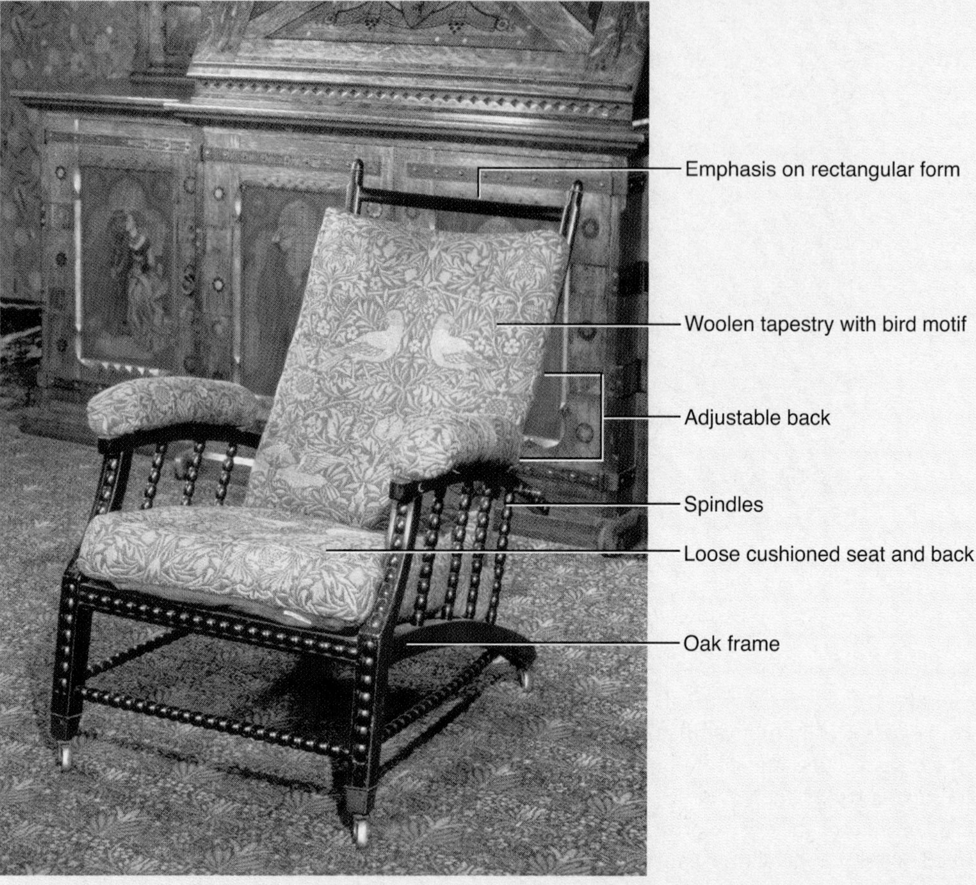

Furniture: The rectangular armchair designed by Philip Webb from a traditional English form, often called the Morris Chair, has spindles, flat arms, and cushioned seat and back. It typifies the suitability of purpose characteristic of Arts and Crafts in its wide arms and adjustable back. The adjustable back is a newly reintroduced concept in design, and one that is much copied in later periods. It is upholstered in the company's textile pattern. The Sussex chair is derived from a country chair supposedly in Sussex. Produced by the firm from 1864 until 1940, it is very popular.

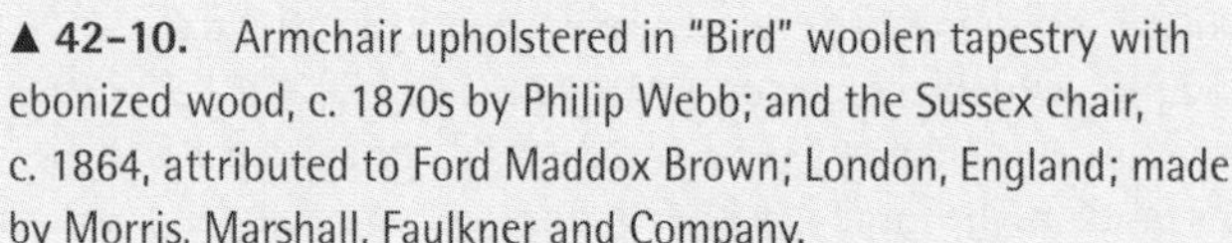

▲ **42-10.** Armchair upholstered in "Bird" woolen tapestry with ebonized wood, c. 1870s by Philip Webb; and the Sussex chair, c. 1864, attributed to Ford Maddox Brown; London, England; made by Morris, Marshall, Faulkner and Company.

▲ **42-11.** Settle, c. 1890s; England; Philip Webb for Morris and Company.

Hand construction is favored and revived. Some designers make furniture to better understand designing to suit material and construction. A few designers, such as Ernest Gimson, achieve the ideal of the craftsperson conceiving and creating the pieces by setting up furniture-making shops in the countryside. More often, the designer creates the piece that is then made commercially or in a cabinetmaking shop.

Designers strive for simplicity with fewer pieces of furniture that blend into the interior so that the room looks and is uncluttered (Fig. 42-2, 42-6, 42-7). Functional arrangements emphasize major architectural elements, and easy maintenance is important. To support a vernacular or rustic tradition, some rooms have a decidedly uncomfortable look with little upholstery and few textiles. Some medieval types, such as settles or dressers, are reintroduced, and antiques are a frequent addition to Arts and Crafts rooms.

Public and Private Buildings

■ *Materials*. Local woods, such as oak or elm, are favored (Fig. 42-10, 42-12, 42-13, 42-14). Some designers use exotic woods for accents, inlay, veneers, and marquetry. Ebonizing and green and brown stains are used earlier. Later pieces have only a shellac finish to reveal the inherent beauty of the wood. Tiles and decorative painting may add color to casepieces.

■ *Seating*. Wood chairs with and without arms are common in all interior spaces (Fig. 42-6, 42-10). Traditional models, such as ladderbacks, are favored, and individual designers adapt these forms to their own design preferences. For example, Voysey's ladderback chairs are tall and slender, sometimes with a heart motif. Some copy past examples such as the Sussex chair (Fig. 42-10), with spindles and rush seat adapted from a country chair. Offered by Morris and Company, it is one of the firm's most commercially successful pieces. One of the most common chairs, offered by nearly every firm, is the Morris chair (Fig. 42-10). Settles (Fig. 42-11) with tall backs and painted decorations are common, but sofas appear less frequently.

▲ **42-12.** Writing desk in oak, 1896; England; Charles F. A. Voysey.

■ *Tables*. Tables are square, rectangular, or round and often have wood plank tops (Fig. 42-6, 42-7). Legs may be straight or curved. Some have inlaid or painted decoration. Trestle tables are used for dining.

■ *Storage*. Cabinets are often built into the wall composition for simplicity and an architectonic appearance. Other types, such as wardrobes and secretaries, reveal a variety of designs (Fig. 42-2, 42-12, 42-13). Some are refined, slender, and tall. They may be raised upon legs to emphasize lightness. Others present a rustic appearance and are composed of heavy planks in the medieval manner. Large dressers with drawer bases and upper shelves often appear in dining rooms or kitchens.

▲ **42-13.** Wardrobe, "The Prioress Tale," 1858–1859; London, England; designed by Philip Webb, painted by Sir Edward Burne-Jones.

■ *Beds*. Rectangular-shaped beds with plain headboards are common. Morris favors Elizabethan-style four-posters with embroidered hangings (Fig. 42-14).

■ *Decorative Arts*. Designers advocate craft or handmade decorative arts, not only English ones, but also those of other cultures including Indian, Japanese, Chinese, and Persian. Arts and Crafts rooms often have historic textiles produced with natural dyes, handmade ceramics, metalwork, and wooden objects. The crafts of embroidery (Fig. 42-14) and book binding are revived.

Artisans, professionals, or hobbyists create handmade products for commercial sales or home use, such as those by Charles F. A. Voysey and Charles R. Ashbee (Fig. 42-15). Seeing crafts as a tool of moral and social reform, some wealthy and upper-class women and philanthropists promote crafts made by the working and lower classes for income and to uplift them. Similar groups seek to preserve or revive regional crafts such as lace making, needlework, and knitting.

▲ **42-14.** Bed, William Morris's bedroom, Kelmscott Manor; bed c. 17th century, embroidered bed hangings 1891; Hammersmith, England; bed hangings by May Morris.

▲ **42-15.** Decorative Arts: Mantel clock, 1896; Charles F. A. Voysey, and decanter, 1901; made by the Guild of Handicraft; Charles R. Ashbee; England.

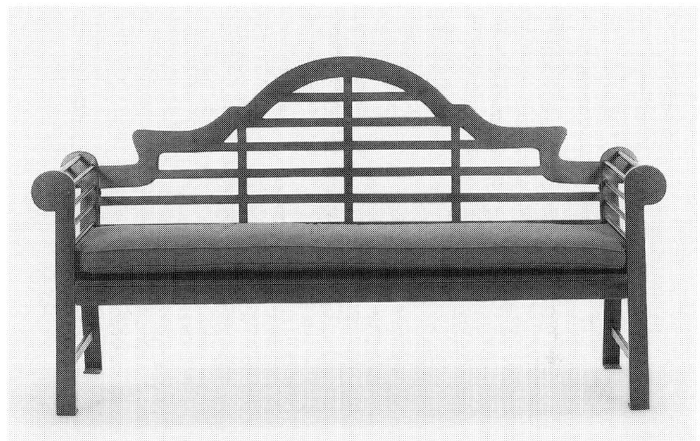

▲ **42-16.** Later Interpretation: Lutyens bench in teak, 2004; Colorado; manufactured by Smith and Hawken. Environmental Modern.

■ *Later Interpretations*. By the 1920s, Modern-style, machine-made furniture replaces Arts and Crafts. Although traditional handcraftsmanship withers, a few struggle to maintain it, mostly in the Cotswolds where life and craft are closely united. The Arts and Crafts Movement is largely forgotten for many years. However, in the 1970s and 1980s, scholars and collectors discover its furniture, which soon becomes fashionable and collectable. Manufacturers begin to reproduce and adapt original designs to suit contemporary tastes. Individual craftspeople begin making furniture according to Arts and Crafts principles. The revival of interest in Arts and Crafts furniture continues in the 1990s and 2000s through works of individuals and various reproductions by furniture companies (Fig. 42-16).

CHAPTER 43

Shingle Style and American Arts and Crafts

1880s–1930s

We have selected for presentation here what we consider the best of the houses designed in The Craftsman Workshops and published in "The Craftsman" during the past five years. Brought together this way in a closely related group, these designs serve to show the development of the Craftsman idea of home building, decoration and furnishing, and to make plain the fundamental principles which underlie the planning of every Craftsman house. These principles are simplicity, durability, fitness for the life that is to be lived in the house and harmony with its natural surroundings. Given these things, the beauty and comfort of the home environment develops as naturally as a flowering plant from the root.

—Gustav Stickley, *Craftsman Homes*, 1909

The Shingle Style, unique to architecture in the United States, evolves from architects' explorations of New England's Colonial architecture combined with aspects of the English Queen Anne style. Buildings are picturesque, rambling, irregular, and covered with wood shingles. Although most examples are architect-designed and found in coastal or resort areas, builder expressions appear across the country.

The American Arts and Crafts Movement follows the principles and tenets of the English Arts and Crafts Movement, but interprets them in a more individualistic way and integrates more diverse influences. Design advocates promote similar ideals and social transformation to a wealthy elite as well as an expanding middle class. The broad style and character of American Arts and Crafts varies by regions of the country and by individual designers, builders, entrepreneurs, or mail-order companies. Examples include Craftsman furniture by Gustav Stickley, Prairie houses in Illinois by Frank Lloyd Wright, individually designed and crafted bungalows in California by Greene and Greene, and smaller bungalows produced by various builders throughout the United States. The overall visual image is one of simplicity and a handmade character.

HISTORICAL AND SOCIAL

A culture of reform dominates the United States during the last two decades of the 19th century. Economic woes, political failures, industrialization, urbanization, and immigration lead to calls on all sides for social and political transformations. Some see the quality of architecture, interiors, and furnishings as indicative of much that is wrong in the nation. Believing that art reflects the nation that creates it and influences the individual user or inhabitant, the reformers look for ways to bring about change in architecture and decorative arts. This atmosphere of change is particularly receptive to the Arts and Crafts agenda of reforming design through handicraft. Many are familiar with its tenets through reading John Ruskin's books or seeing William Morris's ideas in periodicals. English reformers, such as Walter Crane, Charles R. Ashbee, and May Morris, travel the lecture circuit in the United States. Likewise, architects, designers, and artisans from the United States travel to England where they meet Morris and other leaders of the English Arts and Crafts Movement.

The American movement has a greater moral dimension than the one in England, but it is less concerned with the plight of the individual worker. Some manufacturers, such as Gustav Stickley, do try to provide excellent working conditions. The movement is part of continuing efforts to transform the family and the individual by reforming the home and its interiors. As in England, American tools of social reform include guilds, cooperatives, and utopian communities, such as Elbert Hubbard's Roycroft and Rose Valley.

To a greater degree than in England, Americans use craft as a tool for moral and social reform for groups such as immigrants in settlement houses or Native Americans on Indian reservations. This also extends into a strong hobbyist or do-it-yourself component marketed to individual homeowners through magazines such as *Popular Mechanics* and *The Craftsman* and workshop courses for males at high schools. More people have access to the appropriate information to produce reform-inspired furnishings, thereby transforming their lives. Arts and Crafts writings, like others of the period, are couched in a language of virtue that includes such terms as *contentment, simplicity, honesty, truth, sincerity,* and *comfort.* Writings stress the desirability of the simple life, the necessity of rejecting materialism, and a return to nature.

International expositions also acquaint the public with Arts and Crafts beginning with the Centennial International Exhibition of 1876 in Philadelphia and continuing in the World's Columbian Exposition of 1893 in Chicago, the Pan-American Exposition of 1901 in Buffalo, the Louisiana Purchase Exposition of 1904 in St. Louis, the Panama-Pacific International Exposition of 1915 in San Francisco, and the Panama California Exposition of 1915 in San Diego. English architecture books, decorating manuals, and magazines such as the *International Studio* spread Arts and Crafts principles. Numerous American shelter magazines and journals, such as *The Craftsman, The Bungalow Magazine, Lady's Home Journal,* and *House Beautiful* publish articles, plans, and photographs, some by prominent designers and architects. As in England, American Arts and Crafts societies spring up, and some operate like medieval guilds. Unlike in England, these groups are egalitarian and made up of artists, dilettantes, and hobbyists who practice, exhibit, and sell their works; publish journals; listen to lectures; and form discussion groups.

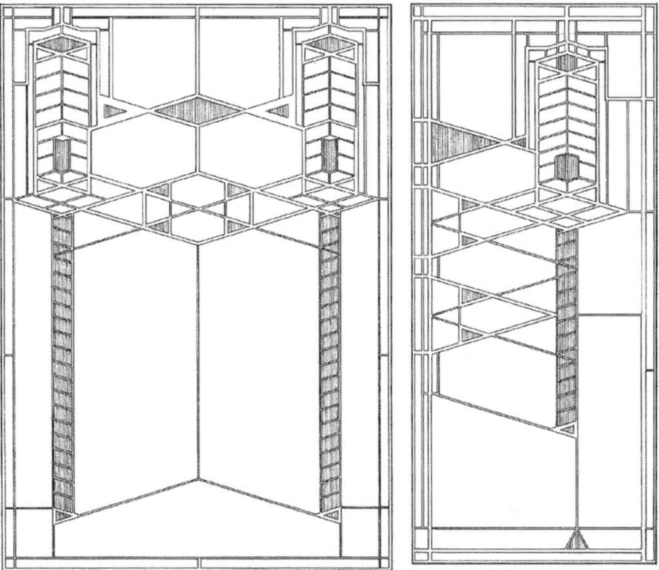

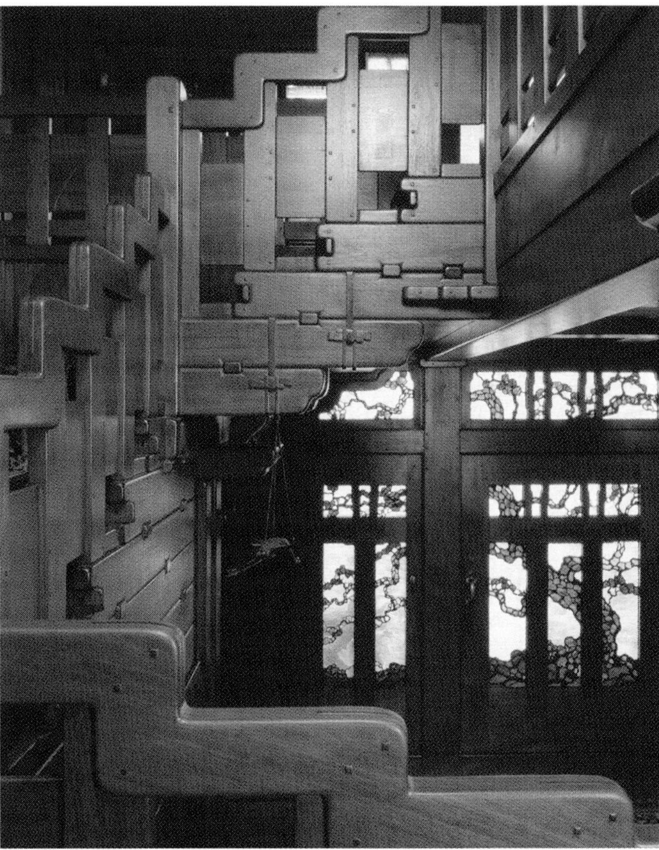

▲ **43-1.** Architectural Details: Stained glass window, Robie House, 1909–1910; Chicago, Illinois; Frank Lloyd Wright, and stair detail, David B. Gamble House, 1907–1908; Pasadena, California; Greene and Greene.

CONCEPTS

■ *Shingle Style.* The roots of Shingle Style are in English Queen Anne architecture and 17th-century buildings of New England. The shingles, additive or rambling qualities, and broad roofs characteristic of early houses become defining elements of this Americanized version of Queen Anne. Designers strive to create order and unity within complex architectural form by using shingles to unify irregular shapes and massing. Further unity is achieved through eliminating and reducing individual details. Because early proponents are trained at *L'École des Beaux-Arts*, many examples display a fundamental geometry and careful relationship of parts. A picturesque image is characteristic; thus, builders often refer to the new houses in Newport, Cape Cod, Long Island, and coastal Maine as "cottages with shingles." Noteworthy examples are high-style homes designed by architects. Although frequently published, there are fewer builder examples of the Shingle Style.

■ *American Arts and Crafts*. American Arts and Crafts derives concepts from Pugin, Ruskin, Morris, and other English design leaders, and manifestations reveal shared principles instead of unified style: honesty, simplicity, regionalism, vernacular traditions, and harmony with the landscape. Within these principles, individual designers strive to create their own American expression. Less cohesive than its English counterpart, the American movement reveals greater diversity in appearance. Like the English, Americans look longingly back to an imaginary preindustrial past. However, the medieval and Gothic are one of many pasts, including regional ones, from which Americans can choose. The English movement's emphasis upon individualism is more appealing to the educated men and women who make up the American movement, giving rise to individualist architects, artisans, and entrepreneurs. Furthermore, the size of the country and its regional differences preclude any real unity.

The American movement also is influenced by other countries such as France, through *L'École des Beaux-Arts* and the writings of Viollet-le-Duc; Japan; and, to a lesser extent, Art Nouveau and other European movements of the period. Unlike their English counterparts, Americans are far less likely to reject the machine while embracing principles of handcraftsmanship and good design. In fact, mechanization democratizes Arts and Crafts. The movement's principles and products are available to any and all consumers through mass production and mass marketing. Thus, the American Arts and Crafts Movement appears in several venues such as elite, custom-designed total environments created for individual clients by architects and designers as well as in less expensive, machine-made and mass-marketed houses and furnishings created for and by the middle class. The style is also identified as Craftsman, Mission, or Prairie style.

CHARACTERISTICS AND MOTIFS

Both the Shingle Style and the American Arts and Crafts Movement favor the styles, forms, and details of the Middle Ages. Common design principles include asymmetry, irregularity, verticality, and simplicity. However, neither strives for a literal interpretation but seeks to capture the essence of the past while reforming design of the present.

■ *American Arts and Crafts*. As in England, American Arts and Crafts architecture, interiors, furniture, and decorative arts display simplicity, honesty through revealed structure and suitability to purpose, truth in materials, vernacular traditions, integrated interiors and exteriors, close ties to the landscape and location, and a handcrafted appearance. A strong thread of back-to-nature is evident in the emphasis upon naturalistic colors and motifs. Local regional traditions are especially strong, which give rise to great diversity of expression. Particularly important are unity of interior and exterior and interior and furnishings; economy of space, furniture, and objects; and efficiency and functionality in planning and organization.

■ *Motifs*. Motifs of the period are flowers, trees, foliage, animals, geometric motifs, Gothic details, and Oriental images (Fig. 43-1, 43-2, 43-3, 43-5, 43-8, 43-9, 43-10).

▲ **43-2.** Old Faithful Inn and interior, Yellowstone National Park, 1903–1904; Wyoming; Robert Reamer. Arts and Crafts.

ARCHITECTURE • SHINGLE STYLE

In the late 1870s, the uniquely American Shingle Style grows out of architects' explorations of Colonial architecture and resort vacations taken by the newly wealthy leisured class. The style appeals because it recalls, but is not shackled by, the past and exhibits freedom of expression, informality, and continuity of texture. The first examples are architect-designed homes in resort areas in New England, but the style spreads quickly across the country through other architects, builders, and publications. Although largely residential, Shingle Style often defines hotels and commercial and retail buildings.

Shingles covering all or nearly all wall surfaces, columns, and details identify the Shingle Style (Fig. 43-4). Other characteristics include asymmetry, irregular massing, horizontal emphasis, a broad gable or gables on one or more façades, towers, bay windows, porches, and multiple roofs. Buildings exhibit more continuity in surface material, texture, line, and form than those in the Stick Style or Queen Anne. Although resembling Queen Anne, the effect is calmer and quieter, while maintaining a free-form character.

The Shingle style's characteristics come from many influences. Its shingles, irregularity, and a picturesque image derive from Queen Anne; rambling additions, gambrel roofs, and Palladian windows come from New England Colonial buildings; Romanesque arches and curved shapes are from Romanesque Revival; and free-flowing space and structural emphasis derive from Japan. The characteristic spatial interplay coming from Japanese architecture is achieved through open, flowing space. Called Queen Anne in its day, art historian Vincent Scully gives it the name Shingle Style in 1955. Shingle Style has no corresponding expression in interiors and furniture.

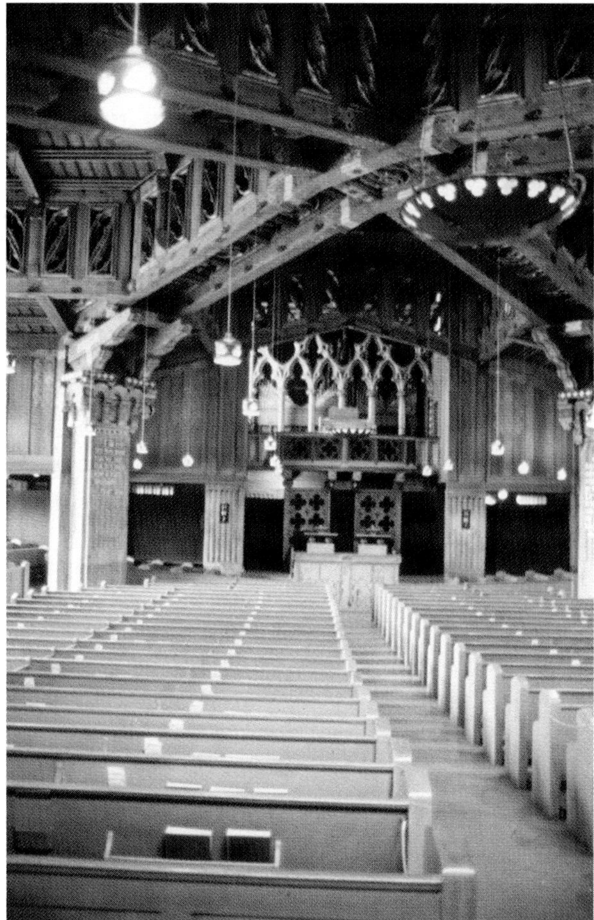

▲ **43-3.** First Church of Christ Scientist and nave, 1910–1912; Berkeley, California; Bernard Maybeck. Arts and Crafts.

DESIGN SPOTLIGHT

Architecture: The Isaac Bell House by McKim, Mead, and White features complex massing, shingled surfaces, and the elimination of details to create order and unity. The composition resembles the character of a New England farmhouse but lacks direct historical references. A large front gable with triple windows dominates the façade but is balanced by a gable to the right and the smaller ones on the porch. The tall chimneys, turret, and two-storied sleeping porch are vertical elements, but the rooflines, projections, and the negative space of the porch emphasize horizontality. Bamboo-like porch supports offer an exotic touch. The entire house is covered with shingles in several forms, including curving ones in the apex of the small gable. The asymmetrical floor plan centers on the living hall with fireplace and inglenook. Broad openings between the rooms on the first floor create greater openness. Private spaces are upstairs. [National Historic Landmark]

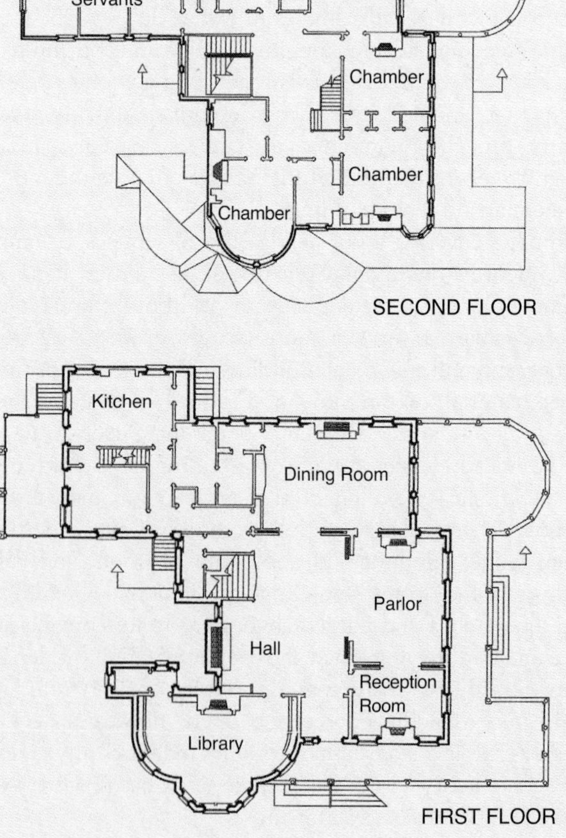

▲ **43-4.** Isaac Bell House and floor plans, 1883; Newport, Rhode Island; McKim, Mead, and White. Shingle Style.

Public and Private Buildings • Shingle Style

■ *Site Orientation*. Most often, houses and hotels are in natural settings with open space and wide expansive views (Fig. 43-2). In resort areas, Shingle Style houses may line streets leading to beaches in New England or group around a lake in the Adirondacks, often with large Shingle-Style hotels nearby. Or houses may be in suburbs in the Midwest and California (Fig. 43-7).

■ *Floor Plans*. Floor plans are usually large and rambling and center on a stair hall (Fig. 43-4). Continuity with the exterior is maintained in the open space planning. Large openings visually connect spaces. Architects sometimes modify the traditional *enfilade* by placing offsetting rooms in sequence to create more dynamic diagonal vistas.

■ *Materials*. Wood is the building material of the Shingle Style. A few examples have stone or rubble ground stories, but their upper stories are shingled (Fig. 43-2). Shingles, although typically square, may be round, hexagonal, or diamond shaped, and most often are left to weather naturally. Roofs are of slate or wooden shingles.

■ *Façades*. Usually asymmetrical, façades are more horizontal with less variation in form and fewer textures than in Queen Anne (Fig. 43-4). A broad triangular gable or gables may dominate one or more sides. Additionally, fronts may have towers, turrets, and bay or oriel windows. Towers often blend into the form of the façade and roofline instead of being separated as in Queen Anne. Most structures have porches that may project or be integrated with the body of the building. Porch supports may be stone arches or shingle-covered piers or columns. Shingles unify the façade. Eliminating corner boards and reducing textures, ornament, and color adds further unity. Elements of American Colonial architecture, such as classical columns and lean-to additions, appear occasionally.

■ *Windows and Doors*. Sash windows with a multipaned upper sash over a single-pane lower sash are common (Fig. 43-4). Windows may vary in size, form horizontal bands across the façade, or be placed symmetrically or asymmetrically. Other window types include casement windows and Palladian windows. Entry doors are usually recessed in the porch. Doors may have transoms and/or side lights.

■ *Roofs*. Most structures have multiple gable or gambrel roofs with dormers (Fig. 43-4). Other roofs include shed, curved, and conical on towers. Dormer windows may take various forms, including curved and eyebrow.

ARCHITECTURE • AMERICAN ARTS AND CRAFTS

As in England, American Arts and Crafts architecture is simple and honest, emphasizing structure and function, vernacular traditions, close ties to the landscape and location, naturalistic colors and motifs, and a handcrafted appearance. Local regional traditions are especially strong, which give rise to great diversity of expression. Single-family houses (Fig. 43-5, 43-6, 43-7) dominate American Arts and Crafts architecture, but there also are Arts and Crafts hotels (Fig. 43-2), vacation houses, churches (Fig. 43-3), and clubs.

Although following English principles, American Arts and Crafts architecture differs greatly in result. Lacking the cohesiveness of England, America produces a wider diversity of expression arising from a strong emphasis upon regionalism and individuality. Each region and individual interprets honesty of structure, harmony with the environment, good craftsmanship, and simplicity in its own fashion. Examples include Craftsman, Prairie, and Bungalow houses.

■ *Craftsman Houses*. Craftsman homes by Gustav Stickley, the great voice and promoter of Arts and Crafts in the United States, vary greatly in type and size. Houses in *The Craftsman* do not illustrate a particular style but their designs conform to his philosophy, which includes the expression of structure and simple, rustic materials used in a natural state and coming from the site or region.

■ *Prairie Houses*. Prairie houses by Frank Lloyd Wright in the Midwest are fully integrated custom designs (Fig. 43-6). The Prairie style, created in the early 20th century, reflects Wright's concepts of Arts and Crafts principles, his admiration of nature, and the art and architecture of Japan. Central to his philosophy is the idea of the house growing from nature, which is revealed in the harmony of form and material with the environment and the integration of exterior and interior. Plans evolve from the inside out, and horizontality is a primary characteristic. Other architects, both in Wright's office and elsewhere, adopt principles of the style. A common manifestation appears on the American four-square, a two-story cubic house type.

■ *The Bungalow*. California popularizes the bungalow (Fig. 43-7), a house type, not a style, based upon rural inns in India. The most common bungalows are small, single-story houses with broad sheltering roofs built for middle-class owners. Bungalows exhibit Arts and Crafts character in their simplicity, functionality, materials, and adaptability to climate. Along with similar small homes, the bungalow fulfills the American dream of home ownership for all. Although the terms are commonly interchanged, not all Craftsman houses are bungalows, nor are all bungalows Craftsman houses. High-style examples are large custom-designed bungalows of Henry Mather Greene and Charles Sumner Greene (Fig. 43-1, 43-5), most of which are in Pasadena, California. Few in number but important, these homes reveal a carpenter approach to design; exquisite craftsmanship inside and out; and influences from Japan, England, and the Spanish missions.

Public and Private Buildings • American Arts and Crafts

■ *Site Orientation*. A sense of place and regional character are important, so structures relate to their sites, whether through form, as in the horizontality of the Prairie style; materials; or style, such as Craftsman examples (Fig. 43-5, 43-6, 43-7). Buildings bring the outside in by using large windows, porches, patios, pergolas, and planters.

■ *Floor Plans*. Plans vary from rectangular to cruciform to T- or L-shaped (Fig. 43-6). Small square or rectangular plans are the most common with cheaper houses exhibiting the least variety in plan. Designers experiment with open planning for efficiency, freedom, and functionality. Open plans usually center on the fireplace as symbolic of home and family. Porches, sleeping porches, and terraces extend living space outdoors.

▲ **43-5.** David B. Gamble House and stair hall, 1907–1908; Pasadena, California; Charles Sumner Greene and Henry Mather Greene. Arts and Crafts.

Arts and Crafts plans, particularly Prairie houses, develop from the inside out with space flowing around the fireplace, which is usually near the center of the house. The elimination of doors and walls allows spaces to interconnect. Changes in floor level and ceiling heights help differentiate spaces. Only the second-story bedrooms and bathrooms are private. California houses by the Greene brothers incorporate these planning principles in designs for wealthy clients (Fig. 43-5). The perception of interior space is enhanced by adding a large entry hall, separating the living and dining rooms, and extending porches or outside living areas.

Bungalow floor plans, most of which are small and rectangular, make the most of limited space by having no separate entry hall and connecting the living and dining rooms with a low or half wall or an arched opening. The kitchen usually is behind the dining room and bathroom, and bedrooms are on the opposite side. Plans for small houses often combine multiple functions in a single room and eliminate unnecessary rooms for greater economy.

■ *Materials*. Materials in natural colors and textures relate buildings to their environments (Fig. 43-5, 43-6, 43-7). Building materials include stone, rubble, brick, wood, clapboard or board and batten siding, shingles, stucco, concrete, and concrete blocks. Stucco in a variety of textures may be tinted beige, tan, or gray. Some houses have stained wooden slats on exterior walls, which resemble half-timbering. Siding stained green or brown gives an informal, rustic appearance to vacation homes and resorts, but often exterior woods are allowed to weather naturally. To further emphasize their characteristic horizontality, Prairie houses are usually constructed of horizontal wooden siding or narrow Roman brick with wood, stone, or concrete trim. Sometimes the mortar in vertical joints is applied flush and tinted the same color as the brick to further increase horizontality. Greene and Greene houses, bungalows, and others may have stone or rubble foundations, sometimes mixed with clinker brick.

■ *Façades*. Arts and Crafts façades frequently give an air of vernacular or rustic origins, simplicity, structural honesty, and good craftsmanship. Decoration comes from materials, forms, and structure rather than applied ornament. Classical elements are rare. Horizontal emphasis, structural repetition, asymmetrical groupings, and a mix of materials are common characteristics.

The Greene brothers use simple elements to form rambling, complex compositions for their houses (Fig. 43-5). Line and form create horizontal emphasis on asymmetrical façades. Structural elements are visible, and the houses have a carpenter/craftsperson appearance in which each joint is carefully articulated. Balconies and porches project from and penetrate the body of the house.

Prairie houses, in contrast to others, are two or three stories with a pronounced horizontality that is further emphasized by bands of windows and trim and the interpenetration of roofs and terraces into the body of the house (Fig. 43-6). A large and broad chimney, usually in the center, and piers at corners and between windows appear to anchor the house to the landscape while providing vertical elements. Some have wings at right angles to the main house. Often cantilevered, porches with massive square or rectangular supports, decks, terraces, and balconies form transitional spaces to the outdoors, and urns, planters, and window boxes are integrated into walls, porches, and terraces.

Bungalows are one or one and a half stories with a front full- or partial-width porch (Fig. 43-7). The two-story variation, which is not considered a true bungalow, may be described as built along bungalow lines or may be called a semi-bungalow or bungaloid. Bungalows have front or side gables with or without dormers. Organization, symmetry, and decorative elements may relate the house to a particular region, such as Colonial for New England or Prairie for the Midwest. Those on the West Coast often reflect a Japanese sensibility. Porch supports may be tapered square columns; short, square columns with large piers beneath; or solid balustrades. Many columns or supports extend to the ground with no break at the floor of the porch.

■ *Windows*. A variety of window types appear on Arts and Crafts houses and commercial buildings. Prairie houses have bands of windows with solid piers between. (Fig. 43-6). Windows may turn corners to give the impression of transparency. Stained glass in geometric patterns depicts local foliage or flowers (Fig. 43-5). Other types of windows include casements with leaded glass or single-pane lower sashes with multipane uppers (Fig. 43-5, 43-7).

■ *Doors*. Prairie house entrances often are hidden to avoid interrupting the horizontality of the house. Generally, entry doors are under porches and often have a geometric balance of natural wood panels, usually oak, and small windows. Art or stained glass often fills the windows and side lights, particularly in the work of Wright and the Greene brothers (Fig. 43-1, 43-5, 43-6). Bungalows have simple paneled doors, sometimes with glass panes.

■ *Roofs*. Arts and Crafts roofs frequently have varying roof levels, sometimes in different shapes, and wide overhangs with exposed rafters (Fig. 43-3, 43-5). Some have decorative beams or braces under the gable. Low-pitched roofs, usually hipped, emphasize horizontality on Prairie houses (Fig. 43-6). A few mix gable roofs with a flat or low-pitched roof. Lower stories may have their own roofs parallel to the main roof. Eaves extend far beyond the wall for shelter and protection from sun and rain. Bungalows have front or side gabled roofs with or without dormers (Fig. 43-7). Side gables usually have a wide dormer with ribbon windows. A few have hipped or cross-gabled roofs.

INTERIORS

Whether elite and architect-designed or builder-designed and more middle class, both Shingle Style and Arts and Crafts interiors integrate architecture, furnishings, and decorative arts into a unified whole. Shingle Style interiors may take influences from English Queen Anne and Japanese architecture, but most are Arts and Crafts in design. Meticulous attention to details and handcrafted work complement the harmonious concept of the parts blended into the whole in the Arts and Crafts house. Like the exteriors, interiors have an informal or vernacular feeling that comes from intimate scale, open space, asymmetrical arrangements, horizontality, rectangular shapes, and straight lines. Japanese influences are prevalent. Architects, designers, and writers, such as Stickley, believe that the room's character should reflect

DESIGN SPOTLIGHT

Architecture: A masterpiece of the Prairie style, the Frederick C. Robie House has a marked horizontality that integrates the structure with the open midwestern landscape. Low, broad, cantilevered hipped roofs and protected courtyards emphasize the home's sheltering nature. In keeping with this concept, Wright disguises the entry on the far side of the house and away from both streets. Bands of windows, narrow Roman brick with the same color mortar, and concrete accents further emphasize horizontality while contrasting with the verticality of the central core, which houses the hearth as center of the home. Numerous large windows and direct access to the terraces bring the outside inside. Characteristically, Wright's designs for the window and doorway glass feature flora and fauna of the prairie. Wright's elongated plan takes advantage of the narrow lot with important public spaces located near the front entry. Like the architecture, the plan centers on the hearth and spaces flow from and around it. The interior design of the dining room also emphasizes horizontality and human scale. The low ceiling with integrated lighting gives a feeling of intimacy, as does the dining set designed by Wright. The tall-back chairs and the corner lights on the table emphasize enclosure and the importance of the ritual of dining for hospitality and family bonding. [National Historic Landmark]

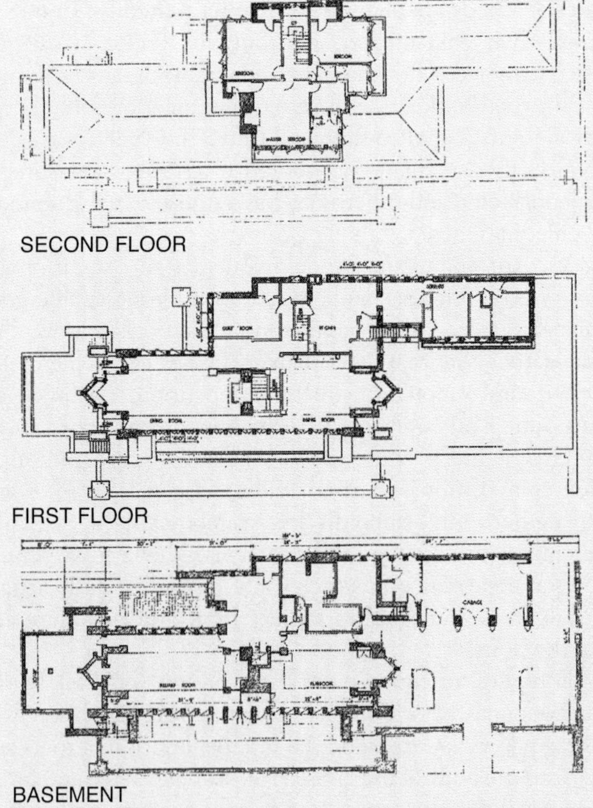

▲ **43-6.** Frederick C. Robie House, floor plans, and dining room, 1909–1910; Chicago, Illinois; Frank Lloyd Wright. Prairie style.

both its function and the individuals who use it. Stickley and others emphasize that the dining room should express warmth and gracious hospitality to support the important ritual of meals, hospitality, and family bonding (Fig. 43-6, 43-10). Equally important design principles are visual continuity among rooms, informal materials and finishes, rough or natural textures, warmth, and light.

Frank Lloyd Wright, the Greene brothers, and other architects create totally designed interior environments for their clients, which may incorporate custom furniture, light fixtures, accessories, and textiles. The middle class seeks assistance from periodicals, such as *The Craftsman* and *House Beautiful*. Prominent architects, such as Wright, occasionally design small houses that are published in these magazines.

▲ **43-7.** Bungalow, 1900s–1920s; California, and "The Winona," 1916; Sears, Roebuck and Company mail-order bungalow.

Public and Private Buildings

- *Color.* Colors of nature characterize the Arts and Crafts interior and include red, yellow, green, ochre, brown, buff, and tan (Fig. 43-2, 43-3, 43-5, 43-9, 43-10). Common wall colors are brown, ochre, buff, and off-white. Color selection may be determined by the room's exposure, with warm colors used in northern rooms and cool colors in rooms facing south. Wallpapers, textiles, and accessories in brighter colors add accents. Wright is known for his earth-tone color palette.
- *Floors.* Wood floors covered with decorative area rugs are common (Fig. 43-2, 43-5, 43-6, 43-9, 43-10), along with painted floors, and tile and linoleum for kitchens and baths. Parquet, with and without borders, is also used. Hand-knotted Oriental rugs,

DESIGN SPOTLIGHT

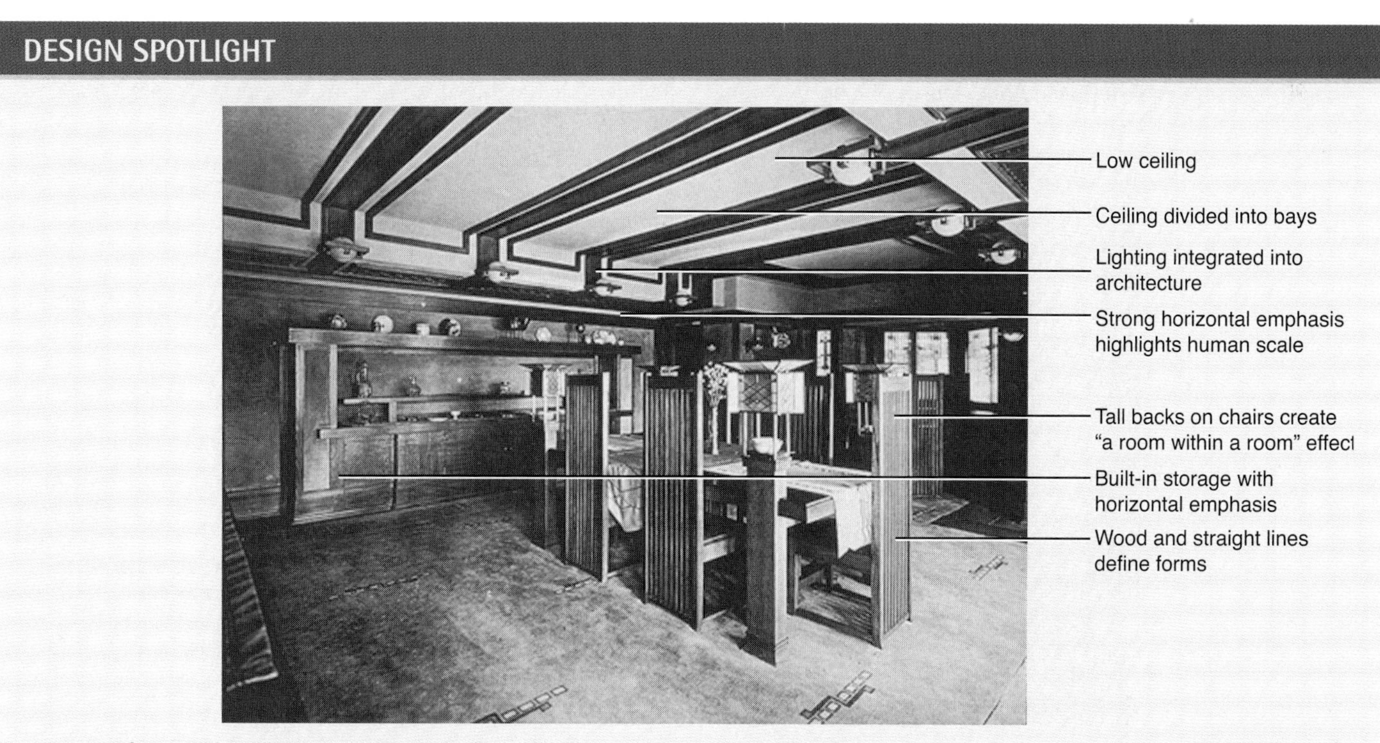

▲ **43-6.** Continued

machine-made Orientals, Native American, druggets, or animal skins cover floors. A few rooms use wall-to-wall carpet in simple patterns or the new plain solid-colored carpets (Fig. 43-2). Magnasite, a concrete-like material, may be used for both flooring and counters in kitchens. Ceramic tile in squares or hexagons and neutral colors covers floors in bathrooms.

■ *Walls*. Stucco walls with wood moldings or slats create a compartmentalized appearance and replicate the structural character of exteriors (Fig. 43-9). Some walls may be of stone or wood to emulate the exterior design. In houses and commercial buildings, natural wood dados or paneling with detailed joinery embellishes the walls (Fig. 43-2, 43-3, 43-8, 43-9, 43-10). Wood paneling is an important design element in Greene brothers' work (Fig. 43-1, 43-5). Rooms occasionally have some built-in seating or storage integrated into the overall interior architectural design. Plain, painted, or wallpaper treatments are common for walls as well. Many rooms have a frieze embellished with wallpaper, painted decoration, fabric, and/or a plate rail to display a limited number of carefully chosen accessories. Friezes and wallpapers have stylized naturalistic, geometric, or abstract patterns and natural colors (Fig. 43-9). Wright often uses a frieze to establish visual continuity between rooms. Alternatives to patterned papers include Lincrusta Walton, felt papers, Japanese grass cloth, denim, burlap, and canvas.

■ *Chimneypieces*. Although the fireplace is no longer needed for heat, living rooms focus on the hearth as the center of home and family. An inglenook often sits adjacent to either side of a fireplace in living rooms or stair halls and supports family unity in larger houses (Fig. 43-5, 43-8) but not in bungalows.

■ *Windows*. Simple drapery treatments of panels suspended from rings hang at windows (Fig. 43-9). Most curtains are sill length and can be tied back to allow in more light. Fabrics are most often plain, natural colored linen or cotton. Naturalistic motifs in brown, gold, green, or coral could be stenciled or embroidered onto plain fabric. Stained glass is a common decorative element (Fig. 43-1, 43-9, 43-10), and half or "Morris" curtains cover the lower half of the window when the upper part is stained glass.

■ *Doors*. Large, wood-planked doors with iron hardware are common. Most are paneled and of gum or oak wood with a clear finish. Some doors have stained glass. *Portières* reach their height of popularity in the last decade of the 19th century. They hang at doors to living rooms, dining rooms, and libraries. Each side matches the room it faces.

■ *Ceilings*. Most ceilings are plain and painted white or cream, but some have beams, planks, or compartments to repeat exterior structural character (Fig. 43-5, 43-6, 43-9). Ceilings may be lower in the inglenook or some rooms to create a cozier atmosphere. Wright sometimes incorporates decorative stained glass ceilings in important rooms.

DESIGN SPOTLIGHT

Interiors: The stair hall in the Samuel Tilton House has the medieval spirit that is common in many Shingle, Queen Anne, and Arts and Crafts houses of the late 19th century. The living hall with staircase, inglenook, and built-in seating is based upon those from English Queen Anne houses. The open and interpenetrating space in which vistas change and flow among the hall, living room, and dining room comes from Japanese architecture. The fireplace design, niches, paneling, and spindles recall 17th- and early-18th-century buildings with which architects McKim, Mead, and White are especially familiar.

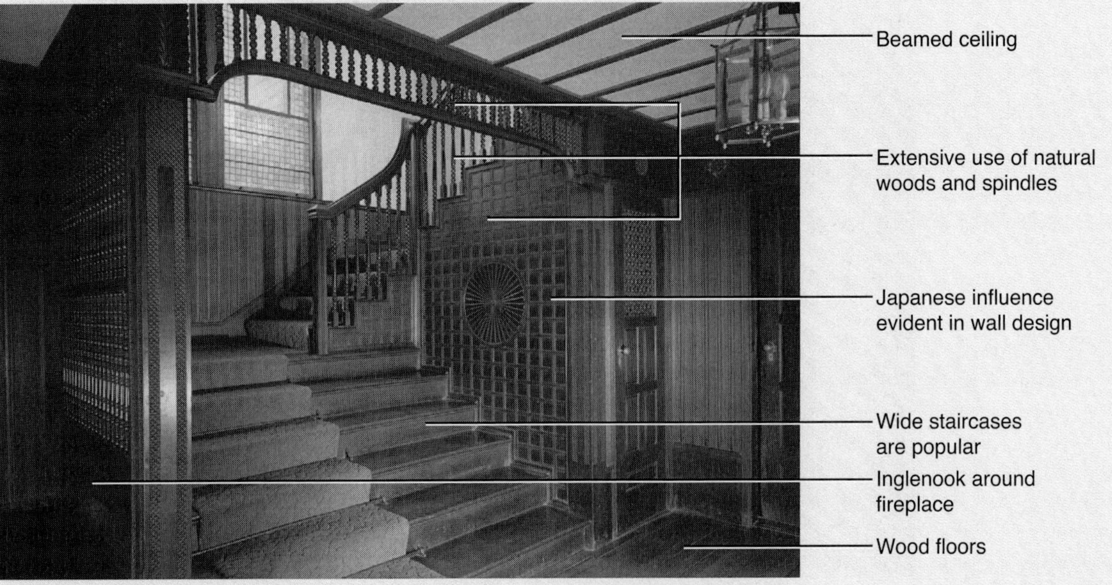

▲ **43-8.** Stair hall, Samuel Tilton House, 1881–1882; Newport, Rhode Island; McKim, Mead, and White.

▲ **43-9.** Living rooms; published in *The Craftsman*, 1905–1909; Gustav Stickley and Harvey Ellis. Craftsman style.

■ *Textiles*. Textile design relies upon geometric patterns; stylized natural objects; and flat, two-dimensional treatments. Common fabrics include cotton, linen, wool, and leather with little decoration. Textiles may be decorated with embroidery, appliqué, cutwork, or stenciling (Fig. 43-9).

■ *Lighting*. Numerous, large windows fill the interiors with natural light. Simple, angular light fixtures, such as chandeliers, table and floor lamps, and wall sconces, convey an image of humble craftsmanship (Fig. 43-5, 43-6, 43-9, 43-11). Iron, copper, brass, and wood combined frequently with opalescent or amber-tinted glass are typical materials.

FURNISHINGS AND DECORATIVE ARTS • AMERICAN ARTS AND CRAFTS

Like architecture, Arts and Crafts furniture may be designed by architects, such as Wright or the Greene brothers, for total environments; or mass-produced in factories like Stickley's; or handcrafted in cooperative or utopian communities, such as Roycroft. Arts and Crafts design principles characterize furniture, whether it is architect-designed, individually handcrafted, or mass-produced. Most furniture is rectangular in form and shape, with no veneers, minimal finishes, and revealed joints and structure. Honest use of materials, structural emphasis, and distinctive joinery also are characteristic. Horizontal in orientation, pieces may show influences from English designers such as Voysey or Mackmurdo. Often limited in quantity, furniture reflects the interior design to reinforce simplicity and openness. Furniture is arranged around major architectural elements.

Prairie furniture, when designed for a particular space in a particular house, is more architectonic and directly linked to the architecture than other furniture is because it relates more to the house instead of the user (Fig. 43-6, 43-10). Furniture by the Greene brothers has rounded edges; tapering forms; and subtle curves in backs, stretchers, legs, and arms. Brackets and stepped-back forms are borrowed from Japanese furniture. Like Prairie furniture, designs of Greene and Greene relate to the architecture but are more human in scale, reveal more careful detailing and joinery, and have softer edges.

As with architecture and interiors, much of American Arts and Crafts furniture is machine-made instead of handcrafted, so it

▲ **43-10.** Living room and dining room, Meyer May House, 1905; Grand Rapids, Michigan; Frank Lloyd Wright with George Niedeken on furniture. Prairie style.

▲ **43-11.** Lighting: Candlesticks, hanging lantern, and lamps, 1900–1915; United States.

reaches a widespread audience. Most examples adhere visibly to Arts and Crafts principles, but lack the philosophical foundation. Some manufacturers create original designs and devote their entire production to Arts and Crafts–style furniture. Others simply add the style to their existing lines and/or copy examples by Stickley and other prominent manufacturers. Stickley's Craftsman furniture is simple in design with an emphasis on straight lines, wood slats that create rhythm, visible joints, and a few subtle curves (Fig. 43-9, 43-13). A well-known variety of Arts and Crafts is Mission furniture, which seems to arise from California and Spanish mission architecture and furniture. It also is inspired by English Cotswold furniture. Mission may also refer to Gustav Stickley's furniture.

Public and Private Buildings

■ *Materials*. Oak is the common wood, but local woods also are used. A few examples use mahogany or rosewood. Greene and Greene favor teak and ebony, particularly for dowels and butterfly joints. Decorative inserts are of more valuable woods such as rosewood or ebony. Hinges and pulls may be of brass, copper, or iron, and hammer marks are characteristic. Simple finishes or no stains are preferred over highly finished shiny surfaces. A wax or lightly shellacked finish is the most common, and oak often is fumed with ammonia for an aged look. Veneer, inlay, and marquetry are uncommon except in work by individual craftspeople, such as Harvey Ellis, or communities, such as the Shop of the Crafters in Cincinnati.

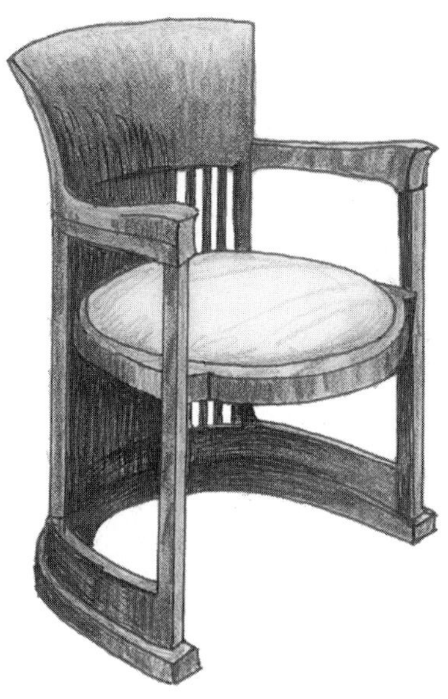

▲ **43-12.** Armchair, Darwin R. Martin House, 1904; Buffalo, New York; Frank Lloyd Wright.

■ *Seating.* Most seating is completely of wood with loose cushions instead of attached upholstery (Fig. 43-2, 43-5, 43-6, 43-9, 43-10, 43-12, 43-13, 43-14). Backs, arms, seats, legs, and stretchers have large, straight components that may be flat planes or quadrangular forms. Backs may have vertical slats, spindles, or pierced splats. Occasionally, curved brackets may support wide, flat arms. The reclining lounge chair, often known as the Morris chair and based on English Arts and Crafts models, is very common in North America. Although most manufacturers have one in their lines, Stickley produces the best-known version of this chair (Fig. 43-13).

■ *Tables.* Tables are square, rectangular, round, or polygonal and often have wooden plank tops (Fig. 43-9, 43-10). Leather, anchored with large nails, or decorative tiles may cover tops. Aprons may be straight or slightly curved. Stretchers may cross and have oversized pegs joining them to legs. Some tables have rectangular spindles between quadrangular legs. Some have planar or flat stretchers, and legs have cutout rectangles or squares. Pegged and mortise and tenon joints are characteristic.

DESIGN SPOTLIGHT

Furniture: Gustav Stickley is the best known and most influential producer of American Arts and Crafts furniture. In 1899, he forms the Gustav Stickley Company in New York, and it produces furniture in many styles. In 1900, Stickley introduces the Craftsman line, consisting of well-designed and well-made furniture in keeping with his Craftsman philosophy, which he absorbs from the English Arts and Crafts Movement. Made of quarter-sawn American white oak, his furniture is simple, rectilinear with mostly straight lines, with revealed construction in pegs and mortise and tenon joints. It is heavy and solid, and the splats give a rhythmic quality. Stickley refuses to use commercial finishes but develops a process he calls fuming to give the wood its characteristic nut-brown color. The company produces quantities of furniture for every room in the house and is widely imitated. The reclining armchair, often known as the Morris Chair, is based on the English Arts and Crafts version produced by Willam Morris and his firm.

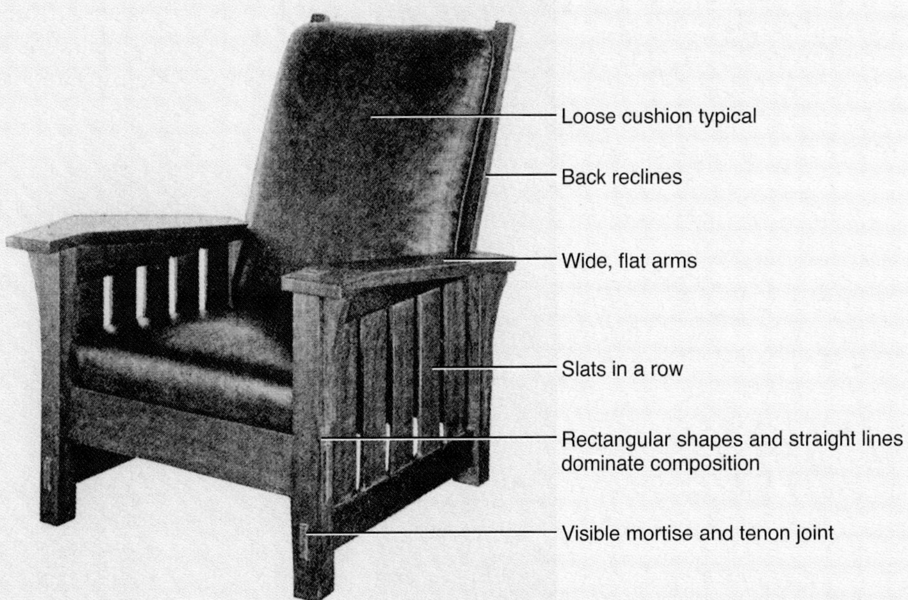

▲ **43-13.** Craftsman armchair, 1905; manufactured by Craftsman Workshops, New York; Gustav Stickley.

▲ **43-14.** Sofa in oak, 1912; United States. Craftsman style.

▲ **43-16.** Art Pottery from Rookwood Pottery and Newcomb College Pottery, c. 1900s–1920s; Ohio and Louisiana.

■ *Storage*. Storage is plain, rectangular, and usually horizontal in orientation (Fig. 43-9, 43-15). Planks compose sides and tops. Brackets and overhangs are typical. Hinges and pulls may be overly large and prominent. Forms emphasize structure with dominant frames composed of rails and stiles. Bookcases have rectangular glazed doors. Many homes have built-in buffets in the dining room (Fig. 43-6, 43-10) and built-in bookcases either separating the living and dining room or flanking the fireplace.

■ *Beds*. Bedroom suites with matching furniture remain fashionable. Beds have simple, plain wood headboards. However simple, painted metal beds or headboards often are used in lesser rooms.

■ *Decorative Arts*. Arts and Crafts rooms usually have fewer decorative accessories than in other styles. Guilds, cooperatives, and manufacturers turn out numerous accessories, including pottery, glass, metal work, baskets, and embroidery. Many objects, however, are handmade by artisans or members of the household. Art education classes, focusing on needlework and pottery, become popular with middle- and working-class women. Many women actively participate in guilds, cooperatives, and societies as designers and makers of ceramics, metal, and work. For some, this remains a fashionable hobby, but for others it becomes an important means of supplementing or earning a living. Some, following Candace Wheeler's example, sell their work. Art Pottery remains a common accessory (Fig. 43-16). Noteworthy examples come from Newcomb College Art School in New Orleans. Pieces feature designs of local flowers, such as magnolias and wisteria. Rookwood Pottery in Cincinnati emphasizes nature, crafts, and an aesthetic image.

■ *Later Interpretations*. In 1989, the L. & J. G. Stickley Company reintroduces Mission furniture that reproduces its earlier pieces. In response to demand, other companies follow suit. Today, individual craftspeople in the United States and England create furniture according to Arts and Crafts design principles (Fig. 43-17).

▲ **43-15.** Display cabinet/bookcase in oak with wrought iron pulls and hinges, c. 1904–1905; Stickley workshops. Craftsman style.

▲ **43-17.** Later Interpretation: Kusaka sideboard in walnut and bubinga, 2002; Massachusetts; John Reed Fox.

N. INNOVATION

During the 1880s through the 1930s, some architects and designers try to integrate design, mechanization, and the idea of modern. Within various countries, individually or in groups, they create forms or styles that strive to express the time in which they are living and thus advance the concept of modern. Although expressions of each individual or group are quite different in appearance, their ideas come from some shared concepts. These include the rejection of historicism as no longer valid or appropriate, the integration of the machine and mechanization, and the adoption of new technologies and new materials. Each group tries to create a new design language to express its world as transformed by industrialization from agrarian to urban, handcrafted to machine-made, and producing to consuming. Additionally they respond to other factors such as the end of the 19th century, World War I, and economic instability.

New ways of living in the period demand new building, interior, and furniture types, as well as forms and designs that respond to the needs of contemporary consumer societies that are no longer based on aristocracy or class. Designers hope to improve life and reform society through their work. Although they share some of the views of the earlier Aesthetic and Arts and Crafts Movements, such as art for art's sake and an emphasis upon craftsmanship, this generation of designers recognizes the failure of the previous one to utilize the machine, the very tool that would enable them to reach the goal of good design that is available for everyone. So they begin to design with mechanization in mind, often using new materials or older ones in new ways. The concepts and work of these groups set precedents for the development and evolution of other modern styles that follow in the 20th century.

As an international style at the end of the 19th century, Art Nouveau has two major trends, one that is curvilinear and organic, and another that is geometric and abstracted. Designers strive for complete unity and total works of art by designing the building, interiors, furniture, and decorative arts. Art Nouveau absorbs influences from many sources, including non-Western ones such as Japan, and past historical styles such as Baroque, Rococo, and Biedermeier. Individuality and creativity of the designer are important.

Members of the Vienna Secession want to create a modern, Viennese style outside academic traditions. The group exhibits its own and others' work and produces architecture, interiors, furniture, and decorative arts in forms, details, and colors generally not popular before. The Vienna Secession advocates simplicity in design, geometric forms, rational construction, and the rejection of ornament, which greatly influences subsequent modern developments, including Art Deco.

A group of progressive architects, known as the Chicago School, introduces the skyscraper in early-20th-century Chicago, Illinois. A new building type, these multistory buildings respond to the spatial needs of modern businesses coupled with the high cost of urban land. Additionally, they take advantage of new technologies such as reinforced concrete, steel frames, and the passenger elevator. Members of the group also grapple with the design and articulation of this new building type for which there is no design precedent.

The Modern Forerunners, a group of individualist architects working in Europe and the United States, seek to create a functional and economically practical architecture that meets the needs of, or even reforms, contemporary society. Their experiments with form and structure reflect diverse approaches, theories, and aesthetics instead of a common movement. The works of these innovators provide important theoretical and functional foundations for the further development of modern architecture.

Founded in Holland by painters and architects around 1917, De Stijl or The Style is an art and design movement that tries to express universal concepts through abstraction; right angles; straight lines; an asymmetrical balance of rectangles; and the primary colors plus black, white, and gray. Members totally reject subject matter, the imitation of nature, and individuality. Although it produces only a handful of examples of architecture, interiors, and furniture, De Stijl significantly influences other avant-garde architects and designers, particularly those of the Bauhaus.

The Bauhaus, a German art and design school founded in 1919 by Walter Gropius, exerts a profound influence upon art education, architecture, interior design, textiles, and decorative arts through its theories, practices, and products. The school's program of study teaches students in both theory and practice to design for modern machine production as opposed to handcrafting. Although rejecting a common style, Bauhaus works have a similar appearance that results from emphasis upon function, mass production, geometry, absence of any ornament, and the use of new materials. Many of its graduates assume important places in industry or become prominent architects, designers, and educators, particularly during the International Style in the 20th century.

CHAPTER 44

Art Nouveau

1880s–1910s

Nature proceeds by continuity, connecting and linking together the different organs that make up a body or a tree; she draws one out of the other without violence or shock.

—Henri van de Velde, *Le Formule de la beauté architectonique moderne*, 1916

The only true modern individual art in proportion, in form and in colour, is produced by an emotion, produced by a frank and intelligent understanding of the absolute and true requirements of a building or object—a scientific knowledge of the possibilities and beauties of material, a fearless application of emotion and knowledge, a cultured intelligence, and a mind artistic yet not too indolent to attempt the task of clothing in grace and beauty the new forms and conditions that modern development of life—social, commercial, and religious—insist upon.

—Charles Rennie Mackintosh, Lectures on "Seemliness," 1902

Art Nouveau is a complex, eclectic international movement made up of various styles in Europe and North America. It has two general trends. One is a stylized, organic, curvilinear form called *Art Nouveau* in France, Belgium, Holland, Czechoslovakia, and the United States; *Stile Liberty* or *Stile Floreale* in Italy; and *Arte Moderno* in Spain. The second, more rectilinear, geometric, and abstract trend, is prominent in Glasgow, Scotland; Scandinavia; Germany; and Austria where it is called *Jugendstil*. Although contributing to it, Great Britain, in the midst of the Arts and Crafts Movement, remains largely outside of Art Nouveau developments.

HISTORICAL AND SOCIAL

Art Nouveau is a conscious attempt to create a new style that rejects historicism and adopts a new visual language. Anticipated first by some artists and writers before 1890, by 1895 it becomes a major force in architecture, followed by the decorative arts. Primarily a style of line and ornament, it is most typically manifested in architecture, interiors, furniture, graphic arts, and the decorative arts, mostly in urban centers. Art Nouveau is dynamic, individualist, but short lived, dominating the arts in Europe and the United States from about 1890 to 1910.

By the end of the 19th century, much of the world has changed dramatically in response to the Industrial Revolution. Population explosions, longer life spans, and scientific and technological progress have transformed lives. Lifestyles are vastly different from even 50 years before, forcing people to look for ways to understand and cope with the changes. Although industrialization has spread to almost all parts of the world, it brings greater change in some countries than in others. A common element in all countries, however, is urbanization in which people leave farming and move to the cities for jobs in industry. Another commonality is the growing power of consumers, who demand more choices in goods. The balance of world power also is changing. Great Britain, the major world power for much of the 18th and 19th centuries, declines, and Germany and the United States become the new industrial and world leaders. Imperialism, in which powerful nations seek to exert control over weaker ones, spurs nations to colonize in Asia, Africa, and the Pacific arenas. Trade and competition become more international.

As the end of the century approaches, some regard it pessimistically, seeing decline and the end of an era. Others who view the change more optimistically see opportunities, particularly to create a new style that reflects the changed, new world of the 20th century. The latter, Art Nouveau represents the first major attempt to portray a visual language as modern, with no allusions to the past.

An exact beginning of the style is difficult to determine because artists, writers, and thinkers anticipate some of Art Nouveau's aspects and character during the 1880s, particularly in England. For example, in 1883, Arthur Heygate Mackmurdo creates an Art Nouveau–like title page for his book on Sir Christopher Wren's churches in London, and later uses curving, organic designs in a side chair (Fig. 44-15). In 1893, the first issue of a new English journal, *The Studio*, carries some of the first Art Nouveau images in work by young illustrator Aubrey Beardsley. Europeans eagerly scrutinize the curvilinear, conventionalized illustrations by Beardsley and others in *The Studio* as well as other English journals. Also influential on the development of Art Noveau are England's Aesthetic Movement, with its focus upon art for its own sake and little or no stress upon morality, and the Arts and Crafts Movement, which advances the individuality of the designer and emphasizes craftsmanship. Images and ideas spread through exhibitions, posters, books, periodicals, trade, and travel.

As a product of various movements, artists, and writers, Art Nouveau emerges full blown in Paris and Brussels in the early 1890s. In 1893 in Brussels, Belgium, Victor Horta designs the *Hôtel Tassel* (Fig. 44-6), the first major expression of the new style to unify architecture and interior design. The façade integrates stone, iron, and glass in a new and very influential design language. In 1895, Belgian Henry van de Velde publishes the important manifesto *Déblaiement d'art* (A Clean Sweep for Art). By identifying key concepts of the movement, it has a significant impact on many designers. In that same year, Siegfried Bing opens a shop and gallery in Paris named *Salon de l' Art Nouveau*. In addition to giving the new style its name, the shop, which displays glass, textiles, and furniture, becomes an international center for Art Nouveau in France. The store also inspires other new galleries, shops, department stores, and companies. Frequently housed in Art Nouveau–style buildings, these retail firms market Art Nouveau ideas, art, and products, including paintings, textiles, furnishings, decorative arts, art glass, ceramics, and jewelry. This helps spread the style and promote individual artists and designers. For a brief period in the early 20th century, Art Nouveau becomes mainstream.

International expositions help the development and spread of Art Nouveau by providing visibility for designers and their products in Europe and England. In 1900, the *Exposition Universelle* in Paris prominently features the versatility and diversity of Art Nouveau. In 1902, the *Prima Esposizione d'Arte Decorativa Moderna* (referred to as the International Exhibition of Decorative Art) in Turin, Italy, showcases the work of designers from France, Belgium, Scotland, Germany, Austria, and Italy. It displays the most comprehensive scope of Art Nouveau to date. In 1905, the *Exposition Universelle* in Liege, Belgium, with its strong representations from France and Belgium, reinforces the notion that Art Nouveau is a public style. Finally, in 1908, the Franco-British Exhibition in London displays the largest collection of French Art Nouveau objects ever seen in England. From 1910 on, international exhibitions no longer represent the style because it has moved in other directions.

In France, Belgium, and the United States, nature and organic motifs are important. Curvilinear forms, whiplash curves, and stylized plants and flowers are typical. In contrast, in Scotland, designs are more linear, geometric, and symbolic. In Czechoslovakia, buildings are decorative but overall plainer than in France or Belgium. Taking its name from Liberty department stores, Italian design is pluralistic and free of eclecticism, and maintains a strong national character. Most examples are curvilinear, with a Neo-Baroque heaviness, and are highly decorative.

■ *Belgium*. Brussels is the center for Belgian Art Nouveau. The style emerges from urban development sponsored by King Léopold II, who desires to transform the city with monumental boulevards, parks, and streets lined with elegant middle-class houses. Patrons of the style see themselves rejecting tradition and conservatism and adopting the avant-garde. Victor Horta (Fig. 44-6, 44-10), Henry van de Velde, and Gustave Serrurier-Bovy are the leading designers.

■ *France*. Two schools of Art Nouveau develop in France, one in the capital of Paris and the other in Nancy. Seeking to maintain France's dominance in art and culture, the French government

▲ **44-1.** Architectural Details: Entrance gate, *Le Castel Béranger*, 1898; Paris, France; Hector Guimard, and stair railing, France; Majorelle.

provides funding to art schools, for exhibitions, and for the reorganization of museums. It also sponsors numerous initiatives to improve living conditions for the French. In Paris, the principal designer is Hector Guimard (Fig. 44-19), who introduces Art Nouveau both in architecture and the Paris Métro (subway) entrances (Fig. 44-4). Consequently, Art Nouveau is briefly called *le style métro*. The Art Nouveau school in Nancy promotes decorative arts, such as furniture, glass, and ceramics, over architecture. Leading practitioners include Émile Gallé, Eugène Vallin, and Louis Majorelle (Fig. 44-20).

■ *Germany*. Germany rapidly industrializes during the second half of the 19th century, becoming affluent with a strong desire for national identity. Munich becomes the major art center following the publication in 1896 of the *Jugend*, a journal with the aim of rejecting historicism and developing a new concept of design for the future. Advocates of these ideas create a German version of Art Nouveau called *Jugendstil*, meaning "young style." Their emphasis upon cooperation among designer, craftsperson, and manufacturer later influences the *Deutsche Werkbund* and the Bauhaus. Leading practitioners include Hermann Obrist, Auguste Endell, Peter Behrens, Bruno Paul, and Richard Riemerschmid.

■ *Spain*. In Spain, Art Nouveau manifests primarily in Barcelona, the leading industrial center. The Spanish government pushes a modernization program for the city to promote political, social, and cultural reform. Spanish Art Nouveau has two trends. The mainstream Art Nouveau, called *Modernismo* or *Arte Moderno*, follows the artistic lead of Belgium and France. The second trend is inspired by the Catholic Church's view of contemporary life, which seeks to mold society both theologically and aesthetically. The idiosyncratic, highly personal, and sometimes bizarre work of Antoni Gaudí i Cornet dominates this trend (Fig. 44-5, 44-9).

▲ 44-2. Shop front, 1897; Brussels, Belgium.

▲ 44-1. Continued

■ *England and Scotland*. Although contributing to it, Great Britain largely rejects Art Nouveau with the exception of Glasgow, Scotland. An industrial city, Glasgow has a healthy economy and close ties to the Continent. Highly influenced by machine precision and the Scottish landscape, Art Nouveau in Glasgow centers on a group of practitioners who are neither teachers nor publicizers of their work. Known as "The Four," the group consists of Charles Rennie Mackintosh (Fig. 44-7, 44-8, 44-11), Herbert McNair, and sisters Margaret and Frances MacDonald. Their work influences Europe, particularly Vienna and Munich.

■ *United States*. Like Britain, the United States does not fully embrace Art Nouveau because Americans are wary of the style's associations with decadence, the erotic, and socialism. The most prominent practitioners are Louis Sullivan, who experiments with Art Nouveau–style architectural ornament, and Will Bradley, who creates and publishes interior and graphic designs. The decorative arts represent some of the best expressions of Art Nouveau in the United States, particularly in art glass, ceramics, and decorative painting. Important designers and firms include Louis Comfort Tiffany and the Tiffany Studios (Fig. 44-14), Frederick Carder and the Steuben Glass Company, and the Durand Art Glass Company.

Art Nouveau succeeds as a creative and imaginative style that creates total works of art. However, many designers are unable to completely divest themselves of the past. Despite an emphasis upon craftsmanship and good design for the masses, many works are not suitable for mass production. Nevertheless, Art Nouveau lays important groundwork for subsequent modern movements in its attempts to throw off the past, its stress on total works of art, and its emphasis upon new technology and contemporary materials.

▲ **44-3.** Glasgow School of Art and library, 1897–1909; Glasgow, Scotland; Charles Rennie Mackintosh.

CONCEPTS

Complex and multifaceted, Art Nouveau has many roots, manifestations, and participants. Various artists, architects, and designers create unique individual and innovative expressions that reflect the geography, governments, economies, lifestyles, and patterns of behavior within their respective countries. A key concept shared by all participants is the desire to create a new style, divorced from those of the past, that expresses a modern urbanized, commercial society. Its genesis often coincides with urban renewals and redevelopments that are part of governmental or social reforms. In the spirit of reform, artists and architects search for a new style, one that expresses their world as transformed by the Industrial Revolution. They want to create a new design language and vocabulary in which buildings and objects look contemporary and are not tied to the past.

A highly eclectic style, Art Nouveau, in reality, does not completely break with the past. Absorbing influences from contemporary art and literature (pre-Raphaelites, Symbolism, and the Nabis), non-Western cultures (Japan, Islam, and China), past styles (Celtic Revival, classicism, Baroque, Rococo, Biedermeier, and Gothic Revival), and vernacular traditions and folk art, Art Nouveau adapts and reinvents them in a spirit of transformation for a modern age. At the heart are the imagination and creativity of the artist or designer.

▲ 44-4. Entrance, Paris Métro station, c. 1900–1910; Paris, France; Hector Guimard.

To an even greater degree than others before them, Art Nouveau designers see no separation between the fine arts of painting and sculpture and architecture and the decorative arts, such as glass and ceramics. They strive for unity in design to create complete expressions, or what they call total works of art. Thus, the architect or designer is called upon to design the building and all its aspects, including the interiors, furniture, and decorative arts, to achieve a synthesis of design. Other shared concepts include an emphasis upon craftsmanship; a reverence for the individuality of the artist or designer; art for its own sake; and art for the masses, not just for the wealthy elite. Rooted in theory, these concepts prove difficult to maintain and contribute to the style's demise.

Individuals see themselves as a vehicle for a transformation of culture. Many designers believe they are developing a completely new art vocabulary and that individuals serve as the vehicles for change. The style sets a precedent for other modern styles that follow in the 20th century.

CHARACTERISTICS AND MOTIFS

Despite individual manifestations, Art Nouveau design has some common characteristics. Line, whether curving and sensuous or straight and geometric, is an important principle that designers explore and exploit. Line combined with form conveys energy, force, dynamism, and/or organic growth. Designers reduce traditional and naturalistic forms and motifs to their essence, transforming them and ascribing to them their design intentions in appearance and meaning. Examples strongly emphasize decoration, particularly surface decoration, which may be linear rather than plastic. Consequently, Art Nouveau often is more successful in interiors, furniture, decorative arts, and graphic arts than in architecture. Design strives for total integration so that architecture, interiors, and furnishings convey the same visual language and are in harmony with each other. Other common characteristics include asymmetry, abstraction of natural forms, free-flowing organic plant forms, whiplash curves, and symmetry with geometric shapes. From Japanese woodblock prints, the Art Nouveau image extracts simplicity, asymmetry, flat pattern, linearity, and color. Also important are the dynamic and exuberant qualities of the Baroque; the asymmetry, naturalism, and cabriole leg of Rococo; the sensuous, curvilinear lines of Islamic art and the Celtic Revival; the restrained classicism of Biedermeier; and Gothic Revival structural theory. New technology and modern materials, such as iron, often are incorporated into designs and frequently drive or inspire design concepts, contrast between function and form, and the dramatic color interpreted by individual designers.

- *Art Nouveau*. In France (Fig. 44-1, 44-4, 44-6, 44-10), Belgium (Fig. 44-2), and the United States (Fig. 44-14), designs emphasize nature and organic motifs. As a result, most works have curvilinear forms and whiplash curves with stylized plants and flowers. In contrast, in Scotland, designs are more linear, geometric, and symbolic (Fig. 44-3, 44-8, 44-9).
- *Jugendstil*. In Germany, the visual language has a strong geometry with whiplash curves and an emphasis upon decoration. The style has minimal impact on architecture but greatly affects textiles, jewelry, and furniture.
- *Stile Liberty or Stile Floreale*. Taking its name from Liberty department stores, Italian design is pluralistic and free of eclecticism, and maintains a strong national character. Most examples are curvilinear with a Neo-Baroque heaviness and are highly decorative.
- *Arte Moderno*. In Spain, work by Antonio Gaudí (Fig. 44-5, 44-9), has a unique organic character, one that is not copied much by others. Work by other designers follows European curvilinear forms and details.
- *Motifs*. Popular motifs stylized from nature include flowers such as the rose, violet, iris, and water lily, and animals such as the dragonfly, butterfly, snail, and peacock (Fig. 44-12, 44-13, 44-14, 44-18).

ARCHITECTURE

Art Nouveau architecture strives to create a modern style free from historicism and academic traditions. Emphasizing the individuality of the architect, this new architecture incorporates new materials and industrial processes and emphasizes structure and function. Influences include Viollet-le-Duc, the French architect and restorer; Gustav Eiffel; and Parisian department stores, such as *Au Printemps* and *Bon Marché*, that have large, open interiors composed of iron and glass. As socialists and political activists, many architects want to improve the quality of life for individuals and society through their designs. However, their work is largely composed of commissions from individuals and groups with little influence.

Art Nouveau defines commercial buildings such as stores (Fig. 44-2), offices, schools (Fig. 44-3), churches (Fig. 44-5), auditoriums, concert halls, and metro stations (Fig. 44-4). Houses (Fig. 44-6, 44-8) and stores are a more frequent expression than other buildings.

Public and Private Buildings

■ *Site Orientation*. As part of urban renewals, most Art Nouveau buildings are located in city centers, with some appearing in suburbs. Because nature is an integral part of the overall design concept, houses may have lawns or garden areas that extend the interior space.

■ *Floor Plans*. Many designs incorporate open plans with free-flowing space to minimize visual separateness and to connect interior spaces to the exterior. Level changes may define and link rooms and circulation areas. Floor plans emphasize important public spaces, stairways, center halls, living rooms, and dining rooms (Fig. 44-6, 44-10). Plans show a logical flow of movement, an axial alignment of windows to help air circulation, defined modules, and rectangular room shapes.

■ *Materials*. Buildings extensively use and/or combine iron, glass, and stone, and some parts may be prefabricated. Iron is used structurally as well as decoratively, both inside and out (Fig. 44-1, 44-2, 44-4, 44-6, 44-10). It may twist and turn to achieve a fluid motion of form and shape. Glass may be clear and layered or stained and decoratively detailed. Other materials include brick, tile, and wood (Fig. 44-3, 44-7, 44-8, 44-11). Each designer conveys his or her individual expression through form and/or decoration to create a unique image.

▲ **44-5.** *Sagrada Familia*, begun 1883; Barcelona, Spain; Antonio Gaudí i Cornet.

■ *Façades*. Exterior façades display horizontal and vertical movement that creates a sculptural, fluid expression (Fig. 44-2, 44-3, 44-5, 44-6, 44-9). Some are plain with little ornamentation, while on others decoration is both an inherent part of the structure and emphasizes structural elements. Compositions may be symmetrical or asymmetrical as determined by the designer, the client, or the site. The façade composition often clearly articulates the interior planning. Verticality, symmetrical and asymmetrical arches, and separation of stories also are characteristic. Elements may appear layered with balconies, grillework, window forms, applied decoration, and bargeboards or decoration in the apexes of gables and dormers. Art Nouveau features include curving details or plant forms reshaped as classical capitals, columns, pilasters, or other elements, displayed in fenestration and grillework; and window mullions with whiplash curves or tendrils.

■ *Windows*. Windows are a distinguishing feature of the style (Fig. 44-2, 44-3, 44-6, 44-9). Generally large, they display verticality. Some are rectangular, but most have symmetrical or asymmetrical rounded arches or curving tops or shapes. A few have a second rounded arch or a teardrop-shaped window above them. Prominent moldings and curving, often whiplashed, grilles give a linear and decorative, organic emphasis. Some of Horta's houses have rows of windows in different heights on each level, with prominent bay windows on the front street side (Fig. 44-6). Windows in Mackintosh's buildings, such the Glasgow School of Art (Fig. 44-3), show great variety in size, height, and prominence. They also convey regularity and simplicity. Gaudí's windows have large areas of glass broken into defined sections with curved wood framing. Window shapes and sizes repeat on large apartment houses. Surrounds often are sculptural and undulate to create movement, like those at Casa Milá (Fig. 44-9).

■ *Doors*. In many countries, entry doors have numerous curves and intricate details, and are often of wood with glass inserts (Fig. 44-6). Three-dimensional curved moldings frame the opening. Elaborate, curving, organically inspired iron gates may provide entry into a small vestibule (Fig. 44-1).

■ *Roofs*. Roofs and rooflines may be downplayed or prominent (Fig. 44-4, 44-5, 44-8, 44-9). Important ones are tall with a marked verticality. Wall and roof dormers with pointed or rounded arches permit light into upper stories and attics. Iron and glass roofs may create light wells over stairways and center halls.

INTERIORS

Like architecture, Art Nouveau interiors are primarily curvilinear with abstracted floral or naturalistic motifs in France, Belgium, and Italy and strongly geometric with rectangular or square shapes dominating the compositions in Germany and Scotland. Rooms of both trends are unified and regarded as works of art. As total

DESIGN SPOTLIGHT

Architecture and Interior: Hôtel Tassel is the first example of fully developed Art Nouveau architecture and interior design in Brussels. One of Victor Horta's most important buildings and his first major commission, this portrait house represents a sophisticated, simple statement of Art Nouveau and establishes the new architectural style through its elegant, restrained façade and three-dimensional form. The symmetrical composition with a vertical emphasis resembles other four-story, narrow townhouses in the area. At first glance, the composition seems classical in its vocabulary and disposition of elements. However, the individual articulation of parts disappears in the masonry skin of the house, which seems to push forward in the semicircular bow oriel windows centered on the façade and the lintels over the flanking windows. The capitals of the first-floor columns are plantlike and curve over the supports above and below them. The iron grilles on the second- and third-floor windows feature Art Nouveau whiplash curves. Important design features include iron columns and balustrades; iron and glass windows and skylights that allow light to penetrate; decorative details accenting architectural elements and arch supports; and a dominant entry door.

The elegant stair hall continues Horta's fascination with organic movement, open flowing space, and decorative design. Enriched through color, materials, and details, the space exemplifies the concept of unity to become a complete, individual work of art, an icon that has transended time. The decorative tile floor, painted walls, and balustrade incorporate various curved lines to convey energy and motion. This repeats in the iron columns, arched opening, and light fixture. Subdued colors derived from nature enhance the impression of unity. Horta uses this design language for both exteriors and interiors, with some variation in overall character and detail, for other clients and for himself. [World Heritage Site]

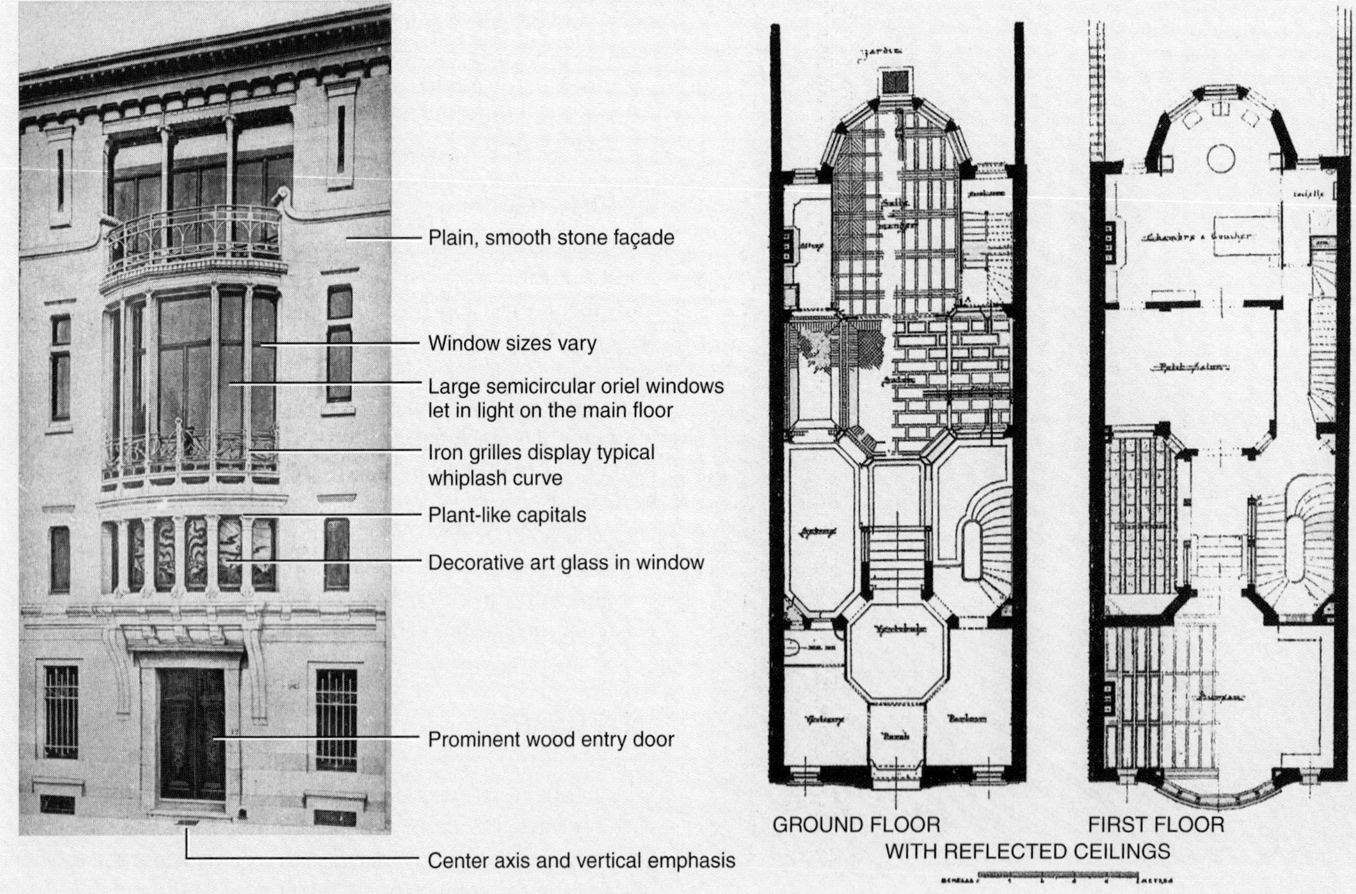

▲ **44-6.** *Hôtel Tassel,* floor plans and stair hall, 1893; Brussels, Belgium; Victor Horta.

works of art, interiors strongly relate to exteriors in form and detail. The designer, usually the architect, creates the exterior, interiors, furniture, and decorative arts with an eye to complete unity in form, color, and decoration. Individually designed, all parts relate to each other and the whole. Designers hope to reform interiors by providing more light and air and through liveliness of form, shape, and color. Rooms may also display a strong relationship to nature in forms, motifs, and color. Complete architect-designed Art Nouveau interiors are uncommon and limited to model rooms at international expositions, commercial interiors, and residences of the affluent (Fig. 44-6, 44-10). Other rooms show the style's influence in one or more of the following: wallpapers, decorative painting, textiles, rugs, furniture, lighting, and decorative accessories (Fig. 44-11, 44-12, 44-13, 44-15, 44-16, 44-18, 44-19, 44-20, 44-21). By the time Art Nouveau becomes mainstream, most of the early practitioners have moved on to other styles or joined other movements.

▲ **44-7.** Front saloon, Ingram Street Tea Room, 1900; Glasgow, Scotland; Charles Rennie Mackintosh.

DESIGN SPOTLIGHT

▲ **44-6.** Continued

No particular room types are associated with Art Nouveau. Room shapes remain traditional rectangles or squares, but balustrades, windows, doors, ceilings, fireplaces, and other details may be composed of organic curves or arches, which gives the impression of movement (Fig. 44-6, 44-10). Ornament and decoration are concentrated on structural elements. Exceptions are the spaces designed by Gaudí in which walls and ceilings often undulate.

Public and Private Buildings

■ *Color.* Nature provides sources for color, including earth tones and pastel shades of blue, green, brown, gold, white, rust, and purple (Fig. 44-6, 44-10, 44-14). Warm colors, such as red, rose, yellow, gold, ochre, and orange, dominate in Belgium. Designers frequently use bright colors to enhance their designs or to make a design statement. Mackintosh interiors often have contrasts between white and black with decorative accents in rose, lilac, and gray, common colors of Scottish landscapes (Fig. 44-7, 44-8, 44-11).

■ *Floors.* Designers use many types of flooring materials to support their design concepts (Fig. 44-6, 44-8, 44-10, 44-11). Wood, a common material, may feature curvilinear or geometric designs repeating those of the walls and furniture. Marble, brick, or ceramic tiles are often used in entries and lower stories. Some department stores have floors of glass tiles to permit light to pass between stories. Rugs are designed in unity with the interior.

■ *Walls.* Walls display a variety of treatments (Fig. 44-3, 44-6, 44-7, 44-8, 44-10, 44-11). Most are stenciled or painted with linear or floral motifs and patterns near the ceiling or highlighting architectural features, such as doors or windows. Many walls have picture moldings at varying heights from the ceiling. Wallpapers may have naturalistic patterns, geometric designs, or women in floral bowers. Some designers favor wallpapers designed by

William Morris or Charles F. A. Voysey. Wood paneling declines in use. When adopted, it may have organic shapes and whiplash curves or geometric and rectangular forms. Paneling may be stained, painted, or lacquered. Wall hangings with *appliqué* or embroidered decorations created by the designer or tapestries also may cover walls. Some designers favor unusual materials, such as ceramic panels or tiles, for wall treatments in important rooms.

■ *Windows and Window Treatments*. Wood moldings frame the upper portion of curved and rectangular windows. Window treatments are usually plain panels hanging from rods by rings. Embroidery, stenciling, or applied decorations of flowers or foliage may embellish the panels. Lace curtains sometimes cover windows.

■ *Doors*. Doorways are three-dimensional and often curve at the top (Fig. 44-10). Doors are usually of wood. Some have plain or stained glass decoration.

DESIGN SPOTLIGHT

Architecture and Interiors: Walter W. Blackie, a prominent businessman and publisher, commissions Hill House. A suburban home for family weekends, Hill House sits on a small hill as its name implies. Charles Rennie Mackintosh, like other Art Nouveau designers, creates a total work of art in this house, his most famous residential project. After observing the Blackie family's daily habits, he designs the house from inside out, concentrating on the functional needs of the users. Borrowing from vernacular Scottish building forms, the exterior reflects the rambling character of traditional designs with its irregular façade, different roof levels, heavy walls, varying window sizes, and subdued personality. The simple exterior with minimal decoration provides contrast to the more refined and carefully articulated interiors.

Within, Mackintosh achieves unity through the repetition of rectangular and square shapes in walls, floors, furnishings, and decorative arts, all of which he designs. To soften and for contrast, he introduces curves and naturalistic forms in details and fabrics. Colors of gray, black, white, purple, and rose also unify the spaces. The entry hall is refined and quiet with its black, gray, and purple color scheme, whereas the bedroom, with its all-white colors, reflects a lighter, more airy aesthetic. Individually, the spaces feel intimate and cozy, portraying a warm and inviting ambience that is enhanced by color and lighting.

▲ 44-8. Hill House, entrance hall, and bedroom, 1902–1903; Helensburgh, Scotland; Charles Rennie Mackintosh.

DESIGN SPOTLIGHT

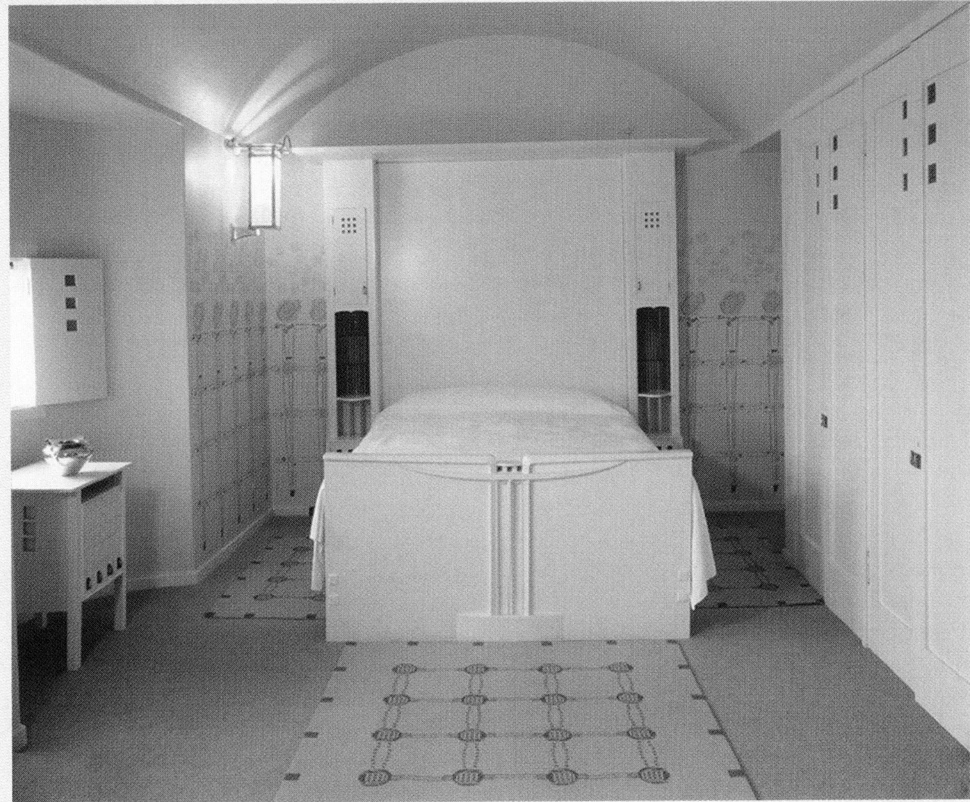

▲ **44–8.** Continued

▲ **44-9.** *Casa Milá (La Pedrera),* 1905–1910; Barcelona, Spain; Antonio Gaudí i Cornet.

■ *Staircases.* Staircases are important conveyors of Art Nouveau character for most designers (Fig. 44-1, 44-6, 44-8, 44-10). Horta places stairs centrally inside iron cages with glass roofs that allow in natural light and offer a decorative medium for his creativity. Columns, supports, rails, banisters, and mullions replicate curving, abstracted naturalistic forms. Others, such as Majorelle, create very ornate rails and banisters with twisting, curving organic forms.

■ *Ceilings.* Ceilings may be flat, curved, coved, or beamed (Fig. 44-7, 44-8, 44-10, 44-11). Treatments include paint, plasterwork, tiles, papers, and glass.

■ *Textiles.* Many architects, designers, and graphic artists create textiles and upholstery to suit the concepts of their interiors, so there is a broad range of patterns, weaves, and colors (Fig. 44-12, 44-16, 44-18). Expressions vary with geography and ethnicity. Some reveal vernacular or folk roots, while others show little influence from the designer's heritage or the past in general. Some revive hand techniques such as batik, embroidery, or lace. Others use sophisticated machine or professional embroiderers.

Fabrics include printed cottons and velvets, silk, and stenciled linens. Designs may be naturalistic and curvilinear or geometric. Colors are strong and contrasting, although some geometric designs are monochromatic. Some interiors use Arts and Crafts textiles by Morris and others.

■ *Lighting.* Natural light from many large windows usually floods Art Nouveau interiors. Light fixtures, candlesticks, and candelabra of wood, iron, copper, brass, silver, and ceramics display curving floral or geometric forms (Fig. 44-6, 44-8, 44-11, 44-13). Usually designed by the creator of the building or interior, they relate to the interior design and furniture.

FURNISHINGS AND DECORATIVE ARTS

Art Nouveau furniture, like interiors, varies in form from whiplash curves, sculptural forms, and elongated shapes with a strong visible relationship to nature, to geometric, hard-edged, and minimal decoration depending upon the country and/or intent of the designer. Even within a nation, there is great diversity of form and design with some revealing strong ties to vernacular or folk traditions. Nevertheless, most furniture is individually designed to suit the space it inhabits. Each piece is conceived in relationship to the other furniture as well as the entire composition.

Designers view furnishings in diverse ways. Some reject traditional forms and methods of construction, while others use them as springboards for their own creations. Many create sculptural, highly decorative, richly appointed designs. Some strive for function over decoration, a strong relationship with architecture, and visible structure. As a style, however, Art Nouveau emphasizes the ability of wood to be carved for furniture, even though it may visually represent another material. Designers use imaginative designs and creative and unique construction methods to achieve their aims. Some designs reveal an awareness and understanding of the material, while pieces with twisted, tortured forms seem to ignore it. Designers often stretch the limitations of the medium and the maker. Subsequent movements will become less dependent upon wood and seek newer materials and technology that can more readily adapt to mass production.

Although some designers, such as Majorelle (Fig. 44-20), attempt to mass-produce their furniture, much Art Nouveau furniture is far too expensive for the general market. An exception is

DESIGN SPOTLIGHT

Interior: Situated in an Art Nouveau neighborhood, the Hôtel van Eetvelde exhibits a similar character as Victor Horta's Hôtel Tassel. The plain, ordered, symmetrical façade has large windows to let light inside and prominent vertical and horizontal structural moldings defining bays. Horta, like other Art Nouveau architects, strives to design interiors with more light and air. Additionally, he dislikes closed spaces that hinder not only air and light but also circulation, so he often places important spaces within an iron framework supporting a glass roof as he has done in this salon. Centrally located, the octagonal hall incorporates a low-domed stained glass ceiling permitting light to enter. Clustered iron columns, an arched arcade with built-in lighting, and a decorative balustrade frame the seating area and define the circulation path at all levels. Naturalistic curving shapes in the glass are repeated in the iron balustrade and accent the upper walls and floor. The color scheme, which uses brown, gold, and pale green, reflects the organic character and the hues of nature. Horta creates complete unity by designing all elements in a light and airy open space. This is one of his most important interiors. [World Heritage Site]

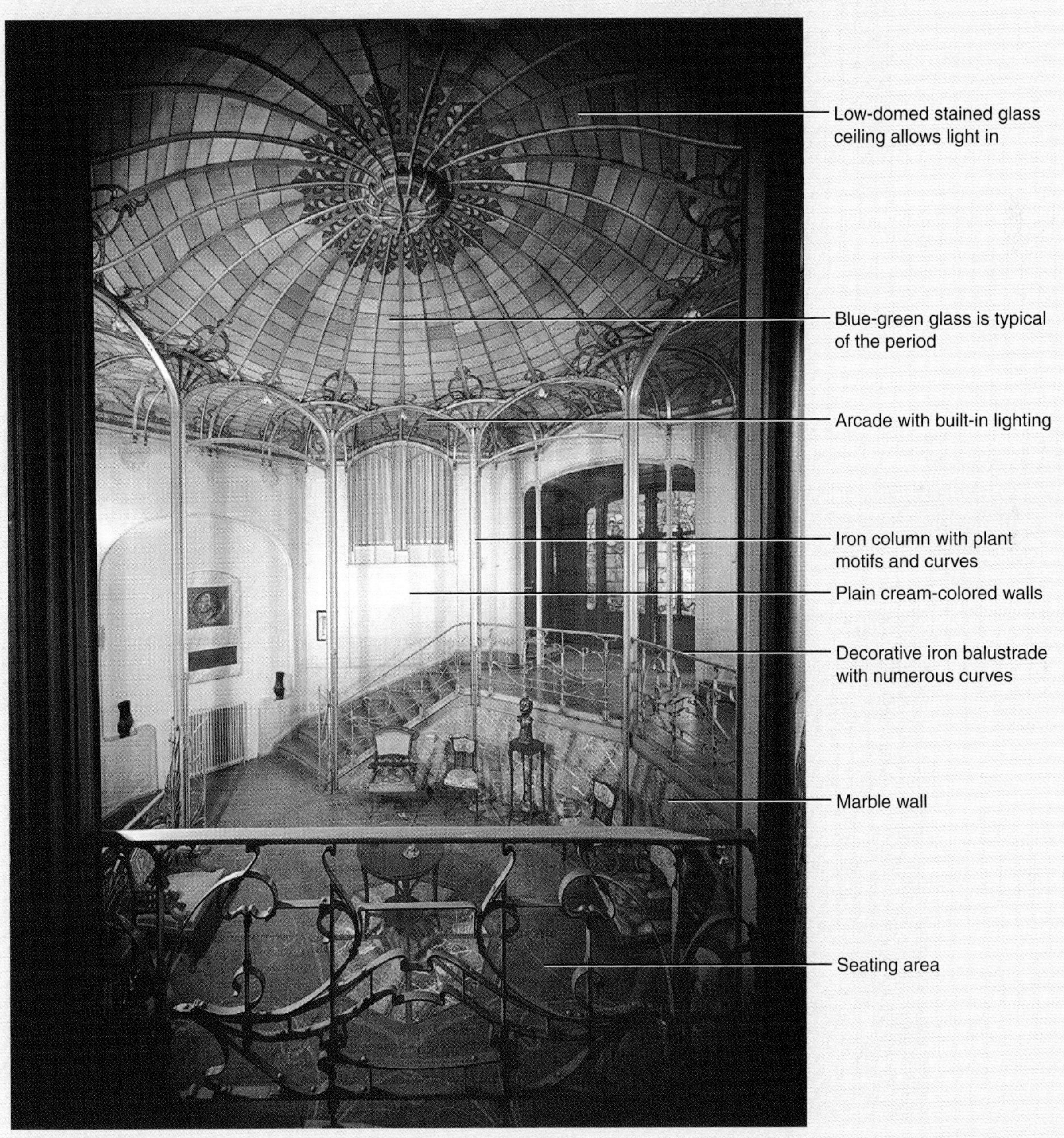

▲ **44-10.** Salon or hall, *Hôtel van Eetvelde*, 1895; Brussels, Belgium; Victor Horta.

▲ **44-11.** Sitting room, C. R. Mackintosh House, 1900, 1906; Glasgow, Scotland; Charles Rennie Mackintosh.

Thonet (Fig. 44-17), whose mass-produced bentwood furniture blends well with Art Nouveau. Thonet's furniture does not, however, arise from Art Nouveau precepts. Rather, its innovations are in its manufacturing processes, which give it simplicity, functionality, and beauty without historic references. Late in the period other manufacturers begin selling furniture with curves and naturalistic ornament.

No particular types of furniture are associated with Art Nouveau, but architects individually design much of it, including small accent pieces such as mirrors, shelves, and music stands.

■ *Belgium*. Belgian furniture reveals influences from past styles such as Baroque, Gothic, and Rococo. Heavier than French, it is dynamic and plastic with abstracted ornament.

■ *France*. French furniture reveals Rococo influence (Fig. 44-16, 44-18, 44-19, 44-20). The Paris School is more individualistic, refined, and restrained. Decoration is stylized and naturalistic. The School of Nancy closely aligns with Rococo. Much of the output is traditional in form with Art Nouveau curvilinear and naturalistic decoration.

▲ **44-12.** Textiles: Fabrics with curves and flowers, c. 1900.

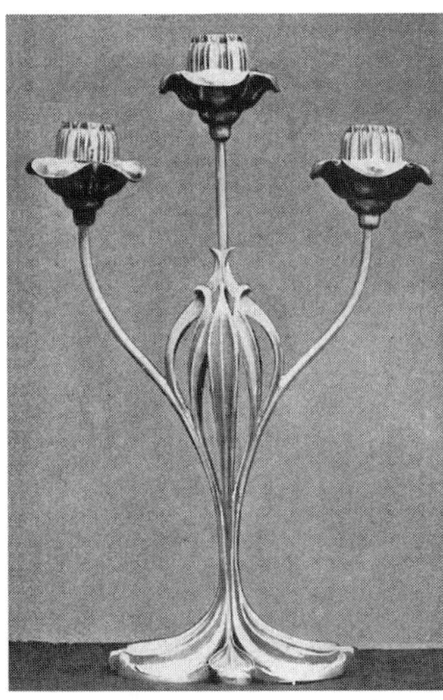

▲ **44-13.** Lighting: *Flambeau, applique électrique,* and *table et lampe,* 1901–1902; France.

■ *Spain.* Spanish furniture usually is sculptural and plastic, eccentric, and idiosyncratic as shown in the work of Gaudí.

■ *Germany.* The Neo-Renaissance and folk art influence German furniture. Nevertheless that which develops in Munich and Darmstadt is remarkably free of historicism. Designers emphasize construction and curving sculptural form.

■ *Scotland.* Mackintosh's work reveals Scottish and Celtic roots (Fig. 44-7, 44-8, 44-11). Individually designed pieces are rectilinear yet softened with gentle curves. Tall and thin, pieces are works of art but are often poorly constructed and uncomfortable. Some furniture is lacquered white or stained black with jewel-tone decorations.

▲ **44-14.** Lighting: Lamp, c. 1906; United States; Louis Comfort Tiffany.

Public and Private Buildings

■ *Materials.* Art Nouveau revives such woods as mahogany and pear. Other common woods include walnut and oak. Some pieces are highly polished, heavily stained, or lacquered as in Scotland, while others are unfinished or unpolished to convey a rustic or vernacular appearance. Carving, gilding, marquetry, and inlay of exotic woods, ceramics, glass, or metals are common decorative techniques.

▲ **44-15.** Dining chair, 1882–1883; England; Arthur Heygate Mackmurdo.

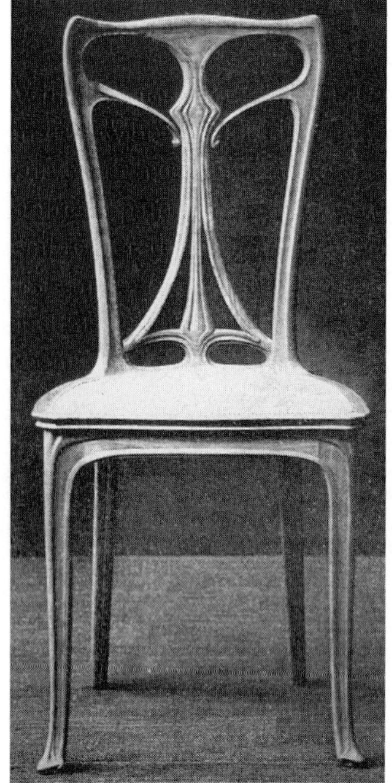

▲ **44–16.** Side chairs, 1899–1901; France; E. Colonna and A. Landry.

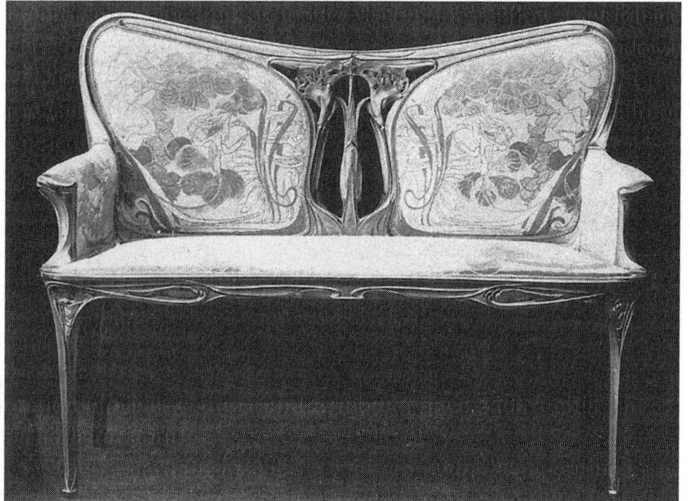

▲ **44–18.** *Canapé* for the Paris Exposition 1900; published in *Art et Décoration*, 1901.

▲ **44–17.** Chairs, settee, and table, c. 1900; Vienna, Austria; Michael Thonet.

■ *Seating.* Art Nouveau's greatest diversity appears in seating, where the individual imagination of the creator can find its fullest expression (Fig. 44-7, 44-11, 44-15, 44-16, 44-18). Some chairs and settees display Rococo roots in the wooden frames around backs and seats, modified cabriole legs ending in plant forms, and continuity of parts. Others reveal a concern for structure and function over historic precedents in their simply curved wooden backs and plain quadrangular legs and arms. Mackintosh designs reveal no evidence of past roots but are rectilinear, often with tall, attenuated backs accented with subtle curves. Although much of it is earlier than Art Nouveau, Thonet's very plain bentwood furniture with its curved lines (Fig. 44-17) appears in many Art Nouveau interiors.

DESIGN SPOTLIGHT

Furniture: Hector Guimard challenges traditional notions of design for cabinets in this undulating cabinet with whiplash curves and plantlike movements. The composition conveys the energy and vitality characteristic of Art Nouveau in France. The asymmetrical form, derived from nature, has two parts blended together, a tall and slender unit on the left and a wider and shorter unit with drawers on the right. Although rectangular in its overall shape, organic curves define and soften the tops, sides, and corners of doors and panels. A vinelike element rises from the side and sweeps across the front, adding dynamism while supporting the upper cabinet. Its curving shape is repeated in the panels and drawers, some of which terminate in stylized floral forms. Door and drawer pulls become part of the overall integrated composition. The various surfaces have numerous intricate, twisted, curving lines and details that convey an organic, fluid design.

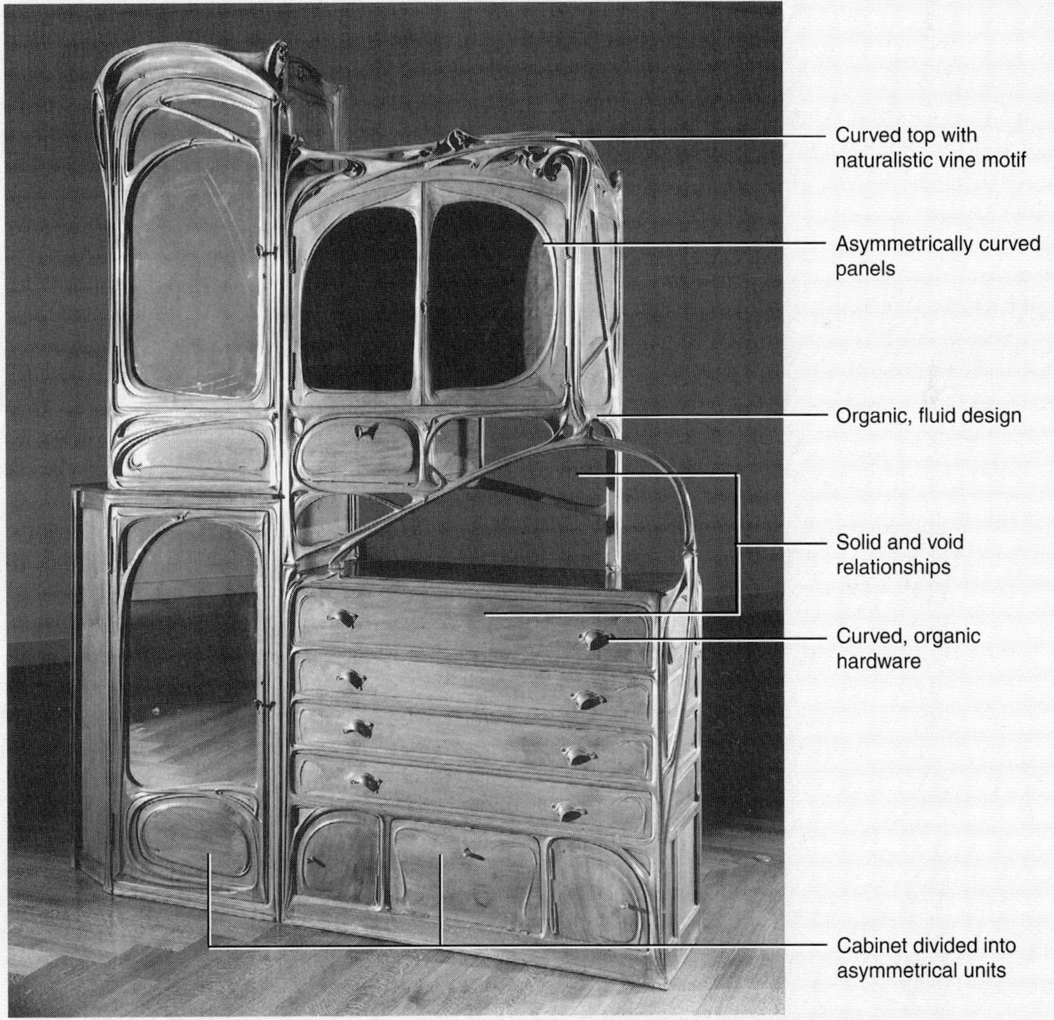

▲ **44–19.** Cabinet, c. 1899; France; Hector Guimard.

■ *Tables*. Tables display a range of forms, designs, and embellishments (Fig. 44-11, 44-17). Some follow Gallé's traditional forms with plant, insect, and floral marquetry or Guimard's round tops and legs of stems or curving tendrils. In contrast, those by Mackintosh have oval and rectangular tops and legs of curving boards, and they may be lacquered white with pink and blue ornament.

■ *Storage*. Storage may have an architectural quality or be sculptural with organic forms and motifs (Fig. 44-11, 44-19). Desks often have whiplash curving tops, sides, and drawers. Sides may be divided into asymmetrical curving panels. Doors and drawers of buffets or china cabinets feature curving corners, tops, glazing, handles, and pulls composed of whiplash tendrils and stems. Some combine open shelves, cabinets, and drawers. Designers may choose woods with strong grains to emphasize the curving organic nature of their design or use marquetry for ornamentation.

■ *Beds*. Beds (Fig. 44-8, 44-20) have curvilinear headboards and footboards but no posts. Like storage pieces, their outlines, composed of flowing moldings, may undulate or curve. Broad surfaces of headboards and footboards often are a particular focus for decoration and may be divided into asymmetrically shaped panels with floral marquetry or contrasting colors of wood and applied ornament.

▲ **44-20.** Bed, c. 1900–1910; France; Louis Marjorelle.

■ *Decorative Arts*. Art Nouveau greatly influences the decorative arts. Many architects and artists, like Riemerschmid, design metalwork in forms, shapes, and motifs that complement their interiors. Similarly, artists and ceramists create ceramics that reflect Art Nouveau design principles, whether curving forms and naturalistic details or geometric with minimal surface decoration (Fig. 44-21). Also evident in ceramics is a shift in hierarchy of importance from porcelain to stoneware or earthenware. Glassmakers revive and exploit traditional techniques such as enameling, cased glass, and iridescence. They also adopt new technologies in color and heating methods and use new materials such as metal foils. Gallé in France, one of the most prolific and innovative of the Art Nouveau glassmakers, uses numerous decorative techniques. He is particularly known for cased glass compositions of leaves, plants, flowers, and insects. Louis Comfort Tiffany in the United States also experiments with glass and creates naturalistic Art Nouveau designs in colored and stained glass. Bohemian glass is also popular during the period, particularly that produced by Johann Loetz.

■ *Later Interpretations*. In the last half of the 20th century, new materials and techniques not previously available allow designers to create works that reflect the whiplash curves of Art Nouveau. Individual craftspeople adopt particular elements, such as its curvilinear or geometric forms and floral ornament. Verner Panton's work in plastics (Fig. 44-22) and Frank Gehry's in bent wood echo the creations of Art Nouveau designers, while not obviously influenced by Art Nouveau.

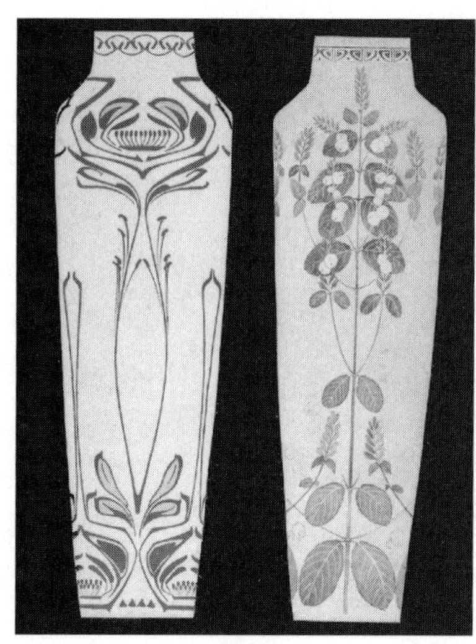

▲ **44-21.** Decorative Arts: Ceramic containers, c. 1902–1906; France.

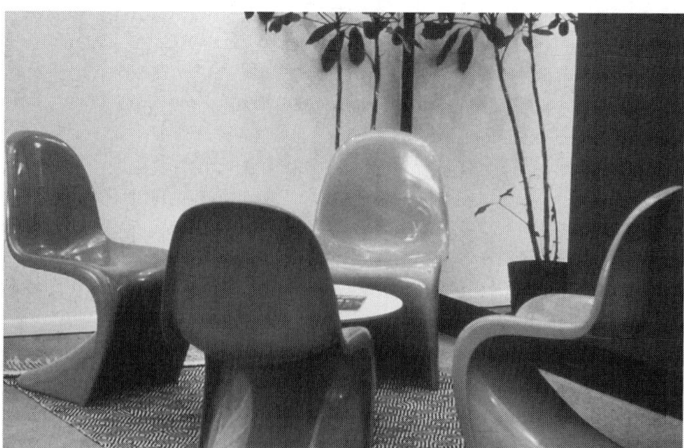

▲ **44-22.** Later Interpretation: Panton stacking chair, 1960–1967; Switzerland and the United States; Verner Panton, manufactured by Vitra and Herman Miller.

CHAPTER 45

Vienna Secession

1897–1920s

> *The exhibition was of prime importance in so far as artistic craftsmanship in Vienna was concerned. . . . One saw for the first time modern interiors arranged in accordance with a new Viennese taste. . . . And, moreover, our works were neither Belgian, nor English, nor Japanese, but Viennese, as the majority of critics indeed acknowledged.*
>
> —Koloman Moser, recollecting the Eighth Secession Exhibition in 1900

Vienna Secession strives to create a modern style devoid of historicism and free of academic stagnation. Founded in 1897 in Vienna, Austria, by a group of artists, sculptors, architects, and designers, it is more influenced by Britain, Scotland, and Germany than by France or Belgium. Rejecting the more flamboyant Art Nouveau expressions, the Secession advocates simplicity, rational construction, and honest use of materials, which will, in turn, influence subsequent modern developments. Members of the Secession form the *Wiener Werkstätte*, a crafts organization similar to a guild. It shares similar beliefs, but puts more emphasis on unity and excellent craftsmanship.

HISTORICAL AND SOCIAL

During the late 19th century, rapid industrialization and a significant increase in population provide the framework for urban growth in Vienna. A bustling, multicultural city, it becomes a center for artistic creativity with far-reaching influences on later design. Architecture in the city favors a strong academic tradition, a hierarchy of importance among buildings, historicism, and expressions of imperial grandeur. The *Künstlerhaus* (Academy of Arts) controls art in Vienna, both who creates it and what it looks like. Otto Wagner, Hans Olbrich, and Josef Hoffmann are members, but they break away from it to show their rejection of its academic position and reliance on traditional theories of art. They, along with Josef Maria Olbrich, Koloman Moser, painter Gustav Klimt, and others, found the Vienna Secession (*Wiener Sezession*) in 1897. This society of avant-garde architects, designers, sculptors, and painters strives to unite art and design, mainly by showcasing their work and that of others in prominent exhibitions. Affected by the concurrent rational construction of architecture and furniture in Munich, Germany, the group also follows, to some degree, the principles of craftsmanship and production promoted by the English Arts and Crafts Movement. Work by Charles Rennie Mackintosh in Scotland provides a major source of design inspiration. The society publishes its own journal, *Ver Sacrum (Sacred Spring)*, from 1897 to 1903. Members also spread their ideas through professorships in various art schools.

The first Secessionist exhibition held in 1898 displays paintings, wallpaper, stained glass designs, and book illustrations. Some of the noteworthy participants include James McNeil Whistler, Walter Crane, and Gustav Klimt, all of whom receive wide acclaim. The exhibition is such a success that later in the year the group builds an exhibition hall, the design of which declares its rejection of academic traditions and illustrates a new architectural language in form and design. Later exhibitions take the form of complete room settings to showcase the talents of the group's members. The eighth exhibition in 1900 is particularly significant because it includes work by C. R. Ashbee's Guild of Handicraft from England and a room by the Glasgow Four (Charles Rennie Mackintosh, Herbert McNair, and the MacDonald sisters, Margaret and Frances) from Scotland. Although the new Viennese style receives critical acclaim, the Secession group begins to lose cohesion as an art movement in 1905 when members move in new directions. It becomes an artists' union and continues exhibitions into the late 20th century.

In 1903, inspired by the success of the Secession group, Hoffmann and Moser form the *Wiener Werkstätte* (Vienna Workshops), a craft studio inspired by Ashbee's Guild of Handicraft and opposed to methods of mass production. Many members of this group are females. Projects, mostly for wealthy patrons, include the decoration of individual rooms, entire houses, or small apartments. Products range from furniture and textile designs, cabinetwork, and lighting to ceramics and silver objects, all bearing a similar unified appearance. The group's passion for unifying all arts extends even to the clothing worn by the lady of the *Wiener Werkstätte* house. The studio initiates artist workshops to promote artistic experimentation in ceramics, woodcarving, enameling, wallpapers, and fashion design. Commercially successful largely because of wealthy patrons and good advertising, the *Werkstätte* continues operations until 1932. Viennese architect Josef Urban opens a New York branch in 1922.

Both the Vienna Secession and *Wiener Werkstätte* make significant contributions to subsequent modern developments. In their quest for a new design language, they explore forms, details, and colors generally not popular before. Additionally, they favor simplicity; rational construction; honest use of materials; and, ultimately, a rejection of ornament.

CONCEPTS

Secession members call for architecture, interiors, and furnishings that develop from contemporary life. Additionally, they strive to dissolve divisions between the fine and decorative arts and design through their exhibitions. Following Otto Wagner in *Moderne Architektur* (1895), the group believes in the expressive power of construction and materials instead of historicism, form over ornament, rationalism, and stylistic simplicity. Like Art Nouveau artists and designers, the Secessionists believe in the power of architecture not only to reform taste, but the very lives of their clients. The *Wiener Werkstätte* shares similar ideals but adds an emphasis on honest use of materials and excellent craftsmanship. They realize that their products are too expensive for most consumers, but they insist that the very exclusivity is evidence of their appeal to the highest tastes and their socially reforming role.

CHARACTERISTICS AND MOTIFS

Designs in architecture, interiors, furniture, textiles, and decorative arts exhibit minimalism, geometric silhouettes, and strong contrasts. All emphasize geometric forms, shapes, repetition, defined outlines, vertical movement, volumes as planes, functionalism, simplicity, and an honest use of materials. Interiors and

▲ **45-1.** Motifs: Poster on the *Wiener Werkstätte* and decorative interior by Leopold Bauer, 1898–1903; Austria.

furniture are plain and stark, with little or no ornament, although often made in rich materials. Quality, details, and human scale also are important. Rectangles or squares and a limited palette of black, white, and gray with occasional accents of brighter colors often characterize designs.

■ *Motifs*. Motifs (Fig. 45-1, 45-2, 45-4, 45-5, 45-7, 45-8, 45-9, 45-10, 45-11, 45-12, 45-13, 45-14) are squares and checker patterns in black and white or in solid and void renditions like repetitive geometric designs, medallions, circles, carved floral ornament, sunflowers, philodendrons, roses, and laurel trees or leaves.

ARCHITECTURE

Secessionist architecture strives to evolve from and, at the same time, reform modern life. Design goals include rectangular and cubic forms that dominate the composition; monumental mass; sparing use of ornament; and an emphasis on function, light, and air. In designing new buildings, architects often strive to transform Vienna's existing classical architecture with simplicity, functionality, and modern materials. These creations are highly individual and often innovative. Projects include offices (Fig. 45-4), railway stations (Fig. 45-3), museums, shops, galleries, churches, large apartment complexes (Fig. 45-5), and tenement houses. Private houses for affluent patrons are important examples of the style. Two of the Secessionists' most famous projects are their own exhibition space, the Secessionist Building (Fig. 45-2), and a sophisticated private house (Fig. 45-6) for millionaire banker and art collector Adolphe Stoclet in Brussels, Belgium.

▲ **45-2.** Vienna Secession Building and entry detail, 1897–1898; Vienna, Austria; Josef Maria Olbrich.

▲ **45-3.** *Karlsplatz Stadtbahn* (railway) Station, 1898; Vienna, Austria; Otto Wagner.

Public and Private Buildings

■ *Site Orientation.* Important buildings, such as banks and churches, sit along prominent streets to provide focal points (Fig. 45-2, 45-4). Tenement houses and apartment complexes are arranged in grid patterns and grouped in neighborhoods that are joined by major streets (Fig. 45-5). Private houses are on residential city blocks or in suburbs (Fig. 45-6).

■ *Floor Plans.* Nonresidential plans reflect the function of the building. Rectangular spaces are arranged to provide maximum light and air and to enhance function and practicality, which are key design principles. To signal their importance, circulation spaces are centrally located in both public and private buildings. Tall apartment complexes feature prominent elevator lobbies, a prestigious addition to enhance vertical circulation. House plans are linear and asymmetrical, with primarily rectangular rooms arranged in a logical sequence (Fig. 45-6).

DESIGN SPOTLIGHT

▲ **45-4.** Post Office Savings Bank, elevation, and main banking room, 1904–1912; Vienna, Austria; Otto Wagner.

DESIGN SPOTLIGHT

Architecture and Interior: Otto Wagner's design wins the competition for the Post Office Savings Bank in 1903, and construction occurs in two phases, in 1904–1906 and again in 1910–1912. The façade is his idea of simplified classicism using new modern materials. Symmetrical rows of slender tall windows and marble tiles held in place with aluminum bolts cover the façade and create a decorative checkered pattern. The bolts are functional as well as decorative. Bold iron columns supporting a glass canopy define the entrance. The roof has picturesque details of figures and carving. The building has a glass vaulted roof over the main banking hall. Innovatively suspended from cables with a second roof above, the glazing allows light into the hall and atrium. Glass block floors permit light to penetrate to the floor below.

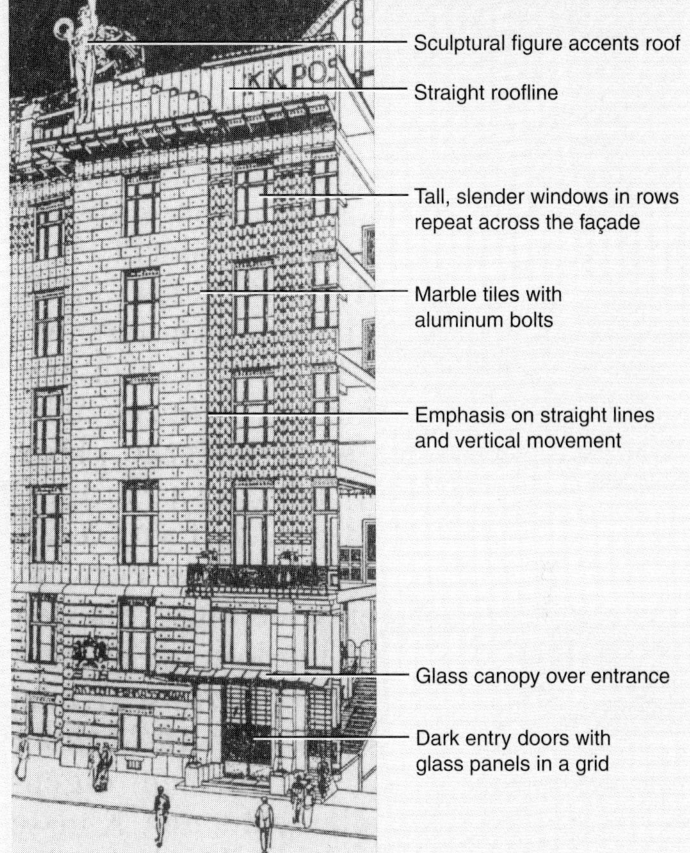

▲ **45–4.** Continued

▲ 45-5. *Majolika Haus* and detail, 1898; Vienna, Austria; Otto Wagner.

■ *Materials*. Designers use a variety of existing and new materials to achieve their concepts. These include marble, granite, brick, glass, steel, and aluminum (Fig. 45-2, 45-3, 45-4, 45-5, 45-6). Some structures have white plaster, colored tile, or brown granite façades. Generally, color evolves from the building materials, but a few structures have elaborate carved, painted, or tile decoration that may be in various colors or have gilded accents. Usual colors include dull shades of green, brown, gold, rust, blue, gray, black, and white.

■ *Façades*. Plain, generally flat façades display smooth surfaces and a strong geometry with an emphasis on rectangular and vertical movement (Fig. 45-2, 45-3, 45-4, 45-5, 45-6). Geometric or organic decorative designs may accent entries, friezes, façades, edges, or important architectural features. Horizontal bands of color in the frieze are a defining characteristic. Patterns of metal bolts or inlays help enliven or accent façades. Iron and glass walls or canopies may announce the entry and establish the design vocabulary. Black or gilded iron balconies are a frequent detail.

■ *Windows*. Most structures have unadorned casement windows with glass panes in grids of different sizes (Fig. 45-2, 45-4, 45-5, 45-6). Windows in the same or various heights repeat across the façade or at corners. Surrounds may include narrow moldings or a prominent lintel and/or sill. In many buildings, the window panes repeat the square or rectangular volumes of the building itself. One example is the Post Office Savings Bank (Fig. 45-4) by Otto Wagner, in which the windows have small and large square panes that not only repeat on the exterior but also in the interior design.

■ *Doors*. Entry doors are generally plain and austere, in natural or painted wood (Fig. 45-2, 45-3, 45-4, 45-5, 45-6). Some have inserts of plain glass arranged in grids or with stained glass panels. Glass awnings and/or other details may set off entries for public buildings.

■ *Roofs*. Roofs are usually hipped or gabled, and lines may be straight or curved, or a combination of the two (Fig. 45-3). Often the roof is not visible from the street level because of the height of the building. Prominent projecting cornices accent roofs and separate them from the façade, as a terminus (Fig. 45-3, 45-4, 45-5, 45-6). Sometimes, the roof has unique design features such as an orb composed of metal vines (as in the Secessionist building; Fig. 45-2), human figures, or triple arches.

INTERIORS

Secessionist and *Werkstätte* members consider interiors as equal in importance to architecture. Designers strive to create total works of art (*Gesamtkunstwerk*) deriving from function, simplicity, geometric forms, defined outlines, and smooth surfaces. Consequently, interiors often reveal similar geometry and linear details to exteriors, and selected geometric details may enrich the simplicity. Private houses usually have a strong connection between interiors and their exteriors, often achieved through the use of transitional terraces connected on axes to main rooms. Rooms are uncluttered and reveal a preference for geometric patterns and details. Designers show simplicity and richness through painted surfaces, colored tile, marble, wood, metal, mirrors, and plain and

DESIGN SPOTLIGHT

Architecture and Interior: *Palais Stoclet*, begun in 1905 from designs by Josef Hoffmann, establishes the visual language of the *Werkstätte* and subsequently becomes an innovative masterpiece of the Modern Movement. A collaboration among Hoffmann, Moser, and artist Klimt, it is a total work of art created through the integration of architecture and interior design, an idea shared by Art Nouveau. Marble tiles held in place by gilded metal define the asymmetrical geometry of the façade. Rectangles dominate the composition from the marble slabs to the pattern of the windows. Circular forms of the entry serve as balance to the severity of the rectangles. A geometric grid leads the eye to the culmination of the composition, the stair tower roof composed of figures supporting a foliage dome that is reminiscent of the Secessionist building. Luxurious materials used throughout the house reflect the unlimited budget. The dramatic and sophisticated interiors glitter with marble, onyx, mosaics, gold, glass, teak, and leather.

The long, narrow dining room walls are white marble. Black lacquered sideboards run the length of the room and over them are frieze panels by Gustav Klimt. The bold mosaics depict stylized figures and scrolling trees of life in copper, tin, coral, semiprecious stones, and gold. Black and white marble tiles cover the floor. Hoffmann designs the furniture, which is composed of large rectangles. [World Heritage Site]

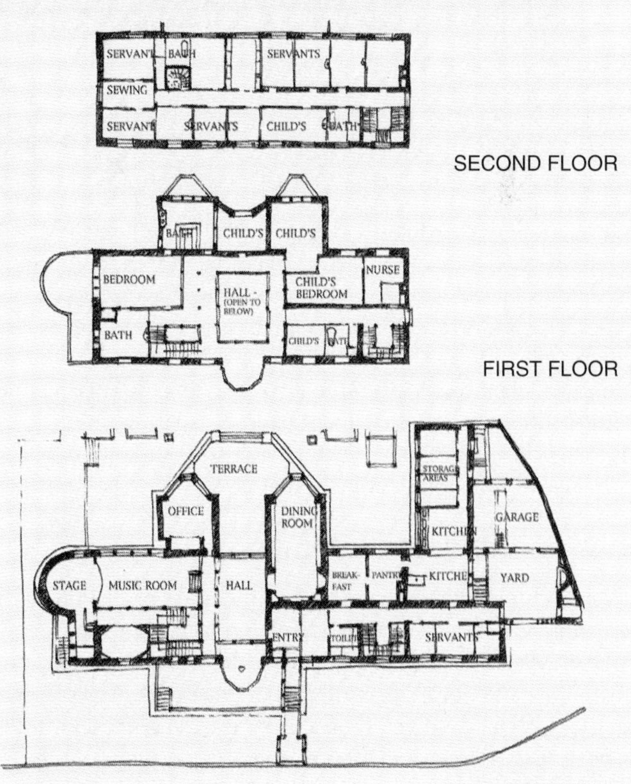

▲ **45-6.** *Palais Stoclet*, floor plans, and dining room (next page), 1905–1911; Brussels, Belgium; Josef Hoffmann, with murals by Gustav Klimt and decorative work by *Wiener Werkstätte*.

DESIGN SPOTLIGHT

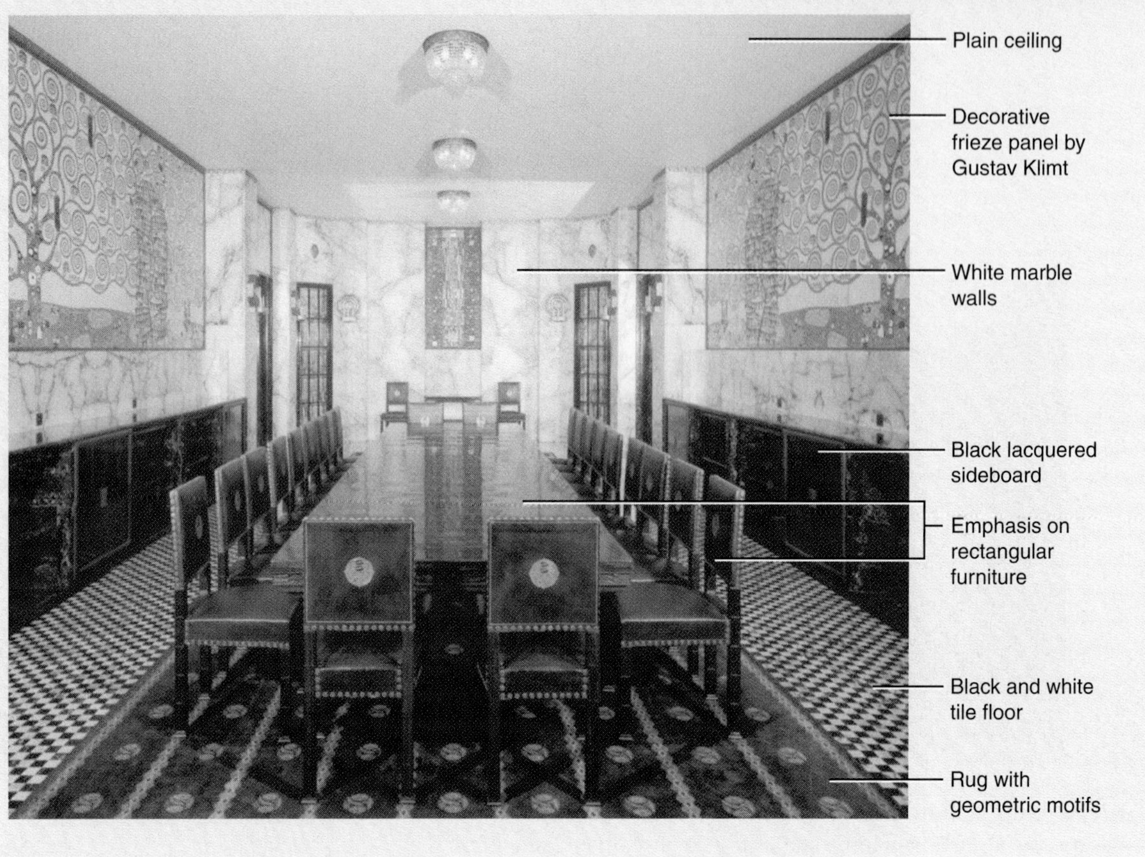

▲ **45-6.** Continued

stained glass. They frequently design the furniture, textiles, and decorative accessories, often of costly materials, for their interiors. Sometimes they use mass-produced furniture. Wagner, for example, uses Thonet furniture in some rooms of the Post Office Savings Bank in Vienna.

No particular spaces are associated with Secessionist public buildings, although designers focus upon circulation and important spaces in public and private houses. Elaborately detailed bathrooms are common in affluent houses.

Public and Private Buildings

■ *Color*. White walls are standard for all interiors, often with doors, trim, and storage areas rendered in black, showing the influence of Mackintosh (Fig. 45-1, 45-4, 45-7, 45-8). Bright red, green, yellow, rose, or blue textiles, floor coverings, artwork, and decorative arts may enliven rooms by punctuating important details. Materials or decoration also may repeat the colors of the exterior. Hoffmann interiors often use white, black, and gray. Gustav Klimt's designs provide ornamental richness with decorative patterning in spirals, rectangles, lozenges, and triangles enhanced with a Byzantine color palette of rich red and blue (Fig. 45-6).

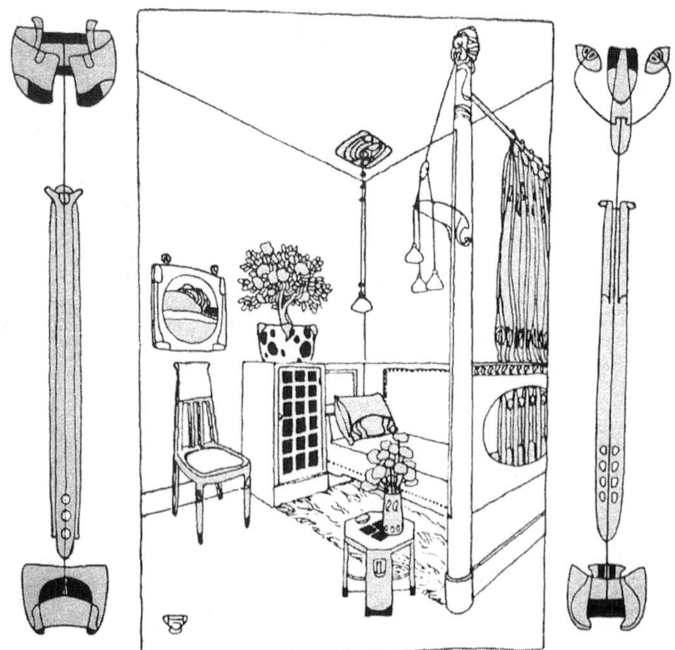

▲ **45-7.** Interior, 1898–1904; Austria; Josef Hoffmann.

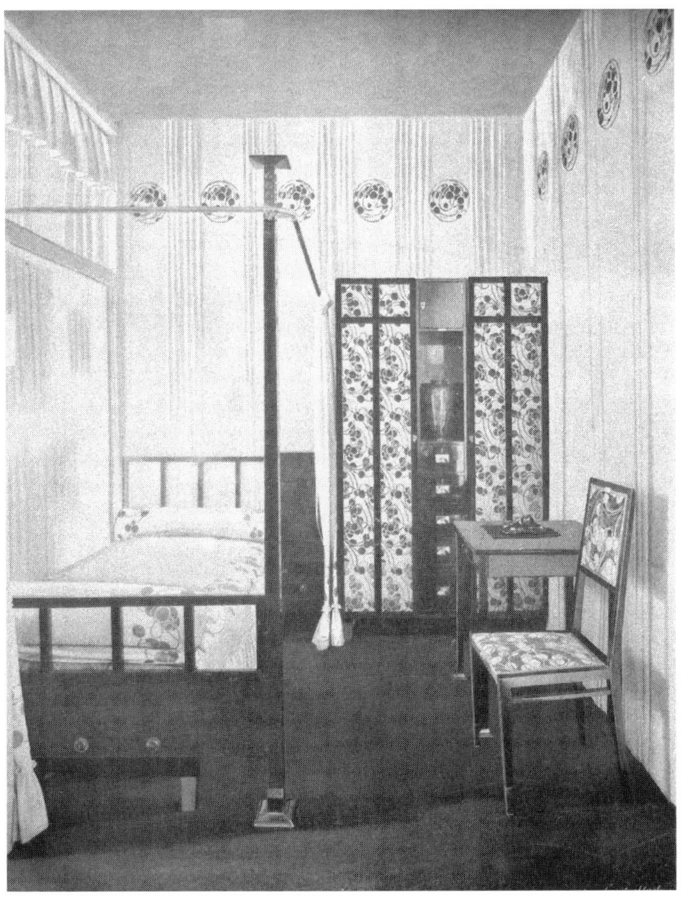

▲ **45-8.** Bedroom, 1901; Austria; Wilhelm Schmidt.

■ *Floors*. Flooring materials include marble, tile, and wood usually in geometric patterns such as rectangles or squares that carry over from the exterior (Fig. 45-4, 45-6, 45-7, 45-8). Black and white patterned floors of marble are especially popular. Similarly, rugs designed by members of the *Wiener Werkstätte* have geometric designs and linear patterns to unify with interiors.

■ *Walls*. Plain, unadorned walls are most common (Fig. 45-4). Tiled dadoes appear in vestibules and stair halls and contrast with white walls. Some interiors have decorative frieze bands in different patterns, although geometric is the most common (Fig. 45-8). Sometimes wallpaper or fabric in geometric or linear patterns designed by members of the Secessionist group or the *Wiener Werkstätte* enlivens a wall treatment (Fig. 45-7). Built-in storage, when present, integrates with the wall design and is arranged in geometric compositions emphasizing rectangles and squares.

■ *Windows and Doors*. Windows are plain, simple, rectangular, and often unadorned, and blend in with the interior architectural arrangement. Drapery, if used, usually has simple panels and a valance, sometimes with a sheer curtain against the glass. The fabric usually is custom designed to match the interior architecture and décor. Interior doors are of wood, either solid with some geometric details or with glass inserts in a grid pattern. They may be painted black or white or stained a very dark mahogany color.

■ *Ceilings*. Ceilings generally are plain, although those in public buildings or important rooms in residences may be coffered or compartmentalized (Fig. 45-4, 45-7). Architects sometimes use glass ceilings in public buildings to enhance the quality of light (Fig. 45-4).

■ *Textiles*. Cotton and wool in plain weaves and velvets are the most common materials (Fig. 45-6, 45-11). Geometric and curved flat, stylized patterns recall architectural forms and nature (Fig. 45-7, 45-8, 45-9, 45-12). Colors, which may repeat those of the architecture, are in dull shades of green, brown, gold, rust, blue, gray, black, and white or bright reds, greens, or yellows.

■ *Lighting*. The simplicity in form and design of lamps, wall sconces, pendant lights, surface-mounted fixtures, and chandeliers integrate with the interior and support concepts of total unity (Fig. 45-4, 45-6, 45-10). Most fixtures are electric.

FURNISHINGS AND DECORATIVE ARTS

The *Wiener Werkstätte*, which designs most of the furniture and decorative arts, is strongly influenced by the craftsmanship of the English Arts and Crafts Movement as well as Charles Rennie Mackintosh's innovative furniture that is individually designed for each space. Equally important are harmony between the exterior and interiors and the creation of total works of art. Consequently, the furniture integrates with the interiors and exteriors.

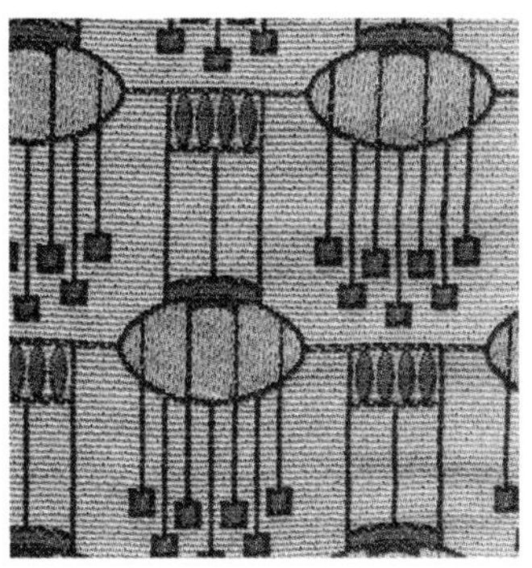

(a)

(b)

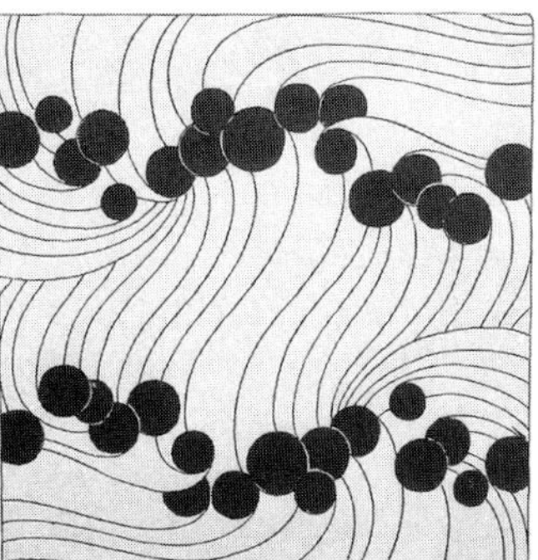

(c)

▲ **45-9.** Textiles: Fabrics, 1901–1908; Austria: (a) Otto Prutscher, (b) Josef Hoffmann, and (c) J. M. Auchentaller.

It reflects an architectonic quality, strong geometry, and rectilinear emphasis like the exterior as well as excellent craftsmanship. Forms are practical and usually severely plain. Surfaces and shapes are unadorned, smooth, and geometric. Checker patterns in black and white or solid and void are common features and may serve as decorative accents.

Truth to materials in design, construction, and use is also a guiding design principle. Designs reveal simplicity, modesty, and classic proportions derived from the earlier Biedermeier style, an unpretentious version of French Empire for the middle class. Although furniture's simplicity looks easily adapted to mass production, *Werkstätte* designers' emphasis on craftsmanship and individuality prevents this. They are not concerned with the relationship of mass production and design, although in several cases their designs are produced in large numbers.

Although usually created for specific spaces, the furniture of individual designers reveals similar characteristics. Both Hoffmann and Moser use structural simplicity, strong purity of form, and geometric repetition. Hoffmann (Fig. 45-11) also includes horizontal and vertical rows of squares in his furniture and decorative accessories. Moser (Fig. 45-13), on the other hand, incorporates cube forms, luxurious materials, and intricate details.

DESIGN SPOTLIGHT

Furniture: Noteworthy for its three-dimensional character, Josef Hoffmann's furniture illustrates his fascination with basic geometric shapes (circles, squares, and rectangles), flat plane surfaces, solid and void patterns, and artistic details. Sometimes large wooden balls or spheres act to reinforce the joints of horizontal and vertical members or to add decoration. Linear elements interact with three-dimensional ones. He considers his furniture as an art object first, and then addresses the functional purpose, a concept common to architects during this period. Much of his furniture draws inspiration from the Biedermeier tradition in Vienna, as well as the work of Michael Thonet and his use of bentwood. Hoffmann mixes the elegance of bentwood with the more traditional English Arts and Crafts character to design furniture that is more avant-garde, refined, unique, and luxurious.

Public and Private Buildings

■ *Materials*. Common woods include beech, spruce, and oak. Rich veneers and mother-of-pearl inlays are typical of furniture designed by Hoffmann and Moser, although some pieces have plywood parts. Wood may be left natural, stained, lacquered, or painted white or black.

■ *Seating*. Seating, particularly chairs, typifies the design vocabulary (Fig. 45-6, 45-8, 45-11, 45-12). Wooden examples are usually tall and slender with smooth surfaces. They are generally rectilinear with an emphasis upon line, like architecture. Curves may appear in backs or seat corners. The straight legs are often

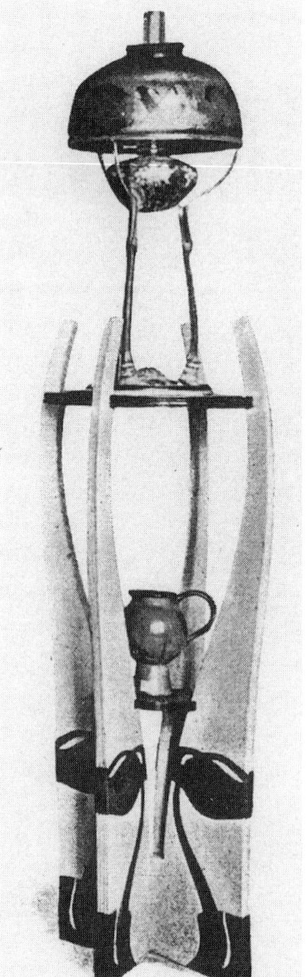

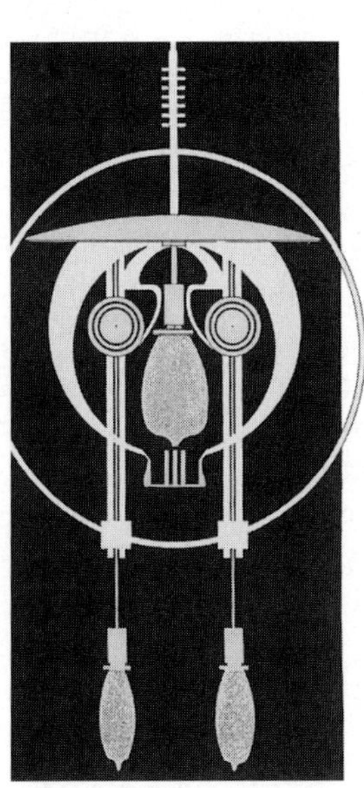

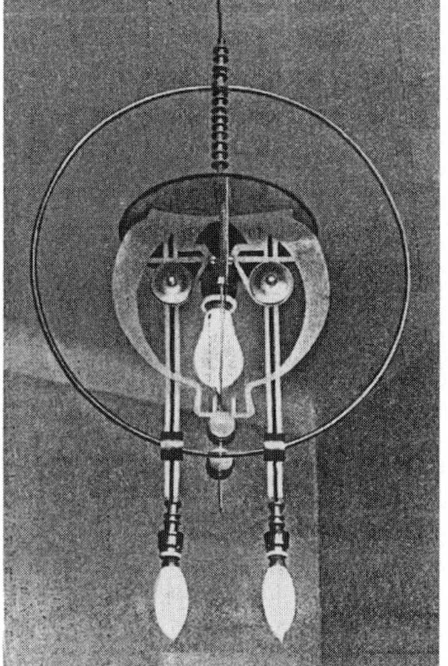

▲ **45-10.** Lighting: Table lamp by Josef Hoffmann and chandelier, c. 1900; Austria.

DESIGN SPOTLIGHT

▲ **45-11.** Chairs and recliner, 1900–1909; Austria; Josef Hoffmann, with much of the furniture manufactured by Thonet Brothers.

▲ 45-12. Armchair, 1901–1904; Austria; Otto Wagner and R. Tropsch.

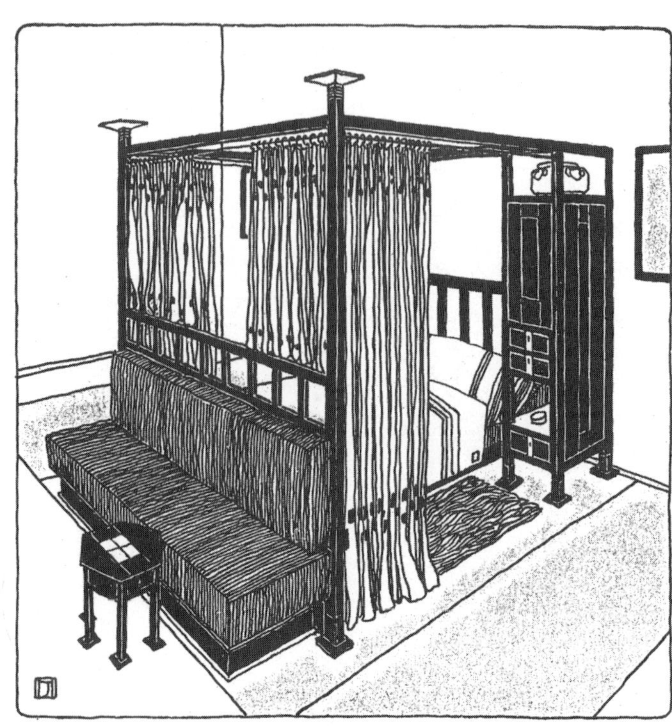

▲ 45-14. Bedroom furnishings; 1901–1904; Austria.

▲ 45-13. Writing desk, c. 1902–1903; Austria; Koloman Moser.

quadrangular. A few examples have metal feet. Designs may recall traditional types, such as ladder-backs or rectangular arm chairs, in a simplified vocabulary with a greater emphasis upon outlines and shape. Squares, rectangles, or circles are the only ornament. Upholstered pieces may be boxy or have simple curves but no carving, inlay, or other ornament. Nails secure fabric to the frame.

■ *Tables*. Tables usually are slender and rectilinear with some curves (Fig. 45-7). Tops may be round or square, and legs are usually straight and quadrangular in form. The *Wiener Werkstätte* vocabulary often redefines traditional types to support new interior design concepts.

■ *Storage*. Storage pieces, such as cabinets and desks, have a rectangular outline (Fig. 45-6, 45-8, 45-13). Inlay or marquetry in repeating patterns of squares, rectangles, ovals, and/or circles may cover fronts. Door and drawer handles are simple, rectangular, and flat to avoid disrupting the composition.

■ *Beds*. Like other furniture, beds have simple rectilinear headboards and footboards (Fig. 45-8, 45-14). Sometimes head- and footboards are embellished with open or veneered squares, rectangles, or other motifs.

■ *Decorative Arts*. Like furniture, decorative arts reflect the *Wiener Werkstätte* design vocabulary. Conceived as part of total works of art, the glass, metalwork, tablewares, and even cutlery feature geometric forms, shapes, and details.

■ *Later Interpretations*. During the 1920s, Art Deco designer Robert Mallet-Stevens, among others, designs furnishings and interiors in character and form that reflect the influence of the Vienna Secessionists. Few interpretations occur after this time until the late 20th century when various manufacturers, such as Knoll International, produce variations of Hoffmann's furniture (Fig. 45-15). Jack Lenor Larson and his designers reinvent the textiles of the period with great success.

▲ **45-15.** Later Interpretation: Armchair model 810, 1982; United States; Richard Meier, manufactured by Knoll International. Modern Historicism.

CHAPTER 46

Chicago School

1880s–1910s

All life is organic. It manifests itself through organs, through structures, through functions. That which is alive acts, organizes, grows, develops, unfolds, expands, differentiates, organ after organ, structure after structure.

—Louis H. Sullivan, *Kindergarten Chats*, 1901–1902

The Chicago School is composed of an intellectually elite group of progressive architects in late-19th-century Chicago, Illinois, who introduce the skyscraper, a new building type for the new 20th century. This multistory structure establishes a new design language for commercial buildings and comes to dominate the urban landscape. Various factors in the United States facilitate the inception and growth of skyscraper construction. These include phenomenal commercial and business growth; the development of huge, national corporations; new technology such as the elevator and the typewriter; an inexpensive process for making steel; and an emerging American architectural theory. The group's work influences similar developments in other cities.

HISTORICAL AND SOCIAL

Following the Civil War, a second wave of the Industrial Revolution begins with America at its forefront. New technology, improvements in communication and transportation, and new or improved manufacturing processes usher in a period of extraordinary growth in industry and commerce. In response, American businesses reorganize and revolutionize how they work. They also recognize that a different framework is needed to conduct business effectively nationally and internationally, so the modern corporation is born. As corporations grow, so does the number of employees and the need for space. Wanting prime locations for their headquarters, they relocate within or move to city centers, creating land shortages and soaring prices for real estate. Consequently, office buildings must grow taller instead of broader. The creation of a new architectural type is not impeded in the United States because it does not share with Europe centuries-old cultural traditions and considerations for the common good. An atmosphere of innovation and the demand for quick profits foster the growth of commercial architecture and offices.

New technologies, some pre–Civil War, also contribute to the skyscraper. Until the invention of the passenger elevator in 1857 by Elisha Graves Otis, buildings are seldom more than four or five stories high. The elevator's use and popularity in the Eiffel Tower sets the stage for its use in skyscrapers. Tall office buildings or skyscrapers of at least 10 stories begin to dominate the urban skyline. In the 1840s and 1850s, cast and wrought iron are used for façades and some structural elements. In the late 1850s England, Sir Henry Bessemer develops an inexpensive process for making steel, which is more fireproof than cast iron is. Other new inventions, such as the typewriter (1868), the telephone (1876), incandescent light (1879), and the dictaphone or gramophone (1888), transform office planning, types of workers, and methods of working.

Chicago, home of the skyscraper, experiences phenomenal growth beginning in the late 1830s. Already known for its stockyards, the city becomes an important railroad hub and manufacturing center in the 1850s. Immigrants flock there for jobs. Many new buildings are constructed with wood frames and cast-iron columns and façades. However, these materials are not fireproof, as proved by the disastrous fire in Chicago in 1871 in which wood buildings are consumed and iron structures collapse. In addition to the economic and commercial growth that creates a demand for more space, Chicago has few established traditions in architecture in the late 19th century, so architects are free to experiment and to produce the skyscraper. William Le Baron Jenney, architect and engineer, creates the prototype. Four architects who work in his office, Daniel Burnham, William Holabird, Martin Roche, and Louis Sullivan, carry his work further. They or their firms become the leaders of the Chicago School, known for tall commercial buildings.

Changes in how businesses operate also affect the development of the skyscraper and its interior planning and furnishing. Before the Civil War, most businesses are small with only a few male employees. Relatively simple office tasks are easily handled individually by hand. Following the Civil War, tasks and paperwork multiply as businesses grow in size and scope. Productivity and profitability begin to drive office work and planning. Companies now require managers to create and oversee a greater variety of jobs, from marketing strategies to transportation arrangements to tracking sales. At the same time, more clerks, typists, and secretaries are needed to process orders and handle correspondence. Managers find that women are well suited for these tasks, so women enter the office workforce in greater numbers. Besides being more socially acceptable than previously, office pay is better than that of factory or domestic work. However, women still are paid considerably less than men are.

CONCEPTS

Need drives the development of the tall commercial structure, which has no precedent in architecture. Once the technology and construction methods are in place and prototypes appear, the architect's dilemma becomes how to articulate a multistory building to reflect a human scale. Also, since there are no historical precedents, architects grapple with the question of an appropriate style. Consequently, these first manifestations of modern architecture often express the structure on the exterior. Additionally, architects and engineers, such as Dankmar Adler and Louis Sullivan, work together to solve structural and architectural problems. These partnerships are less bound by the European Beaux-Arts tradition. Therefore, their ideas and Chicago School traditions of minimal ornament with little historical precedent run counter to the concepts of design promoted in the 1893 World's Columbian Exposition by McKim, Mead, and White and others.

By this time, American architects have more training, both at home and abroad, in architectural theory. They are more keenly aware of a need for design theory based on function, construction, and scale and are better able to create and expand their own ideas. At the forefront in Chicago, architect Louis Sullivan believes that the building's form should express the interior function. "Form follows function" becomes his dictum. Sullivan advances the expressive qualities of the skyscraper using classical precedent and his own unique style of ornament. He creates an architectural language for tall buildings.

▲ **46-1.** Chicago style window, c. 1900; Chicago, Illinois.

▲ **46-2.** Home Insurance Company Building, 1883–1885; Chicago, Illinois; William Le Baron Jenney.

CHARACTERISTICS AND MOTIFS

Early skyscrapers have grid-patterned façades, large windows for light, and little ornament. Verticality is emphasized as façades rise relatively unhindered by horizontals. Lot size and the need for light in interior spaces drive overall shape and configuration. Façades, covered with terra-cotta or masonry, may have bay or oriel windows or, more often, rectangular ones between vertical piers. Lower stories, which house shops, have large plate glass windows to make merchandise visible. At the street level, shops, architectural features, and details provide a human scale. Public interiors reflect the character of the exteriors, with large, impressive spaces.

■ *Motifs*. Some buildings have classical details, such as pilasters or stringcourses. Sullivan incorporates curvilinear plant forms and geometric designs, such as the square, oval, and rectangle (Fig. 46-5, 46-8, 46-10, 46-12, 46-14).

ARCHITECTURE

Significant advances in construction technology affect the structure, form, and composition of buildings in Chicago, New York City, and other metropolitan areas during the second half of the 19th century. Steel skeletons to replace masonry bearing walls or piers, foundations that can support tall buildings, and elevators to access upper floors come together to create the first skyscrapers, or buildings 16 to 20 stories high. Jenney's Home Insurance Company Building (Fig. 46-2) of 1885 in Chicago is the prototype. It uses a metal skeleton composed of cast-iron columns and steel beams that support the masonry walls and floors. To fireproof them, iron beams are usually clad with terra-cotta. Steel frame construction leads to the introduction of curtain or non-load-bearing exterior walls that hang from the metal frame. Curtain walls permit large windows (Fig. 46-1) for more light, a design characteristic exploited by

▲ **46-3.** Auditorium Building (Roosevelt University), 1887–1889; Chicago, Illinois; Dankmar Adler and Louis H. Sullivan.

members of the Chicago School. It ultimately leads to the glass exterior walls that characterize the work of early modern designers and the International Style. Holabird and Roche introduce a reinforced concrete foundation to support a building structure in sandy or muddy soil like that of Chicago. Chicago School and other architects design banks, auditoriums (Fig. 46-3), department stores (Fig. 46-10), and libraries in addition to commercial buildings and skyscrapers (Fig. 46-2, 46-4, 46-6, 46-7, 46-8, 46-9, 46-10).

Construction improvements occur incrementally, so some early skyscrapers retain load-bearing masonry walls combined with wooden or metal beams. However, the thick load-bearing walls take up valuable interior space. The need for more space and profits will soon eliminate masonry walls except as a cladding. In the late 1880s and early 1890s, architects and engineers in other cities begin to employ steel frames extensively, and the modern skyscraper is born. Building lots created by a grid pattern of streets determine the sizes of skyscrapers. Wider lots permit buildings to assume hollow square shapes, whereas narrow ones are rectangular boxes or U-shaped to permit as much light as possible to enter the interiors. Incandescent light, although readily available, is inefficient and unreliable.

Because skyscrapers prevent light from getting to the narrow streets below, New York City and Chicago pass laws requiring upper stories to have a series of setbacks to alleviate the problem. In 1916, New York City passes a setback ordinance mandating that new buildings in selected zoned districts can rise upward two and a half times the street width and then must have a setback. In 1918, a Chicago architectural committee proposes that building heights be limited to 260 feet above grade and that architectural standards be introduced. Consequently, architects design buildings with tall, slender towers for space and height while permitting light and air to filter to the streets below.

Public Buildings

■ *Floor Plans*. Floor plans are generally rectangular or square, so the building forms a rectangular box or sometimes a U shape (Fig. 46-6). Plans often have a central corridor with shallow rectangular rooms on both sides. A typical layout, which usually repeats on every floor, has multiple modules composed of a large office with two smaller ones behind it. Some floors have large open spaces for many workers who usually work at desks in rows.

▲ **46-4.** Wainwright Building, 1890–1891; St. Louis, Missouri; Dankmar Adler and Louis H. Sullivan.

▲ **46-5.** Transportation Building and the Golden Door, World's Columbian Exposition, 1893; Chicago, Illinois; Louis H. Sullivan.

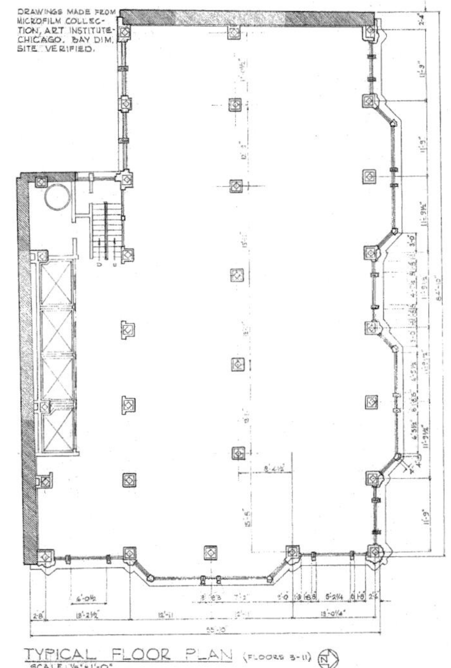

▲ **46-6.** Reliance Building and floor plan, 1890–1891, 1894–1895; Chicago, Illinois; Daniel H. Burnham and John W. Root.

DESIGN SPOTLIGHT

Architecture: In the design of the Guaranty Trust Building, Louis Sullivan captures the expressive power of the skyscraper and exhibits his own theory of skyscraper design in which "form follows function." Like classical architecture, the building has a beginning, middle, and end. Each portion is treated differently to reflect its function within the building. A two-story base houses shops that have large plate glass windows for display. Terra-cotta ornament of triangles, circles, and foliage covers the entrance portals and window surrounds. In the middle section, corner pilasters and piers with reddish terra-cotta geometric and floral ornament rise unimpeded from the base to the top story to emphasize verticality. The ornament in panels between the windows adds interest but does not compete with that of the vertical piers. Identical exterior treatments of this section accentuate the identical floors of offices within. The top story, a service floor, has round windows with low-relief terra-cotta floral ornament. A bold cornice caps the entire composition. [National Historic Landmark]

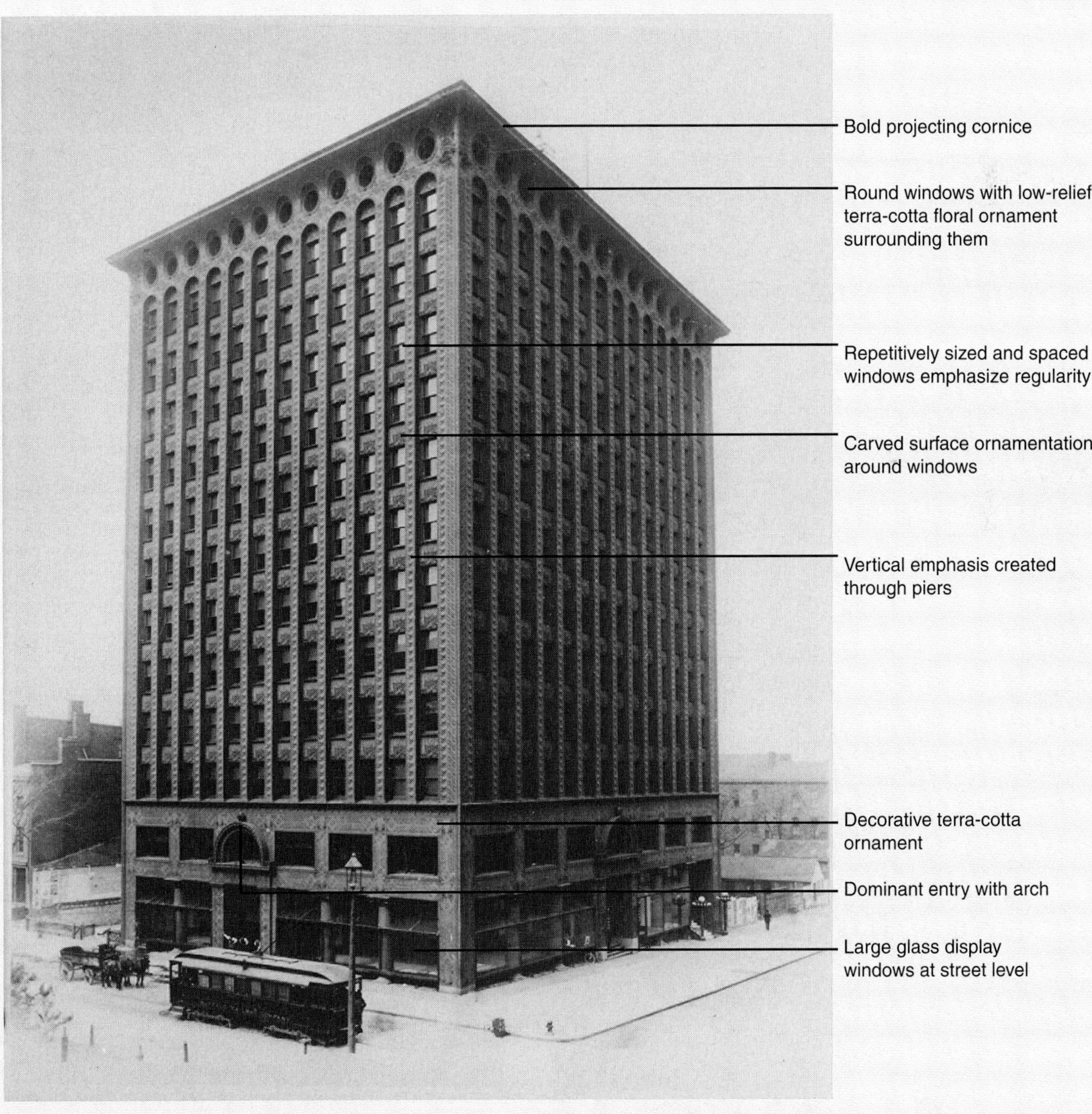

▲ **46-7.** Guaranty Trust Building (later Prudential Building), 1895–1896; Buffalo, New York; Dankmar Adler and Louis Sullivan, with ornamentation designed by Sullivan and George Elmslie.

Heavy metal or steel piers punctuate the plan in a grid system at all levels to support the concentrated weight load. Piers permit more open and spacious interiors with fewer load-bearing walls, an early prototype for later 20th-century high-rise office buildings. Prominent entries lead to vestibules and major public circulation areas, such as hallways, corridors, stairways, and elevators. Architects put vertical circulation on axis with entries and exits, recognizing the importance of fire safety and egress. Elevators, stairways, and bathrooms are centralized.

■ *Materials*. Exterior walls may be of brick, terra-cotta, granite, or other types of stone, giving no hint of the interior metal skeleton (Fig. 46-2, 46-3, 46-4, 46-5, 46-6, 46-7, 46-8, 46-9, 46-10). At first, Adler and Sullivan use granite and limestone to cover load-bearing brickwork. They subsequently adopt steel-skeletal construction covered with brick, terra-cotta, or sandstone, thereby using an outer masonry envelope to cover the skeletal structure.

▲ **46-8.** Flatiron Building (Fuller Building), 1901–1903; New York City, New York; by Daniel H. Burnham.

DESIGN SPOTLIGHT

Interior: Embracing attributes of Richardson Romanesque architecture and new construction technology, Burnham and Root produce the Rookery Building, one of their most important projects and one of the few remaining ones. This picturesque skyscraper, which is 12 stories tall, covers most of the block of a prominent street. The building combines modern construction techniques, such as steel-skeletal framing, with masonry walls of red marble, terra-cotta, and brick to form a bold architectural statement. Horizontal sections separated by stringcourses organize the façade as it ascends to a flat roof, and bold vertical piers define the center and corners. Within the bays are large windows. Smaller rectangular windows surrounded by architectural detailing provide a roofline accent. A large, arched entry at street level indicates the primary entrance.

Root, likely inspired by French department store design, creates a two-story interior court, which was hailed at the time as bold, original, and inspiring. Retail stores surround the court, which is filled with light from a glass roof. Glazed white brick maximizes the light that enters the shops and offices on the first floor and mezzanine. A prominent staircase with cast-iron railing and newel post cantilevers into the space. In 1905, Frank Lloyd Wright gives the space a more modern appearance without altering its essence by replacing the cast iron with white and gold geometric details. [National Historic Landmark]

Color comes from the variety and naturalness of building materials. Sullivan incorporates colored tile to highlight important architectural features such as entryways. Some decorative details are of cast iron. After 1893, skyscrapers often have white terra-cotta or limestone cladding to replicate the image of the White City of the World's Columbian Exposition.

■ *Façades*. Building façades exhibit large scale, verticality, repetition, order, and simplicity (Fig. 46-2, 46-3, 46-4, 46-5, 46-6, 46-7, 46-8, 46-9, 46-10). Speculative buildings, built by developers for rentals, have plain, unadorned exteriors. Corporate headquarters, in contrast, are more lavishly embellished. Piers rising from ground to roof level separate façades into bays, organize the composition, and emphasize verticality when they rise unimpeded by stringcourses. Street-level and second floors, which are tall, provide a heavy base with structural supports acknowledged in the design. Piers are wide and heavy at these levels to support the structure and give the impression of support. Large, wide display windows at this level showcase the merchandise in shops (Fig. 46-4, 46-7, 46-10). Entries are large and prominently placed. Upper floors have many windows arranged in grid patterns around the entire exterior. Rooflines have heavy cornices that are either a plain, flat slab or a projecting form that is more decorated.

Sullivan, who is widely copied, incorporates an aesthetically pleasing façade composition in his office buildings that represents

DESIGN SPOTLIGHT

▲ **46-9.** Rookery Building and main lobby, 1885–1888, 1905; Chicago, Illinois; Daniel H. Burnham and John W. Root, with Frank Lloyd Wright as architect of the lobby renovation in 1905.

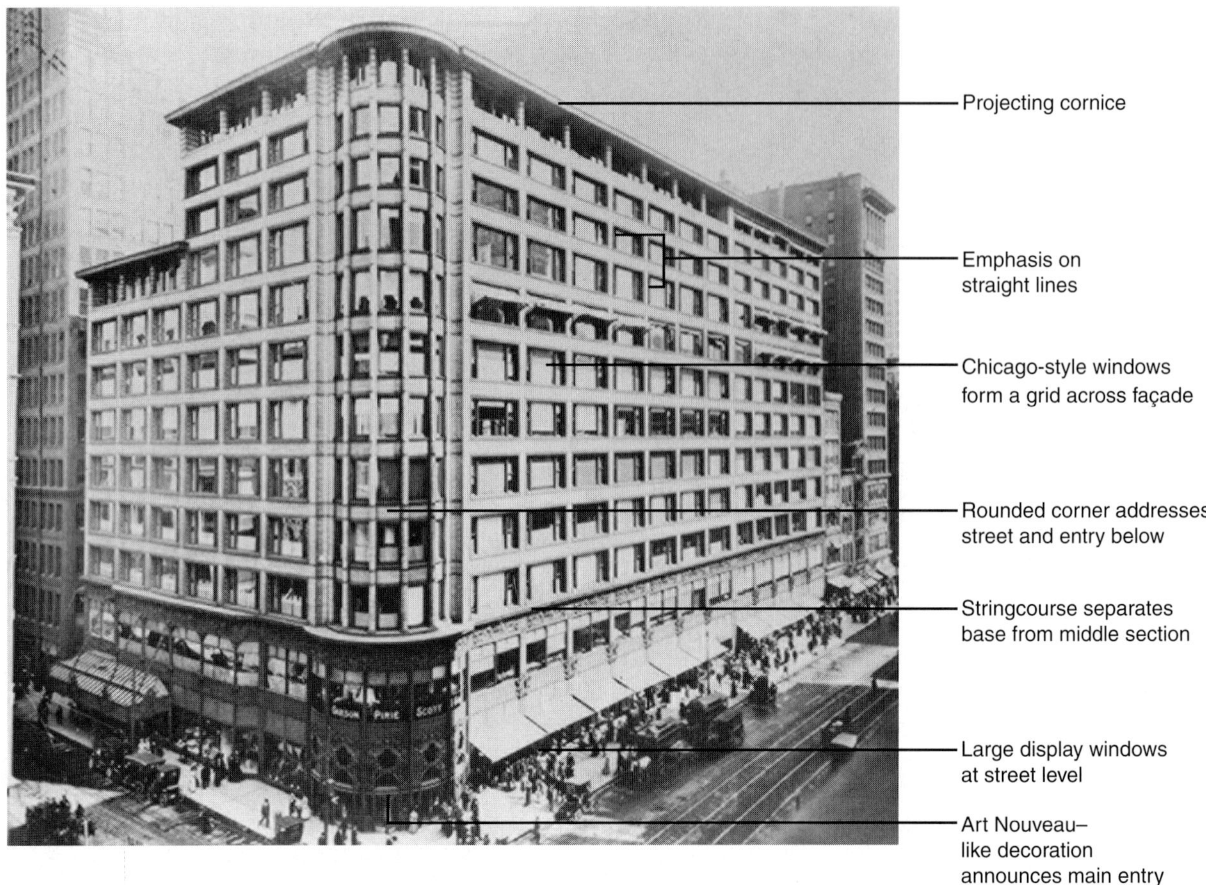

▲ **46-10.** Carson, Pirie, Scott, and Company Department Store (formerly Schlesinger-Mayer Store), 1899–1904, with additions in 1906; Chicago, Illinois; Louis H. Sullivan, and additions by Daniel H. Burnham.

the base, shaft, and capital of a classical column and distinguishes the various functions within the building (Fig. 46-4, 46-5, 46-7, 46-10). His buildings soar upward from the heavy base through prominent piers rising 12 or more stories to the decorated frieze and projecting cornice emphasizing the roofline. Between the piers are large windows (Fig. 46-1, 46-10). Elaborate carved surface decoration accents entries, piers, bays, spandrels, and the frieze, and it may draw attention to the edges of the building. The profuse decoration, a trademark of Sullivan's work, features richly carved geometric and organic motifs. Flower and plant forms are particularly important. Some of his buildings have large, stepped, arched entries framed with a U-shaped surround, all of which are highly ornamented.

■ *Windows*. Buildings have wide expanses of glass windows arranged in rectangular grids that cover most of the façade (Fig. 46-2, 46-3, 46-4, 46-5, 46-6, 46-7, 46-8, 46-9, 46-10). The windows form walls, often referred to as curtain walls, a term reflecting a steel and glass construction system. A few examples have bay or oriel windows that rise from the third or fourth floors to the roofline. A new introduction is the Chicago window (Fig. 46-1), a tripartite composition with a fixed wide center window flanked on one or both sides by double-hung sash windows for light and ventilation, as shown on the Carson, Pirie, Scott Department Store (Fig. 46-10). Windows, taking advantage of new technologies, come in prefabricated, standard sizes. The growing ability to manufacture larger pieces of plate glass is reflected in architecture of the period. The glass itself is most often plain, but Sullivan uses opalescent leaded glass in some of his buildings to accentuate major architectural features such as entryways. The windows of many buildings have adjustable exterior shades.

■ *Doors*. Monumental entries, often with large arches surrounded by heavy architectural features or stonework, lead to major circulation areas (Fig. 46-2, 46-3, 46-4, 46-5, 46-7, 46-9, 46-10). There may be more than one major entry, particularly for buildings on corners.

■ *Roofs*. Roofs usually are not visible because heavy or projecting cornices hide them.

■ *Later Interpretations*. Throughout the 20th and 21st centuries, variations of the high-rise commercial office building proliferate in large urban cities across North America and in other parts of the world. Initially, buildings are often a box shape, which becomes extremely common in the mid-20th century through the influence of Bauhaus designers, such as Walter Gropius and Mies van der Rohe, and later their protégés (Fig. 46-11). But in the 1970s, the building form changes to express design innovations, functional issues, urban context, and/or environmental concerns. By the late 20th century, high-rise commercial buildings become innovative and signature design statements of corporations, countries, and well-known or celebrity architects.

▲ **46-11.** Later Interpretation: Ford Foundation Headquarters, 1967; New York City, New York; Kevin Roche, John Dinkeloo and Associates.

INTERIORS

Entries and lobbies, which are usually two stories and atrium-like, are lavishly decorated with rich materials. Impressive iron or marble staircases lead to upper floors. Major circulation paths from exterior to interior connect important spaces. There is often little design relationship between interior and exterior except in large public spaces, where entries and some spaces may adopt exterior materials. Elevators often are in open cages, at least on the ground floors, with elaborate cast metal doors. Similarly, restaurants, department stores, and shops have open, light-filled spaces and rich finishes to attract customers.

Offices, in contrast, may seem more residential or are strictly utilitarian in appearance. The office hierarchy drives planning, finishes, and furniture with executives having the most space, best treatments, and nicest furniture. Small, private offices maintain a domestic appearance with area rugs, wallpaper, or paneling. In contrast, larger offices, which are planned by managers, are plain and utilitarian with little color and decoration. Furniture defines the spaces. By the turn of the century, the office hierarchy becomes more evident. Sizes and locations of offices identify executives, managers, and workers, with executives and managers in corner offices or offices with windows. Most workers have small, windowless offices or sit in rows of desks in large open spaces, which become known as bull pens (Fig. 46-13).

Public Buildings

■ *Color*. As with the exterior, the primary color palette derives from the architectural materials, including various shades of wood, brick, marble, granite, metal, and stained glass. Staircases and elevator doors display various metals. Walls are often smooth plaster and may be partially painted in an off-white, cream, or light gold. Other colors include earth-tone shades of green, rust, orange, gold, brown, cream, and deep gray. In Sullivan's work, decorative painting may accent friezes, ceilings, and/or a prominent architectural feature such as an arch (Fig. 46-12, 46-14).

■ *Floors*. Common flooring materials include marble, granite, limestone, ceramic tiles, terrazzo, linoleum, and wood. Carpets, such as ingrains or Brussels, cover floors in smaller offices. Individual executive offices may have Oriental rugs.

■ *Walls*. Walls are generally plain, but those in important spaces, such as lobbies, stair halls, or executive offices, may have a marble dado or wainscoting. Some are paneled, and individual offices may have wallpaper. Sullivan decorates some friezes and arches with large-scale carved decoration, infill painting, or stenciling (Fig. 46-12, 46-14). Interior partitions in offices may have glass panels near the ceiling to allow light to penetrate.

■ *Windows and Doors*. Windows and doors in important offices may have moldings around them (Fig. 46-13). Others are more likely to be plain. Doors to offices often have glass panels or transoms above them for light and air. A few doorways have *portières*. Most spaces do not have textile window treatments, although some have roller blinds or shades.

▲ **46-12.** Trading room, Stock Exchange Building, 1893; Chicago, Illinois; Louis H. Sullivan. [Installed in the Art Institute of Chicago]

■ *Ceilings*. Ceilings are high and plainly treated. Many have ceiling-mounted gas or electric light fixtures.

■ *Lighting*. Architects design interior plans to take advantage of natural light. Often in public spaces, the artificial lighting design is integrated into the total interior composition, so it becomes architectonic. The lighting fixture materials usually repeat the interior materials. Gas or electric chandeliers, wall sconces, and lamps are common fixtures in all types of spaces (Fig. 46-12, 46-13, 46-14). Fixtures often are no more than a glass shade with a dropped cord, or a socket with a bare bulb. Portable lamps providing direct task illumination are a critical necessity in offices. In some of Sullivan's major projects, decorative glass panels, often covering a skylight, may be built into an architectural framework in a ceiling of an important space (Fig. 46-12).

FURNISHINGS AND DECORATIVE ARTS

During the last half of the 19th century and into the early 20th century, office furniture differs little in form and appearance from residential furniture. The simple boxlike furniture of the American Arts and Crafts period is common in many offices. Furniture in other more public places reflects the character, scale, and importance of the particular space. Desks are of wood and of three types: rolltops, slant tops, and flat tops with drawers on one or both sides (Fig. 46-13, 46-16). Most are plain, but those used by executives are Renaissance Revival or Eastlake in style. Metal office furniture is introduced in the early 20th century. Desk chairs may have complex iron frames and bases or they may be simple turned or bentwood chairs or Windsor types (Fig. 46-13, 46-15). Although swivel chairs are available, many still use straight chairs. Paper, which comprises the majority of office work, is bound in books or stored in pigeonholes either inside roll-top desks, on open shelves, or in cabinets with doors. Filing cabinets are shown in the 1876 Centennial Exposition but do not become common until the turn of the century. Other office furnishings include tables, safes, bookcases often with glass doors, and built-in counters.

▲ **46-13.** Offices, c. early 1900s; New York and Chicago.

In the early 1900s, standardization becomes the norm for paper, filing systems, furniture, and people. Motion and efficiency studies scrutinize office tasks and procedures to increase productivity and profits. Rows of workers seated at flat-top desks (Fig. 46-13) replace the individual seated at a rolltop or Wooten desk so that managers can more easily monitor work flow, behavior, and productivity. Additionally, office machines, such as typewriters and adding machines, become increasingly common. The typewriter standardizes the paper sheet to 8½ × 11 inches, leading to standard-size manila folders and file cabinets.

▲ **46-14.** Banking hall, National Farmers Bank, 1907–1908; Owatonna, Minnesota; Louis H. Sullivan and George Elmslie.

▲ **46-15.** Office chairs in iron and wood, c. 1850s–1910s.

▲ **46-16.** Desk, Sears, Roebuck & Company catalog, c. 1902; Chicago, Illinois.

CHAPTER 47

Modern Forerunners

1900–1920s

Any deviation from simplicity results in a loss of dignity. Ornaments tend to cheapen rather than enrich; they acknowledge inefficiency and weakness. A house cluttered up by complex ornament means that the designer was aware that his work lacked purity of line and perfection of proportion, so he endeavored to cover its imperfection by adding on detail.

—Irving Gill, "The New Architecture of the West," *The Craftsman*, 1916, p. 147

At the beginning of the 20th century, certain architects advance the search for a modern architecture to express the spirit of a new age. Although unified in purpose, their approaches and aesthetics are diverse, a result of individual experimentation, theory, and personal expression rather than a common, unified style or movement. Collectively, they share a focus upon function, structure, construction, new materials, and urban planning to create new design images. These innovators include Henrik Petrus Berlage of Holland (present-day Netherlands), Frank Lloyd Wright and Irving Gill of the United States, Peter Behrens of Germany, Adolf Loos of Austria, Hans Poelzig of Germany, and August Perret of France. Although they are not the only important designers active during this period, because of their work and influence architecture becomes simpler and less ornamented, and adopts newer materials and construction methods. This sets the stage for future modern movements.

HISTORICAL AND SOCIAL

Industrialization continues unabated in Europe during the early 20th century and is particularly evident in expanded businesses, more factories, mass transportation, and the growth of cities. The period also marks the widespread adoption of electricity as well as an increase in the number of automobiles, telephones, and cinemas. Despite growth in wealth and jobs, the social problems of industrialization and urbanization continue to plague cities and nations. Low pay, long hours, and poor working conditions persist, but now workers are more apt to form labor unions and strike for better wages and work environments. Political and social reforms intensify in various European countries as well as in North America. Important thinkers and theorists, such as Sigmund Freud, Karl Marx, and Friedrich Nietzsche, identify causes of and propose solutions for the problems inherent in modern industrial life.

The chief catalyst of transformation, however, is World War I (the Great War), which breaks out in August 1914. Countries involved are the Allied Powers of the United Kingdom, France, Belgium, Serbia, and Russia and the Central Powers including Germany, Austria, Hungary, Bulgaria, and Japan. The United

States enters the war as an Ally in 1917 after failing to remain neutral. Economic and political policies of Europe in the late 19th century are the basic causes of the war, which mobilizes millions of men as well as the entire populations and economic resources of the countries involved. When the war ends in November 1918, Europe is forever changed politically, socially, and geographically. New nations are created as the boundaries of older ones are changed. The German and Austrian empires collapse, and the war helps bring on the Bolshevik Revolution in Russia. The war's cost in money, people, and physical destruction affects the stability of Europe for many years to come.

Like others before them, the forerunner architects, designers, and theorists search for an architecture that reflects the times in which they live. Unlike many of their predecessors, they do not start movements or schools to achieve their aims. Recognizing the failure of Art Nouveau and previous art movements to come to grips with mechanization, they embrace or celebrate the machine as the means to express modern life and democratize art and architecture. They maintain the belief in the power of buildings to transform what they see as failing societies and are especially concerned with architecturally solving problems of industrialization and, most important, the demand for housing. They begin to challenge the traditional boundaries of architecture and engineering, arguing that the architect can and should design all buildings for a modern society. Because each architect or designer approaches these problems differently, solutions are varied instead of unified. Their opinions and debates center on form versus function, use of new materials and construction methods, innovative planning, and the application of ornament. The forerunners are relatively few in number, and their work has little immediate impact on the public. However, their architecture and ideas give rise to and affect nearly all subsequent modern developments.

As before, books, schools, and organizations play an important role in the dissemination of ideas. Individuals and groups describe their beliefs and theories in treatises and manifestos such as Loos's *Ornament and Crime* and Antonio Sant'Elia's *Messagio*, which are widely read. Design schools refocus their instruction to align with the ideas of progressive directors and professors. For example, in 1903 Peter Behrens becomes the director at the Arts and Crafts School in Dusseldorf and Hans Poelzig assumes the directorship of the Royal Arts and Crafts Academy in Breslau (now Wroclaw, Poland), both in Germany.

CONCEPTS

Individuals working in Europe and North America experiment with form and structure and develop new and diverse ideas in architecture and design. These architects strive to create an architecture that is economically practical and functional, expresses the modern experience, and meets the needs of and even attempts to reform the society of their time. While grappling with how to express new materials and construction methods through structure, volume, and geometry instead of historicism and applied ornament, they draw from many sources and work out solutions that lay important foundations for the further development of modern architecture both theoretically and functionally.

▲ **47-1.** Amsterdam Stock Exchange, 1898–1903; Amsterdam, Holland; Hendrik Petrus Berlage.

Influences upon the forerunners are many, including classicism, Gothic churches, Karl Friedrich Schinkel, Eugène Emmanuel Viollet-le-Duc, C. F. A. Voysey, *L'École des Beaux-Arts*, the Chicago School, Henri van de Velde, the Vienna Secessionists, European vernacular and traditional architecture, factories, and warehouses. Architects sometimes align with or are influenced by early-20th-century avant-garde art movements that reject traditional depictions of visual reality in favor of abstraction. Examples are Expressionism in Germany, which seeks to demonstrate inner thoughts and subjective feelings through painting; Cubism in France, which depicts time and space through multiple images and fractured planes; and Futurism in Italy, a movement that celebrates the machine and motion.

Another source of ideas is urban planning. In 1904, Tony Garnier develops *Cité Industrielle*, a hypothetical industrial city in Lyons, France. This socialist-influenced complex includes housing, government buildings, and industrial structures set along a river valley. Representing a blend of architecture and engineering methods, the buildings are simple, unadorned, and of reinforced concrete. Structures are unified, but there are distinct differences in home and work place, city center and suburbs. Garnier's concepts have a significant impact on those who seek solutions to unmanaged urban growth and the need for decent housing for workers.

MOTIFS

■ *Motifs*. There is no vocabulary for motifs because buildings are generally unadorned. Some architects include unique architectural details that are part of the building structure.

ARCHITECTURE

Architects and engineers, sometimes working together, create a new visual language, one without reference to previous historical styles, except perhaps through classical order or attributes such as symmetry. Form and its manipulation are all important to communicate construction demands, function, new relationships, and a machine aesthetic. Ornament, particularly if derived from the past, is rejected. As a result, most buildings are unadorned, utilitarian, and monumental. Some have industrial features as designers experiment with reinforced concrete construction, metals for structure and surfaces, and larger areas of glass in different sizes. Many designs emphasize solid and void relationships. Mass, form, hard edges, interpenetration of spaces, and minimalism are characteristic. Compositions are volumes with an emphasis on geometry and axial relationships giving a distinctive architectonic quality. Some buildings are more expressive, organic, or sculptural in character or may have parts that curve or move in and out. Common to all is the importance of spatial organization, which is often volumetric. Architecture is reduced to basics with an emphasis on structure and planning.

Architects create individual interpretations based on this new language for design. Some produce buildings with a pure, precise, machinelike appearance (Fig. 47-3, 47-4), while others reveal a stripped-down classicism (Fig. 47-1). Some are more expressionist or evoke traditional, vernacular forms.

Industrial structures provide an opportunity for more experimentation and the use of industrial technology in design. Commercial buildings also are important conveyors of design intentions. They include office buildings (Fig. 47-1, 47-9), city/town halls, railway stations, auditoriums, theaters, libraries, factories (Fig. 47-3, 47-4), department stores, garages, and sometimes churches (Fig. 47-2, 47-12). Residential buildings include apartment and low-cost housing complexes as well as individual houses (Fig. 47-6, 47-7, 47-8).

■ *Nationalist and Regionalist Innovators*. Although the work of this group is often not internationally recognized, it affects local and regional architecture and architects who spread it to others. Henrik Petrus Berlage from Holland introduces a new architectural language that borrows from the vernacular of the country and conveys a simple, unadorned character. One of his most important and influential projects is the Amsterdam Stock Exchange (Fig. 47-1), which is built of brick, glass, and iron and evidences strong spatial organization with attention to details. His emphasis upon exposed construction influences De Stijl and other modernist groups.

■ *American Innovators*. The United States contributes to the modern movement through the work of these innovators. The most influential American architect of the period in Europe is Frank Lloyd Wright. His work is admired for its organic concepts, open planning, integration of structure, geometric forms, horizontality, and natural use of materials. Wright's abstraction of natural forms as ornament is unparalleled in Europe, as are his structural and mechanical innovations, such as textile-block construction in concrete and air conditioning. Unlike most others, Wright designs the building and its furnishings to create a unified and total work of art. Of his many influential projects of the time are Unity Temple (Fig. 47-2) in the Chicago area, one of the first buildings in poured concrete, and the Larkin Building (Fig. 47-9) in Buffalo, which was seen by H. P. Berlage as a great modern work unequaled in Europe. Irving Gill, a former Wright colleague in the office of Louis Sullivan, experiments with reinforced concrete in California. Because of his concern with economy, efficiency, and function, his designs are stark, geometric, and filled with labor-saving devices. Similar to the work of Loos in Vienna, his buildings are unadorned, rectilinear, and white with smooth walls, large glass windows, and flat roofs. Gill's work is comparable to, if not ahead of, other forerunners in Europe, but World War I limits his influence. One of his most important projects is the Walter L. Dodge House (Fig. 47-7) in Los Angeles, a structure whose design simplicity prefigures the later work of Le Corbusier.

■ *Form Innovators*. These innovators introduce new building forms or redesign existing ones that have a broad impact on subsequent architects and architecture. Behrens's design for Germany's A. E. G. Turbine Factory (Fig. 47-3) sets the standard of form for many subsequent buildings. In a first appearance of corporate identity, he also designs the offices, worker housing, logos, advertising, and some products, such as electric fans and light fixtures, for the company. Loos in Vienna vehemently rejects ornament and designs residences with plain, concrete or stucco exteriors and volumetric interiors, as evident in the Steiner House (Fig. 47-6). Because of his work and writings, subsequent modern architecture eschews ornament in any form for a long time.

■ *Expressionist Innovators*. The work of these innovators, while usually plain and unadorned, is unique as they experiment with shape and form to make their design intentions apparent. Poelzig is the most important German architectural expressionist. Characteristics of his work include angular or organic forms and monumental interior volumes. His compositions are highly individual and, occasionally, bizarre. One of his important projects is the Centennial Hall in Breslau. Eric Mendelsohn, another German expressionist, designs the Einstein Tower (Fig. 47-5), an astrophysical observatory in Potsdam, Germany, for experiments related to Einstein's theory of relativity. Sculptural and fluid, its innovative yet eccentric shape intends to reflect the new scientific ideas within. Mendelsohn originally designed it to be of reinforced concrete, hoping to take full advantage of the material, but construction proved difficult. Instead, the building is of brick covered with stucco.

■ *Construction Innovators*. By introducing new or revised construction techniques and uses for new or existing material, this group helps change the form and appearance of later modernist

DESIGN SPOTLIGHT

Architecture and Interior: One of the first buildings of poured concrete, Unity Temple makes a bold and sculptural statement of modern design. Frank Lloyd Wright's idea was to design a religious structure that embodied the Universalists' principles of "unity, truth, beauty, simplicity, freedom, and reason," thereby creating a modern meetinghouse for man. As a result, the building is composed of cubic volumes, each capped with a heavy, flat, interpenetrating roof. The four corner blocks contain the stairs, and the taller volumes comprise the central sanctuary or auditorium. Bold piers with geometric ornament, the only decoration on the plain façade, separate the clerestory windows that illuminate the auditorium during the day. Green, yellow, brown, and white stained glass in these windows provide a soft, mystical light. Wright deliberately inserts no windows in the lower walls for privacy and to muffle noise. The main entry, which is on the side and not on the front, is through an enclosure to create a sense of intimacy and an anticipation of the space within.

Inside, the auditorium has center seating focused to the pulpit with an organ behind it. Additional seating surrounds the central area on three sides. Large piers define the corners. A three-dimensional grid-form ceiling covers the area, incorporates built-in lighting, and allows natural light to penetrate inside. Contrasting bands of wood accent the ceiling, piers, and walls. Light plaster walls and natural colors evoke Wright's organic concepts. Because of the spatial organization, solid and void relationships, and colors, the interior feels warm and inviting. The form and composition of the church are suitable to the materials and construction method; the congregation's limited budget; and Wright's design concept, which is intended to convey the simplicity and power of an ancient temple.

▲ **47-2.** Unity Temple, floor plans, and nave, 1906; Oak Park, Chicago, Illinois; Frank Lloyd Wright.

DESIGN SPOTLIGHT

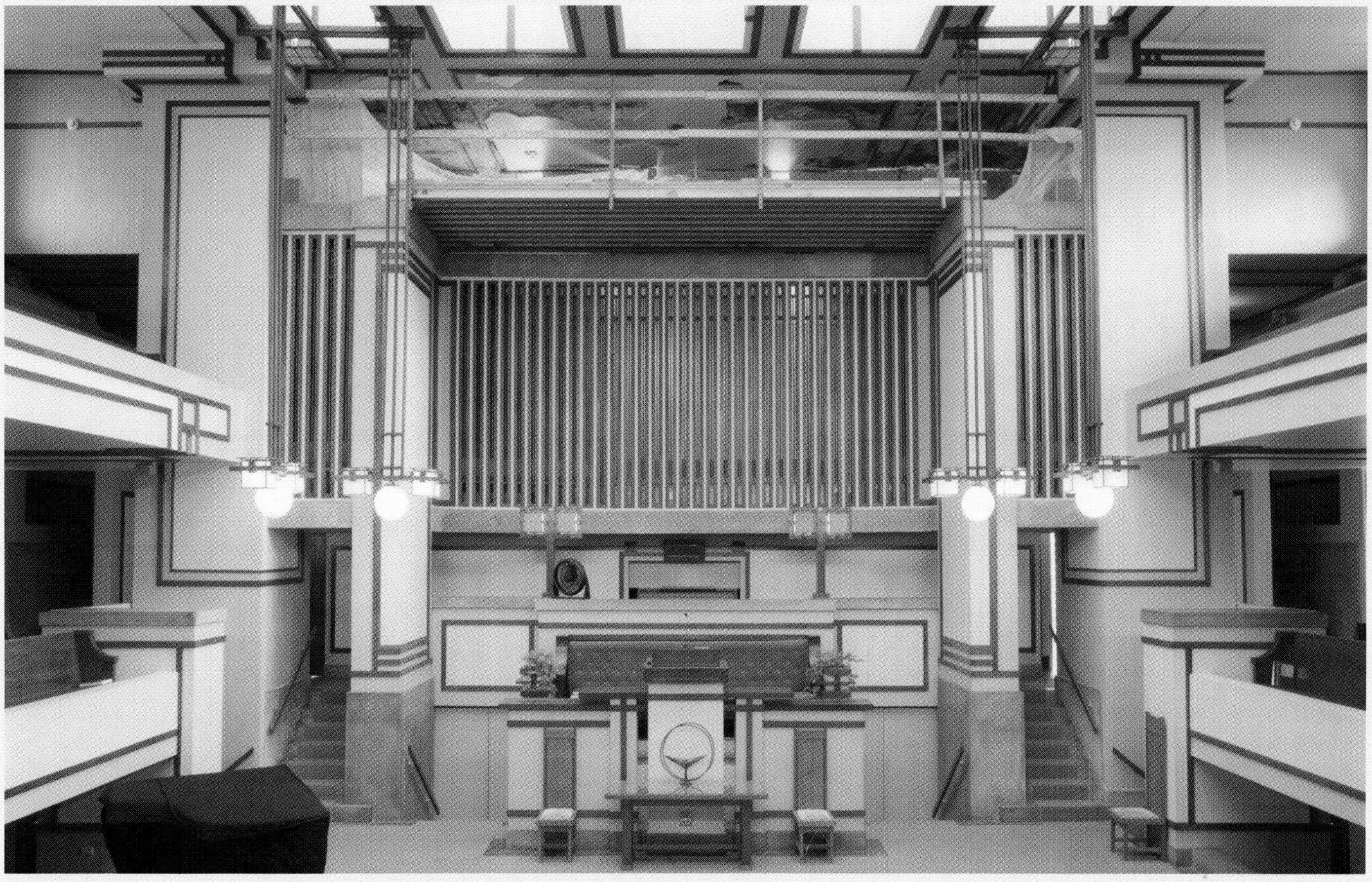

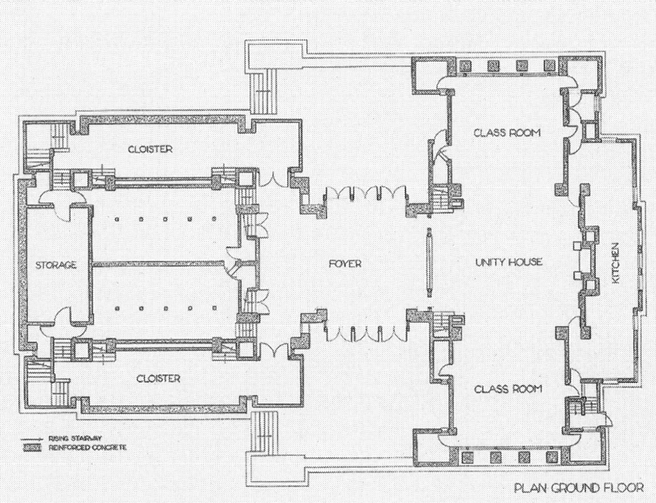

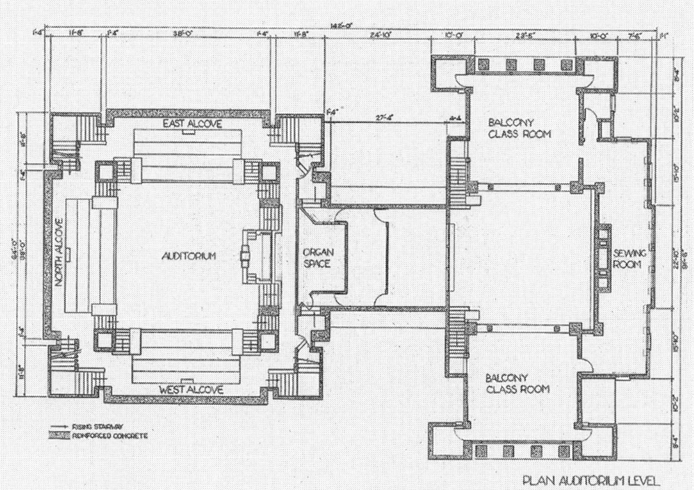

▲ **47-2.** Continued

architecture and interiors. Perret of France is one of the first architects to exploit the potential of reinforced concrete and to use it in an aesthetically pleasing manner. Through his influence, concrete becomes a viable building material. One of his landmark projects is *Notre Dame du Raincy*, a church near Paris that has a precast, pierced concrete façade. Inside, the large, open interior space is shaped by a concrete vaulted ceiling, supported by a minimal number of free-standing solid columns, all of which are unadorned (Fig. 47-12). Henri Sauvage, another French innovator, gains recognition nationally through his low-cost apartment complexes built with reinforced concrete frames and often faced with white and sometimes blue faience tiles. His apartment block on *Rue Vavin* in Paris is noteworthy for its stepped-back form that addresses height requirements while providing interesting sun exposure and balconies on the front.

Public and Private Buildings

■ *Site Orientation.* Architects most often situate commercial buildings on major city streets, in parks, and in commercial zones where they will be accessible to more people. In contrast, they place apartment and mass housing complexes on more private streets where there is less traffic. Because of the urban planning ideas of Garnier and others, some large cities in Europe begin to group buildings by function into separate zones for culture, government, industry, and residences. There also is a strong push to decentralize city centers by creating garden suburbs. Because these new city zones do not emulate the old European city squares, there is little sense of community or intermingling between public and private activities to keep downtowns active and alive. Consequently, downtowns begin to decline.

DESIGN SPOTLIGHT

Architecture: The best known and most influential of the buildings Peter Behrens designs for the A. E. G. Turbine Factory reveals his concern for imbuing technology with a noble spirit by using art. Although not obvious at first glance, the building recalls a spare classical temple that is transformed with modern materials and construction methods into a modern factory. Instead of the orders, tapered steel columns resting on bases composed of rocker hinges form the colonnade of the long side. The spaces between are glazed to permit as much light as possible to enter the work space. The main façade has battered concrete corner piers and a rounded gable roof or pediment. In an unclassical move, the bold central window instead of the piers seems to support the pediment. Additionally, the heavy piers are an illusion because they are not necessary for support. Behrens creates a sense of the modern and the eternal for this expression of industry.

▲ **47-3.** A. E. G. Turbine Factory, 1908–1910; Berlin, Germany; Peter Behrens.

■ *Floor Plans*. Designers pay a lot of attention to building function in shaping the forms and volumes of space in plans. The compositions may be asymmetrical, which is more common, or symmetrical. Plan layouts emphasize geometry (rectangles, squares, circles, half-circles) and axial relationships. Beaux-Arts concepts of order based on hierarchy still influence some plans. Commercial plans usually have open, free space; interpenetrating spaces; nonstructural interior walls; and vertical circulation grouped in one or two locations. Typical areas include open atriums or halls, reception spaces, and service areas in the rear of the building. A central court or hall often opens to skylights above. Tiered, open galleries may surround the hall. Open and structurally exposed stairways, many located in the corners of buildings, are common. In factories, while the manufacturing process determines the plan, there is often a traditional organization with an emphasis on a main building as the headquarters and side pavilions or blocks for the factory operations.

In contrast, Wright develops plans from the inside out. His public buildings of the period often have symmetrical plans with a large, central, inward-looking interior space, like the sanctuary of Unity Temple (Fig. 47-2). This planning intends to foster community among the worshippers and workers. Houses center on the fireplace or hearth and often have a cruciform shape as in the Prairie Style. Exterior compositions express internal organization and functions.

▲ **47-5.** Einstein Tower, 1919–1924; Potsdam, Germany; Eric Mendelsohn.

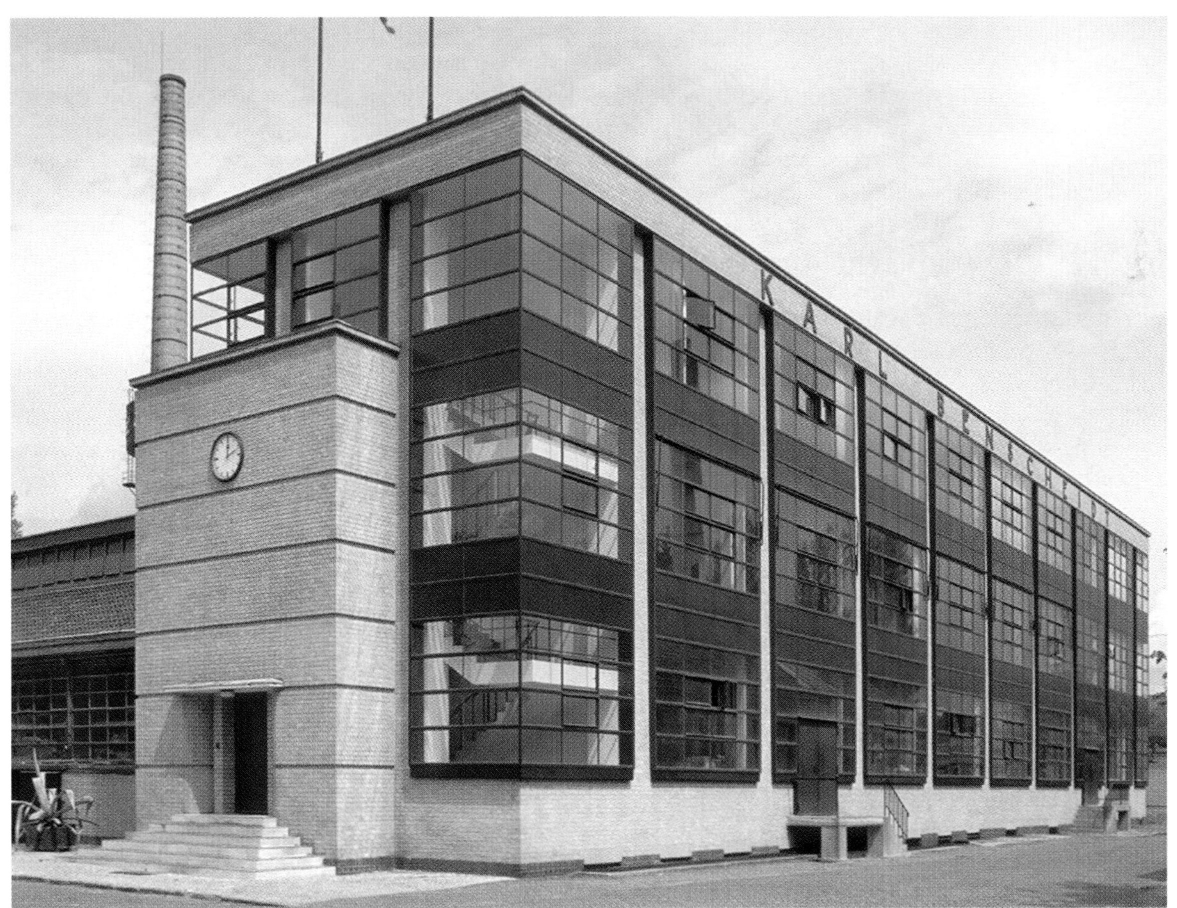

▲ **47-4.** Fagus Shoe Factory, 1911–1913; Alfeld-an-der-Leine, Germany; Walter Gropius and Adolph Meyer.

▲ **47-6.** Steiner House, 1910; Vienna, Austria; Adolf Loos.

▲ **47-7.** Walter L. Dodge House, 1914–1916; Los Angeles, California; Irving Gill.

In general, houses and apartments display a similar plan concept with open space between rooms or areas with vistas between them from large openings. In individual houses, some adopt Loos's emphasis upon volume with changing levels and ceiling heights, and broad openings between and among spaces.

■ *Materials*. New materials for walls are reinforced concrete or brick covering a steel frame and glass walls. Some concrete walls may be precast, stuccoed, or covered with tile. Glazed or polished tiles in blue, green, or other colors may accent the façade. Bricks vary in color with usual selections being red and brown. In commercial structures, large areas of glass or glass blocks often cover façades and stair towers (Fig. 47-1, 47-3, 47-4). Columns or piers may be reinforced concrete or stone, and some are brick, wood, or metal. Exposed structural iron and steel trusses may span an open ceiling. Fireproof terra-cotta, another recent material, may be used on commercial structures with a more traditional look.

Many of Wright's buildings incorporate mechanical systems such as the pioneering air quality control with a built-in duct system that cleans and heats the air in the Larkin Building (Fig. 47-9). This is particularly important because this design seals the building from the heavy air pollution of its industrial location.

■ *Reinforced Concrete*. Perhaps the single most important building material in the early 20th century is reinforced concrete, a concrete incorporating internal metal rods to strengthen it. Although its exact origin is uncertain, its first use appears during the 1850s in France in houses by François Coignet. However, it is not until the 1890s that François Hennebique, also from France, uses the reinforced concrete construction technique in industrial buildings. In 1897, Anatole de Baudot and Paul Cattacin perfect its application in *S. Jean-de-Montmarte*, a novel new church in Paris. Perret, Loos, Gill, and Wright begin using it, and soon others follow suit (Fig. 47-2, 47-7, 47-12). Perret pioneers the use of exposed concrete, a concrete used without the application of tiles or other covering materials. Gill in 1912 develops an insulating core for concrete panels that eliminates condensation and loss of heat. He is also one of the first to use a lift-slab method of construction.

During the 1920s, Wright explores new construction methods using standardized concrete blocks, made and patterned at the site (Fig. 47-8). Called textile-block construction, the blocks are tied together with horizontal and vertical steel rods and reinforced with mortar. Because constructing the blocks is a new process, they are made on site instead of industrially and are, therefore, fragile and porous. They quickly deteriorate, requiring replacement. Nevertheless, textile-block construction gives a structural unity not evident in wood or steel frames.

■ *Façades*. Exteriors display the uniqueness and individualism of the architects as they work with new materials in a new way. Of-

▲ **47-8.** Hollyhock (Barnsdall) House, 1919–1921; Los Angeles, California; Frank Lloyd Wright.

ten unadorned, plain façades have a formal grid or repetitive structural pattern highlighted with focal points created through arches, towers, entryways, balconies, windows, and roofs (Fig. 47-1, 47-2, 47-3, 47-4, 47-6, 47-7, 47-8). This creates three-dimensionality through changes of depth and makes the building seem more active. Many commercial structures show a substantial increase in the use of glass plates set within a metal grid. The glass, which comes in standard sizes, and its frames create a repetition of shape and materials on the exterior. Frequently, these glass walls define the building's character. Some commercial structures have prominent towers that announce and identify the building. Towers sometimes have symbolic meanings and clocks on their fronts (Fig. 47-1). Roofs may be flat and disappear or create a more defined focal point. Any architectural detailing usually is part of the structure, whether it is in concrete, brick, or metal.

Tall apartment complexes may have stepped façades with projecting balconies that punctuate the façade. Windows in groups may project or recede at one or various levels to create movement. Large glass windows may cover the entire perimeter of individual houses.

Loos experiments with extremely plain façades and volumetric planning (Fig. 47-6). Wright's façades are profoundly geometric with interpenetrating volumes. Unlike other designers, he uses stylized ornament to accentuate important architectural features and maintain a sense of place (Fig. 47-2, 47-8). Gill's façades frequently display a series of arches, reflecting the early Spanish influence of Southern California.

■ *Windows.* Size and placement of windows varies according to building use and functions. Designers primarily use double-hung, fixed, and casement windows (Fig. 47-1, 47-3, 47-4, 47-6, 47-7, 47-8). In expressionist compositions, windows may be round, oval, or curvilinear (Fig. 47-5). Sometimes the windows are flat against the façade, and sometimes they project to enhance the composition. Large windows over entryways are particularly noticeable in churches, railway stations, and city halls. Clerestory windows may appear near a roofline (Fig. 47-2). Flat moldings in wood, metal, brick, or glazed tile may frame the window opening.

■ *Doors.* Architects integrate the entry doors into the composition instead of setting them apart (Fig. 47-1, 47-4, 47-5, 47-6, 47-7). Wright often hides the entrance but creates a processonal path to it (Fig. 47-2, 47-8). Usually unadorned and plain, the doors are large, but they do not overly dominate the façade. Some are solid and others have glass panels in the center.

■ *Roofs.* Roofs, which display much variety through experimentation by different architects, may be flat, geometrical, or sculptural (Fig. 47-1, 47-2, 47-3, 47-4, 47-6, 47-7, 47-8). Sometimes the roof is a visual icon or symbol for the building and very expressive in form, such as Einstein Tower (Fig. 47-5) by Mendelsohn. Roofs may be reinforced concrete, sculptural concrete, built-up wood and rolled asphalt, metal with steel supports, glass supported by steel and/or wrought iron trusses, and gables in various materials. A flat band or projecting cornice often separates the roof from the building façade. During this period, Wright develops a new internal roof drainage system that he repeats in his later buildings.

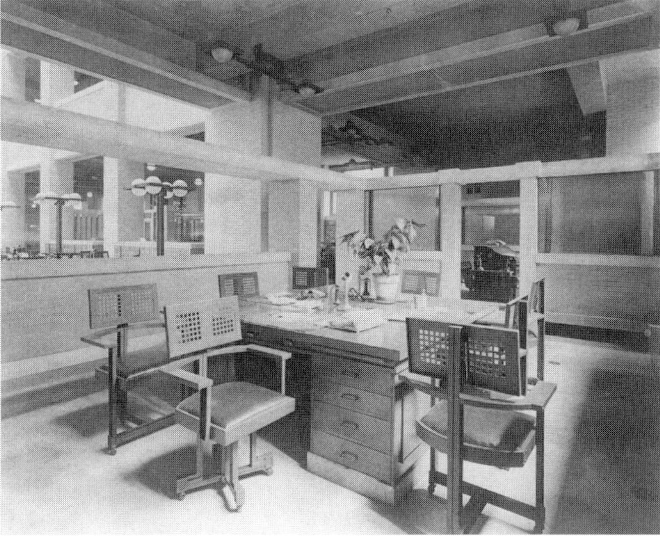

▲ **47-9.** Central atrium and desk and office chairs, Larkin Building, 1903–1906; Buffalo, New York; Frank Lloyd Wright.

INTERIORS

Many architects design interiors for their buildings and contribute to the interiors and furnishings of buildings with which they are not involved. Interiors usually repeat the exterior character and architectural vocabulary in spaces that are functional, simple, utilitarian, and unornamented. Wright designs the interior as an extension of the exterior and to create unity. New construction methods and materials transfer from the exterior to the interior to reinforce a more modern appearance. But the interiors sometimes exhibit formal order and some reference to historical forms, such as columns and vaults, because architects are familiar with these construction features. Most of these architects do not design furniture, but those who do, like Wright, adopt principles of the Arts and Crafts Movement, such as honest construction and minimal applied decoration. Many architects include built-ins as an expression of their own vocabulary.

Public and Private Buildings

■ *Color.* Most of the colors come from the building materials or textiles. Consequently, the palette includes shades of brown, gold, rust, cream, white, gray, and black (Fig. 47-2, 47-9, 47-10). Tiles in these colors and in white with blue and green may enliven the interior.

▲ **47-10.** American Bar, 1907; Vienna, Austria; Adolph Loos.

■ *Floors.* Commonly employed flooring materials include stone, marble, terrazzo, or wood. Gill often uses tan or ochre concrete composition floors in residences.

■ *Walls.* Interior walls and treatments generally repeat those of the exterior, so the structure often is exposed or repeated inside. Walls in some churches and other public buildings are reinforced concrete slabs or poured concrete (Fig. 47-12). Wright frequently articulates walls and other architectural features, such as piers or columns, with simple bands of contrasting materials such as stone or wood (Fig. 47-2). Sometimes materials are left natural or may be covered by stucco. Rarely are wallpaper or other decorative materials applied.

■ *Windows and Doors.* Most often, windows are left plain and unadorned to reflect the design character. If window treatments are used, they are simple curtains or flat shades. Doors, like windows, are plainly treated. Gill introduces frameless doors in 1902.

■ *Ceilings.* The exterior roof structure repeats inside to form the dominant ceiling design, particularly in the most important spaces (Fig. 47-2, 47-9, 47-10, 47-12). Some ceilings are reinforced concrete with curves and vaults. Others may be flat or three-dimensional in the same material, plastered, or a combination of plaster and wood. Still others incorporate central glass skylights with exposed metal trusses over central courts or halls to create light wells above several floors. The skylights may be pitched or curved and/or mounted above glass screens with geometric patterning.

■ *Textiles.* Linens, cottons, and wools are the most common fabrics during the early 20th century. Designs are generally simple, plain, and geometric, with an emphasis on regularity, lines, and shapes. Behrens experiments with tapestry patterns, while Wright provides custom fabric designs for individual clients (Fig. 47-11). His textiles often display the earthy colors associated with his nature-based concepts or derive from ideas related to the building design.

■ *Lighting.* Rooms, by day, are filled with natural light entering through large windows, light wells, or skylights. Artificial lighting primarily includes wall sconces and chandeliers that are architecturally designed to integrate into the interior composition (Fig. 47-2, 47-10, 47-12).

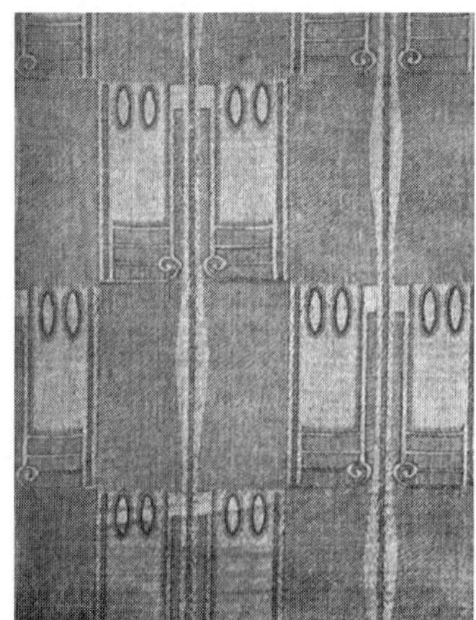

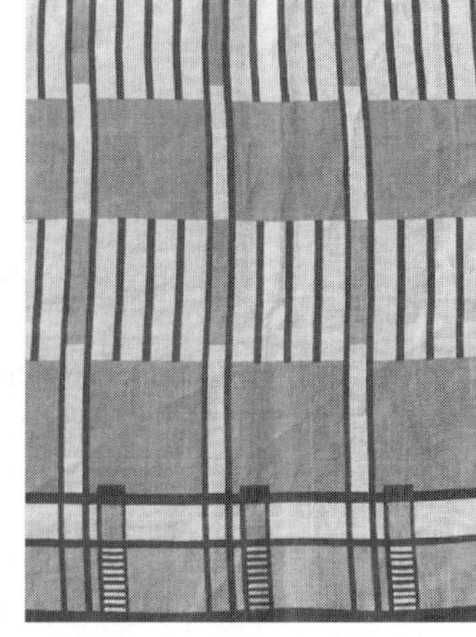

▲ **47-11.** Textiles: Tapestry, 1909; Germany; Peter Behrens, and fabric, 1910s–1920s; United States; Frank Lloyd Wright.

FURNISHINGS AND DECORATIVE ARTS

During this period, these innovative architects often pay little attention to furniture and decorative arts. When they do, however, they select or design furniture that reflects the Arts and Crafts Movement in pieces that are simple, plain, and unadorned. German architect Behrens provides furniture for particular projects with selected examples published internationally in *The Studio Yearbook of Decorative Art*. In North America, Wright creates furnishings and decorative arts for his buildings as part of the whole concept (Fig. 47-9). For example, the backs of the office chairs in his Larkin Building repeat the grid pattern of the interior and the bases repeat the linearity of the overall design. These chairs and the desks are among the earliest mass-produced metal furniture, so are therefore influential. Wright's office chairs, desks, and tables often convey an architectonic quality, simplicity, concern for human scale, and inventiveness. Compositions are severe, angular, and often uncomfortable. Furniture designs usually appear as parts of a whole integrated unit like his interiors.

DESIGN SPOTLIGHT

Interior: At *Notre-Dame du Raincy*, Perret reinvents the traditional church using exposed reinforced concrete and glass. A large concrete vault covers the nave while smaller transverse vaults identify the side aisles. Thirty-five columns in four rows support the roof. The 37′-0″ tall columns taper from 17″ at the base to 14″ at the ceiling and are reminiscent of Gothic cluster or compound columns. Non-load-bearing exterior walls are of precast concrete panels and stained glass. Color is arranged according to the spectrum, changing from yellow at the entrance to purple at the altar. Perret creates rational and pleasing aesthetic solutions for a modern church, but unfortunately, the materials do not live up to their expectations. The exposed concrete begins to crumble and metal reinforcements rust within a few years after construction.

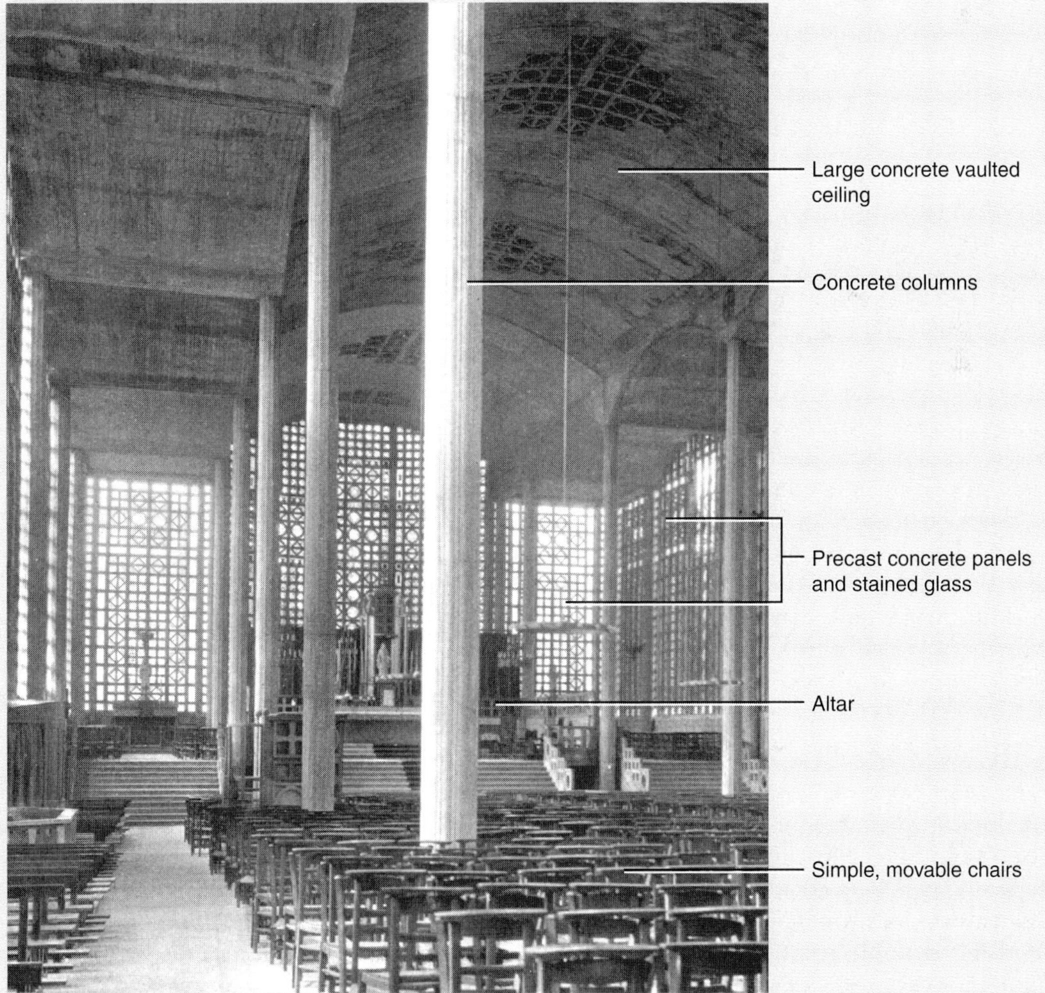

▲ **47-12.** Nave, *Notre-Dame du Raincy*, 1923–1924; Le Raincy near Paris, France; August Perret.

CHAPTER 48

De Stijl

1917–1931

The visual artist orders, multiplies, measures, and determines congruences and proportions of forms and colors and their relation to space. For the artist, every object has a particular relationship to space; it is an image of space. The artist derives his repertoire of color and form from a certain number of objects. With a constantly changing spatial scheme, with a moving object, a space–time framework is generated. It is the artist's function to amalgamate these into a harmonious, melodious unity. I believe the same holds for architecture and that the modern painter, sculptor and architect find each other in this visual consciousness, with only this difference: architecture has to cater not only to spiritual, but also to material needs.

—Theo van Doesburg, "Het Aestetisch Beginsel der Modern Beeldende Kunst" (lecture delivered in Haarlem), in *Drie Voordrachten over de Nieuwe Beeldende Kunst*, 1916

De Stijl, or The Style, is an art and design movement founded in Holland by painters and architects around 1917. The movement strives to express universal concepts through removal, reduction, abstraction, simplification, and a dynamic asymmetrical balance of rectangles, planes, verticals, horizontals, the primary colors, and black, white, and gray. Termed Neo-Plasticism, these principles characterize an art and architecture of spiritual order and harmony, which the followers hope will transform society. The group spreads its philosophies through *De Stijl*, its journal. Although producing few actual works of architecture, interiors, and furniture, De Stijl strongly influences the Modern Movement in art and design by articulating and exploring foundational design principles.

HISTORICAL AND SOCIAL

Until the formation of De Stijl, Holland (today known as the Netherlands) contributes little to the Modern Movement, being less affected by Art Nouveau than other European nations are and producing only one or two innovative architects or designers in the early years of the 20th century. Like other European countries, the country enjoys economic expansion resulting from industrialization, trade, and commerce from the end of the 19th century until World War I. During the war, Holland remains neutral, and this isolation permits building and artistic explorations to continue. After the war, Dutch artists and architects, like others in Europe, react to the upheaval and devastation by seeking means to stimulate universal peace and harmony.

Before the war, painters Piet Mondrian (Fig. 48-1) and Theo van Doesburg (Fig. 48-4, 48-5) are individually exploring principles of abstraction as expressions of universality. They and other like-minded artists come together during the war. Mondrian and van Doesburg continue to work together closely from 1917 to 1919, advancing their own work and formulating the group's philosophy and the tenets of what they call Neo-Plasticism. They issue the group's first manifesto in 1918.

Composed of individualists rather than a unified group, the movement has a basic goal of freeing art from various nonessentials such as subject matter, illusion, ambiguity, and subjectivity. Followers renounce what they consider to be the overdecorated and decadent art of the late 19th and early 20th centuries. Looking toward the future, they want to clear the way for a radical new art form for a modern, industrial society. They believe in a social and artistic revolution where art and daily life would be inseparable.

Mondrian and van Doesburg are the main theorists of the movement, but van Doesburg is its leading spirit. In 1917, he instigates the monthly avant-garde magazine *De Stijl* from which the movement derives its name. *De Stijl* magazine spreads the movement's theory and philosophy to a larger audience and becomes a natural vehicle for expressing the movement's principles in graphic design. As the unifying force for the movement, the magazine highlights the activities and ideas of the artists, architects, designers, and writers who form the De Stijl group. Members include Dutch artists van Doesburg, Mondrian, and Bart van der Leck; architects Gerrit Rietveld (Fig. 48-3, 48-8), Jacobus Johannes Pieter Oud (Fig. 48-3), Robert van't Hoff, and Jan Wils; Belgian sculptor Georges Vantongerloo; and Hungarian painter Vilmos Huszar. Their emphasis is on group interaction through *De Stijl* and shared ideas rather than on individual recognition, group exhibits, or meetings. Membership changes often as members disagree, move in other directions, or simply abandon the principles.

Van Doesburg is the most vocal of the movement's proponents. He spreads De Stijl principles and practices through his writing, travels, and lectures. In 1921, he visits the Bauhaus at Weimar, which significantly affects the students and faculty alike. Additionally, several exhibitions spread the De Stijl aesthetic: one in Berlin in 1920 and another at the Galerie L'Effort Moderne in Paris in 1923. When Van Doesburg dies in 1931, so do the cohesion and force of De Stijl. A few members, such as Mondrian and Rietveld, maintain some of the group's design principles until their deaths.

The movement's total rejection of subject matter, reliance on geometry and color, and deemphasis of individualism is too radical for any real public acceptance during this period. The total artistic output of the movement is small, but it has far-reaching influence upon other avant-garde artists, architects, and designers. De Stijl makes a profound impact upon the development of the International Style.

CONCEPTS

De Stijl seeks to reduce, simplify, and abstract to express concepts of beauty and produce universal, rather than individual, responses. Because they are tied to the past and inappropriate for modern times, visual reality, ornament, and style are rigorously rejected in favor of Neo-Plasticism, harmony, and unity. The individual is subservient to the universal in thought and design. De Stijl compositions seek a dynamic organization through the balance of unequal opposites of the right angle and primary colors (Fig. 48-1, 48-2). Movement or the plastic is achieved through the actions and interactions of form and color instead of the usual means such as linear perspective. Purity of form means the expression of reality without the imitation of nature, references to the past, or decoration. Straight lines and right angles are considered the purest of forms, so pure, in fact, that some of the most vehement arguments among members center on the use of diagonal lines. Rebelling against previous developments focusing on individualism, the proponents emphasize harmony and universal values. Stressing the connections between art and life, they also advocate a clean, pure, and simple design language and lifestyle envisioned through architecture, furniture, painting, and typography. This, they believe, will bring forth order out of the social chaos of the war and universal harmony.

One of the most influential theorists on the movement is mathematician and philosopher M. H. J. Schoenmaekers, who articulates his views in *The New Image of the World* (1915) and *Principles of Plastic Mathematics* (1916). In these books, he states the need for regularity and the harmonious balance between the vertical (male) and the horizontal (female), a relationship that forms a right angle. His ideas, which strongly influence painter Mondrian (Fig. 48-1), also focus on reality as a series of opposing forces and the importance of primary colors, two other concepts readily explored and expanded by Mondrian in painting and van Doesburg in architecture. Mondrian articulates his ideas in *Le Néo-Plasticisme* (1921); van Doesburg does the same in the journal *De Stijl*.

De Stijl followers are well acquainted with avant-garde or modern art and architecture in Europe and America. Concepts come from as well as influence art movements and the work of architects Henrik Petrus Berlage and Frank Lloyd Wright. From the Cubists, such as Pablo Picasso, De Stijl followers learn to break form into planes that interpenetrate and to show multiple views of an object. Russian movements of Constructivism (sculpture and industrial design) and Suprematism (painting), which arrive at abstraction around 1913, push reduction, geometry, and deconstruction of form. The work of fellow Dutch architect Berlage

▲ **48-1.** "Composition with Red, Blue, and Yellow," 1930; Netherlands; Piet Mondrian.

DESIGN SPOTLIGHT

Architecture and Interior: Gerrit Rietveld, architect and furniture designer, epitomizes the language of abstraction in one of his most famous projects, the Schröder House in Utrecht. The house illustrates De Stijl design principles of asymmetry, geometry, flat roof, white or gray walls, and primary colors that highlight details. Originally intended to be constructed of concrete slabs, it is built of brick covered with stucco. Envisioned through models and with the assistance of its owner, Truus Schröder, the house highlights changeable space, interdependent parts, and spatial continuity. It fulfills the concepts of Neo-Plastic architecture by being unmonumental; elementary; functional; formless; and universal, not individual. Color is not decorative but an organic means of expression. Reitveld intends the house to be a model for future middle-class houses, but many of its design elements, such as the open plan and changeable spaces, are adopted later in a variety of other building types.

▲ **48-2.** Schröder House, floor plans, and interior, 1924; Utrecht, Netherlands; Gerrit Thomas Rietveld in association with owner Truus Schröder-Schräder.

DESIGN SPOTLIGHT

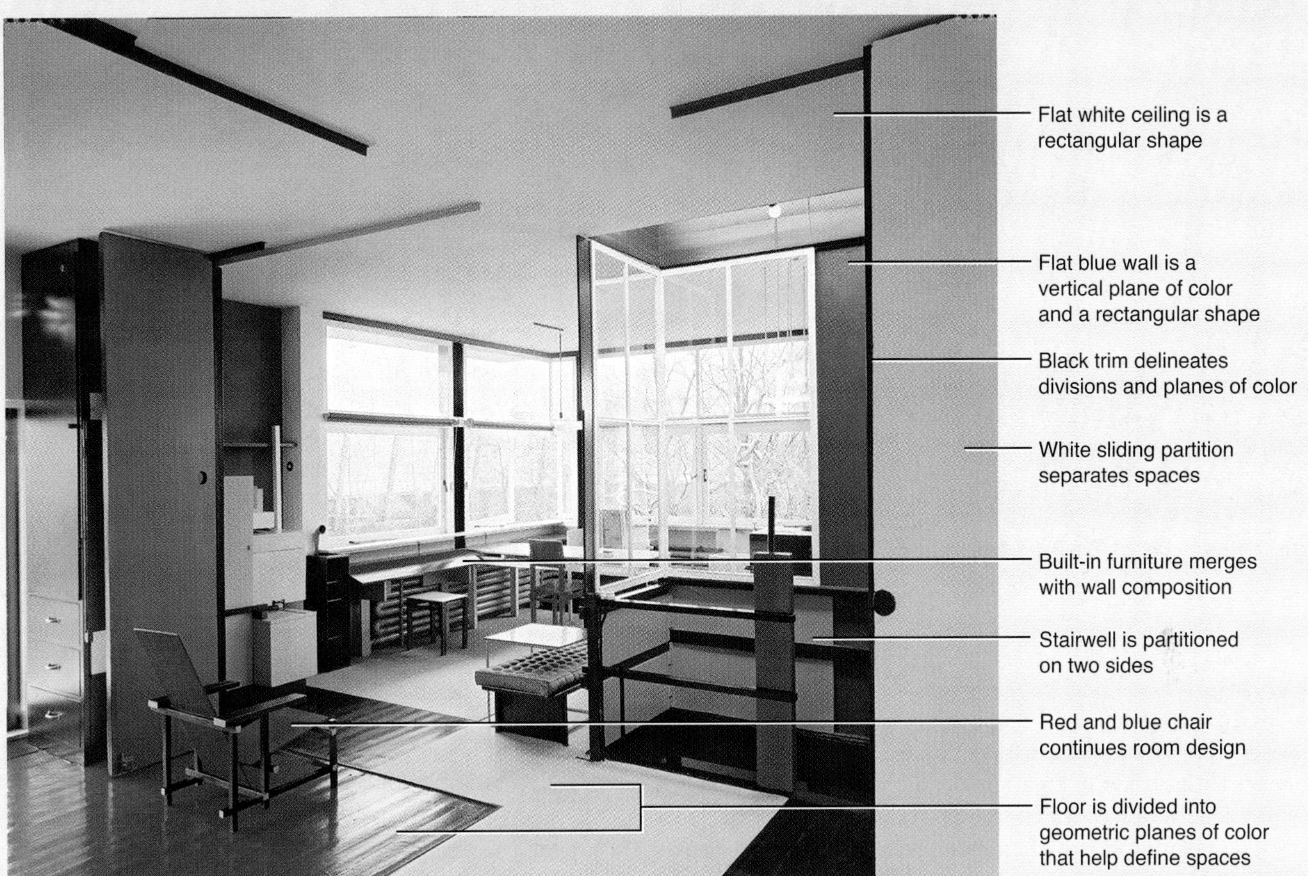

Transformable space characterizes the upper floor of the Schröder House. Rietveld originally conceives it as a large open space with no interior partitions, but Mrs. Schräder wanted the ability to open or close spaces for herself and her children as they desired or as their needs changed. So Rietveld designs the space with sliding or folding partitions similar to those in Japanese houses. The space in the upper floor can take on seven different forms. Rooms are organized into areas by color. Walls are gray or off-white. Exceptions are the blue chimney and a yellow wall in Mrs. Schräder's bedroom. The partitions, painted gray, white, or black, slide on tracks painted the primary colors. Interlocking rectangles of gray, black, white, and red compose the floor. The shapes and forms of panels and furniture merge within walls, ceiling, and floor planes. Much furniture is built in and/or multipurpose. The design utilizes every inch of the limited space with the same color palette as those on the upper floor. The lower floor, by contrast, is conventionally divided into individual rooms with the same color palette as those on the upper floor. [World Heritage Site]

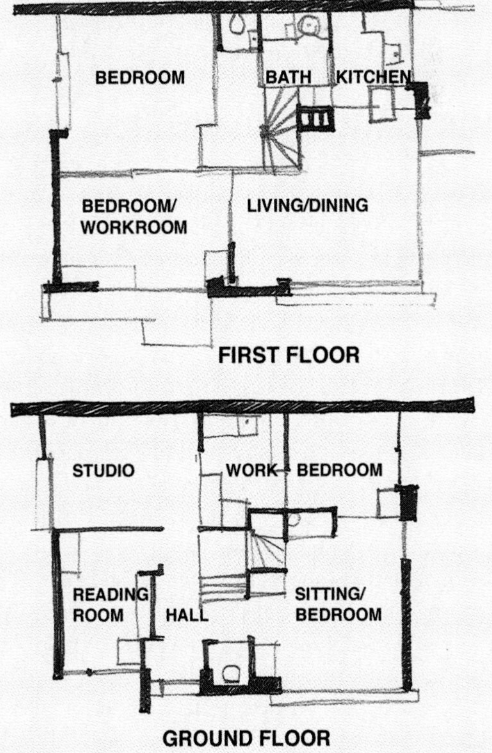

▲ **48-2.** Continued

▲ **48-3.** *Cafe De Unie*, 1924–1925; Rotterdam, Netherlands; J. J. P. Oud.

stresses the importance of interior space, systematic proportions, and walls that create and articulate space. From Wright, De Stijl followers absorb ways to break up the architectural envelope by the interpenetration of wall and roof planes, balconies, and terraces. They admire Wright's rationalism, embrace of the machine, and use of new materials and construction methods. Like Wright and others, they design the building and its contents for total unity and strive for the open, spatial relationships and continuity evident in Wright's Prairie houses.

CHARACTERISTICS AND MOTIFS

The new style has no reference to past history and no connection to visual reality. Abstract, man-made, and calm, it reveals no emotion, but instead embraces simplicity and regularity. Geometry with no parts dominant or subordinate to the whole is important. De Stijl designers discover beauty in art through the straight line arranged as a horizontal, vertical, or right angle and through the primary colors of red, blue, and yellow often placed in concert with black, white, and gray. References to nature are eliminated, an idea in opposition to the traditional and individual Dutch landscapes. Instead, the movement favors a machine vocabulary, one stressing flat shapes, unadorned surfaces, asymmetry, and the purity of the graphic language. The emphasis on two-dimensional flatness shows the need to understand space to achieve pure spatial relationships. Designers transform this idea into three-dimensional, volumetric spaces and furnishings with a focus on solid and void interaction. In buildings, spatial harmony develops through an interpenetration of exterior and interior space so that the proportional relationship of solid and void is emphasized (Fig. 48-2). This same effect, on a smaller scale, is also true in furniture design (Fig. 48-8).

■ *Motifs*. There are no decorative motifs in De Stijl design. Instead, beauty evolves from simple, unadorned surfaces arranged in geometric relationships and from construction detailing (Fig. 48-1, 48-2, 48-3).

ARCHITECTURE

Designers formulate a new language and vocabulary for architecture. To do this, they take the traditional house apart, analyze it like an object, abstract it to eliminate traditional references, and then reassemble it in a new way. The new form emphasizes the cube. However, it is not a solid box but instead opens up from outside to inside with solid and void relationships established through flat planes. Color is important because it articulates the solid planes in opposition to the voids or empty space. Much of pure De Stijl architecture is conceptual because designers find it difficult to persuade their clients to accept it.

Houses for individuals are the most important buildings (Fig. 48-2). Other types include restaurants (Fig. 48-3, 48-4), exhibition spaces, mass housing complexes, apartments, and shopping areas. Characteristics are a flat roof, asymmetry, geometric forms, and white or gray walls with details highlighted by primary colors. However, only Rietveld's Schröder House (Fig. 48-2) reveals all of them. Other buildings may be symmetrical or have pitched roofs. All share the elimination of ornament. The Prairie houses by Wright serve as important models for some De Stijl architects such as van't Hoff and Wils. Compositions incorporate spatial interplay, solid and void relationships, horizontal movements, flat façades, repetitive bands of windows, and overhanging roofs.

Public and Private Buildings

■ *Site Orientation*. Houses usually sit on private streets, with or without yards surrounding them.

■ *Floor Plans*. Plans have an asymmetrical and functional organization of rooms and areas with multifunction spaces common. Rooms are square or rectangular, often with broad openings between them. With the elimination of load-bearing walls, interior space, such as in the Schröder House (Fig. 48-2), can be divided into smaller volumes through sliding panels, allowing the space to change with the function. Vertical circulation is usually in the center of the house.

■ *Materials*. Houses are often brick with stucco cladding to make them smooth. Some are of concrete.

■ *Façades*. Compositions generally emphasize the separation of planes, the application of primary colors, and the spatial relationship of solids to voids (Fig. 48-2, 48-3). Rectangular shapes define the geometric repetition of windows, doors, and blocks of color. Proportional relationships and asymmetrical arrangements are important. Interlocking planes and stepped-back façades identify individual units and provide privacy within mass housing complexes. Individual house façades are not flat; the vertical and horizontal planes composing them advance and recede or interpenetrate. Right angles delineate changes in vertical and horizontal surface movement. Surfaces themselves are flat, painted, and unadorned except to emphasize architectural construction or linear elements. Some buildings have white façades with no primary colors but with a dark gray or black band to define edges. Others boast walls resembling Mondrian paintings. The Schröder House (Fig. 48-2), located within a neighborhood of traditional styles, stands out as a distinctively different three-dimensional visual statement. It completely separates from its surroundings, like a piece of sculpture.

■ *Windows and Doors.* Window sizes vary from large to small on an individual building (Fig. 48-2, 48-3). They may be arranged in patterns or be one unit on a large wall. Casement windows in mass-produced, standard sizes are typical. Architectural moldings are downplayed. In some examples, the De Stijl emphasis upon right angles continues in windows that open only to 90 degrees. The window frames on some brick buildings may be painted primary colors. Some windows have stained glass in geometric, abstract compositions. Entry doors may be solid or incorporate panes of glass. They may be painted black or rendered in a primary color such as red.

■ *Roofs.* Flat roofs are typical and distinctly different from other structures. Some architects use the overhanging roofs of Wright.

INTERIORS

Interiors are important exponents of De Stijl design principles. Interior design emulates the exterior design, so there is a complete interpenetration and repetition of design elements. Houses are generally compact and evolve from a cube form. Volumes of space are interlocked and merged into a complex organization. Architectural surfaces such as floors, walls, and ceilings serve as artistic canvases for De Stijl design principles. Repeating linear or rectangular forms unify structural elements. Rectangular patches of color on walls, floors, and ceilings serve to highlight them and, at the same time, merge structure, ornament, and furnishings. The form and color of structural elements and furnishings are carefully considered in relation to each other horizontally, vertically, and across and between spaces. Architects and painters often collaborate on colors for interiors. This becomes a source of conflict when colors overlap each other or the walls and deconstructs the architectural composition. Furnishings often align against walls so that they become an extension of the architecture.

As shown in the *Café Aubette* (Fig. 48-4), the intent is to place a person inside a painting so that he or she may become one with it. Consequently, all aspects of the interior merge as a total unit. Each component of interior structure serves to emphasize or delineate important features in the painting, but no one item stands

▲ **48-4.** Cinema Dance Hall, Cafe Aubette, 1928–1929; Strasbourg, France; Theo van Doesburg, Jean Arp, and Sophie Taeuber-Arp.

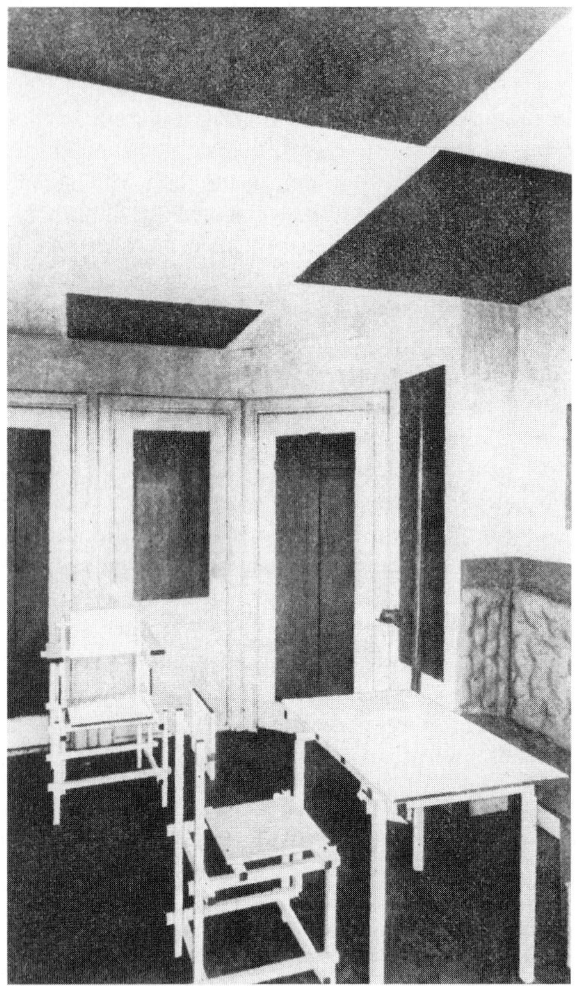

▲ **48-5.** "Example of Coloristic Composition in an Interior," 1919; published in *De Stijl* magazine, 1920; Theo van Doesburg.

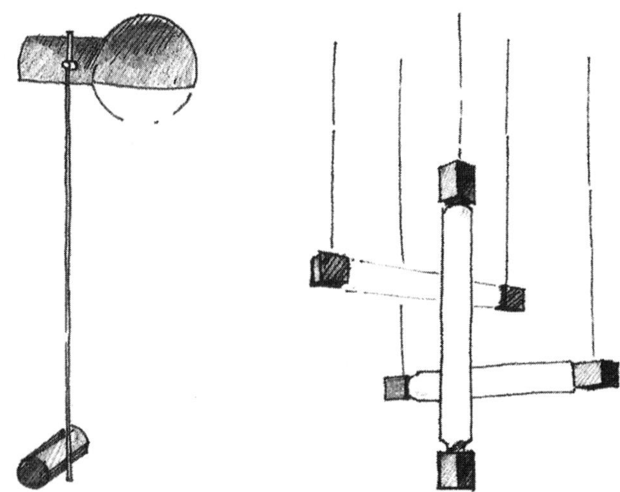

▲ **48-6.** Lighting: Table lamp and hanging light, 1920s; Gerrit Thomas Rietveld.

out more than another. Unity results from the repetition and integration of like components. Furnishings are architectonic to create a seamless blend between fixed structure and mobile objects and to give greater multifunctionalism (Fig. 48-2).

Public and Private Buildings

■ *Color.* The palette has the primary colors of red, blue, and yellow arranged within compositions of white, black, and gray (Fig. 48-1, 48-2, 48-5, 48-8). Occasionally, some designers use the secondary colors of orange, green, and purple.

■ *Floors.* Tile floors in black and white asymmetrical compositions are common. Sometimes other colors are added. Wood floors are less common. Occasionally, colored rectangles or squares compose floors, as they do walls or ceilings (Fig. 48-2).

■ *Walls.* Walls articulate space rather than confine or separate it. They are plain, flat, smooth, and sometimes movable. Usually designers emphasize geometric patches of color, treat walls as separate compositions, align colored planes, and highlight vertical and horizontal elements (Fig. 48-2, 48-4, 48-5).

■ *Windows.* Windows are plain and simple (Fig. 48-2). Most are left bare of coverings. Some have sliding screens to hide the sun or flat treatments, such as roller blinds, that blend in with the wall composition.

■ *Ceilings.* Some ceilings are plain and flat, and painted white or a light gray. Others become artistic canvases with bold geometric designs related to the wall treatments (Fig. 48-2, 48-4, 48-5). Variations in ceiling heights within an individual interior are rare.

■ *Lighting.* Natural light enters the interiors through large windows and sometimes skylights. Light fixtures are architecturally designed and integrated into the walls and ceilings. Examples include chandeliers, surface-mounted globes, and movable floor and table lamps (Fig. 48-6).

▲ **48-7.** Later Interpretation: Atrium, High Museum of Art, 1980–1983; Atlanta, Georgia; Richard Meier. Late Modern.

■ *Later Interpretations.* Bauhaus designers borrow many ideas from the De Stijl group, particularly their concepts for simplicity, geometry, and color. Later the Art Deco period, International Style, and Late Modern developments may use one or more of DeStijl's ideas to define interior space, as expressed in Richard Meier's work (Fig. 48-7).

FURNISHINGS AND DECORATIVE ARTS

Furniture and decorative arts are conceived as one with the architecture and interior design. Designers similarly emphasize structure, construction, proportion, and the balance between solid and void relationships. They carefully place individual parts to develop visual balance and harmony so that all parts are appreciated alone as well as in context with the entire furniture piece. Great attention is given to the size of the part and its construction. Primary colors accent some components. Function is less important than conveying De Stijl concepts of design. Although the furniture and decorative arts look machine-made and some do incorporate machine production, very little is actually mass-produced. Rietveld's furniture (Fig. 48-2, 48-8) is the best known, but others such as Wils and Oud also design furniture for their projects. Chairs and tables are the most important conveyors of De Stijl concepts.

DESIGN SPOTLIGHT

Furniture: Gerrit Rietveld's furniture provides the best illustration of De Stijl concepts. His Red and Blue chair of 1918, the first chair recognized as totally abstract, is a Neo-Plastic icon of order, harmony, and minimalism. Its simple form, flat planes, and primary colors establish Rietveld's design language. The chair is made up of many small-sectioned pieces at right angles to one another that overlap without appearing to be joined. Painted black with yellow ends, they emphasize their supporting function and become the strong horizontals and verticals in a Mondrian painting. The diagonal seat and back are red and blue. Like his other furniture, the chair can also be easily produced by machine. As a craftsperson, Rietveld builds much of his own furniture, which permits him to experiment with form and color. The Red and Blue chair originally is stained wood but after connecting with De Stijl, Rietveld creates its well-known color combination. He also crafts other variations of its form and colors in other furniture, and later repeats these ideas in custom chairs, tables, and built-in furniture developed for the Schröder House.

▲ **48-8.** Red and Blue chair, 1918; Zig Zag chair, 1934; Berlin end table, 1923; and sideboard in beechwood painted with white aniline, 1919; Netherlands; Gerrit Thomas Rietveld. *(continued on next page)*

Public and Private Buildings

■ *Materials*. Most furniture is made of wood. It may be stained a dark color or painted in the De Stijl palette of red, blue, yellow, gray, white, and/or black (Fig. 48-2, 48-5, 48-8).

■ *Seating*. Chairs emphasize geometric components with variations in rectangular shapes and spatial composition (Fig. 48-2, 48-5, 48-8). Most are composed of quadrangular stretchers, legs, and arms that do not intersect but remain separate, especially at the joints. Seats and backs are solid rectangular planes. Color highlights individual parts and unifies with the surroundings for which the piece is intended. Just four planes compose Rietveld's Zig Zag chair. Two are horizontal and two are diagonal. The chair is produced by hand and machine. Rietveld's most commercially successful design is for Crate Furniture, a group composed of flat boards of red spruce. Pieces are bolted together by the purchaser.

■ *Tables and Storage*. Few tables or storage pieces are created. Rietveld designs a sideboard (Fig. 48-8) that resembles the one by E. W. Godwin in 1869. Rietveld adopts the interpenetrating horizontals and verticals in Godwin's design but puts greater emphasis upon them and the rectangular planes that make up the piece. His work also has a greater sense of lightness. The design reduces a traditional form to essential elements of structure. The Berlin end table (Fig. 48-8) by Rietveld, an experimental piece, is composed of four planes: a circular base, two interpenetrating rectangles for support, and a rectangular top. It is painted black, white, and red. The Crate Furniture group includes two occasional tables, a bookcase, and a desk.

■ *Decorative Arts*. Decorative arts are limited in De Stijl houses. Artwork is prohibited because the house itself is a piece of art. Few designers create decorative arts.

DESIGN SPOTLIGHT

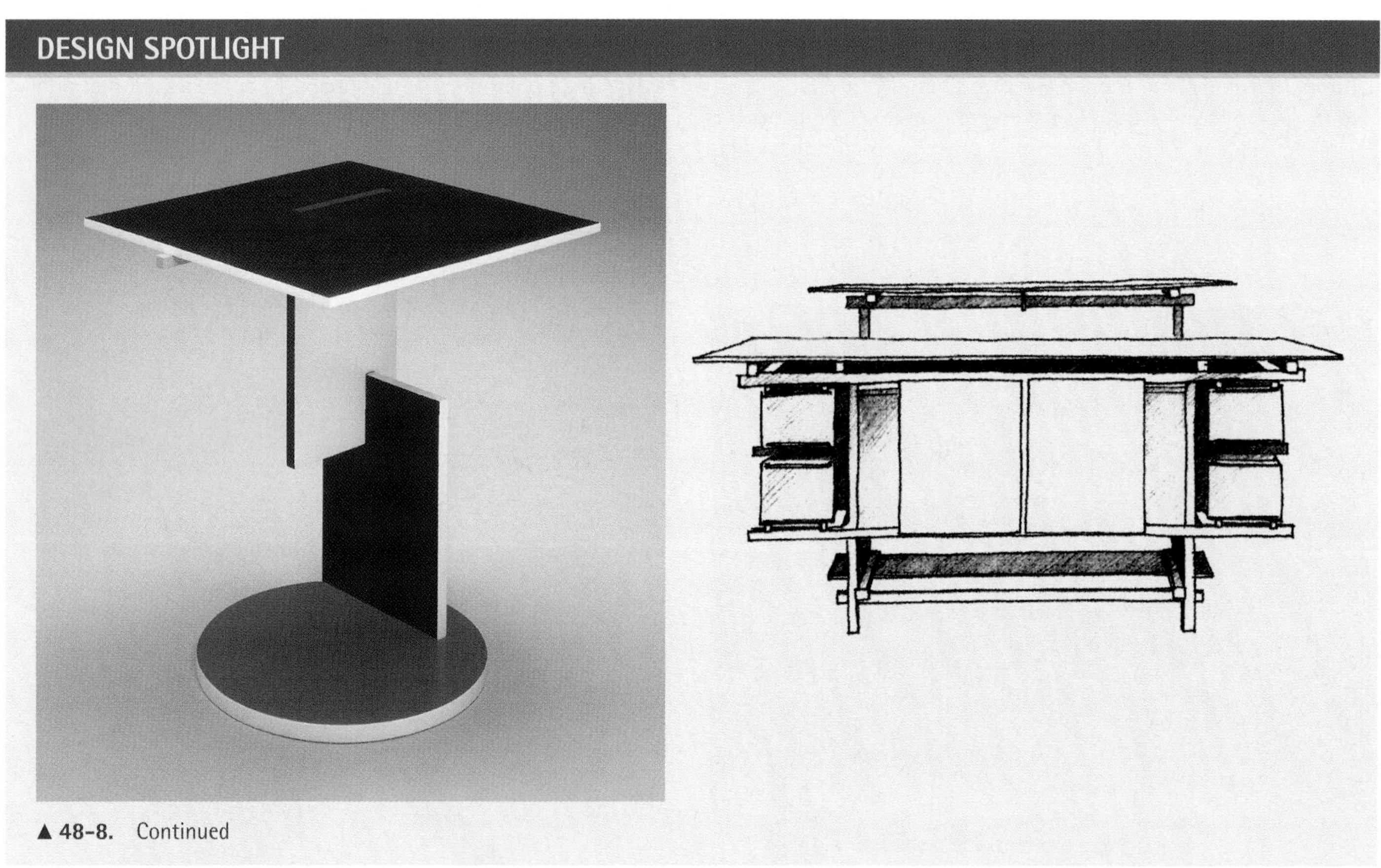

▲ **48-8.** Continued

CHAPTER 49

The Bauhaus

1919–1933

The Bauhaus in Dessau, Institute of Design, has developed more and more into a center for the gathering of all ideas concerning the contemporary intellectual and theoretical foundations of building. . . . The integration of the practical work and instruction at the Institute conveys to the coming architectural generation exactly that which has been missing up to now: an accurate knowledge of new technological inventions, constructions, and materials.

—Walter Gropius, "Request for Contributions to the Bauhaus," 1927

The Bauhaus, an innovative German school of art and design, strives to unite art, craftsmanship, and technology in an aesthetic expression that reflects modern industrial life. Founded in 1919 by Walter Gropius, the school uses a foundations course and workshop experiences to train students in theory and form, materials, and methods of fabrication. This enables them to design for and assume roles in modern industry. Although eschewing historicism and style, Bauhaus works reveal a similar character through emphasis upon function, mass production, geometric form, an absence of applied ornament, and the use of new materials and methods of construction. The Bauhaus has a significant impact on art education, architecture, interior design, textiles, and furniture through its ideas, attitudes, principles, and products.

HISTORICAL AND SOCIAL

In 1919, the armistice of World War I, formalized in the Treaty of Versailles, dissolves the German Empire with its kingdoms and duchies and creates a new government, the Weimar Republic. The treaty also ascribes sole responsibility for the war to Germany, so Germany is required to make restitutions. The resulting inflation, unemployment, food shortages, and widespread destruction of industry and housing set the stage for the growth and acceptance of radical political groups. Although some stability is achieved in the late 1920s, the economic depression of 1929 destroys it. The Weimar Republic is defeated in the 1933 election by the Communist and National Socialist Parties, or Nazis. The Nazis gain control and set up a totalitarian state led by dictator Adolf Hitler.

It is into this culture of disarray, difficulty, and despair that the Bauhaus (literally, "house of building") comes into being. In Weimar, German architect Walter Gropius establishes a new school that merges the Grand Ducal School of Arts and Crafts (originally headed by Henry van de Velde) and the Academy of Fine Arts. The school strives to unite all the arts with craft and technology, to elevate crafts disciplines to the level of the fine arts, and to establish connections with industry. Gropius further envisions a unity of art and technology, an end to historic style imitation, and an establishment of new cultural values.

The Bauhaus program of study uniquely combines academic and craft training. Upon entering the school, students complete a preliminary course (*Vorkurs*) lead by a Master of Form who is an artist. Coursework strives to develop the student's creativity and imagination through theory and experimentation in form and color. The remainder of the course of study consists of workshops in which students become acquainted with materials and techniques of construction by designing and making products. Reminiscent of a medieval guild, a Workshop Master leads the class.

Students (called apprentices or journeymen depending upon their skill levels) collaboratively learn by doing. Craft workshops include furniture, weaving, metalwork, ceramics, mural painting, photography, print and advertising, and theater.

Gropius also strives to establish connections between the school and industry. Links between schools or art associations and industry are stronger in Germany than in other countries. This is a result, in part, of government-sponsored organizations, such as the *Deutscher Werkbund* (German Work Federation), founded in Munich in 1907 by Hermann Muthesius. An association of architects, designers, craftspeople, manufacturers, and writers, the group emphasizes crafts education; tries to unify art and industry; and promotes simplified, machine-made German products internationally. Some architects and designers associated with the Modern Movement are members, including Peter Behrens. Others, such as Le Corbusier, participate in Werkbund conferences or exhibitions. In 1914, the Werkbund has a major exhibition in Cologne, Germany, that showcases the work of numerous designers, including Gropius. Mies van der Rohe heads the 1927 *Wiessenhofsiedlung* exhibit on mass housing. The association continues until 1933, but its influence lasts to the early 1940s, just before the start of World War II.

Although the Bauhaus receives funds from the state, these are never enough for complete autonomy. Workshops create prototypes for industry, which help to provide additional monies through patents, marketing, and sales. Besides providing practical experience, this furthers the goal of creating a new type of designer, one who can work with industry to provide inexpensive well-designed and well-made goods for the middle and working classes.

During the Weimar years, a lack of materials, funds, and facilities hampers the achievement of the school's goals. Nevertheless, it begins to develop a reputation for its work. In 1923, the Bauhaus holds its first formal and public exhibition (Fig. 49-1), which is a huge success. In 1924, the political climate in Weimar changes, resulting in far less support monetarily and socially. Additionally, the state's contract with the Bauhaus ends, so Gropius is forced to move the school.

In 1925, the Bauhaus reopens in Dessau, a larger, more industrial city than Weimar. The program is reorganized. Workshop Masters and Masters of Form become professors, who include Josef Albers, Marcel Breuer (furniture, cabinetmaking), Wassily Kandinsky (basic instruction), Paul Klee (stained glass and basic instruction), Laszlo Moholy-Nagy (metal, lighting), George Muche (weaving), and Gunta Stölz (weaving). Function, geometry, and a design vocabulary that emphasizes mechanization and mass production become the focus of study and production. Some workshops, such as stained glass, are closed because of budget limitations, whereas others, such as cabinetmaking and metalwork, are combined. Ties with industry increase, bringing greater opportunities and more money, although the school is never quite self-supporting. A Bauhaus company to market designs opens, and a school journal and Bauhaus books are published. Most important, the department of architecture opens. Gropius designs new facilities for the school (Fig. 49-2) that announce to the world its modern machine aesthetic and design principles. The Bauhaus begins to achieve an international reputation.

▲ **49-1.** *Staatliches Bauhaus Ausstellung* (National Bauhaus Exhibition), 1923; Josef Schmidt; Weimar, Germany.

Relations with the city and state remain tenuous at best, so in 1928, Gropius resigns as director of the school, hoping a new leader will improve the relationship. New director Hermann Meyer is an architect who strengthens the architecture department so that other workshops become subordinate to it. He also broadens course content to include anatomy, psychology, and economics. Meyer encourages students to become politically active, which increases tensions with the city. These tensions lead to his forced resignation in 1930.

Architect Ludwig Mies van der Rohe succeeds Meyer. Mies strives to regain a positive reputation by ending political activism. He emphasizes architecture more than Meyer did; consequently the school has two main emphasis areas: architecture, which focuses mainly on theory; and interior design, composed of the furniture, metalwork, and mural painting workshops. But all is not well.

In 1931, the Nazis take over Dessau. They regard the anonymous, modern style produced by the Bauhaus as anti-German. Equally suspect are the Jewish teachers and students, so the school is closed in September 1932. After moving to an unused telephone factory in Berlin, it barely survives on student tuition, receiving no state funds. When the National Socialist party takes over the country, the Bauhaus closes in April 1933. However, its pedagogy, design methods and principles, aesthetics, and products live on in its teachers and students who emigrate to other European nations and the United States. Many of its graduates find positions in education and industry. Bauhaus architecture and furniture become and remain statements of the Modern Movement, influencing countless designers and students of design. Projects by leading architects at the school convey a new, original language for architecture that has a significant impact on 20th-century design.

CONCEPTS

Bauhaus design concepts include an emphasis on the functional aspects of the object, an honest statement of form and truth of materials, good design for mass production, use of the machine by the artist, integration of fine art and applied art, and the production of a new kind of beauty based on these factors. A rhetoric of truth, purity, and honesty reveals a moral dimension. Theory develops from practice. Designs grow out of the vocabulary of construction, economy, and practicality. Style, historicism, and applied ornament are rejected in favor of use, purpose, and the visual language of the machine. Designs strive to meet peoples' needs, and designers assume all have the same needs. A belief that democratizing design will, in turn, reform society reveals a utopian outlook. The overarching vision is one of artists and craftspeople collaborating on building projects because this, according to Gropius, is the ultimate goal of all creative activity.

Influences come from other painting and crafts approaches espoused by the Expressionists (demonstration of feelings), the Fauves (expressive color use), the Futurists (action sequences), the Blue Reiter Group (emotion and abstract symbols), the Cubists (deconstruction of three-dimensional compositions), the Dadaists (denying the importance of art), De Stijl (flat plane constructionist compositions), and the Arts and Crafts Movement (handcraft production). Other early influences include Frank Lloyd Wright, the Chicago School, and Far Eastern philosophies. The work of Adolf Loos also serves as a primary influence, particularly his simplicity of design achieved in white, box-shaped buildings.

CHARACTERISTICS AND MOTIFS

Striving to avoid a style, designers emphasize asymmetry, straight lines, rectangles, and flat planes. Parts are arranged in a series of geometric shapes and forms, usually with linear elements. Light and dark relationships are important. A machine aesthetic that includes functionality, simplicity, purity, anonymity, standardization, and flexibility or adjustability is a defining precept. Designers emphasize geometry to unify the whole of a building, interior, or piece of furniture. Other key characteristics are modern industrial materials, such as tubular steel, primary colors, and no applied ornament.

■ *Motifs*. There is no vocabulary for motifs because buildings are generally unadorned. Some architects include unique architectural details that are part of the building structure (Fig. 49-2).

ARCHITECTURE

Bauhaus-designed buildings become modern industrial products with an emphasis on purpose and form. Devoid of any applied decoration, they often are asymmetrical and three-dimensional, so that one must experience the building from all sides. This fairly new concept in design borrows from De Stijl influences. Designers frequently experiment with mass and rectangular form. Equally important is the structural order of a building to achieve regularity, often evident in the placement of interior columns and the use of standardized parts for construction. Most have flat roofs. Because flat roofs neither originate nor have a history of use in Germany, they are controversial and are seen as anti-German.

Although the school has no architecture department until it moves to Dessau in 1925, commissions by Gropius afford opportunities for collaboration in keeping with the goals of the school. One of the earliest is Sommerfeld House in Berlin, designed by Gropius and Meyer with decoration and furnishings by the Bauhaus workshops. More important is the Experimental House (*Haus um Horn*) designed by painter Georg Muche and furnished by Bauhaus workshops for the exhibit of 1923. Intended as a prototype for inexpensive mass-produced housing, it features innovative planning and furnishings of the latest materials. Important commercial buildings include schools (Fig. 49-2), offices, and government buildings. Apartment projects, low-cost housing complexes (Fig. 49-5), and individual houses (Fig. 49-2, 49-4) are equally significant. Architects Gropius and Mies create the best known projects.

Public and Private Buildings

■ *Site Orientation*. Architects orient buildings so that offices, living and dining areas, bedrooms, and roof gardens have the most sun exposure and take advantage of natural light. They place stairways, studios, kitchens, and bathrooms toward the north for softer light. Structures sit on flat plains of grass with limited plantings surrounding them and with only a few trees (Fig. 49-2, 49-4, 49-5). As a result, they stand out from their surroundings like pieces of geometric sculpture. In cities, fronts of buildings most often are parallel to the street. Some large housing complexes may have individual apartment fronts repetitively staggered or at an angle to take advantage of the sun and to increase privacy.

■ *Floor Plans*. Floor plans develop primarily from function, which may divide areas into units. Spatial organization, flexibility, practicality, ventilation, and privacy are very important. Some plans spread out to form open, geometric arrangements, while others are confined to a box shape. Rooms are most often rectangular, vary in size, and align along exterior walls that have large areas of glass. They may connect to interior halls or to each other. Sometimes instead of defined rooms, open spaces penetrate from one to another with only a few carefully positioned walls or vertical planes, as in the German Pavilion (Fig. 49-3). Major circulation paths, such as halls and stairs, are located centrally to support a direct, straight access. In houses, living, dining, and kitchen areas are on the ground floor, while bedrooms and studios occupy upper floors. Terraces and roof gardens extend the interior space.

■ *Materials*. The most important construction materials include steel, glass, and reinforced concrete, sometimes with a brick masonry applied on the face of the concrete (Fig. 49-2, 49-3, 49-4, 49-5). Industrial materials are used frequently.

■ *Façades*. Exteriors are plain, simple, and unornamented (Fig. 49-2, 49-3, 49-4, 49-5). Compositions emphasize asymmetry and repetition through solid and void proportional relationships. Solid, flat concrete surfaces, rendered most often in white, define and support the structure. On commercial buildings, large areas of repetitive windows and glass curtain walls over steel grids cover façades. On houses, windows often vary in size and placement to create interesting asymmetrical arrangements. Some may also have glass curtain walls. Cantilevered balconies or projecting roof terraces may punctuate the façade and add three-dimensional movement.

■ *Windows and Doors*. Windows may be fixed in grid patterns or be repetitions of different types such as casement, awning, and sliding glass (Fig. 49-2, 49-3, 49-4, 49-5). Repeating types of windows are a key characteristic. Groupings of fixed-glass and sliding-glass windows are common. Windows do not interrupt the overall smoothness of the façade, so black or white narrow moldings frame the openings and divide glass areas.

Entry doors, which are often recessed, integrate into the building composition so that they appear unobtrusive. They are plain, flat, and often wider than an interior door. Most are wood painted either black or white.

DESIGN SPOTLIGHT

Architecture and Interior: Rational planning and the primacy of function dictate the organization and appearance of the Bauhaus Buildings designed by Walter Gropius. The various buildings, which are separated by function but unified in appearance, form a sort of swastika, an unusual design in a time when courtyards predominate. Administrative offices join the workshops, auditorium, cafeteria, theater, and studios via a bridge across a road, which was never built. Façades exemplify Bauhaus design principles in the geometric forms punctuated with linear elements, broad windows, and flat roofs. The workshops have glass curtain walls to admit as much light as possible, and balconies identify dormitories. Constructed of reinforced concrete, the buildings are plain, geometric, and industrial. Inside, subdued colors distinguish different areas as a means of wayfinding. Contrasting textures identify load- and non-load-bearing walls. Walls have little articulation, relying on texture or color for interest. Students design and craft much of the furniture and lighting, a great deal of which is multi-functional and of tubular steel.

Gropius designs three semidetached houses for the Bauhaus masters and one detached house for the director. He aims for simple block construction of standardized, prefabricated parts, but limited technology of the day prevents complete realization of his goals. All four houses are cubic in form with interpene-

▲ **49-2.** Bauhaus buildings (studio, administration, classroom, and workshop), detail of workshop wing, Masters' House, 1925; Dessau, Germany; and office of the director, 1923; Weimar, Germany; Walter Gropius.

DESIGN SPOTLIGHT

trating solids and voids of different heights. Vertical windows light stairs and larger windows light the studios, which are placed away from the street. Terraces and balconies also are away from the streets. The semidetached houses have similar floor plans, and all the houses are equipped with Bauhaus-design built-in and free-standing furniture.

The director's office at the Bauhaus in Weimar, also by Gropius, shows common Bauhaus design principles of cubic forms, simplicity, plain walls, large windows, and an industrial appearance. Not only is the space itself cubic and unornamented, but so is the furniture, also designed by Gropius. The wall hanging and area rug supply the only color besides black and white. [World Heritage Site]

▲ **49-2.** Continued

■ *Roofs*. Roofs are mainly flat (Fig. 49-2, 49-3, 49-4, 49-5). A narrow, flat cornice trim surrounds, projects slightly, and defines the perimeter edge. It is usually black against the white façade.

■ *Later Interpretations*. Bauhaus influences and characteristics appear repeatedly in later periods and shape architecture throughout the 20th century. Designers whose work illustrates these influences include Le Corbusier; Philip Johnson, a protégé of Mies; Skidmore, Owings, and Merrill (Fig. 49-6); Richard Meier; and Peter Eisenman. Because many of the Bauhaus design theories and principles still inform education today, there are many practitioners who continue the language of industrialization and simplicity.

INTERIORS

Primarily the work of architects, interiors repeat the exterior vocabulary and are designed with the same goals as exteriors. Consequently, interiors stress simplicity, functionality, standardization, anonymity, and flexibility. They exhibit a similar importance of geometric forms, industrial materials, and no applied decoration. Efficiency, hygiene, and economy of space and time underscore planning and furnishings in much the same manner as factories. New types of rooms derive from new functions or building types, such as cafeterias and workshops in schools and design studios in houses. Many rooms are multipurpose.

DESIGN SPOTLIGHT

Architecture and Interiors: The German Pavilion, built of glass, different kinds of marble, and travertine, illustrates Mies van der Rohe's severely plain, geometric style that relies on careful proportions, precise details, and opulent materials rather than applied ornament for beauty. Clearly this is an architecture of volume, not mass. In the manner of a classical temple, the building rests on a travertine base, which it shares with a reflecting pool. The flat roof extends beyond the walls and is carried by interior columns whose slenderness is accentuated by their sheaths of reflective chrome. The space inside is asymmetrical and fluid. Mies places the walls of glass and marble at right angles to the flow of movement to help move visitors through the space to other parts of the exposition. Richness; strong contrasts of light and dark; and a variety of surfaces and textures, such as marble, glass, chrome, and rugs, characterize the interiors.

Mies designs chairs and other furnishings for the pavilion to accommodate the King and Queen of Spain when they officially open the exposition. Designed for royalty to sit in while signing their names into a guest book, the ample proportions of the famous Barcelona chair (Fig. 49-10) lend dignity and importance. The X shape of shining chrome and warm tufted leather are plain, modern, elegant, and aesthetically pleasing. Despite its machine-made appearance, the chair requires much handcraftsmanship. The frame is almost completely handmade, and the upholstery is composed of 40 individual pieces of leather sewn together. Mies designs the ottomans, which line one wall, in a similar shape and later adapts them to a bench and table. The pavilion is dismantled at the exposition's closing in 1930, but is rebuilt in 1986.

▲ **49-3.** German Pavilion (rebuilt) International Exposition, floor plan, and interiors, 1929; Barcelona, Spain; Ludwig Mies van der Rohe.

The light-filled spaces have minimal furnishings, patterns, and colors. Because most households no longer have servants, Bauhaus interior planning strives to simplify housekeeping and incorporate principles of household management. Breuer's kitchen in the Experimental House of 1923 is one of the first kitchens in Germany with built-in wall and base cabinets. Strictly functional, the design features a continuous work surface that eliminates the need for a table in the middle of the room.

Standardization of parts is characteristic. Often, as in the Masters' Houses at the Bauhaus, room shapes and proportions repeat from one building to another, but with variations in placement and height. Details may also repeat, but they remain simple and industrial looking. Built-in cabinets and storage areas, which are common, order the rooms so that they appear uncluttered and almost empty. Items, such as office supplies, books, glassware, and clothes, are hidden in specially designed compartments. All rooms are sparsely furnished, another factor that adds to the empty appearance. Furnishings arrangements are ordered, geometric compositions that integrate as a design component with the interior architecture. Most furniture is placed in open space, rather than against walls, in some harmonious relationship to the vertical planes (Fig. 49-3, 49-4). Sofas and chairs may be placed perpendicular to a wall to achieve a harmonious balance of form and shape.

DESIGN SPOTLIGHT

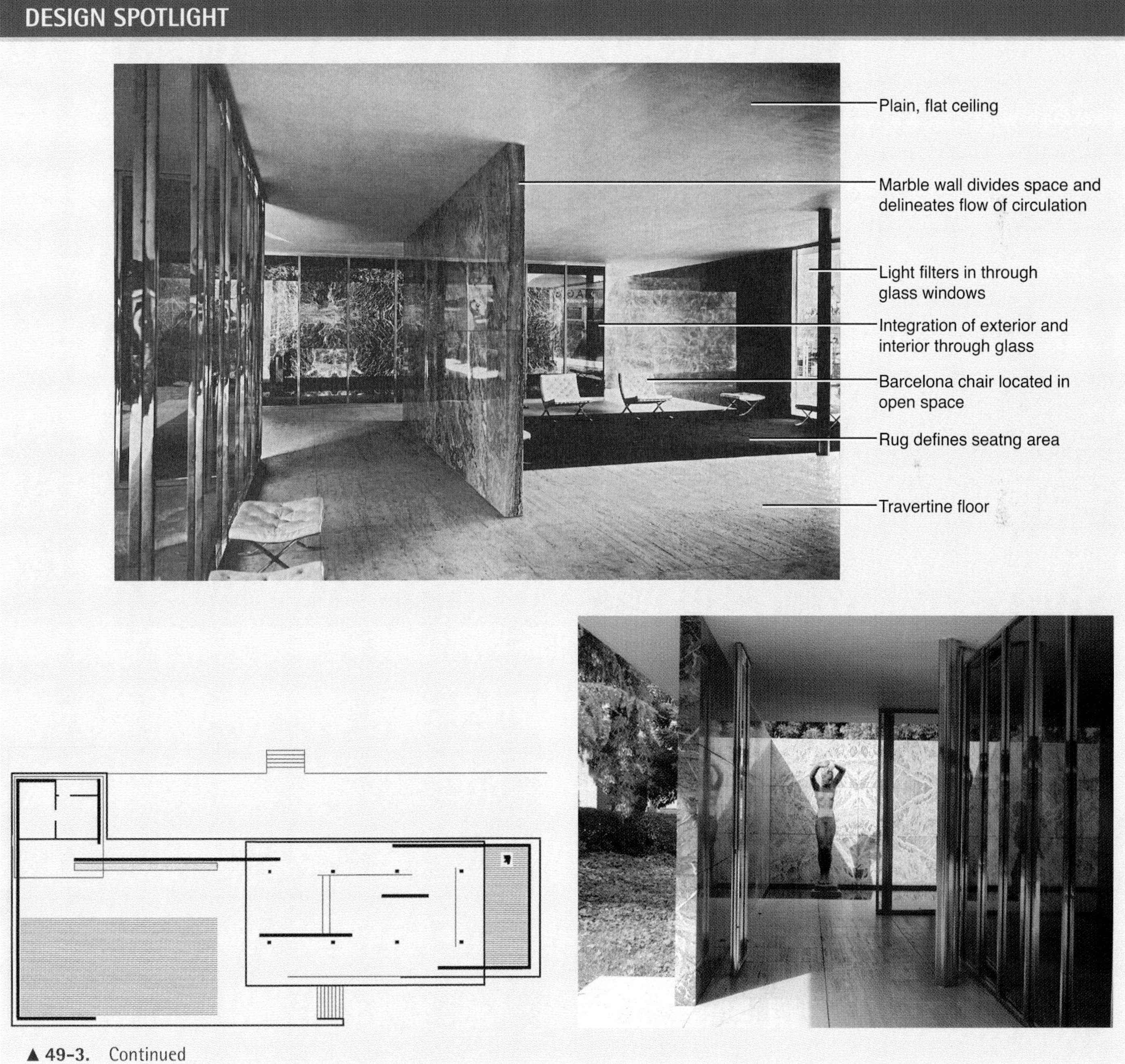

▲ **49-3.** Continued

Until 1928, the mural painting department usually designs interiors at the Bauhaus, while the cabinetmaking workshop supplies furniture. In 1928, Meyer combines mural painting with the metal and furniture workshops to create an interior design department. In addition to furniture, the department creates wallpaper that is sold to the public.

Public and Private Buildings

■ *Color*. Interiors are usually painted white and black, and sometimes gray (Fig. 49-2, 49-3, 49-4). Some walls may be accented with a warm or cool hue or have a large multicolored mural or textile hanging (Fig. 49-7). Large areas of flat color highlight architectural features, such as walls or ceilings. Within the Bauhaus buildings in Dessau, color differentiates areas and provides a means of wayfinding.

■ *Floors*. The most common flooring materials are tile and linoleum. Mies uses richer materials, like travertine, marble, and onyx, more than other Bauhaus designers do (Fig. 49-3, 49-4). Wall-to-wall carpet is rare, but area rugs in brightly colored geometric designs created by the weaving workshop are more common.

■ *Walls*. Most often, solid walls are flat and white with no ornamentation (Fig. 49-2, 49-3, 49-4). They may be broken up into rectangular units or standardized parts for ease of construction. The intent is to achieve an industrial, slick appearance. Some walls are accented in a bright color, while others may feature a mural with geometric designs that becomes an architectural component of the interior. Wallpaper and wall hangings created by the textile workshop appear less commonly in interiors. The mural painting department designs wallpapers with subtle, textural designs that are marketed by several firms and produce consider-

▲ **49-4.** Tugendhat House, living room, and dining room, 1930; Brno, Czechoslovakia; Ludwig Mies van der Rohe.

▲ **49-5.** Apartment complex, Weissenhof Housing Development, 1926–1927; Stuttgart, Germany; Ludwig Mies van der Rohe (planning director) with others.

able income for the school. Large wood, marble, onyx, or travertine walls may serve as focus points to shape and define spaces. Mirrors sometimes cover large wall areas to extend a space. Occasionally walls may be totally of glass so that there is a seamless integration of space from outside to inside, thereby allowing a person to participate with nature. Baseboards and architectural trim are usually painted black. Chrome columns are seen in some structures, such as the Tugendhat House by Mies van der Rohe (Fig. 49-4).

▲ **49-6.** Later Interpretation: Lever House, 1951–1952; New York City, New York; by Gordon Bunshaft at Skidmore, Owings, and Merrill. Geometric Modern.

▲ **49-7.** Textiles: Wall hanging from the weaving workshop at the Bauhaus, c. 1920s; Germany; Benita Otte.

■ *Windows and Doors*. Interior window trims repeat the simplicity of the exterior with narrow moldings used to define and frame the opening (Fig. 49-2, 49-3, 49-4). Some windows are intentionally left bare to enhance the architectural character, while others may have very plain floor-to-ceiling paneled curtains or shades in neutral colors. Interior doors are plain, unpaneled, and usually of wood or metal. They may be stained or painted black or white. Surrounding trim is plain and narrow.

■ *Textiles*. Weavers Gunta Stölzl, Lilly Reich, Anni Albers, and Benita Otte (Fig. 49-7) produce numerous unique and creative pieces. Factory production techniques and processes influence the end products, which include wall hangings, tablecloths, rugs, and upholstery in bright colors and geometric and abstract designs. The most popular upholstery materials are canvas, leather, pigskin, sheepskin, and cowhide, in natural colors.

Because of a lack of materials, early examples display a creative use of nontextile materials such as fur, wire, or beads. These early creations are individually designed and produced; later emphasis switches to designs for mass production. Under the directorship of Meyer, the Bauhaus introduces new concepts for interior textiles by creating fabrics with specific characteristics or to meet functional requirements, an outgrowth of investigations into strength, colorfastness, and other physical qualities. Designers also experiment with fabrics made of aluminum, glass, or cellophane. Structure and texture instead of pattern create interest. Draperies and upholstery fabrics are simply constructed with either a few small pattern repeats or none, and in only one or two colors. In the 1930s, designers create coordinating wallpapers and textiles.

■ *Lighting*. Glass and metal table lamps, task lights, hanging lamps, and ceiling fixtures emphasize form and function (Fig. 49-4, 49-8). Designs, a pleasing combination of curves and straight lines, adopt a machine vocabulary. Most are made of plain, brushed, or lacquered steel, aluminum, or glass with opalescent and frosted glass globes or shades. Lamps and hanging fixtures often have movable arms and shades that offer adjustability. Flexibility for the user is a key consideration.

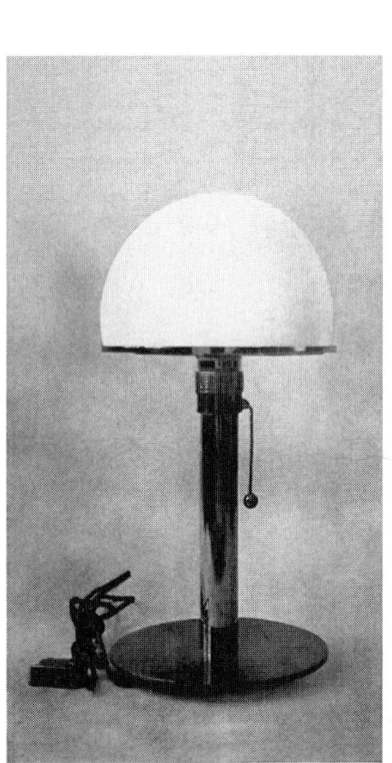

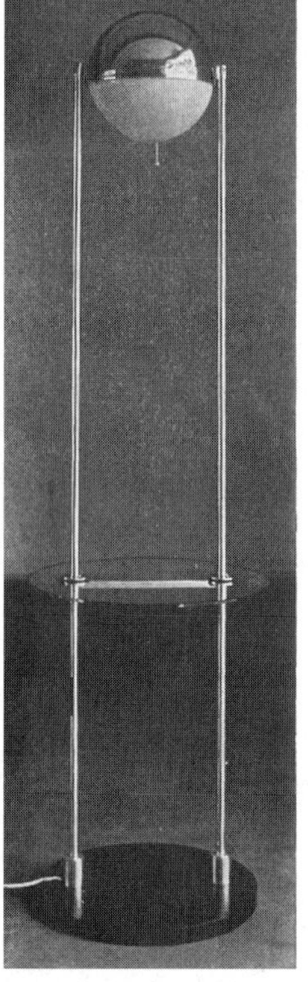

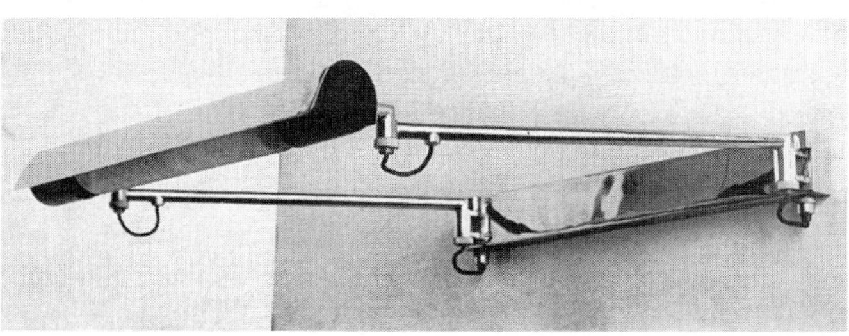

▲ **49-8.** Lighting: Desk lamp, floor lamp, and wall sconce, c. 1920s; Germany.

The lighting workshop, particularly after moving to Dessau, creates many successful and innovative fixtures and lamps that are mass-produced and marketed by various firms. One is the 1927 *Wandarm* (wall arm) wall lamp with its adjustable reading light and push-button switch that is designed for hospital rooms.

■ *Ceilings*. Ceilings are most often flat, plain, and painted either white or black (Fig. 49-2, 49-3, 49-4).

FURNISHINGS AND DECORATIVE ARTS

Unornamented and radically different from others, Bauhaus furnishings suit Bauhaus concepts of the modern home because they share the design goals. Designs, often of metal, are simple and functional with no applied ornament or historical style. Designs stress geometry; anonymity; excellent construction; and hygienic, easy-to-care-for industrial materials. Furniture is lightweight and space saving. That which is not built-in can be easily moved to support flexible arrangements. Because furniture is designed to be machine-made, important design considerations are standardization of form and interchangeable parts. Students investigate user needs as part of the design process so that resulting pieces support diverse user functions.

The furniture workshop opens in 1921 but is hampered by a lack of materials. De Stijl's Gerrit Rietveld or primitive or exotic sources inspire early furniture pieces. Design takes a radical turn from wood to tubular steel under the leadership of Breuer at Dessau. Later, under the direction of Meyer, the target market for furniture changes from the middle class to the worker. As part of the process of creating low-cost furniture for limited spaces, students study workers' possessions to develop appropriate storage furniture.

Leading designers Breuer (Fig. 49-9), Mies (Fig. 49-3, 49-10), and others experiment with tubular steel for construction, cantilevered principles, spatial composition, solid and void relationships, and factory production techniques. This gives rise to a new vocabulary that emulates the machine aesthetic of architecture. Much furniture is designed for Bauhaus buildings, and manufacturers purchase prototypes for mass production. Although less well known, some designers, including Breuer, create children's furniture such as cribs, chairs, and storage pieces that incorporate the newest ideas of child development.

Public and Private Buildings

■ *Materials*. Early prototype furniture and a few later designs are of stained, lacquered, or painted wood. During the 1920s, steel in tubular components or thin strips or sheets takes precedent (Fig. 49-9, 49-10). Besides its hygienic qualities, metal furniture looks machine-made, an important consideration to Bauhaus designers. Glass for tabletops is an innovation.

■ *Seating*. Side and armchairs, sofas, and some stools are the most common types of seating (Fig. 49-2, 49-3, 49-4, 49-9, 49-10). Breuer's fascination with tubular steel, reportedly arising from his bicycle's handlebars, inspires numerous forms of cantilevered

DESIGN SPOTLIGHT

Furniture: The Wassily chair of 1925 is the first one made of tubular steel that Marcel Breuer designs. Named for his friend Wassily Kandinsky, it was created for Kandinsky's home at the Dessau Bauhaus. Seeking a form and material that would be light yet sturdy and adaptable to standardization and mass production, Breuer, like others, explores the possibilities of tubular steel in this chair. For him, the material represents modern technology. The design is intricate as steel tubes intersect with and pass one another. The seat and back originally are of fabric and later of canvas or leather. Breuer chooses a warmer, softer textile to contrast with the cold steel. The chair is one of the most copied of Breuer's designs. The Cesca chair of 1928 uses a new cantilevered principle whereby the base is formed from a curved piece of tubular steel, making it lightweight and very portable. It uses softly curved wood stretchers for the caned seat and back. The nesting tables repeat the use of tubular steel and have laminate tops in primary colors.

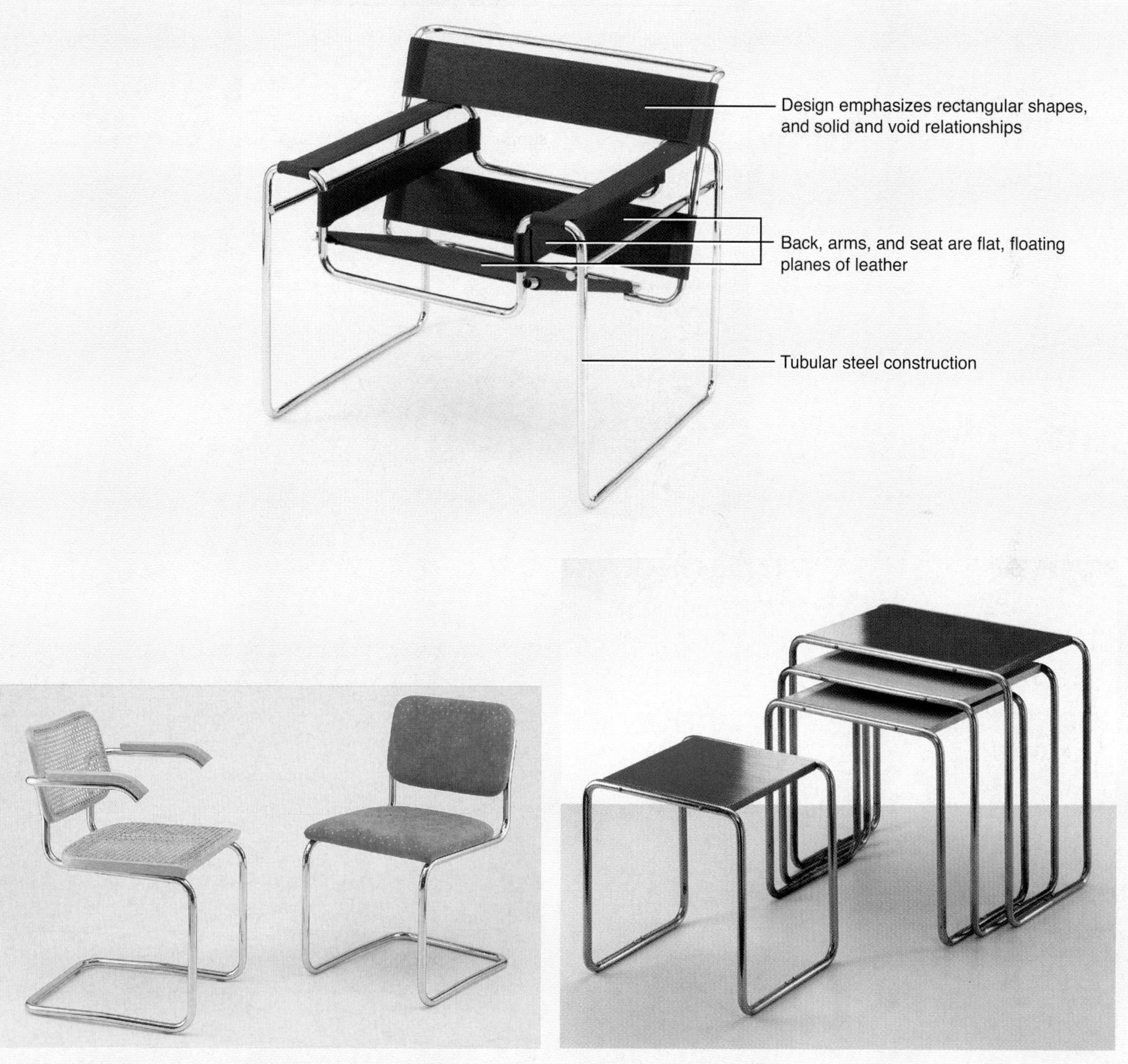

▲ **49-9.** Wassily chair, Cesca chair, and nesting tables, 1925–1929; Germany; Marcel Breuer.

chairs, which have no back legs but instead are supported by a continuous metal loop, an extremely novel idea at the time. Although Breuer promotes the industrial potential of cantilevered metal chairs, Dutch designer Mart Stam is credited with the design of the first one. Breuer's tubular steel chairs are rectangular with rounded corners and have backs and seats of leather or a durable textile developed in the Bauhaus textile workshop. In contrast, Mies's chairs often have broad, sweeping curves. The Bauhaus patents a cantilevered tubular steel work chair with an adjustable wooden seat. The workshop makes some wooden chairs with quadrangular legs and molded plywood seats and backs for adults and children. Fully upholstered chairs, which are less common, are composed of rectangular blocks of upholstery (Fig. 49-2).

▲ **49-10.** MR chair, 1926; Germany; Barcelona chair for the German Pavilion, 1929; Barcelona, Spain; and Brno chair, table with glass top and steel base, and platform couch, 1929–1930; Germany; Ludwig Mies van der Rohe.

Icons of Bauhaus seating design include Breuer's Wassily chair (named after painter Wassily Kandinsky) and Cesca chair (Fig. 49-9), and Mies's MR chair, Barcelona chair produced for the Barcelona Pavilion, and a platform sofa upholstered in leather (Fig. 49-3, 49-4, 49-10).

■ *Tables*. Some tables are of wood with a constructionist appearance. Designs feature interconnecting planes of wood. In the 1920s under Breuer's leadership, the furniture workshop designs round and rectangular cantilevered tubular steel occasional tables with glass tops (Fig. 49-10). Dining tables are simple and functional wood or metal (Fig. 49-4).

■ *Storage*. Bauhaus designers pay great attention to creating storage furniture for both adults and children. The workshop develops unit furniture, storage pieces of glass and metal or wood composed of individual modules with doors or drawers. Modules can be combined to suit the spatial and storage needs of the user. Like all other Bauhaus furniture, storage is plain and geometric with no ornament (Fig. 49-11).

■ *Beds*. Simplicity is a key factor in the design of beds. They are plain and low to the ground, and have tubular steel head- and footboards. Like other Bauhaus furniture, beds are machine produced in standardized units.

■ *Decorative Arts*. After 1923, the metals workshop produces ashtrays, tea and coffee services, kettles, dresser sets, and pitchers in brass, bronze, and silver (Fig. 49-12). Forms are simple and geometric with no applied ornament. Most are machine-made. The ceramics workshop is highly successful in designing industrial prototypes and handmade wares. Early pieces reflect the vernacular tradition in earthenware. Later designs in stoneware are modular, geometric, and plain, often with decorative glazes, and relate to each other without applied decoration. Individual parts could be made in the same molds, a process that approaches mass production.

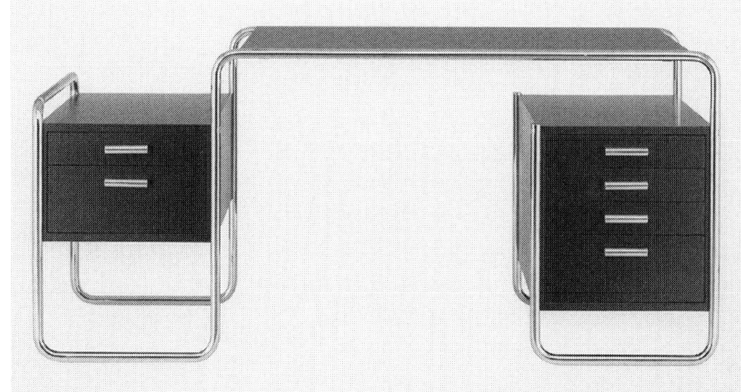

▲ **49-11.** Desk, 1923–1931; Germany; Walter Gropius and Marcel Breuer.

▲ **49-12.** Decorative Arts: Metalwork, 1924–1925; Germany; M. Brandt.

▲ **49-10.** Continued

O. MODERNISM

For the most part, Modernism strives to design for the present and eliminate most traditions, forms, and elements of the past, rejecting historicism, the academic tradition, and the idea of style. Many consider the past obsolete, offering no solutions to modern problems. To seek solutions from the past is to regress, and to look toward modern science and technology is to progress and to be modern. Modernists believe that a new architecture, interiors, and furniture are needed for modern lifestyles, which are hurried, tense, and shaped by the machine. Although Modernism sees itself as separate from what had gone before, in reality it builds upon ideas from 19th-century design reform movements, such as Arts and Crafts; Art Nouveau; De Stijl; the Bauhaus; and innovative designers, such as Frank Lloyd Wright and Peter Behrens. These ideas include honesty of materials, revealed structure, and the use of modern materials and techniques. Much of Modernism rejects ornament or applied decoration and prefers abstraction over objective design, rationality, and geometric forms. Additionally, Modernist designers emphasize functionalism for use and as a design concept, seek universal solutions over individual ones, and embrace a machine aesthetic.

Several movements, each with different ideas or theories of what it means to be modern, occur during the first half of the 20th century. The International Style arises in Europe in the 1920s and gets its name from a 1932 exhibit at the Museum of Modern Art in New York. Evolving from Bauhaus design language, characteristics include regularity, volume over mass, geometry, steel framework and glass curtain walls, smooth white walls, minimal color, and no applied ornament. Although it is most common in architecture, interiors and furniture follow its principles.

Art Deco develops in Paris about 1910. After making a strong impact at the *Exposition Internationale des Arts Decoratifs et Industriels Modernes* held in Paris in 1925, Art Deco quickly becomes a worldwide style in all arts, including architecture, interiors, and furniture. Its manifestations range from highly decorative and lavish to geometric and simple. Unlike other Modern styles, Art Deco retains a respect for the past and relies on capitalism and consumerism to spread its aesthetics. Closely aligned with Art Deco is Art Moderne, a simplified geometric style with more curvilinear forms.

The Scandinavian countries, Denmark, Sweden, Finland, and Norway, create their own version of Modernism called Scandinavian Modern. The style unites elements of the Bauhaus or International Style with Scandinavian traditions. Expressions in architecture, interiors, furniture, and the decorative arts are simple, functional, and often minimal. They feature natural materials, such as wood, and reveal a concern for the individual over the universal. Scandinavian design retains a strong sense of pride in the traditions and collective design identity of Scandinavian countries.

Beginning in the 1930s, Geometric Modern continues the design language and many of the important ideas of the Bauhaus and the International Style in architecture, interior design, and furniture. Definitive characteristics include regularity, rectilinear grids, geometric form, no applied decoration, and functionalism. New materials, technologies, standardization, and prefabrication drive goals and concepts. Modernism aligns with capitalism during this period and becomes the style for office buildings and commercial structures as well as commercial interiors and furnishings.

Paralleling Geometric Modern, Organic and Sculptural Modern rejects its geometry and hard edges and instead looks to sculpture or living organisms for inspiration. It shares simplicity, little applied ornament, and mass production with other modern designs, but it expresses a unified symbolic design language. Designs may be curvilinear, spherical, or parabolic in form. Elongation, abstraction, and asymmetry also are common. Organic and Sculptural Modern becomes very popular in furniture and the decorative arts following World War II.

Although Modernism is mainstream, Historicism and period styles continue to appeal to many people throughout the 20th century and into the 21st. Modern Historicism uses past styles to represent family heritage; express context; or to signal a function, a theme, or a brand. Designers adopt a variety of methods as they make period styles relevant to modern lifestyles and needs. These may include reproducing or replicating the past; suggesting or alluding to the past; or creatively adapting vernacular, historical, or classical principles, elements, and/or attributes. The result often is intrinsically modern, and it usually is evident that this is a building or interior of its time. Common styles, themes, or movements include Historic Preservation, Suburban Modern, Period Interior Decoration, and a new Classical Revival in the late 20th century.

CHAPTER 50

International Style

1920s–1930s

> *The distinguishing aesthetic principles of the International Style as laid down by the authors [Hitchcock and Johnson] are three: emphasis upon volume—space enclosed by thin planes or surfaces as opposed to the suggestion of mass and solidity; regularity as opposed to symmetry or other kinds of obvious balance; and, lastly, dependence upon the intrinsic elegance of materials, technical perfection, and fine proportions, as opposed to applied ornament.*
>
> —Alfred H. Barr, Jr, preface of *The International Style*, 1932

The International Style broadly refers to a modern architectural style appearing in Europe in the 1920s, and in the United States and the rest of the world from the 1930s onward. More narrowly, the term refers to a 1932 exhibit at the Museum of Modern Art in New York City. Synonymous with modernism and evolving from the work of a small group of architects, characteristics of the International Style in architecture include geometric forms, regularity, volume instead of mass, smooth white or glass walls, minimal color, and no applied ornament. The style comes to dominate commercial architecture, factories, and public housing in the United States and Europe. Interiors and furniture exhibit a similar aesthetic.

HISTORICAL AND SOCIAL

The International Style gets its name and identity from "Modern Architecture: An International Exhibition," a 1932 show at the Museum of Modern Art in New York City organized by Alfred Barr, Henry Russell Hitchcock, and Philip Johnson. The exhibit features projects from the late 1920s and 1930s by architects in Germany, France, Czechoslovakia, Switzerland, Holland, Scandinavia, and the United States. The group includes Bauhaus designers Walter Gropius and Ludwig Mies van der Rohe; De Stijl advocate J. J. P. Oud; French architects Charles-Edouard Jeanneret (known as Le Corbusier), Pierre Jeanneret, and Andre Lurcat; and American architects Richard Neutra and Rudolph Schindler.

Published in conjunction with the exhibit is *The International Style Since 1922*, which becomes the definitive treatise on the new architecture. In it, Henry Russell Hitchcock and Philip Johnson give a brief history of style in general and the Modern movement in architecture, and articulate the language and vocabulary that defines the style. Hitchcock and Johnson also emphasize the architect and the industrial designer over the artist and craftsperson. Discussions of planning, structure, materials, and color ensure that the publication becomes a handbook for the International Style. The authors classify architecture as International Style by three broad principles: 1) emphasis upon volume rather than mass; 2) regularity arising from standardized elements rather than axial symmetry; and 3) emphasis on proportions and materials rather than arbitrarily applied decoration. Their choice of buildings for the exhibition based upon these principles promotes a strong homogeneity, yet some individualism is also apparent.

Hitchcock and Johnson identify four leaders of modernism, all Europeans: Walter Gropius, Mies van der Rohe, J. J. P. Oud, and Le Corbusier. Although they acknowledge the pioneer work of Frank Lloyd Wright, they dismiss it as romantic and individualist. The authors include some American work, such as skyscrapers, and that of Europeans who work in the United States—Rudolph Schindler, William Lescaze, and Richard Neutra. By identifying visual characteristics of modern European architecture, Johnson and Hitchcock characterize it as a style instead of a movement. They largely ignore the social and political reforms attached to modernism as well as the idealism and theories of designers such as Le Corbusier. While not well received by the European designers, this omission makes International Style architecture more acceptable in the United States, a country that does not have the social and political upheavals that help inspire modern European architecture.

The exhibit is a seminal event for modern architecture in the United States because it makes modern architecture acceptable to designers and the public. This sets the stage for the United States to become the leading world power and main promoter of modernism in architecture and design following World War II. Although social and economic climates aid this development, the presence of European artists, architects, and designers furthers modernism as well as validates it. Prior to and during the war, many designers, including some from the Bauhaus, migrate to England and the United States, which become safe havens for the nourishment and growth of new ideas.

CONCEPTS

The International Style is a product of converging ideas of early-20th-century architects in Germany, France, and Holland. The group believes that the development and implementation of modern materials and construction methods, including reinforced concrete and steel, demands a new architecture both for new building types, such as public housing, and existing ones, like private dwellings. Instead of reinventing the past or maintaining the status quo, modernist architects challenge traditional ways of designing and construction methods and look for ways to improve life through modern architecture. Additionally, the enormous upheavals and devastation of World War I engender widespread disillusion with European politics and culture, including the Beaux-Arts tradition in architecture. This, in turn, reinforces the earlier idea of an architectural style that expresses modern life and makes good design available to everyone. Many designers envision a functional, rational, and efficient architecture, like the machine, as a critical means to transform European culture by democratizing design and creating new ways of living and working for a modern industrial society. This vision also extends to interior planning and furniture.

Although there are no direct references to the past developments in the International Style, it builds upon the ideas and works of such designers and theorists as Adolf Loos, Peter Behrens, and Auguste Perret. Hitchcock and Johnson specifically cite as important contributors to the style the factory buildings and Bauhaus ideas of Gropius, the clarity and simplicity of Mies, the housing projects of Oud, and the work and writings of Le Corbusier.

CHARACTERISTICS AND MOTIFS

Following a Bauhaus design language, designers emphasize a machine aesthetic that includes functionality, simplicity, purity, anonymity, standardization, and flexibility. Open plans, smooth white surfaces, industrial materials, large areas of glass, geometry, and solid and void relationships are important. Interiors and furnishings complement the exterior design characteristics with an emphasis on simplicity and spaciousness.

■ *Motifs*. There are no motifs because buildings are generally unadorned. Some architects include unique architectural details that are part of the building structure, such as those on the Villa Savoye (Fig. 50-7).

▲ **50-1.** *Pavillon de l'Esprit Nouveau* and hall, *Exposition des Arts Décoratifs et Industriels*, 1925; Paris, France; Le Corbusier and Pierre Jeanneret.

ARCHITECTURE

The International Style emerges from theories, forms, technology, and construction methods developed during the late 19th and early 20th centuries by individuals, movements, and design schools. Of particular importance is the German school, the Bauhaus, where these ideas and methods come together. Bauhaus architecture, interiors, furniture, and other objects have a similar appearance because of the focus on geometry, economy, practicality, function, mass production, new materials and construction methods, and no or minimal applied ornament. Bauhaus designers and students strive to create works that can easily be mass-produced and meet the users' needs, which are assumed to be all the same. Designs spread through regional and international exhibits and the work of students and masters.

Another significant contributor to the International Style is Le Corbusier, who believes in a radical architecture as a tool for social reform and suggests new solutions for houses and urban planning. Key design characteristics of this vision of architecture include rejection of the past and decorative ornament and adoption of functionalism, machine precision, standardization, and purism, a theory that promotes universal forms and anonymity over individualism. Le Corbusier advocates a stronger machine aesthetic in architecture, identifies five important principles for modern buildings, and creates a modular system based upon human scale. He strives to create *objet-types*—universal solutions to problems in design—and looks to industry for models. His dictum that "a house is a machine for living in" summarizes his ideas that the precision, efficiency, and sleekness of the machine should be the example for all architecture, especially residences. His Dom-ino project (Fig. 50-3) of 1914 proposes a faster standardized construction method based upon prefabricated elements of reinforced concrete roof, ceilings, and walls defined and supported by slender columns.

Le Corbusier's "Five Points of New Architecture" include 1) *Pilotis;* 2) free plans because the structural frame is independent of the non-load-bearing walls; 3) a freely designed façade that is independent of structure; 4) strip or band windows; and 5) flat roofs for living space and gardens (Fig. 50-7). The free floor plan permits its organization to be adapted to individual clients. Le Corbusier also develops *Modulor*, a modular system in the tradition of the Greeks, which grows out of the Golden Section and measurements of the human body. His ideas for urban planning are very different from the garden cities proposed by the Arts and Crafts Movement or even the solutions of other modernist archi-

▲ **50-2.** Philadelphia Savings Fund Society (PSFS; now Lowes Philadelphia Hotel) and banking room, 1929–1932; Philadelphia, Pennsylvania; William Lescaze.

tects. Le Corbusier designs multistory towers within green space and working and shopping areas connected by roadways. His 1930 concept called *Ville Radieuse* (Radiant City) illustrates apartment complexes where elite and working classes live in units with an ordered division of functions by zones.

International Style buildings display simplicity; clean lines not obscured by ornament; and purity of forms, which are often cubes, cylinders, or rectangles (Fig. 50-1, 50-2, 50-4, 50-5, 50-6, 50-7). Some reveal floating planes. A skeleton, often of steel and reinforced concrete, carries the structure's load. This permits free and open floor plans that can adapt to any functional requirements and a thin exterior covering with no need to express structure. Thus, the exterior covering can be any material, even glass, and usually has a smooth surface. Because the design of the façade is independent of the structure, fenestration becomes an important design element. Doors and windows are no longer recessed to emphasize mass, and their frames are integrated into the structure. Bands of windows, including corner windows, are common. Some buildings, particularly residences, are raised above the ground on thin columns to take advantage of ground space. Roofs are often flat, sometimes with usable terraces or gardens. Some architects create individual compositions for the client or programmatic requirements, while others advocate one solution for many situations.

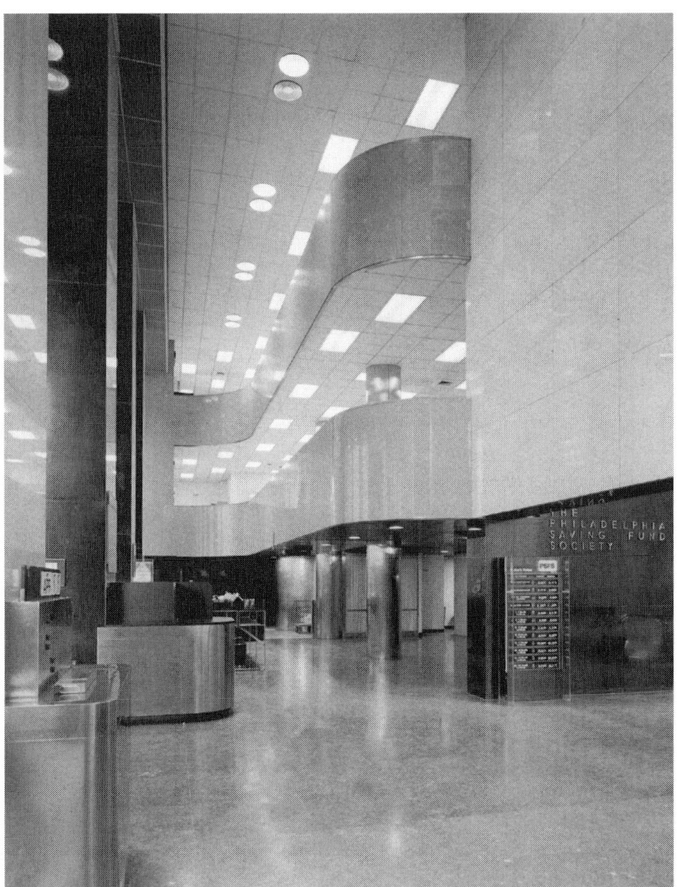

▲ **50-2.** Continued

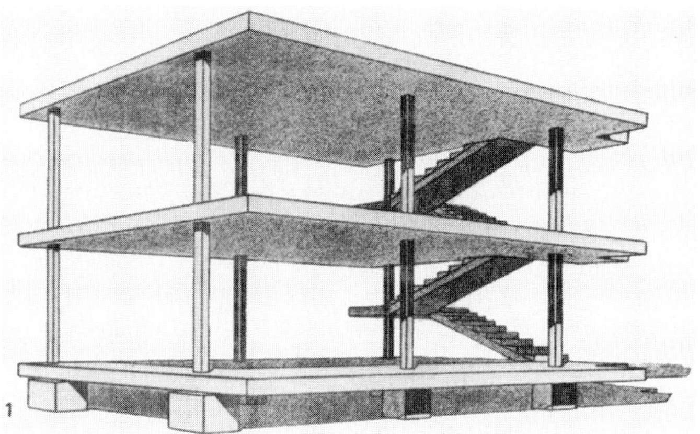

▲ **50-3.** Dom-ino Housing Project, 1914; Le Corbusier.

▲ **50-4.** Lovell Beach House, 1925–1926; Newport Beach, California; Rudolph Schindler.

Commercial building types include exposition pavilions (Fig. 50-1), stores, office complexes, banks (Fig. 50-2), and factories. Residences are a particular focus of the International Style because through them many architects make their ideas concrete. Le Corbusier, Neutra, and Schindler design houses that are a series of white boxy shapes with few architectural details, beautiful proportions, and a relationship of outside to inside, and look like pieces of sculpture within the landscape (Fig. 50-4, 50-6, 50-7).

Public and Private Buildings

■ *Site Orientation.* Architects place buildings to take advantage of the sun, such as locating terraces with southern exposure (Fig. 50-6). Some structures sit on flat plains of grass with only a few plantings around them because the designer wanted to contrast the artificial building with the natural environment (Fig. 50-7). Those in cities line streets and usually have little green space (Fig. 50-5). Urban housing structures are sited to provide the most light and air for each apartment.

■ *Floor Plans*. The structural skeleton permits free and individually determined floor plans (Fig. 50-7). They are usually asymmetrical arrangements with program requirements and room function determining placement. Major circulation paths such as halls and stairs are located centrally for direct access to entries, while private areas maintain spatial separation. Structural supports within interiors exhibit regularity.

Plans emphasize three concepts identified by Hitchcock and Johnson: interior volume, open space, and enclosed rooms. Thin vertical planes define large, three-dimensional, volumetric areas in nonresidential structures, such as exhibition spaces (Fig. 50-1), auditoriums, and stores. Some residences have a mix of one- and two-story open spaces (Fig. 50-6). Open, free-flowing interior space incorporates dividing screens to partition areas but at the same time support unity, interdependence, and continuity between spaces, such as between living and dining areas. Enclosed rooms with rectangular and square shapes vary in size, align along exterior walls with large areas of glass, and may connect to interior halls or to each other. In houses, like the Villa Savoye (Fig. 50-7), exterior and interior spaces flow together through such means as glass windows, ramps, and connected roof terraces. This interconnectivity of space is an important principle of International Style design.

▲ **50-5.** House; Versailles, France; published in *Examples of Modern French Architecture*, 1928; Andre Lurcat.

■ *Materials*. Smooth white stucco with large expanses of windows or glass curtain walls predominates (Fig. 50-1, 50-2, 50-4, 50-5, 50-6, 50-7). Construction materials include steel, glass, reinforced concrete, marble, granite, brick, glazed tile, concrete blocks, terra-cotta blocks, and aluminum.

■ *Façades*. Exteriors of public and private buildings are simple and unornamented, and compositions are independent of and de-emphasize structure (Fig. 50-1, 50-2, 50-4, 50-5, 50-6, 50-7). Walls serve primarily as screens, with an emphasis on transparency or thinness. The organization of elements usually stresses asymmetry and repetition through solid and void proportional relationships. Regularity in window placement helps to reinforce the solid-to-void conections. Large areas of rectangular windows and glass curtain walls with steel grids cover façades on commercial buildings and some houses. To create asymmetrical compositions on houses, designers employ windows varying in shape, size, and placement. Cantilevered balconies or projecting roof terraces accent the façade and create three-dimensionality.

■ *Windows*. Façades have many types of windows. They may be fixed or types that open, such as casement, awning, or sliding glass (Fig. 50-1, 50-4, 50-5, 50-6, 50-7). All are large and horizontal, and their rectangular shapes repeat across the façade but do not interrupt its smoothness. In houses, large windows may afford panoramic views to the outside, while smaller windows may focus to a private space. Corner windows and bands of windows de-emphasize structure and emphasize the thinness of the façade. Black or white narrow metal moldings frame window openings and divide glass areas.

■ *Doors*. Doorways integrate with the rhythm and regularity of the exterior so that they often become an extension of glass walls or solid surfaces (Fig. 50-5, 50-6, 50-7). Plain, flat entry doors may be glass or wood, or a combination of both. Projecting canopies may shield the entry area, or the entry may be recessed to provide protection.

■ *Roofs*. Flat roofs are common (Fig. 50-5, 50-6, 50-7). Sometimes a narrow, flat cornice trim surrounds and defines the perimeter edge. In houses, terraced roofs increase in use following the influence of Le Corbusier. Occasionally, a roof with a single slant is used.

INTERIORS

Primarily architects, who emphasize function, flexibility, efficiency, and practicality, create interiors. Form and proportion are more important than ornament and decoration are. Character comes from geometric forms, asymmetry, free-flowing and open spaces, and no applied ornament. Volume is important, so rooms often have high ceilings, and adjoining spaces may have different ceiling heights. Rooms are light and airy from large windows or glass walls. Spaciousness is important, so furnishings are minimal. There is little texture, pattern, color, and few decorative objects, which contributes to the anonymity. In some environments, exotic woods and stones are used as wall treatments. Furniture may be movable or built-in and of wood or metal with no applied ornament.

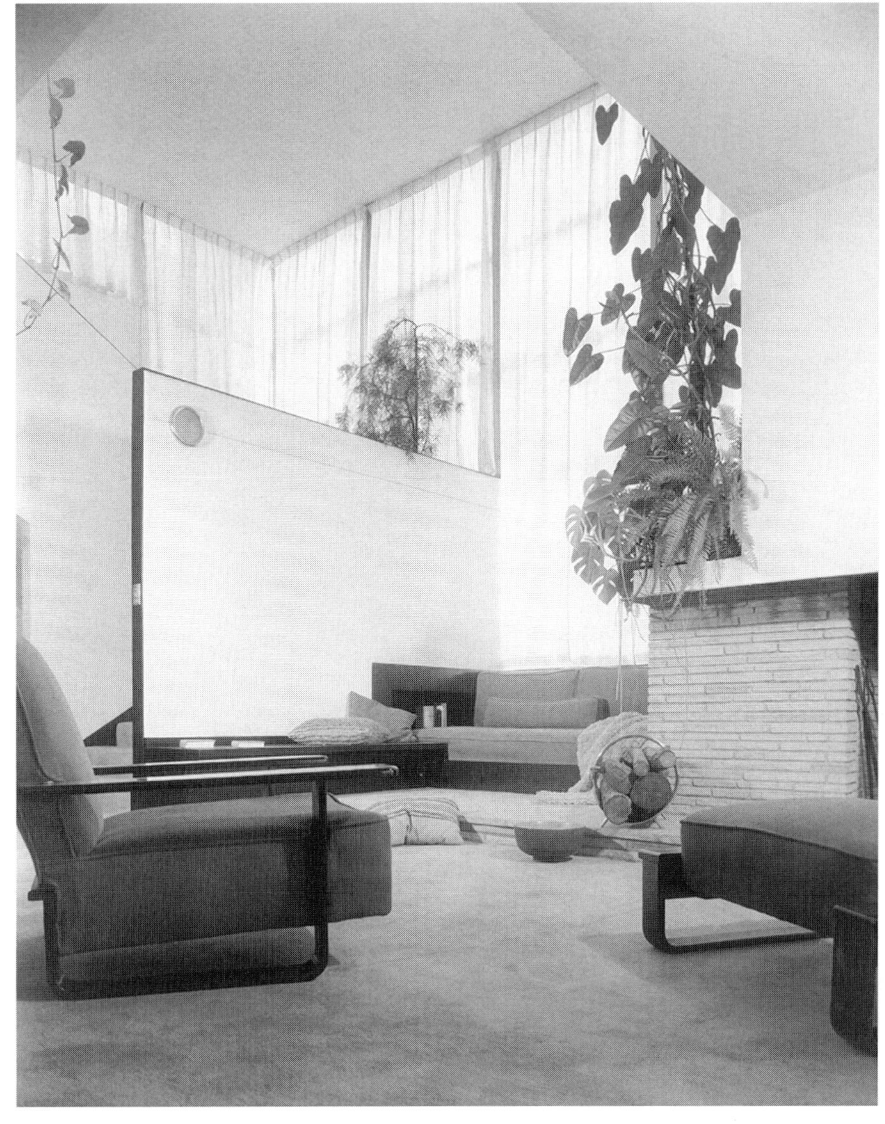

▲ **50-6.** Philip Lovell (Health) House and interior, 1928–1929; Los Angeles, California; Richard Neutra.

DESIGN SPOTLIGHT

Architecture and Interiors: The Villa Savoye is a weekend house for wealthy owner Pierre Savoye and his wife, who use it frequently until 1938. Considered to be one of the finest examples of 20th-century Modern architecture, it is the culmination of Le Corbusier's experimentation and investigations of purest form. In it, he employs his famous "Five Points of the New Architecture." Raised on slender *pilotis* (Principle 1), the house seems weightless and hovers above the ground. Each of the three floors has a different, free, and open plan, permitted by the independent structural frame (Principle 2). Le Corbusier arranges the interior spaces in a carefully planned progression. The ground floor area beneath the raised portion houses a three-car garage, servants' quarters, and entry. A ramp, which is considered one of several architectural promenades, and circular stairs provide vertical circulation. On the first floor is a living space that opens by sliding glass partitions to a terrace.

All four elevations are the same: a freely designed rectangular façade (Principle 3) with full-width strip windows (Principle 4) and curved screen walls on the roof. The stark white cubic form has classical proportions and contrasts with the surrounding landscape. The façade's strip windows frame views to the landscape beyond, permitting an interpenetration of outdoors with indoors. Pastel duck-egg blue and soft coral on living room walls recall the sky and atmosphere outside. The flat roof (Principle 5) provides additional living space, the integration of nature, light, and air, all of which are considered important in early 20th-century Modern residences. Le Corbusier chooses industrial interior finishes, such as ceramic tiles and smooth plaster surfaces, and sleek, industrial-style light fixtures. Similarly, the few pieces of furniture are mostly of modern materials such as tubular steel. Among the furniture is the *Chaise Longue* (1928), designed with Charlotte Perriand.

▲ **50-7.** Villa Savoye, roof deck, floor plan, entry with stairs, and living area, 1928–1931; Poissy, Paris, France; Le Corbusier.

DESIGN SPOTLIGHT

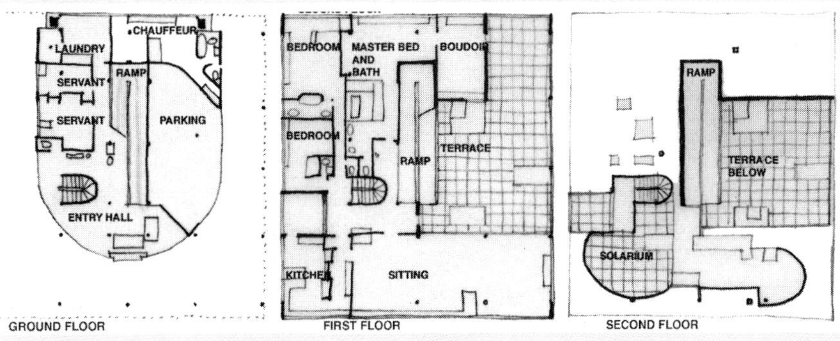

▲ **50-7.** Continued

As in other modern examples, similarity in design principles, organization, and materials create relationships between exteriors and interiors. Glass walls invite the outside into the interior and visually expand it. Important public and private spaces utilize the sun's exposure to take advantage of natural light and to emphasize the interconnectivity of exterior and interior space (Fig. 50-6, 50-7). A harmonious relationship and interplay of forms and shapes between and within exterior and interior are crucial.

Particularly important to the development of modernism and the International Style in housing and residences is the 1927 model housing exhibit *Weissenhofsiedlung*, held in Stuttgart, Germany, and sponsored by the *Deutsche Werkbund*. The exhibit opens the door wider for the acceptance of modernism and brings its principles into the home. The 21 model dwellings by Gropius, Le Corbusier, Oud, and others have open, fluid spaces instead of rooms to be decorated or filled with furnishings; double-height living spaces; and plain, simple furniture and accessories. Kitchens and baths are models with machinelike efficiency because designers plan them according to principles developed by the new discipline of domestic science or home economics. Many of these ideas are worked out in public housing where space is extremely limited.

Public and Private Buildings

■ *Color*. The color palette is simple, usually white and black, and sometimes gray (Fig. 50-6, 50-7). Accents of a single warm or cool hue may be used. In the Villa Savoye, Le Corbusier uses a range of accent colors, including blue, ochre, and coral.

■ *Floors*. Wood, tile, travertine, marble, and linoleum are the most common materials for floors (Fig. 50-7). Wall-to-wall carpet is rare, but area rugs, either plain or in geometric designs, may cover certain sections of the floors. For example, designers put rugs under seating groupings to add visual weight and tie the furnishings together.

■ *Walls*. Most walls are plain, unornamented, and painted white (Fig. 50-1, 50-2, 50-6, 50-7). Some walls are painted a bright accent color, while others may feature a colorful poster or painting with geometric designs. In more formal or expensive rooms, exotic woods or patterned stones may be chosen. Some walls are of glass blocks to allow natural light into a space, while others may have three-dimensional openings to shape and frame space. The interplay of solid and void space is very important, so architects experiment more than earlier with the articulation of interior structure. Walls that are completely glass integrate inside and outside space. Architectural trim is usually black or white to de-emphasize its importance.

■ *Windows and Doors*. Interior window trims are narrow moldings that define and frame the opening (Fig. 50-7). Many windows are bare, but others have plain curtains, blinds, or shades in neutral colors and plain or textured weaves. Doors are plain and usually in wood or sometimes metal. They may be painted black or white, or be stained. Flat, narrow door trims repeat the character of window moldings.

■ *Ceilings*. Ceilings are most often flat, plain, and painted white or sometimes black (Fig. 50-1, 50-2, 50-6, 50-7). Designers occasionally lower ceiling heights to create intimacy and use higher ones to emphasize scale.

■ *Lighting*. Glass and metal table lamps, task lights, wall sconces, hanging lamps, and ceiling fixtures show a machine vocabulary to stress function over ornament (Fig. 50-2). Light fixtures often are unobtrusive and blend in with the interior. Lamps and fixtures are made of plain, brushed, or lacquered steel; aluminum; or glass with opalescent and frosted glass globes or shades following Bauhaus design principles.

■ *Textiles*. International-style interiors usually have few textiles. Those that are used often have minimal texture, although a designer will sometimes use a strong texture for emphasis. Fabrics include canvas or plain, woven cottons or linens and animal skins. Black or natural leather is the most common upholstery material (Fig. 50-1, 50-7, 50-8).

FURNISHINGS AND DECORATIVE ARTS

Furniture and decorative arts follow the concepts and language of design established earlier by the Bauhaus designers and others. Many pieces are by architects. Designs are simple and functional with no applied ornament or references to historical styles. Anonymity, geometry, and hygienic industrial materials are key features. Many pieces incorporate tubular or flat steel for structural support. Although designers want to make well-designed furniture available to everyone, mass production of some of their designs is difficult and/or expensive because of technical innovations in construction that sometimes require hand labor. Furnishings may be built-in or movable to support flexibility in arrangements and different user functions. Modular units and stacking chairs offer additional flexibility. Designers, such as Le Corbusier, sometimes choose bentwood furniture or other simple pieces readily available on the market. Upholstered pieces often are covered in black, brown, or natural leather to coordinate with the stark interiors.

Furniture arrangements relate to the interior architecture. So sofas and chairs may center on a fireplace, and dining tables may align on axis with a window or wall openings.

Public and Private Buildings

■ *Materials*. Steel, aluminum, nickel, and wood are the usual furniture materials.

■ *Seating*. Seating consists of side and armchairs, lounge chairs, and sofas (Fig. 50-1, 50-7, 50-8). Le Corbusier, Pierre Jeanneret, and Charlotte Perriand create room ensembles with an array of tubular and flat steel pieces. Their designs, which emphasize the contours of the human body, are geometric with soft curves. The structural framework is exposed even on fully upholstered chairs and sofas, which is a radical idea at the time. Newly developed flat springs contribute to the development of the simple, uncluttered appearance desired. Some seating is adjustable. Other designers also use tubular steel or metal frames and experiment with different materials for seats. Rene Herbst, for example, uses elastic cords for seats and backs.

■ *Tables*. Square, rectangular, and round tables vary in size and scale based on function (Fig. 50-7, 50-9). Tops are most often glass

DESIGN SPOTLIGHT

Furniture: Furniture by Le Corbusier, Pierre Jeanneret, and Charlotte Perriand incorporates a structural framework, tubular steel, and leather, as shown in these examples. Seating pieces emphasize function and the contours of the human body. Designed initially for the Villa d'Avray, the *Chaise Longue* boasts a complicated construction system consisting of a separate supporting frame and seat to create a fully adjustable lounge chair. The rectangular supporting frame is of flat steel painted with a matte texture. The seat, composed of three planes that contour to the body, provides maximum comfort. It is covered with a light padding and canvas, leather, or pony hide and connected by steel tension springs to a curving tubular steel frame. A rubber covering on the cross members of the support frame permits the seat to be set at any angle chosen by the user, but one must get up to do so. The idea of adjusting the seat in this manner was new and innovative at the time. Le Corbusier noted that the chair's concept is derived from his idea of a cowboy lounging with his feet raised.

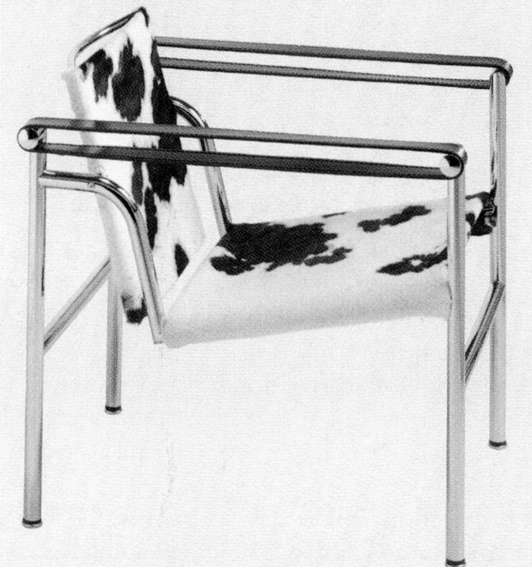

▲ **50–8.** Basculant armchair, *Grand Confort* sofa, and *Chaise Longue* in tubular steel, 1928–1929; France; Le Corbusier, Pierre Jeanneret, and Charlotte Perriand.

▲ **50-9.** E 1027 Occasional table, c. 1927–1928; France; Eileen Gray.

▲ **50-10.** Later Interpretation: Sling Lounge Chair 657, 1960; United States; Charles Pollock, manufactured by Knoll International. Late Modern.

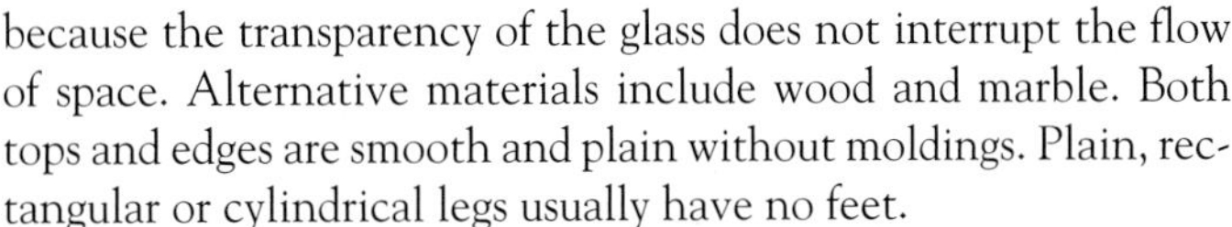

because the transparency of the glass does not interrupt the flow of space. Alternative materials include wood and marble. Both tops and edges are smooth and plain without moldings. Plain, rectangular or cylindrical legs usually have no feet.

■ *Storage*. Movable and built-in storage units help articulate the division of space within interiors (Fig. 50-1, 50-2). Most units integrate with the interior architecture. Made in modular sections, storage is plain, simple, and unadorned except for simple framing and hardware.

■ *Beds*. Beds are of wood or tubular steel with flat, rubber-coated springs. Most often headboards are low and unobtrusive, so the bed looks mainly like a flat horizontal plane and/or a geometric shape in a room. Twin beds may be grouped together to create a larger sleeping surface.

■ *Decorative Arts*. Decorative accessories are limited to a few, usually functional, pieces, such as bowls or ashtrays. Designs, which reveal a machine aesthetic, are simple, geometric, and unornamented.

■ *Later Interpretations*. Numerous designers in the 20th century draw inspiration from work by Le Corbusier and his contemporaries. Some include Donald Deskey, Charles Eames and Ray Eames, George Nelson, Gae Aulenti, Warren Platner, and Charles Pollock (Fig. 50-10).

CHAPTER 51

Art Deco, Art Moderne

1920s–Early 1940s

> *Ours is the era of the Machine. Machinery is creating our style. It is imposing a new tempo and a new mode of life. With shameful sentimentality we still cling to the outgrown "styles" of the past—to houses designed in period styles ridiculously alien to their settings; to gilded gewgaws and polished marbles, to pseudo-period furniture.*
>
> —Paul Frankl, *Form and Re-Form: A Practical Handbook of Modern Interiors*, 1930

Art Deco is an international style with a diversity of expressions in all the design arts, including architecture, interior design, furniture, decorative arts, graphic design, book arts, fashion, and film. Originating in Paris in the 1910s, this decorative, modern style makes a strong design statement at the *Exposition Internationale des Arts Décoratifs et Industriels Modernes* held in Paris in 1925. Art Deco ranges from highly decorative and lavish to geometric and simple. In the 1930s, American designers produce the related Art Moderne or Streamlined Modern, a simplified geometric style with curvilinear forms and modern materials.

HISTORICAL AND SOCIAL

Contrast and change, initiated by the social, political, and economic effects of World War I and continued industrialization, define the years between the two world wars. On one side, there is great growth and prosperity in many countries. Businesses are larger and more complex than ever, factories are producing more new goods, communication is faster and easier, and building booms in many countries provide more employment. Additionally, World War I brings a break with the past, so the world becomes enamored with the idea of Modern. To many people, Modern means the machine; science; business; youth; new roles for women; cityscapes dominated by skyscrapers; speed of the automobile and airplane; and social, economic, and industrial progress. Most people optimistically aspire to change the world so that nothing like the Great War (World War I) can happen again. On the other hand, there is massive devastation, debts, and reparations caused by the war, especially in Germany and its allies. This, along with a consumer culture that encourages people to live beyond their means, and the increasing income separation between the wealthy and the middle class, begin to create economic depression and unemployment around the globe.

Nevertheless, there are many reasons for optimism. The widespread adoption of electricity accelerates industrialization and enhances people's lives. The marketplace showcases new materials, such as Vitrolite or Bakelite and human-made fibers (rayon, nylon); new technologies (electric washing machine and vacuum cleaner); and improved products (radio, phonograph). To market these goods, manufacturers focus their promotions and advertising on the opinions and desires of the middle class, which brings about mass consumerism. Installment buying becomes the norm for many. A media culture emerges from improvements in communications and leads to further developments in the means of communication. Even after the war, the daily newspaper remains important for news, fashion, and entertainment. More people own radios and read magazines, so they are better informed than ever before. Mass entertainment—movies, dance halls, clubs, speakeasies, spectator sports—increases in popularity. Hollywood extends American ideas and culture across the world, first in silent films, and then in "talkies" after 1928. Travel becomes even easier. More highways, automobiles, buses, trains, and airplanes make the world seem smaller. With the growth of transatlantic travel, luxury cruise ships become important venues for displaying new styles and ideas. Art Deco develops from and within this cultural landscape.

In 1901, a group of artist–designers, including Art Nouveau designer Hector Guimard, organizes the *Société des Artistes Décorateurs* (SAD; Society of Decorative Artists). Wanting to promote its work as well as to distinguish it from that of artisans and craftspeople, the group holds exhibitions, which become showcases for new designers; model rooms; and the new, modern style that will be called Art Deco. In 1903, the *Salon d'Automne* is established to spotlight and endorse independent artists whose work is not supported by official salons. Exhibitors include Emile-Jacques Ruhlmann, Le Corbusier, and the *Deutscher Werkbund* (German Work Federation). Elements of Art Deco appear in exhibitions by both of these groups as well as in the furniture and interiors created by individuals, firms, and department stores in early-20th-century Paris. In these early years, examples of Art Deco, which are largely limited to the elite in Paris, follow two forms. One is very decorative and more traditional in form and materials, while the other is more modernist and influenced by the Vienna Secession, the Bauhaus, and Le Corbusier.

From the beginning, members of the *Société des Artistes Décorateurs* want to have an international exhibition to highlight French modern decorative arts, but their idea does not come to fruition until after World War I. In 1925, Paris hosts the *Exposition Internationale des Arts Décoratifs et Industriels Modernes* (Fig. 51-2, 51-3), which is organized by the French government, not the members of SAD, to promote luxury French products to the world and to reestablish France's supremacy in art and decoration. The exhibition, which ushers in the Art Deco style, fosters a forward-looking approach to design, one that fully unites art and industry. Exhibits show examples of Parisian Art Deco or *moderne* and the work of French interior decorators and artists, such as Emile-Jacques Ruhlmann (Fig. 51-23), Maurice Dufrêne, Robert Mallet-Stevens (Fig. 51-15), and René Lalique (Fig. 51-25), who have developed their styles over the previous decade. Although various countries send delegations, the new stylistic movement is essentially initiated and supported by French artists and patrons. There is great worldwide interest in the exhibition because no previous one has had as much publicity in newspapers, journal articles, photographs, and prints. Practitioners of the period denote their work as Modern or *Moderne*; *Art Deco*, the more common term today, does not come into general use until the late 1960s after the publication of *Art Deco of the 20s and 30s* by Bevis Hillier.

Following the exhibition, progressive museums, galleries, and department stores in several countries, including Great Britain and the United States, promote Art Deco by displaying objects from the Paris exhibition. Some of these displays travel, thereby showcasing the work of Art Deco designers to more people. As its

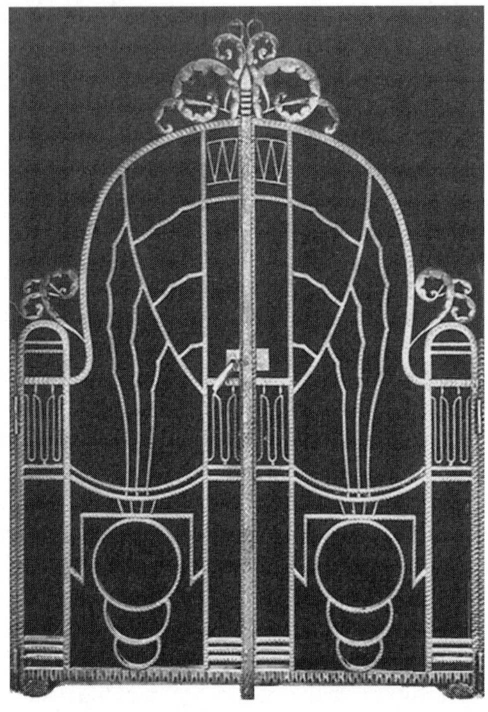

▲ **51-1.** Architectural Details: Iron entry gate portal and elevator doors, c. 1920s–1930s; France and the United States; doors designed by Morgan, Walls, and Clements. (The doors were relocated to the Richfield Oil Building in Los Angeles.)

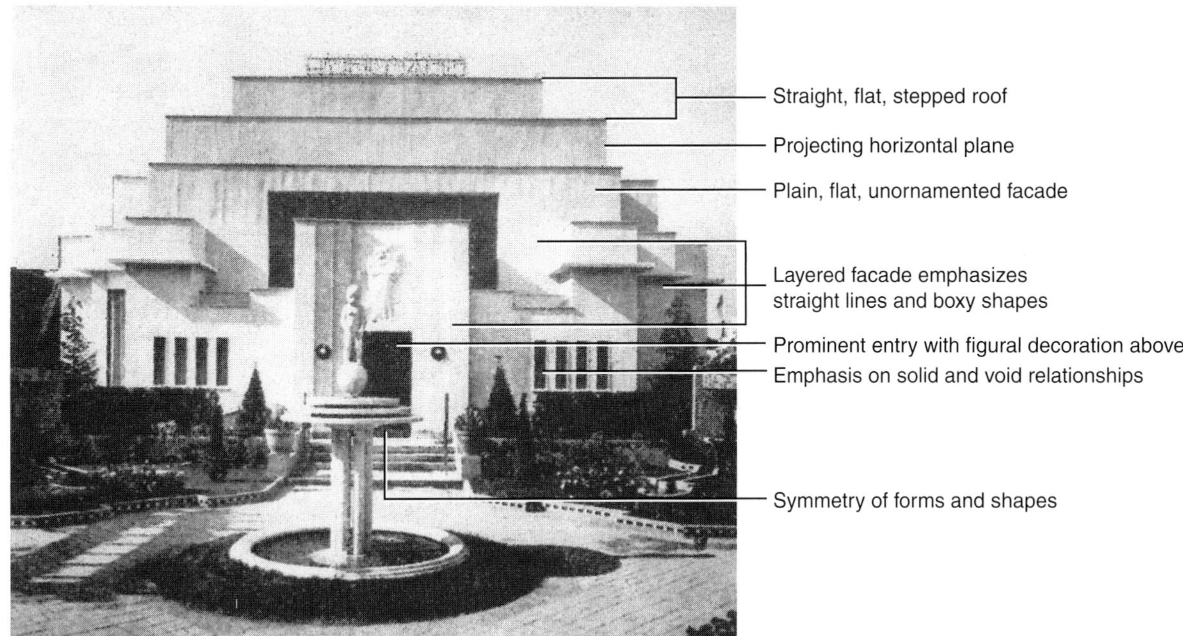

▲ **51-2.** Pavilion of a Rich Collector, published in *Exposition Internationale des Arts Décoratifs et Industriels Modernes*, 1925; Paris, France; Emile-Jacques Ruhlmann and Pierre Patout (Ruhlmann Group). Art Deco.

reputation as a Modern style catches on, Art Deco spreads and begins to assume a variety of forms as designers in Australia, eastern Europe, South America, India, and Japan adapt it to their homelands.

Believing it lacks a modern style, the United States does not participate in the *Exposition Internationale des Arts Décoratifs et Industriels Modernes*. Publicity about the Paris exposition and traveling exhibits of objects from it, imported French furnishings, immigrant French designers, and museum and department store exhibits acquaint American architects, designers, and the public with Art Deco. During the late 1920s and 1930s, the American Art Deco skyscraper becomes a symbol of modernity throughout the world (Fig. 51-4). American designers also democratize the style through adaptations of elite examples in affordable materials for the middle class. In the 1930s, the United States replaces France as the most important purveyor of the Art Deco and the later Art Moderne style. After World War II, she will become the main promoter for modernism, unseating France and Germany.

The American stock market crash in 1929 and subsequent Great Depression end the country's prosperity and building boom and affect the rest of the world. Widespread unemployment slows consumerism. In response, a plainer, more simplified variation of Art Deco emerges. Deriving its imagery from speed and transportation, industrial designs with their stronger machine aesthetic, and the emerging International Style, this variation becomes known as Art Moderne or Streamlined Modern. Stylistic concepts of streamlining come from experiments in aerodynamics and their application to modern means of transportation, such as locomotives and airplanes. Art Moderne is especially important in the United States where its popularity signals a renewed attempt to lessen its aesthetic dependence upon Europe as designers search for an American style. Throughout the 1920s and 1930s, Hollywood and the movies are an important source of information for the public about Art Deco and Art Moderne. Many films feature elaborate sets in both styles. Art Moderne, like Art Deco, also becomes aligned with consumerism. With profits dwindling, manufacturers and advertisers look for new ways to increase sales. One method is to deliberately and quickly outdate a style, leading to planned stylistic obsolescence and yearly introductions of new models, which usually have only minor and/or decorative changes.

Art Deco and Art Moderne gradually decline and eventually disappear with the increasing dominance of the Modern aesthetic, the onset of World War II, and renewed austerity following the war. During the war, architectural and other commissions are few, so many European designers immigrate to the United States. As a result, American designs show a fusion of Art Deco and the new emerging International Style, which will dominate the 1939 World's Fair in New York.

The 30-year popularity of Art Deco and Art Moderne attests to their adaptability and flexibility. Both define a surprising variety of building types, interiors, and furniture for the wealthy and the middle class. They become associated with travel; leisure; entertainment; romance; youth; civic pride; and, in the United States, free trade and commerce. Either one can define a corporation (Fig. 51-4); convey a chic image for a restaurant, a ship, or a boutique; enhance a tropical look for a hotel (Fig. 51-9); form a social backdrop for the wealthy; become a practical, functional living room for a working woman or modern family; or provide a glamorous set for an equally glamorous movie. Most important, both styles convey an image of modernity, progress, and the future while retaining a respect for that which has gone before.

CONCEPTS

During the first decade of the 20th century, elements of Art Deco surface in France in the work of a group of progressive designers. Their work continues some elements of Art Nouveau, such as the minimalism and geometry of the Vienna Secession in Austria and Charles Rennie Mackintosh in Scotland, and the more stylized, naturalistic expressions in Paris. Whereas Art Deco absorbs some ideas of the Bauhaus, Le Corbusier, and the International Style (hereafter referred to as Modernism), such as function and new materials, it rejects others, such as the unornamented aesthetic. Art Deco, like other modern developments, embraces the machine and seeks a machine design vocabulary while maintaining good craftsmanship, like Art Nouveau. Art Deco respects the past in form and ornament and draws from national or regional traditions, unlike Modernism.

Like Art Nouveau and Modernism, Art Deco strives to create a style suitable for the modern age. All three movements acknowledge the importance of unity among the arts and the totality of design. But Art Deco does not share the modernist's faith in the redeeming value of art and it does not have a crusading sprit to improve people's lives. Like Art Nouveau, Art Deco presents a variety of expressions resulting from a diversity of influences. It relies, far more than either Art Nouveau or Modernism, upon capitalism and consumerism for dissemination. Consequently, it pervades all arts, high-style first and then popular ones, in many countries.

Art Deco draws inspiration from many Western and non-Western sources, including avant-garde art, design, and architecture. An important design influence comes from the 1909 *Ballet Russes* in Paris for which costume designer Erté adapts elements from Russian folk art and the brilliant colors of Symbolist painting. His coordinated costumes and sets display naiveté, vivid colors, abstract designs, and Persian and Oriental influences. Avant-garde art movements, such as Cubism, Futurism, Expressionism, and Fauvism, affect Art Deco forms, colors, and use of non-Western elements. The style also adopts exotic influences, particularly from Africa, Egypt, and Latin America. African designs, colors, and concepts come into Art Deco from various exhibitions of African art in Paris, the popularity of jazz music, and the influence of Cubism. In 1923, the opening of King Tutankhamen's tomb in Egypt renews interest in Egyptian designs and motifs. During the 1920s and 1930s, exhibitions, publications, and collections promote the Indian cultures of North and South America. As a result, Native American, Mexican, and Peruvian designs grow increasingly popular, particularly in textiles and pottery.

Avant-garde art movements, particularly abstraction, and some exotic elements also affect Art Moderne, which has less ornament than Art Deco. Among its main influences are the idea of speed, as derived from trains and automobiles, and sleek aerodynamic forms of industrial design.

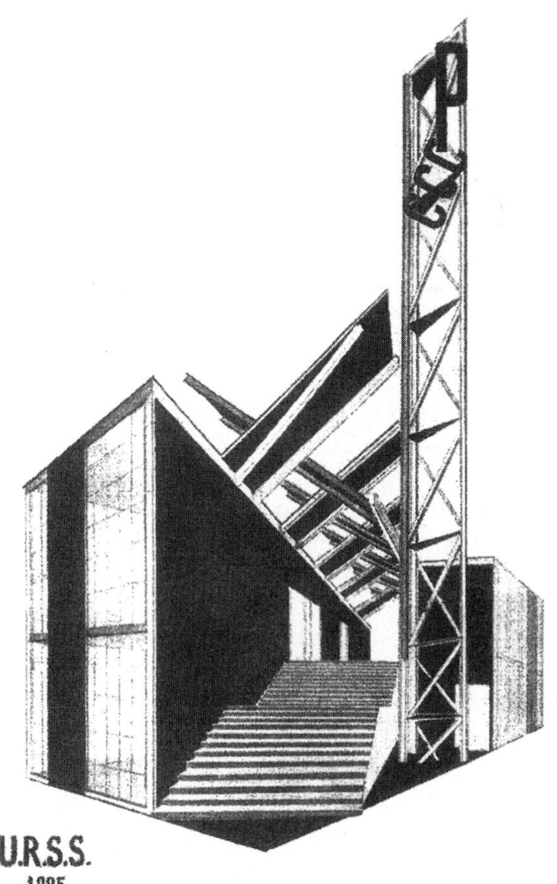

▲ 51-3. USSR Pavilion, published in *Exposition Internationale des Arts Décoratifs et Industriels Modernes*, 1925; Paris, France; Konstantin Melnikov. Art Deco.

CHARACTERISTICS AND MOTIFS

Art Deco modernizes forms and ornament of the past through stylization and contemporary colors and materials. Art Moderne, in contrast, looks to the future and adopts principles of simplification and abstraction based on speed and motion.

- *Art Deco*. Designs reflect a coordinated and integrated approach for total unity. Early examples use extravagant materials, are custom designs, and emphasize asthetics over function. Forms may follow a classical or traditional influence, such as Rococo or Neoclassicism, or reveal a more Modernist approach with simple geometric compositions. Solid and void as well as light and dark relationships are important. Rich decoration in the form of two-dimensional or shallow bas-relief ornament drawn from many sources is a definitive characteristic.
- *Art Moderne*. During the 1920s, buildings, interiors, and objects begin to show influences from trains, automobiles, and airplanes. Forms become simplified, sleek, and efficient. Surfaces are smooth and corners rounded. Horizontality is emphasized through shape and with contour lines. Ornament is kept to a minimum to avoid disturbing an aerodynamic appearance. New materials, such as Vitrolite and tubular steel, are characteristic.
- *Motifs*. Natural motifs (Fig. 51-1, 51-5, 51-11, 51-13, 51-14, 51-16, 51-18, 51-19, 51-20, 51-25) include stylized flowers and garlands, banana leaves, stylized water fountains, feathers, doves,

deer or antelopes, elephants, greyhounds, exotic animals, human figures, sun rays, and sunbursts. Geometric motifs (Fig. 51-1, 51-2, 51-3, 51-4, 51-5, 51-7, 51-8, 51-9, 51-10, 51-12, 51-15, 51-17, 51-18, 51-19, 51-24, 51-25) that are machine-inspired include circles, spirals, squares, rectangles, diamond shapes, chevrons, lightning bolts, parallel lines, and striped bands. Female figures often are focal points in wall murals and decorative arts objects. Exotic motifs derive from the *Ballet Russes*, Egypt, African art, and Oriental influences.

ARCHITECTURE

Art Deco architecture applies stylized and abstracted geometric, floral, and figural decoration and brilliant color to classical and modernistic forms. Many Art Deco architects are classically trained, but modern movements, such as Expressionism or De Stijl, and design trends and ideas of the period, including those of the Bauhaus or theories of Le Corbusier, influence their work. Consequently, some buildings have classical attributes, such as

DESIGN SPOTLIGHT

Architecture: The Chrysler building, designed for the Chrysler Corporation, is an Art Deco architectural icon. The stainless steel pointed tower and spire are among the most recognizable architectural details in New York City. Designed by William Van Alen, the 77-story skyscraper was briefly the world's tallest building. It is of white brick trimmed with gray brick. Entrances are triangular shaped and trimmed with gray. Automobiles inspire the ornament, most of which is almost too small to be seen from the street. At the setback on the 31st story are winged radiator caps and a frieze of stylized hub caps. Stainless steel gargoyles highlight the setback and beginning of the tower at the 59th story. The tower, which rises seven stories, is composed of rounded sunbursts with triangular windows and culminates in a spire. The triangular lobby is an Art Deco masterpiece. The floor is red marble, and the walls are yellow-ochre trimmed with amber and blue. On the ceiling is a fresco by Edward Turnbull titled "Energy, Result, Workmanship, and Transportation." It shows airplanes, buildings, and the Chrysler assembly line. The inlaid wood and metal on the elevator doors repeat elements of the tower with details forming arcs and foliage. [National Historic Landmark]

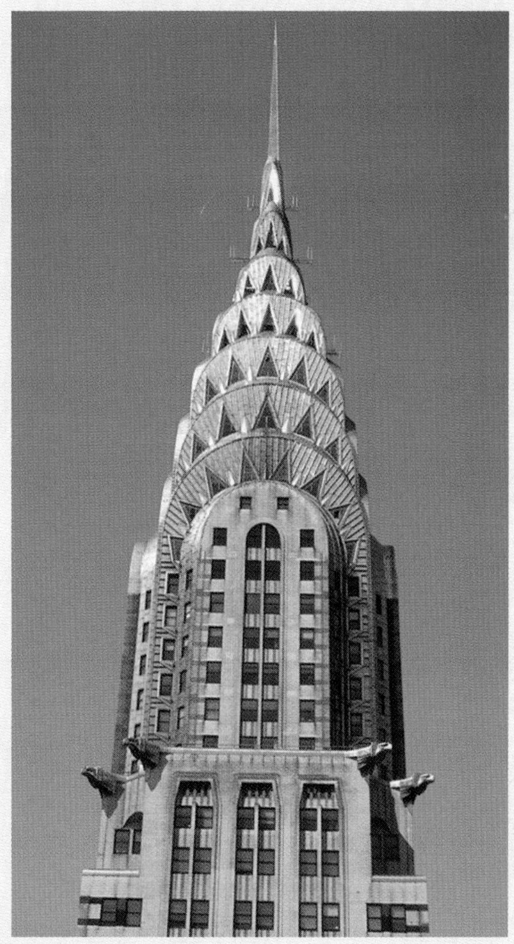

▲ **51-4.** Chrysler Building and tower detail, 1928–1930; New York City, New York; William Van Alen. Art Deco.

symmetry, mathematical proportions, and classical elements and motifs such as columns or pilasters. Others display the symmetrical or asymmetrical geometric, simplified compositions of Modernism. Unlike Modernism, which eschews ornament of any kind, these buildings often have brilliant colors and some applied ornament. The Art Deco architectural vocabulary and its language of ornament prove highly adaptable to any theme, image, or message that a designer anywhere wants to convey in the building image.

Art Deco style architecture is rare before the *Exposition Internationale des Arts Décoratifs et Industriels Modernes* in 1925. At the exposition, the straight lines, cubic and curving forms, layered façades, projecting horizontal planes, prominent entryways, stepped rooflines, and lavish ornament of the French pavilions fascinate visitors and make a strong design statement (Fig. 51-2, 51-3). Because the pavilions are temporary, designers experiment freely with form, color, and unusual materials, such as laminates. Characteristics of the 1925 exhibition buildings become common in architecture in the late 1920s through the early 1930s, primarily in skyscrapers and buildings associated with modern life, such as power stations, movie theaters, and airports.

The plainer, more volumetric Art Moderne or Streamlined Modern appears in the late 1920s. Like Art Deco, Art Moderne defines numerous building types and other structures such as dams and bridge supports. Characteristics are rounded corners, cantilevered eyebrows or projections over doors and windows, glass block or porthole windows, bands of windows, projecting and open linear balustrades, and minimal ornament, most often with an asymmetrical arrangement (Fig. 51-9). Later, Art Moderne residential structures attempt to displace the popularity of the period house in the United States.

A wide variety of building types are Art Deco or Art Moderne. New commercial structures include skyscrapers (Fig. 51-4), movie theaters (Fig. 51-5), office buildings (Fig. 51-6), bus stations (Fig. 51-7), diners (Fig. 51-8), airports, gas stations, and power stations. Other structures include factory buildings, train and subway stations, luxury cruise ships, hotels (Fig. 51-9), restaurants, boutiques, beauty shops, barbershops, department stores, exhibition buildings, churches, schools, civic structures, apartment complexes, and houses (Fig. 51-10).

An important legacy of Art Deco is the use of new and creative lighting designs made possible by the widespread adoption of electricity. Inspired by the spectacular lighting of the Eiffel Tower at the *Exposition Internationale des Arts Décoratifs et Industriels Modernes* in 1925, architects create night architecture in which lighted buildings make strong design statements after dark. Char-

▲ **51-5.** Paramount Theater and lobby, 1931; Oakland, California; Miller and Pflueger. Art Deco.

acteristics include internal illumination made visible through transparent walls and dramatic exterior lighting in which the newly popular neon plays a major role. Colorful neon lighting generates excitement and creates rhythms and focal points. Additionally, uplights, downlights, and concealed lighting emphasize important forms, volumes, and/or ornament.

Public and Private Buildings

■ *American Skyscrapers*. America's significant contribution to architecture during the period is the Art Deco skyscraper (Fig. 51-4). Architects build upon earlier precedents, such as the Woolworth Building (1911–1913), in which ornament at strategic points emphasizes the building's verticality and a richly decorated lobby makes a design statement. Another precedent is the design competition for the Chicago Tribune Tower held in 1921. Although the winning entry is Gothic Revival, submissions reveal the limitations of using historical styles to define modern buildings. A third, more important influence is the 1916 New York zoning law, which requires setbacks on tall buildings to permit light and air to reach the streets below. The number and size of setbacks are dependent upon the height of the building and width of the street. The law challenges architects to produce solutions that meet both their clients' needs for space and the code requirements. Ultimately, they create skyscrapers with sculptural, complicated forms and a variety of volumes. Most typical is the tall, slender, usually pointed, central tower surrounded by wider geometric forms at the base. These forms influence skyscrapers in the rest of the country.

▲ **51-6.** Daily Express Building, Fleet Street, 1930–1932; Herbert Ellis and W. L. Clarke, with Owen Williams. Art Deco.

▲ **51-7.** Greyhound Bus Terminal, 1936–1937; Jackson, Mississippi. Art Moderne.

▲ **51-8.** Diner, c. 1930s; New Jersey. Art Moderne.

■ *Theaters, Cinemas, Movie Palaces*. The film industry is an important and influential purveyor of design in both movies and movie houses (Fig. 51-5). Consequently, cinemas or movie palaces, sometimes dubbed "atmospheric theaters," proliferate as fantasy escape environments across Europe and America. The buildings and interiors often are collaborations of architects, artists, and designers. Some convey a modernist image, while others show exotic cultural influences from countries such as China, Egypt, Africa, and Spain. Still others depict historical periods, nautical environments, fairy tales, and the Wild West in the United States. The intent is to create a theatrical experience that makes a lasting impression.

▲ **51-9.** Century Hotel and Marlin Hotel, 1935–1939; Miami Beach, Florida; Century Hotel by Henry Hohauser. Art Deco and Art Moderne.

■ *America's Miami Beach Art Deco.* Mainly dating to the 1930s when the area was a haven for vacationers, Miami Beach possesses the world's largest collection of more than 400 hotels, theaters, apartment buildings, houses, and other types of structures in the Art Deco and Art Moderne styles (Fig. 51-9). Designs have various combinations of flat and curved walls, circular windows, rows of vertical or horizontal lines, plain walls, surface ornamentation, metal railings, and the use of glass blocks. Compositions are strongly geometric, streamlined, and theatrical with pastel or clear colors, so the architecture is often referred to as Tropical Deco.

■ *Site Orientation.* Large and important buildings in urban areas usually are on major city streets to ensure easy access (Fig. 51-4, 51-5, 51-6, 51-9). Fronts of buildings most often are parallel to the street. Architects usually place exhibition buildings within parklike settings along a well-defined circulation axis (Fig. 51-2, 51-3). Because of the popularity of automobile travel, diners (Fig. 51-8), whose forms are derived from railroad dining cars, sit along roadsides or find havens in city neighborhoods near transportation hubs. In Europe and North America, architects group similarly designed houses together in preplanned neighborhoods in cities or suburbs (Fig. 51-10).

■ *Floor Plans.* Plans vary in size and configuration based on building type and spatial requirements. They may be symmetrical or asymmetrical, but they usually emphasize regularity composed of square and rectangular spaces. Horizontal and vertical circulation patterns are direct, controlled, and centralized. Commercial structures often have a prominent, large entry and lobby to indicate welcome and to support the movement of people. In the 1930s, middle-class houses and apartments have multipurpose spaces, an outgrowth of the continued trend toward smaller residences.

■ *Materials.* Building materials include traditional ones, such as white or colored bricks and stone, and newer materials, such as reinforced concrete and steel, which are mixed with more traditional ones like plaster cladding and glass (Fig. 51-2, 51-3, 51-4, 51-5). Some traditional materials assume more innovative forms. An example is glass, which can be used in sheets as a building covering or for walls as glass blocks. Sold as Carrara glass or Vitrolite, glass panels may be colored, cut, sculpted, or curved (Fig. 51-6). Glass, which gives a new or an older building a sleek and shiny modern look outside and inside, appears on and in many Art Moderne structures in the 1930s. Frequently, buildings have accents of stainless steel, aluminum, or other metals; colorful terracotta tile cladding and/or decoration; gilding; and decorative iron grilles or gates (Fig. 51-1, 51-8, 51-9). Designers of movie theaters sometimes incorporate a wide diversity of materials to create a distinctive and unusual appearance.

■ *Façades.* Building façades vary in design based on the individual architectural need or patron's desire, but they usually are sleek, elegant, and monumental. Compositions maintain a unified yet diverse appearance. Some buildings are boxlike and composed of geometric forms, while others are tall and slender. Generally, Art Deco buildings have a three-dimensionality composed of layered flat surfaces and projecting vertical or horizontal planes (Fig. 51-2, 51-3, 51-4, 51-5, 51-6). Solid and void and light and dark relationships are carefully planned and delineated. Straight lines dominate compositions. Ornament, which is a defining element, is usually low relief and accents important parts. Although many buildings have custom designed decorative concepts with iconographies suited to the owner/client, others have characteristic Art Deco ornament acquired from stock items sold by manufacturers. Some Art Deco buildings are cubic or geometric in form with straight lines, horizontal emphasis, and minimal ornament, like Modernist ones. More extensive use of color, materials, or lighting usually identifies them as Art Deco. Skyscrapers and some office buildings have a strong vertical emphasis, surface enrichment, and stepped rooflines (Fig. 51-4). Decoration in horizontal bands or panels beneath windows establishes a counter rhythm to soaring verticality. Color may infuse the entire building through materials or accentuate important parts, such as corners or entrances, and applied decoration. Ornament consists of sunbursts, stylized fountains, chevrons, zigzags, lightning bolts, overlapping squares or arcs, stylized flowers or foliage, and figures. The decoration may be vertical to emphasize height, and it frequently signals setback portions or changes in height. Other Art Deco buildings, particularly movie theaters (Fig. 51-5), have towers and vertical projections, patterns of vertical ribs organizing the façade, and decorative elements to accent prominent architectural features, such as entries.

Art Moderne buildings are more horizontal and this is emphasized by repeating striped bands that may be horizontal and/or vertical; projecting and open linear balustrades on porches, balconies, or parapets; smooth walls; rounded corners; and bands of windows (Fig. 51-8, 51-9). Compositions may be rectangular blocks or geometric and/or rounded in form. Ornament and color are usually kept to a minimum except when colorful structural glass is used. Houses (Fig. 51-10) may emulate commercial structures in form and design, but in a smaller scale.

■ *Windows.* Window sizes vary but are mass-produced and standardized for efficiency and function. Most windows are framed in flat metal bands set flush against the walls. Common examples include rectangular windows that may be fixed, sliding, casement, or double hung; rows of glass blocks in large wall sections; and porthole windows like those on ships (Fig. 51-2, 51-3, 51-4, 51-7, 51-8, 51-9, 51-10). Corner windows are frequent. Vitrolite panels may frame and/or accentuate windows. Some Art Moderne examples have eyebrows or cantilevered projections over windows.

■ *Doors.* Entry doors are usually simple and blend in with the building design (Fig. 51-2, 51-3, 51-4, 51-6). But some feature decorative metal or ironwork in distinctive compositions. Placement, light and dark contrast, and/or a horizontal canopy may spotlight them on the façade. On some commercial buildings, the area above the entry doors has structural decoration, color variety, large signage, and/or interesting lighting as a way to mark the primary entrance (Fig. 51-5, 51-7, 51-8, 51-9). Colorful Vitrolite panels and details and eyebrows or cantilevered projections often accent entrances of Art Moderne buildings.

■ *Roofs.* Prominent towers and other vertical projections frequently accentuate Art Deco structures (Fig. 51-3). Sometimes unique shapes and distinctive materials define the roof's appearance (Fig. 51-4). Movie theaters with cultural or historical influences may have unusual roof shapes that relate to a particular country or period. Roofs on Art Moderne residences and com-

▲ **51-10.** House, c. 1920s–1930s; San Diego, California. Art Moderne.

mercial buildings are often flat and/or stepped to create a layered look (Fig. 51-8, 51-9). Rather than using large moldings, designers trim the edges with narrow bands or a small projecting ledge that may contrast in color to the main body of the structure.

INTERIORS

Working individually, in partnerships, in design firms, or in department stores, progressive French artistic designers, not architects, create the Art Deco style during the 1910s. Appearing first in individually designed interiors for well-to-do clients, the style emerges from a renewed importance of and emphasis upon decoration and the supremacy of the designer's creativity. The individuality of the client surpasses Modernist universal concepts of interior design. Inspired by French 18th- and 19th-century styles, early Parisian Art Deco interiors have an underlying classical simplicity and organization of forms. Classical motifs may be evident in moldings or ornament. Superb craftsmanship, expensive materials, and lavish decoration from many sources are definitive characteristics.

Interior design, designers, and decorators become more important in the Art Deco period. Because numerous commissions come from the design of custom interiors and furnishings, interior design work may be the responsibility of an architect, interior decorator, artist, furniture designer, theater designer, and/or fashion designer. Sometimes teams of designers collaborate on projects. Designers create furniture, fabrics, rugs, draperies, wallpapers, lighting fixtures, metalwork, glass, ceramics, and numerous decorative arts to support the customized interior designs, especially for large commercial circulation, waiting, gathering, dining, and retail spaces. Such spaces are more important during this period.

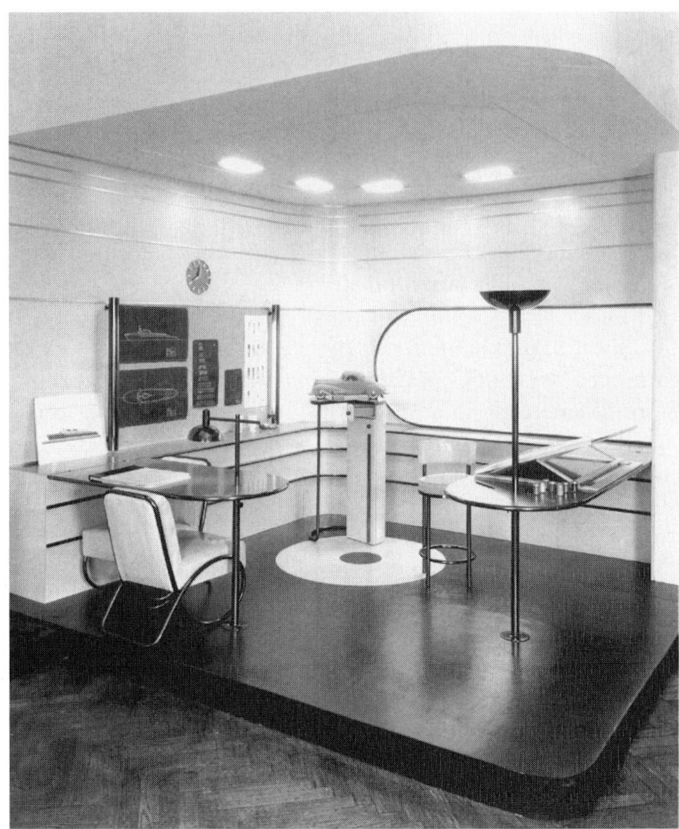

▲ **51-12.** Office, exhibited at the Contemporary American Industrial Art Show at the Metropolitan Museum of Art, 1934; New York City, New York; Raymond Loewry and Donald Deskey. Art Moderne.

▲ **51-11.** Office of Paul Reynaud, Minister of Colonies; 1931; Paris, France; furniture by Emile-Jacques Ruhlmann; frescoes by Louis Bouquet. Art Deco.

DESIGN SPOTLIGHT

Interiors: Radio City Music Hall, an important example of Art Deco, sits within the Rockefeller Center complex of buildings, plazas, and gardens. The center is a significant early-20th-century solution to the integration of structures into and within an urban context. Donald Deskey wins the competition to design the interiors. While designing many interiors, textiles, carpets, wall coverings, and furnishings himself, Deskey also collaborates with artists, painters, sculptors, and craftspeople to complete the more than 30 spaces. Designs incorporate new materials, such as aluminum and Bakelite, and traditional ones, such as copper and cork, often in innovative ways. Deskey calls the style Modern Rococo. In the impressive Grand Foyer, golden draperies, red walls with gold-backed mirrors and sconces, monumental chandeliers, and gold leaf ceiling and walls create a dramatic entry to the Music Hall beyond. A mural by Ezra Winter depicts the Fountain of Youth. [National Historic Landmark]

DESIGN SPOTLIGHT

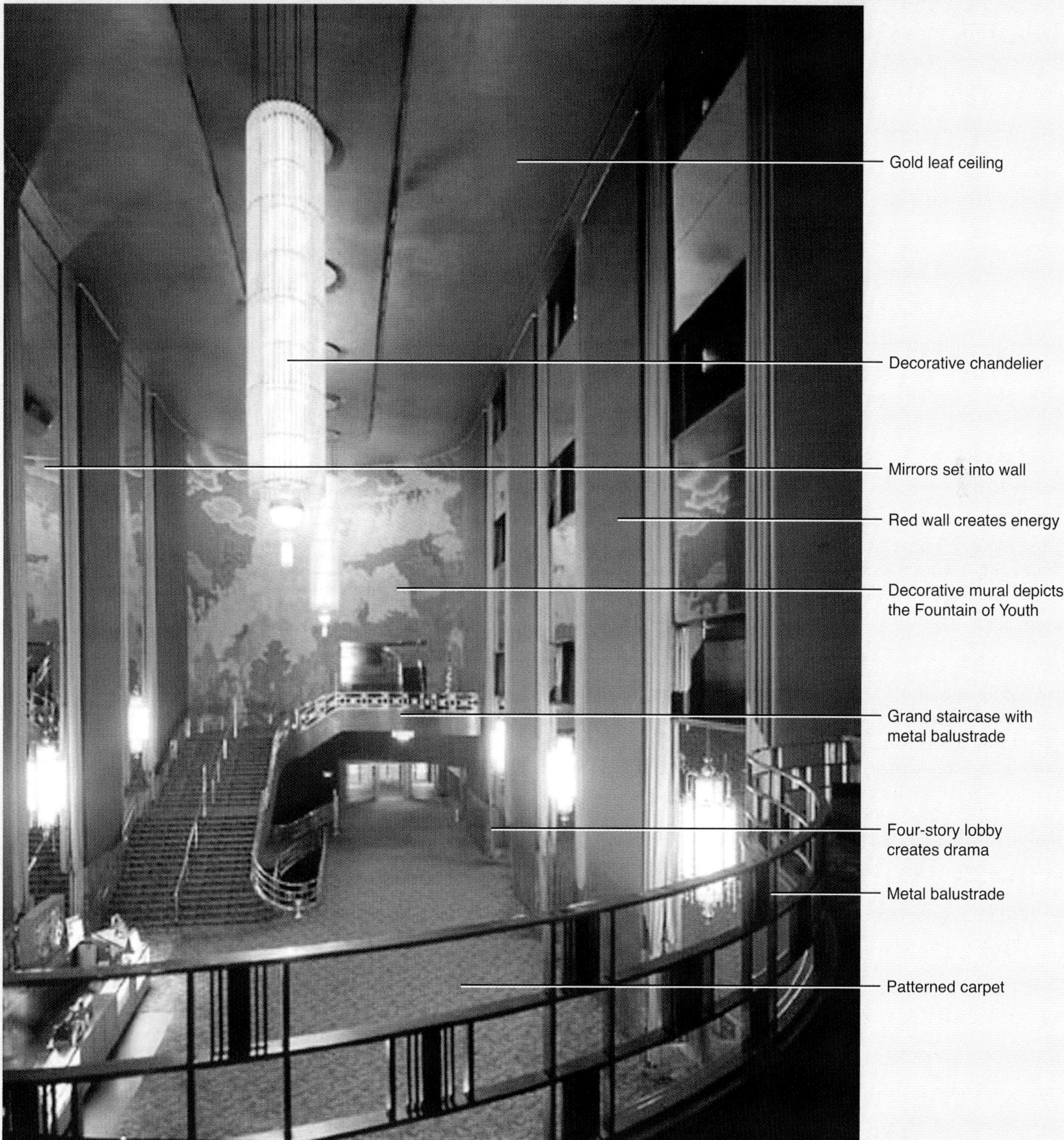

▲ **51–13.** Grand Foyer, Radio City Music Hall, 1931–1940; New York City, New York; Raymond Hood and Edward Durell Stone; Donald Deskey on interior decoration. Art Deco.

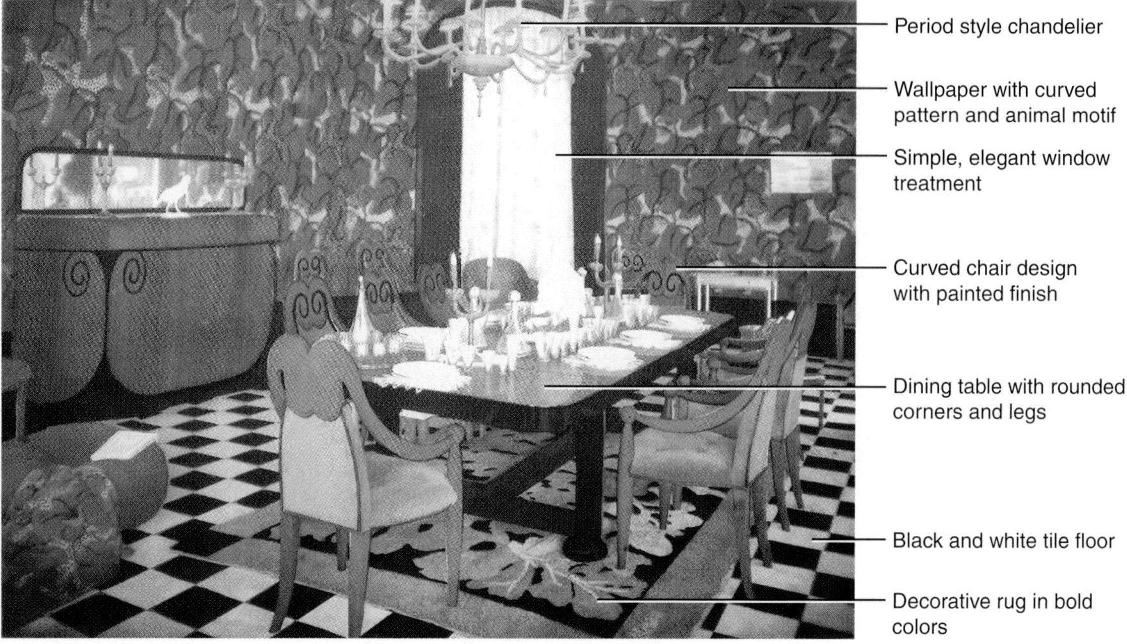

▲ **51-14.** Dining room; published in *Les Arts de la Maison*, 1926; France; Martine. Art Deco.

Art Deco interiors exhibit great variety in style because of the various design approaches used by architects, artists, designers, and decorators. Interiors completed by those with a more architectural emphasis (Fig. 51-12, 51-15) often present more simplicity, starkness, and rectilinear features, while those completed by artistic designers or decorators (Fig. 51-11, 51-13, 51-14, 51-16) incorporate more decoration, patterns, textiles, and stronger colors. Additionally, the latter tend to display more individuality and greater diversity in their work. When the architect is responsible for both the exterior and the interior design, Art Deco and Art Moderne architectural design characteristics repeat in the interiors to achieve a totally integrated concept. Consequently, these Art Deco interiors often have a vertical emphasis, lavish surface enrichment, and stepped lines or forms. Rooms with a modernist approach show simplicity along with a greater emphasis on architectural structure and asymmetry than other Art Deco spaces do. Art Moderne interiors have rounded corners, glass block walls or windows, and projecting horizontal planes. Some interiors, however, may blend aspects of these design approaches.

The Modern Movement inspires a variation of French Art Deco in which the designers reject excessive ornament and adopt new or industrial materials but retain the creativity of the designer and the importance of individuality. In 1930, French designers who support this view and promote mass production form the *Union des Artistes Modernes* (UAM). Members of the organization include Robert Mallet-Stevens (Fig. 51-15, 51-19), Pierre Chareau, François Jourdain, Eileen Gray (Fig. 51-24), and Le Corbusier. Their designs are characterized by a strong geometry, bold forms, and often the use of chrome and steel.

Following the 1925 exhibition, rooms around the world begin to display Art Deco characteristics. In France, Art Deco is more common than Art Moderne, and there is less variety in types of rooms; most are residential. Because of a strong emphasis upon period decoration, Art Deco does not have much impact in Great Britain until the late 1920s. During the 1930s, popularity increases when the Ideal Home exhibits, held in London, begin featuring modern spaces and prominent decorators, such as Betty Joel. The Ideal Home Shows, which continue today, are sponsored by the *Daily Mail* newspaper beginning in 1908. They bring together new technology, furnishings, and planning for the modern home. The United States has the greatest diversity of Art Deco interiors ranging from the glamour of Hollywood shown in the movies, to the cosmopolitan sophistication of the Manhattan skyscraper, to the mass-produced inexpensive middle-class living rooms. By the 1930s, Art Moderne or Streamlined Modern begins to surpass high-style Art Deco in many interiors in the United States and Great Britain. Its simplicity and modernness appeal to many, and it more easily adapts to less expensive products for middle-class interiors.

Art Deco affects many nonresidential and residential interiors, including lobbies and entrance halls (Fig. 51-5, 51-13), lounges, dining areas, and guest suites for luxury cruise ships; ticket, waiting, dining, and service areas in bus stations and airport terminals; passenger and dining cars in trains; beauty and barbershops; dry cleaners; auditoriums in movie houses and theaters; offices (Fig. 51-11, 51-12); particular kinds of retail display spaces; and dining and service areas in diners. Art Deco can be found in any room of the house (Fig. 51-14, 51-15, 51-16, 51-17, 51-24), including kitchens and baths.

■ *Kitchens*. Planning concepts born in the Industrial Revolution are more fully realized in kitchen design during the period. The new discipline of domestic science, or home economics, formulates functional planning concepts for kitchens and baths. This enables designers to better address function, storage, and maintenance in kitchens, along with aesthetics. Layouts are organized to enhance function and aesthetic appeal. Work areas are placed within a triangle for greater efficiency. Built-in cabinets, which are common, provide essential storage and help to reduce clutter. Fixtures, appliances, floors, and countertops have tile and metal surfaces that are more sanitary and easily maintained. And newly available appliances and fixtures support and improve kitchen activities. Many reflect the Art Moderne character of simplicity and streamlined forms.

■ *Bathrooms*. Not until the 1920s do most bathrooms incorporate toilets, tubs, and sinks and support multiple functions, such as shaving, applying makeup, and brushing teeth. Designers strive to transform bathrooms for the well-to-do into aesthetic palaces with lavish materials and decoration. Even baths in middle-class houses reflect new planning concepts as well as new materials and fixtures that are available in many colors, not just white. Stepped forms, simplicity, and streamlining proclaim Art Deco or Art Moderne influences (Fig. 51-17). Because bathrooms and kitchens are a focus for interior schemes, those created by designers appear in shelter magazines, displays at international expositions, and exhibits in department stores.

Public and Private Buildings

■ *Color*. Generally, during the early 1920s colors are brighter and more saturated. Colors include royal blue, rose, pearl white, gray, purple or lavender, lemon yellow, fern green, and Chinese red with accents of black (Fig. 51-14, 51-18). The economic depression in the late 1920s brings a palette of more muted colors, such as gray, bottle green, and brown (Fig. 51-11). Throughout the period in more decorated spaces, colors are often richer and reflect influences from the *Ballet Russes*; avant-garde art; and Persia, the Orient, Egypt, Africa, and Latin America. Pastel hues also are popular in decorative spaces and in Art Moderne interiors. Sometimes brilliant colors are juxtaposed for heightened contrasts. Gold and sliver leaf are common in high-style interiors (Fig. 51-12). In more modernist versions of Art Deco, the dominant color is white (Fig. 51-24). The palette in more architectural spaces may be more monochromatic with textiles providing color enrichment.

■ *Floors*. Floor surfaces include wood, ceramic tile, linoleum, or wall-to-wall carpeting (Fig. 51-5, 51-11, 51-13, 51-14, 51-16, 51-17). Some spaces have glass tile or glass block floors. In Art Deco and Art Moderne rooms, rugs in simple geometric patterns

▲ **51-15.** Dining room, c. 1925–1926; France; Robert Mallet-Stevens. Modernist Art Deco.

provide warmth, color, and pattern. Carpet and rug manufacturers sometimes commission designers and artists to create Art Deco designs for them. Considering them essential to the space, designers, such as Eileen Gray, create rugs and carpets in designs that support the room's concept (Fig. 51-15, 51-24).

■ *Walls*. Walls have many different types of treatments ranging from simple to lavish in ornament and materials. Some are painted or lacquered a single color or richly decorated with custom and individual geometric, abstract, or stylized naturalistic designs (Fig. 51-13, 51-16). Treatments are the most lavish in high-style Art Deco interiors in residences (Fig. 51-14, 51-16); public spaces in ships, hotels, and commercial buildings; and movie theaters (Fig. 51-5). Most walls usually display a strong architectural emphasis with three-dimensional variation in all types of interiors. Designers construct wall compositions with rectangular columns or pilasters, layered planes, panels, and/or alcoves and niches (Fig. 51-5, 51-13). Surfaces may have large areas of solid colors or decorative treatments such as textiles, wallpaper, mosaics, murals, or gold or silver leaf or a combination of both (Fig. 51-11, 51-14). Finishes are smooth, sleek, and shiny. Dark and light contrasts are common, particularly when all of the walls are plain.

Mirrored and glass panels are used in Art Deco or Art Moderne rooms. The latter often have glass block interior partitions. Decorative ironwork may embellish walls and is used for elevator cages and stair balustrades. Nonresidential and residential spaces sometimes have built-in storage as part of the wall design (Fig. 51-12, 51-15). Modernist wall treatments often include industrial materials such as plastic laminate or Vitrolite; other common treatments include cork and metallic finishes. Art Moderne spaces frequently have parallel contour lines, of which three is the most common number (Fig. 51-12).

▲ **51-16.** Interior, published in *Intérieurs au Salon des Artistes Decorateurs*, late 1920s; France. Modernist Art Deco.

▲ **51-17.** Advertisment showing a bathroom, c. 1930s. Art Deco.

■ *Windows and Window Treatments*. Windows often repeat the exterior design, which conveys an architectural simplicity. Glass may be clear, frosted, or etched. Most window treatments are plain or pleated fabric panels hanging from rods, cornices, or padded cornice boards (Fig. 51-11, 51-14, 51-16). They may be sill- or floor-length and may be tied back or hang straight. Most are of plain fabrics, such as velvet or silk, although some are patterned. Because of the cost, fabric window treatments become very simple to use less fabric during and after the Depression. Some Moderne rooms have no curtains, substituting shades or blinds or leaving the windows bare.

■ *Doors*. Simple, plain, rectangular doors are common (Fig. 51-15). Most are glass, wood, or metal or a combination of two materials. They often blend into the wall composition to emphasize an architectonic composition. Some doors have applied moldings in a geometric pattern similar to the wall composition. Surrounds are simple, flat, and narrow.

■ *Textiles*. Designers use a variety of textiles for wall coverings, drapery, and upholstery during the period (Fig. 51-11, 51-14, 51-15, 51-16, 51-24). Synthetic fibers, such as rayon and acetate, join the natural fibers of linen, silk, cotton, and wool. Damask, brocade, brocatelle, lampas, velvet, satin, and plush enhance high-style spaces, whereas plain, often heavily textured, weaves dominate in more modernist interpretations. In addition to other plain and patterned textiles, leather, animal skins, and tapestries are used on Art Deco and Art Moderne furniture. Colors follow period trends with textures becoming more important as colors become more muted in the 1930s. Patterns, which are usually flat instead of three-dimensional, include geometrics, such as squares

▲ **51-18.** Textiles: Woven and printed fabrics in various designs, c. 1920s, France and the United States.

and triangles; abstracts, such as lightning bolts; and stylized naturalistic forms, including the human figure (Fig. 51-18). Some designs reflect avant-garde art, such as Cubism, or exotic or nonindustrial cultures such as Egypt or Africa. Designers frequently custom design textiles in colors and patterns for clients or manufacturers. Art Moderne rooms have fewer patterns than Art Deco ones do. Usually, the only pattern is in an area rug or window treatments.

■ *Lighting.* With the influence of Modernism and new technology after World War I, lighting design changes from a decorative approach to one that is more architectural and integrated harmoniously with the building structure. Designers use fixtures and concealed direct and indirect lighting to accent architectural details or create drama and excitement (Fig. 51-5, 51-12, 51-13). Incandescent lighting is most common, but neon lighting emerges as a new application in interiors like it does on exteriors. Tall panels or grids of lighting often accentuate walls or staircases in important public spaces, such as movie theaters (Fig. 51-5) or dining rooms in cruise ships. Light panels may form supports or newel posts at stairs and may alternate with wood panels or other wall treatments in other spaces.

Individual lighting fixtures and lamps are simple, streamlined, and geometric, showcasing circles, squares, rectangles, and triangles (Fig. 51-12, 51-15, 51-16, 51-19, 51-24). Metal, such as wrought iron, aluminum, and steel, is the most common material for fixtures. Glass shades usually have no applied color but may be etched or sand blasted for decoration. Art Moderne fixtures sometimes have accents of rubber, plastic laminate, or Bakelite. Decorative table and floor lamps have stylized naturalistic or geometric ornamentation, including female figures. In high-style rooms, monumental crystal chandeliers and sconces may dominate the space.

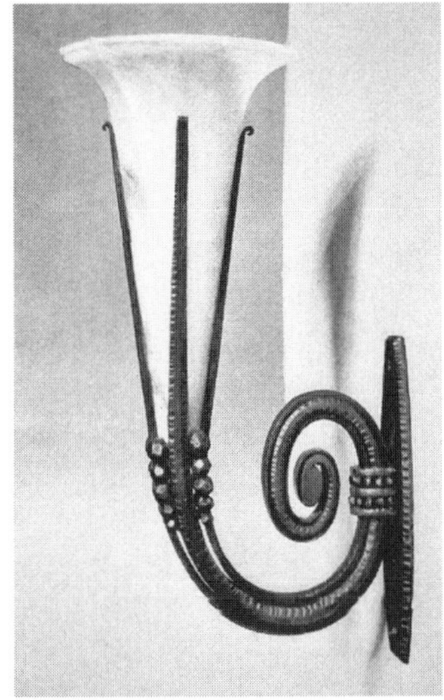

▲ **51-19.** Lighting: *Applique*, table lamp by Robert Mallet-Stevens, and chandelier, c. 1920s–1930s.

■ *Ceilings*. Ceilings may be plainly treated, or they may be decorated with paintings, paper, fabrics, coffers, compartments, layers, or coves (Fig. 51-5, 51-11, 51-12, 51-13, 51-15, 51-16, 51-17, 51-24). A few are glass. Murals and other decoration usually support the room's design concept or iconography. The ceilings in high-style spaces, such as skyscraper lobbies, movie theaters, and bus terminals, often have the most dramatic treatments of prominent recessed, projecting, or concealed lighting; stepped or layered elements; murals; and bold motifs.

FURNISHINGS AND DECORATIVE ARTS

Art Deco and Art Moderne furniture often repeats the architectural and interior character in form and motif. Art Deco furniture and architecture may have similar forms and decoration derived from the same sources. Art Moderne furniture adopts the geometric volumes, standardized forms, and modern or industrial materials of architecture.

Art Deco inspires several types of furniture. High-style French furniture is usually custom designed to suit a particular space for a wealthy and sophisticated clientele who see interiors as settings for social rituals. Elegance, individuality, excellent craftsmanship, and expensive materials define these furnishings. Forms and ornament often are inspired by 18th- and early-19th-century French traditions, particularly Neoclassical. Important traditionalists include Emile-Jacques Ruhlmann (Fig. 51-23) and the Süe et Mare (Fig. 51-20) design firm in France.

Another variation influenced by the Bauhaus and Le Corbusier is more modernist in appearance. This furniture often is custom designed for individual spaces so it relies more on the individuality and creativity of the designer. Typical furnishings have geometric forms and volumes, less ornament, and modern materials, such as tubular steel. Some may be mass produced. Designers include Eileen Gray (Fig. 51-24) and members of the UAM in France.

Art Moderne furniture, usually mass-produced and sometimes created by a designer, has streamlined, geometric, or biomorphic forms; simple contours; and no ornament. Standardization, materials, and functionality give furniture a similar appearance. Furniture in this group responds to consumers and the depressed economic conditions of the late 1920s. Usually inexpensive, it is small-scale and multipurpose to suit modern apartments and houses. Function and practicality are important considerations because households generally have no servants. Additionally, people spend less time at home because they go out to work, travel more, or seek entertainment outside the home. Designers in this group include Donald Deskey and Walter Dorwin Teague in the United States.

Public and Private Buildings

■ *Materials*. Art Deco designers employ a great variety of materials including wood, lacquer, ivory, leather, other animal skins, mother-of-pearl, semiprecious stones, marble, glass, and metal (Fig. 51-11, 51-12, 51-13, 51-14, 51-15, 51-16, 51-21, 51-22, 51-23, 51-24). More modernist Art Deco and Art Moderne furniture uses newer materials such as plastic laminates, Bakelite, Vitrolite, and plywood. Ebony is often the featured wood in Art Deco, but rosewood, mahogany, amboyna, walnut, zebrawood, satinwood, sycamore, beech, and palmwood also are used as solids or veneers. Matched patterned burls are common in panels. Ma-

▲ **51-20.** *Canapé*, c. 1910s–1920s; France; *La Compagnie des Arts Français* (Süe et Mare). Art Deco.

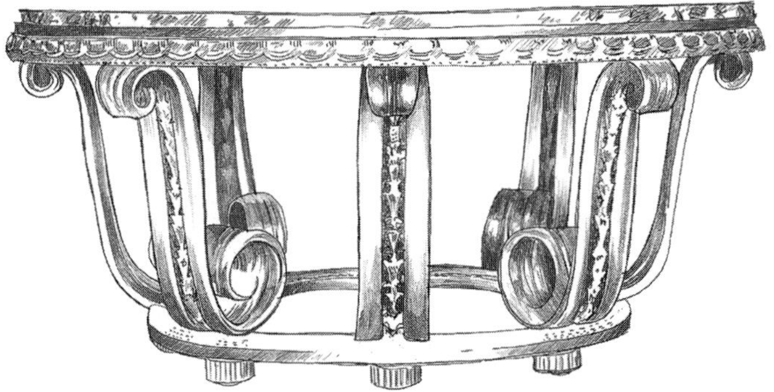

▲ **51-21.** Console table, c. 1920s; France; Edgar Brandt. Art Deco.

terials for inlays include ivory, mother-of-pearl, various woods, tortoiseshell, or metals. Exotic animal skins, such as shagreen, snakeskin, pony hide, and leather cover entire pieces or sides and/or tops. Lacquer treatments, in various colors, cover or accent many different types of furniture. Because lacquer is expensive, furniture manufacturers develop alternative finishes that resemble it. Mirrors or glass panels cover the entire surfaces of some pieces of furniture.

■ *Seating.* Seating has many types and variations, with Art Deco examples showing the greatest variations. Art Deco side and armchairs generally have an underlying traditional form, usually Neoclassical (Fig. 51-11, 51-14, 51-20). Some chairs and stools have a curule or curved X shape. Legs may be slender and tapered, modified cabrioles, or sabers; backs are square, round, or gondola forms; seats are often upholstered trapezoids. Frames may be stained, painted, or gilded with fretwork, inlay, or marquetry ornament. Upholstered chairs often have wood or metal trim and legs. Seating influenced by the Modern Movement has wooden or metal arms and legs or cantilevers (Fig. 51-12, 51-15, 51-16, 51-24). It may be rectangular and blocky in form or have curves to soften corners. Large, comfortable lounge chairs become very popular during the period (Fig. 51-11). Sofas may have curving or stepped ends and/or backs. They may be tufted or plain and have wood or metal trim and/or legs. Sofas, daybeds, and *chaises longues* often have a variety of throw pillows in contrasting fabrics and colors.

■ *Tables.* Like seating, tables come in a wide variety of forms (Fig. 51-11, 51-12, 51-14, 51-15, 51-16, 51-21, 51-24). The most decorative are those in Art Deco spaces. These tables usually have underlying Neoclassical, Directoire, or Empire forms with ornament derived from numerous sources. Simple outlines may be obscured by exuberant decoration. Tops, plain or patterned, may be square, rectangular, round, oval, or kidney-shaped. Legs are straight or modified cabrioles. Consoles and tables have scrolled supports of decorative wrought iron and marble or wooden tops (Fig. 51-21). Some tables, consoles, or desks may be mirrored or have applied or structural glass panels. Dining tables have rectangular wooden or tubular metal legs, or U-shaped trestles of wood and/or metal (Fig. 51-14, 51-15). The rectangular or oval tops are of wood and/or glass. A few examples have lighting built into the tops for drama. Art Moderne tables in wood and metal usually are round or rectangular with plain legs or solid supports and little or no ornament (Fig. 51-12). Usually lamp tables and coffee tables within a room match each other. Desks have much diversity in design, with some that have traditional forms and are soft and feminine looking (Fig. 51-23), while others may follow the aesthetic language of buildings with stepped planes and hard edges. Vanities or dressing tables become fashionable because they are seen in movies. These low tables with mirrors are made to match many bedroom suites. Like other bedroom pieces, night stands and vanities are sometimes made of tubular metal with a metal or glass top.

■ *Storage.* New to the period is the cocktail cabinet to hold liquors, barware, and glasses. Art Deco *commodes* and other storage pieces may adopt the *bombé* or serpentine shapes of 18th-century Rococo (Fig. 51-23). Unlike their elaborate predecessors, decoration sometimes comes from the grain of the wood instead of applied bronze mounts and marquetry or veneer patterns. Alternatively, storage pieces are rectangular and usually have marquetry, inlaid, painted, or lacquered ornament. Paul Frankl creates skyscraper furniture composed of seating and storage

▲ **51-22.** Skyscraper bookcase, c. 1926–1927; United States; Paul Theodore Frankl. Art Deco.

DESIGN SPOTLIGHT

Furniture: Rococo, Neoclassical, Directoire, and Empire styles of the 18th- and early-19th-century furniture inspire Emile-Jacques Ruhlmann's furniture. However, his work does not copy the past, so it is clearly modern. Generally, the forms are simple and reveal a preference for soft curves, which are much harder and more expensive to fabricate. Legs are often straight and tapered or curved. Fronts vary from rectangular to modified serpentine, bow, or kidney-shaped. What sets Ruhlmann's work apart are the richness of materials, such as the ebony, amboyna, and ivory in these pieces; ornament, which may be floral or linear as in the ivory inlay on the desk; and the attention to detail, such as the tassels on the door pulls of the *armoire.* Ruhlmann works in the tradition of the French *ébéniste* of the past, overseeing every step in the design and fabricating process and exerting complete aesthetic control. His furniture is best appreciated in the interior for which it is designed along with his custom textiles, carpet, and decorative arts. As the premier French Art Deco designer, he modernizes past traditions for a wealthy, sophisticated 20th-century clientele.

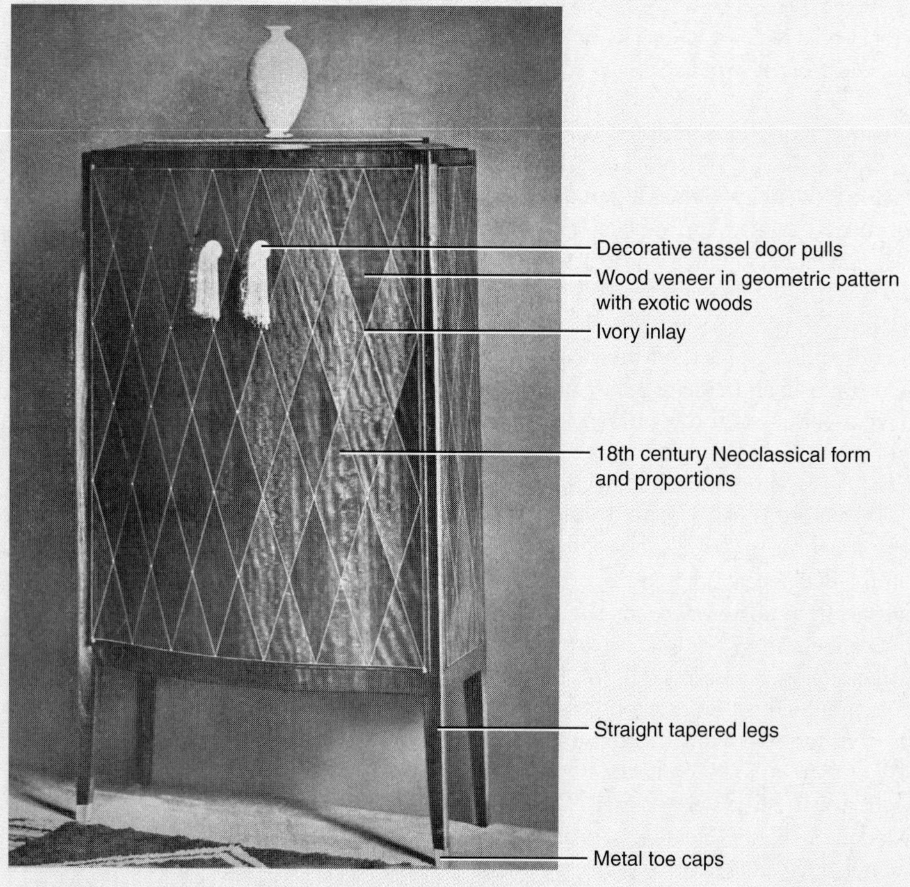

▲ **51-23.** Desk and *armoire,* 1918–1925; France; Emile-Jacques Ruhlmann. Art Deco.

pieces with stepped forms reflecting the setbacks of skyscrapers (Fig. 51-22). He proposes that as the skyscraper solved the urban space problem, so skyscraper furniture will solve space problems in the urban home. Art Moderne storage, in contrast, has no ornament, sometimes relying on the pattern of the wood for decoration. In geometric shapes sometimes with curving corners or ends, most have no moldings or applied decoration. These pieces rely on form and wood grain for interest. Some dressers, chests, and night stands have metal trim to match head- and footboards on beds. Dressers often have circular mirrors.

■ *Beds*. Bedroom suites consisting of bed, dresser, chests, vanities, and night stands in coordinating designs are common in the period. Art Deco beds may be in traditional shapes such as the boat beds of Empire or have one curving end (Fig. 51-24). They are usually of expensive wood veneer or lacquered and can have drapery that falls from a canopy attached to the wall above them or simple curtains hanging at the head of the bed. Wooden Art Moderne beds may have semicircular headboards and no footboards. Also common are semicircular or rectangular headboards and footboards of tubular metal or solid metal.

■ *Decorative Arts*. Designers and consumers choose from a variety of decorative accessories for both Art Deco and Art Moderne rooms. Common accessories include fabric-covered, painted, or lacquered screens (Fig. 51-24); wood, metal, or Bakelite clocks; ceramic, glass, or metal tea, coffee, and cocktail services; candelabra; ceramic or glass vases and bowls (Fig. 51-25); mirrors in wooden or metal frames; wooden and metal sculptures; African masks; Native American baskets and pottery; and posters, prints, and paintings.

Artists, designers, and traditional manufacturers produce ceramics, glass, and metalwork. Unless intended for mass production, the work of artists consists of individual, high-style examples of Art Deco or Moderne. Manufacturers adapt high-style designs for mass production to appeal to consumers. Recognizing the importance of design to sell products, manufacturers sometimes commission artists, designers, and architects to create designs for modern products. However, industrial designers become increasingly important during the period because they create many different types of products for the home that are economical and functional. While influencing the Art Moderne style, they also

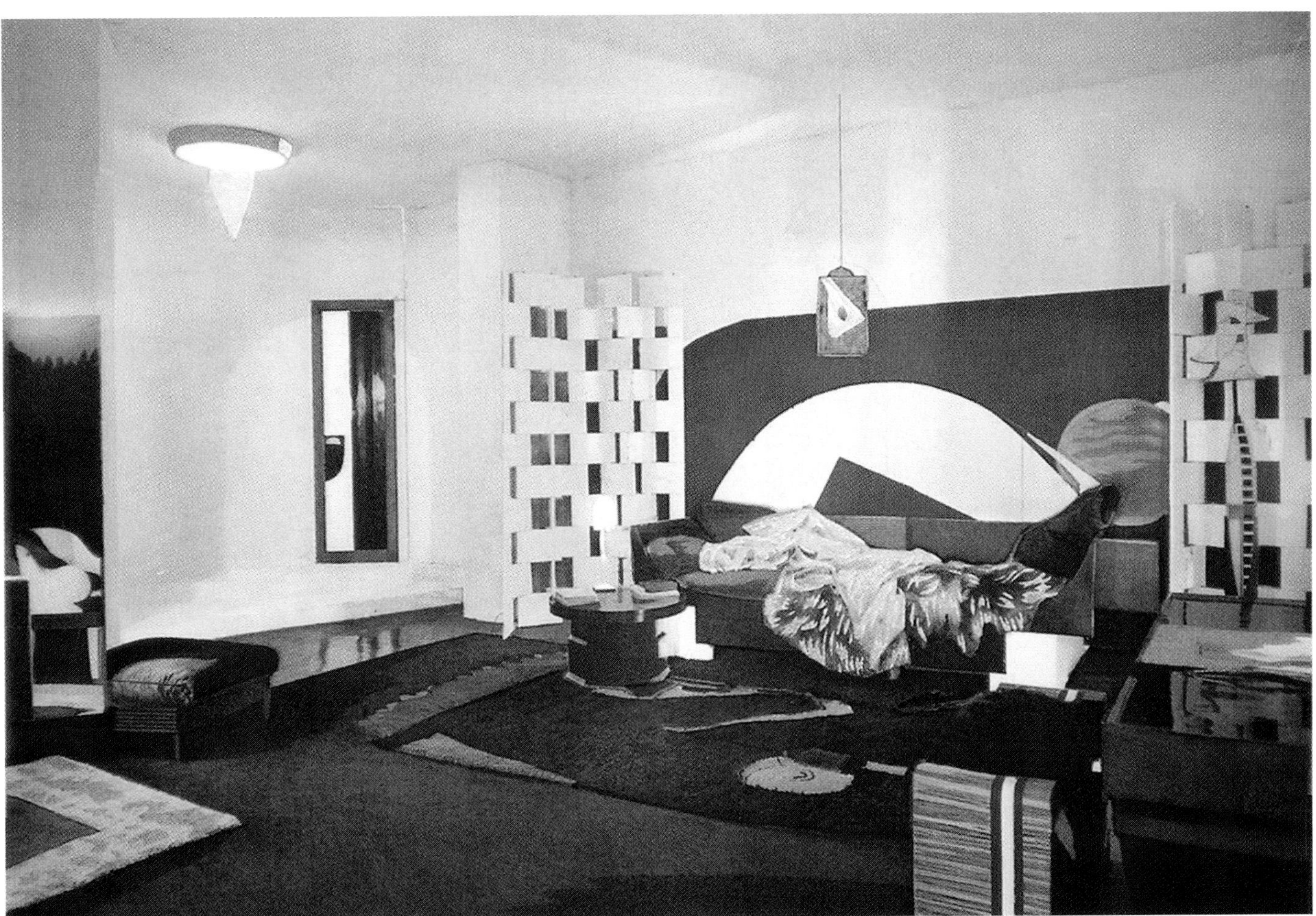

▲ **51-24.** Interior and furnishings, c. 1922; France; Eileen Gray. Modernist Art Deco.

▲ **51-25.** Decorative Arts: Glass vases, c. 1920s; Charles Schneider and René Lalique.

help democratize Modernism. One of the most successful dinner services is Fiesta, introduced by the Homer Laughlin Company in 1927 and created by industrial designer Frederick H. Rhead. Heavy and colorful, Fiesta is still produced.

■ *Later Interpretations*. In the 1970s, Art Deco is rediscovered and becomes an important part of preservation movements in many countries. Buildings are preserved, rehabilitated, and adaptively used. Numerous books and articles describe and promote the style. Art Deco societies hold exhibitions and sponsor lectures and tours. Many begin collecting Art Deco and Art Moderne furniture and decorative arts. Reproductions, adaptations, and interpretations by designers and manufacturers soon appear, and designers continue to experiment with Art Deco or Art Moderne concepts today (Fig. 51-26).

▲ **51-26.** Later Interpretation: Bright City armchair, 1987; Jay Stanger.

CHAPTER 52

Scandinavian Modern

1900s–1960s

> *There is an ulterior motive, too, in architecture, which is always peeping out from around the corner, the idea of creating paradise. It is* **the** *only purpose of our buildings. If we do not carry this idea with us the whole time all our buildings would be simpler, more trivial and life would become—well, would life amount to anything at all? Every building, every work of architecture, is a symbol which has the aspiration to show that we want to build a paradise on earth for ordinary mortals.*
>
> —Alvar Aalto, 1958

Scandinavian Modern describes a specific architecture, interiors, and furnishing from Denmark, Sweden, Finland, and Norway in the early 20th century. Although adopting elements of Bauhaus and International Style modernism, examples are simple, functional, often minimal, yet incorporate a concern for the individual and an emphasis upon natural materials. This shared aesthetic comes from nationalism, folk or vernacular and craft traditions, nature, excellent craftsmanship, and a desire to provide well-designed buildings and objects for all members of Scandinavian society.

HISTORICAL AND SOCIAL

The term *Scandinavian* generally refers to four northwestern European countries that share strong historical, cultural, and linguistic ties. This includes the Scandinavian peninsula countries of Sweden and Norway, plus Denmark and Finland. Although historically Iceland is sometimes included, it has fewer ties to the others. An alternative term referring to these countries is *Nordic*. Because of these ties, Scandinavian architects and designers have similar aesthetic concerns, which embraces a modern appearance strongly grounded in naturalism and vernacular and/or craft traditions.

Scandinavian languages have a common heritage in the Germanic tongues, Western Germanic and Dutch for Finland, and Eastern Germanic for the other countries. Additionally, the histories of Scandinavian countries intertwine with each other, and each is a possession of one or more of the others at some point during their individual pasts. Norway, Denmark, and Sweden share a Viking heritage, so Norse mythology is important in those countries. Southernmost of the Scandinavian countries, Denmark unites with Norway in 1380 and acquires Sweden, on the eastern portion of the Scandinavian peninsula, a few years later. The three countries are united until Sweden gains independence in the early 1500s. In the early 19th century, Denmark's reluctant alliance with Napoleon ultimately forces the country to cede Norway to Sweden. Norway, occupying the western part of the Scandinavian peninsula, gains its independence in 1905. Finland, easternmost of the Scandinavian countries, is a province of Sweden from the 1100s until it is given to Russia as reparations in 1809. It gains its independence during the Russian Revolution and World War I in 1918.

The four countries also have similar climates, which vary from moderate in Denmark to harsher ones in Sweden and Norway where winters are very snowy and windy with periods of little or no sun. Scandinavian landscapes are composed of timber, *fjords*, lakes, streams, mountains, and farmlands. Consequently, adaptations to climate and the importance of the natural environment are important characteristics in Scandinavian design. Scandinavian vernacular forms and craft traditions in building, furniture, textiles, and decorative arts are strong and remain so from their inception to industrialization and into the 21st century. So they inform architectural and design concepts, creating a common visual and aesthetic heritage. Collaborative efforts among artisans, designers, and manufacturers are an important characteristic of architecture, interiors, and decorative arts.

The Scandinavian countries, less densely populated than the rest of Europe, retain an agrarian economy until the end of the 19th century when industrialism begins to take hold. Industrialization is gradual and does not create the monumental upheavals as in Europe or England. Therefore, the Scandinavian countries are able to maintain their rich folk cultures and craft traditions while mechanizing. In the first decades of the 20th century, industrialization ushers in a general move to the cities. Although there are few slums, housing for workers and the general population becomes a governmental concern in all of the Scandinavian countries. During the 1910s, Sweden leads the way in public housing, with improved housing standards, planning guidelines, and government subsidies. By 1945, Sweden, as a social welfare state, provides housing, health care, education, and pensions for its citizens. The government also uses principles of modern design as propaganda tools to inform and improve Swedish public taste. *Möbelråd* (*Furnishing Suggestions*), a government-sponsored design handbook, specifies room sizes, kitchen layouts, materials, and finishes and gives recommendations for well-designed low-cost furniture. The other Scandinavian countries also have government-sponsored housing programs and endorse good design.

The Scandinavian countries spread their design aesthetics in displays and exhibitions at the various World's Fairs in the early 20th century, including the 1925 *Exposition Internationale des Arts Decoratifs et Industriels Modernes* in Paris. The most significant exposition for Scandinavian design, however, is the 1939 New York World's Fair, which is promoted as modern, progressive, and leading to the future. All the Scandinavian countries have pavilions, but the Swedish and Finnish (Fig. 52-8) ones have the most impact, winning international acclaim and generating great interest in Scandinavian furniture and design. Unfortunately, World War II intervenes, delaying further growth and expansion.

Following the war, Scandinavia recovers quickly and strives to make Scandinavian design important both at home and abroad. Working for mostly middle-class societies with few rich or poor, designers concentrate on modest and practical forms, not luxurious ones. Sweden, Finland, and Denmark, more than Norway and Iceland, market themselves and their designs as forward thinking and progressive. To emphasize good design and increase connections between art and industry, Scandinavian design and craft organizations hold exhibitions and competitions at home and display their works at various international design fairs, such as the Milan Triennales. During the 1950s and 1960s, North America embraces architectural principles, furniture, and decorative

▲ **52-1.** Main Railway Terminus, 1904–1914; Helsinki, Finland; Eliel Saarinen, Herman Gesellius, and Armas Lindgren.

▲ **52-2.** Stockholm City Library, 1920–1928; Stockholm, Sweden; Gunnar Asplund.

objects from Scandinavia. Danish and Swedish Modern become indicative of a way of designing buildings, interiors, and furniture that preserves the look of handicrafts while adopting modern manufacturing methods. Designers and manufacturers in North America begin to emulate the look, if not the concepts, of works from Scandinavia.

CONCEPTS

Scandinavian designers and architects are less concerned with design theory than practical and social humanitarian matters. This approach centers on creating designs that are functional yet reflect humanity in planning, scale, and materials. Designers believe that architecture and design are not just about aesthetics, but also must address economical housing and functional living quarters for all citizens and make good design available for the worker as well as the well-to-do. Accordingly, designs are often modest and adaptable, utilizing natural materials and simple construction methods. Scandinavians promote good design through education and collaboration among designers, architects, manufacturers, and, sometimes, the state. Equally important is Nordic or Scandinavian identity, so the vocabulary of design frequently comes from folk or vernacular forms, the natural environment or landscape, and native materials, as well as individual elements from each country or their collective heritage. Designers maintain a sense of nationalism while accepting ideas of modernism.

CHARACTERISTICS AND MOTIFS

Common to Scandinavian design are simplicity, human scale, modesty, practicality, elegance, and excellent craftsmanship. Also evident are such shared Scandinavian traditions as the environment or landscape, respect for materials, and natural materials. Characteristics drawn from the landscape include movement, textures, complex compositions, and/or curvilinear forms. Expressions in architecture, interiors, and furniture are often a reworking of traditional forms in a simplified or refined manner to suit modern aesthetics and lifestyles. Whether purely functional, modernist, or organic, important design characteristics are unity, texture, and light. Designs may be eclectic, adapting elements from other architects, styles, and cultures.

- *Motifs*. Purely modern expressions often have no or minimal applied ornament or decoration, so there are few motifs, except stylized foliage and plants (Fig. 52-9). National Romanticism adapts and stylizes Scandinavian plants and foliage for decoration.

▲ **52-3.** Tuberculosis Sanatorium and Paimio armchair, 1929–1933; Paimio, Finland; Alvar Aalto.

ARCHITECTURE

Scandinavian architecture ranges from rugged stone compositions with steeply pitched roofs and bay windows to plain brick façades composed of geometric forms and rectangular windows, to purely International Style buildings with flat roofs, glass curtain walls or large windows, *pilotis*, and white concrete walls. These come from various national and international influences.

National Romanticism and Neoclassicism dominate architecture during the first decades of the 20th century in Scandinavia. Dating from the late 19th century, National Romanticism draws on folk or vernacular traditions to establish a national identity. Believing that folk traditions are unspoiled by modern life and industry, architects incorporate wood for material and construction methods, handicrafts, and local traditions into building types and forms to devise what they hope is an indigenous design language. Important precursors to National Romanticism include Scandinavian log cabins and other wooden architecture, the Arts and Crafts Movement in England, the architecture of H. H. Richardson in the United States, and Art Nouveau. In Finland, the leading practitioner of National Romanticism, and later Modernism, Eliel Saarinen, is influenced by the Middle Ages, Art Nouveau, and Richardsonian Romanesque.

Dominating architecture through the 1920s, Scandinavian Neoclassicism, like that in the rest of Europe, is made more relevant for the 20th century by simplification and elimination. A spare and stripped-down appearance defines the style, although classical ordering and some classical elements, such as columns, may be used. Geometric forms create the composition, and rules and order are balanced or enhanced by individual creativity. Often eclectic, Scandinavian Neoclassicism borrows from the Renaissance, Baroque, early-19th-century Neoclassicism, and vernacular traditions.

Modernism, or Functionalism as it is called there, makes its appearance in Scandinavia about 1930. There is some awareness of Modernism in the late 1920s evident in Scandinavian publications, especially after the 1927 *Weissenhofsiedlung* housing exhibit in Stuttgart, Germany. Public housing during this period, especially in Sweden and Denmark, begins to follow modernist principles for site and layout. Exterior design may still incorporate traditional forms and materials. Finland leads the way toward Modernism in the work of a group of progressive young architects, including Alvar Aalto and Erik Bryggman. Aalto's Turku Sonomat Building (1927–1929) is considered the first Modern or International Style building in Finland.

DESIGN SPOTLIGHT

Architecture: Small in scale and defined by a central courtyard, Säynätsalo Town Hall has four wings that contain offices, shops, the Council Chamber, and a library. Administration offices are placed around the courtyard to take advantage of the views. Located close to the central marketplace, the structure uses traditional building materials, including uneven red brick for the façade, wood for trim and ceilings, and copper for the roof. Groups of tall windows covered with vertical slats to filter the light repeat along the walls. Custom details in materials, joinery, and hardware add to the effect of a building integrating with its surroundings.

▲ 52-4. Säynätsalo Town Hall, 1949–1952; Jyväskylä, Finland; Alvar Aalto.

The 1930 Stockholm Exhibition is the seminal event in the adoption of Modernism in architecture and interiors, less so in decorative arts and furniture, in Sweden, Denmark, and Norway. Designed by Erik Gunnar Asplund, the buildings exemplify German and French principles of modern architecture and bring together many examples of the International Style in one location. Leaders of Modernism in Scandinavia include Asplund (Fig. 52-2) of Sweden, Eliel Saarinen (Fig. 52-1) and Aalto (Fig. 52-3, 52-4, 52-6) of Finland, and Arne Jacobsen (Fig. 52-5) of Denmark. Although some buildings are purely International Style, some architects, like Aalto, soon move beyond the cubic, flat-roofed forms of the Bauhaus and Le Corbusier to incorporate Scandinavian forms and materials, thereby creating individuality and uniqueness of expression. Aalto's work lays important foundations for postwar Organic and Sculptural Modern architecture in the United States.

Through the middle of the 20th century, Scandinavian architects continue to refine their understanding of the Modern or International Style, adapting concepts, techniques, and material usage from both inside and outside the region. Some, such as Aalto and Jacobsen, are recognized for their creative solutions to design projects in other parts of the world, including North America. Common building types include railway terminals (Fig. 52-1), churches, libraries (Fig. 52-2), town halls (Fig. 52-4), houses (Fig. 52-6), and public housing developments in which standardization, prefabrication, and mass production enable numerous dwellings to be built quickly.

Public and Private Buildings

■ *Site Orientation*. Harmony with the landscape is a governing principle of design. Architects carefully position buildings on the site to capture views and sunlight and to create windbreaks where needed. Urban buildings usually relate to public transportation routes or dominate city centers (Fig. 52-1, 52-2, 52-4, 52-5). Public housing blocks generally are arranged in parallel rows perpendicular to streets and to permit the maximum light and air for each unit. Some developments contain schools, day care centers, community centers, and green spaces. A few are picturesque groups of individual buildings, reflecting a vernacular heritage.

■ *Floor Plans*. Plans may be simple or interlocking rectangles. Some have circular or curvilinear spaces or walls. Open planning permits flexibility in arrangements in both public and private buildings. In public buildings, important entries and circulation spaces are carefully situated for easy access to other spaces. Some public buildings and large residences center on semi-enclosed courtyards (Fig. 52-4). Function and practicality are important

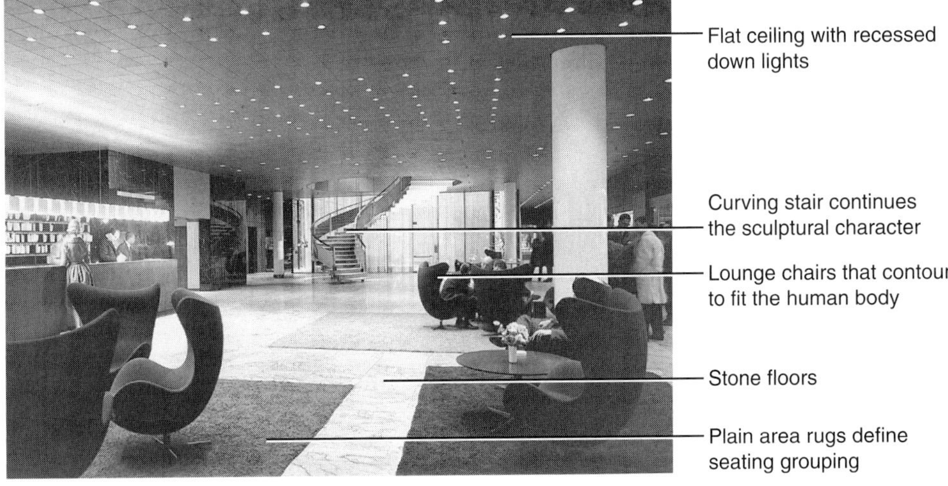

▲ **52-5.** S.A.S. Royal Hotel and lobby, 1959; Copenhagen, Denmark; Arne Jacobsen.

planning concepts, so multifunctional rooms with activity zones characterize residences, which are usually small (Fig. 52-6).

■ *Materials*. Materials include stone, brick, wood, reinforced concrete, steel, and glass (Fig. 52-1, 52-2, 52-4, 52-5, 52-6). Buildings are often white stucco, concrete, or marble that may be mixed with wood planks or logs. Houses in brick and wood are common.

■ *Façades*. National Romantic façades often are asymmetrical with rough stone bases and upper stories of stone or brick. Contrasting colors of stone may define fenestration. Wooden details, such as roof rafters or logs, are important. Geometric forms, symmetry, and simplified details define Neoclassical façades. Modernist façades are plain and clean lined with few applied moldings or stringcourses (Fig. 52-1, 52-2, 52-3, 52-4, 52-5, 52-6). Horizontality is emphasized especially through bands of windows. Façades with environmental or traditional elements mix concrete or stucco with brick, stone, or wood but still have few moldings or other articulation. The harsh Scandinavian climate limits expressions of structure typical of Modernist architecture, and naturalism appears in complex forms that suggest growth and movement. Balconies, stairs, entire or parts of floors, and other elements may project in rectangular or curvilinear forms. Some structures or parts of them are raised on piers, and balconies or porches may have plain metal or wooden railings. Pergolas, found on large residences, act as transition spaces to the exterior.

■ *Windows and Doors*. Neoclassical buildings often have rectangular windows with no moldings surrounding them, whereas National Romantic ones have a variety of windows from bays to arched to rectangular with various surrounds (Fig. 52-1). Window walls or horizontal bands of windows define modern buildings (Fig. 52-3, 52-5, 52-6). Entrances, often covered to protect from the weather, may be either prominent or somewhat hidden. Doors are usually wood with glazing.

■ *Roofs*. Flat roofs dominate modernist or Bauhaus-influenced buildings, although some question their suitability to the Scandi-

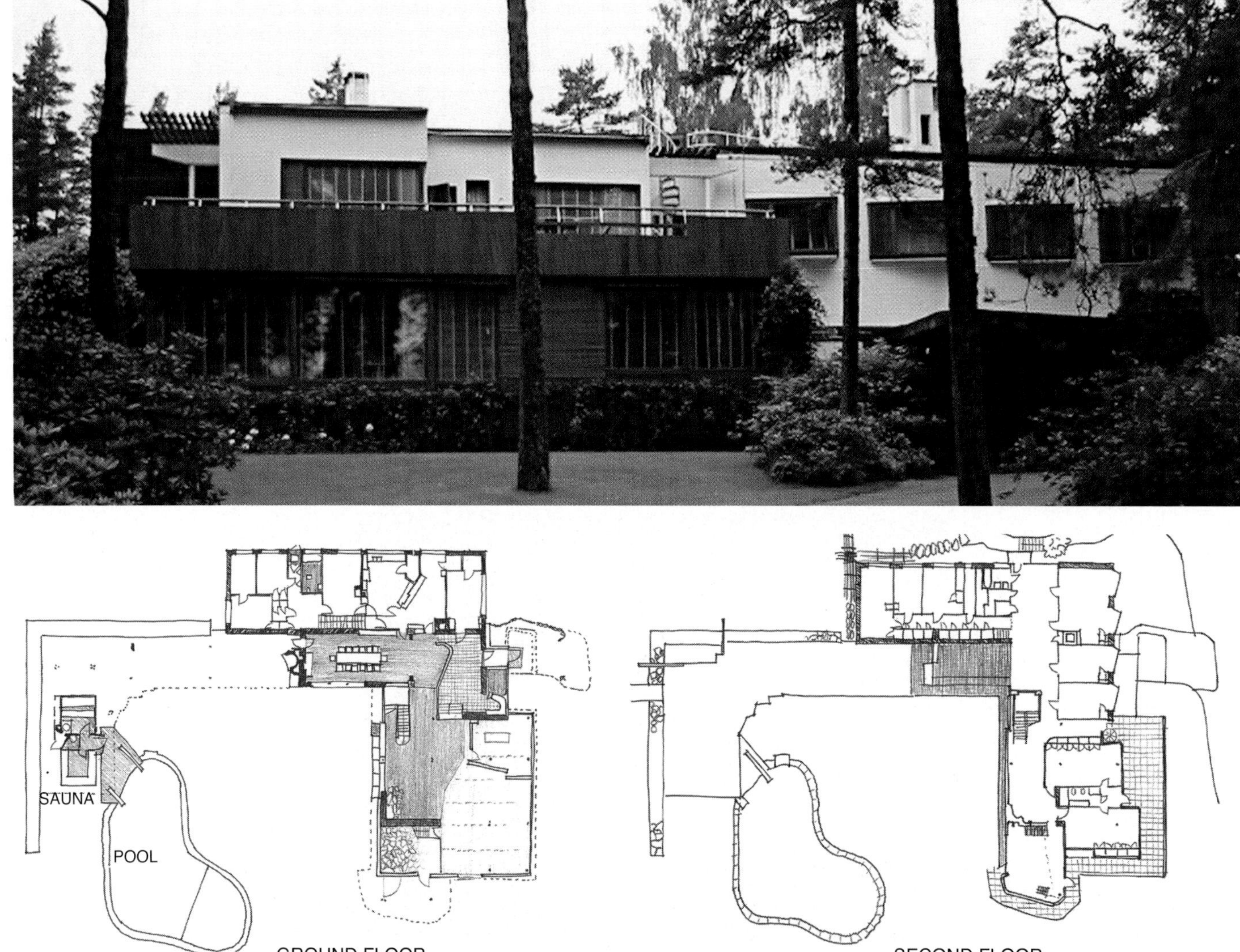

▲ **52-6.** *Villa Mairea,* floor plans, and stair hall, 1937–1938; Noormarkku, Finland; Alvar Aalto.

navian climate (Fig. 52-2, 52-3, 52-4, 52-5, 52-6). Other types of roofs on Scandinavian buildings include single- and double-pitched gables and, later, curved or free-form roofs.

INTERIORS

Most interiors are simple and modest with minimal furnishings. Function, lightness, natural light, and an appreciation for natural materials and textures are more important than applied decoration and/or just filling a space. Interiors designed by architects have the most variety and show greater concern for pleasant sensory experiences through spatial changes, color, light, and texture. Where possible, architects use large windows to maximize light and air and to unite the interior with the landscape. This, together with the long winters, results in interior environments that contrast large glazed openings with more intimate, often fireplace- and hearth-centered alcoves. Wood is an important element whether through its use as a major building component, an interior finish, or in furniture or accessories.

For complete unity, architects often design both the interiors and furnishings (Fig. 52-5, 52-6, 52-7). Interiors, like architecture, reveal a strong sense of nationalism in traditional materials and forms, wood construction, and craftsmanship. To make small spaces seem larger, windows borrow space from outside, colors are light, and high ceilings add volumetric space. Because of the climate, many living areas have fireplaces, and designers, such as Aalto, frequently enhance the Scandinavian hearth with modern, sculptural elements. Furniture arrangements are planned to give the greatest freedom of activity within the usually limited amounts of space. Storage or seating may be built in.

Public and Private Buildings

- *Color*. Most often colors are muted. Reflecting nature and the landscape, hues include shades of brown, green, blue, and yellow, accented with white and black (Fig. 52-9). Occasional spots of bright colors, such as orange or red, add dynamism, variety, and interest.
- *Floors*. Floors are of wood, tile, marble, stone, and concrete (Fig. 52-5, 52-6, 52-7). For color and warmth, designers incorporate white rugs with deep piles and soft patterns, sisal matting, or flat woven or piled rugs with geometric designs in strong colors similar to other modern rooms in other countries (Fig. 52-6). Used extensively, rya rugs originate in Sweden, Norway, and Finland. These hand-knotted rugs with a long pile have colorful geometric or floral patterns.

▲ **52-6.** Continued

■ *Walls*. Walls are plainly treated often with plaster and paint of a single hue or with wood planks or large panels (Fig. 52-5, 52-6, 52-7, 52-8). Rooms often combine several wall treatments, most commonly wood or brick and plaster. Brick walls may be whitewashed. Wallpapers are not common, but fabrics sometimes cover walls. Shelves or other storage may be attached to walls to free the floor space below. Structural supports or pillars of metal or concrete may be covered in wood, rattan, or leather.

■ *Windows and Doors*. Simple metal or wood moldings frame windows (Fig. 52-7). Curtain panels hang straight so that they can open or close easily. Fabrics may be plain, woven solids, open weaves, or heavily textured solids, and usually are in light colors. Alternative treatments include blinds and shades. Where possible, windows are left bare to enhance the view or allow in the most natural light (Fig. 52-6, 52-7). Interior doors are plain or have panels and are surrounded by simple wooden moldings. Some have glazing or transoms.

■ *Ceilings*. Ceilings may be flat, curved, or sloped with a variety of treatments (Fig. 52-5, 52-6, 52-7, 52-8). Wood and plaster are most typical. Some have unique architectural light wells that flood the interiors with natural lighting.

DESIGN SPOTLIGHT

Interior: Surrounded by grass and tall trees, the Municipal Library shows inspiration from the International Style with its stark, smooth, white, plastered exterior walls and rectangular grid windows. The interiors, however, project a more natural, earthy character because of the extensive use of wood, which is introduced by Alvar Aalto with this project. Six different types of wood cover ceilings, walls, floors, and furnishings. The building, composed of two main volumes, develops in plan view from two overlapping blocks, one for the library space and the other for the lecture hall. Unique in concept, the lecture hall features plain wall treatments that emphasize materials; a long row of windows to admit light; and an undulating, wood paneled ceiling that enhances the acoustics of the space. To complete the effect, Aalto designs custom furnishings that include stools, bookcases, wall panels, and light-diffusing lamps. Aalto's custom details are apparent throughout the building.

▲ **52-7.** Discussion and lecture hall, Municipal Library, 1927–1935; Viipuri, Finland; Alvar Aalto.

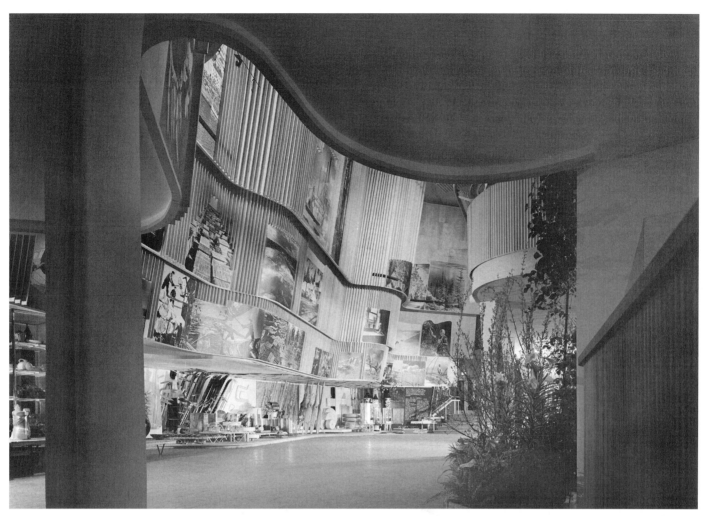

▲ **52-8.** Interior, Finnish Pavilion, World's Fair Exhibition, 1939; New York City, New York; Alvar Aalto.

■ *Textiles*. Natural fibers, such as wool or linen, and handwoven textiles are characteristic. Fabrics may be plain or have Scandinavian patterns and bright colors (Fig. 52-9). Patterns include naturalistic or stylized designs, stripes, or geometric shapes. Texture is important in plain fabrics. Upholstery consists of plain, woven fabrics, often of wool or linen, in muted colors, white, or black, and vinyl, leather, or animal skin (Fig. 52-11, 52-15). Designers prefer woven textiles over printed. Although this in part derives from their hand-weaving tradition and is similar to the Bauhaus aesthetic, Scandinavian designers admire the simple honesty of woven textiles. Some furniture designers use webbing of jute or hemp in place of upholstery.

■ *Lighting*. Natural lighting pervades all types of interiors. A variety of artificial lighting sources, most of which are incandescent, is characteristic. Fixtures, which may be designed by the architect, can be a combination of recessed, surface-mounted, or hanging pendants; floor lamps; and table lamps (Fig. 52-5, 52-6, 52-10). Made of metal, wood, and ceramic, forms harmonize with the rest of the interior.

▲ **52-9.** Textiles: Cottons and linens, c. 1950s–1960s; Sweden and Finland; manufactured by Marimekko and Nordika.

▲ **52-9.** Continued

▲ **52-11.** Blue chair, 1929; Finland; Eliel Saarinen.

▲ **52-10.** Lighting: Chandeliers, c. 1950s; Finland and Denmark; Alvar Aalto and Paul Henningsen.

FURNISHINGS AND DECORATIVE ARTS

Scandinavian furniture ranges from totally handmade to completely mass-produced, with varying increments between the two. As the countries industrialize, especially after World War II, furniture design becomes a collaborative effort among designers, artisans, and manufacturers, a concept that arises from strong craft and cabinetmaker organizations. Furniture designers view themselves as artists to industry, similar to the *Deustche Werkbund,* the Bauhaus, and Le Corbusier. But they do not feel compelled to incorporate machine or industrial imagery into their work. Instead, they emulate the Vienna Secession model of craftsmanship and individuality. As a result, their furniture reflects their crafts heritage in wood through simple but often beautifully detailed forms; contours that fit the human body; and a warm, timeless quality. Often designed for small spaces, furnishings are also economical and practical. Scandinavian designers create all types of furniture but become particularly well known for their lounge and dining chairs and storage units (Fig. 52-3, 52-5, 52-12, 52-13, 52-14, 52-15, 52-16, 52-18). Designers around the world adapt Scandinavian ideas for commercial and residential applications.

Scandinavian furniture can be categorized into three types: designs inspired by or based upon traditional forms that are simplified for the 20th century and adapted to mass production, furniture designed by architects for their projects to achieve total unity, and experiments with new materials and techniques of construction. Preferring the warmth and humanness of wood to steel, designers use such modern techniques as prefabrication, laminated wood, and new materials such as plywood. They also consider the needs of the user, particularly in areas where space is limited and functional requirements are important. Like other modernists, they usually believe that all people have the same basic needs. After World War II, Scandinavian governments, many designers, and architects see furniture as a tool to improve the lives and tastes of the public. They promote simplicity and excellence in design through publications and exhibits.

In the postwar period, Scandinavian furniture becomes extremely popular in modern or contemporary houses, particularly in the United States, and one of several alternatives for furnishings. Sleek and unadorned, the furniture appears up-to-date, and its form is appealing from any angle. The lightness, warmth, and handcrafted appearance appeal to consumers, and it mixes well with traditional furnishings to easily achieve a more contemporary look. Scandinavian furniture is marketed as Danish or Swedish Modern and the Teak Style.

One feature contributing to the worldwide popularity of Scandinavian furniture is flat packaging or knock-down (KD) fittings used by many manufacturers. Both practical and economical, KD allows individual pieces, large or complex storage systems, or entire room furnishings, such as a kitchen, to be shipped in flat cartons and assembled on site with simple tools. The joinings are so uncomplicated that they become almost universal in the manufacturing and shipping of furniture from one part of the world to another. A pioneer in marketing KD furniture is Sweden's IKEA, whose first store opens in 1953. In 1965, the firm opens its first outlet where customers choose furnishings from displays and take the cartons of unassembled furniture with them.

DESIGN SPOTLIGHT

Furniture: These furniture pieces have the simplicity, sophistication, and depth of Hans Wegner's furnishings. Working primarily in wood, he consistently emphasizes naturally finished materials, handcrafted processes, and ergonomically contoured seating. Chairs are noteworthy for their smooth curved surfaces, rounded legs, cane or wood seats, and beautiful proportions. Joints are elegant and well detailed. Based on the traditional 18th-century Windsor chair, the Peacock chair has an ash frame, bentwood hoop back, teak armrests, and wenge dowel splines. Storage units are plain, rectangular, and unadorned. Some have open compartments covered by sliding doors. Emphasis is on the beauty of the wood.

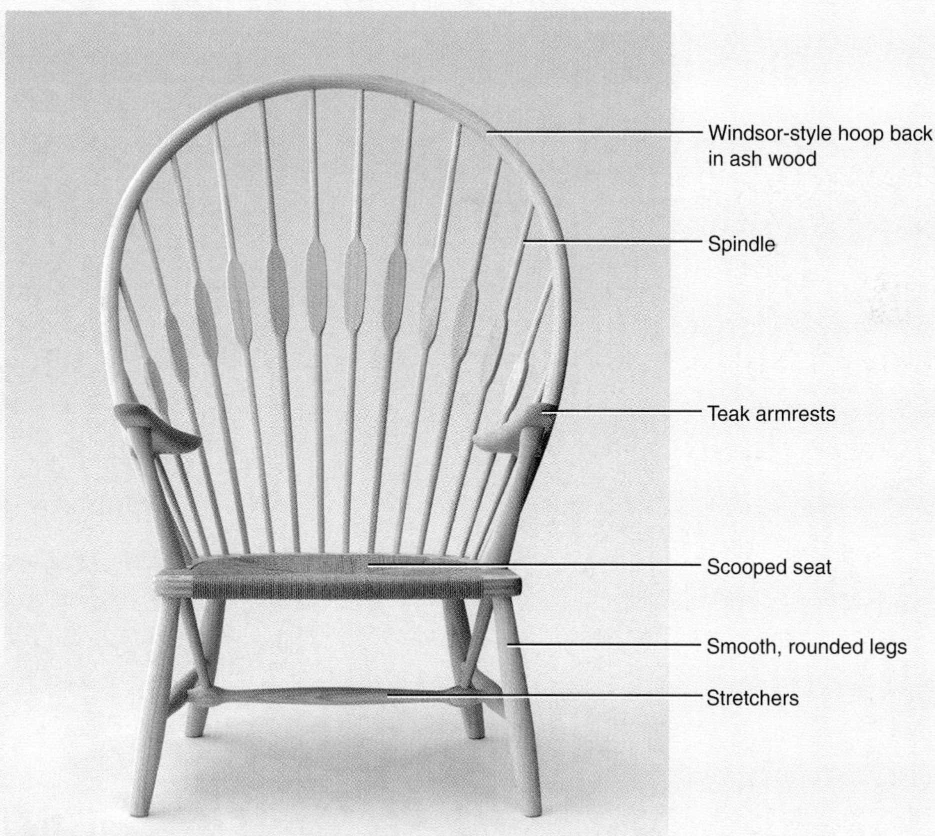

▲ **52-12.** Peacock chair, armchair, and storage cabinet in teak, 1944–1949; Denmark; Hans Wegner. (Continued on next page.)

Public and Private Buildings

■ *Materials*. Early on, a few designers use tubular metal for furniture, but most use common woods native to their individual countries, including oak, fir, birch, beech, and ash (Fig. 52-11, 52-12, 52-13, 52-14, 52-15, 52-16, 52-17, 52-18). For more expensive pieces, designers choose teak; rosewood; mahogany; or wenge, a black wood from Africa. Pieces are lightly stained or left unfinished and simply waxed or polished. A linseed oil finish is the most popular on open-grained woods. Designers sometimes choose light-colored stains in reaction to public tastes for dark, imitation mahogany ones.

Plywood becomes a more common furniture material in Scandinavia after World War I, partly because it can be easily bent and shaped. Although it was previously considered a cheap substitute for solid wood, its use in the construction of airplanes and boats substantially improves the quality. And newly invented glues make it even stronger than before. Designers, such as Aalto (Fig. 52-3), experiment with laminated wood for furniture frames. Laminated wood is stronger than solid wood, may be easily shaped, and is flexible.

After World War II, Scandinavian designers turn to new or industrial materials. Some, such as Poul Kjaerholm (Fig. 52-16), use metal either entirely or for important elements in their pieces. Beginning in the 1960s, Arne Jacobsen (Fig. 52-15) and Eero Aarnio create seating from molded, continuous plastic forms, sometimes covered with padding and upholstery.

■ *Seating*. Seating includes chairs, lounges, stools, and sofas (Fig. 52-3, 52-5, 52-7, 52-11, 52-12, 52-13, 52-14, 52-15, 52-16). In search of forms that fit the human body, many designs grow out of the study of anthropometics and ergonomics. Thus, seating often has a sculptural appearance and is very comfortable. Much seating is of wood with simplified traditional forms or adaptations from other cultures. Legs, arms, and supports may be solid or laminated wood. Solid wood legs are usually straight, rounded, and tapered, while laminated ones are curved for flexibility. Some seating is cantilevered or has continuous, closed curvilinear frames instead of legs. Backs and seats may be lightly upholstered, have fabric webbing, or be of shaped plywood. Seats may be solid wood, cane, rush, rattan, or upholstered. Designs may be distinctive as in Finn Juhl's chairs (Fig. 52-14) and settees in which the back and seat appear to float above the frame instead of being attached to it. Lounge chairs and sofas may have exposed wooden frames that match chairs or may be fully upholstered with or without arms. Sometimes seating consists of a low, built-in platform with a cushion and backrest separated or attached to the wall. Hans Wegner designs a sofa that can easily become a sleep unit and therefore offers great flexibility.

DESIGN SPOTLIGHT

▲ **52-12.** Continued

▲ **52-13.** Eva armchair in laminated beech, 1934; Sweden; Bruno Mathsson.

▲ **52-14.** Armchair, 1945; Denmark; Finn Juhl.

▲ **52-15.** Ant chair/Model 3107-Series 7 chair, 1955; Egg chair, 1956-1957; and Swan Chair, 1956-1957; Denmark; Arne Jacobsen.

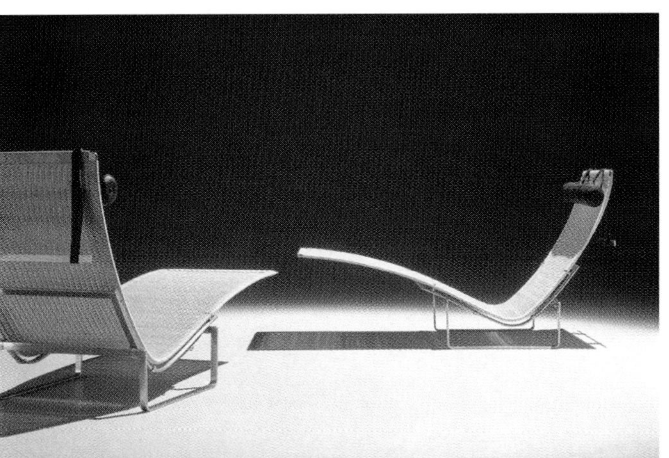

▲ **52-16.** Chaise, Model PK24, 1965; Denmark; Poul Kjaerholm.

▲ **52-17.** Coffee table in teak, 1960s; Denmark; Grete Jalk.

▲ **52-18.** Dining table and chairs, Ørensend Series, 1955; Denmark; Børge Mogensen.

■ *Tables.* Tables, which vary in size and shape, are usually of wood, wood with glass tops, or marble (Fig. 52-17, 52-18). Aalto's tables have curving laminated wooden legs and wooden or glass tops. Dining tables usually extend for greater flexibility, such as one by Bruno Mathsson that extends from only a few inches wide to over 100″ wide.

■ *Storage.* Storage may be free-standing, built-in, or hang on the wall to save floor space (Fig. 52-12). Most storage pieces are rectangular in form with no applied decoration or moldings. Beauty lies in the combination of shapes and the grain of the wood. Pulls may be wood or metal, but they are always simple in design. An innovation is unit furniture in which the user chooses individual modules or units to meet particular storage needs. Unit furniture adapts to any room through a combination of shelves and cabinets with doors and drawers. Designers develop sizes and shapes of individual modules by studying the requirements of the users and the dimensions of the objects to be stored.

■ *Beds.* Beds are low with simple headboards and, sometimes, footboards, relying on proportions and the wood itself for beauty. Headboards are usually rectangular panels or are composed of vertical uprights within a frame. Some unit furniture includes a pull-out bed. Aalto designs a bed resembling a greatly simplified Empire boat bed.

■ *Decorative Arts.* Designers create beauty in everyday objects in ceramics, glass, metal, and wood. Architects, such as Aalto (Fig. 52-19) and Jacobsen, design lighting, glass, and other decorative objects either for specific interiors or for mass production.

■ *Later Interpretations.* Many postwar furniture designers, including Charles and Ray Eames, are inspired by Scandinavian design concepts of lightness, flexibility, good craftsmanship, and use of laminated woods. They develop these ideas further. The Scandinavian craft traditions find many adherents in North America, England, and Japan (Fig. 52-20), including Wharton Eshrick, George Nakashima, and Sam Maloof. Many pieces of furniture by prominent Scandinavian designers are still in production in the early 21st century, a testament to their originality, functionality, and adaptability. Scandinavian furniture designers continue adapting earlier forms and elements and develop new ones to meet contemporary needs and requirements. IKEA stores continue to sell Scandinavian furniture and accessories throughout the world.

▲ **52-19.** Decorative Arts: Savoy vase, c. 1930s; Finland; Alvar Aalto.

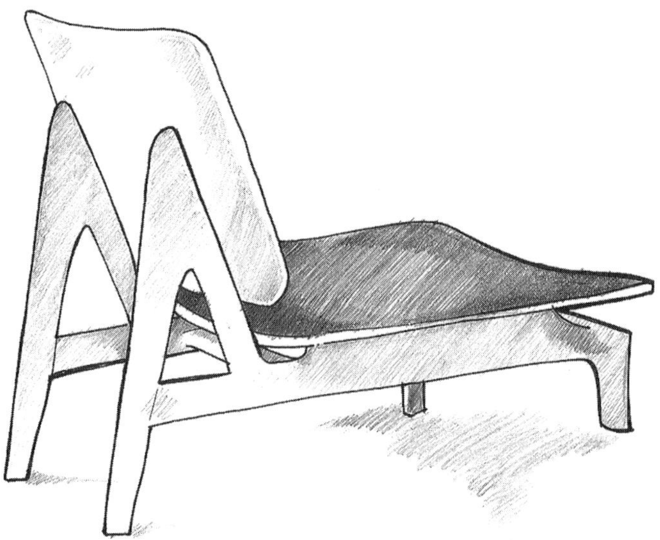

▲ **52-20.** Later Interpretation: Lounge chair, 2002; Japan; Sunao Jindo, manufactured by Goby Works.

CHAPTER 53

Geometric Modern

1930s–1960s

> *The word modern means up to date; and to use the modern style means to take advantage of the technical achievements of the age. It means using the new materials and the new ways of construction that have been developed in recent years. It also means to study changes in our way of living and in our taste.*
>
> —Philip Johnson, ideas derived from "Drama of Decoration," *Arts and Decoration*, February 1935

Geometric Modern continues the design language and many of the ideas of the Bauhaus and International Style through work of the originators and their followers. Key characteristics include functionalism, geometric forms, little applied decoration, and new materials and technologies. During the period, Geometric Modern architecture and design enter the mainstream, particularly in the United States, which becomes the world leader of Modernism. Also important are the development of modern commercial interiors and furnishings and the expansion of the interior design profession.

HISTORICAL AND SOCIAL

From the 1930s through the mid-1940s, the world of design is in turmoil. The rise of Fascism in Germany and Italy and the militaristic expansion of Japan through much of East Asia stifle growth. World War II brings more world involvement and greater destruction across the globe than World War I had. World's Fairs or exhibitions are held in many parts of the United States despite the tragedy unfolding overseas. These exhibitions, all of which feature a streamlined look into the future, are the major outlets for creative expression prior to World War II. Following the war, there is a period of optimism and enthusiasm for the future in the United States, which receives no physical damage from the war. Europe must recover and rebuild following the devastation and destruction.

In the postwar period, United States industries convert quickly from war to civilian production and build upon wartime developments in technology, speed of production, and new materials. Because of this, the United States becomes the leading industrial power, producing half of the world's goods, particularly automobiles, chemicals, and electronics. Americans ship their products and, by extension, their culture, design, and construction expertise all over the world. Spending by the U.S. federal government for veterans' support and education; loans; social programs; and the European Economic Recovery, or Marshall Plan, to help rebuild Europe contribute to the nation's prosperity. The booming economy creates new jobs, so standards of living rise, social mobility is higher, and more people own homes than ever before. The middle class grows larger, and the number of white-collar workers expands. More people go to college as educational opportunities increase. Many women leave factories and return home, but others enter the workforce in greater numbers.

Although it is one of the victors, France does not recover quickly and this causes her to lose artistic supremacy, except in couture fashion. Neither does Modernism become mainstream there. Before the war, the Bauhaus and International Style principles had only minimal acceptance, and following the war, most French designers turn their attention to luxury goods as in the heyday of Art Deco. A few attempt to revive the notion of the *artiste-décorateur*.

Germany recovers quickly despite her defeat, but takes little artistic leadership in modern design. Many of the early Modernist leaders who could have assumed a leading role were forced to emigrate to other countries during the war.

Italy recovers from the war quickly also. Freed from the repression of prewar Fascism, creative energy and innovation burst forth in many areas, and Italy begins to assert supremacy in design and the decorative arts. In 1947, the Milan Triennale resumes, soon becoming the world's leading design show and a platform for Italian designs as well as new and progressive ideas from other countries.

England continues to suffer from shortages in materials. The Utility Scheme, which restricts materials and governs design as it had during the war, encourages practicality and simplicity but little innovation in design. The 1951 Festival of Britain attempts to overcome this problem by promoting excellence in British art, architecture, design, and decorative arts. Not until the 1960s does Britain exert leadership in art, design, and popular culture.

Japan, recovering from its defeat under the guidance of the United States, becomes an industrial power and a major design force. It welcomes a number of European designers in the 1930s and embraces Modernism.

All is not well, however. The Cold War threatens to destroy the hard-won peace. This hostility between the United States and its allies and the Union of Soviet Socialist Republics (USSR) and her allies from the 1940s through the 1980s stops just short of an all-out war and includes the nuclear arms race. Fear of nuclear war prompts some Americans to build home bomb shelters. Anti-Communist concerns arise, and perceived un-American ideas and practices are questioned. In further attempts to stop the spread of Communism, the United States engages in conflicts, such as the Korean War, fought from 1950 to 1953. Consumer debt from mortgages and the new credit cards increases. Minorities, although employed in greater numbers in industry, do not experience the widespread prosperity.

During the postwar period, the United States also becomes the world leader in Modernism. Widespread prosperity and optimism establish a favorable climate for and public acceptance of the Modern image. Also contributing is the significant and lasting impact on the language of the new architecture and architectural education made by prominent Bauhaus practitioners. Beginning in the middle of the 1930s, influential members of the Bauhaus immigrate to the United States to escape the war. Among the first are architects Walter Gropius and Ludwig Mies van der Rohe, who bring Bauhaus ideas and principles to England, and then to the United States. Gropius teaches in, and later chairs, the architecture department at Harvard University in Boston. In 1937, he hires Marcel Breuer, also from the Bauhaus, as a professor, and the two become partners in architectural practice. After his arrival in 1937, Mies van der Rohe becomes director of architecture at the Armour Institute, later the Illinois Institute of Technology (IIT) in Chicago. Through the efforts of Gropius, Breuer, and Mies, the Bauhaus methods of teaching architecture replace the European Beaux-Arts model of studying exemplary buildings of the past. Although Le Corbusier does not come to the United States and designs only one building there, he influences architecture through his work, in which he explores new directions for functionalism, his *Five Points of Architecture*, and his modular systems. He collaborates with architects in the United States and Brazil.

In the early 1950s, critiques of Modernism begin. Some originate in appraisals of modern life and society, particularly the role of consumerism and corporate influences. Others come from individuals and groups, such as *Congres Internationaux d'Architecture Moderne* (CIAM), which challenge the anonymity of Modernism, charging it with lacking community identity and, more important, not providing appropriate monuments or symbols of a particular group or society. Universal solutions and standards for good design and taste are questioned, especially in light of the needs of minorities, the individuality of consumer markets, and the planned obsolescence of yearly models. Designers begin exploring different means to address these issues.

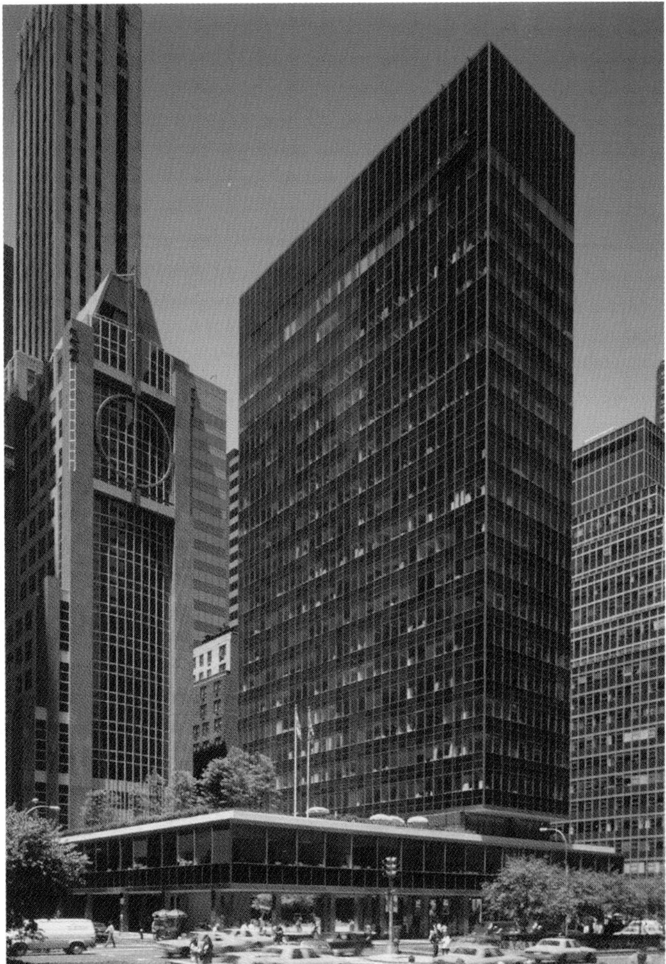

▲ **53-1.** Lever House, 1951–1952; New York City, New York; Gordon Bunshaft at Skidmore, Owings, and Merrill.

DESIGN SPOTLIGHT

Architecture: The Seagram Building, Mies van der Rohe's first commercial building in the United States, shows his usual elegant simplicity in its pure geometric form and richness of material. Raised on columns, the structure is sheathed in amber-tinted glass with bronze I-beams and panels. American fire codes require that steel be covered with fireproof materials, which Mies will not do. So the bronze grid is not the actual structure of the building but covers the steel structure beneath. During the day, the building appears warm and dense, but becomes transparent golden brown at night when lit internally. Placement at the rear of the site focuses greater attention on the building. Spreading before it is a granite plaza with two symmetrical reflecting pools with fountains. The Seagram Building, along with the earlier nearby Lever Building by SOM, establishes the precedent of and sets the design standards for corporate headquarters in the 1950s and 1960s.

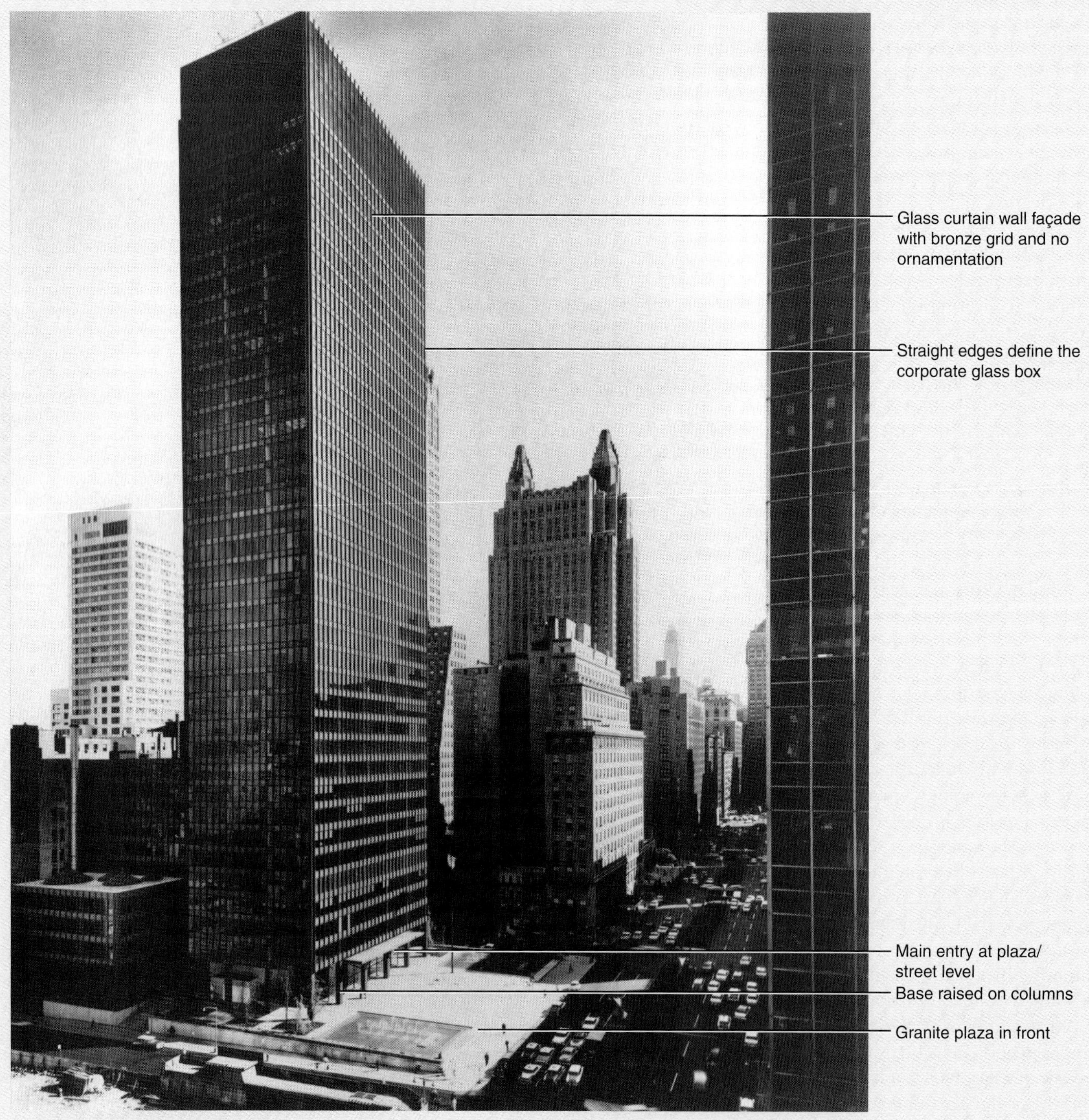

▲ **53-2.** Seagram Building, 1954–1958; New York City, New York; Ludwig Mies van der Rohe and Philip Johnson.

By the end of the 1950s, high-style Modern architecture and design begin to move in different directions as important postwar architects and designers establish their own identities and/or explore new theories and design vocabularies. In the 1960s, a more youth-oriented culture arises, and it craves excitement, novelty, and a faster pace of living supported by inexpensive, disposable items of material culture. The dominance of Geometric Modernism begins to fade but does not completely disappear.

CONCEPTS

Geometric Modernism continues the design vocabulary of the Bauhaus and International Style but not necessarily their political overtones or desire to reform society and culture through architecture and design. In the United States, for example, Geometric Modernism becomes aligned with faith and hope in democracy, egalitarianism, dynamism, and new technologies. The United States design agenda of creating images for itself as a new world power and leader of industry is different from that of Europe, where the priority is rebuilding damaged cities and supplying housing for displaced citizens. The thrust for new and modern construction in the United States comes from the private sector, to which style and image are more important than ideas and theories. Geometric Modernism downplays the Early Modernists' ideas of social reform in deference to the ideals of capitalism in the public arena and the image of the good life in private, reflecting a strong confidence in free enterprise.

In the postwar era, designers and architects embrace standardization, prefabrication, mass production, and new materials and technologies, particularly those developed during the war. The debate is no longer whether these techniques should be used, but how to use them quickly and effectively to produce well-designed goods and architecture for modern society. The inherent character of Geometric Modern offers additional attractive ideas and associations. Some believe that functionalism, efficiency, simplicity, and new materials and techniques point toward a new world where progress and growth fulfill the promises of a better tomorrow today. Elements of Modernism readily adapt to various needs and functions. Furthermore, the efficiency, practicality, and economy of modern architecture, interiors, and furniture appeal to those who revel in a no-nonsense or modest approach to life and design.

The spread of Modern ideas and design is aided by museums, periodicals, and department stores. They sponsor contests, competitions, and exhibitions that promote the principles of Modern design as excellent and demonstrating good taste. For example, beginning in 1951 Good Design competitions and exhibits of winning products are held by the Museum of Modern Art (MOMA) and the Chicago Merchandise Mart. Winners, whose work exemplifies modern design, technical innovation, and unity, include Frank Lloyd Wright and George Nelson. Books and periodicals in the United States and abroad champion modernism, including *Architectural Forum*, *Domus* in Italy, *Form* in Sweden, and *Architectural Review* and *Design* in Britain. Additionally, architectural handbooks, manuals, and graphic standards focused on modern design replace the theories and manifestos of earlier. Through these means, principles of Modernism become institutionalized in the United States, and the term *Modern* comes to mean up-to-date, in step with technical advancements of the time, new materials, new construction methods, new ways of living, and most important, good design. Sometimes designs of modernist character are called Contemporary to further divorce Modernism from its previous political and social reform ideology. Contemporary, like Modern, implies designs that are for today.

CHARACTERISTICS AND MOTIFS

Geometric Modernism incorporates such characteristics of the Bauhaus and International Style as simplicity, geometry, rectilinear grids, regularity but not necessarily symmetry, and minimal applied decoration. New materials, such as aluminum and plastics; standardization; and prefabrication are considered essential elements in achieving design goals.

- *Motifs*. Modern buildings have no motifs or references to the past. Geometric shapes are the dominant motif, with architectural details spotlighted.

ARCHITECTURE

Geometric Modernism defines both public and private architecture because it is economical, easy to construct, and adaptable to a variety of building types and user/client needs. Building types include offices, corporate headquarters (Fig. 53-1, 53-2, 53-5), banks, stores, schools, art galleries, museums, exhibition buildings, churches (Fig. 53-3), apartment buildings (Fig. 53-6, 53-11), transportation terminals, and private dwellings (Fig. 53-7, 53-8, 53-9, 53-10, 53-12, 53-13). Geometric Modern also characterizes some public housing projects from the federally sponsored urban renewal efforts during the 1950s. Work by International Style pioneers Gropius, Breuer, Mies, and Le Corbusier both defines and

▲ **53-3.** Chapel, United States Air Force Academy, 1956–1962; Colorado Springs, Colorado; Skidmore, Owings, and Merrill.

dominates the style. New design leaders emerge, such as Philip Johnson, Louis Kahn, Paul Rudolph, Buckminster Fuller, Oscar Niemeyer, and Luis Barragán, as do architectural firms such as Skidmore, Owings, and Merrill (SOM).

Architects stress newness and modernity in design and purity in form. Most buildings are simple and rectilinear in silhouette. Even those that are more complex are still rectilinear. Also important are simplicity, sleekness, and compatibility between style and materials. Architects often experiment with orientation, form, construction techniques, or materials to suit clients or to move design in different directions. Those buildings that closely follow the International Style have flat, transparent façades, glass curtain walls, and volume as opposed to mass. Other structures maintain the regularity of the grid but use concrete or other materials to express heaviness and monumentality in the manner of Le Corbusier. Their façades may be flat or have projections and recesses, and windows vary between small slits and entire façades.

Most architects emulate purity of form and the "less is more" concepts of Mies, so numerous rectangular buildings with glass curtain walls that become known as "glass boxes" spring up across North America. During the 1960s, prosperity stimulates a desire for more luxurious materials and signature buildings to define a corporate image or express symbolism or monumentality. To achieve these goals, some architects follow the postwar concepts of Le Corbusier while others adopt a more sculptural, expressionist, and personal approach. As always, the work of some individualist architects and designers does not fit into any particular mode.

Geometric Modernism is not widely accepted, especially in some parts of the United States, where concern for site, climate, and materials are more important design goals. Neither is it much in evidence in the numerous suburban developments across the United States, where traditional Cape Cods or Ranch houses predominate.

▲ **53-5.** Salk Institute of Biological Studies, 1959–1966; La Jolla, California; Louis Kahn.

▲ **53-6.** Habitat, EXPO 67, 1967; Montreal, Canada; Moshe Safdie.

▲ **53-4.** Biosphere, United States Pavilion, EXPO 67; Geodesic dome, 1950s–1960s; created by Buckminster Fuller.

■ *New Brutalism.* During the 1950s, New Brutalism, a modern architecture composed of bold concrete in geometric forms, emerges. Combining the logical structure of Mies with Le Corbusier's robust forms, buildings project massiveness and a sense of tension thought to mirror the pressures of modern life. The overtly abstract nature of the style does not tie buildings to their locations, so New Brutalist buildings lack a sense of place, for which they are greatly criticized. The style appears to derive its name from *béton brut*, or raw concrete, a term Le Corbusier uses to describe his work constructed in rough-faced concrete. (Fig. 53-5, 53-6, 53-11). Most examples are in Great Britain, where the style is primarily adopted as a means of swift, inexpensive construction particularly for public housing. Americans Kahn and Rudolph work in the style. An example in the United States is Boston City Hall, the result of a controversial competition.

Public and Private Buildings

■ *Corporate Office Buildings*. The corporate office building, a new building type as defined by Geometric Modernism, is formulated in the United States and spreads to the rest of the world. These buildings take two forms: a high-rise or glass box in an urban context (Fig. 53-1, 53-2), or an expansive single or group of buildings set in a campuslike landscape. Structures contributing to the development of this type after World War II are built in various locations. The Equitable Building in Portland, Oregon, is one of the first tall glass boxes to use aluminum on the exterior and to be fully air-conditioned. The United Nations Secretariat Building in New York City pioneers the use of glass curtain walls for high-rise buildings. Equally important are the Lake Shore Drive apartments and the Illinois Institute of Technology (IIT) campus plan and buildings in Chicago by Mies. The Lake Shore Drive apartments look no different from an office building of the period. The IIT buildings rely on modules and grids for placement within the site and façade design. In these buildings, Mies's use of structural elements, particularly exposed I-beams to add interest, is widely imitated. Throughout the period, high-rises become taller and taller as land-use taxes and clients' need for space increase. Structures compete to be called the world's tallest building.

■ *Geodesic Dome*. An innovative development during this period is the geodesic dome, designed by Buckminster Fuller (Fig. 53-4). The round shape is composed of prefabricated modular parts that easily interlock together. Construction is fairly simple, inexpensive, and fast. Its unique structure offers open interior space, which is large and unhindered by columns. Because of this, the geodesic dome is a popular architectural form for exhibit spaces, theaters, and greenhouses.

■ *Case Study Houses*. To promote Modernism, John Entenza, editor of *Arts and Architecture* magazine, establishes a program to create residential prototypes that can be built quickly and economically for any client anywhere in the United States. Called Case Study Houses, 36 are designed and built largely in California from 1945 to 1966. They are marketed as superior environments that promote practicality and functionality. Most are created for imaginary families of different sizes, budgets, and requirements. Well-known architects and designers such as Richard Neutra, Charles and Ray Eames (Fig. 53-10), and Eero Saarinen, and less well-known ones, such as Pierre Koenig (Fig. 53-13), produce designs. Although varying in design, commonalities normally include a single story, flat roofs, simplicity, open planning, and integration of interior and exterior. Wood construction dominates the first examples, but during the 1950s steel framing and industrial materials become more common. Thousands of people visit the Case Study Houses, which are instrumental in promoting Modernism.

■ *Site Orientation*. Buildings in urban settings are oriented toward the street, sometimes covering an entire block. They often stand in self-contained isolation with no attempt to relate to surrounding structures. Zoning laws in New York no longer require setbacks as long as a percentage of the site is left open or is lower than the tower. Therefore, following Lever House by SOM, most high-rises become rectangular boxes with open piazzas, courtyards, or terraces on one or more sides (Fig. 53-1, 53-2). Some, like Lever House, have broad horizontal lower portions with the tower rising above. Depending upon the site, the long or short side of a rectangular building may face the street.

Architect-planned residences are oriented toward sun, landscape, and views (Fig. 53-8, 53-13). Most compositions adapt to the climate and landscape of the region and requirements of the homeowners. Some are designed around natural features, such as trees or hillsides. Others integrate with the landscape. Suburban houses sit in rows along grids of streets with surrounding lawns. In contrast to earlier, most postwar houses are built on concrete slabs instead of over basements.

■ *Heating and Cooling Systems*. With the increased usage of heating and cooling systems (like air-conditioning) during the 1950s, architects can create glass box buildings that are healthier and more comfortable without the traditional elements, such as high ceilings, thick walls, and building footprints that create cross-ventilation.

▲ **53-7.** Gropius House and living room, 1937–1938; Lincoln, Massachusetts; Walter Gropius and Marcel Breuer.

▲ **53-8.** Kaufmann Desert House, 1945–1947; Palm Springs, California; Richard Neutra.

■ *Floor Plans*. There is no typical floor plan because each develops from function. Most commercial buildings are modular with structural columns forming a geometric grid and organizing the building form, establishing window openings, and defining placement of interior partitions. This permits large open spaces that can be subdivided as necessary, so in many buildings form no longer follows function. In fact, form develops first and functions fit into it. Commercial buildings have centralized service cores and stairwells that may be in the center of the building or on one end.

Residential floor plans exhibit considerable variety and flexibility, particularly in architect-designed examples (Fig. 53-9). Key considerations are the site and zoning. Plans may incorporate features of the site and/or be oriented toward views. Zoning, which places like activities near each other, arises from increased emphasis upon balancing and separating social activities with and from privacy. Because most houses are a single story, plans may be U- or L-shaped or have interior courtyards or swimming or reflecting pools to more easily place living or public areas away from bedrooms and private areas. Open plans with few fixed interior partitions characterize activity and living areas. This suits informal modern lifestyles and makes the most of limited space. Hallways and other circulation spaces are minimized to conserve space.

■ *Materials*. The most common materials, especially in nonresidential buildings, are steel, reinforced and exposed concrete, aluminum, and tinted and plain glass (Fig. 53-1, 53-2, 53-3, 53-4, 53-5). Skyscrapers have structural skeletons and mainly glass walls. Many are prefabricated with modular components and have exposed or covered steel or aluminum frames. Apartment complexes and some houses are similarly constructed with steel framing (Fig. 53-6, 53-11). Like public structures, houses have large expanses of glass but often use other materials such as wood, brick, stone, concrete blocks, ribbed steel decking, and wood (Fig. 53-7, 53-8, 53-9, 53-10, 53-12, 53-13). Use of various materials separates Geometric Modern from Bauhaus and International Style.

■ *Façades*. Most façades on Geometric Modern commercial buildings are modular with large areas of glass in a rectangular grid, which gives a feeling of aloofness or anonymity (Fig. 53-1, 53-2). A rectangular box form is common for all types of buildings, especially skyscrapers. Some are raised on *pilotis* in the manner of Le Corbusier. Others have low horizontal portions to balance verticality and provide open space required by zoning. Architects sometimes incorporate angles to shape and add variety to a building (Fig. 53-3). Mies' use of construction elements to organize the façade and add a decorative element influences many others. Commercial buildings may have green, gray, or amber tinted glass accentuated with black, gray, or amber steel frames or aluminum panels (Fig. 53-1, 53-2). Some incorporate panels of primary colors (Fig. 53-11). New Brutalist buildings feature contrasts of solid and void relationships but retain a strong grid organization (Fig. 53-5, 53-6, 53-11). Most façades have projections, so they are not flat. Although there is considerable variety in residential façades, most are rectangular and horizontal with large

DESIGN SPOTLIGHT

Architecture and Interior: Establishing a dialogue between site and natural environment, Philip Johnson's Glass House integrates the outside with the inside. Placed on a flat manicured lawn, it is a monument to the minimalist machine aesthetic. Translucent window walls frame the open living area and the contrasting brick cylinder bathroom/chimney core. Furnishings with steel frames and leather upholstery designed by Mies van der Rohe replicate the exterior character. In 1957, the architect stated: "I consider my own house not so much as a home (though it is that to me) as a clearinghouse of ideas which can filter down later, through my work or that of others."

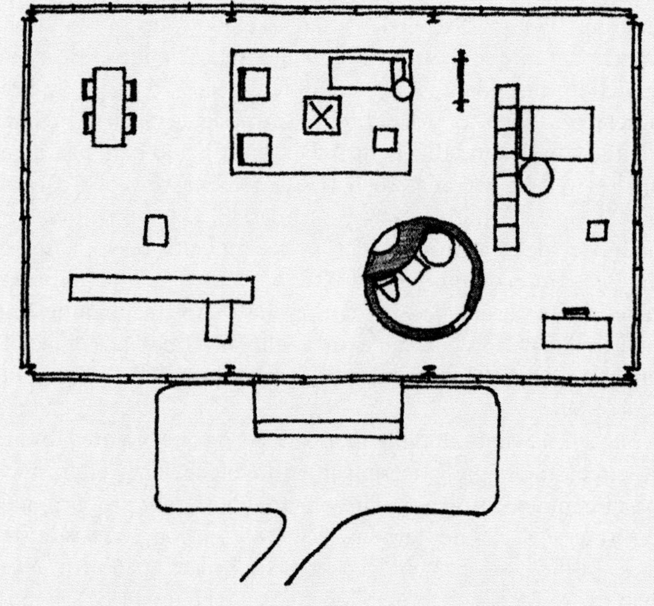

DESIGN SPOTLIGHT

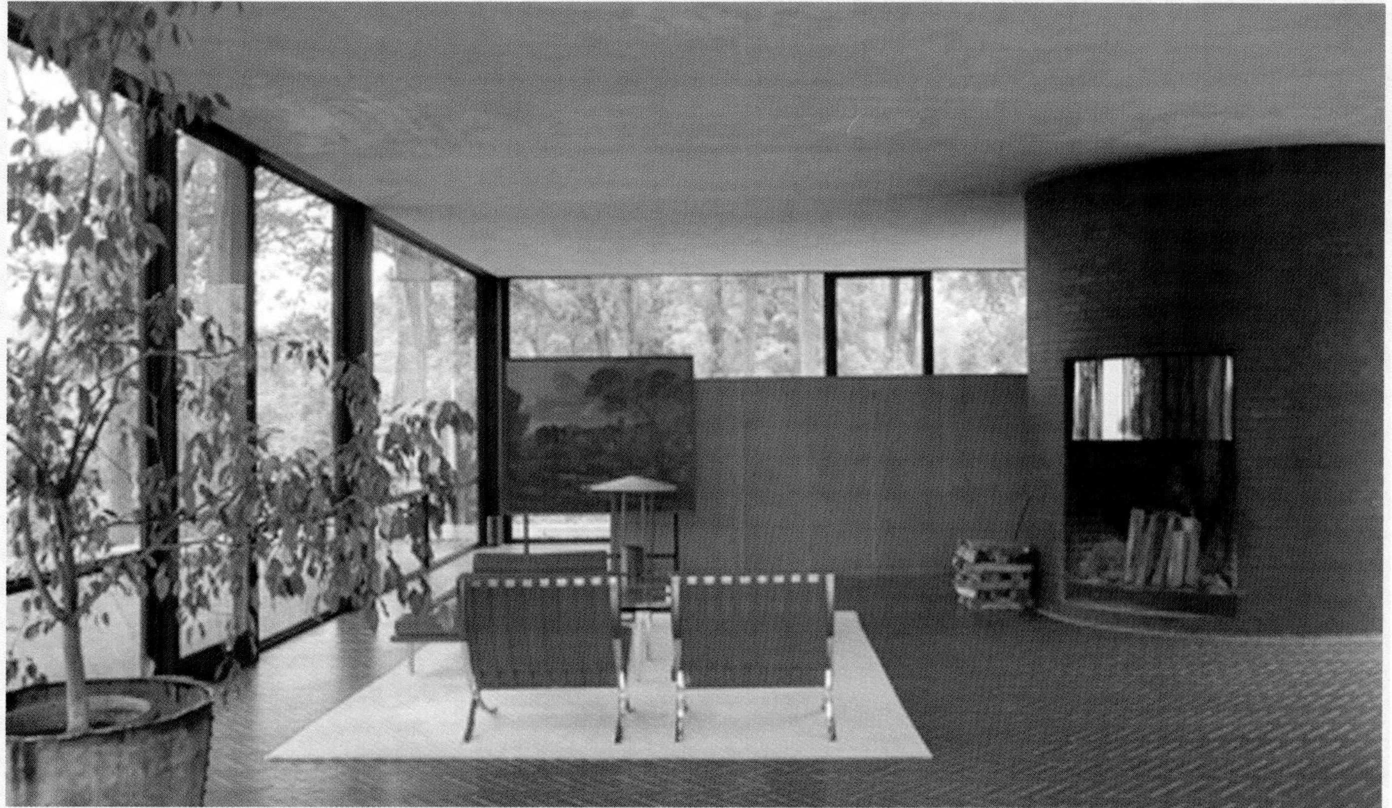

▲ **53-9.** Glass House (Residence of Philip Johnson), floor plan, and living area, 1949; New Canaan, Connecticut; Philip Johnson.

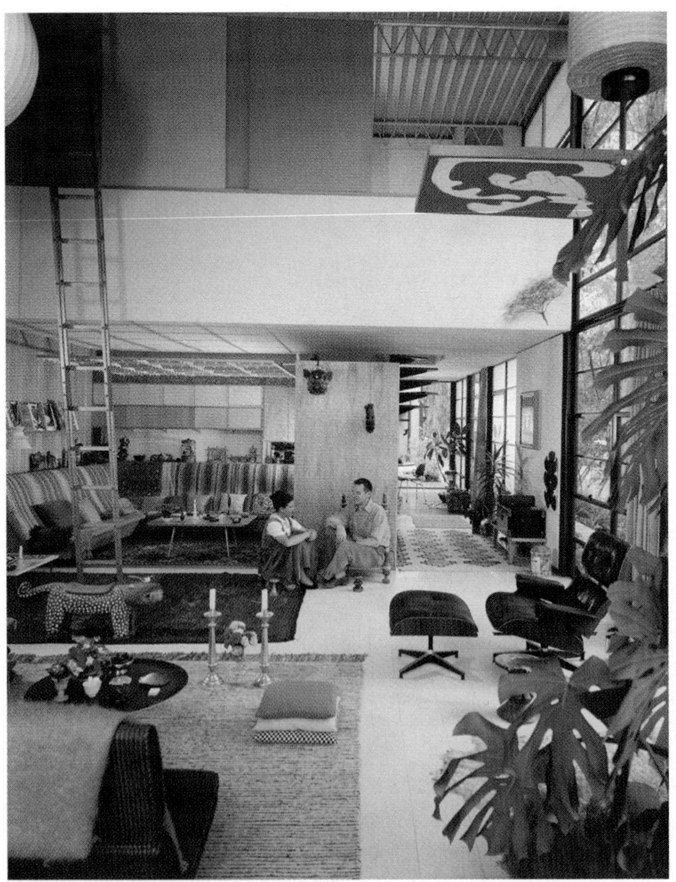

▲ **53-10.** Eames House (Case Study House 8) and interior, 1945–1950; Pacific Palisades, California; Kenneth Acker and Charles Eames.

areas of transparent or translucent glass, which contributes to the feeling of light and openness. Façades are rarely plain white as earlier but usually combine several materials and may incorporate primary colors.

■ *Windows*. Window walls or large areas of glass dominate, aided by the universal incorporation of air-conditioning in commercial buildings (Fig. 53-1, 53-2). New Brutalist buildings have small, slit-like windows or rectangular windows with deep insets (Fig. 53-3, 53-11). Windows on commercial buildings, including New Brutalist, are usually fixed and in grid patterns, while those on houses may include fixed plate glass, sliding glass, casement, and/or awning (Fig. 53-6, 53-7, 53-8, 53-9, 53-10, 53-12, 53-13). On residences, picture windows afford panoramic views to the outside, while smaller ones may focus on a private garden space. Some houses have frameless corner windows with miter joints, which allow in more light and provide uninterrupted views. Windows usually have narrow metal moldings and mullions that frame the openings and divide glass areas. Sometimes moldings are black or bronze to accent the grid effect. Some large plate glass windows have no mullions.

■ *Doors*. Doorways integrate with the rhythm and regularity of the exterior so that they often become an extension of glass walls or solid surfaces (Fig. 53-7, 53-9, 53-12). Entrances on New Brutalist structures often are obscured and difficult to find, which adds to their formidable appearance. Entry doors may be glass or wood, or a combination of both. They are plain, flat, and often wider than an interior door. Projecting canopies or an upper floor may shield the entry area, or it may be recessed to provide protection.

■ *Roofs*. Most roofs are flat with no spires or setbacks, but they may have a slight pitch to allow water to run off (Fig. 53-1, 53-2, 53-5, 53-6, 53-7, 53-8, 53-9, 53-10, 53-11, 53-12, 53-13). Others are single or double pitched, or asymmetrical.

▲ **53-11.** Unité d'Habitation, 1946–1951; Marseilles, France; Le Corbusier.

▲ **53-12.** Farnsworth House, 1950–1952; Plano, Illinois; Ludwig Mies van der Rohe.

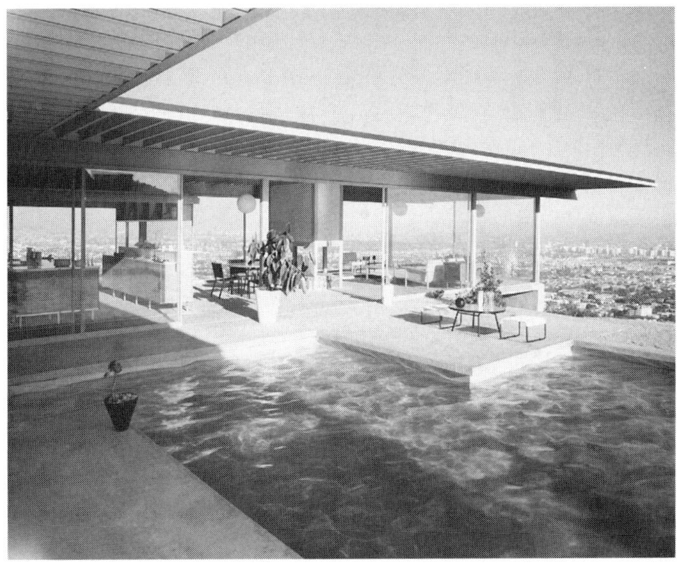

▲ **53-13.** Case Study House 22, 1959–1960; Los Angeles, California; Pierre Koenig.

▲ **53-14.** Later Interpretation: Lloyd's building, 1984–1986; London, England; Richard Rogers and Partners. Late Modern.

■ *Later Interpretations*. In the 1970s and 1980s, the vocabulary of the skyscraper box grid continues in the Late Modern expression, but with changes in form resulting from improved technology. Breaking the box with an inward angle, a more exposed structure, or an angled roofline become common. Important examples include the Sears Tower in Chicago and Pennzoil Place in Houston. The vocabulary expands further through the work of the next generation of innovators, with more changes in building form and with continued advances in technology. Exposed structural elements become common, unusual shapes develop, and buildings reach new heights to garner attention. Two prominent examples of these concepts are the Hong Kong and Shanghai Bank Headquarters in Hong Kong and the Lloyd's Building in London (Fig. 53-14). New Brutalism experiences a reinterpretation at the end of the 20th century in which the roughness of the concrete is covered with stucco or softened with sandblasting or pattern molding.

INTERIORS

Geometric Modern commercial interiors follow Bauhaus and International Style principles that focus on function and reject decoration. Designers stress simple forms, clean lines, architectural structure, open space, and a harmonious integration of parts. Light and airy interiors are mostly rectangular or geometric in form with new materials and technologies highlighted. Large windows or glass curtain walls bring in natural light and help integrate the indoors with the outdoors. In public structures and houses with steel frames, the geometric, usually rectangular, grid of the exterior is often a design feature in the interiors. In commercial buildings, suspended ceilings, which integrate mechanical systems, lighting, and air-conditioning, permit greater freedom in space planning. Many spaces have open plans and are sparsely furnished with modern furniture. Walls are often plain and unadorned. In corporate interiors, pattern and color are usually minimized to help create an architectonic look. Offices dominate commercial interiors (Fig. 53-15, 53-16). With changes in interior design, furniture showrooms emerge as retail venues to market new ideas. They soon multiply because of increased demand for innovative furnishings.

During the 1950s, commercial interior design becomes important, as interior planning grows more complex and specialized. Creating or enhancing image, increasing productivity, and creating pleasant work environments are important design goals, especially to corporations. Architectural firms, such as SOM, establish interiors units, usually headed by men, to design commercial spaces. The Knoll Planning Unit, directed by Florence Knoll, becomes a leader in the design and furnishing of modern commercial interiors, particularly offices for corporate America. Interiors by Knoll and the Planning Unit blend modern furnishings, textiles, and lighting as an integrated whole and are models of simplicity and order (Fig. 53-16). This becomes known as the Knoll look. Other features include open space and furniture lining or at right angles to walls for an architectonic appearance. Knoll also revolutionizes executive office planning when she replaces the customary cluttered and messy table behind the desk with a storage piece or credenza. Following her work, executive offices and lounge areas often resemble living rooms with modern sofas and chairs and a variety of textiles, finishes, and accessories. Furnishings are grouped for informal conversation but align in relationship to walls and windows. Those who work in nonresidential design often describe themselves as space planners or interior designers to separate themselves from decorators who mainly work in residences. To most people, all are decorators.

In houses and apartments, exteriors integrate with interiors through the use of large areas of glass, similar materials and textures, and careful orientation, which also make spaces light and airy (Fig. 53-7, 53-8, 53-9, 53-10, 53-12, 53-13). Most residences have open, free-flowing public spaces with less restriction on room designation. The living room, dining room, and kitchen are frequently one large space subdivided by furniture and/or changes in floor level. Besides providing social interaction for the homemaker, this highlights her prominent role in the home. Open planning also makes meal serving and cleanup easier and increases apparent room size. Family rooms, spaces adjacent to the kitchen where family members and guests gather for informal activities such as watching television, become a mainstay of modern houses during the period. New or experimental materials,

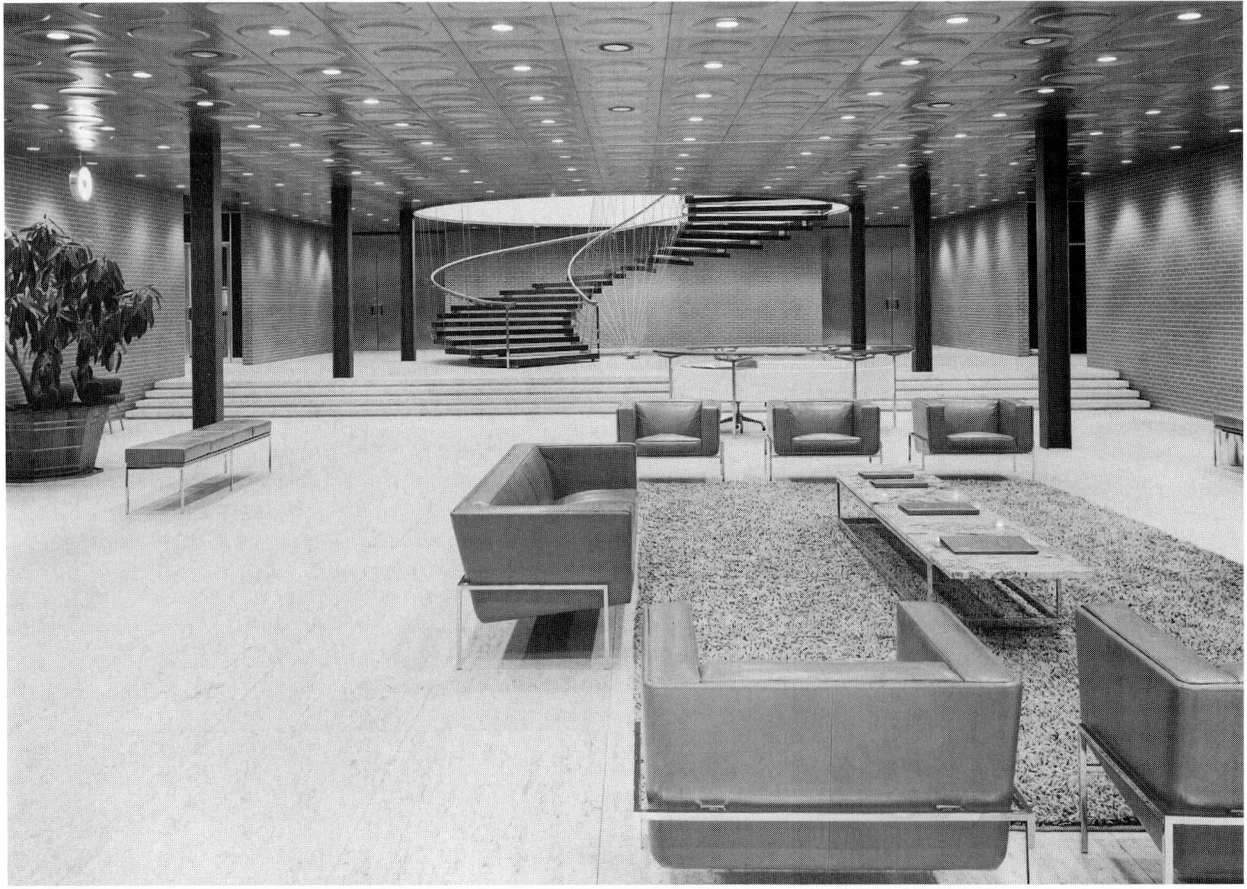

▲ **53-15.** Lobby, General Motors Technical Center, 1951–1956; Warren, Michigan; Eero Saarinen and Associates. [Ezra Stoller © Esto]

DESIGN SPOTLIGHT

Interiors: With its uncluttered appearance, this executive office calls attention to simple forms, clean lines, architectural structure, open space, and a harmonious integration of parts. The ceiling is a suspended grid with acoustical or textured panel inserts, air diffusers, and lighting in a neutral color. Walls are plain, simple, and in a neutral color, and have large windows. Plain, straight casement draperies shield window openings. As was typical of Florence Knoll's work, the space resembles a living room with modern sofas and chairs that are grouped for informal conversation or conferences, but align in relationship to walls and windows. Most furniture designs are by her or her contemporaries. Fabric upholstery or leather covers most seating, with a few pieces accented in bright colors such as red. As usual, there are few accessories.

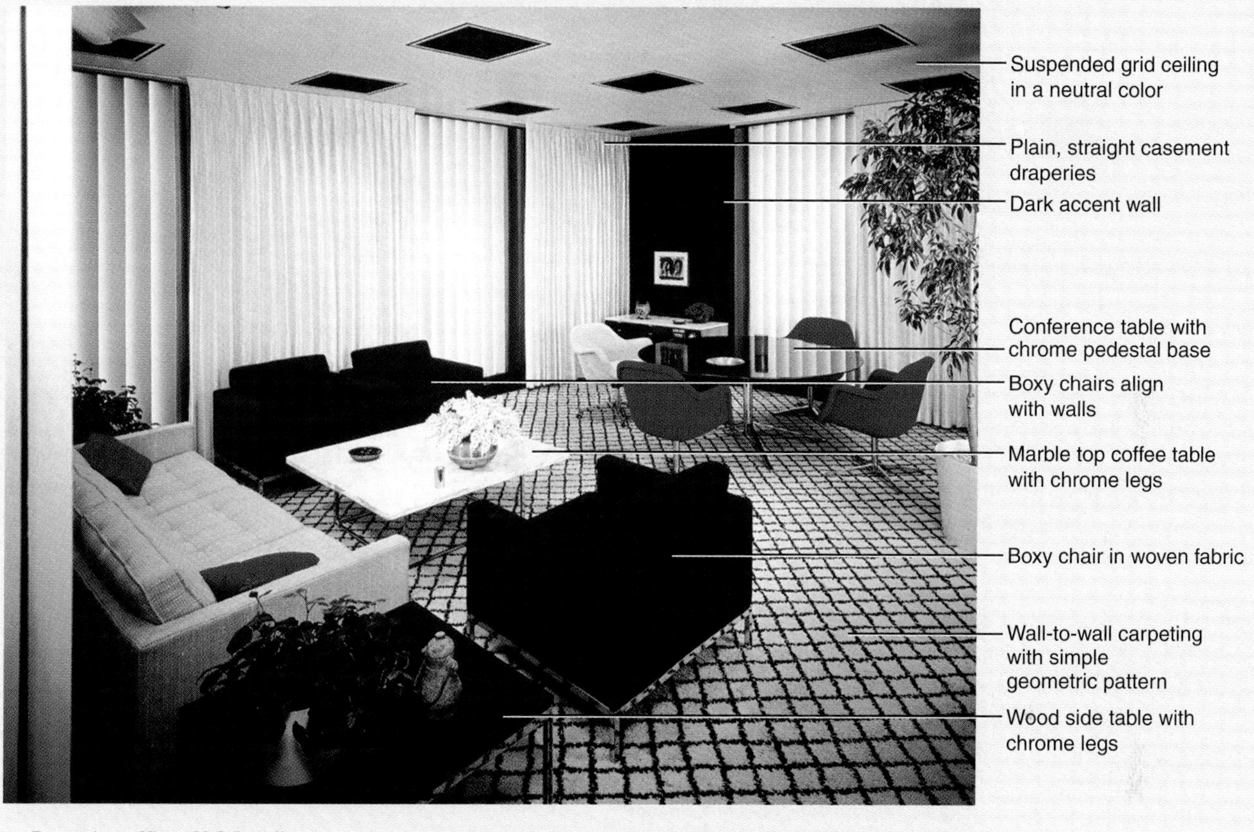

▲ **53-16.** Executive office, CBS Building, c. mid-1960s; New York City, New York; Florence Knoll.

such as fiberglass textiles and plastic laminates, vinyl wall coverings, and aluminum furniture, enhance the Modern look. Furniture groups may be arranged to take advantage of views, landscape, and reflecting pools. Large windows and plants also bring in the outside.

The world strives to emulate modern American kitchens and bathrooms. Efficiently planned around work centers, kitchens are filled with labor-saving appliances. Ranges, ovens, refrigerators, dishwashers, dryers, and washing machines reflect the modern idiom and come in a variety of colors and sizes. Kitchen cabinets in standard sizes have no applied moldings. Less expensive than before, they come in wood or plastic laminate in colors such as the primaries. Countertops are of easy-to-clean materials such as plastic laminate, ceramic tiles, or stainless steel. Similarly, bathrooms are more colorful than before. Fixtures are smaller and more sculptural.

Public and Private Buildings

■ *Offices.* Office hierarchy is still evident in the size, location, number of windows, and type of furniture, which convey status. Bull pens remain the norm for workers, while management and executives have enclosed offices. Many offices have functional open planning with rows of desks between the service core and windows.

During the period, the Knoll Planning Unit introduces the study of user needs and work procedures as part of the design process, a concept that eventually is integrated into programming practice. Knoll and her team collect and analyze information from user interviews to develop office layouts so that their designs relate the interior to the building and the furniture to the interior and human needs. Knoll also pioneers the use of floor plans, elevations, and/or perspectives with textiles and finishes as a means to fully illustrate concepts to the client.

▲ **53-17.** Textiles: Fabrics, c. 1950s–1960s; United States; Alexander Girard.

■ *Color*. A variety of color schemes define Geometric Modern interiors. Open offices are often neutral with spots of dark or bright colors for contrast. Florence Knoll uses a rich or bright color on the wall behind the executive's desk (Fig. 53-16). Additionally, she works out new or innovative color schemes in Knoll's showrooms where there are fewer limitations. Both public and private interiors use natural colors and materials. Color psychology notes that neutrals and grays provide a feeling of rest and quiet.

Bold, highly saturated or primary colors appear in all types of interiors in part as a reaction to the dull and dark colors used during the Depression and war years and to signal optimism (Fig. 53-10). Bright turquoise, orange, pink, and lime green, and red, blue, and yellow with white and black enhance interiors, textiles, tableware, and light fixtures. The so-called harlequin color schemes combine a range of bright tones. Most woods are stained rich warm colors to emulate more expensive woods.

■ *Floors*. The widespread use of central heating allows for the use of materials earlier considered cold, including concrete, marble, terrazzo, ceramic tile, stone, brick, and glass (Fig. 53-7, 53-9, 53-10, 53-15, 53-16). Various rooms, particularly executive offices and living rooms, may feature the warmer patterns of wood blocks, strips, or parquet. Natural and synthetic materials, such as cork, vinyl, rubber, and linoleum, increase in use because they are hygienic and easy to maintain. SOM introduces wall-to-wall carpet for noise suppression in offices in 1959, and it becomes common in important commercial areas. Carpet is popular for bedrooms, whereas in living areas most floors are uncarpeted. Different flooring materials may visually separate space in open rooms in houses. Area rugs in contemporary patterns, asymmetrical designs, curving or rectangular shapes, and plain also subdivide open conversation areas and anchor furniture groupings. Rugs are simpler than other textile or wallpaper patterns and often limited to one or two colors.

■ *Walls*. Drywall (often referred to as gypsum or sheetrock) begins to replace plaster for interior partitions during the period, especially in commercial spaces. Walls are plain and flat with no moldings, except maybe a baseboard. White or neutral painted walls continue, particularly in large office areas (Fig. 53-7, 53-15). Sometimes designers incorporate accent walls in rich or primary colors. Fabric-covered partitions sometimes subdivide open office spaces. Natural materials, such as painted or plain brick, stone, wood panels, and plywood veneer, are favored for the home, but synthetics, such as plastic laminate or vinyl wallpapers, are also used. Wallpapers have abstract, linear, or stylized patterns in varying scales. Borders are out of fashion. Because textures are important, rooms often have different textures on walls, floors, and/or ceilings. Patterns are also important, so two papers with contrasting patterns may cover a single wall or different walls in the same room or in an open space. Patterns relate to the room. For example, kitchen papers have patterns of fruit, vegetables, bottles, and other objects associated with the space.

Built-in storage units integrated with the architecture provide storage and/or subdivide offices and other commercial spaces. In houses, they are often a feature in and/or between living and dining rooms (Fig. 53-10). Staircases, often in conversation areas, are a distinctive element and often have open risers to visually open space (Fig. 53-15).

■ *Fireplaces*. Central heating is now almost universal, but many houses still have fireplaces. No longer centered on a main wall, asymmetry or central placement is the rule. The design usually follows the house style, with a heavy emphasis on straight lines and geometry. The chimney face may be brick or concrete blocks (Fig. 53-7, 53-9).

■ *Window Treatments*. Simple, pleated window treatments hung straight from ceiling to floor are typical (Fig. 53-16). Most are of unpatterned, woven fabrics or sheers in white or natural colors that blend in with the architecture, walls, and surrounding area. Designers strive to keep them unobtrusive and architectural looking. New to the period are casements, which are introduced at Lever House. Some offices and houses have the new vertical blinds inside or large adjustable, angled panels (*brise soleil*) outside to regulate sunlight. Venetian blinds or the newly introduced café curtains cover windows in residences. Wall-to-wall curtains sometimes are used to emulate picture or full-wall windows.

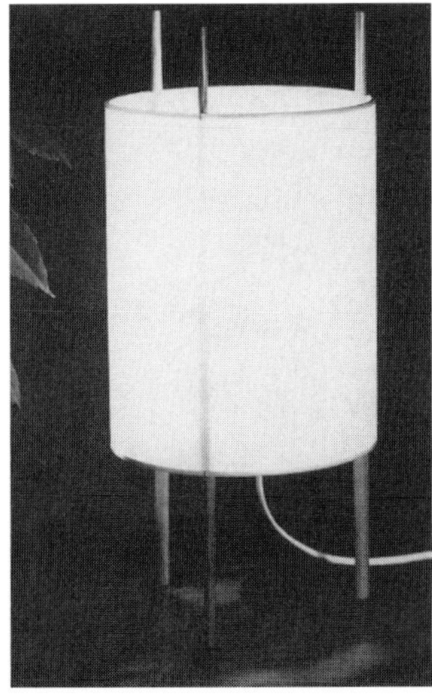

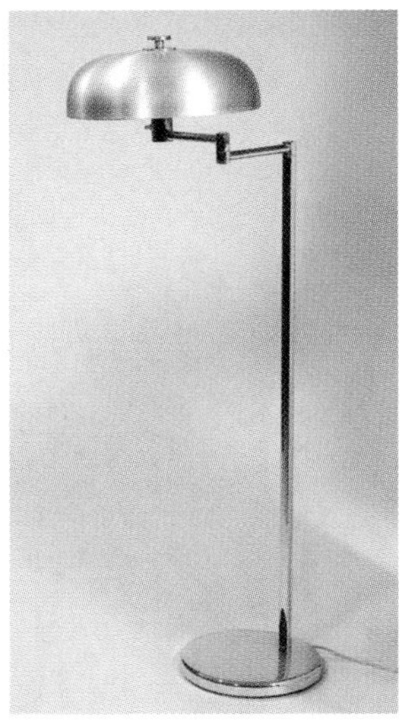

▲ **53-18.** Lighting: Table lamp and floor lamp, c. 1950s–1960s; manufactured by Knoll and Nessen.

■ *Doors*. Doors are flat, plain, usually in wood or sometimes metal, and may be painted black, white, a primary color, or the room color, or stained. Door trims, like window moldings, are flat and narrow and are used to frame the opening.

■ *Ceilings*. Ceilings in all buildings are usually flat and plain (Fig. 53-7, 53-9, 53-10, 53-15, 53-16). Treatments may vary from one space to another, based on function and aesthetic choices, so there is much more variety than earlier. Ceilings in public buildings are painted white or a neutral color; have suspended grids with acoustical or textured panel inserts, air diffusers, and lighting; or are covered with wood strips or a material used in the building design, such as metal. Sometimes architects create unusual ceilings that reflect the building's character. Some living spaces are double height for more openess and may have rooms at half levels like mezzanines.

■ *Textiles*. Textiles (Fig. 53-9, 53-10, 53-15, 53-16, 53-17) in natural and human-made fibers are used less than previously and primarily for window treatments. Some are simple monochromatic woven designs, while others may be linear, geometric, or stylized patterns in bright colors. Newly developed protective finishes, such as Scotchgard, are introduced during the period. Numerous types of fabrics cover furniture, including vinyl (or Naugahyde) and leather. Upholstery fabrics are usually plain, nubby weaves in contrast to other fabrics. Deep tufting and applied trims other than cording are rare. Occasionally, sofas have throw pillows in bright colors for variety and interest.

In 1947, the newly formed Knoll Textiles division opens a showroom exclusively for fabrics in New York, expanding the company's product line and design services. Knoll Textiles strives to create fabrics in appropriate patterns and colors that will withstand the wear of commercial applications. The line includes men's suiting, which Florence Knoll frequently uses in offices; innovative fabrics and patterns and more traditional designs. Marketing innovations in the showroom include the fabric wall and small samples attached to cardboard with descriptive information about the fabric. In 1952, Herman Miller opens a textiles division with designer Alexander Girard in charge (Fig. 53-17). He introduces bright colors and simple stylized or abstract designs inspired by folk and contemporary art. Girard designs more than 300 fabrics, wall hangings, and wallpapers for Herman Miller.

■ *Lighting*. Large windows fill rooms with natural light. Suspended ceiling grids with integrated lighting are common in offices and other commercial spaces, and the illuminated ceiling is introduced (Fig. 53-15, 53-16). Specialists in lighting design emerge during the period, including Richard Kelley, whose luminous ceilings make important design statements in modern corporate buildings. Recessed lighting replaces or supplements surface-mounted ceiling fixtures. Pendant lights, usually in sets of three, are common in houses. Floor and table lamps provide light where needed (Fig. 53-7, 53-18). The Arco floor lamp designed in 1962 is a favored fixture for high-style, modern interiors. Most light fixtures are simple, unadorned, geometric, and flexible with metal stems. Many of the lamp shades are metal, either in silver, white, black, or red. Nelson designs a line of lightweight metal and sprayed plastic lanterns that become very popular.

FURNISHINGS AND DECORATIVE ARTS

Furniture continues the machine aesthetic of the Bauhaus and International Style, blending with the hard-edged geometry of the architecture and interiors. Its rectilinear shape or cubic form reflects interiors, and it is durable and often made of new materials. The lighter scale, airiness, and visual weight eminently suit modern rooms, whether residential or commercial. Most pieces are low and horizontal with hard edges and geometric forms so may not look comfortable. Characteristic features include slender metal or wooden legs and a visual and material separation between functional parts, such as legs and seats. Many pieces are multipurpose and/or modular for flexibility. Architects and the new profession of furniture designers create furnishings in new materials using new construction techniques, most of which emerge during the war. In addition, rooms, especially in houses, also have Scandinavian or Italian Modern furniture.

During the period, offices, especially when planned by office managers, retain a traditional appearance because little moderately priced, well-designed modern furniture is available. Exceptions are custom-designed offices, such as those by the Knoll Planning Unit or SOM (Fig. 53-16). Knoll, Inc. and Herman Miller introduce lines of modern office furniture in the 1940s and 1950s. Although not inexpensive, they are functional and aesthetically pleasing, and they suit modern interiors. Both companies offer pieces with sleek, simple designs in different materials, finishes, and colors. Knoll, Inc. and Herman Miller begin aggressively marketing good design during this period. Florence Knoll (Fig. 53-16) and George Nelson (Fig. 53-20), director of design at Herman Miller, believe that good design is good business and make it the strength of their companies. They hire prominent and relatively unknown designers to create pieces and/or lines for them and give the designers royalties or other creative means of compensation. In this way, both companies become leaders in a reassessment of the relationship of art to industry. Herman Miller Company and Knoll International are the most influential modern furnishing manufacturers of the period.

Manufacturers and designers, like the Herman Miller Company and Florence Knoll, increasingly strive to create or produce office furniture that suits modern offices and aids the process of work. Consequently, suites of office furniture, room dividers, and storage systems are important (Fig. 53-15, 53-16, 53-20, 53-21). New to the period is mass seating such as in airports. Designers modernize traditional furniture types with new forms, materials, and construction for the residential market. Some pieces suit both commerical and residential applications.

▲ **53-19.** Lounge chair, c. 1940s; United States; Jens Risom, manufactured by Knoll International.

▲ **53-20.** Marshmallow sofa, 1956; modular storage unit, and bed, c. 1950s; United States; George Nelson Associates, manufactured by Herman Miller.

Public and Private Buildings

■ *Modular Furniture.* Producing furniture in modular geometric units becomes an important focus for furniture and industrial designers in the mid-1940s. The idea is not a new one. Marcel Breuer designs a component system in 1924 and Le Corbusier's Casiers Standard Units group is shown in the Pavillion Esprit Nouveau in 1925. During the postwar period, modular furniture appeals because it relates to exterior and interior modules while giving flexibility and customization to individual needs. Additionally, standardized parts are easily and inexpensively manufactured and quickly shipped. While working at Herman Miller, top designers Charles and Ray Eames and Nelson explore sectional seating and ways to store numerous modern possessions of various sizes and shapes efficiently. For storage, they create stackable units with exposed construction and interchangeable parts (Fig. 53-20, 53-21). Sizes are standardized but allow flexibility in height, width, depth, materials, and overall arrangement. Materials include various woods, plastic laminate in several colors, and metal grilles. Systems can grow horizontally or vertically. Modular furniture suits both home and office.

■ *Herman Miller Furniture*. In 1942, Herman Miller enters the commercial furniture market with Gilbert Rohde's Executive Office Group (EOG), a suite of interchangeable parts and pieces. The line includes executive and secretarial desks with many choices for finishes, pulls, tops, drawer combinations, and configurations of pedestals. Also offered are matching tables, file cabinets, credenzas, storage units, and conference tables. Although L-shaped desks are known, the EOG's L-shaped executive desk functions more like a workstation and foreshadows later systems furniture. Beginning in the mid-1940s, Herman Miller expands its modern offerings by introducing the work of Nelson and the Eamses for seating, tables, storage units, textiles, decorative arts,

DESIGN SPOTLIGHT

Furniture: Charles and Ray Eames, husband and wife, designed numerous pieces of furniture for Herman Miller. The Aluminum Group has a light aluminum frame and base with a continuous fabric seat and back resting on the frame's side ribs. As a unit, the armchair and ottoman offer flexibility and firmness, showcase a sleek elegant design, and address human contours and proportions. The Eames Storage Units (ESU), inspired by Bauhaus and Japanese aesthetics, have standardized parts made of exposed steel frames with storage portions of perforated, plastic-coated plywood. Completely interchangeable, the system includes open shelves, cabinets, drawer units, and desks. The units, which come in eight colors and black, white, or birch plywood, have an industrial appearance. Originally shipped KD (unassembled), Herman Miller adds cross-wire supports to the frame to begin shipping them assembled in 1952. Conceptually, the units reflect a practical approach to furniture design because they adapt well to a variety of uses. Found in offices as well as houses, the ESU and the Aluminum Group become icons of modern design.

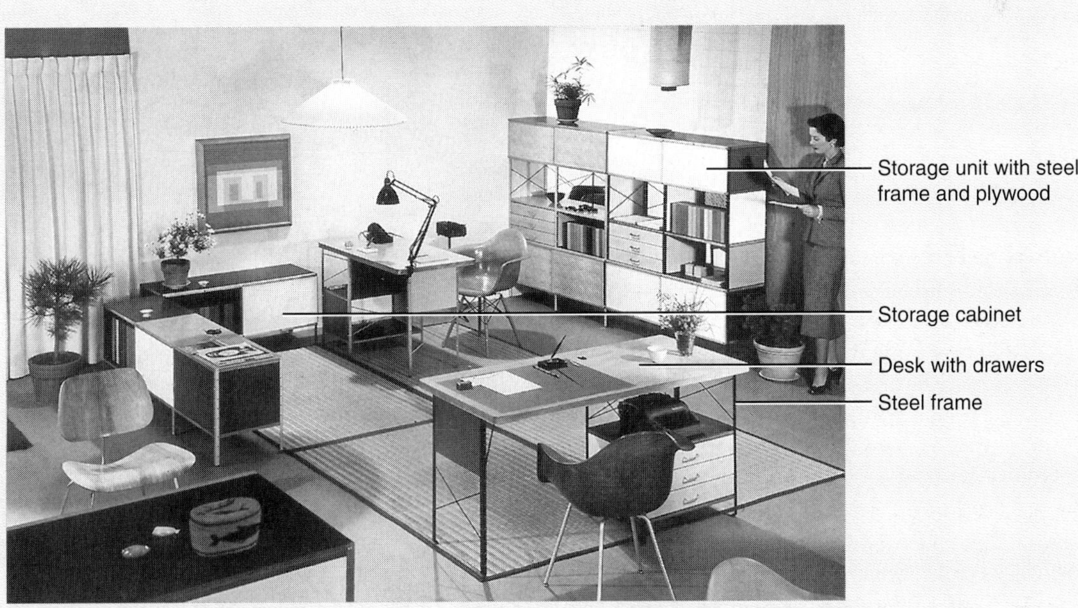

▲ **53-21.** Armchair and stool, Aluminum Group, 1958, 1969; and storage units, 1949–1950; United States; Charles and Ray Eames, manufactured by Herman Miller.

and graphics (Fig. 53-20, 53-21). With examples in geometric, organic, and sculptural forms, their work becomes the standard for office furnishings through the next decades.

■ *Knoll Furniture.* Knoll aligns closely with the International Style and the Bauhaus. Hans Knoll, founder of the company, is German, and Florence Knoll believes that the International Style expression is most suitable for Geometric Modern buildings. In 1948, for example, Knoll becomes the exclusive maker of the Barcelona chair by Mies. Although Knoll claims she isn't a furniture designer, out of necessity she creates what she calls fill-in furniture—sofas, chairs, tables, desks, storage units, and conference tables (Fig. 53-16).

■ *Materials.* Designers use materials previously found only in the manufacturing or aircraft industries, such as rubber, plywood, foam rubber, aluminum, and plastic laminates (Fig. 53-13, 53-16, 53-20, 53-21, 53-22). Tubular metal, usually in thinner gauges than before, remains a core furniture material as does wood. Foam rubber, readily available after 1940, radically changes the overstuffed look of upholstery into one that is sleek, trim, and boxy (Fig. 53-16).

■ *Seating.* With less need for storage and other pieces, chairs become a special concern for furniture designers. User comfort is an important design goal. To address this goal, designers begin to pay more attention to human proportions, relying on the new disciplines of anthropometrics and ergonomics to guide them. The Eamses, for example, study how people actually sit and design accordingly, a new idea in design.

Chairs and sofas are usually long, low, and rectangular with thin wood or metal legs (Fig. 53-13, 53-15, 53-16, 53-19). Knoll designs boxy chairs and sofas that work well in commercial interiors. Most have flat or rectangular metal bases and legs. Loose and attached foam rubber cushions with and without some slight button tufting give a light, refined appearance. Nelson creates modular seating in rectangular forms with numerous options for office or home, building upon industrial designer Rohde's original concepts of sectional sofas for the home. Nelson's whimsical Marshmallow sofa (Fig. 53-20), consisting of round cushions on a metal frame, looks machine made but in reality requires a lot of hand labor.

In 1958, the Eamses produce the Aluminum group for Herman Miller (Fig. 53-21). Originally intended for outdoor furniture, the group, consisting of chairs and tables, has aluminum frames and a four-legged pedestal base. Distinctive is the thin Naugahyde (vinyl) upholstery with horizontal grooves that is one continuous piece. The 1969 Soft Pad Group uses the same frame as the Aluminum Group but has thicker individual cushions on back and seat. In 1962, Herman Miller introduces Eames Tandem Sling Seating, a multiple or mass seating system that was first designed for use in airport waiting areas.

■ *Tables.* Tables (Fig. 53-7, 53-13, 53-15, 53-16, 53-22) are often anonymous in design to permit diverse uses and applications. Size and height distinguish conference tables from lamp tables. Most are of wood and/or metal in geometric shapes emphasizing straight lines. Supports may be straight legs, metal wire in a variety of arrangements, or pedestals. Round, oval, square, or rectangular tops are of wood, glass, or plastic laminate. Laminates may be solid colors or resemble various woods or marbles. As with other furniture, simplicity and flexibility govern table designs. One of the best examples of these principles is the Parson's table. It is square and boxy with straight legs and is available in natural wood, plastic laminate, and painted finishes.

■ *Storage.* Room dividers, prominent features in many open interiors, include a variety of storage elements such as desks. Rectilinear in form with few applied moldings, they have open shelves or cabinets, some of which open on both sides of the unit. They may have glass doors or solid ones in wood grain or colors to contrast with or complement each room's color scheme. Built-ins and room dividers replace the typical china cabinet and sideboard in the dining room.

Between 1949 and 1950, the Eamses design the Eames Storage Units (ESU) with exposed steel frames and storage units of perforated, plastic-coated plywood (Fig. 53-21). Also in 1949, Nelson adapts his earlier storage wall ideas (1945) to mass production and more economical prices in the Basic Storage Components (BSC) made by Herman Miller. One of the first modular storage systems in the United States, the system has a variety of components, including ones for a hi-fi (music) group and television, as well as choices for hardware and lighting. Units attach to a Herman Miller frame or can be custom configured by a carpenter. In 1959, Nelson brings out the Comprehensive Storage System (CSS) for office or home in which components attach to adjustable metal poles stretching from floor to ceiling. Storage units, such as shelves, desks, music center, and file cabinet, could be attached at any height or in any configuration (Fig. 53-20).

■ *Beds.* Modern beds (Fig. 53-20) are low and simple in design, resembling Japanese futons. They may be of metal or wood with or without headboards and footboards. Mattresses are often thin

▲ **53-22.** Cyclone tables, c. 1953–1957; United States; Isamu Noguchi, manufactured by Knoll International.

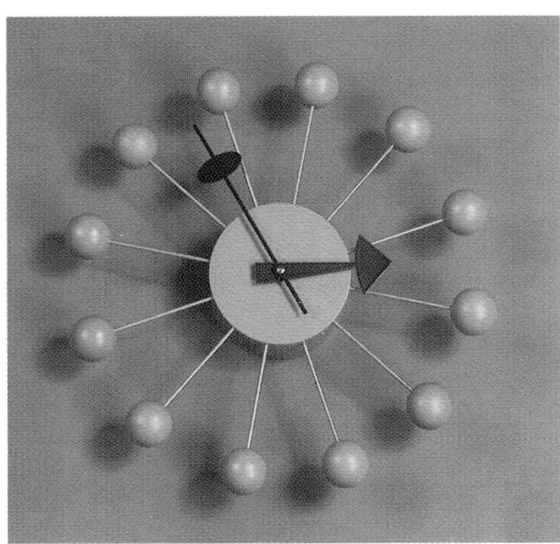

▲ **53-23.** Decorative Arts: Clock, c. 1947; United States; George Nelson, manufactured by Howard Miller.

slabs of foam rubber in keeping with the spare, light, modern aesthetic. Nelson designs a bed with an adjustable headboard to accommodate reading in bed. Bookcase headboards and corner beds are introduced during the period.

■ *Decorative Arts*. The Modern style, sleek and simple with no ornament, extends to the decorative arts, including clocks, glassware, dishes, cutlery, vases, and other accessories (Fig. 53-23). Most commercial spaces have few decorative accessories, while houses have more that are usually in bright colors to coordinate with color schemes. Plants are a common feature in homes (Fig. 53-7, 53-9, 53-10).

CHAPTER 54

Organic and Sculptural Modern

1930s–Early 1970s

By organic architecture I mean an architecture that ***develops*** *from within outward in harmony with the conditions of its being as distinguished from one that is* ***applied*** *from without.*

—Frank Lloyd Wright, *What Is Architecture*, 1937

A design may be called organic when there is an harmonious organization of the parts within the whole, according to the structure, material, and purpose. Within this definition there can be no vain ornamentation or superfluity, but the part of beauty is none the less great—in ideal choice of material, in visual refinement, and in the rational elegance of things intended for use.

—Eliot F. Noyes, *Organic Design in Home Furnishings*, 1941

Organic and Sculptural Modern, inspired by sculptural forms or abstracted living organisms, rejects the hard edges and geometry of the International Style. It seeks total unity within the design or scheme through harmony with nature and a human touch. Following World War II, the style becomes extremely popular in furniture and the decorative arts, whereas the few examples in architecture and interiors are limited to individualistic ones. Although it is a worldwide phenomenon, the design leaders are Scandinavia, the United States, and Italy.

HISTORICAL AND SOCIAL

For much of the industrialized world, the 1950s and 1960s are a time of prosperity, optimism, idealism, and great confidence in the future. The world that had been on the brink of annihilation because of World War II and the subsequent Cold War now strives to prevent this from happening again through conservatism, calmness, and conformity. Radicalism, liberalism, women's rights, and civil rights are suppressed or ignored during the 1950s but return with great force during the 1960s.

Thriving economies demand more buildings and a corresponding need for furnishings, both residential and nonresidential. Consumerism increases, and fashion begins to drive design more than ever before as manufacturers create new products in the latest designs to satisfy the buying public. Television replaces radio as the medium of information and entertainment, and programs center on idealized middle-class families who live in perfect houses, raise model children, and own all the latest appliances. A youth culture develops as teenagers embrace the new music of rock and roll. Beatniks and rebels introduce a deliberate counterculture, which will flourish during the 1960s. Most of the world looks to the United States as design innovator and lifestyle model. The notion of the American dream influences other countries through American movies, television, and exported goods.

Within this cultural landscape, Organic Modernism, an international movement, emerges, deriving its characteristic abstracted curvilinear shapes, undulating lines, and bright colors from avant-garde painters and sculptors of the early 20th century. Amoeboid and asymmetrical curving shapes translate easily into interiors and decorative arts, particularly furniture and textiles. Although examples appear during the 1930s and are seen at World's Fairs, the style's popularity is limited before World War II.

With few exceptions, most early designers in the organic mode are sculptors or associated with painters, so early decorative arts examples are most often conceived of as pieces of sculpture. Frank Lloyd Wright is an early and important advocate of organic concepts and forms in architecture, interiors, and furniture. Architect Alvar Aalto of Finland helps popularize organic form. Before the war, Aalto rejects the linear or boxlike International Style for softer, more curvilinear forms and naturalistic materials in architecture, furniture, and glass. His furniture is exported to North America in the early 1930s, but the 1939 Finnish Pavilion at the New York World's Fair brings Aalto's work to a much broader audience. Also influential is Oscar Niermeyer's 1939 Brazilian Pavilion with its parabolic curves. In 1942, Frederick Kiesler creates a biomorphic interior and furniture for The Art of This Century Gallery owned by Peggy Guggenheim. Open until 1947, the space, which is one of the few completely organic interiors, displays Surrealist and Abstract Expressionist art. A few furniture designers create some organic designs for manufacturers, including Gilbert Rohde at Herman Miller.

Additionally, art schools experiment with organic and biomorphic forms before the war. In the United States, this occurs during the late 1930s at the Cranbrook Academy of Art in Michigan, which produces many important designs and designers. Founded in 1923 by George G. Booth and Eliel Saarinen, Cranbrook is one of the first American schools to adopt the European/Bauhaus model for art and design education. Influential artists, designers, and artisans collaborate with the students and each other. Participating in a working environment for artists and designers, students learn by observation, conversation, and doing. Every student has a studio and a master under whom he or she works. Like the Bauhaus, Cranbrook designers consider the total environment and relate form and function to mass production. Many of the most influential designers of this period study at Cranbrook, including Charles and Ray Eames, Florence (Schust) Knoll, and Eero Saarinen.

Following the war, aided by the renewed creative energy of designers and the availability of new materials and techniques, organic forms explode in popularity, first among the elite, and then the public. Organic and sculptural forms become, for a brief period, synonymous with modern, especially in furniture, textiles, and decorative arts. The style and its forms also express concepts of the future as an important illustration of optimism and progress. Kidney-shaped swimming pools, boomerang tables and desks, and textiles with amoeboid shapes in bright colors fill homes and some offices. Buildings most often are architect designed and not builder interpretations. Similarly, organic interiors are primarily the work of architects, as few interior designers follow the design trend. Furniture designers and architects produce organic furnishings for public and private buildings that are marketed by such manufacturers as Knoll International and Herman Miller in the United States. By the mid-1950s, simpler, less radical forms appear, and the popularity of organic and sculptural design begins to fade. In furniture, there is a brief resurgence of organic forms during the 1960s with the development of plastics.

CONCEPTS

Organic and Sculptural Modern represents a deliberate move away from geometry and hard edges toward asymmetrical, expressionistic designs that are still dependent upon functionalism and mass production. This functionalism, however, emphasizes humans and the human body, expressionism, and symbolism, qualities the designers see lacking in the International Style. However, like International Style and Geometric Modern designers, Organic Modern designers believe that technology, not craft, should drive design concepts and appearances. Accordingly, innovations often come out of designers' experiments with new construction techniques derived from other industries or new materials, which they believe demand new forms. Some concepts are in advance of technology, such as Eero Saarinen's desire for a single molded chair and base, which he had in mind for the Pedestal or Tulip chair (Fig. 54-13). The result is a softer, curvilinear modern that relates to nature or is derived from sculpture. Despite its organic nature, much that is produced is of inorganic materials such as reinforced concrete in architecture or plastic in furniture.

The movement, particularly in the decorative arts, absorbs influences from European and American painters and sculptors, including Jean Arp, Salvador Dali, René Magritte, Joan Miró, Ferdinand Leger, Alexander Calder, and Henry Moore, and Abstract Expressionists such as Jackson Pollock, Willem de Kooning, and Franz Kline. From them come organic or biomorphic forms, abstraction, simplification, energy, and randomness.

CHARACTERISTICS AND MOTIFS

Organic and Sculptural Modern exhibits smooth, curving forms and shapes that are often pierced, abstracted, elongated, attenuated, and asymmetrical like in nature. Also characteristic are exaggerated and abstracted naturalistic forms, such as the tulip, hourglass, amoeba, or kidney. Curves may be long and flowing, asymmetrical, or undulating. Unity is an important design goal. With other modernist expressions, Organic shares simplicity, no applied ornament, and a focus upon designing for mass production. The style creates a new, more expressive or symbolic design language arising from experimentation and energy, one that is conveyed by irregular surfaces, boldness, rhythm, continuous surface, parabolic arches, spherical forms, and oblique angles. Colors come from nature or modern art, including Pop Art of the 1960s.

■ *Motifs*. Common motifs include amoeboid and kidney shapes, spheres, parabolas, atoms, molecules, rockets, satellites, flying saucers, abstracted and stylized fruit, flowers, plants, and objects of daily life (Fig. 54-9, 54-10, 54-16).

ARCHITECTURE

Organic architecture has roots in primitive vernacular forms and a specific architectural language, which also can be seen in Art Nouveau. The meaning of organic architecture evolves over time and within the work of individual architects. Common elements include a focus on humans and humanness in the design, materials and forms derived from nature, and form growing out of the building's site or project constraints. The relationship of a building to its site helps create a sense of place.

In the postwar period, Organic and Sculptural Modern broadens the notion of modern architecture from an assertion of pure form expressed in a straightforward, geometric, hard-edged way to forms that are softer, rounded, and expressive, often monumental

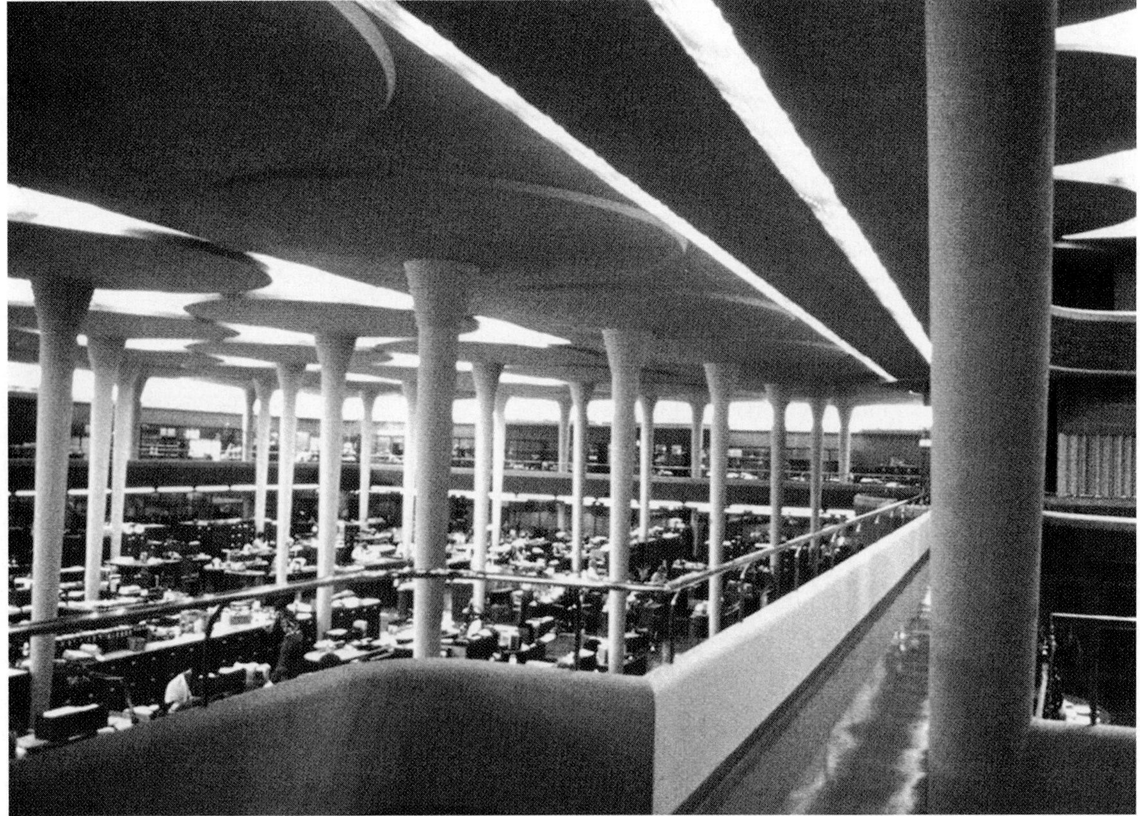

▲ **54-1.** Administration Building, Great Workroom, and office furniture, S. C. Johnson and Son Factory, offices 1936–1939, tower 1947–1950; Racine, Wisconsin; Frank Lloyd Wright.

DESIGN SPOTLIGHT

Architecture and Interior: Sited on a high plateau near Besançon, *Notre-Dame-du-Haut* is a testament to Le Corbusier's goal of "a place of silence, of prayer, of peace, of spiritual joy." Defined by its organic form and monumental scale, the building symbolizes spirituality in form and details. The asymmetrical composition emphasizes light and dark as well as solid and void relationships. White sculptural concrete surfaces contrast sharply with the dark, curved, overhanging roof. The apex of the curving roof leads the eye upward toward heaven. Inside, various sizes and shapes of windows with colored glass and deep reveals cover two walls, creating dramatic and changing light. This enhances spirituality in much the same way as did the stained glass windows in Gothic cathedrals. Le Corbusier innovatively modernizes the medieval techniques of vertically and mystery. Theatrical and inspirational at the same time, the building is unique among churches, as well as a major departure from the architect's other work.

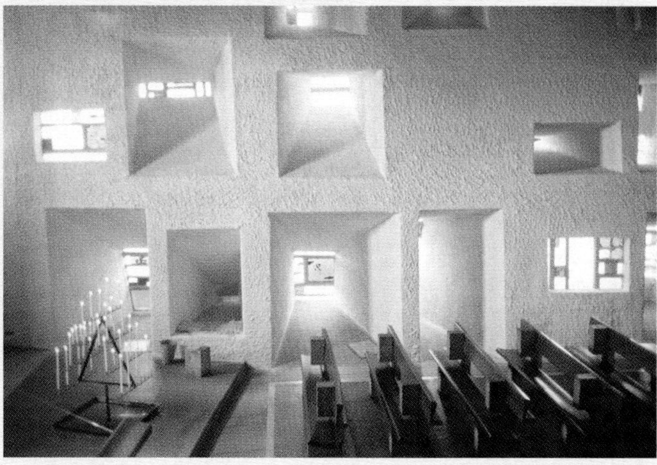

▲ **54-2.** *Notre-Dame-du-Haut* (Pilgrimage Chapel) and interior, 1950–1955; Ronchamp, France; Le Corbusier.

and yet totally unified. Elements of streamlining evident in the late 1930s continue, most notably smooth curves and a sleek outer skin. Organic and Sculptural Modern shares with Geometric Modern an emphasis on function and rejection of applied ornament. Unique to Organic and Sculptural Modern are buildings with fluid, curving forms that evolve from a specific purpose; a desire for a personal architectural statement; or programmatic goals such as symbolism, dynamism, or motion. Consequently, these buildings make bolder, more powerful design statements than Geometric Modern examples do. For example, the TWA Terminal Building (now called Terminal 5; Fig. 54-5) at Kennedy Airport in New York by Eero Saarinen conveys motion, flight, and a sense of the future.

Wright begins to espouse organic concepts during the early 1910s. To Wright, organic means an architecture that evolves from the principles of nature. These principles include unity of site and structure, unity of form and function, and natural materials and colors. Accordingly, Wright's forms frequently develop from the inside out, usually along an axis that may be compared to a tree trunk or plant stem, and the decorative elements evolve from the flora and fauna of the building's location. His Prairie houses exemplify these principles but through geometric forms. Although at that time he rarely designs buildings in the curving naturalistic forms of nature, these principles underlie his own architectural philosophy and influence subsequent organic architectural theory. Wright's most famous work of the 1930s expressing his organic concepts is Fallingwater (Fig. 54-8), a building that embodies a strong sense of place primarily because of its harmonious relationship to nature.

During the 1920s, in Germany, a few architects break with the dominant Bauhaus geometric interpretation of form follows function. The main advocate is Hugo Häring, who believes that structures should develop from explorations of function and place and they should depict this process instead of the designer's personal tastes. He rejects geometry in favor of forms from nature, the site, and/or the individual program. His ideas influence Hans Scharoun, Alvar Aalto, and Louis Kahn. However, there are only a few isolated examples of curvilinear organic forms until after World War II.

As architects move away from geometric purity to expand the meaning of Modernism, two particular buildings influence them. Wright's Guggenheim Museum (Fig. 54-4), conceived in 1947, unites space, function, and sweeping movement in an expanding spiral form. Here, Wright integrates his organic theories with organic form. The second is *Notre-Dame-du-Haut* (Fig. 54-2), a modern church with no references to the past, in which Le Corbusier expresses symbolism through a wavelike roof and curving walls.

Although these works inspire others, Organic structures remain few and specific to some individuals or selected applications. One is Eero Saarinen (Fig. 54-5, 54-6), who strives to create personal, ex-

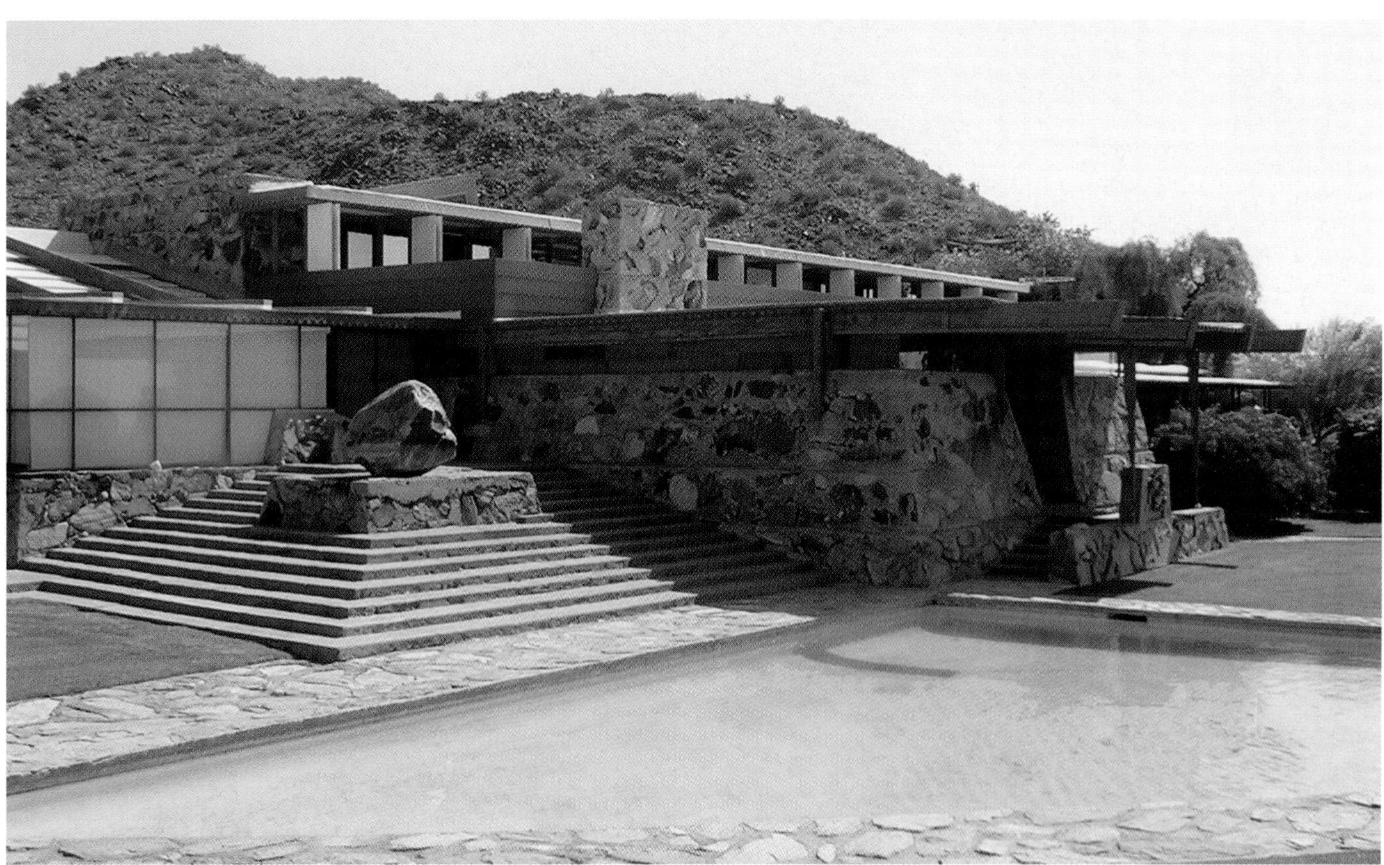

▲ **54-3.** Taliesin West, 1938–1959; Scottsdale, Arizona; Frank Lloyd Wright.

pressionist structures whose forms grow out of function, unity, and symbolism. Not many architects work exclusively in the style, in part because Organic and Sculptural Modern demands extraordinary creativity, technical genius, and innovative construction techniques made possible by reinforced concrete. Despite the limited examples, Organic and Sculptural Modern defines a surprising variety of public buildings, including large corporate headquarters (Fig. 54-1), government complexes, churches (Fig. 54-2), museums (Fig. 54-4), sports facilities, airport terminals (Fig. 54-5, 54-6), train stations, and concert halls (Fig. 54-7). Innovative and unusual houses are the most expressive form of residential construction (Fig. 54-3, 54-8). Concept homes of the future often are organic in form.

▲ **54-4.** Solomon R. Guggenheim Museum, 1957–1959; New York City, New York; Frank Lloyd Wright.

Public and Private Buildings

■ *Site Orientation*. Large corporate, government, transportation, and sports complexes are often situated in expansive planned areas with parklike settings in or just outside major cities (Fig. 54-1, 54-5, 54-6). There may be one or more structures in the complex, with placement based on functional relationships. Architects frequently position churches on large green areas with commanding vistas, sometimes within a large building complex, or near water, or on high plateaus. An example is *Notre-Dame-du-Haut* (Fig. 54-2) by Le Corbusier, which becomes a sculptural monument on its high, flat plateau in France. Sun orientation is important because the design often emphasizes the penetration of light into the interior spaces (Fig. 54-3). Museums, usually in large cities, appear on major streets for easy access (Fig. 54-4). The location and orientation of houses vary depending on the designer, owner, and geography of the area (Fig. 54-8).

■ *Floor Plans*. Floor plans evolve primarily from relationships between particular functional areas. Each building is different and individual, and therefore its planning reflects diversity in approach, programming, and design. Some plans rely on modernist formality in arrangements. More than ever, architects experiment with the interrelationship and transformation of curving two-dimensional shapes into volumetric three-dimensional forms arising from the biomorphic, sculptural, and abstract character of the building design and programmatic needs. Organic or curvilinear forms often are translated into a plan concept that addresses the needs of the users and the artistic expression and creativity of the designer. Sometimes the plans derive from organic shapes, such as the chambered nautilus concept of the Guggenheim Museum (Fig. 54-4) by Wright. Or they may evolve from natural forms, such as the bird's wings concept of Saarinen's TWA Terminal (Fig. 54-5).

■ *Materials*. Architects exploit reinforced concrete in a variety of curvilinear or parabolic shapes that move and undulate in biomorphic and sculptural forms (Fig. 54-2, 54-4, 54-5, 54-6, 54-7). Some buildings, however, are of traditional masonry construction. Structures also incorporate a variety of materials, such as wood, stone, concrete, and steel. Large areas of fixed glass are typical.

■ *Façades*. The most important characteristic of all building façades is their sculptural monumentality shown by their imposing presence on the landscape. Massing and volume define the effect, and a lightweight structure produces a characteristic simplicity of volume and line. Architects' concern for light and dark is expressed in solid and void relationships. Forms curve, undulate, move, and develop in a unified harmony that balances a rhythm of shapes, heights, and contours (Fig. 54-1, 54-2, 54-3, 54-5, 54-6, 54-7, 54-8). Surfaces are often smooth and uninterrupted. Symmetry or asymmetry may characterize individual parts as well as the façade itself. Sometimes large- or small-scale vertical or linear movements repeat in a rhythmic sequence to create architectural texture and/or the interplay of light and dark.

■ *Windows*. Variety in design and type is common. Some buildings feature repeating window styles and shapes, evidence of modernist principles of regularity (Fig. 54-1, 54-6, 54-8). These structures have large areas of fixed glass panes inserted in vertical or horizontal metal grids. On other buildings, randomness or unusual repetitions in window sizes and shapes supports a unified appearance (Fig. 54-2, 54-3, 54-5, 54-7).

■ *Doors*. Commercial buildings, irrespective of type, have large, prominent entryways that are easily recognizable and contribute to user wayfinding (Fig. 54-4). The scale and design may vary based on function and designer, but the entryway always blends in well with the structure. Doors are often of clear glass with metal frames.

■ *Roofs*. Many roofs have curving shapes made possible by reinforced concrete or the use of a cable-hung system. They may blend in or be separate from the building design. On commercial buildings, they are often the most distinctive feature of the design. Shapes vary (Fig. 54-2, 54-3, 54-4, 54-5, 54-6, 54-7, 54-8): some are soft geometric curves, while others have more abstract, undulating, and rounded curves. And still other roofs are flatter, slightly pitched, and hidden behind a sculptural façade. Sometimes skylights pierce the roof surface, allowing natural light to enter.

INTERIORS

Most Organic and Sculptural interior design is done by architects, who continue the exterior design, shapes, and materials into the interior. In Organic and Sculptural buildings, there is a close interrelationship between the exterior design and the interior space because one forms the other. Often exterior materials repeat on the interior either from the inherent, visible construction or by deliberate choice. Interior spaces express the movement, openness, organic, and/or sculptural qualities of the exterior as part of a totally unified design concept. Interiors for airport terminals and sports complexes are some of the newest types of spaces (Fig. 54-5).

Otherwise, most interiors convey a very simple, boxlike appearance with plain walls, minimal trim, and no ornamentation. These minimalist interiors reflect a modernist aesthetic, while their furnishings suggest an artistic and innovative character, much like paintings or pieces of sculpture in a very plain environment. Most commonly, biomorphic, sculptural, or abstract

DESIGN SPOTLIGHT

Architecture and Interior: Eero Saarinen's poetic, expressionist Trans World Airlines Terminal (now Terminal 5) resembles a piece of sculpture on an airport runway—symbolizing a bird in flight. Its reinforced concrete structure undulates and moves so that there is complete fusion between roof, walls, and floor—outside and inside. Four roof vaults with Y-shaped columns blend together to form the composition. Natural light entering from ceiling crevices accents important spaces. Contoured surfaces shape and define circulation paths, terminal desks, and waiting areas. Numerous level changes, bridges, and stairs lead to departure areas, conversation pits, and restaurants. This exciting three-dimensional quality creates an important and memorable structure for TWA. The interior, restricted in color and ornament, appears lively as people enter, move around, and congregate. A circular ceramic tile from Japan covers most interior surfaces.

▲ **54-5.** Trans World Airlines Terminal (TWA, now Terminal 5; Kennedy International Airport) and interior, 1956–1962; New York City, New York; Eero Saarinen and Associates.

▲ **54-6.** Terminal Building, Dulles International Airport, 1958–1962; Chantilly, Virginia; Eero Saarinen and Associates.

concepts are conveyed through the furniture, textiles, lighting, decorative arts, and artwork in many midcentury interiors no matter what the exterior style. Plants, especially rubber plants and others with bold leaf patterns, are important accessories.

Public and Private Buildings

■ *Color.* Most interior walls in public buildings are white or off-white following the modernist aesthetic or are the color, usually neutral, of the exterior building material (Fig. 54-2, 54-5). In contrast, many residential rooms are ablaze with brilliant colors in furniture, finishes, and accessories. Primary and strong secondary colors, often contrasting and mixed with black or white, characterize textiles (Fig. 54-9), wallpapers, area rugs, and decorative arts. By the second half of the 1950s, shocking pink, orange, magenta, brilliant green, dark blue, purple, lemon yellow, mustard, and red appear in all manner of decorative arts and furniture (Fig. 54-10, 54-11, 54-13, 54-14, 54-15). Designers sometimes derive colors and color schemes from modern art and artists such as Mondrian, Paul Klee, Alexander Calder, or Joan Miró.

■ *Floors.* Wood, concrete, ceramic tile, and composition tile floors are common (Fig. 54-1, 54-2, 54-5, 54-8). Different flooring materials may define areas within open spaces. Some floors are covered with area rugs or wall-to-wall carpeting, which again becomes popular during the 1950s. Area rugs may feature abstract or organic patterns in brilliant or subdued colors.

■ *Walls.* Walls are most often plain, bare, and unornamented with no moldings and only a baseboard (Fig. 54-1, 54-2, 54-5, 54-8). Shapes and forms define character and enrich the surface appearance. Architectural features, such as curved walls, windows, and interior columns, add interest and variety. Some, however, may display a textural focal point or a surface enrichment created through the use and design of the building material. In many modern rooms, particularly in residences, wallpapers with amorphous shapes and patterns give an organic quality or display futurist motifs such as rockets. Wallpapers and textiles are rarely in the same pattern because contrast is preferred. Because they cover large areas, wallpaper patterns generally are less demanding and brilliant in color than those of textiles. As in other Modern Style houses, two contrasting wallpapers or paint colors may define some walls, particularly to define and separate individual areas in open plans.

■ *Stoves.* Stoves are an alternative to built-in fireplaces during the period. Usually freestanding, stoves have sculptural or organic shapes and come in white, black, and a range of colors. They may be in the center or at the perimeter of the room. Because of a concern for safety, the walls near stoves are often of a flame-proof material such as brick or stone.

■ *Window Treatments.* Most windows in large public spaces are left bare but often shielded by an architectural feature. Window treatments, when present, are plain, simple, straight panels hanging from ceiling to floor. Made of loosely woven casements or thin sheers in white or natural colors, curtains blend with the space. In houses, printed curtains add interest to spaces with little architectural articulation. Patterns on curtains often have large repeats.

■ *Doors.* Doors are plain, usually in wood, glass, or sometimes metal. Often they are designed to be inconspicuous. Flat, narrow door trims frame the opening.

■ *Ceilings.* Ceilings in Organic and Sculptural buildings usually emulate the character of the architecture and create interest through sculptural form and design (Fig. 54-1, 54-2, 54-5, 54-8). Some may be pierced with skylights in a rhythmic manner. But many ceilings in corporate and residential environments are plain, white or off-white, and unadorned so that they blend in with the wall treatment. This is particularly true if the interior showcases unique furnishings and decorative arts.

■ *Textiles.* Fabrics have abstract, biomorphic, and sculptural designs with figures, symbols, floral motifs, geometric shapes, animals, masks, calligraphy, earth forms, rockets, atoms, and numerous lines and shapes against large areas of background (Fig. 54-9). Sometimes fantasy or humor may dominate the overall character. Some designs relate to modern art or are designed by modern artists such as Pablo Picasso, Raoul Duffy, or Joan Miró. Many fabrics (and wallpapers) are screen printed, which allows large repeats of up to 60" because the process permits pattern and color individuality while keeping costs down. Textile firms market fabrics by collections and/or by individual designers, capitalizing on the period's promotion of good design.

Fibers include cotton, linen, rayon, wool, nylon, polyester, and fiberglass. Colors vary by designer with a range of bright or subdued colors in shades of orange, green, pink, cream, brown, gold, black, yellow, red, and blue. Color is brighter than before because of improvements in dyes and printing processes. In the United States, Knoll and Herman Miller are innovators in the creation and use of brilliant colors in textiles. For example, Knoll introduces the orange and pink color combination, and Herman Miller showcases Alexander Girard's textile and wallpaper designs that combine brilliant colors not seen before. Texture is important, so designers experiment with new textural effects, often aided by new synthetic fibers. To enhance organic or sculptural forms, solids with textural weaves are used.

DESIGN SPOTLIGHT

Architecture and Interior: One of the landmarks of 20th-century architecture, Fallingwater, built for Edgar Kaufman, is a testament to Frank Lloyd Wright's vision of organic architecture. Nestled into a hillside covered with trees, it literally becomes one with nature through site, materials, and structure. Positioned over a rocky waterfall, the house's cantilevered terraces overhang it in horizontal layers. From the living room, there is access to a natural swimming pool below. Materials of natural stone, ochre concrete, and russet-painted steel window frames contribute to the building's earthy character. The terraces and large glass windows and doors support Wright's organic concept of "space flowing outward, space flowing inward." The interiors continue this idea with open spaces, built-in walnut furniture, flagstone floors, large skylights, and earth-toned colors. Natural light enters from all sides. Low ceiling heights and horizontal lines contribute to a sense of human scale. Meandering circulation paths add a feeling of informality. These elements convey Wright's principal themes and help to create a harmonious fusion of parts. [National Historic Landmark]

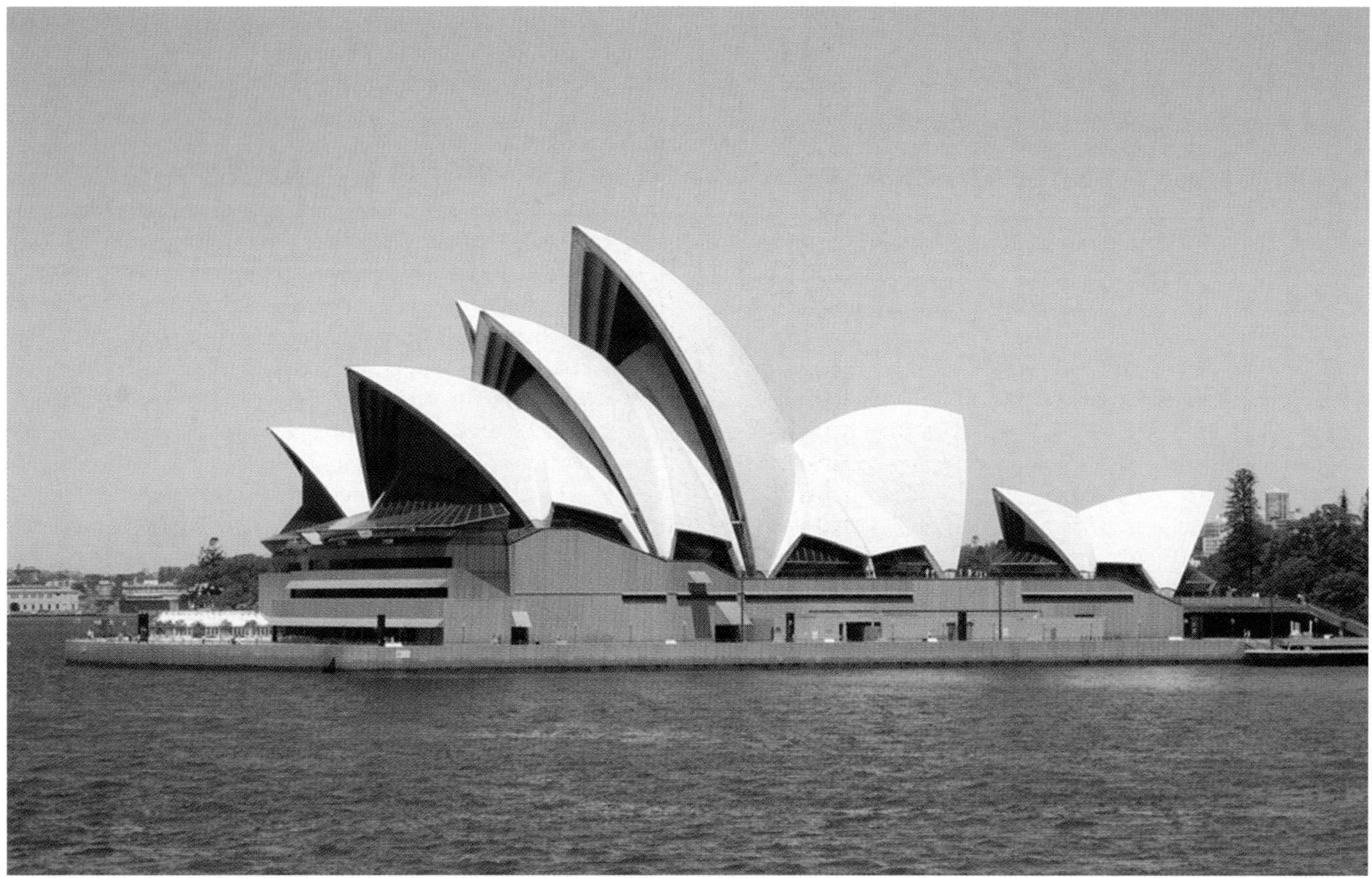

▲ **54-7.** Sydney Opera House, 1956–1973; Sydney, Australia; Jorn Utzon and Peter Hall.

DESIGN SPOTLIGHT

▲ **54-8.** Fallingwater and living room with fireplace, 1935–1937; Bear Run, Pennsylvania; Frank Lloyd Wright.

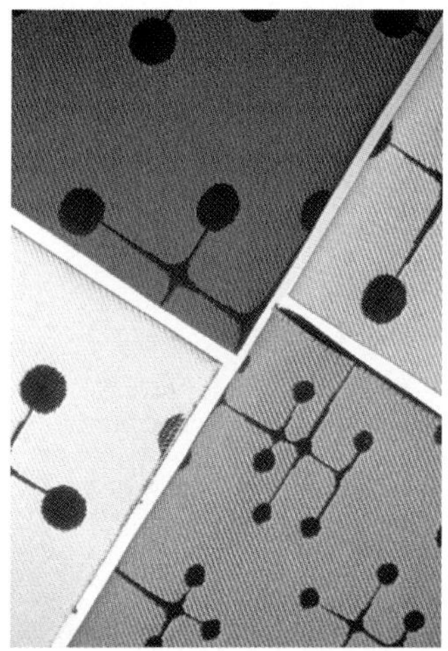

▲ **54-9.** Textiles: Fabrics, c. 1950s–1960s; United States; Ray Eames (with dots) and Alexander Girard (with organic flowers), manufactured by Herman Miller.

■ *Upholstery*. There is an ever-increasing range of upholstery materials produced in an assortment of textures and colors for various applications (Fig. 54-13, 54-14, 54-15). Vinyl often is embossed to simulate leather or other materials, but it begins to lose popularity in the late 1950s because it is not comfortable for the sitter. New in the period is jersey, introduced in the late 1950s. It remains popular until the 1970s. Jersey knits suit new furniture designs that demand stretchable fabrics. Some have upholstery covers that may be removed for cleaning or replacement.

■ *Lighting*. Architects place greater emphasis on built-in architectural lighting, following Modernism and to accent the architectural form (Fig. 54-1). Large, volumetric spaces have a combination of indirect lighting, recessed downlights, and surface-mounted fixtures. Supplementing this in residences or individual offices is an assortment of table lamps, floor lamps, chandeliers, and/or wall sconces that offers flexibility (Fig. 54-10). Sometimes designers create unique and individual fixtures or lighting treatments for a particular project to showcase innovation and creativity as well as add to the personality of the space. Natural lighting is also important, so frequently there are large areas of glass on walls and ceilings (Fig. 54-3, 54-5, 54-6, 54-8).

Lighting specialists, architects, and designers, such as George Nelson, and sculptors, such as Isamu Noguchi, design functional and aesthetically pleasing light fixtures in organic shapes. Nelson's Bubble pendant and wall lamps, originally for Howard Miller, have sprayed plastic shades in various rounded shapes. Akari Light Sculptures by Noguchi have a bamboo frame with a handmade paper covering. They come as floor and table lamps and hanging fixtures.

FURNISHINGS AND DECORATIVE ARTS

Furnishings and decorative arts are some of the best representations of the abstract, biomorphic, and sculptural asthetic. The characteristic fluidity of line; rounded forms; free-form, biomorphic shapes; and lightness of Organic and Sculptural furnishings are made possible by new materials and new construction techniques. Organic furniture, which suits the human frame, usually has long, low proportions. As a result, it relates well to interiors, and its rounded forms contrast with more angular interior spaces. Many pieces, especially seating, are meant to be seen from any angle, so their sculptural qualities are suitable in rooms with broad expanses of glass or when placed away from walls or in the center of a space.

Unlike Geometric Modern furniture, Organic and Sculptural furniture is rarely modular. Although mass produced, examples often offer a variety of choices for chair or table legs and bases, colors, and finishes for individuality or unity within an interior. Most furniture designers are architects or sculptors. They often develop construction techniques to suit their design concepts and pay close attention to comfort.

There are no new types of furniture, but designers focus on furnishings for particular types of spaces, such as airport terminals, school classrooms, executive offices, living and dining rooms, and

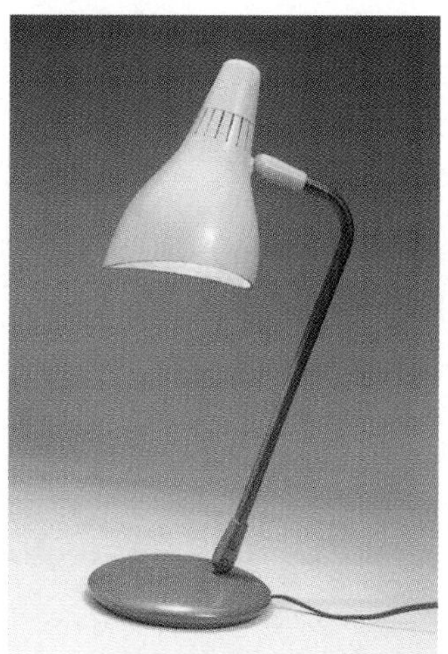

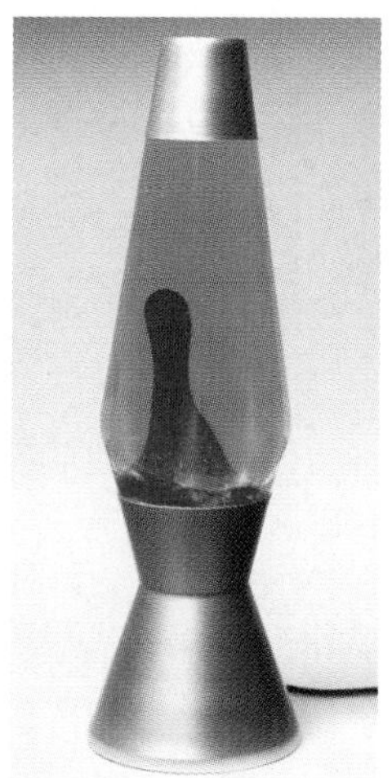

▲ **54-10.** Lighting: Table lamp, desk lamp, and lava lamp, 1940s–1960s; Raoul Raba (sculptural table lamp).

▲ **54-11.** Butterfly or sling chair, 1938; Brazil; Jorge Ferrari-Hardoy, Juan Kurchan, and Antonio Bonet, manufactured by Knoll International.

outdoor areas. Many pieces designed for nonresidential spaces are used in residences because of their excellence in design and reasonable costs. Sometimes designers retrofit existing or new designs to make them adaptable to a different kind of space. Designers usually concentrate on the design of chairs and give their designs colorful names inspired by nature, such as the Coconut chair (Fig. 54-15).

The United States leads the way in Organic and Sculptural Modern furniture, followed by Italy and Scandinavia. Furniture ranges from creations of avant-garde designers to mass-produced pieces by anonymous creators. Along with Herman Miller and Knoll, other furniture manufacturers, such as Baker, Dunbar, and John Widdicomb, commission furniture from less well-known designers. Generally, the furniture-buying public accepts modern design, so manufacturers produce more modern furniture. Designers have difficulty obtaining patents for their designs, so good and bad copies increase. Knockoffs of popular pieces usually resemble the originals but sell for far less because of minimal development and production costs. A common term for these pieces is kitsch, meaning "knockoff" or "trash," that refers to cheap, poorly designed objects made for the mass market.

In 1940, the Museum of Modern Art and Bloomingdale's department store sponsor a competition called "Organic Design in Home Furnishings." Charles Eames and Eero Saarinen enter the competition. Their chairs of plywood, which bend in two directions, win first place. The structurally innovative design consists of compound curves that have to be seen in the round. By using very thin veneers to achieve the curves, Eames and Saarinen give great strength to the design. The resulting exhibit of the same name introduces organic design, total unity, and new advances in furniture design to the public. After the exhibit, some work from it is sold at Bloomingdales, but with limited public success. However, the experimentation and innovation of this early work

DESIGN SPOTLIGHT

Furniture: Charles and Ray Eames experiment with form and materials to create chairs that address the human body. Some of these chairs become important and popular furniture icons of the period. Because they offer flexibility, mobility, and comfort that meets a variety of uses, they are used in schools, cafeterias, offices, and even houses. Charles Eames formulates this lounge chair and ottoman (next page) from concepts first presented in 1940 in the *Organic Designs in Home Furnishings* exhibition at the Museum of Modern Art. The design stresses comfort and luxury, which is achieved through a flexible swivel and tilt-mounted base; contoured and separate seat, back, and headrest; and soft padded leather upholstery. Cushions are of down and foam. Constructed in molded plywood shells with a rosewood veneer, most of the chair is machine produced, except for a few parts that are made by hand. The design resembles a piece of sculpture and presents a quality of elegance in a room, something that is important to Eames.

▲ **54-12.** Side chairs and armchairs in molded plywood, wire, and molded plastic, 1946–1951; Lounge Chair and ottoman, 1956; United States; Charles and Ray Eames, manufactured by Herman Miller.

DESIGN SPOTLIGHT

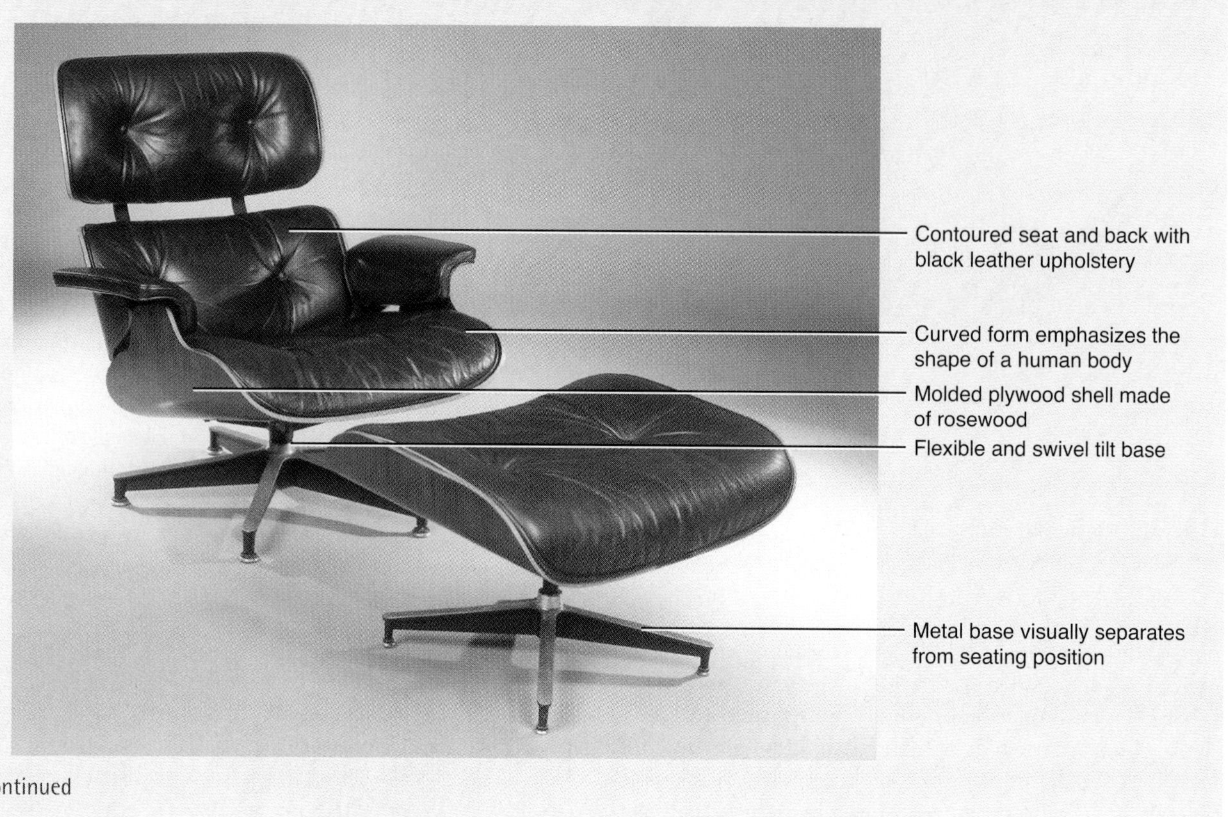

▲ **54–12.** Continued

▲ **54–13.** Pedestal or Tulip chairs and tables, 1956; and Womb chair and ottoman, 1948; United States; Eero Saarinen, manufactured by Knoll International.

▲ **54-14.** Diamond chairs, 1952; United States; Harry Bertoia, manufactured by Knoll International.

influence Eames's and Saarinen's later designs. Eames continues to experiment and explore new materials and constructions throughout his long career. Saarinen searches for his ideal of one-piece construction.

Public and Private Buildings

■ *Materials*. Biomorphic shapes and forms in furniture are made possible by inorganic materials such as fiberglass, plastics, aluminum, polyester resins, and plastic foams. Traditional furniture materials include solid or veneered woods such as ash, walnut, and birch, which may be left natural or stained. Rosewood is also used, but it is expensive. Designers, such as Charles and Ray Eames (Fig. 54-12) and Saarinen (Fig. 54-13), investigate bending laminated plywood into curvilinear shapes.

▲ **54-13.** Continued

■ *Seating*. Seating choices expand substantially during the period, with more variety and experimentation. Seats and bases often are separated visually as well as by the choice of material. Designers test materials not only for variety in design but also to create more comfortable seating. Some early examples use steel frames and construction methods (Fig. 54-1, 54-11), such as the innovative office furniture by Wright. Later ones exploit laminated plywood, metal wire, and plastic (Fig. 54-12, 54-13, 54-14, 54-15). Although lightweight, these chairs are comfortable with well-conceived profiles that appeal from any angle of view. Improvements in wood lamination, molding processes, and welding assist or even drive design ideas. Asymmetry, an organic design goal, appears in a variety of seating pieces, including those with molded steel upholstered shells.

From earlier experiments with Saarinen, the Eamses design side and armchairs with separate seats and backs of plywood bent in two directions to suit the human shape (Fig. 54-12). Rubber shock mounts developed in the automobile industry add flexibility and unite the same or two entirely different materials in seat, back, and supports. Extremely popular and used in a variety of interiors, the chairs come in several versions with choices of materials for legs, seats, and backs, as well as upholstery. Their well-known Lounge Chair, although expensive, is one of Herman Miller's most successful pieces. The Eameses also design a group of chairs with fiberglass-reinforced shells or welded metal wire molded into various shapes that may be upholstered. The chairs come in more than 15 variations, including choices of shell color, upholstery, and various legs or bases, including a rocker.

Similarly, Saarinen designs chairs and sofas of molded fiberglass (Fig. 54-13). His Womb chair is a fiberglass sculptural shell resting on slender metal legs. The shell is upholstered and has a separate seat and back cushion as well as an ottoman. In contrast, the Pedestal or Tulip group, which includes arm and side chairs,

▲ **54-15.** Coconut chair, 1956–1957; United States; George Nelson Associates, manufactured by Herman Miller.

stools, and tables, is composed of a single plastic-coated aluminum stem or pedestal arising from a round base and supporting a fiberglass-reinforced, plastic-molded shell seat and back. Similar in shape, but of transparent plexiglass, is the series of chairs by Erwin and Estelle Laverne. Names, such as Lily, reflect the abstracted naturalistic shapes. Interested in wire construction, Eames and sculptor Harry Bertoia create chairs constructed of welded steel rods. Bertoia also uses welded lattice forms to create seating with more sculptural forms, such as the Diamond chair (Fig. 54-14). Sofas sometimes are expanded chair forms. Others have biomorphic, kidney, or boomerang shapes and resemble a piece of sculpture.

■ *Tables*. Tables come in a wide diversity of types, including dining, conference, end or lamp, and coffee (Fig. 54-8, 54-13, 54-16). Shapes of tops include round, oval, free-form, amoeboid, boomerang, and kidney. Many have glass tops and bases of wood, plastic, or metal. Heights of tables vary depending on function. Eames designs dining and coffee tables to match his plywood chair. Saarinen's Pedestal or Tulip group has matching dining or conference, coffee, and side tables with round or oval tops. Noguchi designs a table with a curved wooden base and a free-form round glass top.

■ *Decorative Arts*. Architects and furniture designers create decorative art objects with organic forms and patterns in glass, ceramic, wood, and metal. The Eameses, for example, create an undulating wooden folding screen based on early plywood experiments with Saarinen. Decorative objects often have rich textures emulating the textural contrasts of interiors. Many glass manufacturers worldwide produce glassware and art glass in biomorphic, undulating, and/or rounded shapes. Forms include bubbles, abstracted flowers, and stems in transparent or translucent clear and/or colored glass. Particularly successful and much copied are the undulating, free-form, handkerchief glass vases by Venini (Fig. 54-17), no two of which have the same shape or decoration. In 1962, the Studio Glass Movement emerges as individual artists work in studios instead of factories. This is made possible by the development of small inexpensive furnaces that can achieve the high temperatures required to make glass. The leaders, Americans Harvey Littleton and Dominic Labino, inspire others, achieve worldwide recognition in their work, and foster the studio glass movement.

Like glass, ceramics display organic shapes influenced by sculpture, abstract patterns, and bright colors. Designers employ a wide range of decorative techniques to give more and varied patterns to pieces. Some patterns come from modern art. Plain dinnerware with fluid organic shapes is preferred over richly decorated and gilded floral porcelains. Industrial designer Russel Wright's American Modern dinnerware of the 1930s for Steubenville is an early

▲ **54-16.** Coffee table, c. 1940s; Isamu Noguchi, manufactured by Herman Miller.

▲ **54-17.** Decorative Arts: Handkerchief vase, mid-1950s–1960s; England.

example of mix-and-match dinnerware. Combining organic and streamlined shapes, the dishes come in seven different but coordinating colors. Similarly, Eva Zeisel's Town and Country dinner service also mixes colors, even among individual pieces. The mix-and-match concept extends to glass as well. Timo Sarpaneva's I-glass series for Iittala includes bottles, drinking glasses, and plates in soft tones of lilac, green, blue, and gray.

■ *Later Interpretations*. During the early 1960s, plastic, solid foam, or foam-covered tubular steel seating sometimes has neo-organic or undulating shapes inspired by Pop Art. Neo-organic shapes frequently repeat in furniture design into the early 21st century as designers continue to experiment with form, materials, and construction techniques (Fig. 54-18). They are not as dominant and pervasive, however, as during the 1950s.

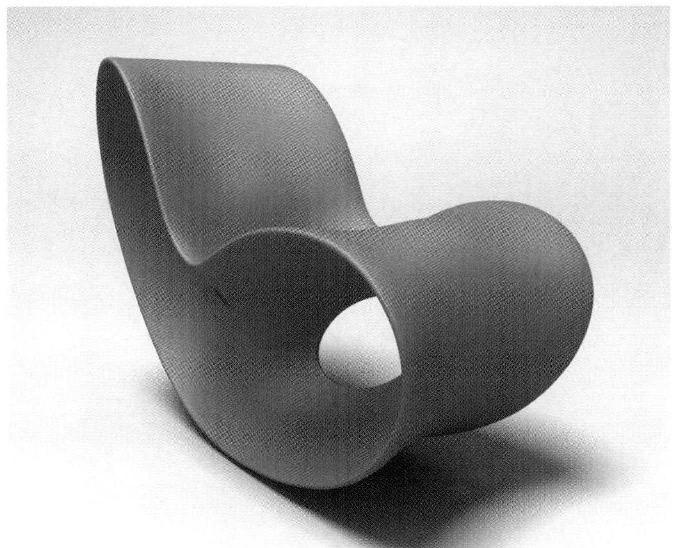

▲ **54-18.** Later Interpretation: Voido rocking chair, 2005; Italy; Ron Arad Associates, manufactured by Magis. Neo-Modern.

CHAPTER 55

Modern Historicism

1930s–2000s

It must be a wonderful thing to be a decorator! Nearly every day somebody makes this remark to me, and I usually reply, "Well it is and it isn't." As a matter of fact, it is wonderful to live your life among beautiful things, and to spend all of your time in an attempt to create beauty, but it would be far more wonderful to be a decorator if the profession had the dignity and authority of an architect's profession—if it were standardized as to the training, experience, and knowledge necessary for admission to its ranks.

—Nancy McClelland, in *An Outline of Careers for Women*, Doris Fleischman, 1929

Developing in the first decades of the 20th century and continuing into the 21st century, Modern Historicism emphasizes the importance of history by using attributes and/or elements from past styles or periods within a modern framework. Recognizing the associative or representative potential of past styles, architects, interior designers, interior decorators, and others look to historical structures, artifacts, and design principles as valid models for and solutions to modern design problems. Modern Historicism includes several styles, themes, and movements, including Suburban Modern, New Urbanism, New Formalism, Regionalism, a new Classical Revival in the late 20th century, and Period Interior Decoration.

HISTORICAL AND SOCIAL

Modern Historicism looks to and uses the past in a variety of ways to express a diversity of themes in the context of contemporary life and requirements. Growing out of the 19th-century Victorian Revivals and Academic Tradition, it both responds to and assimilates influences from design movements and trends of the 20th century, including Bauhaus, Art Deco, International Style, and Historic Preservation Movement.

With the obvious exception of Modernism, nearly all previous styles and periods look to past, especially antiquity, for inspiration. Most often designers attempt to create works that expand, build upon, or further previous theories, ideas, and examples, as in the Renaissance, Baroque, or Neoclassical periods. Although more imaginative and evocative than accurate, revivals of past styles during the Victorian period (1830s–1910s) lay the foundation for using the past in a contemporary context. Victorians associate past styles with wealth, culture, and status. During the last decades of the 19th century, greater historical accuracy in expressions of Classical Eclecticism comes from the new discipline of art history and the study of historical structures and artifacts. Inspired by the academic tradition, architects, artists, furniture makers, and designers look to the best examples of the past to learn design concepts and principles that they can apply to their own situations. As a result, architecture, interiors, and furnishings take on a more accurate historical appearance than in the earlier Victorian revivals. Culture and status remain important associations. Writers of the period, architects, and interior decorators tie good taste to period styles, particularly those of France and Italy. Although Classical Eclecticism is a grand and expensive style, it lays foundations for Modern Historicism in its emphasis upon period rooms and past styles. Unlike Modern Historicism, it regards associations of culture and status that are linked to the classical past as more important than ties to the present.

During the first half of the 20th century, Modern Historicism dominates public and institutional architecture and residences, and it communicates associations of culture, status, and family heritage. Exteriors of both public and private buildings usually maintain at least a period flavor in form and details, but floor plans, interior treatments, and furnishings suit modern functions, building code requirements, and lifestyles. Period styles still are considered expressions of good taste. Interior decorators are the primary purveyors of period-style interiors in the homes of the affluent and some hotels and clubs. With increasing prosperity and greater demand for their services, decorators begin to turn their attention to the rooms of the middle class. At the same time, builders and architects create numerous Modern Historical houses, cottages, and townhouses that fill newly created subdivisions in and around cities.

As the 20th century progresses and architects and designers accept Modern design movements and concepts, so simplification, sleekness, and stylization unite with period influences and styles. The emphasis on historical accuracy diminishes, and eclecticism, combining different styles or mixing period styles with contemporary, becomes the norm. By the late 20th century and into the 21st century, public architecture, particularly corporate, is dominated by Modernism rather than period styles. However, period architectural styles, including Georgian, Colonial Revival, Queen Anne, and Arts and Crafts, maintain some importance in residences, hotels, and other public buildings. Modern Historicism and period styles are a favored choice for interiors and furnishings, especially in residences, so choices of past styles expand to include Victorian styles, the Aesthetic Movement, Arts and Crafts, Art Deco, and Art Moderne. Eclecticism and simplification continue to characterize the majority of expressions, although some strive for greater historical accuracy. By the end of the 20th century, period styles are less often tied to good taste and more commonly tied to individuality, personal choice, and even antiquarianism. Modern Historicism is usually more prominent in areas that have a strong sense of place or history.

Throughout its history, Modern Historicism is affected by events and trends that focus on the past. For example, from its beginning in 1927, the reconstruction and restoration of Colonial Williamsburg in Virginia inspires 18th-century Colonial-style and reproduction houses, interiors, furniture, wallpapers, textiles, and decorative arts in the United States. The Historic Preservation Movement also influences Modern Historicism during the 1970s and 1980s in the United States when federal tax credits and an economic downturn make it far more cost-effective to reuse old buildings than to tear down and build new. Many older structures, including factories and warehouses, experience new life as shops, restaurants, offices, and hotels. Additionally, when people purchase older homes, they often seek ways to decorate them in a period manner. As a result, developers, publishers, and manufacturers produce more products, books, and magazines. History becomes a big business. Toward the end of the 20th century, the environmental movement encourages preservation because, when compared to new construction, preserving is more cost-effective, saves energy, and produces less waste. Late in the first decade of the 21st century, the National Trust for Historic Preservation, along with other groups and the United States Green Building Council (USGBC), begin discussing ways that the LEED standards can be modified to better support preservation of historic and existing buildings.

The media also influence Modern Historicism. In the 1930s, many movies depict Art Deco and Art Moderne interiors, but period movies, such as *Gone with the Wind* of 1939, also help shape design sensibilities. The notions of home, family, and tradition are especially important during the 1950s. Television programs and movies show what they believe are typical American families in period houses with a mixture of period and modern furnishings. In the late 20th and early 21st centuries, period movies and television programs, home decoration and remodeling programs, and important museum exhibitions continue to advance and influence Modern Historicism.

■ *Historic Preservation Movement.* The Historic Preservation Movement (or Heritage Conservation in Canada) recognizes the importance of the past and seeks to save it by protecting and maintaining historic structures and sites. Originating largely as a grassroots movement in the second half of the 19th century in Europe and North America, most early preservation efforts are sporadic. They come from individuals and volunteer groups who identify structures that they believe are important and seek to save them from destruction, usually through purchase and management. Buildings or structures associated with historic events or people are the most common choices. There is minimal local or national government involvement.

Preservation broadens its scope throughout the 20th century to include all types of significant historic structures and sites. Local and national governments become increasingly involved. They work toward creating comprehensive preservation policies that protect important places from inappropriate alterations, destruction, or demolition. They seek to guard significant historic resources by developing comprehensive laws and policies. Among the means they adopt are legal recognition for significant sites, neighborhoods, and individual structures. This includes inventories or lists such as the National Register of Historic Places in the United States. National and local governments pass laws such as the 1966 Historic Preservation Act in the United States that identify and protect historic resources. They also create organizations (National Trust, United Kingdom, and National Trust for Historic Preservation, United States) and assign government bureaus or departments (Department of the Interior and National Park Service, United States) to oversee these resources and provide means to maintain historic resources, such as loans or tax credits.

Even with more government involvement, volunteer organizations still play an important role in historic preservation throughout the 20th century and into the 21st century. They advise individuals, groups, and the government on preservation and restoration and provide educational tools and publications. Some own and maintain historic properties or collections of artifacts. Most important, they create awareness and recognition of the value of history and a sense of place.

Preservation becomes global in 1972 when the United Nations Educational, Scientific, and Cultural Organization (UNESCO) sponsors an international treaty to protect natural and cultural sites and objects around the world. The treaty creates a listing of significant places, the World Heritage List, and requires the home nations to develop policies to protect and manage them with UNESCO's assistance. Sites include the Pyramids of Egypt; Brasilia, Brazil; the Great Wall of China; the Palace and Park of Versailles, France; and the Great Barrier Reef in Australia.

CONCEPTS

Modern Historicism: Reinterpreting the Past

Modern Historicism in architecture, interiors, and furniture uses the past in a variety of ways to express a theme, symbolism, or monumentality while adapting it to modern tastes and needs in architecture, interiors, and furnishings. Past styles appeal to a broad array of people, not just the design elite, so Modern Historicism can represent an expression of self, old money, culture, taste, wealth, and family heritage. It may offer context or a sense of place or signal function and/or monumentality. The past also can be thematic, as at the Disney theme parks, or a branding or marketing tool, as in a Las Vegas hotel. Sometimes period architecture or interiors indicate a rejection or reaction to modern or they may simply be anti-modern. Past styles have an inherent complexity and richness because of their adaptability, which is derived from a multiplicity of elements, details, patterns, colors, and objects.

Architects, decorators, and designers employ many different approaches to use Modern Historical design in architecture and interiors. They may focus on a particular style or aspect of the past, especially as individual styles come in or out of favor. Other methods, which are selective and fluid, may include replicating the past accurately or loosely; using the past as inspiration for new designs; suggesting or alluding to the past; reinventing the past; or creatively adapting vernacular, historical, or classical principles, elements, and/or attributes. Some designers have a more academic attitude to the past. They study its principles and character so as to design in the manner of the past but not necessarily to revive or re-create it. No matter which approach is taken, the result grows out of the designer's creativity, the knowledge and attitudes of the designer and/or client toward the past, and the needs of the project. The result often is intrinsically modern, and it usually is evident that this is a building or interior of its time.

Historic Preservation: Saving the Past

Historic Preservation strives to conserve or retain historic sites, structures, and objects. In doing so it may use one of several methods, such as adaptive use, preservation, rehabilitation, restoration, and reconstruction as the latter four are defined in 1976 and later by the Secretary of the Interior and the National Park Service in the United States. The choice for an approach depends upon many factors, including the historical significance of the structure, its physical condition, budget, available documentation, proposed use, and code requirements.

■ *Preservation*. Preservation, the least invasive or destructive treatment, maintains and sustains the form, details, and materials of a site, building, interior, or object (Fig. 55-19). The process requires repairs instead of rebuilding or replacing and tries to retain the building or interior as it has evolved. Some changes are permitted to update systems and bring structures up to current building codes when required. Adding or rebuilding details can be acceptable.

▲ 55-1. Governor's Palace, 1705–1749, rebuilt in the 1930s; Williamsburg, Virginia. Reconstruction.

■ *Rehabilitation*. Rehabilitation makes a building and/or its interiors usable in a contemporary context (Fig. 55-5). To this end, the treatment repairs and replaces with greater latitude than preservation but tries to retain as many of the significant or defining historic features as possible, such as the façade, the floor plan, a staircase, finishes, or decorative details. More repairs and alterations are permitted to help make the structure meet building codes, update systems, or become more energy efficient or accessible, but the essential character of the building and its interiors is maintained. Details may be added where there is evidence of their original appearance.

■ *Restoration*. Restoration takes a building, interior, site, or object to a significant time in its history by relying on physical and documentary evidence (Fig. 55-14). The result presents a truer period character than the previous approaches do. Accomplishing this may mean removing all parts that do not belong to the chosen time, so restoration can be the most destructive of these approaches. The term *restoration* is most often used when referring to work on historic buildings or interiors, but in reality only parts of most buildings or interiors usually are restored, while other parts are rehabilitated. True restorations generally take place only in house museums, which are taken back, more or less entirely, to particular and significant time periods. Abundant physical and archival documentation is critical to this process. Details may be rebuilt or added where there is evidence.

■ *Reconstruction*. This treatment accurately re-creates a lost building, interior, or site based upon physical and archival evidence, as in the Capitol Building and Governor's Palace in Colonial Williamsburg, Virginia (Fig. 55-1). Missing parts may be reconstructed if there is evidence. This approach is rare and applies specifically to structures, buildings, and interiors instead of details.

■ *Adaptive Use*. Adaptive use, which the Secretary of the Interior's standards do not cover, is the reuse of a building or site that differs from its original purpose, giving the building a new function (Fig. 55-15). Historic forms, details, and materials should be retained when possible, but this is not always the case. Façadism is a particularly destructive variation in which only the façade is retained while the rest of the building is substantially altered or destroyed. Although most architects and designers try to preserve or rehabilitate façades, they frequently alter or even destroy the original interiors to suit the building's function.

These treatments are most easily applied to buildings but also are appropriate and should be used for interiors. In all types of projects, whether exterior or interior or both, the approaches are sometimes mixed because different parts may be preserved, rehabilitated, or restored. For example, a building may be treated as a rehabilitation, but some parts, such as architectural details of the façade or interior, may be preserved or restored. Adaptive use may restore the exterior to a particular period but completely reshape the interiors of a building. Preservation, restoration, rehabilitation, and reconstruction demand meticulous research and analysis of the architecture, its interiors, people who lived or worked there, and the surroundings. Physical and documentary evidence is needed for all-important historical accuracy. Where historical accuracy is not a goal, other approaches, like adaptive use, may be more appropriate.

CHARACTERISTICS AND MOTIFS

Modern Historicism adapts the elements and attributes of many past styles to contemporary buildings, interiors, and/or furniture. They usually reflect attributes, forms, elements, and/or motifs of the particular style or styles so that their specific characteristics vary. However, some general characteristics may be discerned. Expressions change or exploit one or more aspects, such as scale or color, of the original; use them in a new or different way; or combine details from other styles or periods (Fig. 55-12, 55-23, 55-26, 55-27). Simplification and abstraction are the most common changes. The end product may closely approximate the original or bear a range of resemblances to the historic original. For example, buildings and interiors may maintain the form and proportions of a past example but often reduce or eliminate the ornament (Fig. 55-8, 55-20). A Louis XV chair may be wider or taller than the original, or a floral motif on a piece of 18th-century porcelain may be used as a textile pattern. Past styles sometimes define previously unknown types of buildings, rooms, and furniture, such as skyscrapers, bathrooms, or television cabinets (Fig. 55-28). They also may reflect previous associations and uses, such as Gothic Revival for ecclesiastical buildings or ancient temple forms for government buildings or banks (Fig. 55-5, 55-8). Some forms, configurations, and treatments become conventions and are widely accepted as historical whether accurate or not.

Historic Preservation design characteristics are a product of the time and style of the structure or building and the approach chosen. Preservation and restorations reflect as accurately as possible the original style of the building and its interiors, whereas rehabilitation and adaptive use may not.

■ *Motifs*. Modern Historicism features period elements, details, and motifs derived from past styles, such as pediments, columns, pointed arches, flowers, ogee arches, pagodas, birds, leaves, medallions, arabesques, and shells (Fig. 55-6, 55-7, 55-9, 55-10, 55-12, 55-13, 55-14, 55-16, 55-17, 55-18, 55-21, 55-22).

ARCHITECTURE

Throughout the 20th century and, to a lesser extent, into the 21st, many public and private buildings still follow past types or styles. Architects often work in historic styles because of client preference and/or symbolic or associative reasons, such as Gothic for churches or Classical Revival for government buildings. Additionally, many early-20th-century architects are Beaux Arts trained, so they have a thorough grounding in the theories and design language of styles of the past. Several developments or styles centering on the past emerge beginning in the 1950s. Most are inspired by or derived from past forms or styles and do not attempt to replicate the past. These movements or stylistic variations include Historic Preservation, Suburban Modern, New Urbanism, New Formalism, Regionalism, and New Classicism. Modern Historicism, in all its various forms, defines numerous building types including banks, hotels, and motels (Fig. 55-5, 55-10), restaurants, commercial buildings, retail and mixed-use establishments (Fig. 55-2, 55-7), government buildings, university buildings, and residences (Fig. 55-4, 55-6,

55-20). Some architects apply classical styles to buildings not usually associated with those styles, such as supermarkets, as a direct juxtaposition of style with function.

■ *Historic Preservation Approach*. Preservation planning identifies significant structures or areas to be preserved, rehabilitated, or restored usually by individuals, developers, or the government (Fig. 55-1, 55-2). Areas with many significant structures may be designated historic districts to protect their character. Within historic districts, only certain changes are permitted. Rehabilitations and adaptive-use projects convert residential, commercial, religious, and institutional structures to the same or new uses for individuals, retail stores, or commercial firms, sometimes with federal and state tax credits. Schools may become low-income apartments or prestigious condominiums. Churches sometimes are turned into residences, or factories into apartments or artists' studios, and urban townhouses are transformed into restaurants or day spas.

■ *New Formalism*. In the late 1950s, some architects decide to take the International Style in another direction by turning to the past for inspiration. The group includes Edward Durrell Stone (Fig. 55-3); Minoru Yamasaki; and, briefly, Philip Johnson. In a style called New Formalism, the group uses past elements and attributes as springboards for its own creativity. The work is eclectic and characterized by forms and details inspired by the past, particularly classicism but occasionally Gothic or Victorian. The formal style only vaguely recalls the past and is expressed in luxurious materials and increased ornament and applied decoration. Grilles or screens are a common feature.

▲ **55-3.** United States Embassy, 1957–1959; New Delhi, India; Edward Durrell Stone. New Formalism.

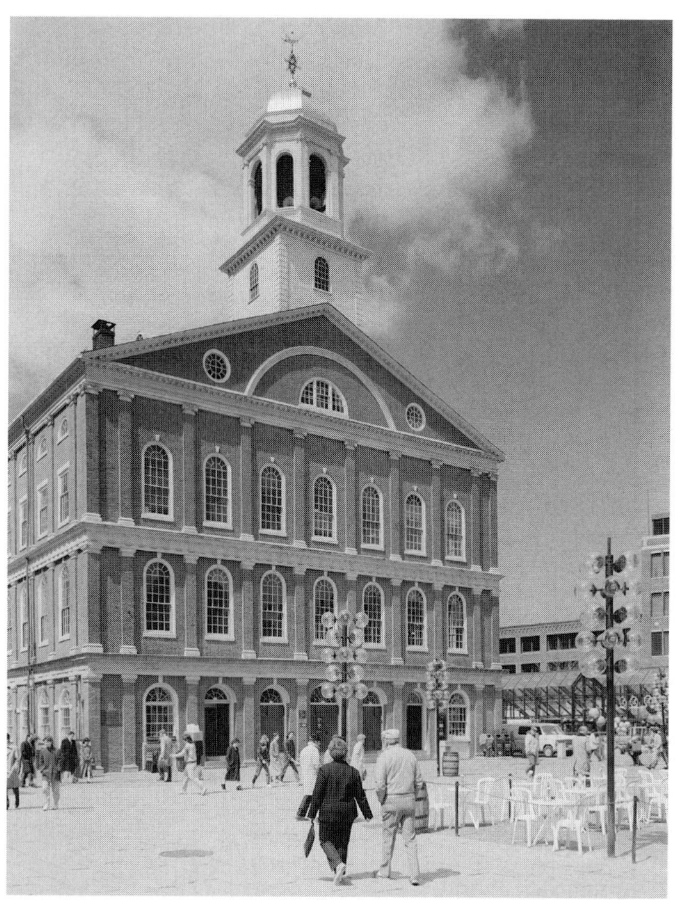

▲ **55-2.** Faneuil Hall Marketplace, 1740–1742, John Smibert; rebuilt after a fire 1761; expanded 1805–1806; Charles Bulfinch; reconstructed 1898–1899; Boston, Massachusetts; 1976, F. A. Stahl & Associates with Benjamin Thompson and Associates; 1992 restored. Restoration and Rehabilitation.

■ *Suburban Modern* (late 1940s–1960s). Following World War II, many countries in Europe and North America experience a housing shortage. Most European countries respond by building government-sponsored public housing. In the United States and Canada (elsewhere later), available land in city centers is limited and expensive, so developers create large suburbs outside many cities. During the 1950s and early 1960s, developers, builders, and some architects construct millions of homes using modern materials and mass-production techniques, such as prefabrication. Tracts, whether small or large, go up quickly and economically. They are filled with houses that are modern and/or derived from period styles or earlier house types. Suburban Modern unites designs that suit popular tastes (often traditional or period style) with rapid construction methods to accomplish the modernist's dream of mass-produced housing for many people. Although not the first such development, Levittown, New York, built by Levitt and Sons in 1949, is one of the best-known of these suburbs. Later subdivisions become more extensive with shopping centers, parks, and community centers, and many have curving streets and cul-de-sacs for variety.

Modern suburban houses usually evolve from past house types and incorporate modern construction techniques; new and modern materials; and contemporary floor plans, kitchens, and baths. American postwar suburban house types include the Ranch, Cape Cod, and split-level (Fig. 55-4). The Ranch house is the most common suburban house after 1945. Assumed to be archetypal of the ranch house of the Old West, these house types first appear in the early 20th century as custom, architect-designed houses sometimes in large subdivisions. The postwar Ranch, also called a rambler, is more compact than its predecessor, with one story in an L- or U-shaped configuration with a garage or carport. The Cape Cod, especially popular on the Eastern seaboard, is a rectangular story-and-a-half house type with a gable roof derived from the hall or half house of the 17th century. Developing somewhat later, the

▲ **55-4.** Suburban houses, split-level and McMansion; c. 1950s–2000s; United States. Suburban Modern.

split-level house has a two-story section inserted about midway in a single-story section to make three living levels.

As the 20th century progresses, more styles and regional expressions begin to dominate suburbs, and their character changes in response to the market and other external factors. New styles include English Georgian, French, Tudor, Victorian, and Arts and Crafts. Some subdivisions have small houses occupying less land to cope with rising costs in land, materials, and construction. These include garden homes, zero lot-line dwellings in which the house sits on or very close to one property line, developments for older adults and retirees, condominiums, and townhouses. In contrast, many suburbanites in the late 20th and early 21st centuries want houses larger than ever. They demand many rooms, such as home offices, exercise or media rooms, gourmet kitchens, and master suites with sitting areas and luxurious baths or spas. In the early 21st century, the popular term for these large homes is *McMansion*, which is adapted from the fast-food giant McDonald's (Fig. 55-4). Sometimes these huge dwellings are inserted in old subdivisions, dwarfing nearby houses.

■ *Regionalism*. Inspired by the Historic Preservation Movement and criticisms that the International Style lacks context, connection, and a sense of place, architects and designers begin to consider the surroundings or locales of their work as well as the area's vernacular buildings. The result is Regionalism, which is defined by buildings and interiors that link to place and the character of a region (Fig. 55-5). Designs address local traditions, vernacular forms, and cultural norms related to the form, elements, ornament, and materials. Expressions of past or vernacular character, such as adobe residences in the Southwest, are common. Some closely copy the existing fabric, while other solutions adopt or adapt elements and attributes of nearby historic structures or the site itself. A few are modernist interpretations with key elements or symbols derived from the site or older buildings. These examples may reflect Critical Regionalism, a design method appearing in the early 1980s, which strives to connect with place in a less visual, more universal or modern manner.

New construction or additions acknowledge surroundings, regional context, and existing structure in a variety of ways, including scale, orientation, massing, articulation, individual elements of the existing building, and materials. Architects use many design devices to achieve the effect including horizontal or vertical orientation, form, shape, height, scale, proportion, roofline, distribution of openings, materials, and/or colors. Consequently, compositions vary from close approximations to unusual designs with only subtle hints of the surroundings or region.

▲ **55-5.** Wigwam Motel, Holbrook, Arizona; and Inn of Loretto, Santa Fe, New Mexico; c. 1950s–1990s; United States. Regionalism.

▲ **55-6.** House; 1981–1987; Seaside, Florida; Andres Duany and Elizabeth Plater-Zyberk. New Urbanism.

■ *New Urbanism.* In the 1970s, new types of suburbs and towns appear in response to the critiques of existing ones by sociologists, ecologists, and designers. Their criticisms include monotony in design; a lack of community spirit; isolation, especially for those who cannot or do not drive; high energy and water consumption; and damage to the environment from land use and the chemicals used to maintain lawns. In the 1980s, designers begin to create small towns with place identity, greater density, and an emphasis upon pedestrians instead of automobiles. Town centers are a key element in this development, which is called New Urbanism. It is the brainchild of architects Andres Duany and Elizabeth Plater-Zyberk (DPZ). One of the first examples is Seaside, Florida, (Fig. 55-10) where DPZ creates both urban codes for planning and building codes derived from traditional and vernacular styles of the Gulf Coast region. The goal was to create a pedestrian town with a sense of place by using small lots surrounding a town center that has shops and stores. Seaside becomes an important model of New Urbanism.

■ *New Classicism.* In the late 1970s, in reaction to Modernism, some architects deliberately return to classicism. Adherents support their cause by citing the importance of maintaining a connection with the past. Classicism is familiar and appealing to many people, not just the design elite. And they maintain that the order and monumentality of classicism are associated with dignity, stability, and permanence. Although a minority, the group studies design principles and significant examples from ancient Greece, ancient Rome, the Renaissance, Neo-Palladian, English Georgian, and English Regency. Generally, compositions, which sometimes reveal an element of nationalism, closely follow the precursors or have some direct quotes from historic monu-

DESIGN SPOTLIGHT

Architecture: Situated on a wide grassy area facing the Thames River, the Richmond Riverside complex houses shops, offices, restaurants, apartments, and gardens. The sloping site and scale of the surroundings dictate several buildings instead of one large structure. Designed by New Classical architect Quinlan Terry, the complex retains two earlier buildings with new façades while adding new ones. Terry uses forms and details from 18th-century English architecture such as red and yellow brick, slate roofs, and sash and casement windows. He takes various details from past classical architects such as Andrea Palladio, Nicholas Hawksmoor, and William Chambers. The complex fits well into its surroundings, appearing as if it has been there for centuries. Proving popular and commercially viable, Richmond Riverside has become an icon of traditional urban design.

▲ **55-7.** Richmond Riverside, 1984–1989; London, England; Quinlan Terry. New Classicism.

ments. Work is often inserted into similarly styled historical sites and areas. Important theorists and practitioners include Demetri Porphyrios, Quinlan Terry, Allan Greenburg, Robert A. M. Stern, and Ricardo Bofill (Fig. 55-7, 55-8).

■ *Themed Environments*. In the tradition of 19th century practice of ascribing particular associations and uses to past architecture, some contemporary buildings and environments, such as theme parks (Fig. 55-9), hotels (Fig. 55-10), restaurants, or retail stores, use the past for thematic branding, or marketing concepts. Often these enviornments give the impression that the users have traveled back in time to a real or imaginary place and/or period. Besides creating a unique and memorable identity, the goal of the design is to give users an emotional experience that usually is enhanced by the integration of site, physical surroundings, food, drink, and activities.

▲ **55-8.** *Teatro Nacionale de Cataluña*, 1997; Barcelona, Spain; Ricardo Bofill. New Classicism.

Public and Private Buildings

■ *Site Orientation*. No particular orientation is associated with Modern Historicism. Preservation practice usually seeks to maintain the integrity of the site and location. Classically styled public buildings usually have prominent entries on axis with the building to create a processional path. Lawns for suburban houses range from expansive to minimal. The broad side of the house usually faces the street for convenient access to the garage or carport. To the rear may be a deck, patio, or courtyard for casual outdoor living. In New Urban developments, houses, townhouses, and condominiums line streets with wide sidewalks and garages as part of the structure or at the rear, sometimes in the alleys. There is usually a town center with shops and restaurants within walking distance for most residents. Sometimes people live in apartments or condominiums above the shops.

■ *Floor Plans*. Plans develop from building function, client preference, and modern needs and requirements. Some plans are based on earlier building types, including vernacular ones. Urban structures often blend older floor plan features, such as symmetry, with modern planning concepts to address codes, functions, circulation, identity, character, and context. Often, areas such as entries, halls, and public spaces are larger than in the prototypes. Most preservation practices require retaining defining features of floor plans.

Suburban house plans support informal lifestyles. They are rectangular, L-, or U-shaped with separate public and private areas. Regarded as quiet living areas, the formal living and dining rooms usually are at the front of the house, and the kitchen is next to the dining room. Kitchens usually open to a family room, considered a noisy living area, which has access to the outside patio or courtyard.

■ *Materials*. Modern Historical buildings often use common materials of the past, such as wood, brick, marble, or stone (Fig. 55-7, 55-10). Alternatives include concrete blocks that may be covered with stucco and scored to resemble stone (Fig. 55-1, 55-3, 55-6, 55-8). Suburban houses display a variety of materials, which are often mixed and may reflect a regional character. Materials include brick; wooden, vinyl, or aluminum horizontal or vertical siding; stone; stucco; and shingles (Fig. 55-4, 55-6). In the second half of the 20th century, paint companies offer collections of historic colors, such as Williamsburg by Martin Senour and Pratt and Lambert and the Preservation Palette by Sherwin Williams.

■ *Façades*. Classical elements, such as rustication, columns, and pediments, identify many public and affluent private examples of Modern Historicism, but these details may be greatly simplified, abstracted, or merely suggested through form (Fig. 55-3, 55-5, 55-7,

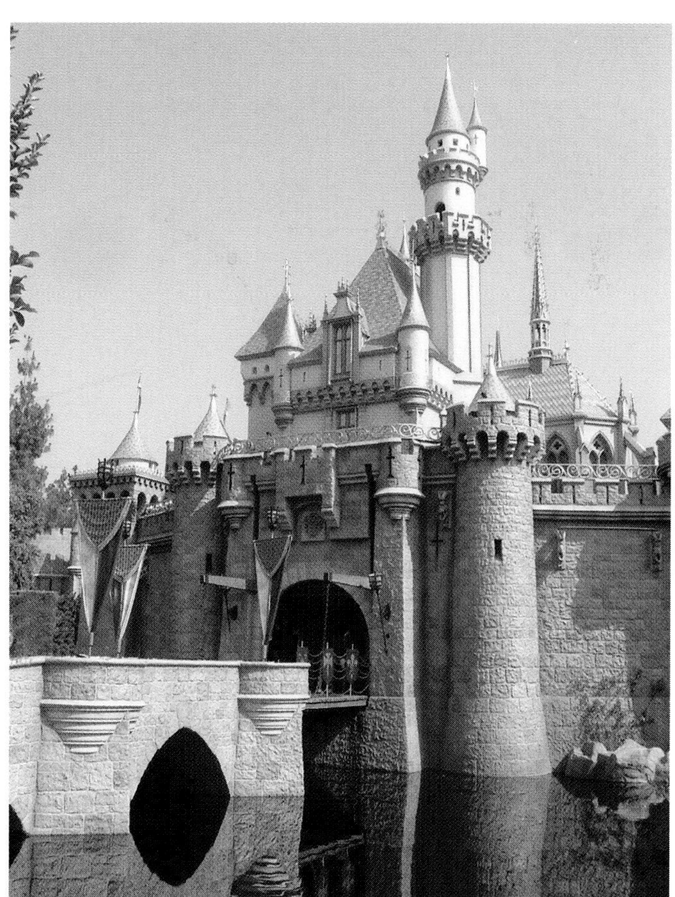

▲ **55-9.** Sleeping Beauty Castle, 1955; Disneyland, Anaheim, California; Walt Disney Imagineering Division. Modern Historicism.

55-8, 55-9, 55-10). Designs may have classical proportions or attributes, such as symmetry. Those following other styles, such as medieval, may feature many of their stylistic forms, attributes, and details. For example, Tudor-style houses are often asymmetrical with an emphasis upon height. Half-timbering and/or a tall gable or gables often dominate the façade.

Façades of ranch style Suburban Modern houses are usually long, low, and horizontal. Others, such as split-levels, are narrower and more vertical (Fig. 55-4). All types may be symmetrical or asymmetrical with a covered full- or partial-width porch. Elements and decoration identify individual styles, when present, and provide variety, but simplicity overrides ornament. Materials may be mixed. Garages or carports sometimes dominate façades.

■ *Windows*. Windows usually are large and rectangular (Fig. 55-1, 55-2, 55-3, 55-4, 55-5, 55-6, 55-7, 55-8, 55-9, 55-10). Most are double hung and subdivided by panes as in their prototypes. Sur-

DESIGN SPOTLIGHT

Architecture and Interior: As a modern, theatrical interpretation of older well-known buildings in Venice, the Venetian Hotel shows one aspect of contemporary popular culture in the United States. Envisioned as a destination playground within a sprawling desert landscape, it offers a fantasy or theme-park-like character, charm, and extreme comfort to pleasure-seeking travelers. The hotel's façade re-creates some of the most famous buildings of Venice, Italy, including the Ducal Palace with its Gothic arches and motifs. The Palace and the Bridge of Sighs surround a Venetian-style canal, complete with gondoliers and other well-known symbols and emblems of the city. Both the elegantly designed exterior and interiors feature marble and painted decoration commonly seen in Venetian buildings. The great hall, by Trisha Wilson and Associates, recalls the *sala* or grand reception room of Italian palaces but on a far more monumental scale. Corinthian columns line the long, narrow space, and the barrel vaulted ceiling features elaborate paintings.

▲ **55-10.** Venetian Hotel and Great Hall, c. 1990s; Las Vegas, Nevada; Veldon Simpson and Marnell Corrao Associates and interiors by Trisha Wilson, Wilson Associates, Texas. Modern Historicism.

rounds are in the building's style. Sizes of windows may become smaller as they ascend the building. Picture windows are a defining feature of most postwar houses, although some have few windows or doors on the front. Also used are awning, jalousie, horizontal sliding or ribbon windows, and bow and bay windows, often with shutters.

■ *Doors*. On all styles or manifestations, main entries may be centered or to one side, and they are often recessed or under a colonnade or porch (Fig. 55-1, 55-3, 55-4, 55-6, 55-8). Most public buildings have prominent entries, often under a portico or pediment. Entry doors, in both public and private buildings, are usually wood panels, sometimes with rectangular or oval glass that may be beveled or stained. Sliding glass or French doors access outdoor living areas.

■ *Roofs*. Roofs include flat (usually with a balustrade), hipped, or gabled (Fig. 55-1, 55-2, 55-3, 55-5, 55-7, 55-8). Significant buildings may have domes or towers. For houses, low-pitched hipped, gabled, side gabled, and cross gabled are common roof types (Fig. 55-4, 55-6). Some homes have shed or flat roofs.

▲ **55-11.** Sales areas, Bonwit Teller Department Stores, 1949–1951; Chicago, Illinois; William Pahlmann. Modern Historicism.

INTERIORS

Public and private interiors express Modern Historicism in various ways. They may closely resemble the past, as in buildings by New Classical architects; be composed of antiques and historic elements, as in period decoration; or have a period/traditional appearance or transitional look. As a result, Modern Historical interiors exhibit great variety in treatments and furnishings depending upon the previously mentioned factors as well as the designer's creativity or understanding of the past. No matter what the design intention, the majority are eclectic, often combining antique and contemporary architectural details, paneling, wallpapers, tapestries, furniture, and artwork. Designers, decorators, and homeowners may mix styles and/or use unexpected elements, patterns, colors, and finishes to create a distinctive and personal look.

Modern Historical interiors are more common in period or period-style buildings, such as residences (Fig. 55-17, 55-18), government buildings, offices, hotels (Fig. 55-10), clubs, banks, restaurants, and institutional buildings such as universities. Occasionally, period-style or traditional interiors are in strictly modern buildings (Fig. 55-13). Modern Historical or period-style decoration may define all room types, but most are in residences (Fig. 55-20). Nonresidential interiors in historic or even modern buildings may be Modern Historical depending upon what the client wishes to communicate about the firm or its employees. Hotels, banks, clubs, government reception rooms, attorneys' offices, and assisted living facilities, for example, are frequently designed in a period style to convey prestige, status, longevity, or continuity or to appeal to a particular market segment.

■ *Period-Style Decoration*. Period decoration—decorating a room or rooms in a particular historical period—includes numerous past styles within a modern context of smaller rooms, antique and/or contemporary furnishings, and modern preferences and manners of living. Thus, many expressions result. Favored high styles include French Provincial, French Rococo, French and English Neoclassical, English Georgian, English Regency, French Empire, and Baroque. These styles come in and out of fashion throughout the 20th and 21st centuries. Rococo is highly esteemed in the early 20th century but less so in the early 21st, for example. Interest in the Victorian styles and *Chinoiserie* appears about midcentury. Also fashionable are the English country house look and theatrical, romantic, or fantasy rooms (Fig. 55-10, 55-12, 55-18).

Period-style decoration in the first decades of the 20th century has a somewhat truer period character resulting from carefully planned details, particularly on walls, floors, and ceilings. The French styles dominate. During the 1930s, Art Deco and Art Moderne help foster a trend toward modernization within period decorating, such as the all-white rooms of Syrie Maugham. Spaces become even more eclectic, frequently mixing antiques with contemporary pieces and adopting colors atypical of the past. The French styles remain popular along with English 18th-century styles.

Some decorators and designers, including William Pahlmann (Fig. 55-11), T. H. Robsjohn-Gibbings, and Edward Wormley, actively strive to create an even more modern interpretation of historicism. They create so-called transitional rooms that have a refined simplicity in keeping with Modernism and a mixture of modern and past or traditional treatments and furniture. Transitional rooms and furniture are neither completely modern nor exact representations of a particular period.

Even greater simplification occurs beginning after World War II and continuing through the rest of the 20th century (Fig. 55-16). Interiors have fewer architectural details, less pattern, and little ornament. Individualism, accomplished with even more eclecticism, and informality define the look, especially in suburban houses. English and American 18th-century, English Country, Arts and Crafts, and Victorian styles surpass French in popularity. Some homeowners and others strive to create period-appropriate settings for their collections of antique furniture or decorative arts. Magazines with glossy and colorful photos, such as *House Beautiful* and *Architectural Digest,* popularize prevailing fashions.

Decorating in styles of the past continues throughout the late 20th and into the 21st century as architects, interior designers, decorators, and homeowners create modern expressions of period rooms, based on budget, preferences or personalities, and the needs of modern lifestyles. They are aided by manufacturers who produce reproductions, adaptations, and modern interpretations of period paints, wallpapers, area rugs, furniture, lighting, and decorative arts. Sometimes designers also create contemporary interpretations within older interiors by renovating the interiors and redecorating the spaces to contrast with the past by using very contemporary floor plans, furnishings, color, and lighting.

Period-style decoration characterizes the work of the early interior decorators whose backgrounds or preparation focuses on historic architecture, antiques, and period styles, mostly European (Fig. 55-12, 55-17, 55-18). They often make buying trips to Europe and import or design entire rooms or paneling and details for their wealthy clients. Some strive for innovation and unusual color schemes to distinguish their work while retaining or reflecting a period character. Others, such as Dorothy Draper and Billy Baldwin, develop a trademark style characterized by signature details. During the post–World War II period, as decorators transform into interior designers, they leave behind their emphasis upon period styles especially when they focus on nonresidential spaces. But some interior designers do not abandon Modern Historical design altogether because they continue to create period-style rooms in a variety of public and private buildings for a diversity of clients (Fig. 55-16).

■ *Historic Preservation and Interiors.* Within the Historic Preservation Movement, interiors, entirely or in part, are preserved, restored, reconstructed, or rehabilitated, the latter being the most common treatment (Fig. 55-12, 55-19). In the United States, interiors are less often preserved or restored than are exteriors because they have fewer protections against demolition or alteration than in other countries, such as the United Kingdom. Additionally, rooms are more likely to be redecorated, refurbished, or renovated in response to events or as fashions, styles, budgets, and modern requirements change (Fig. 55-14). Often, there is far less documentation of interiors, whether physical, archival, or visual.

▲ **55-12.** Metropolitan Museum of Art Restaurant (dubbed The Dorotheum), 1954; New York City, New York; Dorothy Draper. Modern Historicism.

Usually only parts of interiors, such as architectural features and details, are restored. Historically accurate finishes may be applied to them to maintain defining historic features and support the ambiance of the period. Restorations, in contrast, attempt to create a moment in the past as well as the expression of the tastes and preferences of the previous, usually significant, inhabitants. While based upon evidence, documentation is often lacking for some parts or details. For example, there may be physical evidence that a space once had wall-to-wall carpet, but no documentation of the carpet itself. In this case, the curator or designer relies on reproductions appropriate to the period and makes an educated choice of style, pattern, and color. Adaptively used interiors display a wide range of treatments. Some ignore historic materials, while others celebrate them and make them part of the design concept as in the *Museé d'Orsay* (Fig. 55-15) in Paris, which turns a former train station into an art museum.

■ *Suburban Modern.* When the exterior is traditional or a period style, interiors in Suburban Modern houses may display a period flavor in finishes and furniture, such as Mediterranean or Early American. Period decoration is difficult because of the arrangement of most living areas, and rooms are furnished to suit modern activities and casual lifestyles. And furniture usually is arranged around the television instead of the fireplace or the view. In the late 20th century, new rooms unknown in the past emerge, such as the media room, exercise room, hobby room, and master suite. No matter what the exterior design, kitchens and baths usually are contemporary in design and treatment. By the end of the 20th century, however, traditional or period-style cabinets, fixtures, and appliances are available so that even kitchens and baths can have a period look.

■ *Regionalism.* Like architecture, Regional-style interiors reflect the locale in treatments, finishes, and furnishings to highlight a sense of place or heritage (Fig. 55-16). Expressions may be literally or loosely interpreted. Some interior designers become known for Regionalist designs in residential, commercial, and hospitality interiors, such as Trisha Wilson Associates of Texas and Singapore.

■ *New Classicism.* Interiors of New Classical buildings usually reflect the monumentality and formality of the exteriors because they are architect-designed for unity. Classical proportions, architectural details, motifs, and treatments characterize these spaces.

Public and Private Buildings

■ *Color.* Colors in Modern Historical rooms vary, ranging from those that are bright and highly saturated, such as lemon yellow or Chinese red, to rich or dark blues, greens, or browns, to soft pastels thought typical of the Georgian periods (Fig. 55-13, 55-14, 55-18, 55-21, 55-22). Colors are more often suggestive of period styles than the actual colors of the period, which may be imperfectly understood and identified, particularly during the first half of the 20th century. Woods are painted, usually white or a light color, or stained in rich warm tones. Suburban interiors adopt

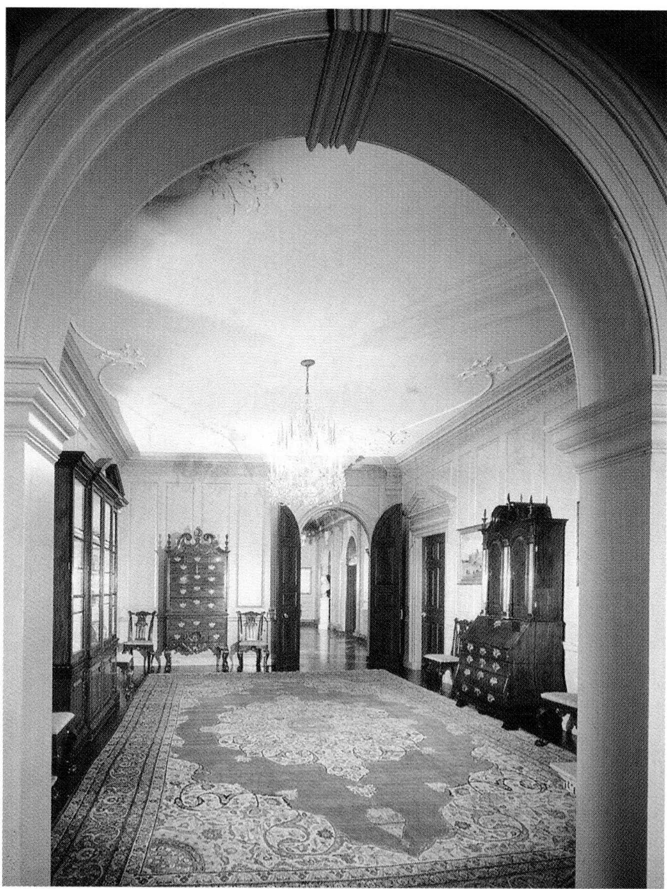

▲ **55-13.** Entrance Hall to the Diplomatic Reception Rooms (before and after images), State Department, 1979–1986; Washington, D.C.; Edward Vason Jones. Modern Historicism. [Courtesy of the Diplomatic Reception Rooms, U.S. Department of State]

DESIGN SPOTLIGHT

Interiors: The original Willard Hotel, built in 1850, was demolished to make way for a new, larger Beaux-Arts structure in 1904. The 1915 lobby is of this early period. After losing business for several years, the hotel closed in 1968. It reopened in 1986 after an extensive restoration and rehabilitation under the direction of the National Park Service. Original blueprints, 1901 photographs by Francis Benjamin Johnston, and paint analysis guided the architects and designer Sarah Tomerlin Lee in accurately re-creating the appearance of original interior spaces. Fragments of damaged moldings were used to replicate the originals, and the chandeliers were recast in Brussels, Belgium. The designers made a few changes, such as using the original yellow marble front desk as the concierge's desk. The old storage cabinet behind it was restored. A large Turkish circular sofa and potted palms dominate the space with its period colors and classical details. In 1999, the firm of Forrest Perkins renovates the guest suites and rooms and other spaces and refurbishes the Ballroom and Willard Rooms.

▲ **55-14.** 1915 lobby and 1986 lobby restoration, Willard Intercontinental Washington Hotel, 1904; Washington, D.C.; 1986 restoration by Henry Janway Hardenbergh, with interiors by Sarah Tomerlin Lee; 1999 renovation and refurbishing of interiors by Forest Perkins. Restoration and Redecoration.

fashionable color schemes dominated by bright and contrasting hues. In the late 20th century, paint companies begin to offer interior paints in historic color collections from museums, restorations, and historic sites, such as the Colors of Historic Charleston and the National Trust Historic Paint Colors by Valspar sold at Lowe's Home Improvement Stores.

■ *Floors*. Floors in homes of the affluent and commercial buildings may be wood parquet, stone, terrazzo, ceramic tiles, brick, marble, or carpet (Fig. 55-10, 55-12, 55-13, 55-14, 55-15, 55-16, 55-17, 55-18, 55-20). Suburban homes incorporate a variety of flooring materials, including wood, terrazzo, ceramic tile, linoleum, vinyl, and carpet. Different materials visually separate different areas in open plans. Area rugs, which define furniture groupings, include Orientals, needlepoint, Aubussons, Savonneries, and contemporary machine-made rugs in traditional or past patterns. Bedrooms are usually carpeted.

Manufacturers offer reproductions of 18th- and 19th-century wall-to-wall carpets and area rugs for restorations and period-style rooms. Some are woven in the narrower widths of earlier carpets. Reproductions of area rugs are sometimes machine-made instead of hand-knotted.

■ *Walls*. Wall treatments may include period treatments (Fig. 55-19), closely copy them, reflect a period flavor, or become simple backgrounds that support the furniture and accessories of the space (Fig. 55-10, 55-12, 55-13, 55-14, 55-15, 55-16, 55-17, 55-18, 55-20). Many types of wall treatments characterize Modern Historical rooms in commercial buildings and homes of the wealthy. Public and important rooms often have paneling or architectural details such as columns or moldings. Paneling and details often are simpler than the prototypes were. When present, cornices, chair rails, and baseboards are stained or painted to match or contrast with wall colors. Paneling may be painted, pickled, or stained. Sometimes moldings simulate paneling. Rooms in affluent homes sometimes have antique paneling imported from Europe. Built-in bookcases and cabinets with a period look are in such spaces as private executive offices and libraries or media rooms in residences.

Most walls are painted, often with shiny finishes, especially when forming a background for artwork. Alternatives are painted decorations, murals, or *faux* finishes such as marbling. Reproductions or adaptations of earlier wallpapers frequently cover walls, especially in dining rooms and bedrooms. Reproduction wallpapers (Fig. 55-21) are usually machine printed, but a few very expensive ones are block printed by hand as in the early 19th century. Reproductions also come in colorways other than those of the original paper. Less common treatments include ceramic tiles, especially in Renaissance or Spanish rooms; tapestries; and stuccowork based upon traditional forms and designs.

In suburban houses, walls may be painted or natural brick, stone, wood panels or planks, plywood veneer, or they may be covered with paint or plastic laminate. Wallpapers with abstract, linear, stylized, and naturalistic patterns also are common. Sometimes contrasting wallpapers are combined within or among rooms to vary the amount and sizes of patterns. By the late 20th century, suburbanites more often use reproductions and adaptations of wallpapers and other wall treatments because they are more readily available and affordable.

▲ **55-15.** Interior, *Musée d'Orsay*, 1980–1987; Paris, France; interiors by Gae Aulenti. Rehabilitation and Adaptive Use.

■ *Windows*. In Modern Historical high-style rooms in public and private buildings, windows often have elaborate moldings surrounding them, whereas other windows have simple surrounds, if any. Window treatments in these rooms sometimes are opulent with a cornice or valance in complicated patterns, under-curtains, and glass curtains, all with rich trims (Fig. 55-18). However, the most common treatments are floor- and sill-length plain panels that are either pleated or hung from rings. Sill-length pleated curtains or café curtains cover kitchen and bedroom windows in many suburban homes. Traditional houses often have Priscilla curtains, ruffled, crossed, and gathered panels of lightweight fabric. Curtains may be of plain fabrics or sheers in white or natural colors, damasks, brocades, silks, or patterned fabrics. Fabrics are reproductions, adaptations, or contemporary designs. Other window treatments include Venetian blinds, shades, interior shutters, and vertical blinds, which are new in the mid-20th century. Windows in restorations may have no window treatments to replicate earlier periods or have curtains copied from period sources. Occasionally, owners of historic houses re-create period window treatments.

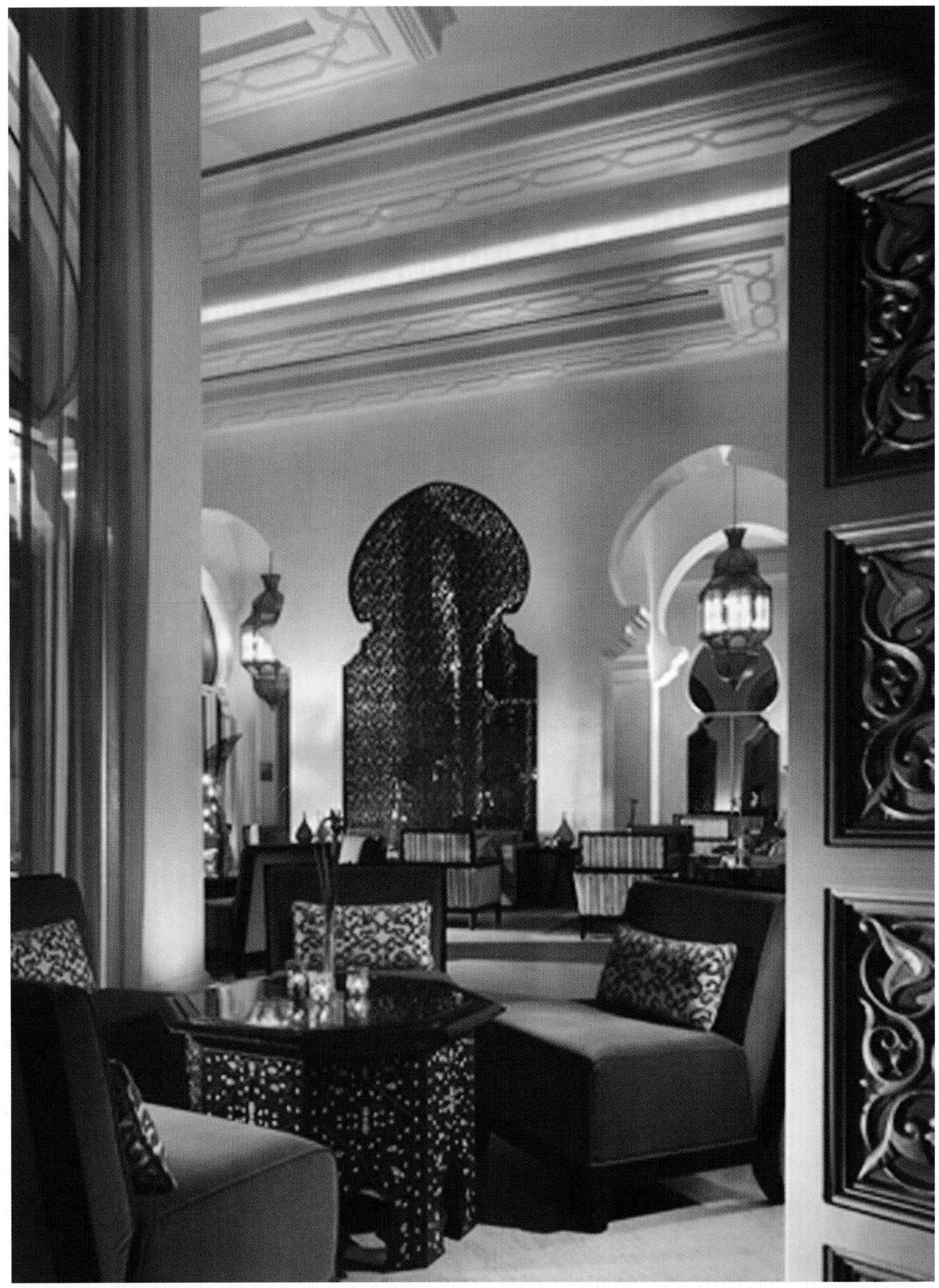

▲ **55-16.** Lobby, Park Hyatt Hotel, 2004–2005; Dubai, United Arab Emirates; Wilson Associates, Singapore and Texas. Regionalism.

▲ **55-17.** Dining room, Mrs. Hugh Mercer Walker residence, 1930s; New York City, New York; Ruby Ross Wood. Period Decoration.

■ *Doors*. Doorways in high-style rooms may have elaborate moldings around the opening, but most are flat, narrow, and simple. Doors are plain or paneled and may be painted or stained. A few high-style rooms have *portières* at their doorways.

■ *Ceilings*. Most ceilings in public and private buildings are plain and flat, and painted white or a light neutral color (Fig. 55-11, 55-17, 55-18, 55-20). Ceilings in important spaces in wealthy homes and public buildings may have coffers, compartments, beams, or painted or stucco decorations (Fig. 55-10, 55-13, 55-14). Some living areas or family rooms in suburban homes have ceilings that are painted, have stained wood boards, or are flat or sloped with or without wooden beams that are left natural wood or painted. A few have skylights.

▲ **55-18.** Nancy Lancaster's Yellow Room, Avery Row, 1960; London, England; John Fowler. Period Decoration.

▲ **55-19.** Stair Hall, Drayton Hall, 1738–1742; Charleston, South Carolina; 1974; a National Trust for Historic Preservation property. Preservation.

▲ **55-20.** Entrance hall, residence, c. 1990s; Santa Barbara, California; John Saladino. Modern Historicism.

■ *Textiles*. Textiles may be plain weaves or traditional weaves, such as damasks or brocades, or have traditional patterns such as stripes and florals. Common fibers include silk, cotton, linen, wool, and synthetics. Patterns, usually in fashionable colors, may be abstract, organic, or naturalistic designs of geometric shapes, figures, animals, foliage, and flowers. Throughout the 20th and 21st centuries, textile companies, such as Scalamandré and Schumacher, offer reproductions and adaptations of fabrics from many periods (Fig. 55-22).

■ *Lighting*. Light fixtures in Modern Historical rooms include chandeliers, wall sconces, and table lamps, which may be copied or adapted from antiques; antiques that are wired for electricity; or modern designs of period styles (Fig. 55-10, 55-11, 55-13, 55-14, 55-16, 55-17, 55-20, 55-23). Because modern lighting requirements are very different from those of the past, new types of lighting, controls, and fixtures, such as fluorescent, dimmers, and recessed or hidden light sources, are integrated into Modern Historical rooms. Table and floor lamps come in many different materials, colors, shapes, and sizes to suit any interior, whether closely or loosely based on the past. Historic buildings, such as house museums, and some owners of historic houses strive to maintain a period look in lighting to preserve antiques and textiles while facilitating activities. In the late 20th century, historic sites begin using lower levels of artificial lighting to more closely simulate original conditions. They also install photo sensors to turn off lights in unoccupied rooms. In some, interpreters can use remote controls to adjust light levels for visitors.

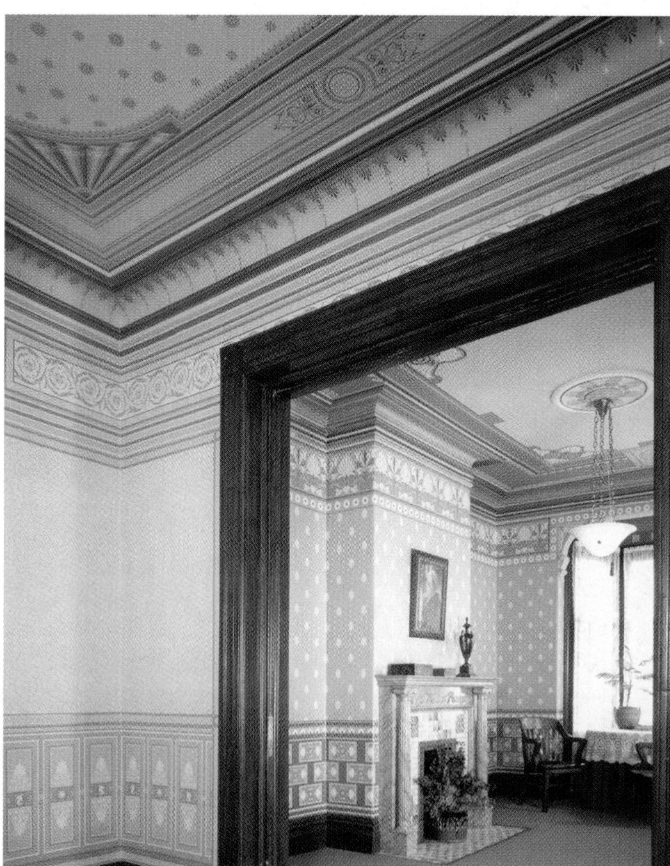

▲ **55-21.** Wallpaper: Victorian influence, c. 1990s–2000s; manufactured by Bradbury and Bradbury. Reproduction.

▲ **55-22.** Textiles: *Toile de Jouy—Panurge Dan l'Ile des Lanternes;* floral—Readbourne Bouquet; and floral—Meissen; c. 1970s–2000s; manufactured by Scalamandré. Modern Historicism and Reproductions.

▲ **55-23.** Lighting: Wall bracket and table lamp, c. 1940s–2000; United States; table lamp by Kartell. Modern Historicism.

FURNISHINGS AND DECORATIVE ARTS

Furniture in Modern Historical rooms in public and private buildings may be antiques or period styles of modern manufacture arranged for modern use. In contrast, period rooms in museums strive to replicate as accurately as possible historic furnishings and arrangements. A piece of furniture may be a loose interpretation, adaptation, reproduction, or invention of a new period style, such as Italian Provincial. Transitional and eclectic spaces may have only contemporary-style furniture or mix contemporary with antiques or period-style furniture. Some designers, decorators, and architects, such as Dorothy Draper, William Pahlmann, Trisha Wilson, and Barbara Barry, design custom furniture for their projects or individual pieces and/or complete lines, sometimes in a period flavor, for manufacturers (Fig. 55-11, 55-12, 55-16, 55-20, 55-24, 55-26).

■ *Period Styles*. Common period furniture styles include the French styles such as Rococo, Neoclassical, Empire, and French Provincial; English Georgian styles such as Chippendale, Sheraton, and English Regency; American Colonial, Federal, and Empire; and Victorian Rococo Revival, as well as invented expressions such as Mediterranean and Early American. Period styles define all types of furniture, even pieces unknown in the precursor period, such as computer desks, file cabinets, and television cabinets (Fig. 55-28).

■ *Reproductions*. *Reproduction*, a term that was imprecisely defined in the first half of the 20th century, now refers to furniture, textiles, finishes, and decorative arts that copy a historical object or document as exactly as possible in scale, form, and details using modern production methods (Fig. 55-21, 55-22, 55-25). For example, a chair may accurately copy a handmade antique but be at least partially machine-made. And original hand-blocked textiles and wallpapers usually are screen printed today.

▲ **55-24.** *Tête-à-tête*, c. 1950s–1960s; United States; Edward Wormley, manufactured by Dunbar. Modern Historicism.

▲ **55-25.** Regency arm chair, c. 1810, England; The Stately Homes Collection, c. 1981; United States; Baker Furniture. Reproduction.

■ *Furniture Manufacturers*. During the mid-20th century, American museums, such as Winterthur in Delaware and Colonial Williamsburg in Virginia, and preservation organizations, such as the Historic Charleston Foundation, license manufacturers such as Kindel, Stickley, and Baker, respectively, to produce adaptations and reproductions of furniture from their collections (Fig. 55-25). Numerous companies produce adaptations, and some take great liberties with period designs or invent new period styles such as Mediterranean, which is vaguely Spanish in dark wood with carving and/or wrought iron.

■ *Contemporary Period Interpretations*. In the late 20th century, various artists and designers mix contemporary and period influences in furnishings to create new interpretations of Modern Historicism, which are distinctly different and reflect new design ideas (Fig. 55-27). An example is "furniture as art," which often includes unusual pieces made for personal expression, exhibition, or display design. These pieces, which may deemphasize functional requirements, have many artistic variations, such as furniture accented with elaborate painted decoration or unique, creative period furniture forms. Some are whimsical and primarily created for artistic enjoyment. In contrast, architects and interior designers usually follow a more practical approach because they

DESIGN SPOTLIGHT

Furniture: Barbara Barry's Oval X-back chair is based on an 18th-century chair type of the Neoclassical period in France or Late Georgian in England. The silhouette, oval back, legs, and arms follow the lines of the original but are greatly simplified to create a contemporary look. The designer's signature X shape inside the oval wooden back frame adds an interesting detail. Barry adapts the scale and eliminates the ornament of the originals to better suit modern tastes and a greater variety of interiors.

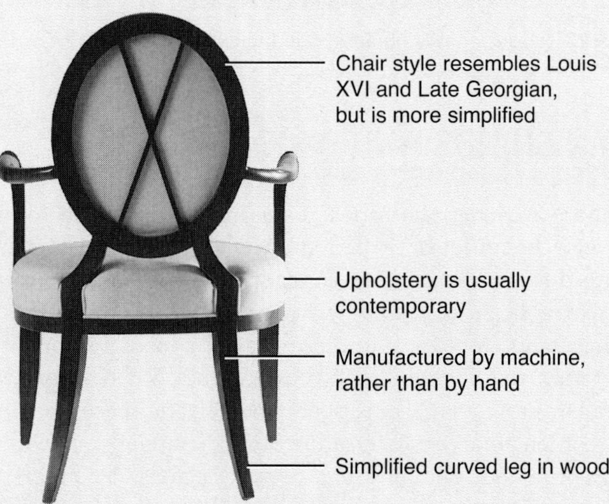

▲ **55-26.** Oval X-back Chair, The Barbara Barry Collection; c. 1980s; United States; Baker Furniture. Modern Historicism.

▲ **55-27.** Table, Wynn Hotel, Las Vegas, c. 2000s; United States. Modern Historicism.

▲ **55-28.** Entertainment unit, late 20th century; The Mission Collection; c. 2000s; L. & J. G. Stickley Furniture. Modern Historicism.

are designing for manufacturers or specific interiors with specific purposes, such as a hotel or retail space, or to create a particular character, themed environment, or regional look. As a result, their creations have abstracted period shapes and forms mixed with contemporary color and/or materials defined by explicit functional requirements.

■ *Materials*. Modern Historical furniture usually is of wood, such as cherry, walnut, maple, or pine, that may be stained, painted, or lacquered. High-style furniture may have veneer patterns, inlay, or marquetry decoration. In less expensive pieces, details and parts may be of plastic finished to resemble wood. A few entire pieces, such as beds, or parts of pieces, such as table bases or legs, are of metal. Decorators and homeowners sometimes strip the finishes of antique furniture to pickle or repaint it; remove, add, or combine portions; or otherwise change the appearance.

■ *Decorative Arts*. Modern Historical interiors may have numerous decorative period accessories including paintings and prints, clocks, screens, mirrors, wall shelves and brackets, ceramics, glass, and metalware (Fig. 55-11, 55-13, 55-14, 55-17, 55-18, 55-20). Accessories may be antiques, reproductions, or modern pieces in traditional or modern styles. Plants and flowers are an integral part of many rooms. Decorators, designers, and homeowners use accessories to support the room's concept; make a statement about the clients, owners, or themselves; or personalize a space.

P. EXPERIMENTATION

Soon after the mid-20th century, architects and designers begin to question and critique the Modern Movement as defined by the International Style. The masters of Modern, such as Mies van der Rohe, are gone, and this new generation of designers does not regard maintaining the Modern Movement's design goals and language as defined and practiced by the masters as important as it once was. Additionally, new technologies, consumerism, and a global community demand new and different approaches to design and even a new design language to express changing contemporary times.

One result of this critique is a plurality of design methods. No longer is there a single design vision, although the notion of modern as forward thinking and promising a new and bright future remains. How to achieve a modern design language and form that expresses its time is open to question, experimentation, and debate. Architects and designers have a greater freedom in how they choose to express their times. No longer is one form of modern preeminent. Some even work outside of modern.

Within the context of a global community united and driven by new technology, architecture, interior design, and furniture design become even more market driven. Niche markets, image, and branding are important concepts that designers cannot ignore. Previously, the Modern Movement had not addressed consumerism, but in the 1980s, many designers begin to create a variety of mass-produced objects. This creates the notion of the designer as celebrity. Architects, interior designers, and others produce various products such as furniture, decorative arts, sheets, towels, carpets, and rugs. Consequently, their names, ideas, and concepts become marketable and recognizable. Previously, architects' and designers' ideas were often ahead of technology, but with new materials, structural techniques, environmental controls, and design tools, they now create what their imaginations can identify. Also driving design are important matters, such as increased regulation, building codes, research and development, and environmental concerns, that give impetus to and provide new ways of doing things.

Late Modern, from the mid-1960s to the 2000s, maintains many of the design goals and language of the International Style but expands and/or exaggerates them to express the complexity and rapidly changing nature of the times. Within Late Modern are several design approaches or appearances. Beginning in the 1970s, High Tech buildings, interiors, and furniture embrace and celebrate technology with complexity and industrial materials and finishes. Pop Modern of the 1960s pursues consumerism and the youth market, especially in interiors and furniture, often in brightly colored plastic. In contrast is Minimalism, which rejects the acquisitive side of consumerism. Architecture, interiors, and furniture are plain and simple with pure forms, few details, and little color, but often with rich textural contrasts.

Beginning in the late 1970s, Post-Modern architects and designers address the lack of context and communication of the International Style through plurality, which may include historicism, complexity, wit, whimsy, and classicism. Designs attempt to connect with and speak to the common person as well as the design elite. Many Post-Modern designers create mass-produced objects as part of that effort. Contemporary with Post-Modern is Memphis, an Italian avant-garde style in interiors and furniture. Memphis confronts traditional notions of design with odd shapes and forms, high-style and common materials, and strong colors and patterns.

Environmental Modern comes from the larger movement that strives to maintain the earth and its resources. Beginning in the late 1970s, architecture, interiors, and furniture respond to the environment with an evolving design process that includes energy conservation, waste management and recycling, land use, climate controls, and wise stewardship of resources. Also called green design or sustainable design, expressions may show little evidence of these concepts or may show a strong contextual relationship to site and location.

In the 1980s, Neo-Modern architects and designers create innovative, unique, and individual buildings, interiors, and furniture that would not be possible without the new technology. Designs, which greatly challenge previous ideas of Modernism, are complex with expressive form, curves and oblique angles, and unusual juxtapositions. This group of designers often disregards context and communication except within their own circle.

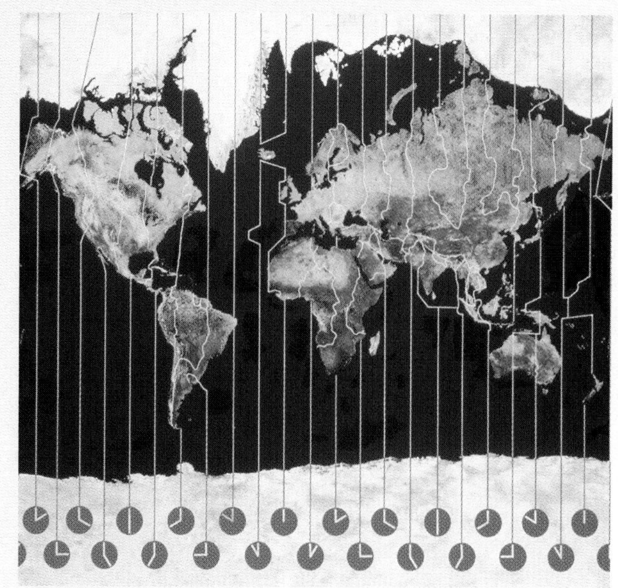

CHAPTER 56

Late Modern • 1

Mid-1960s–Mid-1980s

Late-Modern architecture, "singly coded," takes the ideas and forms of the Modern Movement to an extreme, exaggerating the structure and technological image of the building in its attempt to provide amusement, or aesthetic pleasure.

—Charles Jencks, *Late-Modern Architecture*, 1980

It's truly amazing the number of decisive events and critical dialogues that occur when people are out of their seated, stuffy contexts, and moving around chatting with one another.—The Action Office was supposed to be invisible and embellished with identity and communication artifacts and whatever you needed to create individuation. . . . We wanted this to be a vehicle to carry other expressions of identity.

—Robert Probst, "The Man Behind the Cubicle," *Metropolis*, November 1998

During the 1960s, a new generation of architects and designers reevaluates the value of Modernism and the International Style. Finding them lacking applicability to their times, these designers adopt new approaches to address the complexity, revolutionary changes, plurality, and rampant consumerism of their time. Some expand or exaggerate the language of the International Style. Others turn to Minimalism, a pared-down purist application, while others embrace and celebrate technology. Still others address consumerism and the youth or popular culture in Pop Modern.

HISTORICAL AND SOCIAL

Revolution defines the 1960s and 1970s. Immense social and political transformations in North America and Europe, to which design responds, occur as an outgrowth of the questioning and challenging of traditions and the status quo during the period. Various social and political movements arise or resurface. Particularly significant is the youth movement in which young people strive to change the world. Questioning nearly everything, they reject the values and culture of their parents, what they call the Establishment, in favor of their own ideas. Rejecting the existing political processes to effect change, they demonstrate, protest, and picket. They, along with the Civil Rights, Feminist, and Environmental Movements, bring about significant and long-lasting social and political changes.

By the mid-1960s, increased industrial production, new technologies, and booming economies are creating a more complex and pluralistic world. Consumerism and the emerging global economy become more important. The media, particularly television, rapidly disseminates new ideas, products, trends, and fashions. By doing so, it plays a significant role in defining consumer choices in working, living, dressing, leisure, and entertainment. The huge youth market of the postwar baby boom generation starts to drive production and consumerism. Growing up with plenty, this new generation is unacquainted with the austerity and hardship of the Great Depression and the shortages and sacrifices of World War II. Consummate consumers, many favor contemporary fashions, nontraditional manners of living, the inexpensive and the disposable, television, and rock-and-roll music. London, with its hip and trendy boutiques and restaurants, especially on Carnaby Street, becomes the center for the youth culture and the marketing of design. Design leadership, especially for furniture, passes to Britain and Italy.

During the 1970s, as numerous factors erode American confidence, significant change becomes evident in American culture. The Vietnam War divides the nation more than ever as protests and demonstrations against American involvement mount. Intensification of the fighting and more government social programs raise inflation and interest rates, which signal a weakening of the earlier widespread prosperity. Wage and price controls do not stem the economic decline. For the first time since the 19th century, a trade deficit indicates declining industry. In the early 1970s, the Arab oil embargo sharply increases oil prices, creating a gasoline shortage and energy crisis. At the same time, more immigrants create greater diversity, which tends to undermine national unity. The breakdown of the traditional social system, increased drug use, swelling welfare rolls, and rising crime rates plague the country.

Within the atmosphere of activism and revolution, a new generation of designers begins to question the effectiveness of the International Style. Although being modern and up-to-date is important throughout the period, their definition and appearance change as questions about what it now means to be modern arise. Designers reassess and challenge previous design movements while embracing, rejecting, or reinterpreting their own world. They move away from strict adherence to the vocabulary of the International Style toward a multiplicity of design methods, approaches, and languages.

During the late 1950s and early 1960s, critiques of the International Style and Modernism from inside and outside the design community result as designers and others begin to assess the movements' limitations and question their principles and practices. They recognize that, although the International Style claims to offer universal solutions to architectural problems, in reality it gives similar design solutions to a variety of functions and needs, often at the expense of users. Particularly criticized is the style's anonymity, which results from a limited architectural vocabulary that adopts few, if any, ties with location, the past, or culture. Additionally, creative designers handle a limited vocabulary well, but less inventive ones simply repeat the elements with little originality, and these unfortunately dominate the expression. Thus, large, modern, standardized boxy buildings, produced in assembly-line fashion, repeat the International Style language of buildings, such as the Seagram Building in New York City, in an effort to maintain a purist vocabulary without fully expressing their intended function. Housing units look like office buildings, art galleries appear to be warehouses or hospitals, and collegiate structures resemble factories. Furthermore, they directly contrast with what the public wants, leading to a conflict between designers and users.

Designers also realize that modern buildings are plagued with numerous design flaws and construction problems stemming from the modernist emphasis upon anonymity and the assumption that all users have the same needs. They also question innovations that do not develop from programmatic or user needs. Although technically workable, large expanses of unprotected glass, leaks, air-conditioning difficulties, and a lack of integration of the exterior and interior characterize many buildings. In response, designers begin to look for new methods that better meet human needs and develop from diversity, complexity, and context rather than universal concepts, solutions, and sameness.

All of the International Style's faults seem to come together in 1972 in the failures of two buildings. A technological failure is the John Hancock Center in Boston by the office of I. M. Pei. Intended as a tall glass tower, the windows begin to fail and fall out even before construction is completed. The building stands empty for several years until a solution is found. The second and even more significant design failure is the Pruitt-Igoe Housing complex completed in 1956 in St. Louis by George Hellmuth and Minoru Yamasaki. Composed of several plain modern 14-story boxes, the buildings are devoid of any architectural personality or sense of place, creating a hostile, sterile environment. Hellmuth and Yamasaki make few efforts to address the needs of the inhabitants through the building character, planning, scale, safety, sunlight, or green space. As a result, the residents rebel by constantly

▲ **56-1.** Schulin Jewelry Shop, 1965, 1972–1974; Vienna, Austria; Hans Hollein.

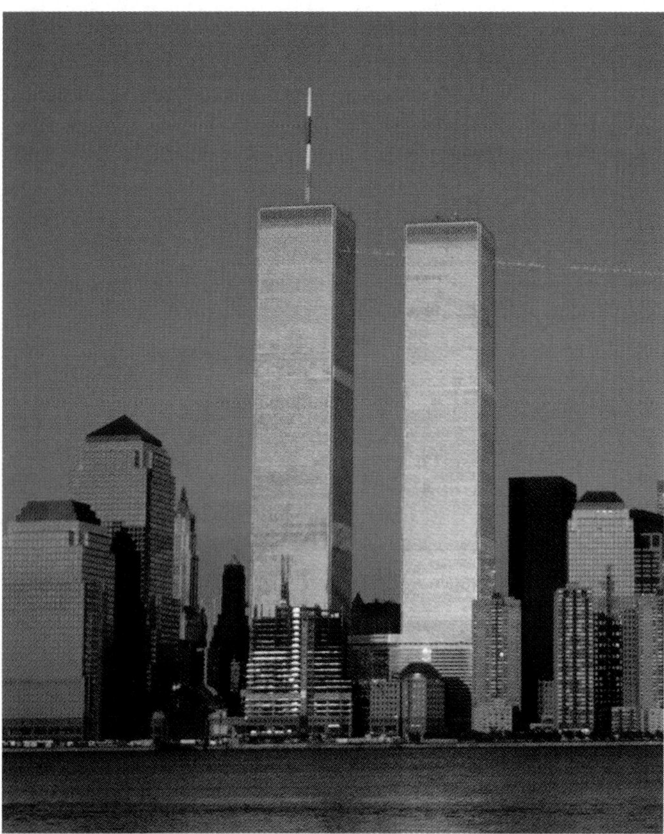

▲ **56-2.** World Trade Center, 1962–1967; New York City, New York; Minoru Yamasaki.

vandalizing and mutilating the structure. Ultimately, the city demolishes the complex in 1972, a signal of the end of Modernism's dominance and the beginning of new design directions and movements that celebrate diversity, communication, and complexity.

CONCEPTS

Shattering the unity of Modernism, as evident in the International Style, is the multiplicity of design methods that surface as architects and designers challenge, reassess, and reinvent its principles and practices. They strive to produce a contemporary expression that addresses the complexity, diversity, and plurality of their time. Underlying their quest are the importance of individuality and rejection of static, uptight formalism. Equally important are customization, identity, and design for the individual. Choices expand, so the design revolution is not a single movement, and neither do architects and designers share a unified viewpoint.

■ *High Tech.* Some designers celebrate technology and early Modern's notion of a building as a machine. The resulting High Tech mode, which combines high style and technology, explores and articulates the relationship of industry, technology, and art. Buildings, interiors, and furniture are creations and expressions of industrial concepts and products. During the 1970s, High Tech is especially fashionable for the home and office.

■ *Minimalism.* Other designers reject rampant consumerism in favor of Minimalism following in the tradition of William Morris's reductivism, Adolf Loos's elimination of ornament, and Mies's idiom of less is more. The term *Minimalism,* first applied to visual art and music, refers to work stripped to its fundamentals. Using the newest technologies, Minimalist designers simplify and eliminate everything they consider nonessential. Closely tied to Minimalism is a resurgence of rationalism. It is especially important in Europe, where its adherents advocate typologies and explore pure form as an expression of beauty.

■ *Pop Modern.* Pop Modern design responds to and takes cues from the youth culture and two art movements of the period. During the late 1950s, Pop Art appears in England and North America as a reaction to the solemnity and intellectualism of avant-garde art movements, such as abstract expressionism. Pop artists transform low art into high art and unite elitist and mass culture. Accordingly, offerings are characterized by images of everyday or popular culture, such as comic books, advertisements, and soup cans; modern materials such as plastic and acrylic paint; and mass-production techniques, such as Andy Warhol's multiple silkscreen images. Pop art affects fashion, graphic design, furniture, and interiors. Also developing in the 1960s is Op Art (Optical Art), a painting movement exploiting optical illusions. Through geometric patterns in black, white, and bright colors, artists create visual effects such as movement, vibrations, and confusion of foreground and background, and manipulate the viewer's perceptions. Op Art affects furniture and interiors, but its greatest influence occurs in fashion, graphic design, wallpapers, and textiles.

CHARACTERISTICS AND MOTIFS

Architecture, interiors, and furniture manifest a variety of expressions with an expanded vocabulary. Function, efficiency, and practicality no longer solely define concepts, so designs are often innovative, individualistic, and monumental, and stand out in their environments. As before, designers continue to use new materials and techniques, prefabrication, and mass production. Characteristics are exaggerated and defined by exposed structure, radical articulation of form, and an impression of stretched skin. Compositions may display extreme and complex technology and a high-tech image. The expression of joints and construction dominates other features, and function and service areas become important design elements. Designs are often anti-historical, with no displays of a base in architecture, and no moldings or transitions of structure in architecture, interiors, and furniture.

■ *High Tech.* Building façades and interiors emphasize the building components and elements of systems, using them to articulate and enhance form. These details, which may be exposed and exaggerated, may be on building corners but can be distributed across the surface. In large open interiors, these components and systems are often in bright colors. Industrial and/or prefabricated components, materials, and furnishings; color coding; and the bright colors of industrial machinery are typical.

■ *Minimalism*. In a purist approach, structure and construction define the clean form through extreme simplicity, repetition, and articulation. Colors, textures, materials, and details are reduced to essentials in architecture, interiors, and furniture.
■ *Pop Modern*. While reflecting many of these characteristics, Pop Modern interiors and furniture are youthful and hip, exciting, novel, colorful, and nontraditional with an emphasis on appealing to the masses. New materials, shiny finishes, and bold patterns create dramatic effects. Colors may be bright or subdued, and patterns range from hard-edged and geometric to the visual effects of Op Art.
■ *Motifs*. There are no specific motifs common to the period. Individual designers use details from projects to emphasize innovative structure, construction, and materials. Pop Modern motifs include elements of popular culture, words or letter forms, human anatomy, rockets, pods, and geometric forms.

▲ **56-4.** Pacific Design Center, Blue Building, 1975–1976, by Victor Gruen Associates, Los Angeles, California.

ARCHITECTURE

A new generation of architects forges diverse design methodologies that create compositions with unique and individual expressions. Architects, developers, and clients alike recognize the importance of identity for corporate headquarters (Fig. 56-2, 56-3), office buildings (Fig. 56-4), and retail stores (Fig. 56-1). They, along with museums (Fig. 56-5, 56-6, 56-7), hotels, libraries, and custom-designed houses (Fig. 56-8), give the best representation of Late Modern • 1 design principles. Experimentation with visual form is common and important because the building often becomes a monument (usually consumerism or capitalism) within its environment.

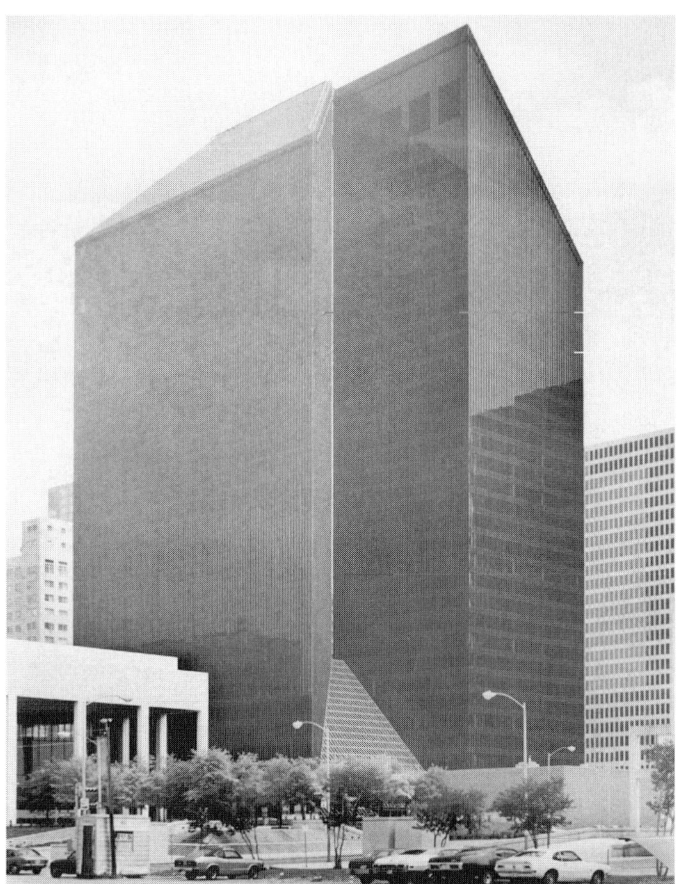

▲ **56-3.** Pennzoil Place, 1974–1976; Houston, Texas; Philip Johnson and John Burgee.

In the most common new approach, the box form of early Modernist buildings disappears through the use of curves, angles, indentations, stepped forms, pitched roofs, and exposed structure, although the elements and design language remain largely the same (Fig. 56-3, 56-4, 56-5). Cutouts in the building are frequent, and designers continue to place a strong emphasis upon solid and void relationships to highlight the building form (Fig. 56-1, 56-6). Although many façades follow a grid concept (Fig. 56-2, 56-3), the grid may be logical or irrational or both within a packaged expression of harmony. Buildings have a slick skin with flat surfaces that may be solid, glass, or a combination of both. Some buildings have an oblique plan axis rather than the usual 90-degree angle. Lessened unity in design is replaced by more experimentation with form and individual expression. As a result, the building structure may be exposed or punctuated to define a new aesthetic language (Fig. 56-5).

■ *High Tech*. High Tech architecture places the building components and systems on the exterior as a celebration or exploration of technology. As if turned inside out, structural parts may sweep across and envelop the façade or only cluster in certain areas. Interior space now is freed from the whims of climate and orientation and can be totally flexible. One of the best examples of this is the Pompidou Centre (Fig. 56-5) in Paris, France.
■ *Minimalism*. In reaction to consumerism and Pop Modern, some architects use a minimalist approach to building in a search for pure form. They explore space through planar geometry and reduce form to its essence. Examples are the Douglas House in Michigan by Richard Meier and *Casa Rotunda;* (Fig. 56-8) in Switzerland by Mario Botta.

Public and Private Buildings

■ *Site Orientation*. Plazas and mixed use facilities surrounding buildings become more common as concepts of urban planning evolve in response to consumerism and the desire to make structures recognizable. To increase prominence and ease of access, urban buildings sit on prominent city streets, waterways, public squares, or malls with green space nearby. Hotels may be in these areas or near beaches and lakes. Buildings often contrast with their surroundings and thereby, it is assumed, acquire greater importance. For example, the John Hancock Center in Chicago and the Pompidou Centre (Fig. 56-5) in Paris are surrounded by older, historical buildings. Houses, usually situated away from urban centers, are often surrounded by green space with only a few plants near the main structure. Richard Meier's buildings look like pieces of white sculpture on a green landscape (Fig. 56-6), and many other architects follow his idea.

■ *Floor Plans*. In a significant change, buildings with a high-tech look have plans that reject the rectangular shapes of earlier periods. Architects move from conceiving a plan as a two-dimensional feature based on a grid to one that is more aesthetically diverse and innovative. They play with interpenetrating geometries, complexity in scale and space, and solid and void relationships. Rather than one dominant building axis, there may be multiple

DESIGN SPOTLIGHT

Architecture: In 1970, French authorities hold an international design competition for a new cultural center and a multiuse facility housing a museum of modern art, a library and research centers, a movie theater, and restaurants. The industrial or high-tech design by Rogers and Piano wins the competition. The Pompidou Centre is one of the best examples of extreme machine articulation with exposed circulation systems, mechanical ducts, and skin and bones structure composed of prefabricated steel supports and trusses. It also features diversity in materials and an exaggerated use of color. Starkly contrasting with buildings around it, a large escalator on the west façade provides movement and carries visitors to the observation deck on the roof. The steel skeleton permits open interiors, and movable partitions allow configurations to meet any requirements. The large open space with little fixed wall space presents a challenge for interior exhibitions. Although a popular attraction, the building is less representational of French culture than it is a monument to industrial technology.

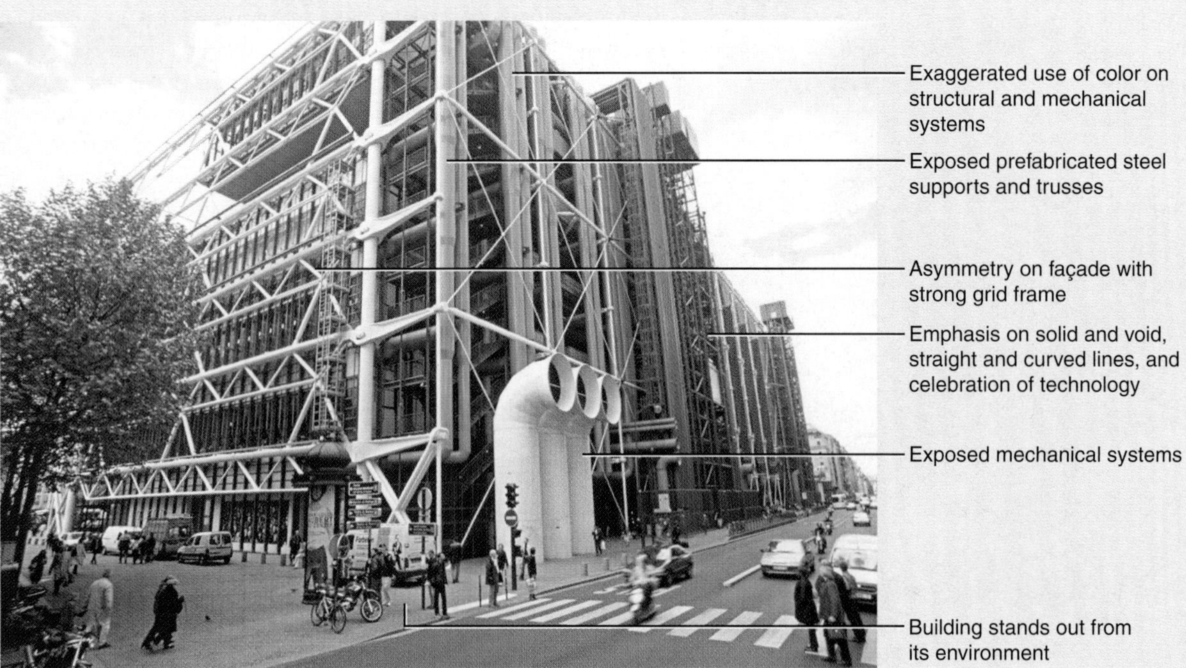

▲ **56-5.** Pompidou Centre, 1971–1977; Paris, France; Richard Rogers and Renzo Piano.

DESIGN SPOTLIGHT

Architecture and Interior: One of the members of the so-called New York Five, Richard Meier reinterprets Le Corbusier's Five Points of New Architecture in the High Museum of Art. He manipulates the structural grid and free plan into complex quadrants that provide the variety of spaces inside required for display and the myriad of functions needed by a museum. The stark, white, layered façade, mainly of white porcelain, enameled steel panels, features curves and bold geometric interpenetrating forms highlighted by grid-patterned ribbon windows. The soaring atrium interior, which allows natural light to penetrate, celebrates the ramp as viewing space as does the Guggenheim Museum, permitting the visitor to glimpse exhibits as he or she ascends. Meier experiments with the "spiritual activity expressed in architectonic forms," the relationships of solid and void, and the use of natural and artifical light to accent interior architecture.

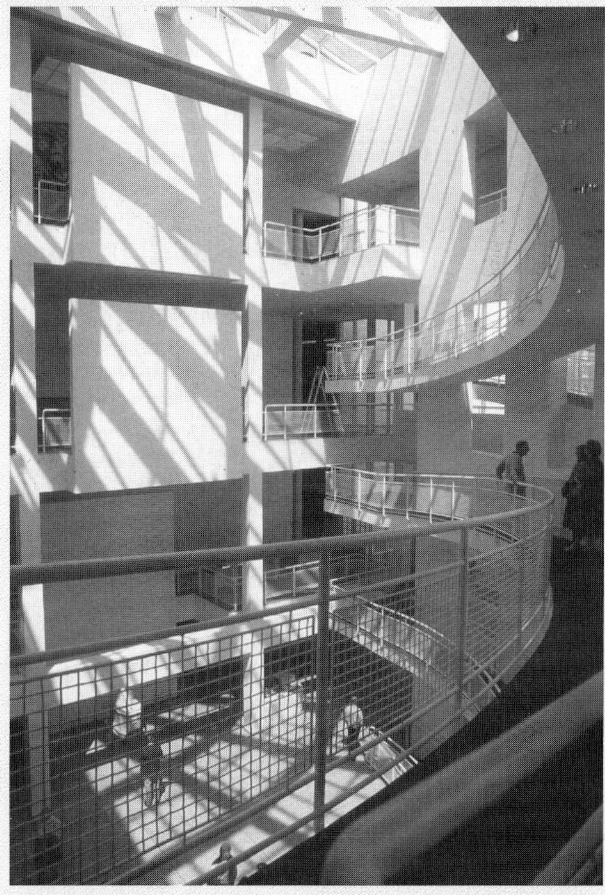

▲ **56-6.** High Museum of Art and atrium interior, 1980–1983; Atlanta, Georgia; Richard Meier.

▲ **56-7.** National Gallery of Art, East Building and atrium interior, 1968–1978; Washington, D.C.; I. M. Pei.

important axes and subdominant ones that define structure, entry, circulation, and function. Although some of these changes begin before the 1960s, they are more fully realized during this period because of technological advancements.

Overall, plans usually have straight edges, but the sides may be angled, curved, or indented with either solid or glass walls (Fig. 56-4, 56-6, 56-7). Or the building may express a variety of these features in the plan, have a circular plan, or have a portion of the building with a circular plan. The connection between the shapes and the solid and void relationships is important. Plan development and interior circulation may be formally or informally organized, two-dimensionally by the placement of spaces and three-dimensionally by the volumetric relationship of spaces, based on aesthetics and function. Centrally located circulation cores continue, but the designs show variety and innovation, particularly in the shapes and placements of stairways. Often interior stairways become major architectural features that continue the building's exterior design language (Fig. 56-6).

The three-dimensional character of spaces changes, too. Rectangular room shapes continue but may be grouped in different ways to create interest and add variety. Spatial shapes that follow the building language are introduced, which increases the angles, curves, and indentations throughout the plan. Interiors may also show spatial layering and level changes to delineate and zone public areas by function, as in hotel lobbies, offices, or living spaces (Fig. 56-9). Or a space may contain more multifunctional areas, a concept that becomes more important as the cost of interior square footage escalates. Plans of hotels, offices, museums, and houses accommodate new interior configurations, such as atriums (Fig. 56-9), that allow in more natural light. Additionally, exterior views become more important, so key spaces orient to them.

■ *Materials.* The most common materials are steel; reinforced and precast concrete; aluminum; and mirrored, tinted, and plain glass (Fig. 56-2, 56-3, 56-4, 56-5). Some also use stone, tile, and brick (Fig. 56-1, 56-6, 56-8). Most construction materials are prefabricated with modular components and may cover the main building surface or accent particular features. Sometimes architects become well known for their repetitive use of certain materials, such as Richard Meier, who uses white tile extensively (Fig. 56-6). The relationship between materials and the exposed building structure is important.

■ *Façades.* Façades exaggerate elements of the International Style, especially the simple, purist, rectangular form or silhouette. Most façades are complex in form and details, especially when compared to earlier Modernist buildings (Fig. 56-1, 56-2, 56-3, 56-4, 56-5, 56-6, 56-7, 56-8). Sometimes, everything is

▲ **56-8.** *Casa Rotunda*, 1980–1982; Stabio, Ticino, Switzerland; Mario Botta.

taken equally to an extreme, but most often one or two attributes, such as shape, are emphasized more than the others. Some office buildings and hotels have glass exterior elevators creating vertical movement and interesting views for passengers. And there is much variety expressed among individual buildings. For example, Pennzoil Place (Fig. 56-3) in Houston, which appears to continue the Modernist form, has twin trapezoidal towers with bronze-tinted glass façades that convey tension and complexity between multiple repetitions, grid exaggerations, and angled rooflines.

■ *Windows and Doors*. Windows on commercial buildings are usually fixed in grid patterns to control air-conditioning and heating systems, whereas those on houses may vary to include fixed plate glass, sliding glass, casement, and/or awning with no molding divisions (Fig. 56-2, 56-3, 56-4, 56-5, 56-6, 56-7). Also following the earlier Modernist language, windows have narrow metal moldings and mullions that frame the openings and divide glass areas. Sometimes they are black or bronze to accent the grid effect.

Some entryways have unique designs that spotlight the entry, the door, and the front façade, as in the Schulin Jewelry Shop (Fig. 56-1) in Vienna. On others, the entry is accented, but it still blends into the design of the building, which is generally a more characteristic expression (Fig. 56-3, 56-6).

■ *Roofs*. Like the façades, roofs may be flat, curved, angled, or punctuated to convey individuality (Fig. 56-2, 56-3, 56-4, 56-5, 56-6, 56-7, 56-8). Experimentation in design is common because there is no accepted standard. Some designs are symmetrical, whereas others are asymmetrical. Designers pay more attention to climate conditions and mechanical requirements.

INTERIORS

Late Modern • 1 interiors often reflect architectural concepts. Designers strive for a strong aesthetic relationship between the exterior and interior of a building so that the design language is complementary. Like the exteriors, the structure of walls and partitions may be exposed, and walls may be curved, angled, punctured, or a combination of these. Architects and interior designers emphasize function; industrial technology; repetition of modular elements; solid and void relationships; spatial layering; and the use of construction, structure, and materials as ornament. Interiors remain light and airy but are more complex. A geometric grid continues to define and shape interior space and primary circulation areas, but it may be regular and symmetrical, irrational and asymmetrical, or both within the same project. Experimentation with space planning leads to new ways to address functional requirements, public and private zoning, and furnishing arrangements. Furniture arrangements reflect this diversity in experimentation, so some arrangements are tightly structured while others illustrate more variety and uniqueness through placement within spaces. Many architects design the interiors of important buildings to achieve an integrated whole. Interior designers primarily address the renovation of existing interiors and the development of new spaces.

There are no new room types, but spaces dedicated to specific uses and multifunctional purposes become more common. Greater attention is given to hotel lobbies (Fig. 56-9, 56-12), offices (Fig. 56-11, 56-13), showrooms, museums (Fig. 56-6, 56-7), kitchens, and bathrooms. Rooms in houses open to each other more than previously. The importance of spaces with more natural light increases as people seek greater bonds with nature.

■ *High Tech*. High Tech incorporates in both commercial and residential spaces prefabricated building components; industrial equipment; and utilitarian materials, such as corrugated aluminum siding, loading dock doors, steel decking, metal shelving, office furniture, rolling metal tables, and industrial carpet (Fig. 56-10, 56-25). Residential spaces look more commercial and industrial than ever before. Furnishings and materials emphasize flexibility, maintenance, and convenience. Dubbed High-Tech in the 1978 book describing its character, this high-style look becomes extremely popular. Various components of it continue to the present but are packaged in a different, more updated way.

■ *Minimalism*. Although designers experiment with shapes, forms, scale, light, color, and some materials, they do so with a common design language, that of minimalism, which simplifies, reduces, and/or eliminates all extraneous visual elements (Fig. 56-11, 56-13, 56-14). Rooms become simple boxes with plain walls, floors, and ceilings and little furniture. With almost no color except black and white, or judiciously placed art, these spaces depend upon rich textures and textural contrasts for interest.

■ *Pop Modern*. Pop Modern defines trendy interiors in boutiques, shops, discotheques, and restaurants, especially those that appeal to young people and residences of the hip and fashionable. Image and branding are important, and interiors change quickly, especially those, such as boutiques, that are free to explore and experiment. This importance and resulting interior designs reflect the new leisure and social activities associated with shopping and eating out. So the style rarely influences corporate or other similar interiors, such as banks or government buildings. Pop Modern interiors, especially when marketed to the young, strive for excitement, novelty, fun, and disposability. Bold and bright colors, shiny finishes, dramatic lighting, and modular plastic or foam furniture are key characteristics (Fig. 56-20, 56-22).

Public and Private Buildings

■ *The Open Plan Office*. One of the most profound changes in office design during this period is the development of the open plan office (Fig. 56-24). It represents a shift from the enclosed office with fixed walls, common up to the mid-20th century, to the open office with flexible wall partitions and modular furniture. The concept stems from a study of the organization and communication patterns of office workers conducted by the Quickborner Team in Germany during the late 1950s. The group found that organizing and placing workers based on communications and paper flow is easier when the workers are grouped together in a free, open space. Additional considerations giving rise to open offices are increasing construction costs; need for greater flexibility; and a desire to improve interoffice communications, work flow, and

DESIGN SPOTLIGHT

Interior: John Portman revives the atrium in his quest to modernize the city hotel with its typical dark, confined lobby. He does so, despite objections from many hoteliers, at the Hyatt Regency in Atlanta. It immediately becomes well known and very successful. Providing both drama and congregating space, the hotel design centers on a large, multistory, open atrium with expansive skylights and illuminated glass elevators. Natural light filters downward from the glass roof to enhance the lobby seating, a bar, a restaurant, hotel corridors, and a large contemporary sculpture. Human scale and soft surroundings are important to the total design concept, so there are various changes in scale, texture, and color within the harmonious environment. Lighting, which is integrated into the architectural design, may accent, brightly illuminate, or soften conversation and circulation areas. Adding to the overall sensory quality and enhancing the spatial ambience, numerous plants are interspersed throughout, and long wind chimes (removed later) tinkle with a soft magical ring. Portman's atrium concept is so unusual that it inspires numerous other projects by Portman as well as other architects.

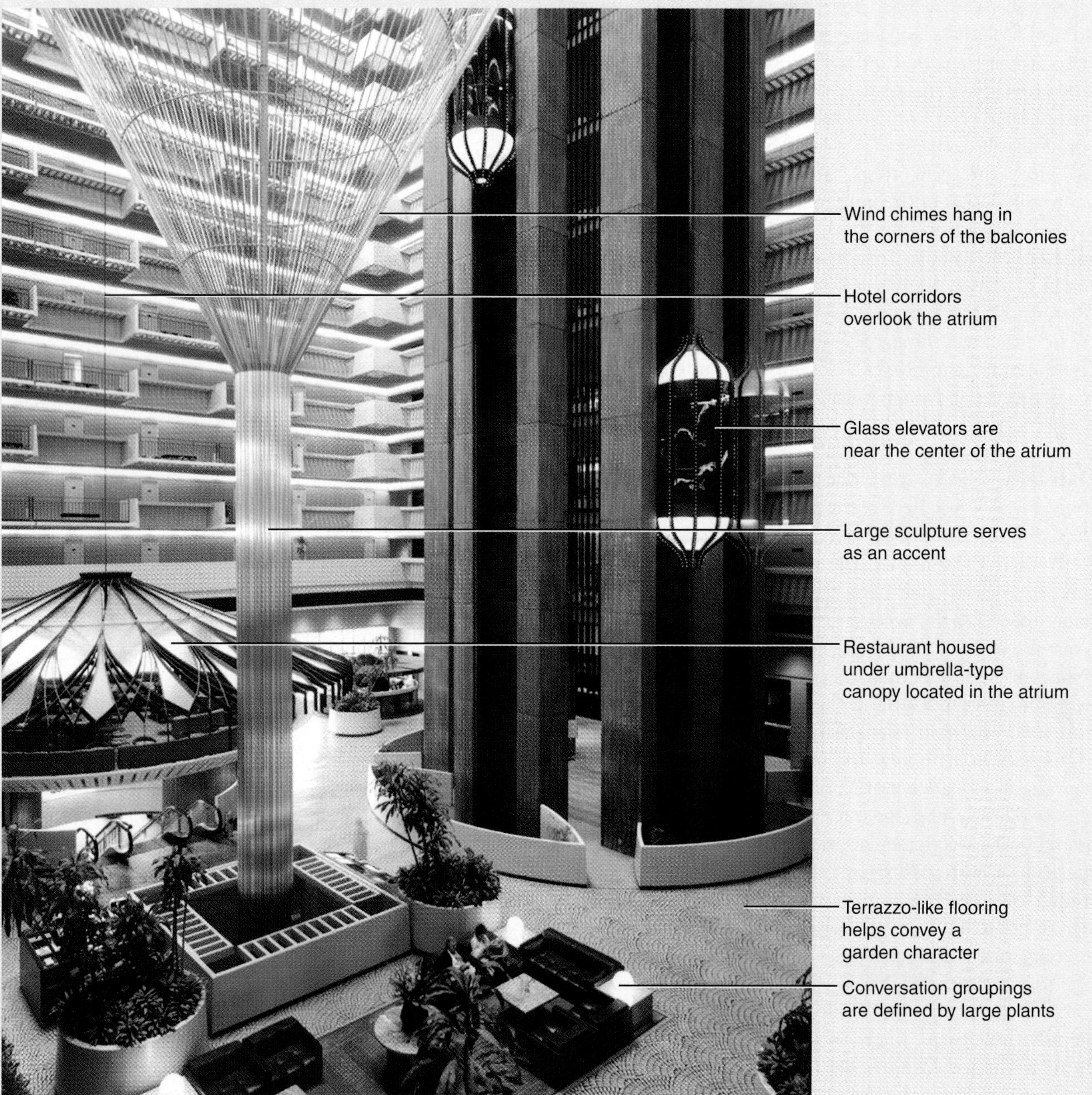

▲ **56-9.** Lobby, Hyatt Regency Hotel, 1967–1972; Atlanta, Georgia; John Portman and Associates.

▲ **56-10.** Interior, Garden Grove Community Church (Crystal Cathedral), 1977–1980; Garden Grove, California; Philip Johnson and John Burgee.

productivity. Open office or landscape planning inspires a broader definition of physical space and how people function in an office environment. This, in turn, initiates a revolution in office furniture design as offices are redefined as workstations. These smaller spaces, defined by low partitions from which hang work surfaces and storage, can be (theoretically) easily expanded, changed, and moved as the needs of the individual or company evolve.

■ *Atrium Hotels*. In the late 1960s, John Portman reintroduces the atrium-style hotel, the Hyatt Regency Hotel (Fig. 56-9) in Atlanta. This innovative idea, an outgrowth of his desire to create interesting spaces for people, results in a hotel with guest rooms and vertical circulation focused around a central atrium, like the Ancient Roman domestic atrium or the late-19th-century department store atrium with a skylight above. Portman's atriums, which extend the full or almost full height of the building, are examples of spatial layering. The spaces strive to be people-friendly through the addition of architectural elements, water features, plants, seating, and moving elevators. The project is so successful that he incorporates atriums in a series of Hyatt hotels designed in various locations. Other hotel chains emulate this idea, and atriums become common features not only in hotels, but also in other commercial facilities including office buildings and museums in North America and elsewhere.

■ *Furnishings, Textile, and Lighting Showrooms*. During the 1960s, furnishings, textile, and lighting showrooms expand tremendously in major metropolitan cities across North America and elsewhere to meet the demands of architects and designers. Building on the previous work of Florence Knoll and others, these showrooms display products available only to the design trade in spaces specifically to attract and support the design community. Some showrooms focus on furnishings, textiles, and lighting by only one manufacturer, while others display products from many of them. This expansion also creates more exposure for the products on display, leading to more concern for the design of the showroom and product presentation. In fact, some designers concentrate their practices in this specialty. In metropolitan areas, manufacturers also enhance their headquarters and manufacturing facilities with showrooms or display spaces. Additionally, major cities in many parts of the world begin to host markets specifically oriented toward the design trade, such as NeoCon in Chicago.

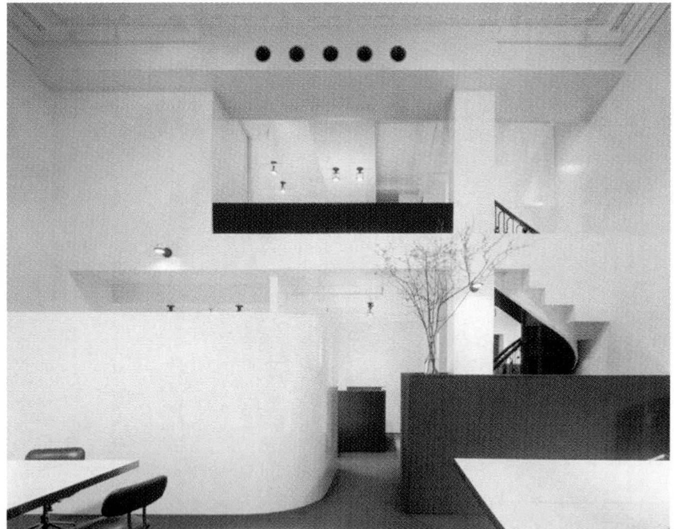

▲ **56-11.** D'Urso office in the minimalist character, 1970s–1980s; New York; office of Joe D'Urso Design.

■ *Color.* High Tech interiors sometimes use primary or secondary colors, blue, yellow or green, to accentuate interior systems or construction elements. Minimalism dictates white interior walls with black, white, or gray trim (Fig. 56-11, 56-12, 56-13, 56-14). Sometimes primary or earth-tone colors appear as accents in carpet and rugs, artwork, and decorative arts. Eye-catching color is a defining feature of Pop Modern. Bright red, blue, yellow, green, orange, and pink are typical (Fig. 56-20). Boutiques sometimes use dark colors and dramatic lighting to highlight merchandise.

■ *Floors.* A wider selection of floor materials inspires more inventiveness in their design application. Concrete, marble, terrazzo, ceramic tile, stone, and brick floors are used along with wood in blocks, strips, and parquet. Resilient flooring—rubber, linoleum, and synthetics such as vinyl—is incorporated more than ever before. Newly developed in Italy, embossed rubber floors with circles, squares, and ribs appear in both commercial and residential spaces for floors as well as walls and desk surfaces. Colors of rubber flooring are black, gray, and red. Embossed metal flooring is new for stairways and other high-traffic areas. Many floors in Pop Modern spaces have shiny finishes to reflect light and heighten the sensory experience. Wall-to-wall carpeting is common in commercial areas and spaces (Fig. 56-11), such as discotheques, where users sit or lie. Carpet again becomes universal in residential spaces as Minimalism and High Tech enter home environments. To enhance the industrial look, commercial carpets—tightly woven level loops—are used in homes as well as offices. Designers also begin to incorporate custom-designed carpets and rugs into projects to create a more individual appearance and emphasize corporate identity. Sisal and cocoa matting become popular as area rugs or in wall-to-wall applications in residences. Oriental rugs and factory-produced area rugs with simple designs also cover uncarpeted floors.

■ *Walls.* Walls may be of plaster, drywall, glass, marble, stone, or exposed concrete (Fig. 56-10, 56-11, 56-12, 56-13, 56-14). They are plain and flat with no moldings except baseboards that, when present, are downplayed as much as possible. White or neutral painted walls are most common, particularly in large office areas, museums, and residences. Other types of wall coverings include embossed metal or rubber, glass blocks, corrugated steel, and perforated metal. Wall-to-wall carpeting in gray or black may be applied to walls to define a particular area, such as over a bed. Cyclone (wire) fencing sometimes divides or partitions High Tech spaces. Some wall treatments develop from a modular system of prefabricated parts and materials to reflect an industrial look. Occasionally, designers deliberately call attention to structural components and/or interior systems by painting them different colors or using a variety of shiny finishes on them.

Pop Modern wall treatments may be subdued or dramatic, depending upon the use of the space. Subdued treatments, common in spaces that focus on merchandise, include plain dark painted or fabric-covered walls, often with shiny finishes. Dramatic treatments include shiny metals; mirrors; brightly colored and boldly patterned or psychedelic wallpapers; and audacious graphics, murals, and other decorations. Op Art wallpapers in geometric patterns in black and white or the primary colors play havoc with the viewer's senses.

■ *Window Treatments.* Simple, plain window treatments hung straight from ceiling to floor are typical. Most are thin sheers in white that blend in with the architecture. Mini blinds and sunscreen shades are new during the period and are used extensively. Vertical blinds continue to be popular.

■ *Doors.* Doors are flat, plain, and usually wood or metal and may be stained or painted black, white, or gray. Borrowing from the Bauhaus aesthetic, door trims, when present, repeat the character of window moldings.

■ *Ceilings.* Ceilings are most often flat, plain; and painted white, black, or a neutral color, especially in Minimalist spaces (Fig. 56-6, 56-11, 56-12, 56-13). Sometimes in High Tech spaces, different colors or finishes emphasize interior systems, such as ductwork or

▲ **56-12.** Lobby, Morgan's Hotel, c. 1985; New York City, New York; Andrée Putman.

sprinklers. Architects often incorporate materials used in the building design for ceiling treatments, such as metal, wood, or glass (Fig. 56-6, 56-9, 56-10). Other types of ceilings include corrugated steel and wood. Treatments may vary from one space to another, based on function and aesthetic choices. Overall, there is much more variety in ceiling treatments than earlier. Some Pop Modern spaces feature dramatic treatments, such as dark or bright colors, mirrors, silvering, graphics, or murals. In offices and other commercial spaces, suspended ceiling grids with textured panel inserts or metal slats are typical.

■ *Textiles*. Designers often select commercial-grade fabrics made of cotton, linen, wool, and synthetic fibers for both commercial and residential interiors because of their low maintenance and durability. Most are simple woven, geometric designs in solid colors. Plain fabrics, such as canvas, and leather and vinyl are common for upholstery especially in Minimalist or High Tech spaces. New to the period are stretch fabrics, made of wool, linen or cotton, that are used on foam upholstery (Fig. 56-19, 56-23). Carpet or matting usually covers platform seating. New companies, such as Maharam Fabrics and Design-Tex, support the growing commercial design market. And furniture manufacturers significantly increase their inventories of commercial textiles samples.

Pop Modern textiles of the early 1960s have controlled and hard-edged geometric and abstract patterns in bold colors. During the middle 1960s, they are replaced by Op Art patterns with static geometric forms such as squares, circles, and lines creating optical illusions. These patterns signal a move away from strictly controlled patterns into the free psychedelic swirling, curving, and moving patterns of the late 1960s.

■ *Lighting*. Designers pay greater attention to lighting and its effects on users. Research on fixture choices and types expands significantly so that designers are better able to select and specify lighting that more fully addresses the needs of the users and the type of space. They also incorporate different types of lighting, including ambient, task, accent, and mood, as well as specialized lighting for specific projects (Fig. 56-9, 56-13, 56-15). Because of the increased complexity in technology, design applications, and client requirements, architects and designers often consult with lighting engineers or lighting designers.

▲ **56-13.** Vignelli Associates Office, 1986; New York City, New York; Vignelli Associates.

▲ **56-14.** Shoe salesroom, Esprit Clothing Company Shoe Showroom, 1988; New York; Michael Vanderbyl, Vanderbyl Design.

▲ **56-15.** Lighting: Tizio desk lamp, 1972, Richard Sapper; and Boalum, c. 1970s, L. Castiglioni and Gianfranco Frattini; both manufactured by Artemide.

With greater demand for natural light, large windows, interior light-filled atriums, and skylights are more common in office buildings, hotels, museums, and houses. Examples include the Hyatt Regency Hotel (Fig. 56-9) in Atlanta and the National Gallery of Art, East Building (Fig. 56-7), in Washington, D.C.

Numerous advances are made in the design of architectural lighting, suspended ceiling systems, track lighting, indirect lighting, and individual fixtures. Suspended ceiling grids with integrated lighting and mechanical systems continue, particularly in offices. Task lighting addresses individual user needs. Track lighting and light fixtures intended for factories, with porcelain-on-steel incandescent light reflectors or fixtures with heavy steel wire cages, also become extremely popular for commercial and residential use because of their flexibility, style, and inexpensive costs. Created in the 1920s and 1930s, they are initially used in factories, museums, and retail spaces. Generally throughout this period, architectural lighting increases, with much variety in design and installation.

There are many innovations in the design of table lamps, wall sconces, and floor lamps. One of the most important new designs is the Tizio desk lamp (Fig. 56-15), a sleek, black linear fixture that offers flexibility to the user. Another is the Luxo drafting lamp, which offers great flexibility because of its adjustable arm, and often incorporates both a fluorescent and an incandescent bulb. Most light fixtures are simple, unadorned, geometric, and flexible with metal stems. Lamp shades are metal or glass to follow the architecturally based aesthetic. In contrast, fixtures for Pop Modern spaces may be of glass, ceramics, paper, metal, or plastic in simple shapes in shiny metallic finishes, bright colors, and/or robust patterns.

FURNISHINGS AND DECORATIVE ARTS

Most furnishings follow two general paths beginning in the 1960s—one focusing on contract furniture, mainly for the office, and the other addressing popular culture. Adopted by major manufacturers, the expanding and changing contract and office furnishings market concentrates primarily on office systems furniture and important office developments, such as changes in the way people work, technology, and the computer. These are regarded as having little applicability to the home. Rationalism, functionalism, flexibility, and durability are important design considerations. Furniture has a refined form and machine-made appearance with no applied ornament, continuing in the traditions of the Bauhaus and International Style. Because of similar materials, form, and/or design, furniture integrates well with the high-tech or minimalist look of the interiors. Sometimes it makes an architectural statement, while at other times it may stand out as a unique feature of a space. Important introductions to contract furniture are office systems furniture (Fig. 56-23, 56-24) that supports open plan offices, office chairs that are more ergonomic, and stackable seating used in auditoriums, schools, and offices (Fig. 56-16).

The other path responds to the domestic, youth, and consumer markets, embracing popular culture, novelty, disposability, and low cost. New materials, human elements, bold forms, large scale, and bright colors distinguish Pop Modern from other furniture (Fig. 56-20, 56-22). Scale often is larger than the previous decade, but furniture retains lightness and flexibility. Pop Modern furniture encompasses many forms, shapes, and materials. Adopting traditional, nontraditional, and neo-organic forms, it conveys newness, fun, and surprise. It may be imaginative, ingenious, flexible, modular, and/or multipurpose. Despite its spontaneous look, Pop Modern furniture fits the human body and may result from experiments with materials and construction methods.

During the 1950s and early 1960s, functionalism is the main consideration in the design of furniture. But as ideas change during this period, some furniture designers choose a different approach because of the demand for high sales volumes. As a result, they consider ease of manufacture, large production runs, short sales periods, and lower prices for the consumer. Additionally, the period's open-minded and less class-conscious consumers want furnishings that convey an image or make a fashion statement instead of communicating permanence and/or status. Lifestyle becomes an important sales concept as designers and marketers strive to fit consumers with products. Retailers, such as Terence Conran's Habitat stores in London and New York, begin to market to customers who plan their own interiors, select furniture from displays, buy it in flat cartons, and assemble it themselves at home.

▲ **56-16.** 40/4 Stacking chair, 1964; United States; David Rowland, manufactured by General Fireproofing, Inc.

Designers also experiment with new ways to organize furnishings based on design trends, evolving functional requirements, and user needs. One result is portable, flexible, and adaptable furniture that can be moved around and positioned or adjusted to fit users (Fig. 56-16, 56-21, 56-23, 56-25). Pieces intended for one purpose may be used in a different way. As industrial products pervade both office and home spaces, factory-styled furniture also becomes significantly more important. Mobility becomes such an important quality that designers create a variety of furniture that is intentionally mobile. Also new in the period is furniture made of solid foam, cardboard or paper, and inflatable plastic, as well as individual seating and storage units that combine several functions (Fig. 56-19, 56-22).

Public and Private Buildings

■ *Materials*. The dominant furniture materials are chrome, glass, wood, a variety of plastics, and plastic laminate (Fig. 56-16, 56-17, 56-20, 56-22, 56-23, 56-25). Many Pop designers abandon traditional furniture materials, such as wood, in favor of plastics, metals, and cardboard. During the 1960s, furniture designers and manufacturers embrace plastics, which are inexpensive, light in weight, strong, and adaptable to many applications. Designers use several types of plastic: acrylics, polyvinyl chloride (PVC), urethane, and ABS (composed of acrylonitrile, butadiene, and styrene). Acrylic is made in sheets that can be bent, cut, folded, and otherwise shaped. PVC is a clear or opaque flexible film used for inflatable furniture. Urethane can be either rigid or flexible, and ABS is moldable, strong, and rigid. It can take any shape and requires no reinforcement.

■ *Seating.* Chairs are the most important pieces of furniture in all environments. Attention is given to their shape, comfort, character, diversity, and mobility (Fig. 56-16, 56-17, 56-18, 56-19, 56-20, 56-21, 56-22, 56-23, 56-24). Side, arm, and lounge chairs are joined by new examples of lightweight folding and stackable chairs, such as the 40/4 chair (Fig. 56-16) designed by David Rowland. Designers and others sometimes use industrial or commercial furniture in atypical applications. Executive chairs or drafting stools may surround a dining table, for example. Previous Modernist and premodernist furniture, such as the Barcelona chair or bentwood chairs, continue to be used in interiors. Restaurants, discotheques, and trendy homes sometimes have elevated or sunken seating.

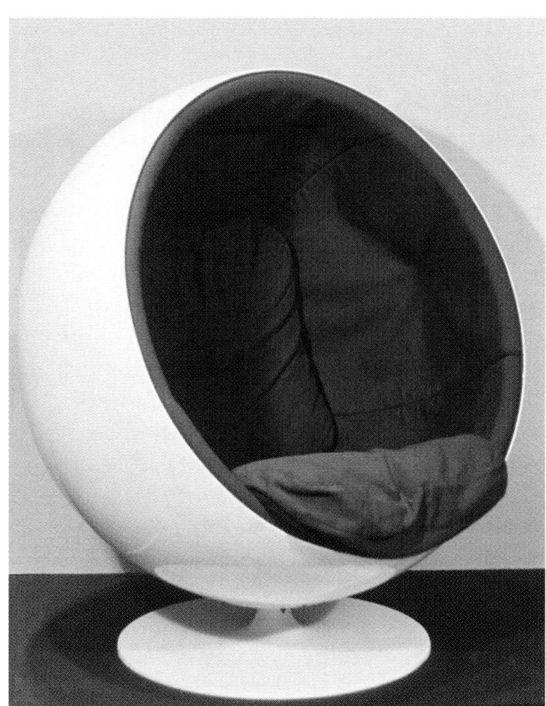

▲ **56-17.** Ball or Globe chair, 1963–1965; Finland; Eero Aarnio.

Plastic chairs reflect the influences of pop culture. One example is Verner Panton's Stacking chair (Fig. 56-20), the first chair to be molded in thermoplastic in a single continuous piece. Achieving total unity in form and material, the chair adapts the cantilever principle to plastic. A common form for seating is the sphere made in plastic or foam, which is reminiscent of the space age. Resting on a pedestal, Eero Aarnio's Ball or Globe chair (Fig. 56-17) has a spherical exterior and upholstered interior that creates an enclosed, cavelike environment for the sitter.

▲ **56-18.** Chairs, 1966; United States; Warren Platner, manufactured by Knoll International.

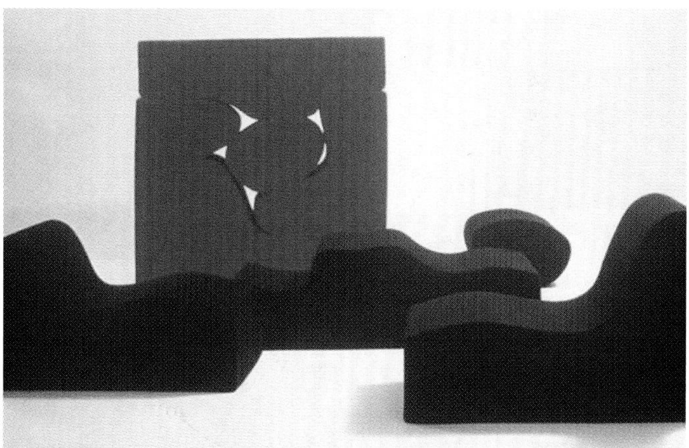

▲ **56-19.** Malitte, 1966; Italy and the United States; Roberto Sebastian Matta, manufactured by Knoll International.

▲ **56-20.** Panton Stacking chair, 1960–1967; Switzerland and the United States; Verner Panton, manufactured by Vitra GmbH and Herman Miller.

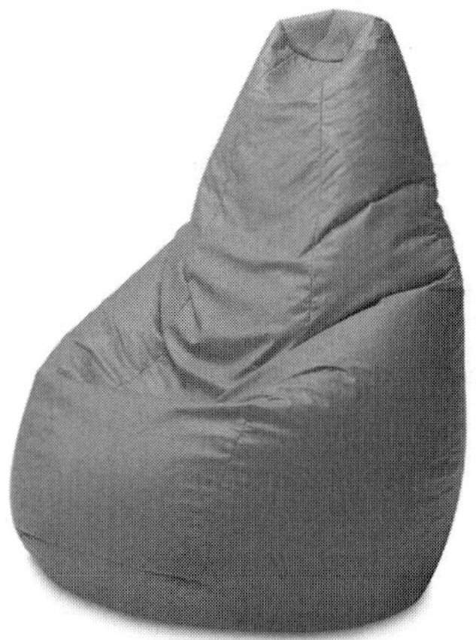

▲ **56-21.** Sacco, 1968; Italy; Piero Gatti, Cesare Paolini, and Fraco Teodoro; manufactured by Zanotta.

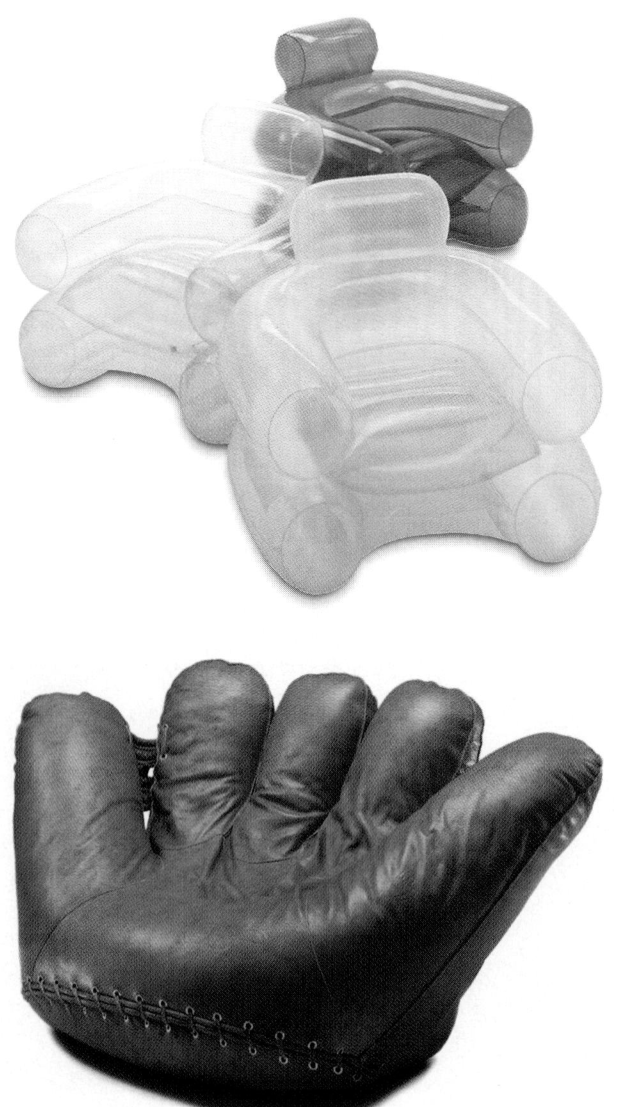

▲ **56-22.** Blow and Joe chairs, 1967, 1970; Italy; De Pas, D'Urbino, and Lomazzi, manufactured by Zanotta and Poltronova.

▲ **56-23.** Ergon chair, 1976; United States; Bill Stumpf, manufactured by Herman Miller.

Some designers adapt elements of nature or the human body to chair designs resulting in a neo-organic character. Examples include those with solid foam or tubular steel frames covered with foam and stretch fabric. Roberto Sebastian Matta designs the Malitte Seating System (Fig. 56-19) composed of solid blocks of urethane foam forming a jigsaw puzzle that when taken apart become four lounge chairs and an ottoman. One of the best known of tubular steel and foam seating is Oliver Mourgue's Dijnn group. Its futurist look prompts use by Stanley Kubrick in his 1968 film *2001: A Space Odyssey*. Another version is the Sacco chair (Fig. 56-21) that has a leather or vinyl sack filled with bits of foam or plastic. Becoming the Pop Modern icon beanbag chair, its shape, which adapts to any sitter, supports casual living.

Designers also create sectional and modular seating using nontraditional materials and construction techniques, such as solid foam in rectangular or undulating shapes and plastic frames with foam upholstery. Also evident in fashionable living rooms and trendy restaurants or discotheques are platform seating in multiple heights and the conversation pit, a sunken or self-contained seating areas. Numerous inflatable chairs appear in the 1960s. The first one to be mass-produced for the home is the Blow chair (Fig. 56-22) by De Pas, D'Urbino, and Lomazzi. Low, bulgy, and transparent, the chair is easily inflated and deflated for maximum transportability. The ultimate in inexpensive and disposable seating is made of cardboard or paper.

■ *Ergonomic Office Chairs*. Contract manufacturers, such as Knoll and Herman Miller, engage in comprehensive studies of ergonomics for the workplace. Consequently, designers more carefully consider clients' needs, creating seating that better suits the comfort and safety requirements of the users in office environments. An important early example of this idea is the executive swivel chair, such as the Pollock chair, designed in 1965 by Charles Pollock for Knoll International. It features a swivel-tilt option, a fully upholstered and contoured leather seat, and an adjustable-height pedestal base with branching leg supports and casters. It is immediately accepted as a standard for corporate offices. Almost a decade later a new type of office chair appears, the Ergon chair (Fig. 56-23). Designed by Bill Stumpf and introduced in 1976 by Herman Miller, it is one of the most important chairs designed to meet ergonomic needs. Based on 10 years of research and development on how people sit, it provides better body support, comfort, and flexibility than earlier designs do. Because of its popularity, it soon becomes standard seating in offices, and many manufacturers replicate its concepts.

■ *Office Systems Furniture*. The new open office concept requires flexible furniture that can be rearranged to support change. Storage units designed earlier by Charles Eames and George Nelson had addressed the modular concept but not the diversity and scope of modular parts needed in the new office environment. In the 1960s, Herman Miller introduces the Action Office system (Fig. 56-24) designed by Robert Probst. As the first of its kind, the modular component system reflects the diversity, complexity, and changing of functional requirements in the new office environment, particularly the beginning impact of technology. This type of furniture flexibility leads to a continuing revolution in office furniture design and the advent of more office systems furniture. Primary manufacturers of systems furniture include Herman

DESIGN SPOTLIGHT

Furniture: After several years of research and development, Herman Miller introduces Action Office, the first modular office furniture system, in 1964. With the concept design by Robert Probst and design details by George Nelson, the group consists of interchangeable components including work surfaces, desks, and storage. Because the system proves unwieldy and difficult to move, in 1968 Herman Miller introduces Action Office 2, the first flexible wall panel office system. It can be reconfigured more easily as the office grows and changes. The group features modular components of writing surfaces, storage units, seating, and support materials that can be adjusted by size and height to fit individual users. Writing surfaces and storage units come in a variety of finishes and can be customized as desired. Like previous Herman Miller designs, the Action Office concept derives from a focus on knowledge-based work; the individual user; and concern for materials, function, and flexibility. The system is so successful that Herman Miller still produces it under other names, evolving the form, components, and design as needs of the modern office change.

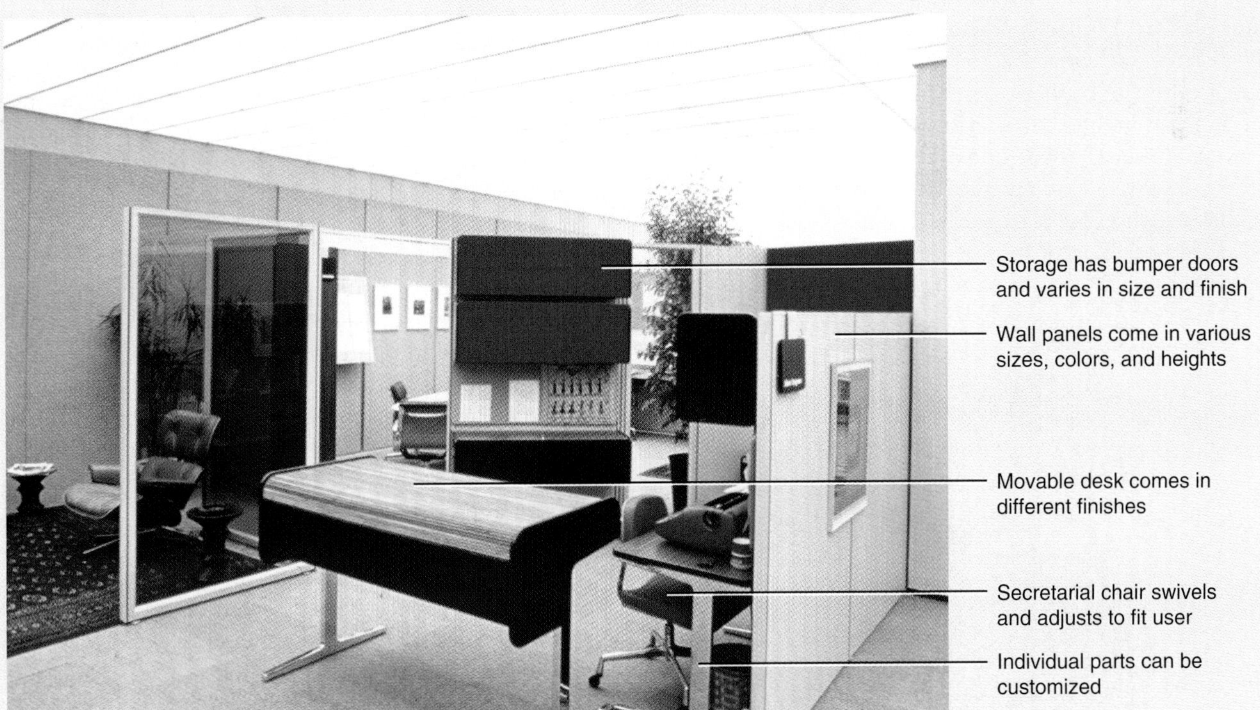

▲ **56-24.** Action Office systems furniture in 1964–1968; United States; Robert Probst with details by George Nelson, manufactured by Herman Miller.

Miller, Steelcase, Haworth, and Knoll International. They compete with each other in variations in design features, character, materials, and costs to satisfy an ever expanding demand.

■ *Tables*. Dining, coffee, and occasional tables with tubular or square metal legs and glass, wood, or laminate tops advance the Bauhaus and International Style aesthetic. New are rolling tables, used in hospitals, factories, restaurants, and institutions. They convey the high-tech, industrial look. Most have metal supports and come with or without adjustable shelves. Tables with pedestal bases in different materials and finishes and top selections appear in homes and commercial spaces. Pop designers create dining, lamp, and coffee tables from ABS plastic and acrylic. Lightweight and easily moved, some retain the traditional legs and tops but are distinguished by their bright colors. Others have nontraditional shapes such as the clear or colored acrylic cubes.

■ *Storage*. The most important changes in nonresidential storage include office systems storage (Fig. 56-24); custom-designed storage; and specialty storage for particular types of interiors, such as retail, hospitality, health care, institutional, and office. New, diverse, and flexible concepts for storage design flourish for all interiors. A major advantage of systems furniture is that most of the materials and supplies needed by an office worker can be stored within arm's reach. Therefore, most groups include numerous compartments and divisions to help organization. Companies, such as Metro Systems, create metal component shelving and storage systems (Fig. 56-25), including bookshelves, wall shelves, and rolling carts. Plastic modular storage units also become very popular, especially in apartments and dormitories, because they are inexpensive, disposable, and very adaptable. White, black, and brightly colored individual units may be open cubes or have shelves or drawers. Designers create mobile units that combine several functions such as storage, serving, and working. Metal lockers in a variety of configurations, file cabinets, open shelves, and wire storage bins and closet systems are also used for storage in homes, retail shops, offices, and other nonresidential applications. The Elfa system from Sweden has plastic-coated bins and baskets that can be inserted into freestanding racks or under counters or other similar locations.

▲ **56-26.** Later Interpretation: Chair One, 2003; Konstantin Grcic, manufactured by Magis in Italy. Neo-Modern.

▲ **56-25.** Chrome shelving, c. 1980s; manufactured by Metro.

■ *Beds*. Designers create beds out of industrial materials such as Metro Systems shelving components, scaffolding, and pipes. New to the period is the platform bed in which a rectangular box or platform, painted or carpeted, supports the mattress. Water beds also become popular but require a more substantial frame.

■ *Decorative Arts*. Accessories in Late Modern • 1 spaces are kept to a minimum and include metal, glass, ceramic, and plastic objects and plants. Metal accessories, common in High Tech or Industrial rooms, include baskets, ashtrays, clocks, and vases. Plastic accessories, usually brightly colored, are also common and include plant and umbrella stands, ashtrays, vases, and dishes. Russel Wright designs a line of melamine dishes that prove extremely popular.

■ *Later Interpretations*. The Late Modern • 1 character continues in furniture through the early 21st century. There are many more varied designs with an industrial look, as well as new concepts that illustrate the use of materials in different ways. One of the most important trends is the geometric grid approach taken by Neo-Modern designer Konstantin Grcic (Fig. 56-26).

CHAPTER 57

Post Modern

1960s–1990s

A Post-Modern building is . . . one which speaks on at least two levels at once: to other architects and a concerned minority who care about specifically architectural meanings, and to the public at large, or the local inhabitants, who care about other issues concerned with comfort, traditional building and a way of life. Thus Post-Modern architecture looks hybrid. . . . The architects can read the implicit metaphors and subtle meanings . . . whereas the public can respond to explicit metaphors and messages. . . . Of course everyone responds somewhat to both codes of meaning, as they do in a Post-Modern building, but certainly with different intensity and understanding, and it is this discontinuity in taste cultures which creates both the theoretical base and "dual coding" of Post-Modernism.

—Charles Jencks, *The Language of Post-Modern Architecture*, 1977

Coalescing in the late 1970s and early 1980s, Post Modern embraces a pluralistic and inclusive approach to design that reflects the modern world. Rejecting concepts and principles of the International Style, designers celebrate complexity, diversity, and historicism and strive to create expressions that communicate with the design elite as well as the common person. Architecture, interiors, furniture, and decorative arts display many different forms, materials, and colors that are often imbued with wit, whimsy, or classicism. Memphis is an avant-garde style based in Italy with an outgrowth of individualism and similar principles to Post Modern. It challenges traditional notions of good design using anti-design—quirky forms and shapes, and strong colors and patterns rendered in both luxurious and common materials.

HISTORICAL AND SOCIAL

Post Modernism attempts to overcome the stylistic void, universality, and loss of context associated with the International Style, as well as respond to the pluralism created by new technologies and the emerging global economy. Concurrent with Late Modern developments, it reacts to them by challenging their notions of Modernism, particularly those shared with the International Style and Geometric Modernism. Instead, it presents a different and more encompassing approach to design, one that stresses period influences, local context, symbolism, and decoration over sleek skin, glass box, and high-tech solutions.

The term *Post Modern* is first used in literature, philosophy, sociology, and other disciplines to describe unique features of the late 20th century such as consumerism and globalization. By 1976, *Post Modern* describes a worldwide architecture that is an avant-garde cultural interpretation reflecting modern influences, but illustrating a symbolic design language of traditional or popular double coding recognizable by the design elite as well as the public. Designs reflect the postindustrial age in which the media, knowledge, and consumerism define modern life. Greater emphasis upon newness, novelty, and quick changes encourage aesthetic experimentation and innovation.

Post Modern architecture in the United States has its foundations in the theories and work of Robert Venturi and his wife, Denise Scott Brown, during the 1960s. During the late 1970s and early 1980s, the style emerges in their work and that of others. The

▲ **57-1.** *La Strada Novissima*—Presence of the Past (street façades), Venice Biennale, 1980; Venice, Italy (as reconstructed in 1982 in San Francisco, California); by Michael Graves, Oswald Mathais Ungers, Joseph Paul Kleues, and Leon Krier.

1980 international exhibition of the Venice Biennale, organized by architect Paolo Portoghesi and called *La Strada Novissima*, displays street façades designed by Americans and Europeans demonstrating that Post Modernism has spread worldwide. Prominent designers include Michael Graves, Robert Venturi, Denise Scott Brown, Charles Moore, Stanley Tigerman, Robert A. M. Stern, and Philip Johnson of the United States; James Stirling, Thomas Gordon Smith, and Terry Farrell of Great Britain; Hans Hollein of Austria; Ricardo Bofill of Spain; and Paolo Portoghesi and Aldo Rossi of Italy. They establish their own personal vocabularies that are widely imitated. Many revive the architectural tradition of designing the building, interiors, and furnishings, in part responding to consumerism. In the United States, Orlando, Las Vegas, New York City, Houston, and Los Angeles become some of the showplaces for these designers' new ideas and work. By the late 1980s, the style is readily copied and popularized by builders and developers so that it becomes one of a variety of available styles, particularly for houses.

Nevertheless, Post Modern is not a universal style. The architectural community debates its appropriateness and applicability. Many individuals reject its historical allusions and eclecticism. Others embrace and promote its various stylistic or theoretical aspects.

CONCEPTS

Post Modernism directly opposes the International Style and Geometric Modernism by adopting a pluralistic, inclusive approach that acknowledges the importance of communication, complexity, and diversity of aesthetics, form, space, and color. Theories and physical elements surface during the late 1960s in response to the perceived failures of Modernism. An early proponent is Robert Venturi who, in *Complexity and Contradiction in Architecture* (1966), describes an architecture that emphasizes intricacy, inconsistency, ambiguity, tension, hybrid elements, and popular culture. All of these attributes are directly opposed to those of the International Style. Additionally, he borrows features and ideas from Antonio Gaudi, Sir Edwin Lutyens, Pop Art, Main Street, and Las Vegas—blending aspects from both the past and the present. Venturi's ideas shake up the architectural world because he challenges the established modernist and International Style traditions. His new architectural principles confront the anonymity, purity, clarity, and simplicity in form and function of Modernism evident in the work of Mies van der Rohe and others. Venturi advocates the reintroduction of individuality, wit, and whimsy. He declares that "less is a bore," in opposition to Mies's dictum that "less is more." Venturi, Denise Scott Brown, and Steven Izenour write *Learning from Las Vegas* (1972), which further challenges designers to learn from and even emulate the glitzy architecture of Las Vegas with its meaningful symbolism and ability to communicate to people.

In Europe, Aldo Rossi's *L'Architectura della Citta* (1966) helps lay the theoretical foundations for Post Modernism. Stressing the importance of restoring monumentality to architecture, Rossi advocates the study and analysis of the development of cities to uncover urban typologies and longstanding social, cultural, and architectural traditions, which can be creatively interpreted in new architecture. Rossi's ideas establish a more political and social foundation along with a greater emphasis upon language. Consequently, Post Modernism in Europe contrasts with that in the United States where the style aligns with consumerism and capitalism.

Post Modernism's principal theorist, architectural historian, and critic is Charles Jencks, who identifies its character in *The Language of Post-Modern Architecture* (1977). Jencks adopts concepts of literary criticism, most notably semiotics and multiple meanings, in his emphasis on visual communication of signs, symbols, and values. According to Jencks, buildings exhibit double coding, meaning that a building speaks on two levels at once, both to the elite modern architects and to the more traditional-leaning public. Accordingly, a modern high-rise office box by Mies van der Rohe may appear intellectually pure and harmonious to the architect, but it represents a symbolic bland, factory-like shoebox to the private citizen. Post Modern architects adopt a variety of means and meanings to achieve this communication goal, including historicism, revivalism, neo-vernacular, urban context, classical populism, metaphor, symbolism, and new extended space.

Jencks advocates eclecticism and stylistic pluralism to counter the abstractness of modernism. He suggests that, through careful selection and rational choice, the designer can use style to visually articulate a particular meaning or meanings unique to the building, location, or client. In this way, the design can produce the desired visual or communicative effects and convey purpose, symbolism, or monumentality. Public and private buildings may illustrate metaphors through a mixture of iconic symbols, traditional features, and cultural accents that speak in the language of popular life. Jencks and others advocate ornament, especially historic, in defiance of Modernism's belief in Loos's equation of ornament and crime. Layering of decoration that is filled with meaning is important.

Architects and designers respond to consumerism in two ways. First, they create designs that are regarded as fine art and thus appeal to the consumer elite. Second, they design everyday objects, such as cutlery and door handles, giving them a distinct image and raising their aesthetic status. This deliberate attempt to create an image is substantially different from the goals of postwar designers. It also creates design celebrities and stars with recognizable design expressions to which the public enthusiastically responds. The media—television, magazines, books, and the Internet—contribute to this new star quality.

CHARACTERISTICS AND MOTIFS

In contrast to International Style and Geometric Modern, Post Modernism embraces individuality, social diversity, and a traditional or period character. Historicism, classicism, and eclecticism are key concepts, and designers creatively manipulate and reinterpret elements from the past to create new, modern, complex compositions. Reflecting the designers' pluralist approach, compositions may be eclectic, whimsical, bizarre, and/or exaggerated (Fig. 57-6). They also may feature creative inventions, fragments, applied ornament, or ironic juxtapositions (Fig. 57-1, 57-2, 57-8, 57-15, 57-18). Variety in size, shape, color, character, and architectural detail expresses diversity and individuality. Designers stress, abstract, imply, or differentiate key compositional features through differences and variations, which sets up a scale of dominance and subordination. Layering of elements, juxtaposition of form, and projecting and receding elements create complexity that is supported or enhanced by contrasts and variations of color and materials. Works reflect an additive design method instead of the integrated one of the International Style. Interior space also is layered, although architects do not necessarily believe that exterior and interior should be connected as earlier modernists did. Sequencing and layering of spaces sometimes creates a sense of procession or infinite extension of space. Designs, even in furniture, look somewhat like stage sets with allusions to the past.

Many Post Modern designers creatively use or manipulate classical attributes such as scale or elements such as columns. Buildings, interiors, and furniture may display classical details and proportioning of base/bottom, column/midsection, and cornice/top (Fig. 57-2, 57-3, 57-4, 57-11). Designers ascribe symbolic meaning to architectural features, even in interiors and furniture. For example, a fireplace or hearth can equate with the

▲ **57-2.** *Piazza d'Italia,* 1975–1980; New Orleans, Louisiana; Charles Moore and William Hersey.

heart, walls may mean territoriality, a roof can symbolize shelter and crown, a column represents a man, and chairs and tables may be symbolic of social interactions. Elements from local, regional, and national architectural history may be expressed in a more modern, symbolic, and distorted way within a small-scale space or a piece of furniture. Buildings, interiors, and furniture may be playful or present fanciful, cartoon-like, or entertainment-like designs and themes (Fig. 57-6, 57-12).

■ *Motifs*. Historically inspired motifs create a multilayered richness. Although many motifs from the past are revived, most come from classicism, including Greece, Rome, Egypt, and the Renaissance. They include columns, pediments, arches, stringcourses, and classical moldings (Fig. 57-1, 57-2, 57-3, 57-4, 57-5, 57-8, 57-11, 57-12). Designers also create motifs from client logos, letters or signs, and abstracted designs.

ARCHITECTURE

Post Modern architecture displays a broad range of interpretations of the design principles identified by Jencks. These principles include ornamentalism or more applied decoration, more and brighter color, contextualism through an identifiable relationship with and reinvention of past historical architecture, and allusionism in which the design relationship of the building relates to its intended purpose. Designs are unique with no rigid guidelines for expression. Designers emphasize figurative, poetic, and symbolic architectural language as opposed to the technical and utilitarian approach of the International Style. Often, the building silhouette, roofline, façade, and main entry convey the historical sources and decoration. Architects make doors and windows human in scale, unlike earlier large-scale Bauhaus or International

DESIGN SPOTLIGHT

Architecture: The Portland Public Services Building is the first major public building of Post Modernism and by Michael Graves. It helps establish Post Modern as a mainstream architectural style. Featuring classical formality, ornament, and implied details, the building is a bold off-white rectangular block resting on a dark green base. Seven-story barred windows with heavy keystones or stylized swags embellish the façades. A change of color suggests the shaft of a column with triangular capital above on the other façades. A grid of small square windows repeats around the perimeter. The small windows do not permit much-needed light into the interiors. Much criticized for the ornament, color, and cramped interiors, Graves's composition nevertheless strives to capture the progressive spirit of the city.

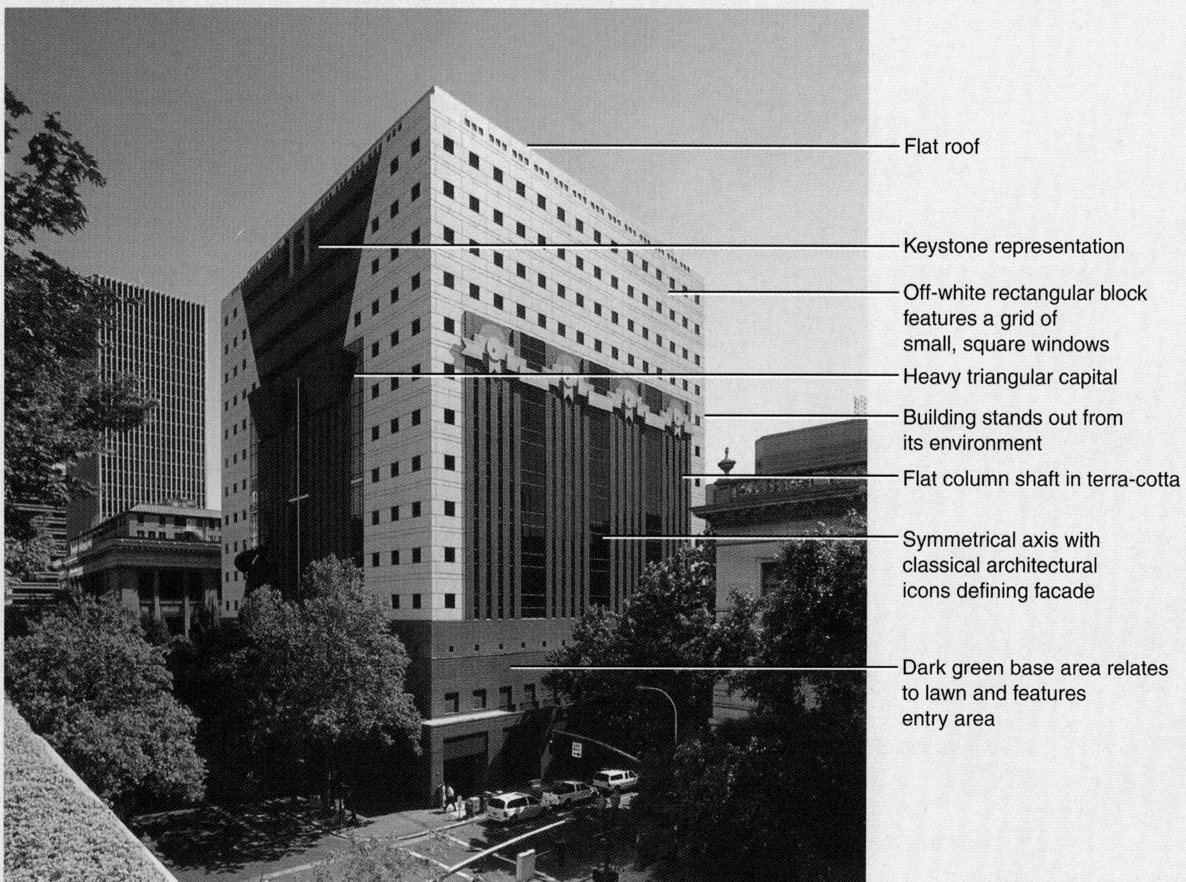

▲ **57-3.** Portland Public Services Building, 1979–1980; Portland, Oregon; Michael Graves.

▲ **57-4.** AT&T (now Sony) Building, 1978–1984; New York City, New York; Philip Johnson and John Burgee.

Modern buildings with continuous window walls having no relation to people. They also distinguish parts of the building, such as walls and doors, through color, material, texture, and design to make them stand out individually and relate to known compositional parts in historic buildings. Wit and whimsy are important, especially in themed hotels and resorts such as Walt Disney World (Fig. 57-6, 57-12). Post Modern public buildings include civic centers, corporate offices (Fig. 57-3, 57-4, 57-5), art museums, libraries, hotels (Fig. 57-6), shopping centers, exhibition displays (Fig. 57-1), expositions, garages, and medical facilities. The most stylistically expressive residential structures are custom-designed houses (Fig. 57-9) and public housing units.

Public and Private Buildings

■ *Site Orientation*. Commercial buildings, often in downtown urban areas, make a visible, distinct statement in their environment, such as Portland Public Services Building (Fig. 57-3) and the AT&T (now Sony; Fig. 57-4) Building. Some, particularly art museums, libraries, and social buildings such as *Piazza d'Italia* (Fig. 57-2) sit in an open or parklike setting, which creates a sort of sanctuary around them. Architect-designed houses and housing units are usually in parklike settings with green and/or water space around them or nearby (Fig. 57-9).

■ *Floor Plans*. Floor plans for both public and private buildings vary considerably based on facility type, user needs, and architectural expression. But several key characteristics shape and define the Post Modern planning. Because of the frequent use of historical allusions, buildings often follow a structured processional development of space with changes in the scale of rooms (small to large), definition of classical features (columns and niches), and articulation of ceiling designs (layered, rounded, and pitched). Mixed with the blended period features are juxtapositions and fragments of new elements, such as the layering of planes, angling of an important axis, distortion of circulation flow, and an extension of abstract space. Because these new components are usually unexpected, they give contrast, ambiguity, and tension—distinctive features of Post Modern plans.

■ *Materials*. Brick, polished marble, and rusticated stone are common building materials, along with wood, concrete, plastic, aluminum, and glass. Painted finishes are prevalent. Post Modernism exhibits a wider range and more decorative use of materials per building than the International Style does (Fig. 57-1, 57-2, 57-3, 57-4, 57-5, 57-6, 57-7, 57-8, 57-9).

■ *Color*. Colors inspired by designers, such as Michael Graves, include dusty pink, mauve, terra-cotta, pale yellow, blue, aqua, and celadon (Fig. 57-2, 57-3, 57-5, 57-6, 57-8). Materials are often selected because of their color impact.

▲ **57-5.** Humana Building, 1982–1985; Louisville, Kentucky; Michael Graves.

▲ **57-6.** The Dolphin Hotel, Walt Disney World, 1989–1990; Lake Buena Vista, Florida; Michael Graves.

■ *Façades*. As the most important and distinguishing feature of a building, the façade establishes the juxtaposition of complexity and contradiction between space and plane, historical allusion and contemporary statement, traditional materials and new ones, formal movement and distorted fragments, and the language of double coding to achieve intellectual as well as popular meaning. Complexities of color and material are important. Façades may be flat with the materials or colored areas defining features or becoming decoration (Fig. 57-3, 57-7). Others are layered with projecting and receding rectangular and rounded elements (Fig. 57-6, 57-8). Often the exterior shows influences of the International Style, such as rectangular fixed glass windows bound in thin metal, mixed with witty, sometimes humorous symbols, such as the Chippendale-style roof with a Palladian arch on the base on the AT&T Building (Fig. 57-4). Sometimes grand classical influences mix with local vernacular ones, creating an interplay of, as well as opposition to, formal and informal organization, architectural features, and construction details. The entry composed of a standardized arch and columns of rusticated wood on the Paulownia House by Thomas Gordon Smith is an example. Pseudohistorical designs are common (Fig. 57-9). Historical influences come from many parts of design history, including classical, regional, and local forms and details. Some architects incorporate surface pattern, letters, signs, and figures into the façade design.

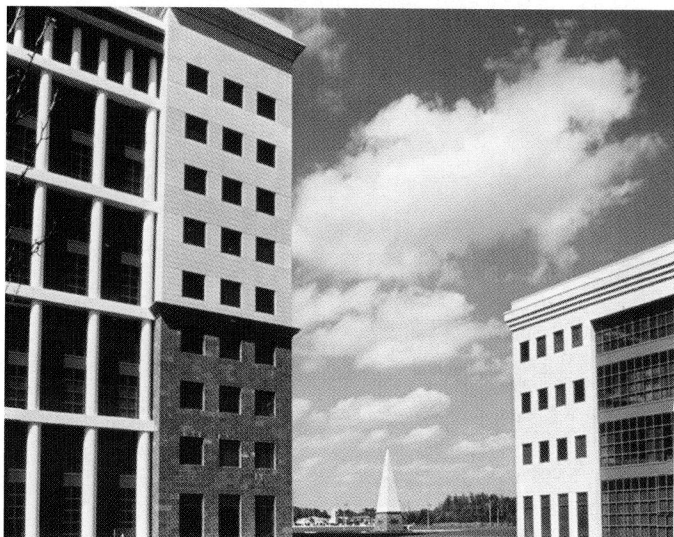

▲ **57-7.** Office complex, 1995; Celebration Place, Florida; Aldo Rossi.

▲ **57-8.** Feature Animation Building, 1995; Burbank, California; Robert Stern.

■ *Windows*. Most windows are of fixed-glass panes or are double-hung and often appear in a modern-style grid (Fig. 57-3, 57-4, 57-5, 57-6, 57-7, 57-8, 57-9). Sizes and shapes vary by individual design, designer, and building type. Compositions are symmetrical or asymmetrical, or there may be a combination of both in one building. Frames are of metal or wood. Moldings may enhance the sill line or the surrounding window area. Some window designs are very plain and nondescript as in the International Style, while others have more historical characteristics related to the particular building.

■ *Entry*. One of the most expressive components of a Post Modern building is the prominent entry because it conveys the building's character and sets the stage for what is to come. Sometimes the entry is an integrated unit within the façade design (Fig. 57-3, 57-4), and at other times it stands out to make a dominant, distinct statement (Fig. 57-5, 57-6, 57-8, 57-9). Designs vary widely by building type as well as designer, so there is no common expression. Graves, Smith, and others often incorporate columns and a classical vocabulary at the entry.

■ *Roofs*. Roofs may be angled, flat, or curved; may come from a historical source; or may have a variety of irregular shapes (Fig. 57-3, 57-4, 57-5, 57-6, 57-7, 57-8, 57-9). As an important component of the building character, they help to convey unique architectural design features, establish the identity, provide wayfinding attributes in a busy skyline, and/or provide a crowning detail at the top of a building. Variety in design distinguishes one building from another and from other modernist influences. Post Modern architects, in reaction to the ubiquitous Modernist flat roof, revive the gabled and shed roof. Roofs were rarely highlighted in the International Style.

INTERIORS

Architects and interior designers create interiors that focus on interior structure, decoration, and color. They use layered, angled, and/or sloped walls and details; color; pattern; and ornament to eliminate the simple, spare rectangular box of the International Style. Interiors may maintain a strong relationship to exteriors by using Post Modern influences such as complexity. Some have a more architectural character, while others are more decorative. Historical allusions and details, especially classical ones, are common, which gives rise to a revival of traditional style and/or revivalist interiors. Some interiors are highly sophisticated while others are kitsch, bizarre, or ironic. Designers mix high-quality materials such as marble (symbolic of wealth) with less sophisticated materials such as plastic laminate (symbolic of the masses) to achieve contradiction and complexity. Some spaces incorporate dramatic elements such as staircases and water features. Some of the most important Post Modern designs are in offices, showrooms (Fig. 57-10, 57-11), lobbies (Fig. 57-12), restaurants, casinos and nightclubs, and exhibition areas as well as all types of residential interior spaces. Architects' own houses often showcase their ideas or are experiments. Jencks explores themes and symbolism in his Thematic House in London, where each room is inspired by a different historical style or particular season.

▲ **57-9.** Vanna Venturi House, 1964; Philadelphia, Chestnut Hill, Pennsylvania; Robert Venturi.

■ *Memphis Design*. The avant-garde Italian group Memphis is launched in Italy in 1981 by Ettore Sottsass (Fig. 57-10, 57-14, 57-21) during the Milan Furniture Fair. Its roots are in the 1970s in the work of Sottsass and others, along with Studio Alchimia in Milan. Memphis takes its name from the Bob Dylan song "Stuck Outside of Mobile with the Memphis Blues." It also alludes to the capital of ancient Egypt and the home of Elvis Presley in a contrast

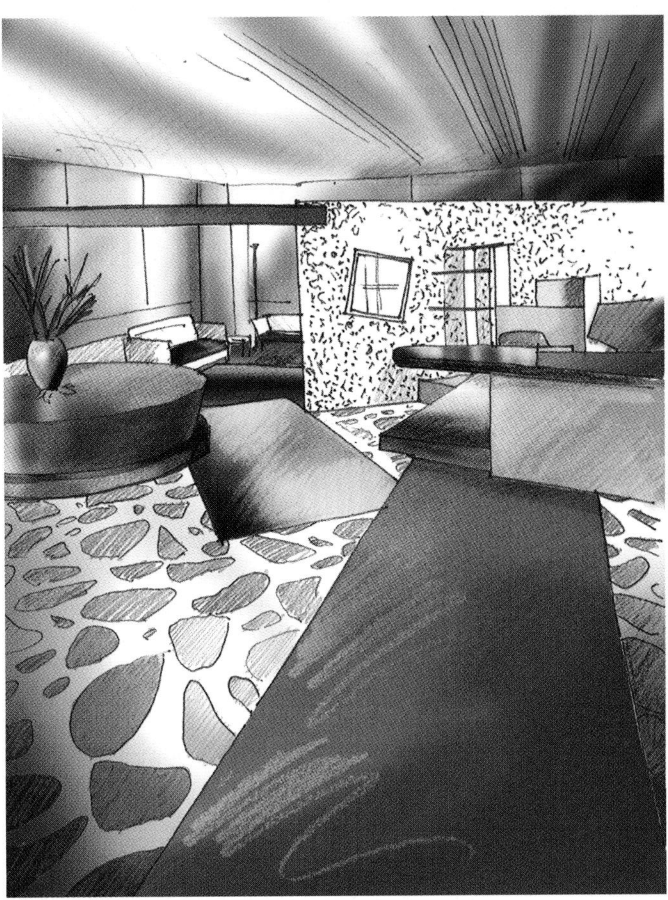

▲ **57-10.** Reception, Esprit showroom, c. 1970s–1980s; Europe; Ettore Sottsass, Memphis.

▲ **57-11.** Sunar Furniture Showroom, 1979–1981; Houston, Texas; Michael Graves.

of high and low, elite and popular culture design. Important Memphis designers include Michele de Lucchi (Fig. 57-16), Nathalie du Pasquier, Marco Zanini, Peter Shire (Fig. 57-17), Javier Mariscal, Matteo Thun, and Andrea Branzi. Their work collectively incorporates fanciful, playful, unexpected designs for interiors and furniture inspired by suburban pop, Asian and Middle Eastern traditions, and the Arts and Crafts Movement. While highly individualistic and quirky, most work is generally unified. Designs favor discontinuity among parts, a new creative expression, use of decoration and color, and the relationship between people and things.

Public and Private Buildings

■ *Color.* Interiors repeat the exterior palette of dusty pink, mauve, terra-cotta, pale yellow, blue, aqua, celadon, and white. Individual colors are usually light and include a combination of earthy tones mixed with pastel ones (Fig. 57-11, 57-12). Sometimes bold colors, including the primaries, are used. Memphis uses pastels and various shades of brighter colors that include yellow-gold, red-orange, blue, and green (Fig. 57-10). Gray, black, and white often become accents to enhance the character of a space.

■ *Floors.* Both commercial and residential interiors reveal substantial changes in the design of floors and in the variety of materials used (Fig. 57-10, 57-11, 57-12). Common flooring materials include ceramic tile, marble, stone, brick, wood, vinyl, and carpet. Architects sometimes design custom wall-to-wall

DESIGN SPOTLIGHT

Interior: Michael Graves's Swan Hotel reflects Walt Disney's emphasis upon architecture as a visual metaphor for American themes, dreams, and myths as well as imagination and entertainment. Using Florida colors of turquoise and coral, with repetition, stylization, and whimsy, Graves creates a themed architecture, inside and out, that communicates Disney's ideals to visitors and supports the theme park experience. His sophisticated, unliteral concept combines Florida beaches and resorts with Disney fun and delight. Looking back to the Baroque, Graves chooses Swans as the main characters instead of Disney cartoon figures or movie motifs. The architecture merges painted stylized triangles and rectangles embellished with square windows on a grid with theatrical and three-dimensional, overscaled cabanas, fish, swans, banana leaves, and fountains. There is constant contrast between sophistication and whimsy, symmetry and asymmetry, and line and form. The Swan lobby is a play on a Victorian conservatory but with giant, stylized banana leaves and a striped ceiling that repeats the cabana theme. Graves also designs carpets, furniture, light fixtures, and tableware to complete the concept for the hotel.

▶ **57-12.** Lobby, the Swan Hotel, 1990; Disney World at Epcot Center, Lake Buena Vista, Florida; Michael Graves.

DESIGN SPOTLIGHT

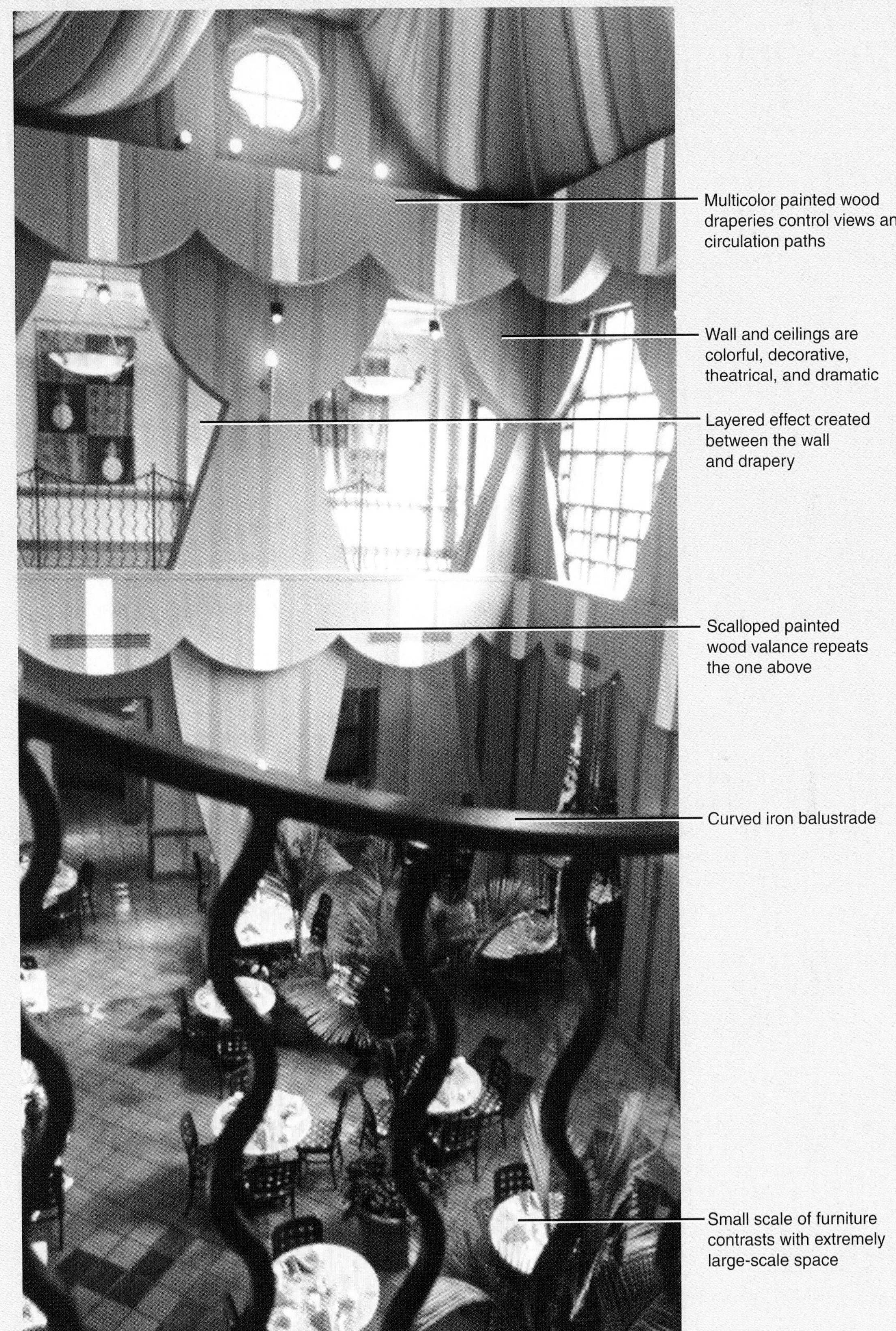
Multicolor painted wood draperies control views and circulation paths
Wall and ceilings are colorful, decorative, theatrical, and dramatic
Layered effect created between the wall and drapery
Scalloped painted wood valance repeats the one above
Curved iron balustrade
Small scale of furniture contrasts with extremely large-scale space

carpets or rugs. Designs may be stylized flowers, architectural elements such as columns and capitals, asymmetrical designs, geometric shapes, blocks of color, or interior elements such as pediments. Memphis carpets have bold colors and patterns that are geometric or abstract and often directional.

■ *Walls*. Walls, especially in Memphis interiors, are plain and white, off-white, or pastels when they serve as backdrops for furnishings and decorative arts objects (Fig. 57-10, 57-11). Blocks of color define or separate walls, architectural features, projections, niches, layering, or progression. Alternative treatments include wood paneling; sometimes rustic, textural contrasts; or decorative murals. Venetian plaster with its multilayered effect also becomes popular. Some designers use architectural delineations that reflect classicism and the tripartite order system of base, shaft, and cornice. Colorful columns, cornice, and trim complement walls that are either plain, have a solid–void square design, or display a decorative mural (Fig. 57-12). Some designers, such as Moore and Graves, like to emphasize vistas, so unique focal points (architectural or painted) often appear on walls at the end of passageways.

■ *Windows*. Arched or rectangular windows support the Post Modern emphasis upon complexity and whimsy (Fig. 57-12). Occasionally, they are surrounded by architectural details, but most have moldings. Window treatments, which are less important than architectural details, especially in commercial interiors, are simple panels, either plain or in colors that support or complement the space.

■ *Ceilings*. Ceilings may be plainly treated; decorated with paintings; or coffers, compartments, layers, or coves (Fig 57-10, 57-11, 57-12). High-style spaces, such as office lobbies, showrooms, hotels, and houses, often have the most dramatic treatments with prominent recessed or concealed lighting, stepped or layered elements, or bold angles.

■ *Textiles and Plastic Laminates*. Memphis textiles (also used for upholstery) and plastic laminates exhibit a funky character, dense patterns, and vibrant colors (Fig. 57-10, 57-13). The palettes and patterns come from video games, television, ethnic textiles, new-wave graphics, and pop culture, and create a lot of energy and tension in the compositions. Patterns are often abstract shapes that look like microbes, zigzags, dots, inkspots, or electronic wavelengths. Each pattern is unique and distinctive. Fabrics, which become immensely popular, include cottons, wools, and synthetics.

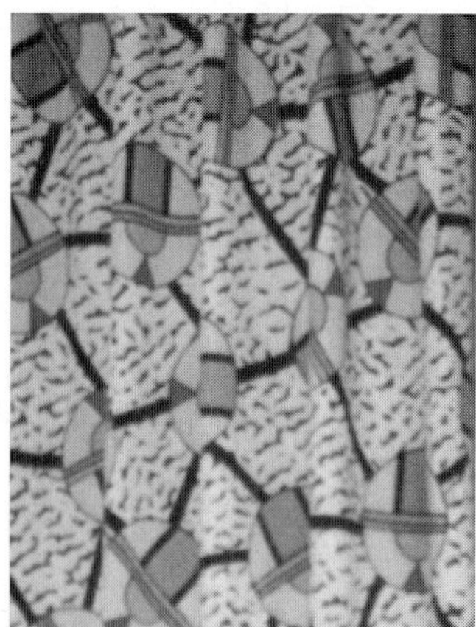

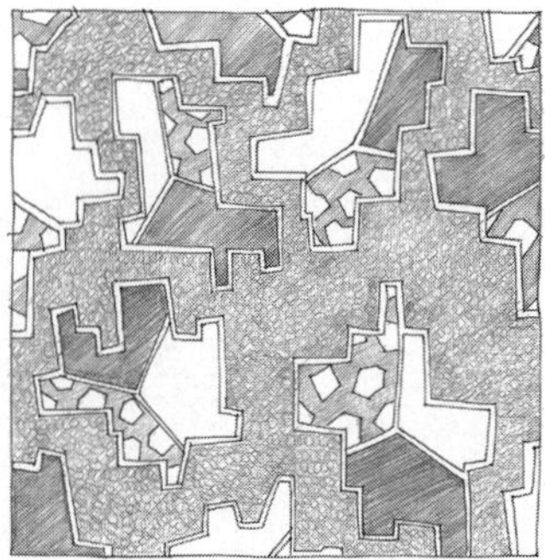

▲ **57-13.** Textiles: Fabrics, c. 1980s; Milan, Italy; Studio Alchimia/Memphis.

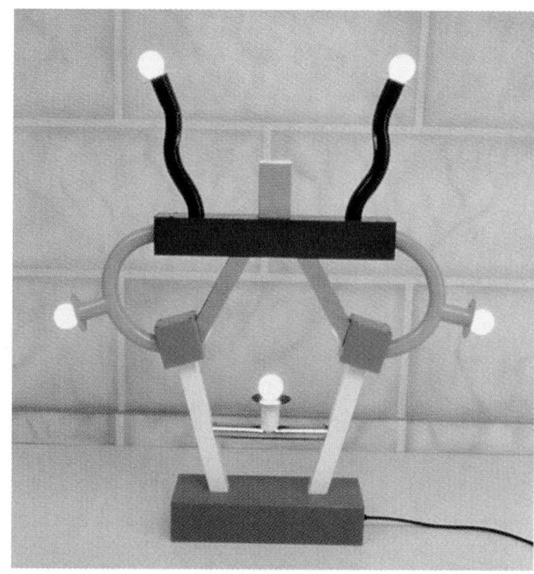

▲ **57-14.** Lighting: Ashoka lamp, 1981; Italy; Ettore Sottsass, Memphis.

■ *Lighting*. Interior lighting incorporates direct and indirect incandescent, fluorescent, neon, and/or halogen lamps. Lighting is often dramatic and highlights architectural elements and interior forms. Graves, for example, often uses indirect lighting hidden in coves, cornices, and brackets (Fig 57-11). Architects design custom light fixtures and applications for specific interiors so that table and floor lamps, sconces, chandeliers, pendant lights, and surface-mounted ceiling fixtures complement the interior in forms, materials, and design. Lighting may be in wood, ceramic, or metal with large, simple round globes. Some look like miniature buildings and feature classical motifs. Memphis designers specialize in table and floor lamps in unique, whimsical, or humorous designs. Usually created in bright, bold colors mixed with black and white, they stand out as art objects in an interior (Fig. 57-14).

FURNISHINGS AND DECORATIVE ARTS

Post Modern architecture inspires Post Modern furniture as designers reject the spare International Style in favor of historicism, color, pattern, and ornament. Reacting to the anonymous machine aesthetic of the Bauhaus and International Style and responding to late-19th-century ideas, designers create furniture as art, which appears as unique objects placed or scattered about an interior, instead of designing for mass production. They want their works to last instead of succumbing to the notion of planned obsolescence exemplified by Pop furniture. No new types of furniture are introduced, but existing ones are redesigned in unusual or odd

▲ **57-15.** Capitello (foam capital chair), 1971; Studio 65, manufactured in Italy.

ways or with traditional forms and motifs. Sometimes individual pieces are blended hybrids serving double functions. Individual furniture pieces are unique and unusual, with no common characteristics other than exhibiting the creativity of the designer.

Post Modernists believe that style is paramount to function, so they select and adapt elements from all past styles but favor classicism, Neoclassicism, Biedermeier, and Art Deco. Other influences include Pop Art, surrealism, and kitsch. Post Modern furniture often playfully reinterprets the forms and motifs of the past using unusual or unexpected materials, exuberant color, and abundant ornament (Fig. 57-15, 57-18). Traditionalism is especially strong among American and British designers, whereas Europeans and the Japanese favor a more futurist approach.

■ *Memphis.* Memphis furniture intentionally mocks Modernism and challenges ideals of traditional decorating, such as a Memphis living room filled with furniture that opposes the notion of status, wealth, and formality. Although often made of inexpensive materials, Memphis furniture is not inexpensive. Furniture has defined planes with large blocks of color or pattern, straight and curved lines, and an asymmetrical emphasis (Fig. 57-16, 57-17, 57-19, 57-20, 57-21). Pieces combine broad areas of color and decoration in geometric shapes, cubes, cones, pyramids, and/or spheres. Contrasts of materials are a key feature and evident in combinations of luxurious materials with inexpensive ones, such as costly wood used with plastic laminate. Structure integrates with decoration and/or color and defines and identifies volume. Memphis designers create patterns that are abstract, repeating, and nondirectional and are often presented as plastic laminates. Color and pattern are defining elements. Bright primaries, pastels, neutrals, black, and white may be combined in a single piece, and each part may be a different color and/or pattern. Examples may look odd because they challenge common or traditional notions of comfort and function. They require people to question how they interact with furniture in an interior and, in essence, question their living patterns.

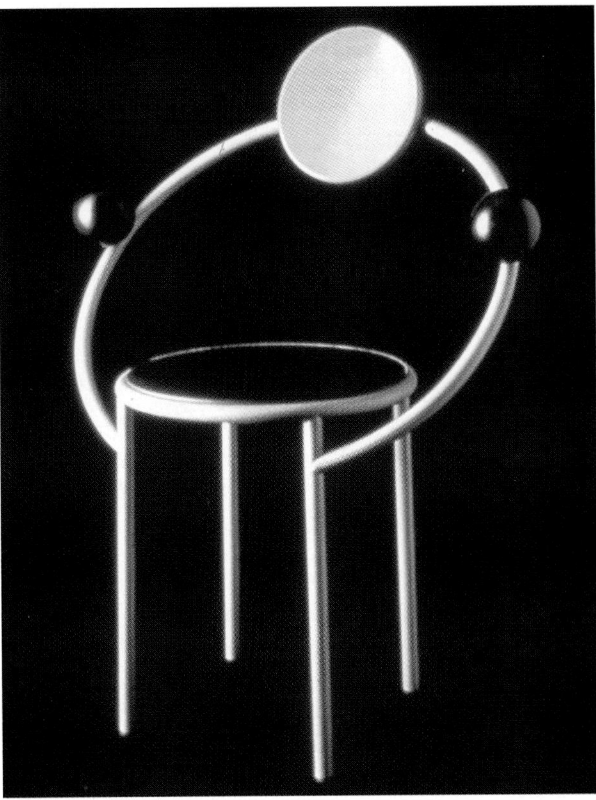

▲ **57-16.** First chair, 1983; Italy; Michele De Lucchi, manufactured by Memphis Milano.

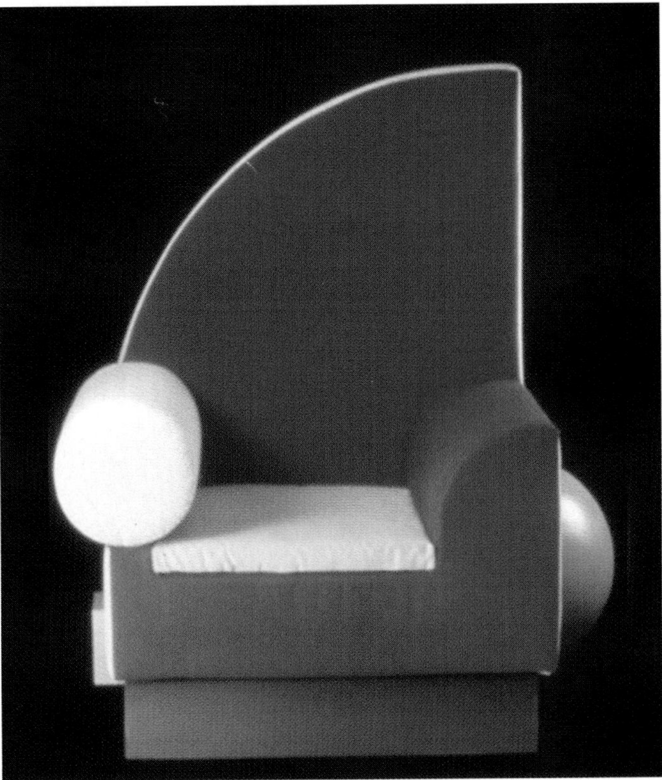

▲ **57-17.** Bel Air armchair, 1982; Italy; Peter Shire, manufactured by Memphis Milano.

Public and Private Buildings

■ *Materials*. Materials include wood (plain, painted, and lacquered), aluminum, steel, plastic laminate, marble, glass, and mirrors (Fig. 57-15, 57-16, 57-17, 57-18, 57-19, 57-20, 57-21). The important innovations of Post Modern and Memphis are the widespread use of plain and decorated plastic laminate and industrial materials, such as sheet metals, industrial paint, neon lighting, colored lights, and decorated glass. Designers especially like materials that imitate other materials. In its use of common materials in high-style designer furniture, Memphis challenges the notion that a particular material conveys a symbolic meaning about living in the world.

■ *Seating*. Seating pieces have wide diversity and uniqueness in design (Fig. 57-16, 57-17, 57-18, 57-19). Designers experiment greatly with form and shape, solid and void relationships, color, character, decoration, and materials. A pseudoperiod vocabulary defines work by Graves, Venturi, and others. Graves often uses expensive veneers and painted finishes. Venturi whimsically interprets historical symbolism in his series of chairs for Knoll International produced in molded plywood covered in laminate or painted, and lacquered (Fig. 57-18). Memphis designers incorporate simpler lines and forms with bright color. Sofas and many chairs are composed of broad planes or geometric volumes of different colors or patterns. Some have wood or laminate trim.

DESIGN SPOTLIGHT

Furniture: As evident in the Kandissi sofa, Memphis designers challenge the intellectual content they see lacking in modern mass-produced objects. Striving to create a new symbolic design language, Mendini redesigns classic pieces such as Breuer's Wassily chair. Here, he attempts to overcome the banality of the traditional sofa by reforming it with innovative colors, patterns, and forms. The Kandissi sofa has lacquered wood in angular forms and a boldly patterned upholstered seat and back.

► **57-19.** Kandissi sofa, 1978; Italy; Alessandro Mendini, from Studio Alchimia/Memphis Milano.

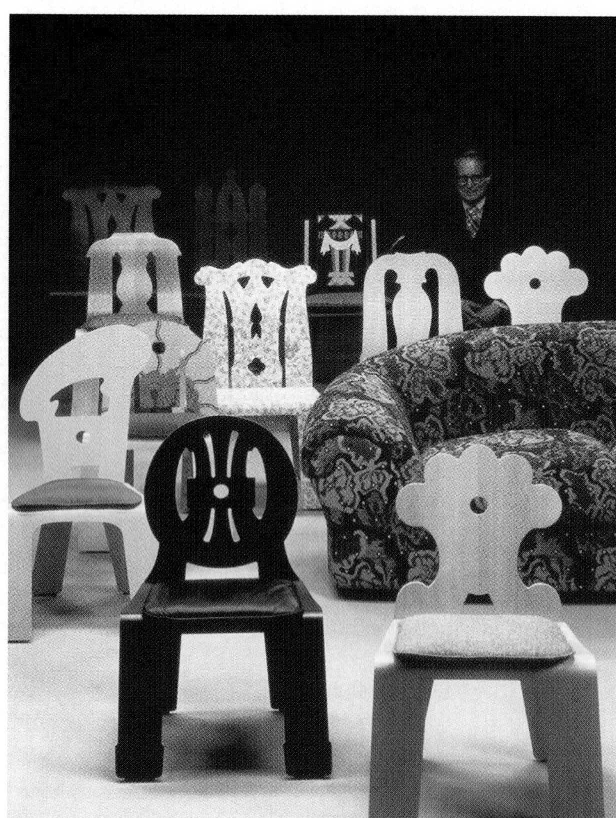

▲ **57-18.** Queen Anne, Sheraton, Art Deco, and other side chairs, 1984; United States; Robert Venturi, manufactured by Knoll International.

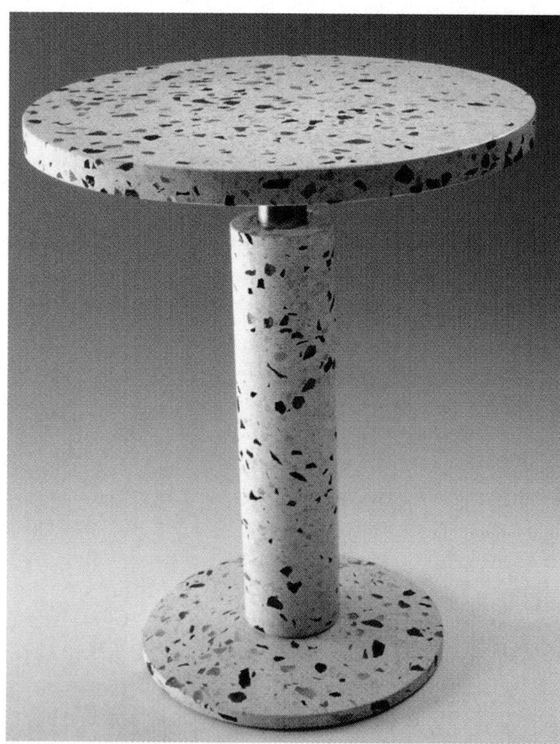

▲ **57-20.** Kyoto end table, c. 1980s; Shiro Kuramata, manufactured by Memphis Milano.

DESIGN SPOTLIGHT

Irregular shapes

Simple flat planes define composition

Bold patterned upholstery

Base has lacquered wood with angled forms

▲ **57-19.** Continued

■ *Tables*. Tables show a wide variety of forms for common uses, such as tea carts or consoles. Some have period features, and others are decidedly simple with no references to the past. Tops, plain or patterned, may be square, rectangular, round, oval, or a fragmented shape with edges that are straight, curved, angled, or broken. Legs are straight, curved, tubular, round and tapered, boxy, and angled (Fig. 57-20). Some Memphis tables look heavy and monumental, while others are light and playful.

■ *Storage*. Memphis storage displays a mixture of bright colors, unusual patterns, and funky materials. The form may follow a conventional model or it may be something distinctively new in concept. Angles, curves, straight lines, and boxy shapes, sometimes all combined, are common. Examples are often humorous or look like a stage-set. Some pieces are designed to be multifunctional, such as the Carlton shelving unit (Fig. 57-21) by Sottsass, which serves as both a room divider and bookshelf.

■ *Beds*. There are only a few new bed designs. The most well known one is the Stanhope by Graves. Because it is expensive, with few in production, it is considered a collector's item. A few Memphis designers create beds composed of geometric planes and solids in contrasting colors.

■ *Decorative Arts*. Post Modern architects including Venturi, Moore, Tigerman, Graves, and Jencks design decorative accessories such as clocks and tea services (Fig. 57-22). Some also design

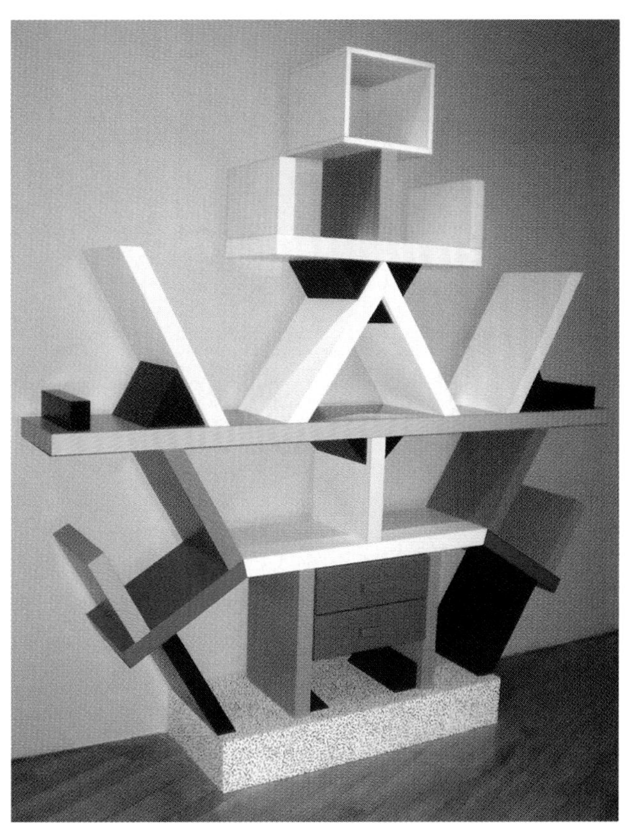

▲ **57-21.** Carlton shelving unit, 1981; Italy; Ettore Sottsass, manufactured by Memphis Milano.

▲ **57-22.** Decorative Arts: Tea kettle; Michael Graves, manufactured by Alessi, and glass vase; Italy; Ettore Sottsass, both c. 1970s–1990s.

flatware, china, and even jewelry. These objects in wood, metal, ceramic, and plastic often have a distinct and recognizable image created by the individual designer. Similar in concept to architecture and featuring an additive approach, forms sometimes resemble small buildings or building types. Classical details are common. In the 1990s, Graves begins to market designs through Target, a discount department store with a progressive design outlook. Memphis designers produce highly unusual clocks, vases, glassware, and accessory items in bright colors and/or shiny metals. They are designed to fit in a Post Modern interior furnished in Memphis and other furniture.

CHAPTER 58

Late Modern • 2

Mid-1980s–2000s

> *Foster + Partners' architecture is driven by the pursuit of quality—a belief that our surroundings directly influence the quality of our lives, whether in the work place, at home or the public spaces in between. It is not just buildings but urban design that affects our well-being. We are concerned with the physical context of a project, sensitive to the culture and climate of their place. . . . The quest for quality embraces the physical performance of buildings.*
>
> —Norman Foster and Partners, firm Web site, 2007

No single look dominates Late Modern • 2, a period that continues the language of Geometric Modern and Late Modern • 1. During this time, design plurality becomes even more common. Designers experiment with form, shape, construction methods, and new materials to express the information age, consumerism, and global economy of their time. Architectural, interior, and furniture forms become even more complex as designers now have the technology and other means to create what they can imagine.

HISTORICAL AND SOCIAL

The 1980s are marked by conservatism and economic prosperity as inflation and unemployment of the 1970s decrease. The Cold War ends as Communism weakens, and the Soviet Union dissolves. In 1989, the Berlin Wall tumbles, uniting East and West Germany once more. However, wars in Latin America and the Middle East and increasing terrorism by radical groups threaten peace across much of the world. During the 1990s, prosperity continues as the global economy expands. Some businesses are forced to make major changes in number of employees, locations, and product lines to compete in world markets. Blue-collar jobs decline as those in the service sector increase. People become more and more dependent upon technology in daily life. A new youth culture is greatly influenced by the media and new technologies, such as cell phones, music videos, and computer games. Increasing violence and vulgarization define popular culture.

The 1980s begin a worldwide shift from an industrial to a postindustrial or information age. This means that technology and information expand, and economies rely more on the service sectors, including managers and technicians, instead of manufacturing. As a result, knowledge, ideas, imagination, and creativity become the raw materials of production instead of steel and iron. This trend also is tied to the development of the personal computer and other personal technologies and an increasingly global economy. There is also a greater disparity between the have and have-not nations. For instance, subsistence countries, primarily in Africa and East Asia, are often in conflict with the developed countries of North America and Europe.

With the miniaturization of room-size computers to desk size and laptops and the introduction of the Internet and cell phones in the 1990s, business is more easily conducted and worldwide connections and communications are nearly instantaneous. Businesses link or partner with each other, or they expand or move their operations overseas to reduce labor costs. Foreigners invest more heavily in the economy of the United States, and vice versa. Countries across the globe enter into trade agreements, such as the Asia Pacific Economic Cooperation Agreement, to ensure the best trade policies are created. As the end of the 20th century

▲ 58-1. State of Illinois Center (now James R. Thompson Center), 1980–1985; Chicago, Illinois; Helmut Jahn.

approaches, fear of the end and the negative influences and failures of technology plague humankind. As the 21st century begins, the world is made up of highly industrial and technological societies with high rates of literacy and standards of living. In contrast, there are many underdeveloped nations with low literacy rates and standards of living and high rates of disease.

CONCEPTS

During the period, architects and designers continue to explore what it means to be modern in the context of the postindustrial age. As in the 1960s, they experiment with various approaches, methods, and means to achieve their individual or collective visions of the information age, new technologies, and the global economy. As before, no single country, movement, style, or look dominates. Alternative expressions are more acceptable than ever before in the history of design. Previously designers' ideas were often ahead of technology, but now new materials, construction techniques, and design tools enable them to construct whatever they imagine. During the 1980s and 1990s, digital technology for design and manufacturing become significant supporting tools that allow imaginations to soar beyond efficiency and standardization.

Typologies, monumentality, and image are important topics for discussion and debate as designers explore how to express power, authority, respectability, and responsibility in an international context. Nevertheless, the individuality of designer and/or client continues to drive concepts, and image and branding are even more important to distinguish one community, corporation, retail outlet, or person from another. Architects and designers find that their work must respond to increased limitations resulting from building codes, concepts of universal design, and environmental considerations. Additionally, research and development provide rules or guidelines for designs for various populations, individuals with special needs, or simply the so-called average human being. More than ever before, architects and designers create and/or lend their names to recognizable buildings and products for consumers.

DESIGN SPOTLIGHT

Architecture and Interior: Designed by Richard Rogers and Partners in a High Tech image similar to the Pompidou Centre in Paris, the Lloyd's building is unusual because insurance companies favor more conservative designs. Rogers places service areas in six towers on the perimeter of the building, which allows the building to fit into the area's medieval streets and gives it a more expressive form. Often concealed, the clearly delineated service areas become part of the design vocabulary and building's image. Covered in stainless steel and glass, the structure rises 14 stories on the north and 7 stories on the south side. The windows refract artificial light, reducing lighting requirements at night. A large glass-covered barrel vault in the center is reminiscent of the Crystal Palace of 1851. The vault covers the full-height atrium on which the building's interiors center. With service areas on the exterior, the interior space is completely open for maximum flexibility to support the major circulation core. Repeating the exterior architectural features, this multileveled open area is surrounded by numerous workstations on all levels. It clearly illustrates the Late Modern • 2 emphasis on function, industrial technology, repetition of modular elements, solid and void relationships, spatial layering, and construction and structure as ornament.

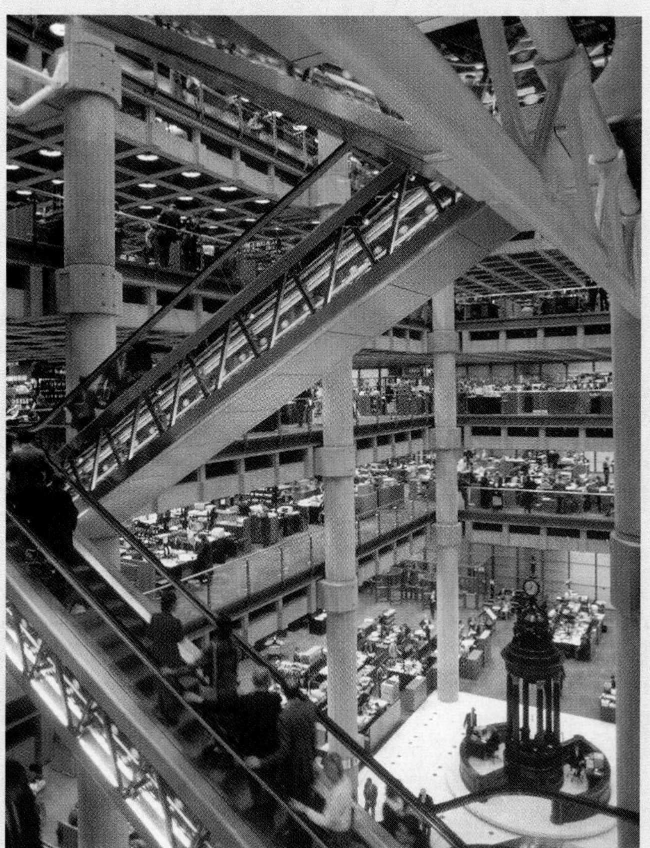

▲ 58-2. Lloyd's building and interior, 1978–1986; London, England; Richard Rogers and Partners.

DESIGN SPOTLIGHT

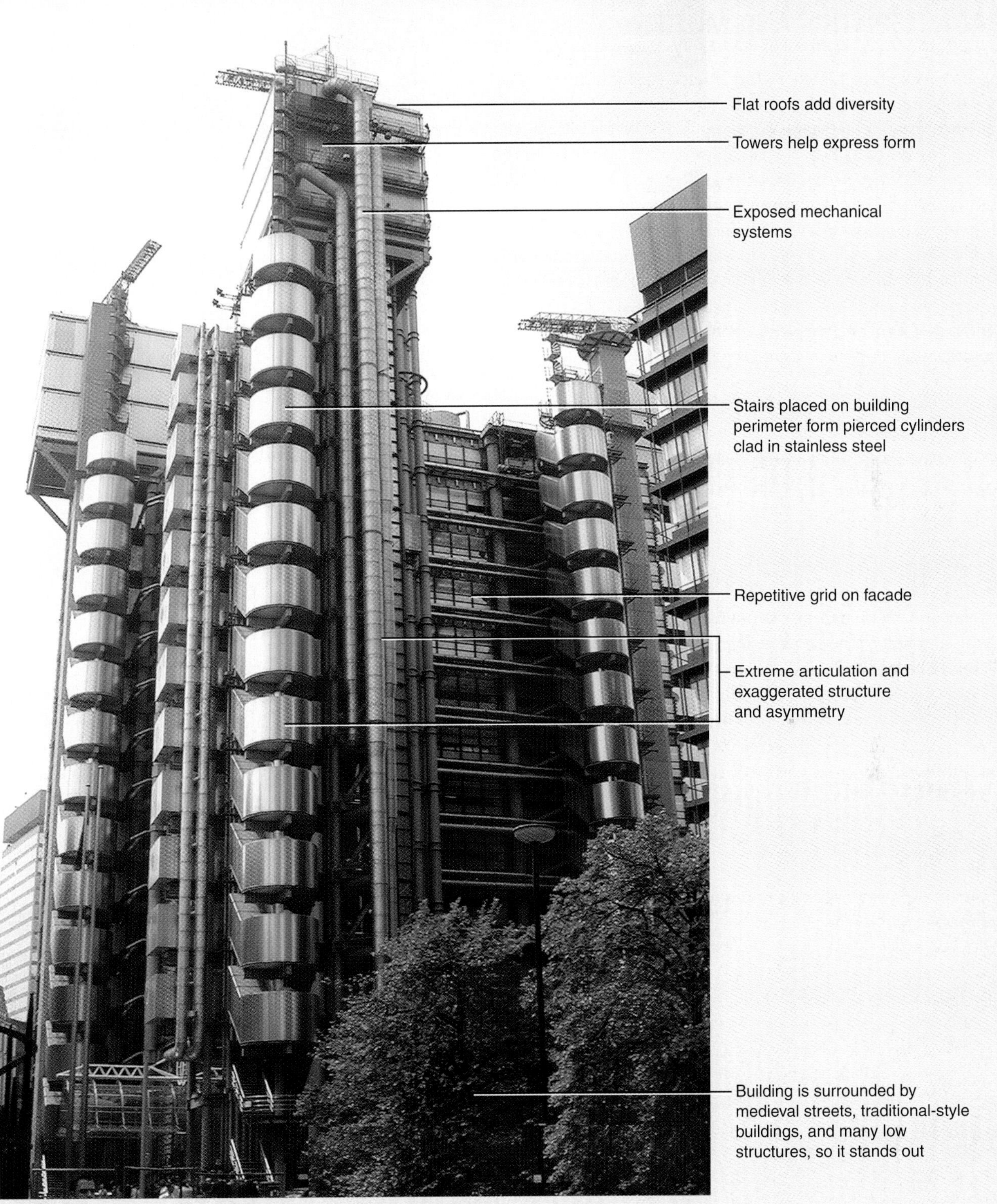
Flat roofs add diversity
Towers help express form
Exposed mechanical systems
Stairs placed on building perimeter form pierced cylinders clad in stainless steel
Repetitive grid on facade
Extreme articulation and exaggerated structure and asymmetry
Building is surrounded by medieval streets, traditional-style buildings, and many low structures, so it stands out

▲ **58-2.** Continued

As a result, architecture, interior design, and furnishings become important aspects of cultural consciousness and global markets.

CHARACTERISTICS AND MOTIFS

As in Late Modern • 1, architecture, interiors, and furniture have varied appearances as designers continue exploring earlier developments and adopt an even more expanded design language. Designers continue to explore, expand, or reinvent principles of the International Style, particularly the grid system. New materials, techniques, and technologies (especially the computer) combine with existing ones, such as prefabrication, to fuel innovation and individualism. As before, expressions may exaggerate characteristics of Modernism such as illustration of joints or structure, geometry, grids or modules, or building as machine. Because of new technologies, form and shape are even more important than they were previously. Form may curve, ripple, layer, or retain the grid, sometimes even in a single composition. Thus, breaking the box is even more common than it was before. Designs are often antihistorical with no visible ties to the past, particularly in reinventions or varied expressions of typologies.

■ *High Tech*. As before, High Tech compositions display extreme and complex technology and the concept of building as machine, and they highlight function and service areas. Lightness and transparency are even more important. Designers push the limits of forms and materials. Interiors become larger and more open.

■ *Minimalism*. Minimalism continues its clean forms, but with extreme simplicity, repetition, articulation, and greater flexibility and emphasis upon form and shape.

■ *Expressionism*. Some designers adopt the Expressionism of the early 20th century in an attempt to depict the spiritual instead of functional or programmatic aspects of design. Expressionism adopts a variety of forms, and most designs are conceived of as sculpture so they are individual and customized.

▲ **58-4.** *Pyramide du Louvre*, Louvre Museum, 1984–1989; Paris, France; I. M. Pei.

■ *Motifs*. There are no specific motifs common to the period. Individual designers use details from projects to emphasize innovative structure, construction, and materials.

ARCHITECTURE

Late Modern • 2 architecture continues the geometry and modularity established in Geometric Modern and Late Modern • 1, which ties them together as sequential developments. In this period, however, the modularity is pushed to an extreme through experimentation with form and structure. Buildings undulate, move, and soar beyond earlier boundaries. This is possible because of enhancements in technology and improvements in engineering

▲ **58-3.** *Institut du Monde Arab*, 1984–1987; Paris, France; Jean Nouvel.

▲ **58-5.** San Francisco Museum of Modern Art, 1989–1995; San Francisco, California; Mario Botta.

and materials that allow architects to achieve new construction innovations. As a result, exposed structure becomes even more common.

On some buildings, modules, grids, and skeletons continue to define the structure, but designs, as a group, are more complicated, more unusual, and more individualistic than earlier. Buildings continue to exhibit a high-tech image, slick skin, extreme repetition, visual layering, and dynamic abstraction (Fig. 58-1, 58-2, 58-8, 58-9, 58-10, 58-11). New features emerge that alter the overall character and imagery. Most notably, architects test complexity through the separation of unusual contiguous parts and through large spaces that demand attention. For example, the building surface and exposed structure may play against one another to create interest and tension (Fig. 58-2, 58-4). Alternatively, mass may be hollowed out to create transitional or negative space within the building form to establish a unique relationship between solid façade and recessed glass openings (Fig. 58-6, 58-7, 58-12). Or two towers may play against each other with negative space between, or the entry area may be unique compared to other parts of the building (Fig. 58-9).

The introduction of digital designing and computer manufacturing tools gives architects more freedom of expression. Standardization is no longer necessary to maintain efficiency, function, and costs. Computerization within the construction industry allows more complex parts to be fabricated more easily. Architects also take advantage of new materials, methods of structural analysis, and environmental control systems to advance new concepts and forms. Freed from restrictions and aided by technology, they can test a design language in a show of creativity that foreshadows Neo-Modern.

Architects also explore new ways to express older themes or associations such as monumentality, civic pride, corporate image, authority, and responsibility. High Tech civic buildings stress lightness and openness, qualities regarded as important in democracies and liberal societies. Becoming more prominent is the mega structure, a new version of the skyscraper seen in expanding markets in the Near East, Asia, and the Pacific. As a new form for commercial buildings, these extremely tall buildings with multiple angles, forms, and towers become symbols of the global economy, power, and authority.

Recognition of mega structures and other buildings is based on the creation of unusual forms and designs, often as shown in façades and roofs. This gives rise to buildings as sculptural entities with little separation between façade and roof (Fig. 58-1, 58-4, 58-8, 58-9, 58-11), a trend that will become more pronounced later in Neo-Modern. In the new global community

▲ **58-6.** Neurosciences Institute, 1995; La Jolla, California; Tod Williams and Billie Tsien.

▲ **58-7.** Getty Museum, 1985–1997; Los Angeles, California; Richard Meier.

with instantaneous communications, design teams of architects, contractors, interior designers, engineers, and project managers from different countries work together on architectural projects. Many firms have multiple offices around the globe.

The most common building types are office buildings (Fig. 58-1, 58-2, 58-8, 58-9), museums (Fig. 58-4, 58-5, 58-7, 58-10), airport and train terminals (Fig. 58-13), and churches. These types contextualize globalization and explore new means of expressing image and monumentality. A few larger residential buildings gain recognition, mainly those that explore theories and themes of form, technology, materials, and color. As earlier, residences often are personal expressions of the architect or client (Fig. 58-12).

Public and Private Buildings

■ *Site Orientation*. Image and recognition drive site orientation, and commercial structures often seek to dominate a skyline or busy highway. Most commercial office buildings and banks are very near the heart of a city. Many stand out because of their height, design, and lack of relationship to surrounding structures (Fig. 58-1, 58-2, 58-4, 58-5, 58-8, 58-9, 58-10, 58-11). Museums frequently are in landscaped parklike settings in urban areas and are often the central focus of their environments. Airport terminals are located on the outskirts of a city center on major thoroughfares in the hub of transportation areas.

DESIGN SPOTLIGHT

Architecture: Located in a busy section of London along the Thames River with open space around it, the London City Hall stands out in its environment due to its distinctive form and shape, and its lack of relationship to surrounding structures. Norman Foster gives the building an asymmetrical shape to reduce the surface for energy conservation. Curved on one side with windows in a grid pattern and layered on the other, the building's glass skin gives maximum transparency and openness suitable for a city's governing body. Each glass pane has a unique shape, which was cut by lasers. In the center of the spherical façade on the river side, the rectangular grid breaks into a pattern of glass triangles that accents the main entry from top to bottom and enhances the graduated and stepped form. Inside, a spiral ramp rises the full height of the building to a viewing gallery on the top floor.

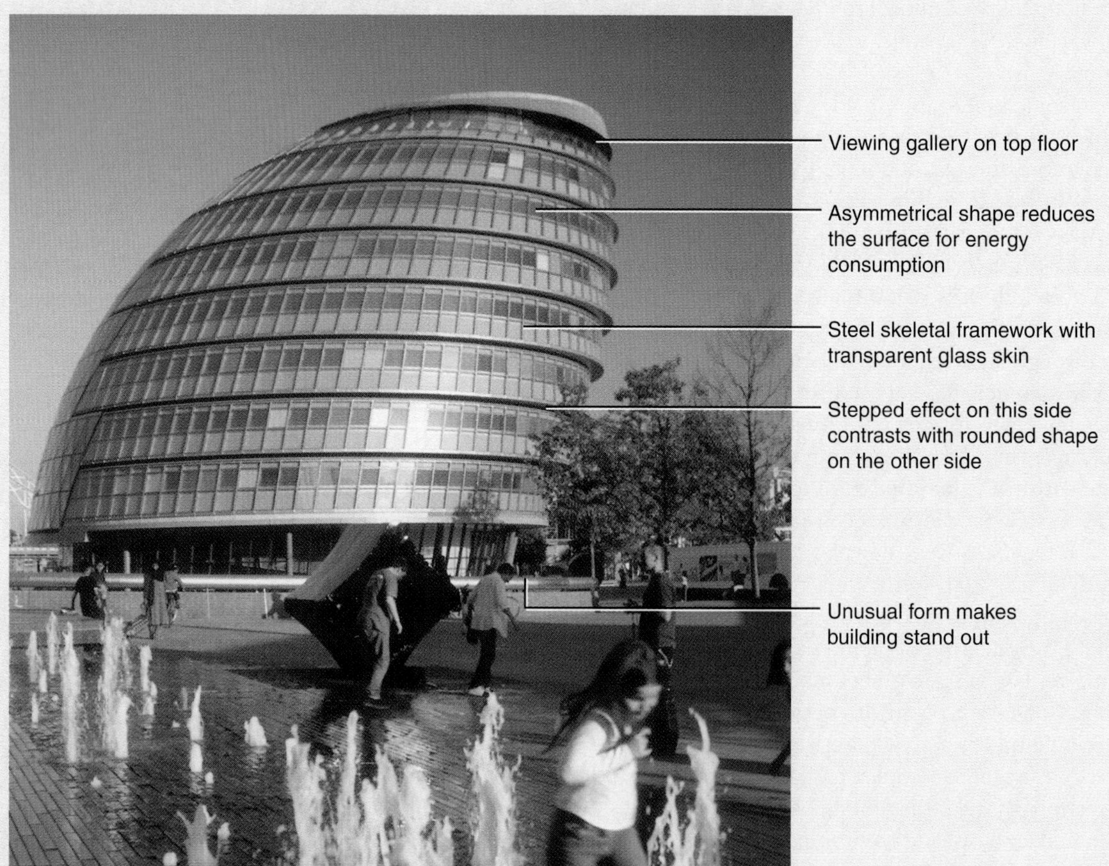

▲ **58-8.** London City Hall, 1998–2002; London, England; Sir Norman Foster.

▲ **58-9.** Swiss Re Tower (30 S. Mary Axe), 1997–2004; London, England; Sir Norman Foster.

■ *Floor Plans*. Building plans follow Late Modern • 1 examples. Designs are aesthetically diverse and innovative with no set pattern for development or layout. Asymmetry in plan arrangement, variety in shape, and a three-dimensional experimentation with form is characteristic and important. Architects continue to play with interpenetrating geometries, complexity in scale and space, and solid and void relationships, but they carry the concepts to an extreme to reflect a three-dimensional relationship to the building envelope. Unusual contiguous parts or areas often are separated to create complexity, which is a dominant design feature. As before, plans exhibit variety with straight edges and sides that may be angled, curved, or indented. The plan and interior circulation may be formally or informally organized horizontally and vertically to establish spatial zones, functional areas, visual layering, and unique design features (Fig. 58-16).

New construction methods and environmental systems liberate architects from previous practices. For example, service cores no longer need to be in the center of a building. They can now be on the exterior, the perimeter, corners, or any other location appropriate to the concept. Centrally located circulation cores continue, but with even more variety and innovation in their designs than earlier. Experimentation with space planning continues with more overlap of functional areas and more multifunctional spaces. Interior spaces no longer require structural supports at regular intervals, which frees interior planning from grids and modules, thus permitting new and innovative interior configurations. As a result, interior architectural forms frequently define and divide space to create unique environments (Fig. 58-14, 58-19, 58-20). For example, some commercial spaces have large, multileveled, open atriums or light-filled corridors defined by exposed structural features that repeat from outside to inside (Fig. 58-2).

▲ **58-10.** Museum of Modern Art, 2004; Ft. Worth, Texas; Tadao Ando.

▲ **58-11.** Apple Store, 2006; New York City, New York; Bohlin, Cywinski, Jackson.

Often open stairways, elevators, walkways, and balconies are inserted in these spaces at various levels and angles, reinforcing their importance as major circulation paths.

■ *Materials*. Steel; reinforced and precast concrete; aluminum; and tinted and plain, clear glass continue to be the dominant construction materials (Fig. 58-1, 58-2, 58-3, 58-4, 58-5, 58-6, 58-7, 58-8, 58-9, 58-10, 58-11). Many are prefabricated with modular components. Reinforced concrete begins to replace steel for structures. Other surfacing materials include stone, brick, and tile. Stainless steel becomes the new marble or stone. New to the period is the use of fabric for walls and/or roofs. Pioneered in the late 1950s, fabrics coated with Teflon or PVC for weatherproofing are lightweight, low-cost alternative materials for roofs and walls. Sometimes architects become well known for their repetitive use of certain materials, such as Tadao Ando (Fig. 58-10), who commonly uses gray concrete and glass. The relationship between materials and exposed building structure continues to be important.

■ *Façades*. Individuality, experimentation, extreme articulation, and exaggerated structure characterize building façades. Because of their shapes and unusual design features, they are even more distinctive than Late Modern • 1 examples. Sides may be angled, curved, or indented with either solid or glass walls. Some buildings exhibit an element of lightness through a stretched outer skin of flat, curved, and/or angled glass or sometimes an asymmetrical building shape (Fig. 58-1, 58-3, 58-4, 58-8, 58-11), while others emphasize more modularity through the interplay of concrete and glass walls (Fig. 58-6, 58-7). In some buildings, the grid is apparent, but it is handled in new, unusual ways. Exposed building structure with an expression of joints and construction (Fig. 58-2, 58-10) is common in all examples and more pronounced than earlier.

Architects continue to emphasize solid and void relationships on the surface of the façade as well as on the attached layered structural parts. The parts undulate and move in either a vertical or horizontal rhythm, which often announces or defines the building's visual image. Sometimes, a shape or repetition of shapes may dominate and define the entire façade or an entry area (Fig. 58-7, 58-12). Other examples exhibit the integration of façade with roof so that the building becomes more like a sculptural object with less separation between façade and roofline or front and back (Fig. 58-4, 58-8, 58-9).

■ *Windows*. Following the earlier modernist language, windows on commercial buildings are usually fixed in grid patterns to control air-conditioning and heating systems (Fig. 58-1). However, new methods of environmental controls allow windows to be opened instead of being hermetically sealed as before (Fig. 58-9). Many are tinted to reduce solar heat gain and loss. As before, windows usually have narrow metal moldings and mullions that frame the openings and divide glass areas (Fig. 58-7, 58-8, 58-12). Sometimes they are black or bronze to accent the grid effect. Flat glass is common, but there is more use of curved glass to relate to the building form.

■ *Doors*. Most entries blend into the design of the building, but some may be accented through a unique architectural feature, unusual scale, or distinctive placement (Fig. 58-5, 58-9). One well-recognized entry is the glass pyramid at the Louvre in Paris (Fig. 58-4). Sometimes, important entries also appear on several sides of the building.

■ *Roofs*. One of the most distinctive characteristics of Late Modern • 2 buildings is the attention paid to roofs, which show much experimentation and individuality in design. Some are symmetrical, while others are asymmetrical. They may be curved, angled, flat, or pointed, or a combination of several shapes to achieve design variety (Fig. 58-1, 58-3, 58-5, 58-8, 58-9, 58-11). They may also have cutouts to emphasize solid and void relationships and to make them more unusual. Some roofs also exhibit exposed construction features derived from the façade design, which provide additional accents. Often roofs serve as visual emblems that announce and personify the building's character and importance, similar to the effect created by the roof of the Art Deco Chrysler Building in New York.

▲ **58-12.** Feinstein House, 2003; Malibu, California; Stephen Kanner of Kanner Architects.

INTERIORS

Interiors by architects continue the design language of the exterior and are often limited to more public spaces, while those by interior designers usually relate to the whole entity but do not interpret it exactly. Large circulation areas (Fig. 58-2, 58-13), reception/lobbies (Fig. 58-15), offices/work areas (Fig. 58-16, 58-17), conference rooms, food services, shops (Fig. 58-18), design showrooms (Fig. 58-14, 58-20), museum spaces, classrooms/training, diagnostic/health/fitness spaces, and important residential spaces, such as media rooms, home offices, kitchens, and bathrooms, often showcase distinctive design ideas, unusual architectural features, ceiling height variations, new furniture arrangements, and experimentation with lighting designs. Office, retail, and health care environments frequently exhibit a wide range of space sizes and types to meet functional and technical requirements.

As in Late Modern • 1, designers strive for a strong aesthetic relationship between the exterior and interior of a building so that the design language is complementary. Interiors emphasize function, industrial technology, repetition of modular elements, solid and void relationships, spatial layering, and the use of construction and structure as ornament. Minimalism and High Tech remain as common interior aesthetic languages but exhibit more individuality and experimentation. The selection and application of materials becomes more important and shows greater variety. The grid continues to define and shape many commercial and some residential interior spaces and primary circulation areas, but there may be more than one axis defining grid directions (Fig. 58-16). Large, open spaces with no structural columns provide opportunities for variety in traditional arrangements and exploration of new ones but at the same time present design challenges.

Some architects custom design the interiors of their buildings to achieve an integrated whole. Others use space planners, interior designers, and other professionals for interiors planning. Some interior designers work on the renovation of existing interiors and the development of new spaces within new or existing buildings, such as large, open office areas; department stores and boutiques; hotel lobbies; and health care facilities. Because of the global context for design and information available through various media, regional differences disappear. Designers still address cultural differences in interior space planning, furniture arrangements, and finish selections. Additionally, regulations, such as the Americans with Disabilities Act (ADA) adopted in the United States in 1992, and health, safety, and welfare codes affect interior planning, furniture, and finishes.

Public and Private Buildings

■ *The Electronic Office and Alternative Offices*. New technologies continue to radically change the office and the ways people work. Because knowledge and ideas are the office's raw material, focus shifts to interaction, collaboration, teaming, and individual autonomy. Desktop computers, introduced in the late 1970s, forever change the work environment. The new technology makes the individual office worker, not the secretary, responsible for typing and primary communication, and redefines the traditional office hierarchy. Computers are essential at all workstations.

With the introduction of laptop computers in the late 1980s, work portability and movable work spaces become even more important and critical to office functions (Fig. 58-15, 58-17, 58-27, 58-28). Fax machines; cell or mobile phones and Smartphones; wireless connections, and file sharing, Internet meetings and e-mail greatly accelerate communication and the speed of work, and profoundly change productivity. Many workers no longer have to come into the office because they can work almost anywhere. Technology changes create a far-reaching revolution, one

▲ **58-13.** Interior and passageway, O'Hare Airport, United Airlines Terminal Building, 1984–1988; Chicago, Illinois; Helmut Jahn.

▲ **58-14.** Interior, Dupont Antron Showroom—Los Angeles, 1991; Los Angeles, California; Eva Maddox at Perkins and Will.

DESIGN SPOTLIGHT

Interior: With offices in the United States and numerous countries worldwide, Gensler is recognized nationally and internationally for its high-quality design, attention to detail, wide diversity of projects, and top-notch clients. Founded in 1965 by Arthur Gensler, the firm focuses on design teamwork and synergy on projects. As stated in its marketing material, the firm's mission is to create "design that empowers people and transforms organizations." Often, the firm's projects anticipate as well as reflect changes affecting the future. Some of the firm's most important work includes office design as in Swiss Re Financial Services. The offices illustrate the use of interpenetrating space, collaborative and zoned work and social areas, well-defined circulation paths, a mix of wall partition systems, innovative lighting solutions, and architecturally inspired ceiling treatments. Comfort, function, technical, and code requirements are fully integrated in design solutions. Organized plan layouts developed through extensive programming techniques are common. Often, standard features include custom furnishings, cabinetry, fixtures, and materials. Creating a strong brand image and corporate identity are often important design responsibilities, particularly in corporate work. Because so many different designers work on projects, there is no specific character or look to the firm's designs other than consistent sophistication and quality developed through harmonious design solutions.

▲ **58-15.** Reception area, Swiss Re Financial Services, 1996–1997; New York City, New York; Gensler.

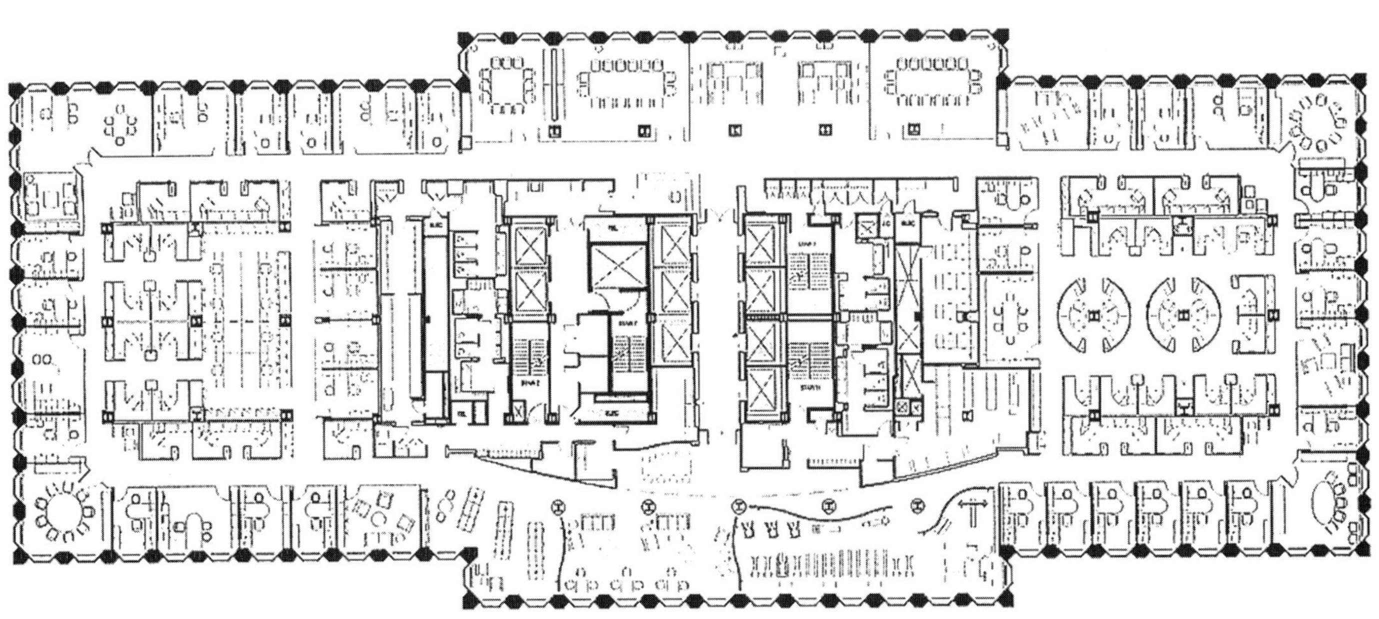

▲ **58-16.** Floor plan, Baron Capital, 1997–1998, New York City; Gensler.

equal to or greater than the Industrial Revolution. But unlike its predecessor, this technology revolution takes place within a short span of 10 to 15 years.

Designers explore new ways to design offices that respond to these changing needs. They focus on how the company and its employees work, the different activities involved, and the ways and means of communicating to develop and enhance appropriate design solutions. A variety of individuals from many disciplines, such as social scientists, behavioral psychologists, ergonomic specialists, facility managers, and designers, work together to generate research on work and productivity. They also formulate new design methods and strategies to better address the physical, technological, and behavioral needs of the users within a corporation or company. As a result, a variety of alternative office strategies for effectively using space to increase productivity, decrease costs, and attract and retain workers make their appearance. Among the alternative officing methods are means for sharing space, facilities, and technology, such as hoteling (providing work space as needed, usually by reservation); and hot desks, which individuals use only for set hours or days. To save time and space and better accommodate workers, companies create satellite offices or centers varying distances away from the main branch. Many allow or encourage workers to telework, or work from home, and/or use a virtual office in which work is conducted in one's car or other convenient, available places.

The open office planning of earlier continues, but responds to changes with greater accommodation for new technology, integrated wiring, and lighting. New design strategies and furnishings produce greater individuality in configuration instead of relying only on grid patterns (Fig. 58-27, 58-28). During the 1990s, as the pace of change within offices accelerates, concepts of office landscaping of the late 1950s reappear. Collaborative spaces, conferencing areas, and neighborhood centers respond to changing work methods. Workstations become smaller and more compact. Individual workspaces, copy centers, and conference areas support numerous technologies, such as multimedia and distance collaboration. With the advent of electronic files and archival methods, storage requirements diminish.

▲ **58-18.** Entry area, Joseph (retail store), 1988 in London, England; Eva Jiricna Architects.

■ *Color.* The color palette during this time varies by individual designer and type of space, so there is no set preference. But more consideration is given to research on color psychology, behavioral aspects, user needs, and cultural contexts in color selections so that the color reflects the intended character and function of the spaces. White walls remain common, but designers more fre-

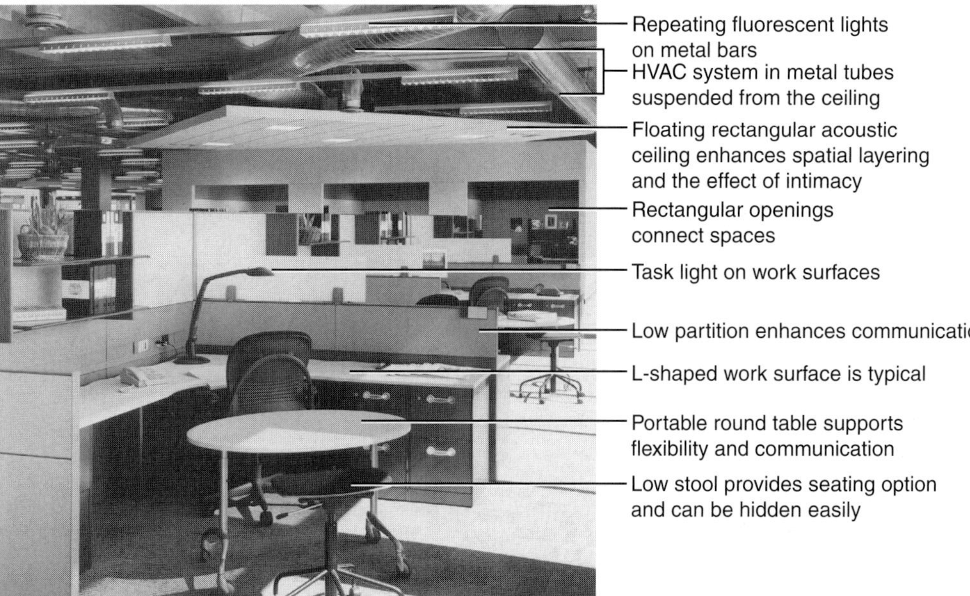

▲ **58-17.** Work area, Temerlin McClain offices, 2002; Irving, Texas; Dallas, Texas; Staffelbach Design Associates.

quently try new and different combinations of color palettes (Fig. 58-13, 58-14, 58-15, 58-18, 58-19, 58-21). Often they select livelier colors for spaces such as hotels, theaters, and boutiques; calming colors for health care and institutional facilities; and more neutral colors with accents for offices. Office color schemes include the combinations of gray, white, and black with accents of red; and cream, rust, gold, and brown. Jewel colors, such as mauve, navy, and burgundy are common in the 1980s. As earlier, carpet and rugs, artwork, and decorative arts contribute to the color schemes.

■ *Floors*. The selection of floor materials continues to expand because of advances in technology. New materials are combined with older ones for better durability and maintenance, and manufacturers offer more choices in design and installation. Concrete, marble, terrazzo, ceramic tile, stone, brick, wood, bamboo, vinyl, laminate, rubber, and linoleum floors in different designs continue as flooring choices (Fig. 58-13, 58-14, 58-18, 58-19). Rugs and wall-to-wall carpeting are common in both commercial and residential spaces. Custom-designed carpets and rugs are typical in high-end projects.

■ *Walls*. Diversity in wall design and the more extensive use of interior architectural features to delineate and articulate interior space (Fig. 58-13, 58-14, 58-15, 58-18, 58-19, 58-20) are more common than any set stylistic features are. Walls may be flat, angled, curved, punctuated, perforated, layered, or transparent. Wall materials include gypsum board (sheet rock), glass, and concrete. Common finishes include paint, metal, ceramic or mirror tiles, fabric, and wall coverings. Some wall treatments continue the earlier modular system of prefabricated parts and materials to reflect an industrial look. Others may be smooth or textured, with or without openings. Wall heights vary, with some to the ceiling, while others may be only partial height. Baseboards are plain or may be nonexistent when wall-to-wall carpeting is used. In Minimalist designs, baseboards, when present, are often the same color as the wall to deemphasize them.

■ *Window Treatments*. Simple window treatments are typical. Unpatterned drapery or curtains, miniblinds, vertical blinds, shutters, and sunscreen shades continue in use. Custom-designed sliding screens are alternative choices. Because of tinted glass or an architectural overhang, some windows have no treatments.

▲ **58-19.** Interior, JSM Music Studios, 1991; New York City, New York; Hariri and Hariri Architecture.

▲ **58-20.** Bolier & Company Furniture Showroom, 2006, High Point, North Carolina; Vanderbyl Design.

■ *Doors*. Doors are often flat and plain but may vary in design as a result of a wider selection of choices available. Custom-designed doors that fit particular projects become more common. Door trims continue to repeat the character of window moldings. Often the doors and trim are integrated as a prefabricated design unit.

■ *Ceilings*. As with wall design, ceilings offer even more variety than earlier. They may be flat, sloped, curved, or stepped and/or have skylights or translucent panels (Fig. 58-13, 58-14, 58-15, 58-17, 58-18, 58-19). Sometimes designers may emphasize pipes and other mechanical items by using contrasting colors. As earlier, many continue to be flat; plain; and painted white, black, or a neutral color. Suspended ceiling grids with integrated lighting and mechanical systems are used extensively in a variety of design installations. To meet growing consumer demands for more variety, manufacturers expand options for ceiling surfaces and materials. These include prefabricated metal and translucent glass. Frequently, designers experiment with custom-designed ceilings that integrate lighting, have visual layering, and create interesting focal points. Treatments may vary from one space or project to another based on function and aesthetic choices. Experimentation is common during this period.

■ *Textiles*. Designers continue to select commercial-grade fabrics made of cotton, linen, wool, and synthetic fibers for commercial and residential use (Fig. 58-19, 58-20, 58-21). Advancements in technology and manufacturing increase variety in designs, textures, and colors. Computer-designed and -manufactured textiles provide even more options for design and customization. Manufacturers and suppliers provide more textiles that meet building and finish codes and regulations and that have improved specifications to help designers address code and wear requirements for interiors. Textile showrooms continue to expand in size with more diverse examples.

▲ **58-21.** Textiles: Upholstery fabrics Cipher (left), Gradual (center), Ply Mesh Black (top right), and Tweed Stripe (right); c. 2000s; United States; manufactured by Maharam.

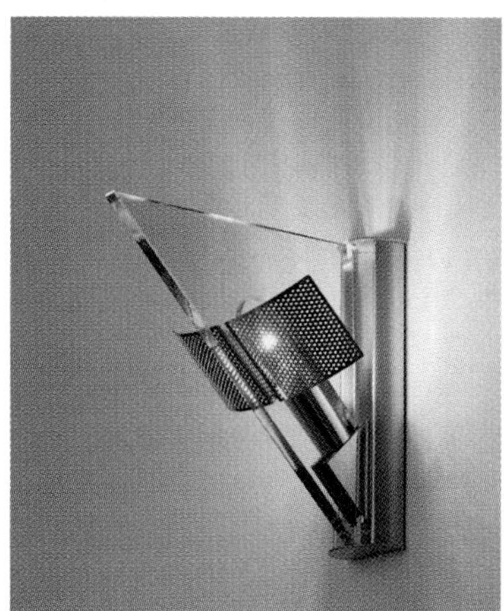

▲ **58-22.** Lighting: Icaro (metal wall sconce), 1985, by Carlo Forcolini; and Mikado Track System, 1991, by F. Porsche; manufactured by Artemide.

■ *Lighting*. Energy conservation and behavioral studies promote greater use of natural light in interiors, as earlier. Lighting installations display diverse fixture or system selections, multifunctional uses, enhanced individual controls, and placement variety (Fig. 58-13, 58-14, 58-15, 58-17, 58-18, 58-19, 58-22). As before, designers take advantage of research on lighting and advances in lighting methods and applications for planning and specifying lighting that more fully meets the needs of users, economics, energy conservation, and the type of space. Because of greater complexity and specificity in applications, more choices, life safety codes, and user needs, designers frequently consult or team with lighting engineers and lighting designers. To create ambient, task, accent, and mood lighting as well as specialized lighting for specific projects, designers incorporate architectual lighting, suspended ceiling systems, track lighting, indirect lighting applications, and individual fixtures into spaces.

Architecturally integrated lighting and custom-designed lighting become more important as interior architectural surfaces break the box shape. For large design projects and small custom ones, architects design the majority of wall sconces, pendants, chandeliers, and dropped lighting units. Manufacturers also expand their lighting choices and allow designers to customize existing items to fit a particular project.

Track systems and task lighting for work surfaces evolve with enhanced features and more flexibility in designs, sizes, and materials. Attention also focuses on indirect lighting such as uplighting (typical in offices or where drama is required), cornice lighting, and architecturally hidden ceiling lighting.

As earlier, there are new innovations in the design of lamps, wall sconces, and floor lamps (Fig. 58-22). The most notable changes are the diversity of shapes, options for flexibility, and new use of materials. There are also more lamp types beyond incandescent and fluorescent, such as halogen and high-intensity discharge. Designs are simple, unadorned, geometric, and flexible, but some may include interesting materials singly or in combination, such as glass, metal, plastic, ceramic, and wood.

FURNISHINGS AND DECORATIVE ARTS

Much commercial and residential furniture continues aspects of the Bauhaus and International Style in a machine-made appearance with no applied ornament. High Tech or industrial factory–style furniture remains a choice, but there are many more design options. The market for individual, avant-garde, and one-of-a-kind furnishings among the affluent expands. Depending upon upholstery color, materials, and/or design, furnishings may blend into the interior environment, emphasize function, appear as art objects or sculpture, or be a combination of all of these. Designs often are more complex because of advancements in technology and materials, and, as in architecture, the interplay of solid form versus negative space is important. With High Tech or International Style–influenced furniture, rationalism, functionalism, durability, and craftsmanship remain important design considerations.

The economic boom of the 1980s increases demand and competition for commercially designed furniture even more than for residential. Corporations and other businesses realize that interior design and furniture choice can create a corporate identity while increasing employee productivity and satisfaction. As a result, contract furniture makers, such as Herman Miller, Knoll, Steelcase, and Vitra, begin focusing on research and development for new furnishings that are ergonomically sound, cost effective, and aesthetically pleasing. Smaller manufacturers with shorter production runs concentrate on the market for avant-garde and custom furniture. They attract designers who want more freedom to express themselves and employ a greater variety of forms, techniques, and materials. Many strive to create furniture with similar visual and aesthetic characteristics as the fine arts, such as painting or sculpture. Because of this, some examples seem like pieces of sculpture in interior environments. These unique and creative expressions, unlike any earlier examples, show greater experimentation by their designers. In the 1990s, independent furniture designers promote their work through special galleries. Their

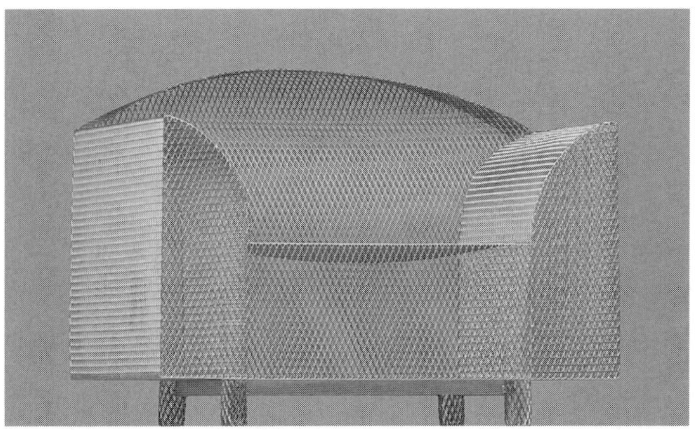

▲ **58-23.** How High the Moon armchair, 1986; Germany; Shiro Kuramata, for Kurosaki in Japan; later reissued by Vitra.

furniture usually is one of a kind, made of unusual materials, and highly expressive of their individual aesthetic sensibilities.

As earlier, designers continue to experiment with multifunctional furniture to address specific functional requirements and with new ways to use furniture. Portability, flexibility, and comfort are important so that furniture can be moved around for greater efficiency, support change, be positioned to fit users, and address ergonomic considerations. There is greater concern for users than there was earlier, so research findings in ergonomics and anthropometrics and principles of universal design drive concepts more than ever before. Many designers attempt to unite the human body and furniture.

DESIGN SPOTLIGHT

Furniture: Designers Don Chadwick and Bill Stumpf set out to design a completely new chair that is ergonomically sound and fits people of many sizes and postures. With strong ideas of what a chair should be and none about how it should look, they conduct field studies, anthropometric studies, mapping, and thermal tests. The result is the Aeron chair exhibiting a completely new look for office chairs. Unlike others, it is not upholstered and reveals no office hierarchy in size. With a unique biomorphic shape, the chair is adjustable in seat height and tilt as well as arm height and angle, and is available in three sizes. Its transparent Pellicle covering supports the sitter, is form fitting, and allows air to penetrate. The covering also is practical and long-wearing. The Aeron chair, which has won numerous design awards, looks and generally is comfortable for all types of users.

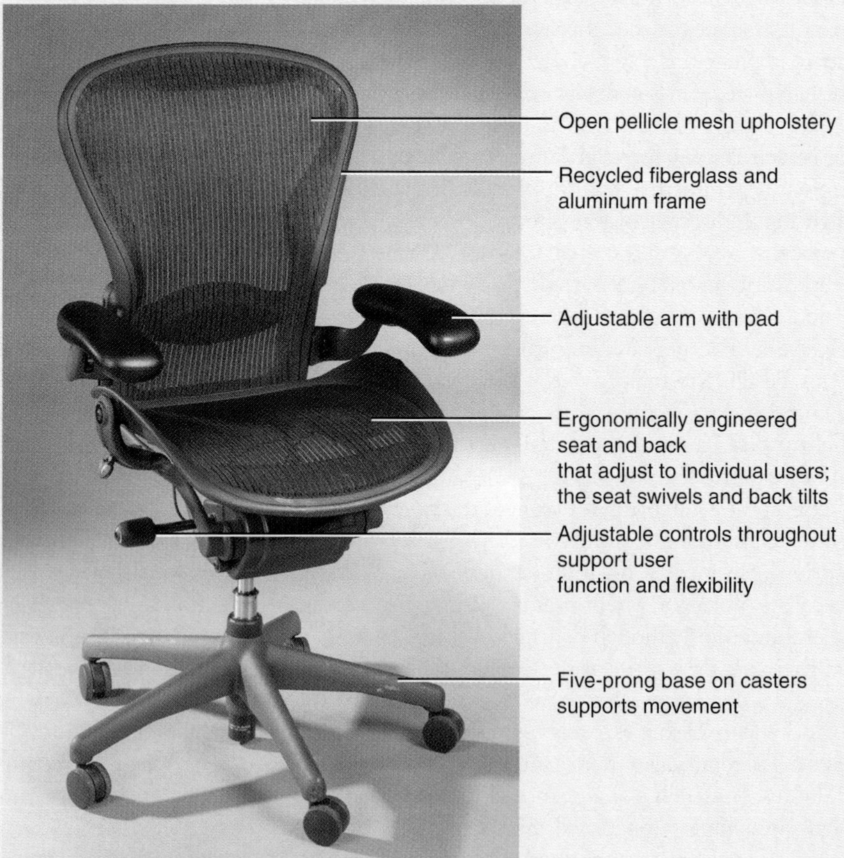

▲ **58-24.** Aeron chair, 1992; United States; Don Chadwick and Bill Stumpf, manufactured by Herman Miller.

▲ **58-25.** Tom Vac chair, 1997; Germany; Ron Arad, for Vitra.

Public and Private Buildings

■ *Materials*. Unlike before, designers experiment with metal above all else. It appears in various forms that may be tubular, thin sheets, perforated, or solid contours. Aluminum and steel are popular materials. Metal in various finishes is often mixed with glass, rubber, laminates, and fabric. Plastic, fiberglass, and other similar materials sometimes are used for furniture. Independent designers employ a variety of materials, many of which are atypical alone or when mixed together, such as glass, concrete, or found objects.

■ *Seating*. Chairs continue to be the most important pieces of furniture in all environments, except retail spaces. Designers continue to explore forms, contours, flexibility, modularity, and ergonomics. The most important new development in ergonomic seating is the Aeron chair (Fig. 58-24), designed by Don Chadwick and Bill Stumpf for Herman Miller and introduced in 1992 after many years of research and development. It represents a more advanced level of ergonomic seating as a result of data about size selection, body contour, and material use than was previously available. Because it is extremely adjustable and comfortable, the chair becomes an instant best-seller with many imitators. New designs emerge in side and stacking chairs for use in schools, institutions, health care facilities, and auditoriums (Fig. 58-25). Some mix metal parts with plastic surfaces or fabric upholstery, while others are entirely of metal or plastic. Carts to store and move them on become very important.

Other new developments in chairs focus on furniture with an artistic look. Examples include the How High the Moon chair (Fig. 58-23) by Shiro Kuramata. These types of chairs address the basic function of sitting but stress appearance and aesthetics of the composition above all else. Sometimes they are comfortable, and sometimes they are not.

■ *Tables*. Most tables are sleek and unornamented, with interesting details conveyed in structural components. Designs stress flexibility, mobility, and simplicity (Fig. 58-14, 58-17, 58-19, 58-26). Office systems tables support multifunctional uses with a wide selection of top sizes, shapes, materials, and colors (Fig. 58-27, 58-28). Most have casters and wire management features, and some have folding components or elements that can be combined. Some designers try out unusual designs for conference, dining, occasional, and coffee tables using glass, wood, metal, granite, or marble tops, and metal legs or bases in various forms and designs.

■ *Systems Furniture*. As the technology revolution evolves and increasingly affects work, office systems furniture must respond to new and different functions, flexibility, and lower costs. Choices increase significantly as more research data and advanced designs address ergonomics, proxemics, communication, and behavioral design (Fig. 58-17, 58-24, 58-27, 58-28). The greatest need is for flexibility. Systems furniture also has to address alternative officing and create work areas that can be reconfigured easily to meet changing business requirements and the needs of those who work on site, in groups, or off site. Although office systems furniture is intended to be mobile, most firms do not take advantage of this, and configurations are largely static grids instead of ones customized to the firm as intended. Manufacturers create new systems that are even easier to reshape and strive to educate designers, clients, office managers, and facility managers about these changes.

Systems furniture supports custom designed offices for each company or user. Units can be arranged at different angles to eliminate the grid and create more asymmetrical patterns that relate to functional needs. Other options include wall panels of different materials and heights; sound-masking systems for more

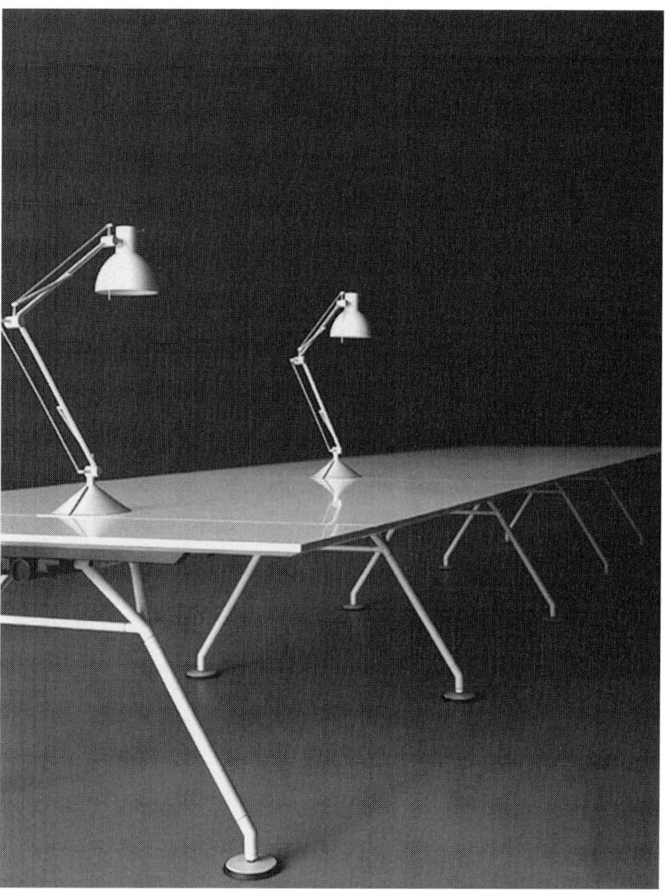

▲ **58-26.** Nomos table, 1989; Italy; Sir Norman Foster, for Tecno.

▲ **58-27.** Personal Harbor office furniture, c. 1992; United States; Paul Siebert, Mark Baloga, and Steve Eriksson; manufactured by Steelcase.

privacy; portable units; more modular components; better storage capabilities; more integrated voice, data, and lighting; more seating options; and more aesthetic choices in colors and materials. With these enhancements, individual work areas can be easily tailored to meet individual needs and personal requirements for

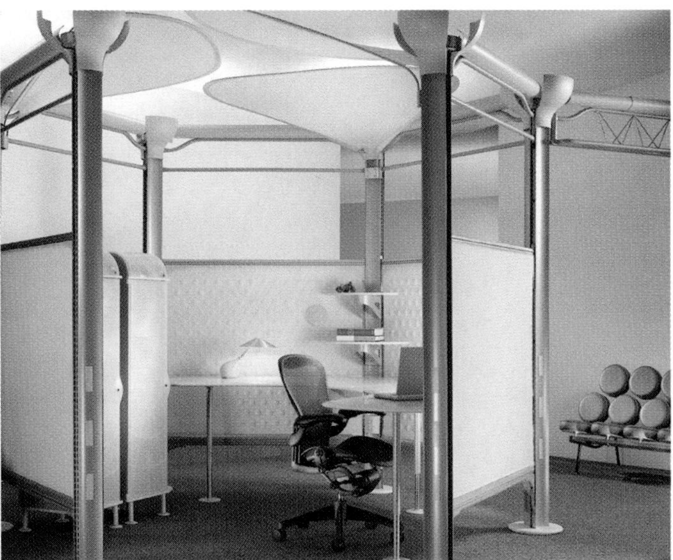

▲ **58-28.** Resolve office system, c. 2006; United States; Douglas Ball, manufactured by Herman Miller.

existing and new employees. One example is Herman Miller's Resolve system (Fig. 58-28), which is pole-based. Resolve has straight and curving components for more openness and greater flexibility. As designs evolve to support functions and the office worker, manufacturers develop small, portable enclosed office units specifically tailored to the worker who is primarily off site, such as Steelcase's Personal Harbor system (Fig. 58-27; no longer in production).

These changes and concepts affect home environments as well. During the 1990s, the number of home offices multiplies to support a more mobile workforce and those who work from home. Teleworkers and others demand the same advantages in their workspaces that are available in commercial office environments. As a result, the design industry begins to offer similar furnishings that are smaller scale, slightly less expensive, and readily available in stores.

CHAPTER 59

Environmental Modern

1960s–2000s

> *Our goal is a delightfully diverse, safe, healthy, just world with clean water, clean air, clean soil, clean power—economically, equitably, ecologically, elegantly enjoyed.*
>
> —William McDonough, Interior Design Educators Council, Annual Conference, 2005

Environmental Modern architecture, interiors, and furnishings respond to the environment, whether macro (building and site) or micro (interiors and furniture), as part of the larger movement that addresses human needs while safeguarding the earth, its climate, and ecological resources. The movement within design is known by various names such as Green Design, Sustainable Design, or Eco Design. Throughout the 20th century, the movement's concepts in the design community evolve, becoming comprehensive design schemes for protection, conservation, and renewal of resources that include energy conservation, waste management, material conservation, land use and reuse, and climate control. In adopting these concepts, buildings, interiors, and furnishings may show little or no evidence of these ideas or they may reflect a strong contextual relationship to nature, site, and place.

HISTORICAL AND SOCIAL

During the late 19th century, a few people, including William Morris, recognize that the Industrial Revolution is creating air and water pollution as well as social evils. However, reforms focus on social problems instead of the environment, in part because there is little understanding of the effects of bad air and water. Early ideas of the Environmental Movement, which influence Environmental Modern, spring from the 19th-century American transcendentalists, such as Henry David Thoreau and his book *Walden*. These writers highlight the significance of nature and link it with spirituality and humanity. They also introduce the notion of nature as teacher, which becomes important for late-20th-century theorists in sustainability.

In the late 19th and early 20th centuries, environmental concerns center on conservation of natural resources. Canada, for example, establishes her first national park, Banff National Park, in 1885. In the United States, John Muir advances the importance of protecting natural resources and the wilderness in his writings. Muir and others found the Sierra Club in 1892, one of the first grassroots environmental organizations. Following Canada's example and influenced by Muir, U.S. President Theodore Roosevelt moves to preserve wilderness lands in national parks, including Yosemite and the Grand Canyon. He also establishes the National Forest Service to safeguard natural resources.

Most environmental efforts are individual, sporadic, and focused on conservation during the first half of the 20th century. Scientists begin investigating the effects of pollution, pesticides, and chemicals on humans and the earth. They and a few individuals who recognize the damaging, long-term effects of air and water pollution, as well as some farming practices and insecticides, begin to call for change. During the period, national governments pass a few laws designed to curb pollution and unsafe practices. Some forward thinkers identify a growing need for energy conservation.

During the early 1960s, spurred by greater industrialization, increased production of chemicals, and nuclear testing of the postwar period, there is a growing awareness of numerous environmental problems. Environmentalism begins to take shape as a distinct movement with cultural and political impact in many countries. An important catalyst is the publication of *Silent Spring* (1962) by Rachel Carson, a book that calls attention to the destructive effects of pesticides on people, organisms, and the environment. It inspires a move toward saving the planet, which is mostly a counterculture trend among young people. Saving the earth suits those who question authority and seek to change the status quo. Although their radicalism helps awareness, it keeps environmentalism from entering the mainstream. In the late 1960s, illnesses and deaths from air pollution and chemicals in the United States and other countries heighten concerns about the increasing environmental problems. At the time, few American designers and architects respond.

▲ **59-1.** Thanksgiving Square Chapel and ceiling detail, 1977; Dallas, Texas; Philip Johnson.

These concerns continue during the next decade as the acute effects of pollution become more apparent in many parts of the world, reflected in famines, droughts, and floods. Scientists, researchers, and thinkers increase their study of the consequences of the unchecked use of chemicals and nuclear testing as well as pollution and other environmental concerns. Some small steps toward curbing the destruction of the environment are made as nations across the world initiate discussions on solving environmental problems. Most important, countries begin to realize that environmental problems require holistic solutions that encompass urban planning and growth, transportation alternatives, and controlled development. More nongovernmental groups focused upon the environment form during the period. For example, in 1971, citizens from Vancouver, British Columbia, protest nuclear testing by the United States. Calling themselves Greenpeace, they form an organization that becomes an effective worldwide force for the environment.

In the early 1970s, concerns about energy conservation come from the shortage of gasoline, which raises prices and limits supply, especially in the United States. The loss of inexpensive petroleum forces a search for ways to lessen dependence on it and to find materials that are not derived from petroleum. Furthermore, some people begin to question unlimited consumption and the throwaway mentality of most citizens of industrialized nations. These practices further deplete energy sources and generate mountains of waste as well as air and water pollution. During this period, architecture and design responses center on energy conservation through passive and active solar design and a search for alternatives to petroleum-based materials.

In 1970, the first Earth Day is held in the United States to educate people about the disastrous effects of industrialization on the earth. One important result is the beginning of a national policy for the environment in the United States, seen in the creation of the Environmental Protection Agency and the National Environmental Protection Act of 1970. Earth Day becomes international within a year, and other nations create governmental departments and ministries focused on the environment. In 1972, the first world conference on the environment is held in Stockholm, Sweden. Sponsored by the United Nations (UN), the event is a global forum for concerns about the environment across the world, especially in Europe. The conference links environmental concerns with economic issues, such as growth and development. Nations begin to work individually and collectively to solve problems of air and water pollution, loss of natural resources, disposal of toxic wastes, and the effects of industrialization and nuclear weapons on the environment. From 1972 onward, numerous international treaties are established in which nations agree to adhere to particular standards for protecting the environment.

By the 1980s, there is greater public, scientific, and governmental awareness around the globe of long-term environmental problems such as acid rain, loss of the rain forests, excess garbage, and toxic waste. Throughout the decade, environmental concerns gain more international attention, aided by several actions of the UN. In 1987, the concept of sustainability comes to the forefront with the publication of the Brundtland report entitled *Our Common Future*. It spreads the concept of sustainable development, which it defines as meeting the "needs of the present without compromising the ability of future generations to meet their own needs." The report also links ecology and the environment with development, economy, and equality. This gives impetus to sustainability as a social and economic movement that centers on the protection and care of the environment in perpetuity. During the 1980s, architects and designers in Europe and North America begin to acknowledge the destructive effects of unchecked development and the negative impact of building upon the environment in terms of loss of green space, destruction of natural resources, pollution, energy consumption, and creation of waste. The first efforts at change are individual and isolated, but they increase as the decade progresses.

During the 1990s, environmental emphasis maintains its comprehensive attitude of economic, political, and social responsibility. Concern for the earth and sustainability enters the mainstream as people around the globe experience the effects of a damaged environment in the form of heat waves, droughts, and more diseases. Global, governmental, and organizational groups continue their efforts to develop effective, long-term solutions. However, an economic recession in the early 1990s halts progress, especially when governments curtail spending. As a result, the marketplace begins to have a greater impact by offering more earth-friendly products. By the end of the decade, the recession ends, and governments renew their spending on environmental efforts. In 1992, people from around the world gather in Rio de Janerio for the first Earth Summit. Participants focus on ecoefficiency, a concept that strives to change attitudes of "take, make, waste" into ones that preserve and protect the environment by doing more with less. They agree on principles of environmentalism and set up Agenda 21, a global program for sustainability.

Also during the 1990s, individuals, corporations, and businesses adopt comprehensive environmental policies and sustainable practices, and the terms *green architecture* and *green design* become more prominent. In 1992, the sustainability movement reveals its effects on design at the World's Exposition in Seville, Spain. The exposition is a showcase for sustainable design, as well as for design solutions that respond to climate and conservation technology used to help, not hurt, the environment. In 1993, the U.S. Green Building Council (USGBC) is founded. Made up of architects, builders, and developers, it strives to promote environmental responsibility, profitability, and healthy living and working spaces.

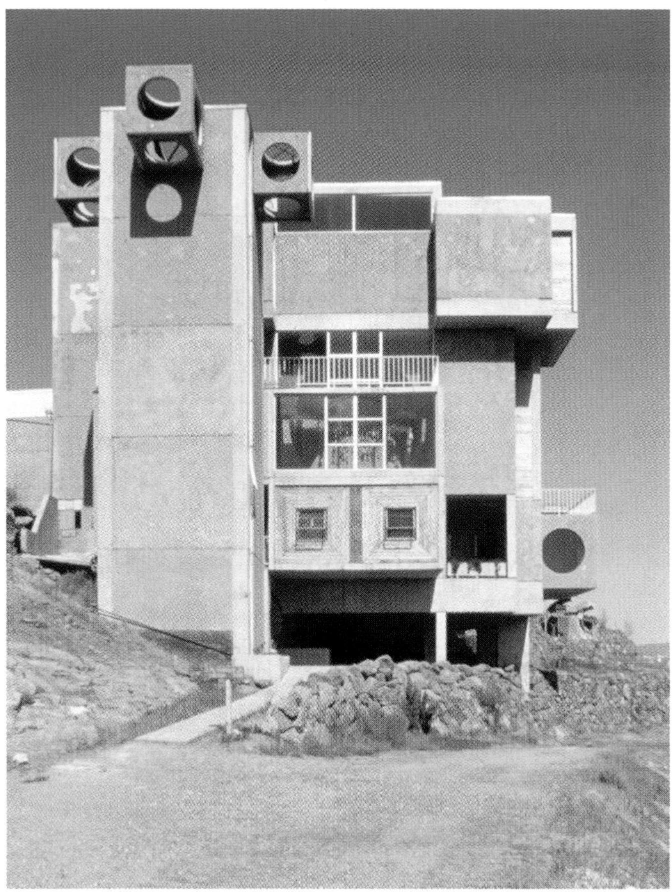

▲ **59-2.** Arcosanti, 1969 to present; Cordes Lakes area, Arizona; Paolo Soleri.

In 1984, the World Health Organization identifies a cluster of symptoms in humans that will become known as Sick Building Syndrome (SBS), which is linked to spending time in certain buildings, either individual rooms or zones. By the 1990s, designers and clients realize that SBS affects the health and productivity of users. SBS is caused by inadequate ventilation, interior and exterior pollutants, allergens, bacteria, and molds, so designers begin to look for ways to eliminate these hazards. Indoor air quality (IAQ) becomes critically important, legally and in design. This complex issue arises from a host of factors from the building envelope, mechanical systems, finishes, and furnishings, and solutions must involve a variety of design professionals including interior designers.

Sustainable efforts within individual nations continue into the 21st century. Most countries have departments or ministries that focus on the environment. Many, including Canada, the United Kingdom, and Australia, adopt sustainable policies and programs and include stringent sustainability requirements in their national building codes. Canada's Department of Commerce pursues energy conservation. Great Britain moves to clean up the Thames River and reduce air pollution. Japan passes some of the world's strictest laws to control air and water pollution. Green Parties, political groups devoted to environmental concerns, arise in nearly all countries with free elections. Global involvement also continues with the aid of the UN.

DESIGN SPOTLIGHT

Architecture and Interior: Thorncrown Chapel, Fay Jones's masterpiece, is a small, elegant chapel nestled in a quiet forested area. The contemporary, Gothic-inspired structure boasts a cross-lattice system of wooden support members that pitch to center and hold the structure together. Reminiscent of construction techniques seen in rural covered bridges, the wooden supports also create a rhythmical quality and emphasize the use of natural materials. Large glass panels inserted between the supports filter ever-changing natural light to reinforce the relationship of solid to void, chapel to nature, and sacred space to setting. The building is at once complex, intimate, and memorable. It exhibits a strong sense of place and spirituality through its form, construction, materials, and details, as it responds to its environmental setting. Voted by the American Institute of Architects as the best building of the 1980s, it is recognized in 2006 with the AIA "Twenty-Five Year Award" for its significant influence on the profession.

▲ **59-3.** Thorncrown Chapel and nave, 1978–1980; Eureka Springs, Arkansas; Fay Jones, with Maurice Jennings.

The design and educational communities broaden and increase their environmental efforts and stewardship. In 2000, the USGBC introduces the Leadership in Energy and Environmental Design (LEED) rating system. LEED is a nationally accepted benchmark for design, construction, and operation of green buildings. Standards address building performance in five areas: site, water savings, energy efficiency, materials, and indoor air quality. In 2004, LEED standards for commercial interiors are established; they are joined by a residential rating system in 2005. By 2007, the USGBC has instituted LEED rating systems for new and existing buildings and has ratings for schools, retail, healthcare, and neighborhoods. LEED also has professional accreditation as LEED Green Associate or LEED AP. Canada has a similar program.

Information about sustainability and environmental design and products are readily available through books; journals; and especially the Internet, which is a major resource not only for education but also for communication. Museums in many countries mount exhibits, and universities offer coursework and degrees in environmentalism and environmental or green design. Architectural and interior design firms, such as HOK in the United States and Penner and Associates in Canada, specialize in green design and planning for all types of buildings and interiors. Professional and shelter magazines highlight environmentally conscious projects and practices. Professional design organizations move to have sustainable concepts become a part of education, standard practice, professional ethics, and social responsibility. ASID partners with USGBC and launches REGREEN in 2008. The program provides guidelines for sustainable remodeling and additions for houses. NeoCon, the Environmental Design Research Association (EDRA), and other organizations host conferences, workshops, and trade markets that highlight the newest sustainable products, technologies, and techniques. These efforts create environmental awareness and promote healthy living and socially responsible consumerism continuing into the early 21st century.

DESIGN SPOTLIGHT

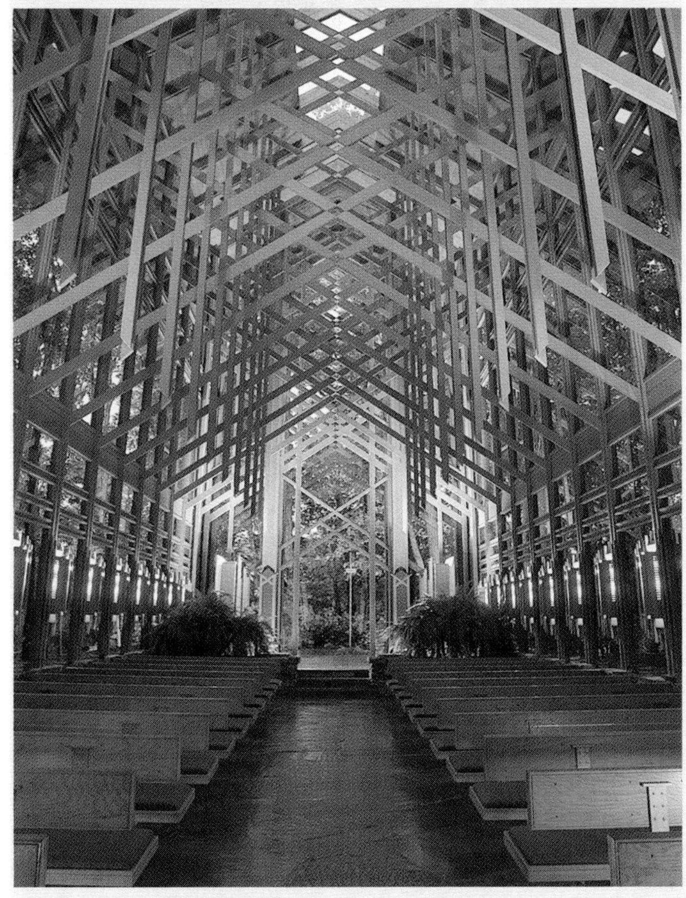

▲ **59-3.** Continued

CONCEPTS

During the late 20th century, a variety of concepts and theories related to environmental and sustainable architecture and design exist internationally. Deriving ideas from science, ecology, philosophy, psychology, and other disciplines, they reflect a comprehensive attitude that strives to limit and/or reverse environmental damage through development and change in thoughts and actions by individuals, designers, businesses, manufacturers, governments, and nations. Most center on conservation, good stewardship, social responsibility, and regeneration of resources. This includes, but is not limited to, eliminating waste, reusing or recycling, minimizing energy consumption, improving indoor air quality, and using only renewable and durable resources. Care and concern for the environment affect economic development, urban planning and land use, architecture, construction techniques, building materials, interior design, interior finishes, textiles, furniture, and decorative arts around the globe. A variety of terms describe environmental concepts.

Definitions

- *Sustainability.* Often used to describe the entire environmental movement, sustainability strives to shape societies, economies, and human activities so that all needs are met to the greatest potential, but resources for the future are maintained. Sustainable design creates products that comply with principles of economic (production, distribution, and consumption of goods and services), societal, and ecological (living organisms and the natural environment) sustainability. The term can be applied to every aspect of life on earth, from natural and built environments to principles, practices, and products that do not deplete resources or harm the environment or users.
- *Green Design, Green Architecture.* Green design refers to architecture, interior design, and related design disciplines that follow sustainable principles, practices, and materials. Practical in concept, green design focuses on energy efficiency, use of renewable resources, and practices and materials that do not harm either the micro environment (building and interiors) or the macro environment (earth). Life cycle costs and durable, local materials with low embodied energy also are important.

▲ **59-4.** Yancey Chapel, c. 1990s; Greensboro, Hale County, Alabama; Auburn University's Rural Studio with Samuel Mockbee.

■ *Environmental Design*. Closely aligned to sustainability and green design is environmental design, which embraces a design process that produces buildings, interiors, and objects that are aesthetically pleasing and functional with a sense of humanity. It encompasses many concepts and principles such as evidence-based design, theories of behavior, universal design, energy efficiency, and sustainability.

Theories and Theorists

By the late 20th century, theories centering on environmental concepts influence leaders of thought and forward-thinking design firms. Using these theories, they produce ideas and processes that address new and smarter ways of planning and designing. Beginning in the late 20th century, designers begin using more comprehensive design methods to achieve sustainability, beginning with problem identification and programming. They often incorporate sophisticated and scientific techniques for data collection and analysis, such as energy and water analyses, and include the latest research findings into their projects and presentations. Some believe that the sustainable and green movements have an equal, if not greater, impact on design than did the Modern Movement of the mid-20th century.

■ *William McDonough*. McDonough is one of the best-known architectural theorists and practitioners of sustainability (Fig. 59-13). He believes that design can solve earth's problems and stop the destructive process of the traditional Industrial Revolution by adopting principles found in nature. McDonough and Michael Braungart advocate what they define as a cradle-to-cradle approach in which products are created using sound economic and sustainable principles. Once these products have reached the end of their life cycles, they are broken down to be reused, recycled, or replenished, thereby eliminating waste. Products that do not fit into this category are stored until ways to reuse them are discovered.

■ *Paolo Soleri*. Architect Soleri popularizes the term *Arcology* (architecture combined with ecology), a theory of urban planning and design dating from the early 20th century, which limits waste of land, energy, and resources and encourages integration between buildings and the surrounding natural environment. Using new technologies, past practices, and ecological concepts, Arcology encourages a rethinking of the city to create huge habitats of living and working environments. Under construction since 1970, Soleri's Arcosanti (Fig. 59-2) in Arizona is an experimental town demonstrating principles of Arcology.

■ *Christopher Alexander*. Theorist and architectural educator Alexander stresses design methods that give context; meet users' needs; and save materials, energy, and labor. In several influential books, he identifies numerous patterns and ideas that people have used to successfully solve problems in design. These patterns can be combined in different ways to create effective, green solutions for cities, neighborhoods, and public and private living and working environments.

■ *Sim Van der Ryn*. Van der Ryn is an architect who believes in the importance of local setting and creating a sense of place. He brings ecology into the design process by stressing that structures should complement climate, nature, and natural processes, such as recycling and reusing. Structures should evolve from the landscape and be responsive to human needs by including the user in the design process.

■ *Other concepts*. Other concepts and principles not directly related to design but informing it include Deep Ecology, which stresses the value of all life, not just human, and Biomimicry, which embraces nature as the model and source of inspiration for business, industry, and design solutions.

CHARACTERISTICS AND MOTIFS

Buildings, interiors, and furnishings can have many different appearances depending upon the views of the designer and client regarding context of site and location, sustainable concepts, and new technologies. Some commonalities include natural materials, earth colors, plants, water features, and an abundance of natural light and air. Usually, sustainable materials, construction techniques, and planning concepts are not visually apparent. Nevertheless, they positively affect the health and productivity of users while keeping energy and maintenance costs down.

Some buildings, interiors, and furniture have a strong modernistic or High Tech appearance, while others embrace vernacular types or organic and sculptural forms. Most High Tech, Minimalist, or Late Modern examples come from designers who see technology as a means to solve both design and environmental problems. Their work embodies new technologies and materials. Designers who regard technology as the cause of environmental problems use it minimally or reject it altogether. Consequently, they usually seek a cultural or contextual fit for their work by adopting or interpreting local or regional, traditional, or vernacular building and interior types and forms and by using local materials and construction methods. Ancient planning methods and philosophies, such as Feng Shui, may be adopted. Compositions may have a simple and natural or vernacular appearance or reflect nature-based images or local environmental relationships.

■ *Motifs*. No particular motifs are associated with Environmental Modern because expressions are varied, but designers may use motifs inspired by the site, the locale, the region, or nature itself.

ARCHITECTURE

Beginning in the late 1960s, some architects try to relate new designs to their surroundings by visible and symbolic links. Influenced by concepts from the Arts and Crafts Movement, Frank Lloyd Wright, Louis Kahn, and Paolo Soleri, they design buildings with a strong, visible contextual relationship to nature, site, and place. As a result, buildings integrate harmoniously with their natural surroundings (Fig. 59-2, 59-3, 59-6, 59-7, 59-11); sit on or near water, woods, or large green spaces (Fig. 59-3, 59-6, 59-7); are oriented to take advantage of the sun and breezes (Fig. 59-1, 59-2, 59-6); and create a strong sense of place within their environment (Fig. 59-3, 59-5). They often become calm, contemplative refuges from the complexity of everyday life. A crafts approach may define, frame, and/or delineate the design aesthetic. Frequently, forms, shapes, scale, and color come from or reflect the surroundings or the locale. Materials and designs blend in with the site to convey the harmonious relationship.

In the second half of the 20th century, architects increasingly consider energy conservation and efficiency in their designs. Comprehensive planning and design schemes have not yet developed. So designers mainly incorporate active and passive solar elements that use climate, orientation, and landscape features to make buildings comfortable but less dependent upon energy sources and more cost efficient (Fig. 59-12). These features may dominate the design or be concealed. A few architects explore solar design, means of greater energy efficiency, and a more effective use and preservation of natural resources. States, such as California, mandate prescriptive standards that include insulation, glazing, space conditions, and lighting, among other concerns.

As environmental concerns intensify and theories of how to solve them increase in the 1980s, architects turn more to the principles of green design, sustainable materials, and socially responsible use of natural resources. This is aided by the mid-20th-century critiques of Modernism's lack of context and perpetuation and glorification of industrialization and technology, which are largely responsible for damaging the environment. Some of the first examples sacrifice aesthetic innovation in the interest of environmental concerns. Later, these two goals unite, producing many aesthetically pleasing and individual works.

In contrast to some other planning methods, green building considers the site and tries to destroy as little of surrounding vegetation as possible while orienting the structure toward views, sunlight, and/or breezes (Fig. 59-6). Some buildings are totally or

▲ **59-5.** Chapel of S. Ignatius, Seattle University, 1997; Seattle, Washington; Steven Holl.

partially underground to enhance energy efficiency. Exterior designs may use local or vernacular building types, materials, and construction methods. Green building features often include structurally insulated panels, photovoltaic panels, and solar heat collectors to increase energy efficiency; geothermal heat pumps to help with heating and cooling; rainwater collectors for cleaning and fire suppression; means of reusing gray water; operable energy-efficient windows for natural ventilation; sun louvers or screens to control natural light; low-flow or waterless composting toilets to reduce water consumption; and natural materials that embody low energy and can be locally obtained, easily replenished, and/or reused or recycled (Fig. 59-6, 59-10, 59-11). Designers often find that compromises are necessary because of client preference, costs, and tradeoffs in choices.

Environmental Modern public building types include museums (Fig. 59-8), chapels (Fig. 59-3, 59-4, 59-5), corporate offices (Fig. 59-6, 59-9, 59-10), hotels, and nature centers, but green concepts appear in all types of buildings. Residences are especially important because architects can test concepts and new technologies in sustainable practice (Fig. 59-11, 59-12). Not all dwellings are or need to be architect-designed. In 2004, Michelle Kaufmann creates the Glidehouse, a prefabricated, sustainable house that can be configured to meet individual site and user needs. Some builders, such as Deltec Homes of North Carolina, specialize in sustainable custom and/or prefabricated houses. Low-income or public housing and apartment complexes with environmental considerations are built in some locations.

Some leading design practitioners include Fay Jones (Fig. 59-3), Steven Holl (Fig. 59-5), Antoine Predock, William McDonough (Fig. 59-13), and Sim Van der Ryn of the United States; Glenn Murcutt of Australia; and Detrich Schwarz of Switzerland. Each structure usually has an individual design expression that emphasizes one or more attributes of the environment. Some, such as Murcutt and Jones, work regionally, while others, such as McDonough, create projects in national and international locations.

DESIGN SPOTLIGHT

Architecture: The Chesapeake Bay Foundation Building is one of the first buildings in the United States to receive a LEED Platinum rating. This innovative office complex sits on 32 acres of shoreline fronting the Chesapeake Bay and is surrounded by native landscaping and vegetation. Conceived with a strong emphasis on environmental conservation and protection, the building incorporates many features common to green design, including a shed roof, operable windows, a rainwater catchment system, natural renewable materials, recycled materials, structurally insulated panels, solar water heating, and composting toilets. The south side has a glazed wall of windows to increase daylight and enhance passive solar heating. Sun louvers and architectural overhangs provide protection as needed. Building materials are mainly wood, galvanized recycled steel (roof and siding), and glass. The spacious, open interiors continue the use of earth-friendly materials with cork and bamboo flooring, linoleum, parallel strand lumber (made from scrap wood), medium density fiberboard, and low VOC paint.

▲ **59-6.** Chesapeake Bay Foundation Building (Philip Merrill Environmental Center; the first building in the United States to receive a LEED Platinum rating), 2000; Annapolis, Maryland; Smith Group, interiors by Cheryl Brown.

▲ **59-7.** The Eden Project, 2001; Bodelva, S. Austell, England; Nicholas Grimshaw.

■ *Contextualism.* Contextualism, also known as Regionalism, which may have elements of green design and sustainable materials, relates to the macro environment. Designs strive for harmony of setting or sense of place and may adopt or adapt elements and attributes of nearby structures, the site, local materials, local traditions, vernacular forms, and cultural norms (Fig. 59-3, 59-6). Links are not always obvious nor are quotations direct, and compositions may be eclectic or aggregates of elements. Some closely copy the existing fabric, while other solutions are modernist interpretations with a few key elements or symbols derived from the context. To achieve their goals, designers use a variety of means, including scale, orientation, articulation, individual elements, colors, and materials.

Public and Private Buildings

■ *Site Orientation.* Orientation is critical for energy efficiency and planning. Architects strive to site urban examples as efficiently as possible with the limitations of city lots and zoning requirements (Fig. 59-8, 59-9, 59-10). Space may allow for green areas and water features. Rural or suburban buildings are often surrounded by native vegetation and oriented to best utilize nature and local resources, including water, trees, and sunlight (Fig. 59-2, 59-3, 59-6, 59-7). Landscapes usually maintain indigenous grasses, wildflowers, rocks or boulders, and native bushes (Fig. 59-6, 59-7, 59-8). Designers try to use plants that require little watering to avoid a need for an irrigation system. Rain gardens or water collectors provide additional water for interior and exterior use. If buildings are in urban areas, local vegetation may surround and frame the building to enhance the human-made setting. Some buildings, such as earth-sheltered ones, emerge directly from or within the landscape.

■ *Floor Plans.* Floor plans vary based on the building function. They are usually simple in organization and design, and may be symmetrical or asymmetrical based on location, geography, or major circulation paths. Some architects regard the design of the plan as a journey of exploration through an open-ended sequence of spatial experiences (Fig. 59-11, 59-12). Others create direct routes that end in important spaces or focal points or lead to specific activity areas (Fig. 59-3). Still others use metaphors from nature, such as shells, plants, and water, to guide the arrangement (Fig. 59-1). Processional or transitional spaces that connect the outside to the inside appear often, sometimes as roofed passages, which may be open or closed (Fig. 59-6). When closed, they have large walls of glass to let in sunlight and show exterior building materials to visually aid the outside-to-inside transition. Water areas may be incorporated to soften the effect. Plan shapes may be rectangular, curved, or angled, or a combination of different shapes. Some are differentiated by their irregularity. Large spaces or rooms, such as conference rooms or naves, may define the shape or project from it to emphasize or increase natural views, focal areas, and/or sun exposure (Fig. 59-3, 59-4, 59-5, 59-8). Open floor plans with minimal wall divisions are common, especially in museums and chapels. Houses feature numerous open areas, sunlit passages, exploratory circulation paths, and contemplative spaces. Public and private areas are defined, but the divisions may be less recognizable (Fig. 59-12).

■ *Materials.* Most buildings incorporate new and recycled natural materials obtained locally or regionally to reduce transportation expenses (Fig. 59-4, 59-12). Sustainable material choices consider durability and maintenance because frequent replacement and frequent or difficult cleaning and repairs harm the environment. Examples of such materials include local stone (Fig. 59-2), galvanized steel siding (Fig. 59-6), medium density fiberboard, parallel strand lumber, insulated precast concrete, fly ash concrete, straw bales, aluminum, limestone, granite, brick, and insulated tinted or patterned glass (Fig. 59-7, 59-9). The use of wood is debated as forests begin to disappear. Alternatives include engineered woods and certified sustainably harvested wood, which is responsibly forested. Color usually comes from the building materials. Sometimes, architects use stains and paints made

▲ **59-8.** National Museum of the American Indian, 2004; Washington, D.C.; Douglas Cardinal, GBQC Architects, Jones & Jones, SmithGroup, Polshek Partnership, and the Native American Design Collaborative.

from natural materials, or ones that are biodegradable or emit low amounts of volatile organic compounds (VOCs). Choices of sustainable materials and finishes continue to increase as more manufacturers, designers, and clients recognize the importance of maintaining the environment.

■ *Façades*. Some buildings, particularly those in an urban context, have a contemporary or even an avant-garde appearance. Green and sustainable features may or may not define their design concepts but are incorporated nevertheless because of designer or client preference or requirements of building codes (Fig. 59-8). Some have an overtly High Tech appearance with glass walls and a dynamic expression of structure (Fig. 59-9, 59-10). Others are Late Modern in style and maintain the grid within varied shapes and with minimal ornament.

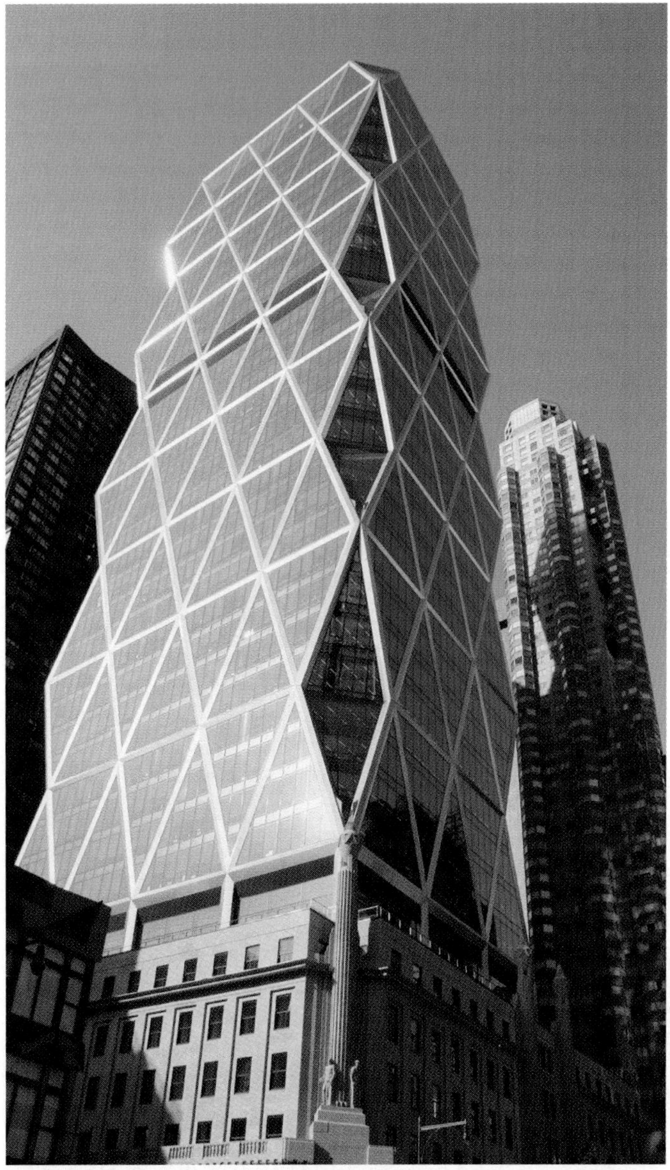

▲ **59-9.** Hearst Building (the first commercial LEED Gold building in the city), 2006; New York City, New York; Foster and Partners with Adamson Associates. Joseph Urban designed the original, old, lower façade of the building in the 1920s.

Some architects often adopt Wright's organic design concepts and consider the building's natural surroundings as they create the individualized façade design. These buildings commonly blend into their environment with materials that usually come from surrounding areas or nearby towns. Façades are simple and often modernistic in appearance, even if complex in organization. Distinctive volumes and shapes define and personalize their character. Some have exposed structural systems that define the building form and become its ornament (Fig. 59-3, 59-6, 59-9). Some integrate the regularity of glass curtain walls with the random placement of wood, concrete, or stone. Several exhibit sculptural forms that move and undulate in an organic rhythm (Fig. 59-1, 59-8). Still others develop from the horizontal layering of rectangular concrete planes with vegetated roofs and open terraces.

Whatever the design, many façades, especially those of Contextualism, are interwoven with the landscape. To achieve this, buildings are one to three stories high, or they appear as such. Solid walls, which may hide level changes, play against glass windows or glass walls. Sometimes the glass walls have structural features that shield, project, or protrude over or in front of them. The interplay of light against dark is an important and a distinguishing feature because it emphasizes the contextual relationship of the building to the environment (Fig. 59-3, 59-4, 59-5, 59-6).

■ *Windows*. Sizes, shapes, and placement of windows vary based on building function, client needs, and green design requirements. Glass walls and windows facing south and east are usual because they increase energy efficiency and provide natural daylight (Fig. 59-6, 59-10). Many buildings incorporate cross-ventilation techniques and operable windows for natural ventilation and to reduce energy costs (Fig. 59-6, 59-12, 59-16). Clerestory windows are also common, particularly in warm climates, because they filter indirect light throughout the interior. Windows become increasingly energy efficient with double and triple glazing and low-emittance (low-E) coatings. New techniques for coating and applying patterns to glass also aid in energy conservation.

■ *Doors*. Overhanging or projecting roofs that blend into the building design spotlight entries on commercial buildings. Doors vary in design and materials, but most blend with the building's composition (Fig. 59-1, 59-3, 59-12). Important doors often have some details that distinguish them from others. Wood or metal frame doors with glass inserts and sliding glass doors are common.

■ *Roofs*. Roofs may be pitched, curved, or somewhat flat (Fig. 59-1, 59-2, 59-3, 59-4, 59-5, 59-6, 59-7, 59-8, 59-9, 59-10, 59-11, 59-12). Shed, gabled, and rounded roofs also are common. They may personalize a building and/or set it apart from others. Wide overhangs shade windows and protect from rain. Some architects, such as Holl, use multiple roofs with different shapes and varying heights. Some buildings have roofs insulated with grass, gardens, or other plantings on top. Others may have a heat-welded thermoplastic olefin roofing system, photovoltaic panels, and/or roofing materials that save or create energy.

INTERIORS

As with other styles, designers of Environmental Modern strive to create interior environments with an appealing aesthetic character that responds to and supports human needs and functions. Interiors, like exteriors, show variations in design that respond to environmental concerns, but more important, especially in nonresidential spaces, are the health, safety, and welfare concerns that inform and define design decisions. Integrating nature-based exteriors with the interiors is another important design principle in Environmental Modern. There are no new types of spaces, but much individuality in the organization and placement of spaces. Open, free-flowing spaces are important because they respond to the environmental considerations. Room layouts are frequently determined by sun orientation, so important spaces and circulation areas are often positioned based on the direct or indirect filtration of sunlight (Fig. 59-16). Like architecture, interiors incorporating sustainable planning and green materials and finishes often look no different from other interiors unless that is the designer's intention.

DESIGN SPOTLIGHT

Architecture and Interior: Alberici's corporate headquarters is a High Tech LEED Platinum building that reflects its construction services and design-build identity. Transformed from a c. 1950s brick office building and a metal fabrication shed, the new complex incorporates sustainability features in its redesign. These include access to convenient transportation, reduction of absorbed heat around the building, reduction of light pollution to neighboring properties, restoration of a native prairie landscape, improvement of water efficiency (through efficient landscaping, wastewater management, and water-use reduction), improvement of energy efficiency (through lighting, HVAC system, operable windows, and renewable energy), use of sustainable building materials and resources, and attention to indoor air quality. As a result, the building has motorized and manual operable windows; a wind turbine system; a reflective white roof membrane; sunshades to block out the sun; low solar heat gain glass; a diversity of open and closed interior spaces; high and low interior ceilings; sound masking systems; and environmentally friendly furnishings, finishes, and materials. The interior color scheme emphasizes the hues of nature to create a calming, quiet atmosphere. All design decisions fully address health, safety, and welfare issues on the exterior and interior. Because of this, the building serves as a model for green design in the community.

▲ **59-10.** Alberici Redevelopment Corporation Headquarters (LEED Platinum rating), 2002; St. Louis, Missouri; Mackey Mitchell Associates with Vertegy as integrated design manager.

▲ **59-11.** House, James Hubbell Compound, c. 1990s; Santa Ysabel, California; James Hubbell designer.

LEED certification of interiors becomes even more important as standards for new and existing interiors are published and more practitioners become LEED AP or LEED Green Associates. Some designers follow McDonough's cradle-to-cradle paradigm and use, in varying levels, sustainable materials, products, and furnishings that are certified (Fig. 59-10, 59-11, 59-13). Others consider the contextual relationship of nature, site, and place by using Feng Shui, earth colors, natural materials, spatial simplicity, and minimalism. The infusion of natural lighting, water, plants, and handcrafted decorative arts enhance the nature-based character (Fig. 59-15). Additionally, designers often try to convey a sense of place. To augment all of these concepts, they sometimes choose second-hand, refurbished, or recycled furniture, and antiques instead of new furnishings.

Many interiors have decidedly High Tech or Late Modern concepts with sleek, simple, industrial-looking forms and little or no applied ornament. They exhibit informal sophistication, rich textural contrast, unique focal points, interesting architectural features, and environmentally friendly finishes and textiles (Fig. 59-10). Some, mainly architect-designed, have built-in furniture that integrates with and emphasizes the architecture. Others have much diversity in furnishing arrangements and selections but adhere to a Zen-based, minimalist environment enlivened with a few decorative objects. Many are intended as refuges or antidotes to the stresses of contemporary life. One of the most recognized designers of this concept is Clodagh (Fig. 59-14). In offices and houses, furnishing arrangements often reflect attention to personal communication and individual work habits, more of a people-centered approach.

By the early 21st century, numerous sustainable products are available, and manufacturers regularly add to their offerings. Various organizations certify products as green, earth-friendly, or eco-friendly. However, most are limited in focus, and there are inconsistencies in standards and the meaning of these terms. Sustainable products often are more costly than others are, but life-cycle costs are generally less when health and well-being of users are considered. Many earn LEED credits.

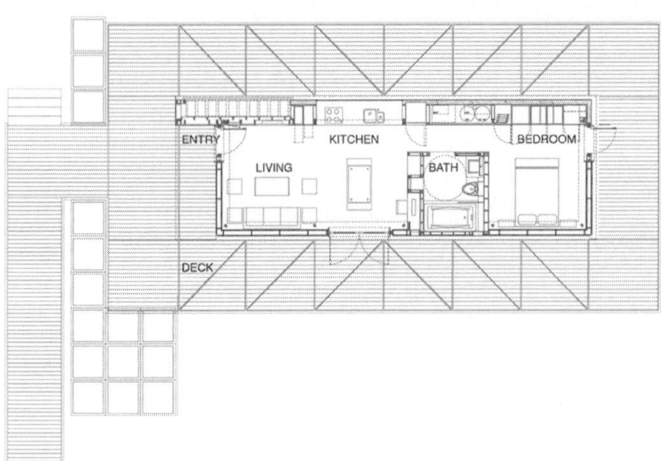

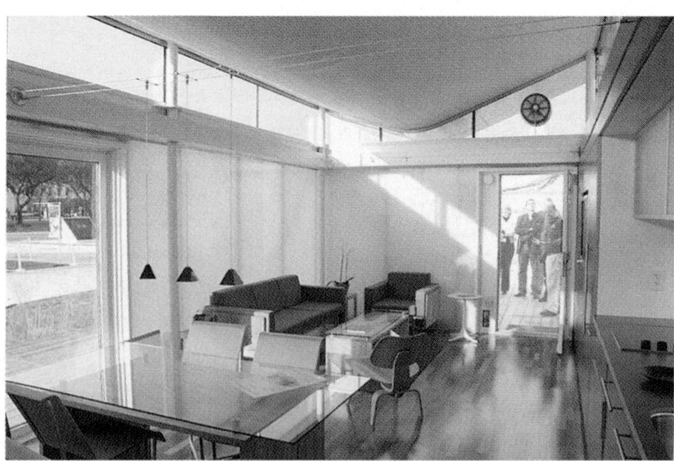

▲ **59-12.** Sustainable House Design Competition, floor plans, and interior, 2005; Blacksburg, Virginia; Virginia Tech University Design Team and Faculty.

Public and Private Buildings

■ *Color*. Color palettes are based on the hues of nature and come from the building materials so that the interiors present a unity of expression with exteriors (Fig. 59-3, 59-10, 59-12, 59-13, 59-14, 59-15). Designers often want to create soothing, calming, or quiet atmospheres, so they use neutral and monochromatic color schemes. Other choices are soft, subdued shades of green, brown, sand, gray, blue, rust, and gold, along with cream. Color accents appear through textural contrast, textiles, and accessories. Black, rich brown, or a rich wood may accent certain features or furnishings.

■ *Floors*. The most appropriate floor materials are of natural materials and include linoleum, recycled rubber, bamboo, cork, wood, limestone, ceramic tile, and concrete (Fig. 59-10, 59-12, 59-13, 59-14, 59-15). Tiles of recycled materials and glass are less common alternatives. Reclaimed, salvaged, and engineered woods are preferred for wood floors.

Carpet is a less desirable green floor covering because it can be a source of off-gassing, or VOCs. Additionally, its short life cycle requires frequent replacement, which creates waste. Carpet also can harbor allergens, molds, and bacteria. Commonly recommended green solutions are carpets of natural fibers (wool, sisal) and carpet tiles. However, rug and carpet manufacturers are among the first to adopt sustainability principles. In the late 20th century, they begin making carpet that can be recycled into new carpet or other products. They also produce carpet with recycled content and backings that do not off-gas, such as those from recycled automobile tires. Carpet also can be installed with recycled padding and adhesives that do not off-gas.

Designs of environmentally friendly floor coverings vary widely, but smooth, simple ones with few patterns and colors are the most common. Many buildings display only one or two floor materials and colors throughout the entire space to create oneness and emphasize simplicity.

■ *Walls*. Most walls are plain, simple, and unadorned. Some slide, pivot, or hinge to open or close spaces. Designers often emphasize architectural features that come from the building, develop from environmental considerations, or highlight Zen-based compositions (Fig. 59-3, 59-10, 59-12, 59-13, 59-14, 59-15). Custom-designed wood surfaces, such as paneling, cabinets, and moldings, frequently define and accent important details and wall compositions. Built-in storage may dominate an entire wall and repeat throughout the interiors. Stone walls are also common. Some walls are made of recycled gypsum board with a variety of coverings including glass, tiles, or concrete. Recycled, reclaimed, or sustainably harvested wood paneling is less common than other wall coverings. Veneers may be used to save materials, particularly endangered or exotic woods. Textiles, especially of natural fibers, and wall coverings are common in homes and some commercial spaces. Wallpapers of natural fibers, like grass, are preferred over vinyl. They and textiles are installed using environmentally friendly adhesives. Paint may be a source of VOCs for years after application, but by the end of the 20th century, more manufacturers offer paint of natural materials, low or zero VOC (emits less than 5 percent). These paints come in a range of colors and finishes so that designers can still create dramatic or subdued effects.

▲ **59-13.** "The Street," Herman Miller "Greenhouse" Factory and Offices, 1995; Holland, Michigan; William McDonough + Partners with VerBurg & Associates.

■ *Window Treatments*. Some windows are tinted and often have no or minimal window treatments to take advantage of the natural light (Fig. 59-12, 59-13, 59-15, 59-16). Others may have sun louvers or exterior shades to control sunlight, along with various types of blinds and shutters. Architectural-style treatments are preferred. However, layered window treatments that cover the entire window save energy and are used in some applications.

■ *Ceilings*. Ceilings in architect-designed buildings may be pitched, angled, curved, or flat (Fig. 59-1, 59-3, 59-10, 59-11, 59-12, 59-13, 59-14, 59-15, 59-16). Architectural features may include indentations, protrusions, beams, and skylights. Exposed structural characteristics from the exterior often reappear in the interior. And each ceiling becomes an individual area for design expression. Interior designers also play with three-dimensional ceiling compositions to repeat architectural features, create movement, and enhance lighting. Designs vary widely by designer, concept, and project. Acoustical ceiling tiles are made of recycled, environmentally friendly materials.

■ *Textiles*. By the end of the 20th century, textile manufacturers around the world are producing environmentally friendly fabrics (Fig. 59-17) using sustainable manufacturing processes for dyeing, weaving, finishing, water and energy conservation, and the production and disposal of waste. Some adopt the cradle-to-cradle protocol. Environmentally friendly textiles are often of natural fibers, but synthetics are used when they can be manufactured in a less harmful way. For example, synthetics can be solution dyed to save waste. Green textiles use natural or nontoxic synthetic dyes and fabric finishes that do not off-gas. Many textile manufacturers market their products with eco-friendly labels. Some sell only green textiles, while others maintain green textiles as part of their regular lines.

Sustainable textiles usually look no different from others, which is important. Designs emphasize textures, weaves, and organic patterns from nature. Colors come primarily from the natural environment but may be other hues.

DESIGN SPOTLIGHT

Interior: Often relying upon the Chinese principles of Feng Shui, Clodagh creates total living environments with a unique sense of place for both commercial and residential spaces. She is known for her sensitive use of materials and textures, the interplay of light, imaginative compositions, and sensual spaces that celebrate the experience of living. Natural woods, metal, stone, and brick, often with unique patterns, frequently define spaces. Subdued colors borrowed from nature display subtle variations of cream, brown, gold, and stone gray, sometimes with an accent of Chinese red, as in this dining room. Important interior design characteristics include the use of custom details, integrated contemporary lighting, and distinctive visual accents, both architectural and decorative. Oriental furniture, ceramics, and flowers sometimes appear as artistic embellishments, all of which are evident here. Her interiors radiate an elegant simplicity achieved through a sophisticated use of space, form, color, light, and materials.

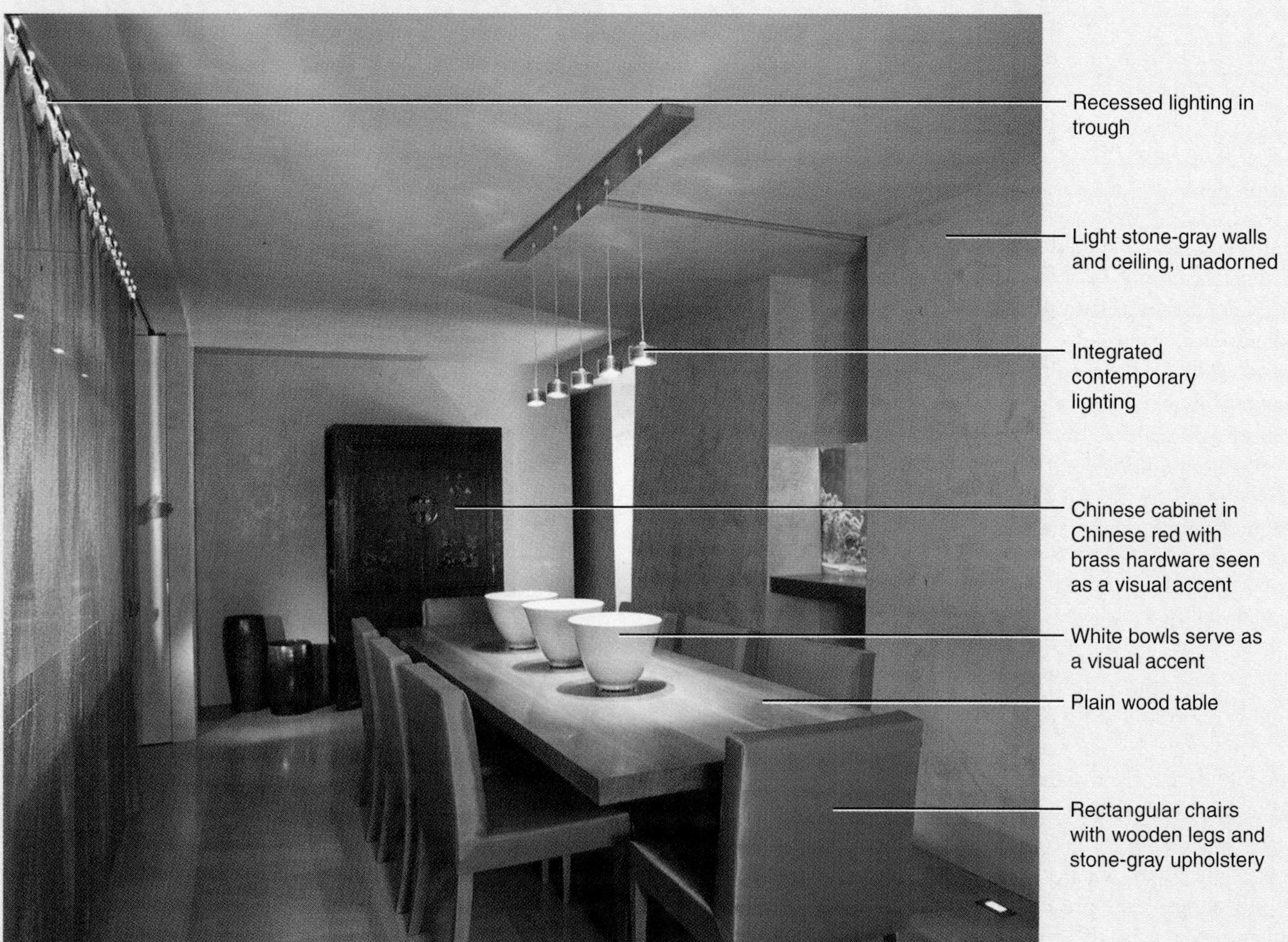

▲ **59-14.** Dining room, Downtown Duplex, 2002; New York City, New York; Clodagh.

▲ **59-15.** Hostess area and Anaconda Bar, El Monte Sagrada Resort (one of the world's first eco-hotels), 2005; Taos, New Mexico; David Sargert, Sargert Design Associates.

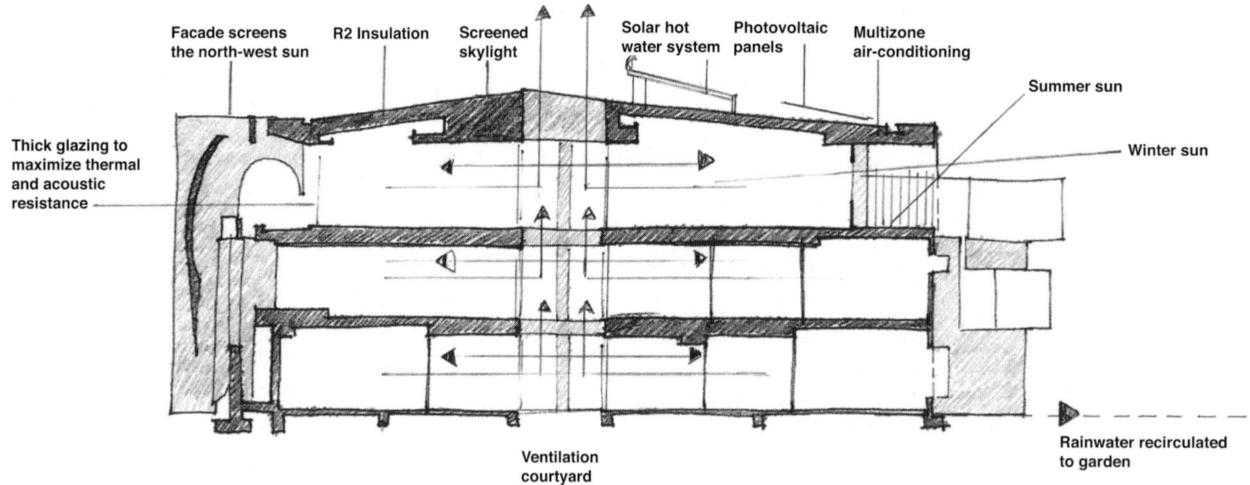

▲ **59-16.** Section, Swart Residence, 2004; Melbourne, Australia; Peter Carmichael.

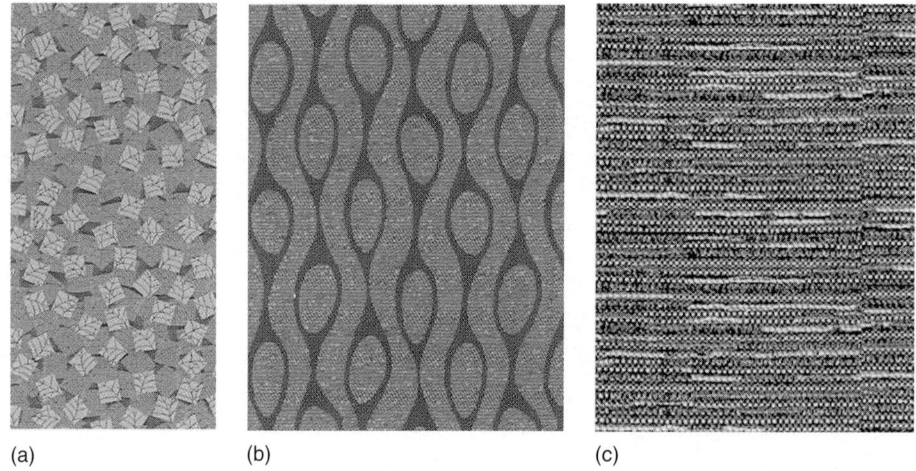

▲ **59-17.** Textiles: (a) Banyon, (b) Finn, and (c) Tibet fabrics, 2007; manufactured by Architex.

■ *Lighting*. The incorporation and manipulation of natural lighting articulates and defines the character of commercial and residential interiors (Fig. 59-1, 59-3, 59-10, 59-12, 59-13, 59-14, 59-15, 59-16). It is often more important than artificial lighting because it costs nothing and saves energy. To create spaces that use only natural light during the day, designers adopt various means, such as leaving windows bare or minimally curtained, and using light-colored and reflective surfaces. For aesthetic appeal, architects and designers may use natural light to create light wells, frame and accent walls, define ceiling compositions, and enhance spaces as artistic compositions. Artificial lighting comes from built-in fixtures that may hang, project, or be surface mounted. Floor and table lamps in interesting designs complement the interior space. There are many choices for fixtures. To minimize energy consumption, designers use new lighting technologies such as fiber optics, compact fluorescent (CFLs), halogen, or LED lights and lighting control systems that may include, but are not limited to, dimmers, timers, and/or occupancy sensors.

FURNISHINGS AND DECORATIVE ARTS

Environmentally friendly furnishings reflect and embrace concepts that include simplicity, vernacular or Late Modern stylistic traditions, minimal use of materials, and eco-friendly production methods. All types of furniture may be completely or partially sustainable. Many are made with natural or nontoxic materials or recycled parts. Some have a handmade, crafts appearance, such as the work of furniture designers George Nakashima (Fig. 59-18) and Sam Maloof (Fig. 59-20). Much furniture is machine-made with a sleek, modern, High Tech appearance, but it incorporates sustainable materials and processes and may even be inspired by nature. Commercial furniture companies quickly embrace sustainability in making and marketing, whereas residential manufacturers are slower to adopt green principles.

During the late 20th century, small and large furniture manufacturers around the world begin to address sustainability issues in the entire manufacturing process, the use, and end of life cycle.

▲ **59-18.** Conoid chair, c. 1970s; New Hope, Pennsylvania; George Nakashima.

Throughout production, they look for ways to reduce, reclaim, reuse, and recycle, and strive for greater energy efficiency, management of air and water quality, and elimination of waste. Manufacturers also move toward natural, biodegradable, and nontoxic durable materials and finishes, including upholstery fillings such as foam; structural materials such as wood or metals; glues and adhesives; and stains, paints, and other finishes. When harmful materials and finishes, such as formaldehyde, are identified, many manufacturers eliminate them whether or not required by law.

Furniture manufacturers and suppliers, like IKEA, commit themselves to providing environmentally friendly furniture. In the United States and Canada, manufacturers, such as Herman Miller and Knoll, produce more furniture that meets LEED ratings. They and others begin to market their products using a green emphasis and emphasizing certifications. Marketing documents and websites describe their efforts to eliminate harmful materials and adopt sustainable practices. Herman Miller, Steelcase, and other companies initiate programs to recycle used products, especially systems furniture (Fig. 59-22, 59-24). Nevertheless, sustainable furniture remains a small portion of the market, although the number of manufacturers and products increases yearly.

Public and Private Buildings

■ *Materials*. Wood, particularly oak, walnut, and teak, is the primary material for construction of handmade items (Fig. 59-18, 59-19, 59-20). Local woods available to the furniture designer, and reclaimed and salvaged woods are preferred and may be applied as veneers. Individuals and firms concerned about the environment use sustainably harvested wood that is certified or veneers of endangered and exotic woods. Easily replenished materials, such as bamboo, often are used, too (Fig. 59-21, 59-23). Mass-produced furniture, especially commercial, is made of steel, glass, engineered wood, laminates, plastics (sometimes recycled), and recycled rubber (Fig. 59-22, 59-24). Stains, paints, adhesives, and applied finishes are biodegradable or nontoxic. Individual parts can be reused or recycled. Some designers avoid glues by using intricate joints. Manufacturers develop upholstery fillings, such as foam, that do not off-gas.

■ *Seating*. Wooden seating pieces often have soft contours (Fig. 59-19). Nakashima designs chairs with vertical spindles and contoured wooden seats. They resemble Windsor chairs of the earlier centuries but with an Asian influence (Fig. 59-18). Maloof borrows from Scandinavian traditions in chairs with smooth, rounded wooden frames that contour to fit the human body (Fig. 59-20). Cushions are sometimes used to add comfort.

Manufacturers produce office seating that is sustainable, ergonomic, and recyclable. For example, Herman Miller's Aeron chair uses pellicle instead of upholstery and parts are recycled aluminum. In 2003, Herman Miller introduces the Mirra chair (Fig. 59-22), the first chair in the United States to be certified Cradle to Cradle by McDonough Braungart Design Chemistry (MBDC). In 2005, Haworth introduces the Zody chair, which is the first task chair to earn the MBDC Gold Cradle to Cradle

▲ **59-19.** Armchair, c. 1970s–1990s; New York; Wendell Castle.

DESIGN SPOTLIGHT

Furniture: Borrowing from Scandinavian traditions, Maloof's chairs are contoured to fit the human body, showing ergonomic considerations, as shown in this low-back armchair. Surfaces are smooth and rounded hardwood, frequently a natural oiled walnut. Saddle seats carved from several joined pieces are common, as here. Hidden dowel joints connect the seat to legs and the back to the legs, and visible ones connect the front legs to the seat. The image conveys expert craftsmanship, human proportions, and attention to details.

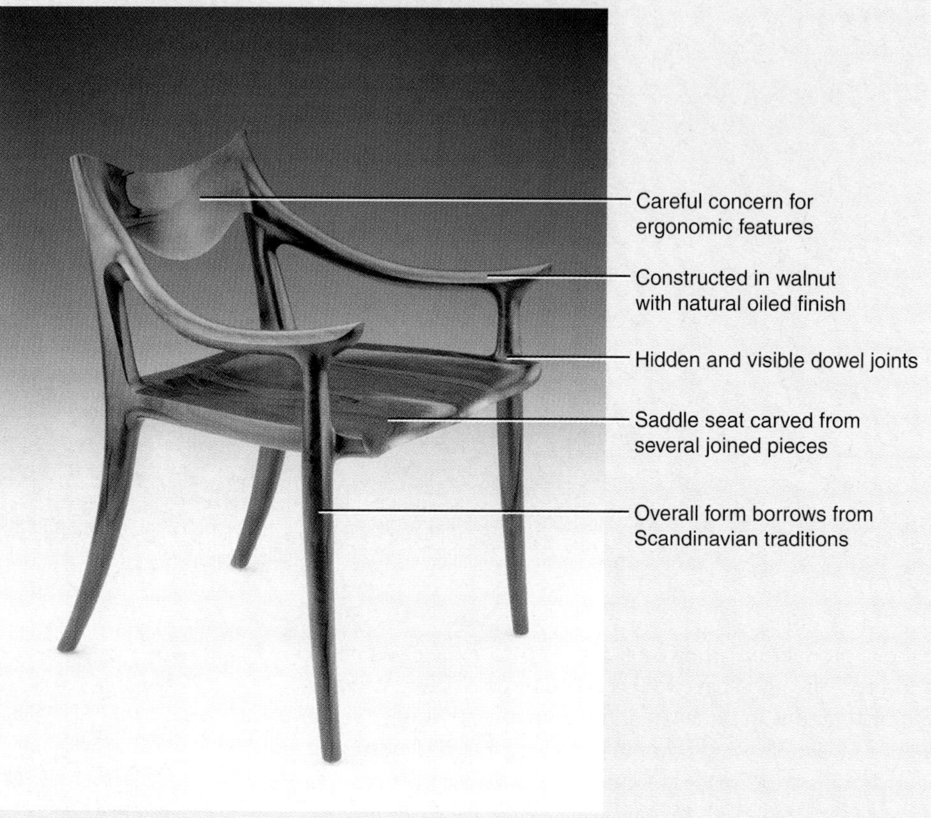

▲ **59-20.** Low-back chair, c. 1990s; California; Sam Maloof.

▲ **59-21.** Bel Air Slipper chair, 2006; Philippines and Indonesia; from Palecek.

(C2C) Product Certification, meaning that it is made with sustainable components and systems. Some earlier seating is already environmentally sound, such as Aalto's Paimio chair. Manufacturers sometimes change the materials of pieces in their lines to make them sustainable. For example, Herman Miller begins making the Eames Lounge Chair in santos palisander, walnut, and cherry instead of endangered rosewood.

■ *Tables*. Tables usually are simple, unadorned, and distinctive in design (Fig. 59-23). Some are made from large slabs of natural wood, while others use nature as a source of inspiration. Still others may be completely made of recycled or salvaged materials. Examples vary widely with individual concepts from the designer or manufacturer.

■ *Storage and Systems Furniture*. Manufacturers make storage cabinets, shelving, and systems furniture that use minimal materials and nontoxic finishes. Many office systems—desks, workstations, and storage—do not harm the environment either during production or use; some can be returned to the manufacturer to be recycled. Examples include Action Office, My Studio Environment (Fig. 59-24), and Ethospace by Herman Miller.

▲ **59-22.** Mirra chair (the first chair in the United States to be certified Cradle to Cradle by MBDC), 2003; Michigan; Studio 7.5, manufactured by Herman Miller.

▲ **59-23.** Moiré square side table with rattan poles, c. 2000s; California; Orlando Diaz-Azcuy, manufactured by McGuire.

▲ **59-24.** My Studio Environment (sustainable systems furniture), 2006; United States; manufactured by Herman Miller.

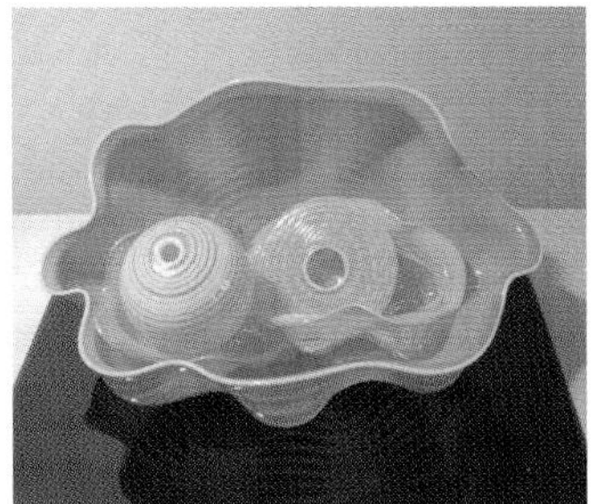

▲ **59-25.** Decorative Arts: Woven basket; and glass bowl by Dale Chihuly, c. late 20th century; United States.

■ *Decorative Arts*. Plants and water features are common in public and private interiors. Decorative objects made of natural materials, such as baskets, glass, ceramics, and some metals, highlight design concepts without harming the micro or macro environments (Fig. 59-25). A few manufacturers create sustainable decorative objects of stone, cane, or wicker.

CHAPTER 60

Neo-Modern

1980s–2000s

Now the New Moderns no longer believe in this humanism; rather they present their work as a self-justifying play with metaphysical ideas. The key architects who follow this agenda are Eisenman, Tschumi, Libeskind, Fujii, Gehry, Koolhas, Hadid, Morphosis, and Hejduk, but not Foster, Rogers, Hopkins, Maki, and Pei.

—Charles Jencks, *The New Moderns, from Late to Neo-Modernism*, 1990

The form is distorting itself. Yet this internal distortion does not destroy the form. In a strange way, the form remains intact. This is an architecture of disruption, dislocation, deflection, deviation and distortion, rather than one of demolition, dismantling, decay, decomposition and disintegration. It displaces structure instead of destroying it.

—Mark Wigley, *Deconstructivist Architecture*, 1988

Neo-Modern architects and designers seek a new design language for the 21st century by challenging the concepts and principles of the International Style, Late Modern, and Post Modern. Their innovative buildings and forms are experimental and creative. Expressive form, curves, oblique angles, a sense of motion, and unusual juxtapositions are characteristic of designs. Complexity becomes the new ornament, and designs often disregard context and historical precedent. New technology is critical to the designing and producing of buildings and objects that become art and individual expressions of the designer.

HISTORICAL AND SOCIAL

At the turn of the 21st century, the worldwide shift to the information age accelerates, and economic, social, and political trends of the 1980s and 1990s continue. Many highly developed countries, such as the United States, the United Kingdom, Japan, and South Korea, experience prosperity, but the gap between the poor and wealthy and developed nations and underdeveloped ones widens. Globalization continues on an unprecedented scale as capitalism spreads. Trade agreements, growth, and consumerism increase substantially, assisted by new technologies and developments in communication. At the end of the 20th century, China and India become important players on the world stage because of their large populations, economic booms, and growth in the middle classes. More and more firms, companies, and businesses operate internationally. The use of technology, computers, and the Internet dominates business, government, and people's lives more than ever. Communication, aided by the Internet and mobile telephones, becomes instantaneous and ubiquitous. People next door or around the globe are readily available to each other.

Many new scientific and medical advances have the potential to make people's lives easier and more healthful, but they create moral and ethical debates. Diseases, such as AIDS and cancer, continue unabated. Conflicts, wars, and terrorism intensify all over the world. Following bombings and acts of violence in numerous countries, some nations undertake military actions to stop terrorism beginning in the early 21st century.

The number of goods and products are at an all-time high, and access to them in many parts of the world is immediate. Consequently, consumers expect and demand instant gratification of their needs and desires. Consumption is regarded as important because it creates jobs and stimulates economies as well as the development of new products that can be marketed around the globe. The media spread an international popular culture characterized by materialism, comfort, and self-interest.

From the late 20th century onward, design is important, and design expressions, styles, and movements are more diverse than ever. Consumers have abundant choices for products as a result of niche marketing that focuses on a particular population segment and planned obsolescence or the throw-away mentality. More people are more aware of design than ever as a result of museum exhibitions, magazines, books, Internet sites, and television programs around the world. The Home and Garden Television (HGTV) in the United States is one of the most popular channels. Contemporary and cutting-edge design is more mainstream than before, and museums for contemporary design and crafts open, such as the Design Museum in London, 1989.

The inception of Neo-Modern ideas is generally acknowledged as 1977 when Peter Eisenman publishes "Post-Functionalism," an editorial in his magazine *Oppositions*. Eisenman's critique of two exhibitions introduces the idea of a new modern that is antihuman and unlike, even antithetical to, the International Style, Late Modern, and Post Modern. Another seminal event takes place in 1982 when Eisenman collaborates with philosopher Jacques Derrida. They submit a design for an architectural competition for the *Parc de la Villette*, a new park on the site of a 19th-century meat market and slaughterhouse in Paris. However, Bernard Tschumi, who also consults Derrida, wins the competition. His design includes a series of Follies (Fig. 60-2), buildings intended to house park activities. The bright red structures grow out of Tschumi's idea that architectural form should be independent of the activities that take place within it, an idea that is counter to much of design history. They also show a relationship to Russia's Constructivist Movement.

In 1988, Philip Johnson and Mark Wigley organize an exhibit entitled Deconstructivist Architecture at the Museum of Modern Art (MOMA) in New York City. The show includes the work of six individuals: Peter Eisenman, Frank Gehry, Zaha Hadid, Rem Koolhaas, Daniel Libeskind, and Bernard Tschumi; and one firm: Coop Himmelblau. The architects have built little, so the exhibit centers on conceptual designs. Much of the theoretical language reveals a concern for images and language derived from Derrida. More important, the show publicizes these new ideas and names and gives form to the new movement in architecture in much the same way as did the 1932 MOMA exhibition on the International Style. Eisenman's (1989) Wexner Center for the Arts (Fig. 60-1) in Ohio is considered the first deconstructivist building. It gives visual form to theories and concepts of the exhibit. By the early 21st century, many of the architects in the show are internationally known with projects around the world. Gradually other architects join the recognized group, and all further the notion of the celebrity architect.

Deconstructivist architecture brings a change through ideology, style, and type, but *Neo-Modern* is the term given to the larger movement centering on a new design language. During the 1980s, the term *New* or *Neo-Modern* is often used in the press to refer to an aggressive attack on and counterpoint to Post Modern evident in the work of Deconstructivist architects. A 1988 article, "Chaos and Machine," by Kazuo Shinohara, uses the term *Modern-Next*. It reaffirms the notion of a new version of modern that is different from, if not in opposition to, the International Style, Late Modern, and Post Modern.

▲ **60-1.** Wexner Center for the Visual Arts, 1983–1989; Columbus, Ohio; Peter Eisenman.

▲ **60-2.** Follies (Pavilions), *Parc de la Villette*, 1986–1989; Paris, France; Bernard Tschumi.

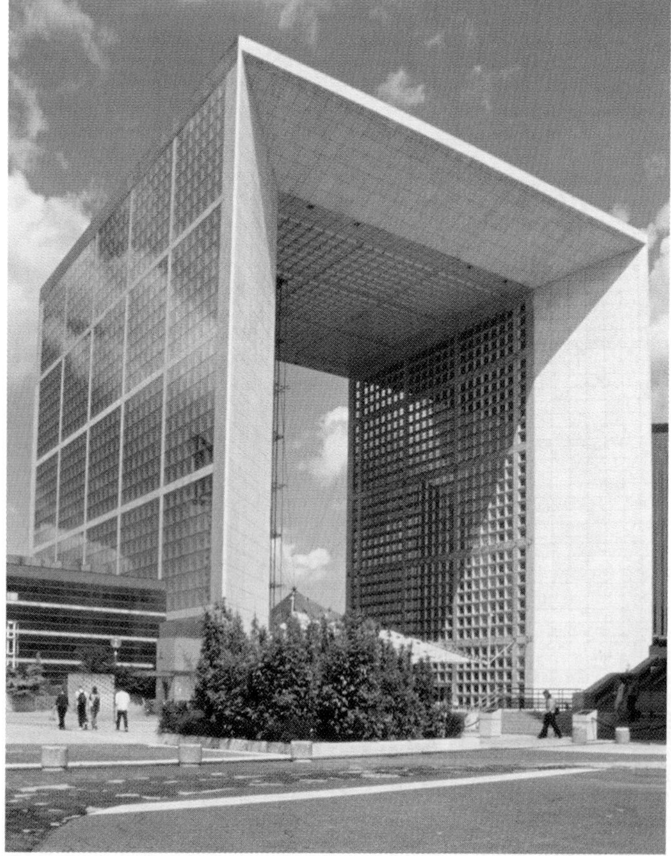

▲ **60-3.** *La Grande Arche, Place de la Defense*, 1982–1990; Paris, France; Johann Otto van Spreckelsen.

CONCEPTS

Neo-Modern, or New Modern, reacts to, rebels against, or rejects International Style, Late Modern, and Post-Modern ideas and imagery. A world movement, Neo-Modern seeks greater diversity of expression and a new design vocabulary for the 21st century. The movement, especially architecture, is influenced by French philosopher Jacques Derrida in his writings of the late 1960s and early 1970s. Derrida develops a method of literary criticism he calls deconstruction, which analyzes text using a process of juxtapositions that value absence over presence. Calling this principle "metaphysics of presence," he sees it as opposing traditional Western philosophy that values written word over speech and seeks an immediate understanding or presence of meaning through the written language. Derrida argues that meanings are absent, not present, because they are ambiguous and changeable. So deconstruction looks for and reinvents hidden or alternative meanings as well as the margins or superficial limits of the text. Deconstruction requires something to play against—a construction to deconstruct.

Other influences include two early-20th-century architectural movements. One is German Expressionism (1910–1925) in which entire buildings are often composed of free-form curving geometries. The other is Russian Constructivism (1913–1921), which contributes the idea of unbalanced geometries. Some modern art movements also influence Neo-Modern, particularly Synthetic Cubism (1913–1920s) with its fragmented images showing multiple views and perspectives. The idea of eliminating context or any references to cultural norms in art and architecture comes from De Stijl and Minimalism. Designs existing only in drawings and models recall Conceptual Art of the 1960s and 1970s.

Neo-Modern architects and designers actively confront accepted norms and precedents by turning them upside down while adopting new design methods. They challenge existing and preconceived notions of all aspects of design and conventional images of what everything should be. Architects and designers dispute or deconstruct the basic concepts of modern such as typology, function, and context as well as its formal design language. Seeing these concepts as changeable, indistinct, and subject to contradiction, they feel free to ridicule or exaggerate them or push them to extremes. In Neo-Modern, the earlier modern adage of form follows function becomes "new and diverse forms express diverse functions" in whatever changing manner the designer chooses. Design is autonomous, whereas function is dependent upon change.

In contrast to earlier Modernist designers, Neo-Modernists do not wish to reform society through design or create a style. They often decenter humanity, making human concerns less important than their own personal design statements are. Neo-Modern does not attempt to communicate or connect with the viewer or user like Post Modern. Symbols, precedents, and meanings are not obvious and usually known only to the designer and his or her select group of peers.

CHARACTERISTICS AND MOTIFS

Neo-Modern architecture and, to some extent, interiors and furniture emphasize distortion, disruption, and deviation. They do not reflect or relate to that which went before them but strive for a completely new appearance for the 21st century. Designs disassociate with location and history, especially the classical or modern traditions with their emphasis upon perfection, order, and rationality. Complicated geometry becomes the ornament of Neo-Modern, and it also devalues what masters of the International Style deemed important—revealed structure, grids, and forms developing from function. Designs stress complexity and contradictions, but with no set requirements and more improvising than planning. The apparent chaos, variety, and disorder reflect the chaotic character of the modern urban environment. Humanity is no longer as important, so designs do not seem to reflect humans.

Façades, forms, and space often are disconnected and discontinuous. Forms move, unfold, soar, rotate, curve, undulate, interpenetrate, open, and close as designers seek to exaggerate elements of earlier modern styles (Fig. 60-1, 60-2, 60-3, 60-4, 60-5, 60-6, 60-7, 60-8, 60-9, 60-10, 60-11, 60-12). Grids disappear, replaced by extreme emphasis on the form of the building or object. Form does not relate to or obviously derive from function, context, or human concerns. Space and mass interpenetrate, and solid and void juxtapose. Also characteristic are fragmentation, extreme abstraction, explosive space, and the separation of unusual contiguous parts to create complexity. Materials vary within a project and by architect and designer.

■ *Motifs*. There are no specific motifs common to Neo-Modern. Individual designers use details from projects to emphasize innovative structure, construction, and materials as substitutes for ornament.

▲ **60-5.** Museum of Glass, 1996; Tacoma, Washington; Arthur Erickson with Nick Milkovich Architects and Thomas Cook Reed Reinvald.

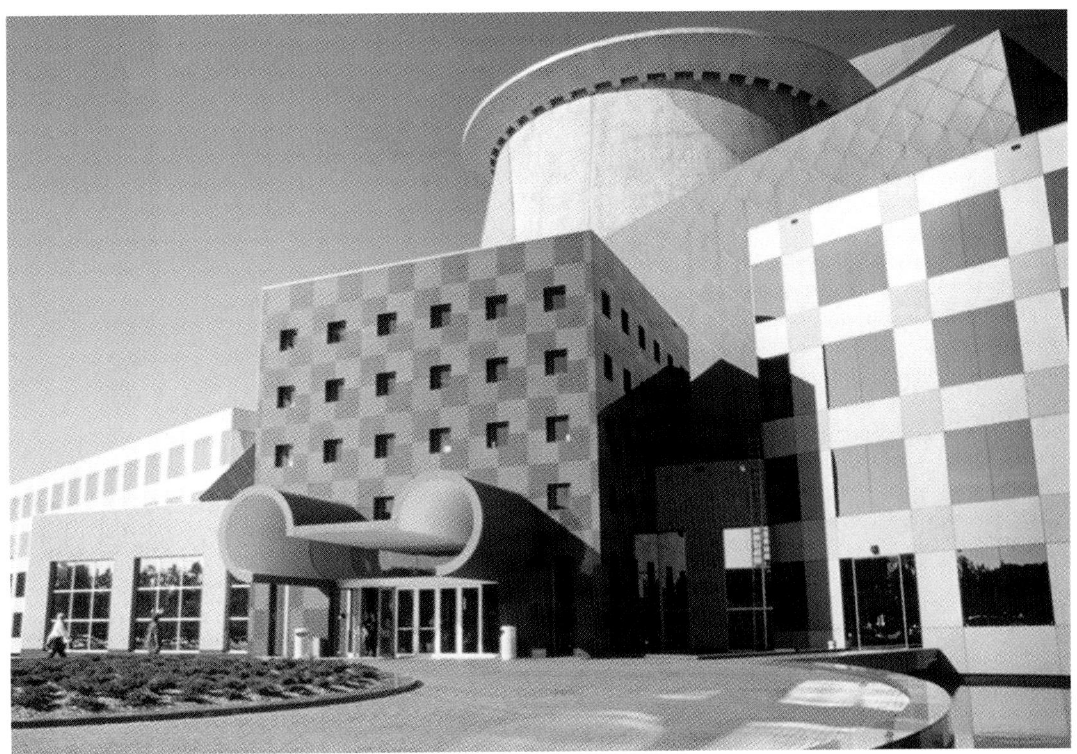

▲ **60-4.** Team Disney Building, 1989–1991; Orlando (in Lake Buena Vista), Florida; Arata Isozaki.

ARCHITECTURE

Through the end of the 20th century and into the 21st, Neo-Modern architects, including those in the 1988 exhibition as well as new design advocates, test and reinvent their own individual languages to express creativity. Buildings are complex, expressionistic, dynamic, ambiguous, distorted, disordered, disjointed, chaotic, inventive, antihuman, and the antithesis of those of the International Style, Late Modern, and Post Modern. Forms are fragmented and often look disconnected. Some buildings are large, while others are small, in contrast to the mega-structures that dominate Late Modern. Architects reject or deconstruct the principles of the International Style and Late Modern, such as expression of structure, pure form, truth to materials, and form follows function. They also discard historic precedent and the importance of context and communication shown in Post Mod-

DESIGN SPOTLIGHT

Architecture: Internationally recognized as the most important building of the late 20th century, the monolithic Guggenheim Museum is located downtown along the main river in Bilbao. The thin, silver titanium surfaces curve and undulate in rhythmical, irregular sequences, creating a dynamic spatial energy. Walls and roof merge as needed. Exterior rectangular elements are covered in limestone. The visual image is at once complex, expressionistic, distorted, disordered, disjointed, chaotic, and inventive. Developed from models and computer drawings, the building illustrates Frank Gehry's design approach in creating spaces, forms, and shapes free of grids. Applying deconstructive theories, he organizes the building through large to small scale, based on the concept of the 19th-century city. To do this, various areas, such as stairs and ramps, are broken down into units of volumetric space that become a metaphor for the Bilbao metropolis. An expansive walkway leads to the museum's main entry, which is glass and partially hidden. Large areas of curved, open space with few columns, because of the underlying steel framework, define interiors. The central atrium is an open, uncluttered area that rises 164 feet in height; it appears even larger because of the white walls and ceiling, where sculptural skylights filter light from top to bottom. Windows that vary in shape, size, and configuration wash the interior walls with light and highlight the overall sculptural quality of the building.

Facade and roof forms move, project, and contour upward
Silver titanium surfaces curve and undulate in rhythmical, irregular sequences
Twisted and distorted forms
Geometric forms offer contrast and disorder to curved elements
Building is a visual icon along the river

▲ **60-6.** Guggenheim Museum, 1997; Bilbao, Spain; Frank Gehry and Partners.

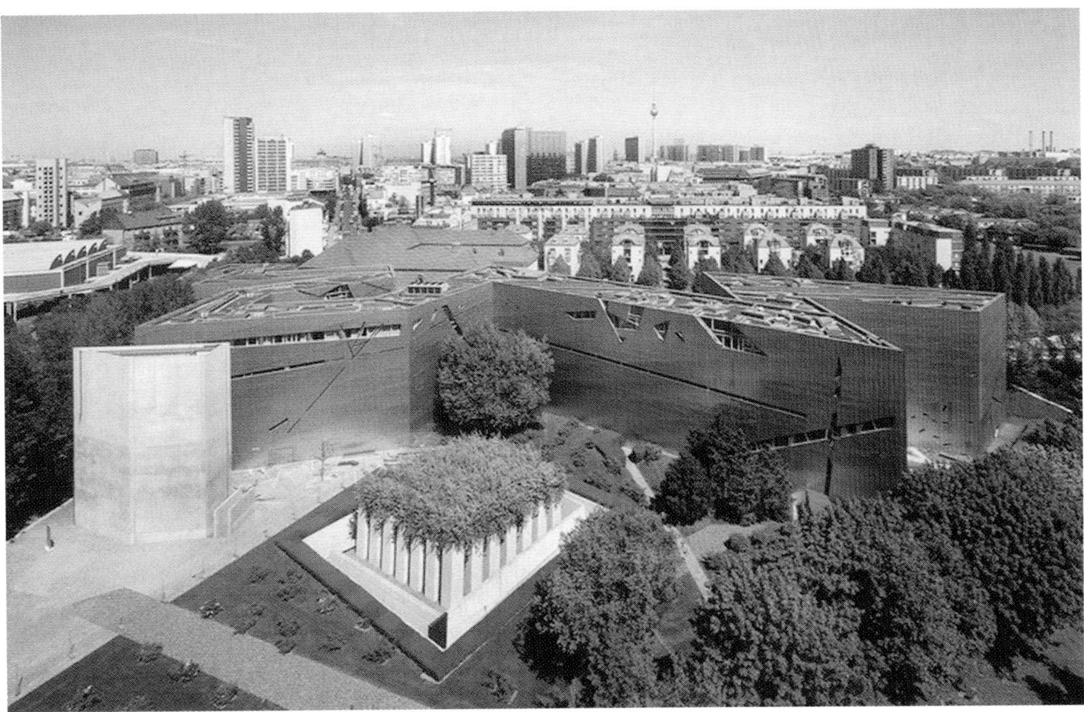

▲ **60-7.** Jewish Museum, 1989–1999; Berlin, Germany; Daniel Libeskind.

ern. Often, architects incorporate symbolic imagery or codes into their designs, but the vocabulary and meanings are difficult to read unless one understands the particular design principles and ideas. Designs often seem deliberately hostile to the public.

Neo-Modern buildings are especially dependent upon computers and software, which speed up the design process and often reduce development costs. No longer limited by process or methods, architects and designers can explore multiple ideas, often in three dimensions, and rely less on hand drawings and handcrafted models. Communication between designer and designer as well as between designer and client is faster and easier. Computers make experimentation with form, proportion, color, and materials far easier; changes can be made with a click of a mouse or stroke of a key. Appearance and performance can be readily tested using computer models, so problems and mistakes can be corrected before construction or production. Additionally, new computer software permits precise laser cutting of material for construction of these design concepts. However, the ability to actually build some structures is questioned and criticized.

Particular types of public buildings are common, specifically structures without a lot of explicit or complex functional requirements. Some of these are buildings where the need for notoriety or public awareness is considered significant. Museums (Fig. 60-1, 60-5, 60-6, 60-7, 60-9), theaters, and concert halls (Fig. 60-11) represent the most important examples. Other types of structures include rail stations, libraries (Fig. 60-10), offices (Fig. 60-3, 60-4), airports, hotels (Fig. 60-8), and houses (Fig. 60-12).

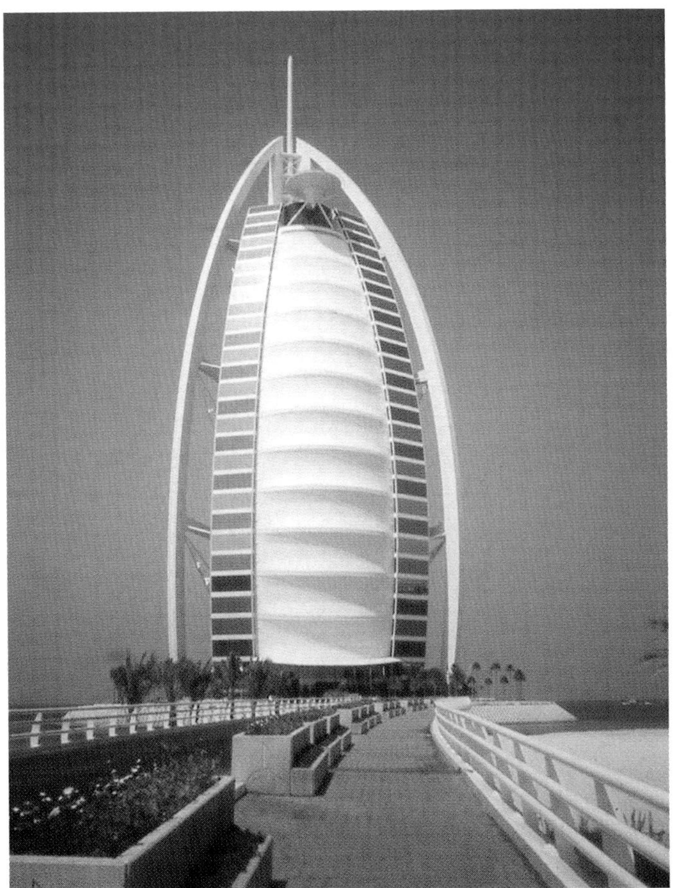

▲ **60-8.** Burj Al Arab Hotel, 1994–1999; Dubai, United Arab Emirates; Thomas Wright.

Public and Private Buildings

■ *Site Orientation*. Most buildings are conspicous because architects often show little respect for location or context. Some dominate and become the site focus through form and scale (Fig. 60-2, 60-3, 60-6, 60-8, 60-11). Others dominate simply by their unusual design (Fig. 60-4, 60-5). The surrounding area may offer a transition through a park, water, or grass area to provide a setting and reinforce vistas. A few may seem to integrate with an urban site and the buildings nearby but also project and protrude to achieve recognition (Fig. 60-9, 60-10).

■ *Floor Plans*. The autonomous forms of the façade are usually juxtaposed to create tension, disorder, and complexity, and the floor plans reflect this. Formal ordering disappears in favor of chaos and disorder. Plans are complex with many layers of interrelationships. They develop from a three-dimensional composition rather than from a two-dimensional drawing, an evolution that springs from architectural experimentation during the late 20th century. Designers play with multiple volumes of interrelated and disconnected scales of space with dominant and subdominant forms. Dominant forms usually have a primary axis along with secondary axes that evidence slight deviations, angled tilts, or disconnections from the main composition. Subdominant forms seem randomly placed as related to the whole plan.

▲ **60-9.** Rosenthal Center for Contemporary Art, 2003; Cincinnati, Ohio; Zaha Hadid.

▲ **60-10.** Seattle Public Library and "Living Room," 1999–2004; Seattle, Washington; Rem Koolhaas.

Designations of functional space on the plans come from a random system of importance, but in a pleasing, poetic, and abstract manner complementary to the aesthetic composition. Large, important spaces, such as auditoriums or exhibit areas, often define the plan and major axis. Curves, half circles, and linear movements are characteristic. Interior circulation is informally organized horizontally and vertically, with a pattern of disorganization. As a result, wayfinding is often difficult.

■ *Materials*. Common materials are steel (galvanized, corrugated, quilted, stainless, smooth sheets), stone, stucco, concrete, aluminum (perforated panels are prevalent), titanium, copper, glass, plastics, tile, wood, and brick (Fig. 60-1, 60-2, 60-3, 60-4, 60-5, 60-6, 60-7, 60-8, 60-9, 60-10, 60-11, 60-12). Architects challenge previous conventional uses of materials and search for new ways to apply them. Sometimes the applications are totally unexpected, incongruous, and contradictory. Color, often intense, may be used to highlight disorder or create order within disorder. It often functions as communication codes or identifiers, which usually are not evident to others. For example, on the Social Housing building in Berlin, Peter Eisenman uses green to represent the surrounding 19th-century buildings and a white, red, and gray grid as the Mercator grid of the world (a universal grid location method).

■ *Façades*. Façades show individuality, complexity, explosive space, chaos, and fragmentation with no expected stylistic imagery as was common in earlier or parallel developments. Forms may be sculptural and filled with motion (Fig. 60-6, 60-8, 60-11) and/or somewhat lyrical or fragmented and jagged with protrusions and projections (Fig. 60-1, 60-4, 60-7, 60-12). Façades exhibit a three-dimensional experimentation with forms, materials, and color (Fig. 60-2, 60-4, 60-6), which are often used to abstractly define particular layers, zones, or functions. Sometimes this contributes to a separation of parts. Façades also emphasize construction to create order, with engineering innovations that support distinctive new forms, unusual heights, and extremely wide spaces. Mass and space as solid and void play against each other to create tension. A juxtaposition of geometries creates disorder, distortion, irregularity, and spatial energy. Curved, straight, and angled lines and forms appear in opposition to each other to create contrast. Most façades are asymmetrical, but some have a central entry with symmetrical ordering.

DESIGN SPOTLIGHT

Architecture: Santiago Calatrava is a creator of architectural icons, such as the City of Arts and Sciences. One of his most famous and dramatic projects, this arts and sciences complex has bold landmark buildings in a newly created city that link to the historic structures in old Valencia using Calatrava-designed bridges. The architect decided "to make water a major element for the whole site using it as a mirror for the architecture," so the buildings are sited on or by large reflecting pools flanked by a meandering walkway that orders the composition. Somewhat reminiscent of work by Eero Saarinen, Jørn Utzon, and Antonio Gaudi, the buildings boast sculptural white forms, emphasizing large scale, lightness, energy, and repetition. They are unusual, eye catching, and conceptually organic, a unified creation that is at once powerful, lyrical, moving, and expressionistic. Constructed of concrete, steel, and glass, the structures blend together and stand out individually. Natural light enters through narrow slits in the roof curves and through glass walls at different levels, and it is supplemented with artificial light that enhances the smooth forms. Large areas of open space flow throughout the interiors, and dramatic ceilings defined by architectural curves shape the spaces.

Roof curves in layers with slits that let in light
White, sculptural concrete form is typical
Windows follow a grid system around a curve
Large glass wall at ground level allows light to enter spaces
Building is a dramatic architectural icon sited by the reflecting pool

▲ **60-11.** The City of Arts and Sciences, 1991–2004; Valencia, Spain; Santiago Calatrava.

■ *Windows and Doors.* There is no standard shape, size, or configuration for windows. Variety within buildings is typical, and diversity within individual forms is expected. Flat, curved, and angled glass shapes are common, as well as glass curtain walls in unusual shapes and windows housed within a grid structure (Fig. 60-3, 60-4, 60-5, 60-8, 60-9). Most windows are fixed glass so they do not open. Some windows are tinted in brown, gray, bronze, or green shades. Narrow metal moldings in neutral colors continue to define edges and shapes.

Entries may blend in with the design of the building to seemingly confuse visitors or they may stand out as if to announce themselves (Fig. 60-1, 60-4, 60-6, 60-11). Size, scale, and design of entries vary by architect. Examples may be lyrical, humorous, or somewhat bland. Usually there is one major entry that sets the stage for more to come, which are unobtrusive secondary entry/exits.

■ *Roofs.* Because buildings are designed like pieces of large sculpture, there may be little separation between roof and façade. Instead, roofs may meet walls to contour upward, angle downward, or diminish in appearance. They may be curved, angled, flat, pointed, or a combination of several shapes to achieve design variety (Fig. 60-2, 60-3, 60-10). Multiple rooflines and cutouts add complexity and interaction (Fig. 60-5, 60-6, 60-11). Some designs are symmetrical, while others are asymmetrical. Often roofs integrate with the building as a visual symbol that proclaims the building's individuality.

INTERIORS

Interiors by architects become the visual extension of the distinctive exterior form so that the building appears as an integrated whole. There is little separation between the two because of the three-dimensional plan. Architectural forms, materials, and colors from the outside repeat within to achieve a unified composition. Growing out of the Neo-Modernist fluid views of function, some interior spaces seem adverse to their intended function and/or the user. Discontinuous space; oblique angles; and juxtapositions of forms, shapes, sizes, and materials are prevalent. Often interiors and circulation are confusing and may exhibit inexplicable details, such as off-center lighting and columns that do not reach the floor.

Interiors by interior designers are far more limited and confined to new construction by others and the remodeling of earlier modernistic spaces. Within these existing shells, designers experiment with architectural forms, colors, materials, lighting, and furnishings as theater to create new visual images. Overall, interiors appear energetic, individualistic, unusual, and distinctive. Creative and original solutions are typical.

Large spaces such as auditoriums, lobbies, and airports (Fig. 60-16) are more common than others because they allow more freedom in expression. Boutique hotels or design hotels frequently hire well-known and prominent designers for name recognition and to create unusual, creative interiors (Fig. 60-14).

▲ **60-12.** Gehry House, 1978; Santa Monica, California; Frank Gehry.

▲ **60-13.** Iridium Restaurant at Lincoln Center, 1994; New York City, New York; Jordan Mozer & Associates.

Public and Private Buildings

■ *Color*. White, black, and gray frame many color palettes, with accents of other colors or materials (Fig. 60-14, 60-15, 60-16). Neutral color schemes give some order to disordered spaces. Some designers use monochromatic colors and materials in various shades to create unity and enhance spatial scale (Fig. 60-13). Others try out a variety of colors to create energy or contrast with structure.

DESIGN SPOTLIGHT

Interior: Located in the heart of Manhattan, the Paramount, a boutique hotel, retains elements of its 19th-century classically articulated exterior, but with modern touches, including distinctive new façade elements, signage, lighting, and handrails. The new additions, juxtaposed against the more traditional building context, offer a prelude to Philippe Starck's innovative, individualistic, and theatrical interiors. In the Paramount, the open lobby features a random placement of unusual and custom furniture in varying colors and materials, angled gray and metal stairs that widen as they ascend to the mezzanine, and elevators illuminated by different floor lights with colored gels. The guest room shown has an enlarged headboard that replicates a small gold-framed Vermeer painting, but with thick padding behind it. Interior colors in white, gray, and black act as a backdrop to spotlight the headboard. Starck's custom-designed furniture with its unusual and distinctive forms enriches the individuality. Lighting is dramatic as well as functional, with up-lighting mounted on a tall movable storage unit to create a kinetic effect, exhibit lighting mounted on top of the gold headboard frame to spotlight it, and task lighting projecting down in a tube shape over the table desk. In the adjacent bathroom, a new conical metal sink and metal-framed mirror offer distinctiveness to a basically simple white space. The interiors are so dramatic and create such lasting visual impressions that one does not fully notice the limited natural light, small-scaled spaces, or lack of some common functional features. Starck manages to cleverly conceal these defects through his inventive, dramatic, and distinctive design.

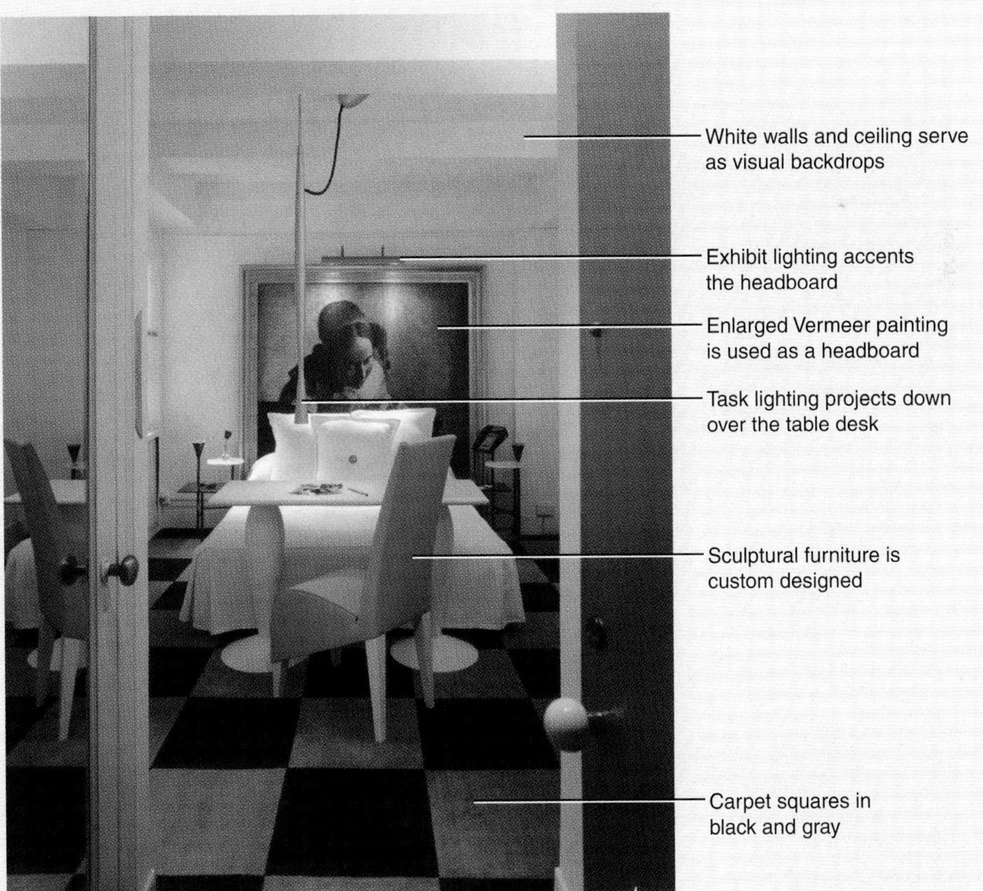
White walls and ceiling serve as visual backdrops
Exhibit lighting accents the headboard
Enlarged Vermeer painting is used as a headboard
Task lighting projects down over the table desk
Sculptural furniture is custom designed
Carpet squares in black and gray

▲ **60-14.** Guest room, Paramount Hotel, 1990; New York City, New York; Philippe Starck.

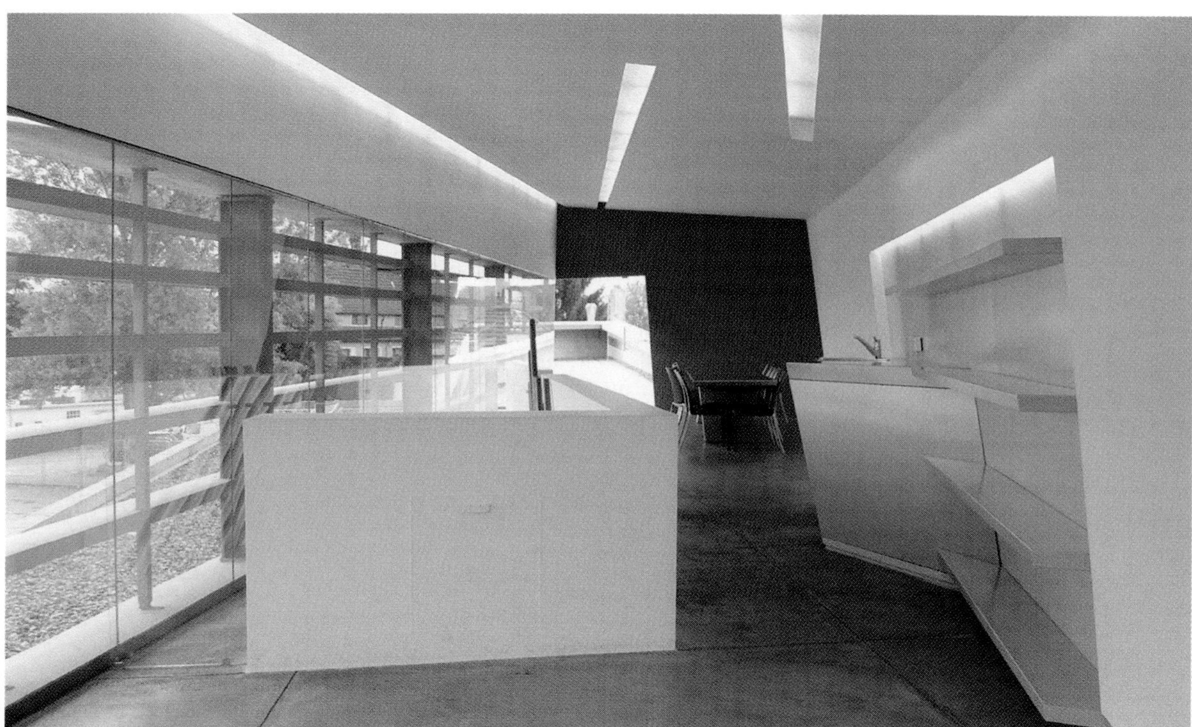

▲ **60-15.** Interior, Vitra Fire Station, 1994; Weil-am-Rhein (near Basel, Switzerland), Germany; Zaha Hadid.

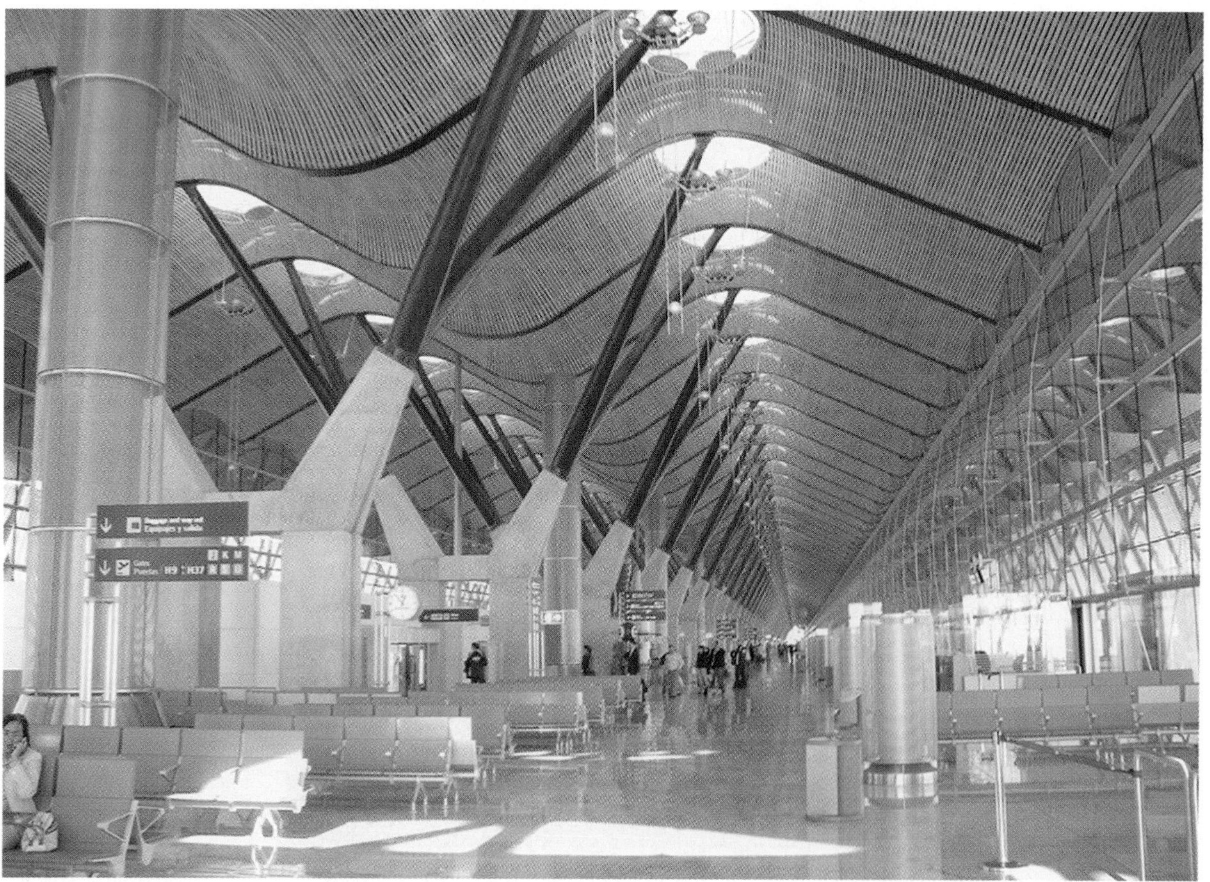

▲ **60-16.** Interior, Barajas Airport, 1998–2006; Madrid, Spain; Richard Rogers Partnership.

■ *Floors*. Concrete, marble, terrazzo, and wall-to-wall carpeting in different colors and designs are the most common floor treatments (Fig. 60-13, 60-14, 60-15, 60-16). Area rugs are less important in some public spaces but are used in homes, private offices, and other similar spaces.

■ *Walls*. Diversity in wall design and the more extensive use of interior architectural features to articulate interior space are characteristic (Fig. 60-10, 60-13, 60-14, 60-15, 60-16). Walls may be flat, angled, curved, broken, perforated, layered, or transparent. Complicated spaces often have little architectural articulation and few details to allow the space to speak for itself. Paint colors may highlight a particular wall or walls and/or significant architectural features. Wallpaper is rare but sometimes used for textural, instead of pattern, contrasts. Sometimes designers use wall hangings or drapery as a backdrop for furniture groups or to soften walls. These are usually of plain, unpatterned, softly draping fabric.

■ *Window Treatments*. Most windows have no window treatments, which can interfere with the concept and complexity. When necessary for privacy, treatments are simple and plain, such as shades, blinds, or pinch-pleated drapery of plain fabrics in white or light neutral colors. Architectural features sometimes protect interiors from glare.

■ *Ceilings*. Designers produce custom-designed ceilings that integrate lighting, have visual layering, and create interesting focal points (Fig. 60-10, 60-13, 60-15, 60-16). Creativity and originality in design composition are the goals.

■ *Lighting*. Natural light enters from various glazed openings in the building. Ongoing research on lighting, enhanced technology, and new types of lighting, such as fiber optics, support new and different lighting designs. Architectural lighting, indirect lighting, and custom fixtures are the most important applications, but so are other types of lighting including ambient, task, and mood, as well as specialized lighting for specific projects (Fig. 60-13, 60-14, 60-15, 60-16, 60-17). Often lighting is unusual or creative to add drama and emphasize circulation or focal points within the interior.

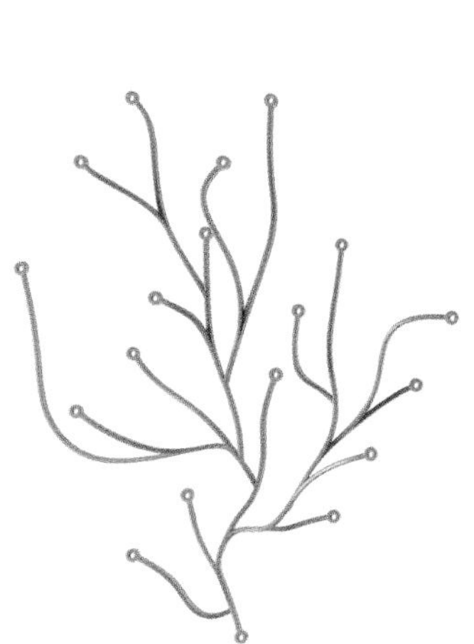

▲ **60-17.** Lighting: Algue lighting (branching light), 2004, Ronan and Erwin Bouroullec, manufactured by Vitra; and candelabra, 2005–2006, by Jordan Mozer & Associates.

▲ **60-18.** Bombo bar stool, 1997; Italy; Stefano Giovannoni, manufactured by Magis.

FURNISHINGS AND DECORATIVE ARTS

Like architecture and interiors, furniture is expressionist, artistic, sculptural, and individualistic in design. There is far less emphasis on function and ergonomics and more on furniture as art. Movement, either physical or visual, and complexity are important design characteristics. Furniture may be conspicuous like a piece of art in the interior or look like an integrated unit so it does not distract from the architecture. Custom-designed furniture continues to be important in all types of spaces but is particularly important in unique interiors.

Like architects, Neo-Modern designers challenge preconceived ideas of seating, what it should be, how it should look, and what it should be made of. Advances in technology, including computers and new materials, allow greater complexity in designs. Designers push the envelope and try out different or new shapes, forms, and materials. Lines and contours are important features, as well as solid and void interplay. Complexity and fragmentation reflect architectural developments. Designers also experiment with atypical materials, such as cardboard. As before, well-known architects and interior designers create individual pieces or furniture groups, textile collections, and decorative arts for various manufacturers. Knoll commissions designs by Gehry (Fig. 60-22) and Eisenman. Some, such as Philippe Starck (Fig. 60-19), design mass-produced objects with lower prices.

Public and Private Buildings

■ *Materials*. The most prevalent materials are laminated wood, cardboard, steel, chrome, aluminum (anodized, enameled, and cast), polypropylene, polycarbonate, other plastics, molded carbon fiber, glass, and polyurethane foam. Metals and wood are often used as frames for upholstered chairs.

■ *Seating*. Chairs continue to be the most important pieces of furniture from the design standpoint (Fig. 60-13, 60-14, 60-18, 60-19, 60-20, 60-21, 60-22). Designers try various forms and contours, but in contrast to Late Modern, they pay far less attention to ergonomics and modularity. This relates to architecture's deemphasis of function. The aesthetic character and uniqueness are more important than anything else. Consequently, some are comfortable, and some are not. Geometry and straight lines become asymmetry, curves, and sculptural features in Neo-Modern. Some pieces have solid compositions, while others are more open or transparent. Designers also explore unusual forms for bar stools, benches, and other types of seating.

▲ **60–20.** Chair One, 2003; Italy; Konstantin Grcic, from Magis.

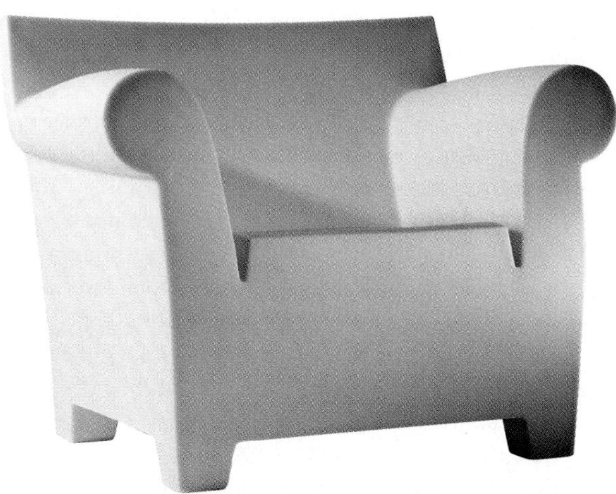

▲ **60–19.** Louis Ghost armchair and Bubble Club chair, 2002; France; Philippe Starck, manufactured by Kartell.

■ *Tables*. Sleek and unornamented in design, most tables exhibit intricate and interesting sculptural forms that relate to the general architectural design of the period. Some examples have pierced surfaces, curved bases, or disconnected parts (Fig. 60-14). As with the architecture, separation of unusual contiguous parts to create complexity is characteristic.

■ *Storage and Furniture Systems*. Storage pieces and furniture systems are not only functional, but they can become unique art objects within their environments (Fig. 60-21, 60-23). Characteristics from Neo-Modern architecture repeat through their curved surfaces, distinctive character, solid and void relationships, and individualistic expression. Sometimes designs challenge the purpose of the piece so that it may look very different from what is expected.

■ *Decorative Arts*. Decorative arts objects repeat the character of Neo-Modern architecture, interiors, and furniture. They are expressionistic, sculptural, unique, and playful. Interior designers often design individualistic pieces to support and enhance the ambiance of a particular space.

DESIGN SPOTLIGHT

Sculptural form suggests an overstuffed upholstered chair
Rounded edge offers comfort and addresses ergonomic contours
Overall massive scale and visual weight
Constructed of glass and carbon fiber laminate that can be fastened at juncture points

Furniture: Defined by his innovative and unique concepts, Ron Arad creates sculptural furniture that shows his experimentation with advanced technologies. Formed of bent and welded steel, his volumetric seating suggests large overstuffed chairs. Simple in shape and form, they dominate interior spaces because of their size, weight, materials, and visual presence. His more recent furniture designs continue these concepts, but the construction materials may be steel, injection-molded plastic, or glass and carbon fiber laminate. With the laminate, as in the Bad Tempered Chair, he is able to pierce the volume, develop more ergonomic contours, and physically and visually lighten the overall form. The Bookworm bookshelf uses the same basic principles and materials, incorporates the curved form, and presents a bit of whimsy through its design. Arad likes solid colors, so often his furniture pieces are executed entirely in red, black, or silver.

▲ **60-21.** Bad Tempered Chair, 2002, and Bookworm bookshelf, 2006; England and Italy; from Vitra and Kartell; Ron Arad Associates.

▲ **60-22.** Red Beaver armchair, 2005, and plastic seating group, 2006–2007; United States and Germany; Frank Gehry, for Vitra and Heller.

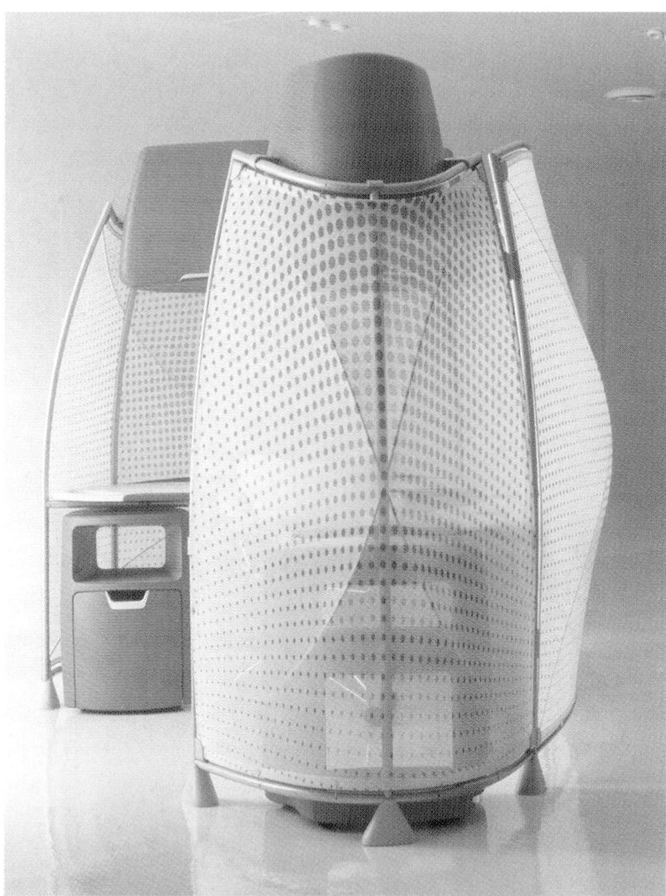

▲ **60-23.** A3 systems furniture, 2002; United States; Hani Rashid at Asymptote, manufactured by Knoll International.

Glossary

***à la Reine* (Fr.)** A flat upholstered chair back.

abacus The block between the capital and the architrave; usually rectangular except in the Corinthian and Composite orders, on which it is concave with cut-off corners.

acanthus A Mediterranean plant with thick scalloped leaves; its stylized forms appear in Greek, Roman, and later architecture, interiors, and furniture.

acropolis The main part of a Greek city, usually on the summit of a hill, housing the main temples and treasuries.

acroterion (*acroteria*, pl.) An ornament placed on the lower parts and apex of a pediment.

adaptation Designs based upon earlier buildings, interiors, and furnishings that change or exploit one or more aspects of the original, such as color; use elements in a new or different way; or combine details from other styles or periods. Simplification and abstraction are the most common changes. The end product may closely approximate the original or show a range of resemblances to the historical original.

adobe Sun-dried clay brick in varying sizes used to build many Spanish missions and dwellings in the southwestern United States. Spanish Colonial Revival re-creates adobe in plaster or stucco.

aedicule (*aedicula*, pl.) A small motif composed of columns or pilasters supporting a pediment. Created by the Romans, it surrounds a niche, window, or door.

aisle Space flanking the nave and separated from it by the arcade in a basilica or Latin cross church.

alfiz (Sp./Arabic) A molding usually in the shape of a rectangular panel that encloses the outward side of an arch and used for embellishment or decoration. Found in Islamic and Spanish architecture influenced by Islam from the 8th century onward.

***ambulantes* (Fr.)** Small or occasional tables.

antae (*anta*, s.) Pilasters marking the ends of the side walls of ancient temples.

***antechamber* (Fr.)** First room of a suite; typically used for eating and waiting.

antefix Ornamental blocks placed at the ends of roof tiles; upright ornament placed on the corners of pediment tops of case pieces in Neoclassical furniture.

anthemion Motif composed of the radiating clusters of stylized leaves and flowers of the honeysuckle.

anthropometrics Study of the measurements and proportions of the human body.

antimacassar Small covering or doily used to protect furniture from soiling by macassar hair oil during the mid to late 19th century.

apartment (*appartement*, Fr.) A series of rooms associated with a single person; introduced in the late 15th century, rooms are usually in a linear sequence and progress from the most public to the most private spaces.

***appartements des bains* (Fr.)** Rooms for bathing.

***appartements de commodité* (Fr.)** Suites of private spaces with bedchambers, *boudoirs*, and *appartement des bains*.

***appartements de parade* (Fr.)** Suites of ceremonial rooms arranged *enfilade* on the garden side; used to receive important people and deal with important matters.

***appartements de société* (Fr.)** Suites of smaller spaces with less formal décor where people of similar status eat, play cards, converse, and socialize.

***applique* (Fr.)** A wall sconce.

***appliqué* (Fr.)** A shaped and worked decoration that is applied to a piece of furniture or textile.

apron A horizontal support under a chair seat, tabletop, bottom frame of a case piece, or window sill; often carved, pierced, or otherwise decorated.

apse A semicircular, polygonal, or rectangular space on the eastern or altar end of a church.

arabesque A decoration composed of flat, geometric patterns and flowing, curving lines and tendrils. Introduced in Hellenic Greece and used in Rome, it becomes a pronounced element of Islamic art and architecture; however, plant forms are less realistic and become formal patterns in Muslim forms.

arabesque or **seaweed marquetry** Veneer in a pattern of small, allover scrolls characteristic of English case pieces in the 17th and early 18th centuries.

arcade A row of arches carried on columns or piers. An arcade may be open, as in a nave, or closed, as on the façade of a building.

arch In architecture, a curved structure composed of wedge-shaped blocks that spans an opening supported on the sides by columns or piers. Arches can take various shapes from round to pointed.

arch order A motif composed of an arch framed by engaged columns carrying a lintel introduced by the Romans.

architectonic Related to or resembling aspects of architecture, such as a space or structure.

architrave The horizontal member (lintel) immediately above columns, posts, or piers.

archivolts Moldings on the face of an arch that define it and follow its shape.

arcuated Construction using arches.

armoire (Fr.) (*amario*, Sp.) French term for a wardrobe; a tall upright cupboard, with or without interior shelves, with a door or doors on its façade.

***armoire à deux corps* (Fr.)** A case piece made in two sections introduced in the French Renaissance; the broader lower section has two paneled doors, while the upper section is narrower and is often topped with a pediment.

***artesonades* (Sp.)** A ceiling of geometric carved wooden panels.

astragal Molding composed of a half-round portion flanked by two flat portions.

atrium Large open space, often glassed or with skylights and plants and greenery, that is derived from the large open entrance hall in Roman houses. In Early Christian and later architecture, a forecourt.

Aubusson A carpet with a coarse tapestry weave, made at the weaving centers in Aubusson, France, established during the Middle Ages. These flat-woven, pileless rugs are characterized by open slits where colors meet.

awning window A window in which the individual panes or sashes are hinged at the top so that they open outward. It may have several panes or sashes.

axial plan A plan that is longitudinal or arranged along an axis.

Axminster Hand-knotted wool cut-pile carpet originating in 18th-century Axminster, England. Later, machine woven on complex looms in an unlimited number of colors.

bailey The courtyard or open area of a castle.

baize A coarse wool or cotton fabric imitating felt that is used to protect carpet, tabletops, and bookcases.

Bakelite Resin similar to plastic available in numerous colors and patterns and used for jewelry and a variety of consumer products especially during the 1920s and 1930s.

***baldacchino* (It.)** A canopy.

ball and claw foot A foot composed of an animal or bird claw grasping a ball; the model supposedly comes from the Asian motif of a dragon claw holding a pearl.

baluster A turned or carved upright, sometimes in the form of a column, that may be used as a leg or arm support, appear in a chair back, or with other balusters in a balustrade.

balustrade A parapet or railing composed of a handrail, balusters, and base.

banquette An upholstered seat that is or appears to be built-in.

baptistery A separate building used for baptismal rites.

bargeboard Decorative board beneath the edge and following a gable roof; also called a vergeboard and characteristic of wooden American Gothic Revival.

barrel vault A semicircular continuous vault used from ancient times to the present.

basilica Originally, a Roman hall of justice with a nave, side aisles, and a circular apse on one end, usually opposite the entrance. During the Early Christian period (3rd–7th centuries), the plan is adapted for Christian churches and becomes a church with a nave and two or more aisles, with or without galleries.

batter Wall that is slanted for stability; usually only on one side; characteristic form in Egyptian and Egyptian Revival architecture and Egyptian Revival furniture.

battlement A parapet consisting of raised rectangular shapes (*merlons*) and openings (*crenellations*); part of early fortification techniques but used decoratively later.

bay A vertical division of an exterior or interior marked by an order, pilasters, fenestration, a vaulting unit as in a nave, or roof component.

bay window An angular window that projects outward at ground level.

beaufat In the 18th century, a closet or cupboard, usually built-in, for storage and display. The term is a mispronunciation of *buffet*. Alternative spellings include beaufait and bowfat.

bed hangings Draperies intended to surround a bed for privacy and protection from drafts, and to demonstrate wealth. A set of hangings includes the **head cloth** that hangs at the head of the bed; **curtains** on all four sides that completely enclosed the bed; the **valances**, shaped or plain fabrics hanging from the tester or cornice; the **ceiler**, the cloth inside the tester or cornice; **bases** that are similar to today's dust ruffles; and the **counterpoint, counterpane**, or **coverlet**.

bead molding Convex molding composed of circular or oval forms.

***bergère* (Fr.)** An upholstered chair with closed arms.

***bergère confessional* (Fr.)** An upholstered chair with closed arms and a high back and wings.

***bergère en gondole* (Fr.)** An upholstered chair with closed arms and an arched horseshoe back that continues to form the arms.

***besso* (Jp.)** A country house.

bifora or biforate window Arched window divided into two lights by a colonette or small column. They are common in medieval and early Renaissance Italian buildings.

billet Romanesque molding composed of regularly spaced short cylinders or square pieces; derives from Norman architecture.

board and batten Exterior wall covering composed of boards with narrow strips applied over the joints between boards.

***boiserie* (Fr.)** Carved wood paneling.

bombé (Fr.) Vertical swelling shape on furniture. Characteristic of French Rococo of the 18th century.

boss An applied circular or oval furniture ornament that grows out of the crossing points of ceiling ribs in Gothic; characteristic of medieval and Renaissance styles and their revivals.

***boudoir* (Fr.)** A dressing room or private sitting room for a woman.

***Boullework* (Fr.)** Form of marquetry composed of tortoiseshell and brass created by André-Charles Boulle in the 17th century and revived later in the Neoclassical period. Thin layers of tortoiseshell and brass are glued together and shaped into complicated designs; when separated, they produce identical images of brass details on a tortoiseshell ground, and vice versa.

bow front A case piece with a convex front shaped like a bow or semicircle; common in the 18th century.

***braccio* (Sp.)** Lantern mounted on iron brackets in Spanish houses.

bracket A projecting support carrying an overhanging element; large, bold brackets beneath the roofline are a defining characteristic of Italianate or Italian Villa architecture.

***briqueté entre poteaux* (Fr.)** Half-timber construction with a brick infill that is covered with plaster.

***brise soleil* (Fr.)** A variety of architectural shading techniques used to regulate sunlight. They range from simple exterior angled panels and horizontal projections to elaborate mechanical or pattern-producing techniques.

brocade Rich, heavy jacquard-woven fabric with a raised pattern that is emphasized by contrasting colors or surfaces; may have satin or twill patterns on a plain, twill, or satin background. The back is distinguished by additional weft threads used in the design but not carried from selvage to selvage. Originally woven in China, some brocades have gold or silver threads.

brocatelle Fabric similar to a brocade, but its design is in higher relief, which gives a distinctive puffed appearance; the jacquard-woven design is in a satin or twill weave on a plain or satin background.

brownstone Red-brown sandstone used as a building material in the eastern United States.

Brussels carpet Looped-pile wool carpet that is first woven in Brussels, Belgium, about 1710. Durable but expensive because of the amount of wool required, Brussels carpet is produced by a weaving process that limits the number of colors in the face to five. The manufacture of Brussels carpet ends in 1930. Today woven looped-pile carpets are made on Wilton looms.

buffet Serving table or cupboard used for serving meals. In medieval times, a buffet was a set of shelves for display and an important piece to demonstrate rank or status because the number of shelves depended upon the rank of the owner.

bull pen Open space with rows of rectangular desks and files sometimes separated by partitions. Common in offices until the 1970s introduction of systems furniture.

bun foot A type of furniture foot of Dutch origin that is round and slightly flattened on top and bottom, resembling a bun.

bungalow Small one- or one-and-a-half-story house with a broad roof with one or two dormers and a porch. As a house type, bungalows have many variations and reflect many stylistic influences. The name is a corruption of a Hindu term that refers to a low house with veranda.

***bureau à cylindre* (Fr.)** A rolltop desk or a cylinder-front desk.

***bureau plat* (Fr.)** A table desk that is oblong in shape with three drawers in the apron.

burl Veneer with a mottled appearance deriving from irregular growths on a tree.

buttress Mass of masonry built against a wall to strengthen it against the pressure of an arch or vault.

***byôbu* (Jp.)** Decorative Japanese screen of two, three, or six panels that adds color and pattern and provides privacy and protection from drafts.

***cabinet* (Fr.)** A small, private space within a suite of rooms used for conducting business.

cabochon An oval ornament with no facets, resembling a polished stone or gem.

cabriole leg A curving form imitating an animal's leg; it curves out to a knee, down and into an ankle, and swells out again to a foot.

café curtains Half-length solid or translucent curtains used alone or with valances.

calico Originally, a printed or painted cotton fabric from India; later the term is applied to a cotton fabric printed in several colors.

calligraphy The art of highly ornamental script.

***camera* (It.)** In residences, the owner's bedroom; often includes a studio (*studiolo*), a small private space in which the owner keeps his most treasured possessions.

***canapé* (Fr.)** A settee or sofa.

candelabrum (*candelabra*, pl.) (Fr.) Multiarm candleholder usually placed on a mantel, table, or stand.

canopy Originally, in the Middle Ages, a fabric or covering hanging over a chair or bed to denote rank. Full canopies are reserved for the person of the highest rank, and lesser persons receive half or partial canopies. During the Renaissance, canopy frames become more elaborate, and eventually the term comes to its present meaning of a framework over a bed on which fabrics hang. It is also called a *tester*.

canterbury An open rack with partitions used to hold music or magazines. Introduced in the 1780s, the canterbury sometimes has drawers beneath the partitions and four short legs usually with casters.

capital The uppermost member of a column or pilaster.

***caquetoire* (Fr.)** A French Renaissance chair with a trapezoid or U-shaped seat and a tall, narrow back with carving and outward-curving arms. Derived from the French term *caqueter*, meaning "to cackle" or "to gossip," it was designed to accommodate the wide skirts of the 16th century.

Carleton House writing table An English writing table with two or three drawers in the apron and a superstructure that sits on top composed of pigeonholes, shelves, small drawers, and doors. Introduced in the 1790s, it is supposedly named for a similar piece in Carleton House, home of the Prince of Wales.

cartouche A tablet or panel, usually oval with an ornamented frame or scrolled edges; usually contains an inscription, coat of arms, or monogram.

Carver chair A 19th-century term for a 17th-century turned chair with wood or rush seat and spindles only in its back; John Carver, first governor of Plymouth Colony, owned one, hence the name.

caryatid A female figure used as a column or furniture support.

cased glass Two or more layers of glass of different colors into which designs are cut; also called cameo glass because it resembles a cameo.

casement window A window hung vertically and opening outward.

casements Modern, loosely woven textiles used as window treatments to block glare.

***cassapanca* (It.)** A chest with an added back used as a seat; a seat of honor when raised on a dais.

***cassone* (It.)** A chest or coffer with a hinged lid; large ones often were part of a bride's dowry and featured elaborate decoration.

caster Small wheel with a swivel on a leg or bottom of a piece of furniture to facilitate moving the piece. Very popular in the Victorian period, casters are invented in the 16th century.

cathedral The main or mother church of a diocese.

celadon Chinese glaze derived from iron that varies from delicate green to gray-blue. In Europe the term refers to Chinese and other porcelain wares with a greenish glaze; origin of the term is uncertain.

cella The main room of a temple, which usually houses the cult statue; also called the *naos*.

centralized plan A plan that radiates from or around a center point.

***certosina* (It.)** Inlay of ivory, bone, metal, or mother-of-pearl in complex geometric patterns on dark wood; found in Italy and Spain. The name comes from a Carthusian order of monks.

***chaînes* (Fr.)** In French architecture, vertical bands of rusticated masonry dividing façades into panels or bays.

chair-back settee A long seating piece composed of a seat and two, three, or more open-work chair backs in whatever style was in fashion during the 17th and 18th centuries. Legs types vary with the style. For example, a Hepplewhite chair-back settee might have three shield-backs, a caned seat, and tapered legs with spade feet.

***chaise* (Fr.)** A side chair.

***chaise longue* (Fr.)** Means literally "long chair"; variation of a daybed consisting of an armchair with a seat long enough for the legs.

***chamber à coucher* (Fr.)** A room within a suite used for receiving and sleeping.

***chamber de parade* (Fr.)** The main reception room for important persons and, consequently, the most formal and lavishly decorated room in the French aristocratic house.

chamfer A flat surface made by smoothing off the angle of a corner where two sides meet; surface can be hollow or concave or have a molding in place of the angle.

***château* (*châteaux*, pl.) (Fr.)** A monumental, luxurious country house or castle of a French aristocrat.

chenille Thick cloth woven with chenille yarns, which are plied.

chevet A circular apse with an ambulatory (walkway) and radiating chapels.

Chicago window Tripartite window with a fixed wide center glass pane flanked on one or both sides by double-hung sash windows for light and ventilation. Introduced by Louis Sullivan at the Carson, Pirie, Scott Store in Chicago, 1899–1904.

chimera A Greek mythological creature with the head of a lion, body of a goat, and tail of a snake.

china clay See *kaolin*.

china stone See *pai-tun-tzu*.

Chinese lacquer Composed of red ornament on a black background with some gold and silver.

Chinoiserie (Fr.) Chinese and pseudo-Chinese motifs that reflect European fanciful, naïve, and/or romantic notions about China.

chintz Originally, painted or printed cotton from India, not like today's glazed and printed cottons. In Hindi, *chint* means spotted cloth; its plural, *chintes*, becomes chintz; used for clothing and furnishings in the 19th century.

***chochin* (Jp.)** An outdoor paper lantern; a portable spiral of thin bamboo covered with rice paper that folds flat when not in use.

choir A location for singers. In a large church, it is usually in the eastern nave or it may be on the east side of the crossing of a cruciform plan. The choir usually has stalls or seats and is partially screened.

choirstall chair Evolves from seating in choirs of churches; a box shape with a tall back and solid paneled arms and bases.

***chumon* (Jp.)** The middle gate of a Buddhist temple. It connects to a kairo or roofed corridor.

***cinquefoil* (Fr.)** Five-lobed form; see also *foils*.

clapboard Weatherboarding on the exterior of a building composed of planks tapering from thick to thin to facilitate horizontal overlapping.

clerestory Windows placed high in a wall, especially near a roof.

clinker brick Bricks fired at higher temperatures, which makes them heavier, denser, and more nonporous than regular brick. Formerly, clinker brick was discarded, but around 1900 Arts and Crafts architects realized that it added an informality and rusticity to buildings.

cloak pin A metal or, later, glass medallion or rod over which drapery may be looped to hold it back from the window glass; also called a holdback.

cloister A covered passage around an open space; in monasteries, connects the church to the chapter house and refectory.

closet Beginning in the 12th century in England, a small inner room used for privacy, retirement, study, or devotions. Closets often were located near the bedchamber of the monarch or owner of the house, who might store his books or collections there.

club foot A plain, round or ovoid, somewhat flat foot terminating a cabriole leg; common in 18th-century England.

cluster column A column with several attached or detached shafts; also called a compound column. Typical of Gothic and Gothic Revival.

coffer A sunken decorative panel in a ceiling, often repeated in a grid.

coffered ceiling A suspended grid of three-dimensional geometric panels developing in the Italian Renaissance.

colonnette A small column used decoratively or as support, such as in an arcade.

colossal order or **colossal column** An order or column that spans two or more stories.

***commode* (Fr.)** A low chest with drawers or doors. Introduced in the 17th century, its name comes from the French term for convenient or accommodation.

***commode-desserte* (Fr.)** An oblong commode with quarter-circle rounded ends with shelves and brass galleries and doors and/or drawers in the center; introduced in Louis XVI period.

common bond A brick pattern consisting of five rows of stretchers (lengths) and one row of headers (ends).

compartmented ceiling A ceiling of rectangular panel grids defined and divided by three-dimensional moldings.

Composite A type of column developed in late Roman times. Its capital is composed of the two pairs of Ionic volutes and the double row of acanthus leaves of the Corinthian; the shaft, which rises from a base, may be fluted or plain.

composite panel In English Renaissance, a regular wainscot panel that is composed of a centered rectangular raised panel, with or without carved decoration, surrounded on all sides by four plain L-shaped panels with molding.

compound column See *cluster column*.

Connecticut or **Wethersfield chest** A 17th-century American oak or pine chest on four short legs with one or more drawers; often painted, its decoration consists of split spindles, applied moldings, and three panels of which the center features stylized Tudor roses (sometimes erroneously called *sunflowers*).

console (Fr.) A table attached to a wall and supported only in the front by legs or a pedestal. Later, any table placed against a wall; only its front portion may be decorated.

console leg A scroll-shaped leg common in French Baroque; may also be called a bracket leg.

corbel A bracket usually supporting a beam of a roof, floor, or other feature.

corbel table Wall projection composed of brackets connected by round arches; characteristic of Romanesque and Romanesque Revival buildings.

Corinthian An order invented by the Greeks. Rising from a base is the slenderest of fluted shafts capped by an inverted bell-shaped capital. Two rows of eight acanthus leaves highlight the lower portion of the capital and stalks rising from them terminate in small scrolls that support the abacus. The abacus curves outward to the corners, ending in a point or chamfer. A carved rosette decorates the center; the entablature resembles that of the Ionic.

cornice Uppermost or crowning portion of a classical entablature; also an ornamental projecting molding along the upper portion of an exterior or interior wall below the roof or the ceiling, respectively.

cornucopia Decorative motif composed of an animal horn with fruit and flowers spilling from it; the horn of plenty symbolizes prosperity and abundance.

Coromandel lacquer Lacquerwork that is made in China and composed of polychrome designs on a black background with incising around motifs.

***cortile* (It.)** A central courtyard surrounded by an arcade in a palace or other building.

***cours d'honneur* (Fr.)** Forecourt of a building.

court cupboard Consists of open shelves with elaborate carving and is no more than 4'-0" tall. Introduced from France at the end of the 16th century, it displays plate (silver and other fine pieces) in the great hall or great chamber of English Renaissance houses; commonly called a *credence* in the period.

cove A ceiling that is rounded instead of rectangular where it joins the wall.

crazing Allover pattern of cracks in glass or a glaze. It may be accidental or intentional.

***credenza* (It.)** A small domestic cupboard; an oblong chest with drawers in the frieze and two or three doors beneath separated by narrow panels or pilasters. During the 15th century, it becomes a common Renaissance piece.

cresting Ornament, often pierced, atop a roof, wall, or chair or sofa back.

cretonne Heavy unglazed, printed cotton common in the late 19th and early 20th centuries.

crewel work Designs embroidered on linen in worsted wool thread in a chain stitch; patterns include trees, flowers, foliage rising from mounds combined with animals. Used in the 17th and 18th centuries primarily for bed hangings.

crockets Blocks of stone carved with foliage that decorate the raking angles of spires or canopies; typical of Gothic and Gothic Revival.

Cromwellian chair Mid-19th-century term for an English and American armless rectilinear chair with turned legs and upholstered or leather seat and back; its name comes from its austerity characteristic during the rule of Oliver Cromwell in England.

cross-banding A border strip of wood veneer running transversely and contrasting in color and grain to the main surface.

cross vault Two barrel vaults intersecting at right angles; also called a groin vault.

crossing A square or nearly square area where the nave, chancel, and transept intersect; four arches corresponding to the four arms of the church define it.

crow-step gable A gable or parapet composed of a series of steps tapering to a single step or apex; common in the Netherlands, Germany, and Scandinavia but also in Gothic, Tudor, Elizabethan, and Jacobean England and their later revivals.

***cubiculum* (L.)** In Roman houses, a bedroom; sometimes refers to other less-defined spaces.

cupid's bow crest A top rail composed of a double ogee curve whose ends turn up into ears; name derives from its supposed resemblance to Cupid's bow.

cupola A small, ornamental structure on a larger roof or dome used to admit light and air, provide a lookout, or serve as a belfry. A cupola may be a small building, such as a little temple, or a small dome or cap on a tower, pavilion, or spire.

curule chair An X-shaped chair with curving legs and arms common in the Neoclassical period. Its ancestors include the Renaissance folding chair, medieval chairs of state, and the *sella curulis*, an X-shaped folding stool used by ancient Roman curules or magistrates.

cusp A projecting point formed by the intersections of curving Gothic tracery.

dado Part of a pedestal between the base and cornice in classical architecture; later, the lower portion of a wall, often decorated to separate it from the upper portion.

dais A raised platform.

damask Fabric with woven designs in contrasting shiny and dull surfaces, which is reversible. Originally made in China, it is imported into Europe through Damascus, hence its name.

Dante A 19th-century term for an Italian X-form chair with four legs curving up to the arms and a leather or fabric seat; sometimes a seat of honor. Author Dante Alighieri owned a chair of this form.

deal A red pine wood used in England; also a general term for woods from softwood evergreen trees with needles or scale-like leaves and cones (coniferous trees).

Delft or **delft** Tin-glazed earthenware made in the Netherlands.

demi-lune A semicircular case piece.

dentil Molding composed of projecting rectangular or toothlike blocks.

dependency A smaller, minor building flanking a larger, major one; modeled after Palladian villas, dependencies are often seen in English Neo-Palladian and American Georgian houses.

dhurrie Hand-woven pileless rug of cotton or wool made in India with a plain, twill, or tapestry weave.

dime novel Mass-produced short stories aimed at young people and sold in dry goods stores and other similar locations between World Wars I and II.

Diocletian window See *thermae* window.

divan Couch without a back or arms intended for lounging appearing in the second half of the 19th century; the name is from the built-in dais covered with pillows and fabrics of Turkish origin for persons of rank.

dome A hemispherical or semielliptical convex covering over a circular, square, or polygonal space; a series of arches rotating in a circle.

***domus* (L.)** In Roman architecture, a single-family dwelling for the well-to-do.

***donjon* (Fr.)** A tall, inner tower of a castle; also called *keep*.

Doric An order introduced by the Greeks and characterized by a thick column with fluted shaft and no base; an echinus and abacus comprise the capital and triglyphs and metopes with relief sculpture define the frieze. Roman Doric columns are more slender than Greek ones and have a base.

dormer Window projecting through the roof.

double-hung or **sash window** Two sliding sashes or panels hold the glass and slide up and down; invented in Holland in the 1640s. Pegs are used to hold the sashes up until they are replaced by cords and counterweights.

dovetail A joint composed of wedge-shaped projections (like a bird's tail) that connects two perpendicular boards together.

drawtop or **draw table** An extension table with two leaves; the two end leaves slide under the center one when closed and pull out when open.

dressing table Any table designed to be used when dressing or applying makeup. During the 17th century, the term refers to a small table with two or three drawers. During the 18th century, dressing tables become more elaborate with drawers, cupboards, and superstructures and are used by both men and women.

***dressoir* (Fr.)** A display piece with open shelves arranged in tiers or steps like a buffet. Introduced in the Middle Ages, it eventually becomes a table with shelves used to dress or prepare food for cooking.

drugget A durable wool or linen and wool fabric used to protect carpet.

***duchesse brisée* (Fr.)** A deep *bergère* with stool.

Dutch cross bond Alternating rows of brick headers (ends) and stretchers (lengths) with colored mortar that creates diamond patterns.

ear A decorative element consisting of a right-angled projection in the top corners of a doorway, fireplace, or other feature; or extensions on both sides of the crest rail of a chair beyond the back upright.

earthenware Pottery or ceramics fired at low temperatures so it does not vitrify. Porous, opaque, and somewhat coarse, it is usually glazed.

easie chair Period name for an upholstered wing chair introduced in the late 17th century.

***ébéniste* (Fr.)** A cabinetmaker who produces furniture with veneers; term comes from the use of ebony as the primary wood used for veneer.

echinus A rounded cushion or projection that is part of the Doric capital.

ecology The study of the relationship between organisms and their environments.

egg and dart or **egg and tongue** or **ovolo** Molding composed of alternating oval or egg-shaped and pointed forms.

***églomisé* (Fr.)** Painting or gilding applied to the reverse side of a piece of glass.

Egyptian faience A glazed, non-clay ceramic made mainly of crushed quartz or sand and small amounts of other ingredients. Before firing, it is coated with a soda-lime and silica glaze that is most often blue-green; other colors, such as white, yellow, red, brown and black, were added later. The Ancient Egyptians used faience to make figurines, jewelry, bowls, and other things. Sometimes it was used for wall tiles.

***égyptiennes en gaine* (Fr.)** An unfluted pillar or column with an Egyptian head for a capital and either feet or a molding for the base. Common in French Consulate and Empire tables and case pieces.

***en cabriolet* (Fr.)** A concave upholstered chair back.

***encoignure* (Fr.)** Low corner cupboard with a bow or flat front that stands on three or four legs; a series of shelves, graduated in size, may fit on top.

***enfilade* (Fr.)** Introduced about 1650, the French system of aligning the interior doors of rooms on an axis so that when they are opened, they create a vista. Doors are placed near windows with fireplaces centered on the same wall as doors.

engaged column A column attached to a wall; vertical member that is circular in section.

English bond A brick pattern of alternating rows of headers and stretchers.

entablature Part of a building above the columns; composed of architrave, frieze, and cornice.

entasis A slight swelling or outward curve of a column shaft; a Greek optical refinement, it is used to counter any inward curve and also gives the appearance that the column is responding to the load it carries.

environmentalism Refers to the principles and methods for reclaiming the natural environment from the destructive effects of industrialization and humanity.

***equipal* (Sp.)** A chair with a circular seat supported by a cylindrical base of cedar splits developed in Mexico; popular for *patios*.

ergonomics An applied science that addresses human fit to environments. Using knowledge from design, psychology, anatomy, and physiology, ergonomics creates objects and systems that people can use comfortably, efficiently, and safely.

***estípite* (Sp.)** A broken pilaster that is composed of stacks of square balusters and a capital that tapers toward the base. Characteristic of Spanish Baroque architecture, they appear in high-style examples of Spanish Colonial Revival.

étagère Display piece consisting of shelves, doors, and/or drawers and mirrored backs. Introduced in the early 19th century, it comes into its own during Rococo Revival; also called a whatnot.

eyebrow dormer A low dormer window with a concave, convex, concave curve like an eyebrow. Unlike a regular dormer, it does not project from the roof.

faience Tin-glazed earthenware made in France after 1600. Wares follow fashionable European styles and copy Chinese ceramics in underglaze blue. Porcelain supersedes it in popularity so faience becomes a peasant art by 1800.

fan vaulting Vaulting that resembles a fan in shape; not structural, it is characteristic of the Perpendicular Gothic and some Gothic Revival in England.

fanlight A semicircular or semielliptical window with radiating mullions, often above a door.

farthingale chair or **back stool** A rectangular side chair common in the English Renaissance with four legs joined by stretchers close to the floor, an upholstered seat, and a slightly raked upholstered back. *Farthingale* is a 19th-century term suggesting that the form developed to accommodate wide hoop skirts; commonly called a *back stool* during the period because of its resemblance to a stool with a back.

fascia Plain, wide bands (usually three), each projecting beyond the other, forming the frieze; often seen in the Ionic and Corinthian orders.

***fauteuil* (Fr.)** Chair with upholstered seat and back and open arms; or an armchair.

feng shui Chinese system of orientation that uses the earth's natural forces to balance yin and yang to achieve harmony.

festoon An ornament depicting a garland of fruit or flowers tied with ribbons and hanging from a rosette or other form; also, a curtain that draws up by tapes on the back, forming a swag shape, introduced in the 18th century.

finial Decorative turned or carved element that terminates a post or corner and accentuates a focal point or crossing of elements.

***flambeau* (Fr.)** A candlestick.

Flemish bond A brick pattern of alternating headers (ends) and stretchers (lengths) on the long side.

***fleur-de-lis* (Fr.)** A motif consisting of three stylized flowers or petals; the center is erect while the two flanking petals curve out and down. Although widely used as a heraldic device in the Middle Ages, it becomes associated with French royalty through French designers' use of it for them.

flock paper Textured wallpaper created by gluing minute textile fibers to the surface; intended to imitate textiles.

fluted Shallow concave channels or grooves in a column, pilaster, chair leg, or other vertical surface.

flying buttress On an exterior, an arch or rounded form extending from the nave wall between the clerestory windows to a separate pier a short distance away. Like a regular buttress, it helps strengthen against pressure from vaults. Common on Gothic and some Gothic Revival cathedrals.

***foils* (Fr.)** Small arc openings or lobes separated by cusps (projecting points at intersections) in Gothic tracery; *trefoils* have three lobes; *quatrefoils* have four; *cinquefoils* have five.

foliated arch An arch that is composed of small arcs or foils; characteristic of Islamic architecture.

four square A two-story cubic-shaped house type in the United States; common in the early 20th century.

***frailero* (Sp.)** Rectangular arm or side chair.

French whorl foot English term for a carved foot composed of an outward and upward scroll. Originating during French Baroque, it becomes very common during the Rococo, where it terminates a cabriole leg. May also be called a *whorl foot* or *French foot*.

French window Casement or fixed window that reaches to floor level and usually opens to a balcony or porch. Also called *French door*.

fresco Water-based painting done on damp lime plaster. After the plaster dries it may be polished. Fresco refers to the technique as well as the painting itself.

fresco paper Wallpaper with decorative borders that appear to divide the wall into vertical panels or compartments. Most centers are plain or have small repeating patterns, but some have landscapes with fountains, statues, and flowers.

fret A Greek ornament composed of intersecting lines at right angles; also called *Greek key*.

fretwork Carved ornament composed of straight lines in geometric patterns. It may be open as in a chair back or in relief as on a seat rail; seen on aprons, legs, stretchers, and arms of furniture with Rococo or Chinese influence.

frieze The middle portion of a classical entablature between the architrave and cornice; may be decorated or plain; also, a decorated band on an interior wall beneath the cornice.

***fulcrum* (L.)** A headrest on a Roman couch; a structure on which the sitter leans, which is often lavishly decorated with animals, busts, and satyrs.

furniture cases Period term for slipcovers that protect upholstery.

***fusuma* (Jp.)** A Japanese opaque interior sliding screen.

***futon* (Jp.)** A thick, rolled comforter that serves as bed and bed covering.

gable-end house A house form in which the narrow or gabled end of the roof forms the façade.

gable roof A roof composed of two sloping sides.

gadrooning Repeating carved decoration consisting of concave flutes or convex reeding on the edges of tables and feet; typical decoration on the cups and covers of Elizabethan and Jacobean furniture.

gambrel roof A roof with two pitches or slopes on either side of a ridge. It is a definitive characteristic of Dutch Colonial Revival.

***garderobe* (Fr.)** A room within a suite used for dressing and storage, as well as sleeping quarters for servants.

gate leg table A 19th-century term for a table with drop leaves supported by hinged gates or frames when raised; introduced in the early 17th century, its contemporary name was *falling table*.

***Ghiordes* knot** See *Turkish knot*.

gingham Light- or medium-weight cotton in a plain weave. It may be a two-color check, multicolor plaid, a stripe, or a solid. Its name may be derived from *ging-gang*, a Malaysian word meaning "striped."

girandole Named for a type of Italian fireworks, an elaborate wall bracket with candleholders and sometimes mirrors, beginning in 17th-century England and France. Mirrors with candleholders are sometimes called *girandoles*.

glass curtain In the 19th century, a curtain of thin or translucent material, such as muslin, beneath panels, next to the window glass.

gondola chair A chair with a low, concave back composed of a sweeping curve that terminates at the seat; introduced in France in the mid-18th century, it is especially fashionable in French Empire.

great chamber Originally, a large room given this name to distinguish it from other chambers. In the later Middle Ages, it becomes a room of state, second in size, importance, and magnificence of decoration to the great hall. The king or lord of the manor and important guests retreat to the great chamber for meals and privacy. Eventually the great chamber surpasses the great hall in size and grandeur.

great hall A communal living space of the Middle Ages used for eating, entertaining, dancing, and, sometimes, sleeping; core of the medieval house.

Greek cross A church plan composed of four arms equal in length. It characterizes Byzantine and some Renaissance churches.

Greek key Motif composed of short, straight, horizontal and vertical lines at right angles to one another; also called *meander* or *fret*.

griffin A mythological creature with the head and wings of an eagle and the body of a lion.

grisaille A *trompe l'oeil* painting that imitates relief sculpture in monochromatic grays.

groin vault Two barrel vaults intersecting at right angles; the groins are the lines of intersection; may be called a *cross vault*.

grotesque Renaissance interpretations of ancient Roman ornament found in grottoes or underground excavations that begin in the last two decades of the 15th century after the discovery of Nero's Golden House in Rome; usually a fanciful ornament in paint and stucco resembling an arabesque with colorful depictions of animals, flowers, mythological creatures, and architecture.

***guéridon* (Fr.)** A floor candle stand that may be sculptural or a small table. See also *torchère*.

guilloche Twisted circular bands or overlapping circular forms of ornament.

gul A repeating octagonal motif originating in Turkoman rugs; derived from the Persian term for flower, it may be a very stylized floral motif or a heraldic device or tribal symbol becuase each tribe had its own distinctive *gul*.

half-timber construction (*columbage*, Fr.; *fackwerk*, Ger.) Consists of a structural wooden frame with an infill of brick, wattle, and daub (clay, mud, and sticks), plaster, or other materials.

hard paste Alternative term for true porcelain, which is made of china clay and china stone.

haremlik In the Middle East, private or women's areas of the home where women, children, and servants dwell; male access is limited to the head of the house and relatives.

hieroglyphs Egyptian picture writing.

highboy American term for a high chest of drawers supported on legs.

high-style Architecture, interiors, and furniture at the forefront of fashion, stylistic, or design trends and usually associated with the aristocracy or the affluent.

hipped roof A roof composed of a single slope on all four sides. The hips are the lines of intersections.

Historicism As applied to architecture, interiors, furniture, and the visual arts, a belief system dominating the 19th century in which historical character becomes the dominant standard of value, thus producing borrowings of ideas and characteristics from past styles.

hood molding Heavy molding over a window originally designed to carry away water. Characteristic of Gothic Revival, Italianate, Renaissance Revival, and Second Empire, hood moldings may be simple moldings or pediments.

horseshoe arch Rounded or pointed arch that is narrower at the bottom like a horseshoe; the top may be round or pointed. Common in Islamic architecture and found in Moorish Revival and Spanish Colonial Revival.

***hosho* (Jp.)** The crowning element or finial of a *pagoda* roof in Japanese architecture.

***hôtel* (Fr.)** Luxurious townhouse of a French aristocrat.

hypostyle hall In Egyptian temples, a covered area or space filled with numerous tightly clustered columns.

***ikebana* (Jp.)** A formal flower arrangement found in the Japanese *tokonoma*; also refers to Japanese art of flower arranging.

***Imari* (Jp.)** Porcelain with crowded, elaborate patterns in strong reds, blues, and golds; patterns come from native Japanese textiles and brocades. Shipped from the port of Imari, Japan, its forms, decoration, and palette are much copied in Europe.

***impluvium* (L.)** A shallow cistern in the floor of the atrium used to catch rainwater from the opening in the roof (*compluvium*) in a Roman house.

impost block A block that separates the capital of a column or pier from the springing of an arch.

incised Cut or carved ornament that is below the surface.

ingrain American term for flat-woven wool carpet with a reversible pattern. Originally made in Kidderminster, England, it is also known as a Scotch carpet.

inlay Decoration created by embedding one material into another to create a flat surface pattern or border.

***insula* (L.)** An apartment house for the middle class in Roman cities.

Ionic A Greek order with slender, fluted shaft and capital composed of two pairs of volutes or spirals, one pair on the front of the column and one pair on the back. The volutes rest on a circular echinus carved with egg and dart and bead moldings; the shallow abacus is carved also. The shaft is more slender than Doric and has a molded base. The architrave may be plain or composed of fascia and may be capped by a dentil or egg and dart moldings.

***iwan* (*liwan*)** In Islamic dwellings, a summer main room, usually on the south side of the principal courtyard and closed on three sides; the open side provides a cool space for entertaining in warm weather.

jalousie Window or door with a series of horizontal panes in a frame. The panes open outward by a hand crank and overlap each other when closed.

***jalousies à la persienne* (Fr.)** Venetian blinds with wooden slats, introduced in the early 18th century.

Japanese lacquer Gold and silver motifs on a black lacquer background.

japanning English and European imitations of Oriental lacquer done mostly on red and black backgrounds, but also on white, blue, yellow, and green backgrounds. Not really a lacquer, it consists of many coats of varnish. Decorations are raised and depict Chinese and pseudo-Chinese scenes and motifs in gold or silver.

Japonisme A style evolving from Japanese prints, decorative arts, and architecture that emerges in late-19th- and early-20th-century Europe and North America.

jerga A flat woven woolen rug in a twill weave of two colors.

jerkinhead roof A roof in which the gable does not rise to a point but is cut off and appears to turn downward, which creates a hipped gable.

jetty An upper story that overhangs a lower one in a timber frame building. First appearing in the Middle Ages, jetties appear in Gothic Revival, Queen Anne, Stick Style, and Colonial Revival in England and the United States.

joined stool An English Renaissance stool with oblong seat, turned or fluted columnar legs, and a continuous stretcher near the floor.

***kairo* (Jp.)** A roofed corridor surrounding the sacred area of a Japanese Buddhist temple complex.

***Kakiemon* (Jp.)** A type of Japanese porcelain with asymmetrical designs in red, yellow, green, and blue with occasional gilding; colors and patterns exploit the white body and adapt to octagonal, hexagonal, and square shapes. *Kakiemon* is the name of the family who develops it in the late 17th century; imported into Europe, it is often copied.

***k'ang* (Ch.)** A built-in or free-standing platform for sitting or reclining in Chinese homes; often has a canopy supported by columns and embellished with carving.

kaolin China clay; a white clay used in porcelain.

***katagami* (Jp.)** Fabric dyed by means of a hand-cut stencil.

keep A tall, inner tower of a castle; also called *donjon*.

kelim or **kilim** A handwoven, heavy, pileless, and reversible rug made in the Middle East and parts of Asia. Typical patterns are geometric and multicolored. The term means "double-faced."

***Ken* (Jp.)** In Japanese architecture, a system of modules for house plans derived from the arrangement of structural pillars; a unit of measurement equal to 5.96′.

***klismos* (Gr.)** A light, simple chair introduced by the Greeks. It has four outward-curving legs and a seat of plaited leather or rushes; the back uprights continue the curve of the back legs and support a horizontal concave board at shoulder height. Usually unornamented, it depends upon its silhouette and proportions for beauty. The *klismos* is the model for numerous Directoire, Empire, Biedermeier, English Regency, and American Empire chairs.

***kodo* (Jp.)** A lecture hall within a Japanese Buddhist temple complex.

***kokera-buki* (Jp.)** Wooden shingles in multiple layers in traditional Japanese architecture.

***kondo* (Jp.)** The main hall of a Japanese Buddhist temple complex in which the images of Buddha are housed.

Kufic Earliest calligraphy of Islamic art; vertical and angular in form, it is particularly suitable for inscriptions on stone or metalware and textiles.

lacquer An opaque finish made from the sap of trees. Lacquering originates in China but is also used in Japan. Following the importation of lacquered wares, the Europeans learn to imitate it and eventually to make it.

lambrequin Decorative window treatment composed of stiffened, unpleated fabric hanging from a cornice. It may be trimmed with tassels or other embellishment. Today it means a decorative treatment framing a window's top and sides.

laminate Several layers of wood glued together with grains at right angles to each other; used extensively in Rococo Revival and some modern furniture for seating backs and other parts.

lampas Patterned fabric with a satin weave in which additional threads create a design in one texture on the background of another with different texture. The effect is a two-color damask.

lancet A slender, pointed window usually with two lights.

***laterna* (Sp.)** A lantern with a metal frame.

Latin cross Cross-shaped plan in which the three upper arms are equal in length and shorter than the lower arm. It becomes the usual plan for churches during the Romanesque period (9th–12th centuries) and afterward.

lattice An open-work grille; in Chinese architecture, a large-scale geometric pattern used on doors.

***lavabo* (L.)** A wall fountain consisting of a wash basin with flaring sides and an upper portion to hold and distribute water.

lean-to A structure with a single pitched roof attached to a taller portion of a building.

***lettiera* (It.)** An Italian Renaissance bed with a high headboard; it rests on a platform composed of three chests for storage, sitting, etc.

linenfold Carving in wood that resembles vertical folds of cloth. Probably introduced in the 15th century by Flemish carvers, it has no architectural prototype. Likely a 19th-century term, it was originally called wavy work.

lintel Horizontal member in post and beam construction; or a horizontal member over an opening that is decorative or carries the wall above it.

list carpet Carpet with strips of cloth, ingrain carpet, or selvages of fabric forming weft threads; called rag rugs in the 19th century.

***lit* (Fr.)** Bed.

***lit d'ange* (Fr.)** A bed with a canopy that is shorter than the bed and is attached to the wall.

***lit à la duchess* (Fr.)** A bed with an oblong tester or canopy as long as the bed attached to the wall or posts.

***lit à la française* (Fr.)** A bed that has a headboard and footboard of equal height; the long side sits against the wall and a canopy above supports hangings.

***lit à la polonaise* (Fr.)** A bed with four iron rods that curve up to support a dome-shaped canopy.

***lit en bateau* (Fr.)** A French Empire bed with scroll or animal-shaped ends. Its name comes from its resemblance to a boat.

***loggia* (It.)** A porch or gallery open on one or more sides.

looking glass From the 17th century onward, common term for a mirror made of glass with reflecting material on one side. Prior to the 17th century, mirrors were made of polished metal because glassmaking was either unknown or unable to produce clear, undistorted glass.

lozenge A diamond-shaped motif or ornament.

***lustre à cristeaux* (Fr.)** A crystal chandelier.

lyre Motif derived from a Greek musical instrument composed of two curving forms with strings between them; common in classical and neoclassical styles.

madrasah A religious school attached to a *mosque*; a collegiate mosque or theological college.

***maiolica* (It.)** Italian tin-glazed earthenware. Introduced in the 14th century in Valencia, Spain, it was imported to Italy where it was made in large amounts during the Renaissance and later. Maiolica has an opaque white body with brightly colored painted decoration that resembles porcelain and is called *faience* in France and delft in Holland and England. Subjects depicted are often historical or mythological.

majolica Type of ceramic produced in the 1850s by Minton; decorated in lead glazes, its colors sometimes resemble Italian *maiolica*.

***manchettes* (Fr.)** Arm pads.

mansard roof A roof with two slopes on all four sides; the lower is more steeply pitched, and the upper is often not visible. The roof may have straight or curved profiles and is usually capped with cresting. Named after French architect François Mansard.

maqsurea A wooden screen or grill near the *mihrab* in a *mosque*, serving to protect dignitaries from crowds.

marquetry Decorative veneer pattern of wood, brass, or other materials applied to furniture.

mausoleum A magnificent tomb usually intended as a monument.

meeting house A building used for assemblies and for Protestant worship.

melon support or **cup and cover** A heavy, elaborately carved, bulbous support typical of Elizabethan and Jacobean furniture; shape resembles a melon or a chalice with a domed lid.

***menuisier* (Fr.)** In France, a craftsperson who works in solid wood with carving.

meri-boteh Derived from the Persian term meaning "cluster of leaves," this rug motif is shaped like a pear or pine cone; it evolves into European paisley.

***méridienne* (Fr.)** A small sofa with one side higher than the other; introduced during the French Empire period and appearing again in Rococo Revival.

metope Flat slabs recessed between triglyphs in a Doric frieze; usually decorated with paintings or sculpture.

mihrab In Islamic architecture, a niche usually in the center of the *qibla* serving to distinguish it; those praying usually face it.

***millefleurs* (Fr.)** Literally, "a thousand flowers"; group of French tapestries made between c. 1480 and c. 1520 with hundreds of scattered flowers, often forming backgrounds for pastoral or courtly scenes.

minaret Tall, slender tower or turret attached to a mosque. It has one or more projecting balconies from which the faithful are called to prayer.

minbar A pulpit in a *mosque* from which the *imam* (leader) declares the *khutba* (sermon) and affirmation of allegiance by the community; may be to the right of the *mihrab*.

modillion Small bracket, usually carved, which, in a series, supports a Corinthian or Composite cornice.

module A unit of measurement that determines the size and/or proportions of a building, interior space, furniture, or other item.

moiré Ribbed wool or silk fabric with a watered design created from uneven pressure of heated rollers.

monopodium (*monopodia*, pl.) Head and chest of a lion attached to a paw. Invented by the Romans, it is common in French Empire and English Regency.

***moquette* (Fr.)** A machine-woven carpet in repeating patterns. Made in narrow widths, the pieces are sewn together for room-sized rugs. Alternative term for *Axminster*.

moreen A wool or mohair fabric that may be plain or embossed with a pattern of flowers or other foliage. Used for upholstery, window curtains, and bed hangings.

mortise and tenon A type of joint composed of a rectangular projection, or tenon, that is inserted into a rectangular cavity with a corresponding shape, or mortise.

mosque In Islamic architecture, a religious building for common prayer; may be used for other purposes.

motte A conical, raised mound of a castle, usually within a bailey.

mudéjar A decoration combining Islamic and Spanish characteristics.

muhaqqaq A form of Islamic calligraphy that is a horizontal script; it is one of six basic styles for calligraphy codified at the end of the 13th century.

multifoil arch An arch composed of a series of small arcs.

muqarnas Small, interlocking, ornamental, corbelled brackets and niches decorating the undersides of arches or vaults in Islamic architecture; these concave segments resemble stalactites.

narthex An arcaded entrance porch of a basilica church.

nave The center portion of a basilica or Latin cross church.

nesting tables Small tables that diminish in size so that they can slide under one another when not in use. Four nesting tables are called *quartetto tables* and three are called *trio tables*.

newel The main post or support for a stair rail.

niche-pilaster A pilaster with a shaft that has a niche with a figure or other decorative element. Characteristic of Spanish Baroque architecture, it appears in high-style examples of Spanish Colonial Revival.

***norens* (Jp.)** Split curtains used for privacy.

obelisk An Egyptian monolithic pillar tapering to a pyramid-shaped point. It is used later in architecture and decorative accessories, especially in Egyptian Revival.

oculus (*oculi*, pl.) A circular opening, usually in the apex of a dome.

ogee arch A pointed arch composed of two curves, one convex and one concave.

ogival arch A pointed arch created by S curves, found in Islamic architecture.

onion dome Pointed bulbous form resembling an onion in shape; not a true dome.

open-well staircase Stairs that rise on the walls of a square, leaving the center open.

order In classical architecture, a column's base, shaft, and capital and the entablature above it treated according to an accepted mode. The Greeks introduce three orders: Doric, Ionic, and Corinthian; the Romans add Tuscan and Composite. The Renaissance codifies these five orders.

oriel window A bay window on an upper story that is supported by brackets, corbels, or pilasters.

***ormolu* (Fr.)** Gilded bronze ornament applied to furniture or used alone, as in a candlestick.

ottoman A small overstuffed seat (or stool) without back or arms for one or more people that is introduced from Turkey into England in the 18th century. By the 19th century, the form becomes circular or octagonal with deep tufting. Ottomans during this period are round with tufted backs and often have a potted palm or sculpture in the center.

oyster veneer A veneer of oval shapes resembling oyster shells that are cut transversely through a small tree branch or trunk.

pad foot A plain, round or ovoid, somewhat flat foot with a disk or pad on the bottom. Like the club foot, it terminates a cabriole leg and is common in 18th-century England.

***pagoda* (Ch.)** A Buddhist temple in the form of a tower; usually polygonal in shape with highly ornamental roofs projecting from its many stories.

***pai-tun-tzu* (*petuntse*) (Ch.)** China stone; a feldspathic rock used in porcelain.

palampore A mordant-printed, resist-dyed cotton with spiraling foliage and flowers (or tree of life motif) from India; composed of a single panel and used for coverlets.

***palazzo* (palazzi, pl.) (It.)** Italian urban palace.

Palladian or **Venetian window** A tripartite window composed of two rectangular lower sections flanking a taller, arched center light; derived from the arch, column, space, and pier combinations seen in the work of Sebastiano Serlio and Andrea Palladio.

palmette A stylized palm leaf in a fan shape that originates in ancient Egypt and subsequently is used by the Greeks and Romans.

***panetière* (Fr.)** A bread cupboard; common in Provence and Normandy.

panorama Continuous painted scenes or landscapes that surround or unroll in front of viewers; popular forms of entertainment in the late 18th and 19th centuries, they usually take place in round buildings especially built to house them. In the mid-19th century, rolled panoramas traveled the country.

***papelera* (Sp.)** An elaborate cabinet similar to a *vargueño*, but without a drop front or a permanent base.

papier-mâché Material composed of paper pulp, resin, and glue; may be pressed into a mold to make ornament or furniture.

parabolic window A parabola-shaped window; a vertical rounded or semipointed arch.

parapet Low retaining wall for support or protection at the edge of a roof or other structure.

pargework Plasterwork in patterns on ceilings or the exteriors of timber frame buildings; originating during the Tudor period, pargework is characteristic of English Queen Anne and Old English–style architecture.

Parian ware Unglazed or biscuit porcelain resembling marble introduced in England in the 1840s. Because it is inexpensive, it becomes enormously popular so that almost no parlor was without a Parian ware bust or figurine.

parquetry Geometric patterned wood inlay used mainly for floors.

***parterres* (Fr.)** Flat terraces near or around a building with flowers and decorative plantings.

paterae An oval or circular form with radiating lines and a rosette in the center, introduced by the ancient Greeks.

patio An open or inner courtyard in Spanish or Spanish-influenced buildings.

pavilion A distinctive, prominent structure marking the ends and center of the façade of a building; characteristic of French architecture including Second Empire.

pedestal A base supporting a column.

pediment In classical architecture, the triangular area formed by the cornice and sloping sides of the roof; also, a similar form over a door, window, or mantel, or surmounting a case piece. Shapes include triangular, segmental (rounded), broken (open at the apex), or swan's neck (double curve).

pelmet Flat, shaped fabric treatment at the top of a window; also called a *valance*.

Pembroke table A small table with two drop leaves, a drawer in its apron, and slender tapering legs, usually with casters; often used as a breakfast table. The name comes from the Countess of Pembroke, who supposedly ordered the first table of this type.

pendentive A triangular curving form that allows construction of a circular dome over a square or rectangular space; originates in Byzantine architecture.

pent roof A roof composed of a single sloping plane, may be between stories; also called a *shed roof*.

peripteral A temple or building surrounded by a single row of columns.

peristyle A row of columns surrounding a temple, other building, or courtyard.

Persian (*Senneh*) knot An asymmetrical knot in which a wool strand encircles one warp and winds loosely around the other; one end pulls through the two warps while the other emerges outside the paired warps. A more difficult knot to tie than the Turkish, it gives a more clearly defined pattern and tightly woven rug.

phoenix A mythological bird, which after living 500+ years, burned itself on a funeral pyre and rose again as a young bird from its own ashes; common in the Far East and also known in classical antiquity and Early Christian times.

photovoltaic panels Solar cells that convert the sun's energy into electricity.

***piano nobile* (It.)** The main floor or first floor above ground level in a residence; the most important rooms in the house are located there, including the owner's state apartments and main entertaining rooms; literally means "floor of the nobles."

***piazza* (It.) (*plaza*, Sp.)** An open space that varies in shape and purpose. It is usually public and surrounded by buildings.

pickle finish Originally a way of treating new wood to make it look old; today pickling is a white or off-white stain.

picture window A window with a large fixed pane of glass to provide a view; some have smaller double-hung windows on either side.

piecrust table Modern term for an 18th-century small table with the top edge carved or molded in a series of small curves resembling a pie crust.

***pied-de-biche* (Fr.)** A cloven-hoof foot.

pier glass A tall, narrow mirror intended to be hung on the wall or pier between windows.

pier table A table originally meant to be placed against the wall or pier between windows. It often has a large matching mirror above or attached to it or may be flanked by candlestands.

***pierrotage* (Fr.)** In France and her colonies, a type of half-timber construction with stones and clay between framing.

***pietra dura* (*pietre dure*, pl.) (It.)** Decorative inlay composed of marble, hard minerals, or semiprecious stones inlaid in wood; used on tabletops and in panels during the Italian Renaissance; because of expense, production limited mostly to Milan and Florence.

pilaster A vertical member attached to a wall with the general form and proportions of a column, but rectangular in section.

***pilotis* (Fr.)** Piers or columns that support and raise a building above the ground. Pilotis lighten visual weight while providing free space beneath the building. Le Corbusier introduces the concept.

pinnacle A terminating element, usually tapering to a point or knob, that resembles a small spire. Common in Gothic and Gothic Revival, pinnacles may be decorative or structural.

piping Variation of tufting that forms a decorative ridge at the edge of a seat or back of a piece of upholstery.

plush Heavy fabric that is similar to velvet but has a longer pile.

podium (*podia*, pl.) A continuous base for a building or a pedestal for a column.

porcelain Ceramic with a translucent white body made of china clay and china stone. **True** or **hard-paste** porcelain contains both ingredients, while artificial or **soft paste** porcelain lacks one of them. True porcelain originates in China. Although true porcelain is made in Germany in the early 18th century, artificial porcelains dominate European production until the middle of the century.

portal An imposing or grand entrance or doorway; also the architectural composition around a church entryway.

portcullis A heavy wood and iron grating in the portal of a castle or other defended building.

***porte cochère* (Fr.)** Porch or covered entrance that is large enough for a carriage or automobile to pass through.

portico Roofed space or porch forming the entrance or center of a façade; may be open or closed and usually has columns.

portière Curtain hanging across a doorway to serve as a door, prevent drafts, or serve as decoration.

post and lintel See *trabeated*.

pouf or ***pouffe*** Stool with deeply tufted coil spring upholstery that is introduced from France about 1830.

Prince of Wales motif Motif composed of three ostrich feathers tied together at the shafts. It is a symbol of the heir to the British throne.

Priscilla curtains Ruffled curtains in solid or sheer fabrics gathered on rods or sometimes crossed and tied back.

pseudo-peripteral A building or temple with surrounding engaged columns creating the impression of a peristyle.

puffing Decorative pleating on the edge of an upholstered seat or back.

pylon Greek word for "gateway;" a monumental gateway shaped like a truncated pyramid found in Egyptian and Egyptian Revival architecture.

qibla A prayer wall in a mosque oriented toward Mecca, the direction in which Muslims must face when praying.

quartetto tables See *nesting tables*.

quatrefoil Four-lobed form; see also *foils*.

quoin Cornerstone that marks the corner of a building because it is different from the wall in its rustication, color, size, or material.

rail On furniture or doors, a horizontal member joining vertical posts (stiles) or framing a panel.

***raku* (Jp.)** Pottery made by hand, featuring a thick, dark lead glaze, and fired at low heat; colors range from dark brown to light red, yellow, green, or cream. Its irregular shape and glaze give it a primitive appearance, but in reality it is highly sophisticated. Raku is used in the tea ceremony.

***ramma* (Jp.)** The transom area above a sliding panel that may be perforated or elaborately carved for air flow and light filtration.

***redodo* (Sp.)** A decorated wall situated behind the altar.

reeded or **reeding** Convex ridges next to each other that cover a surface such as a leg or chair back.

***reja* (Sp.)** An ornate iron grille or screen common in Spanish churches and civic buildings.

relieving arch A segmental arch over the lintel serving to alleviate excess weight; also called a *blind arch*.

reproduction Building, furniture piece, textile, or other object that copies as exactly as possible a historic document or object within the constraints of modern technology.

respond A half-pillar rising from nave arcade columns to the springing (beginning) of the ribs of the vault in Gothic architecture.

***retable* (Fr.) (*retablos*, Sp.)** A screen behind an altar common in Spanish and Spanish-influenced churches; large in scale, the *retable* has many painted or carved panels arranged in successive stories and is a form of altarpiece.

reverse cabriole leg A leg that curves opposite to the cabriole leg; instead of curving out at the top, in down toward the foot, and out again at the foot, it curves inward, then out, then in again to a caster. These legs characterize Victorian Rococo Revival seating.

ribbed vault Vault with structural or decorative projecting bands defining the lines of intersection.

rinceau A linear pattern of scrolling vines, leaves, and foliage.

***rocaille* (Fr.)** Asymmetrical decoration with a profusion of curving tendrils, foliage, flowers combined with shells, and minute details that defines Rococo or Louis XV; originally referred to small rockeries in the artificial grottoes at Versailles, but soon was applied to furniture ornament that resembled small irregular rocks and shells.

rock cairns Heaps of stones or earth and stones piled up as a memorial or landmark.

Roman brick A type of brick that is longer and narrower than other types. Invented by the Ancient Romans, McKim, Mead, and White introduce it to the United States in the late 19th century. Frank Lloyd Wright often uses it in his Prairie-style houses to emphasize horizontality.

Romayne work Motif consisting of a profile of a head within a roundel.

rose window Circular window or motif with tracery that converges in the center like the spokes of a wheel.

rosette Circular stylized floral motif.

runner A horizontal brace for furniture legs at the floor.

rustication Smooth or rough-faced blocks of stone with deeply cut joints that give a rich textural appearance.

saber leg A quadrangular, outward-curving leg with no foot; its name comes from its resemblance to a sword or saber.

sala The main reception room with the most lavish decoration in an Italian or Spanish residence.

***salle á manger* (Fr.)** Dining room.

***salon* (Fr.)** An elegant apartment or living space.

***saltire* stretcher** A flat or raised stretcher in an X shape.

sash or **double-hung window** A window composed of two sliding sashes (the frames that hold the glass); introduced from Holland to England (and America) in the late 17th century.

Savonarola A 19th-century term for an Italian X-form chair with many interlacing slats and a wooden back; often used by scholars, its name comes from Girolamo Savonarola, a Tuscan monk and reformer, executed during the Renaissance.

Savonnerie Hand-knotted cut-pile carpet made at the Savonnerie Factory established in France in 1626.

scagliola Imitation marble composed of plaster or cement and marble chips.

***secrétaire à abattant* (Fr.)** A tall desk with a drop-front writing surface and drawers or door beneath; when open, the drop front reveals small drawers and compartments. Chains or pulls support the drop front when open. Introduced in the 17th century but very fashionable in the 18th century.

***sedia* (It.)** A box-shaped arm chair with runners.

***Seignouret* chair** An American Empire chair created by French cabinetmaker François Seignouret in Louisiana around 1810. The top of the chair's back is made of a single piece of wood and curves forward to form low arms that connect with the seat. In the center of the back is a shaped splat. This type of construction is very strong, so it is adopted by others.

selamlik A public or men's area of the Middle Eastern home where guests, male friends, and business associates are received and entertained.

***sella curulis* (L.)** X-shaped folding stool, sometimes with a back, used by Roman *curules* or city magistrates; *curule* chairs have a back and become the X-form folding chairs of the Middle Ages and the Renaissance.

***Senneh* knot** See *Persian knot.*

serge Durable wool or worsted wool fabric in a twill weave.

serpentine An undulating or curving form; a front or top that is concave, convex, and concave.

serpentine crest The top rail in concave, convex, concave shape that curves down to meet back uprights.

settee An armchair extended to seat two or more; introduced during the 17th century as a more comfortable form of settle.

settle A wooden bench with a back and arms developed during the Gothic period; because it is less portable than a bench, its appearance indicates more stable times.

***sgabello* (It.)** A stool chair; octagonal seat resting on a box with solid supports or trestles for legs and a fan-shaped back; light in weight but uncomfortable; typically used for dining.

***sgraffito* (It.)** Decoration made by scratching or incising a design in the slip (liquid clay) covering of a ceramic so that the color of the body shows through; this process is done before glazing.

shaft The vertical part of the column.

Shagreen Leather made from sharkskin or skin of a ray fish. The rounded scales on the skin are ground to give a rough surface. Shagreen is often dyed green.

shed roof See *pent roof.*

***shibi* (Jp.)** An ornament of a stylized dolphin tail that accents ends of roof ridges in Japanese architecture.

***Shibui* (Jp.)** The highest aesthetic level of traditional Japanese design, reflected in simplicity, implicitness or inner meaning, humility, silence, and use of natural materials; it affects all visual arrangements and daily activities.

***shin-kabe* (Jp.)** A plaster wall with exposed structure; typical of traditional Japanese architecture.

***shoin* style (Jp.)** An aristocratic Japanese style of building that takes its name from the *shoin*, a decorative alcove with window and desk. It features a *tokonoma* and *tana*.

***shoji* (Jp.)** A Japanese sliding screen composed of a wooden lattice grid covered with translucent rice paper; a *shoji* subdivides an interior and/or serves as a door or window.

shotgun house A house type that is one room wide and several rooms deep.

sidelights Two tall, narrow windows flanking a door.

***singerie* (Fr.)** Motif of monkeys dressed in clothing and engaged in human activities.

slip seat A loose, upholstered wooden seat that is set into the seat frame of a chair.

sofa table A tall drop-leaf table with drawers and various types of legs; used for games, sewing, and a variety of activities. Sofa tables were commonly placed in front of sofas after their introduction in the late 18th century, unlike today when they are commonly used behind sofas.

soft paste porcelain Artificial porcelain lacking one of the ingredients of true porcelain; common in England and Europe in the 18th and early 19th centuries.

solar A withdrawing room located around the great hall in a medieval house; a private bed-sitting room for the owner and family. *Solar* derives from French *sol* (floor) and *solive* (beam).

solomonic column A twisted column; name comes from its supposed use on Solomon's temple in Jerusalem.

spade foot A rectangular, tapering foot resembling a spade or shovel.

Spanish foot A tapering, rectangular, ribbed foot terminating in an outward-turned scroll. Originates in Spanish and Portuguese Baroque furniture during the late 17th and early 18th centuries; also known as a Portuguese foot or a paintbrush foot.

sphinx Egyptian mythological creature with a man or woman's head and body of a lion.

spire A tall, tapered structure that terminates in a point and rises from a tower, turret, or roof (usually that of a church); it may be pyramidal, polygonal, or conical in shape.

splat A flat, vertical member in a chair back. An important ornamental element and determinant of style, splats may be shaped, carved, pierced, or otherwise decorated.

split baluster turning A small turned element with curving side out and the flat side applied as decoration to furniture.

spoon back American term for a chair back in which the uprights curve in to fit the human body; term derives from its resemblance to a spoon bowl. Common on some William and Mary chairs, but characteristic of Queen Anne; often found on Chinese chairs.

squinch A small arch or bracket or many projecting arches across the angles of a square or polygonal structure that form a base for a dome.

stereoscope Dating from the mid-19th century, a device that creates the illusion of depth used for viewing stereographic cards. Stereo cards or views have the same image printed side-by-side on a card. When seen through the stereoscope, they appear three-dimensional.

stile A vertical member that frames a back, panel, or door.

stoneware Pottery of clay and fusible stone that vitrifies upon firing so that it becomes impervious to liquids. Glazes are applied for decoration; unlike porcelain, it is not translucent.

straight bracket foot Two brackets with straight sides joining at a right angle under the corner or case piece.

strapwork Ornament composed of flat, curving bands resembling leather thongs or straps; a common Northern European Mannerist motif that is popularized by pattern books.

stretcher A horizontal brace connecting furniture legs for additional support.

string The open side of a stair, beneath the steps.

stringcourse A projecting molding that may be plain or carved, and that runs horizontally on a building; it usually separates stories.

stringing A narrow band of inlay or contrasting wood veneer outlining a leg, drawer, or other element.

stucco Plaster used from antiquity and made of several ingredients; lime stuccos, classified as cements, are used on exteriors, whereas plaster stucco forms interior moldings and applied decoration.

stumpwork Needlework, much of which is in relief, raised on a foundation of wadding or wool; may be embellished with sequins; used on objects that receive little wear and tear.

stylization Simplification; reducing an object to its simplest form or reproducing the essence of its character.

stylobate The upper step on which the columns sit; common in Classical architecture.

***sukiya* style (Jp.)** This style for dwellings and palaces evolves from the tea house and is smaller and simpler than the preceeding shoin style. Constructed of wood, buildings display naturalness, human scale, and rusticity. Details and proportion are important to convey refinement and harmony with nature. The *sukiya* style influences later architects, such as Frank Lloyd Wright.

summer beam In timber frame structure in England and America, the main supporting beam that crosses the ceiling and supports the joists of the floor above.

swag Classical ornament composed of a curving form suspended between two points. The curving form, composed of flowers, fruit, or foliage and tied with ribbons, is lighter on the ends and heavier in the middle. Also, a window treatment composed of fabric draped in a semicircle; also called a *festoon*.

swastika A religious symbol dating to the Bronze Age; a cross with arms of equal length terminated by right-angle extensions lying in the same direction.

***table l'italienne* (Fr.)** During the French Renaissance, a table with a rectangular top and supports of figures, eagles, or griffins joined by a complex stretcher.

***tablinum* (It.)** A room in the atrium, usually on the main axis, used as an office or master bedroom in Roman houses.

tambour A flexible door or shutter composed of strips of wood glued to a cotton or linen backing; front side may be reeded.

***tana* (Jp.)** A series of shelves originally used for Buddhist scrolls that characterizes the *shoin* style in Japanese houses.

***tansu* (Jp.)** Any of a wide variety of chests of drawers in Japan; introduced in early times, *tansu* become more common and specialized forms develop during the Edo period with the rise of a large merchant class.

***tatami* (Jp.)** Woven rice-straw mats with edges of black cloth used in Japanese houses; *tatami*, which are 3'-0" W × 6'-0" L × 3" D, form modules for room dimensions.

tazar The main reception area within a winter or summer hall in an Islamic residence; a step or two up and an imposing arch separate it from the rest of the space.

temple front Composed of columns and a pediment, it replicates the main façade of a temple; may be used decoratively or to form a porch or portico.

term leg A tapering quadrangular support with carving that is sometimes capped with the bust of a human, animal, or mythical creature.

terra-cotta Glazed or unglazed fired clay used in construction and decoration; unglazed tile.

terrazzo Floor composed of small pieces of marble or granite in a concrete mixture.

tesserae Small components of mosaics; may be glass, bone, concrete, marble, etc.

tester Framework over a bed on which fabrics hang. It may fully or partially cover the bed; also called a *canopy*.

tête-à-tête Small S-shaped sofa in which the seats face each other, enabling the two sitters to see each other; common in Rococo Revival.

thermae window An arched window divided into three lights by two mullions; found in Roman baths and adopted later by Palladio and the Neo-Palladians in England; also called a *Diocletian window*.

thimble foot A cylindrical tapering foot characteristic of Hepplewhite or Sheraton furniture.

tie rods or **tie bars** Horizontal metal (or wooden) connectors that give additional support to arches and the outward thrust of vaults.

***toile de Jouy* (Fr.)** White or cream cotton, linen, or silk fabric with monochromatic engraved decoration in red, blue, green, black, or purple.

***tokonoma* (Jp.)** A built-in alcove evolving from private altars that defines the *shoin* style in Japanese houses.

torchère (Fr.) (*torchiera*, It.; *torchere*, Sp.) A floor candle stand; see also *guéridon*.

***torii* (Jp.)** Characteristic main entrance gate to a Japanese shrine or Shinto complex; composed of two posts topped with horizontal beams.

trabeated Post and lintel or post and beam construction; consists of two uprights (post) supporting a horizontal member (beam or lintel).

tracery Curving, ornamental stone or wooden subdivisions in an architectural opening. Common in Gothic stained glass windows, tracery also defines Gothic Revival fenestration, wood paneling, plasterwork, ceilings, textiles, wallpapers, and furniture.

track lighting Individual lighting fixtures attached to an electrified ceiling track; fixtures can move along the track to provide light where needed or desired.

traditional Common term for buildings, interiors, furniture, or decorative arts that are derived closely or loosely from past styles, types, objects, or forms.

transept A space or spaces at right angles to and crossing the nave of a church.

transfer-print A decorative technique in which an impression of the scene, pattern, or motif is made in ink from a copperplate onto transfer paper and applied to the surface of the furniture or ceramic.

transitional Common term for interiors or furniture that is generally modern in style but has elements of the past often in ornament, details, or finishes.

transverse arch An arch or rib formed from pilasters or engaged columns that rises from a pier and crosses the ceiling to the opposite pier in a church or cathedral.

trefoil A three-lobed form; see also *foils*.

trestle A support composed of legs joined by a horizontal beam; legs may be plain, turned, or columnar.

trestle table A table composed of a flat board top supported by trestles; originally developed in the Middle Ages.

triclinium In Roman dwellings, a dining room with three couches on three sides.

trifid foot A carved foot with three (sometimes four) toes or prominent protrusions. Also called a *Drake foot,* it was common in mid-18th-century America and England.

triforium Arches or a gallery above the nave arcade; it may have three arches, which gives it its name.

triglyph A block with three vertical divisions in a Doric frieze.

trio tables See *nesting tables*.

***trompe l'oeil* (Fr.)** Literally, fool the eye; a photographically realistic depiction.

***trumeau* (Fr.)** Over-mantel or over-door treatment typically with a painting in a curving, gilded frame.

trumpet leg A turned leg that tapers from wide to narrow, resembling an upturned trumpet; typical of William and Mary style furniture in England and America.

***tsuitate* (Jp.)** A single-panel screen with legs; although small, it may screen views, partition space, or control drafts in a Japanese interior.

Tudor arch A flattened pointed or four-centered arch.

tufting An effect created when buttons placed between springs create a deep indention and excess fabric gathers into pleats beneath the buttons.

Turkey work or **Norwich work** English Renaissance textile that imitates Oriental rugs; woolen thread is pulled through a loosely woven cotton base and hand knotted.

Turkish (*Ghiordes*) knot A symmetrical hand-tied knot in which a strand of wool encircles two warp threads; the loose ends emerge between the two warps; easier to tie than a Persian knot, but yields a coarser rug.

Tuscan A Roman column with a base and unfluted shaft; an echinus and abacus compose the capital. Architraves are simply treated, usually with moldings.

tympanium In classical architecture, the triangular space formed by the sides of the gable roof and the cornice in the pediment; it usually has relief sculpture. In churches of the Middle Ages, the space between the lintel and the arch in a doorway.

type A domed roof element that lights an interior staircase; common in English Renaissance houses.

***ukiyo-e* (Jp.)** Popular colored woodblock prints created in the 16th century that depict common people, landscapes, and myths; term means "pictures of the floating world" and comes from the images themselves and the asymmetrical arrangements.

valance Today, a flat, shaped fabric treatment at the top of a window; also called a *pelmet*. In the early 19th century, complicated top treatments usually forming swags were called drapery instead of valances.

vanity Alternate, modern term for a dressing table, often with an attached mirror.

***vargueño* (Sp.)** A furniture piece consisting of a drop-front cabinet on a base; the only decorations on the front are wrought-iron mounts and locks, in contrast to the interior, in which the small drawers and doors feature elaborate inlay. The most common base has splayed legs and iron braces; rings or loops on the sides permit mobility.

vault An arched covering of brick or stone; see also *barrel vault, cross vault*, and *groin vault*.

veneer A thin layer of wood or other material attached to another surface, usually to create a decorative effect.

Venetian blind A window treatment composed of horizontal wooden (or other materials later) slats connected by tapes that can be raised or lowered; thought to have been invented near Venice, Venetian blinds appear in the mid-18th century in Italy, then France, England, and the United States. The method of adjusting the angle of the slats is invented in 1841.

Venetian carpet Flat-woven, multicolored, striped carpet.

Venetian window See *Palladian window*.

veranda A gallery or walkway beneath a shed (or single sloping) roof carried by slender columns or piers; may be on one or more sides of the house with French doors allowing access from the main rooms.

vernacular Architecture and material of common people; may reflect and simplify prevailing fashions and styles in form and material.

***vernis Martin* (Fr.)** A shiny lacquer developed in France by the Martin brothers in 1730. Application of many coats of varnish produces a thick surface capable of being carved in low relief; available in many colors, with green being favored.

***verre églomisé* (Fr.)** Decorative painting done mainly in gold, white, and blue on the reverse side of a glass panel to be used in a door, case piece, picture frame, or mirror. Fashionable during the Neoclassical period, the technique is developed by the ancient Romans.

Victrola A brand of gramophone or phonograph; the first device used to record and replay sound. It was popular in the last quarter of the 19th century. *Gramophone* also was a brand of phonograph.

vigas (Sp.) Large beams supporting the flat roof in Spanish, Spanish Colonial, and Spanish Colonial Revival architecture. Vigas may protrude through walls.

villa In Roman architecture, a country farmhouse or mansion; from the Renaissance onward, a country house.

vitrine Originating in the 18th century, a display cabinet with glass doors. The most typical form is a small cabinet on a stand.

Vitrolite A structural, pigmented opaque glass used in buildings during the Art Deco period.

VOC Volatile organic compounds; emitted from solids or liquids, they can be hazardous to health.

volute A spiral scroll reminiscent of a ram's horn or shell, forming the capital of the Ionic order and also part of the capital in Corinthian and Composite orders.

voussoir A wedge-shaped block that, with others, forms an arch.

wainscot chair English, American, and French rectilinear armchair with carved, paneled back; evolves from a seat incorporated into wall paneling during the Gothic period. It may have panels under the arms and all four sides to the floor or only a paneled back.

wainscoting Wooden paneling for walls; derives from a Dutch term for a grade of oak used in fine interior work.

wall dormer A window that rises from the wall below and extends upward into the roof; it may also be called a lucarne.

wall pocket A shelf, pocket, or container made in ceramics, wood, metal, or fabric that hangs on the wall to provide storage or to hold flowers or plants. Wall pockets are common in the second half of the 19th century.

water table A masonry projection, ledge, stringcourse, or molding at the base of a building used to project rainwater away from the foundation.

westwerk A tall façade with two towers or turrets on the west end of a church; inside are multistoried galleries. Characteristic of Carolingian or Romanesque churches and revived in German Baroque.

whorl foot See *French whorl foot*.

Wilton carpet A cut-pile carpet first woven in Wilton, England, in the mid-18th century. It is made in a similar way to Brussels in that face yarns are carried in the backing when not appearing, but the number of colors may be three to six. Today woven carpets are mostly Wilton.

windbreaks A growth or fall of trees or shrubs that break the force of wind.

***yeseria* (Sp.)** Elaborately carved stucco work.

***zabutons* (Jp.)** Square floor cushions used for seating in Japan.

***zapatas* (Sp.)** Bracket capitals found in Spanish, Spanish Colonial, and Spanish Colonial Revival architecture.

Bibliography

Architecture, Art History, Design

Adams, Laura Schneider. *A History of Western Art*. New York: Harry N. Abrams, 1994.

Agnoletto, M. *Masterpieces of Modern Architecture*. New York: Barnes & Noble Publishing, 2006.

Arrigo, Joseph. *The Grace and Grandeur of Natchez Homes*. Stillwater, MN: Voyageur Press, 1994.

The Art Institute of Chicago. *Chicago and New York: Architectural Interactions*. Chicago: The Art Institute of Chicago, 1984.

Asensio, Paco, ed. *The World of Contemporary Architecture*. Cologne: Könemann, 2000.

Baedeker, Karl. *Handbook for Travelers to Paris and Its Environs*. Leipzig: K. Baedeker Publishers, 1891.

Ball, Victoria Kloss. *Architecture and Interior Design: A Basic History through the Seventeenth Century*. New York: John Wiley & Sons, 1980.

———. *Architecture and Interior Design: Europe and America from the Colonial Era to Today*. New York: John Wiley & Sons, 1980.

Banham, Reyner. *Theory and Design in the First Machine Age*. New York: Frederick A. Praeger, 1960.

Bergdoll, Barry. *European Architecture 1750–1890*. Oxford: Oxford University Press, 2000.

Brooks, Alfred M. *Architecture and the Allied Arts*. Indianapolis: Bobbs-Merrill, 1914.

Brownell, Charles, Calder Loth, William M. S. Rasmussen, and Richard Guy Wilson. *The Making of Virginia Architecture*. Richmond: Virginia Museum of Fine Arts, 1992.

Building Images: Seventy Years of Photography at Hedrich Blessing. San Francisco: Chronicle Books, 2000.

Burchard, John, and Albert Bush-Brown. *The Architecture of America: A Social and Cultural History*. Boston: Little, Brown, 1961.

Carley, Rachel. *The Visual Dictionary of American Domestic Architecture*. New York: Henry Holt, 1994.

Ching, Francis D. K. *Building Construction Illustrated*. New York: John Wiley & Sons, 1991.

A Chronology of Western Architecture. New York: Facts on File Publications, 1987.

Clark, Clifford Edward, Jr. *The American Family Home, 1800–1960*. Chapel Hill: University of North Carolina Press, 1986.

Colquhoun, Alan. *Modern Architecture*. New York: Oxford University Press, 2002.

Curl, James Stevens. *Oxford Dictionary of Architecture*. Oxford: Oxford University Press, 1999.

A Dictionary of Terms Used in Architecture and Building. New York: Industrial Publication Co., 1909.

Doordan, Dennis P. *Twentieth-Century Architecture*. New York: Harry N. Abrams, 2002.

Ferguson, Russell, ed. *At the End of the Century, One Hundred Years of Architecture*. New York: Harry N. Abrams, 1998.

Fitch, James Marston. *American Building: The Historical Forces That Shaped It*. New York: Schocken Books, 1966.

Fleming, John, Hugh Honour, and Nikolaus Pevsner. *The Penguin Dictionary of Architecture*. New York: Penguin Books, 1980.

Foley, Mary Mix. *The American House*. New York: Harper and Row, 1980.

Frampton, Kenneth. *Modern Architecture: A Critical History*. London: Thames & Hudson, 1992.

———, and Yukio Futagawa. *Modern Architecture 1851–1919*. New York: Rizzoli, 1983.

———, and David Larkin, eds. *American Masterworks: The Twentieth-Century House*. New York: Universe Publishing, 2002.

French, Hilary. *Architecture: A Crash Course*. New York: Watson-Guptill Publications, 1998.

Gebhard, David, and Robert Winter. *Architecture in Los Angeles: A Compleat Guide*. Salt Lake City, UT: Gibbs Smith, 1985.

Ghirardo, Diane. *Architecture After Modernism*. London: Thames & Hudson, 1996.

Giedion, Sigfried. *Space, Time and Architecture*. Cambridge, MA: Harvard University Press, 1941.

Gillon, Edmund V., Jr. *Pictorial Archive of Early Illustrations and Views of American Architecture*. Mineola, NY: Dover Publications, 1971.

Girouard, Mark. *Life in the English Country House: A Social and Architectural History*. New York: Penguin Books, 1978.

Glancey, Jonathan. *The Story of Architecture*. New York: Dorling Kindersley, 2000.

Goodyear, William Henry. *History of Art for Classes, Art Students, and Tourists in Europe*. New York: A. S. Barnes, 1889.

Gössel, Peter, and Gabriele Liuthäuser. *Architecture in the Twentieth Century*. Germany: Taschen, 1991.

Gowans, Alan. *Images of American Living, Four Centuries of Architecture and Furniture as Cultural Expression*. Philadelphia: J. B. Lippincott, 1964; Harper & Row, 1976.

———. *Styles and Types of North American Architecture: Social Function and Cultural Expression*. New York: Harper Collins, 1992.

Hamlin, Alfred D. F. *History of Architecture*. New York: Longmans, Green, 1902.

Harris, Cyril. M., ed. *Illustrated Dictionary of Historic Architecture*. New York: Dover Publications, 1983.

Hepburn, Andrew H. *Great Houses of American History*. New York: Bramhall House Books, 1972.

History of Architecture. Scranton, PA: International Textbook Company, 1924.

Hitchcock, Henry-Russell. *Architecture: Nineteenth and Twentieth Centuries*. New York: Penguin Books, 1985.

———, and Philip Johnson. *The International Style*. New York: W. W. Norton, 1966.

Howe, Jeffery, ed. *The Houses We Live In: An Identification Guide to the History and Style of American Domestic Architecture*. London: PRC Publishing, 2002.

Jodidio, Philip, ed. *Architecture Now!* New York: Taschen, 2002.

Jones, Inigo. *The Designs of Inigo Jones, consisting of plans and elevations for publick and private buildings*. London: William Kent, 1727.

Kalman, Harold. *A History of Canadian Architecture*, Volume 1. Toronto: Oxford University Press, 1994.

Kelly, J. Frederic. *The Early Domestic Architecture of Connecticut*. New York: Dover Publications, 1952.

Kidney, Walter C. *The Architecture of Choice: Eclecticism in America 1880–1930*. New York: George Braziller, 1974.

Kimball, Fisk, and George Edgell. *A History of Architecture*. New York: Harper & Brothers, 1918.

LeBlanc, Sydney. *The Architecture Traveler: A Guide to 250 Key 20th-Century American Buildings*. New York: W. W. Norton, 2000.

Lemoine, Bertrand. *Architecture in France, 1800–1900*. New York: Harry N. Abrams, 1998.

Lewis, Arnold. *American Country Houses of the Gilded Age*. New York: Dover Publications, 1982.

Maddex, Diane, ed. *All About Old Buildings*. Washington, DC: Preservation Press, 1985.

Matthews, Kevin. *The Great Buildings Collection*. Eugene, OR: Artifice, 1994.

McAlester, Virginia, and Lee McAlester. *A Field Guide to American Houses*. New York: Alfred A. Knopf, 1984.

McGrath, Norman. *Photographing Buildings Inside and Out*. New York: Whitney Library of Design, 1987.

Middleton, Robin, and David Watkin. *Neoclassical and 19th Century Architecture*. 2 vols. New York: Electa/Rizzoli, 1980.

Mignot, Claude. *Architecture of the Nineteenth Century in Europe*. New York: Rizzoli, 1984.

Moffett, Marian, Michael Fazio, and Lawrence Wodehouse. *Buildings Across Time: An Introduction to World Architecture*. New York: McGraw-Hill, 2004.

Morgan, William. *The Abrams Guide to American House Styles*. New York: Harry N. Abrams, 2004.

Musgrove, John, ed. *Sir Banister Fletcher's A History of Architecture*, 19th ed. London: Butterworths, 1987.

Neal, James. *Architecture: A Visual History*. New York: Barnes & Noble Books, 2004.

Nicolson, Nigel. *The National Trust Book of Great Houses of Britain*. Norwich, England: Jarrold & Sons, 1979.

Norwich, John Julius, ed. *Great Architecture of the World*. London: Michael Beazley Publishers Limited, 1991.

Norwich, John J., ed. *The World Atlas of Architecture*. New York: Portland House, 1988.

Perring, Dominic, and Perrin, Stefania. *Then and Now*. New York: MacMillan, 1990.

Pevsner, Nikolaus. *Pioneers of Modern Design, from William Morris to Walter Gropius*. London: Penguin Books, 1991.

———. *The Sources of Modern Architecture and Design*. New York and Toronto: Oxford University Press, 1968.

The Phaidon Atlas of Contemporary World Architecture. New York: Phaidon Press, 2005.

Poesch, Jessie. *The Art of the Old South: Painting, Sculpture, Architecture and the Products of Craftsmen, 1560–1860*. New York: Alfred A. Knopf, 1983.

Poppeliers, John C., and S. Allen Chambers, Jr. *What Style Is It? A Guide to American Architecture*. Hoboken, NJ: John Wiley & Sons, 2003.

Raizman, David. *History of Modern Design*. Upper Saddle River, NJ: Prentice Hall, 2004.

Reiff, Daniel D. *Houses from Books, Treatises, Pattern Books, and Catalogs in American Architecture, 1738–1950: A History and Guide*. University Park: Pennsylvania State University Press, 2000.

Ricciuti, Italo William. *New Orleans and Its Environs, The Domestic Architecture 1727–1870*. New York: Bonanza Books, 1938.

Rifkind, Carole. *A Field Guide to American Architecture*. New York: The New American Library, 1980.

Roth, Leland. *American Architecture: A History*. Boulder, CO: Westview Press, 2001.

Saunders, Ann. *The Art and Architecture of London: An Illustrated Guide*. Oxford: Phaidon Press, 1984.

Saylor, Henry H. *Dictionary of Architecture*. New York: John Wiley & Sons, 1952.

Scully, Vincent. *Architecture: The Natural and the Manmade*. New York: St. Martin's Press, 1991.

Shapiro, Harry L. *Homes Around the World*. New York, NY: The American Museum of Natural History, 1945.

Sharp, Dennis. *Twentieth-Century Architecture: A Visual History*. Victoria, Australia: Images Publishing Group, 2002.

Shipway, Verna Cook, and Warren Shipway. *The Mexican House*. New York: Architectural Book Publishing, 1960.

Smith, G. E. Kidder. *Source Book of American Architecture*. New York: Princeton Architectural Press, 1996.

Smith, Herbert L., ed. *25 Years of Record Houses*. New York: McGraw-Hill, 1981.

Snodin, Michael, and John Styles. *Design and the Decorative Arts in Britain, 1500–1900*. London: Harry N. Abrams, 2001.

Sparke, Penny. *A Century of Design: Design Pioneers of the 20th Century*. Hauppauge, NY: Barron's Educational Series, 1998.

Spong, Dennis J. *The Creative Impulse: An Introduction to the Arts*. New York: Prentice Hall, 1990.

Statham, H. Heathcote. *A Short Critical History of Architecture*. London: B. T. Batsford, 1912.

Steele, James. *Architecture Today*. New York: Phaidon Press, 1997.

Stevenson, Neil. *Architecture: The World's Greatest Buildings Explored and Explained*. New York: Dorling Kindersley, 1997.

Stockstad, Marilyn. *Art History*. 3rd ed. Upper Saddle River, NJ: Pearson Education, 2008.

Stoddard, John. *A Trip Around the World*. N.p., c. 1890.

Sturgis, Russel, et al. *Sturgis' Illustrated Dictionary of Architecture and Building*. New York: Dover Publications, 1989.

Summerson, John. *Architecture of the Eighteenth Century*. New York: Thames & Hudson, 1986.

———. *Architecture in Britain, 1530–1830*, 9th ed. New Haven, CT: Yale University Press, 1993.

———. *The Classical Language of Architecture*. Cambridge: MIT Press, 1966.

———. *Georgian London*. London: Barrie & Jenkins, 1988.

Sutro, Dirk. *San Diego Architecture*. San Diego, CA: San Diego Architectural Foundation, 2002.

Tafuri, Manfredo, and Francesco Dal Co. *Modern Architecture/1*. New York: Rizzoli, 1986.

Traquair, Ramsay. *The Old Architecture of Quebec*. Toronto: The Macmillan Company of Canada Limited, 1947.

Upton, Dell. *Architecture in the United States*. New York: Oxford University Press, 1998.

Vickers, Graham. *Key Moments in Architecture: The Evolution of the City*. New York: Da Capo Press, 1999.

Wallis, Frank E. *How to Know Architecture*. New York: Harper & Brothers, 1910.

Warren, Garnet, and Horace B. Cheney. *The Romance of Design*. New York: Doubleday, Page and Company, 1926.

Watkin, David. *English Architecture*. London: Thames & Hudson, 2001.

———. *A History of Western Architecture*. 3rd ed. New York: Watson-Guptill, 2000.

Whiffen, Marcus, *American Architecture Since 1780: A Guide to the Styles*. Rev. ed. Cambridge, MA: MIT Press, 1992.

———, and Frederick Koeper. *American Architecture, Volume One: 1607–1860*. Cambridge, MA: MIT Press, 1984.

———. *American Architecture, Volume Two: 1860–1976*. Cambridge, MA: MIT Press, 1992.

Widdenhager, Von Graft. *History of Art*. N.p., 1919.

Woodbridge, Sally B. *California Architecture: Historic American Buildings Survey*. San Francisco: Chronicle Books, 1988.

Yarwood, Doreen. *The Architecture of England from Prehistoric Times to the Present Day*. London: B. T. Batsford, 1963.

Zukowsky, John, ed. *Chicago Architecture 1872–1922*. Chicago: The Art Institute of Chicago, 1987.

Interiors, Finishes, and Textiles

Abercrombie, Stanley. *A Century of Interior Design, 1900–2000: The Design, the Designers, the Products, and the Profession*. New York: Rizzoli, 2003.

———, and Sherrill Whiton. *Interior Design Decoration*. 6th ed. Upper Saddle River, NJ: Prentice Hall, 2006.

Art and Design in Europe and America 1800–1900 at the Victoria and Albert Museum. London: Herbert Press, 1987.

Banham, Joanna, Sally MacDonald, and Julia Porter. *Victorian Interior Design*. New York: Crescent Books, 1991.

Beard, Geoffrey W. *Craftsmen and Interior Decoration in England, 1660–1820*. New York: Holmes & Meier, 1981.

———. *The National Trust Book of the English House Interior*. London: Viking, 1990.

———. *Stucco and Decorative Plasterwork in Europe*. New York: Harper & Row, 1983.

———. *Upholsterers and Interior Furnishing in England 1530–1840*. New Haven, CT: Yale University Press, 1997.

Blakemore, Robbie G. *History of Interior Design and Furniture from Ancient Egypt to Nineteenth-Century Europe*. New York: Van Nostrand Reinhold, 1997.

Bossert, Helmuth. *An Encyclopaedia of Colour Decoration from the Earliest Times to the Middle of the XIXth Century*. London: Victor Gollancz, 1928.

Bristow, Ian C. *Architectural Colour in British Interiors 1615–1840*. New Haven, CT: Yale University Press, 1996.

Byron, Joseph. *Photographs of New York Interiors at the Turn of the Century*. New York: Dover, 1976.

Clabburn, Pamela. *The National Trust Book of Furnishing Textiles*. London: Viking, 1988.

Clifford, C. R. *Period Furnishings: An Encyclopedia of Historic Furniture, Decorations and Furnishings*. New York: Clifford and Lawton, 1922.

Cooper, Jeremy. *Victorian and Edwardian Décor: From the Gothic Revival to Art Nouveau*. New York: Abbeville Press, 1987.

Davidson, Marshall B., and Elizabeth Stillinger. *The American Wing at the Metropolitan Museum of Art*. New York: Metropolitan Museum of Art, 1985.

de Wolfe, Elsie. *The House in Good Taste*. New York: Century Company, 1914.

Dutton, Ralph. *The English Interior, 1500 to 1900*. New York, B. T. Batsford, 1948.

Eberlein, Harold Donaldson, Abbot McClure, and Edward Stratton Holloway. *The Practical Book of Interior Decoration*. Philadelphia: J. B. Lippincott, 1919.

Garrett, Elisabeth Donaghy. *At Home: The American Family, 1750–1870*. New York: Harry N. Abrams, 1990.

Gere, Charlotte. *Nineteenth-Century Decoration: The Art of the Interior*. New York: Harry N. Abrams, 1989.

———, and Michael Whiteway. *Nineteenth Century Design: From Pugin to Mackintosh*. New York: Harry N. Abrams, 1994.

Gibbs, Jenny. *Curtains and Drapes: History, Design, Inspiration*. London: Cassell, 1994.

Gore, Alan, and Ann Gore. *The History of English Interiors*. London: Phaidon, 1991.

Holloway, Edward Stratton. *The Practical Book of Furnishing the Small House and Apartment*. Philadelphia: J. B. Lippincott, 1922.

The House Beautiful Furnishing Annual 1926. Boston: Atlantic Monthly Company, 1925.

The Illustrated Dictionary of Twentieth Century Designers. New York: Mallard Press, 1991.

Jakway, Bernard C. *The Principles of Interior Decoration*. New York: Macmillan, 1926.

Jourdain, Margaret. *English Interiors In Smaller Houses, From the Restoration to the Regency, 1660–1830*. London, B. T. Batsford, 1923.

Kurtich, John, and Garret Eakin. *Interior Architecture*. New York: Van Nostrand Reinhold, 1993.

Lewis, Arnold, James Turner, and Steven McQuillin. *The Opulent Interiors of the Gilded Age*. New York: Dover Publications, 1987.

Lowe, David. *Chicago Interiors: Views of a Splendid World*. Chicago: Contemporary Books, 1979.

Lynn, Catherine. *Wallpaper in America from the Seventeenth Century to World War I*. New York: W. W. Norton, 1980.

Malnar, Joy Monice, and Frank Vodvarka. *The Interior Dimension: A Theoretical Approach to Enclosed Space*. New York: Van Nostrand Reinhold, 1992.

Massey, Anne. *Interior Design Since 1900*. 3rd ed. New York: Thames & Hudson, 2008.

Mayhew, Edgar de N., and Minor Myers, Jr. *A Documentary History of American Interiors from the Colonial Era to 1915*. New York: Charles Scribner's Sons, 1980.

McCorquodale, Charles. *History of the Interior*. New York: Vendome Press, 1983.

Montgomery, Florence M. *Printed Textiles: English and American Cottons and Linens, 1700–1850*. New York: The Viking Press, 1970.

———. *Textiles in America, 1650–1870*. New York: W. W. Norton, 1984.

Moss, Roger W., ed. *Paint in America: The Colors of Historic Buildings*. Washington DC: National Trust for Historic Preservation, 1994.

Nylander, Jane C. *Our Own Snug Fireside: Images of the New England Home, 1760–1860*. New Haven, CT: Yale University Press, 1994.

Peck, Amelia, et al. *Period Rooms in the Metropolitan Museum of Art*. New York: Harry N. Abrams, 1996.

Phillips, Barty. *Fabrics and Wallpapers: Sources, Design and Inspiration*. Boston: Bulfinch Press, 1991.

Pile, John. *A History of Interior Design*. 3rd ed. New York: John Wiley & Sons, 2009.

Praz, Mario. *An Illustrated History of Furnishing*. New York: George Braziller, 1964.

Sweeney, John A. H. *The Treasure House of Early American Rooms*. New York: Viking Press, 1963.

Tate, Allen, and C. Ray Smith. *Interior Design in the 20th Century*. New York: Harper & Row, 1985.

Thornton, Peter. *Authentic Décor: The Domestic Interior, 1620–1920*. New York: Random House, 1984.

Trocmé, Suzanne. *Influential Interiors: Shaping 20th Century Style through Key Interior Designers*. New York: Clarkson N. Potter, 1999.

Wheeler, Candace. *Principles of Home Decoration*. New York: Doubleday, Page, 1903.

Whiton, Sherrill. *Interior Design and Decoration*. Philadelphia, New York, Toronto: J. B. Lippincott, 1974.

Yarwood, Doreen. *English Interiors: A Pictorial Guide and Glossary*. Guildford, Surrey: Butterworth Press, 1983.

Furniture and Decorative Arts

Andrews, John. *Victorian and Edwardian Furniture*. Suffolk, England: Antique Collectors' Club, 1992.

Aronson, Joseph. *The Encyclopedia of Furniture*, 3d ed. New York: Crown Publishers, 1965.

Asensio, Paco, ed. *Furniture Design*. New York: teNeues, 2002.

Baker, Fiona, and Keith Baker. *20th Century Furniture*. London: Carlton Books, 2003.

Beard, Geoffrey W. *The National Trust Book of English Furniture*. London: Viking, 1985.

———, and Judith Goodison. *English Furniture, 1500–1840*. Oxford: Phaidon-Christie's, 1987.

———. *Georgian Craftsmen and Their Work*. London: Country Life, 1966.

Benn, R. Davis. *Style in Furniture*. New York: Longmans, Green, 1920.

Boger, Louise Ade. *The Complete Guide to Furniture Styles, Enlarged Edition*. New York: Charles Scribner's Sons, 1969.

———, and H. Batterson Boger. *The Dictionary of Antiques and the Decorative Arts, Enlarged Edition*. New York: Charles Scribner's Sons, 1967.

Brunt, Andrew. *Phaidon Guide to Furniture*. Upper Saddle River, NJ: Prentice Hall, 1983.

Cooke, Edward S., ed. *Upholstery in America and Europe from the Seventeenth Century to World War I*. New York: W. W. Norton, 1987.

Dresser, Charles. *Modern Ornamentation*. New York: American Life Foundation and Study Institute, 1976.

The Dunbar Book of Contemporary Furniture. Berne: Dunbar Furniture Corporation of Indiana, 1956.

Duncan, Alastair. *Modernism: Modernist Design, 1880–1940*. Suffolk, England: Antique Collectors' Club, 1998.

Durant, Stuart. *Ornament*. Woodstock, NY: Overlook Press, 1986.

Encyclopedia of Antiques. New York: Galahad Books, 1976.

Fales, Dean A., Jr. *American Painted Furniture, 1660–1880*. New York: E. P. Dutton, 1979.

Fiell, Charlotte, and Peter Fiell. *Design of the 20th Century*. New York: Taschen, 1999.

———. *1000 Chairs*. New York: Taschen, 2000.

Fitzgerald, Oscar P. *Four Centuries of American Furniture*. Radnor, PA: Wallace-Homestead Book Company, 1995.

Forman, Benno M. *American Seating Furniture, 1630–1730*. New York: W. W. Norton, 1988.

Garner, Philippe. *Twentieth-Century Furniture*. New York: Van Nostrand Reinhold, 1980.

Gloag, John. *British Furniture Makers*. New York: Hastings House, n.d.

———. *A Complete Dictionary of Furniture*. Revised and expanded by Clive Edwards. Woodstock, NY: The Overlook Press, 1991.

Gruber, Alain. *The History of Decorative Arts: The Renaissance and Mannerism in Europe*. New York: Abbeville Press, 1993.

Hanks, David A., and Anne Hoy. *Design for Living: Furniture and Lighting 1950–2000*. New York: Flammarion, 2000.

———, and Donald C. Pierce. *The Virginia Carroll Crawford Collection: American Decorative Arts, 1825–1917*. Atlanta, GA: High Museum of Art, 1983.

Hayward, Helena, ed. *World Furniture*. New York: McGraw-Hill, 1965.

Hurst, Ronald L., and Prown, Jonathan. *Southern Furniture, 1680–1830—The Colonial Williamsburg Collection*. New York: Harry N. Abrams, 1997.

The Italian Chair. Rome: Italian Institute for Foreign Trade, n.d.

Jacobson, Dawn. *Chinoiserie*. London: Phaidon Press, 1999.

Joy, Edward. *The Connoisseur Illustrated Guides: Furniture*. London: Connoisseur Cestergate House, 1972.

Lindquist, David P., and Caroline C. Warren. *Victorian Furniture*. Radnor, PA: Wallace-Homestead Book Company, 1995.

Litchfield, Frederick. *Illustrated History of Furniture*. Boston: Medici Society of America, 1922.

Lucie-Smith, Edward. *Furniture: A Concise History*. London: Thames & Hudson, 1979.

Madigan, Mary Jean, ed. *Nineteenth Century Furniture: Innovation, Revival and Reform*. New York: Roundtable Press, 1982.

Mang, Karl. *History of Modern Furniture*. New York: Harry N. Abrams, 1979.

Miller, R. Craig. *Modern Design in the Metropolitan Museum of Art 1890–1900*. New York: Metropolitan Museum of Art/Harry N. Abrams, 1990.

Morley, John. *The History of Furniture*. Boston: Little, Brown, 1999.

Newman, Harold. *An Illustrated History of Glass*. London: Thames & Hudson, 1977.

Osburne, Harold, ed. *The Oxford Companion to the Decorative Arts*. Oxford: Oxford University Press, 1985.

Payne, Christopher. *19th Century European Furniture*. Suffolk, England: Antique Collectors' Club, 1981.

Sassone, Adriana Boidi, et al. *Furniture from Rococo to Art Deco*. N.p.: Evergreen, 1988.

Savage, George, and Harold Newman. *An Illustrated Dictionary of Ceramics*. New York: Van Nostrand Reinhold Co., 1974.

Sembach, Klaus-Jürgen, Gabriele Leuthäuser, and Peter Gössel. *Twentieth-Century Furniture Design*. Köln, Germany: Taschen, 1991.

Shea, John. *Antique and Country Furniture of North America*. New York: Van Nostrand Reinhold, 1975.

Sollo, John, and Nan Sollo. *American Insider's Guide to Twentieth-Century Furniture*. London: Miller's-Mitchell Beazley, 2002.

Strange, Thomas Arthur. *English Furniture, Decoration, Woodwork, and Allied Arts from the Last Half of the Seventeenth Century to the Early Part of the Nineteenth Century*. London: B. T. Batsford, 1950.

Thornton, Peter. *Authentic Decor: The Domestic Interior, 1620–1920*. New York: Crescent Books, 1985.

———. *Form and Decoration: Innovation in the Decorative Arts, 1470–1870*. New York: Harry N. Abrams, 1998.

Wanscher, Ole. *The Art of Furniture: 5000 Years of Furniture and Interiors*. New York: Reinhold Publishing, 1966.

Wardropper, Ian, and Lynn Springer Roberts. *European Decorative Arts in the Art Institute of Chicago*. Chicago: The Art Institute of Chicago, 1991.

Watson, Sir Francis. *The History of Furniture*. New York: William Morrow, 1976.

East Asia

Kates, George N. *Chinese Household Furniture*. New York: Dover, 1962.
Kawakami, Shiegeki. *Ningyo: The Art of the Human Figurine*. New York: The Japan Society, 1995.
Morse, Edward S. *Japanese Homes and Their Surroundings*. Rutland, VT: Charles E. Tuttle, 1972.
Stierlin, Henri, ed. *China*. Germany: Benedikt Taschen, n.d.
———. *Japan*. Germany: Benedikt Taschen, n.d.

Antiquity

Baker, Hollis S. *Furniture in the Ancient World: Origins and Evolution, 3100–475 BC*. New York: Macmillan, 1966.
Boëthius, Axel. *Etruscan and Early Roman Architecture*. New York: Penguin Books, 1978.
Desroches-Noblecourt, Christiane. *Tutankhamen*. New York: New York Graphic Society, 1963.
Lawrence. A. W. *Greek Architecture*, 4th ed. rev. New York: Penguin Books, 1983.
Linley, David. *Classical Furniture*. New York: Harry N. Abrams, 1993.
Richter, G. M. A. *The Furniture of the Greeks, Etruscans, and Romans*. London: Phaidon, 1989.
Robsjohn-Gibbings, T. H., and Carlton W. Pullin. *Furniture of Classical Greece*. New York: Knopf, 1963.
Roman, James F. *Daily Life of the Ancient Egyptians*. Pittsburgh, PA: Carnegie Museum of Natural History, 1990.
Smith, W. Stevenson. *The Art and Architecture of Ancient Egypt*, 3rd ed. New Haven, CT: Yale University Press, 1998.
Ward-Perkins, J. B. *Roman Imperial Architecture*. New York: Penguin Books, 1985.

Middle Ages

Branner, Robert. *Gothic Architecture*. New York: G. Braziller, 1961.
Conant, Kenneth, John. *Carolingian and Romanesque Architecture, 800 to 1200*, 2nd ed. New York: Penguin, 1979.
Geck, Francis, J. *French Interiors and Furniture: The Gothic Period*. Boulder, CO: Stureck Educational Services, 1988.
Jackson, Thomas Graham, Sir. *Byzantine and Romanesque Architecture*. New York: Hacker Art Books, 1975.
Krautheimer, Richard. *Early Christian and Byzantine Architecture*, 4th ed. New Haven, CT: Yale University Press, 1986.
Kubach, Hans Erich. *Romanesque Architecture*. New York: Abrams, 1975.
Martindale, Andrew. *Gothic Art*. New York: Praeger Publishers, 1967.
Milburn, R. L. *Early Christian Art and Architecture*. Berkeley, CA: University of California Press, 1988.
Radding, Charles M., and William W. Clark. *Medieval Architecture and Medieval Learning: Builders and Masters in the Age of Romanesque and Gothic*. New Haven, CT: Yale University Press, 1992.
Sanderson, Warren. *Early Christian Buildings: A Graphic Introduction*. Champlain, NY: Astrion Publishers, 1993.
Scarce, Jennifer M. *Domestic Culture in the Middle East: An Exploration of the Household Interior*. Richmond, Surrey: Curzon Press, 1996.
Tracy, Charles. *English Medieval Furniture and Woodwork*. London: Victoria and Albert Museum, 1988.
von Simson, Otto Georg. *The Gothic Cathedral: Origins of Gothic Architecture and the Medieval Concept of Order*. 2nd ed. New York: Harper & Row, 1964.
Wilson, Christopher. *The Gothic Cathedral: The Architecture of the Great Church*. New York: Thames & Hudson, 1990.
Wood, Margaret. *The English Medieval House*. London: Ferndale Editions, 1981.

Renaissance

Akerman, James S. *Palladio*. Baltimore, MD: Penguin Books, 1972.
Fleming, John A. *The Painted Furniture of French Canada, 1700–1840*. Camden East, Ontario: Camden House, 1994.
Geck, Francis, J. *French Interiors and Furniture: The Period of Francis I*. Boulder, CO: Stureck Educational Services, 1982.
———. *French Interiors and Furniture: The Period of Henry II*. Boulder, CO: Stureck Educational Services, 1985.
———. *French Interiors and Furniture: The Period of Henry IV*. Boulder, CO: Stureck Educational Services, 1986.
———. *French Interiors and Furniture: The Period of Louis XIII*. Boulder, CO: Stureck Educational Services, 1989.
Girouard, Mark. *Robert Smythson and the Elizabethan Country House*. New Haven, CT: Yale University Press, 1983.
Hutchins, Catherine E. *Arts of the Pennsylvania Germans*. New York: W. W. Norton, 1983.
Kennedy, Roger G. *Mission: The History and Architecture of the Missions of North America*. Boston: Houghton Mifflin, 1993.
Kubler, George, and Martin Soria. *Art and Architecture in Spain and Portugal and Their American Dominions: 1500–1800*. Baltimore: Penguin Books, 1959.
Melor, Michel, Jean Guillaume, Claude d'Anthenaise, Sophie Barthélémy; Marie-Pierre Salé, and Caroline Dubois. *Chateaux of the Loire. Special Issue 55F, Beaux Arts Monuments Historique*. Paris: Publications Nuit et Jour, 1988.
Mowl, Timothy. *Elizabethan and Jacobean Style*. London: Phaidon, 1993.
Odom, William Macdougal. *A History of Italian Furniture from the Fourteenth to the Early Nineteenth Century*, 2nd ed. New York: Archive Press, 1966.
Palardy, Jean. *The Early Furniture of French Canada*. 2nd ed. Translated by Eric McLean. New York: St. Martin's Press, 1965.
Pedrini, Augusto. *Italian Furniture, Interiors, and Decoration of the Fifteenth and Sixteenth Centuries*, new rev. ed. London: A. Tiranti, 1949.
Summerson, John. *Inigo Jones*. Harmondsworth, England: Penguin, 1966.
Thornton, Peter. *The Italian Renaissance Interior, 1400–1600*. New York: Harry N. Abrams, 1991.
Treib, Marc. *Sanctuaries of Spanish New Mexico*. Berkeley: University of California Press, 1993.

Baroque

Beard, Geoffrey W. *The Work of Christopher Wren*. London: Bloomsbury Books, 1987.
———. *The Work of Grinling Gibbons*. Chicago: University of Chicago Press, 1990.
———. *The Work of John Vanbrugh*. London: Batsford, 1986.
Blitzer, Charles. *Age of Kings*. New York: Time, 1967.
Blunt, Anthony, ed. *Baroque and Rococo Architecture and Decoration*. Hertfordshire: Wordsworth Editions, Ltd., 1988.
Geck, Francis, J. *Art and Architecture in France: 1500–1700*. Baltimore, MD: Penguin Books, 1953.
———. *French Interiors and Furniture: The Period of Louis XIV*. Boulder, CO: Stureck Educational Services, 1990.

Hatton, Ragnhild. *Europe in the Age of Louis XIV.* Great Britain: Harcourt, Brace & World, 1969.

Lees-Milne, James. *Baroque in Spain and Portugal and Its Antecedents.* London: B. T. Batsford, 1960.

Mitford, Nancy. *The Sun King: Louis XIV at Versailles.* New York: Harper & Row, 1966.

Norberg-Schultz, Christian. *Baroque Architecture.* New York: Harry N. Abrams, 1971.

Thornton, Peter. *Baroque and Rococo Silks.* London: Faber & Faber, 1965.

———. *Seventeenth-Century Interior Decoration in England, France and Holland.* New Haven, CT: Yale University Press, 1978.

Van der Kemp, Gérald. *Versailles.* New York: Park Lane, 1981.

Wittkower, Rudolf. *Art and Architecture in Italy: 1600–1750.* Baltimore, MD: Penguin Books, 1973.

Rococo

Downs, Joseph. *American Furniture: Queen Anne and Chippendale Periods in the Henry Francis du Pont Winterthur Museum.* New York: Macmillan Company, 1952.

Fowler, John, and John Cornforth. *English Decoration in the Eighteenth Century,* 2nd ed. London: Barrie & Jenkins, 1983.

Geck, Francis J. *French Interiors and Furniture: The Period of Louis XV.* Roseville, MI: Stureck Educational Services, 1993.

———. *French Interiors and Furniture: The Regency Period.* Roseville, MI: Stureck Educational Services, 1992.

Harris, John. *The Palladian Revival: Lord Burlington, His Villa and Garden at Chiswick.* New Haven, CT: Yale University Press, 1994.

Norberg-Schultz, Christian. *Late Baroque and Rococo Architecture.* New York: Rizzoli, 1985.

Parissen, Steven. *Palladian Style.* London: Phaidon Press, 1994.

———. *The Georgian House in Britain and America.* New York: Rizzoli, 1995.

Scott, Katie. *The Rococo Interior: Decoration and Social Spaces in Early Eighteenth-Century Paris.* New Haven, CT: Yale University Press, 1995.

Smith, Charles Saumarez. *Eighteenth-Century Decoration: Design and the Domestic Interior in England.* New York: Harry N. Abrams, 1993.

Whitehead, John. *The French Interior in the Eighteenth Century.* New York: Dutton Studio Books, 1993.

Early Neoclassic

Beard, Geoffrey W. *The Work of Robert Adam.* London: Bloomsbury Books, 1987.

Groër, Léon. *Decorative Arts in Europe 1790–1850.* New York: Rizzoli, 1986.

Irwin, David. *Neoclassicism.* New York: Phaidon Press, 1997.

Kelly, Alison. *Decorative Wedgwood in Architecture and Furniture.* New York: Born-Hawes Publishers, 1965.

Linley, David. *Classical Furniture.* New York: Harry N. Abrams, 1993.

Middleton, Robin, and David Watkin. *Neoclassical and 19th Century Architecture/1.* New York: Rizzoli, 1987.

Montgomery, Charles F. *American Furniture: The Federal Period in the Henry Francis du Pont Winterthur Museum.* New York: Bonanza Books, 1978.

Oglesby, Catharine. *French Provincial Decorative Art.* New York: Scribner, 1951.

Parissien, Steven. *Adam Style.* Washington, DC: The Preservation Press, 1992.

Yarwood, Doreen. *Robert Adam.* London: Dent, 1970.

Revolution

Appelbaum, Stanley. *The Chicago World's Fair of 1893.* New York: Dover Publications, 1980.

The Art Journal Illustrated: The Industry of All Nations. London: Published for the Proprietors, by George Virtue, 1851.

Barlow, Ronald S., ed. *Victorian Houseware, Hardware and Kitchenware.* Mineola, NY: Dover Publications, 1992.

Bicknell, Amos J., and Company. *Bicknell's Victorian Buildings.* New York: Dover Publications, 1979.

Blackie and Son. *The Victorian Cabinet-Maker's Assistant.* New York: Dover Publications, 1970.

Fergusson, James. *History of the Modern Styles of Architecture,* Vol. II. New York: Dodd, Mead, 1899.

Furniture. Grand Rapids, MI: 1890.

Gillon, Edmond V., Jr. *Pictoral Archive of Early Illustrations and Views of American Architecture.* New York: Dover Publications, 1971.

Greeley, William R. *The Essence of Architecture.* New York: Van Nostrand, 1927.

Hamlin, Talbot F. *The American Spirit in Architecture: The Pageant of America.* Vol. 13. New Haven, CT: Yale University Press, 1926.

Harpers Illustrated Weekly, February–March 1872, New York, NY.

Hart, Harold H., ed. *Chairs Through the Ages.* Mineola, NY: Dover Publications, 1971.

Illustrated London News. Vol. XLI, July to December, 1862.

Montgomery Ward Furniture Catalog, 1897.

Palliser, George, and Charles Palliser. *Palliser's American Cottage Homes.* Bridgeport, CT: Palliser, Palliser and Company, 1878.

Sears Roebuck Catalogue. Chicago: Sears, Roebuck & Company, 1902.

Smith, Walter. *Masterpieces of the Centennial Exhibition.* Philadelphia: Gebbie & Barrie, 1876.

Tipping, H. Avray. *English Homes, Period V, Volume I.* London: Offices of Country Life, 1924.

The White City (World's Columbian Exposition catalog). Chicago: 1893.

Williams, Henry T., and Mrs. C. S. Jones. *Beautiful Homes: Or Hints in House Furnishing.* Vol. 4. Williams Household Series. London: Henry T. Williams, 1878.

Late Neoclassic

Ackermann, Rudolf. *Ackermanns's Repository of Arts.* London: R. Ackermann, 1829.

Barron, James. *Modern & Elegant Designs of Cabinet & Upholstery Furniture.* London: 1814.

Cescinsky, Herbert. *Chinese Furniture.* London: Benn Brothers, 1922.

Clute, Eugene. *The Treatment of Interiors.* New York: Pencil Points Press, 1926.

Cooper, Wendy A. *Classical Taste in America, 1800–1840.* New York: Abbeville Press Publishers, 1993.

Cornu, Paul. *Meubles et objets de goût 1796–1830.* Paris: Libraire des Arts Décoratifs, 1833.

Crook, J. Mordaunt. *The Greek Revival: Neoclassical Attitudes in British Architecture, 1760–1870.* London: John Murray, 1972.

Cross, Alfred. *History of Architecture.* London: International Correspondence School, n.d.

Deschamps, Madeleine. *Empire.* New York: Abbeville Press, 1994.

Ellwood, G. M. *English Furniture and Decoration 1680 to 1800.* Stuttgart, Germany: Julius Hoffmann, c. 1930.

Guinness, Desmond, and Julius Trousdale Sadler, Jr. *Mr. Jefferson Architect.* New York: Viking Press, 1973.

Hamlin, Talbot. *Greek Revival in America*. New York: Dover Publications, 1944.

Himmelheber, Georg. *Biedermeier, 1815–1835*. Munich: Prestel-Verlag, 1989.

Hubert, Gerard. *Malmaison*. National Museum of the Château of Malmaison: Editions de la Réunion des Musées Nationaux, 1982.

Irwin, David. *Neoclassicism*. London: Phaidon Press, 1997.

Jackson, Anna. *The V & A Guide to Period Styles*. London: Harry N. Abrams, 2002.

Kennedy, Roger G. *Greek Revival America*. New York: Stewart Tabori and Chang, 1989.

Lévy, Émile, ed. *Art et Décoration*. Paris: Librairie Centrale des Beaux-Arts, Volumes 1897–1906.

Litchfield, Frederick. *Illustrated History of Furniture*. Boston: Medici Society of America, 1922.

Lockwood, Luke Vincent. *Colonial Furniture in America*. New and enlarged ed. New York: Charles Scribner's Sons, 1913.

Morley, John. *Regency Design, 1790–1840*. New York: Harry N. Abrams, 1993.

Nye, Alvan C. *A Collection of Scale Drawings, Details, and Sketches of What Is Commonly Known as Colonial Furniture*. New York: William Helburn, 1895.

Ormsbee, Thomas H. *The Story of American Furniture*. New York: Macmillan, 1934.

Parissien, Steven. *Regency Style*. London: Phaidon Press, 1992.

Percier, Charles, and Pierre Fontaine. *Empire Stylebook of Interior Design*. New York: Dover Publications, 1991.

———. *Recueil de décorations intérieures*. Paris: Jules Didot Pine, 1827.

Pierson, William H. *American Buildings and Their Architects: The Colonial and Neoclassical Styles*. New York: Anchor Books, 1976.

The Room Beautiful: A Collection of Interior Illustrations Showing Decoration and Furniture Details of the Important Furnishing Periods. New York: Clifford and Lawton, 1915.

Shepherd, Thomas H., and James Elmes. *Metropolitan Improvements or London in the Nineteenth Century*. London: Benjamin Blom, 1968.

Smith, George. *The Cabinet Maker and Upholsterer's Guide*. London: 1826.

Speltz, Alexander. *The Styles of Ornament*. New York: Dover, 1959. Reprint of 1904 ed.

Strange, Thomas Arthur. *French Interiors, Furniture, Decoration, Woodwork & Allied Arts During the 17th and 18th Centuries*. New York: Bonanza Books, 1968.

Waissenberger, Robert, ed. *Vienna in the Biedermeier Era, 1815–1848*. London: Alpine Fine Arts Collection, 1986.

Wilkie, Angus. *Biedermeier*. New York: Abbeville Press, 1987.

Victorian Revivals

Aldrich, Megan. *Gothic Revival*. London: Phaidon Press, 1994.

———, et al. *A. W. N. Pugin, Master of Gothic Revival*. New Haven, CT: Yale University Press, 1995.

Artistic Furniture and Architectural Interiors. New York: Clifford & Lawton, 1892.

Atterbury, Paul, and Clive Wainwright. *Pugin: Gothic Passion*. New Haven, CT: Yale University Press, 1994.

Bicknell, A. J., and Company. *Detail, Cottage and Constructive Architecture*. New York: A. J. Bicknell, 1873.

Blum, Stella, ed. *Fashions and Costumes from Godey's Lady's Book*. New York: Dover Publications, 1985.

Blundell, Peter S. *The Marketplace Guide to Oak Furniture, Styles and Values*. Paducah, KY: Collector Books, 1980.

Bridgeman, Harrriet, and Elizabeth Drury, eds. *The Encyclopedia of Victoriana*, New York: Macmillan Publishing, 1975.

Carrott, Richard G. *The Egyptian Revival: Its Sources, Monuments, and Meaning, 1808–1858*. Berkeley: University of California Press, 1978.

Constock, William. *Modern Architectural Design and Detail*. New York: William T. Constock Architectural Publisher, 1881.

Cooper, Jeremy. *Victorian and Edwardian Décor*. New York: Abbeville Publishers, 1987.

Curl, James Stevens. *Victorian Architecture*. London: David & Charles, 1990.

Dixon, Roger, and Stefan Muthesius. *Victorian Architecture*. London: Thames & Hudson, 1978.

Downing, Andrew Jackson. *The Architecture of Country Houses; Including Designs for Cottages, Farm Houses, and Villas*. New York: Dover Publications, 1969. Reprint of original publication by D. Appleton & Co., 1850.

Eastlake, Charles L. *Hints on Household Taste, the Classic Handbook of Victorian Interior Decoration*. New York: Dover Publications, 1986. Reprint of Charles Locke Eastlake, *Hints on Household Taste in Furniture, Upholstery, and Other Details*, 4th ed. London: Longmans, Green 1878.

———. *A History of the Gothic Revival*. London: Longmans, Green, 1872.

Furniture for the Victorian Home, Comprising the Abridged Furniture Sections from A. J. Downing's Country Houses of 1850 and J. C. Louden's Encyclopedia of 1833. Watkins Glen, NY: American Life Foundation, 1968.

Garrett, Wendall. *Victorian America*. New York: Rizzoli, 1993.

Girouard, Mark. *Sweetness and Light: The Queen Anne Movement, 1860–1900*. Oxford, England: Clarendon Press, 1977.

Humbert, Jean-Marcel, Michael Pantazzi, and Christiane Ziegler. *Egyptomania: Egypt in Western Art, 1730–1930*. Ottawa, Canada: National Gallery of Canada, 1994.

Jones, Owen. *Grammar of Ornament*. New York: Van Nostrand Reinhold, 1856. Reprint 1982.

Knight, T., and Son. *Suggestions for Home Decoration*. London: T. Knight and Son, 1880.

Late Victorian Architectural Details. Watkins Glen, NY: American Life Foundation Study Institute, 1978.

Lewis, Michael. *The Gothic Revival*. London: Thames & Hudson, 2002.

Newsom, Samuel, and Joseph Newsom. *Picturesque California Homes*. San Francisco: Samuel and Joseph Newsom, 1884.

Norbury, James. *The World of Victoriana*. New York: Hamlyn Publishing Group, 1972.

Oak Furniture, Styles and Prices. Des Moines, IA: Wallace-Homestead Book Company, 1980. Illustrations from the 1897 Montgomery Ward Furniture catalog.

Pierce, Walter. *Painting and Decoration*. London: 1893.

Prignot, Eugène. *L'Architecture, La Décoration, L'Ameublement Libraire Speciale des Arts Industriels et Décoratifs*. N.p.: 1873.

Pugin, A., and N. Welby. *Fifteenth and Sixteenth Century Ornaments*. Edinburgh: John Grant, 1830.

Seale, William. *The Tasteful Interlude, American Interiors Through the Camera's Eye, 1860–1917*. New York: Praeger Publishers, 1975.

Shoppell, Robert W. *Dining-Room Furniture & Decoration*. New York: Co-Operative Building Plan Association, 1883.

Sloan, Samuel. *Sloan's Homestead Architecture*. Philadelphia: J. P. Lippincott, 1861.

Stevenson, Katherine Cole. *Houses by Mail: A Guide to Houses from Sears, Roebuck and Company*. Washington, DC: Preservation Press, 1986.

Sweetman, John. *The Oriental Obsession: Islamic Inspiration in British and American Art and Achitecture, 1500–1920*. Cambridge, England: Cambridge University Press, 1988.

Talbert, B. J. *Examples of Ancient and Modern Furniture, Metal Work, Tapestries, Decorations*. Boston: James R. Osgood, 1876.

d. Verleger, Eigenthum. *Aus d. Kunstanst d. Bibl. Instit. In Hildbhn.* N.p., n.d.

Winkler, Gail Caskey, and Roger W. Moss. *Victorian Interior Decoration, American Interiors 1830–1900*. New York: Henry Holt, 1986.

Academic Historicism

Anscombe, Isabelle. *A Woman's Touch*. New York: Viking, 1984.

Appleton, Marc. *George Washington Smith: An Architect's Scrapbook*. Los Angeles: Tailwater Press, 2001.

Axelrod, Alan. *The Colonial Revival in America*. New York: W. W. Norton, 1985.

Baca, Elmo. *Romance of the Mission*. Salt Lake City, UT: Gibbs Smith Publisher, 1996.

Brooklyn Museum. *The American Renaissance, 1876–1917*. New York: Pantheon Books, 1979.

Cook, Clarance. *The House Beautiful: Essays on Beds and Tables, Stools and Candlesticks*. New York: Charles Scribner's Sons, 1878.

Cravath, James R., and Van Rensselaer Lansingh. *Practical Illumination*. New York: McGraw-Hill, 1907.

Curran, Kathleen. *The Romanesque Revival: Buildings, Landscapes, and Societies*. University Park: Pennsylvania State University Press, 2003.

Drexler, Arthur, ed. *The Architecture of the École des Beaux-Arts*. New York: Museum of Modern Art, 1977.

Edgell, George H. *American Architecture Today*. New York: Charles Scribner's Sons, 1928.

Elliott, Maud Howe, ed. *Art and Handicraft in the Women's Building of the World's Columbian Expositon*. Chicago: Rand McNally, 1894.

Floyd, Margaret Henderson. *Henry Hobson Richardson: A Genius for Architecture*. New York: Monacelli Press, 1997.

Gellner, Arrol, and Douglas Keister. *Red Tile Style: America's Spanish Revival Architecture*. New York: Viking Studio, 2002.

Hegemann, Werner, and Elbert Peets. *The American Vitruvius: An Architect's Handbook of Civic Art*. New York: 1922.

Hertz, B. Russell. *The Decoration and Furnishing of Apartments*. New York: G. P. Putnam's Sons, 1915.

I.C.S. Reference Library. *Use and Design of Lighting Fixtures*. Scranton, PA: International Textbook Company, 1909.

Jackson, Alice, and Bettina Jackson. *The Study of Interior Decoration*. Garden City, NJ: Doubleday, Doran, 1928.

Jennings, A. S. *Upholstery and Wall Coverings*. N.p., 1903.

Jordy, William H. *American Buildings and Their Architects: Progressive and Academic Ideas at the Turn of the Century*. Vol. 4. Oxford: Oxford University Press, 1972.

Lindquist, David P., and Caroline C. Warren. *Colonial Revival Furniture*. Radnor, PA: Wallace-Homestead, 1993.

May, Bridget A. "Progressivism and the Colonial Revival: The Modern Colonial House, 1900–1920," *Winterthur Portfolio* Vol. 26, No. 2/3, Summer–Autumn 1991, pp. 107–122.

McCelland, Nancy. *The Practical Book of Wall Treatments*. New York: J. P. Lippincott, 1926.

McMillian, Elizabeth. *California Colonial: The Spanish and Rancho Revival Styles*. Atglen, PA: Schiffer Publishing, 2002.

Mizner, Addison. *Florida Architecture of Addison Mizner*. New York: Dover Publications, 1992.

Monograph of the Works of McKim Mead and White 1879–1915. New York: Architectural Book Publishing, 1915–1920.

Nelson, L. H. *View of London Cities*. Portland, ME: 1905.

Nutting, Wallace. *Furniture Treasury*. 2 vols. New York: Macmillan, 1948.

O'Gorman, James F. *H. H. Richardson: Architectural Forms for an American Society*. Chicago: University of Chicago Press, 1987.

———. *Living Architecture: A Biography of H. H. Richardson*. New York: Simon and Schuster, 1997.

Platt, Frederick. *America's Gilded Age: Its Architecture and Decoration*. New York: A. S. Barnes, 1976.

Raymond, Maud Wotring. *The Architecture and Landscape Gardening of the Exhibition*. San Francisco: Paul Elder, 1915.

Renick, Roger, and Michael Trotter. *Monterey: Furnishings of California's Spanish Revival*. Atglen, PA: Shiffer Publishing, 2000.

Rhodes, William B. *The Colonial Revival*. New York: Garland Press, 1977.

Roth, Leland. *McKim, Mead, and White Architects*. New York: Harper & Row, 1983.

Saylor, Henry. *Architectural Styles for Country Houses*. New York: Robert M. McBride, 1919.

———. *Inexpensive Homes*. N.p., 1912.

Scully, Vincent J., Jr. *The Shingle Style and the Stick Style*. Rev. ed. New Haven, CT: Yale University Press, 1971.

Shackleton, Robert, and Elizabeth Shackleton. *The Quest of the Colonial*. New York: Century Company, 1913.

Shapland, H. P. *Style Schemes in Antique Furnishings*. N.p., 1909.

Smith, Jane S. *Elsie de Wolfe: A Life in the High Style*. New York: Atheneum, 1982.

Stein, Susan R., ed. *The Architecture of Richard Morris Hunt*. Chicago: University of Chicago Press, 1986.

Taylor, Lonn, and Dessa Bokides. *New Mexican Furniture, 1600–1940: The Origins, Survival, and Revival of Furniture Making in the Hispanic Southwest*. Santa Fe: Museum of New Mexico Press, 1987.

Thorne, Edward. *Decorative Draperies and Upholstery*. N.p., c. 1900.

Wallis, Frank E. *How to Know Architecture*. New York: Harper & Brothers, 1910.

Van Rensselaer, Marian Griswold. *Henry Hobson Richardson and His Works*. New York: Dover Publications, 1969.

Reforms

Adams, John D. *Arts & Crafts Lamps: How to Make Them*. Chicago: Popular Mechanics, 1911.

Anscombe, Isabelle. *Arts & Crafts Style*. New York: Rizzoli, 1991.

———, and Charlotte Gere. *Arts & Crafts in Britain and America*. New York: Van Nostrand Reinhold, 1978.

Arts and Crafts Movement. New York: Todtri Book Publishers, 2002.

Aslin, Elizabeth. *The Aesthetic Movement: Prelude to Art Nouveau*. New York: Frederick A. Praeger, 1969.

Boris, Eileen. *Art and Labor: Ruskin, Morris, and the Craftsman Ideal in America*. Philadephia: Temple University Press, 1986.

Burke, Doreen Bolger, et al. *In Pursuit of Beauty: Americans and the Aesthetic Movement*. New York: Rizzoli, 1986.

Clark, Robert Judson, ed. *The Arts and Crafts Movement in America 1876–1916*. Princeton, NJ: Princeton University Press, 1972.

Cumming, Elizabeth, and Wendy Kaplan. *The Arts and Crafts Movement.* London: Thames & Hudson, 1991.

Davey, Peter. *Arts and Crafts Architecture.* London: Phaidon Press, 1995.

Duchscherer, Paul, and Douglas Keister. *The Bungalow: America's Arts and Crafts Home.* New York: Penguin Studio, 1995.

The Encyclopedia of Arts and Crafts: The International Arts Movement, 1850–1920. New York: E. P. Dutton, 1989.

Gere, Charlotte, and Lesley Hoskins. *The House Beautiful: Oscar Wilde and the Aesthetic Interior.* London: Geffrye Museum, 2000.

Gordon, Beverly. *Shaker Textile Arts.* Hanover, NH: University Press of New England, 1980.

Harbron, Dudley. *The Conscious Stone: The Life of Edward William Godwin.* New York: Benjamin Blom, 1971.

Johnson, A. P., and Marta K. Sironen. *Manual of the Furniture Arts and Crafts.* Grand Rapids, MI: A. P. Johnson Company, 1928.

Kaplan, Wendy. *"The Art That Is Life": The Arts and Crafts Movement in America, 1875–1920.* Boston: Little, Brown, 1987.

Kardon Janet, ed. *The Ideal Home: 1900–1920.* New York: Harry N. Abrams, 1993.

Lambourne, Lionel. *The Aesthetic Movement.* London: Phaidon Press, 1996.

Limbert Furniture. New York: Turn of the Century Editions, 1981.

Lind, Carla. *The Wright Style.* New York: Simon & Schuster, 1992.

Makinson, Randell L. *Greene and Greene.* Santa Barbara, CA: Peregrine Smith, 1979.

Mission Furniture: How to Make It, Part One. Chicago: Popular Mechanics, 1909.

Mission Furniture: How to Make It, Part Two. Chicago: Popular Mechanics, 1910.

Naylor, Gillian. *The Arts and Crafts Movement.* Cambridge, MA: MIT Press, 1971.

Nicoletta, Julie. *The Architecture of the Shakers.* Woodstock, VT: Countryman Press, 1995.

Pfeiffer, Bruce Brooks, and Gerald Nordland, eds. *Frank Lloyd Wright: In the Realm of Ideas.* Carbondale: Southern Illinois University Press, 1988.

The Radford American Homes. Chicago: Radford Architectural Company, 1903.

Richardson, Margaret. *The Craft Architects.* New York: Rizzoli International Publications, 1983.

Rieman, Timothy D., and Jean M. Burks. *The Complete Book of Shaker Furniture.* New York: Harry N. Abrams, 1993.

Rocheleau, Paul, and June Sprigg. *Shaker Built: The Form and Function of Shaker Architecture.* New York: Monacelli Press, 1994.

Rodel, Kevin P., and Jonathan Binzen. *Arts and Crafts Furniture: From Classic to Contemporary.* Newtown, CT: Taunton Press, 2003.

Roth, Leland M. *Shingle Styles: Innovation and Tradition in American Architecture, 1874–1982.* New York: Harry N. Abrams, 1999.

Scott, M. H. Baillie. *Houses and Gardens—Arts and Crafts Interiors.* Suffolk, England: Antique Collectors' Club, 1995.

Scully, Vincent J., Jr. *The Shingle Style and the Stick Style.* Rev. ed. New Haven, CT: Yale University Press, 1971.

Shea, John G. *The American Shakers and Their Furniture.* New York: Van Nostrand Reinhold, 1971.

Simpson, Duncan. *C. F. A. Vosey: An Architect of Individuality.* New York: Whitney Library of Design, 1981.

Spencer, Robin. *The Aesthetic Movement.* New York: E. P. Dutton, 1972.

Sprigg, June, and David Larkin. *Shaker Life, Work, and Art.* Boston: Houghton Mifflin Company, 1987.

Stickley, Gustav, ed. *Craftsman Bungalows.* New York: Dover Publications, 1988.

———. *Craftsman Homes, Architecture and Furnishings of the American Arts and Crafts Movement.* New York: Dover Publications, 1909.

Talbert, Bruce J. *Victorian Decorative Art.* Watkins Glen, NY: American Life Foundation, 1978.

Tinniswood, Adrian. *The Arts and Crafts House.* New York: Watson/Guptill Publications, 1999.

Watkinson, Ray. *William Morris as Designer.* New York: Reinhold Publishing, 1967.

Watt, William. *Art Furniture from Designs by E. W. Godwin.* London: B. T. Batsford, 1877.

The Work of L & J. G. Stickley. Fayetteville, NY: n.d.

Innovation

Albrecht, Donald, and Chrysanthe B. Broikos, eds. *On the Job: Design and the American Office.* New York: Princeton Architectural Press, 2000.

Amaya, Mario. *Art Nouveau.* New York: E. P. Dutton, 1966.

Blake, Fanny. *Essential Charles Rennie Mackintosh.* Bath, England: Parragon Publishing, 2001.

Boubnova, Iaroslava, Christoph Horst, Robert Fleck, John Miller, and Michel Onfray. *Vienna Secession, 1898–1998: The Century of Artistic Freedom.* Munich: Prestel, 1998.

Brandstätter, Christian. *Wiener Werkstätte: Design in Vienna, 1903–1932.* New York: Harry N. Abrams, 2003.

Crawford, Alan. *Charles Rennie Mackintosh.* London: Thames & Hudson, 1995.

De Wit, Wim., ed. *Louis Sullivan: The Function of Ornament.* New York: W. W. Norton, 1986.

Droste, Magdalena. *Bauhaus 1919–1933.* Köln, Germany: Taschen, 1990.

Duncan, Alastair. *Art Nouveau Furniture.* New York: Crown Publishers, 1982.

Fahr-Becker, Gabriele. *Wiener Werkstätte.* Köln, Germany: Taschen, 1995.

Felderer, Brigitte, Gottfried Fliedl, Otto Kapfinger, Eleonora Louis, and James Shedel. *Secession: The Vienna Secession from Temple of Art to Exhibition Hall.* Ostfildern-Ruit, Germany: Hatje, 1997.

Frazier, Nancy. *Louis Sullivan and the Chicago School.* New York: Crescent Books, 1991.

Friedman, Mildred, ed. *De Stijl: 1917–1931 Visions of Utopia.* New York: Abbeville Press, 1982.

Greenhalgh, Paul, ed. *Art Nouveau, 1890–1914.* London: V&A Publications, 2000.

Johnson, Diane Chalmers. *American Art Nouveau.* New York: Harry N. Abrams, 1981.

Kentgens-Craig, Margret. *The Bauhaus and America: First Contacts, 1919–1936.* Cambridge, MA: MIT Press, 2001.

Macleod, Robert. *Charles Rennie Mackintosh, Architect and Artist.* New York: E. P. Dutton, 1983.

Masini, Lara-Vinca. *Art Nouveau.* Secaucus, NJ: Chartwell Books, 1984.

McCoy, Esther. *Five California Architects.* Los Angeles: Hennessey and Ingalls, 1960.

McQuaid, Matilda. *Lilly Reich: Designer and Architect.* New York: Harry N. Abrams, 1996.

Overy, Paul. *De Stijl.* London: Thames & Hudson, 1991.

Rowland, Anna. *The Bauhaus Sourcebook.* New York: Van Nostrand Reinhold, 1990.

Russell, Frank. *Art Nouveau Architecture.* New York: Rizzoli, 1979.

Saliga, Pauline A., ed. *The Sky's the Limit: A Century of Chicago Skyscrapers*. New York: Rizzoli, 1990.

Schezen, Roberto. *Adolf Loos—Architecture 1903–1933*. New York: Monacelli Press, 1996.

Shimomura, Junichi. *Art Nouveau Architecture: Residential Masterpieces, 1892–1911*. San Francisco: Cadence Books, 1990.

Troy, Nancy J. *The De Stijl Environment*. Cambridge, MA: MIT Press, 1983.

Van Doesburg, Theo. *Principles of Neo-Plastic Art*. New York: Graphic Society, 1966.

Varnedoe, Kirk. *Vienna 1900, Art, Architecture & Design*. New York: Museum of Modern Art, 1986.

Vinci, John. *The Stock Exchange Trading Room*. Chicago: The Art Institute of Chicago, 1977.

Wadsworth, Ginger. *Julia Morgan: Architect of Dreams*. Minneapolis, MN: Lerner Publications Company, 1990.

Waissenberger, Robert. *Vienna Secession*. New York: Rizzoli, 1977.

Warncke, Carsten-Peter. *De Stijl 1917–1931*. Köln, Germany: Taschen, 1990.

Whitford, Frank. *Bauhaus*. London: Thames & Hudson, 1984.

Wichmann, Siegfried. *Jugendstil Art Nouveau: Floral and Functional Forms*. New York: New York Graphic Society, 1984.

Willis, Carol. *Form Follows Finance: Skyscrapers and Skylines in New York and Chicago*. New York: Princeton Architectural Press, 1995.

Wingler, Hans M. *The Bauhaus*. Cambridge, MA: MIT Press, 1979.

Modernism

Abercrombie, Stanley. *George Nelson: The Design of Modern Design*. Cambridge: MA: MIT Press, 1995.

Arwas, Victor. *Art Deco*. New York: Harry N. Abrams, 1980.

Baldwin, Billy. *Billy Baldwin Decorates*. New York: Holt, Rinehart, & Winston, 1972.

Bayer, Patricia. *Art Deco Architecture: Design, Decoration, and Detail from the Twenties and Thirties*. New York: Harry N. Abrams, 1992.

———. *Art Deco Interiors: Decoration and Design Classics of the 1920s and 1930s*. New York: Thames & Hudson, 1990.

Benton, Charlotte, Tim Benton, and Ghislaine Wood. *Art Deco, 1910–1939*. New York: Bulfinch Press, 2003.

Berry, John R. *Herman Miller: The Purpose of Design*. New York: Rizzoli, 2004.

Bony, Anne. *Furniture and Interiors of the 1960s*. Paris: Éditions Flammarion, 2004.

Bréon, Emmanuel, and Rosalind Pepall, eds. *Ruhlmann—Genius of Art Deco*. Paris: Somogy Éditions D'Art, 2004.

Brown, Erica. *Interior Views: Design at Its Best*. New York: Viking Press, 1980.

Brunhammer, Yvonne. *Art Deco Style*. London: Academy Editions, 1983.

Bullock, Orin M., Jr. *The Restoration Manual*. Norwalk, CT: Silvermine Publishers, 1966, 1978.

Calloway, Stephen. *Twentieth-Century Decoration*. New York: Rizzoli, 1988.

Carnard, Florence. *Ruhlmann: Master of Art Deco*. New York: Abrams, 1984.

Carter, Randolph, and Robert Reed Cole. *Joseph Urban: Architecture, Theatre, Opera, Film*. New York: Abbeville Press, 1992.

Le Corbusier. *Towards a New Architecture*. New York: Dover Publications, 1986.

Dietsch, Deborah K. *Classic Modern: Mid-Century Modern at Home*. New York: Simon & Schuster, 2000.

Duncan, Alastair. *Art Deco*. New York: Thames & Hudson, 1988.

———. *Modernism: Modernist Design 1880–1940*. Minneapolis, MN: Norwest Corporation, 1998.

———. *Art Deco Furniture: The French Designers*. New York: Thames & Hudson, 1992.

Dunlop, Beth. *Building a Dream: The Art of Disney Architecture*. New York: Harry N. Abrams, 1996.

The Edward J. Wormley Collection. High Point, NC: Dunbar Furniture, 2003.

Eidelberg, Martin, ed. *Design 1935–1965: What Modern Was*. New York: Harry N. Abrams, 1991.

Fehrman, Cherie, and Kenneth Fehrman. *Postwar Interior Design: 1945–1960*. New York: Van Nostrand Reinhold, 1987.

Fiell, Charlotte, and Peter Fiell. *Modern Furniture Classics since 1945*. Washington, DC: AIA Press, 1991.

Fleig, Karl. *Alvar Aalto*. Basel, Germany: Birkhäuser Verlag, 1999.

Giedion, Sigfried. *Walter Gropius*. New York: Dover Publications, 1992.

Goldstein, Barbara, ed. *Arts & Architecture: The Entenza Years*. Cambridge, MA: MIT Press, 1990.

Greenberg, Cara. *Mid-Century Modern: Furniture of the 1950s*. New York: Harmony Books, 1995.

———. *Op to Pop: Furniture of the 1960s*. Boston: Little, Brown, 1999.

Hampton, Mark. *Legendary Decorators of the 20th Century*. New York: Doubleday, 1992.

Hanks, David A., and Anne Hoy. *Design for Living: Furniture and Lighting, 1950–2000: The Liliane and David M. Stewart Collection*. New York: Flammarion, 2000.

Hanks, David A., and Jennifer Toher. *Donald Deskey: Decorative Designs and Interiors*. New York: E. P. Dutton, 1987.

Hess, Alan. *The Ranch House*. New York: Harry N. Abrams, 2004.

Hillier, Bevis. *The Style of the Century*. New York: E. P. Dutton, 1983.

Hosmer, Charles B. *Presence of the Past*. New York: Putnam, 1965.

———. *Preservation Comes of Age*. Charlottesville, VA: Univ. Press of Virginia, 1981.

Isamu Noguchi. San Francisco: Chronicle Books, 1986.

Jackson, Lesley. *"Contemporary": Architecture and Interiors of the 1950s*. New York: Phaidon Press, 1994.

———. *The New Look: Design in the Fifties*. New York: Thames & Hudson, 1998.

———. *The Sixties: Decade of Design Revolution*. New York: Phaiden, 1998.

Joedicke, Jürgen. *Architecture Since 1945: Sources and Directions*. New York: Frederick A. Praeger, 1969.

Johnson, Stewart J. *American Modern, 1925–1940: Design for a New Age*. New York: Harry N. Abrams, 2000.

Khan, Hasan-Uddin. *International Style: Modernist Architecture from 1925 to 1965*. New York: Taschen, 2001.

Lahti, Louna. *Alvar Aalto*. Los Angeles: Taschen, 2004.

Lupton, Edith, ed. *The ABCs of the Bauhaus and Design Theory*. New York: The Cooper Union, 1991.

McClinton, Katharine Morrison. *Art Deco: A Guide for Collectors*. New York: Clarkson N. Potter, 1972.

Murtagh, William. *Keeping Time*. New York: Wiley, 2005.

Neuhart, John, Marilyn Neuhart, and Ray Eames. *Eames Design: The Work of the Office of Charles and Ray Eames*. New York: Harry N. Abrams, 1989.

Pardo, Vittorio Franchetti. *Le Corbusier*. New York: Grosset & Dunlap, 1971.

Piña, Leslie. *Herman Miller Office*. Atglen, PA: Schiffer Publishing, 2002.

The Radio City Music Hall Art Deco Collection. New York: Schumacher, n.d.

Reed, Peter. *Alvar Aalto: Between Humanism and Materialism*. New York: The Museum of Modern Art, 1998.

Salokorpi, Asko. *Modern Architecture in Finland*. New York: Praeger Publishers, 1970.

Schulman, Julius. *Architecture and Its Photography*. Köln, Germany: Taschen, 1998.

Seale, William. *Recreating the Historic House Interior*. Nashville, TN: American Association of State and Local History, 1979.

Sembach, Klaus-Jürgen. *Contemporary Furniture: An International Review of Modern Furniture, 1950 to the Present*. New York: Architectural Book Publishing Company, 1982.

Serraino, Pierluigi, and Julius Shulman. *Modernism Rediscovered*. Köln, Germany: Taschen, 2000.

Tinniswood, Adrian. *The Art Deco House: Avant-Garde Houses of the 1920s and 30s*. New York: Watson-Guptill, 2002.

Troy, Nancy J. *Modernism and the Decorative Arts in France*. New Haven, CT: Yale University Press, 1991.

Wilson, Kristina. *Livable Modernism: Interior Decorating and Design during the Great Depression*. New Haven, CT: Yale University Press, 2004.

With Heritage So Rich: Special Committee on Historic Preservation, United States Conference of Mayors, 1966.

Experimentation

Anargyros, Sophie. *Le Style des Annes 80: Architecture Decoration Design*. Paris: Rivages, 1986.

Bertoni, Franco. *Minimalist Architecture*. Boston: Birkhäuser, 2002.

———. *Minimalist Design*. Boston: Birkhäuser, 2004.

Blake, Peter. *Form Follows Fiasco: Why Modern Architecture Hasn't Worked*. Boston and Toronto: Little, Brown, 1977.

Collins, Michael. *Towards Post-Modernism: Decorative Arts and Design Since 1851*. New York: New York Graphic Society, 1987.

———, and Andreas Papadakis. *Post-Modern Design*. New York: Rizzoli, 1989.

De Bure, Gilles. *Ettore Sottsass Jr*. Paris: Rivages, 1987.

Edwards, Andres R. *The Sustainability Revolution: Portrait of a Paradigm Shift*. Gabriola Island, Canada: New Society Publishers, 2005.

Friedman, Mildred, ed. *Gehry Talks, Architecture + Process*. New York: Universe Publishing, 2005.

Garofalo, Francesco. *Steven Holl*. New York: Universe Publishing, 2003.

Girardo, Diane. *Architecture After Modernism*. London: Thames & Hudson, 1996.

Horn, Richard. *Memphis: Objects, Furniture, and Patterns*. Philadelphia: Running Press Book Publishers, 1985.

Italy: The New Domestic Landscape. New York: Museum of Modern Art, 1972.

Jencks, Charles. *The Language of Post-Modern Architecture*. 6th rev. ed. New York: Rizzoli, 1991.

———. *Late-Modern Architecture*. New York: Rizzoli, 1980.

———. *The New Moderns: From Late Modern to Neo-Modernism*. New York: Rizzoli, 1990.

———. *The New Paradigm in Architecture: The Language of Post-Modernism*. New Haven, CT: Yale University Press, 2002.

———, ed. *Post-Modern Classicism*. London: Architectural Design, 1980.

Klotz, Heinrich. *The History of Postmodern Architecture*. Cambridge, MA: MIT Press, 1988.

———, ed. *Revision of the Modern*. London: Architectural Design, 1985.

Kron, Joan, and Suzanne Slesin. *High-Tech: The Industrial Style and Source Book for the Home*. New York: Clarkson N. Potter, 1978.

Martinez, Antonio Riggen. *Luis Barragán*. New York: Monacelli Press, 1996.

Mastelli, Rich, and John Kelsey, eds. *Tradition in Contemporary Furniture*. Free Union, NC: Furniture Society, 2001.

McDonough, Michael, and Michael Braungart. "The NEXT Industrial Revolution." *Atlantic Monthly*, October 1998.

Meier, Richard, with introduction by Joseph Rykwert. *Richard Meier Architect*. New York: Rizzoli, 1984.

Miller, Nory. *Johnson/Burgee Architecture*. New York: Random House, 1979.

Nakashima, George. *The Soul of a Tree: A Woodworker's Reflections*. New York: Kodansha International, 1981.

Pearman, Hugh. *Contemporary World Architecture*. New York: Phaidon Press, 2002.

Portoghesi, Paolo. *After Modern Architecture*. New York: Rizzoli, 1980.

———. *Postmodern: The Architecture of the Postindustrial Society*. New York: Rizzoli, 1983.

Radice, Barbara. *Memphis*. New York: Rizzoli, 1984.

Russell, Beverly. *Architecture and Design 1970–1990: New Ideas in America*. New York: Harry N. Abrams, 1989.

———. *Women of Design: Contemporary American Interiors*. New York: Rizzoli, 1992.

Sakellaridou, Irena. *Mario Botta, Architectural Poetics*. New York: Universe Publishing, 2000.

Sottsass Associati. New York: Rizzoli, 1988.

Stang, Alanna, and Christopher Hawthorne. *The Green House: New Directions in Sustainable Architecture*. New York: Princeton Architectural Press, 2005.

Venturi, Robert. *Complexity and Contradiction in Architecture*. New York: Museum of Modern Art, 1966, 1977, 1983.

Wheeler, Karen Vogel, Peter Arnell, and Ted Bickford, eds. *Michael Graves, Buildings and Projects 1966–1981*. New York: Rizzoli, 1982.

Wines, James. *Green Architecture*. London: Taschen, 2000.

Index

(Note: Boldface page numbers indicate illustrations or photographs; italic page numbers indicate inclusive discussions.)

Illustration Credits

NOTE: For greater historical accuracy, some images have been slightly modified digitally from their original appearance to more accurately represent the building or object as it would have appeared upon completion or within its appropriate time frame. These actions include removing automobiles, electrical or telephone wires, and signage that is not of the original period. Older prints and negatives have also had their foxing or spotting removed. These actions have not been taken on images obtained from museums or commercial photographers.

Ackerman, Phyllis, *Wallpaper Its History, Design and Use*, New York: Frederick A. Stokes Co., 1923: Fig. 15-14a, 15-14c.
Ackermann, Rudolf, *Ackermanns's Repository of Arts*, London: R. Ackermann, 1829: Fig. 29-9a, 31-15.
AGE Fotostock: Fig. 54-5b.
Adams, John D., *Arts-Crafts Lamps*, Chicago: Popular Mechanics Co., 1911: Fig. 43-11c.
Ian Aitken © Rough Guides: Fig. 44-5.
Alamy: Fig. I-14, 11-4a (© Mervyn Rees), 39-2 (© Richard Bardwell), 39-6, (© California California), 47-2c, 49-4c (Heidi James), 56-4, 58-12, 58-18.
Courtesy Alessi S.p.a., Crusinalla, Italy: Fig. 55-23b.
Max Alexander © Dorling Kindersley: Fig. 58-3.
Peter Alexander © Dorling Kindersley: Fig. 54-10c.
Alexf, Wikimedia Commons: Fig. 51-9b.
Alsandro, Wikimedia Commons: Fig. 59-9.
© Miroslav Ambrose/GreatBuildings.com: Fig. 49-4b.
Appelton's American Standard Geographies, *Physical Geography*, New York: D. Appelton and Company, 1887: Section B Opener.
Arcaid/Alamy: Fig. 12-8b (Richard Bryant Photographer), 43-1b, 44-3b, 44-8c, 54-2c.
Architectural Association Photo Library, London: Fig. 52-2.
© Architex International: Fig. 59-17a, 59-17b, 59-17c.
Arizona Development Board, Travel Promotion Department: Fig. 16-16.
L'Art Decoratif Francais 1918-1925; Paris: Editions Albert Levy. 1925-1926: Fig. 51-19a, 51-23b.
Artek: Fig. 52-3b, 52-10a.
Courtesy Artemide USA: Fig. 56-15a, 56-15b, 58-22a, 58-22b.
The Art Institute of Chicago, gift of the Antiquarian Society through the Captial Campaign Fund: Fig 28-7.
The Art Journal Illustrated: The Industry of All Nations, London: Published for the Proprietors, by George Virtue, 1851: Fig. 33-13a, 33-15, 34-15a, 34-15b, 34-15d, 46-15a.
Art Resource, NY: Fig. 44-14, 44-15.
Art Resource/The New York Public Library Photographic Services: Fig. 26-19.
© Artists Rights Society (ARS), New York/VG Bild-Kunst, Bonn: Fig. 49-3c.
© 2005, Artists Rights Society (ARS), New York/SOFAM, Brussels: Photo by Ch. Bastin & J. Evrard: Fig. 44-6c.
Artistic Houses, New York: Benjamin Blom, Inc., 1883, Republished 1971: Fig. 32-13, 36-13, 41-5, 41-8, 41-9.
Les Arts de la Maison, Paris, Editions Albert Morancé, c. 1923: Fig. 51-14.
Les Arts de la Maison, Paris, Christian Zervos, 1926: Fig., 51-19b.
Audsley, George A., *The Practical Decorator and Ornamentalist, part 3*, Glasgow, 1892: Fig. 32-1a.
Ayervais, Michael, The Ayervais Collection: Fig. 3-13a, 3-13b, 3-15.
Baedeker, Karl (Ed.), *Baedeker's Egypt*, Leipsec: Karl Baedecker, Publisher, 1902: Fig. 4-5a.
Courtesy Baker Furniture: Fig. 34-21, 55-25, 55-26.
Baneat, Paul, *Le Mobilier Breton*, Paris: Leon Marotte, n.d.: Fig. 23-16.
Benn, H. P. and H. P. Shapland, *The Nation's Treasures*, London: Simpkin, Marshall, Hamilton, Kent, and Co. Ltd. and Benn Brothers, Ltd., 1910: Fig. 24-10c.
Barlow, Ronald S. (Ed.), *Victorian Houseware, Hardware and Kitchenware*, Mineola: Dover Publications, 1992: Fig. 26-17c, 46-15b.
Bauhaus Archive, Berlin, Germany: The Bridgeman Art Library: Fig. 49-7.
Behrens, Peter (1868–1940). "AEG Turbine Factory." 1909. Exterior. Berlin, Germany. © 2006 ARS Artists Rights Society, NY/VG Bild-Kunst, Bonn/Erich Lessing/Art Resource, NY: Fig. 47-3.
Benh Lieu Song, Wikimedia Commons: Fig. 27-2.
Bildarchiv Preussischer Kulturbesitz/Art Resource: Fig. 28-10.
Bildarchiv Monheim GmbH/Alamy: Fig. 28-4.
Used with permission from Biltmore Estate, Asheville, North Carolina: Fig. 37-11b.
© Julian Birbrajer, AGE Fotostock: Fig. 53-11.
Blunt, Ron/Courtesy of the National Trust for Historic Preservation: Fig. 30-14.
Courtesy the Bolduc House Museum: Fig. 16-24.
Victor Borg © Rough Guides: Fig. 58-8.
Photos courtesy of Bradbury & Bradbury Art Wallpapers: Fig. 55-21.
Brightman, Anna: 1-8, 10-2a, 11-1a, 11-6a, 37-19b.
Brooklyn Museum of Art, New York: 34-12 (Gift of John D. Rockefeller, Jr. and John D. Rockefeller III, 46.43).
Brooks, Alfred M., *Architecture and the Allied Arts*, Indianapolis: The Bobb-Merrill Co., 1914/1926: Fig. 6-19, 10-5b.
Bruno Mathsson International AB: Fig. 52-13.
Buffalo and Erie County Historical Society: Fig. 47-9b.
Byrne, Arthur and Mildred Stapley, *Spanish Interiors and Furniture, Vols. I, II, and III*, New York: William Helburn, Inc., 1922: Fig. 13-6a, 13-6b, 13-7, 13-9b, 13-11a, 13-12b.
California Department of Parks & Recreation, Old Town San Diego State Historic Park, Roscoe E. Hazard Collection: Fig. 34-18.
Cambridge University Library. Wikimedia Commons: Map, K. Victorian Opening.
Carolina Art Association, Carl Julian: Fig. 25-7.
Carolus, Wikimedia Commons: Fig. 14-4a.
Cassina USA Inc.: Fig. 48-8a, 48-8b, 48-8c. 50-8a. 50-8c.
Cescinsky, Herbert, *Chinese Furniture*, London: Benn Brothers, Ltd., 1922: Fig. 2-7a, 29-20.
Chachu207, Wikimedia Commons: Fig. 15-5.
Richard Cheek: Fig. 37-16.
Chilli Head, Wikipedia Commons: Fig. 24-4a.
ChrisO, Wikimedia Commons: Fig. 15-6a.
Chuckatuck, Wikimedia Commons: Fig. 19-7, 22-9a.
Clifford, Chandler R., *Period Furnishings: An Encyclopedia of Historic Furniture, Decorations, and Furnishings*, New York: Clifford and Lawton, 1911/1914: Fig. 9-1c, 10-1b, 10-10b, 12-15b, 12-15c, 12-21, 15-14b, 24-7.
Courtesy of Clodagh and Daniel Aubrey Studio: Fig. 59-14.
Clute, Eugene, *The Treatment of Interiors*, New York: The Pencil Point Press, 1926: Fig. 16-11, 27-9, 27-22. 39-17.
© Colefax and Fowler (Photography: English Heritage Millar & Harris Collection): Fig. 30-34c.
Coldwell, Doug, Wikimedia Commons: Fig. 37-11a.
Coro, Wikimedia Commons: Fig. 43-3a.
Cook, Clarence, *The House Beautiful*, New York: Charles Scribner's Sons, 1881: Fig. 41-1.

Cooper-Hewitt, National Design Museum, Smithsonian Institution: Purchased for the Museum by the Advisory Council 1911-28-479, (photo: Scott Hyde): Fig. 29-8a, Gift of Brighton Art Gallery and Museum 1950-59-2, (photo: Scott Hyde): Fig. 4-26a.

Corbis/Bettmann: Fig. I-17, 1-7.

Le Corbusier, Pavillon de l'Esprit Nouveau, International Exposition of Decorative and Modern Industrial Arts, Paris, 1925. From: Le Corbusier, "My Work," London: Architectural Press, 1960, p. 72. © 2005 Artists Rights Society (ARS), New York/ADAGP, Paris/FLC: Fig. 50-1a.

Cornu, Paul, *Meubles et Objets de gout 1796-1830*, Paris: Libraire des Arts Decoratifs, 1833: Fig. 27-10a, 27-12b, 27-16.

Country Life Picture Library, London: England: Fig. 44-8b.

Crane, Walter, *The Basis of Design*, London: G. Bell & Sons Ltd., 1925: Fig. 7-9, 41-10d.

The Craftsman, Vol. 5, October 1903 – March 1904, Syracuse: 1904: Fig. 39-3.

The Craftsman, Vol. 6, April 1904 – September 1904, Syracuse: 1904: Fig. 44-21.

The Craftsman, Vol. 7, October 1904 – March 1905, Syracuse: 1905: Fig. 43-9b.

Cross, A., *History of Architecture*, London: International Correspondence Schools, Ltd. ND: Fig. 4-9, 5-2b, 5-6, 9-8b, 12-11b, 12-13b, 18-2, 27-4a.

Robert Cudmore, Wikimedia Commons: Fig. 58-6.

Daderot, Wikimedia Commons: Fig. 25-4a, 33-7, 53-7a.

Dalbera, Jean-Pierre, Wikimedia Commons: Fig. 27-6.

Daniels, Fred H., *The Teaching of Ornament*, New York: The J. C. Witter Co., 1900: Fig. 6-1d.

Das Interieur II, Ludwig Ables, (Ed.),Vienna: Kunstverlag Anton Schroll & Co., 1901: Fig. 45-8, 45-10a, 45-10b, 45-12, 45-14.

David Skinner & Son Irish Wallpapers Exclusively Through Classic Revivals, Inc., Boston, Mass: Fig. 27-11a.

De Forest, Julia, *A Short History of Art*, New York: Dodd, Mead, and Co., 1881: Fig. 9-6c.

Dehio and von Bezoid, *Die kirchliche Baukunst des Abendlandes*, Stuttgart: 1887-1902: 10-7b.

De Stijl – 11, 9, Leiden/Delft: 1919: Fig. 48-5.

de Wolf, Elsie, *The House in Good Taste*, New York: The Century Co., 1913: Fig 23-9, 37-14, 37-17.

Courtesy Design Within Reach, www.dwr.com.: Fig. 56-16.

Digital Image © The Museum of Modern Art/Licensed by Scala/Art Resource, NY: Fig. 49-9c.

Dilke, Lady, *French Furniture and Decoration in the XVIII Century*, London: George Bell and Sons, 1902: Fig. 20-7, 23-1a.

Dishwasherrat, Wikimedia Commons: Fig. 57-5.

© Dorling Kindersley: Fig. 45-11.

From the archives of Dorothy Draper & Co. Inc. New York: Fig. 55-12.

Downing, Andrew Jackson, *The Architecture of County Houses*, New York: D. Appleton and Company, 1850: Fig. 31-8, 31-17b, 32-7a, 32-7b.

Courtesy Dunbar Furniture: Fig. 55-24.

Dunlap, Deborah Rushan: Fig. 5-17a.

Eastlake, Charles L., *Hints on Household Taste*, London: Longmans, Green & Co., 1878: Fig. 35-25.

Eberlain, Harold D., Abott McClure, Edward Stratton Halloway, and *The Practical Book on Interior Decoration*, Philadelphia: J.B. Lippincott, 1919: Fig. 19-11, 37-20a.

Eberlin, Harold D., *Spanish Interiors, Furniture, and Details*, New York: Architectural Book Publishing, Inc., 1925: Fig. 13-2a, 13-9a, 13-13.

Edgell, George H., *The American Architecture Today*, New York: Charles Scribners Sons, 1928: Fig. 12-10.

Edis, Robert William, *Decoration and Furniture of Town Houses*, NY: Scribner & Welford, 1881: Fig. 35-12.

Endeman, Judith L.: Fig. 1-6b.

Esto Photographics: Fig. 3-11.

Esto: Fig. 34-8b (Roger Straus III), 51-13, 56-11, 60-13 (Peter Mauss).

© Esto for the Ford Foundation: Fig. 46-11.

Esto Photographics, Inc.: Fig. 53-15, 56-3, 60-14.

Exposition Internationale des Arts Décoratifs et Industriels Modernes Paris 1925, Edité Pa L'Art Vivant, Paris: Libraire La Rousse, 1929: Fig. 51-2, 51-3.

Ezra Stoller, Esto/IPNSTOCK: Fig. 52-6c, 52-8.

Fergusson, James, *A History of Architecture in all Countries from the Earliest Times to the Present Day*, London: John Murray, 1874: Fig. 7-2b, 7-2c, 7-5, 11-4d.

Fergusson, James, *History of Modern Styles of Architecture*, New York: Dodd, Mead, 1899: Fig. 6-9, 10-8, 21-3b, 31-3a, 32-2a.

Fiser, Daniel (-df-), Wikimedia Commons: Fig. 49-4a.

flamenc, Wikimedia Commons: Fig. 29-6c.

Bruce Foster © Dorling Kindersley: Fig. 57-3.

Courtesy John Reed Fox: Fig. 43-17.

Fowles, Dorothy L.: Fig. 59-7.

Frankl, Paul, *New Dimension: The Decorative Arts of Today in Words & Pictures*, New York: Payson-Clarke Ltd., 1928: Fig. 47-5, 51-22.

French Embassy: Fig. 50-3.

French Government Tourist Office: Fig. 23-2a.

Frost, David and Roger Sorrell: Fig. 59-25b.

Frye, Alex Everett, *Frye's Complete Geography*, Boston: Ginn & Co., 1895: Section M Opener.

Furniture, Grand Rapids: n.p., June, 1890: Fig. 35-24.

Gagnon, Bernard, Wikimedia Commons: 11-5c.

Gardner, Helen, *Art Through the Ages*, New York: Harcourt, Brace and Co., 1926: Fig. 9-14a, 10-6b.

Gensler Architecture: Fig. 58-15, 58-16.

© J. Paul Getty Trust. Used with permission: Fig. 50-6a, 50-6c.

Getty Images: Fig. 45-6c.

Getty Images/De Agostini Editore Picture Library: Fig. 44-10.

Getty Images, Inc.-Stone Allstock: Fig. 55-5a.

The Getty Research Institute, Research Library, Los Angeles: Fig. 53-8, 53-10b, 53-13.

Giano, Wikimedia Commons: 19-5a.

Gillon, Edmond V. Jr., *Pictoral Archive of Early Illustrations and Views of American Architecture*, New York: Dover Publications, Inc., 1971: Fig. 35-2.

Giraud, Patrick, Wikimedia Commons: Fig. 14-5a.

Glasgow Museums: Fig. 44-7.

Gloag, John, *British Furniture Makers*, New York: Hastings House, n.d.: Fig: 24-10, 24-11, 29-12.

Godey's Ladies Book, New York: Godey's, 1854, 1870: Fig.33-12.

Good, Chris: Fig. 2-2a, 4-4, 6-12, 7-2, 12-12, 14-3b, 15-15a, 15-15b, 16-4, 16-10a, 18-3b, 18-4d, 19-2b, 19-6a, 24-9b, 26-7, 27-3, 27-12a, 27-17, 29-19, 31-16a, 31-20, 32-2b, 33-2c, 35-6, 42-2c, 42-6b, 45-6b, 48-3c, 48-2c, 48-2d, 48-6a, 48-6b, 48-8d, 50-7c, 51-21, 52-3a, 52-6b, 52-20, 53-9b, 56-12, 57-10, 57-13b, 59-16.

Godfrey, Walter H., *A History of Architecture in London*, New York: Charles Scribners Sons, 1911: Fig. 21-2.

Goingstuckey, Wikimedia Commons: Fig. 22-5.

Goodall, John, Wikimedia Commons: Fig. 15-8a.

Goodyear, William Henry, *History of Art for Classes, Art Students, and Tourists in Europe*, New York: A. S. Barnes and Co., 1889: Fig. 5-8c, 6-1e, 6-6, 7-8, 11-1e.

Gotch, J. Alfred, *Old English Houses*, London: Methuen and Co., Ltd., 1925: Fig. 19-4a19-4b

The Great Masters of Decorative Arts, London: The Art Journal Office, 1900: Fig. 42-1.

Guérinet, Armand, *Materials et Documents d'Art Décoratif*, Paris: Libraire d'Architecture et d'Art Décoratif, n.d.: Fig. 20-1a, 20-8c.

Courtesy of the Board of Regents, Gunston Hall Plantation, Mason Neck, VA: Fig. 22-11a, 22-11b.

Halsey, R.T.H. and Elizabeth Tower, *The Home of Our Ancestors*, Garden City: Doubleday & Co. Inc., 1925: Fig. 25-9.

Courtesy of Hamilton Weston Wallpapers, Ltd.: Fig. 33-11b.

Courtesy of Hammond-Harwood House Inc., Annapolis, MD: Fig. 22-9c.

Courtesy Fritz Hansen [www.fritzhansen.com]: Fig. 52-5b, 52-15a, 52-15b, 52-16.

Hansen & Sørensen APS: Fig. 52-14.
Hariri & Hariri – Architecture (Paul Warchol, photography): Fig. 58-19.
Harris, M. and Sons, *A Catalog and Index of Old Furniture and Works of Decorative Art*, Part 1, n.d.: Fig. 19-10b.
Hart, Harold H. (Ed.), *Chairs Through the Ages*, Mineola: Dover Publications, 1971: Fig. 24-10d, 34-19, 35-20.
Harter, Jim (Ed.), *Images of World Architecture*, New York: Bonanza Books, 1990: Figs. 6-11b, 8-3e, 13-4a, 36-2, 36-4.
Harwood, Buie: Fig. I-17, 1-11, 1-13, 1-15a, 2-2d, 4-13, 5-2a, 5-2c, 5-16b, 6-4b, 6-18b, 6-20, 7-3a, 7-3b, 8-1b, 8-1c, 8-2a, 8-3d, 9-1b, 9-1d, 9-2a, 9-13a, 9-13b, 9-13c, 9-14c, 9-15, 9-16a, 9-16b, 10-1c, 10-5a, 10-5c, 11-1b, 11-3a, 11-3b, 11-4b, 11-16a, 12-2b, 13-1a, 13-1b, 13-3, 13-4b, 13-4e, 13-9c, 13-11b, 13-12a, 13-14, 14-2, 14-8, 15-1a, 15-1b, 15-1c, 15-7, 15-10, 15-13, 15-5b, 16-6, 16-10b, 16-20, 16-26, 17-5, 17-6, 17-7, 18-1b, 18-4a, 18-3c, 19-5b, 19-8b, 19-8c, 20-9b, 20-17, 21-1a, 21-1b, 21-1c, 21-5a, 21-8b, 21-15, 22-1a, 22-14a, 22-9b, 23-3a, 24-1b, 24-3, 24-4d, 24-6a, 25-4b, 25-5a, 25-5b, 25-6a, 25-10, 26-14b, 26-16a, 26-17b, 26-18, 27-5, 27-10b, 28-2b, 29-2, 29-5a, 29-6b, 29-8b, 30-1b, 30-5a, 30-17a, 30-17c, 30-22, 31-1, 31-12a, 31-12b, 32-4, 32-10, 32-18, 33-2b, 33-11a, 33-17, 34-5, 34-6a, 34-15c, 35-1a, 35-1b, 35-3, 35-8b, 35-18, 36-1a, 36-5a, 36-8b, 36-8c, 36-9, 37-1b, 37-5, 37-19a, 38-11a, 38-11b, 38-19b, 39-1a, 39-4a, 39-5b, 39-8, 39-11, 40-2b, 40-5b, 40-5c, 40-5f, 40-9, 40-10, 41-12b, 42-2b, 42-4a, 42-4b, 42-5, 42-14, 42-15b, 43-10b, 43-5a, 43-11a, 43-11d, 43-12, 43-15, 44-3a, 44-4, 44-8a, 44-20, 45-1a, 45-2a, 45-3, 45-4a, 45-5a, 45-6a, 45-13, 46-4b, 46-4c, 46-12, 47-6, 47-8, 48-2b, 48-2c, 48-7, , 50-7b, 50-7d, 50-7a, 51-7, 51-25b, 54-2a, 54-2b, 54-4, 55-6, 55-8, 55-19, 56-1, 56-6b, 56-7b, 56-13, 57-11, 57-12, 57-21, 57-22b, 58-4, 58-9, 58-10, 58-13a, 59-1a, 59-1b, 59-10a, 59-10b, 59-25a, 60-2, 60-3, 60-6, 60-11, 60-16.
Hawn, Art: 21-12b.
Heaton, John Adam, *Furniture and Decoration During the Eighteenth Century*, London: John Bumpus, 1789/1892: Fig. 24-1c.
Heck, J. G., and Paul Bacon, *The Complete Encyclopedia of Illustration*, New York: Park Lane/Crown Publishers, 1851/1979: Fig. 5-17b, 8-4b, 12-6, 17-2b, 17-3b, 27-4b.
Hedrich-Blessing Archive, Chicago Historical Society: Fig. 55-11.
Hegemann, Werner and Elbert Peets, *The American Vitruvius: An Architects' Handbook of Civic Art*, New York: 1922, Reissued Benjamin Blom, Inc., 1972: Fig. 12-5b.
The Henry Francis du Pont Winterthur Museum, Inc.: Fig. 38-16, 15-22b.
Courtesy Herman Miller, Inc.: Fig. I-6, 44-22, 53-17a, 53-20a, 53-20b, 53-20c, 53-21a, 53-21b, 53-23, 54-9a, 54-9b, 54-12a, 54-15, 54-16, 56-20, 56-23, 56-24, 58-28, (Hedrich/Blessing photography), 59-21, 59-24, (Hedrich/Blessing Photography).
Hesse, Patrick, Wikimedia Commons: Fig. 17-4.
Hickory Chair, Hickory, N.C.: Fig. 31-21 (Gothcik Bench), 41-22 (Country Occasional Chair).
High Museum of Art, Atlanta, Georgia; Virginia Carroll Crawford Collection: Fig. 41-19.
Hing, Allan: Fig. 29-5b, 52-4, 56-8, 60-8.
Historical Art Furniture, New York, Helburn & Hagen, n.d.: Fig. 11-16b, 14-12, 15-19.
History of Architecture (Editorial staff), Scranton, PA, International Textbook Co., 1924: Fig. 4-2, 5-2d, 5-2e, 5-2f, 6-13, 8-5b.
History of Architecture & Ornament, Scranton, PA, International Textbook Company, 1909: Fig. 5-3, 8-1a.
© Historical Picture Archive/CORBIS: Fig. 1-22.
Holme, Charles (Ed.), *Modern British Domestic Architecture & Decoration "The Studio,"* London: n.p., 1901: Fig. 42-6c, 42-6d.
Holly, H.H., *Modern Dwellings*, London, n.p.,1878: 41-10c.
Hope, Thomas, *Household Furniture and Interior Decoration*, London: Longman, Hurst Rees and Orme (printed by T. Bensey), c. 1807: Fig. 29-1a, 29-1b, 29-7, 29-7, 29-11, 29-14a, 29-14b, 29-17, 29-18,
Hottenroth, Fredrich, *Trachten, Haus- Feld-, und Kriegsgeräthschaften der Völker Alter und Neuer Zeit*, Stuttgart: Verlag von Gustave Weise, 1891: Fig. 5-13, 6-18a, 6-21, 6-22, 6-23, 8-8a, 10-10a.
House Beautiful, Vol. 34, #5, October, 1913: Fig. 38-8.
Reprinted by permission from *House Beautiful*, © September, 1916: Fig. 38-14.
Tim Hursley, photographer: Fig. 59-4.
Hunter, George Leyland, *Decorative Furniture*, Grand Rapids: Good Furniture Magazine, The Dean Hicks Co., 1923: Fig. I-18, 2-11a, 2-11b, 11-1f, 12-17, 12-22, 14-11.
© Hunterian Museum and Art Gallery, University of Glasgow, Mackintosh Collection: Fig. 44-11
Illustrated Postal Card Co., New York: 1907: Fig. 31-2a.
Imagno/Hulton Archive/Getty Images: Fig. 45-6c.
Interfoto, Ognan Borissov, photographer: Fig. 43-5b.
Intérieurs au Salon Des Artistes Décorateurs 6, Paris: Charles Moreau, 1927: Fig. 51-15, 51-16.
Intérieurs Français, Paris: Editions Albert Morancé, 1924: Fig. 51-14.
Intérieurs Français, Paris: Editions Albert Morancé, 1925: Fig. 51-24.
Interior of Ingram Street Tea Room, Charles Rennie Mackintosh. Culture and Sport Glasgow (Museums): Fig. 44-9.
Courtesy InterMetro Industries: Fig. 56-25.
International Library of Technology, Scranton, PA: International Textbook Company, 1905: Section D Opener.
Israel Ministry of Tourism: Fig. 9-3.
Jacquemart, Albert, *A History of Furniture*, London: Reeves and Turner, 1900: Fig. 12-16c, 20-11, 23-14,
JB Flying Eagles, Wikimedia Commons: Fig. 1-14d.
Jeffrey & Co, London: 1876: Fig. 41-10a.
Jennings, A.S. *Upholstery and Wall Coverings*, n,p.,1903: Fig. 38-16.
Jones, Owen, *The Grammar of Ornament*, London: B. Quaritch, 1868: Fig. 2-1b.2-1c, 2-1d, 34-1.
Jordon Mozer and Associates: Fig. 60-13, 60-17b.
J-P Kärnä, Wikipedia Commons: Fig. 52-6a.
Jourdain, M., *English Decoration and Furniture of the Early Renaissance 1500–1650*, London: B.T. Batsford Ltd., 1924: Fig. 15-1d.
Kaldari, Wikimedia Commons: Fig. 30-7.
Karl Andersson & Søner: Fig. 52-18.
Courtesy Kartell: Fig. 60-19a, 60-19b, 60-21b.
Kent, William, *The Designs of Inigo Jones, Consisting of Elevations for Public and Private Buildings*, Volume 1, London: William Kent, 1727: Fig. 15-8c.
Kiesler, Frederick, *Contemporary Art Applied to the Store and Its Display*, New York: Brentano's, Inc., c. 1930: Fig. 48-3, 48-4.
Kimball, Fisk and George Edgell, *A History of Architecture*, New York: Harper and Brothers, Publishers, 1918: Fig. 11-8a, 28-1.
Dave King © Dorling Kindersley: Fig. 5-43.
Photograph by Fred H. Kiser, Portland, Oregon: Fig. 1-4.
Courtesy Knoll, Inc.: Fig. 22-19, 45-15, 49-9a, 49-9b, 49-10a, 49-10b, 49-10c, 49-10d, 49-10e, 50-10, 53-16, 53-18, 53-19, 53-22, 54-11, 54-13a, 54-13b, 54-14, 56-18a, 56-19, 57-18, 60-23.
Lalupa, Wikimedia Commons: Fig. 7-4a.
Lambertini, Paolo. Fotolia: Fig. 2-2b
Latham, Charles, *In English Homes*, Vols. I, II, III, Country Life, 1907, 1908, 1909, Convent Garden, England: Fig. 15-20, 19-5d, 24-4c.
Le Corbusier, Pavillon de l'Espirit Nouveau, International Exposition of Decorative and Modern Industrial Arts, Paris, 1925. From "My Work," London: Architectural Press, 1960, p. 72 © 2005 Artists Rights Society (ARS), New York/ADAGP, Paris/FLC: Fig. 50-1a.
Leixner, Othmar, *Einführung in Die Architektur*, Vienna: Franz Deuticke, 1919: Fig. 45-4b.
Lenygon, Francis, *English Decoration and Furniture of the XVIth–XIXth Centuries*, London: B.T. Batsford, 1924: Fig. 21-12c, 21-17.
Courtesy of Rolande L'Heureux and Archives Nationales du Québec: Fig. 16-21.
Les Arts de la Maison, Paris: Charles Moreau, Spring 1926: Fig. 51-19b.
Les Arts de la Maison, Paris: Editions Albert Morance, c. 1925: Fig. 51-20.
Eric Lessing/Art Resource, NY: Fig. 12-13a, 20-16, 45-4c, 47-10.

Lévy, Albert (Ed.), *L'Art Décoratif Français 1918-1925*, Paris: n.p., 1925-1926: Fig. 51-18b, 51-19a, 51-22b.

Lévy, Albert (Ed.), *Exposition des Art Décoratifs Paris la Ferronnerie*, Paris: Librairie Centrale des Beaux-Arts, 1926: Fig. 51-1a.

Lévy, Émile (Ed.), *Art et Décoration*, Paris: Librairie Centrale des Beaux-Arts, Volumes 1894-1908, 1914, 1920, 1921, 1923: Fig. 27-11b, 27-18, 27-19, 27-21, 44-1a, 44-1b, 44-2, 44-6a, 44-6b, 44-12a, 44-12b, 44-13a, 44-13b, 44-13c, 44-16a, 44-16b, 44-18.

Courtesy of the Library of Congress, American Memory: Fig. 46-2, 46-14, Section C Opener, Section F Opener, Section I Opener, Section L Opener.

Courtesy of the Library of Congress, Prints and Photographs Division: Fig. 11-9, 14-4c, 16-15, 26-4, 26-11 (photography by Carol M. Highsmith), 29-3, 31-9a (photography by Carol M. Highsmith), 31-9c (photography by Carol M. Highsmith), 33-3b, 37-1c (photography by Carol M. Highsmith), 37-13 (photography by Carol M. Highsmith), 55-14a, 55-14b (photography by Carol M. Highsmith), 55-17.

Courtesy of the Library of Congress, Prints and Photographs Division, Historic American Buildings Survey: Fig. I-20, 7-7, 16-14, 16-19, 16-23, 16-22, 16-28, 22-3, 22-4, 22-6b, 22-7b, 22-8b, 25-1c, 25-3, 26-1b, 26-13 (photograph by Cervin Robinson), 26-16b, 26-17d, 26-20 (photograph by Jack E. Boucher), 30-1a, 30-2, 30-3, 30-4a, 30-4b, 30-5b, 30-6, 30-8, 30-9, 30-10a, 30-10b, 30-12, 31-7a, 30-10a, 30-10b, 31-14b, 32-3, 32-5, 32-8, 32-12, 32-14a, 32-14b, 33-1, 33-5, 33-6, 33-8a, 33-8c, 33-8d, 33-13b, 33-18, 34-3, 34-6b, 34-7, 34-8a, 34-8b, 34-10, 35-5b, 35-10, 36-1b, 36-3, 36-7, 36-11a, 36-11b, 36-11c, 37-1a, 37-6, 37-9b, 37-10a, 37-10b, 37-12, 37-18, 37-20b, 38-5a, 38-5b, 39-1b, 39-5a, 39-5c, 39-12a, 39-12b, 40-5a, 40-5d, 40-6, 40-7, 41-4, 41-13a, 41-13b, 43-1a, 43-4b, 43-6b, 43-6c, 43-8, 46-4a, 46-6b, 46-7, 46-9a, 46-9b, 46-10a, 47-2b, 47-7, 50-2a, 50-2b, 50-2c, 50-4, 51-1b, 51-4a, 51-5a, 51-5b, 51-8, 51-9a, 53-7b, 54-8a, 54-8b, 54-8c, 55-2.

Lieu Song, Benh, Wikimedia Commons: Fig. 27-2.

Lipe, Melissa M.: Fig. 54-7.

Litchfield, F., *Illustrated History of Furniture*, Boston, The Medici Society of America, 1922: Fig. 4-16b, 11-15b, 21-10b, 24-16, 38-20.

Lithoderm, Wikimedia Commons: Fig. 25-14.

Courtesy of The Francis Loeb Library, Graduate School of Design, Harvard University: Fig. 36-6.

Longnon & Huard; *French Provincial Furniture*, Philadelphia: Lippencott, 1927: Fig. 23-17, 23-20, 23-21.

Lonpicman, Wikimedia Commons: 19-2c.

Lubke, Wilhelm, *Geschichte der Architekture*, Leipzeg: Verlag Von E.A. Seemann, 1865: Fig. 9-6e, 10-1a, 10-4b, 10-4c.

Courtesy of Lyndhurst, a National Trust Historic Site: Fig. 6-20a (photograph by Carol M. Highsmith), 31-9c (photography by Carol M. Highsmith).

Lyons, David © Dorling Kindersley, Courtesy of Fruitlands Museums, Sudbury, Massachusetts: Fig. 40-11, 40-12.

Courtesy of the Frances Loeb Library, Graduate School of Design, Harvard University: Fig. 36-6.

Los Angeles Public Library, (Security Pacific Collection, Marvin Rand, photography): Fig. 60-12.

Louis Poulsen Lighting, Inc.: Fig. 52-10b.

Lykantrop, Wikimedia: Fig. 43-6a.

David Lyons © Dorling Kindersley, Courtesy of Fruitlands Museums, Sudbury, Massachusetts: Fig. 40-11, 40-12.

Macquoid, Percy, *A History of English Furniture*, Volumes 1 and 2, London: Lawrence and Bullen, Ltd., 1905: Fig. 19-10a, 19-13, 19-15.

Courtesy Eva Maddox Branded Environments, Photographer: Steve Hall, Hedrich Blessing: Fig. 58-14.

Courtesy Magis SPA: Fig. 54-18, 60-18, 60-20.

Courtesy Maharam: 58-21.

MartinVMtl, Wikipedia Commons: Fig. 9-9.

© Mary Evans Picture Library/Alamy: Fig. 51-17.

Mattis, Wikimedia Commons: Fig. 14-4b.

May, Bridget: Fig. 6-1b, 6-1c, 7-1a, 7-1b, 7-1c, 8-2b, 8-2c, 10-1d, 11-1c, 12-2a, 12-2c, 12-3, 12-4, 12-7b, 12-18, 12-19, 15-3, 15-17, 16-1, 16-3, 17-2d, 21-6, 22-1b, 22-10, 22-13b, 22-14b, 22-15b, 22-13a, 31-3b, 32-6, 42-2a, 55-1, 55-7.

Mayer, August L., *Architecture and Applied Arts in Old Spain*, New York: Brentano's, 1921: Fig. 13-2b, 13-8b.

McClleland, Nancy, *Practical Book of Wall Treatments*, New York: J.P. Lippincott Co., 1926: Fig. 38-15.

McDonough, Wisley & Co. Catalog, Chicago: 1878: Fig. 32-16.

Courtesy McGuire Furniture and Orlando Diaz-Azcuy: Fig. 59-23.

Meden, Robert Paul: Fig. 16-18.

Memphis Milano: Fig. 57-14, 57-16, 57-17, 57-20.

The Metropolitan Museum of Art, Gift of Josephine Fiala, 1968; American Wing Restricted Building Fund, 1968; Purchase, Anonymous Gift, 1968 /Art Resource: Fig. 32-11.

_____, Funds from Various Donors, 1970/Art Resource: Fig. 34-17.

_____, Art Resource, Frederick C. Hewitt Fund, 1911, (JP655): Fig. 3-12.

_____, Gift of Mrs. R.W. Hyde, 1943:Fig. 30-18.

_____, Purchase, The Haqtop Kevorkian Fund, 1970/Art Resource: Fig. 9-12.

_____, Purchase, The Jack and Belle Linsky Collection, 1982/Art Resource: Fig. 18-13.

_____, Gift of Richard and Gloria Manney/Art Resource: Fig. 30-13.

_____, Rogers Fund, 1903, (Photography by Schecter Lee): Fig. 6-17.

_____, Rogers Fund, 1906, (06.1335.1a-d): Fig. 17-9.

_____, Rogers Fund, 1939 /Art Resource: Fig. 12-14.

_____, Purchase, Edgar J. Kaufmann, Foundation Gift, 1968 /Art Resource: Fig. 32-18.

_____, Purchase, Edgar Kaufmann, Jr. Gift, 1973/Art Resource: Fig. 51-23a.

_____, photograph, all rights reserved, The Metropolitan Museum of Art: Fig. 51-12.

_____, Gift of John D. Rockefeller Jr., 1935/Art Resource: Fig. 20-14.

_____, The Lesley and Emma Sheafer Collection, Bequest of Emma Sheafer, 1973/Art Resource: Fig. 20-15.

_____, Purchase, Gift of Mrs. Herbert N. Straus, 1942 /Art Resource:. Fig. 23-6.

_____, Mr. and Mrs. Charles Wrightsman Gift, 1963/Art Resource: Fig. 20-2.

Mewes, Wikimedia Commons: Fig. 49-2b.

Miller, Brian K., Photography: Fig. 30-15.

© Judith Miller/Dorling Kindersley: Fig. 9-14b.

© Judith Miller/Dorling Kindersley/Decodame.com: Fig. 51-25a.

© Judith Miller/Dorling Kindersley/Deco Etc.: Fig. 54-10a, 54-10b.

© Judith Miller/Dorling Kindersley/Freeman's: Fig. 40-14, 50-8b, 52-12c, 52-17.

© Judith Miller/Dorling Kindersley/Graham Cooley: Fig. 54-17.

© Judith Miller/Dorling Kindersley/Legacy: Fig. 43-16b.

© Judith Miller/Dorling Kindersley/Lyon and Turnbull Ltd: Fig. I-10, 41-14, 41-18, 41-21b, 50-8c, 54-12c, 58-24.

© Judith Miller/Dorling Kindersley/Mum Had That: Fig. 52-19.

© Judith Miller/Dorling Kindersley/Sloans & Kenyon: Fig. 41-21a.

© Judith Miller/Dorling Kindersley/Wallis and Wallis: Fig. 43-16a.

© Judith Miller/Dorling Kindersley/Woolley and Wallis: Fig. 29-15, 18-52a.

PP Mobler and Brayton International: Fig. 52-12a, 52-12b.

Modern Bauformen-Facaden-Interieurs-Details, Band 2, Stuttgart: Jules Hoffman, 1903: Fig. 45-1b.

Modern World Dictionary of the English Language, New York: P. F. Collier and Sons, 1906: Fig. 11-1d.

Piet Mondrian, (1872–1944), Composition with Red, Blue and Yellow, 1930. 51 × 51 cm. Oil on canvas, 18 1/8" × 18 1/8" Photo: Giraudon/Art Resource © 2004 Mondrian/Holtzman Trust. c/o hcr@hcrinternational.com: Fig. 48-1.

Monograph of the Works of McKim Mead & White 1879-1915, The, New York: The Architectural Book Publishing Co., 1915-1920: Fig. 38-4.

Michael Moran © Dorling Kindersley: Fig. 37-9a.

Morse, Edward S., *Japanese Homes and Their Surroundings*, Boston: Ticknor and Co., 1886: Fig. 3-7a.
Museum of The City of New York, The Byron Collection: Fig. 20-10, 46-13a.
Courtesy of the Museum of Early Southern Decorative Arts, Winston-Salem, NC: Fig. 16-27.
The Museum of Modern Art/Licensed by Scala-Art Resource, NY: Fig. 49-1, 49-2a, 53-2.
Myers, Philip Van Ness, *Ancient History*, Boston: Ginn and Co., 1904: Section C Opener.
_____, *A General History*, Boston: Ginn and Co., 1898: Section F Opener.
Nash, John, *The Mansions of England in the Olden Time*, London: William Heinman, 1912: Fig. 11-15a, 15-11.
National Trust Photo Library, © NTPL/Nadia Mackenzie: Fig. 42-2d.
National Park Service: Fig. 43-2a, 43-2b (J.P. Clum Lantern, photographer).
Needlecraft: Artistic and Practical, New York: The Butterick Publishing Company, 1890: Fig. 41-2b, 41-11, 41-15.
The Netherlands Information Bureau: Fig. 47-1.
Neue Arbeiten der Bauhauswerkstätten, Munich: Albert Langen Verlag, 1925: Fig. 49-2d, 49-8a, 49-12.
Newcomb, Rexford, *The Spanish House for America*, Philadelphia: J.B. Lippincott Co., 1927: Fig. 39-1c, 39-9, 39-15, 39-16, 39-19, 39-20, 39-21.
New Mexico State Tourist Bureau: Fig. 17-32.
New York Convention & Visitors Bureau: Fig. 49-6.
The New York Public Library: Fig. 8-6.
Northend, Mary H., *American Homes and Their Furnishings in Colonial Times*, London: T. Fisher Unwin, 1912: Fig. 16-7.
© Oesterreich Werbung (Austrian National Tourist Office): Fig. 28-3, 28-6.
Ormsbee, Thomas H., *The Story of American Furniture*, New York, The Macmillan Co, 1934: Fig. 30-23.
Oyster House Antiques, Charlottesville, VA: 2-7b, 2-8a, 2-9a, 2-9b, 2-10.
Photolibrary, Glasgow Museums, Glasgow, Scotland: Fig. 44-7.
Picture Desk, Inc./Kobal Collection/Nicolas Sapieha: Fig. 49-3a.
PP Møbler/Brayton International: Fig. 52-13a, 52-13b.
Courtesy of Palacek: Fig. 59-22.
Palladio, Andrea, *The Four Books of Architecture*, London: Isaac Ware, 1738: Fig. 12-8a, 12-9b.
Palliser, George and Charles, *Palliser's American Cottage Homes*, Bridgeport: Palliser, Palliser & Co., 1878: Fig. 26-1b, 26-6, 35-14.
Parker, John Henry, *ABCs of Gothic Architecture*, 2nd Ed., Oxford: Parker and Co., 1882: Fig. 10-2b, 10-2c.
Patche99z, Wikimedia Commons: Fig. 21-3a.
Pavel, Konovalov. Fotolia: 11-7a.
Pencil Points, New York: The Pencil Points Press, Jan. 1–Sept., 1930: Fig. 39-13.
Pennell, E. R., *The Life of James McNeill Whistler*, Philadelphia: J.B. Lippincott, 1911: Fig. 41-6a.
Penor, Rodolphe, *Guide, Artistique & Historique au Palais de Fontainebleau*, Paris: André, Daly Fils & Cie, 1889: Fig. 14-1c.
Percier, C. et P.F.L. Fontaine, *Recueil de Decorations Interieures*, Paris: Jules Didot Pine, 1827: Fig. 27-1, 27-7b, 27-8, 27-13, 27-15.
Pheezy, Wikimedia Commons: Fig. 54-5a.
Pierce, Walter, *Painting & Decoration*, London: n.p., 1893: Fig. 35-15.
Pieniazek, Larry, Wikimedia Commons: Fig. 54-3.
Picture Desk, Inc./Kobal Collection: Fig. 2-4.
PKM, Wikimedia Commons: Fig. 42-8c.
Courtesy Poltronova SRI: Fig. 56-22b.
John Portman & Associates, Inc.: Fig. 56-9.
Practical Handbook on Cutting and Draperies, n.p., 1890: Fig. 35-16.
Postcard, Wikimedia Commons: Fig. 16-2a.
Prignot, Eugène, *L'Architecture, La Décoration, L'Ameublement Soixante Compositions et Dessins Inédit*, Paris: C. H. Claesen, 1873: Fig. 20-9c.
Prignot, Eugène, *L'Architecture, L'Décoration, L'Ameublement Libraire Speciale des Arts Industriels et Decoratifs*, n.p., 1873: Fig. 34-2.
Publishers Photo Service: Fig. 9-12.
Pugin, A. Welby, *Fifteenth and Sixteenth Century Ornaments*, Edinburgh: John Grant, 1830: Fig. 31-14a, 31-16b, 31-17a.
Courtesy of May Frances Ramsey: Fig. 2-5, 59-6.
Réunion des Musées Nationaux/Art Resource, NY: Fig. 23-4, 23-5, 51-11, 57-19.
Ridpath, John Clark, *Cyclopedia of Universal History*, Vol II, Cincinnati: The Jones Bros. Publishing Co,. 1885: Section E Opener.
Gerrit Rietveld (1888–1964). First floor, 1987, view of the stairwell/landing and the living-dining area. In the foreground is the Red and Blue chair. Rietveld Schroderhlis, 1924, Utrecht: The Netherlands. c/o Stichting Beeldrecht, Anstelveen. Collection: Centraal Museum Utrecht/Rietveld-Schroder Archive. Photo: Ernst Moritz, The Hague. © 2005 Artists Rights Society (ARS), New York/Beeldrecht, Amsterdam: Fig. 48-3e.
Ritter-Antik, New York: Fig. 28-8.
© Robert Harding World Imagery/CORBIS All Rights Reserved: Fig. 38-3.
Robertson, Howard and F.R. Yerbury (Ed.), *Examples of Modern French Architecture*, New York: Scribner's Sons, 1928: Fig. 47-12, 50-5.
The Room Beautiful, New York: Clifford & Lawton, 1915: Fig. 28-5.
Rosbach, Hans A., Wikimedia Commons: Fig. I-8, 9-5, 12-9a, 12-9c, 21-4c.
Rosenthal Center for Contemporary Art: Fig. 60-9.
Row 17, Wikimedia Commons: Fig. 15-4a.
Royal Institute of British Architects Library of Photographs Collection: Fig. 42-6a.
Courtesy John Saladino, Saladino Group: Fig. 55-20.
Sale, Edith Tunis, *Interiors of Virginia Houses of Colonial Times*, Richmond, VA: William Byrd Press, Inc., 1927, by Permission of the Library of Congress: Fig. 25-6b.
Sanders, William Bliss, *Half Timbered Houses and Carved Oakwork of the 16th and 17th Centuries*, London: Bernard Quartich, 1894: Fig. 15-16.
Sanderson Wallpapers: Fig. 42-8a, 42-8b.
Sandstein, Wikimedia Commons: Fig. 60-15.
Courtesy Sargert Design Associates – sargertdesign.com: Fig. 59-15a, 59-15b.
Saylor, Henry, *Architectural Styles for Country Houses*, New York: Robert M. McBride & Co., 1919: Fig. 38-9.
© San Diego Historical Society: Fig. 35-4.
SayCheeeeeese, Wikimedia Commons: Fig. 40-3.
Courtesy Scalamandré: Fig. 55-22a, 55-22b, 55-22c.
Courtesy F. Schumaker & Company: Fig. 47-11b.
Sears Roebuck Catalogue, Chicago: 1902: Fig. 35-21, 35-23, 46-16.
Sears, Roebuck and Co., Chicago: 1918: Fig. 30-11.
seier+seier, Wikimedia Commons: Fig. 52-2a.
Shankbone, David, Wikimedia Commons: Fig. 57-4.
Shepherd, T. and James Elmes, *Metropolitan Improvements or London in the Nineteenth Century*, London: Jones & Co., Benjamin Blom, Inc., 1827: Fig. 29-4a, 29-4b.
Sheraton, Thomas, *The Cabinet-Maker and Upholsterer's Drawing Book*, London: L. T. Bensley, 1802: Fig. 24-11.
Sherman, Curt: Fig. I-7, I-12, I-16, 1-2a, 1-2b, 1-2c, 1-2d, 1-2e, 1-2f, 1-6a, 1-10, 1-12, 1-14a, 1-14c, 1-15c, 3-2, 3-3, 3-4, 3-5, 3-6a, 3-6b, 3-6c, 4-1a, 4-1b, 4-1c, 4-3, 5-1, 6-14, 8-8b, 9-1a, 9-1e, 9-6b, 9-6d, 12-2d, 12-7a, 13-4c, 15-5d, 15-9, 16-17a, 16-17b, 18-3a, 18-3d, 22-7a, 23-3b, 26-5, 26-8, 26-10, 26-15, 29-10a, 29-10b, 31-2b, 31-5, 31-6, 35-5a, 35-9, 35-11, 35-19b, 36-8a, 36-12, 36-14a, 36-14b, 38-12, 39-7a, 39-7b, 39-14, 39-18, 40-2a, 40-5e, 40-13a, 40-13b, 43-3b, 43-4a, 43-7a, 43-11b, 43-14, 45-1b, 46-1, 46-3, 46-6a, 46-8, 46-9c, 46-10b, 47-2a, 49-3b, 50-6b, 50-8a, 50-9, 51-4b, 51-6, 51-10, 52-1, 52-9a, 52-9b, 52-11, 53-3, 53-5, 53-9c, 53-10a, 53-14, 53-17b, 54-1a, 54-1b, 54-6, 55-2b, 55-4b, 55-5b, 55-23a, 55-27, 56-6a, 56-17, 56-26, 57-1, 57-2, 57-6, 57-8, 57-9, 57-13a, 57-15, 58-1, 58-2, 58-5, 58-7, 58-11, 58-13b, 59-2, 59-5, 59-11, 59-19, 60-4, 60-5, 60-10a, 60-10b, 60-22b.

Singleton, Esther, *The Collecting of Antiques*, New York: The Macmillan Co., 1926: Fig. 16-13, 21-10a, 24-18.

Skinner, David & Sons, Irish Wallpapers Exclusively Through Classics Revivals, Inc.: Fig. 30-16a, 31-13b.

Skyfox11, Wikimedia Commons, Fig. 59-8.

Courtesy Smith & Hawken: Fig. 142-16.

Smith, G. E. Kidder, New York, NY: Fig. 8-4a.

Smith, G., *Cabinetmaker & Upholstery Guide*, London: n.p., 1826: Fig. 29-9b.

Smith, Walter, *Masterpieces of the Centennial Exhibition*, Philadelphia: Gebbie & Barrie, 1876: Fig. 26-1a, 26-14a, 32-20, 32-21, 34-14, 34-16a, 34-20, 37-22, 41-2a, 41-20, 44-17.

Smithsonian American Art Museum: Fig. 51-26 (Gift of Eleanor T. and Samuel J. Rosenfeld), 59-18 (Gift of Lloyd E. Herman, founding director emeritus of the Renwick Gallery (1971-1986), 59-20 (Gift of Alfreda and Sam Maloof in honor of Michael W. Monroe, curator-in-charge, Renwick Gallery (1986-1995).

Smithsonian Freer Gallery of Art and Arthur M. Sackler Gallery: Fig. 41-6b.

SolarSurfer, Wikimedia Commons: Fig. 55-9.

Speltz, A., *The Colored Ornament of All Historical Styles*, London: B. T. Batsford, Ltd., 1915: Fig. 6-3b, 6-16.

Spanish National Tourist Office: Fig. 9-21.

Courtesy Staffelbach Design Associates: Fig. 58-17.

Staib, Wikimedia Commons: Fig. 53-9a.

Statham, H. Heathcote, *A Short Critical History of Architecture*, London: B. T. Batsford, 1912: Fig. 6-3a, 6-4a, 6-5. 6-7b, 6-8c.

Courtesy Steelcase Inc., Grand Rapids, MI: Fig. I-13, 43-10a, 43-10b, 54-1c, 58-27.

Stephenson, Nathaniel, *An American History*, Boston: Ginn & Co., 1919: Section H Opener.

Stickley, G., *Craftsman Homes*, New York: The Craftsman Publishing Co., 1909: Fig. I-2, 43-9a, 43-13.

L. & J.G. Stickley, Inc.: Fig. 55-28.

Stoddard, John Lawson, *A Trip Around the World*, n.p., n.d.: Fig. I-15, 6-11a, 31-4a, 33-2a, 37-4.

Strange, Thomas Arthur, *An Historical Guide to French Interiors, Furniture and Decoration During the Last Half of the Seventeen Century, the Whole of the Eighteenth Century, and the Earlier Part of the Nineteenth*, New York: Charles Scribners Sons, 1903: Fig. 18-8a, 18-8b, 20-6, 20-9a, 23-1b, 23-1c, 23-8a, 23-8b, 23-8c, 27-12c.

Clive Streeter © Dorling Kindersley: Fig. 57-27a.

Stuart, F.P., *F.P. Stuart Catalog*, n.p., 1900: Fig. 35-19a.

The Studio, an Illustrated Magazine of Fine and Applied Art, Vol. I, No. 6, London: The Studio, 1893: Fig. 42-11.

The Studio, an Illustrated Magazine of Fine and Applied Art, Vol. 7, New York: The Studio, 1899: Fig. 42-3.

The Studio, an Illustrated Magazine of Fine and Applied Art, Vol. 9, New York: The Studio, 1900: Fig. 42-12.

The Studio, an Illustrated Magazine of Fine and Applied Art, Vol. 10, New York: The Studio, 1900: Fig. 42-9a.

The Studio, an Illustrated Magazine of Fine and Applied Art, Vol. 11, New York: The Studio, 1900: Fig. 42-7.

The Studio Yearbook of Decorative Arts, London: The Studio, 1906: Fig. 42-9b, 42-9c.

The Studio Yearbook of Decorative Arts, London, The Studio: 1909: Fig. 47-11a.

Sturgis, Russell, *A Dictionary of Architecture and Building*, New York: The Macmillan Company, 1904: Fig. 11-8b, 20-1b.

SuperStock, Inc./Gala: Fig. 44-8.

Studio Daniel Libeskind, Wikimedia Commons: Fig. 60-7.

Talbert, B.J., *Examples of Ancient and Modern Furniture, Metal Work, Tapestries, Decorations*, Boston: James R. Osgood and Co., 1876: Fig. 31-19a, 31-19b, 41-7.

Targhette, Maurizio, Fotolia: 11-7b.

Tarr, Ralph S. and Frank M. McMurry, *New Geographies*, New York: Macmillan Co., 1913: Section J Opener, Section L Opener.

Courtesy Tecno SPA (Tommaso Sartori, photography): Fig. 58-26.

Courtesy, Texas Pioneer Arts Foundation: Fig. 16-25.

Courtesy Thayer Coggin, Inc.: Fig. 33-19.

The Room Beautiful, New York: Clifford & Lawton, 1915: Fig. 28-5.

Thévene, Cédric, Wikimedia Commons: Fig. 53-4.

Thonet, Frankenberg-Germany: Fig. 49-11.

Thorncrown Chapel, Whit Siemmons, photography: Fig. I-3, 59-3a, 59-3b.

Timms, W. H. and George Webb, *The Thirty-Five Styles of Furniture*, London: Timms & Webb, 1904: Fig. 5-15, 12-16a, 12-16b, 12-20, 19-12.

Tipping, H. Avray, *English Homes, Period II, Volume 1, Early Tudor*, London: Offices of Country Life, 1921: Fig. 15-4b.

———, *English Homes, Period V, Volume 1*, London: Offices of Country Life, 1924: Fig: 21-4a, 21-7, 24-4b, 24-5, 24-9a, 24-17, 26-17a, 29-16.

—, *Grinling Gibbons and the Woodwork of His Age (1648-1720)*, London, Country Life, 1914: Fig. 19-1, 19-14.

Todd, Dorothy and Raymond Mortimer, *The New Interior Decoration: An Introduction to its Principles, and International Survey of its Methods*, New York: Charles Scribner's Sons, 1929: Fig. 49-8b, 49-8c, 50-1b, 51-18a.

Township of Wilmot/Castle Kilbride National Historic Site, Baden, ON, Canada: Fig. 32-9a, 32-9b.

Touriste, Wikimedia Commons: 11-5a.

Tuer, Andrew W., *Japanese Stencil Design*, New York: Scribners, 1892/1967: Fig. 3-1a, 3-1b, 3-1c.

Turkish Ministry of Culture and Tourism: Fig. 8-3a.

U.S. Department of State, Washington, DC: Courtesy of the Diplomatic Reception Rooms: Fig. 30-24, 55-13a, 55-13b.

United Society of Shakers: Fig. 40-4.

Unika Vaev-USA: 45-9a.

University of Texas, Institute of Texan Cultures at San Antonio: Courtesy of Florence Collett Ayres: Fig. 13-10.

Urban, Wikimedia Commons; Fig. 20-5.

Utrecht, Netherlands/The Bridgeman Art Library: Fig. 48-3a.

Courtesy Vanderbyl Design: Fig. 56-14, 58-20.

Mies van der Rohe, Ludwig. German Pavillion, International Exposition, Barcelona. Photograph courtesy of Mies van der Rohe Archive. The Museum of Modern Art/Licensed by Scala-Art Resource, NY. © 1998 Artists Rights Society (ARS), New York: Fig. 24-4a.

Venetian Resort Hotel Casino: Fig. 32-15, 55-10a, 55-10b.

Venturi, Scott Brown and Associates, Inc.: Fig. 57-9 (Photographer, Rollin la France).

Ver Sacrum, No. 8, Vienna: n.p., 1901: Fig. 45-7, 45-9b, 45-9c.

d. Verleger, Eigenthum, *Aus d. Kunstanst d. Bibl. Instit. In Hildbhn*, pre-1900: Fig. 34-4.

Vicens, Wikimedia Commons: Fig. 49-3d.

Victoria & Albert Museum, London/Art Resource, NY: Fig. 31-18, 41-12a, 41-13, 41-17, 42-15a, 45-11.

Victoria & Albert Museum: Fig. 41-10b (V & A Image).

Virginia Tourism Corporation: Fig. 16-2b.

Von Falke, Otto, *Decorative Silks*, New York: William Helburn, Inc., 1922: Fig. 8-7a, 8-7b.

VMtl, Martin, Wikimedia Commons: Fig. 9-9.

Virginia Commonwealth University Libraries, James Branch Cabell Library, Special Collections and Archives: Fig. 38-6.

© Virginia Museum of Fine Arts, Richmond: Gift of Sydney and Frances Lewis, (Katherine Wetzel, photographer): Fig. 44-19.

Virginia Polytechnic Institute and State University: Fig. 59-12a, 59-12b, 59-12c.

Courtesy Vitra (vitra.com): Fig. 58-23 (photography by Andreas Sütterlin), 58-25 (photography by Andreas Sütterlin), 60-17a (photography by Andreas Sütterlin), 60-21a, 60-22a.

VIPlibrary, Wikimedia Commons: Fig. 52-7.

wal, Michael, Wikimedia Commons, Fig. 15-6b.

Ware, William R., *The American Vignola, Part I,* Scranton, PA: International Textbook Co., 1904: Fig. 6-2.

Warren, Garnet and Horace B. Cheney, *The Romance of Design*, New York: Doubleday, Page, and Co., 1926: Fig. 11-14, 12-15a, 13-8a, 13-8c, 20-8a, 23-7, 24-8, 27-11c, 51-18c.

Wasmuth, *An Encyclopaedia of Colour Decoration*, Leipzig, Germany: Poeschel & Trepte, 1928: Fig. 4-7, 4-11, 5-4b, 12-1, 20-1c.

Watt, William, *Art Furniture, from Designs by E.W. Godwin*, London: B.T. Batsford, 1877: Fig. 35-22, 41-18.

Watts & Co., Ltd., *Wallpapers*, London: Watts & Co., Ltd, n.d.: Fig 31-13a.

Courtesy Weissenhofsiedlung.de: Fig. 49-5.

West, Willis Mason, *The Modern World*, Boston: Allyn and Bacon, 1915: Section G Opener.

The White City Beautifully Illustrated, n.p., 1893: Fig. 46-5a, 46-5b.

White, Stanford, *The New York Sketch Book of Architecture*, 1875: Fig. 35-8c.

Linda Whitwam © Dorling Kindersley, Courtesy of Trinity Church, Boston: Fig. 36-5b.

Widdenhager, Von Graft, *History of Art*, 1919: Fig. 6-15, 9-4.

Courtesy of William McDonough and Partners: Fig. 59-13.

William Watt Co. Catalog of Art Furniture, London, 1877: Fig. 41-18.

Courtesy Wilson Associates: 55-16 (Michael Wilson Photography by Lisl Dennis).

Peter Wilson © Dorling Kindersley: Fig. 45-5b.

Winslow, Carlton M. and Bertram G. Goodhue, *The Architecture and the Gardens of the San Diego Exposition*, San Francisco: Paul Elder and Co., 1916: Fig. 39-4b.

Courtesy Winterthur Museum, Winterthur Photographic Services, Winterthur, Delaware: Fig. 16-8, 16-29, 22-1c, 22-12, 22-18, 25-13, 25-11, 25-17, 38-17 (Govin Ashworth, photographer), 40-8.

Courtesy Wittmann Moebelwerkstaetten, Austria, http://www.wittmann.at/: Fig. 45-11b, 45-11d.

World Imaging: Wikimedia Commons: Fig. 18-7.

Zanotta SPA: Fig. 56-21, 56-22b.

zh:user:Munford: Wikimedia Commons: Fig. 55-15.